SPECIAL EDUCATION LAW: CASES AND MATERIALS
Third Edition

SPECIAL EDUCATION LAW: CASES AND MATERIALS

Third Edition

Mark C. Weber
Vincent dePaul Professor of Law
DePaul University College of Law

Ralph Mawdsley
Roslyn Z. Wolf Endowed Chair in Urban Educational Leadership
Cleveland State University College of Education and Human Services

Sarah Redfield
Professor of Law
Franklin Pierce Law Center

ISBN: 978-1-4224-7774-8

Library of Congress Cataloging-in-Publication Data

Weber, Mark C., 1953-
Special education law : cases and materials / Mark C. Weber, Ralph Mawdsley, Sarah Redfield. -- 3rd ed.
p. cm.
Includes index.
ISBN 978-1-4224-7774-8 (hard cover)
1. Special education--Law and legislation--United States--Cases. 2. Children with disabilities--Education--Law and legislation--United States--Cases. I. Mawdsley, Ralph D. II. Redfield, Sarah E. III. Title.
KF4209.3.W428 2010
344.73'0791--dc22   2010022139

This publication is designed to provide accurate and authoritative information in regard to the subject matter covered. It is sold with the understanding that the publisher is not engaged in rendering legal, accounting, or other professional services. If legal advice or other expert assistance is required, the services of a competent professional should be sought.

LexisNexis, the knowledge burst logo, and Michie are trademarks of Reed Elsevier Properties Inc., used under license. Matthew Bender is a registered trademark of Matthew Bender Properties Inc.
Copyright © 2010 Matthew Bender & Company, Inc., one of the LEXIS Publishing companies.
All Rights Reserved.

No copyright is claimed in the text of statutes, regulations, and excerpts from court opinions quoted within this work. Permission to copy material exceeding fair use, 17 U.S.C. § 107, may be licensed for a fee of 10¢ per page per copy from the Copyright Clearance Center, 222 Rosewood Drive, Danvers, Mass. 01923, telephone (978) 750-8400.

Editorial Offices
121 Chanlon Rd., New Providence, NJ 07974 (908) 464-6800
201 Mission St., San Francisco, CA 94105-1831 (415) 908-3200
www.lexisnexis.com

NOTE TO USERS
To ensure that you are using the latest materials available in this area, please be sure to periodically check the LexisNexis Law School web site for downloadable updates and supplements at www.lexisnexis.com/lawschool.

Editorial Offices
121 Chanlon Rd., New Providence, NJ 07974 (908) 464-6800
201 Mission St., San Francisco, CA 94105-1831 (415) 908-3200
www.lexisnexis.com

MATTHEW◆BENDER

(2010–Pub.3189)

Dedication

To Joanne Kinoy — M.W.

To Alice, James and Jonathan Mawdsley — R.M.

To my husband, Stewart Smith, and my children, Alex and Althea Redfield — S.E.R.

Preface

In this book, we undertook the challenging task of developing materials for teaching Special Education Law both in schools of education and in law schools. Instructors in education schools have long complained about the lack of books on the subject that include suitably edited judicial opinions and reliable accounts of how the law operates. Instructors in law schools complained about an absence of any usable books for their courses. Our mission was to satisfy both complaints and meet both needs. We sought to create a book that would be accessible to students whose background is in education rather than law but would still include the original court cases and comprehensive, reliable descriptions of the law, in addition to provocative comments and discussion questions. At the same time, we tried to produce a law school casebook that would challenge second- or third-year students in either classroom or clinical courses and would provide the customary mix of cases, bridge materials, and questions for class discussion. The necessary background information about the theory and practice of special education and disability civil rights is found throughout the cases and in the materials we have contributed.

The first chapter of the book, on Core Concepts, introduces many of the basics of the course and contains a section at the end devoted to sources of law. We envision this latter part of the chapter as an aid to students who do not have formal legal training. We have tried in writing the rest of the book to make the chapters sufficiently independent of each other that an instructor with limited class hours can do some skipping around to cover those topics that are the most useful to the students.

While we were in the final stages of editing the original edition of this book, Congress passed and sent to the President the Individuals with Disabilities Education Improvement Act of 2004, which reauthorizes and amends the basic federal special education law. We knew of the pending legislation, but, like others working in the field, were uncertain which version would ultimately pass both houses, or if anything would pass at all. The new statute became effective, for the most part, July 1, 2005; final regulations were issued in 2006. The Act leaves the core of IDEA intact, and in fact makes fewer changes than many observers anticipated. The Second Edition includes updates for the statutory and regulation changes not covered in the original edition, and includes updates for new caselaw and other developments. This Third Edition updates the Second Edition and draws attention to emerging controversies over matters such as eligibility for special education and services under Section 504 of the Rehabilitation Act.

We owe many debts to others for their assistance with the book. Mark Weber would like to thank his research assistants, Suzanne Shmagin, Sara E. Mauk, Kim Brown and Ben Johnson, as well as Dean Glen Weissenberger, who provided support from the research fund of the DePaul University College of Law. Ralph Mawdsley wishes to thank his research assistant, James L. Mawdsley, as well as Dean James McLoughlin for his encouragement and support of this project. Sarah Redfield thanks Dean John Hutson at Franklin Pierce Law Center and Dean Elizabeth Rindskopf Parker at the University of the Pacific McGeorge School of Law for their unflagging support of this work. She also thanks all of her students whose thinking and work contributed to her own learning, and particularly Krysten Hicks, Julie Robbins, and Janelle Ruley at Pacific/McGeorge and Will Toronto at Pierce for their valuable research assistance. We all thank the good

Preface

people of LexisNexis for their faith in this project and, in particular, Keith Moore for his thoughtful, accurate, and tireless editorial work.

We hope to hear from instructors about experiences with the book and suggestions for improving it. Correspondence may be directed to Mark Weber, mweber@depaul.edu.

TABLE OF CONTENTS

Chapter 1	EDUCATING STUDENTS WITH DISABILITIES: CORE LEGAL CONCEPTS 1

A.	INTRODUCTION TO FUNDAMENTAL PRINCIPLES 1
	NOTES AND QUESTIONS 3
B.	FOUNDATION CASES 3
	P.A.R.C. v. Pennsylvania 3
	Mills v. Board Of Education of The District Of Columbia 10
	NOTES AND QUESTIONS 16
C.	OVERVIEW OF FEDERAL LEGISLATION 16
1.	The Purpose of the Individuals with Disabilities Education Act (IDEA) . 16
2.	Definition of a "Child with a Disability" 17
3.	Definition of "Free Appropriate Public Education" 17
4.	Definition of "Special Education" 18
5.	Section 504 18
6.	Disability Under the Americans with Disabilities Act (ADA) 19
7.	Public Entity Under the Americans with Disabilities Act (ADA) 19
8.	Qualified Individual with a Disability Under the Americans with Disabilities Act (ADA) 20
	NOTES AND QUESTIONS 20
D.	DEFINING CASES 21
1.	Appropriate Education 21
	Board Of Education v. Rowley 21
	NOTES AND QUESTIONS 31
2.	Student Discipline and Maintenance of Placement 32
	Honig v. Doe 32
	NOTES AND QUESTIONS 38
3.	Education for All Children with Disabilities 39
	Timothy W. v. Rochester, New Hampshire, School District 39
	NOTES AND QUESTIONS 47
E.	SOURCES OF LAW 49
1.	Federal and State Constitutions 49
2.	Federal and State Statutes 49
3.	Federal and State Regulations 50
4.	Caselaw 51
5.	Federal and State Court Systems 51

TABLE OF CONTENTS

| Chapter 2 | ELIGIBILITY AND EVALUATION | . . . . | 55 |

A.	INTRODUCTION	. . . .	55
B.	STATUTORY AND REGULATORY REQUIREMENTS	. . . .	55
1.	IDEA	. . . .	55
2.	Section 504 and the Americans with Disabilities Act (ADA)	. . . .	57
C.	DISABLING CONDITIONS GENERALLY	. . . .	58
	Springer v. Fairfax County School Board	. . . .	58
	Johnson v. Metro Davidson County School System	. . . .	62
	NOTES AND QUESTIONS	. . . .	70
D.	BENEFIT FROM SPECIAL EDUCATION	. . . .	72
	J.D. v. Pawlet School District	. . . .	72
	Mr. I. v. Maine School Administrative District No. 55	. . . .	79
	NOTES AND QUESTIONS	. . . .	98
E.	PARTICULAR ACTIVITIES AND CONDITIONS	. . . .	100
	Pottgen v. Missouri State High School Activities Association	. . . .	100
	Rothschild v. Grottenthaler	. . . .	104
	NOTES AND QUESTIONS	. . . .	109
F.	EVALUATION	. . . .	110
	Seattle School District, No. 1 v. B.S.	. . . .	110
	Schoenbach v. District Of Columbia	. . . .	114
	NOTES AND QUESTIONS	. . . .	121

| Chapter 3 | RESIDENCY | . . . . | 127 |

A.	STATUTORY AND REGULATORY REQUIREMENTS	. . . .	127
B.	THE CONSTITUTIONAL PARAMETERS	. . . .	128
	Plyler v. Doe	. . . .	128
	NOTES AND QUESTIONS	. . . .	133
	Martinez v. Bynum	. . . .	134
	NOTES AND QUESTIONS	. . . .	136
C.	RESIDENCY IN CASES INVOLVING STUDENTS WITH DISABILITIES	. . . .	137
1.	Divorce and Joint Custody	. . . .	137
	Linda W. v. Indiana Department Of Education	. . . .	137
2.	State Schools and Homes	. . . .	140
	Sonya C. v. Arizona School For The Deaf And Blind	. . . .	140
	NOTES AND QUESTIONS	. . . .	147
	Manchester School District v. Crisman	. . . .	148
	NOTES AND QUESTIONS	. . . .	154

TABLE OF CONTENTS

Chapter 4   **FREE, APPROPRIATE PUBLIC EDUCATION (FAPE)** . 157

A.   STATUTES AND REGULATIONS 157
  1.   Appropriate Education 157
  2.   Free Education 158
  3.   Public Education 159
B.   COURT DEFINITIONS 160
         Board Of Education v. Rowley 160
         NOTES AND QUESTIONS 162
C.   FAPE FOR CHILDREN WITH SEVERE DISABILITIES 165
         Polk v. Central Susquehanna Intermediate Unit 16 165
         NOTES AND QUESTIONS 171
D.   FAPE AND SPECIFIC SERVICES 172
         Alamo Heights Independent School District v. State Board Of Education
         172
         Sherman v. Mamaroneck Union Free School District 176
         NOTES AND QUESTIONS 182
E.   FAPE AND CHILDREN WITH LESS SEVERE DISABILITIES 183
         NOTES AND QUESTIONS 184
F.   FAPE AND THE LEAST RESTRICTIVE ENVIRONMENT 185
G.   OTHER FAPE ISSUES 185
  1.   Personnel 186
         NOTES AND QUESTIONS 187
  2.   Class Size 187
  3.   Vocational Education 188
  4.   Extracurricular Activities 188
         Dennin v. Connecticut Interscholastic Athletic Association 189
         NOTES AND QUESTIONS 196
  5.   Grading 197
  6.   District-Wide Assessment and Individual High-Stakes Testing 198
         NOTES AND QUESTIONS 199
  7.   Juveniles in Detention Facilities 200
  8.   Charter Schools 200

Chapter 5   **INDIVIDUALIZED EDUCATION PROGRAM** 203

A.   INTRODUCTION 203
B.   STATUTORY AND REGULATORY REQUIREMENTS 205
  1.   IDEA 205
  2.   Section 504 207
C.   SAMPLE IEP 208
         NOTES AND QUESTIONS 211
D.   IEP COURT DECISIONS 211

TABLE OF CONTENTS

1.   The Process as Opportunity to be Heard 211

      White v. Ascension Parish School Board 211

      Burilovich v. Board Of Education Of The Lincoln-Consolidated Schools

      217

      NOTES AND QUESTIONS 222

      Shapiro v. Paradise Valley Unified School District No. 69 222

      NOTES AND QUESTIONS 226

      Sytsema v. Academy School District No. 20 227

      Sytsema v. Academy School District No. 20 235

      NOTES AND QUESTIONS 241

2.   Content and Implementation of the IEP 242

      Houston Independent School District v. V.P. 242

      Notes and Questions 254

3.   The IEP as Controlling (or not) 255

      Michael C. v. Radnor Township School District 255

      NOTES AND QUESTIONS 260

Chapter 6   **THE LEAST RESTRICTIVE ENVIRONMENT** **261**

A.   INTRODUCTION 261

B.   STATUTORY AND REGULATORY PROVISIONS 261

  1.   IDEA 261

  2.   IDEA Regulations 262

  3.   Section 504 Regulations 263

      NOTES AND QUESTIONS 264

C.   PRESUMPTIVE INCLUSION 265

      Roncker v. Walter 265

      NOTES AND QUESTIONS 270

      Daniel R.R. v. State Board Of Education 271

      NOTES AND QUESTIONS 282

D.   APPLYING THE STANDARDS FOR INCLUSION 283

      Sacramento Unified School District v. Rachel H. 283

      NOTES AND QUESTIONS 289

Chapter 7   **RELATED SERVICES** **293**

A.   INTRODUCTION 293

B.   STATUTORY AND REGULATORY REQUIREMENTS 293

      NOTES AND QUESTIONS 294

C.   THE MEDICAL SERVICES EXCEPTION 295

      Irving Independent School District v. Tatro 295

      NOTES AND QUESTIONS 300

      Cedar Rapids Community School District v. Garret F. 300

TABLE OF CONTENTS

NOTES AND QUESTIONS 309

D.   RELATING LEAST RESTRICTIVE ENVIRONMENT TO RELATED
SERVICES 310

        Oberti v. Board Of Education 310

        NOTES AND QUESTIONS 328

Chapter 8   **DUE PROCESS HEARINGS** **331**

A.   HEARING RIGHTS 331

        NOTES AND QUESTIONS 332

  1.   Notice 333

        NOTES AND QUESTIONS 338

  2.   Impartiality Requirements 338

        Mayson v. Teague 339

        NOTES AND QUESTIONS 345

  3.   Participation Rights and Decisions 346

        NOTES AND QUESTIONS 347

  4.   Burden of Persuasion 348

        Schaffer v. Weast 348

        NOTES AND QUESTIONS 358

  5.   Remedies 359

        Burlington School Committee v. Department Of Education 359

        Florence County School District Four v. Carter 367

        Forest Grove School District v. T.A. 372

        NOTES AND QUESTIONS 387

        Draper v. Atlanta Independent School System 388

        NOTES AND QUESTIONS 398

B.   MAINTENANCE OF PLACEMENT 399

        NOTES AND QUESTIONS 399

C.   ISSUES RELATED TO SETTLEMENT 400

  1.   Offers of Judgment 401

        NOTES AND QUESTIONS 402

  2.   Enforcing Settlements 402

  3.   Mediation Procedures and Related Issues 403

        United States General Accounting Office, Special Education: Numbers of
Formal Disputes are Generally Low and States are Using Mediation and
Other Strategies to Resolve Conflicts 1–3 (2003) 404

        NOTES AND QUESTIONS 405

D.   APPEALS AND JUDICIAL REVIEW 406

        NOTES AND QUESTIONS 407

TABLE OF CONTENTS

Chapter 9	**STUDENT DISCIPLINE**	**409**

A. BEHAVIOR INTERVENTION AND APPROPRIATE EDUCATION IN THE
LEAST RESTRICTIVE ENVIRONMENT 409
Neosho R-V School District v. Clark 409
NOTES AND QUESTIONS 415
B. DISABILITY DISCRIMINATION CHALLENGES TO DISCIPLINE .. 415
S-1 v. Turlington 416
NOTES AND QUESTIONS 423
C. PROCEDURAL CHALLENGES TO DISCIPLINE 424
Honig v. Doe 424
NOTES AND QUESTIONS 424
D. THE CURRENT CODIFICATION 425
1. General Provisions and Manifestation Review 426
NOTES AND QUESTIONS 428
2. Children not Yet Classified as Children with Disabilities 430
NOTES AND QUESTIONS 431
3. Drugs, Weapons, and Serious Bodily Injury 432
NOTES AND QUESTIONS 432
4. Interim Alternative Educational Setting Requirements, Appeals, and
Placement During Review Proceedings 433
NOTES AND QUESTIONS 435
5. Seclusion and Restraint 436
NOTES AND QUESTIONS 437

Chapter 10	**COURT PROCEEDINGS**	**439**

A. PROCEEDINGS UNDER SECTION 1415 439
NOTES AND QUESTIONS 439
1. Evidentiary Hearings 441
Town Of Burlington v. Department Of Education 441
Metropolitan Government v. Cook 445
NOTES AND QUESTIONS 449
2. Remedies 449
NOTES AND QUESTIONS 450
B. SECTION 504 AND ADA CLAIMS 450
Baird v. Rose 451
Mark H. v. Lemahieu 460
NOTES AND QUESTIONS 473
C. CONSTITUTIONAL CLAIMS AND IDEA CLAIMS BROUGHT UNDER
SECTION 1983 475
1. Constitutional Claims Brought Pursuant to 42 U.S.C. § 1983 475
2. IDEA Claims Brought Pursuant to 42 U.S.C. § 1983 476

TABLE OF CONTENTS

Padilla v. School District No. 1 479
    NOTES AND QUESTIONS 485
D.   DEFENSES 485
  1.   Exhaustion 485
    Charlie F. v. Board Of Education 486
    NOTES AND QUESTIONS 490
  2.   Limitations 490
  3.   Immunities from Damages Liability 491
    NOTES AND QUESTIONS 491

Chapter 11   **ATTORNEYS' FEES IN SPECIAL EDUCATION LITIGATION** **495**

A.   INTRODUCTION 495
  1.   Procedural Matters 496
  2.   Procedural Victories and Partial Success 496
    G.M. v. New Britain Board Of Education 496
    NOTES AND QUESTIONS 503
  3.   *Buckhannon* Issues 503
    T.D. v. Lagrange School District No. 102 503
    NOTES AND QUESTIONS 515
B.   MEASURE OF FEES 517
  1.   General Considerations 517
  2.   Apportionment of Liability 517
    John T. v. Iowa Department Of Education 517
    NOTES AND QUESTIONS 524

Chapter 12   **CHILDREN IN PRIVATE SCHOOLS** **525**

A.   INTRODUCTION 525
B.   THE CURRENT CODIFICATION 525
  1.   Definition of Private Schools 525
  2.   Proportionate Allocation of Federal IDEA Funds 526
  3.   Child Find and Evaluation 526
  4.   Services Plan Requirement 526
  5.   Absence of an Individual Right to Services 527
  6.   Consultation with Private School Representatives 527
  7.   Personnel Standards 527
  8.   Permissibility of On-Site Services 527
  9.   Transportation 528
  10.   Complaints by Private School Parents 528
    NOTES AND QUESTIONS 528

TABLE OF CONTENTS

C.   PERMISSIVE ACCOMMODATIONS AND THE ESTABLISHMENT
     CLAUSE 530
        Zobrest v. Catalina Foothills School District 530
        NOTES AND QUESTIONS 534
D.   MANDATORY ACCOMMODATIONS AND THE FREE EXERCISE
     CLAUSE 534
        Gary S. v. Manchester School District 535
        NOTES AND QUESTIONS 541
E.   DISCRIMINATION BETWEEN RELIGIOUS SCHOOLS AND OTHER
     PRIVATE SCHOOLS 541
        Peter v. Wedl 541
        NOTES AND QUESTIONS 545

Chapter 13   EARLY CHILDHOOD PROGRAMS **547**

A.   INTRODUCTION 547
        Marie O. v. Edgar 548
        NOTES AND QUESTIONS 556
B.   INDIVIDUALIZED FAMILY SERVICE PLANS 557
        De Mora v. Department Of Public Welfare 561
        NOTES AND QUESTIONS 564
C.   TRANSITION ISSUES 564
        Pardini v. Allegheny Intermediate Unit 565
        D.P. v. School Board 575
        NOTES AND QUESTIONS 586

Chapter 14   POST-SECONDARY EDUCATION **587**

A.   INTRODUCTION 587
        NOTES AND QUESTIONS 588
B.   ELIGIBILITY FOR PROTECTION UNDER TITLE II AND SECTION
     504 588
        NOTES AND QUESTIONS 591
C.   QUALIFIED INDIVIDUAL/REASONABLE ACCOMMODATION ... 591
  1.   In General 591
        Southeastern Community College v. Davis 592
        NOTES AND QUESTIONS 598
        Lane v. Pena 599
        NOTES AND QUESTIONS 612
  2.   Academic Deference 613
        Zukle v. Regents Of The University Of California 613
        Wong v. Regents Of The University Of California 622
        NOTES AND QUESTIONS 635

TABLE OF CONTENTS

D.   TESTING AND TESTING ACCOMMODATIONS 636

         Wynne v. Tufts University School of Medicine ("Wynne I") 639

         Wynne v. Tufts University School of Medicine ("Wynne II") 649

         NOTES AND QUESTIONS 653

E.   HARASSMENT AND HOSTILE ENVIRONMENTS 653

         Guckenberger v. Boston University 653

         NOTES AND QUESTIONS 662

GLOSSARY G-1

TABLE OF CASES TC-1

TABLE OF STATUTES TS-1

INDEX I-1

Chapter 1

EDUCATING STUDENTS WITH DISABILITIES: CORE LEGAL CONCEPTS

A. INTRODUCTION TO FUNDAMENTAL PRINCIPLES

In 1954, the Supreme Court held in *Brown v. Board of Education*, 347 U.S. 483 (1954), that separate but equal was inherently unequal, and then in 1955, determined in its second *Brown* opinion, *Brown v. Board of Education*, 349 U.S. 294 (1955), that desegregation should be accomplished with "all deliberate speed." The Supreme Court told Americans that:

> Today, education is perhaps the most important function of state and local governments. Compulsory school attendance laws and the great expenditures for education both demonstrate our recognition of the importance of education to our democratic society. It is required in the performance of our most basic public responsibilities, even service in the armed forces. It is the very foundation of good citizenship. Today it is a principal instrument in awakening the child to cultural values, in preparing him for later professional training, and in helping him to adjust normally to his environment. In these days, it is doubtful that any child may reasonably be expected to succeed in life if he is denied the opportunity of an education. Such an opportunity, where the state has undertaken to provide it, is a right which must be made available to all on equal terms.

Brown, 347 U.S. at 495.

This was a crucial message for racial desegregation and also a significant message for other groups who had been excluded from equal educational opportunity, including students with disabilities. Prior to the *Brown* decision, and indeed for some time thereafter, state law either permitted or explicitly required the exclusion of the "weak minded" or physically disabled. Many states that did educate such children provided separate facilities that isolated them from their peers. Inspired by *Brown*, families of students with disabilities organized across the country against such exclusion. Of strategic significance at this stage were the lawsuits filed in a large number of states challenging, on equal protection and other grounds, the exclusion of mentally retarded and other students with disabilities from public school classrooms.

Two district court cases decided in favor of these students in the early 1970s set the stage, in both theory and practice, for what would become the federal government's massive entry into the field of special education: *Pennsylvania Association of Retarded Children v. Pennsylvania*, 343 F. Supp. 279 (E.D. Pa. 1972) (*P.A.R.C.*), and *Mills v. Board of Education of the District of Columbia*, 348 F.

Supp. 866 (D.D.C. 1972). The *P.A.R.C.* and *Mills* decisions stand for the propositions that children with mental and other disabilities cannot be excluded wholesale
from free public education and, where exclusion or differential treatment is
considered, due process must be assured. These principles, indeed much of the
language from these very cases, became the core of federal special education
legislation, the Education for All Handicapped Children Act (EAHCA), enacted in
1975 as Public Law 94-142. The rights of children with disabilities to equal
educational opportunity are now fully grounded in statutory law currently codified
federally as the Individuals with Disabilities Education Act (IDEA), 20 U.S.C.
§ 1400, et seq.

In enacting the initial Education for All Handicapped Children Act, Congress
knew that it was changing the face of American education. The impact would be
wide-reaching and profound both for those students who were previously unrecog-
nized and excluded, and for those who would now become their classmates. The
impact on the structure of schools would also be significant as districts adapted to
providing educational services to their new populations in the least restrictive
environment and to implementing the new procedures that they brought with them
for attaining a free appropriate public education through *individualized* educational programs achieved with extensive parental notification and due process
rights.

In instituting this major federal initiative, Congress brought substantial financial
resources to bear on the education of children with disabilities. While the issue of
"full" funding was present and would remain of significant concern, the carrot of
federal money was put in place. Like other federal spending statutes, the basic
schema was (and is) for the federal government to provide funding conditioned on
the states' compliance with the federal legislation and implementing regulations and
directives. States write plans demonstrating their eligibility and compliance in
several major areas focused on providing a free and appropriate public education
for children with disabilities, through individualized education programs and
related services, all as defined by statute, and all subject to accompanying parental
involvement and due process rights. States retain responsibility for overseeing
IDEA's implementation at the local level.

The elements of a free appropriate public education (FAPE) for children with
disabilities through special education and related services have been refined and
amplified through further legislation and through key judicial opinions. Some of
these approaches evoke principles so central to understanding this area of the law
that they are both introduced here and revisited later. In addition to IDEA, of
primary importance on the legislative front are the anti-discrimination provisions of
section 504 of the Rehabilitation Act of 1973, 29 U.S.C. § 794 (section 504), and of
title II of the Americans with Disabilities Act of 1990 (ADA), 42 U.S.C. § 12101, et
seq., relating to state and local government services. Section 504 and title II provide
additional bases for assuring access and appropriate education and include within
their ambit students who, while disabled, do not otherwise fall within the purview
of the IDEA; unlike IDEA, these laws do not provide student-based federal
funding.

In response to these major congressional initiatives, the Supreme Court has addressed special education in a handful of cases. Of these, two are fundamental to understanding the scope of the law: *Rowley,* which set the standard for "appropriate education," and *Honig,* which addressed concerns for exclusion (and staying put) of certain students with disabilities suspended or expelled on disciplinary grounds. *Board of Education v. Rowley,* 458 U.S. 176 (1982); *Honig v. Doe,* 484 U.S. 305 (1988). Also central is an opinion of the First Circuit which firmly articulated the key zero-reject principle of special education law, *Timothy W. v. Rochester, New Hampshire, School District,* 875 F.2d 954 (1st Cir. 1989).

NOTES AND QUESTIONS

1.   Much is written about special education law, including a good deal about its history. *E.g.*, MARK C. WEBER, SPECIAL EDUCATION LAW AND LITIGATION TREATISE § 1.1 (3d ed. 2008 & supps.). For a popular press piece on IDEA's 25th anniversary, with multiple perspectives, see *IDEA 25: Progress and Problems,* EDUCATION WEEK, SPECIAL REPORT, November/December 2000.

2.   The current version of the federal special education law is codified at 20 U.S.C. § 1400, et seq., with implementing regulations at 34 C.F.R. Part 300. Major amendments to the Education for All Handicapped Children Act occurred in 1990 and 1997. The 1990 amendments renamed the law the Individuals with Disabilities Education Act and abrogated Eleventh Amendment immunity in lawsuits brought under the Act. The 1997 amendments made additional significant changes, including limiting requirements for services for children with disabilities in private schools; clarifying that a free and appropriate education was due special education students who had been suspended or expelled; establishing benchmarks for unilateral private placements of special education students; addressing the inclusion of students with disabilities in statewide assessments; and delineating a series of procedural matters. Most recently, Congress enacted the Individuals with Disabilities Education Improvement Act of 2004, reauthorizing and amending IDEA. The new law changes discipline and hearing procedures, alters service delivery and paperwork requirements, coordinates special education law and the No Child Left Behind initiative, and makes a number of other innovations. Specific sections of the current law are reproduced *infra* Section C. For a discussion of the new law, see Mark C. Weber, *Reflections on the New Individuals with Disabilities Education Improvement Act,* 58 FLA. L. REV. 7 (2006).

B.   FOUNDATION CASES

P.A.R.C. v. PENNSYLVANIA
343 F. Supp. 279 (E.D. Pa. 1972)

In a case challenging exclusion of mentally retarded students from Pennsylvania public schools, the court entered a consent judgment providing extensive rights to due process and a free, appropriate public education.

Rule

Masterson, District Judge.

Π's

This civil rights case, a class action, was brought by the Pennsylvania Association for Retarded Children and the parents of thirteen individual retarded children on behalf of all mentally retarded persons between the ages 6 and 21 whom the Commonwealth of Pennsylvania, through its local school districts and intermediate units, is presently excluding from a program of education and training in the public schools. Named as defendants are the Commonwealth of Pennsylvania, Secretary of Welfare, State Board of Education and thirteen individual school districts scattered throughout the Commonwealth. In addition, plaintiffs have joined all other school districts in the Commonwealth as class defendants of which the named districts are said to be representative.

The exclusions of retarded children complained of are based upon four State statutes: (1) 24 Purd. Stat. Sec. 13-1375, which relieves the State Board of Education from any obligation to educate a child whom a public school psychologist certifies as uneducable and untrainable. The burden of caring for such a child then shifts to the Department of Welfare which has no obligation to provide any educational services for the child; (2) 24 Purd. Stat. Sec. 13-1304, which allows an indefinite postponement of admission to public school of any child who has not attained a mental age of five years; (3) Purd. Stat. Sec. 13-1330, which appears to excuse any child from compulsory school attendance whom a psychologist finds unable to profit therefrom; and (4) 24 Purd. Stat. Sec. 13-1326, which defines compulsory school age as 8 to 17 years but has been used in practice to postpone admissions of retarded children until 8 or to eliminate them from public schools at age 17.

Π's Arg

Plaintiffs allege that Sections 1375 (uneducable and untrainable) and 1304 (mental age of 5 years) are constitutionally infirm both on their faces and as applied in three broad respects. First, plaintiffs argue that these statutes offend due process because they lack any provision for notice and a hearing before a retarded person is either excluded from a public education or a change is made in his educational assignment within the public system. Secondly, they assert that the two provisions violate equal protection because the premise of the statute which necessarily assumes that certain retarded children are uneducable and untrainable lacks a rational basis in fact. Finally, plaintiffs contend that because the Constitution and laws of Pennsylvania guarantee an education to all children, these two sections violate due process in that they arbitrarily and capriciously deny that given right to retarded children. Plaintiffs' third contention also raises a pendent question of state law, that is, whether the Pennsylvania Constitution as well as other laws of the Commonwealth already afford them a right to public education.

settlement agreement

On October 7th, 1971 the parties submitted a Consent Agreement to this Court which, along with the June 18th Stipulation, would settle the entire case. Essentially, this Agreement deals with the four state statutes in an effort to eliminate the alleged equal protection problems. As a proposed cure, the defendants agreed, inter alia, that since "the Commonwealth of Pennsylvania has undertaken to provide a free public education for all of its children between the ages of six and twenty-one years" therefore, "it is the Commonwealth's obligation to place each mentally retarded child in a free, public program of education and training appropriate to the child's capacity."

. . . .

The lengthy Consent Agreement concludes by stating that "[e]very retarded person between the ages of six and twenty-one shall be provided access to a free public program of education and training appropriate to his capacities as soon as possible but in no event later than September 1, 1972."

. . . .

The final matter for our consideration is whether to approve the settlement as fair and reasonable. In arriving at such a decision, we must consider its fairness to both the plaintiffs and the defendants since both groups are classes for which this Court assumes the role of guardian. We consider the defendants, particularly the local districts and intermediate units which comprise the vast bulk of this class. When the objectors entered this case, they expressed alarm at the possible burdens, both administrative and financial, which the due process Stipulation and the Consent Agreement would impose. Subsequent changes in the due process Stipulation, however, eliminated most of the administrative burden, and that allayed the fears of all but the Lancaster-Lebanon Unit.

Lancaster-Lebanon continues to object to the basic concept of a prior due process hearing and asserts that injury flows to the school districts because under the Stipulation they will be unable to remove a disruptive retarded child from regular classes immediately. But this danger is more imagined than real. . . . In any case, the Amended Stipulation on hearings provides that in "extraordinary circumstances" the Director of the Bureau of Special Education may authorize tentative assignment to precede the hearing.

. . . .

We have absolutely no hesitation about approving the Agreements as fair and reasonable to the plaintiffs. Approval means that plaintiff retarded children who heretofore had been excluded from a public program of education and training will no longer be so excluded after September 1, 1972. This is a noble and humanitarian end in which the Commonwealth of Pennsylvania has chosen to join. Today, with the following Order, this group of citizens will have new hope in their quest for a life of dignity and self-sufficiency.

ORDER AND INJUNCTION

And now, this 5th day of May, 1972, it is ordered that the Amended Stipulation and Amended Consent Agreement are approved and adopted as fair and reasonable to all members of both the plaintiff and defendant classes.

It is further ordered that the defendants; the Commonwealth of Pennsylvania, the Secretary of the Department of Education, the State Board of Education, the Secretary of the Department of Public Welfare, the named defendant school districts and intermediate units and each of the school districts and intermediate units in the Commonwealth of Pennsylvania, their officers, employees, agents and successors are enjoined as follows:

(a) from applying Section 1304 of the Public School Code of 1949, 24 Purd. Stat. Sec. 1304, so as to postpone or in any way deny to any mentally retarded child access to a free public program of education and training;

. . . .

(g) to provide, as soon as possible but in no event later than September 1, 1972, to every retarded person between the ages of six and twenty-one years as of the date of this Order and thereafter, access to a free public program of education and training appropriate to his learning capacities;

(h) to provide, as soon as possible but in no event later than September 1, 1972, wherever defendants provide a preschool program of education and training for children aged less than six years of age, access to a free public program of education and training appropriate to his learning capacities to every mentally retarded child of the same age;

(i) to provide notice and the opportunity for a hearing prior to a change in educational status of any child who is mentally retarded or thought to be mentally retarded;

(j) to re-evaluate the educational assignment of every mentally retarded child not less than every two years, or annually upon the parents' request, and upon such re-evaluation, to provide notice and the opportunity for a hearing.

APPENDIX A
AMENDED STIPULATION

And now, this 14th day of February, 1972, subject to the approval and Order of the Court, it is agreed by the parties that the Stipulation of June 18, 1971, be amended to provide as follows:

1. Definitions

(a) "Change in educational status" shall mean any assignment or re-assignment based on the fact that the child is mentally retarded or thought to be mentally retarded to one of the following educational assignments: Regular Education, Special Education or to no assignment, or from one type of special education to another.

. . . .

(e) "Regular Education" shall mean education other than special education.

(f) "Special Education" shall mean special classes, special schools, education and training secured by the local school district or intermediate unit outside the public schools or in special institutions, instruction in the home and tuition reimbursement, as provided in 24 Purd. Stat. Secs. 13-1371 through 13-1380.

(g) Wherever the word "Parent" is mentioned, it will include the term "Guardian" and the plural of each where applicable.

2. No child of school age who is mentally retarded or who is thought by any school official, the intermediate unit, or by his parents or guardian to be mentally retarded, shall be subjected to a change in educational status without first being accorded notice and the opportunity of a due process hearing as hereinafter prescribed. This provision shall also apply to any child who has never had an educational assignment.

Nothing contained herein shall be construed to preclude any system of consultations or conferences with parents heretofore or hereafter used by School Districts or Intermediate Units with regard to the educational assignment of children thought to be mentally retarded. Nor shall such consultations or conferences be in lieu of the due process hearing.

3. Within 30 days of the approval of this Stipulation by the Court herein, the State Board of Education shall adopt regulations, and shall transmit copies thereof to the superintendents of the School Districts and Intermediate Units, the Members of their Boards, and their counsel, which regulations shall incorporate paragraphs 1 and 2 above and otherwise shall provide as follows:

(a) Whenever any mentally retarded or allegedly mentally retarded child of school age is recommended for a change in educational status by a School District, Intermediate Unit or any school official, notice of the proposed action shall first be given to the parent or guardian of the child.

(b) Notice of the proposed action shall be given in writing to the parent or guardian of the child either (i) at a conference with the parent or (ii) by certified mail to the parent (addressee only, return receipt requested).

(c) The notice shall describe the proposed action in detail, including specification of the statute or regulation under which such action is proposed and a clear and full statement of the reasons therefor, including specification of any tests or reports upon which such action is proposed.

(d) The notice shall advise the parent or guardian of any alternative education opportunities available to his child other than that proposed.

(e) The notice shall inform the parent or guardian of his right to contest the proposed action at a full hearing before the Secretary of Education, or his designee, in a place and at a time convenient to the parent, before the proposed action may be taken.

(f) The notice shall inform the parent or guardian of his right to be represented at the hearing by any person of his choosing, including legal counsel, of his right to examine before the hearing his child's school records including any tests or reports upon which the proposed action may be based, of his right to present evidence of his own, including expert medical, psychological and educational testimony, and of his right to call and question any school official, employee, or agent of a school district, intermediate unit or the department who may have evidence upon which the proposed action may be based.

(g) The notice shall inform the parent or guardian of the availability of various organizations, including the local chapter of the Pennsylvania

Association for Retarded Children, to assist him in connection with the hearing and the school district or intermediate unit involved shall provide the address and telephone number of such organization in the notice.

(h) The notice shall inform the parent or guardian that he is entitled under the Pennsylvania Mental Health and Mental Retardation Act to the services of a local center for an independent medical, psychological and educational evaluation of his child and shall specify the name, address and telephone number of the MH-MR center in his catchment area.

(i) The notice shall specify the procedure for pursuing a hearing.

If the notice is given at a conference with the parent, the parent may at that conference indicate his satisfaction with the recommendation and may in writing waive the opportunity for a hearing or, if dissatisfied, may in writing request a hearing. In either event, the parent may within five calendar days of the conference change this decision and may then request or waive the opportunity for a hearing by so indicating in writing to the school district or intermediate unit. If the parental decision is indicated at a conference, the parent shall be given a postcard which shall be mailed to the school district or intermediate unit within five calendar days thereafter, if the parent desires to change the decision. There shall be no change in educational assignment during the five day period.

If notice is given by certified mail, the parent must fill in the form requesting a hearing and mail the same to the school district or intermediate unit within ten (10) days of the date of receipt of the notice.

(j) The hearing shall be scheduled not sooner than fifteen (15) days nor later than thirty (30) days after receipt of the request for a hearing from the parent or guardian, provided however that upon good cause shown, reasonable extensions of these times shall be granted at the request of the parent or guardian.

(k) The hearing shall be held in the local district and at a place reasonably convenient to the parent or guardian of the child. At the option of the parent or guardian, the hearing may be held in the evening and such option shall be set forth in the form requesting the hearing aforesaid.

(l) The hearing officer shall be the Secretary of Education, or a person designated by him acting in his stead, but shall not be an officer, employee or agent of any local district or intermediate unit in which the child resides.

(m) The hearing shall be an oral, personal hearing, and shall be public unless the parent or guardian specifies a closed hearing.

(n) The decision of the hearing officer shall be based solely upon the evidence presented at the hearing.

(o) The proposed change in educational status shall be approved only if supported by substantial evidence on the whole record of the hearing. Introduction by the school district or intermediate unit of the official report recommending a change in educational assignment, provided a copy of such report was given to the parent at the time notice was given, shall discharge its burden of going forward with the evidence, thereby requiring the parent to introduce evidence (as contemplated in paragraphs f, r, s, and t herein) in support of his contention.

(p) A stenographic or other transcribed record of the hearing shall be made and shall be available to the parent or guardian or his representative. Said record may be discarded after three years.

(q) The parent or guardian of the child may be represented at the hearing by any person of his choosing, including legal counsel.

(r) The parent or guardian or his representative shall be given reasonable access prior to the hearing to all records of the school district or intermediate unit concerning his child, including any tests or reports upon which the proposed action may be based.

(s) The parent or guardian or his representative shall have the right to compel the attendance of, and to question any witness testifying for the school board or intermediate unit and any official, employee, or agent of the school district, intermediate unit, or the department who may have evidence upon which the proposed action may be based.

(t) The parent or guardian shall have the right to present evidence and testimony, including expert medical, psychological or educational testimony.

(u) No later than twenty (20) days after the hearing, the hearing officer shall render a decision in writing which shall be accompanied by written findings of fact and conclusions of law and which shall be sent by registered mail to the parent or guardian and his representative.

(v) There shall be no change in the child's educational status without prior notice and the opportunity to be heard as set forth herein, except that in extraordinary circumstances the Director of the Bureau of Special Education, upon written request to him by the district or intermediate unit setting forth the parent, may approve an interim change in educational assignment prior to the hearing, in which event the hearing will be held as promptly as possible after the interim change. The Director shall act upon any such request promptly and in any event within three (3) days of its receipt.

(w) Any time limitation herein shall be construed and applied so as to do substantial justice and may be varied upon request and good cause shown.

4. The Department of Education shall revise its regulations to be in accord with the procedures agreed upon herein, shall disseminate the revised regulations to the school districts and intermediate units and shall thereafter file with the court and plaintiffs a statement of how and to whom said regulations and any covering statements were delivered.

5. Notice and the opportunity of a (sic) the reasons therefor and upon notice to due process hearing, as set out in paragraph 3 above, shall be afforded on and after

the effective date of the stipulation to every child who is mentally retarded or who is thought by any school official, the intermediate unit, or by his parents to be mentally retarded, before subjecting such child to a change in educational status as defined herein.

APPENDIX B

. . . .

4. Expert testimony in this action indicates that all mentally retarded persons are capable of benefiting from a program of education and training; that the greatest number of retarded persons, given such education and training, are capable of achieving self-sufficiency, and the remaining few, with such education and training, are capable of achieving some degree of self-care; that the earlier such education and training begins, the more thoroughly and the more efficiently a mentally retarded person will benefit from it; and, whether begun early or not, that a mentally retarded person can benefit at any point in his life and development from a program of education and training.

5. The Commonwealth of Pennsylvania has undertaken to provide a free public education to all of its children between the ages of six and twenty-one years, and further, has undertaken to provide education and training for all of its mentally retarded children.

6. Having undertaken to provide a free public education to all of its children, including its mentally retarded children, the Commonwealth of Pennsylvania may not deny any mentally retarded child access to a free public program of education and training.

7. It is the Commonwealth's obligation to place each mentally retarded child in a free, public program of education and training appropriate to the child's capacity, within the context of the general educational policy that, among the alternative programs of education and training required by statute to be available, placement in a regular public school class is preferable to placement in a special public school class and placement in a special public school class is preferable to placement in any other type of program of education and training.

. . . .

MILLS v. BOARD OF EDUCATION
OF THE DISTRICT OF COLUMBIA
348 F. Supp. 866 (D.D.C. 1972)

The court ruled that the District of Columbia cannot continue to exclude students who have been labeled as behavioral problems, mentally retarded, emotionally disturbed or hyperactive.

WADDY, DISTRICT JUDGE

This is a civil action brought on behalf of seven children of school age by their next friends in which they seek a declaration of rights and to enjoin the defendants from excluding them from the District of Columbia Public Schools and/or denying them publicly supported education and to compel the defendants to provide them with immediate and adequate education and educational facilities in the public schools or alternative placement at public expense. They also seek additional and ancillary relief to effectuate the primary relief. They allege that although they can profit from an education either in regular classrooms with supportive services or in special classes adopted to their needs, they have been labelled as behavioral problems, mentally retarded, emotionally disturbed or hyperactive, and denied admission to the public schools or excluded therefrom after admission, with no provision for alternative educational placement or periodic review. The action was certified as a class action. . . .

[handwritten margin note: Π's Arg]

The defendants are the Board of Education of the District of Columbia and its members, the Superintendent of Schools for the District of Columbia and subordinate school officials, the Commissioner of the District of Columbia and certain subordinate officials and the District of Columbia.

The genesis of this case is found (1) in the failure of the District of Columbia to provide publicly supported education and training to plaintiffs and other "exceptional" children, members of their class, and (2) the excluding, suspending, expelling, reassigning and transferring of "exceptional" children from regular public school classes without affording them due process of law.

The problem of providing special education for "exceptional" children (mentally retarded, emotionally disturbed, physically handicapped, hyperactive and other children with behavioral problems) is one of major proportions in the District of Columbia. The precise number of such children cannot be stated because the District has continuously failed to comply with Section 31-208 of the District of Columbia Code which requires a census of all children aged 3 to 18 in the District to be taken. Plaintiffs estimate that there are ". . . 22,000 retarded, emotionally disturbed, blind, deaf, and speech or learning disabled children, and perhaps as many as 18,000 of these children are not being furnished with programs of specialized education." According to data prepared by the Board of Education, Division of Planning, Research and Evaluation, the District of Columbia provides publicly supported special education programs of various descriptions to at least 3880 school age children. However, in a 1971 report to the Department of Health, Education and Welfare, the District of Columbia Public Schools admitted that an estimated 12,340 handicapped children were not to be served in the 1971-72 school year.

Each of the minor plaintiffs in this case qualifies as an "exceptional" child.

Plaintiffs allege in their complaint and defendants admit as follows:

"PETER MILLS is twelve years old, black, and a committed dependent ward of the District of Columbia resident at Junior Village. He was excluded from the Brent Elementary School on March 23, 1971, at which time he was in the fourth grade. Peter allegedly was a 'behavior problem' and was recommended and approved for exclusion by the principal. Defendants have not provided him with a full hearing or with a timely and adequate review of his status. Furthermore, Defendants have failed to

[handwritten margin note: D's didn't provide w/ a full hearing]

provide for his reenrollment in the District of Columbia Public Schools or enrollment in private school. On information and belief, numerous other dependent children of school attendance age at Junior Village are denied a publicly-supported education. Peter remains excluded from any publicly-supported education.

"DUANE BLACKSHEARE is thirteen years old, black, resident at Saint Elizabeth's Hospital, Washington, D.C., and a dependent committed child. He was excluded from the Giddings Elementary School in October, 1967, at which time he was in the third grade. Duane allegedly was a 'behavior problem.' Defendants have not provided him with a full hearing or with a timely and adequate review of his status. Despite repeated efforts by his mother, Duane remained largely excluded from all publicly-supported education until February, 1971. Education experts at the Child Study Center examined Duane and found him to be capable of returning to regular class if supportive services were provided. Following several articles in the Washington Post and Washington Star, Duane was placed in a regular seventh grade classroom on a two-hour a day basis without any catch-up assistance and without an evaluation or diagnostic interview of any kind. Duane has remained on a waiting list for a tuition grant and is now excluded from all publicly-supported education.

"GEORGE LIDDELL, JR., is eight years old, black, resident with his mother, Daisy Liddell, at 601 Morton Street, N.W., Washington, D.C., and an AFDC recipient. George has never attended public school because of the denial of his application to the Maury Elementary School on the ground that he required a special class. George allegedly was retarded. Defendants have not provided him with a full hearing or with a timely and adequate review of his status. George remains excluded from all publicly-supported education, despite a medical opinion that he is capable of profiting from schooling, and despite his mother's efforts to secure a tuition grant from Defendants.

"STEVEN GASTON is eight years old, black, resident with his mother, Ina Gaston, at 714 9th Street, N.E., Washington, D. C. and unable to afford private instruction. He has been excluded from the Taylor Elementary School since September, 1969, at which time he was in the first grade. Steven allegedly was slightly brain-damaged and hyperactive, and was excluded because he wandered around the classroom. Defendants have not provided him with a full hearing or with a timely and adequate review of his status. Steven was accepted in the Contemporary School, a private school, provided that tuition was paid in full in advance. Despite the efforts of his parents, Steven has remained on a waiting list for the requisite tuition grant from Defendant school system and excluded from all publicly-supported education.

"MICHAEL WILLIAMS is sixteen years old, black, resident at Saint Elizabeth's Hospital, Washington, D.C., and unable to afford private instruction. Michael is epileptic and allegedly slightly retarded. He has been excluded from the Sharpe Health School since October, 1969, at which time he was temporarily hospitalized. Thereafter Michael was excluded from school because of health problems and school absences. Defendants have not provided him with a full hearing or with a timely and adequate review of his status. Despite his mother's efforts, and his attending physician's medical opinion that he could attend school, Michael has remained on a waiting list for a tuition grant and excluded from all publicly-supported education.

"JANICE KING is thirteen years old, black, resident with her father, Andrew King, at 233 Anacostia Avenue, N.E., Washington, D.C., and unable to afford private instruction. She has been denied access to public schools since reaching compulsory school attendance age, as a result of the rejection of her application, based on the lack of an appropriate educational program. Janice is brain-damaged and retarded, with right hemiplegia, resulting from a childhood illness. Defendants have not provided her with a full hearing or with a timely and adequate review of her status. Despite repeated efforts by her parents, Janice has been excluded from all publicly-supported education.

"JEROME JAMES is twelve years old, black, resident with his mother, Mary James, at 2512 Ontario Avenue, N.W., Washington, D.C., and an AFDC recipient. Jerome is a retarded child and has been totally excluded from public school. Defendants have not given him a full hearing or a timely and adequate review of his status. Despite his mother's efforts to secure either public school placement or a tuition grant, Jerome has remained on a waiting list for a tuition grant and excluded from all publicly supported education."

Although all of the named minor plaintiffs are identified as Negroes the class they represent is not limited by their race. They sue on behalf of and represent all other District of Columbia residents of school age who are eligible for a free public education and who have been, or may be, excluded from such education or otherwise deprived by defendants of access to publicly supported education. *Class Action*

Minor plaintiffs are poor and without financial means to obtain private instruction. There has been no determination that they may not benefit from specialized instruction adapted to their needs. Prior to the beginning of the 1971-72 school year minor plaintiffs, through their representatives, sought to obtain publicly supported education and certain of them were assured by the school authorities that they would be placed in programs of publicly supported education and certain others would be recommended for special tuition grants at private schools. However, none of the plaintiff children were placed for the 1971 Fall term and they continued to be entirely excluded from all publicly supported education. After thus trying unsuccessfully to obtain relief from the Board of Education the plaintiffs filed this action on September 24, 1971.

Congress has decreed a system of publicly supported education for the children of the District of Columbia. The Board of Education has the responsibility of administering that system in accordance with law and of providing such publicly supported education to all of the children of the District, including these "exceptional" children.

Defendants have admitted in these proceedings that they are under an affirmative duty to provide plaintiffs and their class with publicly supported education suited to each child's needs, including special education and tuition grants, and also, a constitutionally adequate prior hearing and periodic review. They have also admitted that they failed to supply plaintiffs with such publicly supported education and have failed to afford them adequate prior hearing and periodic review.

Plaintiffs' entitlement to relief in this case is clear. The applicable statutes and regulations and the Constitution of the United States require it.

Section 31-201 of the District of Columbia Code requires that:

> Every parent, guardian, or other person residing [permanently or temporarily] in the District of Columbia who has custody or control of a child between the ages of seven and sixteen years shall cause said child to be regularly instructed in a public school or in a private or parochial school or instructed privately during the period of each year in which the public schools of the District of Columbia are in session. . . .

Under Section 31-203, a child may be "excused" from attendance only when . . . "upon examination the child is found to be unable mentally or physically to profit from attendance at school: Provided, however, That if such examination shows that such child may benefit from specialized instruction adapted to his needs, he shall attend upon such instruction."

Failure of a parent to comply with Section 31-201 constitutes a criminal offense. The Court need not belabor the fact that requiring parents to see that their children attend school under pain of criminal penalties presupposes that an educational opportunity will be made available to the children. The Board of Education is required to make such opportunity available. . . . It has adopted rules and regulations consonant with the statutory direction. . . .

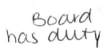

Thus the Board of Education has an obligation to provide whatever specialized instruction that will benefit the child. By failing to provide plaintiffs and their class the publicly supported specialized education to which they are entitled, the Board of Education violates the above statutes and its own regulations.

The Supreme Court in *Brown v. Board of Education*, stated:

> Today, education is perhaps the most important function of state and local governments. Compulsory school attendance laws and the great expenditures for education both demonstrate our recognition of the importance of education to our democratic society. It is required in the performance of our most basic public responsibilities, even service in the armed forces. It is the very foundation of good citizenship. Today it is a principal instrument in awakening the child to cultural values, in preparing him for later professional training, and in helping him to adjust normally to his environment. In these days, it is doubtful that any child may reasonably be expected to succeed in life if he is denied the opportunity of an education. *Such an opportunity, where the state has undertaken to provide it, is a right which must be made available to all on equal terms.* (emphasis supplied)

Bolling v. Sharpe, decided the same day as *Brown*, applied the *Brown* rationale to the District of Columbia public schools by finding that: "Segregation in public education is not reasonably related to any proper governmental objective, and thus it imposes on Negro children of the District of Columbia a burden than constitutes an arbitrary deprivation of their liberty in violation of the Due Process Clause."

Rule

In *Hobson v. Hansen*, Circuit Judge J. Skelly Wright considered the pronouncements of the Supreme Court in the intervening years and . . . concluded "[F]rom these considerations the court draws the conclusion that the doctrine of equal educational opportunity — the equal protection clause in its application to public school education — is in its full sweep a component of due process binding on the District under the due process clause of the Fifth Amendment."

Not only are plaintiffs and their class denied the publicly supported education to which they are entitled many are suspended or expelled from regular schooling or specialized instruction or reassigned without any prior hearing and are given no periodic review thereafter. Due process of law requires a hearing prior to exclusion, termination or classification into a special program. . . .

Due process requires a hearing

The Answer of the defendants to the Complaint contains the following:

These defendants say that it is impossible to afford plaintiffs the relief they request unless:

Δ's Arg

(a) The Congress of the United States appropriates millions of dollars to improve special education services in the District of Columbia; or

insufficient funds.

(b) These defendants divert millions of dollars from funds already specifically appropriated for other educational services in order to improve special educational services. These defendants suggest that to do so would violate an Act of Congress and would be inequitable to children outside the alleged plaintiff class.

This Court is not persuaded by that contention.

The defendants are required by the Constitution of the United States, the District of Columbia Code, and their own regulations to provide a publicly-supported education for these "exceptional" children. Their failure to fulfill this clear duty to include and retain these children in the public school system, or otherwise provide them with publicly-supported education, and their failure to afford them due process hearings and periodical review, cannot be excused by the claim that there are insufficient funds. In *Goldberg v. Kelly*, the Supreme Court, in a case that involved the right of a welfare recipient to a hearing before termination of his benefits, held that Constitutional rights must be afforded citizens despite the greater expense involved. . . . Similarly the District of Columbia's interest in educating the excluded children clearly must outweigh its interest in preserving its financial resources. If sufficient funds are not available to finance all of the services and programs that are needed and desirable in the system then the available funds must be expended equitably in such a manner that no child is entirely excluded from a publicly supported education consistent with his needs and ability to benefit therefrom. The inadequacies of the District of Columbia Public School System whether occasioned by insufficient funding or administrative inefficiency, certainly

Ct rejects arg

Balancing test

Rule

cannot be permitted to bear more heavily on the "exceptional" or handicapped child than on the normal child.

NOTES AND QUESTIONS

P.A.R.C. and *Mills* provided the court-made law which became the basis for the rights which are now afforded by federal and state statutes to students in need of special services, including children with mental retardation. The rights provided by such statutes may be greater than the minimum likely to be secured under a constitutional claim. For example, where rights of persons with mental retardation are raised in a constitutional context, they will be reviewed under a rational basis standard, the courts having found that mental retardation is not a suspect or quasi-suspect class. In *City of Cleburne v. Cleburne Living Center*, 473 U.S. 432 (1985), the Supreme Court considered a challenge to a Texas zoning ordinance which prohibited group homes for mentally retarded persons in a multiple dwelling zone where other groups would be allowed. Finding mentally retarded persons not to be a suspect or quasi-suspect class, the Court held the ordinance unconstitutional on the ground that no rational basis was established to support it. *See also University of Alabama v. Garrett*, 531 U.S. 356 (2001) (finding, in part, that the Fourteenth Amendment generally does not require that states provide special accommodation for persons with disabilities as a matter of equal protection analysis so long as there is a rational basis for the state action). In practical terms, what difference does it make for students with disabilities in public schools whether they are categorized as a quasi-suspect or suspect class?

C. OVERVIEW OF FEDERAL LEGISLATION

1. The Purpose of the Individuals with Disabilities Education Act (IDEA)

In enacting IDEA, Congress spelled out the situation in which children with disabilities found themselves and the Congressional purpose for the federal legislation. IDEA provides:

The purposes of this title are —

(1)(A) to ensure that all children with disabilities have available to them a free appropriate public education that emphasizes special education and related services designed to meet their unique needs and prepare them for further education, employment and independent living;

(B) to ensure that the rights of children with disabilities and parents of such children are protected; and

(C) to assist States, localities, educational service agencies, and Federal agencies to provide for the education of all children with disabilities;

(2) to assist States in the implementation of a statewide, comprehensive, coordinated, multidisciplinary, interagency system of early intervention

services for infants and toddlers with disabilities and their families;

(3) to ensure that educators and parents have the necessary tools to improve educational results for children with disabilities by supporting system improvement activities; coordinated research and personnel preparation; coordinated technical assistance, dissemination, and support; and technology development and media services; and

(4) to assess, and ensure the effectiveness of, efforts to educate children with disabilities.

20 U.S.C. § 1400(d).

2.   Definition of a "Child with a Disability"

(A) In general. The term "child with a disability" means a child —

(i) with mental retardation, hearing impairments (including deafness), speech or language impairments, visual impairments (including blindness), serious emotional disturbance (referred to in this title as "emotional disturbance"), orthopedic impairments, autism, traumatic brain injury, other health impairments, or specific learning disabilities; and

(ii) who, by reason thereof, needs special education and related services.

(B) Child aged 3 through 9. The term "child with a disability" for a child aged 3 through 9 (or any subset of that age range, including ages 3 through 5), may, at the discretion of the State and the local educational agency, include a child —

(i) experiencing developmental delays, as defined by the State and as measured by appropriate diagnostic instruments and procedures, in one or more of the following areas: physical development, cognitive development, communication development, social or emotional development, or adaptive development; and

(ii) who, by reason thereof, needs special education and related services.

20 U.S.C. § 1401(3).

3.   Definition of "Free Appropriate Public Education"

The term "free appropriate public education" means special education and related services that —

(A) have been provided at public expense, under public supervision and direction, and without charge;

(B) meet the standards of the State educational agency;

(C) include an appropriate preschool, elementary, or secondary school education in the State involved; and

(D) are provided in conformity with the individualized education program required under section 614(d) [20 U.S.C. § 1414(d)].

20 U.S.C. § 1401(9).

4.   Definition of "Special Education"

The term "special education" means specially designed instruction, at no cost to parents, to meet the unique needs of a child with a disability, including —

(A) instruction conducted in the classroom, in the home, in hospitals and institutions, and in other settings; and

(B) instruction in physical education.

20 U.S.C. § 1401(29).

5.   Section 504

Section 504 is entitled "Nondiscrimination under Federal Grants and Programs" and provides:

(a) Promulgation of rules and regulations

No otherwise qualified individual with a disability in the United States, as defined in section 705(20) of this title, shall, solely by reason of her or his disability, be excluded from the participation in, be denied the benefits of, or be subjected to discrimination under any program or activity receiving Federal financial assistance or under any program or activity conducted by any Executive agency or by the United States Postal Service. The head of each such agency shall promulgate such regulations as may be necessary to carry out the amendments to this section made by the Rehabilitation, Comprehensive Services, and Developmental Disabilities Act of 1978. Copies of any proposed regulation shall be submitted to appropriate authorizing committees of the Congress, and such regulation may take effect no earlier than the thirtieth day after the date on which such regulation is so submitted to such committees.

(b) "Program or activity" defined

For the purposes of this section, the term "program or activity" means all of the operations of —

(1)(A) a department, agency, special purpose district, or other instrumentality of a State or of a local government; or

(B) the entity of such State or local government that distributes such assistance and each such department or agency (and each other State or local government entity) to which the assistance is extended, in the case of assistance to a State or local government;

(2)(A) a college, university, or other postsecondary institution, or a public system of higher education; or

(B) a local educational agency (as defined in section 7801 of Title 20) system of vocational education, or other school system;

(3)(A) an entire corporation, partnership, or other private organization, or an entire sole proprietorship —

(i) if assistance is extended to such corporation, partnership, private organization, or sole proprietorship as a whole; or

(ii) which is principally engaged in the business of providing education, health care, housing, social services, or parks and recreation; or

(B) the entire plant or other comparable, geographically separate facility to which Federal financial assistance is extended, in the case of any other corporation, partnership, private organization, or sole proprietorship; or

(4) any other entity which is established by two or more of the entities described in paragraph (1), (2), or (3);

any part of which is extended Federal financial assistance.

. . . .

29 U.S.C. § 794.

## 6.	Disability Under the Americans with Disabilities Act (ADA)

The term "disability" means, with respect to an individual —

(A) a physical or mental impairment that substantially limits one or more of the major life activities of such individual;

(B) a record of such an impairment; or

(C) being regarded as having such an impairment.

42 U.S.C. § 12102.

## 7.	Public Entity Under the Americans with Disabilities Act (ADA)

(1) The term "public entity" means —

(A) any State or local government;

(B) any department, agency, special purpose district, or other instrumentality of a State or States or local government; and. . . .

42 U.S.C. § 12131(1).

8.   Qualified Individual with a Disability Under the Americans with Disabilities Act (ADA)

The term "qualified individual with a disability" means an individual with a disability who, with or without reasonable modifications to rules, policies, or practices, the removal of architectural, communication, or transportation barriers, or the provision of auxiliary aids and services, meets the essential eligibility requirements for the receipt of services or the participation in programs or activities provided by a public entity.

42 U.S.C. § 12131(1).

NOTES AND QUESTIONS

1.   Section 504 is codified at 29 U.S.C. § 794, with implementing regulations primarily at 34 C.F.R. Part 104 and 34 C.F.R. Part 104 Appendix A. Section 504, as noted above, predated the Education for All Handicapped Children Act. For the history of the adoption of section 504, see RICHARD K. SCOTCH, FROM GOOD WILL TO CIVIL RIGHTS: TRANSFORMING FEDERAL DISABILITY POLICY (2d ed. 2001). Additional history is found in *Alexander v. Choate*, 469 U.S. 287 (1985), and in the lower court opinion in *Halderman v. Pennhurst State School & Hospital*, 446 F. Supp. 1295 (E.D. Pa. 1977).

2.   Title II of the ADA, which deals with public services from state and local governments, provides, much like section 504, that "no qualified individual with a disability shall, by reason of such disability, be excluded from participation in or be denied the benefits of the services, programs, or activities of a public entity, or be subjected to discrimination by any such entity." This provision is codified at 42 U.S.C. §§ 12131–12132 with implementing regulations primarily at 28 C.F.R. Part 35.

3.   Title III of the ADA, which deals with public accommodations like stores and private, non-religious schools, provides that it shall be discriminatory to "exclude or otherwise deny equal goods, services, facilities, privileges, advantages, accommo-dations, or other opportunities to an individual or entity because of the known disability of an individual with whom the individual or entity is known to have a relationship or association" and specifically prohibits eligibility criteria that screen out individuals with disability, "failure to make reasonable modifications in policies, practices, or procedures, when such modifications are necessary to afford . . . accommodations to individuals with disabilities unless the entity can demonstrate that taking such steps would fundamentally alter the nature of the . . . good, service, facility, privilege, advantage, or accommodation being offered or would result in an undue burden." This part of the ADA is codified at 42 U.S.C. § 12182(b)(1)(E) and (2)(A)(i), with implementing regulations primarily at 28 C.F.R. Part 36. For a discussion of the history of ADA's adoption, see BERNARD D. REAMS JR., PETER J. MCGOVERN & JOHN SCHULTZ, DISABILITY LAW IN THE UNITED STATES: A LEGISLATIVE HISTORY OF THE AMERICANS WITH DISABILITIES ACT OF 1990 (1992). Can you explain how IDEA, section 504, and the ADA provisions fit together? Why would it matter to a school which provision applied to any given student?

4. The 2004 Reauthorization of IDEA added new findings and definitions to specifically address such issues as education of the homeless, education of students with limited English proficiency, and alignment with the Elementary and Secondary Education Act (ESEA/NCLB). These provisions include a definition of highly qualified teachers and core subjects.

5. The 2004 Reauthorization of IDEA changed the purpose section to reflect that special education students are also to be preparing for "further education." 20 U.S.C. § 1400(d)(1)(A). Special education students graduate from high school at low rates as well, just over 32%. Is the change in the law likely to help improve these numbers? *See* Gary Orfield, Daniel Losen, Johanna Wald & Christopher B. Swanson, *Losing Our Future: How Minority Youth are Being Left Behind by the Graduation Rate Crisis*, The Civil Rights Project at Harvard University (Cambridge 2004).

D. DEFINING CASES

Not surprisingly, the statutory provisions concerning the education of special needs students have been much litigated, and many of these cases are discussed throughout the remainder of the text. Here, a few cases are highlighted because they form some very basic parameters of the law of special education around who shall be included and how much education they should receive.

1. Appropriate Education

IDEA revolves around the concept of an appropriate education for students with disabilities. The Supreme Court has provided the key elements for understanding "appropriate" in this context.

BOARD OF EDUCATION v. ROWLEY
458 U.S. 176 (1982)

The school district did not have to provide an interpreter for a deaf student because states are not required to maximize the potential of each handicapped child.   *Rule*

JUSTICE REHNQUIST delivered the opinion of the Court.

This case presents a question of statutory interpretation. Petitioners contend that the Court of Appeals and the District Court misconstrued the requirements imposed by Congress upon States which receive federal funds under the Education of the Handicapped Act. We agree and reverse the judgment of the Court of Appeals.

The Education of the Handicapped Act (Act), provides federal money to assist state and local agencies in educating handicapped children, and conditions such funding upon a State's compliance with extensive goals and procedures. The Act represents an ambitious federal effort to promote the education of handicapped children, and was passed in response to Congress' perception that a majority of handicapped children in the United States "were either totally excluded from schools or [were] sitting idly in regular classrooms awaiting the time when they were old enough to 'drop out.' " The Act's evolution and major provisions shed light on the question of statutory interpretation which is at the heart of this case.

Procedural History

Congress first addressed the problem of educating the handicapped in 1966 when it amended the Elementary and Secondary Education Act of 1965 to establish a grant program "for the purpose of assisting the States in the initiation, expansion, and improvement of programs and projects . . . for the education of handicapped children." That program was repealed in 1970 by the Education of the Handicapped Act, Part B of which established a grant program similar in purpose to the repealed legislation. Neither the 1966 nor the 1970 legislation contained specific guidelines for state use of the grant money; both were aimed primarily at stimulating the States to develop educational resources and to train personnel for educating the handicapped. Dissatisfied with the progress being made under these earlier enactments, and spurred by two District Court decisions holding that handicapped children should be given access to a public education . . . Congress in 1974 greatly increased federal funding for education of the handicapped and for the first time required recipient States to adopt "a goal of providing full educational opportunities to all handicapped children." The 1974 statute was recognized as an interim measure only, adopted "in order to give the Congress an additional year in which to study what if any additional Federal assistance [was] required to enable the States to meet the needs of handicapped children." The ensuing year of study produced the Education for All Handicapped Children Act of 1975.

To qualify under the act:

In order to qualify for federal financial assistance under the Act, a State must demonstrate that it "has in effect a policy that assures all handicapped children the right to a free appropriate public education." 20 U.S.C. § 1412(1). That policy must be reflected in a state plan submitted to and approved by the Secretary of Education, § 1413, which describes in detail the goals, programs, and timetables under which the State intends to educate handicapped children within its borders. §§ 1412, 1413. States receiving money under the Act must provide education to the handicapped by priority, first "to handicapped children who are not receiving an education" and second "to handicapped children . . . with the most severe handicaps who are receiving an inadequate education," § 1412(3), and "to the maximum extent appropriate" must educate handicapped children "with children who are not handicapped." § 1412(5). The Act broadly defines "handicapped children" to include "mentally retarded, hard of hearing, deaf, speech impaired, visually handicapped, seriously emotionally disturbed, orthopedically impaired, [and] other health impaired children, [and] children with specific learning disabilities." § 1401(1).

IEP:

The "free appropriate public education" required by the Act is tailored to the unique needs of the handicapped child by means of an "individualized educational program" (IEP). § 1401(18). The IEP, which is prepared at a meeting between a qualified representative of the local educational agency, the child's teacher, the child's parents or guardian, and, where appropriate, the child, consists of a written document containing

"(A) a statement of the present levels of educational performance of such child, (B) a statement of annual goals, including short-term instructional objectives, (C) a statement of the specific educational services to be provided to such child, and the extent to which such child will be able to participate in regular educational programs, (D) the projected date for initiation and anticipated duration of such services, and (E) appropriate objective criteria and evaluation procedures and schedules for determining, on at least an annual basis, whether instructional objectives are being achieved." § 1401(19).

Local or regional educational agencies must review, and where appropriate revise, each child's IEP at least annually. § 1414(a)(5).

In addition to the state plan and the IEP already described, the Act imposes extensive procedural requirements upon States receiving federal funds under its provisions. Parents or guardians of handicapped children must be notified of any proposed change in "the identification, evaluation, or educational placement of the child or the provision of a free appropriate public education to such child," and must be permitted to bring a complaint about "any matter relating to" such evaluation and education. §§ 1415(b)(1)(D) and (E). Complaints brought by parents or guardians must be resolved at "an impartial due process hearing," and appeal to the state educational agency must be provided if the initial hearing is held at the local or regional level. §§ 1415(b)(2) and (c). Thereafter, "[a]ny party aggrieved by the findings and decision" of the state administrative hearing has "the right to bring a civil action with respect to the complaint . . . in any State court of competent jurisdiction or in a district court of the United States without regard to the amount in controversy." § 1415(e)(2).

Thus, although the Act leaves to the States the primary responsibility for developing and executing educational programs for handicapped children, it imposes significant requirements to be followed in the discharge of that responsibility. Compliance is assured by provisions permitting the withholding of federal funds upon determination that a participating state or local agency has failed to satisfy the requirements of the Act, §§ 1414(b)(2)(A), 1416, and by the provision for judicial review. At present, all States except New Mexico receive federal funds under the portions of the Act at issue today.

This case arose in connection with the education of Amy Rowley, a deaf student at the Furnace Woods School in the Hendrick Hudson Central School District, Peekskill, N.Y. Amy has minimal residual hearing and is an excellent lipreader. During the year before she began attending Furnace Woods, a meeting between her parents and school administrators resulted in a decision to place her in a regular kindergarten class in order to determine what supplemental services would be necessary to her education. Several members of the school administration prepared for Amy's arrival by attending a course in sign-language interpretation, and a teletype machine was installed in the principal's office to facilitate communication with her parents who are also deaf. At the end of the trial period it was determined that Amy should remain in the kindergarten class, but that she should be provided with an FM hearing aid which would amplify words spoken into a wireless receiver by the teacher or fellow students during certain classroom activities. Amy successfully completed her kindergarten year.

As required by the Act, an IEP was prepared for Amy during the fall of her first-grade year. The IEP provided that Amy should be educated in a regular classroom at Furnace Woods, should continue to use the FM hearing aid, and should receive instruction from a tutor for the deaf for one hour each day and from a speech therapist for three hours each week. The Rowleys agreed with parts of the IEP, but insisted that Amy also be provided a qualified sign-language interpreter in all her academic classes in lieu of the assistance proposed in other parts of the IEP. Such an interpreter had been placed in Amy's kindergarten class for a 2-week experimental period, but the interpreter had reported that Amy did not need his services at that time. The school administrators likewise concluded that Amy did not need such an interpreter in her first-grade classroom. They reached this conclusion after consulting the school district's Committee on the Handicapped, which had received expert evidence from Amy's parents on the importance of a sign-language interpreter, received testimony from Amy's teacher and other persons familiar with her academic and social progress, and visited a class for the deaf.

When their request for an interpreter was denied, the Rowleys demanded and received a hearing before an independent examiner. After receiving evidence from both sides, the examiner agreed with the administrators' determination that an interpreter was not necessary because "Amy was achieving educationally, academically, and socially" without such assistance. The examiner's decision was affirmed on appeal by the New York Commissioner of Education on the basis of substantial evidence in the record. Pursuant to the Act's provision for judicial review, the Rowleys then brought an action in the United States District Court for the Southern District of New York, claiming that the administrators' denial of the sign-language interpreter constituted a denial of the "free appropriate public education" guaranteed by the Act.

The District Court found that Amy "is a remarkably well-adjusted child" who interacts and communicates well with her classmates and has "developed an extraordinary rapport" with her teachers. It also found that "she performs better than the average child in her class and is advancing easily from grade to grade," but "that she understands considerably less of what goes on in class than she could if she were not deaf" and thus "isn't learning as much, or performing as well academically, as she would without her handicap". . . . This disparity between Amy's achievement and her potential led the court to decide that she was not receiving a "free appropriate public education," which the court defined as "an opportunity to achieve [her] full potential commensurate with the opportunity provided to other children."

A divided panel of the United States Court of Appeals for the Second Circuit affirmed.

We granted certiorari to review the lower courts' interpretation of the Act. Such review requires us to consider two questions: What is meant by the Act's requirement of a "free appropriate public education"? And what is the role of state and federal courts in exercising the review granted by 20 U.S.C. § 1415? We consider these questions separately.

This is the first case in which this Court has been called upon to interpret any provision of the Act.

. . . .

It is beyond dispute that, contrary to the conclusions of the courts below, the Act does expressly define "free appropriate public education":

> "The term 'free appropriate public education' means special education and related services which (A) have been provided at public expense, under public supervision and direction, and without charge, (B) meet the standards of the State educational agency, (C) include an appropriate preschool, elementary, or secondary school education in the State involved, and (D) are provided in conformity with the individualized education program required under section 1414(a)(5) of this title."

§ 1401(18). . . .

> "Special education," as referred to in this definition, means "specially designed instruction, at no cost to parents or guardians, to meet the unique needs of a handicapped child, including classroom instruction, instruction in physical education, home instruction, and instruction in hospitals and institutions." § 1401(16).

> "Related services" are defined as "transportation, and such developmental, corrective, and other supportive services . . . as may be required to assist a handicapped child to benefit from special education."

§ 1401(17).

Like many statutory definitions, this one tends toward the cryptic rather than the comprehensive, but that is scarcely a reason for abandoning the quest for legislative intent. We think more must be made of it than either respondents or the United States seems willing to admit.

According to the definitions contained in the Act, a "free appropriate public education" consists of educational instruction specially designed to meet the unique needs of the handicapped child, supported by such services as are necessary to permit the child "to benefit" from the instruction. Almost as a checklist for adequacy under the Act, the definition also requires that such instruction and services be provided at public expense and under public supervision, meet the State's educational standards, approximate the grade levels used in the State's regular education, and comport with the child's IEP. Thus, if personalized instruction is being provided with sufficient supportive services to permit the child to benefit from the instruction, and the other items on the definitional checklist are satisfied, the child is receiving a "free appropriate public education" as defined by the Act.

Other portions of the statute also shed light upon congressional intent. Congress found that of the roughly eight million handicapped children in the United States at the time of enactment, one million were "excluded entirely from the public school system" and more than half were receiving an inappropriate education. In addition, . . . the Act requires States to extend educational services first to those children who are receiving no education and second to those children who are receiving an "inadequate education." When these express statutory findings and priorities are read together with the Act's extensive procedural requirements and its definition of "free appropriate public education," the face of the statute evinces a congressional intent to bring previously excluded handicapped children into the public education systems of the States and to require the States to adopt *procedures* which would result in individualized consideration of and instruction for each child.

[handwritten margin note: definition + congression intent]

Noticeably absent from the language of the statute is any substantive standard prescribing the level of education to be accorded handicapped children. Certainly the language of the statute contains no requirement like the one imposed by the lower courts — that States maximize the potential of handicapped children "commensurate with the opportunity provided to other children." That standard was expounded by the District Court without reference to the statutory definitions or even to the legislative history of the Act. Although we find the statutory definition of "free appropriate public education" to be helpful in our interpretation of the Act, there remains the question of whether the legislative history indicates a congressional intent that such education meet some additional substantive standard. For an answer, we turn to that history.

. . . Before passage of the Act some States had passed laws to improve the educational services afforded handicapped children, but many of these children were excluded completely from any form of public education or were left to fend for themselves in classrooms designed for education of their nonhandicapped peers. [T]he House Report begins by emphasizing this exclusion and misplacement, noting that millions of handicapped children "were either totally excluded from schools or [were] sitting idly in regular classrooms awaiting the time when they were old enough to 'drop out.' " One of the Act's two principal sponsors in the Senate urged its passage in similar terms: "While much progress has been made in the last few years, we can take no solace in that progress until all handicapped children are, in fact, receiving an education. The most recent statistics provided by the Bureau of Education for the Handicapped estimate that . . . 1.75 million handicapped children do not receive any educational services, and 2.5 million handicapped children are not receiving an appropriate education."

By passing the Act, Congress sought primarily to make public education available to handicapped children. But in seeking to provide such access to public education, Congress did not impose upon the States any greater substantive educational standard than would be necessary to make such access meaningful. Indeed, Congress expressly "recognize[d] that in many instances the process of providing special education and related services to handicapped children is not guaranteed to produce any particular outcome." Thus, the intent of the Act was more to open the door of public education to handicapped children on appropriate terms than to guarantee any particular level of education once inside.

Mills and *P.A.R.C.* both held that handicapped children must be given *access to* an adequate, publicly supported education. Neither case purports to require any particular substantive level of education. Rather, like the language of the Act, the cases set forth extensive procedures to be followed in formulating personalized educational programs for handicapped children.[1] The fact that both *PARC* and *Mills* are discussed at length in the legislative Reports suggests that the principles which they established are the principles which, to a significant extent, guided the drafters of the Act.

That the Act imposes no clear obligation upon recipient States beyond the requirement that handicapped children receive some form of specialized education is perhaps best demonstrated by the fact that Congress, in explaining the need for the Act, equated an "appropriate education" to the receipt of some specialized educational services. It is evident from the legislative history that the characterization of handicapped children as "served" referred to children who were receiving some form of specialized educational services from the States, and that the characterization of children as "unserved" referred to those who were receiving no specialized educational services. . . .

Respondents contend that "the goal of the Act is to provide each handicapped child with an equal educational opportunity." We think, however, that the requirement that a State provide specialized educational services to handicapped children generates no additional requirement that the services so provided be sufficient to maximize each child's potential "commensurate with the opportunity provided other children."

[handwritten margin note: Π 's Arg.]

The educational opportunities provided by our public school systems undoubtedly differ from student to student, depending upon a myriad of factors that might affect a particular student's ability to assimilate information presented in the classroom. The requirement that States provide "equal" educational opportunities would thus seem to present an entirely unworkable standard requiring impossible measurements and comparisons. Similarly, furnishing handicapped children with only such services as are available to nonhandicapped children would in all probability fall short of the statutory requirement of "free appropriate public education"; to require, on the other hand, the furnishing of every special service necessary to maximize each handicapped child's potential is, we think, further than Congress intended to go. Thus to speak in terms of "equal" services in one instance gives less than what is required by the Act and in another instance more. The theme of the Act is "free appropriate public education," a phrase which is too complex to be captured by the word "equal" whether one is speaking of opportunities or services.

[handwritten margin note: Ct's reasoning]

The legislative conception of the requirements of equal protection was undoubtedly informed by the two District Court decisions referred to above. But cases such as *Mills* and *P.A.R.C.* held simply that handicapped children may not be excluded

---

[1] [FN 16] Like the Act, *P.A.R.C.* required the State to "identify, locate, [and] evaluate" handicapped children, to create for each child an individual educational program, and to hold a hearing "on any change in educational assignment." *Mills* also required the preparation of an individual educational program for each child. In addition, *Mills* permitted the child's parents to inspect records relevant to the child's education, to obtain an independent educational evaluation of the child, to object to the IEP and receive a hearing before an independent hearing officer, to be represented by counsel at the hearing, and to have the right to confront and cross-examine adverse witnesses, all of which are also permitted by the Act. Like the Act, *Mills* also required that the education of handicapped children be conducted pursuant to an overall plan prepared by the District of Columbia, and established a policy of educating handicapped children with nonhandicapped children whenever possible.

entirely from public education. In *Mills*, the District Court said:

> "If sufficient funds are not available to finance all of the services and programs that are needed and desirable in the system then the available funds must be expended equitably in such a manner that no child is entirely excluded from a publicly supported education consistent with his needs and ability to benefit therefrom."

The *P.A.R.C.* court used similar language, saying "[i]t is the commonwealth's obligation to place each mentally retarded child in a free, public program of education and training appropriate to the child's capacity. . . ." The right of access to free public education enunciated by these cases is significantly different from any notion of absolute equality of opportunity regardless of capacity. To the extent that Congress might have looked further than these cases which are mentioned in the legislative history, at the time of enactment of the Act this Court had held at least twice that the Equal Protection Clause of the Fourteenth Amendment does not require States to expend equal financial resources on the education of each child. *San Antonio Independent School Dist. v. Rodriguez.* In explaining the need for federal legislation, the House Report noted that "no congressional legislation has required a precise guarantee for handicapped children, i.e. a basic floor of opportunity that would bring into compliance all school districts with the constitutional right of equal protection with respect to handicapped children." Assuming that the Act was designed to fill the need identified in the House Report — that is, to provide a "basic floor of opportunity" consistent with equal protection — neither the Act nor its history persuasively demonstrates that Congress thought that equal protection required anything more than equal access. . . .

Implicit in the congressional purpose of providing access to a "free appropriate public education" is the requirement that the education to which access is provided be sufficient to confer some educational benefit upon the handicapped child. It would do little good for Congress to spend millions of dollars in providing access to a public education only to have the handicapped child receive no benefit from that education. The statutory definition of "free appropriate public education," in addition to requiring that States provide each child with "specially designed instruction," expressly requires the provision of "such . . . supportive services . . . as may be required to assist a handicapped child *to benefit* from special education." § 1401(17). (emphasis added). We therefore conclude that the "basic floor of opportunity" provided by the Act consists of access to specialized instruction and related services which are individually designed to provide educational benefit to the handicapped child.

The determination of when handicapped children are receiving sufficient educational benefits to satisfy the requirements of the Act presents a more difficult problem. The Act requires participating States to educate a wide spectrum of handicapped children, from the marginally hearing-impaired to the profoundly retarded and palsied. It is clear that the benefits obtainable by children at one end of the spectrum will differ dramatically from those obtainable by children at the other end, with infinite variations in between. One child may have little difficulty competing successfully in an academic setting with nonhandicapped children while another child may encounter great difficulty in acquiring even the most basic of self-maintenance skills. We do not attempt today to establish any one test for determining the adequacy of educational benefits conferred upon all children covered by the Act. Because in this case we are presented with a handicapped child who is receiving substantial specialized instruction and related services, and who is performing above average in the regular classrooms of a public school system, we confine our analysis to that situation.

The Act requires participating States to educate handicapped children with nonhandicapped children whenever possible. When that "mainstreaming" preference of the Act has been met and a child is being educated in the regular classrooms of a public school system, the system itself monitors the educational progress of the child. Regular examinations are administered, grades are awarded, and yearly advancement to higher grade levels is permitted for those children who attain an adequate knowledge of the course material. The grading and advancement system thus constitutes an important factor in determining educational benefit. Children who graduate from our public school systems are considered by our society to have been "educated" at least to the grade level they have completed, and access to an "education" for handicapped children is precisely what Congress sought to provide in the Act.

When the language of the Act and its legislative history are considered together, the requirements imposed by Congress become tolerably clear. Insofar as a State is required to provide a handicapped child with a "free appropriate public education," we hold that it satisfies this requirement by providing personalized instruction with sufficient support services to permit the child to benefit educationally from that instruction. Such instruction and services must be provided at public expense, must meet the State's educational standards, must approximate the grade levels used in the State's regular education, and must comport with the child's IEP. In addition, the IEP, and therefore the personalized instruction, should be formulated in accordance with the requirements of the Act and, if the child is being educated in the regular classrooms of the public education system, should be reasonably calculated to enable the child to achieve passing marks and advance from grade to grade.

Cts reasoning

. . . .

As mentioned in Part I, the Act permits "[a]ny party aggrieved by the findings and decision" of the state administrative hearings "to bring a civil action" in "any State court of competent jurisdiction or in a district court of the United States without regard to the amount in controversy." § 1415(e)(2). The complaint, and therefore the civil action, may concern "any matter relating to the identification, evaluation, or educational placement of the child, or the provision of a free appropriate public education to such child." § 1415(b)(1)(E). In reviewing the complaint, the Act provides that a court "shall receive the record of the [state] administrative proceedings, shall hear additional evidence at the request of a party, and, basing its decision on the preponderance of the evidence, shall grant such relief as the court determines is appropriate."

. . . .

But although we find that this grant of authority is broader than claimed by petitioners, we think the fact that it is found in § 1415, which is entitled "Procedural safeguards," is not without significance. When the elaborate and highly specific procedural safeguards embodied in § 1415 are contrasted with the general and somewhat imprecise substantive admonitions contained in the Act, we think that the importance Congress attached to these procedural safeguards cannot be gainsaid. It seems to us no exaggeration to say that Congress placed every bit as much emphasis upon compliance with procedures giving parents and guardians a large measure of participation at every stage of the administrative process, *see, e.g.*, §§ 1415(a)–(d), as it did upon the measurement of the resulting IEP against a substantive standard. We think that the congressional emphasis upon full participation of concerned parties throughout the development of the IEP, as well as the requirements that state and local plans be submitted to the Secretary for approval, demonstrates the legislative conviction that adequate compliance with the procedures prescribed would in most cases assure much if not all of what Congress wished in the way of substantive content in an IEP.

Thus the provision that a reviewing court base its decision on the "preponderance of the evidence" is by no means an invitation to the courts to substitute their own notions of sound educational policy for those of the school authorities which they review. The very importance which Congress has attached to compliance with certain procedures in the preparation of an IEP would be frustrated if a court were permitted simply to set state decisions at naught. The fact that § 1415(e) requires that the reviewing court "receive the records of the [state] administrative proceedings" carries with it the implied requirement that due weight shall be given to these proceedings. And we find nothing in the Act to suggest that merely because Congress was rather sketchy in establishing substantive requirements, as opposed to procedural requirements for the preparation of an IEP, it intended that reviewing courts should have a free hand to impose substantive standards of review which cannot be derived from the Act itself. In short, the statutory authorization to grant "such relief as the court determines is appropriate" cannot be read without reference to the obligations, largely procedural in nature, which are imposed upon recipient States by Congress.

Therefore, a court's inquiry in suits brought under § 1415(e)(2) is twofold. First, has the State complied with the procedures set forth in the Act? And second, is the individualized educational program developed through the Act's procedures reasonably calculated to enable the child to receive educational benefits? If these requirements are met, the State has complied with the obligations imposed by Congress and the courts can require no more.

In assuring that the requirements of the Act have been met, courts must be careful to avoid imposing their view of preferable educational methods upon the States. The primary responsibility for formulating the education to be accorded a handicapped child, and for choosing the educational method most suitable to the child's needs, was left by the Act to state and local educational agencies in cooperation with the parents or guardian of the child.

We previously have cautioned that courts lack the "specialized knowledge and experience" necessary to resolve "persistent and difficult questions of educational policy." *San Antonio*. We think that Congress shared that view when it passed the

Act. As already demonstrated, Congress' intention was not that the Act displace the primacy of States in the field of education, but that States receive funds to assist them in extending their educational systems to the handicapped. Therefore, once a court determines that the requirements of the Act have been met, questions of methodology are for resolution by the States.

Applying these principles to the facts of this case, we conclude that the Court of Appeals erred in affirming the decision of the District Court. Neither the District Court nor the Court of Appeals found that petitioners had failed to comply with the procedures of the Act, and the findings of neither court would support a conclusion that Amy's educational program failed to comply with the substantive requirements of the Act. On the contrary, the District Court found that the "evidence firmly establishes that Amy is receiving an 'adequate' education, since she performs better than the average child in her class and is advancing easily from grade to grade." In light of this finding, and of the fact that Amy was receiving personalized instruction and related services calculated by the Furnace Woods school administrators to meet her educational needs, the lower courts should not have concluded that the Act requires the provision of a sign-language interpreter. Accordingly, the decision of the Court of Appeals is reversed, and the case is remanded for further proceedings consistent with this opinion.[2]

JUSTICE BLACKMUN filed an opinion concurring in the judgment. [omitted]

JUSTICE WHITE filed a dissenting opinion, in which JUSTICES BRENNAN and MARSHALL joined. [omitted]

NOTES AND QUESTIONS

1.   As the Supreme Court observes, the statute does not offer a "substantive standard" for the level of education to be provided to children with disabilities. Here the Court tells us that "appropriate" does not mean "best." In terms of the purposes of the statute requiring the education of all handicapped students, is this interpretation the most suitable? In terms of the practicalities? States were free to adopt a higher standard, and some have. The standard is discussed further *infra* Chapter 4 (Free, Appropriate Public Education). *Rowley* places heavy reliance on procedure. If the correct procedures are followed, will the right result follow? If the procedures are not followed, should the decision be invalidated on these grounds? Does this approach keep adequate attention focused on the child?

2.   The procedural burdens of IDEA have been the subject of much review and discussion. The President's Commission on Excellence in Special Education, established by Executive Order #13227 by President George W. Bush, concluded "Finding 1: IDEA is generally providing basic legal safeguards and access for children with disabilities. However, the current system often places process above

---

[2]   [FN 32] Because the District Court declined to reach respondents' contention that petitioners had failed to comply with the Act's procedural requirements in developing Amy's IEP, the case must be remanded for further proceedings consistent with this opinion.

results, and bureaucratic compliance above student achievement, excellence and outcomes. The system is driven by complex regulations, excessive paperwork and ever-increasing administrative demands at all levels — for the child, the parent, the local education agency and the state education agency. Too often, simply qualifying for special education becomes an end-point — not a gateway to more effective instruction and strong intervention." *A New Era: Revitalizing Special Education for Children and their Families* (2002), *available at* http://www.ed.gov/inits/commissionsboards/whspecialeducation/reports/index.html. Changes were made in the 2004 Reauthorization of IDEA to respond to some of these concerns.

3.   Computerized legal citation services keep track of the number of times a court opinion is referred to in later opinions. *Rowley* has been discussed (not merely cited) more than 750 times as lower courts attempt to put the Supreme Court's view of "appropriate" into practice in diverse factual situations.

2.   Student Discipline and Maintenance of Placement

HONIG v. DOE
484 U.S. 305 (1988)

In a case involving students with serious behavioral problems, the Supreme Court refused to read into the federal statute a dangerousness exception to the mandate to educate all children with disabilities.

JUSTICE BRENNAN delivered the opinion of the Court [in part].

As a condition of federal financial assistance, the Education of the Handicapped Act requires States to ensure a "free appropriate public education" for all disabled children within their jurisdictions. In aid of this goal, the Act establishes a comprehensive system of procedural safeguards designed to ensure parental participation in decisions concerning the education of their disabled children and to provide administrative and judicial review of any decisions with which those parents disagree. Among these safeguards is the so-called "stay-put" provision, which directs that a disabled child "shall remain in [his or her] then current educational placement" pending completion of any review proceedings, unless the parents and state or local educational agencies otherwise agree. 20 U.S.C. § 1415(e)(3). Today we must decide whether, in the face of this statutory proscription, state or local school authorities may nevertheless unilaterally exclude disabled children from the classroom for dangerous or disruptive conduct growing out of their disabilities. In addition, we are called upon to decide whether a district court may, in the exercise of its equitable powers, order a State to provide educational services directly to a disabled child when the local agency fails to do so.

ISSUE <

In the Education of the Handicapped Act (EHA or the Act) Congress sought "to assure that all handicapped children have available to them . . . a free appropriate public education which emphasizes special education and related services designed to meet their unique needs, [and] to assure that the rights of handicapped children and their parents or guardians are protected." When the law was passed in 1975, Congress had before it ample evidence that such legislative assurances were sorely needed: 21 years after this Court declared education to be "perhaps the most important function of state and local governments," congressional studies revealed that better than half of the Nation's 8 million disabled children were not receiving appropriate educational services. Indeed, one out of every eight of these children was excluded from the public school system altogether, many others were simply "warehoused" in special classes or were neglectfully shepherded through the system until they were old enough to drop out. Among the most poorly served of disabled students were emotionally disturbed children: Congressional statistics revealed that for the school year immediately preceding passage of the Act, the educational needs of 82 percent of all children with emotional disabilities went unmet.

In responding to these problems, Congress did not content itself with passage of a simple funding statute. Rather, the EHA confers upon disabled students an enforceable substantive right to public education in participating States, and conditions federal financial assistance upon a State's compliance with the substantive and procedural goals of the Act. Accordingly, States seeking to qualify for federal funds must develop policies assuring all disabled children the "right to a free appropriate public education," and must file with the Secretary of Education formal plans mapping out in detail the programs, procedures, and timetables under which they will effectuate these policies. Such plans must assure that, "to the maximum extent appropriate," States will "mainstream" disabled children, *i.e.*, that they will educate them with children who are not disabled, and that they will segregate or otherwise remove such children from the regular classroom setting "only when the nature or severity of the handicap is such that education in regular classes . . . cannot be achieved satisfactorily."

The primary vehicle for implementing these congressional goals is the "individualized educational program" (IEP), which the EHA mandates for each disabled child.

Envisioning the IEP as the centerpiece of the statute's education delivery system for disabled children, and aware that schools had all too often denied such children appropriate educations without in any way consulting their parents, Congress repeatedly emphasized throughout the Act the importance and indeed the necessity of parental participation in both the development of the IEP and any subsequent assessments of its effectiveness. Accordingly, the Act establishes various procedural safeguards that guarantee parents both an opportunity for meaningful input into all decisions affecting their child's education and the right to seek review of any decisions they think inappropriate. These safeguards include the right to examine all relevant records pertaining to the identification, evaluation, and educational placement of their child; prior written notice whenever the responsible educational agency proposes (or refuses) to change the child's placement or program; an opportunity to present complaints concerning any aspect of the local agency's provision of a free appropriate public education; and an opportunity for "an impartial due process hearing" with respect to any such complaints.

At the conclusion of any such hearing, both the parents and the local educational agency may seek further administrative review and, where that proves unsatisfactory, may file a civil action in any state or federal court. In addition to reviewing the administrative record, courts are empowered to take additional evidence at the request of either party and to "grant such relief as [they] determine is appropriate." The "stay-put" provision at issue in this case governs the placement of a child while these often lengthy review procedures run their course. It directs that:

> "During the pendency of any proceedings conducted pursuant to unless the State or local educational agency and the parents or guardian otherwise agree, the child shall remain in the then current educational placement of such child. . . ." § 1415(a)(3).

The present dispute grows out of the efforts of certain officials of the San Francisco Unified School District (SFUSD) to expel two emotionally disturbed children from school indefinitely for violent and disruptive conduct related to their disabilities. In November 1980, respondent John Doe assaulted another student at the Louise Lombard School, a developmental center for disabled children. Doe's April 1980 IEP identified him as a socially and physically awkward 17-year-old who experienced considerable difficulty controlling his impulses and anger. Among the goals set out in his IEP was "[i]mprovement in [his] ability to relate to [his] peers [and to] cope with frustrating situations without resorting to aggressive acts." Frustrating situations, however, were an unfortunately prominent feature of Doe's school career: physical abnormalities, speech difficulties, and poor grooming habits had made him the target of teasing and ridicule as early as the first grade, his 1980 IEP reflected his continuing difficulties with peers, noting that his social skills had deteriorated and that he could tolerate only minor frustration before exploding.

On November 6, 1980, Doe responded to the taunts of a fellow student in precisely the explosive manner anticipated by his IEP: he choked the student with sufficient force to leave abrasions on the child's neck, and kicked out a school window while being escorted to the principal's office afterwards. Doe admitted his misconduct and the school subsequently suspended him for five days. Thereafter, his principal referred the matter to the SFUSD Student Placement Committee (SPC or Committee) with the recommendation that Doe be expelled. On the day the suspension was to end, the SPC notified Doe's mother that it was proposing to exclude her child permanently from SFUSD and was therefore extending his suspension until such time as the expulsion proceedings were completed. The Committee further advised her that she was entitled to attend the November 25 hearing at which it planned to discuss the proposed expulsion.

After unsuccessfully protesting these actions by letter, Doe brought this suit against a host of local school officials and the State Superintendent of Public Instruction. Alleging that the suspension and proposed expulsion violated the EHA, he sought a temporary restraining order canceling the SPC hearing and requiring school officials to convene an IEP meeting. The District Judge granted the requested injunctive relief and further ordered defendants to provide home tutoring for Doe on an interim basis; shortly thereafter, she issued a preliminary injunction directing defendants to return Doe to his then current educational placement at Louise Lombard School pending completion of the IEP review process. Doe reentered school on December 15, 51/2 weeks, and 24 schooldays, after his initial suspension.

Respondent Jack Smith was identified as an emotionally disturbed child by the time he entered the second grade in 1976. School records prepared that year indicated that he was unable "to control verbal or physical outburst[s]" and exhibited a "[s]evere disturbance in relationships with peers and adults." Further evaluations subsequently revealed that he had been physically and emotionally abused as an infant and young child and that, despite above average intelligence, he experienced academic and social difficulties as a result of extreme hyperactivity and low self-esteem. Of particular concern was Smith's propensity for verbal hostility; one evaluator noted that the child reacted to stress by "attempt[ing] to cover his feelings of low self worth through aggressive behavior[,] . . . primarily verbal provocations." Based on these evaluations, SFUSD placed Smith in a learning center for emotionally disturbed children. His grandparents, however, believed that his needs would be better served in the public school setting and, in September 1979, the school district acceded to their requests and enrolled him at A.P. Giannini Middle School. His February 1980 IEP recommended placement in a Learning Disability Group, stressing the need for close supervision and a highly structured environment. Like earlier evaluations, the February 1980 IEP noted that Smith was easily distracted, impulsive, and anxious; it therefore proposed a half-day schedule and suggested that the placement be undertaken on a trial basis.

At the beginning of the next school year, Smith was assigned to a full-day program; almost immediately thereafter he began misbehaving. School officials met twice with his grandparents in October 1980 to discuss returning him to a half-day program; although the grandparents agreed to the reduction, they apparently were never apprised of their right to challenge the decision through EHA procedures. The school officials also warned them that if the child continued his disruptive behavior — which included stealing, extorting money from fellow students, and making sexual comments to female classmates — they would seek to expel him. On November 14, they made good on this threat, suspending Smith for five days after he made further lewd comments. His principal referred the matter to the SPC, which recommended exclusion from SFUSD. As it did in John Doe's case, the Committee scheduled a hearing and extended the suspension indefinitely pending a final disposition in the matter. On November 28, Smith's counsel protested these actions on grounds essentially identical to those raised by Doe, and the SPC agreed to cancel the hearing and to return Smith to a half-day program at A.P. Giannini or to provide home tutoring. Smith's grandparents chose the latter option and the school began home instruction on December 10; on January 6, 1981, an IEP team convened to discuss alternative placements.

After learning of Doe's action, Smith sought and obtained leave to intervene in the suit. The District Court subsequently entered summary judgment in favor of respondents on their EHA claims and issued a permanent injunction. . . .

On appeal, the Court of Appeals for the Ninth Circuit affirmed the orders with slight modifications. Agreeing with the District Court that an indefinite suspension in aid of expulsion constitutes a prohibited "change in placement" under § 1415(e)(3), the Court of Appeals held that the stay-put provision admitted of no "dangerousness" exception and that the statute therefore rendered invalid those provisions of the California Education Code permitting the indefinite suspension or expulsion of disabled children for misconduct arising out of their disabilities. The court concluded, however, that fixed suspensions of up to 30 schooldays did not fall within the reach of § 1415(e)(3), and therefore upheld recent amendments to the state Education Code authorizing such suspensions. Lastly, the court affirmed that portion of the injunction requiring the State to provide services directly to a disabled child when the local educational agency fails to do so.

Petitioner Bill Honig, California Superintendent of Public Instruction, sought review in this Court, claiming that the Court of Appeals' construction of the stay-put provision conflicted with that of several other Courts of Appeals which had recognized a dangerousness exception, and that the direct services ruling placed an intolerable burden on the State. We granted certiorari to resolve these questions, and now affirm.

[The court determined that the case was not moot as to Smith, for the wrong was capable of repetition.]

The language of § 1415(e)(3) is unequivocal. It states plainly that during the pendency of any proceedings initiated under the Act, unless the state or local educational agency and the parents or guardian of a disabled child otherwise agree, "the child *shall* remain in the then current educational placement." Faced with this clear directive, petitioner asks us to read a "dangerousness" exception into the stay-put provision on the basis of either of two essentially inconsistent assumptions: first, that Congress thought the residual authority of school officials to exclude dangerous students from the classroom too obvious for comment; or second, that Congress inadvertently failed to provide such authority and this Court must therefore remedy the oversight. Because we cannot accept either premise, we decline petitioner's invitation to rewrite the statute.

Won't rewrite statute

Petitioner's arguments proceed, he suggests, from a simple, commonsense proposition: Congress could not have intended the stay-put provision to be read literally, for such a construction leads to the clearly unintended, and untenable, result that school districts must return violent or dangerous students to school while the often lengthy EHA proceedings run their course. We think it clear, however, that Congress very much meant to strip schools of the *unilateral* authority they had traditionally employed to exclude disabled students, particularly emotionally disturbed students, from school. In so doing, Congress did not leave school administrators powerless to deal with dangerous students; it did, however, deny school officials their former right to "self-help," and directed that in the future the removal of disabled students could be accomplished only with the permission of the parents or, as a last resort, the courts.

As noted above, Congress passed the EHA after finding that school systems across the country had excluded one out of every eight disabled children from classes. In drafting the law, Congress was largely guided by the recent decisions in *Mills v. Board of Education of District of Columbia* and *P.A.R.C.*, both of which involved the exclusion of hard-to-handle disabled students. *Mills* in particular demonstrated the extent to which schools used disciplinary measures to bar children from the classroom. There, school officials had labeled four of the seven minor plaintiffs "behavioral problems," and had excluded them from classes without providing any alternative education to them or any notice to their parents. After finding that this practice was not limited to the named plaintiffs but affected in one way or another an estimated class of 12,000 to 18,000 disabled students, the District

Court enjoined future exclusions, suspensions, or expulsions "on grounds of discipline."

Congress attacked such exclusionary practices in a variety of ways. It required participating States to educate *all* disabled children, regardless of the severity of their disabilities, and included within the definition of "handicapped" those children with serious emotional disturbances. It further provided for meaningful parental participation in all aspects of a child's educational placement, and barred schools, through the stay-put provision, from changing that placement over the parent's objection until all review proceedings were completed. Recognizing that those proceedings might prove long and tedious, the Act's drafters did not intend § 1415(e)(3) to operate inflexibly, and they therefore allowed for interim placements where parents and school officials are able to agree on one. Conspicuously absent from § 1415(e)(3), however, is any emergency exception for dangerous students. This absence is all the more telling in light of the injunctive decree issued in *P.A.R.C.*, which permitted school officials unilaterally to remove students in " 'extraordinary circumstances.' " Given the lack of any similar exception in *Mills*, and the close attention Congress devoted to these "landmark" decisions, we can only conclude that the omission was intentional; we are therefore not at liberty to engraft onto the statute an exception Congress chose not to create.

Our conclusion that § 1415(e)(3) means what it says does not leave educators hamstrung. The Department of Education has observed that, "[w]hile the [child's] placement may not be changed [during any complaint proceeding], this does not preclude the agency from using its normal procedures for dealing with children who are endangering themselves or others." Such procedures may include the use of study carrels, timeouts, detention, or the restriction of privileges. More drastically, where a student poses an immediate threat to the safety of others, officials may temporarily suspend him or her for up to 10 schooldays. This authority, which respondent in no way disputes, not only ensures that school administrators can protect the safety of others by promptly removing the most dangerous of students, it also provides a "cooling down" period during which officials can initiate IEP review and seek to persuade the child's parents to agree to an interim placement. And in those cases in which the parents of a truly dangerous child adamantly refuse to permit any change in placement, the 10-day respite gives school officials an opportunity to invoke the aid of the courts under § 1415(e)(2), which empowers courts to grant any appropriate relief.

Petitioner contends, however, that the availability of judicial relief is more illusory than real, because a party seeking review under § 1415(e)(2) must exhaust time-consuming administrative remedies, and because under the Court of Appeals' construction of § 1415(e)(3), courts are as bound by the stay-put provision's "automatic injunction," as are schools. It is true that judicial review is normally not available under § 1415(e)(2) until all administrative proceedings are completed, but as we have previously noted, parents may bypass the administrative process where exhaustion would be futile or inadequate. While many of the EHA's procedural safeguards protect the rights of parents and children, schools can and do seek redress through the administrative review process, and we have no reason to believe that Congress meant to require schools alone to exhaust in all cases, no matter how exigent the circumstances. The burden in such cases, of course, rests with the school to demonstrate the futility or inadequacy of administrative review, but nothing in § 1415(e)(2) suggests that schools are completely barred from attempting to make such a showing. Nor do we think that § 1415(e)(3) operates to limit the equitable powers of district courts such that they cannot, in appropriate cases, temporarily enjoin a dangerous disabled child from attending school. As the EHA's legislative history makes clear, one of the evils Congress sought to remedy was the unilateral exclusion of disabled children by *schools*, not courts, and one of the purposes of § 1415(e)(3), therefore, was "to prevent *school* officials from removing a child from the regular public school classroom over the parents' objection pending completion of the review proceedings." The stay-put provision in no way purports to limit or pre-empt the authority conferred on courts by § 1415(e)(2), indeed, it says nothing whatever about judicial power.

Holding

In short, then, we believe that school officials are entitled to seek injunctive relief under § 1415(e)(2) in appropriate cases. In any such action, § 1415(e)(3) effectively creates a presumption in favor of the child's current educational placement which school officials can overcome only by showing that maintaining the child in his or her current placement is substantially likely to result in injury either to himself or herself, or to others. In the present case, we are satisfied that the District Court, in enjoining the state and local defendants from indefinitely suspending respondent or otherwise unilaterally altering his then current placement, properly balanced respondent's interest in receiving a free appropriate public education in accordance with the procedures and requirements of the EHA against the interests of the state and local school officials in maintaining a safe learning environment for all their students.

CHIEF JUSTICE REHNQUIST filed a concurring opinion. [omitted]

JUSTICE SCALIA filed a dissenting opinion, in which JUSTICE O'CONNOR joined. [omitted]

NOTES AND QUESTIONS

1. The continued significance of *P.A.R.C.* and *Mills* is evident in this case as is the clear thematic thread of non-exclusion. If students are difficult, then it becomes the obligation of the schools and the states to deal with their difficulties in a manner that continues to provide these students free appropriate public education. In statutory amendments subsequent to *Honig*, behavioral issues attracted increasing attention resulting in explicit statutory definition of processes to address discipline, including the need for a functional behavioral assessment and a particular "manifestation determination" to decide whether the student's behavior was a result of his or her disability, or not. Where the behavior is such a manifestation, discipline is limited by the specific statutory provisions of IDEA; where it is not, the student can be disciplined as other students, as long as the student still receives free, appropriate public education. *See* 20 U.S.C. § 1415(k); *see also* 20 U.S.C. § 1412(a)(1)(A). Not surprisingly, disciplinary issues remain a controversial aspect of the statute and were the subject of extensive debate at the point of the 2004 Reauthorization of IDEA. They are discussed at length in Chapter 9 (Discipline).

2.   In *Honig*, the Court finds that "Congress very much meant to strip schools of the unilateral authority they had traditionally employed to exclude disabled students, particularly emotionally disturbed students, from school." *Honig*, 484 U.S. at 323. The court recognized the importance of students with disabilities being allowed to "stay put" in their current settings pending process to suitably change the student's placement. To exclude special needs students from school beyond a ten-day suspension would either require parental consent or the intervention of a court. Such an approach to the court to remove such students became known as a "*Honig* injunction." To get such an injunction, the school will face what the Supreme Court described as a "presumption in favor of the child's current educational placement which school officials can overcome only by showing that maintaining the child in his or her current placement is substantially likely to result in injury either to himself or herself, or to others." *Honig* at 328. See further discussion *infra* Chapter 9 (Discipline). How does this compare to the way other students will be treated? Does this present any potential problems?

3.   Education for All Children with Disabilities

One of the essential principles of IDEA and its predecessors is to provide public education for all children with disabilities, without exception. As envisioned, and as discussed in *Timothy W.*, the law was intended to reach out to even those with the most severe conditions.

TIMOTHY W. v. ROCHESTER, NEW HAMPSHIRE, SCHOOL DISTRICT
875 F.2d 954 (1st Cir. 1989)

In this case the First Circuit held that Timothy W., a profoundly mentally retarded and multiply disabled student, was included in the purview of the special education statutes and was entitled to a free and appropriate public education "regardless of the severity of the handicap."

BOWNES, CIRCUIT JUDGE.

Plaintiff-appellant Timothy W. appeals an order of the district court which held that under the Education for All Handicapped Children Act, a handicapped child is not eligible for special education if he cannot benefit from that education, and that Timothy W., a severely retarded and multiply handicapped child was not eligible under that standard. We reverse.

BACKGROUND

Timothy W. was born two months prematurely on December 8, 1975 with severe respiratory problems, and shortly thereafter experienced an intracranial hemorrhage, subdural effusions, seizures, hydrocephalus, and meningitis. As a result, Timothy is multiply handicapped and profoundly mentally retarded. He suffers from complex developmental disabilities, spastic quadriplegia, cerebral palsy, seizure disorder and cortical blindness. His mother attempted to obtain appropriate services for him, and while he did receive some services from the Rochester Child Development Center, he did not receive any educational program from the Rochester School District when he became of school age.

On February 19, 1980, the Rochester School District convened a meeting to decide if Timothy was considered educationally handicapped under the state and federal statutes, thereby entitling him to special education and related services.

In a meeting on March 7, 1980, the school district decided that Timothy was not educationally handicapped — that since his handicap was so severe he was not "capable of benefitting" from an education, and therefore was not entitled to one. . . .

In May, 1982, the New Hampshire Department of Education reviewed the Rochester School District's special education programs and made a finding of non-compliance, stating that the school district was not allowed to use "capable of benefitting" as a criterion for eligibility. . . .

On October 9, 1984, the Department of Education issued an order requiring the school district to place him, within five days, in an educational program, until the appeals process on the issue of whether Timothy was educationally handicapped was completed. . . . The school district, however, refused to make any such educational placement. . . .

On November 17, 1984, Timothy filed a complaint in the United States District Court, pursuant to 42 U.S.C. § 1983, alleging that his rights under the Education for All Handicapped Children Act (20 U.S.C. § 1400 et seq.), the corresponding New Hampshire state law (RSA 186-C), section 504 of the Rehabilitation Act of 1973 (29 U.S.C. § 794), and the equal protection and due process clauses of the United States and New Hampshire Constitutions, had been violated by the Rochester School District. The complaint sought preliminary and permanent injunctions directing the school district to provide him with special education, and $175,000 in damages.

. . . On July 15, 1988, the district court rendered its opinion entitled "Order on Motion for Judgment on the Pleadings or in the Alternative, Summary Judgment." The record shows that the court had before it all the materials and reports submitted in the course of the administrative hearings, and the testimony from the two-day hearing. The court made rulings of law and findings of fact. It first ruled that "under EAHCA [the Education for All Handicapped Children Act], an initial determination as to the child's ability to benefit from special education, must be made in order for a handicapped child to qualify for education under the Act." After noting that the New Hampshire statute was intended to implement the EAHCA, the court held: "Under New Hampshire law, an initial decision must be made concerning the ability of a handicapped child to benefit from special education before an entitlement to the education can exist."

The court then reviewed the materials, reports and testimony and found that "Timothy W. is not capable of benefitting from special education. . . . As a result, the school district is not obligated to provide special education under either the federal statute or the New Hampshire statute." Timothy W. has appealed this order. Neither party objected to the procedure followed by the court.

The primary issue is whether the district court erred in its rulings of law. Since
we find that it did, we do not review its findings of fact.

Issue

The Plain Meaning of the Act Mandates a
Public Education for All Handicapped Children

The Education for All Handicapped Children Act, was enacted in 1975 to ensure
that handicapped children receive an education which is appropriate to their unique
needs. In assessing the plain meaning of the Act, we first look to its title: The
Education for *All* Handicapped Children Act. The Congressional Findings section
of the Act states that there were eight million handicapped children, that more than
half of them did not receive appropriate educational services, and that one million
were excluded entirely from the public school system. Given these grim statistics,
Congress concluded that "State and local educational agencies have a responsibility
to provide education for *all* handicapped children."

. . . .

The Act's stated purpose was "to assure that *all* handicapped children have
available to them . . . a free appropriate public education which emphasizes special
education and related services designed to meet their unique needs. . . .

Acts rule

The Act's mandatory provisions require that for a state to qualify for financial
assistance, it must have "in effect a policy that assures all handicapped children the
right to a free appropriate education." 20 U.S.C. § 1412(1). The state must "set forth
in detail the policies and procedures which the State will undertake . . . to assure
that — there is established a goal of providing full educational opportunity to all
handicapped children . . . , [and that] a free appropriate public education will be
available for all handicapped children between the ages of three and eighteen . . .
not later than September 1, 1978, and for all handicapped children between the ages
of three and twenty-one . . . not later than September 1, 1980. . . ." The state must
also assure that "all children residing in the State who are handicapped, regardless
of the severity of their handicap, and who are in need of special education and
related services are identified, located, and evaluated. . . ." The Act further
requires a state to:

> establish priorities for providing a free appropriate public education to all
> handicapped children . . . first with respect to handicapped children who
> are not receiving an education, and second with respect to handicapped
> children, within each disability, with the most severe handicaps who are
> receiving an inadequate education. . . .

Thus, not only are severely handicapped children not excluded from the Act, but
the most severely handicapped are actually given priority under the Act.

. . . .

The language of the Act could not be more unequivocal. The statute is permeated
with the words "*all* handicapped children" whenever it refers to the target
population. It never speaks of any exceptions for severely handicapped children.
Indeed, the Act gives priority to the most severely handicapped. Nor is there any
language whatsoever which requires as a prerequisite to being covered by the Act,

that a handicapped child must demonstrate that he or she will "benefit" from the educational program. Rather, the Act speaks of the *state's* responsibility to design a special education and related services program that will meet the unique "needs" of all handicapped children. The language of the Act in its entirety makes clear that a "zero-reject" policy is at the core of the Act, and that no child, regardless of the severity of his or her handicap, is to ever again be subjected to the deplorable state of affairs which existed at the time of the Act's passage, in which millions of handicapped children received inadequate education or none at all. In summary, the Act mandates an appropriate public education for all handicapped children, regardless of the level of achievement that such children might attain.

Timothy W.: A Handicapped Child Entitled to An Appropriate Education

Given that the Act's language mandates that all handicapped children are entitled to a free appropriate education, we must next inquire if Timothy W. is a handicapped child, and if he is, what constitutes an appropriate education to meet his unique needs.

. . . .

The Act and the implementing regulations define a "free appropriate public education" to mean "special education and related services which are provided at public expense . . . [and] are provided in conformity with an individualized education program."

(a) "Special education" means "specially designed instruction, at no cost to the parent, to meet the unique needs of a handicapped child, including classroom instruction, instruction in physical education, home instruction, and instruction in hospitals and institutions." It is of significance that the Act explicitly provides for education of children who are so severely handicapped as to require hospitalization or institutionalization. Timothy W.'s handicaps do not require such extreme measures, as he can be educated at home. The Act goes on to define "physical education" as the "development of: physical and motor fitness; fundamental motor skills and patterns . . . [and] includes special physical education, adapted physical education, movement education, and motor development." Thus, the Act's concept of special education is broad, encompassing not only traditional cognitive skills, but basic functional skills as well.

(b) "Related services" means "transportation and such developmental, corrective, and other supportive services as are required to assist a handicapped child to benefit from special education, and includes speech pathology and audiology, psychological services, physical and occupational therapy, recreation. . . ." "Physical therapy" means "services provided by a qualified physical therapist." "Occupational therapy" includes "improving, developing or restoring functions impaired or lost through illness, injury, or deprivation; improving ability to perform tasks for independent functioning. . . ." Furthermore, the "comment" to these implementing regulations notes that "the list of related services is not exhaustive and may include other developmental, corrective, or supportive services . . . if they are required to assist a handicapped child to benefit from special education."

. . . .

The record shows that Timothy W. is a severely handicapped and profoundly retarded child in need of special education and related services. Much of the expert testimony was to the effect that he is aware of his surrounding environment, makes or attempts to make purposeful movements, responds to tactile stimulation, responds to his mother's voice and touch, recognizes familiar voices, responds to noises, and parts his lips when spoon fed. The record contains testimony that Timothy W.'s needs include sensory stimulation, physical therapy, improved head control, socialization, consistency in responding to sound sources, and partial participation in eating. The educational consultants who drafted Timothy's individualized education program recommended that Timothy's special education program should include goals and objectives in the areas of motor control, communication, socialization, daily living skills, and recreation. The special education and related services that have been recommended to meet Timothy W.'s needs fit well within the statutory and regulatory definitions of the Act.

We conclude that the Act's language dictates the holding that Timothy W. is a handicapped child who is in need of special education and related services because of his handicaps. He must, therefore, according to the Act, be provided with such an educational program. There is nothing in the Act's language which even remotely supports the district court's conclusion that "under [the Act], an initial determination as to a child's ability to benefit from special education, must be made in order for a handicapped child to qualify for education under the Act." The language of the Act is directly to the contrary: a school district has a duty to provide an educational program for every handicapped child in the district, regardless of the severity of the handicap.

LEGISLATIVE HISTORY

An examination of the legislative history reveals that Congress intended the Act to provide a public education for all handicapped children, without exception; that the most severely handicapped were in fact to be given priority attention; and that an educational benefit was neither guaranteed nor required as a prerequisite for a child to receive such education. These factors were central, and were repeated over and over again, in the more than three years of congressional hearings and debates, which culminated in passage of the 1975 Act.

. . . .

The record is replete with statements by legislators that the Act was in response to this deplorable state of affairs:

> Exclusion from school, institutionalization, the lack of appropriate services to provide attention to the individual child's need — indeed, the denial of equal rights by a society which proclaims liberty and justice for all of its people — are echoes which the subcommittee has found throughout all of its hearings.

> For many years handicapped children have been placed in institutions, or segregated in schools and classes, or left to sit at home, where they have not received the educational opportunity which is their right under the law.

What we are after in this legislation is to rewrite one of the saddest chapters in American education, a chapter in which we were silent while young children were shut away and condemned to a life without hope. This legislation offers them hope, hope that whatever their handicap, they will be given the chance to develop their abilities as individuals and to reach out with their peers for their own personal goals and dreams.

Moreover, the legislative history is unambiguous that the primary purpose of the Act was to remedy the then current state of affairs, and provide a public education for all handicapped children. As the Committee Chairman, Senator Williams stated:

We must recognize our responsibility to provide education for all children which meets their unique needs. The denial of the right to education and to equal opportunity within this Nation for handicapped children — whether it be outright exclusion from school, the failure to provide an education which meets the needs of a single handicapped child, or the refusal to recognize the handicapped child's right to grow — is a travesty of justice and a denial of equal protection of the law.

Most states have legal provisions which authorize school authorities to exclude certain [handicapped] children from public school. . . . [This] act establishes a target date of 1976 for bringing all of the Nation's handicapped children into adequate programs.

Recent court decisions . . . have made it clearer than ever that we have not only a moral but also a legal obligation to provide the opportunity for every handicapped citizen to insure his or her highest educational potential. An important provision of the bill before us today would require that every State have in effect a policy stating the right of all handicapped children to a "free appropriate public education". . . . The bill would also require that each handicapped child be treated as an individual with unique strengths and weaknesses, and not as a member of a category of children all presumed to have the same needs.

. . . .

If the order of the district court denying Timothy W. the benefits of the Act were to be implemented, he would be classified by the Act as in even greater need for receiving educational services than a severely multi-handicapped child receiving inadequate education. He would be in the highest priority — as a child who was not receiving any education at all.

. . . .

In mandating a public education for all handicapped children, Congress explicitly faced the issue of the possibility of the non-educability of the most severely handicapped. The Senate Report stated, "The Committee recognizes that in many instances the process of providing special education and related services to handicapped children is not guaranteed to produce any particular outcome." The report continued: "The Committee has deleted the language of the bill as introduced which required objective criteria and evaluation procedures by which to assure that the short term instructional goals were met."

Thus, the district court's major holding, that proof of an educational benefit is a prerequisite before a handicapped child is entitled to a public education, is specifically belied, not only by the statutory language, but by the legislative history as well. We have not found in the Act's voluminous legislative history, nor has the school district directed our attention to, a single affirmative averment to support a benefit/eligibility requirement. But there is explicit evidence of a contrary congressional intent, that no guarantee of any particular educational outcome is required for a child to be eligible for public education.

We sum up. In the more than three years of legislative history leading to passage of the 1975 Act, covering House and Senate floor debates, hearings, and Congressional reports, the Congressional intention is unequivocal: Public education is to be provided to all handicapped children, unconditionally and without exception. It encompasses a universal right, and is not predicated upon any type of guarantees that the child will benefit from the special education and services before he or she is considered eligible to receive such education. Congress explicitly recognized the particular plight and special needs of the severely handicapped, and rather than excluding them from the Act's coverage, gave them priority status. The district court's holding is directly contradicted by the Act's legislative history, as well as the statutory language.

. . . .

In the 14 years since passage of the Act, it has been amended four times. Congress thus has had ample opportunity to clarify any language originally used, or to make any modifications that it chose. Congress has not only repeatedly reaffirmed the original intent of the Act, to educate all handicapped children regardless of the severity of their handicap, and to give priority attention to the most severely handicapped, it has in fact expanded the provisions covering the most severely handicapped children. Most significantly, Congress has never intimated that a benefit/eligibility requirement was to be instituted.

. . . .

CASE LAW

Subsequent to the enactment of the Act, the courts have continued to embrace the principle that all handicapped children are entitled to a public education, and have consistently interpreted the Act as embodying this principle.

. . . .

The courts have also made it clear that education for the severely handicapped under the Act is to be broadly defined. In *Battle*, 629 F.2d [269,] at 275 [(3d Cir. 1980)], the court stated that under the Act, the concept of education is necessarily broad with respect to severely and profoundly handicapped children, and "[w]here basic self help and social skills such as toilet training, dressing, feeding and communication are lacking, formal education begins at that point."

. . . .

In the instant case, the district court's conclusion that education must be measured by the acquirement of traditional "cognitive skills" has no basis whatso-ever in the 14 years of case law since the passage of the Act. All other courts have consistently held that education under the Act encompasses a wide spectrum of training, and that for the severely handicapped it may include the most elemental of life skills.

The district court relied heavily on *Board of Education of Hendrick Hudson Central School District v. Rowley*, in concluding that as a matter of law a child is not entitled to a public education unless he or she can benefit from it. The district court, however, has misconstrued *Rowley*. In that case, the Supreme Court held that a deaf child, who was an above average student and was advancing from grade to grade in a regular public school classroom, and who was already receiving substantial specialized instruction and related services, was not entitled, in addition, to a full time sign-language interpreter, because she was already benefitting from the special education and services she was receiving. The Court held that the school district was not required to *maximize* her educational achievement.

. . . .

Rowley focused on the level of services and the quality of programs that a state must provide, not the criteria for access to those programs. The Court's use of "benefit" in *Rowley* was a substantive limitation placed on the state's choice of an educational program; it was not a license for the state to exclude certain handicapped children. In ruling that a state was not required to provide the maximum benefit possible, the Court was not saying that there must be proof that a child will benefit before the state is obligated to provide any education at all. Indeed, the Court in *Rowley* explicitly acknowledged Congress' intent to ensure public education to all handicapped children without regard to the level of achievement that they might attain. . . .

And most recently, the Supreme Court, in *Honig v. Doe*, has made it quite clear that it will not rewrite the language of the Act to include exceptions which are not there. The Court, relying on the plain language and legislative history of the Act, ruled that dangerous and disruptive disabled children were not excluded from the requirement of 20 U.S.C. § 1415(e)(3), that a child "shall remain in the then current educational placement" pending any proceedings, unless the parents consent to a change. The Court rejected the argument that Congress could not possibly have meant to allow dangerous children to remain in the classroom. The analogous holding by the district court in the instant case — that Congress could not possibly have meant to "legislate futility," i.e. to educate children who could not benefit from it — falls for the reasons stated in *Honig*. The Court concluded that the language and legislative history of the Act was unequivocal in its mandate to educate all handicapped children, with no exceptions. The statute "means what it says," and the Court was "not at liberty to engraft onto the statute an exception Congress chose not to create."

. . . .

The district court in the instant case, is, as far as we know, the only court in the 14 years subsequent to passage of the Act, to hold that a handicapped child was not entitled to a public education under the Act because he could not benefit from the education. This holding is contrary to the language of the Act, its legislative history, and the case law.

CONCLUSION

The statutory language of the Act, its legislative history, and the case law construing it, mandate that all handicapped children, regardless of the severity of their handicap, are entitled to a public education. The district court erred in requiring a benefit/eligibility test as a prerequisite to implicating the Act. School districts cannot avoid the provisions of the Act by returning to the practices that were widespread prior to the Act's passage, and which indeed were the impetus for the Act's passage, of unilaterally excluding certain handicapped children from a public education on the ground that they are uneducable.

The law explicitly recognizes that education for the severely handicapped is to be broadly defined, to include not only traditional academic skills, but also basic functional life skills, and that educational methodologies in these areas are not static, but are constantly evolving and improving. It is the school district's responsibility to avail itself of these new approaches in providing an education program geared to each child's individual needs. The only question for the school district to determine, in conjunction with the child's parents, is what constitutes an appropriate individualized education program (IEP) for the handicapped child. We emphasize that the phrase "appropriate individualized education program" cannot be interpreted, as the school district has done, to mean "no educational program."

We agree with the district court that the Special Education Act of New Hampshire implements the federal statute. Its policy and purpose is as unequivocal as that of the federal Act:

> It is hereby declared to be the policy of the state that all children in New Hampshire be provided with equal educational opportunities. It is the purpose of this chapter to insure that the state board of education and the school districts of the state provide a free and appropriate public education for *all educationally handicapped children.*

For the reasons already stated, we hold that the New Hampshire statute is not subject to a benefit/eligibility test. The judgment of the district court is reversed, judgment shall issue for Timothy W. The case is remanded to the district court which shall retain jurisdiction until a suitable individualized education program (IEP) for Timothy W. is effectuated by the school district. Timothy W. is entitled to an interim special educational placement until a final IEP is developed and agreed upon by the parties. The district court shall also determine the question of damages.

Costs are assessed against the school district.

NOTES AND QUESTIONS

1.   This excerpt articulates the First Circuit's view of the zero-reject principle underlying the federal law regarding the education of students with disabilities. The opinion was crafted with great care and with exhaustive review of the legislative history and judicial and agency opinion extant at the time (not all of which is

reflected in the excerpt). The law as articulated in the opinion stands in marked contrast to legislation and judicial opinion that existed prior to *P.A.R.C.* and *Mills* and reflects enormous change in societal views. Consider by way of background, *e.g.*, an Illinois case holding: "Existing legislation does not require the State to provide a free educational program, as a part of the common school system, for the feeble minded or mentally deficient children who, because of limited intelligence, are unable to receive a good common school education." *Department of Public Welfare v. Haas*, 154 N.E.2d 265, 270 (Ill. 1958).

2.   At the time this opinion was written, Timothy was 14 years old. Much of his young life had been consumed by the decision-making process around whether or not he would be entitled to special education and related services. In 1980, when Timothy became of school age, the Rochester School District made its first decision that he was not entitled to such services because his disability was "so severe he was not capable of benefitting from an education, and therefore was not entitled to one." Almost ten years later the First Circuit definitively decided otherwise. In the interim there had been orders from the State Department of Education finding Rochester's special education programs to be in non-compliance and mandating that Timothy be provided with special education, appeals of those orders, diagnostic interludes, and complaints in court. In 1988, the District Court finally determined that Timothy was "not capable of benefiting from special education" and thus the district was under no obligation, federal or state, to provide such an education. What made the stakes so high here that the dispute was carried on in so many forums for so many years? What do you think the costs were to the parties for this protracted administrative process and litigation? What were the costs to Timothy?

3.   At each step of this proceeding, as one might expect, there was evidence submitted by a variety of people who knew Timothy, and by some who did not. When Rochester made its first decision, it heard testimony from Timothy's pediatrician, from two occupational therapists, from Timothy's mother, from the Director of the Rochester Child Development Center, and from two other pediatricians. The latter two doctors indicated that part of Timothy's brain had been destroyed and that he had no educational potential. The former testified otherwise, noting that he responded to sounds and that physical occupational therapy would increase Timothy's responses to his environment. Similar experts testified to similar points at later stages of the proceeding. Is this a fact conflict or a conflict over the definition of education? If the latter, is it an issue of law? How is a court to construe conflicting testimony? Upon whom should it rely?

4.   What remedy does the court award in this case? What are the limits to a court's ability to intervene in these kinds of cases? What will Timothy's education look like?

5.   While factual issues were in dispute, the opinion casts itself as interpreting a question of law. In answering a question of law, the court places the usual reliance on the Congressional record both at the time of the passage of the original legislation and in subsequent amendments. Does this mean that Congress is free to change its opinion and redefine the scope of opportunity for education of children with the most profound disabilities?

E.   SOURCES OF LAW

The law applicable to special education comes from a variety of sources: state and federal constitutions; state and federal statutes; administrative agency regulations, orders and polices; administrative agency adjudicatory decisions; and federal and state case law. Different sources of law have different origins in our legal system — legislatures, agencies, and courts — and carry different significance, or weight, in a given situation. In any given case, several sources of law may come together to provide "the answer" to the question presented. *See generally* SARAH REDFIELD, THINKING LIKE A LAWYER: AN EDUCATOR'S GUIDE TO LEGAL ANALYSIS AND RESEARCH (2002).

1.   Federal and State Constitutions

The highest legal authority rests with the constitutions of the states and the United States. Both state and the federal constitutions contain broad rights that protect students, including students with disabilities. Prominent in school settings are cases involving students' rights of free speech, freedom of religion, freedom from overly-intrusive searches, and rights to an education and to due process. *E.g., Morse v. Frederick*, 127 S. Ct. 2618 (2007) (holding that First Amendment does not bar public school discipline of student for display of sign reasonably interpreted as encouraging illegal drug use, at off-campus activity sponsored by school); *Hazelwood Sch. Dist. v. Kuhlmeier*, 484 U.S. 260 (1988) (holding that the First Amendment does not bar school control of school newspaper which has school imprimatur as part of the school curriculum); *Bethel Sch. Dist. v. Fraser*, 478 U.S. 675 (1986) (holding that the First Amendment does not protect lewd speech at school assembly); *New Jersey v. T.L.O.*, 469 U.S. 325 (1985) (establishing constitutional standard for school searches); *Goss v. Lopez*, 419 U.S. 565 (1975) (finding students entitled to procedural due process); *San Antonio Ind. Sch. Dist. v. Rodriguez*, 411 U.S. 1 (1973) (holding that education is not a fundamental right and the Texas system of school financing is constitutional); *Tinker v. Des Moines Indep. Cmty. Sch. Dist.*, 393 U.S. 503 (1969) (holding that the First Amendment protects symbolic student speech in school). Cases involving particular application of some of these rights in the context of special education are discussed in subsequent chapters *infra, e.g.*, Chapter 12 (Children in Private Schools) and Chapters 8 and 9 (Due Process and Discipline).

2.   Federal and State Statutes

Statutes are laws passed by Congress and the various state legislatures. Indeed, most of the law relevant to students with disabilities is derived from statute. In some instances these statutes are prohibitions, for example, it is prohibited to discriminate against students with disabilities under section 504 of the Rehabilitation Act of 1973. States will often have parallel provisions prohibiting discrimination, either generally or specifically. *See, e.g.*, Ohio Rev. Code Chapter 4112. In other cases, these statutes are designed to assure state involvement in providing a public program. For example, the Individuals with Disabilities Education Act (IDEA) calls for states to write plans, and, if necessary, to enact their own parallel statutes so that they have "in effect policies and procedures" to ensure compliance with the requirements of the IDEA, 20 U.S.C. § 1412(a). For an example of such a state statute, see Ohio Rev. Code Chapter 3323.

3.   Federal and State Regulations

When Congress or state legislatures enact major pieces of legislation, they typically delegate to an administrative agency the authority to implement that legislation. *See, e.g.*, 20 U.S.C. § 1221e-3 (rulemaking authority for the Secretary of the Department of Education); *see also* 20 U.S.C. § 1417. Each time Congress enacts a new law, or reauthorizes existing law, statutory changes, in turn, have required DOE to review existing regulations and effect regulatory changes where necessary to comport with new statutory language. Properly adopted, agency regulations have the force and effect of law, and failure to comply with federal statutes and regulations can result in withholding of federal funds.

In the federal system, rulemaking is typically governed by the Administrative Procedure Act, 5 U.S.C. § 553, which applies to so-called "notice and comment" rulemaking. While other specific statutory provisions may apply, in their absence the APA procedures require publication of the proposed rule, opportunity for public comment, consideration of comment, and publication of a final rule. Proposals and regulations appear initially in the Federal Register and then are codified in their final form in the Code of Federal Regulations (C.F.R.).

In addition to regulations, agencies may issue less formal kinds of policies and advice. To provide on-going interpretation of the IDEA, the Office of Special Education Programs (OSEP) periodically issues policy and letter rulings to clarify issues and to respond to questions from school districts. Unlike regulations, such opinions do not carry the force and effect of law. For further discussion, see *infra* Chapter 5 (IEP).

Administrative agencies also typically function in a quasi-judicial capacity and issue adjudicatory orders in individual cases, and IDEA requires state and local educational agencies to provide individual hearings in special education disputes as discussed further *infra* Chapter 8 (Due Process). *See* 20 U.S.C. § 1415(f), (i). Typically there is an appeal from an administrative agency to a court, and there is fairly well-developed law as to how courts are to treat decisions of administrative agencies. However, IDEA has its own provisions as to appeals from hearing officer decisions to courts, and its own standards for what weight is to be given the administrative decision. This topic is discussed further *infra* Chapter 8 (Due Process) and Chapter 10 (Courts). *See* 20 U.S.C. § 1415(f)–(g), (i). IDEA also has its own provisions for alternative dispute resolution through mediation, which is a voluntary, non-adversarial process for addressing conflicts and its success depends on the extent to which the parties are willing to compromise to resolve conflicts. 20 U.S.C. § 1415(e); 34 C.F.R. § 300.506.

In addition to regulations of federal agencies, states have their own rules or regulations regarding enforcement of the IDEA in their state. Frequently, these regulations are published in a state's administrative code and are important for providing detailed interpretations of school district responsibilities. *See, e.g.*, Ohio Admin. Code, §§ 3301-51-01 *et seq.*

4.   Caselaw

When courts are called upon to resolve conflicts among parties regarding rights under federal or state constitutions, statutes, or regulations, the resulting judicial opinions become known as caselaw. Caselaw performs two important functions: first, a court declares the meaning, or interpretation, of a constitutional provision, statute, and/or regulation at issue; and, second, where this interpretation reveals a violation of a person's constitutional, statutory, or regulatory rights, the court determines an appropriate remedy.

In reaching their decisions, courts will generally follow the decisions of other courts in their jurisdiction, particularly those courts in the judicial hierarchy above them. This process of applying judicial precedent is called *stare decisis* and provides a kind of broad predictability that helps attorneys and educators in addressing current legal problems in schools. However, the more that the facts of a current problem differ from the facts of a past case, the less value a prior case will be in predicting how a court might interpret the law.

To further complicate the role of precedent in judicial decision-making, the various federal and state appellate and supreme courts sometimes overrule prior decisions made at the same level, in effect creating a new judicial precedent. The Supreme Court's overruling of some of its education law precedent has had a significant impact on special education. For example, in *Agostini v. Felton*, 521 U.S. 203 (1997), the Supreme Court held that New York's providing Elementary and Secondary Education Act title I services on site at parochial schools was not a violation of the First Amendment establishment clause, overruling its decision on the same subject in *Aguilar v. Felton*, 473 U.S. 402 (1985). *Agostini is* discussed further in Chapter 12 (Children in Private Schools).

5.   Federal and State Court Systems

The United States has 51 different systems of courts, one a hierarchal, three-tiered federal court system, and the others hierarchal court systems in each of the 50 states (some of which systems are three-tiered, but there are variations). The following chart illustrates the general structure.

Federal Court System   **State Court Systems**

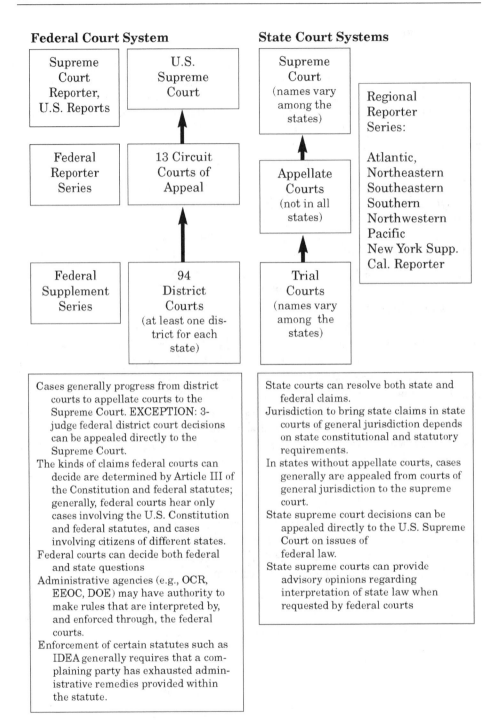

Cases generally progress from district courts to appellate courts to the Supreme Court. EXCEPTION: 3-judge federal district court decisions can be appealed directly to the Supreme Court.

The kinds of claims federal courts can decide are determined by Article III of the Constitution and federal statutes; generally, federal courts hear only cases involving the U.S. Constitution and federal statutes, and cases involving citizens of different states.

Federal courts can decide both federal and state questions

Administrative agencies (e.g., OCR, EEOC, DOE) may have authority to make rules that are interpreted by, and enforced through, the federal courts.

Enforcement of certain statutes such as IDEA generally requires that a complaining party has exhausted administrative remedies provided within the statute.

State courts can resolve both state and federal claims.

Jurisdiction to bring state claims in state courts of general jurisdiction depends on state constitutional and statutory requirements.

In states without appellate courts, cases generally are appealed from courts of general jurisdiction to the supreme court.

State supreme court decisions can be appealed directly to the U.S. Supreme Court on issues of federal law.

State supreme courts can provide advisory opinions regarding interpretation of state law when requested by federal courts

A lawsuit involving IDEA begins in a trial court, either a federal district court or a state trial court. The judgment of that court then may be appealed to an appellate court. Appellate courts do not retry cases and will accept the factual findings of trial courts unless the evidence offered before the trial court clearly does not support the findings. The primary function of appellate courts is to determine that the trial court applied the correct legal principles to the facts and reached a decision consistent with the manifest weight of the evidence. Where an appellate court finds that the trial court incorrectly applied legal principles or that the trial court's legal conclusion is not supported by the facts, the appellate court may choose to reverse the trial court on the merits, remand the case for a trial (or a new trial), or remand the case to the trial court for other proceedings. Appeals to the U.S. Supreme Court or a state supreme court are typically reserved for questions of law. State supreme courts are the final arbiters regarding interpretations of state law, as is the United States Supreme Court on federal law and the United States Constitution.

Chapter 2

ELIGIBILITY AND EVALUATION

A. INTRODUCTION

Factors that determine whether a student is eligible for special education and related services are defined by statute. Simply put, students must first be located (starting with the Child Find requirements, which are applicable at all ages), then evaluated, and, finally, appropriately served. This chapter begins with the statutory and regulatory requirements defining a student's eligibility under IDEA and section 504. Then, cases further illustrating some of the eligibility and evaluation concepts are discussed in regard to particular disabilities, to the IDEA requirement that the student be in need of special education and related services as a result of such disabilities, and to particular conditions and situations where equality of access to programs or services is an issue.

B. STATUTORY AND REGULATORY REQUIREMENTS

Eligibility for special education and related services is defined primarily by federal and state statute and implementing regulations, particularly the Individuals with Disabilities Education Act and section 504 of the Rehabilitation Act of 1973.

1. IDEA

Under the Individuals with Disabilities Education Act the definition of eligibility for special education and related services has three core parameters: age, specified disability, and the need for services. All three are necessary prerequisites. 34 C.F.R. § 300.7(a)(2).

As to age, children aged six through seventeen are squarely within the requirement of IDEA that a free appropriate public education be provided. For children aged three through five and eighteen through twenty-one, services are required to the same extent that children of these ages without disabilities are so served. Beyond these requirements, there is an obligation under Child Find to locate and evaluate *all* children at risk, even those who might not be currently eligible to receive services. The state is specifically obligated to ensure that "all children with disabilities residing in the State, including children with disabilities who are homeless children or are wards of the State, and children with disabilities attending private schools, regardless of the severity of their disability, and who are in need of special education and related services, are identified, located, and evaluated." 34 C.F.R. § 300.111(a)(1)(i). School districts may satisfy the public notice component of this requirement by putting notices in newspapers, posting information on the district web site, making public service announcements on broadcast media, placing posters at public and private school buildings, placing inserts in government mailings, and training private school personnel about referral processes. *See generally P.P. v. West Chester Area Sch. Dist.*, 585 F.3d 727, 731 (3d Cir. 2009) (finding district's child find efforts to be adequate). Additionally, Part C of IDEA, discussed in more detail *infra* Chapter 13 (Early Childhood Programs), establishes a comprehensive program of early intervention for Infants and Toddlers with Disabilities and their families.

As to disabling condition, IDEA defines "child with a disability" as a child "with mental retardation, hearing impairments (including deafness), speech or language impairments, visual impairments (including blindness), serious emotional disturbance, orthopedic impairments, autism, traumatic brain injury, other health impairments, or specific learning disabilities." 20 U.S.C. § 1401(3)(A)(i). Each of these disabilities is further defined by implementing regulation. 34 C.F.R. § 300.8(c). For children aged three through nine, the state may also consider within this definition a child "experiencing developmental delays, as defined by the state and as measured by appropriate diagnostic instruments and procedures, in one or more of the following areas: physical development, cognitive development, communication development, social or emotional development, or adaptive development." 20 U.S.C. § 1401(3)(B)(i), 34 C.F.R. § 300.8(b)(1).

As to need for services, a student with a defined disability must also "by reason thereof" need "special education and related services" to be eligible for a free and appropriate public education and related services under IDEA. 20 U.S.C. § 1401(3)(A)(ii), (B)(ii). Eligibility cannot be based on "lack of appropriate instruction in reading, including the essential components of reading instruction (as defined in [the Elementary and Secondary Education Act], . . . [or] math" or "limited English proficiency" without other qualifying attributes. 34 C.F.R. § 300.306(b).

Under the 2004 IDEA Reauthorization, it is possible for a child to receive services funded under IDEA without being found IDEA-eligible. Under the new law, up to 15% of the school district's federal special education money may be used for early intervening services ("EIS") for children who have not been found to have a disability and a need for special education. 20 U.S.C. § 1413(f). The students to be served are those who need additional academic and behavioral support to succeed in a general education environment. The goal is to improve those children's performance so that they will never need to receive the designation of special education-eligible. The provision is permissive, but if the state determines that an LEA has a significant disproportionality based on race and ethnicity with regard to identification of children with disabilities, placement in particular educational settings of such children, or incidence, duration, and type of disciplinary actions, it shall require the LEA to devote the maximum amount of funding to EIS, in addition to taking other steps to address the disproportion. 20 U.S.C. § 1418(d).

In general terms, eligibility for special education and related services is determined after an evaluation, also defined by statute, regulation, departmental opinion and policies, and case law. *See, e.g.,* 20 U.S.C. § 1414(b); 34 C.F.R. §§ 300.301–.311. Evaluation is discussed further *infra* Part F.

2.   Section 504 and the Americans with Disabilities Act (ADA)

Students who are not found to be eligible for special education under IDEA — for example, because of age or inability to demonstrate a need for special education — may nevertheless fall within the purview of section 504 of the Rehabilitation Act of 1973 or the state and local government provisions of the ADA. Under these provisions, students will be protected from discrimination and entitled to reasonable accommodation to achieve equal access to education. Here, the prohibition bars discrimination against or exclusion of qualified individuals with a disability. 29 U.S.C. § 794; 42 U.S.C. §§ 12131–12132. Individuals with a disability are those with an impairment that "substantially limits a major life activity," or who "have a record of such an impairment," or who are "regarded as having such an impairment." 29 U.S.C. § 705(20)(B); 42 U.S.C. § 12102. Learning is considered a major life activity. 28 C.F.R. § 35.104, 34 C.F.R. § 104.3(2)(j)(ii). Unlike IDEA, eligibility here is not conditioned on age, nor is it conditioned on a need for special education and related services arising out of the impairment. Also unlike IDEA, compliance will not be federally funded.

Congress further expanded the scope of section 504 and the ADA in the ADA Amendments Act of 2008, effective January 1, 2009 (ADAAA), Pub. L. 110-325. This statute overturns Supreme Court decisions that had narrowed the coverage of the original ADA, notably *Sutton v. United Air Lines*, 527 U.S. 471 (1999), which held that impairments had to be evaluated in their mitigated state when determining whether a claimant was a person with a disability covered under the ADA, and *Toyota v. Williams*, 534 U.S. 184 (2002), which held that for a person claiming to be impaired in the ability to perform manual tasks, the court should look to the person's ability to perform activities of central importance in most people's daily lives. *Sutton* also adopted a restrictive view of the definitional prong of a person being regarded as having a disability; the ADAAA disapproves its approach. The ADAAA adopts a non-exclusive list of major life activities, including sleeping, eating, lifting, bending, communicating, thinking, learning, reading, and concentrating. Moreover, it adds a provision stating that the term major life activity includes major bodily functions, such as the functions of the immune system, as well as normal cell growth, digestive, bowel, bladder, neurological, brain, respiratory, circulatory, endocrine, and reproductive functions. The ADAAA defines regarded-as-having-a-disability to encompass being subject to action prohibited because of an actual or perceived impairment, whether or not the impairment is perceived to limit a major life activity. This regarded-as provision does not apply to impairments that are transitory and minor, with transitory being defined as having an actual or expected duration of six months or less.

The definition of disability is to be construed in favor of broad coverage. Specifically, an impairment that is episodic or in remission is a disability if it would substantially limit a major life activity when active, and the determination of whether an impairment substantially limits a major life activity is to be made without regard to the ameliorative effects of mitigating measures such as medication, medical supplies, equipment, appliances, prosthetics, hearing aids, mobility devices, assistive technology, and learned behavioral or adaptive neurological modifications. There is a limited exception for ordinary eyeglasses or contact lenses. Even so, qualification standards for employment based on uncorrected vision must be job-related and consistent with business necessity. A person who is covered merely by being regarded as having a disability is not entitled to reasonable accommodations under the ADA. Coverage under section 504 matches that under the ADA. The new statute is codified in significant part in 42 U.S.C. § 12102.

C. DISABLING CONDITIONS GENERALLY

SPRINGER v. FAIRFAX COUNTY SCHOOL BOARD
134 F.3d 659 (4th Cir. 1998)

Rule

The court held that social maladjustment is not serious emotional disturbance qualifying an eleventh grader for special education.

WILKINSON, CHIEF JUDGE.

Claim

Edward Springer and his parents seek reimbursement from the Fairfax County School Board for tuition paid to a private school in which the Springers enrolled Edward after he failed the eleventh grade. The School Board determined that Edward was not suffering from a "serious emotional disturbance," as the Springers claim, and that he was therefore ineligible for special education services under the Individuals with Disabilities Education Act ("IDEA"). The district court upheld the State Review Officer's determination that Edward was not disabled and that his parents were not entitled to tuition reimbursement. Because the applicable IDEA regulations do not equate mere juvenile delinquency with a "serious emotional disturbance," we affirm.

Facts

During most of his years in the Fairfax County school system, Edward Springer demonstrated no need for special educational services. He progressed successfully from grade to grade in regular education programs. Throughout elementary school his grades were consistently average or above average. He attended a private school from seventh to ninth grade and received no special education services there. When he returned to Fairfax County schools for his tenth grade year, he enrolled in regular education classes at McLean High School and attained a C+ grade point average. Throughout this period, Edward maintained positive relationships with his teachers and peers. During high school he participated in a church group, the Boy Scouts, and the McLean High School wrestling team.

Edward developed significant behavioral problems in his eleventh grade year. He was arrested in August 1993 for possessing burglary tools and tampering with an automobile, offenses for which he was sentenced to one year probation, fifty hours of community service, and a suspended fine of $2,500. Edward would frequently sneak out of his parents' house and stay out all night with friends. He stole from his parents and others. He regularly used marijuana and alcohol. Edward often broke school rules and had a high rate of absenteeism. He was disciplined for driving recklessly on school property, cutting classes, forgery, leaving school grounds without permission, and fighting. Towards the end of the eleventh grade, Edward and his friends stole a fellow student's car. Edward kept the car for a week of joy-riding. In connection with this episode he was sentenced to probation until his eighteenth birthday.

Although he continued to score in the average to superior range of intellectual ability on standardized tests, Edward's eleventh-grade performance suffered because he cut class and frequently failed to complete assignments. During his week of joy-riding, he skipped school and missed his final exams, causing him to fail three of his seven courses for the year. His teachers, his mother, and Edward himself agreed that these difficulties resulted from truancy, lack of motivation, and poor study habits. At the time, Edward recognized that with more effort he could obtain above average grades.

In response to his behavioral problems the Springers enrolled Edward in September 1994 in the New Dominion School, a private residential school located in Dillwyn, Virginia. The Springers requested that the School Board fund this placement, claiming that Edward exhibited a serious emotional disturbance, a qualifying disability under IDEA. See 34 C.F.R. § 300.7(a)(1). A Fairfax County special education eligibility committee evaluated Edward's condition and determined that his behavior indicated a conduct disorder that did not qualify as a serious emotional disturbance. Thus the committee ruled that Edward was ineligible for special education services and tuition reimbursement.

The Springers requested a local due process hearing, which took place on February 9, 1995. The Local Hearing Officer ("LHO") rendered his decision on March 16, 1995. Relying exclusively on a letter written by a psychiatrist, Dr. Joseph Novello, to the Juvenile Court at the time of Edward's second brush with the law, the LHO found that Edward suffered from a conduct disorder and a dysthymic disorder (a moderate depressive disorder). Edward's "inability to get along with his teachers and fellow students and to abide by school rules" was deemed consistent with these diagnoses. The LHO concluded, without elaboration, that Edward "should be considered 'seriously emotionally disturbed' rather than merely 'socially maladjusted,'" and that he thereby qualified for special education services. Finding that Edward was making educational progress at the New Dominion School, the LHO ordered the School Board to reimburse the Springers for tuition there.

The School Board appealed to a State Review Officer ("SRO"), who reversed the LHO and found that Edward did not meet the criteria for a seriously emotionally disturbed student under state and federal special education regulations. The SRO primarily questioned the LHO's reliance on the letter from Dr. Novello. . . . Most critically, the SRO pointed out the abundant psychological evidence that Edward did not have a serious emotional disturbance — evidence that was not even mentioned by the LHO. Several separate evaluations of Edward had uniformly supported the conclusion that, while Edward was "socially maladjusted" and had a "conduct disorder," he exhibited no symptoms of a serious emotional disturbance. . . .

The Springers filed suit in district court, seeking reversal of the SRO's decision. . . . The district court thus agreed with the SRO that Edward was not seriously emotionally disturbed. . . . The Springers now appeal.

A student becomes eligible for special education services if he suffers from a "serious emotional disturbance":

Rule

    (i) The term means a condition exhibiting one or more of the following characteristics over a long period of time and to a marked degree that adversely affects a child's educational performance —

    (A) An inability to learn that cannot be explained by intellectual, sensory, or health factors;

    (B) An inability to build or maintain satisfactory interpersonal relationships with peers and teachers;

    (C) Inappropriate types of behavior or feelings under normal circumstances;

    (D) A general pervasive mood of unhappiness or depression; or

    (E) A tendency to develop physical symptoms or fears associated with personal or school problems.

    (ii) The term includes schizophrenia. The term does not apply to children who are socially maladjusted, unless it is determined that they have a serious emotional disturbance.

34 C.F.R. § 300.7(b)(9); *see also* Regulations Governing Special Education Programs for Children with Disabilities in Virginia Part 1, "Definitions," at p. 9 (restating federal definition of serious emotional disturbance).

Rule to qualify as seriously emotionally disturbed

    The regulatory definition delineates no fewer than four specific conditions a student must satisfy in order to qualify for special education services as seriously emotionally disturbed: the student must demonstrate that he has (1) exhibited one of the five listed symptoms, (2) "over a long period of time," and (3) "to a marked degree," and (4) that this condition adversely affects his educational performance. Finally, the definition pointedly excludes students whose behavior is attributable to social maladjustment, unless they also suffer an independent serious emotional disturbance.

    In interpreting this regulation district courts are required to give deference to the state and local education authorities whose primary duty it is to administer IDEA. . . .

    Courts and special education authorities have routinely declined, however, to equate conduct disorders or social maladjustment with serious emotional disturbance. The fact "that a child is socially maladjusted is not by itself conclusive evidence that he or she is seriously emotionally disturbed." Indeed, the regulatory framework under IDEA pointedly carves out "socially maladjusted" behavior from the definition of serious emotional disturbance. This exclusion makes perfect sense when one considers the population targeted by the statute. Teenagers, for instance, can be a wild and unruly bunch. Adolescence is, almost by definition, a time of social maladjustment for many people. Thus a "bad conduct" definition of serious emotional disturbance might include almost as many people in special education as it excluded. Any definition that equated simple bad behavior with serious emotional disturbance would exponentially enlarge the burden IDEA places on state and local education authorities. Among other things, such a definition would require the schools to dispense criminal justice rather than special education. . . .

As the district court recognized, finding that Edward was socially maladjusted does not end the inquiry. The regulations contemplate that a student may be socially maladjusted and suffer an independent serious emotional disturbance that would qualify him for special education services under IDEA. The Springers insist that Edward's is such a case. Like the district court, we disagree.

First we note the overwhelming consensus among the psychologists who examined Edward. No fewer than three psychologists examined him, and each independently concluded that he was not seriously emotionally disturbed. . . . In her detailed report, which is the most recent psychological analysis of Edward, Dr. Rudolph described him as "a poised and pleasant young man" who is used to being able to " 'figure out' how to make the people around him like him and allow him to have his own way." Even when he was misbehaving, Dr. Rudolph concluded, Edward was getting "his own way"; she testified before the LHO "that last year [in the eleventh grade], in particular, Ed was getting what he wanted. He didn't want to do work, so he didn't. He didn't like going to class, so he didn't do that." Dr. Rudolph thus concluded that during this time Edward was in complete control of his actions, which distinguished him from emotionally disturbed individuals, who may be in "such pain and in such difficulty that they cannot get to their goals." Based on her thorough examination, Dr. Rudolph refused to attribute Edward's behavior, troubling though it was, to any emotional disability or disturbance. Indeed, this case is somewhat remarkable in that the relevant psychological evidence is virtually uncontradicted. . . .

The Springers have given us no reason to doubt this professional consensus. They first attempt to show that Edward exhibited one of the five enumerated symptoms of a serious emotional disturbance by asserting that he was unable "to build or maintain satisfactory interpersonal relationships with peers and teachers," 34 C.F.R. § 300.7(b)(9)(i)(B). However, ample evidence supports the SRO's contrary finding. His father indicated that "Ed has lots of friends across a broad spectrum, from very good students to the academically unsuccessful students." Edward perceived himself as "socially . . . very involved with a large group of people that he considered friends." Dr. Rudolph's observation of him confirmed this self-perception, as did his history of involvement with social and extracurricular activities during his time in the Fairfax County schools. Nor did Edward fail to develop good relationships with teachers. His French teacher from McLean High, Ghislaine Toulu, told the LHO that she "really liked Ed, and . . . still really likes Ed." His history teacher from McLean, Robert Peck, described Edward as "very friendly [with] peers and me." And even Mr. and Mrs. Springer have described Edward as "respectful of teachers and appropriate," and indicated that he "got along well with his teachers." Nothing in the record indicates that an inability to maintain interpersonal relationships existed at all, not to mention persisting "over a long period of time" or "to a marked degree." See 34 C.F.R. § 300.7(b)(9)(i). Thus, neither the SRO nor the district court committed any error in rejecting the contention that Edward was in any way incapable of forming and maintaining relationships with peers or teachers.

The Springers also claim that Edward exhibited a second enumerated symptom, "a general pervasive mood of unhappiness or depression,"

§ 300.7(b)(9)(i)(D). However, we agree with the SRO and the district court that the record simply does not support this contention. . . .

There is one final flaw in the Springers' case for tuition reimbursement. Even if they had been able to demonstrate that Edward exhibited one or more of the five qualifying characteristics for a long period of time and to a marked degree, the Springers still have failed to establish the critical causal connection between this condition and the educational difficulties Edward experienced, the final step in proving a serious emotional disturbance. § 300.7(b)(9)(i). Prior to his eleventh grade year, Edward had made steady educational progress, advancing from grade to grade on schedule. In the eleventh grade Edward stopped attending classes, regularly used drugs and alcohol, and engaged in other criminal activities. The precipitous drop in Edward's grades at this time appears to be directly attributable to his truancy, drug and alcohol use, and delinquent behavior rather than to any emotional disturbance. Particularly given the paucity of evidence that Edward suffered any sort of emotional disorder, it can hardly be said that the record directs a finding that a serious emotional disturbance adversely affected his educational performance. Edward's delinquent behavior appears to be the primary cause of his troubles.

cts holding

JOHNSON v. METRO DAVIDSON COUNTY SCHOOL SYSTEM
108 F. Supp. 2d 906 (M.D. Tenn. 2000)

The court found sufficient evidence to support a decision that student was seriously emotionally disturbed.

WISEMAN, SENIOR DISTRICT JUDGE.

This is a claim filed pursuant to the Individuals with Disabilities Education Act (IDEA), 20 U.S.C. §§ 1401, et seq. Before the Court is Petitioner's Motion for Judgment on Appeal and Request for Court to Receive Additional Evidence.

On 11 November 1996, Tiffiney Johnson ("Petitioner") by and through her parents, Georgianna and Lester Johnson requested a due process hearing. Specifically, Petitioner sought both certification as disabled within the meaning of the IDEA and the resulting benefits from Metropolitan Nashville and Davidson County School System ("Respondent"). . . . On 9 December 1997, an administrative law judge ("ALJ") found that "the student is not eligible for special education and related services under the basis of Health Impairment, Serious Emotional Disturbance, or Learning Disabilities."

Petitioner appealed the ALJ's decision on 9 February 1998.

Tiffiney Johnson was born 22 October 1981 and was adopted by Georgianna and Lester Johnson when she was four months of age. Tiffiney's schooling began with kindergarten at Goodpasture Christian School. Her parents chose Goodpasture because they knew Tiffiney was hyperactive and thought she would benefit from attending school with children she already knew. Johnson did not investigate what public school Tiffiney would have attended.

Tiffiney's first grade teacher at Goodpasture recommended she undergo psychological testing. In concert with Tiffiney's pediatrician, the Johnsons took Tiffiney to The Learning Lab, Inc., for a psychological evaluation on 30 May 1989. Gillian Blair, Ph.D., performed the evaluation. In the background section of Dr. Blair's report, she notes that Tiffiney has always been very active and that Tiffiney is caught between the strong religious beliefs of each of her parents. Dr. Blair also noted that Mr. Johnson feared that he and Mrs. Johnson had contributed to Tiffiney's problems by spoiling her and being too lax in terms of discipline. Dr. Blair noted that Tiffiney's test scores were "unusual, and indicative of a learning disability with an emotional overlay." Dr. Blair additionally noted that Tiffiney demonstrated considerable physiological correlates of anxiety and that her responses to certain tests were "suggestive of high expectations of perfect behavior." In her recommendations, Dr. Blair suggested Tiffiney "should be considered for certification as a child with specific learning disabilities in both reading and mathematics"; that Tiffiney would benefit from both family and individual counseling; and that she should be evaluated "to determine whether she would benefit from a trial of medication to help her attention deficit disorder."

On 15 December 1993, Michael G. Tramontana, Ph.D., performed a psychological/neuropsychological evaluation of Tiffiney. Dr. Tramontana's evaluation suggested "possible frontal lobe dysfunction," but acknowledged that "this impression should be regarded as speculative in the absence of corroborating neurological evidence." Additionally, he noted that "the findings are not entirely consistent with ADHD." Rather, Dr. Tramontana concluded that a "more appropriate diagnostic alternative may be an Impulse Control Disorder NOS." Tiffiney's intelligence testing results from this evaluation were significantly lower than those taken in 1989. This decrease suggested "that Tiffiney's lack of focus and disinhibition have interfered with her keeping optimal pace in her cognitive development." Dr. Tramontana recommended a "fair amount of structure and supervision in promoting on-task performance" for Tiffiney in school. Although she seemed atypical for ADHD, "the type of programming that she will require in school will most closely resemble the needs of an ADHD child."

Tiffiney remained at Goodpasture until 23 October 1995 when she was expelled from the eighth grade. After her expulsion from Goodpasture, the Johnsons did not explore whether or not Metro Davidson County School System could offer Tiffiney the services she required at school due to her learning, behavioral, and emotional problems. Mrs. Johnson explained this decision by noting that she and her husband "did not want to be a burden on Metro if we could provide the proper help." The Johnsons enrolled Tiffiney at Benton Hall School. Ms. Johnson wanted to try Benton Hall because "they said they could work with oppositional youngsters and behavior problems."

On 7 December 1995, Ms. Johnson asked for special education assistance from Metro Public Schools. On 23 January 1996, Ms. Johnson asked Metro to perform an educational evaluation of Tiffiney. . . .

Attending the 1 March 1996 M-Team meeting were Mr. and Mrs. Johnson, Chris

Seibert, a special education teacher, and Dr. Warren Thompson, the Metro school psychologist. The Johnsons were informed of their rights under the special education law. Dr. Thompson reviewed Dr. Tramontana's report and suggested that Tiffiney might be Seriously Emotionally Disturbed ("SED"), but Ms. Johnson suggested that ADHD was a more appropriate diagnosis. The Johnsons discussed Tiffiney's history and her strengths and weaknesses. They noted that Tiffiney had been having severe problems at school and that they had sought help from Johanna Shadoin, a counselor, and Elizabeth Hoover, a psychiatrist. They agreed that a language assessment should be performed and to re-convene on 26 March 1996.

Present at the 26 March 1996 meeting were Mr. and Mrs. Johnson, Chris Seibert, Crystal Lumm, and Warren Thompson. Ms. Lumm, the speech-language pathologist for Metro Schools, reported on her evaluation of Tiffiney. The evaluation indicated that Tiffiney had basically average to low-average language skills. Dr. Thompson suggested that either SED or Health Impaired ADD certificates should be considered. Because the diagnostic picture was unclear, however, they agreed to contract Dr. Hoover, a psychiatrist, for clarification of the certification issues.

. . . During this time in which the M-Team was periodically convening, Dr. Hoover evaluated Tiffiney's condition. Based on her initial psychiatric evaluation, she diagnosed Tiffiney with Oppositional Defiant Disorder and a Parent/Child problem. Dr. Hoover did not feel that medication therapy was warranted nor did she feel that the available data supported certification as Seriously Emotionally Disturbed.

Also during this time period, Dr. Thompson evaluated Tiffiney on 7 February 1996 and 20, 22, and 30 May 1996. . . . Dr. Thompson found that Tiffiney was functioning within the average range of intellectual abilities and that there was no evidence of learning disabilities. He concluded that Tiffiney was impulsive, manipulative, and inclined to be oppositional to authority figures. Dr. Thompson concluded that she was not Seriously Emotionally Disturbed. He did agree with Dr. Hoover, however, that she had Oppositional Defiant Disorder and Parent/Child Problems. He thought that the Johnsons ought to resume family therapy and that Tiffiney had the potential to learn to control her impulses and develop improved problem-solving strategies.

. . . The M-Team determined that Tiffiney was not eligible for special education services under Rule 05 20-1-3.09 of the Rules and Regulations provided by the Department of Education. On 21 June 1996, Metro Schools denied the Johnson's request for an independent evaluation of Tiffiney.

After the M-Team's initial determination and prior to the due process hearing, Petitioner apparently saw three different mental health specialists: Drs. Carol Hersh, Pamela Auble, and Judith Kaas Weiss. On 26 June 1996, Dr. Hersh began treating Tiffiney and provided an initial psychiatric evaluation. After noting that Tiffiney appeared of about average intelligence, Dr. Hersh recorded the following impressions:

AXIS I: 1. OPPOSITIONAL DEFIANT DISORDER
           2. PARENT-CHILD PROBLEM
           3. R/O ANXIETY DISORDER

AXIS II: DEFERRED
AXIS III: NONE KNOWN
AXIS IV: STRESSOR MODERATE (school problems,
            conflict with parents)
AXIS V: GAF 66/55

Dr. Hersh noted that Tiffiney did not need medication at that time; that she did not fit the definition of SED; that the Johnsons needed family counseling; and that Tiffiney needed individual counseling to help develop coping skills and independence.

In a June 1997 deposition, Dr. Hersh indicated that she thought that the Johnsons were substantial contributors to Tiffiney's acting out. Dr. Hersh indicated that the parents set polar opposite limits for Tiffiney — Mr. Johnson setting extraordinarily difficult limits for any adolescent and Mrs. Johnson finding it difficult to set any limits — and that they seemed to use Petitioner as a weapon against each other. . . .

Additionally during this deposition, Dr. Hersh acknowledged that her assessment had changed since June 1996 when she did not believe Tiffiney's history was consistent with a diagnosis of ADD or ADHD. By 1 May 1997, Dr. Hersh had concluded that ADD or ADHD was a reasonable diagnosis. This change in diagnosis resulted from Tiffiney's positive (if not overwhelming) response to Ritalin treatment. Dr. Hersh conceded that providing an absolutely certain diagnosis was difficult. . . .

[handwritten margin note: diagnosed w/ ADD or ADHD]

On 16 November 1996, Dr. Judith Kaas Weiss evaluated Tiffiney. Dr. Weiss concluded that her evaluation supported "attentional deficit with hyperactivity" and "a significant behavior disorder." Dr. Weiss also noted the possibility that a diagnosis of reactive attachment disorder might be appropriate. At the hearing in July 1997, Dr. Weiss stated, "I think [Tiffiney] is one of the most disturbed children that I have ever seen in 35 years." She noted that Tiffiney had several disabilities, "She does have some learning disability. She does have some neurotransmitter problems that are being expressed as Oppositional Defiant Disorder and Attention Deficit Disorder and Hyperactivity, but I think it goes beyond that." Dr. Weiss also testified at the hearing that she felt Tiffiney exhibited inappropriate feelings under normal circumstances. Additionally, she felt that such inappropriate behavior and feelings impacted her performance at school, e.g., she was expelled from school. She also opined that Tiffiney's Reactive Attachment Disorder and Oppositional Defiant Disorder would adversely impact her educational performance in the future. Dr. Weiss further opined that Tiffiney needed an educational environment in which her teachers are compassionate and have a lot of patience, but that a program of behavior modification would fail because of Tiffiney's impulsiveness. She thought that Tiffiney would need to be in a classroom with fifteen students and a teacher and teacher's aide or in a classroom with fewer than fifteen students. Additionally, Dr. Weiss thought that Tiffiney needed medication and probably needed to be in a 24-hour intensive therapeutic situation. Dr. Weiss felt that it would be impossible to educate Tiffiney in a normal classroom. Dr. Weiss also testified that she thought Tiffiney was a sociopath. Dr. Weiss did not think that Tiffiney's problems were the

[handwritten margin note: Dr. Weiss said she had several disabilities]

[handwritten margin note: needed school w/ lots of attention + medication]

result of a dysfunctional family or inadequate parenting; rather the family's problems resulted from Tiffiney's problems.

On 26 March 1997, Pamela Auble, Ph.D., evaluated Tiffiney based on a referral from the Vanderbilt Legal Clinic. In the report based on this evaluation, Dr. Auble concluded that Tiffiney was "suffering from an attention deficit/hyperactivity disorder, an oppositional defiant disorder, and a parent-child problem." She also noted that Tiffiney exhibited some characteristics that were consistent with borderline personality disorder, but it was difficult to diagnose such a disorder until after Tiffiney matured through adolescence. Additionally, Dr. Auble noted her failure to see consistent evidence of reactive attachment disorder or of learning disabilities. Dr. Auble opined that Tiffiney should continue in small classrooms and in individualized instruction to obtain maximum benefit from school. Additionally, family counseling was recommended. Dr. Auble thought that Tiffiney did not meet the criteria for certification as Seriously Emotionally Disturbed. She acknowledged that Tiffiney had a history of and continued to engage in inappropriate behavior, but that she did not believe that Tiffiney's behavior was a manifestation of a disturbing internal emotional state or a misperception of the environment.

When Dr. Auble testified at the due process hearing, she stated that Tiffiney's ADHD would have to be classified as mild due to the extent of the disagreement over the diagnosis, e.g., Drs. Thompson and Tramontana did not diagnose it, and Drs. Blair and Hersh did not make firm diagnoses. In response to a question of whether Tiffiney needed special education services, Dr. Auble replied, "Because of her Attention Deficit Disorder, it is my opinion that she needs small class size and individualized instruction, and that can help her obtain the maximum benefit from school." According to Dr. Auble, the Johnsons' family problems did affect Tiffiney's acting out. Dr. Auble indicated that she disagreed with Dr. Weiss's conclusions that Tiffiney is Seriously Emotionally Disturbed; that she has Reactive Attachment Disorder; and that she has a learning disability. Dr. Auble did agree with Dr. Weiss's opinion that Tiffiney has ADHD. Dr. Auble did note that Tiffiney exhibited some traits that would support Dr. Weiss's diagnosis that Tiffiney was a sociopath, but that such a determination was premature given Tiffiney's age and the fact that her personality was still forming.

A due process hearing was held on 16th and 17th of July 1997 before Administrative Law Judge William Jay Reynolds. ALJ Reynolds issued his opinion and findings of fact denying Petitioner's claim on 9 December 1997.

Between October 1997 and June 1998, Phyleen Ramage, M.D., treated Tiffiney. Dr. Ramage first saw Tiffiney on 22 October 1997. She originally diagnosed Tiffiney with ADHD, but later opined that Tiffiney probably fell within a subset of persons who exhibit ADHD-like symptoms but are actually bipolar. Dr. Ramage said that this diagnosis was verified when she accidentally provided Tiffiney medicine meant to treat her ADHD symptoms but actually precipitated a manic episode. It was one of these manic episodes which resulted in Tiffiney's expulsion from Benton Hall. Dr. Ramage opined that Tiffiney met the criteria for a finding of Emotionally Disturbed which entitled her to additional assistance with school and placement. Additionally, Dr. Ramage stated that Tiffiney was the most impulsive person she had ever met. She stated that after Tiffiney was hospitalized for a second time, that Tiffiney was suffering from an inability to learn and that she would require tight supervision, frequent redirection, and a lot of structure. Dr. Ramage also detailed behavior that supported her diagnosis of bipolar. This includes extremely impulsive behavior, such as sitting in a car at a stop light and striking up a conversation with a man in the next car, chasing a car that cut her off in traffic onto a dark road, running away to Florida with a guy she barely knew, and having a loaded gun at school for no apparent reason. Dr. Ramage noted that she did not notify anyone of her diagnosis of bipolar disorder until 23 January 1998.

After Tiffiney's expulsion from Benton Hall, she enrolled in Williamson County's Page High School. The Williamson County M-Team determined that Tiffiney was eligible for special education because she was Emotionally Disturbed and had a learning disability. This M-Team concluded that she met the state criteria and that her needs could not be met in the regular program without special education.

Enrolled in new school eligible for sped.

In June 1998, Tiffiney was admitted to the New Life Lodge for substance abuse treatment. The psychological evaluation performed by Mary Kathryn Black, Ph.D., on Tiffiney indicated polysubstance abuse, ADHD (combined type), and anxiety disorder. The psychologist did estimate that Tiffiney's intelligence to be within the range of average to high average.

One of the several purposes served by the Individuals with Disabilities Education Act is "to ensure that all children with disabilities have available to them a free appropriate public education that emphasizes special education and related services designed to meet their unique needs and prepare them for employment and independent living."

purpose of Ind w/ disabilities edu.

In reviewing cases brought under 20 U.S.C. § 1415(i)(2), the district court is to engage in a two part assessment: (1) whether the state has complied with the IDEA's procedural requirements and (2) whether the resulting individualized educational program is reasonably calculated to enable the child to receive educational benefits. . . . When considering procedural matters, a court "should 'strictly review technical deviations for procedural compliance.' " Where the procedural requirements are satisfied, the court should give greater deference to the district's placement decision.

cases brought under 2 part assessment

. . . Administrative findings in an IDEA case my be set aside only if the evidence before the court is more likely than not to preclude the administrative decision from being justified based on the agency's presumed educational expertise, a fair estimate of the worth of the testimony, or both. A court should defer to the administrative findings only when educational expertise is relevant to those findings and the decision is reasonable. By so deferring, "due weight" will have been given to the state administrative proceedings.

A court thus gaining jurisdiction (1) "shall receive the records of the administrative proceedings"; (2) "shall hear additional evidence at the request of a party"; and (3) "basing its decision on the preponderance of the evidence, shall grant such relief as the court determines is appropriate." 20 U.S.C. § 1415(i)(2)(B).

The Sixth Circuit has provided guidance to district courts as to when introduction of additional evidence is appropriate. In *Metropolitan Government of Nashville and Davidson County v. Cook*, 915 F.2d 232 (6th Cir. 1990), the court stated that "additional evidence" was not limited to situations such as supplementing or filling in gaps of evidence previously introduced. . . . Thus, it appears that the Sixth Circuit applies a fairly liberal standard for the admittance of evidence to the extent that it sheds light on the reasonableness of the original decision, but not if the evidence brings up new issues.

Applying this standard, the Court grants Petitioner's request for the admission of additional evidence — specifically, evidence of Petitioner's subsequent treatment by Dr. Ramage, Petitioner's subsequent educational records, records of Petitioner's treatment at Vanderbilt's Psychiatric Hospital from December 1997 through February 1998, and medical records from Tiffiney's stay at the New Life Lodge. Pursuant to the above precedent, this Court notes that such evidence is admitted for the narrow and sole purpose of determining whether Tiffiney qualified as disabled at the time of the due process hearing. Thus, subsequent manifestations of disabling traits are relevant only to the extent they confirm that a student was disabled at the time of the final decision. To the extent that the evidence demonstrates a subsequent onset of a disabling condition, it presents a new issue not before the ALJ and, thus, not ripe for determination by this Court.

. . . The IDEA provides a two part definition of child with a disability. *See* 20 U.S.C. § 1401(3)(A). Thus, Tiffiney qualifies as a child with a disability if she meets the following definition:

[A] child —

> (i) with metal retardation, hearing impairments (including deafness), speech or language impairments, visual impairments (including blindness), serious emotional disturbance (hereinafter referred to as "emotional disturbance"), orthopedic impairments, autism, traumatic brain injury, other health impairments, or specific learning disabilities; and

> (ii) who, by reason thereof, needs special education and related services.

. . . Petitioner proffers two arguments that Tiffiney qualifies for special education. First Petitioner argues that she qualifies under the "other health impairments" prong of section 1401(3)(A) due to her ADD and/or ADHD. Second, Petitioner argues that she qualifies as a child with a disability because of her Serious Emotional Disturbance.

Although the ALJ's decision that Tiffiney did not meet the criteria for disability under the IDEA conformed to the preponderance of evidence before him, this Court holds that in light of the additional evidence now before it, that Tiffiney was disabled as of June 1997 when the Respondent made its final determination. The evidence before the court is cloudy; there has been substantial disagreement among the numerous professionals who have evaluated and treated Tiffiney. When considered as a whole — however murky and conflicting — the preponderance of the evidence indicates that Tiffiney then suffered from an Emotional Disturbance as defined under the IDEA.

A finding that a child suffers from an emotional disturbance requires the existence of the following:

> [A] condition exhibiting one of more of the following characteristics over a long period of time and to a marked degree that adversely affects a child's educational performance:
>
> (A) An inability to learn that cannot be explained by intellectual, sensory, or health factors.
>
> (B) An inability to build or maintain satisfactory interpersonal relationships with peers and teachers.
>
> (C) Inappropriate types of behavior or feelings under normal circumstances.
>
> (D) A general pervasive mood of unhappiness or depression.
>
> (E) A tendency to develop physical symptoms or fears associated with personal or school problems.

34 C.F.R. § 300.7(c)(4). Dr. Ramage's testimony provides the greatest support for a determination that Tiffiney was Emotionally Disturbed. Her evaluation, furthermore, indicates that many of the traits and concerns raised by other specialists support a finding of emotional disturbance, even though the specialists themselves did not make such a finding.

The evidence before the ALJ was replete with references to Tiffiney's inappropriate behavior under normal circumstances. Despite the examples of inappropriate behavior, most of the evaluators did not find Emotional Disturbance because they concluded that the behavior lacked emotional roots. Dr. Auble testified that based on her review of prior evaluations Tiffiney did engage in inappropriate behavior. However, she stated that such behavior did not support a finding of emotionally disturbed because it results from a behavioral disorder and is not "a manifestation of a disturbing emotional state or a psychotic process." Dr. Thompson diagnosed Tiffiney with having a behavioral problem known as "Oppositional-Defiant Disorder." Dr. Thompson explained that there must be an emotional disorder to go along with abnormal behavior or feelings under normal circumstances to support a finding of emotional disturbance. Dr. Thompson implied that this underlying emotional disorder was missing from Tiffiney; her behavioral problems were related to social maladjustment, Oppositional Defiant Disorder, and parent-child problems. . . .

Dr. Ramage's testimony, however, indicated that Tiffiney's behavior was, indeed, related to an underlying emotional disorder. She testified that Tiffiney had many traits that were consistent with ADHD, but that in actuality she was bipolar. She testified, "There are a subset of children who look very ADHD-like as little kids, who don't respond well to typical ADHD interventions, behavioral, educational, medication, maybe, who if you follow them into adulthood they were not probably ADHD at all. They were probably bipolar." This sequence of events aptly describes Tiffiney's situation. . . .

When the observations of Tiffiney's inappropriate behavior are combined with Dr. Ramage's persuasive diagnosis of bipolar disorder and opinion that her behavioral patterns result from this disorder, Tiffiney clearly demonstrates one of the characteristics indicative of an emotional disturbance. To qualify as Emotionally Disturbed, however, Tiffiney must have exhibited such inappropriate behavior over an extended period of time to a marked degree and such behavior must have adversely affected her educational performance, *see* 34 C.F.R. § 300.7(c)(4). The first two criteria, the (1) exhibition of the behavior to a marked degree and (2) over a long period of time, are not seriously contested. Certainly, the record demonstrates severe behavioral problems over the course of Tiffiney's lifetime. The parties do dispute whether such behavior has adversely affected Tiffiney's educational performance.

The Special Education Manual of Tennessee discusses the meaning of adverse effect on educational performance and notes that it "pertains to the child's diminished academic performance in the classroom, impaired school learning experience, and/or failure to master skill subjects." The problems caused by emotional disturbance must be "significant enough to require interventions that cannot be provided without special education services." Additionally, the manual notes that if the student is "making reasonable progress and their needs can be accommodated within regular education, the special education services should not be provided to theses students."

Respondent correctly notes that the record indicates in many ways that Tiffiney is making reasonable progress in school. Her grades have been satisfactory in most cases, although it does appear that she performed better and more consistently at Benton Hall. The problem, therefore, is not so much Tiffiney's lack of performance but that she has been unable to remain in school. She has been expelled from both Goodpasture and Benton Hall. This inability to remain in school while in a regular school environment — or even the more controlled environment of Benton Hall — indicates that Tiffiney's needs were not accommodated within the regular education system. Thus, Tiffiney was eligible for special education services under the IDEA due to her Emotional Disturbance.

. . . For the reasons stated above, the Court grants Petitioner's request to submit additional evidence for the limited purpose of establishing that she was disabled as determined by the IDEA at the time of her due process hearing; grants Petitioner's Motion for Judgment on Appeal; and awards Petitioner her tuition expenses for the 1996-97 school year at Benton Hall School.

NOTES AND QUESTIONS

1. As the previous section shows, disabling conditions are very specifically defined by statute and regulation. *Springer* and *Johnson* are examples of the judicial expansion of the definition of disability, reaching different results on the question of whether students were "seriously emotionally disturbed," as those terms are used in IDEA. The regulatory definition quoted in the case itself draws the distinction between serious emotional disturbance and social maladjustment, 34 C.F.R. § 300.8(a)(4)(ii), although it suggests that some children are subject to both and are eligible under the emotional disturbance heading.

2. *Johnson* also involves the often-controversial diagnosis of Attention Deficit Disorder and Attention Deficit Hyperactivity Disorder (ADD/ADHD). The U.S.

Department of Education's regulations on this subject provide that attention deficit disorder or attention deficit hyperactivity disorder may constitute "other health impairment" under IDEA if it is a chronic or acute health problem that results in "limited strength, vitality, or alertness, including a heightened alertness to environmental stimuli, that results in limited alertness with respect to the education environment" and "adversely affects educational performance." 34 C.F.R. § 300.8(a)(9). At the point that the Department adopted this regulatory definition of "other health impairment," it noted that ADD/ADHD may also be categorized as "emotional disturbance" or as "specific learning disability." 64 Fed. Reg. 12406, 12542–43 (1999). The Department also noted: "No child is eligible for services under the Act merely because the child is identified as being in a particular disability category. Children identified as ADD/ADHD are no different, and are eligible for service only if they meet the criteria of one of the disability categories in Part B [of IDEA], and because of their impairment, need special education and related services." 64 Fed. Reg. at 12543. This point is well made by the court in *Johnson.* For general information on dealing with ADD/ADHD in classrooms, see Gerard A. Gioia & Peter K. Isquith, *New Perspectives on Educating Children with ADHD: Contributions of the Executive Functions,* 5 J. HEALTH CARE L. & POL'Y 124 (2002).

3.   Like serious emotional disturbance, ADD/ADHD (which is not a subcategory of serious emotional disturbance) can also present fact patterns where the distinction between disability and poor and disruptive behavior needs to be defined. Cases arise in many contexts. For example, when a fourth-grader with ADHD did not follow the directions for a class project, he was barred from participating in a class field trip which the class earned in a school-wide competition based on the project. What information is needed to determine the propriety of this decision by the school and how should the court evaluate this? *See Sonkowsky v. Board of Educ. for Independent School District No. 721,* 327 F.3d 675 (8th Cir. 2003) (holding that student's refusal to follow instructions was not basis for cognizable First Amendment claim and finding no evidence that ADHD was basis for exclusion).

4.   *Johnson* and the cases that follow in this chapter also illustrate the evidentiary complexity of special education decisions. Virtually the entire text of the opinion as it deals with expert testimony is reproduced here to highlight the many levels of decision-making and hearings as well as the plethora, and confusion, of expert testimony. How many experts evaluated Tiffiney in the course of these proceedings? Was there clear consensus on her condition? Possible diagnoses included ADHD, bipolar disorder, oppositional defiance disorder, serious emotional disturbance, and just plain "manipulative and impulsive" behavior, the latter presumably not a qualifier for special education. Additionally, there is a subtext suggested by the court as to how many, if any, of Tiffiney's problems were attributable to her parents' approach to raising her. Is there a better or easier way to address these questions?

5.   As these cases and others suggest, the demand for residential placement for students with serious emotional and behavioral issues is one of the most controversial areas of special education. One subset of these cases involves students who are drug addicted, and, not surprisingly, find their work at school impaired by drug usage. Some authors are highly critical of the view that IDEA requires school districts to provide these students' placements. *See generally* David S. Doty, *A*

Desperate Grab for Free Rehab: Unilateral Placements under IDEA for Students with Drug and Alcohol Addictions, 2004 B.Y.U. EDUC. & L.J. 249; Beth Hensley Orwick, *"Bartender, I'll Have a Beer and a Disability"; Alcoholism and the Americans with Disabilities Act: Affirming the Importance of the Individualized Inquiry Determining the Definition of Disability*, 20 ST. LOUIS U. PUB. L. REV. 195 (2001).

6. States receiving funds under IDEA are obligated to assure that the McKinney Vento Act provisions relevant to homeless children are met. McKinney Vento provides that "Each State educational agency shall ensure that each child of a homeless individual and each homeless youth has equal access to the same free, appropriate public education, including a public preschool education, as provided to other children and youths." 42 U.S.C. § 11431(1). McKinney Vento further provides that "Homelessness alone is not sufficient reason to separate students from the mainstream school environment." 42 U.S.C. § 11431(3). What unique issues are such students likely to present to local and state policy makers?

D. BENEFIT FROM SPECIAL EDUCATION

As the *Johnson* case in the previous part indicates, the eligibility criterion of needing special education and related services as a result of disability is unique to IDEA. Eligibility depends on evidence of an adverse educational impact as a result of the disability. Litigation in this area, again, involves a good deal of expert opinion on the nature of the disability and its manifestations. Because this is not a specified criterion for section 504, students will often assert eligibility for services under that statute as well as IDEA, and cases will discuss both statutory schemes.

J.D. v. PAWLET SCHOOL DISTRICT
224 F.3d 60 (2d Cir. 2000)

The court found an academically gifted student with emotional and behavioral problems not eligible for special education under IDEA and analogous state law. It ruled that the IEP offering placement at local high school and counseling provided a reasonable accommodation under section 504.

KATZMANN, CIRCUIT JUDGE.

J.D., by his parent J.D., appeals from a final judgment of the United States District Court for the District of Vermont granting the defendants-appellees' motion for summary judgment dismissing the complaint in its entirety. The district court held that: (1) J.D. failed to meet the "adverse effect" eligibility criterion of the Vermont Department of Education Special Education Regulations ("VSER"), which implement the Individuals with Disabilities Education Act ("IDEA"), (2) the defendants-appellees did not discriminate against J.D. in violation of § 504 of the Rehabilitation Act of 1973 and (3) J.D. was not entitled to relief based on alleged violations of certain procedural safeguards in the IDEA. We affirm.

The following facts are undisputed except where noted. J.D., a minor of high school age at all times relevant to this action, is an academically gifted child who also has emotional and behavioral problems. Defendants Bennington-Rutland Supervisory Union and Pawlet School District (collectively, the "School District") are local educational agencies within the meaning of 20 U.S.C. § 1401(a)(8) and receive federal funds. Defendant Vermont Department of Education is a State educational agency within the meaning of 20 U.S.C. § 1401(a)(7) and also receives federal assistance. (The Department and its commissioner, Marc Hull, are collectively referred to as the "State Defendants.")

J.D. attended Pawlet Elementary School through the third grade when he transferred to Poultney Elementary School outside the Pawlet School District for the fourth and fifth grades. Partly because of his academic progress, he skipped the sixth grade and was placed in Poultney High School ("PHS") for the seventh grade, where he was allowed to take ninth grade English. While in the seventh grade, J.D. took an IQ test on which he scored in the top two percent of his age group. In the eighth grade, J.D. took the Comprehensive Test of Basic Skills, a norm-based examination on which he received grade equivalency scores for reading, language, and mathematics that were predominantly in the tenth, eleventh, and twelfth grade levels. Even his lowest score, in spelling, placed him at the mid-eighth grade level. In the ninth grade, he took classes at or above his grade level in a variety of subjects and achieved grades ranging from B to A+.

1. The IDEA Evaluation

During the summer of 1996, between J.D.'s ninth and tenth grade years, J.D.'s parents requested that he be evaluated for special education because they were concerned that PHS was not meeting their son's intellectual or emotional needs. In response, the School District convened an Evaluation and Planning Team (the "EPT") to determine J.D.'s eligibility for special education. The EPT considered J.D.'s results on standardized academic achievement tests, his cumulative school file consisting of grades, progress reports, and teacher comments, and a psychological evaluation conducted by Dr. Roger Meisenhelder, a psychologist selected by J.D.'s parents. According to Dr. Meisenhelder, J.D. had "superior" verbal and language skills, together with good concentration and "highly developed" conceptual and abstract thinking skills. These conclusions were largely consistent with J.D.'s academic record from kindergarten through the ninth grade.

However, Dr. Meisenhelder also observed that J.D. experienced "frustration, boredom, alienation, apathy, and hopelessness" because of an absence of intellectual peers at PHS, and that these feelings persisted despite a "somewhat differentiated curriculum at school," leading to passive resistance as well as aggressive behavior at school. Dr. Meisenhelder recommended that J.D. be: (1) classified as a student with an "emotional and behavioral" disability; (2) placed in a school environment in which he has academically challenging courses and intellectual peers; and (3) given individual and family counseling.

Based on Dr. Meisenhelder's report, the EPT concluded that J.D. had an emotional-behavioral disability within the meaning of Rule 2362.1(h) of the VSER, as further explained below. When the EPT members were unable to reach consensus on whether J.D.'s disability adversely affected his educational performance, the School District, pursuant to Rule 2364.1, offered its decision that J.D. did not meet this criterion and notified J.D.'s parents of their right to challenge this decision.

2. The 504 Evaluation

Having decided that J.D. was ineligible for special education under the IDEA, the EPT referred his request to an evaluation team (the "504 Team") to determine whether he qualified for protection under § 504 of the Rehabilitation Act. In December 1996, the 504 Team informed J.D.'s parents that J.D. was a "qualified individual with a disability" and was eligible for accommodations. On January 10, 1997, the 504 Team offered J.D. a two-part program of support which was to include (1) individual counseling, and (2) training in peer relationship skills in the academic setting. In the same letter, the 504 Team stated that another meeting would be held on January 21, 1997 to determine academic accommodations, if any. Rather than await the outcome of that meeting, J.D.'s parents notified the School District on January 15 that they had unilaterally enrolled their son in Simon's Rock College, an out-of-state boarding school for the academically gifted, and requested funding for his tuition and costs.

Notwithstanding the parents' decision, the 504 Team proceeded with the January 21 meeting and subsequently informed J.D.'s parents that the Team considered three placements: at PHS, which J.D. had been attending since the seventh grade; at Troy Academy, an approved independent local secondary school which is affiliated with PHS; and at Simon's Rock College. The School District recommended PHS, noting that it offered courses in advanced placement biology, chemistry, United States history, and Pacesetter mathematics, with additional access to literature and English courses at a nearby college. The Team specifically rejected Simon's Rock because it is a post-secondary institution, explaining, among other things, that the School District had no duty to provide post-secondary education. The School District did not expressly offer or reject Troy Academy. . . .

II. DISCUSSION

Whether the district court accurately applied the statutory and regulatory terms in the IDEA and the Vermont implementing regulations to J.D.'s educational and emotional history is a mixed question of law and fact, which we review de novo.

We begin with the substantive IDEA claim because its resolution will facilitate our decision as to the procedural IDEA claim. The substantive claim presents a matter of first impression: whether an academically gifted child with an emotional-behavioral disability is eligible for special education under the IDEA and the corresponding Vermont regulations. We agree with the district court that he is not. . . .

Under the IDEA, the term "children with disabilities" means, among others, children with a "*serious emotional disturbance* . . . who, by reason thereof, need special education and related services." § 1401(a)(1)(A) (emphasis added); *see* 34 C.F.R. § 300.7(a)(1). The federal regulations promulgated under the statute further define "serious emotional disturbance" as:

serious emotional disturbance definition

a condition exhibiting one or more of the following characteristics over a long period of time and to a marked degree that adversely affects a child's educational performance. . . .

(B) An inability to build or maintain satisfactory interpersonal relationships with peers and teachers;

(C) Inappropriate types of behavior or feelings under normal circumstances;

(D) A general pervasive mood of unhappiness or depression; or

(E) A tendency to develop physical symptoms or fears associated with personal or school problems.

34 C.F.R. § 300.7(b)(9)(i). However, neither the IDEA nor the federal regulations define the terms "need special education" or "adverse effect on educational performance," leaving it to each State to give substance to these terms.

2. The Vermont Special Education Regulations

The VSER, promulgated by the Vermont Department of Education, have been approved by the U.S. Department of Education. Rule 2362(1) establishes three eligibility criteria for special education that are consistent with the IDEA:

. . . To be determined eligible for special education . . . the Basic Staffing Team must determine that the student:

(a) meets one or more disability categories (Rule 2362.1);

(b) exhibits the adverse effect of the disability on educational performance; and

(c) is in need of special education.

Rule 2362(2)(b) defines "adverse effect of the disability on educational performance" as follows:

that the student is functioning significantly below expected age or grade norms, in one or more of the basic skills. This determination of adverse effect, usually defined as 1.0 standard deviation or its equivalent, shall be documented and supported by two or more measures of school performance. These measures may include but are not limited to: — parent or teacher observation, grades, curriculum-based measures, work or language samples, other test results.

Rule 2362(3) further provides:

Unless otherwise stated in an individual category of disability (Rule 2362.1), basic skill areas are defined as:

(a) oral expression;

(b) listening comprehension;

(c) written expression;

(d) basic reading skills;

(e) reading comprehension;

(f) mathematics calculation;

(g) mathematics reasoning; and

(h) motor skills.

a. "Adverse Effect" Measured by Effect on Basic Skills

Δ's Arg

The defendants contend that J.D. did not meet the "adverse effect" eligibility criterion under Rule 2362(1). Relying on the list of basic skills in Rule 2362(3), the defendants argue that J.D.'s emotional disability had no adverse effect on his educational performance because he consistently performed at or above the level of his age cohorts in each of the enumerated areas. J.D., on the other hand, points out that Rule 2362(3) states that the list of basic skills is used to determine eligibility for special education, "unless otherwise stated in an individual category of disability." J.D. interprets Rule 2362(3) to mean that the basic skills enumerated therein do not apply to a student, such as himself, who has a disability enumerated in Rule 2362.1. . . .

JD's Arg

An emotional-behavioral disability shall be identified by the occurrence of one or more of the following conditions exhibited over a long period of time and to a marked degree:

emotional behavioral disability:

. . . .

2. An inability to build or maintain satisfactory interpersonal relationships with peers and teachers;

3. Inappropriate types of behavior or feelings under normal circumstances;

4. A general pervasive mood of unhappiness or depression.

whether his emotional-behavioral disability has caused an adverse effect

J.D. argues that the 2362.1(1)(h) list, not the 2362(3) list, must be used to discern whether his emotional-behavioral disability has caused an adverse effect.

Based on the language and structure of the VSER, we have no choice but to reject J.D.'s interpretation. . . .

Ct rejects JD's interpretation

JD also Args.

J.D. also argues that his educational performance cannot be measured by his grades and achievement test results alone, which were indisputably at or above the norm for his age group. . . . Based on the overwhelming evidence in the record, the district court did not err in concluding that J.D.'s basic skills, and hence his educational performance, were not adversely affected by his disability within the meaning of the Vermont Rule. *Ct said JD not adversely affected*

JD empha-sizes diff. w/ relationships

J.D., on the other hand, emphasizes his emotional condition, including his difficulty with interpersonal relationships and negative feelings. However, while these are signs of an emotional disability, under the statutory and administrative schemes, they are not measures of an adverse effect on basic skills by which educational performance must be assessed. . . .

Ct says these aren't measures of an adverse effect on basic skills by which edu. performance must be assessed.

The Rehabilitation Act was enacted to promote, among other things, the inclusion and integration of persons with disabilities into mainstream society. *See* 29 U.S.C. § 701. To this end, § 504 of the Rehabilitation Act provides:

> No otherwise qualified individual with a disability in the United States . . . shall, solely by reason of her or his disability, be excluded from the participation in, be denied the benefits of, or be subjected to discrimination under any program or activity receiving Federal financial assistance. . . .

In the education field, the Rehabilitation Act complements the IDEA and the corresponding Vermont regulations. Whereas the latter authorities require federally funded State and local educational agencies to provide special education and related services to students who meet specified eligibility criteria, § 504 of the Rehabilitation Act prohibits such agencies from discriminating against students with disabilities. The federal regulations promulgated under § 504 with respect to education provide:

> A recipient that operates a public elementary or secondary education program shall provide a free appropriate public education to each qualified handicapped person who is in the recipient's jurisdiction, regardless of the nature or severity of the person's handicap.

34 C.F.R. § 104.33(a). An "appropriate education" within the meaning of § 504 means:

> regular or special education and related aids and services that (i) are designed to meet individual educational needs of handicapped persons as adequately as the needs of nonhandicapped persons are met and (ii) are based upon adherence to procedures that satisfy the requirements of §§ 104.34, 104.35, and 104.36.

34 C.F.R. § 104.33(b)(1)

As is apparent from this definition, under the § 504 regulations, a student may have a viable discrimination claim even if his or her academic performance is satisfactory, provided the student establishes that he or she does not enjoy equal access to the school's programs.

On the other hand, the duty to provide a free appropriate public education is not without limits. As the Supreme Court has explained in the higher education context, the Rehabilitation Act distinguishes "between the evenhanded treatment of qualified handicapped persons and affirmative efforts to overcome the disabilities caused by handicaps." While a federal funds recipient must offer "reasonable" accommodations to individuals with disabilities to ensure meaningful access to its federally funded program, § 504 does not mandate "substantial" changes to its program. We have also held that in evaluating the accommodation offered by a defendant, courts should be "mindful of the need to strike a balance between the rights of [the student and his parents] and the legitimate financial and administrative concerns of the School District."

Section 104.33(b)(2) of the federal regulations explains that implementation of an IEP is one way of ensuring the provision of a free appropriate public education. *See* 34 C.F.R. § 104.33(b)(2). Section 104.33(c)(3) requires a student with a disability to be placed in a public or private residential program at no cost to the person or his or her parents if that is necessary to provide a free appropriate public education. On the other hand, if a federal funds recipient "has made available . . . a free appropriate public education to a handicapped person and the person's parents . . . choose to place the person in a private school, the recipient is not required to pay for the person's education in the private school." § 104.33(c)(4).

Furthermore, the federal regulations express a preference for educating qualified persons with disabilities "in the regular educational environment operated by the recipient unless it is demonstrated by the recipient that the education of the person in the regular environment with the use of supplementary aids and services cannot be achieved satisfactorily." § 104.34(a).

The sole issue on appeal with respect to the § 504 claim is whether the proposed IEP constituted a reasonable accommodation. We find that it did.

As explained above, the multi-component IEP that the School District proposed to J.D. responded to the major recommendations of his psychologist. In addition to advanced placement courses at PHS, the program would have given him access to some college-level courses at a nearby college (presumably at the School District's expense). Although the IEP would not have placed J.D. among intellectual peers of his own age, the School District did offer to provide individual counseling and training in peer relationship skills to cope with his feelings of isolation and frustration. We do not think that the School District's refusal to fund J.D.'s enrollment among intellectual peers of his own age, without more, amounts to discrimination. As noted above, the § 504 regulatory scheme expresses a preference for mainstreaming students with disabilities in a school district's regular school environment, unless that objective cannot be achieved even with the aid of supplementary services. Here, the overwhelming uncontroverted evidence shows that J.D.'s academic progress at PHS was exemplary. To the extent he was emotionally troubled, we cannot say that the counseling component of the IEP was an unreasonable accommodation, at least until such time, if ever, that it is proven ineffective.

The heart of J.D.'s opposition to the proposed accommodation is that it was not optimal. However, § 504 does not require a public school district to provide students with disabilities with potential-maximizing education, only reasonable accommodations that give those students the same access to the benefits of a public education as all other students. . . .

In sum, although we sympathize with the understandable desire of J.D.'s parents to provide the best possible education for their academically gifted child, we find no error in the district court's holding that the defendants did not discriminate against J.D. in violation of § 504 by declining to reimburse him for tuition and costs at an out-of-state residential school.

At bottom, in the matter before us, we as a court are constrained because this case involves issues of policy that are the domain of the legislative and administrative branches.

MR. I. v. MAINE SCHOOL
ADMINISTRATIVE DISTRICT NO. 55
480 F.3d 1 (1st Cir. 2007)

The court found that a school district improperly denied IDEA eligibility for a child with Asperger's Syndrome and depressive disorder despite the school's claim that the disability had no adverse effect on educational performance. The court relied in part on state law defining educational performance and on state and federal law establishing broad standards for special education, and tying the need for special education to benefit from special education in adversely affected areas of educational performance rather than overall achievement in school. At the same time, the court affirmed denial of tuition reimbursement and compensatory education remedies.

HOWARD, CIRCUIT JUDGE.

This case presents an issue of eligibility for benefits under the Individuals with Disabilities Education Act, 20 U.S.C. § 1400 et seq. (Supp. 2006) (the "IDEA"). We have previously noted that such issues can require a "difficult and sensitive" analysis. . . . This case is no exception. The appellant, Maine School Administrative District No. 55 ("the district"), appeals the district court's determination that the appellees' daughter ("LI") qualifies as a "child with a disability" eligible for special education and related services under the IDEA as a result of her Asperger's Syndrome. The appellees ("Mr. and Mrs. I" or "the parents") cross-appeal the district court's rulings that (1) even though LI was entitled to IDEA services, her parents were not entitled to reimbursement of their expenses in unilaterally placing LI in a private school following the district's refusal to provide those services and (2) the district would not be separately ordered to provide compensatory education services to reverse the effects of that decision on LI's progress. We affirm the judgment of the district court.

I.

We begin with an overview of the statutory framework. The IDEA provides funding to each state "to assist [it] to provide special education and related services to children with disabilities," 20 U.S.C. § 1411(a)(1), provided that "[a] free appropriate public education is available to all children with disabilities residing in the state. . . ." *Id.* § 1412(a)(1)(A). In this sense, a "free appropriate public education" encompasses "special education and related services," *id.* § 1401(9), including "specially designed instruction, at no cost to parents, to meet the unique needs of a child with a disability. . . ." *Id.* § 1401(29).

To receive special education and related services under the IDEA, a child must qualify as a "child with a disability." In relevant part, a "child with a disability" is a child

    (i) with mental retardation, hearing impairments (including deafness), speech or language impairments, visual impairments (including blindness), serious emotional disturbance (referred to in this chapter as "emotional disturbance"), orthopedic impairments, autism, traumatic brain injury, other health impairments, or specific learning disabilities; and

(ii) who, by reason thereof, needs special education and related services.

Id. § 1401(3)(A). The Secretary of Education has promulgated a regulation defining each of the categories of disability set forth in § 1401(3)(A)(i). Those definitions, so far as they are relevant here, require that each of the enumerated conditions "adversely affect[] a child's educational performance" to constitute a disability. 34 C.F.R. §§ 300.8(c)(1)(i) (2006) (autism), (c)(4)(i) (emotional disturbance), (c)(9)(ii) (other health impairment).

The IDEA places the burden of identifying children with disabilities upon each state. 20 U.S.C. § 1412(a)(3)(A). In deciding whether a particular student has a disability under the IDEA, Maine uses a "pupil evaluation team," or "PET," 05-071-101 Me. Code. R. § 9.4 (2006), consisting of the student's parents, a representative from the school district, and a number of educational and other professionals. *Id.* § 8.6; *see also* 20 U.S.C. § 1414(d)(1)(B). Though the members of the PET attempt to achieve consensus on this issue, the school district retains the "ultimate responsibility to ensure that a student is appropriately evaluated" for IDEA eligibility. 05-071-101 Me. Code. R. § 8.11(C).

The parents of a child deemed ineligible for IDEA benefits can challenge that determination before an impartial hearing officer. 20 U.S.C. §§ 1415(b)(6), (f)(1)(A), (f)(3)(A). After the hearing, the officer issues a final administrative decision, accompanied by findings of fact. *Id.* §§ 1415(h)(4), (i)(1)(A). Any party aggrieved by the decision can then file a civil action in federal district court. *Id.* § 1415(i)(2)(A). Then the "trial court must make an independent ruling based on the preponderance of the evidence, but the Act contemplates that the source of that evidence generally will be the administrative hearing record, with some supplementation at trial." *Town of Burlington v. Dep't of Educ.*, 736 F.2d 773, 790 (1st Cir. 1984), *aff'd sub nom. Sch. Comm. v. Dep't of Educ.*, 471 U.S. 359 (1985) ("*Burlington*"); *see also* 20 U.S.C. § 1415(i)(2)(C).

In keeping with this approach, the district court referred the case to a magistrate judge for proposed findings and a recommended disposition, *see* 28 U.S.C. § 636(b)(1)(B) (2006), which were made based on the facts adduced at the due process hearing and supplemental evidence submitted by the parents. The district court, in the absence of an objection from either side, accepted the magistrate's proposed findings wholesale. In the continued absence of any challenge to these factual findings, we take the same tack.

II.

A.

LI's
school
history

LI attended Cornish Elementary School in Cornish, Maine, until 2003. Though she excelled academically, by the fourth grade she began to experience sadness, anxiety, and difficulty with peer relationships. These problems persisted into the fifth grade, when LI sought to distance herself physically from most of her classmates. Her parents sought psychological counseling for LI and she started taking a prescription anti-depressant. Her grades also dropped from "high honors" to "honors." As the school year progressed, however, LI became more successful at interacting with her peers and participating in class.

During the summer recess preceding sixth grade, LI asked her mother, as she had the previous summer, to allow her to be home-schooled. LI also expressed her desire to attend The Community School ("TCS"), a private school in South Tamworth, New Hampshire, where her older sister had matriculated. Nevertheless, LI started the 2003-2004 school year at Cornish, where Mrs. I believed her daughter would benefit, in particular, from her assigned sixth grade teacher.

By mid-September, however, LI was "slacking off" in her academic work and regularly missing school, prompting a meeting between her teacher and Mrs. I. At this meeting, also attended by LI, Mrs. I noticed cuts or scratches on her daughter's arms; the teacher offered that LI might have inflicted those wounds on herself during her "lengthy bathroom breaks" from class. According to the teacher, LI was also having continued trouble relating with her peers due to a "serious lack of awareness" of their social and emotional states, which bordered on "hostility." The teacher added that she could not "reach" LI, who had refused to complete assignments and shown a "passive resistance to meeting learning goals." Yet the teacher considered LI "a very bright young girl with strong language and math skills . . . capable of powerful insights in her reading and writing. . . ."

The teacher and Mrs. I came up with a "contract" that would have entitled LI to study more advanced topics in her areas of interest in November if she satisfactorily completed her assignments for October. As October approached, however, LI refused to sign the contract and stayed home from school on both September 30 and October 1. On October 1, following an argument with Mrs. I over one of LI's academic assignments, LI deliberately ingested excessive quantities of one her prescription drugs and two over-the-counter medications in a suicide attempt.

LI spent the balance of the day in the emergency room at a nearby hospital and was discharged with instructions to remain out of school for two days under high safety precautions. The hospital social worker also directed Mr. and Mrs. I to "share with [LI] something that would change in her life, and produce a positive impact on her emotional functioning." Based on LI's comments to hospital personnel that she hated school, Mr. and Mrs. I told her that she would not have to return to Cornish Elementary and discussed enrollment at TCS as an alternative.

In the wake of her attempted suicide, LI met with a new counselor, who, suspecting that LI might suffer from Asperger's Syndrome, referred her to Dr. Ellen Popenoe for neuropsychological testing.[1] Mr. and Mrs. I conveyed this information, as well as the news of LI's suicide attempt, to the district's director of special services, Jim McDevitt. They added that LI would not return to Cornish Elementary "for the time being" and that they were looking at other options,

---

[1] [FN 2] "Asperger's disorder is a developmental disability on the autism spectrum that is associated with significant misperceptions of otherwise routine elements of daily life. It is a permanent condition that is not treatable with medication." *Greenland [Sch. Dist. v. Amy N.]*, 358 F.3d [150] at 154 [(2004)].

including TCS. McDevitt explained the process for seeking reimbursement from the district for placing LI in a private school and also told the parents that the district planned to convene a pupil evaluation team for LI at the end of the month. At that meeting, the PET decided that LI should receive up to ten hours of tutoring outside of school each week pending completion of her neuropsychological testing.

The testing, finished by early November, further suggested that LI had Asperger's Syndrome, as well as adjustment disorder with depressed mood. Popeneo, the neuropsychologist, observed that LI "experiences significant limitations in many areas of adaptive skills" and executive skills, "which likely contribute[s] to her behavioral and emotional difficulties." These behavioral difficulties, particularly LI's poor pragmatic language abilities and restricted range of social interests, supported a diagnosis of Asperger's. Popeneo recommended that LI begin seeing both a social skills coach, who would help her develop social abilities and judgment, and a therapist familiar with Asperger's, who would use a cognitive-behavioral approach.

Popeneo also recommended that LI undergo a speech-language evaluation, which was completed in January 2004 by Amber Lambke, a speech-language pathologist. Lambke observed that LI suffered "significant social understanding deficits which impact her overall emotional and social well-being." Like Popeneo, Lambke recommended that LI receive direct teaching of social skills.

In the meantime, McDevitt told Mrs. I that he would attempt to find LI a tutor in accordance with the PET's decision. Mrs. I had not heard back from him by November 10, however, so she started home-schooling LI. Despite additional prodding by Mrs. I in November and December, the district never provided a tutor as ordered by the PET, nor explained its failure to do so. While LI preferred home-schooling to attending Cornish Elementary, Mrs. I was having trouble getting LI to complete her assignments, and her counselor believed that LI should resume formal schooling.

On January 5, 2004, LI began attending TCS. Although she was withdrawn and isolated at the outset, over time LI developed positive relationships with some of her peers. She also thrived academically, completing assignments at the seventh- and eighth-grade level with ease. TCS, however, provided LI with neither the direct teaching of social skills nor the cognitive behavioral therapy that had been recommended as treatment for her Asperger's.

When the PET reconvened in early March, it accepted Popenoe's conclusion that LI suffered from both Asperger's and adjustment disorder with depressed mood. The PET also agreed that LI needed social skills and pragmatic language instruction. The PET, however, could not reach consensus on whether LI qualified as a "child with a disability" under the IDEA. The district's representatives argued that LI's condition, whether denominated "autism," "emotional disturbance," or "other health impairment," 20 U.S.C. § 1401(3)(A)(i), had not affected her academic performance "to a marked degree" or "over a long period of time," which they deemed essential to IDEA eligibility. The district then issued a "prior written notice," id. § 1415(b)(3), announcing its refusal to offer special education services on the stated basis of "no significant adverse effect on education." The district instead

District said to see if qualifies under Rehab. Act

asked the PET to consider LI's eligibility for services under the Rehabilitation Act, 29 U.S.C. § 794 (2000).

PET said aid quality

At its next meeting, the PET identified LI as a "qualified individual with a disability" under the Rehabilitation Act, *id.* § 794(a), and recommended an array of services. These included close supervision throughout the school day; instruction in "social pragmatics"; access to the district's existing gifted and talented programming as well as additional programming provided through a consultant to be hired by the district; and placement in any elementary school within the district. The district also offered to supply a tutor to work with LI for three hours each day to ease her eventual transition back to the classroom.

provided tutor

Mr. and Mrs. I objected to this proposal as inadequate and unduly restrictive, given LI's success in a classroom environment at TCS and her apprehension over returning to public school. They wanted LI to remain at TCS for the balance of the academic year with a view toward beginning her transition back to public school in September 2004, and notified the district that they intended to seek reimbursement under the IDEA for LI's attendance at TCS. LI completed the 2003-2004 academic year at TCS, and stayed on for the 2004-2005 and 2005-2006 school years as well. While she has done well academically, she continues to experience "atypical" peer relationships and spent the summer of 2004 shunning her TCS classmates in favor of solitary pursuits. LI also generally refuses to go outdoors or to eat more than a severely limited variety of foods. Her current social worker believes that, without social skills coaching, LI is unlikely to master the flexible thinking, problem solving, teamwork, and communication abilities she will need for employment in the future.

B.

Parents requeste due process hearing for not qualifying under IDEA

After the final PET decision, Mr. and Mrs. I requested a due process hearing to challenge the district's refusal to identify LI as a child with a disability under the IDEA. The hearing officer upheld the district's decision that LI was ineligible for IDEA services. The hearing officer noted the parties' agreement that LI had Asperger's and a depressive disorder, making her "a troubled young woman," but further observed that she was not entitled to IDEA benefits unless these disabilities " 'adversely affect[ed]' [her] educational performance."

The hearing officer recognized that both the IDEA and Maine's implementing regulations define "educational performance" to include more than just academic proficiency, but concluded that the IDEA does not call for services "to address social and emotional needs when there are no academic needs." Accordingly, because LI "completes homework independently, is well behaved in class, is successful at test taking and successfully completes projects," the hearing officer determined that "neither the [IDEA] nor the Maine Special Education Regulations require a school district to provide special education services to address what is essentially a mental health issue."

In response, Mr. and Mrs. I commenced an action in the district court, which, as we have noted, referred the case to a magistrate judge. The magistrate judge determined that the hearing officer erred in treating LI's lack of academic needs as dispositive of her IDEA eligibility when the correct standard, he believed, is whether a disability "manifest[s] itself in an adverse effect on the child's ability to learn." Nevertheless, the magistrate judge ruled that LI did not meet this standard because her condition did not adversely affect her achievements as measured by any of the criteria Maine uses to define "educational performance." While the magistrate judge recognized that LI had fallen short of these benchmarks during the period in the fall of 2003 when she had repeatedly missed school and attempted suicide, he considered this episode too short-lived "to trigger eligibility for special-education services."

The district court, however, rejected the magistrate judge's recommended decision, concluding that LI's "condition did adversely affect her educational performance as Maine defines that term and that the events of the fall of 2003 cannot be isolated from [her] underlying condition." The district court determined that LI's Asperger's had exerted an adverse effect on her educational performance as measured by state criteria, most significantly in the areas of socialization and communication. The district court also disagreed with the view that any downturn in LI's educational performance was too fleeting to constitute an "adverse effect." Reasoning that neither the Maine regulations defining the disabilities listed in § 1401(3)(A)(i) nor their federal counterparts used any restrictive modifier in conjunction with the term "adversely affects," the district court ruled that "any negative effect should be sufficient" to constitute a disability under the IDEA.

Turning to the second prong of the IDEA's eligibility standard, 20 U.S.C. § 1401(3)(A)(ii), the district court concluded that LI needed special education and related services by reason of her disability. First, the district court found that the PET had agreed to provide LI with a number of accommodations that fit the definition of "special education" under both the IDEA and Maine law, including one-on-one tutoring and instruction in social pragmatics. Second, observing that "the PET, the experts, the School District and the parents all initially believed that [LI] 'needed' the identified services," the district court decided to "hold the parties to their original understandings" and therefore treated "need" as an uncontested issue. Based on its determination that LI satisfied both elements of the IDEA eligibility test, the district court ordered the district "to convene a PET meeting . . . to develop an IEP for [LI] that meets her unique needs as a student with Asperger's Syndrome and a depressive disorder."

The district court also considered the parents' requests for additional relief: reimbursement of their expenses in unilaterally placing LI at TCS, and compensatory education to make up for the district's failure to identify her as eligible under the IDEA. Though the district court found that Mr. and Mrs. I had given the requisite notice of the unilateral placement under Maine law, the court also ruled that their decision to enroll LI at TCS was not "'reasonably calculated to enable [her] to receive educational benefits'" so as to entitle them to reimbursement. Finally, reasoning that LI's "IEP will necessarily take into account the effect of the school district's failure to identify and offer [LI] special education services earlier," the district court did not separately grant the parents' request for compensatory education.

III.

The district challenges the district court's conclusion that LI qualifies as a "child with a disability" under the IDEA. While we have never expressly set forth our standard of review for a district court's decision on IDEA eligibility, we have treated "ultimate determinations in cases under the Act" as mixed questions of fact and law. We agree with the parties that whether a student qualifies as "a child with a disability" under § 1401(3) also poses a mixed legal and factual inquiry. Mixed questions generally "fall along a degree-of-deference continuum, ranging from non-deferential plenary review for law-dominated questions, to deferential review for fact-dominated questions." *In re PolyMedica Corp. Sec. Litig.*, 432 F.3d 1, 4 (1st Cir. 2005). But we need not decide at the moment where along the continuum the question of IDEA eligibility falls, as the parties agree that we should review the question for clear error.

The district maintains, however, that the district court arrived at its conclusion that LI is a "child with a disability" only through a series of legal errors. First, the district argues that the district court misread the terms "adversely affects" and "educational performance" as they appear in the regulatory definitions of the disabilities attributed to LI, improperly extending the breadth of § 1401(3)(A)(i). Second, the district claims that the district court similarly misinterpreted the term "special education" as it appears in § 1401(3)(A)(ii), the second prong of the test for IDEA eligibility. The district also challenges the determination that it effectively waived the opportunity to dispute LI's need for special education. We review these rulings of law de novo.

A.

1.

Though the IDEA "establishes a basic floor of education" for children with disabilities, guaranteeing them "[a] free appropriate public education," 20 U.S.C. § 1412(a)(1)(A), it does not displace the states from their traditional role in setting their own educational policy. Each state thus remains free to calibrate its own educational standards, provided it does not set them below the minimum level prescribed by the statute.

As we have seen, the right to special education and related services under the IDEA extends to children "with" one or more of a variety of disabilities, 20 U.S.C. § 1401(3)(A)(i), "who, by reason thereof, need[] special education and related services." *Id.* § 1401(3)(A)(ii). The IDEA does not itself define any of the qualifying disabilities listed in § 1401(3)(A)(i), though the Department of Education has issued a regulation fleshing them out. 34 C.F.R. § 300.8(c). The regulatory definitions, with one exception not relevant here, state, among other requirements, that each condition must "adversely affect[] a child's educational performance." *Id.* § 300.8(c)(1)–(c)(13). In keeping with the IDEA's respect for state policy judgments, however, the regulation does not expand upon this phrase, "leaving it to each state to give substance to these terms."

It is here that the district's argument as to the proper scope of § 1401(3)(A) begins to encounter difficulty. While Maine's Department of Education has promulgated its own regulation defining the disabilities recognized under the IDEA, those definitions simply ape their federal counterparts, including the requirement that a disability "adversely affect[] the student's educational performance." 05-071-101 Me. Code. R. §§ 3.2–3.14 (2006). The regulation, like its federal cousin, also does not further elaborate on this phrase, although Maine has adopted its own definition of "educational performance" for IDEA purposes:

> The term "educational performance" includes academic areas (reading, math, communication, etc.), non-academic areas (daily life activities, mobility, etc.), extracurricular activities, progress in meeting goals established for the general curriculum, and performance on State-wide and local assessments.

Id. § 2.7. Despite this expansive notion of educational performance, and in the absence of any regulatory guidance as to the term "adversely affects," the district asks us to hold that a child meets the first criterion of IDEA eligibility in Maine "only if the student's condition imposes a significant negative impact on the child's educational performance . . . limited to those areas of performance actually being measured and assessed by the local unit, in accordance with law." We decline to do so.

At the outset, Maine does not look only at "areas of performance actually being measured and assessed by the local unit" when determining whether a child has a disability under the IDEA. That much is clear from the regulatory definition of "educational performance" itself, which counts "performance on state-wide and local assessments" as just one of a number of different indicators embraced by the concept. As the district points out, the term "general curriculum," which also appears in the definition of educational performance, has a narrower meaning under the regulations, i.e., "the school administrative unit's local curriculum for grades K-12 which incorporate the content standards and performance indicators of the Learning Results." 05-071-101 Me. Code. R. § 2.11. Based on this definition, the district argues that "educational performance" encompasses only those "performance indicators" measured as part of the local curriculum. Even if the district's reading of "general curriculum" is correct, however, the fact remains that a student's progress in that regard comprises but one of the aspects of "educational performance" as defined by the regulation. More far-ranging measurements, such as "academic areas" and "non-academic areas," are also included.

As the magistrate judge and the district court observed, Maine's broad definition of "educational performance" squares with the broad purpose behind the IDEA: "to ensure that all children with disabilities have available to them a free and appropriate public education that emphasizes special education and related services designed to meet their unique needs and prepare them for further education, employment, and independent living." 20 U.S.C. § 1400(d)(1)(A). We have likewise held that the IDEA entitles qualifying children to services that "target 'all of [their] special needs,' whether they be academic, physical, emotional, or social." It is true that we have also stated that IDEA services need not address "problems truly 'distinct' from learning problems." *Gonzalez v. P.R. Dep't of Educ.*, 254 F.3d 350, 352 (1st Cir. 2001); *see also Rome Sch. Comm. v. Mrs. B.*, 247 F.3d 29, 33 n.3 (1st Cir.

2001) (noting that, in determining adequacy of IEP for emotionally disturbed boy, "[t]he question is whether [his] behavioral disturbances interfered with the child's ability to learn"). But it does not follow, as the hearing officer wrongly concluded, that a child without "academic needs" is per se ineligible for IDEA benefits, especially when the state has conditioned eligibility on a standard that explicitly takes "non-academic areas" into account. In other words, as the district admits, "educational performance in Maine is more than just academics."

In light of Maine's broad notion of "educational performance" as the standard of IDEA eligibility, we see no basis for restricting that standard to "areas of performance actually being measured and assessed by the local unit." Indeed, "there is nothing in IDEA or its legislative history that supports the conclusion that . . . 'educational performance' is limited only to performance that is graded." *See* Robert A. Garda, Jr., *Untangling Eligibility Requirements Under the Individuals with Disabilities Education Act*, 69 Mo. L. Rev. 441, 471 (2003). To be sure, some states have adopted more circumscribed criteria for identifying children with disabilities under the IDEA, requiring, for example, that a student perform poorly in a specific area of "basic skills." Maine, however, has chosen not to do so.[2] We therefore decline the district's invitation to reformulate state educational policy by narrowing the indicia of educational performance used as the test for IDEA eligibility under Maine law. The district court properly articulated this standard as "whether [LI's] condition adversely affected her performance in any of the educational areas Maine has identified."

The district also argues that the district court misconstrued the "adversely affects" component of the test to include disabilities with "any adverse effect on educational performance, however slight. . . ." The correct formulation, the district urges, requires "some significant impact on educational performance." In rejecting this proposal, the district court reasoned that the phrase "adversely affects," as it appears in the relevant regulations, "has no qualifier such as 'substantial,' 'significant,' or 'marked,'" and declined to infer such a limitation "from Maine's regulatory silence." We agree with this interpretation of the "adversely affects" standard.

Though the district marshals a number of arguments in support of its contrary position, they all sound a common theme: that an unlimited definition of "adversely affects" will qualify every child with one of the listed disabilities — no matter how minor — for IDEA benefits. This contention, however, overlooks the structure of the IDEA's eligibility standard, which requires not only that a child have one of the listed conditions, § 1401(3)(A)(i), but also that, "by reason thereof," the child "needs special education and related services," *id.* § 1401(3)(A)(ii). So a finding that a child

---

[2] [FN 10] The Maine Department of Education has proposed amending its special education regulations to insert, inter alia, a requirement that "[a] child's disability must result in an adverse affect [sic] on the child's ability to learn and/or perform the academic, daily living, and/or age-relevant tasks required to demonstrate educational progress in the general curriculum." Maine Unified Special Education Regulation § VII.3 (proposed Nov. 2006), to be codified at 05-071-101 Me. Code R. § 1 et. seq., available at http://www.maine.gov/education/rulechanges.htm (last visited Feb. 21, 2006). The proposed regulations also restrict the definition of "educational performance" for children older than five to "academic areas (written literacy skills, math, communication, etc.) [and] functional areas of performance (daily life activities). . . ." *Id.* § II.9. These draft regulations, still in the public comment period, are not before us.

meets the first criterion because his or her disability adversely affects educational performance — to whatever degree — does not itself entitle the child to special education and related services under the IDEA. *See* Mark C. Weber, Special Education Law and Litigation Treatise § 2.2(1), at 2:4 (2d ed. 2002); Garda, *supra*, at 490–91. The child must also need special education and related services by reason of the disability.

In fact, an adverse effect on educational performance, standing alone, does not even satisfy the first prong of the eligibility test. The child's condition must also possess the additional characteristics required by the regulatory definitions of each of the disabilities enumerated in § 1401(3)(A)(i). *See* 34 C.F.R. §§ 300.8(c)(1)–(c)(13); 05-071-101 Me. Code. R. §§ 3.2–3.14. For example, to meet the first part of the eligibility standard on the basis of autism, a child must have "[1] a developmental disability [2] significantly affecting [3] verbal and [4] nonverbal communication and [5] social interaction, [6] generally evident before age three, [7] that adversely affects a child's educational performance." 34 C.F.R. § 300.8(c)(1)(i); 05-071-101 Me. Code. R. § 3.2. Thus, the "adversely affects educational performance" requirement serves as but one of a list of factors that must be present for a child's condition to qualify as a disability under § 1401(3)(A)(i) — and, to receive IDEA benefits, the child must also need special education and related services by reason of the disability under § 1401(3)(A)(ii). The district court's interpretation of "adversely affects," then, is unlikely to loose the torrent of IDEA claims forecast by the district and its amici.

The district's specific arguments fare no better. The district contends that § 1401(3)(A)(i) fails to put the states on notice that, as a condition of accepting federal money under the IDEA, they are required to provide benefits to children whose conditions have merely an "adverse effect" on their educational performance. It is true that "when Congress attaches conditions to a State's acceptance of federal funds" pursuant to its Spending Clause authority, "the conditions must be set out unambiguously" so that each state can intelligently decide whether to take the money and its accompanying obligations. *Arlington Cent. Sch. Dist. Bd. of Ed. v. Murphy*, 126 S. Ct. 2455, 2459 (2006) (internal quotation marks omitted). Based on this principle, the Supreme Court has held that whether the IDEA imposes a particular obligation on the states depends, at the outset, on whether the IDEA "furnishes clear notice regarding the liability at issue. . . ." *Id.*

The principal place to look for such notice, of course, is the text of the IDEA itself. The district asserts that the language of § 1401(3)(A)(i) fails to clarify that a state's duty to provide IDEA benefits extends to children with disabilities having only an adverse effect on educational performance. In fact, the district argues, the statute — through its use of the term "disability" — limits that duty to children whose conditions "significantly impact educational performance." We disagree.

To properly understand "disability" as it appears in the IDEA, we do not, as the district implores, resort to dictionary definitions of the word "disable," but to § 1401(3)(A)(i), which functions as the first part of the statutory definition of "child with a disability." Section 1401(3)(A)(i), as the district court observed, does not include the qualifying language urged upon us by the district, but simply defines "child with a disability" as a child "with" one of a number of specific conditions.

The district also directs us to the more restrictive meaning of the term "disability" under Title II of the Americans with Disabilities Act and the Rehabilitation Act. Because the IDEA contains its own definition of the term, however, its appearance in other acts of Congress is of little moment. . . .

Given the express definition of "disability" set forth in § 1401(3)(A)(i), we need look no further to conclude that the statute sufficiently articulates the first prong of the standard for IDEA eligibility and, in so doing, adequately informs the states of the extent of their obligations. The district and its amici nevertheless argue that this standard, as interpreted by the district court, flies in the face of congressional admonishments against identifying too many students as "children with disabilities" under the IDEA. It is true that, in amending the Act in 1997, Congress voiced concern about "over identifying children as disabled when they may not be truly disabled . . . particularly in urban schools with high proportions of minority students. . . ." H.R. Rep. No. 105-95, at 89 (1997), reprinted in 1997 U.S.C.C.A.N. 78, 86. To remedy this problem, Congress changed the formula for calculating the funds due each state under the IDEA from one "based on the number of children with disabilities to a formula based on census and poverty. . . ."

Notably, though, Congress thought this shift — rather than any alteration to the eligibility criteria — sufficient to address the over-identification problem. Congress specifically stated, in fact, that the change to the funding formula "should in no way be construed to modify the obligation of educational agencies to identify and serve students with disabilities." *Id.* at 88, 1997 U.S.C.C.A.N. at 85. Congress eschewed any change to the eligibility standard not only in 1997, but also in 2004, when it amended the IDEA again. Individuals with Disabilities Education Improvement Act of 2004, Pub. L. No. 108-446, § 602(3)(A), 118 Stat. 2647, 2652, codified at 20 U.S.C. § 1401(3)(A). The Department of Education similarly declined, by and large, to tinker with its definitions of the § 1401(3)(A)(i) disabilities when it issued regulations in response to the amended Act. 71 Fed. Reg. 46,540, 46,549–46,551 (Aug. 14, 2006). Thus, although the district and its amici argue that an over-identification problem persists, we cannot tighten the standard for IDEA eligibility when Congress itself has chosen not to do so.[3]

The legislative history, then, only strengthens our conviction that § 1401(3)(A)(i), as construed by the district court, does not offend the Spending Clause by springing hidden liabilities upon participating states. Furthermore, as the district acknowledges, states deciding whether to enter into the IDEA bargain also have the benefit of the federal regulation defining the disabilities set forth in § 1401(3)(A)(i). Those definitions, again, specifically require that each disability (save one) "adversely affect[] a child's educational performance." 34 C.F.R. §§ 300.8(c)(1)–(c)(13). They do

---

[3] [FN 13] Moreover, Congress took this course of action despite the presidential committee report touted by the district and its amici in support of their proffered standard. President's Comm'n on Excellence in Special Educ., A New Era: Revitalizing Special Education for Children and Their Families (2002), available at http://www.ed.gov/inits/commissionsboards/whspecialeducation/index.html (last visited Jan. 19, 2007). This report not only further expressed concern about over-identification, as the district and its amici point out, but strongly criticized the regulatory definitions of the disabilities recognized by the IDEA. *Id.* at 22. Because neither Congress nor the Department of Education appears to have acted on the commission's recommendations, however, the report is of little use in construing the eligibility standards that have endured.

not contain the limiting language urged by the district, i.e., "significantly impacts educational performance."

We reject the district's argument that such a limitation lurks in the term "adversely," which the district equates with "calamitously" or "perniciously" on the authority of an unabridged dictionary. We think it considerably more likely that federal regulators used "adverse" in its ordinary sense, namely "against." *Black's Law Dictionary* 58 (8th ed. 2004); *see also* Webster's Third New International Dictionary of the English Language (Unabridged) 31 (1993) (giving primary definition of "adverse" as "acting against or in a contrary direction"). In this way, the regulation sensibly demands that a disability cannot qualify a child for IDEA benefits unless it has a negative effect on educational performance; no effect, or a positive one, will not do. The regulation does not, however, put any quantitative limit, "significant" or otherwise, on the disability.

Maine's regulation, cribbed from 34 C.F.R. § 300.8, also requires no particular degree of impact on educational performance. 05-071-101 Me. Code. R. §§ 3.2–3.14. This fact alone distinguishes this case from the decisions of other courts, cited by the district, which derived a higher standard from state law. See *J.D.*, 224 F.3d at 66–67; *Gregory M. ex rel. Ernest M. v. State Bd. of Educ.*, 891 F. Supp. 695, 702 (D. Conn. 1995); *Doe ex rel. Doe v. Bd. of Educ.*, 753 F. Supp. 65, 70 & n.9 (D. Conn. 1990). In *J.D.*, for example, the Second Circuit considered a Vermont regulation that defined "adverse effect of the disability on educational performance" to require a determination "that the student is functioning significantly below expected age or grade norms, in one or more of the basic skills." 224 F.3d at 66 (internal quotation marks omitted). This provision further required that the "determination of adverse effect, usually defined as 1.0 standard deviation or its equivalent, shall be documented and supported by two or more measures of school performance," which were themselves specified by the regulation. *Id.* Based on this standard, the Second Circuit concluded that the child did not qualify for IDEA benefits because he was "unable to identify at least two school performance measures that point to an adverse effect," despite his emotional-behavioral disability. *Id.* at 67.

The Second Circuit reached its decision in *J.D.*, then, by applying the highly specific definition of "adversely affects educational performance" set forth in state law, not by imposing its own gloss on that language, as the district invites us to do here. For the reasons we have stated, we decline that invitation. States wishing to put meat on the bones of the "adversely affects" standard are free to do so — provided, of course, they do not transgress the "floor" of substantive protection set by the IDEA.[4] On its own, however, the federal regulation does not contain the

---

[4] [FN 17] Maine recently passed emergency legislation, effective May 30, 2006, defining "child with a disability," in relevant part, as: "[f]or children at least 3 years of age and under 20 years of age evaluated in accordance with [20 U.S.C. §§ 1414(a)–(c)] as measured by both standardized, norm-referenced diagnostic instruments and appropriate procedures with delays or impairments such that the children need special education . . . with at least one" of a number of specified conditions. An Act To Improve Early Childhood Education, 2006 Me. Legis. Serv. 662, sec. A-15, § 7001(1–B)(B), to be codified at Me. Rev. Stat. Ann. tit. 20-A, § 7001(1–B)(B). The Maine Department of Education has also proposed a regulation imposing a number of requirements, similar to Vermont's, on the adverse effect determination. *See* Maine Unified Special Education Regulation, *supra*, § VII.3. These versions of the Maine definitions are not before us, however, and we express no opinion on them.

"significant impact" requirement the district desires, and we cannot put it there. The district court correctly ruled that any negative impact, regardless of degree, qualifies as an "adverse effect" under the relevant federal and state regulations defining the disabilities listed in § 1401(3)(A)(i).

2.

Because the district court applied the right standard, we review its determination that LI has one of the disabilities included in § 1401(3)(A)(i) "for clear error on the record as a whole." We find none. As the hearing officer noted, the parties agree that LI suffers from Asperger's, manifested in her poor pragmatic language skills and social understanding difficulties, as well as from a depressive disorder brought on by the stress of managing these problems; indeed, the district has never questioned the opinions of LI's neuropsychologist and speech therapist in this regard. The parties disagree, however, on whether these conditions have adversely affected LI's educational performance in light of her strong grades, generally nondisruptive classroom behavior, and what the district court called her "undisputed intellectual ability." In a lengthy written opinion, the district court tackled this issue head on, ultimately finding that, despite LI's above-average academic performance, "many of [her] social and communication deficits, including her isolation, inflexibility, and self-mutilation during schooltime, are precisely in the content areas and skills that Maine mandates educationally." This finding, the district court reasoned, compelled the conclusion that LI's disability had exerted an adverse effect on her educational performance under the governing standard.

Much of the district's challenge to this outcome relies on its contention that the district court applied the "adversely affects educational performance" test too leniently, which we have already rejected. A few of the district's supplemental points, however, merit additional discussion. First, the district argues that the district court mistakenly gauged LI's educational performance on the basis of selected "performance indicators," see 05-071-131 Me. Code R. §§ 1–8, that Maine has developed to measure students' proficiency in various "content standard subject areas." Me. Rev. Stat. Ann. tit. 20-A, § 6209. This was error, the district asserts, because Maine does not mandate the actual use of the performance indicators by local school districts, but has simply instructed them to develop their own "local assessment systems." Id. § 6202-A. While we have our doubts about this proposition, see 05-071-127 Me. Code R. § 4.02 (requiring each district to "implement a local assessment system as the measure of student progress on achievement of the content standards of the system of Learning Results established in" 05-071-131 Me. Code R. §§ 1–8), the district court did not assess LI's educational performance solely by reference to the performance indicators. Our review of the record convinces us that, even if the district court erred by also using the performance indicators to measure LI's educational performance, the error did not affect the outcome of its analysis.

In particular, the district court found that LI had difficulty with "communication," an area of "educational performance" specifically incorporated in Maine's definition of that term for IDEA purposes. The district disputes this finding, emphasizing certain aspects of both her educators' observations and the results of the testing conducted by Popeneo and Lambke. The district court, however, focused on other aspects of those materials, such as the educators' reports of LI's "distancing" herself from her teachers and peers and, most significantly, the experts' express conclusions that LI had "poor pragmatic language skills" and "significant social understanding deficits." The district court was by no means required to second-guess these conclusions, especially after they had been unreservedly accepted by both the districts' representatives at the PET and the hearing officer. Though the record of the administrative hearing might permit a different view, the district court did not commit clear error in finding that LI's Asperger's has impaired her ability to communicate.

Moreover, the district court's ruling that LI had demonstrated an adverse effect on her educational performance did not rest solely on her deficits in communication, but also on other difficulties implicating "the career preparation component of the Maine general curriculum." The district does not question that "career preparation" — which comprises one of the "content standards" dictated by statute, Me. Rev. Stat. Ann. tit. 20-A, § 6209(2)(A), rather than one of the "performance indicators" established by regulation — is irrelevant to the "educational performance" inquiry for purposes of the IDEA. Indeed, the IDEA exists, in part, to ensure children with disabilities receive an education preparing them for employment. 20 U.S.C. § 1400(d)(1)(A). Nor does the district question the lower court's specific finding, consistent with the opinion of LI's current social worker, that a number of LI's symptoms have hindered her in this area. 416 F. Supp. 2d at 162. This finding was itself an adequate basis for the district court's conclusion that LI's educational performance has suffered, even if, as the district argues, her condition has not impacted her communication skills.

Second, the district argues that the impact of LI's condition on her educational performance, which it sees as limited to her suicide attempt and the events immediately preceding it in the fall of 2003, was not sustained enough to constitute an adverse effect. Though the magistrate judge accepted this point of view, the district court disagreed, treating the suicide attempt as simply the darkest point in the spectrum of LI's educational difficulties. There is ample support for this approach in the record. . . .

Third, the district charges that the district court "committed legal error" by ruling that LI met the first prong of the standard for IDEA eligibility without assigning her one of the disabilities listed in § 1401(3)(A)(i). As we have pointed out, that a condition "adversely affects a child's educational performance" functions as just one of the essential elements of each of the qualifying disabilities as defined in the regulation, so a determination that a child has one of those disabilities would ordinarily demand a showing as to each of those elements. Here, however, the district court specifically noted that, while the parties were at odds as to whether LI's condition adversely affected her educational performance, they were in agreement that her condition otherwise "fit[] within those enumerated" by § 1401(3)(A)(i). The district has not questioned this observation. . . .

B.

The district also argues that the district court misapplied § 1401(3)(A)(ii), which requires that a child "need[] special education and related services" as a result of his or her disability in order to qualify for them under the IDEA. The district asserts two errors: first, the district court used the wrong definition of "special education," and, second, it found that the district had waived any argument that LI does not "need" special education based on the position it took before the PET and the hearing officer. We believe the district court correctly defined "special education" under § 1401(3)(A)(ii). We do not decide, however, whether the district court properly treated the "need" issue as waived, because the district has not adequately explained to us why LI does not need special education, even under its view of the proper standard for making that determination.

1.

The IDEA defines "special education," in relevant part, as "specially designed instruction, at no cost to parents, to meet the unique needs of a child with a disability. . . ." 20 U.S.C. § 1401(29). A federal regulation, promulgated by the Department of Education, elaborates:

> Specially designed instruction means adapting, as appropriate to the needs of an eligible child . . . , the content, methodology, or delivery of instruction —
>
> (i) To address the unique needs of the child that result from the child's disability; and
>
> (ii) To ensure access of the child to the general curriculum, so that the child can meet the educational standards within the jurisdiction of the public agency that apply to all children.

34 C.F.R. § 300.39(b)(3) (2006). As the district court noted, Maine law also contains its own definition of "special education": "classroom, home, hospital, institutional or other instruction; educational diagnosis and evaluation; transportation and other supportive assistance, services, activities, or programs, as defined by the commissioner [of education], required by exceptional students."[5] Me. Rev. Stat. Ann. tit. 20-A, § 7001(5) (1993).

The district court ruled that a number of the interventions recommended by Popeneo and Lambke, and included in the services offered by the PET under the Rehabilitation Act, were "special education" within the meaning of federal law as well as "under Maine's broader definition." In challenging this conclusion, the district principally argues that the district court misinterpreted Maine law to exceed IDEA requirements as to the definition of "special education." We have little

---

[5] [FN 19] This definition is set forth as part of a statute requiring each school district to, inter alia, "[p]rovide special education for each exceptional student within its jurisdiction." Me. Rev. Stat. Ann. tit. 20-A, § 7202(5) (1993). The statute defines "exceptional student" as a person between the ages of five and twenty who "[r]equires special education because of an impairment in one or more" specified functions. *Id.* § 7001(2). As we have observed, *supra* note 17, this provision was recently amended, as were §§ 7001(5) and 7202(5), but the amended versions are not before us.

trouble with the district court's interpretation, given the expansive language of Me. Rev. Stat. Ann. tit. 20-A, § 7001(5), but, in any event, that provision was not essential to the district court's view that LI needs special education. The district court also specifically ruled that certain of the services recommended for LI constituted "special education" as defined by federal law.

Most significantly, the district court reasoned that "extra instructional offerings such as social-skills and pragmatic-language instruction are 'specially designed instruction' to ensure [LI's] 'access . . . to the general curriculum.'" The district protests that its proffered "social pragmatics instruction," which "was aimed more at counseling LI at how she could better interact with others" than at traditional "speech services," qualifies as a "related service," not "special education," under the IDEA. The district has it backwards, however. While "speech-language pathology services" comprise a category of "related services," 20 U.S.C. § 1401(26)(A), directly teaching social skills and pragmatic language to LI amounts to adapting the content of the usual instruction to address her unique needs and to ensure that she meets state educational standards, viz., those defining educational performance to include "communication" and requiring progress in "career preparation."[6] The district court did not err in ruling that the services recommended for LI by her neuropsychologist and speech-language pathologist, and agreed to by the PET as part of its Rehabilitation Act plan, are "special education."

2.

The district also challenges the district court's resolution of whether LI "needs" the special education in question. The district court made no finding on this point, electing to "hold the parties to their original understandings" that "'[n]eed' is not a contested issue." In support of this course of action, the district court noted that "the factual record on need is poorly developed" because "the PET meetings proceeded on the basis that everyone agreed that LI 'needed' and should be afforded what the experts recommended for her" and because the district gave no indication that it disputed LI's need for special education in either the prior written notice heralding its denial of IDEA benefits or its brief filed in advance of the due process hearing. Accordingly, the district court reasoned that "[w]hether or not waiver is the correct term," it had no sensible option but to conclude that LI "'needed' the identified services" as the parties "all initially believed."

The district insists that it preserved the issue of LI's need for special education by presenting argument and evidence on that score at the due process hearing. We agree with the district that it adduced some evidence at the hearing, in the form of testimony from McDevitt, as to LI's need for special education. . . .

We need not decide whether this presentation came too late to raise the issue of

---

[6] [FN 20] Contrary to the district's reading, the Second Circuit in *J.D.* did not "conclude" that "training in peer relationship skills . . . is more akin to a related service rather than special education." Rather, as we have discussed, the court in *J.D.* ruled that the student did not qualify for IDEA benefits because his condition did not adversely affect his educational performance in the manner required for IDEA eligibility under Vermont law. 224 F.3d at 67–68. The court in *J.D.* therefore had no occasion to define "training in peer relationship skills," which the defendant had offered as part of a Rehabilitation Act plan, as either special education or a related service under the IDEA, and did not do so.

LI's need for special education, as the district court ruled, because the district does not explain why LI does not need special education under the standard it urges us to follow in making that determination. The district contends that "whether a child needs special education for IDEA eligibility should depend on whether that child requires special education to benefit in those areas of educational performance that are adversely affected," but does not argue that LI does not pass that test. Instead, the district argues, based on McDevitt's testimony and LI's performance at TCS, that she does not need special education "to benefit from school" or "to do well in school."

But whether a child requires special education "to do well in school," or even "to benefit from school," presents a different question from whether the child requires special education "to benefit in those areas of educational performance that are adversely affected by her disability." The former inquiry considers the effect of special education on the child's overall achievement in school, while the latter focuses on the effect of special education on the components of that achievement hampered by the child's disability. *See* Garda, *supra*, at 498–99 (positing "which of the child's performance areas must need special education?" as a crucial question in developing the test for IDEA eligibility under § 1401(3)(A)(ii)). Indeed, a child may "do well in school" without special education, accumulating a high grade point average, but may nevertheless perform below acceptable levels in other areas, such as behavior. *See, e.g., In re Monrovia Unified Sch. Dist.*, 38 Inds. with Disabilities Educ. L. Reptr. (LRP Publ'ns) 84, at 342–43 (Cal. State Educ. Agency Nov. 27, 2002) (finding student to "require special education to address social, behavioral, and written expression needs" despite "good academic work"). The questions of whether such a child "needs special education" under a proper interpretation of § 1401(3)(A)(ii) — and how to articulate that interpretation in the first instance — have generated a cacophony of different answers. *See* Garda, *supra*, at 491–507 (surveying divergent authority).

We do not attempt to compose the correct standard of "need" here. We simply note the significant variance between the standard the district urges us to adopt and the standard it argues has been satisfied. McDevitt's testimony may have supported a finding that LI does not require special education "to do well in school," had the district court not ruled that the issue had been waived. But the district does not explain how such a finding would support the conclusion that LI does not "need special education" under the IDEA and, in fact, argues that the proper inquiry incorporates a substantially different standard, i.e., whether LI "requires special education to benefit in those areas of educational performance that are adversely affected." Conversely, the district does not explain how the evidence received at the due process hearing falls short of that standard. The district has therefore failed to show that the district court's treatment of the "need" issue as settled had any effect on its ultimate conclusion that LI qualified for IDEA benefits. . . .

The district has not directed us to any error undermining the district court's determination that LI meets the second prong of the standard for IDEA eligibility, 20 U.S.C. § 1401(3)(A)(ii).

Having found that the district court's ruling as to the first prong also holds up,

Part III.A, *supra*, we affirm the district court's decision that LI is eligible for services under the IDEA.

IV.

In their cross-appeal, the parents challenge the adequacy of the relief given as a remedy for the district's failure to provide LI with IDEA benefits. First, they argue that the district court wrongfully denied them reimbursement for the costs of enrolling LI at TCS on the ground that it is not an educationally appropriate placement. Second, they argue that the district court should have explicitly ordered the district to provide LI with a compensatory education as a remedy for its denial of IDEA services, rather than leaving that matter for the PET to decide in the first instance. We address these contentions in turn.

A.

The IDEA authorizes a district court reviewing the outcome of a due process hearing to "grant such relief as the court determines is appropriate." 20 U.S.C. § 1415(i)(2)(C)(iii). The Supreme Court has read this provision, as it appeared in the predecessor to the IDEA, as empowering a court "to order school authorities to reimburse parents for their expenditures on private special education for a child if the court ultimately determines that such placement, rather than a proposed IEP, is proper under the Act." *Burlington*, 471 U.S. at 369. In accordance with this holding, parents "are entitled to reimbursement only if a federal court concludes both that the public placement violated IDEA and that the private school placement was proper under the Act." *Florence County [Sch. Dist. Four v. Carter by & Through Carter]*, 510 U.S. [7] at 15 [(1993)]. . . .

[T]he right to reimbursement of private special education expenses depends in the first instance on whether the private school placement was "proper." We consider this threshold inquiry, like other conclusions demanded by the IDEA, as a mixed question of fact and law. As we did with the question of LI's eligibility for IDEA benefits, we will review the propriety of her enrollment at TCS for clear error based on the parties' accession to that standard.

. . . .

We do not see . . . how the decision to reject public education in favor of enrolling a child in private school can be described as "reasonably calculated to enable the child to receive educational benefit" if the private school does not offer at least "some element of special education services in which the public school placement was deficient." To hold otherwise would, in essence, embrace the argument we explicitly rejected in *Rafferty*: that the IDEA entitles a parent, at public expense, to "seek any alternative school she wishes if the public education is inadequate."

Accordingly, the district court did not apply the wrong standard in finding that TCS is not an appropriate private school placement under the IDEA because it "does not offer any of the special education services recommended by the experts or the PET." We are left, then, to review this finding for clear error, and discern none. Although both of the experts who examined LI, as well as her present social worker, have stressed that LI needs direct teaching of social skills to manage the effects of her Asperger's, it is undisputed that TCS has never provided her with this service, or any roughly equivalent intervention. TCS has also not supplied the cognitive behavioral therapy recommended by Popeneo or the close supervision or one-on-one tutoring offered by the PET as part of the Rehabilitation Act plan. The district court did not clearly err in judging TCS an inappropriate private placement in the absence of any of these special education services.

. . . .

B.

Finally, Mr. and Mrs. I challenge the district court's refusal to order the district to provide LI with compensatory education. We have recognized that, as another form of "appropriate relief" available under § 1415(i)(2)(C)(iii), a court may require "compensatory education" in the form of "further services, in compensation for past deprivations" of IDEA benefits. Compensatory education, like reimbursement, is a form of equitable relief. Accordingly, we review the district court's decision on compensatory education for abuse of discretion.

The district court considered the parents' request for compensatory education in light of the other relief granted, namely its order to the district "to convene a PET meeting in accordance with State and Federal law to develop an IEP for [LI] that meets her unique needs as a student with Asperger's Syndrome and a depressive disorder." Noting that "[t]he IEP necessarily will take into account the effect of the School District's failure to identify and offer special education services earlier," the district court declined to order compensatory education on the theory that the PET could better assess "what special education [LI] needs at this point. . . ."

This approach strikes us as sensible and, moreover, not an abuse of the district court's discretion. As the parents acknowledge, it is not unheard of for a compensatory education claim to be remanded to the responsible educational authority for consideration, particularly where "the district court does not believe that the record is sufficient to permit it to make the highly nuanced judgments necessary to resolve the claim. . . ." The parents, in fact, do not appear to object to such an approach here, provided we "ensure at the very least that guidelines governing the type, form, intensity, and duration of services are specified to assist the parties in moving forward without confusion or acrimony." This is a worthy objective, to be sure, but we are not up to the task.

Like the district court, we confront an administrative record naturally devoid of any evidence as to the effect of the district's failure to offer IDEA services to LI over the past two years and counting, since LI's eligibility for those services was precisely what was at issue in the due process hearing. As a result, any "guidelines" that we might set forth to "govern" the resolution of the compensatory education claim would amount to an improper advisory opinion, just as it would have been a highly speculative exercise for the district court to attempt to resolve the claim on its merits. The district court ordered the district to convene a PET, in accordance with applicable law, for the purpose of formulating an IEP for LI that meets her needs, and further recognized that this task would necessarily require resolution of the compensatory education inquiry. We do not view this as an abuse of discretion, and Mr. and Mrs. I have not provided us with any authority to the contrary.

V.

For the foregoing reasons, we affirm the judgment of the district court in its entirety.

NOTES AND QUESTIONS

1. *J.D.* offers a good example of three crucial relationships: first, the interplay between statutory and regulatory provisions; second, the relationship between federal and state law; and third, the relationship between special education and related services under IDEA and reasonable accommodation under section 504. Gifted students are only one of several examples where students who do not qualify for special education under IDEA might be entitled to certain services under section 504 or the ADA. Of course some students may be covered under IDEA as well as section 504 and the ADA. *See, e.g., Weixel v. Board of Educ.*, 287 F.3d 138 (2d Cir. 2002) (student with chronic fatigue syndrome and fibromyalgia may be covered under IDEA and section 504/ADA). For an interesting discussion, particularly on the relationship of 504 and the ADA, see Ruth Colker, *The Americans with Disabilities Act: The Death of Section 504*, 35 U. MICH. J.L. REF. 219 (2002).

2. *J.D.* is consistent with other court decisions that find that academic giftedness is not a disabling condition, though some state statutes explicitly make gifted students eligible for services. For example, Louisiana's special education statute provides: "A 'child with an exceptionality' is any child who is located, identified, and evaluated according to R.S. 17:1945 and is defined in the regulations developed pursuant to R.S. 17:1944 with mental disabilities, hearing impairments (including deafness), multiple disabilities, deaf-blindness, speech or language impairments, visual impairments (including blindness), emotional/behavioral disorders, orthopedic impairments, other health impairments, specific learning disabilities, which include perceptual disabilities, brain injury, minimal brain dysfunction, developmental aphasia and dyslexia, traumatic brain injury, or autism, or as being gifted or talented, and as a result may require special education and related services. This may also include a child with a disability, aged three through nine experiencing developmental delays." La. R.S. 17:1943. The services provided would presumably need to be funded by some means other than federal IDEA dollars, unless the gifted student were eligible for IDEA on some other basis.

3. *J.D.* also is typical of other court decisions outlining the parameters of a state or district obligation under section 504, which is to provide an evenhanded, equal access to a free appropriate public education. The basic standard for section 504 was enunciated by the Supreme Court in *Southeastern Community College v. Davis*, 442 U.S. 397 (1979). Deciding against a claim by a deaf student for accommodations in admission to an associate-degree nursing program, the Court observed that Congress recognized a distinction between evenhanded treatment and affirmative efforts and specifically concluded that "Section 504 imposes no requirement upon an educational institution to lower or to effect substantial modifications of standards to

accommodate a handicapped person." Where the accommodation of the student would have required reducing a clinical program to an academics-only program or otherwise drastically altering the method of instruction, the Court found such "a fundamental alteration in the nature of a program is far more than the 'modification' the regulation requires." For further discussion of issues of particular relevance to section 504 claims regarding higher education, see *infra* Chapter 14 (Post-Secondary Education). Additional sources include Ruth Colker, Et. al., The Law of Disability Discrimination, Chapter 4 (4th ed. 2003); Laura Rothstein, Disability Law: Cases, Materials, and Problems, Chapter 6 (3d ed. 2002).

4. *Mr. I.* concludes that the child at issue is eligible for services under IDEA. How does its approach differ from that of the *J.D.* court? Are the differences between Vermont law and Maine law significant enough to explain the difference in the courts' views? Does it make sense for the same child to meet eligibility standards under one state's implementation of a federal program and not meet eligibility standards under another state's rules?

5. The court in *Mr. I.* mentions at several points that Maine has now changed its laws. From the court's description of the new changes, do you think that L.I. is still eligible for services? Should a state be permitted to amend its rules to eliminate eligibility for children it previously would have been required to serve?

6. In another case involving a gifted child, the court in *Hood v. Encinitas Union School District*, 486 F.3d 1099 (9th Cir. 2007), affirmed administrative and district court determinations that a child with a section 504 plan was not eligible for services under IDEA on the basis of specific learning disability or other health impairment. Accordingly, it rejected a tuition reimbursement claim for a unilateral private placement undertaken by the parents. Anna's intellectual ability was high, but she had a seizure disorder and had to take medication for attention deficit disorder. Her section 504 accommodations plan in public school included preferential seating, use of a graphic organizer and a keyboard, simplified directions, visual support for instruction, frequent checks for understanding of material, and daily teacher checks of homework. On the issue of eligibility on the basis of learning disability, the parents pointed to the discrepancy between Anna's high ability and her achievement of merely average grades in her classes, but the court relied on a state law provision that conditioned eligibility on the requirement that a discrepancy between ability and achievement not be able to be corrected through regular or categorical services offered within the regular instruction program. The court went on to state that cases such as *Board of Education v. Rowley*, 458 U.S. 176 (1982), are instructive in assessing whether the "correctability" standard is satisfied, and emphasized that under *Rowley*, services need not be maximized but rather provide a basic floor of opportunity. There may be grounds to criticize *Hood* for relying on *Rowley*, which as the *Hood* court admitted, is a case about the appropriate education of a child achieving at grade level who was clearly eligible for special education. The United States Department of Education has consistently interpreted IDEA as barring the public school from imposing any eligibility requirement that the child fail to progress from grade to grade. *Letter to Anonymous*, 41 Individuals with Disabilities Educ. L. Rep. 212 (U.S. Dep't of Educ., Off. of Special Educ. & Rehabilitative Servs. 2004). Is the result in *Hood* nevertheless a sensible one? Interestingly, the opinion reports that when Anna reached high school two years later, the new school

district found her eligible for special education.

7. The facts of *Mr. I.* are illustrative of students whose disabilities may be multiple. For an example of disabilities and behavior changing over time, see *Alvin Independent School District v. A.D.*, 503 F.3d 378 (5th Cir. 2007). In *Alvin*, the student originally received special education in elementary school based on ADHD and a speech impediment, then on agreement stopped receiving services, then in seventh grade exhibited behavioral, mood, and alcohol-abuse issues culminating in a theft charge. While disciplinary charges were pending, A.D.'s mother asked for him to again receive special education services, which the school district refused, based in part on the finding that his academic performance ranged between average and high, his "cognitive abilities were found to be in the average range . . . [and] symptoms of ADHD did not prevent him from making age-appropriate academic and social progress." The reviewing courts agreed with the school district. *Id.* at 380–81.

8. In recent scholarship, Professor Garda calls for greater attention to whether a child needs special education and related services by reason of the child's disabling condition, arguing for a more limited eligibility standard under IDEA. Robert A. Garda, *Who Is Eligible Under the Individuals with Disabilities Education Improvement Act?*, 35 J.L. & EDUC. 291, 332 (2006). Professor Weber argues for a laxer reading of the needs-special-education-by-reason-of-the-disability term, and for a broader understanding of IDEA eligibility. Mark C. Weber, *The IDEA Eligibility Mess*, 57 BUFF. L. REV. 83 (2009). Both articles collect and analyze recent caselaw on the eligibility topic.

E.   PARTICULAR ACTIVITIES AND CONDITIONS

POTTGEN v. MISSOURI STATE HIGH SCHOOL ACTIVITIES ASSOCIATION
40 F.3d 926 (8th Cir. 1994)

The court found that a nineteen year old who was still in high school because of learning disabilities was not entitled to waiver of an athletic association's age eligibility requirements under section 504 or ADA where the rule was "an essential eligibility standard" and its waiver would "constitute a fundamental alteration in the nature of the baseball program."

BEAM, CIRCUIT JUDGE.

The Missouri State High School Activities Association (hereinafter "MSHSAA") appeals the issuance of a preliminary injunction which restrains it from enforcing its age limit for interscholastic sports against Edward Leo Pottgen. . . .

After Pottgen repeated two grades in elementary school, the school tested him to see whether he needed special classroom assistance. When the school discovered that Pottgen had several learning disabilities, it placed him on an individualized program and provided him with access to special services. With these additional resources, Pottgen progressed through school at a normal rate. . . . He played interscholastic baseball for three years in high school and planned to play baseball his senior year as well. However, because he had repeated two grades, Pottgen turned nineteen shortly before July 1 of his senior year. Consequently, MSHSAA By-Laws rendered Pottgen ineligible to play. . . .

Pottgen petitioned MSHSAA for a hardship exception to the age limit since he was held back due to his learning disabilities. Pottgen struck out. MSHSAA determined that waiving the requirement violated the intent of the age eligibility rule.

Pottgen then brought this suit, alleging MSHSAA's age limit violated the Rehabilitation Act of 1973 (the "Rehabilitation Act"), the Americans with Disabilities Act (the "ADA"), and section 1983. The district court granted a preliminary injunction enjoining MSHSAA from "(i) preventing [Pottgen] from competing in any Hancock High School baseball games or district or state tournament games; and (ii) imposing any penalty, discipline or sanction on any school for which or against which [Pottgen] competes in these games." . . .

Pottgen has now played his last game of high school baseball. Thus, the portion of the injunction permitting him to play is moot. However, a live controversy still exists regarding the portion of the injunction which prohibits MSHSAA from imposing sanctions upon a high school for whom or against whom Pottgen played.

. . . MSHSAA appeals the district court's finding that Pottgen could potentially prevail under the Rehabilitation Act. MSHSAA contends Pottgen is not an "otherwise qualified individual" under section 504 of the Rehabilitation Act.

Section 504 states that "No otherwise qualified individual with a disability . . . shall, solely by reason of her or his disability, be excluded from the participation in, be denied the benefits of, or be subjected to discrimination under any program or activity receiving Federal financial assistance." . . . [I]ndividuals with disabilities need only meet a program's necessary or essential requirements.

A Rehabilitation Act analysis requires the court to determine both whether an individual meets all of the essential eligibility requirements and whether reasonable modifications exist. . . . We find that MSHSAA has demonstrated that the age limit is an essential eligibility requirement in a high school interscholastic program. An age limit helps reduce the competitive advantage flowing to teams using older athletes; protects younger athletes from harm; discourages student athletes from delaying their education to gain athletic maturity; and prevents over-zealous coaches from engaging in repeated red-shirting to gain a competitive advantage. These purposes are of immense importance in any interscholastic sports program.

Even though Pottgen cannot meet this essential eligibility requirement, he is "otherwise qualified" if reasonable accommodations would enable him to meet the age limit. Reasonable accommodations do not require an institution "to lower or to effect substantial modifications of standards to accommodate a handicapped person." Accommodations are not reasonable if they impose "undue financial and administrative burdens" or if they require a "fundamental alteration in the nature of [the] program."

Since Pottgen is already older than the MSHSAA age limit, the only possible accommodation is to waive the essential requirement itself. Although Pottgen contends an age limit waiver is a reasonable accommodation based on his disability, we disagree. Waiving an essential eligibility standard would constitute a fundamental alteration in the nature of the baseball program. Other than waiving the age limit, no manner, method, or means is available which would permit Pottgen to satisfy the age limit. Consequently, no reasonable accommodations exist.

Since Pottgen can never meet the essential eligibility requirement, he is not an "otherwise qualified" individual. . . .

Title II provides that "no qualified individual with a disability shall, by reason of such disability, be excluded from participation in or be denied the benefits of the services, programs, or activities of a public entity, or be subjected to discrimination by any such entity." . . .

To determine whether Pottgen was a "qualified individual" for ADA purposes, the district court conducted an individualized inquiry into the necessity of the age limit in Pottgen's case. Such an individualized inquiry is inappropriate at this stage. Instead, to determine whether Pottgen is a "qualified individual" under the ADA, we must first determine whether the age limit is an essential eligibility requirement by reviewing the importance of the requirement to the interscholastic baseball program. If this requirement is essential, we then determine whether Pottgen meets this requirement with or without modification. It is at this later stage that the ADA requires an individualized inquiry.

. . . Pottgen alleges he can meet the eligibility requirement if MSHSAA waives it for him. In conformity with our previous finding, we conclude that this is not a reasonable modification.

Dissent: RICHARD S. ARNOLD, CHIEF JUDGE.

In my view, the courts are obligated by statute to look at plaintiffs as individuals before they decide whether someone can meet the essential requirements of an eligibility rule like the one before us in the present case. Such an individualized inquiry, I believe, shows that the age requirement, as applied to Ed Pottgen, is not essential to the goals of the Missouri State High School Activities Association. I therefore respectfully dissent.

. . . For me, this case is largely controlled by the words of the Americans With Disabilities Act of 1990, 42 U.S.C. § 12132, and by regulations issued under the Act. The statute provides, in relevant part, that

> no qualified individual with a disability shall, by reason of such disability, be excluded from participation in or be denied the benefits of the services, programs, or activities of a public entity, or be subjected to discrimination by any such entity.

There is no doubt that Ed Pottgen has a learning disability (for which he is now adequately compensating), and that, by reason of this disability, he has become unable to meet the Activities Association's age requirements. The Court today holds, however, that Ed is not a "qualified individual."

The statute itself defines this term. "Qualified individual with a disability" means:

> an individual with a disability, who, with or without reasonable modifica-
> tions to rules, policies, or practices . . . meets the essential eligibility
> requirements for . . . participation in programs or activities provided by a
> public entity.

42 U.S.C. § 12131(2). So, by the express words of Congress, it is not necessary for a person to meet all eligibility requirements. Instead, if a proposed modification of those requirements is "reasonable," a person can be a "qualified individual." The question therefore is whether it is "reasonable" to require the Activities Association to modify or waive the age requirement in the case of Ed Pottgen. The age criterion would not have to be abandoned completely: Ed would have been eligible if the requirement had been modified by only thirty-five days. He was that close to complete and literal compliance with all of the Activities Association's rules.

I agree with the Court that if a requirement is "essential" to a program or activity, a waiver or modification of that requirement would not be "reasonable" within the meaning of the statute. But how do we determine what is "essential"? The regulations interpreting the statute are of some help in answering that question. Under 28 C.F.R. § 35.130(b)(7) (1994),

> A public entity shall make reasonable modifications in policies, practices, or
> procedures when the modifications are necessary to avoid discrimination on
> the basis of disability, unless the public entity can demonstrate that making
> the modifications would fundamentally alter the nature of the service,
> program, or activity.

Was high-school baseball competition in Missouri fundamentally altered when Ed Pottgen was allowed to play one more year? I think not, and here the District Court's findings of fact become important. According to the Activities Association itself, there are three reasons for the age requirement. First, there is a desire to protect the safety of younger athletes against whom an older athlete might compete. Second, the Association wishes to reduce the competitive advantage that results when older students play, because of their presumed greater maturity. And third, the Association wishes to discourage students from delaying their education to gain athletic maturity. There is no contention whatever in the present case that Ed Pottgen deliberately repeated the first and third grades in order to make himself eligible to play baseball another year at age nineteen. The District Court found, moreover, "that any competitive advantage resulting from plaintiff's age is de minimis." The Court further found that the Activities Association made no individu-alized review of plaintiff's circumstances and gave no consideration to the issue of safety when it denied plaintiff's request for a waiver of the age rule. Finally, the Court found that "plaintiff does not appear to constitute a threat to the safety of others." Plaintiff is not appreciably larger than the average eighteen-year-old.

In other words, the age requirement could be modified for this individual player without doing violence to the admittedly salutary purposes underlying the age rule. But instead of looking at the rule's operation in the individual case of Ed Pottgen, both the Activities Association and this Court simply recite the rule's general justifications (which are not in dispute) and mechanically apply it across the board.

But if a rule can be modified without doing violence to its essential purposes, as the District Court has found in the present case, I do not believe that it can be "essential" to the nature of the program or activity to refuse to modify the rule.

The Court avoids this issue by holding that "an individualized inquiry into the necessity of the age limit in Pottgen's case . . . is inappropriate. . . ." With respect, I find no such principle in the words of the statute. If an eligibility requirement can be reasonably modified to make someone eligible, that person is a qualified individual. In determining this issue, it seems to me entirely appropriate to focus on the effect that modification of the requirement for the individual in question would have on the nature of the program. When the case is looked at from this point of view, it becomes clear that the Association could easily bend to accommodate Ed Pottgen without breaking anything essential. For these reasons, I would affirm the preliminary injunction entered by the District Court.

ROTHSCHILD v. GROTTENTHALER
907 F.2d 286 (2d Cir. 1990)

The court ruled that under section 504, the school must provide sign language interpreter services to hearing-impaired parents of nondisabled children for certain school-initiated meetings and activities.

ALTIMARI, CIRCUIT JUDGE.

The central question presented on this appeal is whether a public school district which receives federal financial assistance must provide sign-language interpreter services, at school district expense, to deaf parents of non-hearing impaired children at certain school-initiated activities. Defendants-appellants Ramapo Central School District ("School District") and the School District Superintendent, Charles Grottenthaler, appeal from a judgment, entered in the United States District Court for the Southern District of New York declaring the School District's refusal to provide sign-language interpreter services to the Rothschilds to be a violation of section 504 of the Rehabilitation Act of 1973, 29 U.S.C. § 794(a) ("Rehabilitation Act").

The parties stipulate that plaintiffs-appellees Kenneth and Karen Rothschild are deaf parents of two non-hearing impaired children who attend schools operated by defendant-appellant Ramapo Central School District. It is also stipulated that the Rothschilds use American Sign Language as their primary method of communication. The parties further stipulate that the Rothschilds have been invited to attend meetings with School District teachers and counselors "to discuss their children's academic program, disciplinary problems, or other matters." In addition, the Rothschilds have been invited to attend various group events, such as "Back to School Night" and orientation meetings, at their children's schools. The Rothschilds contend that, without the services of a sign-language interpreter, they cannot effectively communicate with teachers and other School District personnel at these meetings, conferences, and events. Thus, while they are concerned about their children's educational development and, like other parents in the School District, are invited to participate in such activities, the Rothschilds often do not attend.

Since September 1981, the Rothschilds have made numerous requests that the School District provide a sign-language interpreter, at School District expense, for various school-initiated activities related to their children's education. However, the School District has consistently refused to provide such services, citing its belief that the Rothschilds are not "qualified" under section 504. On occasion, the Rothschilds have hired a sign-language interpreter to facilitate communication with teachers and other School District personnel. In these instances, the School District has refused to pay the interpreter bills submitted by or on behalf of the Rothschilds. The School District has, however, provided special seating arrangements at school functions for the Rothschilds and their privately-hired sign-language interpreters.

The Rothschilds commenced this action in May 1989, seeking declaratory and injunctive relief, as well as damages, under section 504 of the Rehabilitation Act and 42 U.S.C. § 1983. The Rothschilds contended that, although they are invited to attend School District meetings, conferences, and other events concerning their children's education, they cannot effectively communicate with teachers and other School District personnel at these activities without the services of a sign-language interpreter. They claimed that, without a sign-language interpreter, the opportunity afforded them to participate in School District activities concerning their children's education is not equal to the opportunity afforded non-hearing impaired parents.

. . . This case presents a matter of first impression: Whether section 504 requires a public school district receiving federal financial assistance to provide sign-language interpreter services, at school district expense, to deaf parents of non-hearing impaired children at certain school-initiated activities. . . .

Our inquiry begins, as it must, with the language of section 504.

> No otherwise qualified individual with handicaps in the United States, as defined in section 706(8) of this title, shall, solely by reason of her or his handicap, be excluded from the participation in, be denied the benefits of, or be subjected to discrimination under any program or activity receiving Federal financial assistance. . . .

In this Circuit, it is settled that a private right of action against recipients of federal financial assistance may be implied from section 504. To establish a *prima facie* violation of section 504, a plaintiff must prove that: 1) he or she is a "handicapped person" as defined in the Rehabilitation Act; 2) he or she is "otherwise qualified" to participate in the offered activity or to enjoy its benefits; 3) he or she is being excluded from such participation or enjoyment solely by reason of his or her handicap; and 4) the program denying the plaintiff participation receives federal financial assistance. Once a *prima facie* violation of section 504 has been established, "the defendant must present evidence to rebut the inference of illegality."

In the present case, the School District concedes that the Rothschilds are handicapped persons within the meaning of the Rehabilitation Act, and that the School District receives federal financial assistance. The School District does not seriously contest that the Rothschilds are denied the opportunity to participate in school-initiated activities concerning their children's education by reason of their handicaps. Rather, the heart of the School District's argument is that the Rothschilds are not "otherwise qualified" for the offered activities. According to the

School District, "Section 504 does not apply to plaintiffs because public schools are for children, not their parents and Section 504 was designed to protect children, not their parents." The School District seriously misapprehends the import of section 504.

. . . An "otherwise qualified" handicapped individual is one "who is able to meet all of a program's requirements in spite of his handicap." A recipient of federal financial assistance may consider an individual's handicap if it "could reasonably be viewed as posing a substantial risk that the applicant would be unable to meet [the recipient's] reasonable standards." However, where an individual's handicap is unrelated to reasonable requirements for participation in the activity, section 504 prohibits denying that individual's participation on the sole basis of his or her handicap. If the Rothschilds are "otherwise qualified" for the parent-oriented activities offered by the School District, the Rothschilds must be afforded an equal opportunity to participate in those activities.

The Rothschilds are "otherwise qualified" for the parent-oriented activities incident to their children's education that are offered by the School District. The Rothschilds are parents of school children enrolled in the School District. They are concerned with their children's educational development. They are interested in meeting with teachers and other School District personnel and are able to meet them at the scheduled times and locations. The Rothschilds' inability to effectively communicate without the services of a sign-language interpreter simply has no bearing on the reasonable requirements for participating in school-initiated activities incident to their children's education. The fact that they have expended some $2,000 on privately-hired sign-language interpreters is evidence of their concern. Their use of privately-hired sign-language interpreters is also evidence that it is solely the Rothschilds' inability, as deaf persons, to effectively communicate with teachers and other School District personnel that prevents their participation in parent-teacher conferences and other School District activities. With the assistance of a sign-language interpreter, the Rothschilds are able to participate in school-initiated meetings and conferences concerning their children's education.

This conclusion is supported by the DOE regulations interpreting the term "otherwise qualified" contained in section 504. These regulations, promulgated pursuant to 29 U.S.C. § 794(a), are "an important source of guidance on the meaning of § 504." Regulation 104.3(k) defines "qualified handicapped person" as:

(1) With respect to employment, a handicapped person who, with reasonable accommodation, can perform the essential functions of the job in question;

(2) With respect to public preschool[,] elementary, secondary, or adult educational services, a handicapped person (i) of an age during which nonhandicapped persons are provided such services, (ii) of any age during which it is mandatory under state law to provide such services to handicapped persons, or (iii) to whom a state is required to provide a free appropriate public education under section 612 of the Education of the Handicapped Act; and

(3) With respect to postsecondary and vocational education services, a handicapped person who meets the academic and technical standards requisite to admission or participation in the recipient's education program or activity;

(4) *With respect to other services, a handicapped person who meets the essential eligibility requirements for the receipt of such services.*

34 C.F.R. 104.3(k)(1989) (emphasis added).

The School District and Superintendent Grottenthaler contend that the Rothschilds are not "otherwise qualified" because they are not eligible to receive educational services under Regulation 104.3(k)(2). They argue that this provision alone applies to the School District and that none of its related provisions address the rights of persons, such as parents, not actually receiving educational services. However, the School District's proposed interpretation of Regulation 104.3(k) is inconsistent with its plain language. Regulation 104.3(k) does not define "qualified handicapped person" with regard to the category of institution receiving federal financial assistance, but rather the category of service offered by the recipient institution. The fact that a particular recipient institution is primarily engaged in the provision of one category of service does not exempt it from Regulation 104.3(k) in its provision of other services. Thus, while the School District is subject to section 504 in providing educational services, that is not the only area in which it must refrain from discrimination on the basis of handicap. In hiring employees, for example, the School District is obviously subject to the definition of qualified handicapped person in Regulation 104.3(k)(1). So too, the School District is subject to the definition of qualified handicapped person in Regulation 104.3(k)(4) with respect to "other services" which, in this case, include parent-teacher conferences, meeting with School District personnel, and other parent-oriented services related to the education of its students. The Rothschilds are not excluded from the protection of section 504 merely because they are parents and not school children.

The School District has failed to articulate any reason that the Rothschilds should not be considered eligible to participate in school-initiated activities designed to involve parents in their children's education. That the Rothschilds meet the "essential eligibility requirements" for participation in the School District's parent-oriented activities is bolstered by the DOE's own interpretation of Regulation 104.3(k)(4). The DOE has determined that, under section 504, schools are required to afford handicapped parents of non-handicapped school children the same opportunity to participate in school activities as that afforded non-handicapped parents. It is instructive to note that, after the district court rendered its judgment, the OCR determined that the School District's refusal to provide a sign-language interpreter to the Rothschilds violates section 504. According to the OCR:

> As parents, the [Rothschilds] meet the essential eligibility requirements for participation in meetings with school teachers and administrators and in other school events since they have been invited or requested to attend. . . . The Section 504 statute and the regulation make clear that the [School] District owes a duty . . . to parents who are handicapped and seek to participate in their children's education in the same manner as nonhandicapped persons.

Case No. 02-88-1108 (Ramapo Central School District). The DOE's interpretation of Regulation 104.3(k)(4), a regulation which it promulgated, is "controlling unless it is plainly erroneous or inconsistent with the regulation." In this case, we find the DOE's interpretation to be neither plainly erroneous nor inconsistent with Regulation 104.3(k). Accordingly, we hold that the Rothschilds are "otherwise qualified" for the parent-oriented activities offered by the School District.

As "otherwise qualified handicapped individuals," the Rothschilds are entitled to "meaningful access to" the activities that the School District offers parents. However, our determination must be "responsive to two powerful but countervailing considerations — the need to give effect to the statutory objectives and the desire to keep § 504 within manageable bounds." Accommodations to permit access to handicapped persons should not impose "undue financial and administrative burdens." *Southeastern Community College.* Thus, a recipient of federal financial assistance should not be "required to make 'fundamental' or 'substantial' modifications to accommodate the handicapped." A recipient may, however, be required to make "reasonable" modifications to accommodate an otherwise qualified handicapped individual. "Section 504 of the Rehabilitation Act requires some degree of positive effort to expand the availability of federally funded programs to handicapped persons otherwise qualified to benefit from them."

Mindful of the need to strike a balance between the rights of the Rothschilds and the legitimate financial and administrative concerns of the School District, the district court limited the scope of activities for which the School District would be required to provide a sign-language interpreter. It stated:

> We take pains, however, to emphasize that the [school] district's obligation, and, correspondingly, the plaintiffs' entitlement, is limited to "school-initiated conferences incident to the academic and/or disciplinary aspects of their child's education." To the extent that the plaintiffs wish to voluntarily participate in any of the plethora of extra-curricular activities that their children may be involved in, we think they, like other parents, must do so at their own expense.

This seems a "reasonable accommodation," which permits the Rothschilds to be involved in their children's education while preserving the responsible administration of the School District. It is an accommodation which fosters the Rothschilds' interest in their children's educational development by facilitating their involvement in that development, without requiring the School District to subsidize parental involvement in extracurricular activities. The reasonableness of providing the Rothschilds with sign-language interpreters at certain school-initiated activities is demonstrated by the contemplation of such an accommodation in related DOE regulations promulgated pursuant to section 504. *See, e.g.,* 34 C.F.R. § 104.12(b)(2) (1989) (with regard to employment practices, "reasonable accommodation may include . . . the provision of readers or interpreters"); 34 C.F.R. § 104.44(d)(2) (1989) (in postsecondary education services, appropriate "auxiliary aids may include taped texts, interpreters or other effective methods of making orally delivered materials available to students with hearing impairments"); 34 C.F.R. § 104.52(d)(3) (1989) (with regard to health, welfare and other social services, appropriate "auxiliary aids may include . . . interpreters, and other aids for persons with impaired hearing"). The School District's refusal to modify its program to accommodate the Rothschilds' handicap is "unreasonable and discriminatory." The Rothschilds' entitlement to sign-language interpreter services provided at School District expense is limited, however, to those activities directly involving their children's academic and/or disciplinary progress.

Finally, it appears that the district court's Judgment is partially inconsistent with its Opinion and with this opinion. . . . The Judgment should not have included the requirement that the School District provide a sign-language interpreter at a child's graduation ceremony. Graduation does not seem directly related to a child's academic and/or disciplinary progress and, absent a factual determination to the contrary, should not have been included in the district court's Judgment. Accordingly, we vacate that part of the district court's Judgment which orders the School District to provide a sign-language interpreter for a child's graduation.

NOTES AND QUESTIONS

1. *Pottgen* directly sets out the analysis for claims of discrimination in availability of programs or activities. This is an area where section 504 and the ADA may provide remedies that IDEA does not. By regulation, "A recipient to which this subpart applies shall provide non-academic and extracurricular services and activities in such manner as is necessary to afford handicapped students an equal opportunity for participation in such services and activities." 34 C.F.R. § 104.37. The focus is on opportunity to participate. Accommodation, including services, is discussed further *infra* Chapter 14 (Post-Secondary Education).

2. Like *Pottgen*, *Rothschild* offers insight into the difference between section 504 and IDEA as to age and applicability, but in a case where services are for parents, not directly for students. It also offers an outline of the section 504 analysis as to a recipient's general obligations not to discriminate.

3. As *Pottgen* and *Rothschild* illustrate, the question is whether the claimant, with or without reasonable accommodation, meets the essential eligibility requirements for participation in a given activity. 34 C.F.R. § 104.3(k)(4). For athletics, the Casey Martin case offers guidance from the Supreme Court. *PGA Tour, Inc. v. Martin*, 532 U.S. 661 (2001) (holding that allowing a golfer with degenerative circulatory disorder that prevents his walking to use a golf cart is a reasonable modification and not a fundamental alteration of the golf tour requirements). For students, questions arise where a student may lack a physical attribute (such as a leg) but still seek to participate in school athletics and where students who, because of their disability, may have been held back but still want to participate in school athletics beyond the relevant state athletic association's age limits. As these cases indicate, reasonable accommodation will not require fundamental alteration of the program, and will not require the school to bear an undue financial burden, considering all available resources. What does this mean for a particular sport? For a particular athlete? Is the dissent in *Pottgen* persuasive? Issues around athletics are discussed further *infra* Chapter 4 (Free Appropriate Public Education). For more on athletics, see, e.g., Susan M. Denbo, *Disability Lessons in Higher Education: Accommodating Learning-Disabled Students and Student-Athletes under the Rehabilitation Act and the Americans With Disabilities Act*, 41 AM. BUS.

L.J. 145 (2003); Laura F. Rothstein, *Don't Roll in My Parade: The Impact of Sports and Entertainment Cases on Public Awareness and Understanding of the Americans with Disabilities Act*, 19 REV. LITIG. 399 (2000); John T. Wolohan, *Are Age Restrictions a Necessary Requirement for Participation in Interscholastic Athletic Programs?* 66 UMKC L. REV. 345 (1997).

F. EVALUATION

Evaluation is addressed by statute and implementing regulations. 20 U.S.C. § 1414(a)–(c); 34 C.F.R. §§ 104.35, 300.301–.311. The IDEA process typically starts from a referral, followed by an evaluation and determination of eligibility for special education and related services. There are strict timelines for the processes of evaluation and determination of eligibility and, if the child is eligible, developing an IEP. 34 C.F.R. § 300.323(c) (requiring IEP meeting within 30 days of eligibility determination and provision of services as soon as possible after development of IEP). Unless the state has its own time limit, evaluations must be competed within 60 days of when parental consent is received, unless the child has moved schools after the timeline began and the parent agrees to an extension. 20 U.S.C. § 1414(a)(1)(C). There is also an exception to the time limit if the parent repeatedly fails or refuses to produce the child for the evaluation. 20 U.S.C. § 1414(a)(1)(C)(ii)(II). This exception has prompted some states to consider imposing a separate 30 day time limit from referral to parent consent; if the parents have not consented at the end of 30 days, the district can request a due process hearing.

An initial evaluation commences with notice to, and consent from, parents. Evaluation is done by a team, specified by statute and regulation, to assure participation of parents and qualified professionals. *See* 34 C.F.R. § 300.321(a); *see also* § 300.321(e) (allowing excuse from attendance for team members under some circumstances, with parent consent). The evaluation team first reviews existing data and then determines (and obtains, as necessary) additional data or testing to define the category of disability, level of present performance, and student needs for special education and related services. If the student is determined eligible, the student's needs are defined, an IEP is developed for the student, a placement is determined, and a free appropriate public education is provided. Reevaluation occurs before any determination of change in eligibility, or upon parental or teacher request or, in any case, at least every three years, unless the parent and the school district agree that reevaluation is unnecessary.

SEATTLE SCHOOL DISTRICT, NO. 1 v. B.S.
82 F.3d 1493 (9th Cir. 1999)

The court found that the school district failed to provide FAPE and to follow proper procedures for an emotionally and behaviorally disabled student. The district was ordered to reimburse the parents for the cost of an independent evaluation and placement at an out of state facility as well as for attorney's fees and costs.

Fletcher, Circuit Judge.

This case involves a dispute over the appropriate educational placement of a disabled child, A.S., under the Individuals with Disabilities and Education Act ("IDEA"), 20 U.S.C. § 1400–1490. The Seattle School District appeals the decision of the district court affirming the Administrative Law Judge's decision that the School District violated the procedural requirements of the IDEA and failed to provide A.S. a free appropriate public education under the Act. Accordingly, the School District was ordered to reimburse A.S.'s parent the cost of an independent evaluation, to pay for A.S.'s placement at a residential facility in Montana, and to pay the parent's attorneys' fees and costs. We have jurisdiction, 28 U.S.C. § 1291, and affirm.

After A.S. was expelled from school and temporarily hospitalized in a psychiatric facility for severe behavioral and emotional problems, the Seattle School District identified her as emotionally and behaviorally disabled and thereby qualifying for special education and related services under the IDEA. The School District did not propose placing A.S. in a residential school, contending that mainstreaming in the regular school environment was preferable.

Dissatisfied with this assessment, A.S.'s parent, B.S., requested an independent evaluation at public expense. The School District denied this request and initiated an administrative proceeding to establish the appropriateness of its evaluation and, consequently, that it did not have a duty to pay for an independent evaluation at the parent's request. The parent requested a hearing to challenge the School District's refusal to place A.S. in a residential school. The matters were consolidated and a 5-day administrative hearing held.

The parent prevailed on all claims. The ALJ found that the School District's evaluation was deficient, that B.S. was entitled to reimbursement of the cost of the independent evaluation, that the School District's proposal for educating A.S. was deficient, that Intermountain Children's Home in Montana was an appropriate placement, and that the School District must pay for A.S.'s residential placement at Intermountain (except for the costs of medical care).

The School District appealed the decision. . . . [T]he district court affirmed the ALJ's decision in its entirety. In its oral ruling, the district judge commented that her "decision is not one that was a close call." The district court awarded B.S. attorneys' fees and costs.

A.S. was born on October 7, 1982. She has a history of early neglect, physical and sexual abuse, abandonment, and placement in several foster homes, which experts have identified as a cause of her emotional and behavior problems. She has been diagnosed as having an attachment disorder, an oppositional defiant disorder, a conduct disorder, and a histrionic personality. She has resided with her adoptive mother, B.S., within the Seattle School District, since September 1989.

At school, A.S. exhibited frequent behavioral problems, including physical and verbal aggression, oppositionality, tantrums, attention difficulties, and the showing of inappropriate affection toward adults. A.S. was referred to the School District for evaluation of a suspected disability in April 1990, but the District's assessment team did not identify a disability. Nonetheless, the School District attempted to cope with

A.S.'s difficulties by providing individual staff attention, reinforcement for positive behavior, and other means of intervention. A.S. was placed in a special education classroom for students with serious behavioral disabilities. B.S. privately secured individual and family counseling for A.S.

In spite of these and other attempts at intervention, A.S.'s problems at school worsened. A.S. continued to exhibit physical and verbal aggression, lying, stealing, and oppositional behavior.

A.S.'s therapists ultimately concluded that a day program supplemented by counseling was insufficient. They recommended a residential facility with a thera- peutic environment. In March 1992, B.S. sought an evaluation by Dr. Vera Fahlberg, a physician, who recommended placing A.S. in a residential setting employing strategies to address A.S.'s attachment difficulties and behavioral concerns. She identified Intermountain Children's Home in Montana as the nearest known program which met A.S.'s needs. This recommendation was supported by A.S.'s therapists.

By the fall of 1992, A.S.'s behavioral problems had escalated. School staff gave A.S. individual attention and attempted various interventions, including removal from class. A.S. became isolated from other children. Her problems seriously affected her ability to benefit from classroom instruction. In December 1992, A.S. became so verbally and physically assaultive that she was placed in restraints and taken to Fairfax Hospital. Based on her behavior, A.S. was expelled from school. She was discharged from the hospital in March 1993. As the School District had expelled her, A.S. remained out of school through the end of the school year. In May 1993, Dr. Springer, A.S.'s pediatrician, wrote the School District recommending that A.S. be placed in a residential facility to allow her to acquire the emotional skills necessary for attachment to others and to make use of her cognitive abilities.

In May 1993, the School District reevaluated A.S. and concluded that she was seriously behaviorally disabled and eligible for special services. It noted that in spite of A.S.'s age-appropriate academic scores on standardized tests, A.S. had long exhibited behaviors which adversely affected her educational performance. The evaluation did not address the question of A.S.'s need for residential placement.

B.S. and the School District failed to agree on A.S.'s placement during two individualized education program (IEP) meetings held in June 1993. The School District rejected residential schooling, proposing instead a specialized self- contained behavioral classroom with counseling services, to be provided during the regular school day. Disagreeing with this recommendation, and believing the School District's evaluation to be deficient, B.S. sought an independent assessment from Dr. Ulrich Schoettle, a child psychiatrist. The School District refused to pay for this assessment. Dr. Schoettle concluded that A.S. was unable to progress outside a residential school environment.

As of the time of the administrative hearing, A.S. had received no educational services for six months. B.S. asked the School District to provide private tutoring pending the hearing decision. The School District refused, and B.S. obtained an order from the ALJ requiring the District to provide tutoring.

At the administrative hearing, Drs. Fahlberg, Schoettle, and Springer testified that the severity of A.S.'s disability affected her ability to participate in learning activities at school and to make productive use of what she might learn. Each recommended placement in a residential school as soon as possible, noting that they rarely made such a recommendation. Each concluded that A.S. was unlikely to derive any meaningful educational benefit from the School District's proposed day program, as only a residential school could provide the intensity, structure, and consistency necessary for A.S. to progress. The ALJ agreed, and ordered the School District to pay for A.S.'s placement at Intermountain.

The School District filed suit in district court, seeking to overturn the ALJ's decision. Shortly thereafter, A.S. enrolled at Intermountain, where she has gradually made progress. At the time of trial before the district court, A.S. had been enrolled at Intermountain for seven months.

The district court reviewed the administrative record and entertained additional testimony. The School District introduced the testimony of one medical expert, Dr. William Sack, whom the district court found to be well-qualified but not as familiar with A.S. as the parent's experts. The School District's primary witness was Jody Decker, the tutor that the ALJ had ordered the School District to hire. Although Decker testified that the tutoring situation with A.S. was progressing, the district court found this situation irrelevant to predicting A.S.'s future, as the School District proposed mainstreaming, not private one-on-one tutoring. The district court agreed with the conclusions reached by the ALJ and affirmed the administrative decision.

The School District had the burden of proving compliance with the IDEA at the administrative hearing, including the appropriateness of its evaluation, 34 C.F.R. § 300.503(b), and its proposed placement for A.S. As the party challenging the administrative ruling, the School District also had the burden of proof in district court.

. . . This appeal presents three primary issues: (1) whether the School District was required to pay for Dr. Schoettle's independent evaluation of A.S.; (2) whether the School District was required to pay for A.S.'s placement at Intermountain or whether an alternative proposal provided A.S. a free appropriate public education; and (3) whether A.S.'s parent was entitled to attorneys' fees.

The School District challenges the district court's conclusion that its evaluation of A.S. was deficient and, therefore, that B.S. was entitled to reimbursement of the cost of an independent evaluation by Dr. Schoettle.

The IDEA imposes an affirmative obligation on the School District to identify and evaluate children with disabilities. See 34 C.F.R. § 300.128; Wash. Admin. Code § 392-171-341. The district court and ALJ properly concluded that the School District failed to include on the assessment team anyone with knowledge in the disorders known to be the cause of A.S.'s problems. This was contrary to the School District's duty to "ensure . . . [that the] evaluation [of the student] is made by a multidisciplinary team . . . including at least one teacher or other specialist with knowledge in the area of suspected disability." Moreover, the School District failed to reconcile the parent's experts' recommendation that A.S. be placed in a residential facility. The District summarily concluded that a day program was educationally appropriate for A.S. without even addressing the fact that medical experts had concluded residential placement was necessary. *See* Wash. Admin. Code § 392-171-366 (requiring reconciliation of inconsistent opinions).

Because A.S.'s parent disagreed with the School District's evaluation and the District was unable to establish the appropriateness of its evaluation, A.S. was entitled to an independent evaluation at public expense. 34 C.F.R. § 300.503(b). Accordingly, the district court properly affirmed the ALJ's order that the School District reimburse B.S. for the costs of Dr. Schoettle's evaluation.[7]

. . . The district court properly concluded that the School District's evaluation of A.S. was inadequate, its day-schooling proposal was unlikely to provide A.S. educational benefit, a residential program was the least restrictive alternative appropriate to A.S.'s needs, and Intermountain Children's Home was an appropriate placement. Accordingly, the IDEA required the School District to pay for an independent assessment of A.S. and to pay the nonmedical costs of A.S.'s placement at Intermountain.

SCHOENBACH v. DISTRICT OF COLUMBIA
309 F. Supp. 2d 71 (D.D.C. 2004)

The court recognized the significance of evaluation in determining correct placement for student with Asperger Syndrome, but refused reimbursement for a private placement where the parents did not raise objections and concerns at the appropriate time.

KENNEDY, DISTRICT JUDGE.

Plaintiffs, Anna Schoenbach ("Anna"), a minor with Asperger's Syndrome and Attention Deficit and Hyperactivity Disorder, and her parents Andrew Schoenbach and Daryl Kade ("Anna's parents"), appeal a District of Columbia Public Schools ("DCPS") hearing officer's decision that they are not entitled to reimbursement for tuition incurred in sending Anna to the Kingsbury Day School. Defendants are the District of Columbia and Paul Vance, former Superintendent of DCPS, sued in his official capacity. Plaintiffs allege that the Individuals with Disabilities in Education Act ("IDEA"), 20 U.S.C. §§ 1400–1461, the Rehabilitation Act of 1973, 29 U.S.C. § 701 *et seq.*, and 42 U.S.C. § 1983 provide the bases for obtaining the relief they seek.

Before this court are the parties' cross-motions for summary judgment. Upon consideration of the motions, the oppositions thereto, and the record of this case, the court concludes that defendants' motion should be granted and plaintiffs' motion should be denied.

---

[7] [FN 3] The School District's suggestion that Dr. Schoettle's evaluation did not ultimately support the diagnosis advocated by the parent and that therefore the parent is not entitled to reimbursement is without merit. The parent is entitled to an independent evaluation if the school district's evaluation is deficient. What conclusion the independent expert reaches is irrelevant. In any event, Dr. Schoettle supported the parent's contentions in essential respects: he found that A.S. had severe disorders and he recommended residential placement.

A. IDEA Background

Congress passed IDEA to "ensure that all children with disabilities have available to them a free appropriate public education that emphasizes special education and related services designed to meet their unique needs." 20 U.S.C. § 1400(d)(1)(A). IDEA provides funding and assists states in implementing a "comprehensive, coordinated, multidisciplinary, interagency system of early intervention services for infants and toddlers with disabilities and their families." 20 U.S.C. § 1400(d)(2). In order to receive funding under IDEA, states must also ensure that "[a]ll children with disabilities residing in the State, including children with disabilities attending private schools, regardless of the severity of their disability, and who are in need of special education and related services, are identified, located, and evaluated," 34 C.F.R. § 300.125(a)(1)(i). IDEA's free appropriate public education ("FAPE") provision entitles each disabled student to an individualized education program ("IEP"), educational services tailored to the unique needs of each disabled child. 20 U.S.C. § 1414(d)(2)(A) ("At the beginning of each school year, each [state] shall have in effect, for each child with a disability in its jurisdiction, an individualized education program."); 34 C.F.R. § 300.300(a)(3)(ii).

A full evaluation of a child is an integral part of developing an appropriate IEP. Therefore, IDEA requires states to "conduct a full and individual initial evaluation . . . before the initial provision of special education and related services to a child with a disability." 20 U.S.C. § 1400(d)(2). Once a child has been evaluated and identified as disabled, the school district must annually create an IEP tailored to the disabled child's needs. The IEP is developed in a periodic, but no less than annual, meeting of an IEP team including parents, faculty, and evaluators. 20 U.S.C. § 1414(d)(1)(B). The IEP must meet a number of standards set out in 20 U.S.C. § 1414(d)(1)(A).

By definition, a "free" appropriate public education means that services, including evaluations, must be "provided at public expense, under public supervision and direction, and without charge." 20 U.S.C. § 1401(8)(A). If the proposed educational services cannot be provided by the school district, the IDEA requires the child's placement in a private school at public expense. 20 U.S.C. § 1413(a)(4). Parents who disagree with their child's evaluation or placement may request an administrative hearing, before an impartial hearing officer, to challenge the IEP. 20 U.S.C. § 1415(b)(2). The hearing officer's determination ("HOD") may be challenged in federal district court. 20 U.S.C. § 1415(e)(2).

Anna Schoenbach, now thirteen years old, attended Murch Elementary School ("Murch") from kindergarten through the fifth grade — through the 2001-02 school year. At the end of third grade, Anna had some psychological evaluations, which indicated the presence of a learning disability in fine motor skills, an anxiety disorder, Oppositional Defiant Disorder, and a provisional diagnosis of ADHD (Inattentive Type). Terry Edelstein & Lynnwood Andrews, Psychological Assessment: Anna Schoenbach at 2 (Dec. 19, 2001). DCPS provided her with a Section 504 plan pursuant to the Rehabilitation Act, but not for IDEA services. Anna's last Section 504 plan, revised in September 2001, provided for certain classroom accommodations (e.g., "reducing homework," "allowing student to tape record lessons") and prescribed medication for Anna's ADHD.

Despite the Section 504 plan, Anna continued to have problems. In October 2001, Anna's parents made arrangements to have Anna evaluated by psychologists, Dr. Terry Edelstein and Dr. Lynnwood Andrews, "due to her difficulties with social interactions, anxiety, oppositional behavior and problems in school." Dr. Andrews confirmed the ADHD diagnosis but also found that Anna had Asperger's, an autism-spectrum disorder that combines high cognitive ability with impairment of social relations and restrictive, repetitive patterns of behavior. Anna's parents gave DCPS the report, which a DCPS-hired psychologist reviewed and largely agreed with.

On February 19, 2002 and March 26, 2002, DCPS held IEP meetings with a multidisciplinary team ("MDT") consisting of Anna's parents, DCPS officials, Anna's teachers at Murch, and psychologists. Based on the Edelstein Report and input from Anna's Murch teachers and parents, the team agreed that Anna was eligible for special educational services under IDEA. Most of the team agreed that Anna should be eligible for IDEA services under the category of "autism," although Anna's parents objected, arguing that she should also be eligible under another category as well. This is the sole instance, on the record, of Anna's parents objecting to anything at the IEP meetings. The team also agreed that Anna should receive one hour of specialized instruction and thirty minutes of counseling every week, and, in addition, that DCPS should hire a full-time, in-class aide to assist Anna. The parents took the IEP home. Plaintiffs apparently had every opportunity to request changes and make objections, and any changes they did request were incorporated into the Initial IEP. Nothing appears to have stopped Anna's parents from requesting different goals than those in the Initial IEP or recommending a private placement.

On April 4, 2002, Anna's parents signed and submitted the proposed IEP along with a letter stating that they accepted the IEP for the remaining months of the 2001-02 school year, but that otherwise they felt the IEP inadequate. They claimed that the proposed IEP failed to provide small group instruction available daily across all subject areas, staff knowledgeable about children with severe social disabilities, training integrated into the wider curriculum, small structured and supervised activity groups, and an individualized educational plan that allows Anna to practice new skills and demonstrate her competency within the confines of her limited range of interests — in summary, a "coordinated social, communications, and adaptive skills curriculum and behavior management approach."

. . . Anna's parents claim that they signed the Initial IEP "to get something in place as soon as possible for the remainder of the school year." The letter itself, however, contained no request for a private school placement, and no attempt to notify DCPS that they had applied to private schools.

On April 12, 2002, plaintiffs submitted DCPS a letter indicating that Anna had been accepted at the Kingsbury Day School, a private school for disabled children, for the 2002-03 school year. The letter simply announced, as fact, that Anna would attend Kingsbury. . . .

. . . In July 2002, plaintiffs requested a due process hearing, alleging that Anna's IEP was inappropriate and was not even implemented as written. Plaintiffs requested "that DCPS be ordered (or agree) to place and fund Anna at Kingsbury for school year 2002-03, with tuition, related services, and transportation." DCPS held a hearing before an impartial officer on September 9, 2002. The hearing officer denied plaintiffs' request for relief, finding that DCPS "developed an appropriate IEP that provides educational benefits to Anna, that it has implemented that IEP and that Murch is an appropriate placement for Anna."

Under IDEA, parents who unilaterally decide to place their disabled child in private school, without consent of local school officials, "do so at their own risk." *Florence County Sch. Dist. Four v. Carter*, 510 U.S. 7, 15 (1993). Parents may receive tuition reimbursement if a court finds that (1) "the public placement violated IDEA" *and* (2) "the private school placement was proper under the Act.

. . . The threshold question in this case is whether Anna's proposed public school placement at Murch was appropriate. This inquiry turns on two further sub-issues: (1) whether DCPS has complied with IDEA's administrative procedures and (2) whether or not the IEP generated by the MDT was reasonably calculated to provide some educational benefit to Anna. . . .

A school district must comply with the procedural requirements and safeguards listed in 20 U.S.C. § 1415. Claims of procedural violations of IDEA do not, in themselves, inexorably lead a court to find a child was denied FAPE. [The court rejects the procedural arguments.]

Plaintiffs contend that DCPS offered an inappropriate public school placement for Anna by proposing to keep her at Murch. Specifically, they argue that DCPS "neglected to propose a number of critical goals, objectives and services for this troubled student, as identified by her parents in their April 4, 2002 letter." Based on the record before the hearing officer, and its obligation to give a hearing officer's decision due weight, the court would not have disturbed the HOD. However, evidence unavailable to the hearing officer — the 2003-04 IEP — indicates that the Initial IEP was inappropriate. The court therefore finds Anna's Initial IEP inappropriate.

The analysis of whether Anna's IEP was appropriate begins with the hearing officer's determination. *Rowley*, which the hearing officer cites in his report holds that IDEA was intended to provide a "basic floor of opportunity" and an individualized plan "designed to provide educational benefit to the handicapped child." 458 U.S. 176, 201 (1982). . . . The analysis of the appropriateness of a public school placement "is not comparative." *Jenkins v. Squillacote*, 935 F.2d 303, 305 (D.C. Cir. 1991).

After considering oral testimony and the written record, the hearing officer found that the proposed IEP met the *Rowley* standard, finding DCPS "developed an appropriate IEP that provides educational benefits to Anna, that it has implemented that IEP and that Murch is an appropriate placement for Anna," and the hearing officer relied on evidence that while at Murch, Anna had advanced in grade every year and received, in some classes, higher-than-average marks at "one of the best academically performing schools in the DCPS system." *Rowley* indicates that academic progress is strong, though not probative, evidence that an IEP provides educational benefit. Not only did Anna progress academically at Murch, but according to the hearing officer, the IEP "included goals and objectives on most of the issues raised by the parents and the assessment including social-emotional, organizational skills, interpersonal social skills, coping skills, and attending skills." Further, the hearing officer identified evidence that Anna had made social and emotional progress.

On the other hand, there is written and testimonial evidence by Drs. Andrews and Edelstein, indicating that Anna requires a small classroom setting, unavailable at Murch, to make any progress in coping with Asperger's. ("Anna requires placement in a school which has small classrooms where individual, and small group (3–4 students or fewer) is available daily across all subject areas. . . ."); (stating that "it's not possible for [the Murch classroom curriculum] to be individualized to meet Anna's needs, in my opinion. So it's not a criticism of the teacher. It's not possible to do that in a large class that is a mainstream setting."); ("I think . . . that the identification of strengths and weaknesses is fairly correct. What disturbs me . . . is that the goals are well meaning and well intended, but there is no sensitivity, from my perspective, as to what Asperger's [sic] children require."). Indeed, Dr. Edelstein testified that while Anna has progressed academically, such progress in children with Asperger's can be misleading because they cannot effectively use information they seem to have mastered. Finally, testimony suggested that Anna's "social" progress at Murch — fewer students teasing her — was also deceptive, and that Anna's condition had not improved and would not improve at Murch. ("[Anna's] behaviors are seriously atypical. The atypicality does not allow children to embrace her."); (indicating that Murch provided "a counterproductive set of circumstances for a child who has a hopeful prognosis if the right intervention is available").

Based solely on the record before the hearing officer, the court would not overturn the HOD. . . .

However, plaintiffs present evidence — Anna's IEP for the 2003-04 school year — not available to the hearing officer when he made his decision. The new IEP team recommends, in essence, her current Kingsbury placement. At the July 23, 2003 IEP meeting for Anna, the multi-disciplinary team agreed that Anna should be placed in a full-time special educational program. . . .

In this situation, the New IEP Notes are relevant in determining whether the Initial IEP, placing Anna at Murch, was appropriate. Nothing in the new notes suggests that Anna's needs changed in a year, or that the team thought the Initial IEP was appropriate at the time it was formulated. Furthermore, no evidence suggests that Anna's condition deteriorated suddenly between 3/26/02, the date of the Initial IEP, to 7/23/03, when the new IEP was released. Rather, the simple, unexplained reversal by the new IEP team is evidence that the Initial IEP was wrong, even when formulated in 2002. . . .

The New IEP Notes are important not because they contain new information about Anna, but because they contain new information about the judgments of those with greater educational expertise than this court. The current consensus among those who know Anna is that a public school placement is simply inappropriate for her. The court does not "substitute [its] own notions of sound educational policy for those of school authorities." The court therefore concludes that the Initial IEP, recommending Anna's placement at Murch, was inappropriate. It does not, and need not, reach the issue of whether DCPS failed to implement the Initial IEP, since in any case, the IEP was inappropriate. . . .

Once a plaintiff establishes that the proposed public school placement was inappropriate, the second inquiry is whether or not the private school placement is appropriate. No one seriously disputes the appropriateness of Kingsbury as a private school placement. The new IEP team recommends Kingsbury unreservedly. . . .

As a result, under *Rowley*, the court finds that (1) Anna's public school placement at Murch was inappropriate and violated FAPE; and (2) Anna's private placement at Kingsbury is appropriate.

Even when a court finds parents of a disabled child eligible for tuition reimbursement under *Carter*, the 1997 IDEA Amendments allow a court to reduce or deny reimbursement under certain circumstances. The purpose of these "exceptions to reimbursement" provisions is to "give the school system an opportunity, before the child is removed, to assemble a team, evaluate the child, devise an appropriate plan, and determine whether a [FAPE] can be provided in the public schools."

A court may reduce or deny tuition reimbursement if, *inter alia*, a disabled child's parents, prior to or during the most recent IEP meeting before removing their child from school, failed to "inform the IEP team that they were rejecting the placement proposed by the public agency to provide a [FAPE] to their child including stating their concerns and their intent to enroll their child in a private school at public expense. . . ." 20 U.S.C. § 1412(a)(10)(C)(iii)(I)(aa). A court may also reduce or deny tuition reimbursement "upon a judicial finding of unreasonableness with respect to actions taken by the parents." § 1412(a)(10) (C)(iii)(III). The court finds that plaintiffs both failed to provide adequate notice and acted unreasonably, and therefore denies the equitable remedy of tuition reimbursement. . . .

The Edelstein Report — especially the way Anna's parents reacted to it and presented it to others — is central to this analysis. Anna's parents profess to have been greatly moved by the report since reading it in December 2001. The report first alerted Anna's parents that Anna had Asperger's and also recommended Anna for full-time special educational services. Anna's parents claim that the report "has been an eye-opener," that they "refer to the report continuously, in terms of how we need to modify the environment, what sort of attention to be placed on Anna, where her strengths and weaknesses are," and that it has "has been [their] bible" with regard to Anna's condition.

The report suggests, but does not directly say, that Anna should be in a private school. Specifically, it indicates that "Anna requires placement in a school which has small classrooms where individual, and small group (3–4 students or fewer) instruction is available daily across all subject areas and which has a staff knowledgeable about children with severe social disabilities." Murch did not offer small classroom teaching. Nevertheless the report's implication — that Anna should be in private school — was not self-evident. Anna's parents testified that Drs. Edelstein and Andrews had to convince them that public school was inappropriate; once converted, Anna's parents quickly applied to private schools:

[W]e argued very strongly with Dr. Andrews and Dr. Edelstein about that: why it had to be a small school; couldn't it be supplement to a regular school. And we argued about that. And they were very clear why. And frankly, I have to tell you, we weren't completely convinced that that was the only way, because we really do love Murch so much. But we felt we had — *We know in order to apply, you have to apply a year ahead. So we started to apply.*

Anna's parents gave the report to DCPS which, in turn, gave the report to another psychologist, who presented her review of the report on February 15, 2002. The reviewer seemed to agree with the report's diagnosis and recommended that the IEP team "consider all additional up to date data presented by parents, current teachers, and other personnel." Dr. Vincent's review did not recommend a private school placement and did not seem to read the Edelstein Report as requiring such a placement. Yet the evidence available on the record suggests DCPS agreed with all findings in the report, and nothing suggests DCPS, before the Initial IEP meeting, favored or disfavored a private school placement.

Critical to the finding that Anna's parents' actions contributed to the inappropriateness of the Initial IEP is the dog that did not bark at the March 26, 2002 IEP meeting. Dr. Edelstein and Anna's parents testified that they strongly believed, before the IEP meeting, that public school was inappropriate; yet they failed to object when the IEP team simply recommended precisely that — a public school placement, albeit with certain special services and accommodations.

First, Dr. Edelstein conceded that, while she attended perhaps half of the IEP meeting on March 26, 2002, she never commented on, much less criticized, the goals and objectives proposed by the Initial IEP. Her silence is striking given the apparent depth of her conviction, also expressed to Anna's parents, that a public school setting was radically inappropriate and even likely to cause Anna's conditions to worsen. During her oral testimony, Dr. Edelstein's had difficulty justifying her silence:

> Q: . . . [I]f you heard goals and objectives that you now say are inappropriate being drafted at an IEP meeting, you didn't at any point say that, "maybe you need to revisit these"? . . .
>
> A: I do remember one thing I did says, and that was . . . I was in complete agreement with all of [Dr. Andanitis's] conclusions.

The Initial IEP explicitly rejected full-time special education and proposed a general classroom placement with just 5% of Anna's time outside that setting. But at the meeting when these proposals were made, Dr. Edelstein failed to criticize a plan she later repudiated as having "no sensitivity . . . as to what Asperger's children require." This inconsistency struck, unfavorably, the hearing officer. ("Dr. Edelstein went to the IEP meeting which lasted over three hours, but she did not participate in a discussion on the IEP goals and objections and offered no recommendations on the IEP.").

 . . . In sum, the record and oral testimony indicates that (1) DCPS and the Initial IEP team took the Edelstein Report seriously; (2) that the team took the concerns of Anna's parents seriously and accepted their requests; (3) that the

Edelstein Report did not make clear, on its own, that Anna needed to be in private school; (4) that at the March 26, 2002 IEP meeting, or anytime before April 12, 2002, Anna's parents, and Dr. Edelstein, did not mention their conviction that Anna required a private placement. The Initial IEP team may have made a fundamental mistake in believing that the Edelstein Report could be read to allow for a public school placement, or that Anna's condition could improve in a regular classroom with the piecemeal addition of services (1 1/2 hours of out-of-class instruction, the full time aide). If alerted, the Initial IEP team might have agreed with Anna's parents and changed the IEP, if the new IEP (recommending Anna's placement at Kingsbury) is any indication. Though strongly convinced before the IEP meeting that such piecemeal services in a general classroom setting were simply *not* sufficient to help Anna progress, neither Anna's parents nor Dr. Edelstein objected to the public school placement at the IEP meeting. Such silence, despite their genuine conviction that Anna needed to be in private school, is inexplicable and unreasonable.

The court concludes that the Initial IEP proposed an inappropriate public school placement in significant part because of the failure of Anna's parents to object to the IEP when given the opportunity to do so. Therefore, plaintiffs are not entitled to tuition reimbursement.

CONCLUSION

IDEA expects strong parental input at IEP meetings. Such input is critical in assuring that disabled children get the services they need. *Rowley*, 458 U.S. at 209 ("[I]ndividualized planning conferences are a way to provide parent involvement and protection to assure that appropriate services are provided to a handicapped child."). But parents must talk, or complain, when given the chance. Timely input can allow a school district to respond meaningfully to parental requests. A disabled child's parents are not entitled to reimbursement for an inappropriate IEP when their input may have made the plan appropriate. An appropriate order accompanies this memorandum opinion.

NOTES AND QUESTIONS

1.   For an overview of the issues and caselaw on evaluation, see MARK C. WEBER, SPECIAL EDUCATION LAW AND LITIGATION TREATISE, Chapter 4 (3d ed. 2008 & supps.).

2.   The 2004 Reauthorization of IDEA adds to the prior law's obligation on the state and local agencies to conduct evaluations that ". . . either a parent of a child, or a State educational agency, other State agency, or local educational agency may initiate a request for an initial evaluation to determine if the child is a child with a disability." 20 U.S.C. § 1414(a)(1)(B). This new section then refers to the new provisions for parental consent, discussed in the next note.

3.   Parental rights are strong in the evaluation process, including the right to be notified in an understandable format of the evaluation and the requirement of parental written consent for initial evaluation. *See* 20 U.S.C. §§ 1415(b)–(d) (notice), 1414(a)(1)(D) (consent); 34 C.F.R. §§ 300.503 (notice),.300(a) (consent). Notice puts the parents on alert and involves them in the identification of what may be a

disability and also serves to keep the school on track where parents may think the district's response insufficient. What should the result be if a parent does not consent? IDEA separates consent for initial evaluation and consent for services, saying that consent for the former shall not be considered consent for the latter. 20 U.S.C. § 1414(a)(1)(D)(ii). There are specific provisions for situations involving wards of the state. The absence of consent is then also separately addressed for each point as well. In the absence of consent for initial evaluation, the agency may pursue evaluation following the procedures in § 1415. In the absence of consent for services, the LEA shall not provide special education and related services by utilizing the due process hearing procedure, and the local agency will then not be required to convene an IEP meeting and will not be considered in violation of its obligations to provide FAPE. The ability to override parental refusal to consent to evaluation is limited to children who remain in the public schools. The Eighth Circuit Court of Appeals has ruled that a school district lacks the power to compel the evaluation of a child when the parents do not consent to the evaluation and withdraw the child from public school and opt for home-schooling. *Fitzgerald v. Camdenton R-III Sch. Dist.*, 439 F.3d 773 (8th Cir. 2006). In 2008, the Department of Education revised the IDEA regulations to clarify parental rights to revoke consent, and to restrict the powers and duties of school districts with regard to children whose parents exercise the right not to consent or the right to withdraw consent previously given. *See* 34 C.F.R. 300.300 (2009). The amended provisions are reproduced in the Statutes and Regulations Pamphlet.

4. *Seattle* is a combined review of a request for independent evaluation at public expense, which the school opposed, and placement in a residential setting, which the school also opposed. *Seattle* outlines a situation where the evaluation process and resultant decisions are found lacking upon review by the court and describes the sometimes-controversial issue presented by parents' desire to obtain independent evaluations. Note that this is not a case where there is an issue as to whether the student's disability is preventing her from getting educational benefit. What could have been done in this situation before the point of expulsion, hospitalization, and litigation?

5. If students' problems are not identified accurately and in a timely way, their educational opportunities will indeed be harmed. Mistakes are costly for school districts as well; they will be faced with remediating a perhaps more difficult situation, or they will be faced with claims for reimbursement where parents place their children elsewhere. Given the significance of this determination, it is not surprising that regulations under IDEA provide that parents have the "right" to obtain "an independent educational evaluation of the child" at public expense where the parents disagree with the evaluation obtained by the school unless the school demonstrates at a hearing that its evaluation is appropriate. Even where the school shows that its evaluation is appropriate, parents have the right to an independent evaluation at private expense, and the results from that evaluation must be considered. 34 C.F.R. § 300.502. *See generally* Robert A. Garda, Jr., *Untangling Eligibility Requirements Under the Individuals with Disabilities Education Act*, 69 Mo. L. Rev. 441 (2004). For a discussion of the role of parents in evaluation and more generally, see Philip T.K. Daniel, *Education for Students with Special Needs: The Judicially Defined Role of Parents in the Process*, 29 J.L. & Educ. 1 (2000).

6. Like other cases in this chapter, the facts in *Schoenbach* illustrate the significance of evaluation — here, an evaluation sought by parents and later an evaluation by a school psychologist who apparently agreed. While parents did not prevail in their quest for reimbursement, their insistence on an evaluation was crucial in securing an appropriate outcome for the student. One parent attorney explains, "Without comprehensive and appropriate assessment and measures serving to properly identify a child's unique needs, one might as well be playing 'Pin the Tail on The Donkey.'" GARY MAYERSON, HOW TO COMPROMISE WITH YOUR SCHOOL DISTRICT WITHOUT COMPROMISING YOUR CHILD: A FIELD GUIDE FOR GETTING EFFECTIVE SERVICES FOR CHILDREN WITH SPECIAL NEEDS (2004).

7. Evaluation, as mandated by statute and implementing regulation, must include all areas of disability, must be nondiscriminatory, and must follow certain specified procedures and be properly administered and reviewed by trained professionals. 34 C.F.R. §§ 300.304–.305. Where the evaluation contemplates identification for a specific learning disability, additional requirements apply for an expanded team and evaluation and written reports addressing the specifics of the designation. 34 C.F.R. §§ 300.307–.311. IDEA specifically provides that the LEA shall not be "required to take into consideration whether a child has a severe discrepancy between achievement and intellectual ability. . . ." 20 U.S.C. § 1414(b)(6)(A).

8. Eligibility determinations cannot be based on a single criterion, must be tailored to individual needs and not "merely those that are designed to provide a single general intelligence quotient." 34 C.F.R. § 300.304(c)(2). Where tests are used, they must be valid for the purpose used, administered in a child's native language (unless unfeasible to do so), and racially or culturally unbiased. These requirements reflect some of the court decisions regarding fairness in testing. *Larry P. v. Riles*, 793 F.2d 969 (9th Cir. 1984) (invalidating California's use of IQ tests to evaluate and to place students in classes for the educable mentally retarded, which resulted in disproportionate numbers of black students being placed in such classes); *Parents in Action on Special Education (PASE) v. Hannon*, 506 F. Supp. 831 (N.D. Ill. 1980) (recognizing some questions culturally biased against black children but not enough to support invalidation even though more black children in mentally retarded placements).

9. Among the provisions of the 2004 Reauthorization of IDEA) is a general provision regarding the states' role overall in what the statute terms "overidentification and disproportionality" in regard to race and ethnicity. 20 U.S.C. § 1412(a)(24). What polices and procedures might a state implement to meet this standard?

10. Evaluation of students with learning disabilities is particularly controversial, and the federal regulations contain a set of additional procedures that must be used for identifying children with specific learning disabilities as opposed to other disabling conditions. 34 C.F.R. §§ 300.307–.311. A method traditionally used to screen for disabilities is to compare the child's scores on subtests of an intelligence test and probe for discrepancies between the subtest scores. In reaction to some dissatisfaction over that approach, the 2004 IDEA Reauthorization provides that a school district cannot be required to take into consideration whether a child has a

severe discrepancy between achievement and intellectual ability in oral expression, listening comprehension, written expression, basic reading skill, reading comprehension, mathematical calculation, or mathematical reasoning. Instead, the school district is permitted to use a process that determines if the child responds to scientific, research-based intervention. 20 U.S.C. § 1414(b)(6). The background materials published with the final regulations embodying these requirements discuss the use of a "Response to Intervention" (RTI) approach in contributing to the assessment of students suspected of having learning disabilities. *See* 71 Fed. Reg. 46647–59 (Aug. 14, 2006); *see also* 34 C.F.R. § 300.307 (permitting use of process based on child's response to "scientific, research-based intervention").

One writer makes the following observations about the controversy over evaluation for learning disabilities and the RTI response:

> Between 1976 and 1996, the number of students identified under the category of specific learning disabilities (SLD or LD) increased 283% to 2,259,000. The number currently stands at 2,710,476, making SLD the largest disability category, with about 45% of all IDEA-eligible children. . . . Critics contend that methods dependent on IQ testing magnify the effects of IQ measurement errors and make the unjustified assumption that IQ is a good ability measure. They challenge the reliability (that is, the stability from testing session to testing session) of discrepancy measurements. Moreover, they observe that there are wide variations from state to state concerning how much discrepancy will support a conclusion that a learning disability exists. IQ-discrepancy methodology has its defenders, however, and there are also some authorities who take a middle position, suggesting that both IQ-discrepancy and other means should be employed in determining the existence of learning disability.

> [V]irtually all authorities recognize the existence of genuine cases of LD. [But] the fact that learning disabilities actually exist and have a physiological basis may not be crucial for educational decision making. A consensus is emerging that effective instruction does not depend on the results of the psychological testing that has traditionally been used in LD diagnosis. And this may mean that the controversies over testing and categorical integrity need never be resolved if children who need assistance can be identified sufficiently that they can be given instruction that meets their educational needs.

> One attempt to provide that form of instruction is Response to Intervention (RTI) methodology. RTI is a process by which children in early grades who are not achieving at a level commensurate with their class or the norms for their grade receive more individualized and more intense instruction with methods that have been validated as effective, while at the same time continuing to attend their general education classes during the lengthy periods of intervention. Those children who do not make adequate progress when exposed to these progressively more intense methods over a set number of weeks are deemed to have a learning disability. . . . The specialized instruction includes phases (sometimes called tiers) of intervention. The first phase is nothing more than high quality instruction and

careful assessment of the learning progress of all students on the classroom curriculum. Students who are below a proficiency criterion are referred for a second phase of more intense instruction to meet the weaknesses their assessments display; these interventions are implemented by the classroom teacher over a period of perhaps six weeks. Students whose progress is not adequate enter a third phase, in which they receive a specially designed set of educational interventions for a period of eight or more weeks. This phase may or may not be designated special education. Children who do not respond to intervention after this intensive intervention may be designated as having a learning disability on the basis of the failure to respond or on that basis plus other indicators.

IDEA does not require the use of RTI, but amendments made in the 2004 Reauthorization pave the way for RTI by forbidding states from forcing school districts to use discrepancy criteria when determining if a child has a specific learning disability. The Reauthorization also creates a funding stream for RTI by permitting school districts to use up to 15% of federal special education funding to provide services to children who have not been found to be eligible under IDEA but who need additional support to succeed in general education. The final regulations repeat the statutory language permitting non-discrepancy methods for determining LD, including methods relying on the child's response to scientific, research-based intervention. Moreover, they omit a provision in the earlier regulations stating that a child could be determined to have a specific learning disability if he or she "has a severe discrepancy between achievement and intellectual ability in one or more" areas of learning. The regulations modify the prior rule's reference to achievement commensurate with age "and ability levels" and make it achievement adequate for age or meeting state-approved grade-level standards.

Even those who defend discrepancy methodology may have to agree that there are virtues to an RTI approach. First, it delivers instructional intervention to children who need it, and it does so before test score discrepancies emerge, which typically occurs in grade three Second, even for students who eventually are found to be special education-eligible, the method gives data about which educational interventions do or do not produce progress for a specific child, something discrepancy testing methods do not achieve, and which will likely be useful in designing a special education program. Third, RTI may help keep students who do not actually have learning disabilities out of special education, while at the same time conferring educational benefit on them. These are children who may be characterized as "instructional casualties" (the victims of poor teaching practices who could learn if exposed to good teaching), or who come from troubled home environments, or who have other non-disability related circumstances that keep them from learning as well as they can.

Balanced against the possible benefits of RTI are a number of anticipated difficulties with it. The first is that of the bright child who achieves at grade level despite dyslexia or some other learning disability who could nevertheless benefit from special education. Dyslexia, for example, can be present in a child with high general intelligence. Estimates of the percentage of children with learning disabilities who are gifted range from 2–5%. These students tend to use their general intelligence to compensate for weaknesses in phonics, memorization, computation, or other tasks, and are likely not to be identified as having learning disabilities until later in their schooling than other students with learning disabilities.

A second problem is simply that of compliance with RTI requirements when the program is implemented on a large scale. The method mandates that teachers use only scientifically supported instructional techniques; school personnel must monitor individual children's progress rigorously. . . . Exacerbating compliance problems is the reality that the evidence supporting the effectiveness of RTI interventions across the curriculum and across age ranges is surprisingly incomplete. . . . [I]nterventions directed to reading comprehension have proven ineffective, and specialized instruction in other areas remains unproven. . . . Research is limited regarding appropriate protocols for RTI for children beyond their first few years in school.

A third problem is that of affording parents and children their important procedural protections while implementing RTI. For example, under IDEA parents are entitled to notice and the opportunity to give or withhold consent to evaluation. RTI is a method of evaluation, and the fact that the regulations providing for RTI are listed under the "Evaluation" heading implies that notice of use of RTI evaluation methods must be provided. . . . RTI is an educational methodology, not an interpretation of legal requirements, so there is no clear point at which notice must be given to parents in the RTI protocols themselves. Timelines are an important part of IDEA procedural protections. The general time limit for evaluation is sixty days after receipt of parental consent. . . . RTI can be a lengthy process, even if the lapse of time is to some degree compensated by educational benefit some children will receive.

The fourth problem with RTI is the interaction of disciplinary protections with delays in identification of the child as a child with a disability. . . . These rights in connection with the discipline process are extremely important to children and their parents. Though the law says that the rights apply in limited instances for a child who has not yet been determined to be a child with a disability when the school had knowledge that the child was a child with a disability, the applicability of that provision [to RTI] is far from certain.

Mark C. Weber, *The Special Education Eligibility Mess*, 57 BUFF. L. REV. 83, 123–42 (2009). Do you think the RTI approach is superior to one based on comparison of IQ subtests?

Chapter 3

RESIDENCY

A. STATUTORY AND REGULATORY REQUIREMENTS

Where a student resides determines who is responsible for providing the requisite public education. Residency does not necessarily determine the location of services, but rather it determines the source of responsibility for those services. Because the costs are significant this is a seriously contested issue.

IDEA provides that students with disabilities be identified and evaluated and that a free appropriate public education be made available to them. 20 U.S.C. § 1412(a). This obligation extends to students residing in the jurisdiction; identification, evaluation, and some service obligations apply as well to those attending private schools there. *See* 34 C.F.R. §§ 300.131–132. The relationship of IDEA to private schools is discussed *infra* Chapter 12 (Children in Private Schools).

Similar obligations arise under regulations that implement section 504 of the Rehabilitation Act of 1973, 29 U.S.C. § 794, where each recipient of federal funds "that operates a public elementary or secondary education program or activity" must provide a free appropriate public education to each "qualified handicapped person who is in the recipient's jurisdiction, regardless of the nature or severity of the person's handicap." 34 C.F.R. § 104.33(a). Indeed, section 504 is interpreted to require that no recipient of federal funds can refuse to provide services to a child with a disability because of another entity's failure to assume the related financial responsibility:

> Under § 104.33(a), a recipient is responsible for providing a free appropriate public education to each qualified handicapped person who is in the recipient's jurisdiction. The word "in" encompasses the concepts of both domicile and actual residence. If a recipient places a child in a program other than its own, it remains financially responsible for the child, whether or not the other program is operated by another recipient or educational agency. Moreover, a recipient may not place a child in a program that is inappropriate or that otherwise violates the requirements of Subpart D. And in no case may a recipient refuse to provide services to a handicapped child in its jurisdiction because of another person's or entity's failure to assume financial responsibility.

34 C.F.R. Part 104 Subpart D, Appendix A at 23.

Within constitutional parameters set by the Supreme Court in two education-related cases, *Plyler* and *Bynum*, the issues of residency are generally questions of state statutory and common law. However, while residency itself may be disputed, as illustrated in the cases in this chapter, the obligation to serve all students with disabilities remains.

B. THE CONSTITUTIONAL PARAMETERS

PLYLER v. DOE
457 U.S. 202 (1982)

While finding neither a fundamental right nor a suspect class, the Supreme Court invalidated a Texas statute that would refuse free public education to undocumented school-age children.

JUSTICE BRENNAN delivered the opinion of the Court.

The question presented by these cases is whether, consistent with the Equal Protection Clause of the Fourteenth Amendment, Texas may deny to undocumented school-age children the free public education that it provides to children who are citizens of the United States or legally admitted aliens.

Since the late 19th century, the United States has restricted immigration into this country. Unsanctioned entry into the United States is a crime, and those who have entered unlawfully are subject to deportation. But despite the existence of these legal restrictions, a substantial number of persons have succeeded in unlawfully entering the United States, and now live within various States, including the State of Texas.

In May 1975, the Texas Legislature revised its education laws to withhold from local school districts any state funds for the education of children who were not "legally admitted" into the United States. The 1975 revision also authorized local school districts to deny enrollment in their public schools to children not "legally admitted" to the country.

This is a class action, filed in the United States District Court for the Eastern District of Texas . . . on behalf of certain school-age children of Mexican origin residing in Smith County, Tex., who could not establish that they had been legally admitted into the United States. . . . The Superintendent and members of the Board of Trustees of the School District were named as defendants; the State of Texas intervened as a party-defendant. After certifying a class consisting of all undocumented school-age children of Mexican origin residing within the School District, the District Court . . . enjoined defendants from denying a free education to members of the plaintiff class. . . . The Court of Appeals for the Fifth Circuit upheld the District Court's injunction.

. . . .

The Fourteenth Amendment provides that "[no] State shall . . . deprive any person of life, liberty, or property, without due process of law; nor deny to *any person within its jurisdiction* the equal protection of the laws." (Emphasis added.) Appellants argue at the outset that undocumented aliens, because of their immigration status, are not "persons within the jurisdiction" of the State of Texas, and that they therefore have no right to the equal protection of Texas law. We reject this argument. Whatever his status under the immigration laws, an alien is surely a "person" in any ordinary sense of that term. Aliens, even aliens whose presence in this country is unlawful, have long been recognized as "persons" guaranteed due process of law by the Fifth and Fourteenth Amendments. Indeed, we have clearly held that the Fifth Amendment protects aliens whose presence in this country is unlawful from invidious discrimination by the Federal Government.

Appellants seek to distinguish our prior cases, emphasizing that the Equal Protection Clause directs a State to afford its protection to persons *within its jurisdiction* while the Due Process Clauses of the Fifth and Fourteenth Amendments contain no such assertedly limiting phrase. In appellants' view, persons who have entered the United States illegally are not "within the jurisdiction" of a State even if they are present within a State's boundaries and subject to its laws. Neither our cases nor the logic of the Fourteenth Amendment supports that constricting construction of the phrase "within its jurisdiction." We have never suggested that the class of persons who might avail themselves of the equal protection guarantee is less than coextensive with that entitled to due process. To the contrary, we have recognized that both provisions were fashioned to protect an identical class of persons, and to reach every exercise of state authority.

> "The Fourteenth Amendment to the Constitution is not confined to the protection of citizens. It says: 'Nor shall any state deprive any person of life, liberty, or property without due process of law; nor deny to any person within its jurisdiction the equal protection of the laws.' *These provisions are universal in their application, to all persons within the territorial jurisdiction*, without regard to any differences of race, of color, or of nationality; and the protection of the laws is a pledge of the protection of equal laws." *Yick Wo* [*v. Hopkins*, 118 U.S. 356, 369 (1886)].

. . . .

Our conclusion that the illegal aliens who are plaintiffs in these cases may claim the benefit of the Fourteenth Amendment's guarantee of equal protection only begins the inquiry. The more difficult question is whether the Equal Protection Clause has been violated by the refusal of the State of Texas to reimburse local school boards for the education of children who cannot demonstrate that their presence within the United States is lawful, or by the imposition by those school boards of the burden of tuition on those children. It is to this question that we now turn.

The Equal Protection Clause directs that "all persons similarly circumstanced shall be treated alike." But so too, "[the] Constitution does not require things which are different in fact or opinion to be treated in law as though they were the same." The initial discretion to determine what is "different" and what is "the same" resides in the legislatures of the States. A legislature must have substantial latitude to establish classifications that roughly approximate the nature of the problem perceived, that accommodate competing concerns both public and private, and that account for limitations on the practical ability of the State to remedy every ill. In applying the Equal Protection Clause to most forms of state action, we thus seek only the assurance that the classification at issue bears some fair relationship to a legitimate public purpose.

But we would not be faithful to our obligations under the Fourteenth Amendment if we applied so deferential a standard to every classification. The Equal Protection Clause was intended as a restriction on state legislative action inconsistent with elemental constitutional premises. Thus we have treated as presumptively invidious those classifications that disadvantage a "suspect class," or that impinge upon the exercise of a "fundamental right." With respect to such classifications, it is appropriate to enforce the mandate of equal protection by requiring the State to demonstrate that its classification has been precisely tailored to serve a compelling governmental interest. In addition, we have recognized that certain forms of legislative classification, while not facially invidious, nonetheless give rise to recurring constitutional difficulties; in these limited circumstances we have sought the assurance that the classification reflects a reasoned judgment consistent with the ideal of equal protection by inquiring whether it may fairly be viewed as furthering substantial interest of the State. We turn to a consideration of the standard appropriate for the evaluation of § 21.031.

. . . .

Sheer incapability or lax enforcement of the laws barring entry into this country, coupled with the failure to establish an effective bar to the employment of undocumented aliens, has resulted in the creation of a substantial "shadow population" of illegal migrants — numbering in the millions — within our borders. This situation raises the specter of a permanent caste of undocumented resident aliens, encouraged by some to remain here as a source of cheap labor, but nevertheless denied the benefits that our society makes available to citizens and lawful residents. The existence of such an underclass presents most difficult problems for a Nation that prides itself on adherence to principles of equality under law.[1] The children who are plaintiffs in these cases are special members of this underclass. Persuasive arguments support the view that a State may withhold its beneficence from those whose very presence within the United States is the product of their own unlawful conduct. These arguments do not apply with the same force to classifications imposing disabilities on the minor *children* of such illegal entrants. . . . Even if the State found it expedient to control the conduct of adults by acting against their children, legislation directing the onus of a parent's misconduct against his children does not comport with fundamental conceptions of justice.

---

[1] [FN 19] We reject the claim that "illegal aliens" are a "suspect class." No case in which we have attempted to define a suspect class, has addressed the status of persons unlawfully in our country. Unlike most of the classifications that we have recognized as suspect, entry into this class, by virtue of entry into this country, is the product of voluntary action. Indeed, entry into the class is itself a crime. In addition, it could hardly be suggested that undocumented status is a "constitutional irrelevancy." With respect to the actions of the Federal Government, alienage classifications may be intimately related to the conduct of foreign policy, to the federal prerogative to control access to the United States, and to the plenary federal power to determine who has sufficiently manifested his allegiance to become a citizen of the Nation. No State may independently exercise a like power. But if the Federal Government has by uniform rule prescribed what it believes to be appropriate standards for the treatment of an alien subclass, the States may, of course, follow the federal direction.

. . . .

Public education is not a "right" granted to individuals by the Constitution. *San Antonio Independent School Dist. v. Rodriguez*, 411 U.S. 1, 35 (1973). But neither is it merely some governmental "benefit" indistinguishable from other forms of social welfare legislation. Both the importance of education in maintaining our basic institutions, and the lasting impact of its deprivation on the life of the child, mark the distinction. The "American people have always regarded education and [the] acquisition of knowledge as matters of supreme importance." *Meyer v. Nebraska*, 262 U.S. 390, 400 (1923). We have recognized "the public schools as a most vital civic institution for the preservation of a democratic system of government," *Abington School District v. Schempp*, 374 U.S. 203, 230 (1963) (Brennan, J., concurring), and as the primary vehicle for transmitting "the values on which our society rests." *Ambach v. Norwick*, 441 U.S. 68, 76 (1979). "[As] pointed out early in our history . . . some degree of education is necessary to prepare citizens to participate effectively and intelligently in our open political system if we are to preserve freedom and independence." *Wisconsin v. Yoder*, 406 U.S. 205, 221 (1972). . . . In addition, education provides the basic tools by which individuals might lead economically productive lives to the benefit of us all. In sum, education has a fundamental role in maintaining the fabric of our society. We cannot ignore the significant social costs borne by our Nation when select groups are denied the means to absorb the values and skills upon which our social order rests.

In addition to the pivotal role of education in sustaining our political and cultural heritage, denial of education to some isolated group of children poses an affront to one of the goals of the Equal Protection Clause: the abolition of governmental barriers presenting unreasonable obstacles to advancement on the basis of individual merit. Paradoxically, by depriving the children of any disfavored group of an education, we foreclose the means by which that group might raise the level of esteem in which it is held by the majority. But more directly, "education prepares individuals to be self-reliant and self-sufficient participants in society." *Wisconsin v. Yoder*, 406 U.S. at 221. Illiteracy is an enduring disability. The inability to read and write will handicap the individual deprived of a basic education each and every day of his life. The inestimable toll of that deprivation on the social, economic, intellectual, and psychological well-being of the individual, and the obstacle it poses to individual achievement, make it most difficult to reconcile the cost or the principle of a status-based denial of basic education with the framework of equality embodied in the Equal Protection Clause. What we said 28 years ago in *Brown v. Board of Education* still holds true:

> Today, education is perhaps the most important function of state and local governments. Compulsory school attendance laws and the great expenditures for education both demonstrate our recognition of the importance of education to our democratic society. It is required in the performance of our most basic public responsibilities, even service in the armed forces. It is the very foundation of good citizenship. Today it is a principal instrument in awakening the child to cultural values, in preparing him for later professional training, and in helping him to adjust normally to his environment. In these days, it is doubtful that any child may reasonably be expected to succeed in life if he is denied the opportunity of an education. Such an

opportunity, where the state has undertaken to provide it, is a right which must be made available to all on equal terms. [347 U.S. 483, 493 (1954).]

These well-settled principles allow us to determine the proper level of deference to be afforded § 21.031. Undocumented aliens cannot be treated as a suspect class because their presence in this country in violation of federal law is not a "constitutional irrelevancy." Nor is education a fundamental right; a State need not justify by compelling necessity every variation in the manner in which education is provided to its population. *See San Antonio Independent School Dist. v. Rodriguez*, 411 U.S. at 28–39. But more is involved in these cases than the abstract question whether § 21.031 discriminates against a suspect class, or whether education is a fundamental right. Section 21.031 imposes a lifetime hardship on a discrete class of children not accountable for their disabling status. The stigma of illiteracy will mark them for the rest of their lives. By denying these children a basic education, we deny them the ability to live within the structure of our civic institutions, and foreclose any realistic possibility that they will contribute in even the smallest way to the progress of our Nation. In determining the rationality of § 21.031, we may appropriately take into account its costs to the Nation and to the innocent children who are its victims. In light of these countervailing costs, the discrimination contained in § 21.031 can hardly be considered rational unless it furthers some substantial goal of the State.

It is the State's principal argument, and apparently the view of the dissenting Justices, that the undocumented status of these children *vel non* establishes a sufficient rational basis for denying them benefits that a State might choose to afford other residents. . . .

Appellants argue that the classification at issue furthers an interest in the "preservation of the state's limited resources for the education of its lawful residents." Of course, a concern for the preservation of resources standing alone can hardly justify the classification used in allocating those resources. The State must do more than justify its classification with a concise expression of an intention to discriminate. . . . We discern three colorable state interests that might support § 21.031.

First, appellants appear to suggest that the State may seek to protect itself from an influx of illegal immigrants. While a State might have an interest in mitigating the potentially harsh economic effects of sudden shifts in population, § 21.031 hardly offers an effective method of dealing with an urgent demographic or economic problem. There is no evidence in the record suggesting that illegal entrants impose any significant burden on the State's economy. To the contrary, the available evidence suggests that illegal aliens underutilize public services, while contributing their labor to the local economy and tax money to the state fisc. . . .

Second, while it is apparent that a State may "not . . . reduce expenditures for education by barring [some arbitrarily chosen class of] children from its schools," appellants suggest that undocumented children are appropriately singled out for exclusion because of the special burdens they impose on the State's ability to provide high-quality public education. But the record in no way supports the claim that exclusion of undocumented children is likely to improve the overall quality of education in the State. . . .

Finally, appellants suggest that undocumented children are appropriately singled out because their unlawful presence within the United States renders them less likely than other children to remain within the boundaries of the State, and to put their education to productive social or political use within the State. Even assuming that such an interest is legitimate, it is an interest that is most difficult to quantify. The State has no assurance that any child, citizen or not, will employ the education provided by the State within the confines of the State's borders. In any event, the record is clear that many of the undocumented children disabled by this classification will remain in this country indefinitely, and that some will become lawful residents or citizens of the United States. It is difficult to understand precisely what the State hopes to achieve by promoting the creation and perpetuation of a subclass of illiterates within our boundaries, surely adding to the problems and costs of unemployment, welfare, and crime. It is thus clear that whatever savings might be achieved by denying these children an education, they are wholly insubstantial in light of the costs involved to these children, the State, and the Nation.

If the State is to deny a discrete group of innocent children the free public education that it offers to other children residing within its borders, that denial must be justified by a showing that it furthers some substantial state interest. No such showing was made here. Accordingly, the judgment of the Court of Appeals in each of these cases is *Affirmed*.

[Concurring and dissenting opinions omitted]

NOTES AND QUESTIONS

1. Does *Plyler* stand for the proposition that a state can never restrict educational opportunities for children of illegal aliens?

2. What does this case tell us about the relationship of the state and federal governments in regard to education? This relationship plays out more specifically under the statutory mandates of IDEA; in special education, the federal law carries funding with it, and to attain that funding states must come in line with the federal directives.

3. The dissent begins as follows: "Were it our business to set the Nation's social policy, I would agree without hesitation that it is senseless for an enlightened society to deprive any children — including illegal aliens — of an elementary education. I fully agree that it would be folly — and wrong — to tolerate creation of a segment of society made up of illiterate persons, many having a limited or no command of our language. We trespass on the assigned function of the political branches under our structure of limited and separated powers when we assume a policymaking role as the Court does today." The final sentence in the dissent is: "The solution to this seemingly intractable problem is to defer to the political processes, unpalatable as that may be to some." What does this case tell us about the relationship between the courts and the Congress or state legislature? Is it the same situation for educating students with special needs?

MARTINEZ v. BYNUM
461 U.S. 321 (1983)

The Supreme Court upheld a Texas statute which required the child's parent, guardian, or person having lawful control of the child to reside in the school district for tuition-free admission and which disallowed free admission where the child lives apart from such caretakers "for the primary purpose of attending the public schools free."

POWELL, J., delivered the opinion of the Court.

This case involves a facial challenge to the constitutionality of the Texas residency requirement governing minors who wish to attend public free schools while living apart from their parents or guardians.

Roberto Morales was born in 1969 in McAllen, Texas, and is thus a United States citizen by birth. His parents are Mexican citizens who reside in Reynosa, Mexico. He left Reynosa in 1977 and returned to McAllen to live with his sister, petitioner Oralia Martinez, for the primary purpose of attending school in the McAllen Independent School District. Although Martinez is now his custodian, she is not — and does not desire to become — his guardian. As a result, Morales is not entitled to tuition-free admission to the McAllen schools. Sections 21.031(b) and (c) of the Texas Education Code would require the local school authorities to admit him if he or "his parent, guardian, or the person having lawful control of him" resided in the school district, but denies tuition-free admission for a minor who lives apart from a "parent, guardian, or other person having lawful control of him under an order of a court" if his presence in the school district is "for the primary purpose of attending the public free schools." Respondent McAllen Independent School District therefore denied Morales' application for admission in the fall of 1977.

In December 1977 Martinez, as next friend of Morales, and four other adult custodians of school-age children instituted the present action in the United States District Court for the Southern District of Texas against the Texas Commissioner of Education, the Texas Education Agency, four local School Districts, and various local school officials in those Districts. . . . The District Court denied a preliminary injunction. . . . In an appeal by two plaintiffs, the United States Court of Appeals for the Fifth Circuit affirmed. In view of the importance of the issue, we granted certiorari. We now affirm.

This Court frequently has considered constitutional challenges to residence requirements. On several occasions the Court has invalidated requirements that condition receipt of a benefit on a minimum period of residence within a jurisdiction, but it always has been careful to distinguish such durational residence requirements from bona fide residence requirements.

. . . .

We specifically have approved bona fide residence requirements in the field of public education. The Connecticut statute before us in *Vlandis v. Kline*, 412 U.S. 441 (1973), for example, was unconstitutional because it created an irrebuttable presumption of nonresidency for state university students whose legal addresses were outside of the State before they applied for admission. The statute violated the Due Process Clause because it in effect classified some bona fide state residents as nonresidents for tuition purposes. But we "fully recognize[d] that a State has a legitimate interest in protecting and preserving . . . the right of its own bona fide residents to attend [its colleges and universities] on a preferential tuition basis." This "legitimate interest" permits a "State [to] establish such reasonable criteria for in-state status as to make virtually certain that students who are not, in fact, bona fide residents of the State, but who have come there solely for educational purposes, cannot take advantage of the in-state rates." Last Term, in *Plyler v. Doe*, we reviewed an aspect of Tex. Educ. Code Ann. 21.031 — the statute at issue in this case. Although we invalidated the portion of the statute that excluded undocumented alien children from the public free schools, we recognized the school districts' right "to apply . . . established criteria for determining residence."

A bona fide residence requirement, appropriately defined and uniformly applied, furthers the substantial state interest in assuring that services provided for its residents are enjoyed only by residents. Such a requirement with respect to attendance in public free schools does not violate the Equal Protection Clause of the Fourteenth Amendment. It does not burden or penalize the constitutional right of interstate travel, for any person is free to move to a State and to establish residence there. A bona fide residence requirement simply requires that the person does establish residence before demanding the services that are restricted to residents.

There is a further, independent justification for local residence requirements in the public-school context. As we explained in *Milliken v. Bradley*, 418 U.S. 717:

> "No single tradition in public education is more deeply rooted than local control over the operation of schools; local autonomy has long been thought essential both to the maintenance of community concern and support for public schools and to quality of the educational process. . . . [L]ocal control over the educational process affords citizens an opportunity to participate in decision-making, permits the structuring of school programs to fit local needs, and encourages 'experimentation, innovation, and a healthy competition for educational excellence.' "

The provision of primary and secondary education, of course, is one of the most important functions of local government. Absent residence requirements, there can be little doubt that the proper planning and operation of the schools would suffer significantly. The State thus has a substantial interest in imposing bona fide residence requirements to maintain the quality of local public schools.

The central question we must decide here is whether 21.031(d) is a bona fide residence requirement. Although the meaning may vary according to context, "residence" generally requires both physical presence and an intention to remain. As the Supreme Court of Maine explained over a century ago:

> "When . . . a person voluntarily takes up his abode in a given place, with intention to remain permanently, or for an indefinite period of time; or, to speak more accurately, when a person takes up his abode in a given place, without any present intention to remove therefrom, such place of abode

becomes his residence. . . ." *Inhabitants of Warren v. Inhabitants of Thomaston* 43 Me. 406, 418 (1857).

This classic two-part definition of residence has been recognized as a minimum standard in a wide range of contexts time and time again.

Section 21.031 is far more generous than this traditional standard. It compels a school district to permit a child such as Morales to attend school without paying tuition if he has a bona fide intention to remain in the school district indefinitely, for he then would have a reason for being there other than his desire to attend school: his intention to make his home in the district. Thus 21.031 grants the benefits of residency to all who satisfy the traditional requirements. The statute goes further and extends these benefits to many children even if they (or their families) do not intend to remain in the district indefinitely. As long as the child is not living in the district for the sole purpose of attending school, he satisfies the statutory test. For example, if a person comes to Texas to work for a year, his children will be eligible for tuition-free admission to the public schools. Or if a child comes to Texas for six months for health reasons, he would qualify for tuition-free education. In short, 21.031 grants the benefits of residency to everyone who satisfies the traditional residence definition and to some who legitimately could be classified as nonresidents. Since there is no indication that this extension of the traditional definition has any impermissible basis, we certainly cannot say that 21.031(d) violates the Constitution.

The Constitution permits a State to restrict eligibility for tuition-free education to its bona fide residents. We hold that 21.031 is a bona fide residence requirement that satisfies constitutional standards. The judgment of the Court of Appeals accordingly is

Affirmed.

[Concurring and dissenting opinions omitted.]

NOTES AND QUESTIONS

1. *Martinez* answers the question left open in *Plyler*; that is, some bona fide residency requirements imposed by states are acceptable. Each state will have its own statute. Why are residency provisions so important?

2. Who decides how to treat various other situations such as children of divorced parents, wards of the state, temporary residents, homeless residents, etc.? Some states have complicated provisions to ascertain residency in such situations. *See, e.g.*, N.H. R.S.A. 193:12 Legal Residence Required. The New Hampshire statute starts with the provision that "Notwithstanding any other provision of law, no person shall attend school, or send a pupil to the school, in any district of which the pupil is not a legal resident, without the consent of the district or of the school board except as otherwise provide . . ." and then provides for children of divorced or separated parents, children in state institutions, children living with relatives on state recommendation, homeless children, etc. In some cases the federal government has imposed limits on state law residency requirements, for example, for homeless children. *See, e.g.*, McKinney Vento Homeless Assistance Act, 42 U.S.C.

§ 11431(2) (discussed *supra* Chapter 2). The way some of these issues present themselves in special education is discussed in the next section. The 2004 Reauthorization of IDEA addresses the education of homeless children in need of special education and related services in several sections. *E.g.*, 20 U.S.C. §§ 1401(11), 1415(b)(2)(A)(ii).

C.   RESIDENCY IN CASES INVOLVING STUDENTS WITH DISABILITIES

The concept of residency evokes two particular legal terms, domicile and residency. Generally domicile means one's permanent, established home, while residency, a place of current residence, may have a more temporary aspect. As *Martinez* indicates, the principles of residency are physical presence and intention to remain. Many issues involving the relationship of children to their parents and families also involve residency questions, for example, divorce, custody, guardianship, or foster or residential placement. In many states some of these issues will be answered by statute, with or without additional judicial interpretation.

1.   Divorce and Joint Custody

LINDA W. v. INDIANA DEPARTMENT OF EDUCATION
927 F. Supp. 303 (N.D. Ind. 1996), *aff'd*, 200 F.3d 504 (7th Cir. 1999)

In this case the minor child, Ryan, lived with his mother 75% of the time and with his father 25% of the time. The Court analyzed the state statute and concluded that since a court had granted his parents joint custody, Ryan was deemed to be living with both parents, that is, in both school districts in which his parents resided.

MILLER, DISTRICT JUDGE.

This cause comes before the court on the motion of all the defendants to either dismiss for want of subject matter jurisdiction . . . or for summary judgment.

Linda W., Eric W. and Steven V.D. bring this suit under the Individuals with Disabilities Education Act, 20 U.S.C. § 1400 *et seq.* (the "IDEA"), contending, among other things, that the individual education program provided for their son,[2] Ryan V.D., is legally inadequate.

Ryan has dyslexia. The plaintiffs seek review of several administrative decisions, and request compensation for their expenses incurred for Ryan's education and for attorneys' fees. Before bringing this suit, the parties engaged in an extensive administrative process, including two hearings and two appeals to the Indiana Board of Special Education Appeals. In this motion, the defendants contend, apparently for the first time, that this suit should not have been brought, either in

---

[2] [FN 2] Ryan's natural parents, Linda W. and Steven V.D., are now divorced. Both Linda W. and Steven V.D. have remarried; Ryan's stepfather, Eric W., is a plaintiff, but his stepmother, Linda V.D., is not.

this court or in the administrative proceedings, against defendants Mishawaka-Penn-Harris-Madison Joint Services ("MPHM Joint Services") and the Board of Education of School City of Mishawaka ("Mishawaka School City"), since Ryan's "legal settlement," as Indiana law defines that term, is not within the confines of Mishawaka School City. Because this is so, the defendants claim: (1) the court lacks subject matter jurisdiction over the case; and/or (2) summary judgment is warranted.

The defendants' theory as to why the court should either dismiss the cause or award summary judgment relies solely upon the contention that the defendants owe no duty to Ryan under applicable Indiana law and therefore cannot be sued under the IDEA. Under the defendants' view of the facts, Ryan lives with his mother and stepfather 75% of the time, while living with his father only 25% of the time. Ryan's mother and stepfather reside within the boundaries of the South Bend School Corporation, while his father lives within the boundaries of Mishawaka School City. The IDEA requires school corporations to provide for the education of only those children "residing within the jurisdiction of the local educational agency of the intermediate educational unit." 20 U.S.C. § 1414(a)(1)(A). Thus, the defendants claim that Ryan has sued the wrong party[.]

. . . .

The defendants' motion misses its mark. The plaintiffs brought this case under the authority of 20 U.S.C. § 1415(c) as a result of decisions made by the Indiana Board of Special Education Appeals, which in turn was reviewing the decisions of the independent hearing officers stemming from two hearings held under the authority of 20 U.S.C. § 1415(b). . . . The plaintiffs brought this claim under § 1415(e)(2) as "parties aggrieved by the findings and decisions" under the administrative proceedings, and thus, regardless of whether Ryan's legal settlement is within the confines of Mishawaka School City, the defendants have no valid objection to this court's subject matter jurisdiction. Accordingly, the motion for dismissal for lack of subject matter jurisdiction is denied.

. . . .

The defendants' theory supporting their summary judgment motion is the same as that used to support the dismissal motion: that the plaintiffs have no claim against the defendants since Ryan's legal settlement is not within Mishawaka School City. Even when accepting as true the defendants' own view of the facts, and thus assuming that Ryan lives with his father only 25% of the time, the defendants' theory does not support summary judgment.

The IDEA requires school corporations to provide for the education of only those children "residing within the jurisdiction of the local educational agency of the intermediate educational unit." 20 U.S.C. § 1414(a)(1)(A). The parties agree that the IDEA leaves the determination of a student's residency to state law. At first blush, Indiana appears to mirror the simple residency language of the IDEA, because Ind. Code § 20-1-6-14(a), which designates which school corporations will be responsible for the education of children covered under the IDEA, provides that "the school corporation *in which a child with a disability resides* is primarily responsible for providing the child with a disability with an appropriate special education program."

(emphasis added). Since Ind. Code § 10-8.1-6.1-1(e) provides that "for the purposes of calculating the amount of state distribution of money to any school corporation, a student is a resident of a school corporation if the student's legal settlement is in its attendance area," the parties appear to agree that the ultimate determination of where a student "resides" for purposes of the IDEA is governed in Indiana by where his "legal settlement" is.

Ind. Code § 20-8.1-6.1-1, which sets forth the applicable standards for determining a student's legal settlement, states in part:

> (a) The legal settlement of a student shall be governed by the following provisions:
>
>> (1) If the student is under eighteen (18) years of age, or is over that age but is not emancipated, the legal settlement of the student is in the attendance area of the school corporation where the student's parents reside.
>
>> (2) Where the student's mother and father, in a situation otherwise covered in subdivision (1), are divorced or separated, the legal settlement of the student is the school corporation whose attendance area contains the residence of the parent with whom the student is living, in the following situations:
>
>> (A) Where no court order has been made establishing the custody of the student.
>
>> (B) Where both parents have agreed on the parent or person with whom the student shall live.

Since this portion of the statute bases legal settlement on the residency of the parents, the statute defines the term as follows:

> (b) The words "residence", "resides", or other comparable language when used in this chapter with respect to legal settlement . . . means a permanent and principal habitation which a person uses for a home for a fixed or indefinite period, at which the person remains when not called elsewhere for work, studies, recreation, or other temporary or special purpose. These terms are not synonymous with legal domicile. Where a court order grants a person custody of a student, the residence of the student is where that person resides.

Ind. Code § 20-8.1-6.1-1(b).

. . . .

The court is left with the conclusion that neither subsection (a)(2)(A) or (a)(2)(B) applies in Ryan's case, and the analysis thus returns to subsection (a)(1): "the legal settlement of the student is in the attendance area of the school corporation where the student's parents reside." Although Ryan's parents are divorced and living separately, this subsection would appear to suggest that Ryan's legal settlement lies in both school corporations where his parents reside. Further, subsection (b), which defines the words "residence," and "resides," explicitly states that "where a court order grants a person custody of a student, the residence of the student is where that person resides." The court notes that, with the exception of subsections (a)(4) and (a)(6), which apply only if the student is still a minor but married and living with his spouse or if the student is emancipated, the student's residence is not an issue in determining where that student's legal settlement is located. Nevertheless, the clear implication of the language is that if a court grants a person custody of a student, the student is deemed to reside, or live, with that person. Ryan's parents have been granted joint custody of Ryan by a court order, so (unless further facts come to light) Ryan is deemed to be living with both parents (which indeed he is), and his legal settlement is located in the two school corporations in which his parents reside.

Although this may be an awkward reading of the statute, it is the only logical way to interpret the statute, which does not explicitly address a situation in which the student lives at the homes of two parents with joint custody. . . . Therefore, the defendants have not carried their burden on summary judgment of demonstrating that they are "entitled to judgment as a matter of law."

2.   State Schools and Homes

SONYA C. v. ARIZONA SCHOOL FOR THE DEAF AND BLIND
743 F. Supp. 700 (D. Ariz. 1990)

Sonya C., a deaf child, was born in Arizona to parents who were Mexican citizens. Sonya lived in Mexico, but moved back to Arizona at age 12 to live with family friends. When Sonya's residency was questioned in regard to her tuition at the Arizona School for the Deaf and Blind, the court found her citizenship, wardship and physical presence, where guardianship was not obtained to avoid tuition, to be evidence of residence and domicile, entitling her to a free public education.

Marquez, District Judge.

This is a judicial review of an administrative decision of the Arizona Department of Education (ADOE), pursuant to the Education of the Handicapped Act (EHA), 20 U.S.C. § 1401 *et seq.*, relating to the free education of Sonya Castro, a deaf student at the Arizona School for the Deaf and Blind (ASDB).

In July 1988, an initial administrative hearing was held to determine if Sonya, then a minor, was a resident of Arizona for the purpose of receiving tuition-free education at ASDB. It was a "change of placement" due process evidentiary hearing. The Impartial Hearing Officer decided that Sonya was an Arizona resident.

ASDB appealed the decision to the ADOE. The Appeals Hearing Officer reversed the decision below, finding that Sonya was not an Arizona resident. Her court-appointed guardians, Francisco and Elva Olivas, then filed this action, seeking judicial review of the ADOE decision, and a declaratory judgment that Sonya has been since 1984 an Arizona resident entitled to free educational services. Defendants ASDB, Arizona State Board of Education, and C. Diane Bishop, Superintendent of Public Instruction, brought a pendent state counter-claim, seeking payment for out-of-state tuition for the years Sonya had been enrolled tuition-free at ASDB.

The Court finds that Sonya is a named plaintiff, with or without her guardians, and that judicial review of the ADOE decision is authorized. Sonya's legal right to this review continues despite her reaching the age of majority. She continues to receive an education at ASDB. One of the issues for review is her status as an Arizona resident. If she is not a resident, she is subject to a tuition payment obligation imposed by state statute. Tuition at ASDB exceeds $30,000.00 per year.

The Court further finds that the Olivas' have standing to litigate this action. As Sonya's guardians they admitted her to ASDB, and they would be adversely affected if this Court were to determine that she was not entitled to free tuition between 1984 and 1989. They could be required to reimburse ASDB $122,939.00 for tuition and residential care.

Sonya C. was born in Yuma, Arizona on December 17, 1971. She is significantly hearing impaired, and is a handicapped child for purposes of the EHA. For purposes of A.R.S. § 15-1343 (defining persons entitled to education at ASDB) she is sensory impaired. Her parents are Mexican citizens who reside in Puerto Penasco, Mexico. Sonya was raised in Puerto Penasco until 1984, when she was sent to live with long-time family friends Francisco and Elva Olivas in Ajo, Arizona. At this time she was twelve years old.

In late August 1984, Mr. Olivas attempted to enroll Sonya in the Ajo public schools. He was advised by school personnel that they did not have a suitable program for Sonya. The Ajo public schools recommended ASDB. Mr. Olivas was told by either the Ajo public schools or by ASDB personnel that a guardianship would be necessary, so that a responsible person living in the United States could make decisions for Sonya's welfare. On September 4, 1984, Olivas contacted attorney Peter Brown in Ajo to arrange for a guardianship.

On September 5, 1984, an Application for Enrollment at ASDB was submitted on Sonya's behalf. No one in the Ajo public schools or at ASDB ever discussed or mentioned any tuition payment obligations to the Olivas' or to Brown.

. . . .

No one was misled, nor was there an attempt to mislead anyone, regarding Sonya's parents' residence in Mexico. The Olivas' were appointed as Sonya's guardians by the Honorable Lillian Fisher on September 28, 1984. Sonya was officially admitted to ASDB, tuition-free, on that same day. She has been a boarding student at ASDB since the fall of 1984.

The guardianship was sought primarily so that Sonya could attend school in the United States and learn skills sufficient to reside here. Since obtaining guardianship of Sonya, the Olivas' have received no financial support from her natural parents. Sonya is listed as a dependent on Mr. Olivas' state and federal tax returns since 1984. Olivas maintains health and dental insurance for Sonya. Sonya receives monthly SSI checks in the amount of $235.00, for which Elva Olivas is the representative payee.

The Appeals Hearing Officer found that during school holiday recesses and summer vacation, Sonya resided with her family in Puerto Penasco, and that the Olivas' had had Sonya reside with them for short periods of time, ordinarily on weekends and short holiday recesses. When Sonya goes to Mexico to visit her parents, she is usually accompanied by Mr. or Mrs. Olivas. She needs a visa to travel to Mexico.

In Mr. Olivas' opinion, he and his wife are responsible for Sonya's welfare. They consider her part of their family. They make many decisions concerning her education at ASDB, and have had many contacts with ASDB authorities.

In these conversations, staff ask the Olivas' for permission to discipline Sonya; to release her for field trips and to spend the weekend with friends. Other privileges such as extended curfew hours, leaving campus to shop, or inviting male students to her room, are discussed. The Olivas' consent to certain of these and refuse consent to others. Sonya asks the Olivas' to send her money, and asks for permission to buy certain things. There are also communications concerning who will pick Sonya up for vacations, and when. The Olivas' call to advise they will be coming to visit Sonya. Many of the conversations close with "I Love You" and "I Love You Too" or words to that effect. In two or three of the conversations, mention is made that Sonya will travel to her home in Puerto Penasco, or that her mother rather than the Olivas' will pick her up for vacation.

In September 1984, the ASDB admissions policy was based on age, residency and evidence of sensory disability. With regard to residency, the policy was to admit any ward of an Arizona resident, upon presentation of a Superior Court order. The assumption was that the residence of the child was the same as that of the guardian, and it was the policy of the school not to question or look beyond the guardianship order.

During the time this admissions policy was in effect, minors from other states attended ASDB as tuition-paying students. Their tuition was paid for by their parents or by their state government. They were not required to obtain a local guardian as a prerequisite to enrollment.

Sometime in the summer of 1985 the Arizona Attorney General's office questioned ASDB officials regarding the propriety of admitting to ASDB children from Mexico who had guardians appointed in Arizona.

By letter dated July 28, 1986, Arizona Assistant Attorney General Sarah Bailey advised ASDB Superintendent Dr. Barry Griffing that the admission of Sonya and six other children to ASDB was improper and could result in personal liability of ASDB personnel for approximately $289,000.00 in back tuition. This issue was discussed at an executive session of an ASDB Board meeting on August 21, 1986. After that meeting the children were ordered removed from ASDB, until it was determined (as a result of legal action initiated by their guardians) that the removal had violated their due process rights under the EHA. They were then reinstated at ASDB.

After this incident, Dr. Griffing and Board President Edward Berger contacted outside legal counsel to determine whether existing admissions practice was proper. Griffing was advised by three different attorneys that under existing law the current ASDB policies were appropriate, and that the correct solution to the problem would be to change the state legislation which governed admission procedures at ASDB. The Attorney General's office later reimbursed Griffing and Berger for the costs of this legal advice.

Immediately after receiving this legal advice, Griffing spoke to Bailey and others in the Attorney General's office about how to change A.R.S. § 15-1346, which authorized state residents to attend ASDB free of charge. The Attorney General's office eventually drafted new legislation, A.R.S. § 15-1343, which was adopted by the Arizona legislature and became effective in May 1987. It requires payment of tuition in cases where guardian/ward relationships were created for the primary purpose of circumventing the payment of tuition.

The ASDB policy concerning admission of wards of Arizona guardians changed following adoption of this legislation. The new admission policy established procedures for testing the intent of each guardianship, including an ASDB Domicile/Residence Affidavit. . . .

The affidavit asked "Who is the child presently living with?" Elva Olivas answered that "She is living with my family." Another question was: "When school is not in session, (i.e. summer vacation, Christmas vacation) where and with whom will the child stay?" Elva Olivas answered that "She goes with her mother." The affidavit also contained the question: "What was your reason for assuming custody?" Six options were given as answers, including "to assure enrollment in ASDB tuition-free." This was the option checked by Elva Olivas when she completed the affidavit.

As part of the new policy of testing guardianships, Dr. Griffing, Associate Superintendent Kenneth Rislov, James Keller, Director of ASDB Department of the Deaf, and TUSD employee Gene Webber and his assistant reviewed all existing guardianships to test the intent of the parties when they were created. This process included interviews of the guardians, which were conducted by Griffing, Rislov, and the two TUSD employees.

. . . .

On March 1, 1988, Acting Superintendent Rislov wrote to the Olivas', informing them of the Board's decision, and that they were liable for back tuition in excess of $85,000.00. The Olivas' were further informed that unless tuition payments of approximately $35,000.00 for the 1987-88 school year were made by April 1, Sonya would not be allowed to return to ASDB following spring break.

On April 14, it was decided that Sonya could return to ASDB pending further action, again after the Olivas' (through their attorney) had asserted violation of her due process rights under the EHA.

. . . .

The Impartial Hearing Officer found that under Arizona law in 1984, Sonya's guardianship was legitimately sought and granted, pursuant to statutory language and existing precedent. He further found that ASDB officials, the Olivas', and their attorney acted in the good faith belief that the guardianship entitled Sonya to tuition-free attendance at ASDB; and that all parties proceeded according to existing custom and consistent with generally understood principles of law in

Arizona. The Hearing Officer found no evidence whatsoever that Sonya's admission was effected conspiratorially to defraud the State of Arizona; in fact, he called this theory "nonsensical."

Having found that Sonya was entitled to a tuition-free education at ASDB in 1984, the Hearing Officer examined the effect of the 1987 adoption of A.R.S. § 15-1343 on her eligibility for free services. He concluded that the legislation did not remove Sonya's eligibility for services, because a denial of her residency through the guardianship would deprive her of the benefits of her United States citizenship. As a minor child of non-citizens, all that Sonya could do to establish access to public schooling and her residency in Arizona was to seek a guardian who was a resident citizen. Indeed, when she first joined the family that was later appointed her guardians, they expected that she would live with them and attend local schools in Ajo. It is solely because those schools could not provide an appropriate education that she came to attend ASDB . . . it is clear that she did intend to leave her family, enter the United States, and enjoy the benefits of her citizenship.

The Court finds that in 1984, Sonya's United States citizenship, physical presence in Arizona and wardship to long time family friends was prima facie evidence of residence/domicile, entitling her to a free public education among other benefits and privileges.

In *Vlandis v. Kline*, 412 U.S. 441 (1973), the Supreme Court approved a rigorous domicile test as a reasonable standard for determining the residential status of a college student who wished to qualify for resident tuition. The test contemplated that

> in general, the domicile of an individual is his true, fixed and permanent home and place of habitation. It is the place to which, whenever he is absent, he has the intention of returning.

In *Martinez v. Bynum*, 461 U.S. 321 (1983), the Court declared that this strict standard may not be applied to school-age children in the same way as to college students. Instead, the Court found that a school district

> . . . generally would be justified in requiring school-age children or their parents to satisfy the traditional, basic residence criteria — *i.e.*, to live in the district with a bona fide intention of remaining there — before it treated them as residents.

Martinez, 461 U.S. at 332. The Court pointed out that

> the "intention to remain" component of the traditional residency standard does not imply an intention never to leave. Given the mobility of people and families in this country, changing a place of residence is commonplace. The standard accommodates that possibility as long as there is a bona fide present intention to remain. . . . In most cases, of course, it is the intention of the parent *or guardian* on behalf of the child that is relevant. (emphasis supplied).

. . . .

The Court upheld the statute in *Martinez* as a bona fide residence requirement. Justice Brennan, in a concurrence, emphasized that the Court did not address the question of the statute's constitutionality *as applied* to the subject minor, a United States citizen child of non-resident alien parents:

> if this question were before the Court, I believe that a different set of considerations would be implicated which might affect significantly an analysis of the statute's constitutionality.

The Olivas' guardianship of Sonya was validly granted in 1984. Under *Martinez*, the Olivas' intent at that time that Sonya reside with them in the State of Arizona and attend school there can be imputed to her. By means of her wardship to the Olivas', Sonya became an Arizona resident in 1984, and the State of Arizona therefore became liable for the expenses of her tuition at ASDB.

The Court finds that the Olivas' guardianship of Sonya was validly granted after a full hearing and with full disclosure of Sonya's Mexican parentage. At the time that the guardianship proceedings were instituted, ASDB officials were provided with copies of all relevant court pleadings and documents. Should they have chosen to do so they could have sought to intervene in the guardianship proceedings.

. . . .

In this case, the primary purpose for obtaining the guardianship was the Olivas' desire to enroll Sonya in school. This is a permissible purpose. The guardianship was also important for a myriad of reasons bearing on Sonya's physical, mental, moral and emotional health. Without it the Olivas' could not obtain insurance benefits for Sonya; consent to medical treatment; or consent to evaluation and placement pursuant to the EHA. The Court takes judicial notice that life in the United States offers greater opportunity in general, than life in Mexico. This is especially true for a handicapped child like Sonya.

The Olivas' guardianship of Sonya was not obtained in order to circumvent the payment of tuition at ASDB, because they were unaware of any such payment obligation. Rather, the guardianship was obtained because, *after* the Olivas' had attempted to enroll Sonya in the Ajo public schools and had instead been directed to ASDB, they were told that a guardianship would be necessary so that a responsible person living in the United States could make decisions for her welfare. No one in the Ajo public schools or at ASDB ever discussed or mentioned any tuition payment obligations to the Olivas' or to their attorney.

. . . .

In view of the Court's finding that the guardianship was legitimately obtained in 1984, the Court need not address the issue of retroactivity of A.R.S. § 15-1343. The Court finds that the enactment of this legislation in 1987 did not affect Sonya's subsequent eligibility to receive services at ASDB. School officials investigated the circumstances of Sonya's guardianship, and although there was some difference of opinion among them, the presentation they made to the Board convinced the Board that Sonya was properly eligible for tuition-free education at ASDB, at least until the Board was confronted with the threat of personal liability for that tuition.

. . . .

Under the EHA, Arizona is required to provide special education services to Sonya, tuition-free, regardless of her residency status. The EHA provides federal funds to assist state and local agencies in educating handicapped children. To qualify for federal assistance, a state must submit a detailed plan which demonstrates a policy assuring all handicapped children the right to a "free appropriate public education." 20 U.S.C. § 1412(1). The state is also obligated to "identify, locate and evaluate all children residing in the state who are handicapped. . . ." 20 U.S.C. § 1412(2)(C). The federal regulations which implement the EHA provide that "in no case may a recipient [state] refuse to provide services to a handicapped child in its jurisdiction because of another person's or entity's failure to assume financial responsibility." 34 C.F.R. § 104, App. A, n. 23.

In *Rabinowitz v. New Jersey State Board of Education*, 550 F. Supp. 481 (D.N.J. 1982), the New Jersey State Board of Education was ordered to provide a free education to a handicapped child whose natural parents resided in New York state. The *Rabinowitz* court examined closely the EHA, its legislative history and the federal regulations which implement it. The court concluded that

> the will of Congress could not have been more clearly expressed: if states are to accept funding under the Act, then they have an obligation to educate the handicapped children "within [their] borders."

. . . .

Defendants here argue that Sonya's "parents sought admission [to ASDB] by guardians because someone told them the school would then be free." This cited passage does not exist in the record by statement or inference. Rather, the record reflects that the Olivas' on behalf of Sonya and her parents only approached ASDB after being directed to do so by their local school district in Ajo.

The Court finds that Sonya was within the borders of the state of Arizona, a recipient of EHA funds, for bona fide reasons and was therefore entitled to a free appropriate public education at ASDB.

. . . .

Attendance at ASDB tuition-free is and should be one of the benefits of Sonya's United States citizenship. Although not essential to the disposition of this case, the Court includes the following discussion as illustrative of the constitutional principles guiding other courts' resolutions of similar cases.

. . . .

The *Plyler* Court noted the importance of educating undocumented children who may one day be eligible for citizenship, or who may never be deportable. The Court recognized a need to prepare these children to lead productive lives in this country:

> by denying these children a basic education, we deny them the ability to live within the structure of our civic institutions, and foreclose any realistic way that they will contribute in even the smallest way to the progress of our Nation.

. . . .

The rationale articulated in *Plyler* holds even more true for a United States citizen child. If Sonya's parents were also United States citizens, the family could move to any state in the union, and Sonya would be eligible for free public education (and for free "special" education under the EHA, assuming the state was a recipient of EHA funds).

It is not reasonable that Sonya be denied this benefit, and the benefit of SSI payments, and any other benefits of her United States citizenship, because she cannot enter the United States with her parents or as an unemancipated minor. This in effect would penalize her for her parents' status, in violation of her fourteenth amendment equal protection rights.

The only way that Sonya can claim the benefits of her United States citizenship before reaching adulthood is if a guardianship is established for her. It is illogical that Sonya could enter the United States at the age of eighteen and start receiving SSI payments, but could not receive them any sooner. It is even more illogical that upon reaching eighteen she could qualify for other welfare benefits such as Aid to Families with Dependent Children or General Assistance, but that prior to that time she could not receive an education which would help her to become self-sufficient and less likely to require a "hand-out" of this kind. *See Plyler*, 457 U.S. at 230 ("It is difficult to understand precisely what the State hopes to achieve by promoting the creation and perpetuation of a subclass of illiterates within our boundaries. . . .").

The Court finds that plaintiffs have demonstrated by a preponderance of the evidence that the decision of the Impartial Hearing Officer was correct, and that Sonya Castro has been an Arizona resident entitled to free educational services since 1984.

NOTES AND QUESTIONS

1.   Indiana may be unique in its statutory focus on "legal settlement." But the attention the court pays to state law provisions is consistent with other residency cases.

2.   In *Rabinowitz v. New Jersey State Board of Education*, 550 F. Supp. 481 (D.N.J. 1982), Abby Rabinowitz, a child with Downs syndrome, age 11 at the time of the litigation, sought a free and appropriate public education in New Jersey where she had lived all her life in foster homes. Her parents lived in New York. Because Abby was not domiciled in New Jersey, New Jersey believed it was not obligated to provide her education. The court recognized the potential harm to the children as the various players involved dispute their own legal and financial obligations and found that the obligation to serve comes first, and answered issues of residency and financial responsibility come second: "Here, all that is sought by plaintiff is what the Supreme Court recognized that the Act required: access to an education. The court therefore holds that under these circumstances, where a handicapped child has been living in the state since she was two months old, and where the reasons for her being placed here were bona fide and not for purposes of obtaining a free education, and where to uproot her would be traumatic and dysfunctional, then the state has an obligation to provide the child with a free appropriate education pursuant to the dictates of the Act. Whether New Jersey is

entitled to be reimbursed by New York for the cost of the education is not before the court. Instead, the court only decides that New Jersey has an obligation for providing the education. It is inconceivable that Congress would have intended any other result." While it is clear that Congress would want the student to be provided with services while the various government entities involved dispute the financial responsibility questions, is Congress clear on what principles should apply as between jurisdictions? How, as a practical matter, will these obligations be worked out?

3. The 2004 Reauthorization of IDEA adds to the definitional section a definition of ward of the state:

(A) IN GENERAL. — The term "ward of the State" means a child who, as determined by the State where the child resides, is a foster child, is a ward of the State, or is in the custody of a public child welfare agency.

(B) EXCEPTION. — The term does not include a foster child who has a foster parent who meets the definition of a parent. . . .

20 U.S.C. § 1401(36). Will this help resolve any of the residency problems raised in this chapter?

MANCHESTER SCHOOL DISTRICT v. CRISMAN
306 F.3d 1 (1st Cir. 2002)

Five months after she was born in Colorado, while her family was in Manchester, New Hampshire, Kimberli was in a serious accident that left her blind and severely developmentally delayed. Kimberli was placed in a home for children in Pittsfield, N.H. Her parents moved to South Carolina and by the time of the litigation, were divorced. Her father, by then in Ohio, was awarded "residential and legal custody" of Kimberli and her siblings. Manchester sought to have another district bear the costs of Kimberli's education, but the court ultimately applied state law and held Manchester responsible.

CAMPBELL, SENIOR CIRCUIT JUDGE.

At issue in this appeal is whether the Manchester School District ("MSD"), a school district within the State of New Hampshire, has a continuing duty to pay for the special education expenses of Kimberli M.

Kimberli, now fourteen years old, is a developmentally delayed child. Since the age of seven months she has lived at the Brock Home, a state licensed home for children located in Pittsfield, New Hampshire. Because the home for children where Kimberli lives is located within the Pittsfield School District, she attends school there; and because of her disabilities she receives special education services under provisions of federal and state law. But because state educational authorities have determined that MSD was Kimberli's "sending district," as that term is used in the relevant New Hampshire statutes, the New Hampshire Department of Education ("NHDOE") requires MSD to reimburse the Pittsfield School District for the cost of the educational services furnished by the latter to Kimberli.

MSD strenuously objects to being held financially responsible for Kimberli's educational expenses. It points out that Kimberli's parents are not New Hampshire residents. Born in Colorado, Kimberli came, as an infant, with her parents to Manchester, New Hampshire in 1989, where she was severely injured in an accident. At the age of seven months, while her parents were still in Manchester, she was placed, with the assistance of New Hampshire officials, in the Brock Home in Pittsfield, New Hampshire. Soon thereafter her parents left New Hampshire, leaving Kimberli in the Brock Home where she has since resided. . . . Neither parent appears to be involved with her or to contribute to her support.

In the view of MSD, Kimberli's residence has, by operation of law, become that of her father, making her an Ohio resident. MSD resents being forced to pay for the educational expenses of a minor whom it regards as an out-of-state resident. MSD challenges the correctness of the NHDOE's interpretation of New Hampshire statutory law so as to charge MSD for Kimberli's educational expenses.

After failing over a period of years to convince New Hampshire education authorities that it should not be held responsible for Kimberli's educational expenses, MSD sued under 20 U.S.C. § 1415(i)(2)(A), in the United States District Court for the District of New Hampshire. Acting on cross motions for summary judgment, the district court agreed with the NHDOE's interpretation of state law imposing liability for Kimberli's educational expenses upon MSD in the present circumstances. This appeal followed. We affirm.

Because of her several disabilities, Kimberli was entitled under federal and New Hampshire law to receive special education services beginning at the age of three. *See* 20 U.S.C. § 1412(a)(1)(A); N.H. Rev. Stat. Ann. § 186-C:1. In May 1992, the Moore Center Services, Inc., on behalf of Kimberli, requested the NHDOE to make a so-called "district of liability" determination to decide which school district in New Hampshire, if any, was responsible to pay for the expenses of Kimberli's education. In a letter dated May 15, 1992, the NHDOE, quoting N.H. Rev. Stat. Ann. § 193:29 notified MSD that MSD was the district of liability for Kimberli because it was the district in which Kimberli had "most recently resided" prior to her placement in the Brock Home. Unhappy with this determination, MSD appealed to the Commissioner of Education, Charles H. Marston. The Commissioner affirmed the NHDOE's decision, and MSD sought no further review of the decision at this time although entitled to do so. Therefore, as matters stood, while Kimberli would attend school in the Pittsfield School District where the Brock Home was located, MSD had to pay for her special education costs.

In 1993, James M., Kimberli's father, relocated from South Carolina to Akron, Ohio with his remaining children. On February 1, 1993, Kimberli, along with Mrs. Brock of the Brock Home and an assistant, traveled to Ohio to visit her family. According to MSD (but not appellees), there was some thought at the time to place Kimberli in a facility located in Ohio. The attempted Ohio placement, if it was such, failed, and on February 4, 1993, Kimberli was returned to the Brock Home. MSD believed that the out-of-state trip formed a basis for once again challenging the 1992 NHDOE's district of liability determination. MSD argued, in a letter to the NHDOE, that the four-day trip constituted a move that altered Kimberli's residence, thereby relieving MSD of further liability. The NHDOE rejected MSD's characterization. It determined that the trip to Ohio was a mere visit that did not constitute a change in residence. Thus, the NHDOE determined that MSD remained liable for Kimberli's educational expenses. MSD did not seek review of this decision.

Also in 1993, the NHDOE appointed an educational surrogate parent, Margaret "Peggy" Crisman, to act in the place of Kimberli's parents for purposes of making educational decisions. *See* N.H. Rev. Stat. Ann. § 186-C:14 III. Since her appointment, Ms. Crisman has acted on Kimberli's behalf in all matters related to her education. In May 2000, Ms. Crisman became Kimberli's legal guardian.

In 1995, James and Paula M. were divorced. James M. was awarded "residential and legal custody" of their four children, including Kimberli. Focusing on the 1995 divorce decree, MSD petitioned the NHDOE for yet another district of liability determination. MSD argued that, because James M. had been awarded "residential" custody, Kimberli, a minor, had become a resident of Akron, Ohio, where her father resided. MSD reasoned that Akron, and not Manchester, was liable financially for Kimberli's education. Consistent with this theory, MSD administratively discharged Kimberli from special education in 1996, reiterating that her residence, like her father's, was in Akron, Ohio. In response, Ms. Crisman requested a due process hearing before a hearing officer of the NHDOE. That request had the effect of temporarily maintaining the status quo as to Kimberli's placement and MSD's liability for her education expenses.

In January 1997, the hearing officer issued a decision that the doctrines of res judicata and collateral estoppel prevented MSD from re-litigating Kimberli's residency. The hearing officer determined that the NHDOE's 1992 district of liability decision constituted a final order binding upon MSD.

. . . .

MSD thereupon brought this action in the district court against Crisman, as Kimberli's surrogate parent, and the Pittsfield School District, contesting the hearing officer's conclusion. MSD sought a determination that it was no longer financially liable for the special education costs associated with Kimberli's education. While the case was pending in district court, New Hampshire amended its state residency laws as they related to school attendance. The district court remanded the case to the hearing officer to determine whether the 1998 amendments to RSA 193:12 (in conjunction with the 1995 divorce decree) operated to effectuate a "change in circumstances" (i.e. changed the legal residence of a minor child), rendering Kimberli M. no longer legally resident in New Hampshire for educational purposes, therefore relieving MSD of any future obligation to fund her special education (i.e. thereby justifying MSD's decision to prospectively discharge Kimberli from its educational responsibility).

On remand, the hearing officer concluded that "MSD remains legally liable for Kimberli's educational costs based on her placement in a home for children pursuant to RSA 193:27–29."

. . . .

The basic question on appeal, as it was below, is whether MSD is financially liable for the costs of the special education being furnished to Kimberli by the Pittsfield School District. All parties agree that, while she is living at the Brock Home, Kimberli will attend school in the Pittsfield School District. The only issue remaining, as a practical matter, is which school district pays for the costs associated with the "free appropriate public education" guaranteed to children with educational disabilities. While MSD contends that Kimberli is an Ohio resident and that Ohio should therefore provide and finance her special education, there is no Ohio party involved here and no form of relief of this nature is being sought or is available in this proceeding.

. . . .

Because this case involves only questions of law — the interpretation of federal and state statutes — we review the district court's conclusions de novo. While our review is plenary, New Hampshire, like most states, gives some deference to the reasonable interpretation of a state statute by the state administrative agency charged with the responsibility of enforcing that statute. On issues lacking an overriding federal concern, both federalism and comity suggest we look at the NHDOE's interpretations in a similar light. The Supreme Court of the United States has admonished federal courts, when reviewing cases under the IDEA, to take great care not to displace the educational policy judgments made by state and local public education officials.

. . . .

Contrary to MSD's position, however, the IDEA contains no provision dictating which district or agency within a state must assume financial liability for special education services. The IDEA nowhere purports to allocate financial liability among the multitude of school districts housed within the fifty states. And while the IDEA, as a condition of federal funding for any state, requires a state to provide a free appropriate public education to children with disabilities "residing in the State," § 1412(a)(1)(A), it does not purport to limit the provision of such an education to children who fit that standard, however interpreted. "Residing in" could, of course, include children like Kimberli, who have resided since infancy in a New Hampshire home. But even if the phrase were interpreted to exclude a minor like Kimberli the IDEA does not forbid a state from providing and funding a free appropriate public education to a disabled child who may not be a domiciliary of that state even if, arguably, the state is not required to do so and the child may in fact be a charge under the IDEA upon the custodial parent's state.

. . . .

The federal statute, as we say, leaves the assignment and allocation of financial responsibility for special education cost of local school districts to each individual state's legislature. The IDEA provides states with federal funds to help defray the costs of educating children with disabilities. It requires, as a condition of the receipt of federal financial assistance, that a State enact the policies and procedures necessary to ensure that the mandates of the statute are met. See 20 U.S.C. § 1412; 34 C.F.R. § 300.600(b). This duty includes the allocation of financial responsibility for certain special education services. § 1412(a)(12)(A)(ii). But it is the New Hampshire legislature, and not Congress, that assigns and allocates liability for the expenses incurred by a school district administering the mandates of the IDEA.

. . . .

Put another way, it is to New Hampshire law, not federal law, to which we must look to determine whether MSD must pay for Kimberli's special education costs.

The New Hampshire legislature has provided a statutory framework for assigning responsibility for special education costs as part of the state's responsibility to ensure that children with educational disabilities receive a free appropriate education as mandated by federal law. Section 186-C:13, entitled "Liability for Expenses," provides that when a child with educational disabilities is placed in a "home for children" the liability for expenses is determined in accordance with section 193:29. Section 193:29 states that for any child "placed and cared for in a home for children, the sending district shall make payments to the receiving district." The statute defines sending and receiving district as follows:

193:27 Definitions

4. "Sending district" means the school district in which the child most recently resided other than in a home for children, the home of a relative or friend in which the child is placed by the department of health and human services or a court of competent jurisdiction . . . , health care facility, or state institution, if such child is not in the legal custody of a parent or if the parent resides outside the state; if the child is retained in the legal custody of a parent residing within the state, "sending district" means the school district in which the parent resides. . . .

5. "Receiving district" means the school district in which the home for children or health care facility is located. . . .

6. "School district" means a school district in the state.

The district court concluded that MSD was the "sending district" and thus liable for the special education services that Kimberli receives from the Pittsfield School District. MSD attacks the district court's determination that it is the "sending district" in three ways. First, MSD argues that it can no longer be considered the "sending district" because the 1998 amendments to section 193:12 establish that Kimberli is not a "legal resident" of New Hampshire. Second, MSD avers that it is not the "sending district" because, based on the new definition of "legal resident" contained in 193:12, Kimberli never "resided" in Manchester prior to her placement at the Brock Home. Third, it contends that Kimberli was not "placed" in the Brock Home within the meaning of the statute because her placement was not facilitated by the New Hampshire Department of Health and Human Services or by court order.

MSD's first two arguments, that the amendments to section 193:12 relieve it of liability, are without merit. MSD's attempt to make section 193:12, and the definition of "legal resident" for purposes of school attendance, the focal point of the financial liability determination for special education costs is a red herring. The definition of legal resident contained in section 193:12 does not affect the particular statutory provisions on which MSD's liability to Kimberli turns.

Section 193:12 makes provisions for where students may attend school. The 1998 amendments to 193:12 provided that a child may not attend a school in a district in which he or she is not a legal resident except in defined circumstances. One of the defined circumstances, of particular relevance to Kimberli's situation, is that a child placed and cared for in a home for children may attend the public school in which the home for children is located. § 193:12 V. Thus, pursuant to section 193:12, Kimberli is appropriately attending school in the Pittsfield School District — an issue not in dispute.

Contrary to MSD's position, the definition of "sending district" explicitly accounts for a situation in which a child attends school in New Hampshire and the parents reside outside the state. In those cases, the "sending district" is the school district in which the child "most recently resided" prior to placement in the home for children. The New Hampshire Supreme Court has interpreted the phrase "most recently resided" to mean the district in which the child lived prior to his or her placement — regardless of legal residency. *See In re Gary B.*

. . . .

MSD's third argument, that Kimberli was not "placed" in the Brock Home within the meaning of the statute because her placement was not facilitated by the New Hampshire Department of Health and Human Services or by court order, is not supported by the statute or the record.

. . . .

Given New Hampshire's statutory framework, we find ourselves in accord with the rulings of the district court. . . . In 1992, the NHDOE determined that Manchester was the district of liability and financially responsible for the costs of Kimberli's special education. It found that "the most recent residence of Kimberli other than a licensed home was 213 Pine Street, Manchester, where she lived with her parents from birth to April 11, 1989." MSD concedes that it did not, as it could have, appeal from this decision to the State Board of Education or to a court of competent jurisdiction. Consequently, the NHDOE's decision became a final order and is binding upon MSD.

Not only has there been no change in the New Hampshire statutory landscape that would alter the NHDOE's original determination, MSD has not proffered any relevant change in circumstances since the NHDOE's 1992 decision that would entitle it to a different finding. MSD, moreover, is also now collaterally estopped from challenging the NHDOE's 1992 district of liability determination. . . . Pursuant to this doctrine, MSD is not now free to challenge NHDOE's finding, made a decade ago, that the district in which Kimberli most recently resided prior to her placement in the Brock Home was Manchester. The doctrine of res judicata has also been applied to administrative decisions in New Hampshire. Under this doctrine, MSD is barred from challenging the NHDOE's conclusion that it was the district of liability for the costs associated with Kimberli's special education.

Appendix

[The court includes the entire statutory reference, NH RSA §§ 171-A:18, 186:C:1-16, 193:12-29.]

NOTES AND QUESTIONS

1. In this case as in *Linda W.*, consider the care with which the court parses the relevant state statutes. Consider also the layers of administrative proceedings and legal appeals. Should decisions like this require this type of effort? Could there be a uniform rule and, if so, what might it look like? A recent decision in which a court analyzes New Hampshire law to determine that a district in which neither parent lived at the time of the decision was nonetheless the "sending district" is *In re Juvenile*, 897 A.2d 940 (N.H. 2006) (ruling that when mother left child who was subject of neglect proceedings in care of neighbor in Manchester, where mother and child lived, then mother entered nursing home in Unity School District, and then court awarded legal supervision of child to state Division for Children, Youth and Families, which first kept child with neighbor in Manchester and eventually placed child in Nashua Children's Home, state law makes Manchester "sending district" subject to financial liability for special education costs).

2. In 2006, the New Hampshire legislature amended the definition of "sending district" by deleting the following language: "When custody is transferred subsequent to the original placement of a child in a home for children . . . , the 'sending district' shall be from the change in legal custody or guardianship forward, that district in which the child resided at the time of the original jurisdiction." However, the legislature retained the following sentence: "An award of legal custody by a court of competent jurisdiction, in this state or in any other state, shall determine legal custody under this paragraph." N.H. Stat. Ann. § 193.27(IV). Since the father in *Manchester* was granted legal custody after Kimberli had been placed in the Brock Home, does this change create a stronger argument that the Akron school district should be responsible for the cost of Kimberli's education at the Brock Home?

3. The specifics of state law are also carefully analyzed in an Illinois Supreme Court case deciding that a school district was not obligated to pay for the educational portion of a residential placement. D.D. had been adjudicated a delinquent minor and was on probation. His mother was apparently unable to make sure that D.D. attended school or counseling or probation appointments. The juvenile court continued probation with a condition of residential placement. The school district was the home district of the student prior to his being so placed. After a review of the purpose of IDEA and the relevant provisions of the Illinois School Code and Juvenile Court Act, the Illinois Supreme Court concluded that the school district was not involved in the placement but rather the placement "was ordered as a result of D.D.'s probation violation under the Juvenile Court Act and not as a remedy for D.D.'s special education needs." The court found that the school district "cannot be held liable for funding the educational component of the placement. . . ." *In re D.D.*, 819 N.E.2d 300, 308–09 (Ill. 2004). Is this the right result for a delinquent student? What about the question of whether the behavior

which contributed to the delinquency was part of the student's disability? See further discussion on this point in Chapter 9 (Discipline).

Chapter 4

FREE, APPROPRIATE PUBLIC EDUCATION (FAPE)

A. STATUTES AND REGULATIONS

The Individuals with Disabilities Education Act establishes a right to a free, appropriate public education for all children with disabilities. The statute contains provisions that define the concept of free, appropriate public education and other related terms.

1. Appropriate Education

IDEA defines free appropriate public education (FAPE) as:

[S]pecial education and related services that:

>   (A) have been provided at public expense, under public supervision and direction, and without charge;

>   (B) meet the standards of the State educational agency;

>   (C) include an appropriate preschool, elementary, or secondary school education in the State involved; and

>   (D) are provided in conformity with the individualized education program required under section 1414(d).

20 U.S.C. § 1401(9); *see* 34 C.F.R. § 300.17.

A number of the components of this definition of FAPE are further defined in the statute. IDEA defines "special education" as:

> specially designed instruction, at no cost to parents, to meet the unique needs of a child with a disability, including — (A) instruction conducted in the classroom, in the home, in hospitals and institutions, and in other settings; and (B) instruction in physical education.

20 U.S.C. § 1401(29).

"[R]elated services" are defined as:

> transportation, and such developmental, corrective, and other supportive services (including speech pathology and audiology services, interpreting services, psychological services, physical and occupational therapy, recreation, including therapeutic recreation, social work services, school nurse services designed to enable a child with a disability to receive a free appropriate public education as described in the individualized education program of the child, counseling services, including rehabilitation counsel-

ing, and medical services, except that such medical services shall be for diagnostic and evaluation purposes only) as may be required to assist a child with a disability to benefit from special education, and includes the early identification and assessment of disabling conditions in children.

20 U.S.C. § 1401(26).

An "individualized education program" (IEP) "means a written statement for each child with a disability that is developed, reviewed, and revised in accordance with section 1414(d)." 20 U.S.C. § 1401(14).

2.   Free Education

IDEA requires that special education services provided pursuant to the statute be "provided at public expense" and "without charge," 20 U.S.C. § 1401(9)(A) and "at no cost to parents," 20 U.S.C. § 1401(29). Thus, parents cannot be required to pay for any part of the special education of their children. *Miener v. Missouri*, 800 F.2d 749 (8th Cir. 1986). The term "at no cost" "does not preclude incidental fees that are normally charged to nondisabled students or their parents as a part of the regular education program" 34 C.F.R. § 300.39(b)(1). States vary as to whether school districts are authorized under state constitutions to charge fees to students. These fees can include such items as rental of textbooks or musical instruments and participation in extracurricular activities or fieldtrips. For example, Ohio provides that "the board of education of a city, exempted village, or local school district shall not be required to furnish, free of charge, to the pupils attending the public schools any materials used in a course of instruction with the exception of the necessary textbooks or electronic textbooks required to be furnished without charge pursuant to section 3329.06 of the Revised Code." Ohio Rev. Code § 3313.642. The Ohio statute contains no exemption for students with disabilities. The statute permits, but does not require remission of fees for "materials used in a course of instruction to such pupils as it determines are in serious financial need of such materials." Assuming that a student with disabilities has an IEP provision that the student participate in a fall and spring extracurricular sport to meet a goal for socialization and that the child's parent, who can otherwise afford a participation fee, refuses to pay it, should the student with disabilities be entitled to participate without paying the fee charged to all other participants? Since the IDEA regulation permits the charging of "incidental fees," how would you define that term? How much of a financial charge can be made for educational materials or services for a student with disabilities and still have a public education that is free and appropriate?

The IDEA regulations permit school districts to ask parents to file a claim with their medical insurer to help defray costs, but parents must provide "informed consent" before a public agency can access private insurance funds. 34 C.F.R. § 300.154(e). School districts can use parent consent to access insurance only if there is no realistic threat that parents will experience a financial loss. *See* 34 C.F.R. § 300.154(d)(2), (e). Courts have prohibited recovery of insurance proceeds from parents where the effect would be to decrease lifetime coverage, increase premiums, discontinue the policy, or increase an out-of-pocket expense such as a deductible. *See Shook v. Gaston County Board of Education*, 882 F.2d 119 (4th Cir.

1989). Parents can consent to a school district billing their insurance company but failure of a consent form to adequately notify parents that the billing program is voluntary or that the billing can result in potential financial loss violates section 504 of the Rehabilitation Act. Chicago (Ill.) Pub. Schs., 17 EHLR 124 (U.S. Dep't of Educ., Office for Civil Rights 1990).

The restrictions relating to billing parents do not prevent school districts and other public agencies from seeking reimbursement from Medicaid or permissible third party payments. *See Bowen v. Massachusetts*, 487 U.S. 879 (1988). However, the Third Circuit Court of Appeals held in *Chester County Intermediate Unit v. Pennsylvania Blue Shield*, 896 F.2d 808, 810 (3d Cir. 1990), that IDEA does not obligate insurance companies to make third-party payments for related services at the direction of parents where the language of the insurance contract between the parents and the company states that services are excluded for which the parent was "not legally obligated to pay" or which the parent was entitled to receive from a governmental unit or agency "without cost." Likewise, a county that provides services to pre-school and school-age children that are required to be free under the IDEA cannot impose Medicaid liens on personal injury awards for reimbursement of moneys paid. *Andree v. County of Nassau*, 311 F. Supp. 2d 325 (E.D.N.Y. 2004).

Parties who claim that third party payments have been used improperly to pay for IDEA services must exhaust administrative remedies under IDEA before bringing a claim in court. In *Gean v. Hattaway*, 330 F.3d 758 (6th Cir. 2003), juveniles adjudged delinquent and placed in various live-in detention facilities claimed that their right to a free education had been denied because the state Department of Children's Services had obtained without their consent their Social Security benefits and applied them toward their maintenance, including the cost of education. The Sixth Circuit determined that whether a school district's acceptance of Social Security benefits in this case violated its obligation under the IDEA to provide a free education had to first be addressed through the statutorily-prescribed administrative process.

3.   Public Education

FAPE under IDEA requires that special education services be provided "under public supervision and direction." 20 U.S.C. § 1401(9)(A); 34 C.F.R. § 300.17(a). While these services will usually be provided in public schools or at other public sites, children placed in private schools by public agencies are also considered under IDEA to be receiving a public education and have "all of the rights the children would have if served by such agencies." 20 U.S.C. § 1412(a)(10)(B)(ii); *see* 34 C.F.R. § 300.146(c). However, local education agencies (LEAs) have no responsibility to pay for special education and related services on-site in private schools where parents have elected private placements for their children, provided that the public agency has made FAPE available at its public site. 34 C.F.R. § 300.148(a). Nonetheless, children placed in private schools by parents have some rights regarding special education services. For the special education rights of students with disabilities placed in private schools by parents, see *infra* Chapter 12 (Children in Private Schools).

B. COURT DEFINITIONS

In the absence of a clearer definition of "appropriate" in the IDEA statute or its regulations, the Supreme Court in *Board of Education v. Rowley* defined the term, in part, as "some educational benefit."

BOARD OF EDUCATION v. ROWLEY
458 U.S. 176 (1982)

The school district did not have to provide an interpreter for a deaf student because states are not required to maximize the potential of each handicapped child.

[The majority opinion in this case is reproduced in Chapter 1 (Core Concepts), *supra*.]

JUSTICE BLACKMUN, concurring in the judgment.

Although I reach the same result as the Court does today, I read the legislative history and goals of the Education of the Handicapped Act differently. Congress unambiguously stated that it intended to "take a more active role under its responsibility for equal protection of the laws to guarantee that handicapped children are provided *equal educational opportunity*."

As I have observed before, "[it] seems plain to me that Congress, in enacting [this statute], intended to do more than merely set out politically self-serving but essentially meaningless language about what the [handicapped] deserve at the hands of state . . . authorities." *Pennhurst State School v. Halderman, 451 U.S. 1, 32 (1981)* (opinion concurring in part and concurring in judgment). The clarity of the legislative intent convinces me that the relevant question here is not, as the Court says, whether Amy Rowley's individualized education program was "reasonably calculated to enable [her] to receive educational benefits," measured in part by whether or not she "[achieves] passing marks and [advances] from grade to grade," Rather, the question is whether Amy's program, *viewed as a whole*, offered her an opportunity to understand and participate in the classroom that was substantially equal to that given her nonhandicapped classmates. This is a standard predicated on equal educational opportunity and equal access to the educational process, rather than upon Amy's achievement of any particular educational outcome.

In answering this question, I believe that the District Court and the Court of Appeals should have given greater deference than they did to the findings of the School District's impartial hearing officer and the State's Commissioner of Education, both of whom sustained petitioners' refusal to add a sign-language interpreter to Amy's individualized education program. I would suggest further that those courts focused too narrowly on the presence or absence of a particular service — a sign-language interpreter — rather than on the total package of services furnished to Amy by the School Board.

[P]etitioner Board has provided Amy Rowley considerably more than "a teacher with a loud voice." By concentrating on whether Amy was "learning as much, or performing as well academically, as she would without her handicap," the District

Court and the Court of Appeals paid too little attention to whether, on the entire record, respondent's individualized education program offered her an educational opportunity substantially equal to that provided her nonhandicapped classmates. Because I believe that standard has been satisfied here, I agree that the judgment of the Court of Appeals should be reversed.

JUSTICE WHITE, with whom JUSTICE BRENNAN and JUSTICE MARSHALL join, dissenting.

In order to reach its result in this case, the majority opinion contradicts itself, the language of the statute, and the legislative history. Both the majority's standard for a "free appropriate education" and its standard for judicial review disregard congressional intent.

. . . .

The Act itself announces it will provide a *"full* educational opportunity to all handicapped children." This goal is repeated throughout the legislative history, in statements too frequent to be "passing references and isolated phrases."[1] . . . According to the Senate Report, for example, the Act does "guarantee that handicapped children are provided *equal* educational opportunity." This promise appears throughout the legislative history. Indeed, at times the purpose of the Act was described as tailoring each handicapped child's educational plan to enable the child "to achieve his or her maximum potential." Senator Stafford, one of the sponsors of the Act, declared: "We can all agree that education [given a handicapped child] should be equivalent, at least, to the one those children who are not handicapped receive." The legislative history thus directly supports the conclusion that the Act intends to give handicapped children an educational opportunity commensurate with that given other children.

The majority opinion announces a different substantive standard, that "Congress did not impose upon the States any greater substantive educational standard than would be necessary to make such access meaningful." While "meaningful" is no more enlightening than "appropriate," the Court purports to clarify itself. Because Amy was provided with *some* specialized instruction from which she obtained *some* benefit and because she passed from grade to grade, she was receiving a meaningful and therefore appropriate education.[2]

This falls far short of what the Act intended. The Act details as specifically as

---

[1] [FN 1] The Court's opinion relies heavily on the statement, which occurs throughout the legislative history, that, at the time of enactment, one million of the roughly eight million handicapped children in the United States were excluded entirely from the public school system and more than half were receiving an inappropriate education. But this statement was often linked to statements urging equal educational opportunity. That is, Congress wanted not only to bring handicapped children into the schoolhouse, but also to benefit them once they had entered.

[2] [FN 2] As further support for its conclusion, the majority opinion turns to *Pennsylvania Assn. for Retarded Children v. Commonwealth (PARC)*, and *Mills v. Board of Education of District of Columbia*. That these decisions served as an impetus for the Act does not, however, establish them as the limits of the Act. In any case, the very language that the majority quotes from *Mills* sets a standard not of *some* education, but of educational opportunity equal to that of nonhandicapped children. . . .

possible the kind of specialized education each handicapped child must receive. It would apparently satisfy the Court's standard of "access to specialized instruction and related services which are individually designed to provide educational benefit to the handicapped child," for a deaf child such as Amy to be given a teacher with a loud voice, for she would benefit from that service. . . . The basic floor of opportunity is instead, as the courts below recognized, intended to eliminate the effects of the handicap, at least to the extent that the child will be given an equal opportunity to learn if that is reasonably possible. Amy Rowley, without a sign-language interpreter, comprehends less than half of what is said in the classroom — less than half of what normal children comprehend. This is hardly an equal opportunity to learn, even if Amy makes passing grades.

. . . .

The Court's discussion of the standard for judicial review is as flawed as its discussion of a "free appropriate public education." According to the Court, a court can ask only whether the State has "complied with the procedures set forth in the Act" and whether the individualized education program is "reasonably calculated to enable the child to receive educational benefits." Both the language of the Act and the legislative history, however, demonstrate that Congress intended the courts to conduct a far more searching inquiry.

The majority assigns major significance to the review provision's being found in a section entitled "Procedural safeguards." But where else would a provision for judicial review belong? The majority does acknowledge that the current language . . . was substituted at Conference for language that would have restricted the role of the reviewing court much more sharply. It is clear enough to me that Congress decided to reduce substantially judicial deference to state administrative decisions. . . . The Conference Committee directs courts to make an "independent decision." The deliberate change in the review provision is an unusually clear indication that Congress intended courts to undertake substantive review instead of relying on the conclusions of the state agency. On the floor of the Senate, Senator Williams, the chief sponsor of the bill, Committee Chairman, and floor manager responsible for the legislation in the Senate, emphasized the breadth of the review provisions at both the administrative and judicial levels. . . .

Under the judicial review provisions of the Act, neither the District Court nor the Court of Appeals was bound by the State's construction of what an "appropriate" education means in general or by what the state authorities considered to be an appropriate education for Amy Rowley. Because the standard of the courts below seems to me to reflect the congressional purpose and because their factual findings are not clearly erroneous, I respectfully dissent.

NOTES AND QUESTIONS

1.   The *Rowley* Court refused to adopt the federal district court definition of appropriateness, which would have required "an opportunity to achieve . . . full potential commensurate with the opportunity provided to other children." *Rowley v. Board of Educ.*, 483 F. Supp. 528, 534 (S.D.N.Y. 1980). Instead, the Supreme Court opined that Congress had not intended to establish a standard of education beyond

access, *Rowley*, 458 U.S. at 192, reasoning that maximizing each disabled child's potential was "further than Congress intended to go." *Id.* at 198–99. The Court concluded that, based on the record of Amy Rowley's academic progress, she was "receiving an 'appropriate education.' " *Id.* at 209–10. Assuming that the Court had adopted the district court's higher standard, would a sign-language interpreter have been required in order for Amy Rowley to receive FAPE?

2. How would special education services be different if the majority had adopted the views of Justice Blackmun? Of Justice White and the dissenters? The majority had concerns that an equality-based standard would be unworkable. Would the standards proposed by these separate opinions be workable?

3. In the 1997 amendments to the IDEA, Congress made findings that the education of children with disabilities could be more effective if they are provided with properly trained personnel who can provide the skills and knowledge necessary for children with disabilities

> to meet developmental goals and, to the maximum extent possible, those challenging expectations that have been established for all children; and to be prepared to lead productive, independent, adult lives, to the maximum extent possible.

20 U.S.C. § 1400(c)(5)(E). A number of federal circuit courts of appeals have interpreted this language as not overruling the *Rowley* standard in favor of a higher maximum-possible-extent standard. *Lt. T.B. v. Warwick Sch. Comm.*, 361 F.3d 80, 83 (1st Cir. 2004); *Missouri Dep't of Elementary and Secondary Educ. v. Springfield R-12 Sch. Dist.*, 358 F.3d 992, 999 n. 7 (8th Cir. 2004); *Evanston Cmty. Consol. Sch. Dist. No. 65 v. Michael M.*, 356 F.3d 798, 802, 804 (7th Cir. 2004); *A.B. v. Lawson*, 354 F.3d 315, 319 (4th Cir. 2004). *Contra J.L. v. Mercer Island Sch. Dist.*, No. C06-494P, 2006 U.S. Dist. LEXIS 89492, at *11 (W.D. Wash. Dec. 8, 2006) ("In defining the applicable standard, the District and the ALJ place much reliance on the Supreme Court case of *Hendrick Hudson District Bd. of Education v. Rowley*, a case which interprets the EHA. To the extent that the Supreme Court at that time was interpreting a statute which had no requirement (1) that programming for disabled students be designed to transition them to post-secondary education, independent living or economic self-sufficiency or (2) that schools review IEPs to determine whether annual goals were being attained, the Court must consider that opinion superseded by later legislation, and the District's and ALJ's reliance on it misplaced."), *amended in part on reconsideration*, 2007 U.S. Dist. LEXIS 10343 (W.D. Wash. Feb. 10, 2007), *rev'd*, 575 F.3d 1025 (9th Cir. 2009). In *N.B. v. Hellgate Elementary Sch. Dist.*, 541 F.3d 1202 (9th Cir. 2008), a panel of the Ninth Circuit declared that the 1997 IDEA Amendments required that children with disabilities be provided with a meaningful educational benefit, which the court understood as a standard higher than *Rowley*'s standard of some educational benefit. Less than a year later, another panel of the Ninth Circuit declared that the Amendments did not supersede *Rowley* and reversed and remanded the decision of a district court whose "analysis was clearly infected by its interpretation of the 1997 Individuals with Disabilities Education Act amendment." *J. L. v. Mercer Island Sch. Dist.*, 575 F.3d 1025, 1037 n.9 (9th Cir. 2009). Although the *J.L.* court minimized the differences between its approach and that in *N.B.*, *see J.L.*, 2009 U.S. App. LEXIS 17513, at *

34 n.10, there appears to be an internal split in the Ninth Circuit regarding *Rowley*'s current validity.

4. *Rowley* does not prohibit states from setting a higher standard. However, only four states (Michigan, New Jersey, North Carolina, Tennessee) have established a definition of appropriateness higher than that found in *Rowley.* Mich. Comp. L. § 380.1701(a) (state, intermediate and local agencies "shall provide for the delivery of special education programs and services designed to develop the maximum potential of each handicapped person"); N.J. Stat. Ann. §§ 18:46-13, 18A:46-19.1 (obligation to provide "suitable facilities and programs of education" must assure children with disabilities "the fullest possible opportunity to develop their intellectual capacities"); N.C. Gen. Stat. § 115C-106(a) ("[T]he policy of the State is to ensure every child a fair and full opportunity to reach his full potential."); Tenn. Code Ann. § 49-10-101(a)(1) ("It is the policy of this state to provide, and to require school districts to provide, as an integral part of free public education, special education services sufficient to meet the needs and maximize the capabilities of children with disabilities."). Two states that had higher standards have recently replaced them with the *Rowley* standard. Mass. Gen. Laws, ch. 71B, § 3 (effective in 2002, deleting requirement that program "benefit the child to the maximum extent feasible" and replaced standard for hearing officer from "child's maximum possible development" to "child receives a free and appropriate education."); Mo. Ann. Stat. § 162.670 (in 2002, replacing requirement to "maximize capabilities" with obligation to provide an "appropriate education consistent with the provisions set forth in state and federal regulations implementing the Individuals with Disabilities Education Act (IDEA)"). For an illuminating discussion of this issue, see Gary L. Monserud, *The Quest for a Meaningful Mandate for the Education of Children with Disabilities*, 18 St. John's J. Legal Comment 675 (2004). A Florida federal court recently ruled that language in the state constitution providing for high quality education did not create an elevated standard for appropriate education for children with disabilities. *School Bd. of Lee County, Fla. v. M.M.*, Nos. 2:05-cv-5-FtM-29SPC, 2:05-cv-7-FtM-29SPC (M.D. Fla. Mar. 27, 2007). In the states with a higher standard than that contained in *Rowley*, the higher standard does not apply to schools on federal military bases located within those states. *See G. v. Fort Bragg Dependent Schs.*, 343 F.3d 295 (4th Cir. 2003).

5. In cases about providing FAPE, to what extent should courts defer to local school officials' decisions to conserve scarce resources where less expensive program placements are available? In *Age v. Bullitt County Pub. Schs.*, 673 F.2d 141, 145 (6th Cir. 1982), the Sixth Circuit upheld a local school district's new program for the hearing impaired as applied to a student with a severe to profound hearing disability who had in previous years been transported to a school in another county that used the oral/aural approach for instruction and communication. The student's parents objected to the new program because it involved their child being in the same room with another student who was taught using sign language, their objection being that the mixing of these two approaches would interfere with their child's language development pursuant to his IEP. However, in affirming the school district's use of two different approaches to dealing with hearing disability, the Sixth Circuit agreed with the school district that, because the presence of two approaches in the same room would not adversely affect the student's language development,

the district did not have to bear the expense of transporting the student to his previous school. Similarly, in *Bales v. Clarke*, 523 F. Supp. 1366, 1371 (E.D. Va. 1981), a federal district court rejected parents' request for reimbursement for their placement of a severely disabled child in a private academy summer school when the child had made satisfactory progress over a two-year-period in a public regional school and when the parents had failed to prove that the summer school was necessary to prevent severe regression. In *Thompson R2-J School District v. Luke P.*, 540 F.3d 1143 (10th Cir.2008), *cert. denied*, 129 S. Ct. 1356 (2009), the court upheld the school district's program for a child with autism over a residential program chosen by the parents. The court noted that the child made educational progress in public school, and, citing *Rowley*, it found the program sufficient despite its failure in addressing his inability to generalize functional behavior learned at school to home and other environments. *Id.* at 1150.

6.   In some situations, parents contend that they should be reimbursed for placing their children in psychiatric hospitals, citing evidence that the placement is needed for the child to learn. *See, e.g., Richardson Indep. Sch. Dist. v. Michael Z.*, 580 F.3d 286 (5th Cir. 2009) (vacating decision below and remanding for determination whether child's treatment at psychiatric facility was primarily oriented toward enabling her to receive meaningful educational benefit); *Mary T. v. School Dist.*, 575 F.3d 235 (3d Cir. 2009). Should the parents be entitled to reimbursement? This topic is discussed again in Chapter 7.

7.   Although private special education placements are sometimes blamed for contributing disproportionately to educational costs, a recent study published by the Hoover Institution concludes that "the evidence contradicts the private placement myth. Only a very small fraction of disabled students are placed in private schools at public expense. And contrary to claims that this is increasingly common, the likelihood that disabled students will be placed in a private school has not grown in the last 15 years. While some of those private placements are indeed expensive, the overall cost of private placement nationwide constitutes a tiny portion of public school spending." Jay P. Greene & Marcus A. Winters, Debunking a Special Education Myth, Education Next (2007), http://www.hoover.org/publications/ednext/6018321.html.

C.   FAPE FOR CHILDREN WITH SEVERE DISABILITIES

POLK v. CENTRAL SUSQUEHANNA INTERMEDIATE UNIT 16
853 F.2d 171 (3d Cir. 1988),
cert. denied, 488 U.S. 1030 (1989)

In Polk, the Third Circuit held that appropriateness under Rowley as applied to a student with severe disabilities means more than trivial educational benefit.

BECKER, CIRCUIT JUDGE.

This appeal requires that we examine the contours of the "free appropriate public education" requirement of the Education of the Handicapped Act . . . as it touches on the delivery of physical therapy, which is a "related service" under the EHA. Ronald and Cindy Polk are parents of Christopher Polk, a child with severe mental and physical impairments. They claim that defendants, the local school district and the larger administrative Intermediate Unit (which oversees special education for students in a five-county area) violated the EHA because they failed to provide Christopher with an adequate program of special education. Specifically, plaintiffs contend that defendants' failure to provide direct "hands-on" physical therapy from a licensed physical therapist once a week has hindered Christopher's progress in meeting his educational goals.

The district court granted summary judgment in favor of defendants. The court held that because Christopher derived "some educational benefit" from his educational program, the requirements of the EHA, as interpreted by the Supreme Court in *Board of Education v. Rowley*, . . . have been met. . . .

We will reverse the district court's grant of summary judgment for two reasons. First, we discern a genuine issue of material fact as to whether the defendants, in violation of the EHA procedural requirement for individualized educational programs, have refused, as a blanket rule, to consider providing handicapped students with direct physical therapy from a licensed physical therapist. Second, we conclude that the district court applied the wrong standard in evaluating the appropriateness of the child's education. . . . More specifically, we believe that the district court erred in evaluating this severely handicapped child's educational program by a standard under which even trivial advancement satisfied the substantive provisions of the EHA's guarantee of a free and appropriate education. There is evidence in the record that would support a finding that the program prescribed for Christopher afforded no more than trivial progress. We will therefore reverse and remand for further proceedings consistent with this opinion.

. . . .

Christopher Polk is severely developmentally disabled. At the age of seven months he contracted encephalopathy, a disease of the brain similar to cerebral palsy. He is also mentally retarded. Although Christopher is fourteen years old, he has the functional and mental capacity of a toddler. All parties agree that he requires "related services" in order to learn. He receives special education from defendants, the Central Susquehanna Intermediate Unit # 16 (the IU) and Central Columbia Area School District (the school district). Placed in a class for the mentally handicapped, Christopher has a full-time personal classroom aide. His education consists of learning basic life skills such as feeding himself, dressing himself, and using the toilet. He has mastered sitting and kneeling, is learning to stand independently, and is showing some potential for ambulation. Christopher is working on basic concepts such as "behind," "in," "on," and "under," and the identification of shapes, coins, and colors. Although he is cooperative, Christopher finds such learning difficult because he has a short attention span.

Although the record is not clear on this point, until 1980, the defendants apparently provided Christopher with direct physical therapy from a licensed physical therapist. Since that time, however, under a newer, so-called consultative model, . . . Christopher no longer receives direct physical therapy from a physical therapist. Instead, a physical therapist (one of two hired by the IU) comes once a month to train Christopher's teacher in how to integrate physical therapy with Christopher's education.

. . . Although the therapist may lay hands on Christopher in demonstrating to the teacher the correct approach, he or she does not provide any therapy to Christopher directly, but uses such interaction to teach the teacher. Plaintiffs do not object to the consultative method per se, but argue that, to meet Christopher's individual needs, the consultative method must be supplemented by direct ("hands on") physical therapy. . . .

. . . .

In support of this position, plaintiffs adduced evidence that direct physical therapy from a licensed physical therapist has significantly expanded Christopher's physical capacities. In the summer of 1985, Christopher received two weeks of intensive physical therapy from a licensed physical therapist at Shriner's Hospital in Philadelphia. According to Christopher's parents, this brief treatment produced dramatic improvements in Christopher's physical capabilities.[3] A doctor at Shriner's prescribed that Christopher receive at least one hour a week of direct physical therapy. Because the defendants were unwilling to provide direct physical therapy as part of Christopher's special education program, the Polks hired a licensed physical therapist, Nancy Brown, to work with Christopher at home. At the time of the hearing, she was seeing Christopher twice a week. . . .

Plaintiffs first challenged Christopher's IEP before a Commonwealth of Pennsylvania Department of Education Hearing Officer. . . . The Hearing Officer found that Christopher was benefiting from his education, and that his education was appropriate. . . . This finding was affirmed by the Pennsylvania Secretary of Education. . . .

After exhausting administrative remedies to their dissatisfaction, the Polks brought suit in the district court for the Middle District of Pennsylvania. . . . Relying on the Supreme Court's decision in *Rowley*, . . . the court held that the provisions of EHA had been met because Christopher had received *some* benefit from his education. This appeal followed.

Plaintiffs present two arguments on appeal. First, they submit that the defendants violated EHA's procedural requirements because Christopher's program is not truly individualized. . . . Plaintiffs rely, in this regard, on the defendants' failure to provide direct ("hands on") physical therapy from a licensed physical therapist to any of the children in the intermediate unit (a fact they learned during Christopher's due process hearing before the state examiner). This failure, they contend, is evidence that the defendants have an inflexible rule prohibiting direct

---

[3] [FN 4] Mrs. Polk testified that after Christopher's 13-day intensive experience in Shriner's he was much better able to feed himself; that his weight bearing, control over his body, and use of a walker were improved; and that he began kneeling on his own.

therapy and that such a rigid rule conflicts with the EHA's mandate of providing *individualized* education.

. . . .

Second, plaintiffs assert that Christopher's education is inadequate to meet his unique needs. They claim that the district court found Christopher's education appropriate only because it applied an erroneous legal standard in judging the educational benefit of Christopher's program.

. . . .

As we noted above, the plaintiffs have offered to prove that the defendants never genuinely considered Christopher's unique needs because of a rigid policy of providing only consultative physical therapy. . . .

. . . .

In our view, a rigid rule under which defendants refuse even to consider providing physical therapy . . . would conflict with Christopher's procedural right to an individualized program. Drawing all reasonable inferences in favor of the non-moving party, . . . we believe that a genuine dispute exists over whether the defendants would consider, under any circumstances, offering direct physical therapy, and that this dispute is over material facts, precluding summary judgment. Concomitantly, we believe that plaintiffs should be given an opportunity to continue their discovery into this question because the existence of a rigid rule prohibiting such therapy would violate the EHA. Therefore, we will reverse and remand the district court's decision for inquiry into whether defendants possess a rigid policy prohibiting the provision of direct physical therapy to children in the IU.

. . . .

We begin our discussion of the substantive protections of the EHA with the Supreme Court's opinion in *Board of Education v. Rowley* because the parties' arguments are so closely tied to that case; only in the context of *Rowley* can we intelligently present the parties' contentions and the district court's opinion.

. . . .

Although the tenor of the *Rowley* opinion reflects the Court's reluctance to involve the courts in substantive determinations of appropriate education and its emphasis on the procedural protection of the IEP process, it is clear that the Court was not espousing an entirely toothless standard of substantive review. Rather, the *Rowley* Court described the level of benefit conferred by the Act as "meaningful." . . . As the Court explained:

> By passing the Act, Congress sought primarily to make public education available to handicapped children. But in seeking to provide such access to public education, Congress did not impose upon the States any greater substantive educational standard than would be necessary to make such access meaningful.

. . . After noting the deference due to states on questions of education and the theme of access rather than a guarantee of any particular standard of benefit, the

Court acknowledged that:

> Implicit in the congressional purpose of providing access to a "free appropriate public education" is the requirement that the education to which access is provided be sufficient to confer some educational benefit upon the handicapped child. It would do little good for Congress to spend millions of dollars in providing access to a public education only to have the handicapped child receive no benefit from that education. The statutory definition of "free appropriate public education," in addition to requiring that States provide each child with "specially designed instruction," expressly requires the provision of "such . . . supportive services . . . as may be required to assist a handicapped child to benefit from special education." § 1401(17). We therefore conclude that the "basic floor of opportunity" provided by the Act consists of access to specialized instruction and related services which are individually designed to provide educational benefit to the handicapped child.
>
> . . . .

We hold that the EHA calls for more than a trivial educational benefit. That holding rests on the Act and its legislative history as well as interpretation of *Rowley*.

. . . The opinion of the district court, anchored to the "some benefit" language of *Rowley* . . . explained its holding as follows:

> The fact that Christopher would advance more quickly with intensive therapy rather than the therapy he now receives does not make the School District's program for Christopher defective. Programs need only render some benefit; they need not maximize potential. . . . The Supreme Court has determined that the Act is primarily a procedural statute and does not impose a substantive duty on the state to provide a student with other than some educational benefits. Increased muscle tone may well fall outside of the scope of the requirement that Christopher receive some educational benefits from the program in which he is enrolled.

. . . Plaintiffs argue on appeal that the district court applied the wrong standard in measuring the educational benefit of Christopher's program and that the case should be remanded for further proceedings consistent with the correct standard, one that requires more than a *de minimis* benefit. Defendants rejoin that *Rowley's* announcement of a "some benefit" test precludes judicial inquiry into the substantive education conferred by the Act, so long as the handicapped child receives any benefit at all. Noting that Christopher's parents acknowledge that he derives some benefit from his education, defendants submit that the inquiry is over and that the district court's summary judgment must be affirmed.

Our review of the legal standard applied by the district court is plenary. . . .

Because *Rowley* is a narrow decision, our decision must perforce also be informed by the text of the EHA and the legislative history of the 1975 amendments. Accordingly, we turn to a discussion thereof. Our interpretation of "educational benefit" is informed by the text of the EHA and by the legislative history concerning the passage of the 1975 amendments. The self-defined purpose of the EHA is to provide *"full* educational opportunity to all handicapped children." 20 U.S.C. § 1412(2)(A) (emphasis added). Similarly, the Senate Report on the 1975 amendments defined related services as "transportation, developmental, corrective, and supportive services (specifically including at least speech pathology and audiology, psychological services, counseling services, physical and occupational therapy, and recreation) necessary for a handicapped child to *fully* benefit from special education." . . . (emphasis added). The House Report echoes this language, citing the EHA's "goal of providing each handicapped child with a free, *full*, public education." . . . (emphasis added).

. . . .

Implicit in the legislative history's emphasis on self-sufficiency is the notion that states must provide some sort of meaningful education — more than mere access to the schoolhouse door. We acknowledge that self-sufficiency cannot serve as a substantive standard by which to measure the appropriateness of a child's education under the Act. . . . Indeed, Christopher Polk is not likely ever to attain this coveted status, no matter how excellent his educational program. Instead, we infer that the emphasis on self-sufficiency indicates in some respect the quantum of benefits the legislators anticipated: they must have envisioned that significant learning would transpire in the special education classroom — enough so that citizens who would otherwise become burdens on the state would be transformed into productive members of society. Therefore, the heavy emphasis in the legislative history on self-sufficiency as one goal of education, where possible, suggests that the "benefit" conferred by the EHA and interpreted by Rowley must be more than *de minimis*.

We believe that the teaching of *Rowley* is not to the contrary. As discussed above, the *Rowley* Court described the education that must be provided under the EHA as "meaningful." The use of the term "meaningful" indicates that the Court expected more than *de minimis* benefit.

. . . .

To summarize, in our view, the danger of the district court's formulation is that under its reading of *Rowley* the conferral of any benefit, no matter how small, could qualify as "appropriate education" under the EHA. Under the district court's approach, carried to its logical extreme, Christopher Polk would be entitled to no physical therapy because his occupational therapy offers him "some benefit." . . . We do not believe that such a formulation reflects congressional intent in light of the importance of related services (particularly physical therapy) in the statutory and regulatory scheme. Just as Congress did not write a blank check, neither did it anticipate that states would engage in the idle gesture of providing special education designed to confer only trivial benefit. Put differently, and using *Rowley*'s own terminology, we hold that Congress intended to afford children with special needs an education that would confer meaningful benefit.

We further conclude that *Rowley*, although it prescribes restraint and warns that Congress did not intend the Act to maximize a child's potential, does not militate against the standard we have announced. Because the test employed by the district court ostensibly could have allowed only a *de minimis* benefit, we must remand in light of our interpretation. Finally, we do not read the Supreme Court's salutary warnings against interference with educational methodology as an invitation to abdicate our obligation to enforce the statutory provisions that ensure a free and appropriate education to Christopher. . . .

Obviously, this court is in no position to determine the factual question whether the treatment the defendants currently provide for Christopher is appropriate. We are, however, obligated to correct errors of law on appeal, and we hold that the district court applied the wrong standard in granting summary judgment for defendants when it allowed for the possibility of only *de minimis* benefit.

. . . .

We recognize the difficulty of measuring levels of benefit in severely handicapped children. Obviously, the question whether benefit is *de minimis* must be gauged in relation to the child's potential. However, we believe that the extent of the factual dispute concerning the level of benefit Christopher received from his educational program precludes summary judgment under the standard that we announce today. The judgment of the district court will therefore be reversed and the case remanded for further proceedings consistent with this opinion.

NOTES AND QUESTIONS

1. *Polk* addresses one of the questions left unanswered under *Rowley*, namely how the "some educational benefit" test should be applied to a child with severe disabilities. A "meaningful" education for purposes of FAPE in this case could not be provided under a rigid school district rule regarding how a particular service (physical therapy) was to be delivered to students. Does *Polk* suggest that such rigid rules are suspect in terms of providing FAPE because they do not allow for individual differences among students?

2. The meaningfulness of services has become a particular issue for children with autism where programs of discrete trial therapy (DTT), such as Lovaas therapy, have been demanded by parents. Cases arise both under Part C (children under the age of three) and under Part B of IDEA. Where parents have home-instructed children using a DTT program, courts are divided as to whether the parents should be reimbursed. One court ordered reimbursement for parents where a school district could not present evidence that its program had a number of individual interventions adequate to address the level of severity of a child's autism. *T.H. v. Board of Educ. of Palatine Cmty. Consol. Sch. Dist.*, 55 F. Supp. 2d 830 (N.D. Ill. 1999), *aff'd sub nom. Board of Educ. v. Kelly*, 207 F.3d 931 (7th Cir. 2000) (requiring reimbursement under IDEA Part B); *see Bucks County Dep't of Mental Health/Mental Retardation v. Pennsylvania*, 379 F.3d 61 (3d Cir. 2004) (requiring reimbursement of Lovaas services under IDEA Part C). In recent years, numerous other cases have overturned decisions by school districts to deny Lovaas and similar programs to children with autism. *E.g., County Sch. Bd. v. Z.P.*, 399 F.3d 298 (4th Cir. 2005); *Deal v. Hamilton County Bd. of Educ.*, 392 F.3d 840 (6th Cir. 2004); *L.B. v. Nebo Sch. Dist.*, 379 F.3d 966 (10th Cir. 2004); *G. v. Fort Bragg Dependent Schs.*, 343 F.3d 295 (4th Cir. 2003). However, many courts have refused

reimbursement for home-based autism programs. *E.g.*, *Gill v. Columbia 93 Sch. Dist.*, 217 F.3d 1027 (8th Cir. 2000); *Burilovich v. Board of Educ. of Lincoln*, 208 F.3d 560 (6th Cir. 2000). Some courts have considered programs for autism to be methodologies and, thus, have deferred to the expertise of school district personnel in choosing educational methods most suitable to a child's needs. *Deal v. Hamilton County Dep't of Educ.*, 259 F. Supp. 2d 687 (E.D. Tenn. 2003), *rev'd*, 392 F.3d 840 (6th Cir. 2004); *Tyler v. Northwest Indep. Sch. Dist.*, 202 F. Supp. 2d 557 (N.D. Tex. 2002); *Pitchford v. Salem-Keizer Sch. Dist. No. 24J*, 155 F. Supp. 2d 1213 (D. Or. 2001); *see Thompson R2-J School District v. Luke P.*, 540 F.3d 1143 (10th Cir. 2008) (upholding school district program despite child's failure to generalize behavioral skills in out-of-school settings), *cert. denied*, 129 S. Ct. 1356 (2009); *Bradley v. Arkansas Dep't of Educ.*, 443 F.3d 965 (8th Cir. 2006) (upholding school district program despite challenges to program content and implementation).

When dealing with expensive pre-existing programs, to what extent should courts defer to local school officials' decisions to conserve scarce resources where less expensive program placements are available? In *Lt. T.B. v. Warwick School Committee*, 361 F.3d 80 (1st Cir. 2004), the First Circuit upheld a school district's modified TEACCH program that contained considerable one-on-one instruction, over a more expensive private placement that emphasized DTT. Professor Seligmann observes that autism cases "present a particularly timely and dramatic prism through which to examine" *Rowley*'s "principles of restraint and deference." Terry Jean Seligmann, *Rowley Comes Home to Roost: Judicial Review of Autism Special Education Disputes*, 9 U.C. DAVIS J. JUV. L. & POL'Y 217, 218 (2005) (collecting and analyzing recent IDEA cases concerning autism, including *Lt. T.B.*). For further discussion of this topic, see *infra* Chapter 13 (Early Childhood Programs).

3.   Some courts have used an individualization approach and required extensive services for students with severe disabilities. *Capistrano Unified Sch. Dist. v. Wartenberg*, 59 F.3d 884 (9th Cir. 1995) (ordering intensive services at private placement for child with learning disability); *Union Sch. Dist. v. Smith*, 15 F.3d 1519 (9th Cir. 1994) (holding that an autistic child's placement in communicatively handicapped class at school was inappropriate under IDEA because it was insufficiently individually designed to meet his special needs). For a definition of "individualization," see *infra* this Chapter, "FAPE and Children with Less Severe Disabilities."

D.   FAPE AND SPECIFIC SERVICES

ALAMO HEIGHTS INDEPENDENT SCHOOL DISTRICT v. STATE BOARD OF EDUCATION
790 F.2d 1153 (5th Cir. 1986)

In Alamo Heights, the Fifth Circuit required that specific services, in this case summer school and transportation, be provided as FAPE under the Rowley test where a student would severely regress without them.

RUBIN, CIRCUIT JUDGE.

The primary issues presented by this appeal are whether, under the Education for All Handicapped Children Act (EAHCA) . . . , Steven G., a multiply handicapped child, is entitled to educational services beyond the usual 180-day school year and whether after-school transportation of Steven a short distance out of his school district to his only available custodian is a "related service" required by the EAHCA. The district court . . . concluded that (1) Steven G. would experience significant regression without some sort of summer program, and that, therefore, the School District was required to include in Steven's "individualized education program" (IEP) a provision for structured summer services; and (2) the School District was required to provide out-of-district transportation for Steven from his educational placement so that his working mother could rely on a custodian to care for Steven until she could pick him up. Because the court's findings of fact are supported by the record and its application of the EAHCA was correct, we affirm its judgment.

I.

Steven G. was born July 30, 1972. He lives with his mother, Beverly G., within the boundaries of the Alamo Heights Independent School District. Steven suffers from cerebral dysplasia or hyperplasia, which is an abnormal development of the brain. Steven's hands and face are deformed. He has an unusual laxity in his joints, an uncoordinated gaze, a significant lack of muscle tone, and can walk only with assistance. He has been diagnosed as severely mentally retarded, has frequent tantrums, and cannot communicate by oral expression, although he does communicate by means of pointing to pictures and symbols on a "communication board." Because of Steven's mental and physical handicaps, he is not, in education terminology, considered "educable," but rather is "trainable," that is, he can be taught to communicate with others and to take care of his physical needs.

From September 1975 to May 1977, Steven attended a Head Start program which operated on a twelve-month basis. In September 1977, he was enrolled in a half-day program at the Cerebral Palsy Center and then in September 1978 he was enrolled in the first grade in an elementary school in the Northside School District. In the summer of 1979, when Steven was seven, his mother moved into the Alamo Heights Independent School District. That school year Steven attended a special education program at Cambridge Elementary School. In the late spring of 1980, Mrs. G. requested that the Alamo Heights Independent School District provide summer services for Steven.

For seven years prior to 1980 the Alamo Heights School District had offered a summer program to all special education students who were moderately or severely handicapped. The decision to offer the program was made on the administrative level, as a matter of district policy, and any moderate to severely handicapped child was eligible to attend. In the summer of 1980, when Steven would have been eligible for this program, however, the School District changed its policy and offered only a half-day one-month program, without providing transportation.

. . . .

During that summer, Steven stayed with a baby-sitter who had no training in special education. There was testimony that Steven's behavior deteriorated that summer and that he suffered regression in his ability to stand, point, and feed himself.

The next year Mrs. G.'s request for summer services and transportation was refused by school officials, without consultation with Steven's Admission, Review and Dismissal (ARD) Committee or with his teacher. The only caretaker Mrs. G. could find for Steven lived a mile outside of the district boundary, and even during the school year, the School District would not provide out-of-district transportation.

Mrs. G. then employed legal counsel and appealed the denial of services to the Texas Education Agency. . . . [The final administrative order] required the School District to provide Steven with full summer services and transportation for all succeeding summers. In February 1982, the School District filed its complaint in federal district court.

In the interim, the School District did not provide summer services comparable to those provided Steven during the regular school year. In the summer of 1981, Steven was enrolled at The Learning Tree, a child care center in San Antonio. Some adaptive equipment was provided by the School District, and state regional consultants provided indirect speech, occupational and physical therapy services through the Learning Tree staff. The evidence proffered suggested that during the 1981 summer Steven advanced in his ability to communicate by using his "communication boards" and in his social and feeding skills. However, the evidence suggested that, because Steven lacked structured physical training, he regressed in his development of motor skills and mobility.

. . . .

In the summer of 1982, Mrs. G. arranged for Steven's placement at the Warm Springs Rehabilitation Hospital in Gonzalez, Texas, from the first week of June until the third week in July. He was given an educational program with a special education teacher, and received physical, occupational, and speech therapy twice each day. While at Warm Springs, Steven developed the ability to walk approximately thirty feet between parallel bars and could walk perhaps twenty feet in a "walker." He also made substantial progress in his communication skills.

After trial, in 1984, the district court rendered its final judgment for Mrs. G. and Steven. The court found that the School District had a policy of denying summer services to handicapped children regardless of their needs and issued an injunction against the further implementation of such a policy. The district court also made the following finding of fact:

> Without some kind of continuous, structured educational program during the summer months, Steven G. will regress in skills learned and knowledge gained in the previous 180-day academic year. Although the Court has insufficient evidence to conclude that Steven G. would definitely suffer severe regression after a summer without such a program, neither can it conclude that he would not and there is evidence that shows that Steven G. has suffered more than the loss of skills in isolated instances, and that he has required recoupment time of more than several weeks after structured

programming. *A summer without continuous, structured programming would result in substantial regression of knowledge gained and skills learned, and, given the severity of Steven G.'s handicaps, this regression would be significant.* (Emphasis added.)

Pursuant to this finding, the court ordered injunctive relief requiring Steven's ARD Committee to recommend, and the School District to provide free of charge, structured summer programming for Steven. . . .

In response to the preliminary and permanent injunctive relief granted by the district court, the School Board has since provided Steven with a full summer program, with a teacher, an aide, and state regional consultative services.

II.

The School District argues that it has a legal duty to provide summer placement only if a handicapped child will suffer "severe regression in cognitive skills gained and disciplines learned" due to an interruption of programming. They assert that the evidence presented before the district court did not show that Steven did or would suffer such severe regression, and that, accordingly, the district court had no basis to order the relief it did.

. . . .

A.

Pursuant to the provisions of the EAHCA, the School District is required to provide Steven with a "free appropriate public education." . . . That mandate includes "the requirement that the education to which access is provided be sufficient to confer some educational benefit upon the handicapped child." . . . The some-educational-benefit standard does not mean that the requirements of the Act are satisfied so long as a handicapped child's progress, absent summer services, is not brought "to a virtual standstill." . . . Rather, if a child will experience severe or substantial regression during the summer months in the absence of a summer program, the handicapped child may be entitled to year-round services. The issue is whether the benefits accrued to the child during the regular school year will be significantly jeopardized if he is not provided an educational program during the summer months. . . .

B.

. . . .

The testimony concerning Steven's particular regression-recoupment tendencies was directly conflicting: the School District's employees and consultants were unanimous that they observed no significant regression, while the doctors, therapists, and former teachers who testified on behalf of Steven all agreed that Steven required a continuous structured program in order to prevent significant regression. The record thus clearly supports, although it does not compel, the district court's assessment of the facts presented — "that Steven G. would suffer at least substantial regression without continuous, structured programming." . . . The general injunctive relief granted by the court was appropriate to ensure that Steven receives the summer programming to which he is entitled under the Act.

III.

With respect to out-of-district transportation for Steven G., the district court found that transportation is included in the definition of "related service" under 20 U.S.C. § 1401(a)(17) and that such transportation does not cease to be a related service simply because a parent requests transportation to a site a short distance beyond the district boundaries.

. . . .

Section 1401(a)(17) of Title 20 specifically provides: "The term 'related services' means transportation, and such . . . other supportive services . . . as may be required to assist a handicapped child to benefit from special education." The Act does not further define "transportation." . . .

. . . The district court implicitly found Mrs. G.'s request for one-mile out-of-district transportation for Steven reasonable. The School District has not argued that the transportation would in any way create a burden, much less an unfair burden, on the School District or on other children being transported. . . . Unless the transportation request is shown to be unreasonable, the Act requires that such transportation be provided as a related service. . . .

SHERMAN v. MAMARONECK UNION FREE SCHOOL DISTRICT
340 F.3d 87 (2d Cir. 2003)

In Sherman v. Mamaroneck Union Free School District, the Second Circuit held that IDEA did not require that an advanced math calculator be provided to a student who could pass the class in a manner consistent with the education goals of the class' curriculum.

WINTER, CIRCUIT JUDGE.

The Mamaroneck Union Free School District ("School District") appeals from Judge Brieant's decision that it violated the Individuals with Disabilities Education Act ("IDEA"). . . . The issue on appeal is whether the district court erred when it concluded that appellant had denied Grant Nishanian ("Grant") a free appropriate public education by denying him use of an advanced calculator in a particular mathematics class. Because the district court failed to give proper deference to the administrative rulings of the Impartial Hearing Officer ("IHO") and State Review Officer ("SRO"), we vacate and order entry of judgment for appellant.

BACKGROUND

Origins of the Dispute

Prior to entering high school, Grant was classified by the School District's Committee on Special Education ("CSE") as "learning disabled" because of a disorder affecting his ability in mathematics. As required by federal regulations, 34 C.F.R. §§ 300.300, 300.343–300.347, the CSE met at least annually to fashion an Individualized Education Program ("IEP") designed to provide Grant with a free appropriate public education consistent with the IDEA. . . .

Grant successfully completed freshman and sophomore mathematics courses using several assistive technology devices, including a Texas Instruments Model 82 calculator ("TI-82"). The TI-82 is a scientific/graphing calculator that can be cable linked to a computer. On March 6, 1998, in the spring of Grant's sophomore year, the School District's CSE prepared an IEP for his junior year that again allowed Grant to have use of a scientific/graphing calculator and a cable link to a computer. The IEP did not name a specific model of calculator, however.

Sometime thereafter, but apparently before receiving the IEP, Grant's mother, appellee Eleanor Sherman ("Sherman"), requested that the School District allow Grant to use a more advanced calculator, the Texas Instruments Model 92 ("TI-92"), in his upcoming Math 3A class. Notes from a meeting held in May, 1998, indicate that it was agreed that Grant's teachers would determine whether use of the TI-92 during tests would be appropriate.

On or about June 16, 1998, Sherman received the IEP for Grant's junior year. Although Sherman signed a form indicating that she consented to implementation of the IEP, she also noted that she did so "under protest regarding study in Biology, and Geometry Sketch pad instruction only." Sherman did not raise the issue of Grant's use of a TI-92 calculator in her consent to the implementation of the IEP, but she subsequently contacted the New York State Department of Education about whether the TI-92 would be an acceptable testing modification for her son. She was told that a TI-92 with a qwerty keyboard was an acceptable testing modification on a state examination and that one state school used the TI-92 with all its disabled students.

When the school year started, it remained unclear whether the School District would allow Grant to use the TI-92. Appellees viewed the lack of a definitive decision as permission to use it, and Grant began using the TI-92 about three weeks into the fall semester. When Ms. Elaine Peikes, Grant's Math 3A teacher, discovered that Grant was using the TI-92 on a test, she contacted the high school building and house principals and the mathematics department chairperson. Ms. Peikes and these other school officials proposed a compromise in which Grant would retake the test using the TI-82 to show his work but could use the TI-92 to check his answers. Appellees rejected the compromise and Grant received an "Incomplete" in Math 3A for the first marking period.

At around this time, Sherman informed the School District that Grant needed the TI-92 to factor. In the Math 3A curriculum, factoring requires the student to demonstrate the steps followed to arrive at the correct mathematical answer.

Factoring constitutes a significant component of the Math 3A curriculum. It is undisputed that the TI-92 provides the final answer but not the steps leading to it whereas the TI-82 requires the student to engage in the various steps of analysis to get to the right answer. In a letter dated October 27, 1998, Unit Principal Anne Garcia-Murruz informed Sherman that Grant's teachers were of the opinion that Grant could learn to factor and that use of the TI-92 was not appropriate because it would circumvent this part of the learning process. The letter stated in part:

> All three teachers agree that Grant can learn to factor. Ms. Peikes assures me that he is learning to factor. On his most recent quiz, Grant factored eleven out of twelve expressions correctly. . . . [By contrast] the TI-92 does the factoring, rather than allow Grant to demonstrate that he knows how to factor. It is educationally beneficial for Grant to acquire new skills, well within his capability. It would, therefore, be inappropriate for him to retake tests using the TI-92 to factor.

School District Proceedings

On December 18, 1998, following communications with members of the Board of Education and an unsuccessful appeal to the School District's superintendent, Grant and his parents met with the building principal, the School District's Assistant Superintendent for Administration and Personnel, the Assistant Supervisor of Special Education, and Grant's resource room teacher. They discussed, *inter alia*, the procedures to be followed when Grant took tests and quizzes, his use of a calculator and laptop computer, and the method of grading to be applied in his math class.

In a letter dated December 18, 1998, Principal Mark P. Orfinger summarized the results of the meeting, namely, that Grant would not be allowed to use the TI-92 either in class or during exams. The letter also stated that Grant's first marking period grades would not count towards his final grade in Math 3A and that he would be given an alternative assessment — limited to use of the TI-82 — in order to allow him to demonstrate mastery of the topics taught prior to December 18, 1998. Ms. Peikes testified that she provided Grant with this alternative assessment over the Christmas holiday period but that he never turned in the work.

Administrative Proceedings

Following receipt of Principal Orfinger's letter, Sherman sent letters to the building principal and the superintendent of schools expressing dissatisfaction with the outcome and alleging that her son was being discriminated against on the basis of his disability. Sherman had already requested an impartial hearing on December 16, 1998, for the purpose of amending Grant's IEP. Sherman reiterated this request in a December 23, 1998 letter, alleging, in relevant part, violations of the IDEA and Section 504 of the Rehabilitation Act of 1973. . . .

Hearings pursuant to IDEA before [an] IHO . . . focused on the educational goals of the Math 3A curriculum, whether the TI-92 was consistent with these goals, whether Grant could answer factoring questions without the TI-92, and whether use of the TI-82 was sufficient to allow Grant to succeed in Math 3A.

The teachers and administrators were in agreement that success in Math 3A involved more than simply arriving at the right answer. For example, Ms. Peikes testified that students also had "to show the mathematical steps to solve a problem." Several of the School District witnesses also testified that the TI-92 was not an appropriate assistive learning device in this regard because it would allow Grant to answer questions without demonstrating any understanding of the underlying mathematical concepts. For example, Ms. Geraldine Brause, Grant's ninth-grade algebra teacher, testified, "I worry about the TI-92 stopping that [process of understanding] and it would be just hitting a button, you get an answer and there's no convincing argument that shows me that the student understands the process and has learned something." Ms. Garcia-Marruz stated that "[t]he calculator model [TI-92] denies us the ability to see if G[rant] knows what he's doing and has taken the steps necessary to solve the problem."

There was also universal agreement among the School District teachers and administrators that the TI-82 struck the right balance between educational assistance and the need for Grant to show mastery of the underlying mathematical concepts. Grant's math teachers demonstrated at the hearing how the TI-82 — in a step-by-step approach — could be used in a manner consistent with the educational goals of the Math 3A curriculum to assist a student in answering questions that required factoring and multi-step operations. Moreover, three of the School District's witnesses testified that Grant was capable of factoring based upon their prior observations of his math assignments and exams.

Grant himself testified that the TI-82 was sufficient for him to answer questions in Math 3A: "Using the TI 82 I could prove my work to Ms. Peikes by writing the steps she would like me to show. On some examples it takes me a very, very, long time to find the answer." Additionally, Ms. Brause testified that if an assistive technology device proved incapable of directing a student to the right answer, then some form of alternative assessment would be devised to measure and assess the student's performance. There was also testimony that Grant's resistance to solving problems without the TI-92 was a major factor in his poor performance. As the IHO stated:

> Then why is [Grant] failing Course 3A? His teachers believe that he is purposely failing. More importantly, [Grant] is not performing the tasks required so that the teachers can properly evaluate his understanding of the work. For example, he wrote on an assessment: "do not remember how to do without the TI 92." When asked to take a quiz without the TI 92, he wrote, "this is in violation of my rights." He stated again on the math midterm: "cannot be done with the TI 82." The grade of 15 that he received was because he didn't attempt the problems or show his work, according to his resource room teacher.

In addition to the testimony at the impartial hearing, a Student Technology Consultation was performed in March 1999 by David L. Grapka, a Certified Assistive Technology Practitioner. This consultation confirmed many of the views offered by the School District's witnesses. During one part of the consultation, Grapka had Grant review his wrong answers on an earlier math midterm. In three instances, without the assistance of a calculator, Grant solved problems he had gotten wrong or partially wrong on the midterm. He solved another question by using the TI-92, but conceded that his entry of the data "only shows that I know[ ] how to press buttons. I know more than that." On two other questions, Grant attempted the problem with the TI-82, but it yielded an answer in decimal form whereas the question required that it be expressed in radical terms. Grant explained the steps he would use to solve the problem, used the TI-82 to assist with multiplication, and then got the right answer using the TI-92. Based upon his observations of Grant's problem-solving abilities with the TI-82 and TI-92, Grapka concluded that

> Because Grant has demonstrated that he understands and can explain the steps needed to solve problems on the math course 3A mid term, and because the TI-92 does not require a student to demonstrate his or her problem-solving steps, it is not necessary for Grant to use the TI-92 to actually solve the problems for him and then copy the answers from the TI-92 to the test answer sheet.

Grapka recommended that Grant continue using the TI-82 as a tool to solve problems, and that his use of the TI-92 be limited to checking answers because "[h]e is capable of demonstrating mastery without it."

In his decision, the IHO concluded that: (i) the IEP for Grant's junior year was reasonable; (ii) the School District had implemented the IEP's test modification and accommodations requirements; and (iii) the School District had met its requirements under the IDEA and Section 504 of the Rehabilitation Act with regard to Grant's effective participation in Math 3A by providing him with appropriate assistive technology, extra assistance from professionals, note takers, and study notes.

Sherman appealed the IHO's decision to the SRO [and] . . . the SRO concluded that the School District had: (i) not denied Grant a free appropriate public education in his Math 3A course when it required him to use the TI-82 rather than the TI-92; (ii) properly implemented the IEP; and (iii) provided proper instruction in Math 3A.

District Court Decision

Sherman then instituted the present action, asserting four claims against the School District and other defendants under both the IDEA and Section 504 of the Rehabilitation Act of 1973. The district court granted summary judgment for appellants on the Section 504 claim and dismissed all IDEA claims against individual defendants on qualified immunity grounds. . . . The district court also granted summary judgment to all defendants on the claim that the School District had failed to comply with the procedural requirements of IDEA by failing to convene a meeting of the CSE to revise Grant's IEP before changing his testing modifications.

However, the district court granted appellees summary judgment on their claim that the School District had violated Section 1412(a)(12)(B)(i) of the IDEA by not providing Grant with the assistive technology — the TI-92 — necessary to ensure a free appropriate public education. The court concluded that the TI-92 was necessary for Grant's educational success because "[w]ithout the T.I.92, Grant did not and could not pass." . . .

The district court also concluded that the evidence did not support the findings of the IHO and the SRO that Grant's lack of effort had contributed to his failing grade in Math 3A. The court found that Grant's nearly perfect attendance record contradicted his teachers' assertions that he was choosing not to learn, and that Grant's comments on his exam stating that he could not solve the problem without the TI-92 and that his rights were being violated did not clearly demonstrate a lack of motivation to learn.

The district court awarded Sherman $28,391.25, which included attorneys' fees and damages. This appeal followed. The only issue before us is the IDEA claim with regard to use of the TI-92.

DISCUSSION

We review the district court's grant of summary judgment *de novo*. . . . One of the requirements under the IDEA is that an IEP be "reasonably calculated" to confer "educational benefits." *Board of Education v. Rowley*. . . . The School District bears the burden of proving that it has met this requirement. . . . The core issue before us, therefore, is whether the School District's denial of the use of a TI-92 in Grant's Math 3A course, confirmed by the decisions of the IHO and SRO, deprived him of a free appropriate public education.

. . . .

[I]t is undisputed that Grant ultimately failed his Math 3A course and that access to the TI-92 would have — under most circumstances — provided correct answers on his Math 3A exams. Passing grades are, of course, often indicative of educational benefit. . . . Grant's failing grades are therefore evidence of a denial of educational benefit.

Nevertheless, failing grades are not dispositive. The IDEA does not require school districts to pass a student claiming a disability when the student is able, with less than the assistive aids requested, to succeed but nonetheless fails. If a school district simply provided the assistive devices requested, even if unneeded, and awarded passing grades, it would in fact deny the appropriate educational benefits the IDEA requires.

In this case, therefore, the failing grades must be viewed in light of the evidence as a whole. The IHO and SRO found that Grant was able to pass Math 3A without using the TI-92 and that learning to factor would provide him with educational benefits; they further found that his failing grades in Math 3A were due to his failure to make a sufficient effort. These conclusions find ample support in the record.

Several of Grant's teachers testified that he was capable of factoring with the assistance of the TI-82. The only testimony to the contrary was from Grant himself, but even this testimony was undermined by his admission that the TI-82 was sufficient for him to answer questions in Math 3A. Moreover, Grant's Math 3A teacher demonstrated how the TI-82 could be used to factor, albeit in a step-by-step process. There was also evidence that Grant was responsible for his failing grades in Math 3A. The School District provided Grant with an alternative assessment in December 1998, but he never completed the work. In other exams, he refused even to attempt to answer questions, although his own testimony and his work with Grapka showed at least some ability to factor with regard to those questions.

In rejecting the conclusions of the IHO and SRO, the district court relied upon the Grapka Report as suggesting that Grant needed access to the TI-92 to succeed in Math 3A. However, this is a misreading of the report. The report recommended only that Grant be allowed to use the TI-92 to *check* his math problem-solving "as needed." Grapka also concluded that the TI-82 was the appropriate assistive technology device for *solving* problems because Grant was capable of demonstrating mastery of the Math 3A materials without the aid of the TI-92. As noted, the School District indicated a willingness to provide an "alternative assessment" where the limitations of the TI-82 actually prevented Grant from competing equally with his peers. However, the dispute at all times concerned appellees' demand that the TI-92 be used to solve Math 3A problems. In fact, they rejected a compromise proposal that the TI-92 be used only to check answers.

Therefore, the administrative proceedings were thorough and arrived at a conclusion that is amply supported by the record. Given the deferential standard of review, summary judgment should have been granted to appellant.

For the reasons stated, we vacate and order entry of judgment for appellant.

NOTES AND QUESTIONS

1.   *Alamo Heights Independent School District* is the leading case for determining eligibility for extended year services, and its test, "severe or substantial regression," is still the predominant test in determining whether such a service should be provided. However, the Tenth Circuit, in *Johnson v. Independent Sch. Dist. No. 4*, 921 F.2d 1022 (10th Cir. 1990), has proposed a more individualized standard that would allow courts to consider "the degree of impairment and the ability of the child's parents to provide the educational structure at home, . . . the child's rate of progress, his or her behavioral and physical problems, the availability of alternative resources, the ability of the child to interact with non-handicapped children, the areas of the child's curriculum which need continuous attention, and the child's vocational needs." *Id.* at 1027. Since nothing in the text of IDEA requires use of the "severe or substantial regression" test in determining whether an extended year is required, some courts are likely to opt for an individualization approach that provides greater flexibility in determining the appropriateness of summer school. In *Reusch v. Fountain*, 872 F. Supp. 1421 (D. Md. 1994), the court endorsed an individualized standard that considered "nonregression-based factors," such as the child being on the brink of being able to read, in requiring an extended year.

2.   In *Alamo Heights*, the Fifth Circuit held that FAPE under the IDEA required school district transportation of the child to a caretaker outside the school district's boundaries, despite a district policy prohibiting out-of-district transportation. However, other courts have found that transportation beyond district

boundaries is not a matter of right under the IDEA. In *Fick v. Sioux Falls School District*, 337 F.3d 968 (8th Cir. 2003), the Eighth Circuit, in upholding denial of out-of-district transportation under a policy similar to *Alamo Heights*, viewed the requested transportation as a matter of preference or convenience for the parent and unrelated to the child's educational needs. In *Timothy H. v. Cedar Rapids Community Sch. Dist.*, 178 F.3d 968 (8th Cir. 1999), the Eighth Circuit upheld, under a section 504 challenge, an intra-district transfer policy that required parents to pay for the cost of transportation outside assigned school attendance areas.

The court reasoned that even if the policy had a negative effect on children with disabilities, an accommodation requiring a change in the policy would constitute a financial burden for the district and would amount to a fundamental alteration in the nature of the intra-district transfer program.

3.   *Sherman* suggests that the nature of a student's services for a course can be related to the essential function(s) of the course. In this case, an essential function of the math course was factoring. If the student had not been able to perform the function of factoring, would the student then have been entitled to the use of the TI-92 calculator? How does the court's reference to an "alternate assessment" relate to the use of a TI-92 calculator? Can the New York Department of Education's permitting use of the TI-92 on its statewide test be reconciled with the school district's denial of use of the calculator for a course? Considering that the cost of the TI-92 is relatively low and that the student would be able to use the TI-92 anyway when he took the state Regents exam, does the school district's incurring considerable expense to litigate this case seem to be an appropriate use of school resources? Why or why not?

E.   FAPE AND CHILDREN WITH LESS SEVERE DISABILITIES

The *Rowley* Court cautioned that it was not holding that "every handicapped child who is advancing from grade to grade in a regular public school system is automatically receiving a 'free appropriate education.'" *Rowley*, 458 U.S. at 203. The notion of enhanced services as a requirement under FAPE is consistent with the concept of individualization, "the idea that children with disabilities should be treated as individuals with unique needs requiring specially tailored services." Mark C. Weber, Special Education Law and Litigation Treatise § 3.1(3) (3d ed. 2008 & supps.).

Consistent with the concept of individualization, the *Rowley* standard has been applied to children with less than severe disabilities to require extra services even though a child is passing academic subjects. In *Blazejewski v. Board of Educ.*, 560 F. Supp. 701 (W.D.N.Y. 1983), a federal district court issued a preliminary injunction directing a school board to identify a 17-year-old student as eligible so that he could receive special education instruction in a learning disabilities resource room, because without special assistance the student would continue to have deficient communicative skills. Even in cases where student progress has been very similar to that of Amy Rowley, courts have ordered additional services to allow a child to perform closer to the level of nondisabled children. In most of these cases, services have been ordered so that a student could be in a regular classroom. In *Tokarcik v. Forest Hills Sch. Dist.*, 665 F.2d 443 (3d Cir. 1981), the Third Circuit ordered clean intermittent catheterization to keep a child in a regular classroom. Similarly, in *Board of Education, Sacramento Unified Sch. Dist. v. Rachel H.*, 14 F.3d 1398 (9th Cir. 1994), the Ninth Circuit ordered a school board to provide an in-class aide and special education consultant so that a moderately mentally disabled student would receive appropriate services without detracting from other students' learning or teacher time.

NOTES AND QUESTIONS

1. A number of cases support the notion that courts can order special education services even though a student is making some educational progress. *E.g., Draper v. Atlanta Indep. Sch. Sys.*, 518 F.3d 1275 (11th Cir. 2008) (ordering remedy when child in eleventh grade was reading at third-grade level after misidentification as individual with intellectual disabilities and failure to receive promised services while passing from grade to grade); *Hall v. Vance County Bd. of Educ.*, 774 F.2d 629, 636 (4th Cir. 1985) (in ordering private tutoring for a dyslexic child with above-average intelligence, citing *Rowley* for the principle that "FAPE must be tailored to the individual child's capabilities" and a showing of minimal improvement on test results was not sufficient); *Community Consol. Sch. Dist. No. 93 v. John F.*, 33 IDELR 210 (N.D. Ill. 2000) (rejecting presumption that student with a behavior disorder who had almost all As and was advancing from grade to grade in a regular public school system was automatically receiving FAPE; where student was not mainstreamed during home placement pending manifestation determination result and where his grades dropped, the student did not receive the educational benefit required under *Rowley*); *Max M. v. Illinois State Bd. of Education*, 629 F. Supp. 1504 (N.D. Ill. 1986) (ruling that a school district denied FAPE to a high school student when it failed to provide psychotherapy as recommended by district's psychologist in order for student to "experience success socially, emotionally or academically," even though by the end of student's senior year he had earned more than the required amount of credits to graduate and was ranked 455 out of 546 students in the senior class). *But see Lyons v. Smith*, 829 F. Supp. 414, 418 (D.D.C. 1993) (refusing to find that a child with a disability affecting social adjustment who was passing his courses had a disability that adversely affected educational performance because "[t]he achievement of passing marks is one important factor in determining educational benefit.").

2. Parents of students with higher than average IQs who had been performing satisfactorily in public schools with some special education services are not entitled to reimbursement for placement in a private school simply because the student has been performing at a higher level in the private school. As the Fourth Circuit observed in *A.B. v. Lawson*, 354 F.3d 315, 330 (4th Cir. 2004), "IDEA's FAPE standards are far more modest than to require that a child excel or thrive." Is it consistent with IDEA that some students with disabilities will not have the opportunity to thrive?

F. FAPE AND THE LEAST RESTRICTIVE ENVIRONMENT

The *Rowley* appropriateness standard has taken on expanded meaning when courts have applied it to the least restrictive environment, a topic covered more thoroughly in Chapter 6. Although *Rowley* spoke of duties to provide access to an educational benefit, such cases as *Roncker v. Walter*, 700 F.2d 1058 (6th Cir. 1983), have indicated an open-ended obligation for school boards to provide services to enable a child to learn in a general education classroom, even if the classroom setting is an environment in which the child has never been served before. Subsequent case law recognizes "the overlap, and sometime[s] tension, between the IDEA's FAPE and LRE requirements," *A.S. v. Norwalk Bd. of Educ.*, 183 F. Supp. 2d 534, 541 (D. Conn. 2002), but still applies *Rowley* to require an assessment by school boards of the adequacy of services being provided in a mainstreamed setting before considering a more restrictive placement outside the regular classroom. In *Springdale Sch. Dist. No. 50 v. Grace*, 693 F.2d 41 (8th Cir. 1982), the Eighth Circuit held that providing a sign-language interpreter in a regular classroom was appropriate for purposes of FAPE even though the child would have learned more quickly in a school for the deaf.

Consistent with the discussion above, the U.S. Department of Education has adopted a regulation imposing an unlimited responsibility on school boards to provide supplementary services and aids. The regulation requires that:

Each public agency shall ensure that —

(i) To the maximum extent appropriate, children with disabilities, including children in public or private institutions or other care facilities, are educated with children who are nondisabled; and

(ii) Special classes, separate schooling or other removal of children with disabilities from the regular educational environment occurs only if the nature or severity of the disability is such that education in regular classes with the use of supplementary aids and services cannot be achieved satisfactorily.

34 C.F.R. § 300.114(a)(2).

G. OTHER FAPE ISSUES

FAPE includes a galaxy of issues surrounding and related to the delivery of special education services. The issues that have received attention include: qualifications of personnel, class size and age of students, vocational instruction, extracurricular activities, grading, district-wide assessment and high-stakes testing, and juveniles in detention facilities. IDEA does not provide guidance on all of these areas, so claims are frequently brought under section 504 or ADA challenging whether students with disabilities have been unfairly treated.

1.   Personnel

The quality of personnel providing services to students with disabilities is addressed in a number of ways. IDEA requires that states establish personnel standards, 20 U.S.C. § 1412(a)(14); 34 C.F.R. § 300.156. Local school districts must ensure that all personnel needed to carry out IDEA obligations are appropriately and adequately prepared subject to the state personnel standards. 34 C.F.R. § 300.207.

The Strengthening and Improvement of Elementary and Secondary Schools Act (No Child Left Behind Act, or NCLB), enacted in 2002, 20 U.S.C. §§ 6301, *et seq.*, requires that all teachers teaching in core academic areas in programs supported by title I funds be "highly qualified" by the 2005-06 school year. *See* 20 U.S.C. §§ 6319(a), 7801(23). The highly-qualified-teacher standard requires teachers to have a bachelor's degree, state certification, and demonstrated subject-matter competence in core subjects. Methods of demonstrating competence vary with grades taught and between new and existing teachers. 20 U.S.C. § 6319(a); 34 C.F.R. § 200.56. Core academic subjects are English, reading or language arts, mathematics, science, foreign languages, civics and government, economics, arts, history, and geography. 20 U.S.C. § 7801(11); 34 C.F.R. § 200.55(c).

A goal of the 2004 IDEA amendments was to coordinate IDEA and NCLB. Under the new definition provisions in IDEA, a highly qualified public elementary or secondary school special education teacher is one who has obtained full state certification or passed a special education licensing exam, holds a license (though charter school teachers may be treated differently), has not had the licensure provisions waived, and holds at least a bachelor's degree. 20 U.S.C. § 1401(10)(B). If the individual teaches core academic subjects exclusively to children who receive assessment against alternate achievement standards, that teacher either may meet qualification standards set out in 20 U.S.C. § 7801 for an elementary, middle, or secondary school teacher who is new or not new to the profession or may meet the requirements for a highly qualified teacher as defined by 20 U.S.C. § 7801(23)(B) or (C) as applied to an elementary school teacher. As applied to a teacher providing instruction above the elementary level, the teacher may meet the standard by having "subject matter knowledge appropriate to the level of instruction provided, as determined by the State, needed to effectively teach to those standards." 20 U.S.C. § 1401(10)(C)(ii).

Special education teachers who provide instruction in two or more core academic subjects exclusively to children with disabilities may qualify under 20 U.S.C. § 7801, or, if not new to the profession, may demonstrate competence in all the core academic subjects that the teacher teaches in the same way that applies to an experienced teacher under 20 U.S.C. § 7801(23)(C)(ii) (including under a single standard of evaluation covering multiple subjects), or if new and highly qualified in mathematics, language arts, or science, make the demonstration under 20 U.S.C. § 7801(23)(C)(ii) in the other core academic subjects no later than two years after starting employment. 20 U.S.C. § 1401(10)(D). The Department of Education has emphasized that special educators who do not "directly instruct students in core academic subjects or who provide only consultation to highly qualified teachers in adapting curricula, using behavioral supports and interventions or selecting appropriate accommodations, do not need to demonstrate subject-matter competency in those subjects." U.S. Dep't of Educ., Fact Sheet, New *No Child Left Behind* Flexibility: Highly Qualified Teachers (2004), *available at* http://www.ed.gov/nclb/methods/teachers/hqtflexibility.html.

NCLB also sets standards for instructional paraprofessionals. *See* 20 U.S.C. § 6319(c); 34 C.F.R. § 200.56(d)–(f). The paraprofessionals must have a high school diploma, two years of post-secondary education, and have at least an associate's degree or have demonstrated competence on a formal academic assessment in "reading/language arts, writing, and mathematics" or "reading readiness, writing readiness, and mathematics readiness." 34 C.F.R. § 200.58; *see also* 34 C.F.R. § 200.59. Under the IDEA amendments, paraprofessionals must meet state qualification standards, 20 U.S.C. § 1412(a)(14)(B).

NOTES AND QUESTIONS

There is strong evidence that instruction by highly qualified teachers has a significant impact on student achievement, and that often the least qualified teachers work with the students most in need. *See, e.g.*, Heather G. Peske & Kati Haycock, Teaching Inequality — How Poor and Minority Students Are Shortchanged on Teacher Quality: A Report and Recommendations by the Education Trust, *at*

> http://www2.edtrust.org/NR/rdonlyres/010DBD9F-CED8-4D2B-
> 9E0D-91B446746ED3/0/TQReportJune2006.pdf

Is this as likely to be true for special education as for core subjects? Is the IDEA approach well-calculated to assure the qualification of special education teachers? What other policy or regulatory approaches can best address these needs?

2.   Class Size

States are responsible for determining the class size and age range for students with various disabilities. *See e.g.*, Ohio Admin. Code, § 3301-51-09(G)(3)(c). The Office for Civil Rights (OCR) of the U.S. Department of Education has suggested that failure of a school to comply with state class-size ratios denies the student FAPE and states a claim under section 504 of the Rehabilitation Act and title II of the Americans with Disabilities Act. Conecuh County (AL) Sch. Dist., 21 IDELR 805 (U.S. Dep't of Educ., Office for Civil Rights 1994). A few courts have considered FAPE implications regarding the age of the students in a group with which a student might be placed. *See Hines v. Pitt County Bd. of Educ.*, 497 F. Supp. 403 (E.D.N.C. 1980) (holding that placement of 10-year-old child with children 11–17 years of age deprived the child of FAPE where evidence showed that his behavior worsened; child needed to be placed in a setting where he would not be the youngest).

3. Vocational Education

The IDEA regulations include vocational education among special education's "specially designed instruction" to meet "the unique needs of a child with disabilities." 34 C.F.R. § 300.39(a)(2)(iii). Vocational education means:

> organized educational programs that are directly related to the preparation of individuals for paid or unpaid employment, or for additional preparation for a career requiring other than a baccalaureate or advanced degree.

34 C.F.R. § 300.39(b)(5).

Vocational education can become part of a child's coordinated set of activities designed to "facilitate the child's movement from school to post-school activities. . . ." 20 U.S.C. § 1401(30). The IEP in effect when the child turns 16 and those IEPs that follow must include appropriate post-secondary goals and transition services. § 1414(d)(1)(A)(i)(VIII). Preferences and interests of students need to be taken into consideration in determining transition services, 20 U.S.C. § 1401(30)(B), and failure to provide a transition plan is a violation of IDEA, *J.B. v. Killingly Bd. of Educ.*, 990 F. Supp. 57 (D. Conn. 1997).

4. Extracurricular Activities

The IDEA regulations provide that students with disabilities must be provided "an equal opportunity" to participate in nonacademic and extracurricular activities. 34 C.F.R. § 300.107(a). Although the regulations identify a range of services activities available for students with disabilities, (a list of services is found at 34 C.F.R. § 300.107(b)), most litigation has concerned modification of ordinary rules to permit participation in athletics by students with disabilities. State athletic associations typically limit eligibility for participation in high school athletics under their eight-semester (or four years) and/or 19-year-old rules. Thus, an athlete may be eligible to compete for no more than eight semesters or only until reaching his or her nineteenth birthday. *See* CHARLES RUSSO & RALPH MAWDSLEY, EDUCATION LAW § 7.02[2] (2010).

Litigation involving eligibility for extracurricular activities generally has involved section 504 or ADA and courts have been divided as to whether these rules can be waived for students with disabilities who allege that their lack of eligibility (usually for their senior year) is disability-related because of their having repeated an earlier grade. MARK C. WEBER, SPECIAL EDUCATION LAW AND LITIGATION TREATISE § 3.9 (3d ed. 2008 & supps.). In essence, the question is whether waiver of such rules would amount to a reasonable accommodation for purposes of section 504 of the Rehabilitation Act or title II of ADA. *See Pottgen v. Mo. State High Sch. Activities Ass'n*, 40 F.3d 926 (8th Cir. 1994), reproduced *supra* Chapter 2 (Eligibility).

Extracurricular participation can be part of a student's IEP.

DENNIN v. CONNECTICUT INTERSCHOLASTIC ATHLETIC ASSOCIATION

913 F. Supp. 663 (D. Conn.), *judgment vacated and appeal dismissed as moot,* 94 F.3d 96 (2d Cir. 1996)

In Dennin, a federal district court held that refusal of a state athletic association to waive its 19-year-old eligibility rule for a 19-year-old special education student whose IEP required participation on the school's swim team violated section 504 and the ADA.

RULING ON MOTION FOR PRELIMINARY INJUNCTION

DORSEY, CHIEF JUDGE.

Plaintiffs move for a preliminary injunction to prevent defendant from denying plaintiff David Dennin ("Dennin") a waiver of its age eligibility rule. The parties were fully heard. An order granted a preliminary injunction with this full discussion of the issues to follow.

I. BACKGROUND FACTS

Dennin is a nineteen-year old student at Trumbull High School with Down Syndrome. He is eligible for special education pursuant to the Individuals with Disabilities Education Act ("IDEA"). . . .

Defendant, The Connecticut Interscholastic Athletic Conference, Inc. ("CIAC"), is a Connecticut non-profit corporation organized to supervise, direct and regulate interscholastic athletics in Connecticut with 175 public and private secondary schools. Trumbull High School is a CIAC member and must abide by its rules.

Due to his special education needs, Dennin spent four, rather than three, years in middle school, commencing high school in 1992 at sixteen. For the past three years, plaintiff was a fully eligible member of the Trumbull High School swim team. Although his times were slow, his relay teams at times scored points. Plaintiff's competition on the swim team is specified in his Individualized Education Program ("IEP"), developed as required by 20 U.S.C. § 1414(a)(5).

CIAC's eligibility rules provide that a player may not compete at age nineteen unless he reaches his nineteenth birthday on or after September 1. The purposes of the rule are to prevent competitive advantage for older athletes; to protect younger athletes from older athletes; to discourage students from delaying their education for athletic purposes; to prevent coaches from "red-shirting" athletes to gain competitive advantage; and to avoid younger athletes from preemption by older athletes.

Plaintiff turned nineteen before September 1, 1995. Without a waiver, he is not eligible for the 1995-96 season.

Dennin requested a waiver of the age eligibility rule. CIAC denied a waiver, but allowed him to swim as a non-scoring exhibition swimmer. He may swim in all regular season meets, but he and his relay team cannot earn points.

Dennin is aware of his ineligibility. Being treated no differently then others is important in his relations with the community. The absence of differential treatment fosters his sense of self-esteem and self-confidence and in turn, nurtures his belief in his ability and willingness to function in a community, most of whose members are not afflicted with his limitations.

Participation on the Trumbull swim team is open to all. No one is cut on the basis of ability. Co-plaintiff, the Trumbull Board of Education joins in Dennin's requested relief and fully supports his claim to full eligibility and participation which it would allow but for CIAC's eligibility rules.

II. DISCUSSION

To issue a preliminary injunction, it is well-settled that movant must show (a) irreparable harm; and (b) either (1) probable success on the merits, or (2) sufficiently serious questions going to the merits to make them a fair ground for litigation and a balance of hardships tipping decidedly toward the party seeking injunctive relief. . . .

A. *Irreparable Harm*

If the requested injunction does not issue, Dennin will swim in meets as an exhibition swimmer. He is not listed on Trumbull High School's eligibility list submitted to the CIAC, nor on the team roster or the team score book. He cannot score points for the team and his relay team is ineligible to score points.

Plaintiff's competition on the swim team has increased his self-esteem and social skills. It is considered sufficiently important to his development to be included in his IEP. The limitations on Dennin deprive him of essential badges and indicia of full team membership and participation. Plaintiff is able to understand this difference in treatment. It may diminish his swimming in meets, and in turn his sense of parity with his teammates. Such differential treatment will negatively impact his self-esteem and thereby his IEP goals.

Any relay team plaintiff swims on cannot earn points. Potentially he will be eliminated if his relay team cannot score points which might otherwise be scored despite Dennin's slowness. His relay teammates cannot earn points without a fully eligible team member. These points are necessary to earn varsity letters. Such losses of points would negatively impact plaintiff's self-esteem. In a close meet, the coach may be placed in the position of having to choose between allowing Dennin to swim or losing the meet.

The harm is immediate and irreparable. The swim season is progressing. Meets are occurring and are not awaiting a decision here. Accordingly, plaintiffs have established irreparable harm that cannot be compensated by monetary damages nor recouped.

B. *Probability of success on the merits*

Plaintiffs allege defendant's waiver denial violates the Rehabilitation Act, 29 U.S.C. § 794, the Americans with Disabilities Act ("ADA"), 42 U.S.C. § 12101 *et seq.*, and 42 U.S.C. § 1983 and the IDEA.

1. *Rehabilitation Act*

To establish a claim under the Rehabilitation Act, plaintiff must prove:

(1) he has a disability as defined by the Act;

(2) he is "otherwise qualified" to participate in interscholastic high school athletics as regulated by the [CIAC] or that he may be "otherwise qualified" via "reasonable accommodations";

(3) he is being excluded from participating in interscholastic high school athletics solely because of his disability; and

(4) the [CIAC] receives federal financial assistance. . . .

a. *Individual with a disability*

An individual with a disability is defined as "any person who . . . has a physical or mental impairment which substantially limits one or more of such person's major life activities." 29 U.S.C. § 706. Down Syndrome is such a disability. Plaintiff is covered by the Rehabilitation Act.

b. *Receipt of federal financial assistance*

CIAC receives federal financial assistance indirectly through fees paid by 150 public schools which receive federal assistance. Programs receiving indirect federal financial assistance are subject to the Rehabilitation Act. *See Pottgen v. Missouri High School Activities Association*, 857 F. Supp. 654, 663 (E.D. Mo. 1994), *rev'd on other grounds*, 40 F.3d 926 (8th Cir. 1994). . . . CIAC is a program which receives federal financial assistance indirectly from its members "which delegate to it a portion of their responsibilities for regulation of interscholastic activities." *Pottgen*, 857 F. Supp. at 663. In addition, it holds competitions in facilities receiving federal financial assistance, and most of the team coaches participating in the competitions are employed by schools receiving federal financial assistance. . . .

c. *"Otherwise qualified" individual*

Dennin is an "otherwise qualified" individual if with "reasonable accommodation" he can meet the "necessary" or "essential" requirements of the program. . . . An "otherwise qualified" individual is one who meets all the essential requirements of a program in spite of his disability. . . . To be "otherwise qualified," defendant argues that Dennin must meet the age requirement.

However, if the individual does not meet an essential requirement because of his disability, it must be determined if a "reasonable accommodation" would enable the individual to become "otherwise qualified." . . . In this case, the question is whether CIAC's waiver of the age requirement would be a reasonable accommodation. An accommodation is not "reasonable" if it imposes "undue financial or administrative burdens" or "fundamentally alters the nature of the program." . . . Thus, the question presented is whether waiver of the age requirement fundamentally alters the program or imposes undue burdens.

Courts disagree on this issue. In *Pottgen*, plaintiff was disabled and ineligible to play interscholastic baseball because he was nineteen. The *Pottgen* court found the age rule was essential to prevent competitive advantage, to protect younger athletes from harm, to discourage athletes from delaying their education, and to prevent red-shirting. . . . The court held that waiver of an essential eligibility standard in that case would constitute a fundamental alteration in the nature of the baseball program. . . . Since no reasonable accommodation could be made, plaintiff was not "otherwise qualified." . . .

The *Sandison* [*v. Michigan High School Athletic Association*, 863 F. Supp. 483 (E.D. Mich. 1994), *rev'd in part on other grounds*, 64 F.3d 1026 (6th Cir. 1995),] court followed *Pottgen*, determining that waiving the age requirement for nineteen-year old disabled students fundamentally altered the nature of the track and cross-country program because more mature and competitive students would be competing. . . . It also determined that waiving the age requirement would constitute an undue burden, as a case-by-case analysis would be necessary to determine unfair competitive advantage. . . .

Other courts have rejected this analysis. In *Johnson* [*v. Florida High School Activities Association*, 899 F. Supp. 579 (M.D. Fla. 1995)], the court considered whether a disabled student could be excluded from football and wrestling because he was not age eligible. Rather than a blanket holding that the requirement was essential, and that *any* waiver would be unreasonable, *Johnson* undertook an individualized analysis of the requirement and its underlying purposes. . . . In analyzing the requirement,

> the relationship between the age requirement and its purposes must be such that waiving the age requirement *in the instant case* would necessarily undermine the purposes of the requirement. . . . "[I]f a rule can be modified without doing violence to its essential purposes . . . it cannot be essential to the nature of the program or activity. . . ." *Id.* at 585 (quoting *Pottgen*, 40 F.3d at 932–33 (Arnold, C.J., dissenting)) (emphasis added).

Plaintiff there was found not a safety hazard, was a mid-level player without competitive advantage, and had less experience than other players. . . . Therefore, waiving the age requirement was found not to fundamentally alter the nature of the program. . . .

Similar individual analyses have found an age requirement waiver to be a reasonable accommodation. [citations omitted].

The reasoning of *Johnson* and the dissent in *Pottgen* is persuasive. It would be an anathema to the goals of the Rehabilitation Act to decline to require an individualized analysis of the purposes behind the age requirement as applied to Dennin. Failure to perform such an analysis would exalt the rule itself without regard for the essential *purposes* behind the rule.

So analyzed, waiver of the rule for Dennin could not undermine any of the purposes of the CIAC rule. Plaintiff has no competitive advantage. He is, without dispute, always the slowest swimmer in the pool. He is no safety risk to himself or others. Swimming is not a contact sport. His education was not delayed to gain a competitive advantage but only because of his disability. He is not a red-shirt threat. Granting him a waiver would not alter the nature of the swimming program.

Additionally, a waiver for Dennin does not impose an undue burden upon defendant. CIAC claims that a waiver in this case will result in a flood of waiver applications which will be administratively impossible to handle. CIAC is not required to grant waivers to *all* students who fail to meet the age requirement. However, it would be required under the Rehabilitation Act to give the disabled individual consideration, including to Dennin, as he falls within the Act. . . . The holding of this case only affects CIAC's consideration of the disabled, not its consideration of all students failing to meet the age requirement.

In Dennin's case, such consideration would be relatively simple. In some cases it would be more complex, depending on the sport in question, the size, agility, strength and endurance of the individual, and whether the quality of his/her athletic capacity/capability is enhanced by his/her age beyond eighteen. That it may prove difficult in some cases does not substantiate the claim that it would be unduly burdensome or destructive of the purpose of the rule.[4]

Assuming, arguendo, a waiver for plaintiff does increase applications for waivers of disabled students, the cost may be passed onto the schools through fees.

Defendant argues that it has already made a reasonable accommodation by granting Dennin exhibition status. This status treats Dennin fundamentally differently from fellow teammates. The Rehabilitation Act seeks full participation and equality of the disabled to the extent reasonable accommodations can be made. Thus a reasonable accommodation of full participation of Dennin is required.

d. *Discrimination "solely because of" disability*

Finally, it must be determined whether Dennin is being excluded from participating "solely because of" his disability. Defendant argues that the age eligibility rule is a neutral rule neutrally applied to him. Therefore, defendant claims, he is not being excluded solely because of his handicap, but because of his age. . . .

This argument ignores the fact that the *sole* reason that Dennin is in school at nineteen is due to his disability. But for his disability, his fourth year of athletic participation (provided in CIAC's rules) would not have been when he had become nineteen but at age eighteen. . . . Defendant's argument would result in the rule insulating itself from scrutiny.

---

[4] [FN 1] CIAC has in place a waiver mechanism for eligibility requirements. There is no limitation on which rules are waivable. Subjective case-by-case analysis must have been foreseen for considering such waivers. In fact, transfer waivers are routinely considered. The presence of this mechanism weakens CIAC's argument that case-by-case consideration of waivers constitutes an undue burden. The ruling here does not mandate the grant of a waiver in any case but this one.

The Supreme Court noted in *Alexander v. Choate*, 469 U.S. 287 (1985), that under the Rehabilitation Act, the question of whether an individual is "otherwise qualified" and whether he is a victim of "discrimination" were "two sides of a single coin." *Id.* at 299, n. 19. The ultimate question, was whether reasonable program modifications were required to accommodate the disabled. . . .

The sole reason plaintiff is in school at nineteen is his disability. Since plaintiff is "otherwise qualified" due to the availability of a reasonable accommodation, under the Rehabilitation Act, defendant must grant a waiver to plaintiff.

2. *ADA*

To establish a claim under Title III of the ADA, 42 U.S.C. § 12182, plaintiff must prove

(1) he is disabled;

(2) the [CIAC] is a "private entity" which [owns, leases (or leases to), or operates] a "place of public accommodation"; and

(3) he was denied the opportunity to "participate in or benefit from services or accommodations on the basis of his disability," and that reasonable accommodations could be made which do not fundamentally alter the nature of [CIAC] accommodations.

. . . .

A "private entity" is defined as "any entity other than a public entity. . . ." 42 U.S.C. § 12181(6). "Place of public accommodation" is defined in 42 U.S.C. § 12181(7), which lists private entities considered "public accommodations." Such private entities include "a place of exhibition or *entertainment*," § 12181(7)(c), "a . . . secondary, undergraduate, or postgraduate private school, or *other place of education*," § 12181(7)(J), or "a gymnasium . . . or other place of exercise or *recreation*," § 12181(7)(L) (emphasis added).

CIAC's purposes include "to supervise, direct and control interscholastic athletics in Connecticut," and "to develop intelligent recognition of the proper place of interscholastic athletics in the *education* of our youth." *See* CIAC Handbook, Sec. 1.3. Member schools delegate significant control and authority to CIAC in regulating this athletic component of education. Additionally, CIAC sponsors athletic competitions and tournaments. By managing and controlling the aforementioned, it "operates" places of public accommodation, i.e., a place of education, entertainment and/or recreation. The fact that some of these facilities might be owned by a public entity, i.e., a public school, does not affect the conclusion that CIAC "operates" the facilities for purposes of athletic competition. . . .

Assuming arguendo that CIAC is not a private entity operating a place of public accommodation, to establish a claim under Title II of the ADA, 42 U.S.C. § 12132, plaintiff must prove

(1) the [CIAC] is a "public entity";

(2) he is a "qualified individual with a disability"; and

(3) he has been excluded from participation from or denied the benefits of the public entity. . . .

A "public entity" is defined as "(A) any State or local government; (B) any department, agency, special purpose district, or other instrumentality of a State or States or local government. . . ." 42 U.S.C. § 12131(1). Public schools delegate authority to CIAC to direct and control their athletic programs. Public schools play a substantial role in determining and enforcing CIAC policies. Therefore, CIAC is an "instrumentality of a State."

Once defendant is found to be covered by ADA, then it must be determined if Dennin falls under the second element of Title II or the third element of Title III. The Rehabilitation Act analysis for an "otherwise qualified" individual is utilized to determine these elements under the ADA. . . . Since Dennin is "otherwise quali-fied" under the Rehabilitation Act, he has met all the elements under Title III, or alternatively, Title II of the ADA.

C. § 1983

Dennin also contends that the enforcement of the age requirement deprives him of his constitutional rights. To state a cause of action under § 1983, he must show (1) the conduct complained of was committed by a person acting under color of state law; and (2) such conduct deprived him of rights, privileges or immunities secured by the Constitution or laws of the United States.

. . . Actions of voluntary interscholastic athletic associations, of which public schools comprise part of the membership, constitute state action. . . .

Although there generally is no constitutional right to participate in interscho-lastic sports, it has been held that inclusion of such activity in an IEP transforms it into a federally protected right. . . . Accordingly, due process is required before Dennin can be deprived of that right. Due process requires a "meaningful, individualized inquiry into [plaintiff's] request for a waiver." . . . This includes consideration of whether any of the stated purposes behind the rule are implicated by plaintiff's participation. . . .

CIAC declined to inquire meaningfully and consider whether Dennin's partici-pation would undercut the purposes behind the rule. A waiver for Dennin was simply not considered. In fact, CIAC officials could provide no reason that an individualized inquiry would not permit a waiver to be granted to plaintiff. As earlier noted, his participation was not shown to undermine any of the stated purposes of the rule. Since, upon individualized inquiry, no reason not to grant the waiver exists, the waiver should be granted.

III. CONCLUSION

Plaintiff has established irreparable harm absent an injunction, and probability of success on the merits. The record here reflects no justification under the Rehabilitation Act, the ADA, and § 1983 and the IDEA for defendant to refuse to waive the age requirement for Dennin. The motion for preliminary injunction is granted. Without disagreement from the parties, this ruling is dispositive of the merits of plaintiff's claims for relief. The only issue flagged as possibly to be raised is that if defendant ultimately prevails on appeal, it may impose penalties or attorney's fees pursuant to its bylaws upon Trumbull High School.

SO ORDERED.

NOTES AND QUESTIONS

1.   Cases involving extracurricular participation as FAPE are still quite rare. Although FAPE is not explicitly mentioned in *Dennin*, one can argue that it is implicit in the IEP team's inclusion of participation on the swim team as part of the student's IEP. Because of the school's open participation rule regarding the swim team, there was no competition for places on the squad. To date, no reported case has arisen where a student's athletic participation as part of FAPE conflicts with a limit on the number of participants in a sport. Assuming that such a conflict does occur and that some students who try out will not make the team, what arguments might be raised under the IDEA or section 504 and the ADA to support participation of a student with the skill level of the student in *Dennin*?

2.   The athletic association (CIAC) appealed the district court's finding of the student's claims under section 504, the ADA, and section 1983. The Second Circuit Court of Appeals dismissed as moot the CIAC's appeal because the swim season for which the injunction had been sought had been completed. The CIAC argued that the case was not moot if the student did not graduate because other litigation was possible under the association's three-year rule which prohibited competition for more than three years in grades 10–12 in the same sport. However, because the student graduated at the end of the school year represented in the case (which also was his third year of high school competition), the three-year rule never became an issue. If plaintiff had not yet graduated at the end of this third high school year, what arguments could you make that he should still be entitled as part of his FAPE under the IDEA to another year's waiver from the CIAC's 19-year-old rule, plus a waiver from the three-year rule?

3.   Of special note in *Dennin* is that, according to the district court, the inclusion of plaintiff's extracurricular participation in his IEP creates a federally protected right under the Fourteenth Amendment's due process clause. While the court indicates that Fourteenth Amendment due process could be invoked against CIAC before it deprived Dennin of extracurricular participation, the court is not clear what due process standard could be invoked if Dennin's IEP team were to decide not to include extracurricular activities in his IEP. Would Dennin's statutory recourse through IDEA's due process hearing route be equivalent to due process under the Fourteenth Amendment? *See* MARK C. WEBER, SPECIAL EDUCATION LAW AND LITIGATION TREATISE § 21:6(2) (3d ed. 2008 & supps.) (listing cases both recognizing and rejecting constitutional due process claims involving IDEA).

4.   Involvement of students with disabilities in extracurricular activities can present issues of accessibility. In *Logwood v. Louisiana Department of Education*, 197 Fed. Appx. 302 (5th Cir. 2006) (not precedential), a student who used a wheelchair enrolled in the drama club. His IEP provided him with an aide to move him throughout the school. The court held that he was not denied an appropriate

education even though the school auditorium, where plays usually were staged, was not wheelchair accessible. The student did not audition for or participate in any activity that required access to the stage during the relevant time period. Had he done so, the school district would have moved any production to the school gymnasium, which was accessible. Since a gymnasium is not likely to have the accoutrements associated with an auditorium stage, does this seem like a fair resolution for both the student with the disability and those without disabilities?

5. Grading

IDEA requires that students' individualized education programs contain a description of how the child's progress toward meeting measurable annual goals, including academic and functional goals will be measured, and when periodic reports on the progress the child is making toward the goals will be provided. The reporting may be through the use of quarterly or other periodic reports, concurrent with the issuance of report cards. 20 U.S.C. § 1414(d)(1)(i)(II)–(III), Grading of students with disabilities is frequently different from grading students in general education and often relies less on letter grades and competitive tests. Challenges to grading have frequently occurred under section 504, and the following grading practices have been found to be discriminatory: failure to modify testing procedures to accommodate disabilities, *Kittle*, 14 EHLR 353:120 (U.S. Dep't of Educ., Office for Civil Rights 1988); *Yorktown Cent. Sch. Dist.*, 16 EHLR 771 (N.Y. Comm'r of Educ. 1990); failure to give grades on disabled students' mainstreamed academic work, *Scarnato*, 1978-88 EHLR 352:156 (U.S. Dep't of Educ., Office for Civil Rights 1986); *Myers*, 1978-88 EHLR 352:112 (U.S. Dep't of Educ., Office for Civil Rights 1985); excluding special education students from academic honors, *Hornstine v. Township of Moorestown*, 263 F. Supp. 2d 887 (D.N.J. 2003); and weighting courses taken by special education students with lower multipliers, *id.* at 895, 907.

In *Hornstine*, a New Jersey federal district court found that a school board effort to retroactively apply a new valedictorian rule served to deprive a student with a disability from being the sole valedictorian and violated both section 504 and the ADA. While *Hornstine* did not involve the awarding of grades to the student as such, the effect of the school board's proposal to enforce a new joint valedictorian policy served to subject the student's grades to a higher scrutiny than for the grades of students without disabilities and, thus, to dilute Hornstine's higher weighted GPA. In comparing the relationship between FAPE under the IDEA and nondiscrimination under section 504 and ADA, the court observed that

> The IDEA focuses on the appropriateness of the public education afforded special needs students whereas both the Rehabilitation Act and the ADA focus on disability-based discrimination against special needs students and are intended to reach "grosser kinds of misconduct" than the IDEA.

Id. at 901. While the court did not hold that Hornstine had been deprived of FAPE under the IDEA, it found that she was deprived of "fully enjoying a benefit she rightfully earned," namely the right under existing school board policy to be named the sole valedictorian. *Id.*

6.   District-Wide Assessment and Individual High-Stakes Testing

Under the 1997 amendments to IDEA, Congress sought to increase participation by students with disabilities in district and state-wide assessments. However, school districts had discretion in determining whether special education students were required to participate in state and district-wide assessments or, instead, could use alternate assessments.

The 2002 law popularly known as No Child Left Behind (NCLB) required that every state administer a state-wide assessment to all students in English, math and, starting in the 2005-2006 school year, science, with results reported to parents and on state and district report cards. 20 U.S.C. § 6311(b)(3), (d), (h); 34 C.F.R. § 200.8. The state must provide for the participation of all students in these assessments, and must make "reasonable adaptations and accommodations for students with disabilities . . . necessary to measure the academic achievement of such students relative to State academic content and State student academic achievement standards." 20 U.S.C. § 6311(b)(3)(C)(ix)(II). Department of Education regulations require the state to provide appropriate accommodations for students as determined by a student's IEP team under IDEA or placement team under section 504. 34 C.F.R. § 200.6(a)(1). States must also provide for alternative assessments where the IEP team determines the student "cannot participate in all or part" of the state assessment even with accommodations. 34 C.F.R. § 200.6(a)(2). The 2004 IDEA Reauthorization modified these provisions to align them more closely with NCLB.

Assessment results are to be disaggregated within each state, school district and school and by "gender, by each major racial and ethnic group, by English proficiency status, by migrant status, by students with disabilities as compared to nondisabled students, and by economically disadvantaged students as compared to students who are not economically disadvantaged." 20 U.S.C. § 6311(b)(3)(C)(xiii); 34 C.F.R. § 200.7. For each group, 95% of the students must take the assessments, consistent with applicable "accommodations, guidelines, and alternative assessments provided in the same manner as those provided under . . . § 1412(a)(17)(A) of IDEA." 20 U.S.C. 6311(b)(2)(I)(i); 34 C.F.R. § 200.6. Each group must make appropriate annual yearly progress toward proficiency if a school or district is to be found to be making appropriate progress under NCLB. 20 U.S.C. § 6311(b)(2)(C), (G)(i); 34 C.F.R. §§ 200.13–.21. Such disaggregation serves to call attention to each group, including students with disabilities, especially where that group may be the cause for a school to fail to make annual yearly progress and be designated as a school in need for improvement. 20 U.S.C. §§ 6311(h)(C)(viii), 6316(b); 34 C.F.R. §§ 200.33–.53. Given such attention, the practice of assessment of students with disabilities and counting their scores toward proficiency totals has proved controversial. Department of Education Regulations issued in 2007 establish that alternate academic achievement standards may be used for the proficient and advanced scores of children with the most significant cognitive disabilities, provided that the number of those scores at LEA and state levels, separately, does not exceed 1% of all students in the grades assessed in reading/language arts and mathematics. Modified academic achievement standards may be used for the proficient and advanced scores of other students with disabilities, provided that the number of those scores at the LEA and the state levels, separately, does not exceed 2% of all the students in the grades assessed in reading/language arts and mathematics. 34 C.F.R. § 200.13(c)(2). Very limited flexibility is permitted to exceed these caps. 34 C.F.R. § 200.13(c)(3)–(7). Accommodations and alternate assessments are also covered under a new regulation promulgated under the authority of the 2004 IDEA Reauthorization, 34 C.F.R. § 300.160.

Other aspects of IDEA as it was amended in 2004 also connect with NCLB's requirements for assessment of students. State performance goals must be the same as the state's definition of adequate yearly progress under NCLB. 20 U.S.C. § 1412(a)(15)(A)(ii). Children with disabilities are to be included in state and district assessment programs, including those for NCLB. 20 U.S.C. § 1412(a)(16)(A). Students with disabilities are to be given appropriate accommodations and alternate assessments where necessary and as indicated in their respective IEPs, and the state (or for district-wide assessments, the district) must develop guidelines for the provision of accommodations. 20 U.S.C. § 1412(a)(16)(A)–(B). Alternate assessments are to be aligned with the state's challenging academic content standards and challenging academic achievement standards; if the state has adopted alternate academic achievement standards pursuant to NCLB, the alternate assessments must also measure achievement against those standards. 20 U.S.C. § 1412(a)(16)(C)(ii). Reporting of assessment results is also mandatory. 20 U.S.C. § 1412(a)(16)(D).

NOTES AND QUESTIONS

1.   What are the advantages and disadvantages of including students with disabilities in state-wide assessments and disaggregating the data that is reported about this group? What impact could accommodations and alternative assessments have on comparative data? Why is the testing of students with disabilities so controversial?

2.   Statewide assessment under NCLB is only part of increasing accountability and assessment efforts. Many states now have requirements for so-called "high stakes" tests that link high school graduation to test scores. *E.g.*, Cal. Educ. Code, § 60851; Mass. Gen. Laws, ch. 69, § 1D; Ohio Rev. Code, § 3301.0710. These tests have proven controversial. Claims have been made that such tests violate constitutional or statutory rights of students with disabilities. Are such tests inherently unfair? How would you argue that such tests represent violations of substantive or procedural due process? Are they apt to have a particularly negative impact for students with disabilities? *See Rene v. Reed*, 751 N.E.2d 736 (Ind. Ct. App. 2001) (upholding a graduation exam against a challenge by students with disabilities). *See generally* Ralph Mawdsley and Jacqueline Cumming, *School District Accountability, Special Education Students, and the Dilemma of High Stakes Testing: An Australia-United States Comparison*, 188 ED. LAW REP. 1 (2004).

3.   In challenges to high stakes testing that contend that such tests have a disparate impact on minority groups, courts have used an approach that balances the students' and state's interests. *See Debra P. v. Turlington*, 730 F.2d 1405 (11th

Cir. 1084) (upholding a state's denial of diplomas to students who had not passed the state competency exam despite disproportionate impact on African-American students); *G.I. Forum v. Texas Educ. Agency*, 87 F. Supp. 2d 667 (W.D. Tex. 2000) (upholding the Texas Assessment of Academic Skills exam). *See generally* Jay P. Heubert, *Nondiscriminatory Use of High-Stakes Tests: Combining Professional Test-Use Standards with Federal Civil-Rights Enforcement*, 133 ED. LAW REP. 17 (1999). With increasing attention to accountability and assessment, more litigation can be expected. What is the appropriate role for the courts?

7.   Juveniles in Detention Facilities

Students in juvenile detention facilities are entitled to special education services provided that they are otherwise eligible. In *Green v. Johnson*, 513 F. Supp. 965 (D. Mass. 1981), a federal district court issued an injunction requiring that the State of Massachusetts provide special education services for incarcerated juveniles. In effect, the court determined that failure of the state to provide the services had denied the juveniles FAPE under the IDEA.

However, the 1997 amendments to the IDEA restricted the services required for students who have been convicted as adults and are incarcerated in adult prisons. 20 U.S.C. § 1414(d)(7)(A). The services not required are participation in general assessments and transition planning and services. 20 U.S.C. § 1414(d)(7)(A). In addition, a juvenile's IEP team can modify the IEP or placement without following the requirements of 20 U.S.C. §§ 1412(a)(5)(A) and 1414(d)(1)(A) "if the State has demonstrated a bona fide security or compelling penalogical interest that cannot otherwise be accommodated." 20 U.S.C. § 1414(d)(7)(B).

In the absence of state law to the contrary, juvenile courts function independently from school districts. One state court has held that juvenile courts can change the disposition arrangements of juvenile delinquents without being subject to the stay-put and manifestation determination requirements that apply to school districts changing educational placements. *In re P.E.C.*, 211 S.W.3d 368 (Tex. Ct. App. 2006).

8.   Charter Schools

Children in charter schools are entitled to special education services the same as children in other public schools. Nevertheless, the enrollments of children with disabilities, particularly those with severe disabilities, tend to be lower than the enrollments at other public schools, and parents have leveled charges that some charters steer away students with disabilities who are difficult or costly to serve. *See* Mark C. Weber, *Special Education from the (Damp) Ground Up: Children with Disabilities in a Charter School-Dependent Educational System*, LOY. J. PUB. INT. L. (forthcoming 2010), *available at*

http://papers.ssrn.com/sol3/papers.cfm?abstract_id=1487667

(discussing principles for providing adequate services for children with disabilities in public education system making extensive use of charter schools, citing example of New Orleans). If charter schools discourage hard-to-serve children from enrolling, can charters be viewed as a valid example of a successful school choice initiative? *See generally* Jay P. Heubert, *Schools Without Rules? Charter Schools, Federal Disability Law, and the Paradoxes of Deregulation*, 32 HARV. C.R.-C.L. L. REV. 301, 312 (1997) ("If a charter school's educational success depended on whether it could exclude students who have special educational needs or who are costly to educate, the school could hardly be a good model for traditional public schools, which must serve all children. Certainly this would defeat a central charter school objective.").

Chapter 5

INDIVIDUALIZED EDUCATION PROGRAM

A. INTRODUCTION

The Individualized Education Program or IEP is the core of special education law. The U.S. Department of Education describes the IEP as "the cornerstone of a quality education for each child with a disability." U.S. Department of Education, A Guide to the Individualized Education Program, *available at* http://www.ed.gov/parents/needs/speced/iepguide/index.html. The IEP is a single written document that provides an individually-tailored blueprint with goals and objectives for each student and with delineation of methods for achieving and measuring those goals through special education and related services. Central concepts are 1) the individual student's involvement and progress in the general curriculum with appropriate special education and related services and consistent with high academic standards and expectations for all students; 2) the involvement of parents and consideration of views and information provided by them in developing the education placement and plans for the student; and 3) the preparation of students for transition from high school to adult life. In outline form, the IEP process involves referral to a school's multidisciplinary team, evaluation for disability that adversely affects educational performance, and, upon determination of eligibility, an IEP meeting to establish an IEP, educational placement and implementation. 20 U.S.C. § 1414(d), (f). Once developed, an IEP is subject to review "periodically, but not less than annually to determine whether the annual goals for the child are being achieved." 20 U.S.C. § 1414(d)(4).

BASIC SPECIAL EDUCATION PROCESS UNDER IDEA[1]
Identification as possibly needing special education and related services by Child Find or referral or request for evaluation by parent or teacher
Consent to evaluation
Evaluation provided.　　　　**OR**　　　**If not mediation/due process.**
Evaluation in all areas related to the suspected disability
Eligibility determined by group of qualified professionals and parents.
If finding of eligibility, **IEP teams meets** within 30 days to write an IEP for the child. **IEP meeting** scheduled by the school with appropriate notice to the parents.
IEP meeting held & **IEP written and parental consent obtained** for placement (required before special education can be provided for the first time).
Consent
Services provided　　　**OR**　　　If not agreed, **mediation or due process may resolve.**
Progress toward annual goals measured and reported to parents
IEP is **reviewed**, annually at least.
Child is fully **reevaluated** at least every three years.

As *Rowley* set out, an IEP, the adoption of which is procedurally correct and the content of which is substantively adequate, fulfills the obligations of the school to provide a free appropriate public education to a student with disabilities. *Board of Educ. v. Rowley*, 458 U.S. 176, 207 (1982). Like other parts of special education law, the process and content are defined by statute and implementing regulations as well as by judicial opinion to make clear the who, what, and when requirements of the process. Not surprisingly, the adequacy of both process and substance is often the subject of litigation.

[1] Table adapted from Office of Special Education and Rehabilitative Services, U.S. Department of Education, A Guide to the Individualized Education Program (July 2000); *see also* **Letter from Stephanie S. Lee, Director, Office of Special Education Programs to Mr. Geoffrey A. Yudien, Legal Counsel, Vermont Department of Education (March 20, 2003) (regarding consent).**

B. STATUTORY AND REGULATORY REQUIREMENTS

1. IDEA[2]

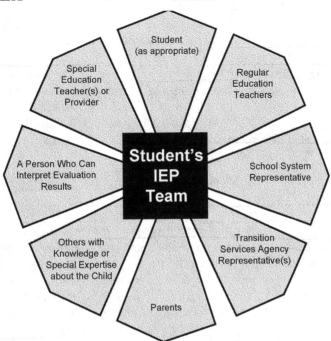

IDEA provides explicitly for who is to be involved in the process of developing an IEP. The school district has the responsibility for initiating and conducting meetings of the IEP team, which includes:

> "(i) the parents of a child with a disability; (ii) not less than 1 regular education teacher of such child (if the child is, or may be, participating in the regular education environment); (iii) not less than 1 special education teacher, or where appropriate, not less than 1 special education provider of such child; (iv) a representative of the local educational agency who — (I) is qualified to provide, or supervise the provision of, specially designed instruction to meet the unique needs of children with disabilities, (II) is knowledgeable about the general curriculum; and (III) is knowledgeable about the availability of resources of the local educational agency; (v) an individual who can interpret the instructional implications of evaluation results. . . ."

20 U.S.C. § 1414(d)(1)(B). In the parent's or agency's discretion, "other individuals who have knowledge or special expertise regarding the child, including related services personnel" may be included "as appropriate." The child with a disability is also to be included "whenever appropriate." 20 U.S.C. § 1414(d)(1)(B)(vi)–(vii); *see*

---

[2] Diagram from Office of Special Education and Rehabilitative Services, U.S. Department of Education, A Guide to the Individualized Education Program (July 2000).

34 C.F.R. § 300.321(a)(7). In addition, where transition services are being considered, the student is to be invited; if the student does not attend, the agency has to take other steps to ensure the student's preferences and interests are considered. 34 C.F.R. § 300.321(b). The 2004 Reauthorization of IDEA added new provisions regarding mandatory attendance at IEP meetings, providing that an IEP team member will not be required to attend if the parent and agency agree that attendance is not necessary because "the member's area of the curriculum or related services is not being modified or discussed at the meeting," 20 U.S.C. § 1414(d)(1)(C)(i), or if the parent consents to excusal and the member submits written input prior to the meeting, 20 U.S.C. § 1414(d)(1)(C)(ii)–(iii). These agreements must be in writing. The 2004 Reauthorization of IDEA also explicitly permits video conferences and conference calls, if agreed to by the parents and LEA for IEP meetings. 20 U.S.C. § 1414(f).

The IEP team and the development of the IEP proceed on a specific timeline set out in federal law, with possible additional requirements under state law. Unless the state has its own timeframe, the determination whether the child is eligible must be done within 60 days of when the district received parental consent to evaluation, unless the child has moved schools after the timeframe began and the parent agreed to an extension. 20 U.S.C. § 1414(a)(1)(C). (There is also an exception to the timeframe if the parent repeatedly fails or refuses to produce the child for the evaluation. 20 U.S.C. § 1414(a)(1)(C)(ii)(II).) For initial IEPs, the IEP meeting is to follow within 30 days of the determination of eligibility. 34 C.F.R. § 300.323(c)(1). There must be an IEP in place at the beginning of each school year for each student, 20 U.S.C. § 1414(d)(2)(A), and that IEP must be known and accessible to each special and regular education teacher and service provider responsible for implementation, 34 C.F.R. § 300.323(d). Implementation of the IEP must begin as soon as possible after the IEP meeting. 34 C.F.R. § 300.323(c)(2).

As to formulation of the IEP, the IDEA requires that consideration be given to the child's strengths and the parents' concerns as well as to certain specific factors, where applicable, for children with behavioral problems, limited English language skills, visual or hearing impairments (including communication needs and opportunities for direct instruction in the child's mode of language and communication), and in need of assistive technology. 20 U.S.C. § 1414(d)(3)(B); 34 C.F.R. § 300.324(a)(1)–(2).

As to content of the IEP, IDEA provides an explicit definition of an "individualized education program" or "IEP" as "a written statement for each child with a disability that is developed, reviewed, and revised" as specified in section 1414. Section 1414(d)(1)(A) provides that an IEP include the description of the child's "present levels of educational performance" together with "a statement of measurable annual goals, including academic and functional goals. . . ."

The IEP must also specify what is to be provided for the child in terms of special education, related services, supplementary aids and services, together with their dates, frequency, location and duration. 20 U.S.C. § 1414(d)(1)(A)(IV); 34 C.F.R. § 300.320(a)(4), (7). It must specify program modifications or supports for school personnel and delineate treatment of the student in terms of district assessments. 34 C.F.R. § 300.320(a)(4). The 2004 Reauthorization of IDEA specifically addresses assessments, accommodations, alternative assessments, and reporting, all in an effort to align IDEA with NCLB. *See* 20 U.S.C. § 1414(d)(1)(A)(i)(VI). Consistent with the legislative intent to provide appropriate education and involve children and their parents in the process, the IEP must indicate how the child's progress will be measured and reported to the parents. 20 U.S.C. § 1414(d)(1)(A)(i)(III); 34 C.F.R. § 300.320(a)(3). Congress was also concerned that children with disabilities be integrated into schools and society and no longer be excluded and thus hidden away and invisible. To address these concerns, the IEP must include a statement of special education, related services and supplementary aids and services and program modifications or supports for school personnel to be involved with and make progress in the general education curriculum, and be educated with other children, both disabled and nondisabled, and an explanation if the child will not participate with nondisabled children in the regular class. 20 U.S.C. § 1414(d)(1)(A)(i)(IV)(bb)–(cc), (V); 34 C.F.R. § 300.320(a)(4)(ii)–(iii), (5). It must also address transition from school to adult life 20 U.S.C. § 1414(d)(1)(A)(i) (VIII); 34 C.F.R. § 300.320(b).

Amendments to the IEP made after the annual review may be made, upon the agreement of the parents, without the convening of the IEP team, and may be placed in separate documents. 20 U.S.C. § 1414(d)(3)(D).

2.   Section 504

Section 504 assures that students with disabilities are not discriminated against in education programs receiving federal financial assistance. 29 U.S.C. § 794; 34 C.F.R. § 104.31. Regulations adopted pursuant to section 504 require that to achieve this objective public elementary or secondary education programs or activities receiving federal funds provide free appropriate public education "to each qualified handicapped person who is in the recipient's jurisdiction, regardless of the nature or severity of the person's handicap." 34 C.F.R. § 104.33(a). Such regular or special education is to be provided consistent with applicable procedures and "to meet individual educational needs of handicapped persons as adequately as the needs of nonhandicapped persons are met." 34 C.F.R. §§ 104.33–.36. *One* of the ways that this standard can be met is by providing an IEP consistent with IDEA. 34 C.F.R. §§ 104.33(a)(2). Another approach is through the implementation of section 504 accommodation or service plans.

C. SAMPLE IEP

The sample which follows was taken from the U.S. Department of Education website and integrates references to regulatory requirements into the form.[3]

ANNOTATED SAMPLE FORM

THE INDIVIDUALIZED EDUCATION PROGRAM (IEP) IS A WRITTEN DOCUMENT THAT IS DEVELOPED FOR EACH ELIGIBLE CHILD WITH A DISABILITY. THE PART B REGULATIONS SPECIFY, AT 34 CFR §§ 300.320–300.328, THE PROCEDURES THAT SCHOOL DISTRICTS MUST FOLLOW TO DEVELOP, REVIEW, AND REVISE THE IEP FOR EACH CHILD. THE DOCUMENT BELOW SETS OUT THE IEP CONTENT THAT THOSE REGULATIONS REQUIRE.

A STATEMENT OF THE CHILD'S PRESENT LEVELS OF ACADEMIC ACHIEVEMENT AND FUNCTIONAL PERFORMANCE INCLUDING:

- **HOW THE CHILD'S DISABILITY AFFECTS THE CHILD'S INVOLVEMENT AND PROGRESS IN THE GENERAL EDUCATION CURRICULUM (I.E., THE SAME CURRICULUM AS FOR NONDISABLED CHILDREN) OR FOR PRESCHOOL CHILDREN, AS APPROPRIATE, HOW THE DISABILITY AFFECTS THE CHILD'S PARTICIPATION IN APPROPRIATE ACTIVITIES. [34 CFR § 300.320(A)(1)]**

```
┌──────────────────────────────────────────────────┐
│                                                    │
│                                                    │
└──────────────────────────────────────────────────┘
```

A STATEMENT OF MEASURABLE ANNUAL GOALS, INCLUDING ACADEMIC AND FUNCTIONAL GOALS DESIGNED TO:

- **MEET THE CHILD'S NEEDS THAT RESULT FROM THE CHILD'S DISABILITY TO ENABLE THE CHILD TO BE INVOLVED IN AND MAKE PROGRESS IN THE GENERAL**
- **EDUCATION CURRICULUM. [34 CFR § 300.320(A)(2)(I)(A)]**

MEET EACH OF THE CHILD'S OTHER EDUCATIONAL NEEDS THAT RESULT FROM THE CHILD'S DISABILITY. [34 CFR § 300.320(A)(2)(I)(B)]

```
┌──────────────────────────────────────────────────┐
│                                                    │
│                                                    │
└──────────────────────────────────────────────────┘
```

FOR CHILDREN WITH DISABILITIES WHO TAKE ALTERNATE ASSESSMENTS ALIGNED TO ALTERNATE ACHIEVEMENT STANDARDS (IN ADDITION TO THE ANNUAL GOALS), A

```
┌──────────────────────────────────────────────────┐
│                                                    │
│                                                    │
└──────────────────────────────────────────────────┘
```

---

[3] The regulations referenced and incorporated are those referenced in the USDOE form. U.S. Department of Education, Model Form: Individualized Education Program, *at* http://idea.ed.gov/static/modelForms.

DESCRIPTION OF BENCHMARKS OR SHORT-TERM OBJECTIVES. [34 CFR § 300.320(A)(2)(II)]

A DESCRIPTION OF:

- HOW THE CHILD'S PROGRESS TOWARD MEETING THE ANNUAL GOALS WILL BE MEASURED. [34 CFR § 300.320(A)(3)(I)]
- WHEN PERIODIC REPORTS ON THE PROGRESS THE CHILD IS MAKING TOWARD MEETING THE ANNUAL GOALS WILL BE PROVIDED SUCH AS THROUGH THE USE OF QUARTERLY OR OTHER PERIODIC REPORTS, CONCURRENT WITH THE ISSUANCE OF REPORT CARDS. [34 CFR § 300.320(A)(3)(II)]

A STATEMENT OF THE SPECIAL EDUCATION AND RELATED SERVICES AND SUPPLEMENTARY AIDS AND SERVICES, BASED ON PEER-REVIEWED RESEARCH TO THE EXTENT PRACTICABLE, TO BE PROVIDED TO THE CHILD, OR ON BEHALF OF THE CHILD, AND A STATEMENT OF THE PROGRAM MODIFICATIONS OR SUPPORTS FOR SCHOOL PERSONNEL THAT WILL BE PROVIDED TO ENABLE THE CHILD:

- TO ADVANCE APPROPRIATELY TOWARD ATTAINING THE ANNUAL GOALS. [34 CFR § 300.320(A)(4)(I)]
- TO BE INVOLVED IN AND MAKE PROGRESS IN THE GENERAL EDUCATION CURRICULUM AND TO PARTICIPATE IN EXTRA-CURRICULAR AND OTHER NONACADEMIC ACTIVITIES. [34 CFR § 300.320(A)(4)(II)]
- TO BE EDUCATED AND PARTICIPATE WITH OTHER CHILDREN WITH DISABILITIES AND NONDISABLED CHILDREN IN EXTRA-CURRICULAR AND OTHER NONACADEMIC ACTIVITIES. [34 CFR § 300.320(A)(4)(III)]

AN EXPLANATION OF THE EXTENT, IF ANY, TO WHICH THE CHILD WILL NOT PARTICIPATE WITH NONDISABLED CHILDREN IN THE REGULAR CLASSROOM AND IN EXTRACURRICULAR AND OTHER NONACADEMIC ACTIVITIES. [34 CFR § 300.320(A)(5)]

A STATEMENT OF ANY INDIVIDUAL APPROPRIATE ACCOMMODATIONS THAT ARE NECESSARY TO MEASURE THE ACADEMIC ACHIEVEMENT AND FUNCTIONAL PERFORMANCE OF THE CHILD ON STATE AND DISTRICTWIDE ASSESSMENTS. [34 CFR § 300.320(A)(6)(I)]

IF THE IEP TEAM DETERMINES THAT THE CHILD MUST TAKE AN ALTERNATE ASSESSMENT INSTEAD OF A PARTICULAR REGULAR STATE OR DISTRICTWIDE ASSESSMENT OF STUDENT ACHIEVEMENT, A STATEMENT OF WHY:

- THE CHILD CANNOT PARTICIPATE IN THE REGULAR ASSESS- MENT. [34 CFR § 300.320(A)(6)(II)(A)]
- THE PARTICULAR ALTERNATE ASSESSMENT SELECTED IS APPROPRIATE FOR THE CHILD. [34 CFR § 300.320(A)(6)(II)(B)]

THE PROJECTED DATE FOR THE BEGINNING OF THE SERVICES AND MODIFICATIONS AND THE ANTICIPATED FREQUENCY, LOCATION, AND DURATION OF SPECIAL EDUCATION AND RELATED SERVICES AND SUPPLEMENTARY AIDS AND SERVICES AND MODIFICATIONS AND SUPPORTS. [34 CFR § 300.320(A)(7)]

SERVICE, AID OR MODIFICA-TION	FREQUENCY	LOCATION	BEGINNING DATE	DURATION

TRANSITION SERVICES

BEGINNING NOT LATER THAN THE FIRST IEP TO BE IN EFFECT WHEN THE CHILD TURNS 16, OR YOUNGER IF DETERMINED APPRO- PRIATE BY THE IEP TEAM, AND UPDATED ANNUALLY THEREAFTER, THE IEP MUST INCLUDE:

- APPROPRIATE MEASURABLE POSTSECONDARY GOALS BASED UPON AGE-APPROPRIATE TRANSITION ASSESSMENTS RE- LATED TO TRAINING, EDUCATION, EMPLOYMENT, AND WHERE APPROPRIATE, INDEPENDENT LIVING SKILLS. [34 CFR § 300.320(B)(1)]

- THE TRANSITION SERVICES (INCLUDING COURSES OF STUDY) NEEDED TO ASSIST THE CHILD IN REACHING THOSE GOALS. [34 CFR § 300.320(B)(2)]

TRANSITION SERVICES (INCLUDING COURSES OF STUDY)

RIGHTS THAT TRANSFER AT AGE OF MAJORITY

- **BEGINNING NOT LATER THAN ONE YEAR BEFORE THE CHILD REACHES THE AGE OF MAJORITY UNDER STATE LAW, THE IEP MUST INCLUDE A STATEMENT THAT THE CHILD HAS BEEN INFORMED OF THE CHILD'S RIGHTS UNDER PART B OF THE IDEA, IF ANY, THAT WILL, CONSISTENT WITH 34 CFR § 300.520, TRANSFER TO THE CHILD ON REACHING THE AGE OF MAJORITY.**

NOTES AND QUESTIONS

1. The IEP process and content, as illustrated by the U.S. Department of Education sample, is highly regulated and highly detailed. Is this amount of regulatory control useful? Necessary?

2. The operative word in IEP is supposed to be individualized. Does the use of a sample, fill-in-the-blank form help or hinder such individualization?

3. The 2004 Reauthorization of IDEA provides that up to 15 states may, with approval of the Secretary of Education, use multi-year (up to three years) IEPs set to "natural transition points" under a pilot program. 20 U.S.C. § 1414(d)(5). Participation by parents is voluntary. If you were the advisor to your state education agency, would you want to do this? If you were the advisor to a parent group, what position would you recommend the group take in its advocacy efforts with the state?

D.   IEP COURT DECISIONS

1.   The Process as Opportunity to be Heard

Given the scope of the IEP process and the IEP itself, it is not surprising that various aspects of IEP development find their way to court as illustrated by the cases in this part. IEP cases, such as *White* and *Burilovitch*, could, of course, also be read as placement cases; they are included here because the IEP meetings and discussions are important to the courts' analyses and decisions.

WHITE v. ASCENSION PARISH SCHOOL BOARD
343 F.3d 373 (5th Cir. 2003)

The court held that the school system has the authority to decide that a child with a hearing impairment will attend a centralized school rather than the neighborhood school requested by his parents.

Barksdale, Circuit Judge.

For this interlocutory appeal from injunctive and other relief awarded parents of a child, pursuant to the Individuals with Disabilities Education Act, primarily at issue is whether, consistent with IDEA, a school system has the right to select a centralized location for providing services to a hearing-impaired child, notwithstanding the child's parents' request that services be provided instead at his neighborhood school (site-selection issue).

Dylan White (Dylan), a hearing-impaired student, identified and qualified under IDEA as disabled, attends school in Ascension Parish, Louisiana. Under the IDEA, he is qualified for special education and related services by Ascension Parish Schools (Ascension). Dylan uses a cochlear implant in one ear and a hearing aid in the other to receive sound input. He does not require communication assistance outside of the classroom environment, but uses a person — a cued speech transliterator — to assist him in processing spoken information in class. (A cued speech transliterator does not translate from spoken language to a sign language, but supplements lip-reading and residual or assisted hearing by hand and finger motions to distinguish between elements of speech that would otherwise appear identical.)

Ascension provides a system through which certain services are provided at centralized school sites. For hearing-impaired students who need cued speech transliterators, Ascension provides those services at three centralized schools (a primary school, a middle school, and a high school). These centralized schools are regular education campuses, and hearing-impaired students are "mainstreamed" (educated in regular classrooms). (Deaf students who use American Sign Language attend neighborhood, rather than centralized, schools.)

Dylan attends one of the centralized schools, Gonzales Primary, and has done so since he began attending Ascension schools. It is undisputed that Dylan has achieved substantial academic benefit and success at the centralized school.

In May 2000, when Dylan was in the second grade, the annual, IDEA-required conference for his individualized education program (IEP) was held. Dylan's parents requested his transfer from the centralized school to his neighborhood school, Dutchtown Primary, along with his transliterator (provided by Ascension). Gonzales Primary, the centralized school, is approximately five miles further from Dylan's home than the neighborhood school. Dylan's parents felt that transferring him to his neighborhood school would enhance his social development, including allowing him to attend school with neighborhood children.

Lengthy discussions were held at the IEP conference between the Whites and other IEP committee members regarding the school site selection. Ascension refused the transfer request pursuant to its policy of centralizing the cued speech program and because it believed Dylan was being provided an appropriate education at the centralized school.

The Whites requested an administrative due process hearing. After an evidentiary hearing, including live testimony, the hearing officer addressed whether Ascension "can determine placement for a hearing impaired child excluding parental input" and ruled in favor of Ascension. The Whites appealed the decision to a three-judge administrative panel, which affirmed.

The Whites then filed this action, seeking review of the administrative decision, as well as asserting violations of the IDEA, 20 U.S.C. § 1400, et seq.; the Americans with Disabilities Act (ADA), 42 U.S.C. § 12101, et seq.; the Rehabilitation Act (section 504), 29 U.S.C. § 794; 42 U.S.C. § 1983; and various state laws. The parties stipulated that the dispute was essentially a legal issue and filed cross motions for summary judgment. Under the stipulation, the *only issue* was whether the School Board has the right to select the school that a student shall attend.

. . . .

Our role under the IDEA is purposefully limited.

Congress left the choice of educational policies and methods where it properly belongs — in the hands of state and local school officials. Our task is not to second guess state and local policy decisions; rather it is the narrow one of determining whether state and local school officials have complied with the Act. Moreover, the IDEA creates a presumption in favor of a school system's educational plan, placing the burden of proof on the party challenging it. The Whites frame the issue as whether, under the IDEA and state law, the school board may, *at its sole discretion*, reject placement in the school the child would attend if not disabled and the school closest to the student's home (the neighborhood school) *without parental involvement* in that decision and where the IEP can be feasibly and appropriately implemented there. However, the school district did not stipulate (at least in district court) that *no* parental input was allowed on the issue of school selection. . . . Nor does such a stipulation fit the evidence: Dylan's mother testified before the hearing officer that, "during the IEP meeting we discussed at length [Dylan's] going to Dutch Town [the neighborhood school] and why this had to continue for him to be at Gonzales Primary [the centralized school]."

The Whites, in essence, ask us to do one of two things: (1) render an advisory opinion based on a situation that is not before us (parents not given opportunity to offer any input concerning school selection); or (2) as the district court apparently did, equate giving input with dictating the outcome. Of course, we cannot render advisory opinions. Moreover, we reject the assertion that parents are denied input into a decision *if* their position is not adopted.

Although Ascension and the Whites dispute whether there was "input," there is no genuine issue of material fact. Indeed, the parties do not dispute any facts, but instead dispute what constitutes the requisite parental input under the IDEA. Thus, based upon the input described by Mrs. White (discussions at the IEP meeting), we will address the question that is before us in this case: whether the school district violated the IDEA in assigning Dylan to a centralized school, notwithstanding his parents' request that he be assigned to his neighborhood school.

Ascension first asserts that the IDEA was not violated. . . . The cornerstone of the IDEA is the IEP, which is produced by a team that includes: the child's parents or guardian; a qualified representative of the local education agency who is knowledgeable about, *inter alia*, the resources of the school district; a regular education teacher of the child; a special education teacher of the child; other individuals at the discretion of the agency or the parent; and, where appropriate, the child. The written IEP specifies the program of benefits to which the student is entitled in order to receive a FAPE. Once a child's educational program is determined, the school must attempt to place the child in the "least restrictive environment" (LRE) (*e.g.*, as best it can, it must educate the child among not disabled children).

When an action is brought under the IDEA, or the appropriateness of an IEP challenged, our inquiry is two-fold: (1) whether "the [IEP] developed through the Act's procedures [is] reasonably calculated to enable the child to receive educational benefits"; and (2) whether the school district has "complied with the procedures set forth in the [IDEA]." *Rowley.* "If these requirements are met, the State has complied with the obligations imposed by Congress and the courts can require no more."

Of course, a primary purpose of the IDEA is to ensure that disabled children receive a FAPE. *See* 20 U.S.C. § 1412(a). A school satisfies that requirement by providing personalized instruction with sufficient support services to permit the child to benefit educationally from that instruction. Such instruction and services must be provided at public expense, must meet the State's educational standards, must approximate the grade levels used in the State's regular education, and must comport with the child's IEP. In addition, the IEP, and therefore the personalized instruction, should be formulated in accordance with the requirements of the Act and . . . should be reasonably calculated to enable the child to achieve passing marks and advance from grade to grade. A FAPE need not maximize the child's potential; it must guarantee "a basic floor of opportunity." Under this prong of *Rowley*, the focus of our inquiry is on academic achievement; and, while the IDEA requires the school to provide services to allow the child the requisite basic floor of opportunity, it does not require the school to make special accommodations at the parent's request (no matter how well intentioned), particularly where the request is not related to helping the child achieve *academic* potential. As noted, it is undisputed that Dylan was succeeding academically at the centralized school; thus, his IEP clearly met the requirements of FAPE. It is also undisputed that the parents' request that Dylan attend his neighborhood school was primarily social — they wanted him to be able to attend school with other neighborhood children; this concern is beyond the scope of the "educational benefit" inquiry courts make under the IDEA.

Regarding whether the IDEA's procedural requirements were followed, as stated, the Whites first assert that they were improperly denied input into the site selection. They also maintain the decision otherwise contravened the IDEA.

As noted, the IDEA requires that the parents be part of the team that creates the IEP and determines the educational placement of the child, 20 U.S.C. § 1414(d)(1)(B); and the IEP is to include location, 20 U.S.C. § 1414(d)(1)(A)(vi) (IEP must include the projected date for the beginning of services and their anticipated frequency, location, and duration). Additionally, 20 U.S.C. § 1414(f) requires the local education agency to ensure that the parents are members of any group that makes decisions on educational placement.

These statutory provisions do not, however, explicitly require parental participation in site selection. "Educational placement," as used in the IDEA, means educational program — not the particular institution where that program is implemented. Thus, contrary to the Whites' position, that parents must be involved in determining "educational placement" does not necessarily mean they must be involved in site selection. Moreover, that the parents are part of the IEP team and that the IEP must include location is not dispositive. The provision that requires the IEP to specify the location is primarily administrative; it requires the IEP to include such technical details as the projected date for the beginning of services, their anticipated frequency, and their duration. *See* 20 U.S.C. § 1414(d)(1)(A)(vi).

The Whites also rely on the IDEA's implementing regulations. 34 C.F.R. § 300.552 provides:

> In determining the educational placement of a child with a disability
>
> . . . each public agency shall ensure that —
>
> (a) The placement decision —
>
>> (1) Is made by a group of persons, including the parents, and other persons knowledgeable about the child, the meaning of the evaluation data, and the placement options; and
>>
>> (2) Is made in conformity with the LRE provisions . . .
>
> (b) The child's placement —
>
>> (1) Is determined at least annually;
>>
>> (2) Is based on the child's IEP; and
>>
>> (3) Is as close as possible to the child's home;
>
> (c) Unless the IEP of a child with a disability requires some other arrangement, the child is educated in the school that he or she would attend if nondisabled. . . .

The Whites note that "placement" in 34 C.F.R. § 300.552 appears to have a broader meaning than just educational program (thus, the requirement that "placement" be based on the IEP, which contains the educational program, along with other requirements) and to relate in some way to location (thus, the reference to distance from the child's home). Ascension responds that "placement" does not mean a particular school, but means a setting (such as regular classes, special education classes, special schools, home instruction, or hospital or institution-based instruction). It cites 34 C.F.R. § 300.551, which describes "placement" options as such. This is the better view.

In any event, even assuming *arguendo* that the regulations contemplate a parental right to provide input into the location of services, the facts are undisputed that the Whites did so as part of the IEP team that discussed location at length and that ultimately selected the centralized site. To accept the Whites' view of "input" would grant parents a veto power over IEP teams' site selection decisions. Congress could have included that power in the IDEA; it did *not* do so. The right to provide meaningful input is simply not the right to dictate an outcome and obviously cannot be measured by such. Absent any evidence of bad faith exclusion of the parents or refusal to listen to or consider the Whites' input, Ascension met IDEA requirements with respect to parental input. In short, on this record, Ascension complied with this procedural component.

The question then becomes whether Ascension was otherwise required by the IDEA to defer to the Whites' wishes that their son be transferred, along with his support services, to the neighborhood school. The Whites point to two main provisions that they contend support neighborhood school selection: (1) the child's placement is determined at least annually, is based on the child's IEP, and *is as close as possible to the child's home*, 34 C.F.R. § 300.552(b) (emphasis added); and (2) unless the IEP requires some other arrangement, the child is educated in the school that he or she would attend if not disabled, 34 C.F.R. § 300.552(c).

Regarding these provisions, their qualifying language is critical. 34 C.F.R. § 300.552(b) only requires that the student be educated as close *as possible* to the child's home. 34 C.F.R. § 300.552(c) specifies that the child is educated in the school he would attend if not disabled *unless the IEP requires some other arrangement*. Here, it was not possible for Dylan to be placed in his neighborhood school because the services he required are provided only at the centralized location, and his IEP thus requires another arrangement.

Of course, as the Whites point out, neighborhood placement is not possible and the IEP requires another arrangement only because Ascension has elected to provide services at a centralized location. This is a permissible policy choice under the IDEA. Schools have significant authority to determine the school site for providing IDEA services.

State agencies are afforded much discretion in determining which school a student is to attend. . . . The regulations, not the statute, provide only that the child be educated "as close as possible to the child's home." However, this is merely *one of many factors* for the district to take into account in determining the student's proper placement. *It must be emphasized that the proximity preference or factor is not a presumption that a disabled student attend his or her neighborhood school.*

IDEA expressly authorizes school districts to utilize regional day schools such as the one at issue here, and we think the importance of these regional programs is obvious. Undoubtedly there are a limited number of interpreters, speech pathologists with backgrounds in deaf education, and deaf education teachers; and by allocating these limited resources to regional programs, the state is better able to provide for its disabled children. Additionally, by placing these educators at regional centers, those centers are better able to provide further training for those educators and make substitutions for absent educators.

All of our sister circuits that have addressed the issue agree that, for provision of services to an IDEA student, a school system may designate a school other than a neighborhood school.

. . . Administrative agency interpretations of the regulations confirm that the school has significant authority to select the school site, as long as it is educationally appropriate. The Office of Special Education Programs (OSEP), the Department of Education branch charged with monitoring and enforcing the IDEA and its implementing regulations, has explained:

> If a public agency . . . has two or more equally appropriate locations that meet the child's special education and related services needs, the assign-

ment of a particular school . . . may be an administrative determination, provided that the determination is consistent with the placement team's decision.

Letter from Office of Special Education Programs to Paul Veazey (26 Nov. 2001). The Whites insist that 1997 amendments to the IDEA enlarged parents' role. Nevertheless, the amendments do not state — and the Whites do not cite any post-amendment authority for the proposition — that parents may alter a school's good faith policy decision regarding site selection. Moreover, the 2001 OSEP letter (interpreting the current version of the IDEA) is contrary to the Whites' position.

The Whites also urge that there is simply no reason the transliterator cannot move to Dylan's neighborhood school, because she provides services only for Dylan. Again, our task is not to question educational policy decisions; rather, it is to determine whether state and local officials have complied with the IDEA. This principle is unquestionably applicable here:

> Whether a particular service or method can feasibly be provided in a specific special education setting is an administrative determination that state and local school officials are far better qualified and situated than are we to make.

Regardless, Ascension has proffered numerous, sound reasons for its centralization policy, including: (1) ability to cover absences and scheduling difficulties; (2) training and staff development; (3) effective use of limited resources; and (4) educational and social advantages. Concerning Dylan's placement, it notes: (1) while Dylan is the only student now served by the transliterator, another student needing to share the transliterator could move into the district; and (2) making an exception to the centralization policy for Dylan would not be fair to other students who share transliterators and must attend the centralized school.

Ascension also disputes that Louisiana law requires the school to place Dylan in his neighborhood school.

. . . .

In sum, neither the IDEA nor state law prevents Ascension from selecting the centralized school site for the implementation of Dylan's IEP, notwithstanding parental input to the contrary. For the foregoing reasons, the summary judgment in favor of the Whites and the concomitant order granting the injunction and other relief are VACATED; judgment is RENDERED for Defendants on the site-selection issue; and this matter is REMANDED to the district court for further proceedings consistent with this opinion.

BURILOVICH v. BOARD OF EDUCATION OF THE LINCOLN-CONSOLIDATED SCHOOLS
208 F.3d 560 (6th Cir. 2000)

The court held that the school system may determine the substantive program provided for a child with disabilities where procedures followed were appropriate.

Norris, Circuit Judge.

Plaintiffs Edwin Burilovich and Dr. Linda Burilovich ("plaintiffs"), acting on behalf of their autistic son Bradley ("B.J."), sued the Board of Education of the Lincoln Consolidated Schools and its special education director ("defendants") under the Individuals with Disabilities Education Act. Plaintiffs challenge the district court's grant of summary judgment for defendants, maintaining that a proposal to place B.J. in a mainstream kindergarten violated procedural and substantive provisions of the IDEA. For the following reasons, we affirm the judgment of the district court.

B.J. was born on November 15, 1990. At an early age, his parents noticed that his language skills were significantly delayed. When he was three, plaintiffs sought assistance from their local school district, Lincoln Consolidated Schools. B.J. was evaluated by a Multidisciplinary Evaluation Team ("MET") at Willow Run Community Schools, which was providing Preprimary Impaired ("PPI") services for Lincoln. The MET generated an Individualized Education Program ("IEP"), providing B.J. with nonclassroom PPI services, along with speech and language therapy.

On February 24, 1994, B.J. was evaluated by Dr. Luke Tsai at the University of Michigan Adult/Child Psychiatric Hospitals. Suzanne Boyer, B.J.'s teacher, was present for the last part of the appointment. Dr. Tsai diagnosed B.J. as autistic; Dr. Burilovich later hand-delivered a copy of Dr. Tsai's evaluation to Ms. Boyer. This evaluation was not placed in B.J.'s school file.

Plaintiffs began researching educational approaches to treating autism. They learned of an approach developed by Dr. Ivar Lovaas, called discrete trial training ("DTT"). DTT emphasizes heavy parental involvement, early intervention, and treatment in the home and elsewhere in the community, rather than in professional settings. Plaintiffs started a home-based DTT program for B.J.

In June 1994, Dr. Burilovich wrote to Willow Run's Superintendent, Dr. Yomtoob, expressing her concerns about the downsizing of the Willow Run infant-toddler program and B.J.'s being given only three hours of instruction a week. That letter also indicated that B.J. was autistic.

In September 1994, Lincoln notified B.J.'s parents that it was transferring B.J. from the Willow Run program to the Lincoln PPI program. On October 1, 1994, the parents consulted with Dr. Patricia Meinhold, a psychology professor at Western Michigan University, who concluded that B.J. was an appropriate candidate for DTT and suggested the parents request assistance from their school district. An IEP Committee meeting ("IEPC") was held with the school. The resulting IEP placed B.J. in the district's PPI program 2.5 hours a day, four days a week, with 40–80 minutes per week of speech and language therapy. The parents requested that part of B.J.'s school time be used for DTT, but the district did not include DTT in the IEP. B.J.'s teacher Betsy McMillin offered to, and did, provide DTT therapy for a half hour before the school day began.

B.J.'s home program continued to develop. By Thanksgiving he was receiving at least 20 hours per week of DTT. The parents decided to reduce B.J.'s school participation to two days a week following Christmas vacation; his time spent on

DTT increased to 20–25 hours a week. According to plaintiffs, in the first half of 1995, B.J. made progress with his language and imitative skills, but was not involved in classroom activities. By the last half of 1995, B.J. was averaging 25–30 hours of home-based DTT. On November 28, 1995, Mr. Burilovich visited B.J.'s classroom and made a videotape. The parents maintain that the behavior on the videotape confirmed Dr. Burilovich's concerns that B.J.'s behavior in school was more regressed than at home.

On July 1, 1995, defendant Ronald Greiner became the Director of Special Education for the Lincoln Consolidated Schools. He began working with the Burilovich family in the fall of 1995 and an IEPC for B.J. was held on December 1, 1995. On December 7, 1995, Mr. Greiner sent a letter to plaintiffs memorializing conversations he had with them and setting out the district's perspective on an appropriate program for B.J. The letter also indicated that the parents had mentioned they were having some medical evaluations completed addressing autism, and asked for access to that information. In response, plaintiffs requested an independent educational evaluation ("IEE") by Dr. Meinhold. Plaintiffs later provided Mr. Greiner with a copy of Dr. Tsai's March 1994 evaluation. In January 1996, Mr. Greiner initiated an evaluation of B.J. for autism. The evaluation included some home observation by the school psychologist, school social worker, and Mr. Greiner.

Another IEPC was scheduled for March 18, 1996. Before that meeting, Dr. Meinhold submitted a report that included a formal written program proposal for B.J. At the meeting, Mr. Greiner proposed a program predominantly consisting of DTT, accepting the goals and objectives developed by Dr. Meinhold, and providing for staff training by Dr. Meinhold. According to Mr. Greiner, he proposed the plan involving DTT because he wanted to avoid conflict and a due process hearing. The staff, however, did not support the proposal. While most of the meeting was taped, the proposal was not written in a formal IEP. The parties disagree over the reason why there was no written document. Nonetheless, the participants left with the understanding that Dr. Meinhold would begin training the staff the next week. That training session was later canceled, according to Mr. Greiner, because of recent snow days.

Proposal not written in a formal IEP. ←

After the meeting, Mr. Greiner realized that the staff did not think DTT was a good program for B.J. Mr. Greiner met privately with his staff on April 16 and 26, 1996 to discuss DTT and develop a new proposal. A proposal was drafted and sent to the parents, with goals similar to those proposed by Dr. Meinhold, but without any DTT. Instead, the proposal placed B.J. in a mainstream kindergarten class with one-to-one support from a trained paraprofessional.

New proposal staff saw fit

An IEPC was scheduled for May 17, 1996, to which Dr. Meinhold was not invited. At the May IEPC, plaintiffs had serious concerns about placing B.J. in a mainstream kindergarten program without any DTT and discussed why the proposal differed from the March proposal for B.J. According to defendants, Mr. Greiner tried to explain the rationale for the proposal, but the parents were not interested in hearing details. Plaintiffs signed the IEPC, noting their disagreement, on May 23, 1996.

IEPC – Dr. not invited parents had concerns

Pursuant to the IDEA, the parents requested an impartial due process hearing before a local hearing officer ("LHO"). The LHO decided in favor of B.J.'s parents, finding that the March 1996 oral proposal was an IEP that should be implemented, and directing the district to reimburse the parents for the expenses of providing DTT at home. . . .

Plaintiffs filed a complaint in district court appealing the SHO's determination and alleging violations of the IDEA, the Rehabilitation Act of 1973, the Americans with Disabilities Act, 42 U.S.C. § 1983, and the Michigan Handicappers' Civil Rights Act. Defendants filed a motion for summary judgment addressing all counts of the complaint; plaintiffs filed a motion for partial summary judgment addressing their IDEA claim. . . .

The IDEA was designed to give children with disabilities a free appropriate public education designed to meet their unique needs. There are two parts to a court's inquiry. . . . First, the court determines whether the state has complied with the procedures set forth in the IDEA. *See Rowley.* Second, the court assesses whether the IEP developed through the act's procedures is reasonably calculated to enable the child to receive educational benefits. Michigan has added to this standard by requiring that an IEP be designed to develop the "maximum potential" of a child.

This court reviews both the procedural and substantive matters under a standard of "modified de novo review."

. . . .

With regard to procedural matters, a court should "strictly review an IEP for procedural compliance," although technical deviations will not render an IEP invalid. The Supreme Court has emphasized the importance Congress attached to the IDEA's procedural safeguards. . . . Furthermore, "if the procedural requirements of the IDEA are met, greater deference is to be afforded to the district's placement decision."

. . . .

[W]e hold that administrative findings in an IDEA case may be set aside only if the evidence before the court is more likely than not to preclude the administrative decision from being justified based on the agency's presumed educational expertise, a fair estimate of the worth of the testimony, or both. A court should defer to the administrative findings only when educational expertise is relevant to those findings and the decision is reasonable. . . .

Plaintiffs raised numerous issues in their brief. With regard to procedural matters, plaintiffs argue that an IEP was finalized in March, not May, of 1996; two meetings in April 1996 were IEPC meetings from which the parents were excluded; the school district failed to consult with knowledgeable professionals regarding B.J.'s placement; he was not properly evaluated; and he was not timely recertified as autistic. Plaintiffs contend that even if the procedural requirements of the IDEA were met, the IEP was substantively invalid because it failed to address B.J.'s unique needs and was not designed to allow him to attain his maximum potential.

Plaintiffs argue that the district court erred in determining that there never was a March 1996 IEP. They maintain that despite the absence of a written document the evidence shows that Mr. Greiner did not intend his proposal to be tentative and planned to implement the IEP. Federal law and Michigan regulation, however, both indicate that an IEP is a written document. Therefore, plaintiffs cannot prevail on their claim that an IEP existed in March when there was no written document until May. . . .

Next, plaintiffs argue that they were denied meaningful parental participation in the IEPC process because they were not invited to two meetings in April 1996. Defendants counter that the meetings on April 16 and 26 were staff meetings that plaintiffs were not entitled to attend. The SHO and district court agreed with defendants' characterization of the meetings and plaintiffs do little to suggest that the meetings were in fact IEP meetings. Plaintiffs have not indicated how they were prevented from participating in the development of the IEP. . . .

Plaintiffs also argue that the district failed to consult with knowledgeable professionals regarding B.J.'s placement as required by IDEA regulations. Plaintiffs maintain that because they preferred Lovaas-style DTT therapy, at least one decision-maker should have been well-versed in that treatment. More specifically, plaintiffs argue that the district should have, but did not, consult Dr. Meinhold.

This court has rejected "the contention that [a school district] must include an expert in the particular teaching method preferred by the parents in order to satisfy the requirement that the IEPC include persons knowledgeable about 'placement options.'" Furthermore, the record indicates that Marianne Miller, a teacher consultant for the district, had experience using DTT. The district also had Dr. Meinhold's report and was able to consider it at the IEPC.

. . . .

Plaintiffs suggest that the IEP failed to take B.J.'s unique needs into consideration, asserting that the district proposed the IEP because its personnel had insufficient experience for any other program. . . .

The district court and the SHO correctly determined that defendants' program took B.J.'s unique needs into consideration. As the district court pointed out, defendants' program set goals for B.J. and created a detailed daily schedule to address each of the goals with a program including both group instruction and one-on-one therapy. In contrast, the court noted that it did not see how the parents' proposed "standard" 40 hours of DTT therapy "was tailored to B.J.'s needs." The court later stated that the "school's proposal is the only one which took into consideration B.J.'s goals and abilities, and developed a plan specifically to accommodate him." After reviewing the record, and giving due weight to the SHO's opinion, we agree with the district court that the IEP did take into account B.J.'s unique needs.

Plaintiffs also suggest that the IEP did not address B.J.'s unique needs because it did not mention B.J.'s home program of DTT or his potential for regression. They rely on a case in which a district court ruled against a change in placement due to a risk of regression. We do not read the case as saying that an IEP always will be defective if it fails specifically to address regression, nor do plaintiffs posit any argument that would persuade this court that we should so hold.

. . . .

NOTES AND QUESTIONS

1.   A bedrock principle of the formulation of an IEP is the involvement of the parents and, where appropriate, the student, making the role of the parent a recurring theme in IEP decisions. The school has the responsibility to take steps to have parents at the IEP team meetings. Parents are to be notified as to the time, place, and location of the meeting and efforts are to be made to accommodate parent schedules and special needs and allow for their participation by phone or otherwise. Where a parent does not attend an IEP meeting, the meeting may proceed, but the school needs to precisely document its efforts to assure parental attendance. 34 C.F.R. § 300.322(d). As a matter of policy and practice, how much responsibility should the school bear for obtaining meaningful parental participation? To what extent and at what point should parents be allowed to waive services?

2.   While the law requires involvement of parents, as *White* and *Burilovich* indicate, parents' participation does not equate with parent control of the substantive decisions. Nor will parents necessarily prevail on claims of substantive defects where parents have actively participated, but have failed to provide relevant information or raise timely objections. *S.M. v Weast*, 240 F. Supp. 2d 426 (D. Md. 2003) (tuition reimbursement denied).

SHAPIRO v. PARADISE VALLEY UNIFIED SCHOOL DISTRICT NO. 69
317 F.3d 1072 (9th Cir. 2003)

The court held that the district's IEP decision as to where to place a child will not be valid when the IEP team is not properly constituted; parents held entitled to tuition reimbursement.

PAEZ, CIRCUIT JUDGE.

Defendant-Appellant and Cross-Appellee Paradise Valley Unified School District No. 69 ("PVUSD") appeals the district court's ruling that it did not provide Plaintiff-Appellee and Cross-Appellant Isadora Shapiro ("Dorie"), a profoundly deaf seven year old child with a cochlear implant, a free appropriate public education ("FAPE").[4] The district court determined that the PVUSD violated several procedural mandates required by the Individuals with Disabilities Education Act in creating Dorie's individualized education program ("IEP") and that Dorie's parents were therefore entitled to reimbursement for the costs of sending her to a private out-of-district school. By failing to include a teacher from Dorie's private educational placement and her parents in her June 8, 1994 IEP meeting, the PVUSD denied Dorie a FAPE. We therefore agree with the district court that

---

[4] [FN 1] A cochlear implant is a "device for treating severe deafness that consists of one or more electrodes implanted by surgery inside or outside the cochlea (an organ in the inner ear that transforms sound vibrations into nerve impulses for transmission to the brain). . . . [As the electrodes are implanted], a miniature receiver is implanted under the skin, either behind the ear or in the lower part of the chest. A wire connecting the electrodes to the receiver is implanted at the same time. Directly over the implanted receiver, the patient wears an external transmitter, which is connected to a sound processor and a microphone." AMERICAN MEDICAL ASSOCIATION, ENCYCLOPEDIA OF MEDICINE 286 (1989).

Dorie's parents are entitled to reimbursement for the costs of sending her to a private out-of-district school for the 1994-1995 school year. We have jurisdiction under 28 U.S.C. § 1291, and we affirm.

As part of a study on children with cochlear implants, Dorie attended a private, out-of-state school called the Central Institute for the Deaf ("CID") tuition-free for the 1991-1992, 1992-1993, and 1993-1994 school years. In the fall of 1993, as the study's three-year grant period was ending, Dorie's parents approached the PVUSD to seek authorization for her continued placement at CID for the 1994-1995 school year because the PVUSD did not have a program for Dorie in its district.

In March 1994, however, the PVUSD obtained permission to create an oral self-contained program[5] for children with hearing impairments at Sonoran Sky Elementary, a PVUSD school located about a mile from the Shapiros' home. The PVUSD notified Dorie's parents about this new program, and on April 13, 1994, representatives from the school district met with Dorie's parents to discuss the appropriateness of the program for Dorie. Dorie's parents expressed concern that the program was not yet "up and running" and that it may not continue past the 1994-1995 school year. Moreover, Dorie was the only child with a cochlear implant identified for the program.

The parties agreed to meet again on May 4, 1994, to continue to discuss the proposed program at Sonoran Sky Elementary. During the May 4 meeting, the district psychologist began drafting an IEP for Dorie. At the conclusion of the meeting, Dorie's parents expressed concern that the PVUSD had not yet hired a classroom teacher, that in the draft IEP the district had not specified related services to which Dorie would have access, and that Dorie would be a "guinea pig" in the PVUSD's new program. They again requested a placement at CID, which the PVUSD rejected, stating that the program at Sonoran Sky would be appropriate for Dorie.

The district's refusal to place Dorie at CID prompted Dorie's parents to initiate a due process hearing to determine Dorie's school placement for the 1994-1995 school year. Prior to the hearing, the PVUSD notified Dorie's parents that it planned to convene a meeting on June 8, 1994, to develop an IEP for Dorie. In response, Dorie's mother informed the district that she and her husband would be unavailable to meet on June 8 and requested a postponement. The PVUSD claimed it could not postpone the meeting because at least two of its IEP team members would be unavailable to meet after June 10.

The PVUSD convened a meeting on June 8, 1994, without Dorie's parents or a representative from CID. At the meeting, the district representatives drafted an IEP relying solely on information they had gathered from prior meetings with Dorie's parents. The PVUSD did not independently evaluate Dorie.

After the due process hearing began, Dorie's parents enrolled her at CID for the

---

[5] [FN 2] In his findings of fact, the hearing officer noted that "oral education" relies solely on speech language and lip reading. It contrasts with "total communication," which teaches both sign language and speech language. Dorie's parents wanted her to receive oral education.

1994-1995 school year and the PVUSD commenced its program at Sonoran Sky Elementary.

The hearing officer concluded that the oral self-contained program at Sonoran Sky Elementary complied with the IDEA and that under the stay-put provision of the IDEA, the district had to reimburse Dorie's parents for the costs of educating Dorie at CID for the 1994-1995 school year. Dorie's parents appealed this decision to the Arizona Department of Education. The state appellate hearing officer affirmed the hearing officer's decision that the PVUSD's oral self-contained classroom provided Dorie with a FAPE but reversed the decision regarding reimbursement.

Dorie's parents then commenced this action. The district court issued an order reversing the decision of the appellate hearing officer.

. . . .

Holding

We agree with the district court that the PVUSD violated the IDEA's procedural mandates in its development of Dorie's June 8 IEP, and thereby denied Dorie a FAPE, by not including a representative from CID or Dorie's parents at the June 8 meeting. We address each procedural error in turn.

. . . .

Rule re: teacher from schol

We have held that a school district's failure to include a representative from a private school that a child is currently attending violates the procedural mandates of the IDEA. IDEA requires the persons most knowledgeable about the child to attend the IEP meeting. The PVUSD made no attempt to include a representative from CID at the June 8 IEP meeting. As a result, the teachers most knowledgeable about Dorie's special education levels and needs did not attend the meeting, in violation of the IDEA

. . . .

As noted, the district court held that the PVUSD's failure to include Dorie's parents at the June 8 IEP meeting was a violation of the IDEA. We agree.

failure to have parents @ Mtg rule)

The importance of parental participation in the IEP process is evident. . . . It seems to us no exaggeration to say that Congress placed every bit as much emphasis upon compliance with procedures giving parents and guardians a large measure of participation at every stage of the administrative process . . . as it did upon the measurement of the resulting IEP against a substantive standard. The PVUSD argues that despite the IDEA's emphasis on parental participation in the IEP formulation process, the IDEA does not require parents to attend every IEP meeting. It relies on 34 C.F.R. § 300.345(d) for this proposition. This regulation states that "[a] meeting may be conducted without a parent in attendance if the public agency is unable to convince the parents that they should attend." According to the PVUSD, because Dorie's mother chose not to attend the June 8 IEP meeting but had a sufficient opportunity to do so, it was acceptable to hold the meeting without her. The PVUSD misinterprets § 300.345.

Under the regulation, before it can hold an IEP meeting without a child's parents, the school district must document phone calls, correspondence, and visits

to the parents demonstrating attempts to reach a mutually agreed upon place and *Rule*
time for the meeting. 34 C.F.R. § 300.345(d)(1)–(3). Here, the Shapiros asked to
reschedule the June 8 IEP meeting; they did not refuse to attend. The PVUSD's
reliance on § 300.345 therefore misses the mark. The school district simply
prioritized its representatives' schedules over that of Dorie's parents.

The PVUSD also contends that Dorie's parents contributed adequately to the
June 8 IEP because the PVUSD mailed the IEP to them for their approval and they
participated in prior IEP meetings. We disagree. The IDEA "imposes upon the
school district the duty to conduct a meaningful meeting *with* the appropriate ← *Rule*
parties." We have made clear that those individuals, like Dorie's parents, "who have
first-hand knowledge of the child's needs and who are most concerned about the
child must be involved in the IEP *creation* process." After-the-fact parental
involvement is not enough. Nor does the PVUSD's inclusion of the Shapiros in
certain parts of the process excuse the district's failure to include the Shapiros in
the June 8 IEP meeting; involvement in the "creation process" requires the PVUSD
to include the Shapiros unless they affirmatively refused to attend. By proceeding
with the June 8 IEP meeting without Dorie's parents, the PVUSD violated the
IDEA.[6]

We engage in a two-part inquiry to determine whether the PVUSD afforded   *2 part*
Dorie a FAPE. First, we must determine whether the PVUSD complied with the *inquiry*
procedures set forth in the IDEA. Second, we must determine whether the IEP
developed through the IDEA's procedures was reasonably calculated to confer
educational benefit upon Dorie.

We agree with the district court's ruling that the PVUSD's violations of the
IDEA's procedural mandates resulted in lost educational opportunity for Dorie. We
have held that:

> Procedural flaws do not automatically require a finding of a denial of a
> FAPE. However, procedural inadequacies that result in the loss of educa-   *Ct held*
> tional opportunity, or seriously infringe the parents' opportunity to partici-
> pate in the IEP formulation process, clearly result in the denial of a FAPE.

The PVUSD's failure to include the persons most knowledgeable about Dorie's
educational levels and needs — namely, a representative from CID and Dorie's

---

[6] [FN 6] We also agree with the district court that the PVUSD violated the IDEA's substantive
requirements by failing to include in its draft IEP a statement of Dorie's present educational levels and
procedures for determining whether the instructional objectives had been achieved. *See* 20 U.S.C.
§ 1401(a)(2)(C) (requiring that an IEP contain "a statement of the specific educational services to be
provided to such child"); 20 U.S.C. § 1401(a)(20)(F) (requiring that an IEP contain "appropriate objective
criteria and evaluation procedures and schedules for determining . . . whether instructional objectives
are being achieved"). The PVUSD argues that it did not include a statement of Dorie's present
educational levels because CID was delinquent about providing Dorie's educational records in response
to its requests, but this is inconsistent with its statutory obligation. *See* (2)(C); 34 C.F.R. § 300.531
("Before any action is taken with respect to the initial placement of a child with a disability in a program
providing special education and related services, a full and individual evaluation of the child's educational
needs must be conducted. . . ."). Because we conclude, however, that the PVUSD violated the IDEA's
procedural mandates by failing to include a representative from CID and Dorie's parents at the June 8
IEP meeting, which contributed significantly to its creation of a defective IEP and denied Dorie a FAPE,
we need not address the PVUSD's substantive violations of the IDEA.

parents — at the June 8 IEP meeting and its concomitant creation of a defective IEP resulted in lost educational opportunity for Dorie.

Because we conclude that the PVUSD's procedural violations of the IDEA resulted in a loss of educational opportunity for Dorie, it is unnecessary for us to address the second prong of the FAPE analysis. On the basis of the first prong of the FAPE two-part inquiry, which is a procedural analysis, we conclude that the PVUSD denied Dorie a FAPE. . . .

NOTES AND QUESTIONS

1. Parent involvement supports another core principle of IDEA, that proper participation and procedures will go a long way to assuring an appropriate IEP and education for students with disabilities. Given the essential nature of this principle, courts look closely for proper adherence to the procedures mandated for IEP formulation and review. As *Shapiro* indicates, proper constitution and participation of the IEP team is crucial. So too are the other procedural standards established in IDEA. Courts have invalidated district programs for children where school systems have failed, for example, to convene an IEP team, to explain specific services, to lay out a method for measuring progress, to have an IEP in place at the beginning of the school year, to fashion an individual program rather than recycle parts of previous programs used for other students, or to provide for transition services. *E.g., Deal v. Hamilton County Bd. of Educ.*, 392 F.3d 840 (6th Cir. 2004) (finding that failure to have regular classroom teacher of student attend IEP meetings when integration was at issue violated IDEA); *Knable v. Baxley*, 238 F.3d 755 (6th Cir. 2001) (failure to convene an IEP conference, failure to provide FAPE); *Cleveland Heights-University Heights City Sch. Dist. v Boss*, 144 F.3d 391 (6th Cir. 1998) (IEP shortcomings not harmless); *Gerstmyer v. Howard County Pub. Schs.*, 850 F. Supp. 361 (D. Md. 1994) (IEP not in place for most of first grade for student with specific developmental dyslexia).

2. Even where proper procedures are not followed, courts will recognize that procedural irregularities must be more than de minimis. For example, where an IEP did not provide adequate specificity on related services, the court accepted it where it appeared that the student had not been denied services and was making progress. *O'Toole v. Olathe Dist. Schs. Unified Sch. Dist. No. 233*, 144 F.3d 692 (11th Cir. 1998).

3. An IEP must be developed and implemented for each student with a disability, including eligible students who are placed in or referred to a private school or facility by a public agency. 34 C.F.R. §§ 300.323(a); .325. In such cases, an IEP must be developed, with the participation of the private school or facility, before the public agency places or refers the child to a private school or facility. 34 C.F.R. § 300.325(a). Once a child is in a private facility, that facility may conduct IEP meetings at the discretion of the public agency; where this is done, parents and the agency must be involved and responsibility remains with the public agency. 34 C.F.R. § 300.325(b). Responsibility for compliance with the IEP requirements remains with the public agency placing the child and the state educational agency. 34 C.F.R. § 300.325(c).

SYTSEMA v. ACADEMY SCHOOL DISTRICT NO. 20
538 F.3d 1306 (9th Cir. 2008)

In a case involving a child with autism, the court ruled that failure to offer a complete IEP did not necessarily deny the child appropriate public education when the parents obtained private services before completion of the IEP process. An IEP, even if incomplete, should be evaluated without considering outside evidence of the school district's position. The court upheld the following year's IEP.

EBEL, CIRCUIT JUDGE.

Plaintiff-Appellant Nicholas Sytsema brought suit, by and through his parents, against the Academy School District for reimbursement for his educational expenses pursuant to the Individuals with Disabilities Education Act. The district court concluded that the Sytsemas were entitled to reimbursement for their expenses for the 2001-2002 academic year because the school district violated the Act's procedural requirements by never finalizing the draft IEP it provided to the Sytsemas. The court also concluded that the individualized education plan for the 2002-2003 academic year complied with all of the Act's requirements, and thus denied the Sytsemas' request for reimbursement for that period. Both parties now appeal.

We conclude that the district court erred in awarding relief to the Sytsemas for procedural differences in the 2001 IEP and we remand for the district court to consider whether the 2001 draft IEP substantively denied Nicholas a free appropriate public education (FAPE). In conducting this review, the district court should restrict its review to the draft IEP as written without considering any oral discussions that occurred between the respective parties. We further conclude that the 2002-2003 IEP complied with the IDEA requirements. Accordingly, we REVERSE the district court's decision granting the Sytsemas reimbursement for their expenses for the 2001-2002 academic year and we REMAND for consideration of whether the written draft 2001 IEP denied Nicholas a FAPE. We AFFIRM the denial of reimbursement expenses to the Sytsemas for the 2002-2003 academic year.

I

Nicholas Sytsema was born in July 1998. Approximately two and a half years later he was diagnosed with autism. Autism is a condition that "affects all areas of essential human behaviors such as social interactions, the ability to communicate ideas and feelings, imagination, fine and gross motor skills, and the establishment of relationship[s] with others." As a result of his condition, Nicholas has "severely delayed communication skills." This delay manifests itself in several ways, including the fact that "[Nicholas is] very much in his own world, [does] not respond to his name, [does] not make eye contact, and [does] not want to be part of any of the groups that [are] around him." Nicholas also has a short attention span and is easily distracted by movements outside.

During the period from Nicholas's diagnosis until his third birthday, Resources for Young Children and Families provided funding for an in-home program pursuant to the IDEA. As part of this in-home program, Nicholas received 16.5 hours of one-on-one therapy per week. When Nicholas turned three, the responsibility for complying with the IDEA's requirements shifted to his local school district. Pursuant to these requirements, the District assessed Nicholas's learning skills during a "play-based assessment." . . .

Subsequent to the assessment, Nicholas's parents met with District employees to review a draft IEP for the 2001-2002 school year ("2001 IEP") in May 2001. The District's director of special education, a special education teacher, an occupational therapist, a social worker, and the District's autism specialist all attended the IEP meeting. The draft IEP documented several items, including: (i) the data gathered during the assessment; (ii) Nicholas's levels of functioning, achievement, and performance; (iii) a statement of educational needs; (iv) a statement of goals and objectives; (v) a statement of special education needs and related services; and (vi) a recommended placement. To provide Nicholas with a FAPE, the IEP proposed a total of 10.75 hours of services per week. A significant portion of that total — 9.5 hours per week — would occur in an education placement in an integrated preschool classroom, while the remainder — 1.25 hours per week — would consist of additional educational services, such as speech and language services.

Nicholas's parents rejected the draft IEP's suggested placement due to their concerns about Nicholas's educational experience in an integrated classroom. The Sytsemas believed that the suggested placement would not have benefitted Nicholas. To support their position, the Sytsemas provided the District with letters from two behavior specialists, a neurologist, and a staff member at the JFK Center for Developmental Disabilities.

The District and the Sytsemas held another meeting on August 2, 2001. This meeting did not constitute an official IEP team meeting because several team members were out of town. At this meeting, the District offered to increase the total service hours to 20 hours per week. The District, however, never formally amended the IEP to reflect this offer. Due to their continued concerns about Nicholas's placement, the Sytsemas rejected the draft IEP shortly after the August 2, 2001 meeting. They instead continued Nicholas's at-home program at their own expense. The District did not complete a final IEP for Nicholas for the 2001-2002 academic year.

The District and the Sytsemas began discussions regarding an IEP for the 2002-2003 school year ("2002 IEP") in October 2002. In preparation for this IEP, the District evaluated Nicholas using both the Mullen Scales of Early Learning and the Vineland Adaptive Behavior Scales. The Sytsemas and the District employees on the IEP team met on November 20, 2002, to discuss the 2002 IEP. The 2002 IEP proposed a total of 25 hours of services per week. The plan included 20 hours per week in an integrated classroom, and 5 hours per week of one-on-one discrete trial training.

Unlike the previous year, the District finalized the 2002 IEP and delivered it to the Sytsemas; however, the Sytsemas neither agreed to nor signed the 2002 IEP. Instead, they continued the at-home program that consisted primarily of one-on-one instruction. Beginning in November 2002, Nicholas's parents also enrolled him in a private preschool for nine hours per week. Nicholas attended the private school with the help of an aide. The Sytsemas paid for both the at-home program and the private school.

On November 15, 2002, the Sytsemas submitted their demand for an Impartial Due Process Hearing. . . . After a five-day hearing, the independent hearing officer ("IHO") determined that the 2001 IEP and the 2002 IEP were appropriate and that the District did not deny Nicholas a FAPE for either school year. The IHO thus denied the Sytsemas' request for reimbursement.

The Sytsemas appealed the IHO decision to a Colorado administrative law judge ("ALJ"). In the course of reaching his decision, the ALJ adopted substantially all of the IHO's factual findings. . . .

Following the ALJ's decision, the Sytsemas filed a civil action in the United States District Court. . . . After reviewing the administrative record and the applicable law, the district court reversed the ALJ in part. The court held that the 2001 IEP was procedurally deficient because the District failed to present the Sytsemas with a final IEP. Based on this deficiency, the court ordered the District to reimburse the Sytsemas for the expenses they incurred during the 2001-2002 school year. Both in the district court and here on appeal, the District did not dispute the reimbursement amount of $38,503.45, nor did it dispute that the at-home program provided Nicholas some educational benefit.

The district court affirmed the ALJ's ruling for the 2002-2003 school year. The court first determined that the 2002 IEP was not procedurally defective. The court then reviewed the portion of the administrative record addressing whether the 2002 IEP was "reasonably calculated" to provide Nicholas with educational benefits. In light of the administrative record, the court held that the 2002 IEP did not deny Nicholas a FAPE, and thus affirmed the ALJ's denial of the reimbursement claim for that year.

The Sytsemas appeal the district court's order affirming the ALJ's denial of reimbursement for the 2002-2003 school year. The District has filed a cross-appeal seeking reversal of the district court's reimbursement order for the 2001-2002 school year.

II

. . . .

An IEP's failure to clear all of the Act's procedural hurdles does not necessarily entitle a student to relief for past failures by the school district. Instead, this court must determine whether the procedural error resulted in "substantive harm to the child or his parents"; "deprive[d] an eligible student of an individualized education program"; or "result[ed] in the loss of [an] educational opportunity." *Knable ex rel. Knable v. Bexley City Sch. Dist.*, [238 F.3d 755,] 765–66 (6th Cir. 2001). In sum, then, the courts inquire whether the violation resulted in the denial of a FAPE.

If a school district has complied with the procedural requirements for the IEP, the court must turn its attention to whether the IEP was "reasonably calculated" to provide the child with "educational benefits." [*Bd. of Educ. v.*] *Rowley*, 458 U.S. 176,

206–07 (1982). The IEP complies with the Act's substantive standards if it provides the disabled student with "[a] 'basic floor of opportunity' . . . [that] consists of access to specialized instruction and related services which are individually designed to provide educational benefit. . . ." *Rowley*, 458 U.S. at 201. This court has interpreted the *Rowley* standard to require an educational benefit that is more than de minimis. We have also recognized, however, that the Act focuses on providing disabled children access to public schools, and thus, does not require an education "guaranteed to maximize the child's potential." As a result, we apply the "some benefit" standard the Supreme Court adopted in *Rowley*.

III

A

The parties do not dispute that the District violated the Act by failing to provide the Sytsemas with a final 2001 IEP. This failure, however, does not necessarily entitle the Sytsemas to reimbursement. . . . We . . . conclude that the district court wrongly decided that the lack of a final IEP denied Nicholas a FAPE.

As noted above, the Act provides for reimbursement for procedural violations only where that violation effectively denied the student a FAPE. Although we have not yet had the occasion to consider the effect of a parent's conduct in this context, two of our sister circuits have concluded that a procedural violation does not deny a student an educational opportunity where the parents did not meaningfully participate in the IEP development process.

In *MM ex rel. DM v. School Dist.*, the Fourth Circuit considered whether the Act entitled a student to reimbursement for a procedural violation similar to the one at issue in the case at bar. 303 F.3d [523,] 533–34 [(4th Cir. 2002)]. In that case, the parents opted out of the IEP development process before the IEP team finalized the plan. The parents then sought reimbursement for their at-home program based, in part, on the alleged procedural violation. The Fourth Circuit's analysis focused on two factors. First, the court noted that the IEP development process conducted by the school district allowed for complete participation by the parents. Second, the court observed that there was nothing in the record to indicate that the parents would have accepted any IEP that did not include reimbursement for the at-home instruction. Based on the parents' "lack of cooperation" with the IEP development process, the court concluded that the absence of a finalized IEP did not result in lost educational opportunities for the student.

The Seventh Circuit recently reached a similar result. *See Hjortness ex rel. Hjortness v. Neenah Joint Sch. Dist.*, 507 F.3d 1060, 1065–66 (7th Cir. 2007). In *Hjortness*, the parents and the school district initially worked to develop an IEP. The parents, however, refused to discuss any options other than placing their son as a residential student at a private school. Thus, the school district drafted the IEP without the parents' participation.

The parents then sought reimbursement for the private school expenses by claiming that the school district had violated the Act's procedures because it had not allowed the parents to participate in the IEP development process. The Seventh Circuit flatly rejected the parents' claim because "they chose not to avail themselves" of the opportunity to participate in the development process. *Id.* at 1066. Under those circumstances, the court held that the district did not deny the student a FAPE. *See id.* ("[T]he parents' intransigence to block an IEP that yields a result contrary to the one they seek does not amount to a violation of the procedural requirements of the IDEA.").

MM ex rel. DM and *Hjortness* cast doubt on the Sytsemas' claim that the lack of a final IEP deprived Nicholas of a FAPE. The hearing officer's findings of fact indicate that the Sytsemas unilaterally terminated the IEP development process due to their concerns about the District's plan to place Nicholas in an integrated classroom. The Sytsemas made this decision in spite of the fact that the District had not yet finalized its offer for educational services. While we do not fault the Sytsemas for making a difficult decision regarding which educational resources they believed would best benefit Nicholas, that decision precluded them from meaningfully participating in the complete IEP development process. Thus, we conclude that the lack of a final IEP did not substantively harm Nicholas.

B

Because the district court found a procedural defect with regard to the 2001 IEP, it did not take the next step of determining whether the draft 2001 IEP was substantive[ly] defective in denying Nicholas a FAPE. We think that matter is best addressed by the district court in the first instance. Accordingly, we remand this issue to the district court. However, before doing so, we address one legal matter that pertains to this inquiry which has been adequately presented to us in this appeal to assist the district court in its substantive analysis of the adequacy of the draft 2001 IEP. Specifically, we consider whether the district court should consider only the IEP itself, or whether it should extend its review to the offers made by the District during the August 2, 2001 meeting. The Sytsemas contend that the court must analyze only whether the provisions of the IEP, as written, substantively comply with the Act. The District, on the other hand, asserts that the court should consider both the written IEP as well as the subsequent offers. Based on the Act and the relevant case law, we conclude that the court should consider only the written IEP during its review.

Our consideration of this issue begins with the Act itself. The IDEA specifically defines an IEP as a written document: "The term 'individualized education program' or 'IEP' means a *written statement* for each child with a disability that is developed, reviewed and revised in accordance with this section. . . ." 20 U.S.C. § 1414(d)(1)(A)(i) (emphasis added). This statutory definition is significant in light of the Supreme Court's direction that federal courts must determine whether a school district substantively complied with the Act by focusing on whether "the *individualized educational program* developed through the Act's procedures [is] reasonably calculated to enable the child to receive educational benefits[.]" *Rowley*, 458 U.S. at 207 (emphasis added). Taken together, the statutory definition of an IEP and the Court's command that the courts must focus the inquiry on the draft IEP as written.[7]

_____

[7] [FN 8] The fact that the Sytsemas did not sign the draft 2001 IEP does not affect its status as an

Our sister circuits' careful analysis of this issue supports our conclusion. The Ninth Circuit addressed a similar question in *Union School District v. Smith*, 15 F.3d 1519 (9th Cir. 1994). The school district in that case argued that the court should incorporate, as part of the court's substantive evaluation of the IEP, a placement offer not included in the IEP itself. The placement offer was not included in the IEP because the parents had refused to consider that placement. The court rejected the district's argument and held that it must restrict its analysis to the written document because doing so would eliminate difficult factual disputes about the specifics of an oral offer. *See id.* at 1526 ("We find that this formal requirement has an important purpose that is not merely technical, and we therefore believe it should be enforced rigorously. The requirement of a formal, written offer creates a clear record that will do much to eliminate troublesome factual disputes many years later. . . .").

More recently, the Sixth Circuit agreed with the decision in *Union* and explained, in dicta, that substantive analysis of an IEP should be confined to the written document. *Knable*, 238 F.3d at 768. The parents in *Knable* refused to agree to the district's proposed placement, and thereafter, the district never finalized the draft IEP. In spite of this lack of cooperation from the parents, the court noted that the terms and underlying policies of the IDEA required the school district to provide the parents with a written IEP. Thus, the court held that it would consider only the draft IEP as written to decide whether the district substantively complied with the Act.

Finally, a recent decision from the Fourth Circuit also supports our conclusion. *See A.K. ex rel. J.K. v. Alexandria City Sch. Bd.*, 484 F.3d 672 (4th Cir. 2007). In *A.K. ex rel. J.K.*, the school district offered the parents an IEP that did not specify a placement for the student. The court held that it could not consider placement offers not included in the written IEP because "[e]xpanding the scope of a district's offer to include a comment made during the IEP development process would undermine the important polices served by the requirement of a formal written offer. . . ." *Id.* at 682. One of these policies included assisting the parents' evaluation of the proposed IEP.

Lastly, we take comfort that our conclusion is correct because the facts of the case at bar provide a perfect example of why the court should restrict its analysis to the draft IEP as written. At the August 2001 meeting, the District offered to amend several material aspects of the 2001 IEP in an attempt to resolve the impasse. The offer, however, was plagued by generalities; at best, it presented vague, hypothetical possibilities for settling the dispute between the District and the Sytsemas. In fact, according to the District, the offer provided no greater specificity than an increase in the aggregate number of service hours.

The courts cannot analyze the substance of an IEP based on such a factual record. Instead of embracing the difficult task of determining whether the draft 2001 IEP, as supplemented by the August 2001 offer, complied with the IDEA, we echo the language in *Smith*: "The requirement of a formal, written offer creates a clear record that will do much to eliminate troublesome factual disputes many years

---

IEP. The statutory definition of an IEP does not require a parent's signature. . . .

later about [the specifics of the offer]." 15 F.3d at 1526. Moreover, given our own hesitancy to analyze the substantive deficiencies of an oral offer, we are reluctant to require parents to make a similar judgment regarding a proposed IEP without a final written offer. Therefore, we conclude that when analyzing the substantive compliance of an IEP, the court should restrict our examination to the written document.[8]

IV

We now turn to the 2002 IEP. The Sytsemas do not assert that the 2002 IEP development process violated any of the Act's procedural safeguards, and thus, we focus solely on their claim that the IEP's substantive shortcomings denied Nicholas a FAPE. The Sytsemas contend that the 2002 IEP was substantively deficient because the IEP's sole teaching method was ineffective for Nicholas and because the IEP did not provide Nicholas with generalization skills. We disagree. The Sytsemas' first argument fails because the record indicates that the IEP incorporated several teaching techniques, which in total, would have provided Nicholas with some educational benefit. The Sytsemas' second argument fails because the 2002 IEP provided adequate generalization services for Nicholas to receive some educational benefit. Thus, we affirm the district court's decision to deny the Sytsemas reimbursement because the 2002 IEP provided Nicholas with a FAPE.

The Sytsemas first assert that the 2002 IEP denied Nicholas a FAPE because the IEP relied exclusively on the errorless learning method, which had previously proved ineffective for Nicholas during his at-home tutoring. Errorless learning is a teaching technique often used with autistic children. The basic method teaches children through the use of successful learning experiences. A teacher creates these successful experiences by providing both the correct answer and reinforcement to the child as part of the learning process. Although this method can be enormously helpful for children that frustrate easily and are resistant to demands, it can also hamper the learning progress of more passive children. Thus, in certain circumstances, the exclusive use of the errorless learning technique might deprive a student of a FAPE.

In the case at bar, however, the use of this method did not deprive Nicholas of a FAPE. The record demonstrates that the errorless learning method was one of several methods included in the IEP. In addition to errorless learning, the IEP provided that the District would utilize: (i) discrete trial training; (ii) various "reinforcement strategies"; (iii) "communication temptations"; (iv) "[t]ask analysis of multi step actions"; and (v) "shaping procedures" to achieve the goals set forth in

---

[8] [FN 9] We recognize that with this determination we are splitting with the First Circuit's holding in *C.G. ex rel. A.S. v. Five Town Community School District*, 513 F.3d 279, 286 (1st Cir. 2008). There, the First Circuit held that if parents obstruct an IEP development process, then a reviewing court must be able to consider evidence extrinsic to the written IEP. Although we understand the First Circuit's rationale, we conclude that the statute's language and the policy concerns raised above trump the reasons underlying the totality of the circumstances review the court adopted in *Five Town*. Further, this bright-line rule should not disadvantage a diligent school district because it is always able to tender to recalcitrant parents a final IEP that incorporates any rejected oral offers that it may have extended during the consultative process.

the IEP. Although errorless learning had proved ineffective for Nicholas during his at-home tutoring, nothing in the record suggests that combining this teaching method with several other techniques would render the IEP substantively deficient. The 22.5 hours of instruction per week — which included five hours of one-on-one discrete trial training similar to the methods used in the at-home tutoring — would have provided Nicholas with some educational benefit, and thus, we do not question the District's selected methodologies. Accordingly, the 2002 IEP did not deprive Nicholas of a FAPE in this regard.

The Sytsemas' second argument rests on the 2002 IEP's generalization plans, and proceeds in three parts. First, they argue that the 2002 IEP's inadequate generalization plans — including plans for both parent training and coordination with Nicholas's at-home program-deprived Nicholas of a FAPE. In the instant case, the 2002 IEP explicitly listed "[g]eneralization programs" as one necessary accommodation or modification. Therefore, the Sytsemas' argument can prevail only if they can demonstrate that the lack of specific generalization plans would have limited Nicholas to a de minimis (or less) educational benefit.

The IHO, the ALJ, and the district court all recognized that the Sytsemas had significant experience and knowledge regarding autism and that they were directly involved with Nicholas's education. The IEP also provided for quarterly progress reports, an annual IEP meeting, and a parent-teacher conference once per semester. The combination of the Sytsemas' knowledge and experience with the IEP's provisions to keep the Sytsemas informed and engaged with Nicholas's education demonstrates that the lack of specific generalization plans would not have deprived Nicholas of a FAPE. We thus agree with the ALJ's and the district court's decisions that the lack of a specific reference to parent training and coordination with Nicholas's at-home program did not deny Nicholas a FAPE.

Second, the Sytsemas assert that *Luke P.* supports their argument. In that case, the parents of an autistic student sought reimbursement for placing their son in a residential school. *See Thompson R2-J Sch. Dist. v. Luke P.*, No. 05-cv-2248, 2007 U.S. Dist. LEXIS 47043 (D. Colo. June 28, 2007). The student faced significant generalization problems and was completely unable to apply the lessons he learned at school in any other environment. The student's significant generalization difficulties prevented him from gleaning any on-going benefit from his education, and thus, the district court concluded that the school district denied the student a FAPE.

Luke P. is inapposite to the instant case. Nothing in the record intimates that Nicholas faces generalization problems of the same magnitude and character as the student in *Luke P.* Accordingly, *Luke P.* does not persuade us that the lack of a specific reference to parent training and coordination in the 2002 IEP denied Nicholas a FAPE.

The Sytsemas' final generalization argument is similarly unconvincing. Beginning in 2002, the District employed the Denver Model for educating autistic students. The Sytsemas contend that the 2002 IEP did not address the model's requirement that each education plan coordinate between a student's activities at school and home, and therefore denied Nicholas a FAPE. Ultimately, this argument raises the same issue we considered above — whether the IEP's lack of a specific reference to coordination plans limited Nicholas to a de minimis educational benefit — but does not present us with persuasive grounds to reach the opposite conclusion. Admirably, the Sytsemas have exhibited a great degree of knowledge and involvement with their son's education. This involvement would have augmented Nicholas's educational experience and makes clear that he would have received some educational benefit if he had enrolled with the district. Accordingly, the district court correctly determined that the Sytsemas were not entitled to reimbursement for their expenses for the 2002-2003 academic year.

CONCLUSION

We REVERSE the district court's reimbursement of expenses to the Sytsemas based on the procedural failure of the school district to deliver a final IEP for 2001-02. We REMAND for the district court to consider whether the draft IEP, as written, for 2001-02 provides Nicholas with a FAPE. We AFFIRM the district's denial of reimbursement expenses to the Sytsemas for the 2002-03 academic year.

SYTSEMA v. ACADEMY SCHOOL DISTRICT NO. 20
No. 03-cv-2582-RPM, RPM, 2009 U.S. Dist. LEXIS 105978 (D. Colo. Oct. 30, 2009)

The District Court found on remand that the written IEP proposed by the school for 2001-02 did not provide meaningful benefit to the student.

RICHARD P. MATSCH, SENIOR DISTRICT JUDGE.

Plaintiffs Jack and Rebecca Systema brought this suit on behalf of their minor son Nicholas Sytsema, claiming that the Individualized Education Plans ("IEP") developed for Nicholas by Academy School District No. 20 for the 2001-02 and 2002-03 academic years denied Nicholas his right to a free appropriate public education ("FAPE") under the Individuals with Disabilities Education Act, 20 U.S.C. § 1400 *et seq.* ("IDEA"). In the memorandum opinion and order dated June 7, 2006, this court concluded that the written IEP proposed by the District for the 2001-02 academic year was procedurally defective and awarded the Plaintiffs $38,503.45 as reimbursement for the cost of the private education they provided for Nicholas during that school year. The court denied the Plaintiffs' claim for reimbursement of their expenses for the 2002-03 academic year, concluding that the IEP developed by the District for that year would have provided Nicholas with a FAPE. Both parties appealed the judgment. The United States Court of Appeals for the Tenth Circuit reversed the judgment as to the 2001-02 academic year and affirmed as to the 2002-03 academic year. *Sytsema ex rel. Sytsema v. Academy School District No. 20*, 538 F.3d 1306 (10th Cir. 2008). The Tenth Circuit remanded with directions to determine whether the 2001-02 IEP complied with the IDEA's substantive requirements, based solely on the written document.

The sole issue to be determined is whether the services described in the written 2001-02 IEP were reasonably calculated to enable Nicholas to receive some educational benefit. *See Board of Education v. Rowley*, 458 U.S. 176 (1982). "The IEP complies with IDEA's substantive standards if it provides the disabled student with '[a] basic floor of opportunity' . . . [that] consists of access to specialized instruction and related services which are individually designed to provide educational benefit. . . ." *Sytsema*, 538 F.3d at 1313 (quoting *Rowley*, 458 U.S. at 201). In its opinion in this case, the Tenth Circuit Court of Appeals explained:

> This court has interpreted the *Rowley* standard to require an educational benefit that is more than *de minimis*. . . . We have also recognized, however, that the Act focuses on providing disabled children access to public schools, and thus, does not require an education "guaranteed to maximize the child's potential." . . . As a result, we apply the "some benefit" standard the Supreme Court adopted in *Rowley*.

The Sytsemas contend that the IDEA requires the school district to provide a "meaningful benefit" whereby the disabled student achieves "significant learning." The Tenth Circuit has addressed that argument, noting:

> Admittedly, it is difficult to distinguish between the requirements of the "some benefit" and the "meaningful benefit" standards. We have applied the "some benefit" standard, and thus evaluate the case at bar with that standard in mind.

The role of the District Court in an action under the IDEA is as follows:

> Pursuant to the statute, a district court must independently review the administrative record and apply a preponderance of the evidence standard to decide if the requirements of the IDEA have been met. . . . During its review of the administrative record, the district court must "give "due weight" to the hearing officer's findings of fact, which are considered *prima facie* correct.

This standard has been described as a "modified de novo" review. *See Murray ex rel. Murray v. Montrose County Sch. Dist. RE-1J*, 51 F.3d 921, 927 (10th Cir.1995).

There have been two administrative hearings in this action, the first conducted by an Impartial Hearing Officer ("IHO") and the second by an Administrative Law Judge ("ALJ"). The IHO and the ALJ did not make any findings as to the educational benefit to be provided by the draft IEP because they considered the IEP to include services that the District offered orally during meetings with the Sytsemas in May and August, 2001. The IHO concluded that the 2001-02 IEP, as modified orally, was appropriately designed to meet Nicholas's needs and was therefore reasonably calculated to confer a meaningful benefit on Nicholas. The ALJ affirmed the IHO's opinion, finding that the District's oral offers were not vague and the Systemas had rejected those offers because the Sytsemas were unwilling to consider any program for Nicholas other than in-home services. Under the statutory structure it would be appropriate to remand this case for another administrative hearing with the findings to be reviewed under the modified de novo standard.

On February 12, 2009, the Sytsemas moved for entry of judgment, arguing that the adequacy of the 2001-02 IEP should be decided by this court without remand to the state administrative process and without consideration of any additional evidence. The District responded with a request to present additional evidence in support of the written draft IEP.

At a hearing held on April 2, 2009, the parties agreed that because of the long delay the adequacy of the IEP should be determined by this court, without further administrative proceedings. The court permitted the submission of additional evidence by affidavits.

It is the Sytsemas' burden to show that the services described in the IEP would not have provided Nicholas with a FAPE. *See Schaffer ex rel. Schaffer v. Weast*, 546 U.S. 49 (2005) (holding that the party challenging an IEP in a due process hearing bears the burden of proof). The preponderance of the evidence supports their claim. The services described in the written 2001-02 IEP were not appropriate for Nicholas's individual educational needs.

An IEP must contain, in relevant part:

> (I) a statement of the child's present levels of academic achievement and functional performance, including —
>
> . . .
>
>> (bb) for preschool children, as appropriate, how the disability affects the child's participation in appropriate activities; . . .
>
> (II) a statement of measurable annual goals, including academic and functional goals . . . ;
>
> (III) a description of how the child's progress toward meeting the annual goals described in subclause (II) will be measured and when periodic reports on the progress the child is making toward meeting the annual goals . . . will be provided;
>
> (IV) a statement of the special education and related services and supplementary aids and services, based on peer-reviewed research to the extent practicable, to be provided to the child, or on behalf of the child, and a statement of the program modifications or supports for school personnel that will be provided for the child . . . ;
>
> (V) an explanation of the extent, if any, to which the child will not participate with nondisabled children in the regular class . . . ;
>
> . . .
>
> (VII) the projected date for the beginning of the services and modifications described in subclause (IV), and the anticipated frequency, location, and duration of those services and modifications. . . .

20 U.S.C. § 1414(d)(1)(A).

The IEP for the 2001-02 school year is dated May 11, 2001. Nicholas was approximately 34 months old when the IEP was prepared. The evaluation data were taken from a play-based observation of Nicholas conducted by District representatives on May 4, 2001, information from a parent interview and information from Resources for Young Children and Families ("RYCF"). Nicholas was determined to have a disability and to be eligible for special education services. The IEP states that Nicholas had been diagnosed with autism. Developmental delays were identified, particularly in the areas of communication and socialization. Areas of concern were "decreased eye contact, decreased attention to task, decreased receptive/ expressive language skills and decreased functional communication." The IEP stated that Nicholas did not follow instructions and expressed himself using sounds and gestures and occasional random words. The accuracy of the evaluation data is not in dispute.

The written IEP includes a statement of goals. The overall goals included development of appropriate classroom behaviors, improvement of functional communication skills, and improvement of self-help skills. Under each of those categories, the IEP listed short-term instructional objectives and benchmarks. Under the heading "Early Childhood Transition Plan," the IEP identified improved communication and socialization skills as the transition priorities and listed activities to address Nicholas's identified language problems and for improving his motor skills and social interactions. The statement of goals and objectives in the IEP is not a subject of dispute. The dispute between the Sytsemas and the District arose out of disagreement about the appropriate educational setting for Nicholas and whether the District's methods of instruction were adequate for him.

The written IEP stated, "Nicholas will attend an integrated preschool setting with support from Speech/Language. Occupational Therapy will provide consultation on an as-needed basis." An integrated preschool classroom includes disabled and non-disabled students, taught by a special education teacher, assisted by special education para-professionals. The IEP designated 10.75 hours of services per week, with 9.5 hours provided solely by the classroom teacher and para-professionals and 1.25 hours provided by those persons with support from a speech and language specialist. Ten hours (including one hour of speech and language services) were identified as "direct" services and.75 of an hour (including.25 of speech and language) correlated to "indirect" services. Deb Montgomery, the District's Director of Special Education during the relevant time period, testified that direct services are services provided during interaction with the student and indirect services are services that do not involve student interaction, such as consultations among the special education teacher, the speech and language pathologist and the autism specialist. In sum, the written IEP proposed that Nicholas would receive ten hours of instruction in a classroom setting, including one hour of speech and language services. The IEP did not require any individual instruction outside the integrated classroom.

During the administrative proceedings, the Sytsemas' primary claim was that the District violated the IDEA by refusing to fund Nicholas's in-home education, which in May 2001 consisted of one-on-one instruction using techniques known as Applied Behavior Analysis ("ABA").[9] The Systemas argued that the 2001-02 IEP was deficient in the following ways: (1) the services described in the IEP did not utilize

---

[9] [FN 1] ABA is an instructional method that emphasizes one-on-one instruction and behavioral modification techniques to reinforce desired behavior. *See* Ex. 19 (summarizing methods of instruction recognized by experts in the field of autism) and Ex. J-1, National Research Council, EDUCATING CHILDREN WITH AUTISM, 148–49 (National Academy Press 2001).

proven methodology; (2) the IEP did not contain sufficient service hours; (3) the IEP did not include necessary services, such as a personal aide, home instruction, and family training and counseling; (4) the proposed preschool setting was not appropriate for Nicholas, and (5) the District staff charged with implementing the services did not have sufficient training or experience to address Nicholas's needs. The Plaintiffs' motion for judgment, dated February 12, 2009, narrows the focus of their challenge. The Sytsemas now argue that the IEP was inadequate because it did not provide enough hours of instruction or any one-on-one instruction outside the classroom.

The number of classroom hours proposed in the written IEP (10 hours per week) represented a significant reduction from the level of instruction (16 1/2 hours per week) that Nicholas was receiving in May 2001. Montgomery testified that the ten hours shown on the IEP was based on information the District had received from RYCF, which showed that Nicholas was receiving 10 hours per week of in-home ABA therapy. The RYCF intake form (Exhibit 1) reflects that Nicholas was receiving 10 hours of in-home ABA instruction in February 2001, but that number had increased by May 2001. In May 2001, Nicholas was receiving 16 1/2 hours of one-on-one instruction each week. RYCF provided funding for most of that instruction because Nicholas qualified for services under Part C of the IDEA until his third birthday in July 2001.

The failure to provide any one-on-one services in the IEP and the small number of instructional hours show that the District did not give adequate consideration to Nicholas's individual needs in preparing the IEP. Nicholas was making progress with one-on-one instruction. The change to an integrated classroom setting was a drastic move which required some transitional services to assist him in adjusting to a new environment.

At the hearing before the IHO, the District did not offer any evidence or elicit any testimony regarding the appropriateness of the services described in the written IEP. The District characterized the written IEP as a draft and represented that those services "were never on the table or at issue in this case." Montgomery testified that the written document "was just kind of a starting point." Montgomery testified that at the first meeting with the Sytsemas in May 2001, the District recognized the need to increase the hours of instruction and include some one-to-one services. This evidence shows that the District acknowledged that the services described in the written IEP were not adequate to meet Nicholas's needs.

Even now the District cannot clearly describe the services proposed in the written IEP. . . .

Montgomery states in her affidavit that "the services proposed in Nicholas's IEP were reasonably calculated to enable Nicholas to make some progress towards the goals and objectives contained in his IEP. The services offered would have provided much more than a de minimis educational benefit to Nicholas." That opinion is based on Montgomery's current description of the preschool setting as one that would have provided Nicholas with significant individual attention. Montgomery states in her affidavit, "During the entire time [Nicholas] was in school, either an early childhood special education teacher, a para-professional, or a speech language provider would be directly working with Nicholas. Some of this time would be spent doing ABA one-on-one training." The written IEP does not support those statements. There is no indication in the written IEP that the classroom instruction or the language services identified in that document would have provided Nicholas with ABA training or constant one-on-one attention. There is no provision in the IEP for an individual aide or teacher for Nicholas.

In response to the (school's) affidavits, the Sytsemas submitted the affidavit of Diane Osaki. Osaki is a licensed occupational therapist with expertise in autism. . . . Osaki's affidavit states the opinion she would have provided if she had been allowed to answer counsel's question about the written IEP. Osaki opines that the special education services proposed in the written 2001-02 IEP were not appropriate for Nicholas's individual needs. Osaki states, "The lack of 1:1 systematic instruction leads me to conclude that Nicholas would have likely made little to no progress towards most, if not all, of the goals and objectives set forth in the written IEP."

Osaki's opinion carries more weight. . . . During the 2001-02 school year, Osaki worked for JFK Partners and assisted the District with its effort to implement an educational program for children with autism based on the Denver Model. During the administrative proceedings in this action, the District presented Osaki as an expert in education programs for autistic children. The opinion that Osaki expresses in her affidavit is consistent with her testimony about the components of an effective preschool education program for autistic children. Osaki testified that one-on-one instruction is critical for children with autism, in addition to instruction in group situations.

The testimony of the Plaintiffs' expert, Dr. Susan Hepburn, supports the conclusion that the 2001-02 IEP was not appropriate for Nicholas. Dr. Hepburn testified that in June 2001, Nicholas still needed a large component of one-on-one instruction. In a letter dated June 8, 2001, Dr. Hepburn stated that Nicholas lacked the skills to respond to group instruction and needed one-on-one instruction to benefit from instruction in a group setting. That assessment, although dated a month after the District's evaluation of Nicholas, is consistent with information that was available to the District when it prepared the written IEP.

Under the IDEA, children with disabilities are to be educated with children who are not disabled, to the maximum extent appropriate. 20 U.S.C. § 1412(5). The term "least restrictive environment" embodies that policy. "Least restrictive environment" means:

> programs used to educate a child with a disability using the delivery system most appropriately meeting the needs of the child. To the maximum extent appropriate, as determined by the child's IEP team, subject to the appeals procedures outlined in section 22-20-108(3), the term means an environment in which a child with a disability is educated with children without disabilities, unless the nature or severity of the disability is such that education in general education classes with the use of supplementary aids and services cannot be achieved satisfactorily, or, when provided with supplementary aids and services, the nature or severity of the disability is so disruptive that the education of other children in such classes would be significantly impaired.

C.R.S. § 22-20-103(18). In accordance with this definition, the services or combination of services set forth in an IEP must appropriately meet the needs of the disabled child. The goal of educating the disabled child alongside children who are not disabled does not allow a school district to shortchange the individual needs of the disabled child.

The written 2001-02 IEP did not provide Nicholas a FAPE. The preponderance of the evidence shows that for the 2001-02 school year, Nicholas needed one-on-one instruction for him to obtain more than a de minimis benefit from group participation in a preschool classroom.

Exhibit P summarizes the expenses the Sytsemas incurred from July 14, 2001 through July 13, 2002, for the services of two therapists and two consulting groups. The Plaintiffs are entitled to recover the amounts set forth in Exhibit P that relate to the 2001-02 academic year.

In any action or proceeding brought under 20 U.S.C. § 1415, "the court, in its discretion, may award reasonable attorneys' fees as part of the costs to a prevailing party who is the parent of a child with a disability." 20 U.S.C. § 1415(i)(3)(B)(i)(I). The Plaintiffs are the prevailing party with respect to their request for reimbursement for educational expenses for the 2001-02 school year.

Upon the foregoing, it is

ORDERED, judgment will enter for the Plaintiffs in the amount of $ 38,503.45 to reimburse them for their costs and expenses for the education of Nicholas Sytsema during the 2001-02 school year, and it is

FURTHER ORDERED that the Plaintiffs shall recover their costs upon the filing of a bill of costs within 10 days after the entry of judgment. The Plaintiffs shall submit their request for attorneys' fees for this claim. . . .

NOTES AND QUESTIONS

1.   As the court of appeals indicates, courts frequently fault parents for failing to cooperate fully with the IEP process. Does it make sense to consider outside evidence of the school district's position when the parents have not pursued the IEP process to completion? What are the reasons that parents might stop cooperating with the school district? Do you agree with the court of appeals regarding generalization in the 2002-03 school year?

2.   The final decision in the case seems almost accidental; could the decision just as easily have gone the other way if the school had put some of its oral positions in writing? Once the Tenth Circuit determined that the adequacy of the plan depended on what was written, the school's statement that the IEP as written "was just kind of a starting point" presaged the result. What does this say about the focus (or not) on the needs of the student and the purpose of IDEA?

3.   The award to the parents of $38,503 plus attorneys fees was a significant amount, but they had been engaged in the controversy for several years by the time this decision was reached. Prior to the 2006 litigation, they had been involved in the administrative hearing process, first before an Impartial Hearing Officer and then

before an Administrative Law Judge, both of whom concluded for the school that the IEP, as modified orally, was reasonably calculated to confer a meaningful benefit on Nicholas. The appeal to the District Court in 2006 reached a mixed result with the parents prevailing regarding 2001-02 and the school district regarding 2002-03, *Sytsema v. Acad. Sch. Dist. No. 20*, No. 03-cv-02582-RPM, 2006 U.S. Dist. LEXIS 98192 (D. Colo. June 7, 2006).

4.   This sequence offers a good view of the kinds of issues and process that parents of a young child with autism are likely to face as they try to make decisions for their child, with or without school district support, or perhaps without knowing if the school district's actions are supportive. Was there a better way here?'

5.   The message of the significance of what is written versus what is orally offered or discussed is a clear one. Why do you think the case played out as it did in practice?

2.   Content and Implementation of the IEP

HOUSTON INDEPENDENT SCHOOL DISTRICT v. V.P.
582 F.3d 576 (5th Cir. 2009)

The Fifth Circuit upheld the parents' placement of their child in a private school when the IEPs prepared by a public school district failed to satisfy the meaningful educational benefit requirement under FAPE.

Leslie H. Southwick, Circuit Judge:

. . . .

The Houston Independent School District (HISD) initiated the present action in the district court as an appeal of an administrative decision that HISD had denied a child a free appropriate public education. The relevant statute is the Individuals with Disabilities Education Act (IDEA), 20 U.S.C. § 1400, et seq. Reimbursement for a year of private school placement was awarded. The district court affirmed the decision. The court denied reimbursement for the private school placement during a second school year that occurred during the pendency of the proceedings. Both parties were aggrieved and appeal. We AFFIRM as to the reimbursement for the first school year, REVERSE and RENDER as to the second year, and REMAND for further proceedings as to attorney's fees.

I. FACTUAL AND PROCEDURAL BACKGROUND

The child whose needs are at the center of this dispute is referred to as V.P. to protect her privacy. At the time of the administrative hearing, V.P. was an eight-year-old student within the jurisdictional boundaries of HISD. V.P. qualified as a child with a disability entitled to receive special education services under the IDEA due to her auditory and speech impairments. HISD first identified V.P. as a child eligible for special education when she was four years old.

Accordingly, HISD placed V.P. in the Preschool Program for Children with

Disabilities at Garden Oaks Elementary. It developed an individualized education plan (IEP) to address her language delays. After three weeks at Garden Oaks, V.P.'s mother obtained a transfer for her daughter to Wainwright Elementary School, where V.P.'s mother was employed. V.P. remained in a regular education, pre-kindergarten classroom at Wainwright Elementary for the remainder of the 2001-2002 school year.

A. 2002-2003 School Year

In 2002, V.P. began kindergarten in a regular education classroom at Wainwright. In October 2002, an Admission, Review, and Dismissal Committee ("IEP Committee" or "Committee") met to develop an IEP for V.P.'s kindergarten year. The IEP Committee continued the identification of V.P. as a child with a speech impairment and approved two hours per week of speech therapy, along with classroom modifications. In the spring of 2003, V.P.'s parents obtained hearing aids for V.P., including a pair of loaner hearing aids in February 2003 and her own custom aids in May 2003.

In May 2003, V.P.'s IEP Committee met to evaluate V.P.'s progress under her current IEP and to prepare for the next school year. The Committee considered whether V.P. had a hearing impairment that would qualify her for special education services as a student with an auditory impairment. Finding that she did, it developed an IEP for audiological management for the 2003-2004 school year recommending that V.P. remain in a regular education classroom with modifications and teaching strategies designed to accommodate her hearing impairment. The Committee continued V.P.'s identification as a child with a speech impairment and continued two hours of speech therapy per week. Additionally, in May 2003, V.P. was provided with an FM loop system in her classroom for the last week of her kindergarten year.

B. 2003-2004 School Year

In October 2003, which was six weeks into V.P.'s first-grade year, her IEP Committee was convened to review her IEP in light of concerns expressed by V.P.'s mother and also by her classroom teacher, Ms. Williams, regarding V.P.'s academic performance and progress and whether a more restrictive educational placement was needed. The Committee continued V.P.'s identification as a child with auditory and speech impairments. The Committee further determined that V.P. should remain in a regular education classroom, but it approved the implementation of additional special education services and modifications within the regular education setting, including in-class support, frequent breaks, content mastery, and speech therapy. In addition to other recommendations, it requested additional testing, including a new audiological evaluation, new achievement testing, and an observation by an auditory impairment specialist.

The IEP Committee met again in January 2004 to discuss V.P.'s progress and the results of the additional testing. The Committee continued V.P.'s classification as a child with auditory and speech impairments. She would remain in the regular education classroom. The Committee continued V.P.'s placement in two hours of speech therapy per week and approved additional classroom modifications, including amplification, visual cues, having the teacher try to face V.P., preferential classroom seating, and questioning to check understanding. The Committee also developed an IEP to address V.P.'s language and listening skills. Under this IEP, an itinerant teacher for the auditory-impaired was to work with V.P. for one hour per week. Additionally, the Committee incorporated Earobics computer software as a special education service to address V.P.'s auditory-processing weakness. The Committee requested a new speech and language assessment.

In May 2004, V.P.'s IEP Committee met to evaluate V.P.'s progress and consider her placement for V.P.'s second-grade year, starting that fall. The Committee continued V.P.'s identification as a child with auditory and speech impairments. It then developed an IEP for the remainder of the 2003-2004 school year and the full 2004-2005 school year. For 2004-2005, which was V.P.'s second-grade year, the Committee recommended that V.P. remain in a regular education classroom with special education and related services similar to those provided during the prior school year, including two hours per week of speech therapy, one hour per week with the itinerant teacher for the auditory-impaired, amplification, visual cues, teacher facing student, preferential classroom seating, and questioning to test understanding. V.P.'s mother disagreed with the proposed IEP for 2004-2005 and indicated that she wished to withdraw V.P. from HISD and place her in a private institution. The Committee held a "recess meeting" in an effort to resolve the situation, but V.P.'s parents ultimately decided to withdraw V.P. one week before the end of the 2003-2004 school year.

C. 2004-2005 School Year

In September 2004, V.P.'s parents enrolled V.P. in a kindergarten/first-grade class at the Parish School, a private school for children with language-learning disabilities. At the Parish School, V.P. was in a small classroom with ten students, a teacher, and an assistant teacher. Through the Parish School, V.P. also worked with the Carruth Center, which provided language services to Parish School students. V.P. received ten hours of group speech/language therapy per week. Speech pathologists provided therapy addressing V.P.'s receptive and expressive language skills. V.P. also received phonemic awareness training, auditory memory training, and gap-detection training through the Fast ForWord computer program. Additionally, the Parish School attempted to minimize V.P.'s exposure to ambient noise whenever possible in an effort to promote noise desensitization. V.P.'s Parish School curriculum also included sequencing exercises to improve her auditory-processing skills.

In addition to the 2004-2005 school year, V.P. remained at the Parish School for the 2005-2006 school year during the district court's review of the hearing officer's decision. No issues regarding later years are raised.

D. Procedural History

In August 2004, V.P.'s parents requested a special education due process hearing before the Texas Education Agency to address whether HISD failed to provide V.P. with a free appropriate public education, failed to develop or implement IEPs reasonably calculated to provide V.P. with educational benefit, and failed to consider an appropriate placement for V.P. The Texas Education Agency hearing officer held a due process hearing in December 2004 and issued a decision in February 2005. The hearing officer concluded that V.P. has extensive language development and auditory-processing problems stemming from sensory hearing loss and an auditory-processing disorder. The hearing officer found that V.P. requires auditory training, memory training, phonemic awareness training, noise desensitization, sequencing ability training, gap-detection training, onset-time training, visual instruction, and an FM loop system to meet her educational needs. The hearing officer concluded that HISD failed to include many of these necessary services in V.P.'s IEPs, including noise desensitization training, gap-detection training, and sequencing training. Ultimately, the hearing officer determined that HISD did not provide V.P. with a free appropriate public education and that the Parish School was an appropriate placement for V.P. Accordingly, the hearing officer awarded V.P.'s parents reimbursement for V.P.'s 2004-2005 placement at the Parish School.

In May 2005, HISD appealed the hearing officer's decision to the district court. V.P. filed an answer and counterclaim in June 2005, appealing the hearing officer's decisions on the issues for which she did not prevail at the due process hearing. . . .

In March 2007, the district court granted partial summary judgment in V.P.'s favor. The court affirmed the hearing officer's determination that HISD failed to provide V.P. with a free appropriate public education, failed to develop educationally beneficial IEPs, and failed to consider an appropriate placement for V.P. It further affirmed the hearing officer's decision that V.P. is entitled to reimbursement for the 2004-2005 Parish School placement. With respect to the 2005-2006 Parish School costs, the court refrained from addressing that issue because V.P. had not moved for summary judgment on it.

The court then requested additional record development regarding the appropriate amount of reimbursement to be awarded. The parties stipulated that $16,125.30 was the proper reimbursement for the 2004-2005 school year and the amount would also be appropriate should reimbursement for the 2005-2006 placement be awarded. After the filing of cross motions for summary judgment, the Court denied reimbursement for the 2005-2006 school year.

V.P. now appeals, arguing that the district court erred in failing to award reimbursement for V.P.'s 2005-2006 Parish School placement and the attorney's fees and costs expended in seeking such reimbursement. HISD has filed a cross-appeal alleging that the district court erred in concluding that it failed to provide V.P. with a free appropriate public education.

II. DISCUSSION

A. Free Appropriate Public Education

. . . .

When a parent challenges the appropriateness of an IEP, a reviewing court's inquiry is twofold. The court must first ask whether the state has complied with the procedural requirements of the IDEA, and then determine whether the IEP developed through such procedures was "reasonably calculated to enable the child to receive educational benefits." *Board of Educ. of Hendrick Hudson Central School Dist v. Rowley*, 458 U.S. 176, 206–07 (1982). If the court finds that the state has not provided an appropriate educational placement, the court may require the school district to reimburse the child's parents for the costs of sending the child to an appropriate private school or institution. *Town of Burlington, Mass. v. Dep't of Educ. of Mass.*, 471 U.S. 359, 369–70 (1985); *[Cypress-Fairbanks Indep. Sch. Dist. v.] Michael F.*, 118 F.3d [245] at 248 [(1997)]. Reimbursement may be ordered only if it is shown "that (1) an IEP calling for placement in a public school was inappropriate under the IDEA, and (2) the private school placement . . . was proper under the Act." *Cypress-Fairbanks Indep. Sch. Dist. v. Michael F.*, 118 F.3d 245, 247 (5th Cir.1997) (citations omitted).

HISD argues that the district court erred in concluding that it failed to provide V.P. with a free appropriate public education. Despite V.P.'s disabilities, HISD asserts she was receiving a meaningful educational benefit, including earning a promotion from first to second grade under the same standards that apply to non-disabled first graders. HISD further contends that the IDEA does not require it to provide V.P. with an education designed to remediate her disability or to ensure optimal performance, and it maintains that the district court erred in concluding that it should have implemented every aspect of the program recommended by V.P.'s expert witness.

We have set out four factors that serve as "indicators of whether an IEP is reasonably calculated to provide a meaningful educational benefit under the IDEA," and these factors are whether "(1) the program is individualized on the basis of the student's assessment and performance; (2) the program is administered in the least restrictive environment; (3) the services are provided in a coordinated and collaborative manner by the key 'stakeholders'; and (4) positive academic and non-academic benefits are demonstrated." *Id.* at 253; *see also Adam J. ex rel. Robert J. v. Keller Indep. Sch. Dist.*, 328 F.3d 804, 810 (5th Cir.2003). Both the hearing officer and the district court found that all of these considerations militated in favor of finding that HISD failed to provide V.P. with a free appropriate public education. We will deferentially review the district court's fact findings with respect to each of these factors. We will also give de novo consideration to any legal issues that arise under each.

1. Individualized program on the basis of V.P.'s assessment and performance

The district court found that V.P.'s IEPs were not sufficiently individualized to her needs. The court pointed to these deficiencies: as of May 2004, more than a year after V.P.'s IEP Committee recommended an audiological evaluation, the evaluation still had not been completed; V.P.'s IEPs were not specific enough with regard to V.P.'s auditory-processing or audiological deficiencies because they lacked strategies to assist with sequencing, gap detection, and noise desensitization; although the Committee recognized that V.P.'s most significant problems were speech and language deficiencies due to hearing loss, it did not integrate special education sessions with a teacher for hearing-impaired students until January 2004; and the

Committee did not address problems that developed with V.P.'s FM loop system in September 2003.

HISD argues that each of the bases for the district court's finding are erroneous. Initially, it asserts that a school district is not required to furnish every special service necessary to maximize a child's potential. Consequently, HISD's failure to provide V.P. with sequencing training, gap detection, and noise desensitization did not render V.P.'s IEP inadequate. Instead, HISD maintains that these services were programs suggested by V.P.'s expert witness to remediate V.P.'s speech and auditory-processing disorder, and the fact that HISD failed to provide these services does not mean that V.P.'s needs were not being addressed. HISD further maintains that it should not be penalized for failing to include an explanation concerning the problems with V.P.'s FM loop system in the IEP Committee minutes. HISD points out that the problem was caught and corrected, and there is no requirement that the Committee's notes include all issues that arise on a day-to-day basis.

V.P.'s IEP included several accommodations and modifications to address her general speech and auditory impairments, such as limited speech therapy (two hours per week), visual cues, preferential classroom seating, questioning to check understanding, an FM loop system, content mastery classes, and limited instruction by an itinerant teacher for the auditory impaired (one hour per week). However, these services failed adequately to address V.P.'s distinct auditory-processing disorder.

V.P.'s expert witness, Dr. Ray Battin, a neuropsychologist and audiologist, testified that he performed an advanced audiological evaluation on V.P. in October 2004. Battin's evaluation revealed that V.P. has moderate to severe sensory hearing loss and severe auditory-processing problems. To address these problems, Battin explained that V.P. requires noise desensitization, sequencing training, and gap-detection work and that V.P.'s May 2004 IEP did not address those needs. Battin noted that although the May 2004 IEP was good for V.P.'s expressive language delay problems, it was inappropriate to address her auditory-processing disorder. In fact, Battin testified that V.P. needed a separate IEP for her auditory-processing disorder.

In light of Battin's testimony, we find no clear error with the district court's finding that noise desensitization, sequencing training, and gap-detection work were necessary to address V.P.'s specific auditory-processing problems. Further, there was evidence to support that they were not offered merely as a means of maximizing her potential or making her more competitive with the other members of her class. Based on the valid fact-finding concerning what was necessary to address her auditory needs, and applying our de novo review, we accept that her IEP was insufficiently individualized.

2. Program administered in the least restrictive environment

The IDEA requires that children with a disability be provided a free appropriate public education in the least restrictive environment:

To the maximum extent appropriate, children with disabilities . . . [should be] educated with children who are not disabled, and special classes, separate schooling, or other removal of children with disabilities from the regular educational environment [should occur] only when the nature or severity of the disability of a child is such that education in regular classes with the use of supplementary aids and services cannot be achieved satisfactorily.

20 U.S.C. § 1412(a)(5)(A).

The district court concluded that V.P.'s IEP did not provide her with sufficient supplementary services to be successful in the general education classroom. In reaching this conclusion, the court explained that it was not concerned with whether V.P. was mainstreamed to the maximum extent possible; instead, it was addressing whether V.P. was mainstreamed beyond her capabilities. The court noted several deficiencies in V.P.'s ability to benefit satisfactorily from her education in the regular classroom, including her failure to attend content mastery training after the fall of 2003. There was evidence that although V.P. paid attention to the teacher's portion of a lesson, she was unable to participate in the group portion of a lesson. Further, she could remain focused on her assignment only for short periods of time without redirection. The court also explained that V.P.'s FM system did not allow her the benefit of class discussion.

There is no record evidence that the proposed solution to this problem (having the teacher pass the microphone around the class during discussion) was ever implemented. The court also noted that when the loop component of the system was unavailable, V.P.'s use of headphones further limited her ability to hear her classmates and participate in class discussions. Finally, the court pointed out that after V.P. lost her hearing aids on the playground, she regularly took them off before going out for recess. Nothing in the record suggests that the IEP Committee attempted to address this problem with V.P. or her parents. Thus, V.P. was restricted in her ability to communicate and socialize with other students during recess.

Without conceding the point, HISD maintains that even if the district court was correct in finding V.P.'s placement improper, the appropriate remedy would be to require the school to provide additional supplementary aids and services in the general education environment or to allow V.P. to attend a combination of regular and special education classes. Additionally, HISD contends that because of the nature of V.P.'s disability, exposure to the language models of non-disabled peers is important to V.P.'s progress.

V.P.'s regular education placement was certainly a less restrictive environment than her Parish School placement. However, the IDEA mandates that a child be placed in the least restrictive environment in which the child can achieve an appropriate education. *See* 20 U.S.C. § 1412(a)(5)(A). The IDEA's strong preference in favor of mainstreaming must "be weighed in tandem with the Act's principal goal of ensuring that the public schools provide [disabled] children with a free appropriate public education." *Daniel R.R. v. State Bd. of Educ.*, 874 F.2d 1036, 1044–45, 1048 (5th Cir.1989) (internal quotation marks and citation omitted).

Though HISD tried to accommodate V.P. in a regular education classroom, the district court concluded that V.P. was not receiving a meaningful educational benefit from such placement. Although exposure to the language models of V.P.'s non-disabled peers is important, V.P.'s interaction with her peers within the regular education classroom was significantly limited. Under the FM loop system, only V.P.'s teacher wore a microphone. Accordingly, V.P. was not receiving amplification of her peers during class and group discussions. Additionally, because V.P. removed her hearing aids during recess, she was not able to interact effectively with her peers during a significant portion of her time outside of class. The district court's fact-finding regarding the difficulties that arose due to her placement in the general classroom, including that there were insufficient supplemental services, is not clearly erroneous. Applying a de novo review, we agree that V.P.'s IEP failed to provide her with the least restrictive environment appropriate to her condition.

3. Coordinated and collaborative services provided by key stakeholders

The district court concluded that the services HISD provided V.P. were not coordinated and collaborative. The court explained that although V.P.'s IEP Committee meetings were well attended and generally included the key stakeholders, the participants failed to communicate and collaborate outside of the meetings. For example, the special education chair never discussed V.P.'s progress with her classroom teacher outside of the meetings, and V.P.'s classroom teacher never discussed V.P.'s progress with V.P.'s writing teacher or other school staff outside of the Committee meetings. Furthermore, when V.P.'s classroom teacher missed a meeting in January 2004, the record does not reflect that anyone informed her of the modifications made in that meeting, even though their implementation required the teacher's involvement. Additionally, the special education chair instructed V.P.'s classroom teacher to modify V.P.'s regular tests and assignments, but no such modifications were adopted by the Committee.

The district court also noted that the HISD staff "struggled with training and followup." The court concluded that the one-page flyer provided to train school staff on working with hearing-impaired students was inadequate. Furthermore, the school nurse who was assigned to maintain V.P.'s FM system received little training and provided little training to the other staff members. The nurse did not attend the IEP Committee meetings and did not adequately communicate with others to repair V.P.'s FM loop system in a timely fashion. Finally, school staff did not follow up on V.P.'s failure to attend content mastery for more than two months or on an October 2003 Committee plan to try proposed modifications at Wainwright for thirty days before revisiting the possibility of placing V.P. in Sutton Elementary's oral deaf program.

HISD maintains that these isolated occurrences are insufficient to show that it failed to implement substantial or significant provisions of V.P.'s IEP, that the services it provided were sufficient to confer an educational benefit upon V.P., and that the district court's determination that it failed to implement the content mastery provision of V.P.'s IEP is not supported by the record evidence. According to HISD, V.P.'s mother made the decision to prohibit V.P. from attending content mastery, and it could not force her to attend over her mother's instructions to the contrary. HISD further responds that the IEP Committee met multiple times during the school year to discuss V.P.'s progress and adjust her program accordingly, and that there was testimony from other teachers indicating that they communicated frequently about V.P., including testimony from V.P.'s classroom teacher that she often talked with V.P.'s mother and testimony from V.P.'s speech teacher that she worked closely with all of V.P.'s teachers. "[A] party challenging the implementation of an IEP must show more than a de minimis failure to implement all elements of that IEP, and, instead, must demonstrate that the school board or other authorities failed to implement substantial or significant provisions of the IEP." *Houston Indep. Sch. Dist. v. Bobby R.*, 200 F.3d 341, 349 (5th Cir.2000). What provisions are significant in an IEP should be determined in part based on "whether the IEP services that were provided actually conferred an educational benefit." *Id.* at 349 n. 2.

The fact-findings by the district court that are fundamental to the conclusions on this factor are sound. First, we find no clear error that poor communication and collaboration between the Wainwright school nurse and others assigned to monitor the system led to the problems with the FM loop system being out of service for approximately two months. Furthermore, while the FM loop was broken, school personnel allowed V.P. to wear the alternative headphone system over her hearing aids. There was no error in finding that to be improper and potentially harmful.

Further, there is evidence that the special education chair instructed V.P.'s classroom teacher to provide testing and assignment modifications without such modifications being included in V.P.'s IEP. The special education chair's unilateral decision to change the IEP suggests a lack of coordination and collaboration with V.P.'s other key stakeholders. Next, it was not clearly erroneous for the court to find that the IEP Committee did not communicate effectively and collaborate to address V.P.'s failure to attend content mastery. Although there is evidence that V.P.'s mother made the decision to remove V.P. temporarily from the service, the school staff failed to follow up on V.P.'s extended absence. Finally, V.P.'s classroom teacher testified that in November 2003, V.P.'s one-on-one aide stopped coming to work with V.P. for approximately three to four weeks at the direction of the school principal, despite the fact that V.P.'s IEP called for one-on-one assistance.

In addition to problems with the implementation of V.P.'s IEP, the district court did not clearly err in finding that V.P.'s key stakeholders received inadequate training. Although the school provided its personnel with a one-page tip sheet for working with an auditory or speech impaired child, such minimal training was insufficient. Moreover, despite such training, V.P.'s classroom teacher, one of the most important stakeholders, explained that she was unable to communicate effectively with V.P. and evaluate her progress.

4. Demonstration of positive academic and non-academic benefits

Perhaps one of the most critical factors in this analysis is the final one. This factor seeks to determine whether the student was obtaining benefits from the IEP. *Michael F.*, 118 F.3d at 252. There are subordinate components of the fact-finding, perhaps best thought of as evaluating the validity of the various measures of the progress that were offered. It is difficult analytically to compartmentalize all the determinations as ones of fact and ones of law, but we will proceed to make that effort.

The district court concluded that V.P. made only minimal progress, and the benefits she received were not meaningful. The court noted that there was conflicting testimony regarding V.P.'s progress at Wainwright-V.P.'s mother and classroom teacher were not encouraged by V.P.'s progress; V.P.'s speech therapist included both positive and negative impressions of V.P.'s advancement; and V.P.'s standardized speech and language test scores did not improve over time. The court explained that V.P. failed language arts and reading during the first two nine-weeks of the fall semester. Her grades then improved when her teacher implemented test and assignment modifications; however, her teacher testified that she would not have achieved passing grades without the modifications. Furthermore, although V.P. met the promotion standards for second grade, based on her grades with the modifications and the district standards for standardized testing with modifications, her classroom teacher testified that V.P. had not mastered the curriculum necessary to be successful in second grade.

HISD contends that V.P. demonstrated academic advancement because she achieved passing grades in her regular education program sufficient to advance to the next grade, her standardized scores show that she achieved the level of educational benefit required by the IDEA, and she mastered the high frequency words required for promotion. HISD maintains that the district court improperly considered V.P.'s standardized speech and language test scores. HISD notes that such scores are percentile scores that merely compare V.P.'s scores to those of other children who took the test, and V.P.'s development should be measured with respect to her individual progress, not her abilities in relation to the rest of the class. HISD also points to objective evidence indicating that V.P. was receiving an educational benefit from her HISD placement, arguing that V.P.'s speech and language skills suggested three years of progress in the three years she was in HISD, and achievement testing in November 2003 indicated that V.P. was performing at or near the first-grade level in most areas.

HISD further alleges that the IDEA does not require a school district to ensure that a disabled child is able to advance at a rate faster than non-disabled peers. Even when a disabled child falls further behind her peers, she may still be receiving some educational benefit from the placement. HISD attributes V.P.'s speech therapist's equivocal responses regarding her progress to the requirement that the therapist assess both V.P.'s strengths and weaknesses in the classroom. HISD asserts that V.P.'s weaknesses show that V.P. continues to have a disability and do not indicate that she has not received a free appropriate public education. Finally, HISD argues that the testimony of V.P.'s teacher that V.P. would need modifications to perform well in second grade does not support the district court's conclusion that V.P.'s progress was minimal.

Urged strongly upon us as a controlling precedent, particularly in light of the point about test scores, is a 2000 decision of this court also involving HISD. *See Bobby R.*, 200 F.3d 341. In that case, we considered whether HISD provided a free appropriate public education to a student with speech disabilities. Only the third and fourth factors that we have discussed here were at issue in *Bobby R.*: were the services required in the child's IEP provided in a coordinated and collaborative manner, and had the child demonstrated academic and non-academic benefits from his IEP? *Id.* at 348. What is most relevant here is the discussion of this last factor. We will review our prior analysis.

We start with context. In applying *Bobby R.*, it is of some relevance that the court was considering whether the district court clearly erred in finding that a child was receiving a meaningful educational benefit. Here, the issue is whether the district court clearly erred in finding that V.P. was not receiving a meaningful educational benefit.

The student, Bobby R., argued that where he stood in relation to his non-disabled peers was the best measure of his academic performance, whereas HISD maintained that passing scores and advancement from grade to grade was the proper indicia of academic progress. *Id.* We sided with HISD:

> a disabled child's development should be measured not by his relation to the rest of the class, but rather with respect to the individual student, as declining percentile scores do not necessarily represent a lack of educational benefit, but only a child's inability to maintain the same level of academic progress achieved by his non-disabled peers.

Id. The court pointed out that the test scores and grade levels in a number of subjects had improved during the child's years in HISD. *Id.* It concluded that the improvements were not trivial and that no clear error existed in the district court's factual determination that the child was receiving educational benefits from his IEP. 200 F.3d at 350. It was not necessary for the child "to improve in every area to obtain an educational benefit," as maximization of a disabled student's educational potential is not required. *Id.*

HISD argues that just as in *Bobby R.*, V.P. had improved test scores and advanced to a new grade level. Therefore, the district court is said to have erred in determining that she did not receive more than a minimal educational benefit from her IEP. Even though her test scores improved and she was advanced only after her teacher implemented modifications in her assignments and tests, HISD argues that such modifications are permitted under the IDEA. HISD also submits that a failure to master curriculum cannot be determined by comparing V.P.'s success to that of her non-disabled peers.

We find the district court's rulings on this fourth factor to be consistent with *Bobby R.* In the present case, passing grades and yearly advancement were not found to be adequate measures because V.P.'s teacher testified that the improved grades and advancement resulted from modifications the special education director unilaterally imposed. The IEP Committee itself never evaluated the changes and determined whether they were consistent with the requirements of the IDEA. V.P.'s teacher testified that V.P. would not have made passing grades and advanced to a new grade-level without these unauthorized modifications.

Modifications to an IEP legally can and likely often must be made in response to the experiences of a child in the classroom. However, before acceptable test scores and advancement in class grade can be seen as supporting that educational benefits are being received, those indicia must arise from compliance and not deviation from the IEP.

In evaluating this evidence, we are guided by the requirement that HISD is to provide V.P. with a "basic floor of opportunity" that "consists of access to specialized instruction and related services" individually designed to provide V.P. with educational benefit. *Rowley*, 458 U.S. at 201. HISD did not need to provide V.P. with the best possible education or one that will maximize her potential; however, the education benefits it provides cannot be de minimis. *Michael F.*, 118 F.3d at 247 (citing *Rowley*, 458 U.S. at 188–89). This distinction may well be the key to the dispute before us. HISD clearly was taking steps to provide educational benefits to V.P. The question is not whether there was more that could be done, but only whether there was more that had to be done under the governing statute.

Passing grades and advancement from year to year are factors that indicate a child is receiving meaningful educational benefit. As a legal matter, we find that such evidence should be rejected when it is found to be the product of unapproved deviations from the IEP. V.P.'s classroom teacher, the stakeholder most familiar with V.P.'s performance, testified that although V.P. did not do well the first or second semester of her first-grade year, her grades improved near the end of the year only because the teacher started modifying more work product for her, including giving her fewer test items. Without these modifications, the teacher stated, V.P. could not have done work on the curriculum level with the non-disabled students in her class and could not have made passing grades. The teacher explained that she made these modifications because the special education chair told her that they were part of V.P.'s IEP. However, V.P.'s IEP did not provide for modified curriculum or tests, and her teacher stated that she would have been concerned about making the modifications if she knew they were not in V.P.'s IEP. Finally, the teacher testified that despite V.P.'s passing grades, she did not believe V.P. mastered the curriculum necessary to move on to second grade.

Considering the testimony of V.P.'s teacher, the district court did not clearly err in concluding that the test scores were not reliable evidence of progress. The district court's factual determination that the child was not receiving educational benefits from her IEP was not clear error. As we said in *Bobby R.*, it is not necessary for the child "to improve in every area to obtain an educational benefit," 200 F.3d at 350, but there was no evidence here that had to be accepted that V.P. was improving in many areas at all.

The ultimate legal issue under this factor is whether V.P. was receiving a meaningful educational benefit from the services provided for her under her IEP. We find that she was not.

Therefore, we sustain the district court's finding that under the four factors, HISD was not providing a free appropriate public education. Consequently, V.P.'s move to the Parish School was justified.

[In the remainder of this opinion, the Fifth Circuit found that because the parents' 2004-05 private school placement was determined by the administrative hearing officer and the federal district court judge to be the appropriate one, the parents were entitled to reimbursement for 2004-05 and, in addition, were entitled to reimbursement for 2005-06 under the stay-put provision of the law.]

Notes and Questions

1. *V.P.* indicates that courts can consider both the design and implementation of a student's IEP in determining whether the student has been provided a FAPE. The Fifth Circuit found that the student's test results were not a reliable measure of meaningful benefits because the test modifications used by the teacher had not been part of the IEP. Would the "meaningful benefits" criterion be satisfied if the IEP team (plus the parent) had incorporated the modifications into the IEP, even if the student had still not mastered the curriculum?

2. *V.P* is a good example of the role of the expert witness in the IEP process. The failure of the IEP team to address the recommendations of Dr. Battin regarding the specific needs of V.P. demonstrated that the IEP had not been individualized. Does the importance of this expert's testimony suggest that Congress should amend the IDEA to overrule *Arlington Central School District Board of Education v. Murphy*, 548 U.S. 291 (2006), and permit prevailing parents to recover witness fees as costs?

3. The Fifth Circuit found that the school district's FM loop system in the general classroom had failed to provide the student with the least restrictive environment appropriate to her condition. Yet, the court of appeals upheld as the least appropriate environment V.P.'s placement by her parents in a private school for children with language-learning disabilities, in a classroom with ten students, a teacher, and an assistant teacher. At the private school, V.P. received speech therapy, phonemic training, auditory memory training, gap-detection training, and noise desensitization. In light of the requirement of the IDEA that students with disabilities be included with typical students to the maximum extent appropriate, would the school district have been successful if it had placed V.P. in a segregated classroom similar to that in the private school?

4. IDEA states that the IEP must include "a statement of the special education and related services and supplementary aids and services, based on peer-reviewed research to the extent practicable, to be provided to the child, or on behalf of the child. . . ." 20 U.S.C. § 1414(d)(1)(A)(i)(IV) (added 2004). The requirement that services be based on peer-reviewed research could be a far-reaching duty that would call into question teaching practices that are traditionally used but have little research support. Without specifically relying on the statutory provision, the court in *Waukee Community School District v. Douglas L.*, 51 IDELR 15 (S.D. Iowa 2008), ruled that the services given to a child with pervasive developmental disorder failed the standard for appropriate education because the restraint-type interventions and extended time-outs used to control the child's behavior reinforced the problem behavior and were contraindicated by professional research. In *Joshua A. v. Rocklin Unified Sch. Dist.*, 2008 U.S. Dist. LEXIS 26745 (E.D. Cal. 2008), *aff'd*, 319 F. Appx. 692 (9th Cir. 2009), however, a different court held that the "peer-reviewed research" provision did not in and of itself raise the appropriate education standard, and ruled that the failure of a school district to provide services based on peer-reviewed research did not automatically constitute a denial of appropriate education. For an illuminating discussion of the peer-reviewed research

provision, see Perry A. Zirkel, *Have the Amendments to the Individuals with Disabilities Education Act Razed* Rowley *and Raised the Substantive Standard for "Free Appropriate Public Education?,"* 28 J. NAT'L ASS'N ADMIN. L. JUDICIARY 397, 410–15 (2008).

5.   The IDEA regulations state that "As soon as possible following development of the IEP, special education and related services are [to be] made available to the child in accordance with the child's IEP." 34 C.F.R. § 300.323(c)(2). Nevertheless, delays in implementation of IEPs occur frequently. One court ruled that IDEA requires actual compliance, not substantial compliance, with the implementation requirement, but nevertheless ruled that the plaintiffs in a class action suit were not entitled to receive all required services immediately upon development of their IEPs or within a specific period of time. *D.D. v. New York City Bd. of Educ.*, 465 F.3d 503 (2d Cir. 2006) (vacating order denying preliminary injunction and remanding for reconsideration).

3.   The IEP as Controlling (or not)

MICHAEL C. v. RADNOR TOWNSHIP SCHOOL DISTRICT
202 F.3d 642 (3d Cir. 2000)

The court held that when a student moved from one state to another, the district in the new state is not obligated to provide an identical IEP.

This appeal has its genesis in social legislation enacted by Congress designed to encourage states to provide meaningful education to individuals with disabilities. The specific question before us is whether the Individuals with Disabilities Education Act requires a Pennsylvania school district to provide a student with disabilities who relocates from another state with an interim educational program identical to the program the student received in his or her prior state of residence. Michael C., a student with disabilities, attended a private school in Washington, D.C. under an Individualized Education Plan ("IEP") formulated by Washington educational authorities. Michael and his father moved from Washington to Radnor Township, Pennsylvania in the summer of 1997, and requested special educational treatment from the Radnor Township School District ("Radnor"). Radnor responded with specific educational proposals but Michael's father rejected them, and unilaterally placed Michael in a private school. Michael remained in this school for 41 days, after which his family again moved, this time to New Jersey.

Michael's father later initiated administrative proceedings seeking reimbursement for tuition costs incurred while Michael attended the private school in Pennsylvania. After unsuccessfully pursuing his administrative remedies, Michael's father filed this action in the United States District Court for the Eastern District of Pennsylvania against Radnor and the Pennsylvania Department of Education ("PDE"), seeking tuition reimbursement and claiming violations of the IDEA, 20 U.S.C. § 1415(j), the Rehabilitation Act, 29 U.S.C. § 794, and the Civil Rights Act of 1871, 42 U.S.C. § 1983. He also claimed that Michael's and his family's right to travel interstate under the Fourteenth Amendment to the United States Constitution had been violated. On cross-motions for summary judgment, the district court entered summary judgment in favor of Radnor and PDE as to all claims. . . . We will affirm.

The facts of this case are undisputed. Michael, 17 years old at the time events relevant to this case occurred, is learning disabled and suffers from severe hemophilia. Prior to August 1997, Michael and his father lived in Washington, D.C. Pursuant to the IDEA, Washington public educational authorities had developed an IEP for Michael. This IEP recommended placement at a "public/private separate school." Accordingly, Michael attended a small private school for learning disabled students called the LAB School. The LAB School served only students with disabilities, and therefore its students were segregated from their non-disabled peers. Michael attended the LAB School for three years.

When Michael and his father moved to Pennsylvania in 1997, the father contacted Radnor educational authorities to obtain appropriate placement for Michael. Radnor convened an "IEP meeting" to develop an interim program for Michael for the 1997-98 school year. At this time, Radnor had not yet completed its own evaluation of Michael's educational needs. By letter dated August 26, 1997, Radnor offered Michael two interim programming options pending completion of its own evaluation of Michael's needs. Both of these options placed Michael at Radnor High School ("Radnor High"), a large public high school with a total enrollment of approximately 800 students, where Radnor believed it could effectively implement the substance of Michael's Washington IEP. The first option, which Radnor characterizes as the "learning support" or "LS" option, involved enrolling Michael in mainstream English, science, social studies and elective classes, and in special education mathematics and written expression classes. This option also involved provision of support for homework and test preparation, and the development of study skills through a special education resource program. The second option, which Radnor characterizes as the "emotional support" or "ES" option, involved enrolling Michael in an "Emotional Support Program" for English, science, social studies, health and physical education classes, in "learning support" for mathematics, and in mainstream elective courses.

Michael's father rejected these options, and unilaterally decided to place Michael at the Hill Top School, a small private school for children with disabilities. In the fall of 1997, before Radnor had completed Michael's evaluation, Michael and his father again relocated, this time to New Jersey, for reasons related to the father's job. Michael had attended Hill Top for 41 days, during which time his father incurred tuition expenses in the amount of $4299.31. Because Michael left Pennsylvania before Radnor officials had completed their own evaluation of Michael's educational needs, Radnor never developed its own IEP for Michael.

. . . .

The plaintiffs then instituted the present action against Radnor and PDE. PDE moved to dismiss their § 1983 claim against it based on the Eleventh Amendment. In addition, the parties agreed that all claims could be decided on the administrative record without further evidence, and cross-moved for summary judgment. On February 5, 1999, the district court granted PDE's motion to dismiss the § 1983 claim as to it, and also granted the defendants' motion for summary judgment as to all claims and denied the plaintiffs' cross-motion, relying heavily on the OSEP policy memorandum.

In enacting the IDEA, Congress made known its strong preference for integrating students with disabilities into regular classrooms, and against segregating such students from their non-disabled peers unless absolutely necessary to provide them with an educational benefit. Nevertheless, cases presenting the reverse situation occasionally arise, where the complaint is the school district's failure to segregate a child from his or her non-disabled peers by placing that child in a learning environment serving only disabled students. This is such a case.

The plaintiffs contend that the defendants' refusal to adopt Michael's Washington IEP and to implement that IEP by placing him in the segregated Hill Top school, as opposed to a more integrated learning program at Radnor High, violated the IDEA's "pendency" or "stay-put" provision. This provision, found at 20 U.S.C. § 1415(j), states in pertinent part:

> . . . During the pendency of any proceedings conducted pursuant to this section, unless the State or local educational agency and the parents or guardian otherwise agree, the child shall remain in the then-current educational placement of such child, or, if applying for initial admission to a public school, shall, with the consent of the parents or guardian, be placed in the public school program until all such proceedings have been completed.

Plaintiffs argue that when Michael moved to Radnor Township, the LAB School in Washington was Michael's "then-current educational placement," and Radnor educational authorities' process of evaluating his educational needs constituted pending proceedings. Accordingly, plaintiffs contend that Radnor was obligated during this time to implement Michael's Washington IEP, and that this required placing him at Hill Top, a private school, which they assert provided the educational program most similar to the one Michael received at the LAB School.

The district court agreed with the local hearing officer, the state appeals board, and the defendants that the IDEA is silent on how to apply the pendency provision when a student transfers from another state. It therefore accorded deference to the federal OSEP Policy Memorandum 96-5. That memorandum states in pertinent part:

> Entitlement to a [free appropriate public education, or] FAPE, by its terms, encompasses an appropriate educational program that is individually-designed for each student in accordance with the requirements of Part B [of IDEA] and the educational standards of the State in which the student's parents reside. In addition, under 34 C.F.R. § 300.600, each State must exercise a general supervision over all programs in the State that provide educational services to disabled students, and must ensure that all such programs meet State education standards and Part B requirements.

>> When a student moves from a school district in State A to a school district in State B, the State B school district first must ascertain whether it will adopt the most recent evaluation and IEP developed for the student by the State A school district. Since the State A school district's evaluation

and IEP were based in part on the educational standards and eligibility requirements of State A, the student's evaluation and IEP developed by the State A school district might not necessarily be consistent with the educational standards of State B. Therefore, the State B school district must determine, as an initial matter, whether it believes that the student has a disability and whether the most recent evaluation of the student conducted by the school district in State A and the State A school district's IEP meet the requirements of Part B and well as the educational standards of State B.

OSEP Policy Memorandum 96-5, reprinted in 24 Indiv. Disabil. Educ. L. Rptr. 320 (U.S. Dep't Educ. Dec. 6, 1995). The district court therefore held that the pendency provision did not require implementation of Michael's Washington IEP.

In interpreting a congressional enactment, a court must first " 'determine whether the language at issue has a plain and unambiguous meaning with regard to the particular dispute in the case.' " . . . The IDEA is silent on how its pendency provision is to be applied to students who transfer interstate versus students who transfer intrastate, and the plain language of the pendency provision is at best ambiguous with respect to this issue. . . . For example, a student's prior place-ment no longer seems "current" after he or she withdraws from that placement and moves away. Moreover, it is impossible for the student's new school district in Pennsylvania to keep the student in his or her previous school as required by the "stay put" provision where that school is in another state. Therefore, we must look beyond the isolated text of section 1415(j) for guidance on how to apply this provision in this case.

OSEP is the agency charged with principal responsibility for administering the IDEA. 20 U.S.C. § 1402(a). The portion of OSEP Policy Memorandum 96-5 relevant to this case is properly characterized as an interpretive rule because it imposes no substantive obligations, but rather clarifies that the IDEA's pendency provision does not apply to situations where a student moves from one state to another.

The district court deferred to OSEP Policy Memorandum 96-5, citing *Chevron, U.S.A. Inc. v. Natural Resources Defense Council, Inc.*, 467 U.S. 837 (1984). This court has held that the level of deference to be accorded such interpretive rules depends upon their persuasiveness. "Admittedly, [they] do not rise to the level of a regulation and do not have the effect of law. A court is not required to give effect to an administrative interpretation. . . . Instead, the level of deference given to an interpretive bulletin is governed by the bulletin's persuasiveness."

The conclusion expressed in OSEP Policy Memorandum 96-5 that one state need not automatically accept and implement an IEP developed by another state does not appear to conflict with any previous or subsequent position taken by that agency. As we now discuss in greater detail, because this aspect of the policy memorandum is well-reasoned and persuasive in that it comports with the IDEA's statutory and regulatory scheme and with precedent interpreting that scheme, we are persuaded that the district court did not err in its thoughtful analysis and conclusion to defer to the memorandum.

. . . .

Because Congress left primary responsibility for providing a FAPE and for implementing the IDEA to the states, we believe it unlikely that Congress intended the stay-put provision, which dates back to 1975 and the IDEA's predecessor statute, to impose a requirement on states that they must implement an IEP established in another state without considering how consistent that IEP is with the policies and mandates of the student's new residential state. . . .

We hold that the IDEA's overall scheme and the precedent interpreting that scheme leads inexorably to the conclusion that when a student moves from State A to State B, any prior IEP in effect in State A need not be treated by State B as continuing automatically in effect. This interpretation of the inapplicability of the stay-put provision may, as plaintiffs claim, lead to the initial result that "disabled students like Michael with comprehensive and long-standing IEP's . . . can be forced upon an interstate move to somehow cope in regular education without supports while the district and the parent resolve any IEP dispute." But if parents believe that private school placement remains the only way to provide the student with the educational benefit required by the IDEA, or otherwise disagree with an IEP proposal, they can place the child in a private school, initiate a due process hearing, and seek reimbursement from educational authorities later. Of course, they act at their own financial risk, and will recover only if they are correct that local authorities have failed to provide the educational program to which their child is entitled under the IDEA. [School Comm. of Town of] Burlington [v. Department of Educ. of Commonwealth of Mass.], 471 U.S. [359,] at 373–74 [(1985)]. The plaintiffs' contention that these parents would have to keep paying private school tuition out of pocket for "years" is meritless, as federal and state regulations impose strict timing requirements on the completion of evaluations, the development and implementation of IEPs, and review of challenges to a local educational authority's proposal or refusal to initiate or change the identification, evaluation, or educational placement of a child or the provision of FAPE to a child. See 34 C.F.R. §§ 300.504(a), 300.512; 22 Pa. Code §§ 14.25(m), 342.25(p) (timeline for completion of multidisciplinary evaluations); 22 Pa. Code. § 14.32(i) (timeline for preparation and implementation of IEPs); 22 Pa. Code §§ 14.63, 14.64(o) (timelines for requesting and holding prehearing conference or due process hearing). We are mindful that this interpretation may bind the hands of parents who cannot afford to pay private school tuition out-of-pocket and await future reimbursement. This same result, however, can occur where parents of a student who transfers intrastate disagree with the new school district's placement of their child, and appears to be an unfortunate reality of the system Congress created.

Accordingly, we hold that the interpretation adopted by OSEP in Policy Memorandum 96-5 is a reasonable accommodation of the stay-put provision and the overriding purposes and structure of the IDEA, and we are persuaded that this interpretation deserves deference.

Michael has a right, established by the IDEA and defined by state law, to a free, appropriate public education. Radnor has done nothing to alter or deny Michael that right. It has not imposed different standards on the type of education Michael may receive versus the type of education a disabled student who moves from one school district to another within Pennsylvania may receive. Thus, Michael cannot claim that Radnor's action in this case violated his right to travel under the Equal

Protection Clause of the Fourteenth Amendment, and consequently, cannot claim a violation of 42 U.S.C. § 1983.

NOTES AND QUESTIONS

1. As the *Michael C.* opinion indicates, if the child moves from district to district within the state, the IEP from the previous school remains in force until a new one is adopted. Is there any policy reason that the rule should differ when the child moves out of state?

2. The 2004 Reauthorization of IDEA provides specific provisions for transfer of students in and out of state and transmittal of records. In-state districts must provide FAPE and services comparable to those in the old IEP until, in consultation with the parents, a new IEP is adopted. 20 U.S.C. § 1414(d)(2)(C)(i)(I); 34 C.F.R. § 300.323(e). Out-of state districts must provide FAPE and comparable services in consultation with parents until evaluation is conducted if the new LEA wants one, and a new IEP is developed. 20 U.S.C. § 1414(d)(2)(C)(i)(II); 34 C.F.R. § 300.323(f).

3. In addition to addressing the situation which arises when students move from jurisdiction to jurisdiction, *Michael C.* highlights important administrative law aspects of special education law. The United States Department of Education has adopted extensive implementing regulations for IDEA and section 504, which regulations, under general principles of administrative law, carry the force and effect of law. *See* 20 U.S.C. § 1406. The statutory delegation of power nevertheless states that "the Secretary shall issue regulations under this title only to the extent that such regulations are necessary to ensure that there is compliance with the specific requirements of this title." 20 U.S.C. § 1406(a). The Department also issues individual investigatory and policy letters and policy rulings. As discussed in *Michael C.*, Congress has specifically addressed the legal status and significance of these policy interpretations providing that: "The Secretary may not, issue policy letters or other statements . . . that — establish a rule that is required for compliance with, and eligibility under, this title without following the requirements of section 553 of title 5." 20 U.S.C. § 1406(d). The Secretary may address questions informally but the response must indicate that it is informal guidance and not legally binding. 20 U.S.C. § 1406(e). Policy memoranda can be on very significant topics. For example, the issue of assessment for special education students, now the subject of No Child Left Behind and its implementing guidance, was discussed much earlier in the Joint Policy Memorandum on Assessments, 27 IDELR 138 (U.S. Dep't of Educ. 1997) (discussing inclusion of children with disabilities in districtwide assessments).

Chapter 6

THE LEAST RESTRICTIVE ENVIRONMENT

A. INTRODUCTION

One of the principal goals of the federal special education law is to bring children with disabilities into the mainstream of life, and out of situations in which they are locked away out of sight, and, if seen at all, viewed only as the manifestation of disabling medical conditions. One of the sponsors commented that the law was to end both kinds of invisibility:

> [A]s much as any other action of Congress in the two hundred years of the Republic, the Education for All Handicapped Children Act represents a gallant and determined effort to terminate the two-tiered invisibility once and for all with respect to exceptional children in the Nation's school systems.

Robert T. Stafford, *Education for the Handicapped: A Senator's Perspective*, 3 Vt. L. Rev. 71, 72 (1978).

Relevant to discussions of least restrictive environment are the underlying statutes and regulations, caselaw that interprets these rules either to establish a presumption of a mainstreamed setting or to shy away from making that presumption, and caselaw that develops contemporary standards for evaluating claims that children are not being offered placements in the least restrictive setting.

B. STATUTORY AND REGULATORY PROVISIONS

IDEA and its regulations, and section 504 and its regulations, insist that children with disabilities should be served in settings that have children without disabilities, that is, that they should be placed in "mainstream" educational settings. These provisions further provide that within the range of possible settings, from more restrictive (and less integrated) to less restrictive (and more integrated), the less restrictive is to be preferred. Consider the following excerpts from IDEA, its regulations, and the regulations adopted to enforce section 504.

1. IDEA

The following provisions of IDEA establish a right to education in the least restrictive environment:

> To the maximum extent appropriate, children with disabilities, including children in public or private institutions or other care facilities, [must be] educated with children who are not disabled, and special classes, separate

schooling, or other removal of children with disabilities from the regular educational environment [must occur] only when the nature or severity of the disability of a child is such that education in regular classes with the use of supplementary aids and services cannot be achieved satisfactorily.

20 U.S.C. § 1412(a)(5)(A).

A State funding mechanism shall not result in placements that violate the requirements of subparagraph (A), and a State shall not use a funding mechanism by which the State distributes funds on the basis of the type of setting in which a child is served that will result in the failure to provide a child with a disability a free appropriate public education according to the unique needs of the child as described in the child's IEP.

20 U.S.C. § 1412(a)(5)(B)(i).

2.   IDEA Regulations

The United States Department of Education adopted the following regulations to implement the statutory provisions:

[The IEP] must include —

(1) A statement of the child's present levels of academic achievement and functional performance, including —

(i) How the child's disability affects the child's involvement and progress in the general education curriculum (i.e., the same curriculum as for nondisabled children); . . .

(2)(i) A statement of measurable annual goals, including academic and functional goals designed to —

(A) Meet the child's needs that result from the child's disability to enable the child to be involved in and progress in the general curriculum . . .

(4) A statement of the special education and related services and supplementary aids and services, based on peer-reviewed research to the extent practicable, to be provided to the child, or on behalf of the child, and a statement of the program modifications or supports for school personnel that will be provided to enable the child — . . .

(ii) To be involved in and progress in the general education curriculum . . . and to participate in extracurricular and other nonacademic activities; and

(iii) To be educated and participate with other children with disabilities and nondisabled children in the activities described in this section;

(5) An explanation of the extent, if any, to which the child will not participate with nondisabled children in the regular class and in the activities described in paragraph (a)(4) of this section.

34 C.F.R. § 300.320(a).

34 C.F.R. § 300.114 (recapitulating statutory LRE requirements).

34 C.F.R. § 300.115 (requiring a "continuum of alternative placements" and "provision for supplementary services (such as resource room or itinerant instruction) to be provided in conjunction with regular class placement").

34 C.F.R. § 300.116(b) ("The child's placement — (3) [must be] as close as possible to the child's home").

34 C.F.R. § 300.116(c) ("Unless the IEP of a child with a disability requires some other arrangement, the child [must be] educated in the school that he or she would attend if nondisabled").

34 C.F.R. § 300.116(d) ("In selecting the LRE, consideration [must be] given to any potential harmful effect on the child or on the quality of services that he or she needs").

34 C.F.R. § 300.116(e) ("A child with a disability [must] not [be] removed from education in age-appropriate regular classrooms solely because of needed modifications in the general education curriculum.").

> In providing or arranging for the provision of nonacademic and extracurricular services and activities, including meals, recess periods, and activities set forth in § 300.107[(b): "counseling services, athletics, transportation, health services, recreational activities, special interest groups or clubs sponsored by the public agency, referrals to agencies that provide assistance to individuals with disabilities, and employment, including both employment by the public agency and assistance in making outside employment available"], each public agency must ensure that each child with a disability participates with nondisabled children in the extracurricular services and activities to the maximum extent appropriate to the needs of that child. The public agency must ensure that each child with a disability has the supplementary aids and services determined by the child's IEP Team to be appropriate and necessary for the child to participate in nonacademic settings.

34 C.F.R. § 300.117.

34 C.F.R. §§ 300.118–.120 (imposing implementation, training, technical assistance, monitoring, and corrective action responsibilities on state educational agencies in connection with least restrictive environment obligations with regard to institutions and local educational agencies).

3.   Section 504 Regulations

Regulations promulgated to enforce section 504 of the Rehabilitation Act of 1973 are also relevant. The relevant regulations are:

> A recipient to whom this subpart applies shall educate, or shall provide for the education of, each qualified handicapped person in its jurisdiction with persons who are not handicapped to the maximum extent appropriate to the needs of the handicapped person. A recipient shall place a handicapped person in the regular educational environment operated by the recipient

unless it is demonstrated by the recipient that the education of the person in the regular environment with the use of supplementary aids and services cannot be achieved satisfactorily. Whenever a recipient places a person in a setting other than the regular educational environment pursuant to this paragraph, it shall take into account the proximity of the alternate setting to the person's home.

34 C.F.R. § 104.34(a).

In providing or arranging for the provision of nonacademic and extracurricular services and activities, including meals, recess periods, and the services and activities set forth in 104.37(a)(2) [substantially identical to § 300.306(b)], a recipient shall ensure that handicapped persons participate with nonhandicapped persons in such activities and services to the maximum extent appropriate to the needs of the handicapped person in question.

34 C.F.R. § 104.34(b).

If a recipient, in compliance with paragraph (a) of this section, operates a facility that is identifiable as being for handicapped persons, the recipient shall ensure that the facility and the services and activities provided therein are comparable to the other facilities, services, and activities of the recipient.

34 C.F.R. § 104.34(c).

NOTES AND QUESTIONS

1. The Supreme Court has interpreted Fourteenth Amendment due process and a regulation promulgated under title II of the Americans with Disabilities Act, *see* 28 C.F.R. § 35.130(d), to require placement in the least restrictive environment for people with disabilities in publicly run institutions. *See Youngberg v. Romeo*, 457 U.S. 307 (1982) (requiring that confinement of person with mental disability be in reasonably nonrestrictive conditions); *see also Olmstead v. L.C.*, 527 U.S. 581 (1999) (ruling that ADA requires persons involuntarily confined for mental impairments to be placed in least restrictive setting). Is there a constitutional obligation to provide public educational services to children with disabilities in the least restrictive setting?

2. The Report of the President's Commission on Excellence in Special Education made the finding: "Children placed in special education are general education children first. Despite this basic fact, educators and policy-makers think about the two systems as separate. . . ." A New Era: Revitalizing Special Education for Children and Their Families 3 (2002), *available at* http://www.ed.gov.inits/commissionsboards/whspecialeducation/reports.html. Think back to your own experience in grade school and high school. Were the school systems following the laws quoted above and educating children with disabilities in the same settings as children without disabilities to the maximum extent appropriate? If the answer is no, what are the reasons? Are there other regulations that ought to be adopted?

3. Despite 34 C.F.R. § 300.116(b)(3) and (c), courts have been reluctant to require schools to replicate in the child's neighborhood school programs available somewhere a reasonable distance from his or her home. *See, e.g., White v. Ascension Parish Sch. Bd.*, 343 F.3d 373, 380–82 (5th Cir. 2003); *McLaughlin v. Holt Pub. Schs. Bd. of Educ.*, 320 F.3d 663, 670 n.2, 671–72 (6th Cir. 2003). How would you argue in favor of, or against, the creation of a program at the school the child would otherwise attend when the same program exists at a school several miles away?

C. PRESUMPTIVE INCLUSION

Roncker v. Walter is perhaps the most influential early decision on the topic of least restrictive environment.

RONCKER v. WALTER
700 F.2d 1058 (6th Cir. 1983)

In this case, the court overturned a decision approving placement of a child with severe mental retardation at a specialized school and required a determination whether the services the child needed could be provided in a more integrated setting.

CONTIE, CIRCUIT JUDGE.

In this appeal, the plaintiff challenges the placement of her retarded son under the Education for All Handicapped Children Act of 1975, 20 U.S.C. § 1401 *et seq.* (the Act). As a condition for receiving federal aid, the Act provides that a free appropriate education must be provided to all children. 20 U.S.C. § 1412. It further requires states to establish "procedures to assure that, to the maximum extent appropriate, handicapped children, including children in public or private institutions or other care facilities, are educated with children who are not handicapped and that special classes, separate schooling, or other removal of handicapped children from the regular educational environment occurs only when the nature or severity of the handicap is such that education in regular classes with the use of supplementary aids and services cannot be achieved satisfactorily." 20 U.S.C. § 1412(5)(B).

The Supreme Court recently decided what "free appropriate education" means in the context of the Act. *Bd. of Ed. of the Hendrick Hudson Central School District v. Rowley*, 458 U.S. 176 (1982). In this case, we examine the Act's requirement that handicapped children be educated with non-handicapped children to the "maximum extent appropriate."

I

The plaintiff's son, Neill Roncker, is nine years old and is severely mentally retarded. He is classified as Trainable Mentally Retarded (TMR), a category of children with an IQ of below 50. Less severely retarded students are classified as Educable Mentally Retarded (EMR) and are generally educated in special classes within the regular public schools.

There is no dispute that Neill is severely retarded and has a mental age of two to three with regard to most functions. Neill also suffers from seizures but they are not convulsive and he takes medication to control them. No evidence indicates that Neill is dangerous to others but he does require almost constant supervision because of his inability to recognize dangerous situations.

In 1976, Neill was evaluated and recommended for the Arlitt Child Development Center. It was believed that he would benefit from contact with non-handicapped children. In the spring of 1979, a conference was held to evaluate Neill's Individual Education Plan (IEP) as required by the Act. Present at the conference were Neill's parents, school psychologists, and a member of the Hamilton County Board of Mental Retardation. After evaluating Neill, the school district decided to place him in a county school. Since these county schools were exclusively for mentally retarded children, Neill would have received no contact with non-handicapped children.

The county schools receive part of their funding through tuition for individual students, which is paid by the school district. The county schools also receive partial funding through the state by virtue of a mental retardation tax levy. Funds from this levy are not available to public schools.

The Ronckers refused to accept the placement and sought a due process hearing before an impartial hearing officer pursuant to the Act. 20 U.S.C. § 1415(b)(2). The hearing officer found that the school district had not satisfied its burden of proving that its proposed placement afforded the maximum appropriate contact with non-handicapped children. He ordered that Neill "be placed within the appropriate special education class in the regular elementary school setting."

The school district appealed to the Ohio State Board of Education pursuant to 29 U.S.C. § 1415(c). The State Board found that Neill required the educational opportunities provided by the county school. It also found, however, that he needed interaction with non-handicapped children during lunch, recess and transportation to and from school. Accordingly, the State Board held that Neill should be placed in a county school so long as some provision was made for him to receive contact with non-handicapped children. The State Board did not indicate how this split program was to be administered.

While the dispute over placement continued, Neill began attending a class for the severely mentally retarded at Pleasant Ridge Elementary School in September 1979. Pleasant Ridge is a regular public school which serves both handicapped and non-handicapped children. Neill's contact with non-handicapped children at Pleasant Ridge is limited to lunch, gym and recess. Neill has remained at Pleasant Ridge during the pendency of this action.

In January 1980, Neill's mother filed this action against the state and the school district. The claims against the state were settled. . . .

At trial, both parties presented expert testimony. Both agreed that Neill required special instruction; he could not be placed in educational classes with non-handicapped children. The plaintiff, however, contended that Neill could be provided the special instruction he needed in a setting where he could have contact with non-handicapped children. The school district contended that Neill could not benefit significantly from mainstreaming and that any minimal benefits would be greatly outweighed by the educational benefits of the county school.

The district court found in favor of the school district. The court interpreted the Act's mainstreaming requirement as allowing school districts broad discretion in the placement of handicapped children. In this case, the district court found that the school district did not abuse its discretion in placing Neill Roncker in a school where he would receive no contact with non-handicapped children. This conclusion was supported by the district court's finding that Neill had made no significant progress after 18 months at Pleasant Ridge. . . .

II

We find that the district court erred in reviewing the school district's placement decision under an "abuse of discretion" standard.

The Act provides that a district court "shall receive the records of the [state] administrative proceedings, shall hear additional evidence at the request of a party, and, basing its decision on the preponderance of the evidence, shall grant such relief as the court determines is appropriate." 20 U.S.C. § 1415(e)(2). The school district contends that this provision only gives courts the limited authority to determine if the district has complied with the procedural requirements of the Act. The plaintiff, on the other hand, contends that the Act requires a *de novo* review not limited to the Act's procedural requirements.

This exact dispute over standard of review was presented and decided in *Rowley*, 458 U.S. 176. The Supreme Court rejected the notion that courts were strictly limited to reviewing for procedural compliance with the Act. However, the Court also rejected the argument that the Act gave the courts broad power to review and upset placement decisions, stating that "the provision that a reviewing court base its decision on the 'preponderance of the evidence' is by no means an invitation to the courts to substitute their own notions of sound educational policy for those of the school authorities which they review." The court concluded that the proper balance is to give greater deference to the state's placement decision if the procedural requirements of the Act are met. In this way, the court's encroachment on the basically legislative decisions involving the distribution of educational resources is kept to a minimum.

The first inquiry in the two-step test mandated by *Rowley* is whether the state has complied with the Act's procedural requirements. These requirements clearly have been satisfied in this case. The second inquiry is whether "the individualized educational program developed through the Act's procedures [is] reasonably calculated to enable the child to receive educational benefits?"

In *Rowley*, the Supreme Court found that the state had complied with the Act's procedural requirements and had developed an IEP reasonably calculated to lead to educational benefits. Accordingly, the Act was satisfied. The present case differs from *Rowley* in two significant ways.

First, this case involves the mainstreaming provision of the Act while *Rowley* involved a choice between two methods for educating a deaf student. In the latter case, the dispute is simply one of methodology and the Supreme Court has emphatically stated that such questions should be left to the states. In the present case, the question is not one of methodology but rather involves a determination of whether the school district has satisfied the Act's requirement that handicapped children be educated alongside non-handicapped children to the maximum extent appropriate. The states accept federal aid in return for compliance with the Act. Since Congress has decided that mainstreaming is appropriate, the states must accept that decision if they desire federal funds.

Second, in this case, the district court failed to give "due weight" to the state administrative proceedings. Both the impartial hearing officer and the State Board of Education found that the school district's placement did not satisfy the Act's mainstreaming requirement. Under such circumstances, the district court erred in reviewing the school district's placement under the deferential abuse of discretion standard. Such a standard of review renders the administrative hearings provided for by the Act virtually meaningless. By way of contrast, in *Rowley*, the administrative hearings unanimously concurred with the original placement but the district court found the placement to be inappropriate.

In sum, the abuse of discretion standard of review utilized by the district court was improper under the Act. We further find that the standard of review as set out in *Rowley* requires a *de novo* review but that the district court should give due weight to the state administrative proceedings in reaching its decision.

III

Since the district court employed an improper standard of review, we remand this case in order to allow the district court to re-examine the mainstreaming issue in light of the proper standard of review.

The Act does not require mainstreaming in every case but its requirement that mainstreaming be provided to the *maximum* extent appropriate indicates a very strong congressional preference. The proper inquiry is whether a proposed placement is appropriate under the Act. In some cases, a placement which may be considered better for academic reasons may not be appropriate because of the failure to provide for mainstreaming. The perception that a segregated institution is academically superior for a handicapped child may reflect no more than a basic disagreement with the mainstreaming concept. Such a disagreement is not, of course, any basis for not following the Act's mandate. *Campbell v. Talladega City Bd. of Education*, 518 F. Supp. 47, 55 (N.D. Ala. 1981). In a case where the segregated facility is considered superior, the court should determine whether the services which make that placement superior could be feasibly provided in a non-segregated setting. If they can, the placement in the segregated school would be inappropriate under the Act. Framing the issue in this manner accords the proper respect for the strong preference in favor of mainstreaming while still realizing the possibility that some handicapped children simply must be educated in segregated facilities either because the handicapped child would not benefit from mainstreaming, because any marginal benefits received from mainstreaming are far outweighed by the benefits gained from services which could not feasibly be provided in the non-segregated setting, or because the handicapped child is a disruptive force in the non-segregated setting. Cost is a proper factor to consider since excessive spending on one handicapped child deprives other handicapped children. *See Age v. Bullitt County Schools*, 673 F.2d 141, 145 (6th Cir. 1982). Cost is no defense, however, if the school district has failed to use its funds to provide a proper continuum of alternative placements for handicapped children. The provision of such alternative placements benefits all handicapped children.

In the present case, the district court must determine whether Neill's educational, physical or emotional needs require some service which could not feasibly be provided in a class for handicapped children within a regular school or in the type of split program advocated by the State Board of Education. Although Neill's progress, or lack thereof, at Pleasant Ridge is a relevant factor in determining the maximum appropriate extent to which he can be mainstreamed, it is not dispositive since the district court must determine whether Neill could have been provided with additional services, such as those provided at the county schools, which would have improved his performance at Pleasant Ridge.

We recognize that the mainstreaming issue imposes a difficult burden on the district court. Since Congress has chosen to impose that burden, however, the courts must do their best to fulfill their duty. The district courts are not without guidance inasmuch as they have the benefit of two state administrative proceedings and may justifiably give due weight to those administrative findings.

. . . .

The judgment of the district court is VACATED and the case is REMANDED for further proceedings consistent with this opinion.

KENNEDY, CIRCUIT JUDGE, dissenting.

. . . .

The whole record of the District Court is devoted to the question of whether Neill Roncker's needs can be met in the self-contained handicapped classroom in the elementary school he has been attending or whether he needs to be taught with other children closer to his chronological age and learning level with the support services that can presently only be provided in the 169 program at a separate school. Appellant argues that the finding that Neill could not benefit from continued placement in his present classroom is clearly erroneous. The panel's opinion does not so find and I would not so find. These findings of fact are independent of the District Court's legal conclusions. Neill Roncker was not progressing in his present placement but was regressing. His ability to interact with the non-handicapped children was at best minimal. His opportunity to interact with non-handicapped children there was also very minimal. Yet, despite these findings, the panel's decision requires the District Court to determine on remand whether it would be "feasible" to provide an equivalent of what is now provided in the 169 schools in classrooms located in regular elementary schools. The District Court has admittedly not made such a finding. I do not believe, however, that such an inquiry is authorized by section 1412(5) or the "mainstreaming" concept it embodies. . . .

Congress has expressed a clear preference for educating handicapped children in the regular classrooms of the public schools. Handicapped children should be removed from regular classes only when their education cannot be achieved satisfactorily with the use of supplementary aids and services. Despite this preference for "mainstreaming," however, the statute clearly contemplates that there will be some separate schools and schooling. *Rowley*, 458 U.S. 176, [181] n. 4 (1982). Section 1412(5) does not require that classrooms for the severely mentally retarded, such as Neill Roncker, whose only interaction with non-handicapped children is to observe them, be located in the regular elementary school. Rather, this section is directed to the handicapped child who can spend some time in the regular classroom if given special aids or assistance. . . .

Rowley held that Congress did not intend the courts to overturn a state's educational policy once the statutory requirements have been met. . . . When Congress imposes a requirement in legislation enacted pursuant to the spending power, it must do so unambiguously. Section 1412(5), far from unambiguously requiring that school districts place severely handicapped children in the regular school environment even if they cannot be satisfactorily educated in that environment, requires only that handicapped children be "mainstreamed" to the maximum extent *appropriate*. For those more severely retarded children, such as Neill Roncker, who are unable to be satisfactorily educated in any respect in a regular classroom, the statute does not prohibit the school district from making the judgment as to where their classrooms should be located. . . .

Finally, I am unable to agree that the District Court failed to give "due weight" to the state administrative proceedings. The disposition by the District Court was based upon Neill Roncker's progress and lack of progress in a special classroom. The administrative hearing officers did not have this actual information concerning Neill's progress but could only anticipate what his progress might be. Further, the two administrative decisions cannot themselves be fully reconciled. . . .

I would affirm the judgment of the District Court that Neill Roncker's placement satisfies the requirements of section 1412(5).

NOTES AND QUESTIONS

1. Does the majority opinion establish a presumption in favor of mainstream placements? If so, what is needed to overcome the presumption? How does the view of the dissent differ on this issue? What evidence would you expect the parties to present to support their positions when the case returns to the trial court?

2. The *Roncker* court distinguished *Rowley*'s holding that deference must be given to school district decisions about educational methodology on the ground that *Rowley* was interpreting the term "appropriate education" rather than the mainstreaming requirement. Is this distinction persuasive? Many courts have ruled that the limits *Rowley* placed on the duty to provide appropriate education do not control in controversies over mainstreaming. *E.g.*, *Board of Educ. v. Illinois State Bd. of Educ.*, 184 F.3d 912, 916 n.1 (7th Cir. 1999); *Greer v. Rome City Sch. Dist.*, 950 F.2d 688, 695–96 & n.25 (11th Cir. 1991), *withdrawn*, 956 F.2d 1025, *reinstated in part*, 967 F.2d 470 (1992); *Daniel R.R. v. State Bd. of Educ.*, 874 F.2d 1036, 1045 (5th Cir. 1989); *A.W. v. Northwest R-1 Sch. Dist.*, 813 F.2d 158, 163 n.7 (8th Cir. 1987); *see also*

Department of Educ. v. Katherine D., 727 F.2d 809, 815 (9th Cir. 1983) (finding entitlement to aids and services to promote mainstreaming to be open ended). Courts have ordered school districts to provide very extensive levels of services in order to enable children to be educated in less restrictive settings. *See, e.g., L.B. v. Nebo School District*, 379 F.3d 966 (10th Cir. 2004) (requiring in-class aide and program with thirty-five to forty hours of applied behavioral analysis services delivered primarily at home to enable child with autism to remain in mainstreamed preschool class).

3. The question of cost is a recurring one in disputes over provision of specialized services in mainstream settings. Is there a basis in IDEA for imposing a cost limit on efforts to educate children in settings with non-disabled peers? If so, what should the limit be?

On facts not dissimilar to those of *Roncker*, the court in *Daniel R.R.* affirmed a district court decision upholding a non-mainstreamed placement for a child with disabilities.

DANIEL R.R. v. STATE BOARD OF EDUCATION
874 F.2d 1036 (5th Cir. 1989)

Here, the court affirmed a district court decision upholding a due process hearing officer's ruling that a child with developmental disabilities would not receive educational benefit from education in a mainstreamed placement. The court thus concluded that the child was not entitled to education in the mainstreamed setting.

GEE, CIRCUIT JUDGE.

Plaintiffs in this action, a handicapped boy and his parents, urge that a local school district failed to comply with the Education of the Handicapped Act. Specifically, they maintain that a school district's refusal to place the child in a class with nonhandicapped students violates the Act. The district court disagreed and, after a careful review of the record, we affirm the district court.

I. *Background*

A. General

In 1975, on a finding that almost half of the handicapped children in the United States were receiving an inadequate education or none at all, Congress passed the Education of the Handicapped Act (EHA or Act). *See* 20 U.S.C.A. § 1400(b) (1988 Supp.); S. Rep. No. 168, 94th Cong., 1st Sess. 8 (1975), *reprinted in* 1975 U.S. Code Cong. & Admin. News 1425, 1432. Before passage of the Act, as the Supreme Court has noted, many handicapped children suffered under one of two equally ineffective approaches to their educational needs: either they were excluded entirely from public education or they were deposited in regular education classrooms with no assistance, left to fend for themselves in an environment inappropriate for their needs. *Hendrick Hudson District Board of Education v. Rowley*, 458 U.S. 176, 191

(1982). To entice state and local school officials to improve upon these inadequate methods of educating children with special needs, Congress created the EHA, having as its purpose providing handicapped children access to public education and requiring states to adopt procedures that will result in individualized consideration of and instruction for each handicapped child.

The Act is largely procedural. It mandates a "free appropriate public education" for each handicapped child and sets forth procedures designed to ensure that each child's education meets that requirement. 20 U.S.C.A. §§ 1412(1) and 1415(a)–(e). School officials are required to determine the appropriate placement for each child and must develop an Individualized Educational Plan (IEP) that tailors the child's education to his individual needs. The child's parents are involved at all stages of the process. *See generally* § 1415(b). In addition, the Act requires that handicapped children be educated in regular education classrooms, with nonhandicapped students — as opposed to special education classrooms with handicapped students only — to the greatest extent appropriate. § 1412(5)(B). Educating a handicapped child in a regular education classroom with nonhandicapped children is familiarly known as "mainstreaming," and the mainstreaming requirement is the source of the controversy between the parties before us today.

B. Particular

Daniel R. is a six year old boy who was enrolled, at the time this case arose, in the El Paso Independent School District (EPISD). A victim of Downs Syndrome, Daniel is mentally retarded and speech impaired. By September 1987, Daniel's developmental age was between two and three years and his communication skills were slightly less than those of a two year old.

In 1985, Daniel's parents, Mr. and Mrs. R., enrolled him in EPISD's Early Childhood Program, a half-day program devoted entirely to special education. Daniel completed one academic year in the Early Childhood Program. Before the 1986-87 school year began, Mrs. R. requested a new placement that would provide association with nonhandicapped children. Mrs. R. wanted EPISD to place Daniel in Pre-kindergarten — a half-day, regular education class. Mrs. R. conferred with Joan Norton, the Pre-kindergarten instructor, proposing that Daniel attend the half-day Pre-kindergarten class in addition to the half-day Early Childhood class. As a result, EPISD's Admission, Review and Dismissal (ARD) Committee met and designated the combined regular and special education program as Daniel's placement.

This soon proved unwise, and not long into the school year Mrs. Norton began to have reservations about Daniel's presence in her class. Daniel did not participate without constant, individual attention from the teacher or her aide, and failed to master any of the skills Mrs. Norton was trying to teach her students. Modifying the Pre-kindergarten curriculum and her teaching methods sufficiently to reach Daniel would have required Mrs. Norton to modify the curriculum almost beyond recognition. In November 1986, the ARD Committee met again, concluded that Pre-kindergarten was inappropriate for Daniel, and decided to change Daniel's placement. Under the new placement, Daniel would attend only the special education, Early Childhood class; would eat lunch in the school cafeteria, with nonhandicapped children, three days a week if his mother was present to supervise him; and would have contact with nonhandicapped students during recess. Believing that the ARD had improperly shut the door to regular education for Daniel, Mr. and Mrs. R. exercised their right to a review of the ARD Committee's decision.

As the EHA requires, Mr. and Mrs. R. appealed to a hearing officer who upheld the ARD Committee's decision. *See* § 1415(b)(2). After a hearing which consumed five days of testimony and produced over 2500 pages of transcript, the hearing officer concluded that Daniel could not participate in the Pre-kindergarten class without constant attention from the instructor because the curriculum was beyond his abilities. In addition, the hearing officer found, Daniel was receiving little educational benefit from Pre-kindergarten and was disrupting the class — not in the ordinary sense of the term, but in the sense that his needs absorbed most of the teacher's time and diverted too much of her attention away from the rest of the class. Finally, the instructor would have to downgrade 90 to 100 percent of the Pre-kindergarten curriculum to bring it to a level that Daniel could master. Thus, the hearing officer concluded, the regular education, Pre-kindergarten class was not the appropriate placement for Daniel.

Dissatisfied with the hearing officer's decision, Mr. and Mrs. R. proceeded to the next level of review by filing this action in the district court. *See* § 1415(e). Although the EHA permits the parties to supplement the administrative record, Daniel's representatives declined to do so; and the court conducted its de novo review on the basis of the administrative record alone. The district court decided the case on cross motions for summary judgment. Relying primarily on Daniel's inability to receive an educational benefit in regular education, the district court affirmed the hearing officer's decision.

. . . .

IV. *Substantive Violations*

A. Mainstreaming Under the EHA

The cornerstone of the EHA is the "free appropriate public education." As a condition of receiving federal funds, states must have "in effect a policy that assures all handicapped children the right to a free appropriate public education." § 1412(1). The Act defines a free appropriate public education in broad, general terms without dictating substantive educational policy or mandating specific educational methods. In *Rowley*, the Supreme Court fleshed out the Act's skeletal definition of its principal term: "a 'free appropriate public education' consists of educational instruction specially designed to meet the unique needs of the handicapped child, supported by such services as are necessary to permit the child 'to benefit' from the instruction." *Rowley*, 458 U.S. at 188–89. The Court's interpretation of the Act's language does not, however, add substance to the Act's vague terms; instruction specially designed to meet each student's unique needs is as imprecise a directive as the language actually found in the Act.

The imprecise nature of the EHA's mandate does not reflect legislative omission. Rather, it reflects two deliberate legislative decisions. Congress chose to leave the

selection of educational policy and methods where they traditionally have resided —
with state and local school officials. *Rowley*, 458 U.S. at 207. In addition, Congress's
goal was to bring handicapped children into the public school system and to provide
them with an education tailored to meet their particular needs. *Id.* at 189. Such
needs span the spectrum of mental and physical handicaps, with no two children
necessarily suffering the same condition or requiring the same services or
education. *Id.* Schools must retain significant flexibility in educational planning if
they truly are to address each child's needs. A congressional mandate that dictates
the substance of educational programs, policies and methods would deprive school
officials of the flexibility so important to their tasks. Ultimately, the Act mandates
an education for each handicapped child that is responsive to his needs, but leaves
the substance and the details of that education to state and local school officials.

In contrast to the EHA's vague mandate for a free appropriate public education
lies one very specific directive prescribing the educational environment for handicapped children. Each state must establish

> procedures to assure that, to the maximum extent appropriate, handi-
> capped children . . . are educated with children who are not handicapped,
> and that special education, separate schooling or other removal of handi-
> capped children from the regular educational environment occurs only
> when the nature or severity of the handicap is such that education in
> regular classes with the use of supplementary aids and services cannot be
> achieved satisfactorily.

§ 1412(5)(B). With this provision, Congress created a strong preference in favor of
mainstreaming. *Lachman v. Illinois State Board of Education*, 852 F.2d 290, 295
(7th Cir. 1988); *A.W. v. Northwest R-1 School District*, 813 F.2d 158, 162 (8th Cir.
1987); *Roncker v. Walter*, 700 F.2d 1058, 1063 (6th Cir. 1983).

By creating a statutory preference for mainstreaming, Congress also created a
tension between two provisions of the Act. School districts must both seek to
mainstream handicapped children and, at the same time, must tailor each child's
educational placement and program to his special needs. §§ 1412(1) and (5)(B).
Regular classes, however, will not provide an education that accounts for each
child's particular needs in every case. The nature or severity of some children's
handicaps is such that only special education can address their needs. For these
children, mainstreaming does not provide an education designed to meet their
unique needs and, thus, does not provide a free appropriate public education. As a
result, we cannot evaluate in the abstract whether a challenged placement meets
the EHA's mainstreaming requirement. "Rather, that laudable policy objective
must be weighed in tandem with the Act's principal goal of ensuring that the public
schools provide handicapped children with a free appropriate public education."
Lachman, 852 F.2d at 296; *Wilson v. Marana Unified School District*, 735 F.2d
1178, 1183 (9th Cir. 1984) (citations omitted).

Although Congress preferred education in the regular education environment, it
also recognized that regular education is not a suitable setting for educating many
handicapped children. *Rowley*, 458 U.S. at 181 n. 4; *Lachman*, 852 F.2d at 295. Thus,
the EHA allows school officials to remove a handicapped child from regular
education or to provide special education if they cannot educate the child satisfac-

torily in the regular classroom. § 1412(5)(B). Even when school officials can mainstream the child, they need not provide for an exclusively mainstreamed environment; the Act requires school officials to mainstream each child only to the maximum extent appropriate. *Id.* In short, the Act's mandate for a free appropriate public education qualifies and limits its mandate for education in the regular classroom. Schools must provide a free appropriate public education and must do so, to the maximum extent appropriate, in regular education classrooms. But when education in a regular classroom cannot meet the handicapped child's unique needs, the presumption in favor of mainstreaming is overcome and the school need not place the child in regular education. *See Lachman*, 852 F.2d at 295; *A.W.*, 813 F.2d at 163; *Roncker*, 700 F.2d at 1063. The Act does not, however, provide any substantive standards for striking the proper balance between its requirement for mainstreaming and its mandate for a free appropriate public education.

B. Determining Compliance With the Mainstreaming Requirement

Determining the contours of the mainstreaming requirement is a question of first impression for us. In the seminal interpretation of the EHA, the Supreme Court posited a two-part test for determining whether a school has provided a free appropriate public education: "First, has the State complied with the procedures set forth in the Act. And second, is the individualized educational program developed through the Act's procedures reasonably calculated to enable the child to receive educational benefits." *Rowley*, 458 U.S. at 206–07 (footnotes omitted). Despite the attractive ease of this two part inquiry, it is not the appropriate tool for determining whether a school district has met its mainstreaming obligations. In *Rowley*, the handicapped student was placed in a regular education class; the EHA's mainstreaming requirement was not an issue presented for the Court's consideration. Indeed, the Court carefully limited its decision to the facts before it, noting that it was not establishing a single test that would determine "the adequacy of educational benefits conferred upon all children covered by the Act." *Id.* at 202. Faced with the same issue we face today, both the Sixth and the Eighth Circuit concluded that the *Rowley* test was not intended to decide mainstreaming issues. *A.W.*, 813 F.2d at 163; *Roncker*, 700 F.2d at 1063. Moreover, both Circuits noted that the *Rowley* Court's analysis is ill suited for evaluating compliance with the mainstreaming requirement. *A.W.*, 813 F.2d at 163; *Roncker*, 700 F.2d at 1062. As the Eighth Circuit explained, the *Rowley* test assumes that the state has met all of the requirements of the Act, including the mainstreaming requirement. *A.W.*, 813 F.2d at 163 n. 7 (citations omitted). The *Rowley* test thus assumes the answer to the question presented in a mainstreaming case. Given the *Rowley* Court's express limitation on its own opinion, we must agree with the Sixth and Eighth Circuits that the *Rowley* test does not advance our inquiry when the question presented is whether the Act's mainstreaming requirement has been met.

Although we have not yet developed a standard for evaluating mainstreaming questions, we decline to adopt the approach that other circuits have taken. In *Roncker*, visiting the same question which we address today, the Sixth Circuit devised its own test to determine when and to what extent a handicapped child must be mainstreamed. According to the *Roncker* court,

[t]he proper inquiry is whether a proposed placement is appropriate under the Act. . . . In a case where the segregated facility is considered superior, the court should determine whether the services which make that placement superior could be feasibly provided in a non-segregated setting. If they can, the placement in the segregated school would be inappropriate under the Act.

Roncker, 700 F.2d at 1063 (citation and footnote omitted); *accord, A.W.*, 813 F.2d at 163.[1] We respectfully decline to follow the Sixth Circuit's analysis. Certainly, the *Roncker* test accounts for factors that are important in any mainstreaming case. We believe, however, that the test necessitates too intrusive an inquiry into the educational policy choices that Congress deliberately left to state and local school officials. Whether a particular service feasibly can be provided in a regular or special education setting is an administrative determination that state and local school officials are far better qualified and situated than are we to make. Moreover, the test makes little reference to the language of the EHA. Yet, as we shall see, we believe that the language of the Act itself provides a workable test for determining whether a state has complied with the Act's mainstreaming requirement.

Nor do we find the district court's approach to the issue the proper tool for analyzing the mainstreaming obligation. Relying primarily on whether Daniel could receive an educational benefit from regular education, the district court held that the special education class was the appropriate placement for Daniel. According to the court, "some children, even aided by supplemental aids and services in a regular education classroom, will never receive an educational benefit that approximates the level of skill and comprehension acquisition of nonhandicapped children." In these cases, regular education does not provide the child an appropriate education and the presumption in favor of mainstreaming is overcome. As no aspect of the Prekindergarten curriculum was within Daniel's reach, EPISD was not required to mainstream him.[2] Given the nature and severity of Daniel's handicap at the time EPISD placed him, we agree with the district court's conclusion that EPISD was not required to mainstream Daniel. We disagree, however, with the court's analysis of the mainstreaming issue, finding it troublesome for two reasons: first, as a prerequisite to mainstreaming, the court would require handicapped children to learn at approximately the same level as their nonhandicapped classmates. Second, the court places too much emphasis on the handicapped student's ability to achieve an educational benefit.

First, requiring as a prerequisite to mainstreaming that the handicapped child be able to learn at approximately the same level as his nonhandicapped classmates fails to take into account the principles that the Supreme Court announced in *Rowley.* Our public school system tolerates a wide range of differing learning abilities; at the same time, it provides educational opportunities that do not

---

[1] [FN 5] When the court conducts this inquiry, it may consider cost and the handicapped child's educational progress. *Roncker*, 700 F.2d at 1063 (citation omitted). It appears that the court also should compare the benefits the child would receive in special education to the benefits he would receive in regular education. *Id.*

[2] [FN 6] In addition, it was relevant to the court, but not dispositive, that Daniel's presence in the regular classroom was disruptive in that he required too much of the teacher's attention.

necessarily account for all of those different capacities to learn. As the *Rowley* Court noted, "[t]he educational opportunities provided by our public school systems undoubtedly differ from student to student, depending upon a myriad of factors that might affect a particular student's ability to assimilate information presented in the classroom." *Rowley*, 458 U.S. at 198.

With the EHA, Congress extended the states' tolerance of educational differences to include tolerance of many handicapped children. States must accept in their public schools children whose abilities and needs differ from those of the average student. Moreover, some of those students' abilities are vastly different from those of their nonhandicapped peers:

> [t]he Act requires participating states to educate a wide spectrum of handicapped children, from the marginally hearing impaired to the profoundly retarded and palsied. It is clear that the benefits obtainable by children at one end of the spectrum will differ dramatically from those obtainable by children at the other end, with infinite variations in between. One child may have little difficulty competing successfully with nonhandicapped children while another child may encounter great difficulty in acquiring even the most basic of self maintenance skills.

Rowley, 458 U.S. at 202. The *Rowley* court rejected the notion that the EHA requires states to provide handicapped children with educational opportunities that are equal to those provided to nonhandicapped students. *Id.* at 189. Thus, the Court recognized that the Act draws handicapped children into the regular education environment but, in the nature of things, cannot always offer them the same educational opportunities that regular education offers nonhandicapped children. States must tolerate educational differences; they need not perform the impossible: erase those differences by taking steps to equalize educational opportunities. As a result, the Act accepts the notion that handicapped students will participate in regular education but that some of them will not benefit as much as nonhandicapped students will. The Act requires states to tolerate a wide range of educational abilities in their schools and, specifically, in regular education — the EHA's preferred educational environment. Given the tolerance embodied in the EHA, we cannot predicate access to regular education on a child's ability to perform on par with nonhandicapped children.[3]

We recognize that some handicapped children may not be able to master as much of the regular education curriculum as their nonhandicapped classmates. This does not mean, however, that those handicapped children are not receiving any benefit from regular education. Nor does it mean that they are not receiving all of the benefit that their handicapping condition will permit. If the child's individual needs make mainstreaming appropriate, we cannot deny the child access to regular education simply because his educational achievement lags behind that of his classmates. Second, the district court placed too much emphasis on educational

---

[3] [FN 7] We emphasize, however, that school officials are not obligated to mainstream every handicapped child without regard for whether the regular classroom provides a free appropriate public education.

benefits.[4] Certainly, whether a child will benefit educationally from regular education is relevant and important to our analysis. Congress's primary purpose in enacting the EHA was to provide access to education for handicapped children. *Rowley*, 458 U.S. at 192, 193 n. 15. Implicit in Congress's purpose to provide access is a purpose to provide meaningful access, access that is sufficient to confer some educational benefit on the child. *Id.* at 200. Thus, the decision whether to mainstream a child must include an inquiry into whether the student will gain any educational benefit from regular education. Our analysis cannot stop here, however, for educational benefits are not mainstreaming's only virtue. Rather, mainstreaming may have benefits in and of itself. For example, the language and behavior models available from nonhandicapped children may be essential or helpful to the handicapped child's development. In other words, although a handicapped child may not be able to absorb all of the regular education curriculum, he may benefit from nonacademic experiences in the regular education environment. As the Sixth Circuit explained "[i]n some cases, a placement which may be considered better for academic reasons may not be appropriate because of the failure to provide for mainstreaming." *Roncker*, 700 F.2d at 1063. As we are not comfortable with the district court or the Sixth Circuit's approach to the mainstreaming question, we return to the text of the EHA for guidance. As we use the term "educational benefits" here, we, like the hearing officer and the district court, refer to the academic benefits available through education — as opposed to the overall growth and development benefits gained from education.

Ultimately, our task is to balance competing requirements of the EHA's dual mandate: a free appropriate public education that is provided, to the maximum extent appropriate, in the regular education classroom. As we begin our task we must keep in mind that Congress left the choice of educational policies and methods where it properly belongs — in the hands of state and local school officials. Our task is not to second-guess state and local policy decisions; rather, it is the narrow one of determining whether state and local school officials have complied with the Act. Adhering to the language of the EHA, we discern a two part test for determining compliance with the mainstreaming requirement. First, we ask whether education in the regular classroom, with the use of supplemental aids and services, can be achieved satisfactorily for a given child. *See* § 1412(5)(B). If it cannot and the school intends to provide special education or to remove the child from regular education, we ask, second, whether the school has mainstreamed the child to the maximum extent appropriate. *See id.* A variety of factors will inform each stage of our inquiry; the factors that we consider today do not constitute an exhaustive list of factors relevant to the mainstreaming issue. Moreover, no single factor is dispositive in all cases. Rather, our analysis is an individualized, fact-specific inquiry that requires us to examine carefully the nature and severity of the child's handicapping condition, his needs and abilities, and the schools' response to the child's needs.

In this case, several factors assist the first stage of our inquiry, whether EPISD can achieve education in the regular classroom satisfactorily. At the outset, we must

---

[4] [FN 8] As we use the term "educational benefits" here, we, like the hearing officer and the district court, refer to the academic benefits available through education — as opposed to the overall growth and development benefits gained from education.

examine whether the state has taken steps to accommodate the handicapped child in regular education. The Act requires states to provide supplementary aids and services and to modify the regular education program when they mainstream handicapped children. *See* § 1401(17), (18), § 1412(5)(B); *Rowley*, 458 U.S. at 189; 34 C.F.R. Part 300, App. C Question 48; *see also* Tex. Admin. Code Tit. 19 § 89.223(a)(4)(C). If the state has made no effort to take such accommodating steps, our inquiry ends, for the state is in violation of the Act's express mandate to supplement and modify regular education. If the state is providing supplementary aids and services and is modifying its regular education program, we must examine whether its efforts are sufficient. The Act does not permit states to make mere token gestures to accommodate handicapped students; its requirement for modifying and supplementing regular education is broad. *See* 34 C.F.R. Part 300, App. C Question 48; *see, e.g., Irving Independent School District v. Tatro*, 468 U.S. 883 (1984). Indeed, Texas expressly requires its local school districts to modify their regular education program when necessary to accommodate a handicapped child. Tex. Admin. Code Tit. 19 § 89.223(a)(4)(C).

Although broad, the requirement is not limitless. States need not provide every conceivable supplementary aid or service to assist the child. Furthermore, the Act does not require regular education instructors to devote all or most of their time to one handicapped child or to modify the regular education program beyond recognition. If a regular education instructor must devote all of her time to one handicapped child, she will be acting as a special education teacher in a regular education classroom. Moreover, she will be focusing her attentions on one child to the detriment of her entire class, including, perhaps, other, equally deserving, handicapped children who also may require extra attention. Likewise, mainstreaming would be pointless if we forced instructors to modify the regular education curriculum to the extent that the handicapped child is not required to learn any of the skills normally taught in regular education. The child would be receiving special education instruction in the regular education classroom; the only advantage to such an arrangement would be that the child is sitting next to a nonhandicapped student.

Next, we examine whether the child will receive an educational benefit from regular education. This inquiry necessarily will focus on the student's ability to grasp the essential elements of the regular education curriculum. Thus, we must pay close attention to the nature and severity of the child's handicap as well as to the curriculum and goals of the regular education class. For example, if the goal of a particular program is enhancing the child's development, as opposed to teaching him specific subjects such as reading or mathematics, our inquiry must focus on the child's ability to benefit from the developmental lessons, not exclusively on his potential for learning to read. We reiterate, however, that academic achievement is not the only purpose of mainstreaming. Integrating a handicapped child into a nonhandicapped environment may be beneficial in and of itself. Thus, our inquiry must extend beyond the educational benefits that the child may receive in regular education.

We also must examine the child's overall educational experience in the mainstreamed environment, balancing the benefits of regular and special education for each individual child. For example, a child may be able to absorb only a minimal amount of the regular education program, but may benefit enormously from the language models that his nonhandicapped peers provide for him. In such a case, the benefit that the child receives from mainstreaming may tip the balance in favor of mainstreaming, even if the child cannot flourish academically. *Roncker*, 700 F.2d at 1063. On the other hand, placing a child in regular education may be detrimental to the child. In such a case, mainstreaming would not provide an education that is attuned to the child's unique needs and would not be required under the Act. Indeed, mainstreaming a child who will suffer from the experience would violate the Act's mandate for a free appropriate public education.

Finally, we ask what effect the handicapped child's presence has on the regular classroom environment and, thus, on the education that the other students are receiving. A handicapped child's placement in regular education may prove troublesome for two reasons. First, the handicapped child may, as a result of his handicap, engage in disruptive behavior. " '[W]here a handicapped child is so disruptive in a regular classroom that the education of other students is significantly impaired, the needs of the handicapped child cannot be met in that environment. Therefore regular placement would not be appropriate to his or her needs.' " 34 C.F.R. § 300.552 Comment (quoting 34 C.F.R. Part 104 — Appendix, Paragraph 24). Second, the child may require so much of the instructor's attention that the instructor will have to ignore the other students' needs in order to tend to the handicapped child. The Act and its regulations mandate that the school provide supplementary aids and services in the regular education classroom. A teaching assistant or an aide may minimize the burden on the teacher. If, however, the handicapped child requires so much of the teacher or the aide's time that the rest of the class suffers, then the balance will tip in favor of placing the child in special education.

If we determine that education in the regular classroom cannot be achieved satisfactorily, we next ask whether the child has been mainstreamed to the maximum extent appropriate. The EHA and its regulations do not contemplate an all-or-nothing educational system in which handicapped children attend either regular or special education. Rather, the Act and its regulations require schools to offer a continuum of services. 34 C.F.R. § 300.551; *Lachman*, 852 F.2d at 296 n. 7 (citing *Wilson v. Marana Unified School District No. 6 of Pima County*, 735 F.2d 1178, 1183 (9th Cir. 1984)). Thus, the school must take intermediate steps where appropriate, such as placing the child in regular education for some academic classes and in special education for others, mainstreaming the child for nonacademic classes only, or providing interaction with nonhandicapped children during lunch and recess. The appropriate mix will vary from child to child and, it may be hoped, from school year to school year as the child develops. If the school officials have provided the maximum appropriate exposure to non-handicapped students, they have fulfilled their obligation under the EHA.

C. EPISD's Compliance with the Mainstreaming Requirement

After a careful review of the voluminous administrative record, we must agree with the trial court that EPISD's decision to remove Daniel from regular education does not run afoul of the EHA's preference for mainstreaming. Accounting for all of the factors we have identified today, we find that EPISD cannot educate Daniel satisfactorily in the regular education classroom. Furthermore, EPISD has taken creative steps to provide Daniel as much access to nonhandicapped students as it can, while providing him an education that is tailored to his unique needs. Thus, EPISD has mainstreamed Daniel to the maximum extent appropriate.

EPISD cannot educate Daniel satisfactorily in the regular education classroom; each of the factors we identified today counsels against placing Daniel in regular education. First, EPISD took steps to modify the Pre-kindergarten program and to provide supplementary aids and services for Daniel — all of which constitute a sufficient effort. Daniel contends that EPISD took no such steps and that, as a result, we can never know whether Daniel could have been educated in a regular classroom. Daniel's assertion is not supported by the record. The Pre-kindergarten teacher made genuine and creative efforts to reach Daniel, devoting a substantial — indeed, a disproportionate — amount of her time to him and modifying the class curriculum to meet his abilities. Unfortunately, Daniel's needs commanded most of the Pre-kindergarten instructor's time and diverted much of her attention away from the rest of her students. Furthermore, the instructor's efforts to modify the Pre-kindergarten curriculum produced few benefits to Daniel. Indeed, she would have to alter 90 to 100 percent of the curriculum to tailor it to Daniel's abilities. Such an effort would modify the curriculum beyond recognition, an effort which we will not require in the name of mainstreaming.

Second, Daniel receives little, if any, educational benefit in Pre-kindergarten. Dr. Bonnie Fairall, EPISD's Director of Special Education, testified that the Pre-kindergarten curriculum is "developmental in nature; communication skills, gross motor [skills]" and the like. The curriculum in Kindergarten and other grades is an academic program; the developmental skills taught in Pre-kindergarten are essential to success in the academic classes. Daniel's handicap has slowed his development so that he is not yet ready to learn the developmental skills offered in Pre-kindergarten. Daniel does not participate in class activities; he cannot master most or all of the lessons taught in the class. Very simply, Pre-kindergarten offers Daniel nothing but an opportunity to associate with nonhandicapped students.

Third, Daniel's overall educational experience has not been entirely beneficial. As we explained, Daniel can grasp little of the Pre-kindergarten curriculum; the only value of regular education for Daniel is the interaction which he has with nonhandicapped students. Daniel asserts that the opportunity for interaction, alone, is a sufficient ground for mainstreaming him. When we balance the benefits of regular education against those of special education, we cannot agree that the opportunity for Daniel to interact with nonhandicapped students is a sufficient ground for mainstreaming him. Regular education not only offers Daniel little in the way of academic or other benefits, it also may be harming him. When Daniel was placed in Pre-kindergarten, he attended school for a full day; both Pre-kindergarten and Early Childhood were half-day classes. The experts who testified before the hearing officer indicated that the full day program is too strenuous for a child with Daniel's condition. Simply put, Daniel is exhausted and, as a result, he sometimes falls asleep at school. Moreover, the record indicates that the stress of regular education may be causing Daniel to develop a stutter. Special education, on the other hand, is an educational environment in which Daniel is making progress. Balancing the benefits of a program that is only marginally beneficial and is somewhat detrimental against the benefits of a program that is clearly beneficial, we must agree that the beneficial program provides the more appropriate placement.

Finally, we agree that Daniel's presence in regular Pre-kindergarten is unfair to the rest of the class. When Daniel is in the Pre-kindergarten classroom, the instructor must devote all or most of her time to Daniel. Yet she has a classroom filled with other, equally deserving students who need her attention. Although regular education instructors must devote extra attention to their handicapped students, we will not require them to do so at the expense of their entire class.

Alone, each of the factors that we have reviewed suggests that EPISD cannot educate Daniel satisfactorily in the regular education classroom. Together, they clearly tip the balance in favor of placing Daniel in special education. Thus, we turn to the next phase of our inquiry and conclude that EPISD has mainstreamed Daniel to the maximum extent appropriate. Finding that a placement that allocates Daniel's time equally between regular and special education is not appropriate, EPISD has taken the intermediate step of mainstreaming Daniel for lunch and recess. This opportunity for association with nonhandicapped students is not as extensive as Daniel's parents would like. It is, however, an appropriate step that may help to prepare Daniel for regular education in the future. As education in the regular classroom, with the use of supplementary aids and services cannot be achieved satisfactorily, and as EPISD has placed Daniel with nonhandicapped students to the maximum extent appropriate, we affirm the district court. . . .

VI. *Conclusion*

When a parent is examining the educational opportunities available for his handicapped child, he may be expected to focus primarily on his own child's best interest. Likewise, when state and local school officials are examining the alternatives for educating a handicapped child, the child's needs are a principal concern. But other concerns must enter into the school official's calculus. Public education of handicapped children occurs in the public school system, a public institution entrusted with the enormous task of serving a variety of often competing needs. In the eyes of the school official, each need is equally important and each child is equally deserving of his share of the school's limited resources. In this case, the trial court correctly concluded that the needs of the handicapped child and the needs of the nonhandicapped students in the Pre-kindergarten class tip the balance in favor of placing Daniel in special education. We thus

AFFIRM

NOTES AND QUESTIONS

1. To what extent do the *Roncker* and *Daniel R.R.* cases conflict with each other? Could both have been decided correctly, or is one of them (or are both) wrong? Does *Daniel R.R.* support the idea that there is a presumption in favor of a mainstreamed placement? If it does, how strong is the presumption and what is needed to overcome it? A recent law review article questions the wisdom of a presumption in favor of integrated settings for students in special education. Ruth

Colker, *The Disability Integration Presumption: Thirty Years Later*, 154 U. Pa. L. Rev. 789 (2006). A partial response is found in Mark C. Weber, *Reflections on the New Individuals with Disabilities Education Improvement Act*, 68 Fla. L. Rev. 7, 44–45 (2006).

2.   Does the court's discussion convince you that the requirements of appropriate education and the least restrictive environment may conflict? Many courts have relied on concerns over appropriate education in denying parents' requests for less restrictive placements for their children. *See, e.g., Beth B. v. Van Clay*, 282 F.3d 493 (7th Cir. 2002). Are there ways to resolve or avoid the conflict short of abandoning inclusion? An interesting debate over whether services appropriate for a child can be delivered in a less restrictive setting is found in *Pachl v. Seagren*, 453 F.3d 1064 (8th Cir. 2006) (upholding administrative decision and district court judgment that placement of sixth-grade child with multiple disabilities, including epilepsy, Dandy Walker syndrome, autism spectrum disorder, scoliosis, and bilateral hearing loss in self-contained classroom 30% of school day met least restrictive environment standard). The dissent in *Pachl* emphasized that the requirement for inclusion should compel consideration of the quality of a student's inclusion experience. For example, the dissent lamented that the student in this case did not interact with other students in the lunchroom or her social studies classroom. *Id.* at 1071 (Heaney, J., dissenting). If the quality of inclusive education were deemed guaranteed by IDEA, what might be the implications for public school personnel in administering IEPs?

D.   APPLYING THE STANDARDS FOR INCLUSION

In the *Rachel H.* case, the Ninth Circuit Court of Appeals determined that the law dictated an inclusive placement for a child with mental retardation who was making little progress in her mainstream placement.

SACRAMENTO UNIFIED
SCHOOL DISTRICT v. RACHEL H.
14 F.3d 1398 (9th Cir. 1994)

In this case, the court affirmed a district court decision that required a placement in a full-day mainstream setting, with supplemental services, for a second grader with mental retardation.

SNEED, CIRCUIT JUDGE.

The Sacramento Unified School District ("the District") timely appeals the district court's judgment in favor of Rachel Holland ("Rachel") and the California State Department of Education. The court found that the appropriate placement for Rachel under the Individuals with Disabilities Act ("IDEA") was full-time in a regular second grade classroom with some supplemental services. The District contends that the appropriate placement for Rachel is half-time in special education classes and half-time in a regular class. We affirm the judgment of the district court.

I.
FACTS AND PRIOR PROCEEDINGS

Rachel Holland is now 11 years old and is mentally retarded. She was tested with an I.Q. of 44. She attended a variety of special education programs in the District from 1985-89. Her parents sought to increase the time Rachel spent in a regular classroom, and in the fall of 1989, they requested that Rachel be placed full-time in a regular classroom for the 1989-90 school year. The District rejected their request and proposed a placement that would have divided Rachel's time between a special education class for academic subjects and a regular class for non-academic activities such as art, music, lunch, and recess. The district court found that this plan would have required moving Rachel at least six times each day between the two classrooms. The Hollands instead enrolled Rachel in a regular kindergarten class at the Shalom School, a private school. Rachel remained at the Shalom School in regular classes and at the time the district court rendered its opinion was in the second grade.

The Hollands and the District were able to agree on an Individualized Education Program ("IEP") for Rachel. Although the IEP is required to be reviewed annually, see 20 U.S.C. § [1414(d)(4)(A)(i)], because of the dispute between the parties, Rachel's IEP has not been reviewed since January 1990.[5]

The Hollands appealed the District's placement decision to a state hearing officer pursuant to 20 U.S.C. § 1415(b)(2). They maintained that Rachel best learned social and academic skills in a regular classroom and would not benefit from being in a special education class. The District contended Rachel was too severely disabled to benefit from full-time placement in a regular class. The hearing officer concluded that the District had failed to make an adequate effort to educate Rachel in a regular class pursuant to the IDEA. The officer found that (1) Rachel had benefitted from her regular kindergarten class — that she was motivated to learn and learned by imitation and modeling; (2) Rachel was not disruptive in a regular classroom; and (3) the District had overstated the cost of putting Rachel in regular education — that the cost would not be so great that it weighed against placing her in a regular classroom. The hearing officer ordered the District to place Rachel in a regular classroom with support services, including a special education consultant and a part-time aide.

The District appealed this determination to the district court. Pursuant to 20 U.S.C. § 1415(e)(2), the parties presented additional evidence at an evidentiary hearing. The court affirmed the decision of the hearing officer that Rachel should be placed full-time in a regular classroom.

In considering whether the District proposed an appropriate placement for Rachel, the district court examined the following factors: (1) the educational benefits available to Rachel in a regular classroom, supplemented with appropriate

[5] [FN 3] The 1990 IEP objectives include: speaking in 4- or 5-word sentences; repeating instructions of complex tasks; initiating and terminating conversations; stating her name, address and phone number; participating in a safety program with classmates; developing a 24-word sight vocabulary; counting to 25; printing her first and last names and the alphabet; playing cooperatively; participating in lunch without supervision; and identifying upper and lower case letters and the sounds associated with them.

aids and services, as compared with the educational benefits of a special education classroom; (2) the non-academic benefits of interaction with children who were not disabled; (3) the effect of Rachel's presence on the teacher and other children in the classroom; and (4) the cost of mainstreaming Rachel in a regular classroom.

1. *Educational Benefits*

The district court found the first factor, educational benefits to Rachel, weighed in favor of placing her in a regular classroom. . . . The court noted that the District's evidence focused on Rachel's limitations but did not establish that the educational opportunities available through special education were better or equal to those available in a regular classroom. Moreover, the court found that the testimony of the Hollands' experts was more credible because they had more background in evaluating children with disabilities placed in regular classrooms and that they had a greater opportunity to observe Rachel over an extended period of time in normal circumstances. The district court also gave great weight to the testimony of Rachel's current teacher, Nina Crone, whom the court found to be an experienced, skillful teacher. Ms. Crone stated that Rachel was a full member of the class and participated in all activities. Ms. Crone testified that Rachel was making progress on her IEP goals: She was learning one-to-one correspondence in counting, was able to recite the English and Hebrew alphabets, and was improving her communication abilities and sentence lengths.

The district court found that Rachel received substantial benefits in regular education and that all of her IEP goals could be implemented in a regular classroom with some modification to the curriculum and with the assistance of a part-time aide.

2. *Non-Academic Benefits*

The district court next found that the second factor, non-academic benefits to Rachel, also weighed in favor of placing her in a regular classroom. The court noted that the Hollands' evidence indicated that Rachel had developed her social and communications skills as well as her self-confidence from placement in a regular class, while the District's evidence tended to show that Rachel was not learning from exposure to other children and that she was isolated from her classmates. The court concluded that the differing evaluations in large part reflected the predisposition of the evaluators. The court found the testimony of Rachel's mother and her current teacher to be the most credible. These witnesses testified regarding Rachel's excitement about school, learning, and her new friendships and Rachel's improved self-confidence.

3. *Effect on the Teacher and Children in the Regular Class*

The district court next addressed the issue of whether Rachel had a detrimental effect on others in her regular classroom. The court looked at two aspects: (1) whether there was detriment because the child was disruptive, distracting or unruly, and (2) whether the child would take up so much of the teacher's time that the other students would suffer from lack of attention. The witnesses of both parties agreed that Rachel followed directions and was well-behaved and not a distraction in class. The court found the most germane evidence on the second aspect came from Rachel's second grade teacher, Nina Crone, who testified that Rachel did not interfere with her ability to teach the other children and in the future would require only a part-time aide. Accordingly, the district court determined that the third factor, the effect of Rachel's presence on the teacher and other children in the classroom weighed in favor of placing her in a regular classroom.

4. *Cost*

Finally, the district court found that the District had not offered any persuasive or credible evidence to support its claim that educating Rachel in a regular classroom with appropriate services would be significantly more expensive than educating her in the District's proposed setting.

The District contended that it would cost $109,000 to educate Rachel full-time in a regular classroom. This figure was based on the cost of providing a full-time aide for Rachel plus an estimated $80,000 for school-wide sensitivity training. The court found that the District did not establish that such training was necessary. Further, the court noted that even if such training were necessary, there was evidence from the California Department of Education that the training could be had at no cost. Moreover, the court found it would be inappropriate to assign the total cost of the training to Rachel when other children with disabilities would benefit. In addition, the court concluded that the evidence did not suggest that Rachel required a full-time aide.

In addition, the court found that the District should have compared the cost of placing Rachel in a special class of approximately 12 students with a full-time special education teacher and two full-time aides and the cost of placing her in a regular class with a part-time aide. The District provided no evidence of this cost comparison.

The court also was not persuaded by the District's argument that it would lose significant funding if Rachel did not spend at least 51% of her time in a special education class. The court noted that a witness from the California Department of Education testified that waivers were available if a school district sought to adopt a program that did not fit neatly within the funding guidelines. The District had not applied for a waiver.

By inflating the cost estimates and failing to address the true comparison, the District did not meet its burden of proving that regular placement would burden the District's funds or adversely affect services available to other children. Therefore, the court found that the cost factor did not weigh against mainstreaming Rachel.

The district court concluded that the appropriate placement for Rachel was full-time in a regular second grade classroom with some supplemental services and affirmed the decision of the hearing officer.

. . . .

IV.

DISCUSSION

. . . .

B. *Mainstreaming Requirements of the IDEA*

1. *The Statute*

The IDEA provides that each state must establish:

> [P]rocedures to assure that, to the maximum extent appropriate, children with disabilities . . . are educated with children who are not disabled, and that special classes, separate schooling, or other removal of children with disabilities from the regular educational environment occurs only when the nature or severity of the disability is such that education in regular classes with the use of supplementary aids and services cannot be achieved satisfactorily. . . .

20 U.S.C. § 1412(5)(B).

This provision sets forth Congress's preference for educating children with disabilities in regular classrooms with their peers. *Department of Educ. v. Katherine D.*, 727 F.2d 809, 817 (9th Cir. 1983); *see also Oberti v. Board of Educ.*, 995 F.2d 1204, 1213 (3d Cir. 1993); *Greer v. Rome City Sch. Dist.*, 950 F.2d 688, 695 (11th Cir. 1991), *withdrawn*, 956 F.2d 1025 (1992), and *reinstated*, 967 F.2d 470 (1992); *Daniel R.R.*, 874 F.2d at 1044.

. . . .

3. *Test for Determining Compliance with the IDEA's Mainstreaming Requirement*

We have not adopted or devised a standard for determining the presence of compliance with 20 U.S.C. § 1412(5)(B). The Third, Fifth and Eleventh Circuits use what is known as the *Daniel R.R.* test. *Oberti*, 995 F.2d at 1215; *Greer*, 950 F.2d at 696; *Daniel R.R.*, 874 F.2d at 1048.[6] The Fourth, Sixth and Eighth Circuits apply the *Roncker* test. *Devries v. Fairfax County Sch. Bd.*, 882 F.2d 876, 879 (4th Cir. 1989); *A.W. v. Northwest R-1 Sch. Dist.*, 813 F.2d 158, 163 (8th Cir. 1987); *Roncker v. Walter*, 700 F.2d 1058, 1063 (6th Cir. 1983).[7]

Factors the courts consider in applying the first prong of this test are (1) the

---

[6] [FN 5] First, the court must determine "whether education in the regular classroom, with the use of supplemental aids and services, can be achieved satisfactorily. . . ." *Daniel R.R.*, 874 F.2d at 1048. If the court finds that education cannot be achieved satisfactorily in the regular classroom, then it must decide "whether the school has mainstreamed the child to the maximum extent appropriate." *Id.*

[7] [FN 6] According to the court in *Roncker*: "[W]here the segregated facility is considered superior, the court should determine whether the services which make that placement superior could be feasibly provided in a non-segregated setting. If they can, the placement in the segregated school would be inappropriate under the Act." 700 F.2d at 1063.

steps the school district has taken to accommodate the child in a regular classroom; (2) whether the child will receive an educational benefit from regular education; (3) the child's overall educational experience in regular education; and (4) the effect the disabled child's presence has on the regular classroom. *Daniel R.R.*, 874 F.2d at 1048–49; *see also Oberti*, 995 F.2d at 1215–17; *Greer*, 950 F.2d at 696–97. In *Greer* the court added the factor of cost, stating that "if the cost of educating a handicapped child in a regular classroom is so great that it would significantly impact upon the education of other children in the district, then education in a regular classroom is not appropriate." 950 F.2d at 697.

Regarding the second factor, the *Oberti* and *Greer* courts compared the educational benefits received in a regular classroom with the benefits received in a special education class. *Oberti*, 995 F.2d at 1216; *Greer*, 950 F.2d at 697.

Courts are to (1) compare the benefits the child would receive in special education with those she would receive in regular education; (2) consider whether the child would be disruptive in the non-segregated setting; and (3) consider the cost of mainstreaming. *Id.*

Although the district court relied principally on *Daniel R.R.* and *Greer*, it did not specifically adopt the *Daniel R.R.* test over the *Roncker* test. Rather, it employed factors found in both lines of cases in its analysis. The result was a four-factor balancing test in which the court considered (1) the educational benefits of placement full-time in a regular class; (2) the non-academic benefits of such placement; (3) the effect Rachel had on the teacher and children in the regular class; and (4) the costs of mainstreaming Rachel. This analysis directly addresses the issue of the appropriate placement for a child with disabilities under the requirements of 20 U.S.C. § 1412(5)(B). Accordingly, we approve and adopt the test employed by the district court.

4. *The District's Contentions on Appeal*

The District strenuously disagrees with the district court's findings that Rachel was receiving academic and non-academic benefits in a regular class and did not have a detrimental effect on the teacher or other students. It argues that the court's findings were contrary to the evidence of the state Diagnostic Center and that the court should not have been persuaded by the testimony of Rachel's teacher, particularly her testimony that Rachel would need only a part-time aide in the future. The district court, however, conducted a full evidentiary hearing and made a thorough analysis. The court found the Hollands' evidence to be more persuasive. Moreover, the court asked Rachel's teacher extensive questions regarding Rachel's need for a part-time aide. We will not disturb the findings of the district court.

The District is also not persuasive on the issue of cost. The District now claims that it will lose up to $190,764 in state special education funding if Rachel is not enrolled in a special education class at least 51% of the day. However, the District has not sought a waiver pursuant to California Education Code § 56101. This section provides that (1) any school district may request a waiver of any provision of the Education Code if the waiver is necessary or beneficial to the student's IEP, and (2) the Board may grant the waiver when failure to do so would hinder compliance with federal mandates for a free appropriate education for children with disabilities. Cal. Educ. Code § 56101(a) & (b) (Deering 1992).

Finally, the District, citing *Wilson v. Marana Unified Sch. Dist.*, 735 F.2d 1178 (9th Cir. 1984), argues that Rachel must receive her academic and functional curriculum in special education from a specially credentialed teacher.

Wilson does not stand for this proposition. Rather, the court in *Wilson* stated:

> The school district argues that under state law a child who qualifies for special education *must* be taught by a teacher who is certificated in that child's particular area of disability. We do not agree and do not reach a decision on that broad assertion. We hold only, under our standard of review, that the school district's decision was a reasonable one under the circumstances of this case.

735 F.2d at 1180 (emphasis in original). More importantly, the District's proposition that Rachel must be taught by a special education teacher runs directly counter to the congressional preference that children with disabilities be educated in regular classes with children who are not disabled. *See* 20 U.S.C. § 1412(5)(B).

We affirm the judgment of the district court. While we cannot determine what the appropriate placement is for Rachel at the present time, we hold that the determination of the present and future appropriate placement for Rachel should be based on the principles set forth in this opinion and the opinion of the district court.

NOTES AND QUESTIONS

1.   The court notes the differences between the circuit courts regarding the standard to be applied in disputes over the least restrictive environment. Do you think that results will be much different under the two standards? What is the Ninth Circuit standard for evaluating disputes over mainstreaming after *Rachel H.*? Will results in future Ninth Circuit cases differ from those of other circuits, and if so, how?

2.   The district court opinion contains an account of the evidentiary proceedings, in which two witnesses described Rachel holding a book upside down in a Hebrew class in a private school. The school district witness said that the incident demonstrated that Rachel was not benefiting from mainstreamed instruction. The parents' witness pointed out that another child helped Rachel turn the book over and find her place in the text; the witness described this as an example of the positive peer interaction that Rachel needed to experience in developing her ability to live in the world. *See Board of Educ. v. Holland*, 786 F. Supp. 874, 881 (E.D. Cal. 1992). One author views the interchange as "a parable about least restrictive environment ideas in general." Mark C. Weber, *The Least Restrictive Environment Obligation as an Entitlement to Educational Services: A Commentary*, 5 U.C. Davis J. Juv. L. & Pol'y 2 (2001).

3.   IDEA and its regulations appear to recognize that a mainstreamed setting is not appropriate for all children. For example, the regulations discuss residential placements and specify that they be provided free of cost to parents when they are

needed. 34 C.F.R. § 300.104. Just as courts have frequently rejected parents' requests for placements in less restrictive settings, as described in note 2 following *Daniel R.R., supra,* so they have frequently upheld parents' requests for more restrictive settings than school districts proposed. *E.g., Independent Sch. Dist. No. 284 v. A.C.,* 258 F.3d 769 (8th Cir. 2001) (ordering residential placement for chronically truant child displaying oppositional behavior); *S.C. v. Deptford Township Bd. of Educ.,* 248 F. Supp. 2d 368 (D.N.J. 2003) (requiring specialized placement for child with autism). For a recent review of the arguments on inclusion in the context of the reauthorized IDEA, see Stacey Gordon, *Making Sense of the Inclusion Debate under IDEA,* 2006 BYU EDUC. & L.J. 189.

4. Parents have challenged systemic failures by school districts to implement procedures guaranteeing that children will receive placement in the least restrictive setting, and that related services will be provided in mainstreamed settings to keep children from being moved to more restrictive placements. *See, e.g., Gaskin v. Pennsylvania,* 389 F. Supp. 2d 628 (E.D. Pa. 2005) (approving class action settlement promoting placement in mainstream settings, expanding related services and accommodations, and creating monitoring procedures); *Corey H. v. Board of Educ.,* 995 F. Supp. 900 (N.D. Ill. 1998) (requiring compliance plan from state to force municipal school district to comply with least restrictive environment obligations), 27 IDELR 688 (N.D. Ill. 1998) (entering consent decree establishing procedures to promote school based intervention and enable children to learn in mainstreamed settings); *J.G. v. Board of Educ.,* 26 IDELR 114 (W.D.N.Y. 1998) (entering consent decree with extensive inclusion provisions). What sort of evidence would you expect to see presented in proceedings of this type? What systemic practices would lead to or prevent placement of children in less restrictive settings? Would you expect some parents to oppose the positions taken by other parents? *See generally Reid L. v. Illinois State Bd. of Educ.,* 289 F.3d 1009 (7th Cir. 2002) (affirming denial of motion to intervene in *Corey H.*). What would their arguments be?

5. Numerous cases deny reimbursement to parents for unilateral placements they made for their children on the basis that the placements were in a setting more restrictive than required to educate the child. *See, e.g., M.S. v. Yonkers Board of Educ.,* 231 F.3d 96 (2d Cir. 2000) (overturning reimbursement award on ground, among others, that placement chosen by parents failed test of least restrictive environment); *Linda W. v. Indiana Dep't of Educ.,* 200 F.3d 504 (7th Cir. 1999) (denying reimbursement on ground that district's proposed modification of program would have provided appropriate education in less restrictive environment than that chosen by parent). Nevertheless, some courts have recognized that a parent whose child is offered an inappropriate placement by the school district frequently cannot buy special education services in a mainstreamed setting. The parent cannot simply place the child in a public school in another district, but typically must enroll the child in a private school that specializes in the disability that the child has. *See, e.g., Cleveland Heights-University Heights City Sch. Dist. v. Boss,* 144 F.3d 391 (6th Cir. 1998) (not holding parent to least restrictive environment standard for unilateral placement when district violated IDEA). Is there any middle ground between these two positions?

6. As *Rachel H.* demonstrates, a child may need extensive related services in order to succeed in a mainstreamed educational setting, and failure to make progress without those services does not mean that the effort at mainstreaming should be abandoned. *See, e.g., A.S. v. Norwalk Bd. of Educ.*, 183 F. Supp. 2d 534 (D. Conn. 2002) (upholding hearing officer decision requiring mainstreaming with extensive related services for child with neurological and visual impairments). For this reason, the topic of related services is closely tied to that of least restrictive environment. In fact, it is no exaggeration to say that the obligation to provide education in the least restrictive environment imposes a positive entitlement to related services. For a discussion of related services and the connection to the entitlement to placement in the least restrictive environment, see *infra* Chapter 7 (Related Services).

Chapter 7

RELATED SERVICES

A. INTRODUCTION

The federal special education law worked a major innovation by providing specifically that children are entitled not just to specialized instruction, but also to aids and services that are not strictly educational in nature, but facilitate learning. The entitlement may be studied by considering first, the statutory and regulatory requirements; second, the scope of an exception to the entitlement for services that are medical in nature but not diagnostic; and third, the intimate relationship between the entitlement to related services and the obligation to provide education in the least restrictive setting.

B. STATUTORY AND REGULATORY REQUIREMENTS

The term "related services" is defined to mean "transportation and such developmental, corrective, and other supportive services as are required to assist a child with a disability to benefit from special education." 34 C.F.R. § 300.34(a); *see* 20 U.S.C. § 1401(26). Those services include, but are not intended to be limited to, the following:

> speech-language pathology and audiology services, interpreting services, psychological services, physical and occupational therapy, recreation, including therapeutic recreation, early identification and assessment of disabilities in children, counseling services, including rehabilitation counseling, orientation and mobility services, and medical services for diagnostic purposes. Related services also include school health services and school nurse services, social work services in schools, and parent counseling and training.

34 C.F.R. § 300.34(a). Students of interest-group politics may infer the working of particular groups of professionals to insure that their specialties are mentioned, but the list as a whole is more a testament to the breadth of services that a child may need in order to make educational progress than anything in the way of a serious effort to increase demand for a particular service.

As a component of free, appropriate public education, these services must be provided without cost to parents or children. *See* 20 U.S.C. § 1401(9). Efforts to recover funding from public aid or other third-party payors may occur only when the parents and child face no realistic threat of financial loss from decreases in available lifetime coverage or any other source. *See Seals v. Loftis*, 614 F. Supp. 302 (E.D. Tenn. 1985). Many cases deal with claims for reimbursement or compensatory services because of denial of specific related services. For an overview of the caselaw, see Mark C. Weber, Special Education Law and Litigation, Chapter 8 (3d ed. 2008 & supps.).

NOTES AND QUESTIONS

1. Does the *Board of Education v. Rowley*, 458 U.S. 176 (1982), operate as a limit on the entitlement to special education or to related services or to both? Are there ways in which parents can argue for extensive related services even for a child who is advancing from grade to grade in a timely way without the requested services?

2. Under 20 U.S.C. § 1401(1)–(2) and 34 C.F.R. §§ 300.5–.6, school districts have to provide assistive technology devices, defined as items, pieces of equipment, or product systems that are used to maintain or improve functional capabilities of children with disabilities. States have the option to deem assistive technology special education or related services. Policy Letter, 16 EHLR 1317 (U.S. Dep't of Educ., Office of Special Educ. Programs 1990). Could the assistive technology entitlement be relied on to argue for enhanced services (other than implanted devices) despite *Rowley* (or despite the exception for medical services discussed below)?

3. The entitlement to an individual assessment and determination has been enforced in a variety of cases. In one, the court required a school district to pay for mapping sessions for a child's cochlear implant. *Stratham Sch. Dist v. Beth P.*, 2003 DNH 22; 2003 U.S. Dist. LEXIS 1683 (D.N.H. Feb. 5, 2003). The 2004 Amendments to IDEA exclude coverage of medical devices that are surgically implanted (such as cochlear implants) from the definition of assistive technology devices. 20 U.S.C. § 1401(1)(B). This change would not affect the outcome in the *Beth P.* case, but the regulations appear to do so by providing that "Related services do not include a medical device that is surgically implanted, the optimization of that device's functioning (e.g. mapping), maintenance of that device, or the replacement of that device." 34 C.F.R. § 300.34(b)(1). Some limits apply to this exclusion. *See* 34 C.F.R. § 300.34(b)(2). Do you think that the exclusion of mapping services is a sensible interpretation by the Department of Education of the congressional exclusion of the device itself from the definition of assistive technology devices?

4. It would appear that a child would have to be covered under IDEA in order to be entitled to related services. *See Dubois v. Connecticut State Bd. of Educ.*, 727 F.2d 44 (2d Cir. 1984) (finding that child not eligible under IDEA lacked entitlement to transportation). The picture is not so simple; a child with a disabling condition who is not eligible for special education under IDEA may still be covered under section 504 of the Rehabilitation Act of 1973 or other laws, and entitled to related services as a reasonable accommodation. *See Kennedy v. Board of Educ.*, 337 S.E.2d 905 (W. Va. 1985) (holding that equal protection requires district to provide specialized transportation across private dirt road for children with spina bifida enrolled in general education). One difficulty school districts then face is the obligation to provide the service without a specific funding stream to pay for it. This gives districts an incentive to find a child eligible for special education services (if only for adaptive physical education) in order to obtain state and federal funding for services given the child.

C. THE MEDICAL SERVICES EXCEPTION

The statute and regulations restrict "medical services" specified in the list of related services to those for diagnostic and evaluation purposes. In *Tatro*, one of the first cases the Supreme Court decided under the federal special education law, the Court ruled that clean, intermittent catheterization was a covered related service, rather than one excluded by the definition of medical services.

IRVING INDEPENDENT SCHOOL DISTRICT v. TATRO
468 U.S. 883 (1984)

The Court ruled that the exception to covered related services for medical services does not reach the service of clean, intermittent catheterization for a child who cannot urinate normally.

CHIEF JUSTICE BURGER delivered the opinion of the Court.

We granted certiorari to determine whether the Education of the Handicapped Act or the Rehabilitation Act of 1973 requires a school district to provide a handicapped child with clean intermittent catheterization during school hours.

I

Amber Tatro is an 8-year-old girl born with a defect known as spina bifida. As a result, she suffers from orthopedic and speech impairments and a neurogenic bladder, which prevents her from emptying her bladder voluntarily. Consequently, she must be catheterized every three or four hours to avoid injury to her kidneys. In accordance with accepted medical practice, clean intermittent catheterization (CIC), a procedure involving the insertion of a catheter into the urethra to drain the bladder, has been prescribed. The procedure is a simple one that may be performed in a few minutes by a layperson with less than an hour's training. Amber's parents, babysitter, and teenage brother are all qualified to administer CIC, and Amber soon will be able to perform this procedure herself.

In 1979 petitioner Irving Independent School District agreed to provide special education for Amber, who was then three and one-half years old. In consultation with her parents, who are respondents here, petitioner developed an individualized education program for Amber under the requirements of the Education of the Handicapped Act, as amended significantly by the Education for All Handicapped Children Act of 1975. The individualized education program provided that Amber would attend early childhood development classes and receive special services such as physical and occupational therapy. That program, however, made no provision for school personnel to administer CIC.

Respondents unsuccessfully pursued administrative remedies to secure CIC services for Amber during school hours. In October 1979 respondents brought the present action in District Court against petitioner, the State Board of Education, and others. *See* § 1415(e)(2). They sought an injunction ordering petitioner to provide Amber with CIC and sought damages and attorney's fees. First, respondents invoked the Education of the Handicapped Act. Because Texas received funding under that statute, petitioner was required to provide Amber with a "free appropriate public education," §§ 1412(1), 1414(a)(1)(C)(ii), which is defined to include "related services," § 1401(18). Respondents argued that CIC is one such "related service." Second, respondents invoked § 504 of the Rehabilitation Act of 1973, 87 Stat. 394, as amended, 29 U.S.C. § 794, which forbids an individual, by reason of a handicap, to be "excluded from the participation in, be denied the benefits of, or be subjected to discrimination under" any program receiving federal aid.

The District Court denied respondents' request for a preliminary injunction. *Tatro v. Texas*, 481 F. Supp. 1224 (N.D. Tex. 1979). That court concluded that CIC was not a "related service" under the Education of the Handicapped Act because it did not serve a need arising from the effort to educate. It also held that § 504 of the Rehabilitation Act did not require "the setting up of governmental health care for people seeking to participate" in federally funded programs. *Id.* at 1229.

The Court of Appeals reversed. *Tatro v. Texas*, 625 F.2d 557 (C.A.5 1980) (*Tatro I*). First, it held that CIC was a "related service" under the Education of the Handicapped Act, 20 U.S.C. § 1401(17), because without the procedure Amber could not attend classes and benefit from special education. Second, it held that petitioner's refusal to provide CIC effectively excluded her from a federally funded educational program in violation of § 504 of the Rehabilitation Act. The Court of Appeals remanded for the District Court to develop a factual record and apply these legal principles.

On remand petitioner stressed the Education of the Handicapped Act's explicit provision that "medical services" could qualify as "related services" only when they served the purpose of diagnosis or evaluation. The District Court held that under Texas law a nurse or other qualified person may administer CIC without engaging in the unauthorized practice of medicine, provided that a doctor prescribes and supervises the procedure. The District Court then held that, because a doctor was not needed to administer CIC, provision of the procedure was not a "medical service" for purposes of the Education of the Handicapped Act. Finding CIC to be a "related service" under that Act, the District Court ordered petitioner and the State Board of Education to modify Amber's individualized education program to include provision of CIC during school hours. It also awarded compensatory damages against petitioner. *Tatro v. Texas*, 516 F. Supp. 968 (N.D. Tex. 1981).

The Court of Appeals affirmed. *Tatro v. Texas*, 703 F.2d 823 (C.A.5 1983) (*Tatro II*). That court accepted the District Court's conclusion that state law permitted qualified persons to administer CIC without the physical presence of a doctor, and it affirmed the award of relief under the Education of the Handicapped Act. In affirming the award of attorney's fees based on a finding of liability under the Rehabilitation Act, the Court of Appeals held that no change of circumstances since *Tatro I* justified a different result.

We granted certiorari, and we affirm in part and reverse in part.

II

This case poses two separate issues. The first is whether the Education of the Handicapped Act requires petitioner to provide CIC services to Amber. The second is whether § 504 of the Rehabilitation Act creates such an obligation. We first turn to the claim presented under the Education of the Handicapped Act.

States receiving funds under the Act are obliged to satisfy certain conditions. A primary condition is that the state implement a policy "that assures all handicapped children the right to a free appropriate public education." 20 U.S.C. § 1412(1). Each educational agency applying to a state for funding must provide assurances in turn that its program aims to provide "a free appropriate public education to all handicapped children." § 1414(a)(1)(C)(ii).

A "free appropriate public education" is explicitly defined as "special education and related services." § 1401(18). The term "special education" means

> "specially designed instruction, at no cost to parents or guardians, to meet the unique needs of a handicapped child, including classroom instruction, instruction in physical education, home instruction, and instruction in hospitals and institutions." § 1401(16).

"Related services" are defined as

> "transportation, and such developmental, corrective, and other supportive services (including speech pathology and audiology, psychological services, physical and occupational therapy, recreation, and medical and counseling services, except that such medical services shall be for diagnostic and evaluation purposes only) as may be required to assist a handicapped child to benefit from special education, and includes the early identification and assessment of handicapping conditions in children." § 1401(17).

The issue in this case is whether CIC is a "related service" that petitioner is obliged to provide to Amber. We must answer two questions: first, whether CIC is a "supportive servic[e] . . . required to assist a handicapped child to benefit from special education"; and second, whether CIC is excluded from this definition as a "medical servic[e]" serving purposes other than diagnosis or evaluation.

A

The Court of Appeals was clearly correct in holding that CIC is a "supportive servic[e] . . . required to assist a handicapped child to benefit from special education." It is clear on this record that, without having CIC services available during the school day, Amber cannot attend school and thereby "benefit from special education." CIC services therefore fall squarely within the definition of a "supportive service."[1]

---

[1] [FN 7] The Department of Education has agreed with this reasoning in an interpretive ruling that specifically found CIC to be a "related service." 46 Fed. Reg. 4912 (1981). *Accord, Tokarcik v. Forest Hills School District,* 665 F.2d 443 (C.A.3 1981), *cert. denied sub nom. Scanlon v. Tokarcik,* 458 U.S. 1121 (1982). The Secretary twice postponed temporarily the effective date of this interpretive ruling, *see* 46 Fed. Reg. 12495 (1981); *id.* at 18975, and later postponed it indefinitely, *id.* at 25614. But the Department

As we have stated before, "Congress sought primarily to make public education available to handicapped children" and "to make such access meaningful." *Board of Education of Hendrick Hudson Central School District v. Rowley*, 458 U.S. 176, 192 (1982). A service that enables a handicapped child to remain at school during the day is an important means of providing the child with the meaningful access to education that Congress envisioned. The Act makes specific provision for services, like transportation, for example, that do no more than enable a child to be physically present in class, *see* 20 U.S.C. § 1401(17); and the Act specifically authorizes grants for schools to alter buildings and equipment to make them accessible to the handicapped, § 1406; *see* S. Rep. No. 94-168, p. 38 (1975), U.S. Code Cong. & Admin. News 1975, p. 1425; 121 Cong. Rec. 19483–19484 (1975) (remarks of Sen. Stafford). Services like CIC that permit a child to remain at school during the day are no less related to the effort to educate than are services that enable the child to reach, enter, or exit the school.

We hold that CIC services in this case qualify as a "supportive servic[e] . . . required to assist a handicapped child to benefit from special education."

B

We also agree with the Court of Appeals that provision of CIC is not a "medical servic[e]," which a school is required to provide only for purposes of diagnosis or evaluation. *See* 20 U.S.C. § 1401(17). We begin with the regulations of the Department of Education, which are entitled to deference. The regulations define "related services" for handicapped children to include "school health services," 34 C.F.R. § 300.13(a) (1983), which are defined in turn as "services provided by a qualified school nurse or other qualified person," § 300.13(b)(10). "Medical services" are defined as "services provided by a licensed physician." § 300.13(b)(4).[2] Thus, the Secretary has determined that the services of a school nurse otherwise qualifying as a "related service" are not subject to exclusion as a "medical service," but that the services of a physician are excludable as such.

This definition of "medical services" is a reasonable interpretation of congressional intent. Although Congress devoted little discussion to the "medical services" exclusion, the Secretary could reasonably have concluded that it was designed to spare schools from an obligation to provide a service that might well prove unduly expensive and beyond the range of their competence. From this understanding of congressional purpose, the Secretary could reasonably have concluded that Congress intended to impose the obligation to provide school nursing services.

Congress plainly required schools to hire various specially trained personnel to help handicapped children, such as "trained occupational therapists, speech therapists, psychologists, social workers and other appropriately trained personnel." S.

---

presently does view CIC services as an allowable cost under Part B of the Act. *Ibid.*

[2] [FN 10] The regulations actually define only those "medical services" that are owed to handicapped children: "services provided by a licensed physician to determine a child's medically related handicapping condition which results in the child's need for special education and related services." 34 C.F.R. § 300.13(b)(4) (1983). Presumably this means that "medical services" not owed under the statute are those "services by a licensed physician" that serve other purposes.

Rep. No. 94-168, *supra*, at 33, U.S. Code Cong. & Admin. News 1975, p. 1457. School nurses have long been a part of the educational system, and the Secretary could therefore reasonably conclude that school nursing services are not the sort of burden that Congress intended to exclude as a "medical service." By limiting the "medical services" exclusion to the services of a physician or hospital, both far more expensive, the Secretary has given a permissible construction to the provision.

Petitioner's contrary interpretation of the "medical services" exclusion is unconvincing. In petitioner's view, CIC is a "medical service," even though it may be provided by a nurse or trained layperson; that conclusion rests on its reading of Texas law that confines CIC to uses in accordance with a physician's prescription and under a physician's ultimate supervision. Aside from conflicting with the Secretary's reasonable interpretation of congressional intent, however, such a rule would be anomalous. Nurses in petitioner School District are authorized to dispense oral medications and administer emergency injections in accordance with a physician's prescription. This kind of service for nonhandicapped children is difficult to distinguish from the provision of CIC to the handicapped.[3] It would be strange indeed if Congress, in attempting to extend special services to handicapped children, were unwilling to guarantee them services of a kind that are routinely provided to the nonhandicapped.

To keep in perspective the obligation to provide services that relate to both the health and educational needs of handicapped students, we note several limitations that should minimize the burden petitioner fears. First, to be entitled to related services, a child must be handicapped so as to require special education. *See* 20 U.S.C. § 1401(1); 34 C.F.R. § 300.5 (1983). In the absence of a handicap that requires special education, the need for what otherwise might qualify as a related service does not create an obligation under the Act. *See* 34 C.F.R. § 300.14, Comment (1) (1983).

Second, only those services necessary to aid a handicapped child to benefit from special education must be provided, regardless how easily a school nurse or layperson could furnish them. For example, if a particular medication or treatment may appropriately be administered to a handicapped child other than during the school day, a school is not required to provide nursing services to administer it.

Third, the regulations state that school nursing services must be provided only if they can be performed by a nurse or other qualified person, not if they must be performed by a physician. *See* 34 C.F.R. §§ 300.13(a), (b)(4), (b)(10) (1983). It bears mentioning that here not even the services of a nurse are required; as is conceded, a layperson with minimal training is qualified to provide CIC. *See also, e.g.,*

---

[3] [FN 12] Petitioner attempts to distinguish the administration of prescription drugs from the administration of CIC on the ground that Texas law expressly limits the liability of school personnel performing the former, *see* Tex. Educ. Code Ann. § 21.914(c) (Supp. 1984), but not the latter. This distinction, however, bears no relation to whether CIC is a "related service." The introduction of handicapped children into a school creates numerous new possibilities for injury and liability. Many of these risks are more serious than that posed by CIC, which the courts below found is a safe procedure even when performed by a 9-year-old girl. Congress assumed that states receiving the generous grants under the Act were up to the job of managing these new risks. Whether petitioner decides to purchase more liability insurance or to persuade the State to extend the limitation on liability, the risks posed by CIC should not prove to be a large burden.

Department of Education of Hawaii v. Katherine D., 727 F.2d 809 (C.A.9 1983).

Finally, we note that respondents are not asking petitioner to provide equipment that Amber needs for CIC. Tr. of Oral Arg. 18–19. They seek only the services of a qualified person at the school.

We conclude that provision of CIC to Amber is not subject to exclusion as a "medical service," and we affirm the Court of Appeals' holding that CIC is a "related service" under the Education of the Handicapped Act.

. . . .

It is so ordered.

JUSTICE BRENNAN, with whom JUSTICE MARSHALL joins, concurring in part and dissenting in part [omitted].

JUSTICE STEVENS, concurring in part and dissenting in part [omitted].

NOTES AND QUESTIONS

1.   The last portion of the majority opinion and the separate opinions of Justices Brennan and Stevens address claims for attorneys' fees and other relief advanced under the Rehabilitation Act of 1973. Although *Smith v. Robinson*, 468 U.S. 992 (1984), made these claims unavailable, that determination was congressionally overruled in the Handicapped Children's Protection Act, now codified at 20 U.S.C. § 1415(*l*).

2.   The concerns over liability raised in note 12 of the majority opinion are very real for school districts and may induce them to balk at providing services that children need to learn. Are there any measures that a state may undertake to ease districts' fears of liability? Are there reasons not to adopt measures such as governmental immunities from tort liability?

Fifteen years later, in *Garret F.*, the Court built upon *Tatro* in ruling that a school needed to provide a variety of services, including tracheotomy suctioning and ventilator maintenance, to a child with quadriplegia.

CEDAR RAPIDS COMMUNITY SCHOOL DISTRICT v. GARRET F.
526 U.S. 66 (1999)

This case established that extensive services to enable a child with quadriplegia who uses a ventilator are related services that must be provided under the federal special education law, rather than excluded medical services.

JUSTICE STEVENS delivered the opinion of the Court.

The Individuals with Disabilities Education Act (IDEA) was enacted, in part, "to assure that all children with disabilities have available to them . . . a free appropriate public education which emphasizes special education and related services designed to meet their unique needs." 20 U.S.C. § 1400(c). Consistent with this purpose, the IDEA authorizes federal financial assistance to States that agree to provide disabled children with special education and "related services." *See* §§ 1401(a)(18), 1412(1). The question presented in this case is whether the definition of "related services" in § 1401(a)(17) requires a public school district in a participating State to provide a ventilator-dependent student with certain nursing services during school hours.

I

Respondent Garret F. is a friendly, creative, and intelligent young man. When Garret was four years old, his spinal column was severed in a motorcycle accident. Though paralyzed from the neck down, his mental capacities were unaffected. He is able to speak, to control his motorized wheelchair through use of a puff and suck straw, and to operate a computer with a device that responds to head movements. Garret is currently a student in the Cedar Rapids Community School District (District), he attends regular classes in a typical school program, and his academic performance has been a success. Garret is, however, ventilator dependent,[4] and therefore requires a responsible individual nearby to attend to certain physical needs while he is in school.[5]

During Garret's early years at school his family provided for his physical care during the schoolday. When he was in kindergarten, his 18-year-old aunt attended him; in the next four years, his family used settlement proceeds they received after the accident, their insurance, and other resources to employ a licensed practical nurse. In 1993, Garret's mother requested the District to accept financial responsibility for the health care services that Garret requires during the schoolday. The District denied the request, believing that it was not legally obligated to provide continuous one-on-one nursing services.

---

[4] [FN 2] In his report in this case, the Administrative Law Judge explained: "Being ventilator dependent means that [Garret] breathes only with external aids, usually an electric ventilator, and occasionally by someone else's manual pumping of an air bag attached to his tracheotomy tube when the ventilator is being maintained. This later procedure is called ambu bagging."

[5] [FN 3] "He needs assistance with urinary bladder catheterization once a day, the suctioning of his tracheotomy tube as needed, but at least once every six hours, with food and drink at lunchtime, in getting into a reclining position for five minutes of each hour, and ambu bagging occasionally as needed when the ventilator is checked for proper functioning. He also needs assistance from someone familiar with his ventilator in the event there is a malfunction or electrical problem, and someone who can perform emergency procedures in the event he experiences autonomic hyperreflexia. Autonomic hyperreflexia is an uncontrolled visceral reaction to anxiety or a full bladder. Blood pressure increases, heart rate increases, and flushing and sweating may occur. Garret has not experienced autonomic hyperreflexia frequently in recent years, and it has usually been alleviated by catheterization. He has not ever experienced autonomic hyperreflexia at school. Garret is capable of communicating his needs orally or in another fashion so long as he has not been rendered unable to do so by an extended lack of oxygen."

Relying on both the IDEA and Iowa law, Garret's mother requested a hearing before the Iowa Department of Education. An Administrative Law Judge (ALJ) received extensive evidence concerning Garret's special needs, the District's treatment of other disabled students, and the assistance provided to other ventilator-dependent children in other parts of the country. In his 47-page report, the ALJ found that the District has about 17,500 students, of whom approximately 2,200 need some form of special education or special services. Although Garret is the only ventilator-dependent student in the District, most of the health care services that he needs are already provided for some other students. "The primary difference between Garret's situation and that of other students is his dependency on his ventilator for life support." The ALJ noted that the parties disagreed over the training or licensure required for the care and supervision of such students, and that those providing such care in other parts of the country ranged from nonlicensed personnel to registered nurses. However, the District did not contend that only a licensed physician could provide the services in question.

The ALJ explained that federal law requires that children with a variety of health impairments be provided with "special education and related services" when their disabilities adversely affect their academic performance, and that such children should be educated to the maximum extent appropriate with children who are not disabled. In addition, the ALJ explained that applicable federal regulations distinguish between "school health services," which are provided by a "qualified school nurse or other qualified person," and "medical services," which are provided by a licensed physician. *See* 34 C.F.R. §§ 300.16(a), (b)(4), (b)(11) (1998). The District must provide the former, but need not provide the latter (except, of course, those "medical services" that are for diagnostic or evaluation purposes, 20 U.S.C. § 1401(a)(17)). According to the ALJ, the distinction in the regulations does not just depend on "the title of the person providing the service"; instead, the "medical services" exclusion is limited to services that are "in the special training, knowledge, and judgment of a physician to carry out." App. to Pet. for Cert. 51a. The ALJ thus concluded that the IDEA required the District to bear financial responsibility for all of the services in dispute, including continuous nursing services.

The District challenged the ALJ's decision in Federal District Court, but that court approved the ALJ's IDEA ruling and granted summary judgment against the District. The Court of Appeals affirmed. 106 F.3d 822 (C.A.8 1997). It noted that, as a recipient of federal funds under the IDEA, Iowa has a statutory duty to provide all disabled children a "free appropriate public education," which includes "related services." *See id.* at 824. The Court of Appeals read our opinion in *Irving Independent School Dist. v. Tatro*, 468 U.S. 883 (1984), to provide a two-step analysis of the "related services" definition in § 1401(a)(17) — asking first, whether the requested services are included within the phrase "supportive services"; and second, whether the services are excluded as "medical services." 106 F.3d at 824–825. The Court of Appeals succinctly answered both questions in Garret's favor. The Court found the first step plainly satisfied, since Garret cannot attend school unless the requested services are available during the schoolday. *Id.* at 825. As to the second step, the court reasoned that *Tatro* "established a bright-line test: the services of a physician (other than for diagnostic and evaluation purposes) are subject to the medical services exclusion, but services that can be provided in the school setting by a nurse or qualified layperson are not." 106 F.3d at 825.

In its petition for certiorari, the District challenged only the second step of the Court of Appeals' analysis. The District pointed out that some federal courts have not asked whether the requested health services must be delivered by a physician, but instead have applied a multifactor test that considers, generally speaking, the nature and extent of the services at issue. *See, e.g., Neely v. Rutherford County School*, 68 F.3d 965, 972–973 (C.A.6 1995); *Detsel v. Board of Ed. of Auburn Enlarged City School Dist.*, 820 F.2d 587, 588 (C.A.2) *(per curiam)* (1987). We granted the District's petition to resolve this conflict.

II

The District contends that § 1401(a)(17) does not require it to provide Garret with "continuous one-on-one nursing services" during the schoolday, even though Garret cannot remain in school without such care. However, the IDEA's definition of "related services," our decision in *Irving Independent School Dist. v. Tatro*, 468 U.S. 883 (1984), and the overall statutory scheme all support the decision of the Court of Appeals.

The text of the "related services" definition, broadly encompasses those support-ive services that "may be required to assist a child with a disability to benefit from special education." As we have already noted, the District does not challenge the Court of Appeals' conclusion that the in-school services at issue are within the covered category of "supportive services." As a general matter, services that enable a disabled child to remain in school during the day provide the student with "the meaningful access to education that Congress envisioned." *Tatro*, 468 U.S. at 891 (" 'Congress sought primarily to make public education available to handicapped children' and 'to make such access meaningful' " (quoting *Board of Ed. of Hendrick Hudson Central School Dist., Westchester Cty. v. Rowley*, 458 U.S. 176, 192 (1982))).

This general definition of "related services" is illuminated by a parenthetical phrase listing examples of particular services that are included within the statute's coverage. § 1401(a)(17). "[M]edical services" are enumerated in this list, but such services are limited to those that are "for diagnostic and evaluation purposes." *Ibid.* The statute does not contain a more specific definition of the "medical services" that are excepted from the coverage of § 1401(a)(17).

The scope of the "medical services" exclusion is not a matter of first impression in this Court. In *Tatro* we concluded that the Secretary of Education had reasonably determined that the term "medical services" referred only to services that must be performed by a physician, and not to school health services. 468 U.S. at 892–894. Accordingly, we held that a specific form of health care (clean intermittent catheterization) that is often, though not always, performed by a nurse is not an excluded medical service. We referenced the likely cost of the services and the competence of school staff as justifications for drawing a line between physician and other services, *ibid.*, but our endorsement of that line was unmistakable.[6] It is thus

---

[6] [FN 6] "The regulations define 'related services' for handicapped children to include 'school health services,' 34 C.F.R. § 300.13(a) (1983), which are defined in turn as 'services provided by a qualified school

settled that the phrase "medical services" in § 1401(a)(17) does not embrace all forms of care that might loosely be described as "medical" in other contexts, such as a claim for an income tax deduction. *See* 26 U.S.C. § 213(d)(1) (1994 ed. and Supp. II) (defining "medical care").

The District does not ask us to define the term so broadly. Indeed, the District does not argue that any of the items of care that Garret needs, considered individually, could be excluded from the scope of 20 U.S.C. § 1401(a)(17). It could not make such an argument, considering that one of the services Garret needs (catheterization) was at issue in *Tatro*, and the others may be provided competently by a school nurse or other trained personnel. As the ALJ concluded, most of the requested services are already provided by the District to other students, and the in-school care necessitated by Garret's ventilator dependency does not demand the training, knowledge, and judgment of a licensed physician. While more extensive, the in-school services Garret needs are no more "medical" than was the care sought in *Tatro*.

Instead, the District points to the combined and continuous character of the required care, and proposes a test under which the outcome in any particular case would "depend upon a series of factors, such as [1] whether the care is continuous or intermittent, [2] whether existing school health personnel can provide the service, [3] the cost of the service, and [4] the potential consequences if the service is not properly performed."

The District's multifactor test is not supported by any recognized source of legal authority. The proposed factors can be found in neither the text of the statute nor the regulations that we upheld in *Tatro*. Moreover, the District offers no explanation why these characteristics make one service any more "medical" than another. The continuous character of certain services associated with Garret's ventilator dependency has no apparent relationship to "medical" services, much less a relationship of equivalence. Continuous services may be more costly and may require additional school personnel, but they are not thereby more "medical." Whatever its imperfections, a rule that limits the medical services exemption to physician services is

---

nurse or other qualified person,' § 300.13(b)(10). 'Medical services' are defined as 'services provided by a licensed physician.' § 300.13(b)(4). Thus, the Secretary has [reasonably] determined that the services of a school nurse otherwise qualifying as a 'related service' are not subject to exclusion as a 'medical service,' but that the services of a physician are excludable as such.

. . . .

"... *By limiting the 'medical services' exclusion to the services of a physician or hospital,* both far more expensive, the Secretary has given a permissible construction to the provision."

468 U.S. at 892–893 (emphasis added) (footnote omitted); *see also id.* at 894 ("[T]he regulations state that school nursing services must be provided only if they can be performed by a nurse or other qualified person, not if they must be performed by a physician").

Based on certain policy letters issued by the Department of Education, it seems that the Secretary's post-*Tatro* view of the statute has not been entirely clear. We may assume that the Secretary has authority under the IDEA to adopt regulations that define the "medical services" exclusion by more explicitly taking into account the nature and extent of the requested services; and the Secretary surely has the authority to enumerate the services that are, and are not, fairly included within the scope of § 1407(a)(17). But the Secretary has done neither; and, in this Court, she advocates affirming the judgment of the Court of Appeals. We obviously have no authority to rewrite the regulations, and we see no sufficient reason to revise *Tatro*, either.

unquestionably a reasonable and generally workable interpretation of the statute. Absent an elaboration of the statutory terms plainly more convincing than that which we reviewed in *Tatro*, there is no good reason to depart from settled law.

Finally, the District raises broader concerns about the financial burden that it must bear to provide the services that Garret needs to stay in school. The problem for the District in providing these services is not that its staff cannot be trained to deliver them; the problem, the District contends, is that the existing school health staff cannot meet all of their responsibilities and provide for Garret at the same time. Through its multifactor test, the District seeks to establish a kind of undue-burden exemption primarily based on the cost of the requested services. The first two factors can be seen as examples of cost-based distinctions: Intermittent care is often less expensive than continuous care, and the use of existing personnel is cheaper than hiring additional employees. The third factor — the cost of the service — would then encompass the first two. The relevance of the fourth factor is likewise related to cost because extra care may be necessary if potential consequences are especially serious.

The District may have legitimate financial concerns, but our role in this dispute is to interpret existing law. Defining "related services" in a manner that *accommodates* the cost concerns Congress may have had, *cf. Tatro*, 468 U.S. at 892, is altogether different from using cost *itself* as the definition. Given that § 1401(a)(17) does not employ cost in its definition of "related services" or excluded "medical services," accepting the District's cost-based standard as the sole test for determining the scope of the provision would require us to engage in judicial lawmaking without any guidance from Congress. It would also create some tension with the purposes of the IDEA. The statute may not require public schools to maximize the potential of disabled students commensurate with the opportunities provided to other children, *see Rowley*, 458 U.S. at 200; and the potential financial burdens imposed on participating States may be relevant to arriving at a sensible construction of the IDEA, *see Tatro*, 468 U.S. at 892. But Congress intended "to open the door of public education" to all qualified children and "require[d] participating States to educate handicapped children with nonhandicapped children whenever possible." *Rowley*, 458 U.S. at 192; *see id.* at 179–181; *see also Honig v. Doe*, 484 U.S. 305, 310–311, 324 (1988); §§ 1412(1), (2)(C), (5)(B).[7]

-----

[7] [FN 10] The dissent's approach, which seems to be even broader than the District's, is unconvincing. The dissent's rejection of our unanimous decision in *Tatro* comes 15 years too late, *see Patterson v. McLean Credit Union*, 491 U.S. 164, 172–173, (1989) (*stare decisis* has "special force" in statutory interpretation), and it offers nothing constructive in its place. Aside from rejecting a "provider-specific approach," the dissent cites unrelated statutes and offers a circular definition of "medical services." Moreover, the dissent's approach apparently would exclude most ordinary school nursing services of the kind routinely provided to nondisabled children; that anomalous result is not easily attributable to congressional intent. *See Tatro*, 468 U.S. at 893.

In a later discussion the dissent does offer a specific proposal: that we now interpret (or rewrite) the Secretary's regulations so that school districts need only provide disabled children with "health-related services that school nurses can perform as part of their normal duties." The District does not dispute that its nurses "can perform" the requested services, so the dissent's objection is that District nurses would not be performing their "normal duties" if they met Garret's needs. That is, the District would need an "additional employee." This proposal is functionally similar to a proposed regulation — ultimately withdrawn — that would have replaced the "school health services" provision. *See* 47 Fed. Reg. 33838,

This case is about whether meaningful access to the public schools will be assured, not the level of education that a school must finance once access is attained. It is undisputed that the services at issue must be provided if Garret is to remain in school. Under the statute, our precedent, and the purposes of the IDEA, the District must fund such "related services" in order to help guarantee that students like Garret are integrated into the public schools.

The judgment of the Court of Appeals is accordingly

Affirmed.

JUSTICE THOMAS, with whom JUSTICE KENNEDY joins, dissenting.

The majority, relying heavily on our decision in *Irving Independent School Dist. v. Tatro*, 468 U.S. 883 (1984), concludes that the Individuals with Disabilities Education Act (IDEA), 20 U.S.C. § 1400 *et seq.*, requires a public school district to fund continuous, one-on-one nursing care for disabled children. Because *Tatro* cannot be squared with the text of IDEA, the Court should not adhere to it in this case. Even assuming that *Tatro* was correct in the first instance, the majority's extension of it is unwarranted and ignores the constitutionally mandated rules of construction applicable to legislation enacted pursuant to Congress' spending power.

I

As the majority recounts, IDEA authorizes the provision of federal financial assistance to States that agree to provide, *inter alia*, "special education and related services" for disabled children. § 1401(a)(18). In *Tatro*, *supra*, we held that this provision of IDEA required a school district to provide clean intermittent catheterization to a disabled child several times a day. In so holding, we relied on Department of Education regulations, which we concluded had reasonably interpreted IDEA's definition of "related services" to require school districts in participating States to provide "school nursing services" (of which we assumed catheterization was a subcategory) but not "services of a physician." *Id.* at 892–893. This holding is contrary to the plain text of IDEA, and its reliance on the Department of Education's regulations was misplaced.

A

Before we consider whether deference to an agency regulation is appropriate, "we first ask whether Congress has 'directly spoken to the precise question at issue. If the intent of Congress is clear, that is the end of the matter; for the court, as well as the agency, must give effect to the unambiguously expressed intent of Congress.'"

33854 (1982) (the statute and regulations may not be read to affect legal obligations to make available to handicapped children services, including school health services, made available to nonhandicapped children). The dissent's suggestion is unacceptable for several reasons. Most important, such revisions of the regulations are better left to the Secretary, and an additional staffing need is generally not a sufficient objection to the requirements of § 1401(a)(17).

Unfortunately, the Court in *Tatro* failed to consider this necessary antecedent question before turning to the Department of Education's regulations implementing IDEA's related services provision. The Court instead began "with the regulations of the Department of Education, which," it said, "are entitled to deference." *Tatro, supra,* at 891–892. The Court need not have looked beyond the text of IDEA, which expressly indicates that school districts are not required to provide medical services, except for diagnostic and evaluation purposes. 20 U.S.C. § 1401(a)(17). The majority asserts that *Tatro* precludes reading the term "medical services" to include "all forms of care that might loosely be described as 'medical.'" The majority does not explain, however, why "services" that are "medical" in nature are not "medical services." Not only is the definition that the majority rejects consistent with other uses of the term in federal law, it also avoids the anomalous result of holding that the services at issue in *Tatro* (as well as in this case), while not "medical services," would nonetheless qualify as medical care for federal income tax purposes.

The primary problem with *Tatro*, and the majority's reliance on it today, is that the Court focused on the provider of the services rather than the services themselves. We do not typically think that automotive services are limited to those provided by a mechanic, for example. Rather, anything done to repair or service a car, no matter who does the work, is thought to fall into that category. Similarly, the term "food service" is not generally thought to be limited to work performed by a chef. The term "medical" similarly does not support *Tatro*'s provider-specific approach, but encompasses services that are "of, *relating to, or concerned with* physicians *or* with the practice of medicine." *See* WEBSTER'S THIRD NEW INTERNATIONAL DICTIONARY 1402 (1986) (emphasis added); *see also id.* at 1551 (defining "nurse" as "a person skilled in caring for and waiting on the infirm, the injured, or the sick; *specif:* one esp. trained to carry out such duties under the supervision of a physician").

IDEA's structure and purpose reinforce this textual interpretation. Congress enacted IDEA to increase the *educational* opportunities available to disabled children, not to provide medical care for them. *See* 20 U.S.C. § 1400(c) ("It is the purpose of this chapter to assure that all children with disabilities have . . . a free appropriate public education"); *see also* § 1412 ("In order to qualify for assistance . . . a State shall demonstrate . . . [that it] has in effect a policy that assures all children with disabilities the right to a free appropriate public education"); *Board of Ed. v. Rowley,* 458 U.S. 176, 179 (1982) ("The Act represents an ambitious federal effort to promote the education of handicapped children"). As such, where Congress decided to require a supportive service — including speech pathology, occupational therapy, and audiology — that appears "medical" in nature, it took care to do so explicitly. *See* § 1401(a)(17). Congress specified these services precisely because it recognized that they would otherwise fall under the broad "medical services" exclusion. Indeed, when it crafted the definition of related services, Congress could have, but chose not to, include "nursing services" in this list.

B

Tatro was wrongly decided even if the phrase "medical services" was subject to multiple constructions, and therefore, deference to any reasonable Department of

Education regulation was appropriate. The Department of Education has never promulgated regulations defining the scope of IDEA's "medical services" exclusion. One year before *Tatro* was decided, the Secretary of Education issued proposed regulations that defined excluded medical services as "services relating to the practice of medicine." 47 Fed. Reg. 33838 (1982). These regulations, which represent the Department's only attempt to define the disputed term, were never adopted. Instead, "[t]he regulations actually define only those 'medical services' that *are* owed to handicapped children," *Tatro*, 468 U.S. at 892, n. 10 (emphasis in original), not those that *are not.* Now, as when *Tatro* was decided, the regulations require districts to provide services performed " 'by a licensed physician to determine a child's medically related handicapping condition which results in the child's need for special education and related services.' " *Ibid.* (quoting 34 C.F.R. § 300.13(b)(4) (1983), recodified and amended as 34 C.F.R. § 300.16(b)(4) (1998)).

Extrapolating from this regulation, the *Tatro* Court presumed that this meant that " 'medical services' not owed under the statute are those 'services by a licensed physician' that serve other purposes." *Tatro, supra,* at 892, n. 10 (emphasis deleted). The Court, therefore, did not defer to the regulation itself, but rather relied on an inference drawn from it to speculate about how a regulation might read if the Department of Education promulgated one. Deference in those circumstances is impermissible. We cannot defer to a regulation that does not exist.

II

Assuming that *Tatro* was correctly decided in the first instance, it does not control the outcome of this case. Because IDEA was enacted pursuant to Congress' spending power, *Rowley, supra,* at 190, n. 11, our analysis of the statute in this case is governed by special rules of construction. We have repeatedly emphasized that, when Congress places conditions on the receipt of federal funds, "it must do so unambiguously." *Pennhurst State School and Hospital v. Halderman,* 451 U.S. 1, 17 (1981). *See also Rowley, supra,* at 190, n. 11. . . . It follows that we must interpret Spending Clause legislation narrowly, in order to avoid saddling the States with obligations that they did not anticipate.

The majority's approach in this case turns this Spending Clause presumption on its head. We have held that, in enacting IDEA, Congress wished to require "States to educate handicapped children with nonhandicapped children whenever possible," *Rowley, supra,* at 202. Congress, however, also took steps to limit the fiscal burdens that States must bear in attempting to achieve this laudable goal. These steps include requiring States to provide an education that is only "appropriate" rather than requiring them to maximize the potential of disabled students, *see* 20 U.S.C. § 1400(c); *Rowley, supra,* at 200, recognizing that integration into the public school environment is not always possible, *see* § 1412(5), and clarifying that, with a few exceptions, public schools need not provide "medical services" for disabled students, §§ 1401(a)(17) and (18).

For this reason, we have previously recognized that Congress did not intend to "impos[e] upon the States a burden of unspecified proportions and weight" in enacting IDEA. *Rowley, supra,* at 190, n. 11. These federalism concerns require us to interpret IDEA's related services provision, consistent with *Tatro,* as follows:

Department of Education regulations require districts to provide disabled children with health-related services that school nurses can perform as part of their normal duties. This reading of *Tatro*, although less broad than the majority's, is equally plausible and certainly more consistent with our obligation to interpret Spending Clause legislation narrowly. Before concluding that the district was required to provide clean intermittent catheterization for Amber Tatro, we observed that school nurses in the district were authorized to perform services that were "difficult to distinguish from the provision of [clean intermittent catheterization] to the handicapped." *Tatro*, 468 U.S. at 893. We concluded that "[i]t would be strange indeed if Congress, in attempting to extend special services to handicapped children, were unwilling to guarantee them services of a kind that are routinely provided to the nonhandicapped." *Id.* at 893–894.

Unlike clean intermittent catheterization, however, a school nurse cannot provide the services that respondent requires, and continue to perform her normal duties. To the contrary, because respondent requires continuous, one-on-one care throughout the entire schoolday, all agree that the district must hire an additional employee to attend solely to respondent. This will cost a minimum of $18,000 per year. Although the majority recognizes this fact, it nonetheless concludes that the "more extensive" nature of the services that respondent needs is irrelevant to the question whether those services fall under the medical services exclusion. This approach disregards the constitutionally mandated principles of construction applicable to Spending Clause legislation and blindsides unwary States with fiscal obligations that they could not have anticipated.

For the foregoing reasons, I respectfully dissent.

NOTES AND QUESTIONS

1. Concerns about cost seem paramount in the discussion of Justice Thomas. Assuming that the majority view prevails, are there any means states might use to ease the burden placed on specific school districts by the need to provide services that are expensive? State statutes typically provide for state assistance to districts for unusually expensive placements, such as those in private residential schools. Should the state also make money available for unusually expensive related services that may be needed to educate a child in a school within the district? What is the socially optimal way to finance services to children with disabilities as severe as those Garret has?

2. Cost factors sometimes create the prospect of pitting parents of children with disabilities against parents of children who do not receive special education services. The parents of children with severe disabilities tend to bear very high costs for their children's care and maintenance outside of school, and reason that the costs of education and related services should be considered as merely one more part of the ordinary cost of conducting affairs for school districts. Those parents seeking funding for other priorities, from Advanced Placement programs to football, may think of themselves in competition with the parents looking for related services for their children. What should a school administrator do when faced with these types of conflicting demands for resources?

3. After *Garret F.*, is there any service that need not be provided by a physician that a school district does not have to furnish? Assume that you are an attorney for a state department of education giving technical assistance to school districts, and that *Garret F.* has just come down. What advice will you give to the districts about what they must do to comply with the ruling?

4. Although courts have generally been reluctant to view psychiatric hospitalizations as either special education or related services, at least one case holds that a hospitalization for diagnostic and evaluative purposes was a covered related service, and so should have been paid for by the child's school district. *Department of Educ. v. Cari Rae S.*, 158 F. Supp. 2d 1190 (D. Haw. 2001). How would you challenge or defend that holding if it were appealed? Recent cases on reimbursement for psychiatric hospitalization for non-diagnostic purposes include *Richardson Indep. Sch. Dist. v. Michael Z.*, 580 F.3d 286 (5th Cir. 2009) (vacating decision below and remanding for determination whether child's treatment at psychiatric facility was primarily oriented toward enabling her to receive meaningful educational benefit); *Mary Courtney T. v. School Dist.*, 575 F.3d 235 (3d Cir. 2009) (distinguishing between stay in residential school and one in psychiatric hospital, rejecting a reimbursement claim for the latter and holding that services provided child while she was in psychiatric crisis were excluded medical services). Are there circumstances under which the parents should be entitled to reimbursement for a psychiatric hospital placement? *See generally* Ralph D. Mawdsley, *Applying the* Forest Grove *Balancing Test to Parent Reimbursement for Placement in Residential Treatment Medical Facilities*, 253 EDUC. L. REP. 521 (2010).

D. RELATING LEAST RESTRICTIVE ENVIRONMENT TO RELATED SERVICES

Neither the entitlement to related services nor the least restrictive environment requirement stands alone. The point is perhaps too apparent to be mentioned, but in order for a child to succeed in the mainstream, the child may need extensive related services, far more than might be required in a more restrictive setting. In the following case, parents obtained a less restrictive placement for their child. The court develops with some specificity the obligation of the school district to provide related services to make an inclusive placement work.

OBERTI v. BOARD OF EDUCATION
995 F.2d 1204 (3d Cir. 1993)

The court in this case affirmed a district court decision requiring the education of a child with severe disabilities in a general education classroom.

BECKER, CIRCUIT JUDGE.

The Individuals with Disabilities Education Act (IDEA), 20 U.S.C. §§ 1400–1485 (formerly the "Education for All Handicapped Children Act"), provides that states receiving funding under the Act must ensure that children with disabilities are educated in regular classrooms with nondisabled children "to the maximum extent appropriate." 20 U.S.C. § 1412(5)(B). Plaintiff-appellee Rafael Oberti is an eight year old child with Down's syndrome who was removed from the regular classroom by defendant-appellant Clementon School District Board of Education (the "School District") and placed in a segregated special education class. In this appeal, we are asked by the School District to review the district court's decision in favor of Rafael and his co-plaintiff parents Carlos and Jeanne Oberti concerning Rafael's right under IDEA to be educated in a regular classroom with nondisabled classmates. This court has not previously had occasion to interpret or apply the "mainstreaming" requirement of IDEA.[8]

We construe IDEA's mainstreaming requirement to prohibit a school from placing a child with disabilities outside of a regular classroom if educating the child in the regular classroom, with supplementary aids and support services, can be achieved satisfactorily. In addition, if placement outside of a regular classroom is necessary for the child to receive educational benefit, the school may still be violating IDEA if it has not made sufficient efforts to include the child in school programs with nondisabled children whenever possible. We also hold that the school bears the burden of proving compliance with the mainstreaming requirement of IDEA, regardless of which party (the child and parents or the school) brought the claim under IDEA before the district court.

Although our interpretation of IDEA's mainstreaming requirement differs somewhat from that of the district court, we will affirm the decision of the district court that the School District has failed to comply with IDEA. More precisely, we will affirm the district court's order that the School District design an appropriate education plan for Rafael Oberti in accordance with IDEA, and we will remand for further proceedings consistent with this opinion. . . .

I. FACTUAL AND PROCEDURAL BACKGROUND

A. *Rafael Oberti's educational history*

Rafael is an eight year old child with Down's syndrome, a genetic defect that severely impairs his intellectual functioning and his ability to communicate. Now and throughout the period in question, Rafael and his parents have lived within the Clementon School District, in southern New Jersey. Prior to his entry into

---

[8] [FN 1] Integrating children with disabilities in regular classrooms is commonly known as "mainstreaming." *See Daniel R.R. v. State Bd. of Educ.*, 874 F.2d 1036, 1039 (5th Cir. 1989); *Board of Educ. Sacramento City Unified School Dist. v. Holland*, 786 F. Supp. 874, 878 (E.D. Cal. 1992). The Obertis point out that some educators and public school authorities have come to disfavor use of the term "mainstreaming" because it suggests, in their view, the shuttling of a child with disabilities in and out of a regular class without altering the classroom to accommodate the child. They prefer the term "inclusion" because of its greater emphasis on the use of supplementary aids and support services within the regular classroom to facilitate inclusion of children with disabilities. *See Winners All: A Call for Inclusive Schools*, Report to the National Association of State Boards of Education by Study Group on Special Education (October 1992). While "inclusion" may be a more precise term, we will nonetheless use the term "mainstreaming" because it is currently the common parlance. Moreover, as we discuss below, "mainstreaming" as required under IDEA does *not* mean simply the placement of a child with disabilities in a regular classroom or school program. *See infra* Part II.

kindergarten, Rafael was evaluated in accordance with federal and state law by the School District's Child Study Team (the "Team"). Based on its evaluation, the Team recommended to Rafael's parents that he be placed in a segregated special education class located in another school district for the 1989-90 school year. The Obertis visited a number of special classes recommended by the School District and found them all unacceptable. Thereafter the Obertis and the School District came to an agreement that Rafael would attend a "developmental" kindergarten class (for children not fully ready for kindergarten) at the Clementon Elementary School (Rafael's neighborhood school) in the mornings, and a special education class in another school district in the afternoons.

The Individualized Education Plan (IEP) developed by the School District for Rafael for the 1989-90 school year assigned all of Rafael's academic goals to the afternoon special education class. In contrast, the only goals for Rafael in the morning kindergarten class were to observe, model and socialize with nondisabled children.

While Rafael's progress reports for the developmental kindergarten class show that he made academic and social progress in that class during the year, Rafael experienced a number of serious behavioral problems there, including repeated toileting accidents, temper tantrums, crawling and hiding under furniture, and touching, hitting and spitting on other children. On several occasions Rafael struck at and hit the teacher and the teacher's aide.

These problems disrupted the class and frustrated the teacher, who consulted the school psychologist and other members of the Child Study Team to discuss possible approaches to managing Rafael's behavior problems. The teacher made some attempts to modify the curriculum for Rafael, but Rafael's IEP provided no plan for addressing Rafael's behavior problems. Neither did the IEP provide for special education consultation for the kindergarten teacher, or for communication between the kindergarten teacher and the special education teacher. In March of 1990, the School District finally obtained the assistance of an additional aide, which had been requested by the parents much earlier in the school year, but the presence of the extra aide in the kindergarten class did little to resolve the behavior problems. According to Rafael's progress reports for the afternoon special education class, and as the district court found, Rafael did not experience similar behavior problems in that class.

At the end of the 1989-90 school year, the Child Study Team proposed to place Rafael for the following year in a segregated special education class for children classified as "educable mentally retarded." Since no such special education class existed within the Clementon School District, Rafael would have to travel to a different district. The Team's decision was based both on the behavioral problems Rafael experienced during the 1989-90 school year in the developmental kindergarten class and on the Team's belief that Rafael's disabilities precluded him from benefiting from education in a regular classroom at that time.

The Obertis objected to a segregated placement and requested that Rafael be placed in the regular kindergarten class in the Clementon Elementary School. The School District refused, and the Obertis sought relief by filing a request for a due process hearing. The parties then agreed to mediate their dispute, pursuant to New

Jersey regulations, as an alternative to a due process hearing. *See* N.J.A.C. 6:28-2.6. Through mediation, the Obertis and the School District came to an agreement that for the 1990-91 school year Rafael would attend a special education class for students labeled "multiply handicapped" in a public elementary school in the Winslow Township School District ("Winslow"), approximately 45 minutes by bus from Rafael's home. As part of the agreement, the School District promised to explore mainstreaming possibilities at the Winslow school and to consider a future placement for Rafael in a regular classroom in the Clementon Elementary School.

The special education class in Winslow that Rafael attended during the 1990-91 school year was taught by an instructor and an instructional aide and included nine children. Although Rafael initially exhibited some of the same behavioral problems he had experienced in the Clementon kindergarten class, his behavior gradually improved: he became toilet trained and his disruptiveness abated. Rafael also made academic progress. However, by December of 1990, Rafael's parents found that the School District was making no plans to mainstream Rafael. The Obertis also learned that Rafael had no meaningful contact with nondisabled students at the Winslow school.

B. *The due process hearing*

In January of 1991, the Obertis brought another due process complaint, renewing their request under IDEA that Rafael be placed in a regular class in his neighborhood elementary school. A three-day due process hearing was held in February of 1991 before an Administrative Law Judge (ALJ) of the New Jersey Office of Administrative Law. On March 15, 1991, the ALJ affirmed the School District's decision that the segregated special education class in Winslow was the "least restrictive environment" for Rafael. Based on the testimony of Rafael's kindergarten teacher and other witnesses for the School District who described Rafael's disruptive behavior in the developmental kindergarten class, the ALJ found that Rafael's behavior problems in that class were extensive and that he had achieved no meaningful educational benefit in the class.[9] The ALJ concluded that

---

[9] [FN 7] The School District presented eight witnesses before the ALJ. Melinda Reardon, the teacher of the developmental kindergarten class, testified to Rafael's behavioral problems that disrupted the class throughout the year, including repeated toileting accidents, touching and hitting other children, throwing objects, not following instructions, and running and hiding from the teacher and the aides. She also testified that throughout the year she had great difficulty communicating with Rafael, and that she had consulted with the school psychologist to come up with methods of controlling Rafael's behavior. Karen Lightman, the speech therapist at the Clementon Elementary School, testified that Rafael regularly disrupted her small-group speech therapy sessions during the 1989-90 school year. She testified that Rafael slapped her on one occasion, refused to follow instructions, threw paper, and touched other students. She stated that these behaviors disrupted the session and took away therapy time from the other students. William Sherman, the superintendent of Schools for the School District and acting principal of the Clementon Elementary School in May and June of 1990 testified that he was called to Rafael's kindergarten class several times by the teacher to help her address Rafael's disciplinary problems. Valeria Costino, an instructional aide for that class, corroborated the testimony of the teacher and the acting principal regarding Rafael's behavior problems.

Peggy McDevit, the Clementon Elementary School psychologist, a member of the Child Study Team, and a qualified expert in child placement and child psychology, testified that she had observed Rafael engaging in disruptive behavior in the kindergarten class and that, in her opinion, placement in a regular

Rafael was not ready for mainstreaming.[10]

In reaching this conclusion, the ALJ discounted the testimony of the Obertis' two expert witnesses. Dr. Gail McGregor, a professor of education at Temple University and an expert in the education of children with disabilities, testified that Rafael could be educated satisfactorily in a regular class at the Clementon Elementary School with supplementary aids and services, and that Rafael would learn important skills in a regular classroom that could not be learned in a segregated setting.[11] The ALJ disregarded Dr. McGregor's testimony because, unlike the School District's witnesses, she did not have daily experience with Rafael. Likewise, the ALJ discounted the testimony of the Obertis' other expert witness, Thomas Nolan, a teacher and special education specialist who had taught a child with Down's syndrome in a regular classroom, because he too had not had day-to-day experience with Rafael.[12] The ALJ thus concluded that the Winslow placement was in

---

classroom would not be feasible for Rafael at that time because of his behavior problems. David Hinlicky, the principal of the Clementon Elementary School, described a visit he paid to a summer school class Rafael attended in 1991 in which he observed Rafael misbehaving and disrupting the class. In contrast, Nancy Leetch, Rafael's speech therapist at Winslow, and Lisa Mansfield, the special education teacher at Winslow, both testified that Rafael had made significant academic and social progress in the Winslow special education class.

[10] [FN 8] Although the ALJ upheld the School District's decision to place Rafael in the segregated class in Winslow, he added:

> This is not to say that the time may not come when mainstreaming in Winslow Tp. and/or Clementon will not be called for. The present record discloses only that *now* is not such a time.

(emphasis in original).

[11] [FN 9] Based on her observation of Rafael in the Winslow program, observation of the Clementon Elementary School, review of Rafael's education records, and her expertise in this area, Dr. McGregor testified that there were no aspects of Rafael's disability that would preclude him from being educated in a regular classroom with supplementary aids and services. She testified that many of the educational aids and techniques that were provided for Rafael at Winslow could be transferred to a regular classroom. She described various types of special support that could be provided to enable Rafael to learn in a regular classroom, including use of a behavior modification plan to address Rafael's specific behavior problems, working in small groups with tutoring by peers, and multisensory instructional techniques that are often used in special education classes.

As to the behavioral problems Rafael experienced in the kindergarten class in 1989-90, Dr. McGregor testified that those problems could be contained through use of adequate supplementary aids and services (such as those described above), which, she explained, had not been provided for Rafael in the kindergarten class.

Dr. McGregor also testified that it is extremely important for a child like Rafael to learn to work and communicate with nondisabled peers, and that this type of learning could only be provided by including him as much as possible in a regular classroom. Finally, Dr. McGregor testified that she did not observe any opportunities for Rafael to interact with nondisabled students in the Winslow program.

[12] [FN 10] In addition to the two experts, the Obertis presented the testimony of both of Rafael's parents, who testified that from their experience with and understanding of their son, they were convinced that Rafael would be successful in a regular classroom with adequate aids and services. Jeanne Oberti testified that she believed the segregated Winslow class had a negative emotional impact on Rafael, who would cry regularly before boarding the bus for the 45 minute trip to Winslow. She also testified that she and her husband understood that Rafael could not be expected to master the curriculum in a regular class in the same way as the nondisabled students, but that they did not believe Rafael should be excluded for that reason. Michelle Zbrozek, a neighbor of the Obertis and a parent of a nondisabled child in the Clementon kindergarten class, testified that her son played with Rafael and other neighborhood children and that she believed Rafael and the nondisabled children learned from

compliance with IDEA.

C. *The proceedings before the district court*

Seeking independent review of the ALJ's decision pursuant to 20 U.S.C. § 1415(e)(2), the Obertis filed this civil action in the United States District Court for the District of New Jersey. . . .

In May of 1992, the district court held a three-day bench trial, receiving new evidence from both parties to supplement the state agency record. *See* 20 U.S.C. § 1415(e)(2). The Obertis presented the testimony of two additional experts who had not testified in the administrative proceedings: Dr. Lou Brown, a professor of special education at the University of Wisconsin, and Amy Goldman, an expert in communication with children with developmental disabilities.

Dr. Brown, who over the past twenty years has been a consultant to hundreds of school districts throughout the country regarding the education of severely disabled children, interviewed and evaluated Rafael on two occasions, and reviewed Rafael's educational records, as well as a set of videotapes showing Rafael at age seven working with his mother, being taught by a language professional, and participating in a Sunday school class with nondisabled children. Dr. Brown testified that he saw no reason why Rafael could not be educated at that time in a regular classroom with appropriate supplementary aids and services. He told the court that if such aids and services were provided, he had no reason to believe that Rafael would be disruptive at that time (more than two years after the experience in the Clementon kindergarten class). He also stated that integrating Rafael in a regular class at his local school would enable Rafael to develop social relationships with nondisabled students and to learn by imitating appropriate role models, important benefits which could not be realized in a segregated, special education setting.

Dr. Brown outlined a number of commonly applied strategies which could be used, in combination, by the School District to integrate Rafael in a regular classroom, including: (1) modifying some of the curriculum to accommodate Rafael's different level of ability; (2) modifying only Rafael's program so that he would perform a similar activity or exercise to that performed by the whole class, but at a level appropriate to his ability; (3) "parallel instruction," i.e., having Rafael work separately within the classroom on an activity beneficial to him while the rest of the class worked on an activity that Rafael could not benefit from; and (4) removing Rafael from the classroom to receive some special instruction or services in a resource room, completely apart from the class. Dr. Brown explained that with proper training, a regular teacher would be able to apply these techniques and that, in spite of Rafael's severe intellectual disability, a regular teacher with proper training would be able to communicate effectively with Rafael. Dr. Brown also testified that many of the special educational techniques applied in the segregated Winslow class could be provided for Rafael within a regular classroom.

Based on her evaluation of Rafael and her expertise in developing communication

---

each other by working and playing together. *See infra* n. 24. The ALJ considered this testimony but was nonetheless convinced by the School District's witnesses that Rafael's behavior problems in the kindergarten class during the 1989-90 school year precluded an integrated placement at that time.

skills for disabled children, Amy Goldman testified that the speech and language therapy Rafael needs could be most effectively provided within a regular classroom; otherwise, she explained, a child with Rafael's disabilities would have great difficulty importing the language skills taught in a separate speech therapy session into the regular class environment, where those skills are most needed. She testified that language and speech therapy could easily be provided by a therapist inside the regular class during ongoing instruction if the therapist were able to collaborate ahead of time with the instructor regarding the upcoming lesson plans.

In addition, Dr. McGregor reaffirmed her prior opinion in the administrative proceedings that placement in a regular classroom was not only feasible but preferable for Rafael. Further, she testified that, given the resources and expertise available to public schools in New Jersey, the School District should be able to design an inclusive program for Rafael with assistance from professionals who have experience integrating children with disabilities in regular classes.

The Obertis also offered the videotape evidence that had been reviewed by Dr. Brown, the testimony of Jeanne Oberti, and the testimony of Joanne McKeon, the mother of a nine year old child with Down's syndrome who had been successfully mainstreamed in a regular classroom.

To counter the Obertis' experts, the School District offered Dr. Stanley Urban, a professor of special education at Glassboro State College. After observing Rafael in a special class for perceptually impaired children at the St. Luke's School (a private school that Rafael attended for two months in the fall of 1991), observing Rafael for two hours in his home, reviewing the programs available at the Clementon Elementary School, reviewing Rafael's education records, and reviewing the written evaluations of the Obertis' experts, Dr. Urban testified that in his opinion Rafael could not be educated satisfactorily in a regular classroom, and that the special education program at Winslow was appropriate for Rafael.

More specifically, Dr. Urban testified that Rafael's behavior problems could not be managed in a regular class, that a regular teacher would not be able to communicate with a child of Rafael's ability level, and that it would be difficult if not impossible to adapt a first grade-level curriculum to accommodate Rafael without adversely affecting the education of the other children in the class. Dr. Urban, however, also stated that if Rafael did not have serious behavior problems, integration in a regular classroom might be feasible.

The School District presented several additional witnesses, including the teacher and teacher's aide of a non-academic summer school class for elementary school children which Rafael attended in the summer of 1991, and the teacher of the St. Luke's class, which Rafael attended for two months in the fall of 1991. These witnesses recounted examples of Rafael's disruptive behavior, including pushing and hitting other children, disobeying and running away from the instructors, and throwing books.

In August of 1992, after reviewing all of this new evidence along with the evidence that had been adduced at the administrative proceedings, the district court issued its decision, finding that the School District had failed to establish by a preponderance of the evidence that Rafael could not at that time be educated in a regular classroom with supplementary aids and services. The court therefore concluded that the School District had violated IDEA.

In particular, the court was persuaded by the Obertis' experts that many of the special education techniques used in the Winslow class could be implemented in a regular classroom. The court also found that the School District did not make reasonable efforts to include Rafael in a regular classroom with supplementary aids and services (e.g., an itinerant teacher trained in aiding students with mental retardation, a behavior management program, modification of the regular curriculum to accommodate Rafael, and special education training and consultation for the regular teacher); that Rafael's behavior problems during the 1989-90 school year in the developmental kindergarten class were largely the result of the School District's failure to provide adequate supplementary aids and services; and that the record did not support the School District's contention that Rafael would present similar behavior problems at that time (more than two years after the kindergarten class) if included in a regular classroom setting with adequate aids and services. The court declined to defer to the findings of the ALJ because it found that "they were largely and improperly based upon Rafael's behavior problems in the developmental kindergarten as well as upon his intellectual limitations, without proper consideration of the inadequate level of supplementary aids and services provided by the School District."

In addition to finding a violation of IDEA, the court concluded that by refusing to include Rafael in a regular classroom, the School District was discriminating against Rafael in violation of § 504 of the Rehabilitation Act. Accordingly, the court ordered the School District "to develop an inclusive plan for Rafael Oberti for the 1992-93 school year consistent with the requirements" of IDEA and § 504 of the Rehabilitation Act. This appeal followed. . . .

II. THE MAINSTREAMING REQUIREMENT OF IDEA

. . . .

In addition to the free appropriate education requirement, IDEA provides that states must establish

> procedures to assure that, to the maximum extent appropriate, children with disabilities . . . are educated with children who are not disabled, and that special classes, separate schooling, or other removal of children with disabilities from the regular educational environment occurs only when the nature and severity of the disability is such that education in regular classes with the use of supplementary aids and services cannot be achieved satisfactorily. . . .

20 U.S.C. § 1412(5)(B). As numerous courts have recognized, this provision sets forth a "strong congressional preference" for integrating children with disabilities in regular classrooms. *See, e.g., Devries v. Fairfax County School Bd.*, 882 F.2d 876, 878 (4th Cir. 1989); *Daniel R.R. v. State Bd. of Educ.*, 874 F.2d 1036, 1044 (5th Cir. 1989); *A.W. v. Northwest R-1 School Dist.*, 813 F.2d 158, 162 (8th Cir. 1987); *Roncker v. Walter*, 700 F.2d 1058, 1063 (6th Cir. 1983); *Board of Educ. Sacramento City Unified School Dist. v. Holland*, 786 F. Supp. 874, 878 (E.D. Cal. 1992).

One of our principal tasks in this case is to provide standards for determining when a school's decision to remove a child with disabilities from the regular classroom and to place the child in a segregated environment violates IDEA's presumption in favor of mainstreaming. This issue is particularly difficult in light of the apparent tension within the Act between the strong preference for mainstreaming, 20 U.S.C. § 1412(5)(B), and the requirement that schools provide individualized programs tailored to the specific needs of each disabled child, 20 U.S.C. §§ 1401, 1414(a)(5). *See Daniel R.R.*, 874 F.2d at 1044; *Greer v. Rome City School Dist.*, 950 F.2d 688, 695 (11th Cir. 1991).

The key to resolving this tension appears to lie in the school's proper use of "supplementary aids and services," 20 U.S.C. § 1412(5)(B), which may enable the school to educate a child with disabilities for a majority of the time within a regular classroom, while at the same time addressing that child's unique educational needs. We recognize, however, that "[r]egular classes . . . will not provide an education that accounts for each child's particular needs in every case." *Daniel R.R.*, 874 F.2d at 1044; *see also Devries*, 882 F.2d at 878–80 (holding that 17-year-old autistic student could not benefit from "monitoring" regular high school academic classes and was appropriately placed at county vocational center).

We also recognize that "[i]n assuring that the requirements of the Act have been met, courts must be careful to avoid imposing their view of preferable educational methods upon the States." *Rowley*, 458 U.S. at 207. We are mindful that the Act leaves questions of educational policy to state and local officials. *Id.* On the other hand, as the Supreme Court recognized in *Rowley*, the Act specifically "requires participating States to educate handicapped children with nonhandicapped children whenever possible." *Rowley*, 458 U.S. at 202; *see also Honig v. Doe*, 484 U.S. 305, 311 (1988). It is our duty to enforce that statutory requirement. *See Polk [v. Central Susquehanna Intermediate Unit 16]*, 853 F.2d [171] at 184 [(1988)] ("We do not read the Supreme Court's salutary warnings against interference with educational methodology as an invitation to abdicate our obligation to enforce the statutory provisions [of the Act].").[13]

---

[13] [FN 20] In its *Fourteenth Annual Report to Congress on the Implementation of the Individuals with Disabilities Act* (1992), the U.S. Department of Education (DOE) reported that nearly two-thirds of the state plans submitted for DOE approval in 1991 under the Act were not in compliance with the mainstreaming requirements of IDEA. Specifically, nearly two-thirds of the state plans reviewed by the DOE "failed to include . . . an adequate description of how the [state educational agency] makes arrangements with public and private institutions to ensure that the least restrictive environment (LRE) requirements [of IDEA] are effectively implemented." *Id.* at 119. Half of the states reviewed "did not ensure that their public agencies removed children with disabilities from the regular educational environment only when the nature or severity of the disability was such that education in regular classes with the use of supplementary aids and services could not be achieved satisfactorily." *Id.* at 136. Further, over half of the state plans reviewed "did not include . . . procedures to ensure that in providing or arranging for nonacademic or extra-curricular services and activities, each public agency will ensure that each child with a disability participates with children who do not have disabilities to the maximum extent appropriate to the needs of that child." *Id.* at 119.

The statistics reported in the *Fourteenth Annual Report* also reflect a wide variation in the percentage of disabled children who are mainstreamed in regular classes among the different states. For the 1989-90 school year, the DOE reported that among all the states, 26% of children with mental retardation between the ages of 6 and 21 were placed in regular classes for at least 40% of the school day. *Id.* at 25. But in New Jersey, which has one of the lowest mainstreaming rates, only 2.35% of children with mental

In *Daniel R.R.*, the Fifth Circuit derived from the language of 20 U.S.C. § 1412(5)(B) a two-part test for determining whether a school is in compliance with IDEA's mainstreaming requirement. First, the court must determine "whether education in the regular classroom, with the use of supplementary aids and services, can be achieved satisfactorily." 874 F.2d at 1048. Second, if the court finds that placement outside of a regular classroom is necessary for the child to benefit educationally, then the court must decide "whether the school has mainstreamed the child to the maximum extent appropriate," i.e., whether the school has made efforts to include the child in school programs with nondisabled children whenever possible. *Id.* We think this two-part test, which closely tracks the language of § 1412(5)(B), is faithful to IDEA's directive that children with disabilities be educated with nondisabled children "to the maximum extent appropriate," 20 U.S.C. § 1412(5)(B), and to the Act's requirement that schools provide individualized programs to account for each child's specific needs, 20 U.S.C. §§ 1401, 1414(a)(5). *See Greer*, 950 F.2d at 696 (adopting the *Daniel R.R.* test); *Liscio v. Woodland Hills School Dist.*, 734 F. Supp. 689 (W.D. Pa. 1989) (same).

The district court in this case adopted the somewhat different test set forth by the Sixth Circuit in *Roncker v. Walter*, 700 F.2d 1058 (6th Cir. 1983), the first federal court of appeals case to interpret IDEA's mainstreaming requirement. *See Oberti II*, [*Oberti v. Board of Education*] 801 F. Supp. [1392] at 1401 [(1992)]. In *Roncker*, the court stated:

> In a case where the segregated facility is considered superior [academically], the court should determine whether the services which make that placement superior could be feasibly provided in a non-segregated setting. If they can, the placement in the segregated school would be inappropriate under the Act.

700 F.2d at 1063; *see also A.W. v. Northwest R-1 School Dist.*, 813 F.2d 158, 163 (8th Cir. 1987) (adopting *Roncker* test). We believe, however, that the two-part *Daniel R.R.* test is the better standard because the *Roncker* test fails to make clear that even if placement in the regular classroom cannot be achieved satisfactorily for the major portion of a particular child's education program, the school is still required to include that child in school programs with nondisabled children (specific academic classes, other classes such as music and art, lunch, recess, etc.) whenever possible. We therefore adopt the two-part *Daniel R.R.* test rather than the standard espoused in *Roncker.*

In applying the first part of the *Daniel R.R.* test, i.e., whether the child can be educated satisfactorily in a regular classroom with supplementary aids and services, the court should consider several factors. First, the court should look at the steps that the school has taken to try to include the child in a regular classroom. *See Greer*, 950 F.2d at 696; *Daniel R.R.*, 874 F.2d at 1048. As we have explained, the Act and its regulations require schools to provide supplementary aids and services

---

retardation within that age group were mainstreamed, while in Massachusetts, a state with one of the highest mainstreaming rates, 74.97% of children with mental retardation were placed in regular classes. *Id.* at A-62; *see also* Alan Gartner & Dorothy Kerzner Lipsky, *Beyond Special Education: Toward a Quality System for All Students*, 57 HARV. EDUC. REV. 367, 374–76 (1987) (children with similar disabilities are provided widely divergent degrees of mainstreaming depending on where they reside).

to enable children with disabilities to learn whenever possible in a regular classroom. *See* 20 U.S.C. §§ 1401(a)(17), 1412(5)(B); 34 C.F.R. § 300.551(b)(2). The regulations specifically require school districts to provide "a continuum of placements . . . to meet the needs of handicapped children." 34 C.F.R. § 300.551(a). The continuum must "[m]ake provision for supplementary services (such as resource room or itinerant instruction) to be provided in conjunction with regular class placement." 34 C.F.R. § 300.551(b).

Accordingly, the school "must consider the whole range of supplemental aids and services, including resource rooms and itinerant instruction," *Greer*, 950 F.2d at 696, speech and language therapy, special education training for the regular teacher, behavior modification programs, or any other available aids or services appropriate to the child's particular disabilities. The school must also make efforts to modify the regular education program to accommodate a disabled child. *See* 34 C.F.R. Part 300, App. C. Question 48. If the school has given no serious consideration to including the child in a regular class with such supplementary aids and services and to modifying the regular curriculum to accommodate the child, then it has most likely violated the Act's mainstreaming directive. "The Act does not permit states to make mere token gestures to accommodate handicapped students; its requirement for modifying and supplementing regular education is broad." *Daniel R.R.*, 874 F.2d at 1048; *see also Greer*, 950 F.2d at 696.

A second factor courts should consider in determining whether a child with disabilities can be included in a regular classroom is the comparison between the educational benefits the child will receive in a regular classroom (with supplementary aids and services) and the benefits the child will receive in the segregated, special education classroom. The court will have to rely heavily in this regard on the testimony of educational experts. Nevertheless, in making this comparison the court must pay special attention to those unique benefits the child may obtain from integration in a regular classroom which cannot be achieved in a segregated environment, i.e., the development of social and communication skills from interaction with nondisabled peers. *See Daniel R.R.*, 874 F.2d at 1049 ("a child may be able to absorb only a minimal amount of the regular education program, but may benefit enormously from the language models that his nonhandicapped peers provide"); *Greer*, 950 F.2d at 697 (language and role modeling from association with nondisabled peers are essential benefits of mainstreaming); *Holland*, 786 F. Supp. at 882 (benefits obtained by child with mental retardation as result of placement in a regular classroom include development of social and communications skills and generally improved self-esteem).[14] As IDEA's mainstreaming directive makes clear, Congress understood that a fundamental value of the right to public education for children with disabilities is the right to associate with nondisabled peers.[15]

---

[14] [FN 23] In passing the Act, Congress recognized "the importance of teaching skills that would foster personal independence . . . [and] dignity for handicapped children." *Polk*, 853 F.2d at 181 (discussing Act's legislative history). Learning to associate, communicate and cooperate with nondisabled persons is essential to the personal independence of children with disabilities. The Act's mainstreaming directive stems from Congress's concern that the states, through public education, work to develop such independence for disabled children.

[15] [FN 24] Courts should also consider the reciprocal benefits of inclusion to the nondisabled students in the class. Teaching nondisabled children to work and communicate with children with disabilities may

Thus, a determination that a child with disabilities might make greater *academic* progress in a segregated, special education class may not warrant excluding that child from a regular classroom environment. We emphasize that the Act does *not* require states to offer *the same* educational experience to a child with disabilities as is generally provided for nondisabled children. *See Rowley*, 458 U.S. at 189, 202. To the contrary, states must address the unique needs of a disabled child, recognizing that that child may benefit differently from education in the regular classroom than other students. *See Daniel R.R.*, 874 F.2d at 1047. In short, the fact that a child with disabilities will learn differently from his or her education within a regular classroom does not justify exclusion from that environment.

A third factor the court should consider in determining whether a child with disabilities can be educated satisfactorily in a regular classroom is the possible negative effect the child's inclusion may have on the education of the other children in the regular classroom. While inclusion of children with disabilities in regular classrooms may benefit the class as a whole, *see supra* n. 24, a child with disabilities may be "so disruptive in a regular classroom that the education of other students is significantly impaired." 34 C.F.R. § 300.552 *comment* (citing 34 C.F.R. part 104 — Appendix, Para. 24); *see Greer*, 950 F.2d at 697; *Daniel R.R.*, 874 F.2d at 1048–49. Moreover, if a child is causing excessive disruption of the class, the child may not be benefiting educationally in that environment. Accordingly, if the child has behavioral problems, the court should consider the degree to which these problems may disrupt the class. In addition, the court should consider whether the child's disabilities will demand so much of the teacher's attention that the teacher will be required to ignore the other students. *See Daniel R.R.*, 874 F.2d at 1049.

We emphasize, however, that in considering the possible negative effect of the child's presence on the other students, the court must keep in mind the school's obligation under the Act to provide supplementary aids and services to accommodate the child's disabilities. *See Greer*, 950 F.2d at 697. An adequate individualized program with such aids and services may prevent disruption that would otherwise occur. *See id.* With respect to the concerns of nondisabled children in the regular classroom, we note that the comment to 34 C.F.R. § 300.552 (citing 34 C.F.R. part 104 — Appendix, Para. 24) reads: "[I]t should be stressed that, where a handicapped child is so disruptive in a regular classroom that the education of other students is significantly impaired, the needs of the handicapped child cannot be met in that environment. Therefore, regular placements would not be appropriate to his or her needs. . . ." On the other hand, "a handicapped child who merely requires more teacher attention than most other children is not likely to be so disruptive as to significantly impair the education of other children." *Greer*, 950 F.2d at 697.

---

do much to eliminate the stigma, mistrust and hostility that have traditionally been harbored against persons with disabilities. *See* Minow, *Learning to Live with the Dilemma of Difference*, 48 LAW & CONTEMP. PROBS. at 160, 202–11; *Winners All: A Call for Inclusive Schools*, Report to the National Ass'n of State Bds. of Educ., at 14 (1992); *Oberti II*, 801 F. Supp. at 1404 (nondisabled children are likely to benefit and learn from children with disabilities who are included in regular classroom).

At the state administrative hearing in this case, a parent of a nondisabled child in the Clementon Elementary School kindergarten class was asked by counsel for the Obertis whether she would have any concerns if Rafael were included in a class with her child. She responded, "No," explaining that she believed disabled and nondisabled children learned from each other by working and playing together. *See supra* n. 10.

In sum, in determining whether a child with disabilities can be educated satisfactorily in a regular class with supplemental aids and services (the first prong of the two-part mainstreaming test we adopt today), the court should consider several factors, including: (1) whether the school district has made reasonable efforts to accommodate the child in a regular classroom; (2) the educational benefits available to the child in a regular class, with appropriate supplementary aids and services, as compared to the benefits provided in a special education class; and (3) the possible negative effects of the inclusion of the child on the education of the other students in the class.[16]

If, after considering these factors, the court determines that the school district was justified in removing the child from the regular classroom and providing education in a segregated, special education class, the court must consider the second prong of the mainstreaming test — whether the school has included the child in school programs with nondisabled children to the maximum extent appropriate. *See Daniel R.R.*, 874 F.2d at 1048, 1050. IDEA and its regulations "do not contemplate an all-or-nothing educational system in which handicapped children attend either regular or special education." *Id.* at 1050. The regulations under IDEA require schools to provide a "continuum of alternative placements . . . to meet the needs of handicapped children." 34 C.F.R. § 300.551(a). As the Fifth Circuit stated:

> the school must take intermediate steps wherever appropriate, such as placing the child in regular education for some academic classes and in special education for others, mainstreaming the child for nonacademic classes only, or providing interaction with nonhandicapped children during lunch and recess. The appropriate mix will vary from child to child and, it may be hoped, from school year to school year as the child develops.

Daniel R.R., 874 F.2d at 1050. Thus, even if a child with disabilities cannot be educated satisfactorily in a regular classroom, that child must still be included in school programs with nondisabled students wherever possible.

III. BURDEN OF PROOF UNDER IDEA'S MAINSTREAMING REQUIREMENT

Before we apply the two-part analysis discussed above to the facts in this case, we must address the School District's argument that the district court improperly placed the burden of proof under the Act on it. In the School District's view, while it may have had the initial burden at the state administrative level of justifying its educational placement, once the agency decided in its favor, the burden should have shifted to the parents who challenged the agency decision in the district court. Courts must place the burden on the party seeking to reverse the agency decision, the School District argues, in order to effectuate IDEA's requirement that "due

---

[16] [FN 25] Additional factors may be relevant depending on the circumstances of the specific case. For example, other courts have considered cost as a relevant factor in determining compliance with the Act's mainstreaming requirement. *See, e.g., Greer*, 950 F.2d at 697; *Roncker*, 700 F.2d at 1063. Since the parties have not raised cost as an issue, we do not consider it here. *See Daniel R.R.*, 874 F.2d at 1049 n. 9.

weight shall be given to [the state administrative] proceedings," *Rowley*, 458 U.S. at 206 (interpreting 20 U.S.C. § 1415(e)). We disagree.

IDEA instructs district courts and state trial courts reviewing the decisions of state educational agencies to "receive the records of the administrative proceedings . . . hear additional evidence at the request of a party, and, basing its decision on the preponderance of the evidence, . . . grant such relief as the court determines is appropriate." 20 U.S.C. § 1415(e)(2). As construed by the Supreme Court in *Rowley*, § 1415(e)(2) requires courts to give "due weight" to the agency proceedings. *Rowley*, 458 U.S. at 206. However, neither *Rowley* nor the Act itself specifically addresses which party bears the burden of proof at the district court level, an issue which we believe is quite different from the district court's obligation to afford due weight to the administrative proceedings.

The School District points to several cases that hold, either directly or implicitly, that even if the school district bears the burden of proving compliance with IDEA in the state administrative proceedings, the burden of proof shifts to the party challenging the agency decision at the district court level. *See Roland M. v. Concord School Comm.*, 910 F.2d 983, 991 (1st Cir. 1990); *Kerkam v. McKenzie*, 862 F.2d 884, 887 (D.C. Cir. 1988); *see also Briggs v. Bd. of Educ.*, 882 F.2d 688, 692 (2d Cir. 1989) (placing burden on parents challenging state agency decision to prove that their child's educational needs could be met in a less segregated setting). We find these cases unpersuasive.

In reviewing the decision of a state agency under IDEA, the district court "must make an independent determination based on a preponderance of the evidence." *Geis v. Bd. of Educ.*, 774 F.2d 575, 583 (3d Cir. 1985). Given that the district court must *independently* review the evidence adduced at the administrative proceedings and can receive new evidence, we see no reason to shift the ultimate burden of proof to the party who happened to have lost before the state agency, especially since the loss at the administrative level may have been due to incomplete or insufficient evidence or to an incorrect application of the Act.

The purpose of the "due weight" obligation is to prevent the court from imposing its own view of preferable educational methods on the states. *See Rowley*, 458 U.S. at 207. Accordingly, the due weight is owed to the *administrative proceedings*, not to the party who happened to prevail in those proceedings. Moreover, the amount of deference to be afforded the administrative proceedings "is an issue left to the discretion of the district court. . . . [T]he district court must consider the administrative findings of fact, but is free to accept or reject them." *Jefferson County Bd. of Educ. v. Breen*, 853 F.2d 853, 857 (11th Cir. 1988). The district court can give due weight to the agency proceedings (i.e., refrain from imposing its own notions of educational policy on the states), while the ultimate burden of proof remains on the school.

Underlying the Act is "an abiding concern for the welfare of handicapped children and their parents." *Lascari v. Board of Education*, 560 A.2d [1180] at 1188 [(N.J. 1989)]; *see* 20 U.S.C. § 1400(c). Requiring parents to prove at the district court level that the school has failed to comply with the Act would undermine the Act's express purpose "to assure that the rights of children with disabilities and their parents are protected," 20 U.S.C. § 1400(c), and would diminish the effect of the provision that enables parents and guardians to obtain judicial enforcement of the Act's substantive and procedural requirements, *see* 20 U.S.C. § 1415(e). In practical terms, the school has an advantage when a dispute arises under the Act: the school has better access to the relevant information, greater control over the potentially more persuasive witnesses (those who have been directly involved with the child's education), and greater overall educational expertise than the parents. *See Lascari*, 560 A.2d at 1188 (placing burden of proof on school is "consistent with the proposition that the burdens of persuasion and production should be placed on the party better able to meet those burdens."); Engel, *Law, Culture, and Children with Disabilities*, 1991 DUKE L.J. at 187–94 (arguing that parents are generally at a disadvantage vis-a-vis the school when disputes arise under IDEA because parents generally lack specialized training and because their views are often treated as "inherently suspect" due to the attachment to their child).

In light of the statutory purpose of IDEA and these practical considerations, we believe that when IDEA's mainstreaming requirement is specifically at issue, it is appropriate to place the burden of proving compliance with IDEA on the school. Indeed, the Act's strong presumption in favor of mainstreaming, 20 U.S.C. § 1422(5)(B), would be turned on its head if parents had to prove that their child was worthy of being included, rather than the school district having to justify a decision to exclude the child from the regular classroom. *See supra* Part II. We therefore hold that the district court correctly placed the burden on the School District to prove that the segregated placement proposed for Rafael was in compliance with the mainstreaming requirement of IDEA.

IV. DID THE SCHOOL DISTRICT COMPLY WITH IDEA?

We now reach the dispositive question in this case: whether the district court erred in holding that the School District failed to comply with IDEA's mainstreaming requirement. Initially, applying the first part of the two-part test set forth above, *supra* Part II, we consider whether the School District has met its burden of proving that Rafael could not be educated satisfactorily in a regular classroom with supplementary aids and services.

. . . .

B. *Application of the* Daniel R.R. *test*

In Part II of this opinion, we outlined three factors that should be considered by a court in determining whether a child with disabilities can be educated satisfactorily in a regular classroom (the first part of the *Daniel R.R.* test): (1) whether the school district has made reasonable efforts to accommodate the child in a regular classroom with supplementary aids and services; (2) a comparison of the educational benefits available in a regular class and the benefits provided in a special education class; and (3) the possible negative effects of inclusion on the other students in the class. We now consider each of these factors, looking to the relevant fact findings of the district court to determine whether those findings are clearly erroneous, and if not, whether they support the district court's ultimate legal conclusion that the School District violated the mainstreaming requirement of IDEA.

As to the first factor, the district court found that the School District made only negligible efforts to include Rafael in a regular classroom. Specifically, the court found that during the 1989-90 school year, the only period during which the School District mainstreamed Rafael in a regular classroom, the School District placed Rafael in the developmental kindergarten class "without a curriculum plan, without a behavior management plan, and without providing adequate special education support to the teacher." *Oberti II*, 801 F. Supp. at 1402; *see also id.* at 1396, 1398. Further, the court found that the School District has since refused to include Rafael in a regular classroom largely based on the behavioral problems experienced by Rafael in the kindergarten class during the 1989-90 school year. *Id.* at 1396, 1403. For the 1990-91 year, the court found that Rafael was placed in a segregated class with "no meaningful mainstreaming opportunities," *id.* at 1397, and that "[t]he School District's consideration of less restrictive alternatives for the 1990-91 school year was perfunctory." *Id.* at 1396.

There is very little evidence in the record that conflicts with these findings. The School District produced some evidence that the kindergarten teacher and the school psychologist attempted to modify the curriculum in that class and to come up with methods of controlling Rafael's behavior problems. However, the record reflects that the School District had access to information and expertise about specific methods and services to enable children with disabilities like Rafael to be included in a regular classroom, but that the School District did not provide such supplementary aids and services for Rafael in the kindergarten class.

Rafael's IEP for the 1989-90 school year included no provisions for supplementary aids and services in the kindergarten class aside from stating that there will be "modification of regular class expectations" to reflect Rafael's disability. The only goal provided for the regular kindergarten teacher was to "facilitate Rafael's adjustment to the kindergarten classroom." After reviewing this IEP along with the rest of Rafael's education records, Dr. McGregor testified that no supplementary aids and services were provided for Rafael in the 1989-90 kindergarten class.

Moreover, there is no evidence in the record that the School District gave any serious consideration to including Rafael in a regular classroom with supplementary aids and services *after* the 1989-90 school year; and the School District does not appear to dispute this fact. Further, Nancy Leech, the Winslow speech therapist (and one of the School District's witnesses) admitted that Rafael had not been included in any school programs with nondisabled children at Winslow, apart from attending lunch and school assemblies.

In view of the foregoing, the district court's finding that the School District has not taken meaningful steps to try to include Rafael in a regular classroom with supplementary aids and services is not clearly erroneous. We also note that the district court did not fail to give "due weight" to the agency proceedings on this issue since the ALJ did not even consider whether the School District had made efforts to include Rafael in a regular classroom with supplementary aids and services, as is required by IDEA. *See Greer*, 950 F.2d at 698 (school district's determination that child with Down's syndrome would receive more benefit in a segregated special education class "is due no deference because school officials failed to consider what benefits she would receive from education in a regular classroom *with appropriate supplemental aids and services.*") (emphasis in original). Accordingly, the School District's failure to give adequate consideration to including Rafael in a regular classroom with supplementary aids and services supports the district court's legal conclusion that the School District violated IDEA.

As to the second factor — a comparison of the educational benefits of the segregated placement in Winslow with the benefits Rafael could obtain from placement in a regular classroom — the district court found that "[v]arious experts who testified on Rafael's behalf have convincingly refuted the School District's assertion that such services could not be delivered within the matrix of a regular education class without disrupting the class or converting it into a special education class." *Oberti II*, 801 F. Supp. at 1403 n. 17. The court also found that Rafael would benefit academically and socially from inclusion in a regular classroom. *Id.* at 1404. Moreover, the district court found, based on expert testimony, that "nondisabled children in the class will likewise benefit" from the inclusion of Rafael in a regular classroom. *Id.* at 1404; *see also supra* n. 24.

The School District points to some evidence in the record that conflicts with these findings. Specifically, Dr. Urban testified for the School District that, in his opinion, a regular teacher would not be able to communicate with Rafael and that a regular curriculum would have to be modified beyond recognition to accommodate Rafael. *See supra* Part I.C. However, the Obertis' experts, Drs. Brown and McGregor, described various commonly applied methods that could be used to educate Rafael in a regular classroom and testified that, although Rafael has severe intellectual disabilities, a regular teacher with appropriate training would be able to communicate effectively with Rafael. *See supra* Parts I.B & C. They testified that many of the special education techniques used in the segregated Winslow class could be imported successfully into a regular classroom and that the regular teacher could be trained to apply these techniques. *Id.* Further, the Obertis' experts testified at length that inclusion in a classroom with nondisabled students would benefit Rafael substantially. *Id.* In addition, Amy Goldman testified that speech and language therapy not only could be provided in a regular classroom, but would be more effective for Rafael in an integrated setting. *See supra* Part I.C.

In short, the parties' experts disagreed on the respective benefits of a segregated versus an integrated placement for Rafael, and the district court was in a better position than we are to evaluate their testimony. We therefore defer to that court's findings, which, at all events, are not clearly erroneous. We note also that the district court did not fail to give due weight to the agency proceedings on this factor since the court's findings were based largely on new expert testimony that was not before the ALJ. Additionally, we agree with the district court's legal conclusion that, although including Rafael in a regular classroom would require the School District to modify the curriculum, the need for such modification is "not a legitimate basis upon which to justify excluding a child" from the regular classroom unless the education of other students is significantly impaired. *Oberti II*, 801 F. Supp. at 1403; *see also* 34 C.F.R. Part 300, App. C Question 48 (school must set forth in the IEP any modifications of the regular education program necessary to accommodate a disabled child). Thus, a comparison of the educational benefits of a segregated versus an integrated placement for Rafael supports the district court's conclusion that the School District's selection of a segregated placement did not comply with IDEA.

As to the third factor — the potentially disruptive effect of Rafael's presence on the other children in a regular classroom — the record again contains conflicting evidence. The School District presented numerous witnesses before both the ALJ and the district court who testified to Rafael's extremely disruptive behavior in the 1989-90 kindergarten class and in several other teaching environments. *See supra* Parts I.B & C. In contrast, the Obertis' experts Drs. McGregor and Brown evaluated Rafael and testified that in their opinion he would not at that point in time (nearly two years after Rafael's experience in the kindergarten class) cause any significant disruption in a regular classroom if provided with adequate supplementary aids and services, such as the assistance of an itinerant instructor with special education training, special education training for the regular teacher, modification of some of the academic curriculum to accommodate Rafael's disabilities, parallel instruction to allow him to learn at his academic level, and use of a resource room.

After evaluating the evidence on both sides, the district court found that "[t]here is nothing in the record which would suggest that *at this point in time* Rafael would present similar behavior problems if provided with an adequate level of supplementary aids and related services within the matrix of a regular education class. In fact, the record supports the opposite conclusion." *Oberti II*, 801 F. Supp. at 1403 (emphasis added). The court found that the behavioral problems Rafael experienced during the 1989-90 school year in the developmental kindergarten class "were exacerbated and remained uncontained due to the inadequate level of services provided there," that Rafael's behavioral problems were diminished in settings where an adequate level of supplementary aids and services were provided, and that both the School District and the ALJ "improperly justified Rafael's exclusion from less restrictive placements in subsequent years based upon those behavior problems." *Id.*

Although the School District presented ample evidence of Rafael's disruptive behavior in the 1989-90 kindergarten class, the Obertis' evidence supports the district court's finding that Rafael would not have had such severe behavior problems had he been provided with adequate supplementary aids and services in that kindergarten class, and that Rafael (who at the time of the district court trial was two years older than when he attended the kindergarten class) would most likely not present such problems if he were included in a regular class at that time. We therefore conclude that the district court's findings on this issue are not clearly erroneous, and, accordingly, that consideration of the possible negative effects of Rafael's presence on the regular classroom environment does not support the School District's decision to exclude him from the regular classroom.

We also conclude that the district court did not abuse its discretion in deciding not to defer to the findings of the ALJ on the issue of whether Rafael would significantly disrupt a regular classroom. As the court noted, the ALJ's findings "were largely and improperly based upon Rafael's behavior problems in the developmental kindergarten, as well as upon his intellectual limitations, *without proper consideration of the inadequate level of supplementary aids and services provided by the School District." Oberti II*, 801 F. Supp. at 1404 (emphasis added).

For all of these reasons, we agree with the district court's conclusion that the School District did not meet its burden of proving by a preponderance of the evidence that Rafael could not be educated satisfactorily in a regular classroom with supplementary aids and services. We will therefore affirm the district court's decision that the School District has violated the mainstreaming requirement of IDEA. Because we have come to this conclusion based on application of the first part of the *Daniel R.R.* two-part test, we need not apply the second part of the test (whether the child has been included in programs with nondisabled children whenever possible). We note, however, that in the event that the Child Study Team were to determine in designing an IEP for Rafael in the future that education in a regular classroom with supplementary aids and services could not be achieved satisfactorily at that time and therefore would not be required under IDEA, the Team would then have to satisfy the second part of the *Daniel R.R.* test, ensuring that Rafael is included in regular school programs with nondisabled students whenever possible.[17]

Finally, in affirming the district court's order that the School District develop a more inclusive program for Rafael in compliance with IDEA for the upcoming school year, we emphasize that neither this court nor the district court is mandating a specific IEP for Rafael. The development of Rafael's IEP, and the specific nature of his placement, is, of course, the job of the Child Study Team.

The order of the district court will be affirmed.

NOTES AND QUESTIONS

1. The obligation to provide services in the least restrictive environment is sometimes thought of as a "negative" right, that is, the right to be free from unnecessary restraint. Examples of such negative rights are those to be free from all but the minimally required restrictions on freedom for persons residing in state facilities for persons with developmental disabilities. *See, e.g., Olmstead v. L.C.*, 527 U.S. 581 (1999) (requiring placement in community settings on basis of Americans with Disabilities Act); *Youngberg v. Romeo*, 457 U.S. 307 (1982) (upholding constitutional right to be free from unneeded restraint). *Oberti* and *Rachel H.* suggest that under IDEA, the right is more of a positive entitlement: a child must be given the services in a mainstreamed setting to permit her to succeed there, and thus avoid a more restrictive placement. The language of § 1412(a)(5)(A) supports this view. For a more detailed exposition of this interpretation and its implications, see Mark C. Weber, *The Least Restrictive Environment Obligation as an Entitlement to Educational Services: A Commentary*, 5 U.C. Davis J. Juv. L. & Pol'y 147

---

[17] [FN 30] We also note that, as the Obertis' counsel acknowledged at oral argument, inclusion in regular academic classes may become less appropriate for Rafael, given his cognitive disability, as he reaches the higher grades. Dr. Brown testified before the district court:

> . . . as Rafael — children [with similar disabilities] all over this country, as they increase in chronological age, they spend more and more of their time learning to function in non-school settings; in respected, valued integrated settings like vocational environments. Rafael, as he gets older, will have to leave school and learn how to function in a real job as part of his school program.

(2001). Does it make sense to describe *Garret F.* as a least restrictive environment case, arguing that the extensive services were required to enable him to learn at school with peers rather than in a program at home or in a hospital?

2. The Second Circuit has endorsed *Oberti's* approach to least restrictive environment issues. *P. v. Newington Bd. of Educ.*, 546 F.3d 111, 120 (3d Cir. 2008). Some other cases that are quite explicit in requiring the provision of related services to permit the child to be placed in a less restrictive setting are: *Hunt v. Bartman*, 873 F. Supp. 229 (W.D. Mo. 1994) (compelling consideration of supplemental aids and services before referral of child for state school placement); *Mavis v. Sobol*, 839 F. Supp. 968 (N.D.N.Y. 1993) (requiring placement of child with moderate mental retardation in general education classroom with aids and services). Behavior management plans or modification of ordinary disciplinary rules may also be required if a child is to remain in a more inclusive setting without facing suspension or other exclusion. *See infra* Chapter 9 (Student Discipline).

3. Chapter 6, *supra*, notes that many courts have analyzed the least restrictive environment requirement as imposing obligations that are not restricted by the limits on the duty of appropriate education found in the *Rowley* case. Cases concerning parents' demands for related services to facilitate mainstreaming are key examples of instances when levels of services that rise above a floor of opportunity must be provided. An interesting recent example is *L.B. v. Nebo School District*, 379 F.3d 966 (10th Cir. 2004), in which the court rejected a school district's proposal to place a young child with autism in a largely non-mainstreamed class with eight to fifteen hours of applied behavioral analysis services, and upheld the parents' position that she should continue in her private, mainstreamed preschool class (paid for by the parents) but with an in-class aide and with thirty-five to forty hours of applied behavioral analysis services delivered primarily at home, paid for by the public school district. The court reasoned that the aide and applied behavioral analysis services were needed to enable the child to succeed in a mainstreamed setting and so had to be provided by the school district.

4. The expense of certain related services, such as a one-on-one aide, raises concern among some school districts. See the discussion *supra* regarding *Garret F.* When should provision of a one-on-one aide be required in order to enable a child to be educated in a mainstreamed setting? Scholarly discussions of broader least restrictive environment issues display a range of positions. *Compare, e.g.*, Daniel H. Melvin II, Comment, *The Desegregation of Children with Disabilities*, 44 DEPAUL L. REV. 599 (1995), *with* Anne Proffitt Dupre, *Disability and the Public Schools: The Case Against "Inclusion,"* 72 WASH. L. REV. 775 (1997).

Chapter 8

DUE PROCESS HEARINGS

A. HEARING RIGHTS

In *Mills v. Board of Education*, 348 F. Supp. 866, 880 (D.D.C. 1972) (reprinted *supra* Chapter 1), a principal case leading to passage of the federal special education law, the court required that parents receive notice and the right to an impartial hearing before their child could be placed in a special education program. When Congress codified federal special education law, one of the main concerns of parents was that school officials were making decisions about placing children in special education, or refusing to do so, without giving the parents enough opportunity to participate in these determinations that so deeply affected their children's futures. Accordingly, the drafters of the Education for All Handicapped Children Act, now the Individuals with Disabilities Education Act, drafted elaborate notice and hearing provisions, adopting the processes imposed on the District of Columbia school system in *Mills* and going somewhat beyond them. By calling the procedure the "due process hearing," the Act's drafters suggested that the hearing rights the Act created were sufficient, and perhaps necessary, to satisfy the requirements of the Fourteenth Amendment due process clause in the context of special education disputes.

Of course, process-style protections are only effective if individual parents are able to use them effectively. Some broad-scale problems regarding special education persist despite the existence of individual procedural rights. Children with disabilities drop out of school at a vastly disproportionate rate compared to the school population as a whole, and there is a low rate of children with disabilities who move on to higher education. Concern remains that some children may be inappropriately placed into special education, particularly in light of the disproportionately large number of non-Hispanic African-American children in special education. *See generally* U.S. Dep't of Educ., 23d Annual Report to Congress on Implementation of IDEA II-27 (2002) (noting that non-Hispanic African-American students constitute 20.3% of children in special education but only 14.5% of the population, with even higher disproportionate representation in mental retardation and developmental delay categories). While over-identification of children may be taking place in some instances, there are also children who need services who are not receiving them, or not receiving them in the proper setting. Whether parents could solve these collective problems by exercising individual hearing rights is unclear. Parents may not know what to ask for their children. Those who do often feel ambivalence in requesting hearings or otherwise insisting on the programs or placements they want in the face of school district opposition. Working from interviews with parents of children in special education, one researcher concluded that parents feel at a disadvantage participating in special education processes, and are reluctant to disturb existing relationships with schools and communities by asserting special education rights. David M. Engel, *Law Culture, and Children with Disabilities: Educational Rights and the Construction of Difference*, 1991 DUKE L.J. 166.

For parents who exercise due process rights, the results are, predictably, mixed. One study of due process hearings in Illinois reports that over a five year period, parents won (in the sense of achieving any success at all) 30.5% of the due process hearings that went to decision. Three of 20 hearing officers decided 100% of their cases in favor of school districts. Parents had attorney representation in only 44% of cases, in contrast to school districts, which had attorneys in 94% of cases. When a lawyer represented the parent, the rate of parents prevailing rose to 50.4%, in contrast to a success rate of 16.8% for parents without attorneys. MELANIE ARCHER, ACCESS AND EQUITY IN THE DUE PROCESS SYSTEM: ATTORNEY REPRESENTATION AND HEARING OUTCOMES IN ILLINOIS, 1997-2002, at 4–7 (2002). More study would be needed to determine whether the greatly higher success rate for parents represented by attorneys is because lawyers present cases more effectively or because they select only the strongest cases, or some combination of the two.

NOTES AND QUESTIONS

1. In *Burlington School Committee v. Department of Education*, 471 U.S. 359, 370 (1985), the Supreme Court described the special education due process hearing and judicial review procedure as "ponderous," with final decisions usually coming a year or more after the school year covered by the individualized education program being challenged. What, if any, harms result from these delays? What could be done to expedite hearings and appeals?

2. The hearing procedure is a key example of the legalization of special education. "Legalization" is the term that describes the pervasive role that law plays in delivery of special education services, in contrast to the weaker role that law plays in general education. *See generally* David Neal & David L. Kirp, *The Allure of Legalization Reconsidered: The Case of Special Education*, LAW & CONTEMP. PROBS., Winter, 1985, at 63 (describing legalization phenomenon). What conditions led to the legalization of special education? Should changes be made to decrease the significance of law in special education? To increase it? Do you agree with the claim that "The culture of compliance has often developed from the pressures of litigation, diverting much energy of the public schools' first mission: educating every child." President's Commission on Excellence in Special Education, A New Era: Revitalizing Special Education for Children and Their Families 3 (2002), *available at* http://www.ed.gov.inits/commissionsboards/whspecialeducation/reports.html. In contrast to the views of the President's Commission about the overuse of litigation, an independent report by the General Accounting Office summarized its conclusions in its title: Special Education: Numbers of Formal Disputes Are Generally Low and States Are Using Mediation and Other Strategies to Resolve Conflicts (U.S. Gen. Accounting Office 2003).

3. The rights provided by the special education law are examples of procedural due process protections. Lawyers distinguish procedural due process from substantive due process. Generally speaking, the distinction is that under procedural due process doctrine, government must provide notice, an opportunity to be heard, or

other measures to insure fairness and accuracy in making individual determinations that will result in the loss of a person's life, liberty, or property. Thus the government must afford a welfare recipient the opportunity for a fair hearing before cutting off assistance on the basis of his alleged ineligibility, *Goldberg v. Kelly*, 397 U.S. 254 (1970), and it must pay for a blood test for an indigent defendant to insure an accurate determination in a paternity case, *Little v. Streater*, 452 U.S. 1 (1981). The Supreme Court applied procedural due process doctrine to public schooling when it ruled in *Goss v. Lopez*, 419 U.S. 565 (1975), that school authorities had to afford some kind of notice and hearing to a child facing a suspension of ten days for violating school rules. Would you say that the statutory due process rights provided by IDEA exceed the minimum due process that the Constitution requires, or would a proper interpretation of the Fourteenth Amendment provide parents the same procedural rights in special education disputes that IDEA's due process provisions establish? Stated another way, are there any procedural protections now afforded parents that Congress could repeal without violating the Constitution?

4. In contrast to procedural due process, which requires minimum factfinding or other steps that the government must take to insure fairness before disadvantaging someone, substantive due process doctrine establishes that the government cannot take away some life, liberty or property interests at all, or at least without adequate reasons. Thus the government must afford a woman the liberty to have an abortion in the period before the viability of the fetus, *Planned Parenthood v. Casey*, 505 U.S. 833 (1992), and it may not institutionalize an individual on the basis of mental retardation without providing the person habilitation, adequate food, shelter, clothing, and medical care, and reasonable personal safety and freedom from restraint, *Youngberg v. Romeo*, 457 U.S. 307 (1982). There is little or no necessary connection between contemporary procedural and substantive due process doctrines apart from their origin in the same constitutional language, though some writers contend that there should be a closer link. *See, e.g.*, Jane Rutherford, *The Myth of Due Process*, 72 B.U. L. REV. 1 (1992). For a concise discussion of the distinction between procedural and substantive due process, see ERWIN CHEMERINSKY, CONSTITUTIONAL LAW: PRINCIPLES AND POLICIES 523–25 (2d ed. 2002).

1.   Notice

The statutory provision in IDEA specifies in some detail the notice that must be afforded parents so that they can decide if, when, and how to influence or contest special education decisions made by school districts:

(a) Establishment of procedures. Any State educational agency, State agency, or local educational agency that receives assistance under this part shall establish and maintain procedures in accordance with this section to ensure that children with disabilities and their parents are guaranteed procedural safeguards with respect to the provision of a free appropriate public education by such agencies.

(b) Types of procedures. The procedures required by this section shall include the following:

(1) An opportunity for the parents of a child with a disability to examine all

records relating to such child and to participate in meetings with respect to the identification, evaluation, and educational placement of the child, and the provision of a free appropriate public education to such child, and to obtain an independent educational evaluation of the child.

(2) (A) Procedures to protect the rights of the child whenever the parents of the child are not known, the agency cannot, after reasonable efforts, locate the parents, or the child is a ward of the State, including the assignment of an individual to act as a surrogate for the parents, which surrogate shall not be an employee of the State educational agency, the local educational agency, or any other agency that is involved in the education or care of the child. . . .

(B) The State shall make reasonable efforts to ensure the assignment of a surrogate not more than 30 days after there is a determination by the agency that the child needs a surrogate.

(3) Written prior notice to the parents of the child, in accordance with subsection (c)(1), whenever the local educational agency —

(A) proposes to initiate or change; or

(B) refuses to initiate or change, the identification, evaluation, or educational placement of the child, or the provision of a free appropriate public education to the child.

(4) Procedures designed to ensure that the notice required by paragraph (3) is in the native language of the parents, unless it clearly is not feasible to do so.

(5) An opportunity for mediation, in accordance with subsection (e).

(6) An opportunity for any party to present a complaint —

(A) with respect to any matter relating to the identification, evaluation, or educational placement of the child, or the provision of a free appropriate public education to such child; and

(B) which sets forth an alleged violation that occurred not more than 2 years before the date the parent or public agency knew or should have known about the alleged action that forms the basis of the complaint, or, if the State has an explicit time limitation for presenting such a complaint under this part, in such time as the State law allows, except that the exceptions to the timeline described in subsection (f)(3)(D) shall apply to the timeline described in this subparagraph.

(7) (A) Procedures that require either party, or the attorney representing a party, to provide due process complaint notice in accordance with subsection (c)(2) (which shall remain confidential) —

(i) to the other party, in the complaint filed under paragraph (6), and forward a copy of such notice to the State educational agency; and

(ii) that shall include —

(I) the name of the child, the address of the residence of the child (or available contact information in the case of a homeless child), and the name of the school the child is attending;

(II) in the case of a homeless child or youth . . . , available contact information for the child and the name of the school the child is attending;

(III) a description of the nature of the problem of the child relating to such proposed initiation or change, including facts relating to such problem; and

(IV) a proposed resolution of the problem to the extent known and available to the party at the time.

(B) A requirement that a party may not have a due process hearing until the party, or the attorney representing the party, files a notice that meets the requirements of subparagraph (A)(ii).

(8) Procedures that require the State educational agency to develop a model form to assist parents in filing a complaint and due process complaint notice in accordance with paragraphs (6) and (7), respectively.

(c) Notification requirements.

(1) Content of prior written notice. The notice required by subsection (b)(3) shall include —

(A) a description of the action proposed or refused by the agency;

(B) an explanation of why the agency proposes or refuses to take the action and a description of each evaluation procedure, assessment, record, or report the agency used as a basis for the proposed or refused action;

(C) a statement that the parents of a child with a disability have protection under the procedural safeguards of this part and, if this notice is not an initial referral for evaluation, the means by which a copy of a description of the procedural safeguards can be obtained;

(D) sources for parents to contact to obtain assistance in understanding the provisions of this part;

(E) a description of other options considered by the IEP Team and the reason why those options were rejected; and

(F) a description of the factors that are relevant to the agency's proposal or refusal.

(2) Due process complaint notice.

(A) Complaint. The due process complaint notice required under subsection (b)(7)(A) shall be deemed to be sufficient unless the party receiving the notice notifies the hearing officer and the other party in writing that the receiving party believes the notice has not met the requirements of subsection (b)(7)(A).

(B) Response to complaint.

(i) Local educational agency response.

(I) In general. If the local educational agency has not sent a prior written notice to the parent regarding the subject matter contained in the parent's due process complaint notice, such local educational agency shall, within 10 days of receiving the complaint, send to the parent a response that shall include —

(aa) an explanation of why the agency proposed or refused to take the action raised in the complaint;

(bb) a description of other options that the IEP Team considered and the reasons why those options were rejected;

(cc) a description of each evaluation procedure, assessment, record, or report the agency used as the basis for the proposed or refused action; and

(dd) a description of the factors that are relevant to the agency's proposal or refusal.

(II) Sufficiency. A response filed by a local educational agency pursuant to subclause (I) shall not be construed to preclude such local educational agency from asserting that the parent's due process complaint notice was insufficient where appropriate.

(ii) Other party response. Except as provided in clause (i), the non-complaining party shall, within 10 days of receiving the complaint, send to the complaint a response that specifically addresses the issues raised in the complaint.

(C) Timing. The party providing a hearing officer notification under subparagraph (A) shall provide the notification within 15 days of receiving the complaint.

(D) Determination. Within 5 days of receipt of the notification provided under subparagraph (C), the hearing officer shall make a determination on the face of the notice of whether the notification meets the requirements of subsection (b)(7)(A), and shall immediately notify the parties in writing of such determination.

(E) Amended complaint notice.

(i) In general. A party may amend its due process complaint notice only if —

(I) the other party consents in writing to such amendment and is given the opportunity to resolve the complaint through a meeting held pursuant to subsection (f)(1)(B); or

(II) the hearing officer grants permission, except that the hearing officer may only grant such permission at any time not later than 5 days before a due process hearing occurs.

(ii) Applicable timeline. The applicable timeline for a due process hearing under this part shall recommence at the time the party files an amended notice, including the timeline under subsection (f)(1)(B).

(d) Procedural safeguards notice.

(1) In general.

(A) Copy to parents. A copy of the procedural safeguards available to the parents of a child with a disability shall be given to the parents only 1 time a year, except that a copy also shall be given to the parents —

(i) upon initial referral or parental request for evaluation;

(ii) upon the first occurrence of the filing of a complaint under subsection (b)(6); and

(iii) upon request by a parent.

(B) Internet website. A local educational agency may place a current copy of the procedural safeguards notice on its Internet website if such website exists.

(2) Contents. The procedural safeguards notice shall include a full explanation of the procedural safeguards, written in the native language of the parents (unless it clearly is not feasible to do so) and written in an easily understandable manner, available under this section and under regulations promulgated by the Secretary relating to —

(A) independent educational evaluation;

(B) prior written notice;

(C) parental consent;

(D) access to educational records;

(E) the opportunity to present and resolve complaints, including —

(i) the time period in which to make a complaint;

(ii) the opportunity for the agency to resolve the complaint; and

(iii) the availability of mediation;

(F) the child's placement during pendency of due process proceedings;

(G) procedures for students who are subject to placement in an interim alternative educational setting;

(H) requirements for unilateral placement by parents of children in private schools at public expense;

(I) due process hearings, including requirements for disclosure of evaluation results and recommendations;

(J) State-level appeals (if applicable in that State);

(K) civil actions, including the time period in which to file such actions; and

(L) attorneys' fees.

20 U.S.C. § 1415.

NOTES AND QUESTIONS

1. Why do you think Congress wrote such an elaborate provision? Do you suspect that there is something that parents of children with disabilities were especially worried about, and that they asked their congressional representatives to address?

2. The current codification, amended in 2004, places significant responsibilities on parents when they initiate requests for due process hearings. The hearing request must specify the child's name and address; the name of the school the child attends; a description of the problem of the child that relates to initiation or change of identification, evaluation, educational placement, or free, appropriate public education, including facts relating to the problem; and the proposed way of resolving the problem, to the extent that is known and available to the parent. Will parents be able to comply with these requirements in any useful way without hiring a lawyer?

2. Impartiality Requirements

The current special education regulation provides:

(c) Impartial hearing officer.

(1) At a minimum, a hearing officer —

(i) Must not be —

(A) An employee of the SEA or the LEA that is involved in the education or care of the child; or

(B) A person having a personal or professional interest that conflicts with the person's objectivity in the hearing;

(ii) Must possess knowledge of, and the ability to understand, the provisions of the Act, Federal and State regulations pertaining to the Act, and legal interpretations of the Act by Federal and State courts;

(iii) Must possess the knowledge and ability to conduct hearings in accordance with appropriate, standard legal practice; and

(iv) Must possess the knowledge and ability to render and write decisions in accordance with appropriate, standard legal practice.

(2) A person who otherwise qualifies to conduct a hearing under paragraph (c)(1) of this section is not an employee of the agency solely because he or she is paid by the agency to serve as a hearing officer.

34 C.F.R. § 300.511; *see* 20 U.S.C. § 1415(f)(3)(A).

MAYSON v. TEAGUE
749 F.2d 652 (11th Cir. 1984)

In this case, the court ruled that individuals working for school districts other than the one involved in the hearing and state university employees who formulate special education policies lack the impartiality to serve as hearing officers in due process hearings.

JOHNSON, CIRCUIT JUDGE.

In this case, Superintendent Wayne Teague and the Alabama Board of Education appeal from an order enjoining Superintendent Teague from selecting as due process hearing officers under the Education for All Handicapped Children Act individuals who are officers or employees of local school systems which the child in question does not attend, or university personnel who have been involved in the formulation of state policies on educating handicapped children. Appellants argue that the district court's order should be vacated, as it was based upon an unacceptably broad interpretation of the requirements of the Education for All Handicapped Children Act (EAHCA), 20 U.S.C.A. § 1415(b)(2), and its implementing regulations, 34 C.F.R. § 300.57. Because we conclude that the order of the district court is supported by both the requirements of the EAHCA and those opinions which have construed them, we affirm.

I. THE FACTS

In Alabama, officers responsible for conducting due process hearings under the EAHCA are selected by the Superintendent of the State Board of Education. The three officers who compose a due process panel are selected from the areas of college teaching, school administration and local supervisors of special education. These individuals may be officers or employees of a local school system where the child involved is not attending school and they may be employees of an institution of higher education. Since late in 1979, panels have typically been composed of one university educator and two officers or employees of local school systems.

A. *Mayson et al. v. Teague*

Appellees Lisa Mayson and William Dean Carpenter are handicapped children who are enrolled in the Mobile Public Schools. In December 1978 appellees, who were dissatisfied with the educational plans that had been prescribed for them, sought and were accorded due process hearings. Prior to the time of these hearings, the Maysons and Carpenters filed written objections to the method used by the state for selecting due process hearing officers. In their written objections, appellees alleged that the selection of hearing officers who are officers or employees of local school systems in which the child in question is not enrolled or who are university personnel involved in the formulation of state policies concerning special education violates the EAHCA and its implementing regulations. Due process hearings were subsequently conducted, and in each case a determination adverse to appellees was reached. Appellees' claims were then evaluated by a review panel, which was selected according to the same method as the due process panel. Prior to the second hearing, the Maysons and Carpenters filed a second set of written objections to the method of selecting hearing officers.

When the review panel affirmed the adverse ruling of the due process panel, the Maysons and Carpenters filed separate civil actions in the United States District Court for the Southern District of Alabama, alleging violations of the EAHCA and its implementing regulations. On August 11, 1979, the district court granted the motions of the parties to consolidate. On September 22, 1980, the court adopted a magistrate's recommendation that a class be certified, composed of all children who are, have been or will be enrolled in the Mobile Public School System who are affected by a learning disability, an educable mental retardation, a behavioral or emotional disturbance or a speech impediment.

On June 1, 1983, the court approved a partial settlement that had been reached by the parties, and issued a Consent Decree, Order and Judgment. The sole remaining issue in the case was whether the selection as hearing officers of officers or employees of local educational systems in which the child is not enrolled, and of university personnel who helped formulate state policy on educating handicapped children violates EAHCA and its implementing regulations. These regulations prohibit a hearing from being conducted

   1) by a person who is an employee of a public agency which is involved in the education or care of the child or

   2) by any person having a personal or professional interest which would conflict with his or her objectivity in the hearing.

34 C.F.R. § 300.57.

On October 5, 1983, the court issued an opinion to the effect that the selection procedure employed by the Alabama Board of Education violated the EAHCA and its implementing regulations. In accordance with this conclusion, the court entered an order enjoining defendants from selecting as hearing officers:

   1) a Superintendent of Schools or Assistant Superintendent of Schools for any county or local public school system in the State

   2) any employee of any (non-university) public school system in the State

   3) any employee of the university system of the State who has participated in the formulation of regulations and policies of the State affecting handicapped children.

From this order Superintendent Teague and the Board of Education appeal.

   . . . .

II. "IMPARTIALITY" UNDER THE EDUCATION FOR
ALL HANDICAPPED CHILDREN ACT

A. Issues Framed by the Parties

The district court held that local educational agency personnel are "very closely aligned with" and "to some extent under the direct or indirect supervision of" the State Superintendent and the State Board of Education. For this reason, the court concluded that these individuals are employees of an agency "involved in the education or care of the child" and are not impartial within the meaning of the EAHCA. The court also found that the university personnel who have actively participated in the formulation of state educational policies affecting handicapped children do not meet the impartiality requirements of the Act. . . .

Appellants claim that the court adopted an inappropriately expansive interpretation of the statutory phrase "involved in the education or care of the child." They argue that this phrase refers only to officers or employees of the specific school district in which the child is enrolled. While appellants concede that there have been several court opinions holding that officers or employees of the *State Board of Education* may not serve as hearing officers, indicating that the state may also be understood as being "involved in the education or care of the child," they argue that these opinions reach no farther than state board employees and do not implicate employees of local school systems. Appellants claim that Congress, which was concerned only with the exclusion of the specific groups noted above, expressed no concern over the "supervisory control" cited by the court or the "appearance of impropriety" relied upon by appellees. Appellants finally note that to view university personnel who help formulate state programs as being "involved with the education or care of the child" would require the court to consider handicapped children as a group, rather than as individuals, in direct contravention of the intended (and judicially-sanctioned) emphasis of the Act.

Appellees endorse the district court's interpretation of the phrase "involved in the education or care of the child." They claim that under the State Constitution, the state (through its Board of Education) is the governmental unit charged with the education and care of handicapped children. Furthermore, while employees of local school systems are not technically employees of the State Board of Education, appellees argue that they should be considered as such for purposes of the Act, both because they are under the supervision of the Superintendent and the State Board of Education, and because in other legal contexts employees of local school systems have been considered to be agents of the state.

Appellees also claim that employees of local school systems have "personal or professional interest[s] which would conflict with [their] objectivity in the hearing." The position of the local school employee within the larger state system of education makes it unlikely that he could be objective in evaluating a claim involving a local school system. As an adverse due process hearing can sometimes lead to the withdrawal of state funds, appellees note, employees of local education systems might be concerned about retribution and about being subjected to adverse decisions, or they might be reluctant to set a high standard with which they too would have to comply. Appellees describe such attitudes not as hypothetical possibilities, but as motives which have been at work in recent years in the State system of education. They cite a situation, involving concerted action by local school officials and Superintendent Teague, which they claim produced a change in the selection of hearing officers.

In October 1979, Lance Grissett, Superintendent of the Talladega County Board of Education, wrote a letter to Superintendent Teague, expressing surprise and disappointment over the way that State Department of Education employees had been participating in the due process hearings in his county. Stating that his school system had "endured six such hearings" in the preceding eighteen months, Superintendent Grissett complained that there had been a lack of professionalism in the Department's response. He claimed that Department employees had offered placement recommendations and advice, often on the phone and on the basis of scant evidence, to the parents of handicapped children. He also noted that Department employees had given "minimal" input and assistance to his school system. Grissett stressed his understanding that "a primary function of, if not the overriding purpose for the existence of the State Department of Education, is to operate as a service agency to local school districts," and urged Teague to take action on the problem. Following this letter, Teague attended a regularly scheduled meeting with local superintendents, at which other administrative complaints were raised. Teague then appointed a select committee of local superintendents, including Superintendent Grissett, to consider administrative problems in special education.

On October 23, 1979, one day after the first meeting of this select committee, Grissett wrote Superintendent Teague a letter commending the attention Teague and his staff had given to Grissett's "recently expressed serious concerns." He noted that the problems facing local school systems in administering special education programs were "serious and complex in nature," but added that "much of the solution to this significant educational problem begins with getting 'our team' together, i.e., state Board and its staff, local Board and its staff, appropriate college and university personnel, etc." Stating that he appreciated " 'our kind' of State Superintendent exemplified in yesterday's discussions," Grissett offered his services in " 'getting our act together' subject to your direction and request."

After the October 22, 1979, meeting, a precipitous change took place in the composition of the due process and review panels selected by the Superintendent. Before the October 1979 meeting, panels most often contained a majority of university personnel. A compilation of panel composition figures stipulated by the parties indicates that 47 out of 54 panels appointed in 1977 and 1978 contained such a majority. After October 1979, however, not a single panel contained a majority of university personnel; all of these subsequent panels contained a majority of local educational system employees as hearing officers.

Finally appellees argue that university personnel who are involved in the formulation of state policies affecting the education of handicapped children are no more fit than local educational employees to serve as "impartial" due process hearing officers. Appellees note that a university employee who had had a role in formulating a state policy would inevitably find it difficult to overturn that policy, though the claim of a particular handicapped child might require it.

B. Local School System Personnel

1. "Involved in the Education or Care of the Child"

Appellees correctly note that the Alabama Constitution charges the State Superintendent and the State Board of Education with responsibility for providing a public education for Alabama's children, a responsibility which presumably includes care for the educationally handicapped. Yet appellees need not rely solely on the Alabama Constitution to support their claim that the phrase "involved in the education or care of the child" extends beyond the local school system in which the child is enrolled. At least two recent cases, one citing the "clear legislative history of the statute," have held that this language cannot be construed as narrowly as appellants suggest. See *Robert M. v. Benton*, 634 F.2d 1139 (8th Cir. 1980); *Vogel v. School Board of Montrose*, 491 F. Supp. 989 (W.D. Mo. 1980). Though these cases technically hold that officers of a state board of education are barred from serving as hearing officers, the opinions also address the specific interpretive claim raised by appellants here: that the phrase in question refers only to the school system in which the child is enrolled. In *Robert M. v. Benton, supra*, the court stated:

> The Senate Conference Report therefore indicates that the Act, promulgated as the conference substitute for differing House and Senate versions of the bill and passed November 1975 by both Houses, intentionally expanded its prohibition to include employees of state educational agencies not directly involved in the education of the child and so to disqualify them from serving as hearing officers under Section 1415(b)(2).

634 F.2d at 1142. *See also Vogel v. School Board, supra*, 491 F. Supp. at 995. While it is not clear that the court intended to include local school boards under the heading of "state educational agencies," such a construction seems plausible, as the term is as likely to connote educational agencies within the state as it is to refer to the State Board of Education. But even if the inclusion of local school boards was not intended or considered by the court in *Robert M. v. Benton*, these cases still offer persuasive evidence that the narrow interpretation proposed by appellants should be rejected. It remains only to consider whether officers and employees of local school boards can be considered agents or employees of the State Board of Education for purposes of the Act.

Appellees argue that for purposes of tort immunity, employees of local school boards are considered to be agents of the state of Alabama. See, e.g., *Hickman v. Dothan City Board of Education*, 421 So. 2d 1257 (Ala. 1982); *DeStafney v. University of Alabama*, 413 So. 2d 391 (Ala. 1982). While immunity from tort actions need not be determinative of a question of federal statutory interpretation, these immunity opinions contain broader language which is relevant to the role played by local school board employees in the educational scheme of the state. In *Enterprise City Board of Education v. Miller*, 348 So. 2d 782 (Ala. 1977), the court stated that the extension of sovereign immunity to the local school board employees was appropriate because city boards of education, like county boards of education, are "agencies of the state, empowered to administer public education within the cities." 348 So. 2d at 783.

The role described by the Alabama Supreme Court appears to be borne out, moreover, by the performance of both state and local school board employees over the past several years. Superintendent Teague's appointment of a select committee of local superintendents and the changes which followed in the state's administration of special education claims suggest that local educational employees do not act independently on questions of special education, but follow policies arrived at collectively by employees on both state and local levels. Indeed the gravamen of Superintendent Grissett's highly effective complaint to Superintendent Teague was that he had not seen sufficient evidence of the coordination between state and local officials that he believed to be the rule in the administration of the state's educational programs. Thus whether the relationship between state and local educational officials is supervisory, as the district court maintained, or cooperative, as appellees allege, the district court did not err in finding that officers and employees of local school boards are employees of agencies "involved in the education and care of the child."

2. "Personal or Professional Interest[s]" Affecting Impartiality

The district court did not consider the applicability of the second criterion of exclusion under the Act: a "personal or professional interest which would interfere with . . . objectivity in the hearing." Appellees, however, present this factor as an equally persuasive basis for affirming the district court's order. Not only do they identify influences, such as fear of retaliation or reluctance to set high statewide standards, which would seem to interfere with objectivity on the part of local educational employees, they present evidence suggesting that in Alabama, at least, these potential sources of conflict have had palpable practical ramifications. The way in which the special education problem was addressed in Grissett's second letter to Teague — " 'our kind' of State Superintendent," "appropriate university personnel," "getting 'our team' together" — suggests that educators at both state and local levels had developed and intended to advance a common attitude about the provision of educational assistance for the handicapped. The precipitous drop in the number of university personnel appointed to due process panels after the meeting between Teague and the Select Committee suggests the willingness of educators at both levels to permit these attitudes to shape their administration of the Act. While appellees do not present evidence of bias in operation at a specific hearing, they provide ample evidence of a "professional interest" which had interfered with the impartiality of local school system employees in other phases of their administration of the Act, and might reasonably be expected to interfere with their objectivity during hearings. Though the district court did not rely on this ground, it provides additional support for the judgment entered by that court.

C. University Personnel Involved in State Policymaking

Appellants also challenge the district court's conclusion that university personnel who have been actively involved in the formulation of state policy in the area of special education are not sufficiently impartial to serve as hearing officers under the Act. However, appellants' claim, that the district court's position is untenable because it requires the court to consider handicapped children as a group, is undermined by cases such as *Robert M. v. Benton* and *Vogel v. School Board, supra.* In holding that the state school board is an agency "involved in the education and care of the child" because it is responsible for the education and care of all handicapped children, these cases clearly — and acceptably — view handicapped children as a group.

The district court's order regarding university personnel is supported by the same type of attitudinal argument which buttressed its order regarding local educational employees. When a university professor has taken an active part in formulating a state policy in the area of special education, it seems entirely plausible that he could become sufficiently personally or professionally invested in the policy that he would find it difficult to reverse or modify it as a due process hearing officer. Though this potential conflict has had fewer practical ramifications than the attitudes attributed to local educators,[1] given the comparatively narrow scope of the district court's order with respect to university personnel and the fact that appellants offer no persuasive ground for finding that the district court erred, it provides sufficient ground to require affirmance.

. . . .

NOTES AND QUESTIONS

1.   Not all decisions are in accord with *Mayson. See, e.g., L.B. v. Nebo Sch. Dist.,* 379 F.3d 966 (10th Cir. 2004) (finding employment by district other than that involved in hearing not to disqualify hearing officer). As a general matter, should school district employees be barred from presiding over cases involving other districts? Does the peculiar history of the state policy described in *Mayson* influence the outcome of the case? Should the case's approach be applied in other states that may not have the same history? Or does the history simply illustrate the unfairness in any state of having as hearing officers people with a potentially cozy or at least sympathetic peer relationship to the school district officials defending a hearing?

2.   Impartiality principles generally forbid ex parte contact between the hearing officer and the parties or their attorneys on anything but scheduling or similar administrative matters not going to the merits of the case. *See, e.g., Hollenbeck v. Board of Educ.,* 699 F. Supp. 658 (N.D. Ill. 1988) (disqualifying hearing officer on basis of ex parte contact). Try your hand at drafting guidelines for conduct by hearing officers. Would your guidelines permit review of draft decisions by a specialist hearing officer who does not preside in the case? *See generally Jones v. Washington County Bd. of Educ.,* 15 F. Supp. 2d 783 (D. Md. 1998) (allowing practice). Would they permit consultation between the hearing officer and subject matter experts in the state educational agency?

3.   Though hearing officers must be impartial, and the courts have proven

---

[1] [FN 3] Superintendent Grissett's reference to "appropriate university personnel" supports the proposition that university professors may vary in the degree to which they are disposed to favor state policies for educating the handicapped; professional association would seem to be one of the most influential factors leading university personnel to support such policies.

willing to enforce that requirement, courts have been reluctant to enforce, or even to admit to, any requirement that hearing officers know what they are doing. *See, e.g., Carnwath v. Grasmick,* 115 F. Supp. 2d 577, 583 (D. Md. 2000) ("[T]here is no federal right to a competent or knowledgeable ALJ."). Can you construct a constitutional argument in support of the proposition that a hearing officer must have some threshold level of competence? In 2004, Congress imposed a competence requirement, embodied in the regulatory language of 34 C.F.R. § 300.511(c)(ii)–(iii) quoted above.

4. Some states have systems in which specialized hearing officers hear only special education cases. Others use a state corps of administrative law judges who may hear special education cases on one day and environmental enforcement actions or insurance regulation matters the next. While the former system may stimulate the development of expertise among hearing officers, the latter may promote impartiality. Which system is superior?

3. Participation Rights and Decisions

The current federal regulation provides:

Hearing rights.

(a) General. Any party to a hearing conducted pursuant to §§ 300.507 through 300.513 or §§ 300.530 through 300.534, or an appeal conducted pursuant to § 300.514, has the right to —

    (1) Be accompanied and advised by counsel and by individuals with special knowledge or training with respect to the problems of children with disabilities;

    (2) Present evidence and confront, cross-examine, and compel the attendance of witnesses;

    (3) Prohibit the introduction of any evidence at the hearing that has not been disclosed to that party at least five business days before the hearing;

    (4) Obtain a written, or, at the option of the parents, electronic, verbatim record of the hearing; and

    (5) Obtain written, or, at the option of the parents, electronic findings of fact and decisions.

(b) Additional disclosure of information.

    (1) At least five business days prior to a hearing conducted pursuant to § 300.511(a), each party must disclose to all other parties all evaluations completed by that date and recommendations based on the offering party's evaluations that the party intends to use at the hearing.

    (2) A hearing officer may bar any party that fails to comply with paragraph (b)(1) of this section from introducing the relevant evaluation or recommendation at the hearing without the consent of the other party.

(c) Parental rights at hearings. Parents involved in hearings must be given the right to —

(1) Have the child who is the subject of the hearing present;

(2) Open the hearing to the public; and

(3) Have the record of the hearing and the findings of fact and decisions described in paragraphs (a)(4) and (a)(5) of this section provided at no cost to parents.

34 C.F.R. § 300.512.

With regard to timeliness of decision and convenience of the hearing, the regulation states further:

Timelines and convenience of hearings and reviews.

(a) The public agency must ensure that not later than 45 days after the expiration of the 30 day period under § 300.510(b), or the adjusted time periods described in § 300.510(c) —

(1) A final decision is reached in the hearing; and

(2) A copy of the decision is mailed to each of the parties.

(b) The SEA must ensure that not later than 30 days after the receipt of a request for a review —

(1) A final decision is reached in the review; and

(2) A copy of the decision is mailed to each of the parties.

(c) A hearing or reviewing officer may grant specific extensions of time beyond the periods set out in paragraphs (a) and (b) of this section at the request of either party.

(d) Each hearing and each review involving oral arguments must be conducted at a time and place that is reasonably convenient to the parents and child involved.

34 C.F.R. § 300.515.

NOTES AND QUESTIONS

1.   The hearing rights provided by IDEA cause a due process hearing to resemble nothing so much as a bench trial in a civil case. Is this degree of procedural formality a good thing? Can it be avoided while still affording adequate safeguards to parents?

2.   The guarantee of a right to confront and cross-examine witnesses would appear to bar the use of hearsay in due process hearings, but at least one court, relying on state law, has permitted the admission of hearsay evidence at the due process hearing when it is not the sole basis of the hearing officer's decision. *See Glendale Unified Sch. Dist. v. Almasi*, 122 F. Supp. 2d 1093 (C.D. Cal. 2000). Should all hearsay be prohibited?

3.   Hearing structures under IDEA may be one-tier or two-tier. If there is no appeal from the hearing before the case is ripe to go to court, the one-tier system is to be conducted by the state. If there is appeal to a state-appointed hearing officer, then the local education agency is to conduct the initial hearing. *See* 34 C.F.R. § 300.510(b). State-level reviews are discussed in greater detail *infra* section D. As 34 C.F.R. § 300.511 indicates, timeliness standards vary depending upon whether the decision is at the state level (in a one or two tiered system) or the local one (in a two-tiered system). In any instance, the hearing officer may grant extensions of time at the request of either party. What would be proper grounds for extension of time? Improper grounds? Timeliness standards differ in some discipline cases. *See generally infra* Chapter 9 (Student Discipline).

4.   In 2008, the Department of Education altered 34 C.F.R. § 300.512 to provide that the right to be accompanied and advised by counsel and by individuals with special knowledge or training applies "except that whether parties have the right to be represented by non-attorneys at due process hearings is determined under State law." 34 C.F.R. § 300.512(a)(1) (2009). This may signify the ever increasing legal formality of hearings (see Note 1), or it may demonstrate concern over the quality of representation provided by some non-attorney representatives, or it may represent the efforts of lawyers to grab a larger share of the business of representation. The amended provision is reproduced in the Statutes and Regulations Pamphlet.

4.   Burden of Persuasion

SCHAFFER v. WEAST
546 U.S. 49 (2005)

In this case, the Supreme Court ruled that in due process hearings assessing the appropriateness of an IEP, the burden of persuasion falls on the party seeking relief. In the typical case, that will be the parent.

JUSTICE O'CONNOR delivered the opinion of the Court.

The Individuals with Disabilities Education Act (IDEA or Act) is a Spending Clause statute that seeks to ensure that "all children with disabilities have available to them a free appropriate public education," § 1400(d)(1)(A). Under IDEA, school districts must create an "individualized education program" (IEP) for each disabled child. § 1414(d). If parents believe their child's IEP is inappropriate, they may request an "impartial due process hearing." § 1415(f). The Act is silent, however, as to which party bears the burden of persuasion at such a hearing. We hold that the burden lies, as it typically does, on the party seeking relief.

I

A

Congress first passed IDEA as part of the Education of the Handicapped Act in 1970, and amended it substantially in the Education for All Handicapped Children Act of 1975. At the time the majority of disabled children in America were "either totally excluded from schools or sitting idly in regular classrooms awaiting the time when they were old enough to 'drop out,' " H. R. Rep. No. 94-332, p 2 (1975). IDEA was intended to reverse this history of neglect. As of 2003, the Act governed the provision of special education services to nearly 7 million children across the country. *See* Dept. of Education, Office of Special Education Programs, Data Analysis System, http://www.ideadata.org/tables27th/ar_aa9.htm (as visited Nov. 9, 2005, and available in Clerk of Court's case file).

IDEA is "frequently described as a model of 'cooperative federalism.' " *Little Rock School Dist. v. Mauney*, 183 F.3d 816, 830 (8th Cir. 1999). It "leaves to the States the primary responsibility for developing and executing educational programs for handicapped children, [but] imposes significant requirements to be followed in the discharge of that responsibility." *Board of Ed. of Hendrick Hudson Central School Dist., Westchester Cty. v. Rowley*, 458 U.S. 176, 183 (1982). For example, the Act mandates cooperation and reporting between state and federal educational authorities. Participating States must certify to the Secretary of Education that they have "policies and procedures" that will effectively meet the Act's conditions. 20 U.S.C. § 1412(a). (Unless otherwise noted, all citations to the Act are to the pre-2004 version of the statute because this is the version that was in effect during the proceedings below. We note, however, that nothing in the recent 2004 amendments, 118 Stat. 2674, appears to materially affect the rule announced here.) State educational agencies, in turn, must ensure that local schools and teachers are meeting the State's educational standards. 20 U.S.C. §§ 1412(a)(11), 1412(a)(15)(A). Local educational agencies (school boards or other administrative bodies) can receive IDEA funds only if they certify to a state educational agency that they are acting in accordance with the State's policies and procedures. § 1413(a)(1).

The core of the statute, however, is the cooperative process that it establishes between parents and schools. *Rowley, supra*, at 205–206, 102 S. Ct. 3034, 73 L. Ed. 690 ("Congress placed every bit as much emphasis upon compliance with procedures giving parents and guardians a large measure of participation at every stage of the administrative process, . . . as it did upon the measurement of the resulting IEP against a substantive standard"). The central vehicle for this collaboration is the IEP process. State educational authorities must identify and evaluate disabled children, §§ 1414(a)–(c), develop an IEP for each one, § 1414(d)(2), and review every IEP at least once a year, § 1414(d)(4). Each IEP must include an assessment of the child's current educational performance, must articulate measurable educational goals, and must specify the nature of the special services that the school will provide. § 1414(d)(1)(A).

Parents and guardians play a significant role in the IEP process. They must be informed about and consent to evaluations of their child under the Act. § 1414(c)(3).

Parents are included as members of "IEP teams." § 1414(d)(1)(B). They have the right to examine any records relating to their child, and to obtain an "independent educational evaluation of the[ir] child." § 1415(b)(1). They must be given written prior notice of any changes in an IEP, § 1415(b)(3), and be notified in writing of the procedural safeguards available to them under the Act, § 1415(d)(1). If parents believe that an IEP is not appropriate, they may seek an administrative "impartial due process hearing." § 1415(f). School districts may also seek such hearings, as Congress clarified in the 2004 amendments. They may do so, for example, if they wish to change an existing IEP but the parents do not consent, or if parents refuse to allow their child to be evaluated. As a practical matter, it appears that most hearing requests come from parents rather than schools.

Although state authorities have limited discretion to determine who conducts the hearings, § 1415(f)(1), and responsibility generally for establishing fair hearing procedures, § 1415(a), Congress has chosen to legislate the central components of due process hearings. . . . Congress has never explicitly stated, however, which party should bear the burden of proof at IDEA hearings.

B

This case concerns the educational services that were due, under IDEA, to petitioner Brian Schaffer. Brian suffers from learning disabilities and speech-language impairments. From prekindergarten through seventh grade he attended a private school and struggled academically. In 1997, school officials informed Brian's mother that he needed a school that could better accommodate his needs. Brian's parents contacted respondent Montgomery County Public Schools System (MCPS) seeking a placement for him for the following school year.

MCPS evaluated Brian and convened an IEP team. The committee generated an initial IEP offering Brian a place in either of two MCPS middle schools. Brian's parents were not satisfied with the arrangement, believing that Brian needed smaller classes and more intensive services. The Schaffers thus enrolled Brian in another private school, and initiated a due process hearing challenging the IEP and seeking compensation for the cost of Brian's subsequent private education.

In Maryland, IEP hearings are conducted by administrative law judges (ALJs). After a 3-day hearing, the ALJ deemed the evidence close, held that the parents bore the burden of persuasion, and ruled in favor of the school district. The parents brought a civil action challenging the result. The United States District Court for the District of Maryland reversed and remanded, after concluding that the burden of persuasion is on the school district. Around the same time, MCPS offered Brian a placement in a high school with a special learning center. Brian's parents accepted, and Brian was educated in that program until he graduated from high school. The suit remained alive, however, because the parents sought compensation for the private school tuition and related expenses.

Respondents appealed to the United States Court of Appeals for the Fourth Circuit. While the appeal was pending, the ALJ reconsidered the case, deemed the evidence truly in "equipoise," and ruled in favor of the parents. The Fourth Circuit vacated and remanded the appeal so that it could consider the burden of proof issue along with the merits on a later appeal. The District Court reaffirmed its ruling that the school district has the burden of proof. On appeal, a divided panel of the Fourth Circuit reversed. Judge Michael, writing for the majority, concluded that petitioners offered no persuasive reason to "depart from the normal rule of allocating the burden to the party seeking relief." 377 F.3d 449, 453 (2004). We granted certiorari to resolve the following question: At an administrative hearing assessing the appropriateness of an IEP, which party bears the burden of persuasion?

II

A

The term "burden of proof" is one of the "slipperiest member[s] of the family of legal terms." 2 J. Strong, McCormick on Evidence § 342, p 433 (5th ed. 1999) (hereinafter McCormick). Part of the confusion surrounding the term arises from the fact that historically, the concept encompassed two distinct burdens: the "burden of persuasion," *i.e.*, which party loses if the evidence is closely balanced, and the "burden of production," *i.e.*, which party bears the obligation to come forward with the evidence at different points in the proceeding. We note at the outset that this case concerns only the burden of persuasion, as the parties agree, and when we speak of burden of proof in this opinion, it is this to which we refer.

When we are determining the burden of proof under a statutory cause of action, the touchstone of our inquiry is, of course, the statute. The plain text of IDEA is silent on the allocation of the burden of persuasion. We therefore begin with the ordinary default rule that plaintiffs bear the risk of failing to prove their claims. McCormick § 337, at 412 ("The burdens of pleading and proof with regard to most facts have and should be assigned to the plaintiff who generally seeks to change the present state of affairs and who therefore naturally should be expected to bear the risk of failure or proof or persuasion"); C. Mueller & L. Kirkpatrick, Evidence § 3.1, p 104 (3d ed. 2003) ("Perhaps the broadest and most accepted idea is that the person who seeks court action should justify the request, which means that the plaintiffs bear the burdens on the elements in their claims").

Thus, we have usually assumed without comment that plaintiffs bear the burden of persuasion regarding the essential aspects of their claims. For example, Title VII of the Civil Rights Act of 1964, 42 U.S.C. § 2000e-2 *et seq.*, does not directly state that plaintiffs bear the "ultimate" burden of persuasion, but we have so concluded. *St. Mary's Honor Center* v. *Hicks*, 509 U.S. 502, 511 (1993); *id.*, at 531 (SOUTER, J., dissenting). In numerous other areas, we have presumed or held that the default rule applies. *See, e.g., Lujan* v. *Defenders of Wildlife*, 504 U.S. 555, 561 (1992) (standing); *Cleveland v. Policy Management Systems Corp.*, 526 U.S. 795, 806 (1999) (Americans with Disabilities Act); *Hunt v. Cromartie*, 526 U.S. 541, 553 (1999) (equal protection); *Wharf (Holdings) Ltd. v. United Int'l Holdings, Inc.*, 532 U.S. 588, 593 (2001) (securities fraud); *Doran v. Salem Inn, Inc.*, 422 U.S. 922, 931 (1975) (preliminary injunctions); *Mt. Healthy City Bd. of Ed. v. Doyle*, 429 U.S. 274, 287 (1977) (First Amendment). Congress also expressed its approval of the general rule when it chose to apply it to administrative proceedings under the Administrative Procedure Act, 5 U.S.C. § 556(d).

The ordinary default rule, of course, admits of exceptions. See McCormick § 337, at 412–415. For example, the burden of persuasion as to certain elements of a plantiff's claim may be shifted to defendants, when such elements can fairly be characterized as affirmative defenses or exemptions. Under some circumstances this Court has even placed the burden of persuasion over an entire claim on the defendant. *See Alaska Dept. of Environmental Conservation v. EPA*, 540 U.S. 461, 494 (2004). But while the normal default rule does not solve all cases, it certainly solves most of them. Decisions that place the *entire* burden of persuasion on the opposing party at the *outset* of a proceeding — as petitioners urge us to do here — are extremely rare. Absent some reason to believe that Congress intended otherwise, therefore, we will conclude that the burden of persuasion lies where it usually falls, upon the party seeking relief.

B

Petitioners contend first that a close reading of IDEA's text compels a conclusion in their favor. They urge that we should interpret the statutory words "due process" in light of their constitutional meaning, and apply the balancing test established by *Mathews v. Eldridge*, 424 U.S. 319 (1976). Even assuming that the Act incorporates constitutional due process doctrine, *Eldridge* is no help to petitioners, because "[o]utside the criminal law area, where special concerns attend, the locus of the burden of persuasion is normally not an issue of federal constitutional moment." *Lavine v. Milne*, 424 U.S. 577, 585 (1976).

Petitioners next contend that we should take instruction from the lower court opinions of *Mills v. Board of Education*, 348 F. Supp. 866 (D.D.C. 1972), and *Pennsylvania Association for Retarded Children v. Commonwealth*, 334 F. Supp. 1257 (E.D. Pa. 1971) (hereinafter *PARC*). IDEA's drafters were admittedly guided "to a significant extent" by these two landmark cases. As the court below noted, however, the fact that Congress "took a number of the procedural safeguards from *PARC* and *Mills* and wrote them directly into the Act" does not allow us to "conclude . . . that Congress intended to adopt the ideas that it failed to write into the text of the statute." 377 F.3d, at 455.

Petitioners also urge that putting the burden of persuasion on school districts will further IDEA's purposes because it will help ensure that children receive a free appropriate public education. In truth, however, very few cases will be in evidentiary equipoise. Assigning the burden of persuasion to school districts might encourage schools to put more resources into preparing IEPs and presenting their evidence. But IDEA is silent about whether marginal dollars should be allocated to litigation and administrative expenditures or to educational services. Moreover, there is reason to believe that a great deal is already spent on the administration of the Act. Litigating a due process complaint is an expensive affair, costing schools approximately $8,000-to-$12,000 per hearing. *See* Department of Education, J. Chambers, J. Harr, & A. Dhanani, What Are We Spending on Procedural Safeguards in Special Education 1999-2000, p 8 (May 2003). Congress has also repeatedly amended the Act in order to reduce its administrative and litigation-related costs. For example, in 1997 Congress mandated that States offer mediation for IDEA disputes. In 2004, Congress added a mandatory "resolution session" prior to any due process hearing. It also made new findings that "[p]arents and schools should be given expanded opportunities to resolve their disagreements in positive and constructive ways," and that "[t]eachers, schools, local educational agencies, and States should be relieved of irrelevant and unnecessary paperwork burdens that do not lead to improved educational outcomes." §§ 1400(c)(8)–(9).

Petitioners in effect ask this Court to assume that every IEP is invalid until the school district demonstrates that it is not. The Act does not support this conclusion. IDEA relies heavily upon the expertise of school districts to meet its goals. It also includes a so-called "stay-put" provision, which requires a child to remain in his or her "then-current educational placement" during the pendency of an IDEA hearing. § 1415(j). Congress could have required that a child be given the educational placement that a parent requested during a dispute, but it did no such thing. Congress appears to have presumed instead that, if the Act's procedural requirements are respected, parents will prevail when they have legitimate grievances.

Petitioners' most plausible argument is that "[t]he ordinary rule, based on considerations of fairness, does not place the burden upon a litigant of establishing facts peculiarly within the knowledge of his adversary." *United States v. New York, N. H. & H. R. Co.*, 355 U.S. 253, 256, n. 5 (1957). But this "rule is far from being universal, and has many qualifications upon its application." *Greenleaf's Lessee v. Birth*, 31 U.S. 302, 6 Pet. 302, 312 (1832); *see also* McCormick § 337, at 413 ("Very often one must plead and prove matters as to which his adversary has superior access to the proof"). School districts have a "natural advantage" in information and expertise, but Congress addressed this when it obliged schools to safeguard the procedural rights of parents and to share information with them. As noted above, parents have the right to review all records that the school possesses in relation to their child. § 1415(b)(1). They also have the right to an "independent educational evaluation of the[ir] child." *Ibid.* The regulations clarify this entitlement by providing that a "parent has the right to an independent educational evaluation at public expense if the parent disagrees with an evaluation obtained by the public agency." 34 C.F.R. § 300.502(b)(1) (2005). IDEA thus ensures parents access to an expert who can evaluate all the materials that the school must make available, and who can give an independent opinion. They are not left to challenge the government without a realistic opportunity to access the necessary evidence, or without an expert with the firepower to match the opposition.

Additionally, in 2004, Congress added provisions requiring school districts to answer the subject matter of a complaint in writing, and to provide parents with the reasoning behind the disputed action, details about the other options considered and rejected by the IEP team, and a description of all evaluations, reports, and other factors that the school used in coming to its decision. 20 U.S.C. § 1415(c)(2)(B)(i)(I) (Supp. 2005). Prior to a hearing, the parties must disclose evaluations and recommendations that they intend to rely upon. 20 U.S.C. § 1415(f)(2). IDEA hearings are deliberately informal and intended to give ALJs the flexibility that they need to ensure that each side can fairly present its evidence. IDEA, in fact, requires state authorities to organize hearings in a way that guarantees parents and children the procedural protections of the Act. *See* § 1415(a). Finally, and perhaps most importantly, parents may recover attorney's fees if they prevail. § 1415(i)(3)(B). These protections ensure that the school bears no unique informational advantage.

III

Finally, respondents and several States urge us to decide that States may, if they wish, override the default rule and put the burden always on the school district. Several States have laws or regulations purporting to do so, at least under some circumstances. *See, e.g.*, Minn. Stat. § 125A.091, subd. 16 (2004); Ala. Admin. Code Rule 290-8-9-.08(8)(c)(6) (Supp. 2004); Alaska Admin. Code tit. 4, § 52.550(e)(9) (2003); Del. Code Ann., Tit. 14, § 3140 (1999). Because no such law or regulation exists in Maryland, we need not decide this issue today. JUSTICE BREYER contends that the allocation of the burden ought to be left *entirely* up to the States. But neither party made this argument before this Court or the courts below. We therefore decline to address it.

We hold no more than we must to resolve the case at hand: The burden of proof in an administrative hearing challenging an IEP is properly placed upon the party seeking relief. In this case, that party is Brian, as represented by his parents. But the rule applies with equal effect to school districts: If they seek to challenge an IEP, they will in turn bear the burden of persuasion before an ALJ. The judgment of the United States Court of Appeals for the Fourth Circuit is, therefore, affirmed.

It is so ordered.

THE CHIEF JUSTICE took no part in the consideration or decision of this case.

JUSTICE STEVENS, concurring [omitted].

JUSTICE GINSBURG, dissenting.

When the legislature is silent on the burden of proof, courts ordinarily allocate the burden to the party initiating the proceeding and seeking relief. As the Fourth Circuit recognized, however, "other factors," prime among them "policy considerations, convenience, and fairness," may warrant a different allocation. 377 F.3d 449, 452 (2004) (citing 2 J. Strong, McCormick on Evidence § 337, p 415 (5th ed. 1999) (allocation of proof burden "will depend upon the weight . . . given to any one or more of several factors, including: . . . special policy considerations . . . [,] convenience, . . . [and] fairness")); see also 9 J. Wigmore, Evidence § 2486, p 291 (J. Chadbourn rev. ed. 1981) (assigning proof burden presents "a question of policy and fairness based on experience in the different situations"). The Court has followed the same counsel. For reasons well stated by Circuit Judge Luttig, dissenting in the Court of Appeals, 377 F.3d, at 456–459, I am persuaded that "policy considerations, convenience, and fairness" call for assigning the burden of proof to the school district in this case.

The Individuals with Disabilities Education Act (IDEA) was designed to overcome the pattern of disregard and neglect disabled children historically encountered in seeking access to public education. Under typical civil rights and social welfare legislation, the complaining party must allege and prove discrimination or qualification for statutory benefits. The IDEA is atypical in this respect: It casts an affirmative, beneficiary-specific obligation on providers of public education. School districts are charged with responsibility to offer to each disabled child an individualized education program (IEP) suitable to the child's special needs. The proponent of the IEP, it seems to me, is properly called upon to demonstrate its adequacy.

Familiar with the full range of education facilities in the area, and informed by "their experiences with other, similarly-disabled children," 377 F.3d, at 458 (Luttig, J., dissenting), "the school district is . . . in a far better position to demonstrate that it has fulfilled [its statutory] obligation than the disabled student's parents are in to show that the school district has failed to do so," id., at 457. Accord Oberti v. Board of Ed. of Borough of Clementon School Dist., 995 F.2d 1204, 1219 (3d Cir. 1993) ("In practical terms, the school has an advantage when a dispute arises under the Act: the school has better access to relevant information, greater control over the potentially more persuasive witnesses (those who have been directly involved with the child's education), and greater overall educational expertise than the parents."); Lascari v. Board of Ed. of Ramapo Indian Hills Regional High School Dist., 560 A.2d 1180, 1188–1189 (N.J. 1989) (in view of the school district's "better access to relevant information," parent's obligation "should be merely to place in issue the appropriateness of the IEP. The school board should then bear the burden of proving that the IEP was appropriate. In reaching that result, we have sought to implement the intent of the statutory and regulatory schemes.").

Understandably, school districts striving to balance their budgets, if "[l]eft to [their] own devices," will favor educational options that enable them to conserve resources. Deal v. Hamilton County Bd. of Ed., 392 F.3d 840, 864–865 (6th Cir. 2004). Saddled with a proof burden in administrative "due process" hearings, parents are likely to find a district-proposed IEP "resistant to challenge." 377 F.3d, at 459 (Luttig, J., dissenting). Placing the burden on the district to show that its plan measures up to the statutorily mandated "free appropriate public education," will strengthen school officials' resolve to choose a course genuinely tailored to the child's individual needs.

The Court acknowledges that "[a]ssigning the burden of persuasion to school districts might encourage schools to put more resources into preparing IEPs." Curiously, the Court next suggests that resources spent on developing IEPs rank as "administrative expenditures" not as expenditures for "educational services." Costs entailed in the preparation of suitable IEPs, however, are the very expenditures necessary to ensure each child covered by IDEA access to a free appropriate education. These outlays surely relate to "educational services." Indeed, a carefully designed IEP may ward off disputes productive of large administrative or litigation expenses.

This case is illustrative. Not until the District Court ruled that the school district had the burden of persuasion did the school design an IEP that met Brian Schaffer's special educational needs. Had the school district, in the first instance, offered Brian a public or private school placement equivalent to the one the district ultimately provided, this entire litigation and its attendant costs could have been avoided.

Notably, nine States, as friends of the Court, have urged that placement of the burden of persuasion on the school district best comports with IDEA's aim. If allocating the burden to school districts would saddle school systems with inordinate costs, it is doubtful that these States would have filed in favor of petitioners.

One can demur to the Fourth Circuit's observation that courts "do not automatically assign the burden of proof to the side with the bigger guns," 377 F.3d, at 453, for no such reflexive action is at issue here. It bears emphasis that "the vast majority of parents whose children require the benefits and protections provided in the IDEA" lack "knowledg[e] about the educational resources available to their [child]" and the "sophisticat[ion]" to mount an effective case against a district-proposed IEP. *Id.*, at 458 (Luttig, J., dissenting). In this setting, "the party with the 'bigger guns' also has better access to information, greater expertise, and an affirmative obligation to provide the contested services." 377 F.3d, at 458 (Luttig, J., dissenting). Policy considerations, convenience, and fairness, I think it plain, point in the same direction. Their collective weight warrants a rule requiring a school district, in "due process" hearings, to explain persuasively why its proposed IEP satisfies IDEA's standards. *Ibid.* I would therefore reverse the judgment of the Fourth Circuit.

JUSTICE BREYER, dissenting.

As the majority points out, the Individuals with Disabilities Education Act (Act) requires school districts to "identify and evaluate disabled children, . . . develop an [Individualized Education Program] for each one . . . , and review every IEP at least once a year." A parent dissatisfied with "any matter relating [1] to the identification, evaluation, or educational placement of the child," or [2] to the "provision of a free appropriate public education," of the child, has the opportunity "to resolve such disputes through a mediation process." 20 U.S.C. §§ 1415(a), (b)(6)(A), (k) (Supp. 2005). The Act further provides the parent with "an opportunity for an impartial due process hearing" provided by the state or local education agency. § 1415(f)(1)(A). If provided locally, either party can appeal the hearing officer's decision to the state educational agency. § 1415(g). Finally, the Act allows any "party aggrieved" by the results of the state hearing(s), "to bring a civil action" in a federal district court. § 1415(i)(2)(A). In sum, the Act provides for school board action, followed by (1) mediation, (2) an impartial state due process hearing with the possibility of state appellate review, and, (3) federal district court review.

The Act also sets forth minimum procedures that the parties, the hearing officer, and the federal court must follow. *See, e.g.,* § 1415(f)(1) (notice); § 1415(f)(2) (disclosures); § 1415(f)(3) (limitations on who may conduct the hearing); § 1415(g) (right to appeal); § 1415(h)(1) ("the right to be accompanied and advised by counsel"); § 1415(h)(2) ("the right to present evidence and confront, cross-examine, and compel the attendance of witnesses"); § 1415(h)(3) (the right to a transcript of the proceeding); § 1415(h)(4) ("the right to written . . . findings of fact and decisions"). Despite this detailed procedural scheme, the Act is silent on the question of who bears the burden of persuasion at the state "due process" hearing.

The statute's silence suggests that Congress did not think about the matter of the burden of persuasion. It is, after all, a relatively minor issue that should not often arise. That is because the parties will ordinarily introduce considerable evidence (as in this case where the initial 3-day hearing included testimony from 10 witnesses, 6 qualified as experts, and more than 50 exhibits). And judges rarely hesitate to weigh evidence, even highly technical evidence, and to decide a matter on the merits, even when the case is a close one. Thus, cases in which an administrative law judge (ALJ) finds the evidence in precise equipoise should be few and far between.

Nonetheless, the hearing officer held that before him was that *rara avis* — a case of perfect evidentiary equipoise. Hence we must infer from Congress' silence (and from the rest of the statutory scheme) which party — the parents or the school district — bears the burden of persuasion.

One can reasonably argue, as the Court holds, that the risk of nonpersuasion should fall upon the "individual desiring change." That, after all, is the rule courts ordinarily apply when an individual complains about the lawfulness of a government action. On the other hand, one can reasonably argue to the contrary, that, given the technical nature of the subject matter, its human importance, the school district's superior resources, and the district's superior access to relevant information, the risk of nonpersuasion ought to fall upon the district. My own view is that Congress took neither approach. It did not decide the "burden of persuasion" question; instead it left the matter to the States for decision.

The Act says that the "establish[ment]" of "procedures" is a matter for the "State" and its agencies. § 1415(a). It adds that the hearing in question, an administrative hearing, is to be conducted by the "State" or "local educational agency." 20 U.S.C. § 1415(f)(1)(A) (Supp. 2005). And the statute as a whole foresees state implementation of federal standards. § 1412(a); *Cedar Rapids Community School Dist. v. Garret F.*, 526 U.S. 66, 68 (1999); *Board of Ed. of Hendrick Hudson Central School Dist., Westchester Cty. v. Rowley*, 458 U.S. 176, 208 (1982). The minimum federal procedural standards that the Act specifies are unrelated to the "burden of persuasion" question. And different States, consequently and not surprisingly, have resolved it in different ways. See, *e.g.*, Alaska Admin. Code, tit. 4, § 52.550(e)(9) (2003) (school district bears burden); Ala. Admin. Code Rule 290-8-9.08(8)(c)(6)(ii)(I) (Supp. 2004); (same); Conn. Agencies Regs. § 10-76h-14 (2005) (same); Del. Code Ann., tit. 14, § 3140 (1999) (same); 1 D. C. Mun. Regs., tit. 5, § 3030.3 (2003) (same); W. Va. Code Rules § 126-16-8.1.11(c) (2005) (same); Ind. Admin. Code, tit. 511, 7-30-3 (2003) (incorporating by reference Ind. Code § 4-21.5-3-14 (West 2002)) (moving party bears burden); 7 Ky. Admin. Regs., tit. 707, ch. 1:340, Section 7(4) (2004) (incorporating by reference Ky. Rev. Stat. Ann. § 13B.090(7) (Lexis 2003)) (same); Ga. Comp. Rules & Regs., Rule 160-4-7-.18(1)(g)(8) (2002) (burden varies depending upon remedy sought); Minn. Stat. Ann. § 125A.091, subd. 16 (West Supp. 2005) (same). There is no indication that this lack of uniformity has proved harmful.

Nothing in the Act suggests a need to fill every interstice of the Act's remedial scheme with a uniform federal rule. And should some such need arise — *i.e.*, if non-uniformity or a particular state approach were to prove problematic — the Federal Department of Education, expert in the area, might promulgate a uniform federal standard, thereby limiting state choice.

Most importantly, Congress has made clear that the Act itself represents an exercise in "cooperative federalism." Respecting the States' right to decide this procedural matter here, where education is at issue, where expertise matters, and where costs are shared, is consistent with that cooperative approach. And judicial respect for such congressional determinations is important. Indeed, in today's technologically and legally complex world, whether court decisions embody that kind of judicial respect may represent the true test of federalist principle.

Maryland has no special state law or regulation setting forth a special IEP-related burden of persuasion standard. But it does have rules of state administrative procedure and a body of state administrative law. The state ALJ should determine how those rules, or other state law applies to this case. Because the state ALJ did not do this (*i.e.*, he looked for a federal, not a state, burden of persuasion rule), I would remand this case.

NOTES AND QUESTIONS

1. As the Court's opinion and Justice Breyer's dissent note, the burden that this case is concerned about is who bears the risk of losing when the evidence is equally drawn, and that question should arise only in the rare case where the evidence is, in fact, equally strong on both sides. Practically speaking, though, is there a broader effect when the hearing officer knows that one side or the other bears the burden of proof? Do you expect that the *Schaffer* decision will affect the results in many cases or only a few?

2. In determining which side should have the burden of persuasion, one might ask the following questions: (1) Which party has greater access to evidence? (2) Which party is, in the run of litigated cases, more likely to be right? (3) Are there considerations of policy that favor one party or the other? *See generally* Edward Cleary, *Presuming and Pleading: An Essay in Juristic Immaturity*, 12 STAN. L. REV 5 (1959) (discussing issue of assignment of burdens). Does the Court's approach to the burden or proof issue jibe with this understanding of how to approach the question?

3. The Court's opinion restricts itself to the burden in hearings assessing the appropriateness of IEPs. Should the approach differ when the case involves an issue other than appropriate education, for example, one involving the presumption in favor of less restrictive educational environments? Do you expect *Schaffer* to influence those cases? *See generally Van Duyn v. Baker Sch. Dist. 5J*, 502 F.3d 811 (9th Cir. 2007) (holding that burden falls on party objecting to implementation of IEP, even if not challenging IEP's content).

4. If the state has a statute or administrative rule assigning the burden of persuasion to the school district, should that provision control, or should the burden be placed on the parent because of the operation of the federal law, as interpreted in *Schaffer*? Justice O'Connor's opinion leaves this issue open, and the lower courts have only begun to address it. *See M.M. v. Special Sch. Dist. No. 1*, No. CIV 05-2270, 2006 U.S. Dist. LEXIS 63255 (D. Minn. Sept. 5, 2006) (finding that administrative law judge properly placed burden of proof on school district in accordance with Minnesota law despite *Schaffer*).

5.   Remedies

In hearings, parents may ask for remedial measures such as evaluations, revisions to individualized education programs, new placements, institution of services, or correction of records. The remedies that have been controversial have not been these forms of prospective relief, but rather orders that school districts pay money or provide compensatory services to make up for deficiencies of services in the period before the hearing. Initially, lower courts split on the question whether hearing officers could order school districts to reimburse parents for the bills of private schools in which they unilaterally placed their children after the school district failed to offer adequate services. In a pair of cases, however, the Supreme Court established that the federal special education law encompasses tuition reimbursement as a remedy for denial of free, appropriate public education. The cases have been codified in part and superseded in part by the current statutory provisions on the subject.

<h1 style="text-align:center">BURLINGTON SCHOOL
COMMITTEE v. DEPARTMENT OF EDUCATION</h1>

471 U.S. 359 (1985)

In this case, the Supreme Court determined that the federal special education law permitted courts, and by implication, hearing officers, to provide retrospective relief in the form of tuition reimbursement.

JUSTICE REHNQUIST delivered the opinion of the Court.

The Education of the Handicapped Act (Act), 84 Stat. 175, as amended, 20 U.S.C. § 1401 *et seq.*, requires participating state and local educational agencies "to assure that handicapped children and their parents or guardians are guaranteed procedural safeguards with respect to the provision of free appropriate public education" to such handicapped children. § 1415(a). These procedures include the right of the parents to participate in the development of an "individualized education program" (IEP) for the child and to challenge in administrative and court proceedings a proposed IEP with which they disagree. §§ 1401(19), 1415(b), (d), (e). Where as in the present case review of a contested IEP takes years to run its course — years critical to the child's development — important practical questions arise concerning interim placement of the child and financial responsibility for that placement. This case requires us to address some of those questions.

Michael Panico, the son of respondent Robert Panico, was a first grader in the public school system of petitioner Town of Burlington, Mass., when he began experiencing serious difficulties in school. It later became evident that he had "specific learning disabilities" and thus was "handicapped" within the meaning of the Act, 20 U.S.C. § 1401(1). This entitled him to receive at public expense specially designed instruction to meet his unique needs, as well as related transportation. §§ 1401(16), 1401(17). . . .

In the spring of 1979, Michael attended the third grade of the Memorial School, a public school in Burlington, Mass., under an IEP calling for individual tutoring by a reading specialist for one hour a day and individual and group counselling. Michael's continued poor performance and the fact that Memorial School was not equipped to handle his needs led to much discussion between his parents and Town school officials about his difficulties and his future schooling. Apparently the course of these discussions did not run smoothly; the upshot was that the Panicos and the Town agreed that Michael was generally of above average to superior intelligence, but had special educational needs calling for a placement in a school other than Memorial. They disagreed over the source and exact nature of Michael's learning difficulties, the Town believing the source to be emotional and the parents believing it to be neurological.

In late June, the Town presented the Panicos with a proposed IEP for Michael for the 1979-1980 academic year. It called for placing Michael in a highly structured class of six children with special academic and social needs, located at another Town public school, the Pine Glen School. On July 3, Michael's father rejected the proposed IEP and sought review under § 1415(b)(2) by respondent Massachusetts Department of Education's Bureau of Special Education Appeals (BSEA). A hearing was initially scheduled for August 8, but was apparently postponed in favor of a mediation session on August 17. The mediation efforts proved unsuccessful.

Meanwhile the Panicos received the results of the latest expert evaluation of Michael by specialists at Massachusetts General Hospital, who opined that Michael's "emotional difficulties are secondary to a rather severe learning disorder characterized by perceptual difficulties" and recommended "a highly specialized setting for children with learning handicaps . . . such as the Carroll School," a state-approved private school for special education located in Lincoln, Mass. Believing that the Town's proposed placement of Michael at the Pine Glen School was inappropriate in light of Michael's needs, Mr. Panico enrolled Michael in the Carroll School in mid-August at his own expense, and Michael started there in September.

The BSEA held several hearings during the fall of 1979, and in January 1980 the hearing officer decided that the Town's proposed placement at the Pine Glen School was inappropriate and that the Carroll School was "the least restrictive adequate program within the record" for Michael's educational needs. The hearing officer ordered the Town to pay for Michael's tuition and transportation to the Carroll School for the 1979-1980 school year, including reimbursing the Panicos for their expenditures on these items for the school year to date.

The Town sought judicial review of the State's administrative decision in the United States District Court for the District of Massachusetts pursuant to 20 U.S.C. § 1415(e)(2) and a parallel state statute, naming Mr. Panico and the State Department of Education as defendants. In November 1980, the District Court granted summary judgment against the Town on the state-law claim under a "substantial evidence" standard of review, entering a final judgment on this claim under Federal Rule of Civil Procedure 54(b). The court also set the federal claim for future trial. The Court of Appeals vacated the judgment on the state-law claim, holding that review under the state statute was pre-empted by § 1415(e)(2), which establishes a "preponderance of the evidence" standard of review and which permits the reviewing court to hear additional evidence. 655 F.2d 428, 431–432 (C.A.1 1981).

In the meantime, the Town had refused to comply with the BSEA order, the District Court had denied a stay of that order, and the Panicos and the State had moved for preliminary injunctive relief. The State also had threatened outside of the judicial proceedings to freeze all of the Town's special education assistance unless it complied with the BSEA order. Apparently in response to this threat, the Town agreed in February 1981 to pay for Michael's Carroll School placement and related transportation for the 1980-1981 term, none of which had yet been paid, and to continue paying for these expenses until the case was decided. But the Town persisted in refusing to reimburse Mr. Panico for the expenses of the 1979-1980 school year. When the Court of Appeals disposed of the state claim, it also held that under this status quo none of the parties could show irreparable injury and thus none was entitled to a preliminary injunction. The court reasoned that the Town had not shown that Mr. Panico would not be able to repay the tuition and related costs borne by the Town if he ultimately lost on the merits, and Mr. Panico had not shown that he would be irreparably harmed if not reimbursed immediately for past payments which might ultimately be determined to be the Town's responsibility.

On remand, the District Court entered an extensive pretrial order on the Town's federal claim. In denying the Town summary judgment, it ruled that 20 U.S.C. § 1415(e)(3) did not bar reimbursement despite the Town's insistence that the Panicos violated that provision by changing Michael's placement to the Carroll School during the pendency of the administrative proceedings. The court reasoned that § 1415(e)(3) concerned the physical placement of the child and not the right to tuition reimbursement or to procedural review of a contested IEP. The court also dealt with the problem that no IEP had been developed for the 1980-1981 or 1981-1982 school years. It held that its power under § 1415(e)(2) to grant "appropriate" relief upon reviewing the contested IEP for the 1979-1980 school year included the power to grant relief for subsequent school years despite the lack of IEPs for those years. In this connection, however, the court interpreted the statute to place the burden of proof on the Town to upset the BSEA decision that the IEP was inappropriate for 1979-1980 and on the Panicos and the State to show that the relief for subsequent terms was appropriate.

After a 4-day trial, the District Court in August 1982 overturned the BSEA decision, holding that the appropriate 1979-1980 placement for Michael was the one proposed by the Town in the IEP and that the parents had failed to show that this placement would not also have been appropriate for subsequent years. Accordingly, the court concluded that the Town was "not responsible for the cost of Michael's education at the Carroll School for the academic years 1979-80 through 1981-82."

In contesting the Town's proposed form of judgment embodying the court's conclusion, Mr. Panico argued that, despite finally losing on the merits of the IEP in August 1982, he should be reimbursed for his expenditures in 1979-1980, that the Town should finish paying for the recently completed 1981-1982 term, and that he should not be required to reimburse the Town for its payments to date, apparently because the school terms in question fell within the pendency of the administrative and judicial review contemplated by § 1415(e)(2). The case was transferred to another District Judge and consolidated with two other cases to resolve similar issues concerning the reimbursement for expenditures during the pendency of review proceedings.

In a decision on the consolidated cases, the court rejected Mr. Panico's argument that the Carroll School was the "current educational placement" during the pendency of the review proceedings and thus that under § 1415(e)(3) the Town was obligated to maintain that placement. *Doe v. Anrig*, 561 F. Supp. 121 (1983). The court reasoned that the Panicos' unilateral action in placing Michael at the Carroll School without the Town's consent could not "confer thereon the imprimatur of continued placement," *id.* at 129, n. 5, even though strictly speaking there was no actual placement in effect during the summer of 1979 because all parties agreed Michael was finished with the Memorial School and the Town itself proposed in the IEP to transfer him to a new school in the fall.

The District Court next rejected an argument, apparently grounded at least in part on a state regulation, that the Panicos were entitled to rely on the BSEA decision upholding their placement contrary to the IEP, regardless of whether that decision were ultimately reversed by a court. With respect to the payments made by the Town after the BSEA decision, under the State's threat to cut off funding, the court criticized the State for resorting to extrajudicial pressure to enforce a decision subject to further review. Because this "was not a case where the town was legally obliged under section 1415(e)(3) to continue payments preserving the status quo," the State's coercion could not be viewed as "the basis for a final decision on liability," and could only be "regarded as other than wrongful . . . on the assumption that the payments were to be returned if the order was ultimately reversed." *Id.* at 130. The court entered a judgment ordering the Panicos to reimburse the Town for its payments for Michael's Carroll placement and related transportation in 1980-1981 and 1981-1982. The Panicos appealed.

In a broad opinion, most of which we do not review, the Court of Appeals for the First Circuit remanded the case a second time. 736 F.2d 773 (1984). The court ruled, among other things, that the District Court erred in conducting a full trial *de novo*, that it gave insufficient weight to the BSEA findings, and that in other respects it did not properly evaluate the IEP. The court also considered several questions about the availability of reimbursement for interim placement. The Town argued that § 1415(e)(3) bars the Panicos from any reimbursement relief, even if on remand they were to prevail on the merits of the IEP, because of their unilateral change of Michael's placement during the pendency of the § 1415(e)(2) proceedings. The court held that such unilateral parental change of placement would not be "a bar to reimbursement of the parents if their actions are held to be appropriate at final judgment." *Id.* at 799. In dictum the court suggested, however, that a lack of parental consultation with the Town or "attempt to achieve a negotiated compromise and agreement on a private placement," as contemplated by the Act, "may be taken into account in a district court's computation of an award of equitable reimbursement." *Ibid.* To guide the District Court on remand, the court stated that "whether to order reimbursement, and at what amount, is a question determined by balancing the equities." *Id.* at 801. The court also held that the Panicos' reliance on the BSEA decision would estop the Town from obtaining reimbursement "for the period of reliance and requires that where parents have paid the bill for the period, they must be reimbursed." *Ibid.*

The Town filed a petition for a writ of certiorari in this Court challenging the decision of the Court of Appeals on numerous issues, including the scope of judicial review of the administrative decision and the relevance to the merits of an IEP of violations by local school authorities of the Act's procedural requirements. We granted certiorari only to consider the following two issues: whether the potential relief available under § 1415(e)(2) includes reimbursement to parents for private school tuition and related expenses, and whether § 1415(e)(3) bars such reimbursement to parents who reject a proposed IEP and place a child in a private school without the consent of local school authorities. We express no opinion on any of the many other views stated by the Court of Appeals.

Congress stated the purpose of the Act in these words:

"to assure that all handicapped children have available to them . . . a free appropriate public education which emphasizes special education and related services designed to meet their unique needs [and] to assure that the rights of handicapped children and their parents or guardians are protected." 20 U.S.C. § 1400(c).

The Act defines a "free appropriate public education" to mean

"special education and related services which (A) have been provided at public expense, under public supervision and direction, and without charge, (B) meet the standards of the State educational agency, (C) include an appropriate preschool, elementary, or secondary school education in the State involved, and (D) are provided in conformity with [an] individualized education program." 20 U.S.C. § 1401(18).

To accomplish this ambitious objective, the Act provides federal money to state and local educational agencies that undertake to implement the substantive and procedural requirements of the Act. *See Hendrick Hudson District Bd. of Education v. Rowley*, 458 U.S. 176, 179–184 (1982).

The *modus operandi* of the Act is the already mentioned "individualized educational program." The IEP is in brief a comprehensive statement of the educational needs of a handicapped child and the specially designed instruction and related services to be employed to meet those needs. § 1401(19). The IEP is to be developed jointly by a school official qualified in special education, the child's teacher, the parents or guardian, and, where appropriate, the child. In several places, the Act emphasizes the participation of the parents in developing the child's educational program and assessing its effectiveness. *See* §§ 1400(c), 1401(19), 1412(7), 1415(b)(1)(A), (C), (D), (E), and 1415(b)(2); 34 CFR § 300.345 (1984).

Apparently recognizing that this cooperative approach would not always produce a consensus between the school officials and the parents, and that in any disputes the school officials would have a natural advantage, Congress incorporated an elaborate set of what it labeled "procedural safeguards" to insure the full participation of the parents and proper resolution of substantive disagreements. Section 1415(b) entitles the parents "to examine all relevant records with respect to the identification, evaluation, and educational placement of the child," to obtain an independent educational evaluation of the child, to notice of any decision to initiate or change the identification, evaluation, or educational placement of the child, and to present complaints with respect to any of the above. The parents are further entitled to "an impartial due process hearing," which in the instant case was the

BSEA hearing, to resolve their complaints.

The Act also provides for judicial review in state or federal court to "[a]ny party aggrieved by the findings and decision" made after the due process hearing. The Act confers on the reviewing court the following authority:

> "[T]he court shall receive the records of the administrative proceedings, shall hear additional evidence at the request of a party, and, basing its decision on the preponderance of the evidence, shall grant such relief as the court determines is appropriate." § 1415(e)(2).

The first question on which we granted certiorari requires us to decide whether this grant of authority includes the power to order school authorities to reimburse parents for their expenditures on private special education for a child if the court ultimately determines that such placement, rather than a proposed IEP, is proper under the Act.

We conclude that the Act authorizes such reimbursement. The statute directs the court to "grant such relief as [it] determines is appropriate." The ordinary meaning of these words confers broad discretion on the court. The type of relief is not further specified, except that it must be "appropriate." Absent other reference, the only possible interpretation is that the relief is to be "appropriate" in light of the purpose of the Act. As already noted, this is principally to provide handicapped children with "a free appropriate public education which emphasizes special education and related services designed to meet their unique needs." The Act contemplates that such education will be provided where possible in regular public schools, with the child participating as much as possible in the same activities as nonhandicapped children, but the Act also provides for placement in private schools at public expense where this is not possible. *See* § 1412(5); 34 CFR §§ 300.132, 300.227, 300.307(b), 300.347 (1984). In a case where a court determines that a private placement desired by the parents was proper under the Act and that an IEP calling for placement in a public school was inappropriate, it seems clear beyond cavil that "appropriate" relief would include a prospective injunction directing the school officials to develop and implement at public expense an IEP placing the child in a private school.

If the administrative and judicial review under the Act could be completed in a matter of weeks, rather than years, it would be difficult to imagine a case in which such prospective injunctive relief would not be sufficient. As this case so vividly demonstrates, however, the review process is ponderous. A final judicial decision on the merits of an IEP will in most instances come a year or more after the school term covered by that IEP has passed. In the meantime, the parents who disagree with the proposed IEP are faced with a choice: go along with the IEP to the detriment of their child if it turns out to be inappropriate or pay for what they consider to be the appropriate placement. If they choose the latter course, which conscientious parents who have adequate means and who are reasonably confident of their assessment normally would, it would be an empty victory to have a court tell them several years later that they were right but that these expenditures could not in a proper case be reimbursed by the school officials. If that were the case, the child's right to a *free* appropriate public education, the parents' right to participate fully in developing a proper IEP, and all of the procedural safeguards would be less than complete. Because Congress undoubtedly did not intend this result, we are confident that by empowering the court to grant "appropriate" relief Congress meant to include retroactive reimbursement to parents as an available remedy in a proper case.

In this Court, the Town repeatedly characterizes reimbursement as "damages," but that simply is not the case. Reimbursement merely requires the Town to belatedly pay expenses that it should have paid all along and would have borne in the first instance had it developed a proper IEP. Such a *post hoc* determination of financial responsibility was contemplated in the legislative history:

> "If a parent contends that he or she has been forced, at that parent's own expense, to seek private schooling for the child because an appropriate program does not exist within the local educational agency responsible for the child's education and the local educational agency disagrees, that disagreement and *the question of who remains financially responsible* is a matter to which the due process procedures established under [the predecessor to § 1415] appl[y]." S. Rep. No. 94-168, p. 32 (1975), U.S. Code Cong. & Admin. News 1975, pp. 1425, 1456 (emphasis added).

See 34 CFR § 300.403(b) (1984) (disagreements and question of financial responsibility subject to the due process procedures).

Regardless of the availability of reimbursement as a form of relief in a proper case, the Town maintains that the Panicos have waived any right they otherwise might have to reimbursement because they violated § 1415(e)(3), which provides:

> "During the pendency of any proceedings conducted pursuant to [§ 1415], unless the State or local educational agency and the parents or guardian otherwise agree, the child shall remain in the then current educational placement of such child. . . ."

We need not resolve the academic question of what Michael's "then current educational placement" was in the summer of 1979, when both the Town and the parents had agreed that a new school was in order. For the purposes of our decision, we assume that the Pine Glen School, proposed in the IEP, was Michael's current placement and, therefore, that the Panicos did "change" his placement after they had rejected the IEP and had set the administrative review in motion. In so doing, the Panicos contravened the conditional command of § 1415(e)(3) that "the child shall remain in the then current educational placement."

As an initial matter, we note that the section calls for agreement by *either* the *State or* the *local educational agency.* The BSEA's decision in favor of the Panicos and the Carroll School placement would seem to constitute agreement by the State to the change of placement. The decision was issued in January 1980, so from then on the Panicos were no longer in violation of § 1415(e)(3). This conclusion, however, does not entirely resolve the instant dispute because the Panicos are also seeking reimbursement for Michael's expenses during the fall of 1979, prior to the State's concurrence in the Carroll School placement.

We do not agree with the Town that a parental violation of § 1415(e)(3) constitutes a waiver of reimbursement. The provision says nothing about financial responsibility, waiver, or parental right to reimbursement at the conclusion of judicial proceedings. Moreover, if the provision is interpreted to cut off parental rights to reimbursement, the principal purpose of the Act will in many cases be defeated in the same way as if reimbursement were never available. As in this case, parents will often notice a child's learning difficulties while the child is in a regular public school program. If the school officials disagree with the need for special education or the adequacy of the public school's program to meet the child's needs, it is unlikely they will agree to an interim private school placement while the review process runs its course. Thus, under the Town's reading of § 1415(e)(3), the parents are forced to leave the child in what may turn out to be an inappropriate educational placement or to obtain the appropriate placement only by sacrificing any claim for reimbursement. The Act was intended to give handicapped children both an appropriate education and a free one; it should not be interpreted to defeat one or the other of those objectives.

The legislative history supports this interpretation, favoring a proper interim placement pending the resolution of disagreements over the IEP:

> "The conferees are cognizant that an impartial due process hearing may be required to assure that the rights of the child have been completely protected. We did feel, however, that the placement, or change of placement should not be unnecessarily delayed while long and tedious administrative appeals were being exhausted. Thus the conference adopted a flexible approach to try to meet the needs of both the child and the State." 121 Cong. Rec. 37412 (1975) (Sen. Stafford).

We think at least one purpose of § 1415(e)(3) was to prevent school officials from removing a child from the regular public school classroom over the parents' objection pending completion of the review proceedings. As we observed in *Rowley*, 458 U.S. at 192, the impetus for the Act came from two federal-court decisions, *Pennsylvania Assn. for Retarded Children v. Commonwealth*, 334 F. Supp. 1257 (E.D. Pa. 1971), and 343 F. Supp. 279 (1972), and *Mills v. Board of Education of District of Columbia*, 348 F. Supp. 866 (D.C. 1972), which arose from the efforts of parents of handicapped children to prevent the exclusion or expulsion of their children from the public schools. Congress was concerned about the apparently widespread practice of relegating handicapped children to private institutions or warehousing them in special classes. *See* § 1400(b)(4); 34 CFR § 300.347(a) (1984). We also note that § 1415(e)(3) is located in a section detailing procedural safeguards which are largely for the benefit of the parents and the child.

This is not to say that § 1415(e)(3) has no effect on parents. While we doubt that this provision would authorize a court to order parents to leave their child in a particular placement, we think it operates in such a way that parents who unilaterally change their child's placement during the pendency of review proceedings, without the consent of state or local school officials, do so at their own financial risk. If the courts ultimately determine that the IEP proposed by the school officials was appropriate, the parents would be barred from obtaining reimbursement for any interim period in which their child's placement violated § 1415(e)(3). This conclusion is supported by the agency's interpretation of the Act's application to private placements by the parents:

"(a) If a handicapped child has available a free appropriate public education and the parents choose to place the child in a private school or facility, the public agency is not required by this part to pay for the child's education at the private school or facility. . . .

"(b) Disagreements between a parent and a public agency regarding the availability of a program appropriate for the child, and the question of financial responsibility, are subject to the due process procedures under [§ 1415]." 34 CFR § 300.403 (1984).

We thus resolve the questions on which we granted certiorari; because the case is here in an interlocutory posture, we do not consider the estoppel ruling below or the specific equitable factors identified by the Court of Appeals for granting relief. We do think that the court was correct in concluding that "such relief as the court determines is appropriate," within the meaning of § 1415(e)(2), means that equitable considerations are relevant in fashioning relief.

The judgment of the Court of Appeals is

Affirmed.

FLORENCE COUNTY SCHOOL DISTRICT FOUR v. CARTER
510 U.S. 7 (1993)

Here, the Court elaborated on Burlington's approval of tuition reimbursement as a remedy, and further held that the absence of the private school from the state list of approved placements did not rule out reimbursement relief.

Justice O'Connor delivered the opinion of the Court.

The Individuals with Disabilities Education Act (IDEA or Act), 84 Stat. 175, as amended, 20 U.S.C. § 1400 *et seq.* (1988 ed. and Supp. IV), requires States to provide disabled children with a "free appropriate public education," § 1401(a)(18). This case presents the question whether a court may order reimbursement for parents who unilaterally withdraw their child from a public school that provides an inappropriate education under IDEA and put the child in a private school that provides an education that is otherwise proper under IDEA, but does not meet all the requirements of § 1401(a)(18). We hold that the court may order such reimbursement, and therefore affirm the judgment of the Court of Appeals.

I

Respondent Shannon Carter was classified as learning disabled in 1985, while a ninth grade student in a school operated by petitioner Florence County School District Four. School officials met with Shannon's parents to formulate an individualized education program (IEP) for Shannon, as required under IDEA. 20 U.S.C. §§ 1401(a)(18) and (20), 1414(a)(5) (1988 ed. and Supp. IV). The IEP provided that Shannon would stay in regular classes except for three periods of individualized instruction per week, and established specific goals in reading and mathematics of four months' progress for the entire school year. Shannon's parents were dissatisfied, and requested a hearing to challenge the appropriateness of the IEP. *See* § 1415(b)(2). Both the local educational officer and the state educational agency hearing officer rejected Shannon's parents' claim and concluded that the IEP was adequate. In the meantime, Shannon's parents had placed her in Trident Academy, a private school specializing in educating children with disabilities. Shannon began at Trident in September 1985 and graduated in the spring of 1988.

Shannon's parents filed this suit in July 1986, claiming that the school district had breached its duty under IDEA to provide Shannon with a "free appropriate public education," § 1401(a)(18), and seeking reimbursement for tuition and other costs incurred at Trident. After a bench trial, the District Court ruled in the parents' favor. The court held that the school district's proposed educational program and the achievement goals of the IEP "were wholly inadequate" and failed to satisfy the requirements of the Act. App. to Pet. for Cert. 27a. The court further held that "[a]lthough [Trident Academy] did not comply with all of the procedures outlined in [IDEA]," the school "provided Shannon an excellent education in substantial compliance with all the substantive requirements" of the statute. *Id.* at 37a. The court found that Trident "evaluated Shannon quarterly, not yearly as mandated in [IDEA], it provided Shannon with low teacher-student ratios, and it developed a plan which allowed Shannon to receive passing marks and progress from grade to grade." *Ibid.* The court also credited the findings of its own expert, who determined that Shannon had made "significant progress" at Trident and that her reading comprehension had risen three grade levels in her three years at the school. *Id.* at 29a. The District Court concluded that Shannon's education was "appropriate" under IDEA, and that Shannon's parents were entitled to reimbursement of tuition and other costs. *Id.* at 37a.

The Court of Appeals for the Fourth Circuit affirmed. 950 F.2d 156 (1991). The court agreed that the IEP proposed by the school district was inappropriate under IDEA. It also rejected the school district's argument that reimbursement is never proper when the parents choose a private school that is not approved by the State or that does not comply with all the terms of IDEA. According to the Court of Appeals, neither the text of the Act nor its legislative history imposes a "requirement that the private school be approved by the state in parent-placement reimbursement cases." *Id.* at 162. To the contrary, the Court of Appeals concluded, IDEA's state-approval requirement applies only when a child is placed in a private school by public school officials. Accordingly, "when a public school system has defaulted on its obligations under the Act, a private school placement is 'proper under the Act' if the education provided by the private school is 'reasonably calculated to enable the child to receive educational benefits.'" *Id.* at 163, quoting *Board of Ed. of Hendrick Hudson Central School Dist. Westchester Cty. v. Rowley,* 458 U.S. 176, 207 (1982).

The court below recognized that its holding conflicted with *Tucker v. Bay Shore Union Free School Dist.*, 873 F.2d 563, 568 (1989), in which the Court of Appeals for the Second Circuit held that parental placement in a private school cannot be proper under the Act unless the private school in question meets the standards of the state education agency. We granted certiorari to resolve this conflict among the Courts of Appeals.

II

In *School Comm. of Burlington v. Department of Ed. of Mass.*, 471 U.S. 359, 369 (1985), we held that IDEA's grant of equitable authority empowers a court "to order school authorities to reimburse parents for their expenditures on private special education for a child if the court ultimately determines that such placement, rather than a proposed IEP, is proper under the Act." Congress intended that IDEA's promise of a "free appropriate public education" for disabled children would normally be met by an IEP's provision for education in the regular public schools or in private schools chosen jointly by school officials and parents. In cases where cooperation fails, however, "parents who disagree with the proposed IEP are faced with a choice: go along with the IEP to the detriment of their child if it turns out to be inappropriate or pay for what they consider to be the appropriate placement." *Id.* at 370. For parents willing and able to make the latter choice, "it would be an empty victory to have a court tell them several years later that they were right but that these expenditures could not in a proper case be reimbursed by the school officials." *Id.* Because such a result would be contrary to IDEA's guarantee of a "free appropriate public education," we held that "Congress meant to include retroactive reimbursement to parents as an available remedy in a proper case." *Id.*

As this case comes to us, two issues are settled: (1) the school district's proposed IEP was inappropriate under IDEA, and (2) although Trident did not meet the § 1401(a)(18) requirements, it provided an education otherwise proper under IDEA. This case presents the narrow question whether Shannon's parents are barred from reimbursement because the private school in which Shannon enrolled did not meet the § 1401(a)(18) definition of a "free appropriate public education." We hold that they are not, because § 1401(a)(18)'s requirements cannot be read as applying to parental placements.

Section 1401(a)(18)(A) requires that the education be "provided at public expense, under public supervision and direction." Similarly, § 1401(a)(18)(D) requires schools to provide an IEP, which must be designed by "a representative of the local educational agency," 20 U.S.C. § 1401(a)(20) (1988 ed., Supp. IV), and must be "establish[ed]," "revise[d]," and "review[ed]" by the agency, § 1414(a)(5). These requirements do not make sense in the context of a parental placement. In this case, as in all *Burlington* reimbursement cases, the parents' rejection of the school district's proposed IEP is the very reason for the parents' decision to put their child in a private school. In such cases, where the private placement has necessarily been made over the school district's objection, the private school education will not be under "public supervision and direction." Accordingly, to read the § 1401(a)(18) requirements as applying to parental placements would effectively eliminate the right of unilateral withdrawal recognized in *Burlington.* Moreover, IDEA was intended to ensure that children with disabilities receive an education that is both appropriate and free. *Burlington, supra,* at 373. To read the provisions of § 1401(a)(18) to bar reimbursement in the circumstances of this case would defeat this statutory purpose.

Nor do we believe that reimbursement is necessarily barred by a private school's failure to meet state education standards. Trident's deficiencies, according to the school district, were that it employed at least two faculty members who were not state-certified and that it did not develop IEP's. As we have noted, however, the § 1401(a)(18) requirements — including the requirement that the school meet the standards of the state educational agency, § 1401(a)(18)(B) — do not apply to private parental placements. Indeed, the school district's emphasis on state standards is somewhat ironic. As the Court of Appeals noted, "it hardly seems consistent with the Act's goals to forbid parents from educating their child at a school that provides an appropriate education simply because that school lacks the stamp of approval of the same public school system that failed to meet the child's needs in the first place." 950 F.2d at 164. Accordingly, we disagree with the Second Circuit's theory that "a parent may not obtain reimbursement for a unilateral placement if that placement was in a school that was not on [the State's] approved list of private" schools. *Tucker*, 873 F.2d at 568 (internal quotation marks omitted). Parents' failure to select a program known to be approved by the State in favor of an unapproved option is not itself a bar to reimbursement.

Furthermore, although the absence of an approved list of private schools is not essential to our holding, we note that parents in the position of Shannon's have no way of knowing at the time they select a private school whether the school meets state standards. South Carolina keeps no publicly available list of approved private schools, but instead approves private school placements on a case-by-case basis. In fact, although public school officials had previously placed three children with disabilities at Trident, *see* App. to Pet. for Cert. 28a, Trident had not received blanket approval from the State. South Carolina's case-by-case approval system meant that Shannon's parents needed the cooperation of state officials before they could know whether Trident was state-approved. As we recognized in *Burlington*, such cooperation is unlikely in cases where the school officials disagree with the need for the private placement. 471 U.S. at 372.

III

The school district also claims that allowing reimbursement for parents such as Shannon's puts an unreasonable burden on financially strapped local educational authorities. The school district argues that requiring parents to choose a state approved private school if they want reimbursement is the only meaningful way to allow States to control costs; otherwise States will have to reimburse dissatisfied parents for any private school that provides an education that is proper under the Act, no matter how expensive it may be.

There is no doubt that Congress has imposed a significant financial burden on States and school districts that participate in IDEA. Yet public educational authorities who want to avoid reimbursing parents for the private education of a disabled child can do one of two things: give the child a free appropriate public education in a public setting, or place the child in an appropriate private setting of the State's choice. This is IDEA's mandate, and school officials who conform to it need not worry about reimbursement claims.

Moreover, parents who, like Shannon's, "unilaterally change their child's placement during the pendency of review proceedings, without the consent of state or local school officials, do so at their own financial risk." *Burlington, supra,* at 373–374. They are entitled to reimbursement *only* if a federal court concludes both that the public placement violated IDEA and that the private school placement was proper under the Act.

Finally, we note that once a court holds that the public placement violated IDEA, it is authorized to "grant such relief as the court determines is appropriate." 20 U.S.C. § 1415(e)(2). Under this provision, "equitable considerations are relevant in fashioning relief," *Burlington,* 471 U.S. at 374, and the court enjoys "broad discretion" in so doing, *id.* at 369. Courts fashioning discretionary equitable relief under IDEA must consider all relevant factors, including the appropriate and reasonable level of reimbursement that should be required. Total reimbursement will not be appropriate if the court determines that the cost of the private education was unreasonable.

Accordingly, we affirm the judgment of the Court of Appeals.

———————

Congress has modified IDEA to conform to the principles applied in the two Supreme Court cases, and it has added some other provisions. The current law provides for tuition reimbursement for unilateral placements, but specifies conditions and limits:

> (C) Payment for education of children enrolled in private schools without consent of or referral by the public agency.

> (i) In general. Subject to subparagraph (A), this part does not require a local educational agency to pay for the cost of education, including special education and related services, of a child with a disability at a private school or facility if that agency made a free appropriate public education available to the child and the parents elected to place the child in such private school or facility.

> (ii) Reimbursement for private school placement. If the parents of a child with a disability, who previously received special education and related services under the authority of a public agency, enroll the child in a private elementary school or secondary school without the consent of or referral by the public agency, a court or a hearing officer may require the agency to reimburse the parents for the cost of that enrollment if the court or hearing officer finds that the agency had not made a free appropriate public education available to the child in a timely manner prior to that enrollment.

> (iii) Limitation on reimbursement. The cost of reimbursement described in clause (ii) may be reduced or denied —

> > (I) if —

> > > (aa) at the most recent IEP meeting that the parents attended prior to removal of the child from the public school, the parents did not inform the IEP Team that they were rejecting the placement proposed by the public agency to provide a free appropriate public

education to their child, including stating their concerns and their intent to enroll their child in a private school at public expense; or

(bb) 10 business days (including any holidays that occur on a business day) prior to the removal of the child from the public school, the parents did not give written notice to the public agency of the information described in item (aa);

(II) if, prior to the parents' removal of the child from the public school, the public agency informed the parents, through the notice requirements described in section 615(b)(3) [20 USCS § 1415(b)(3)], of its intent to evaluate the child (including a statement of the purpose of the evaluation that was appropriate and reasonable), but the parents did not make the child available for such evaluation; or

(III) upon a judicial finding of unreasonableness with respect to actions taken by the parents.

(iv) Exception. Notwithstanding the notice requirement in clause (iii)(I), the cost of reimbursement —

(I) shall not be reduced or denied for failure to provide such notice if —

(aa) the school prevented the parent from providing such notice;

(bb) the parents had not received notice, pursuant to section 615 [20 USCS § 1415], of the notice requirement in clause (iii)(I); or

(cc) compliance with clause (iii)(I) would likely result in physical harm to the child; and

(II) may, in the discretion of a court or a hearing officer, not be reduced or denied for failure to provide such notice if —

(aa) the parent is illiterate or cannot write in English; or

(bb) compliance with clause (iii)(I) would likely result in serious emotional harm to the child.

20 U.S.C. § 1412(a)(10).

FOREST GROVE SCHOOL DISTRICT v. T.A.
129 S. Ct. 2484 (2009)

The Court ruled that 20 U.S.C. § 1412(a)(10)(C)(ii) does not prevent a court or hearing officer from ordering tuition reimbursement when a child has not previously received special education and related services under the authority of a public agency.

Justice Stevens delivered the opinion of the Court.

The Individuals with Disabilities Education Act requires States receiving federal funding to make a "free appropriate public education" (FAPE) available to all children with disabilities residing in the State. We have previously held that when a public school fails to provide a FAPE and a child's parents place the child in an appropriate private school without the school district's consent, a court may require the district to reimburse the parents for the cost of the private education. *See School Comm. of Burlington v. Department of Ed.*, 471 U.S. 359, 370 (1985). The question presented in this case is whether the IDEA Amendments of 1997 (Amendments), categorically prohibit reimbursement for private-education costs if a child has not "previously received special education and related services under the authority of a public agency." § 1412(a)(10)(C)(ii). We hold that the Amendments impose no such categorical bar.

I

Respondent T. A. attended public schools in the Forest Grove School District from the time he was in kindergarten through the winter of his junior year of high school. From kindergarten through eighth grade, respondent's teachers observed that he had trouble paying attention in class and completing his assignments. When respondent entered high school, his difficulties increased.

In December 2000, during respondent's freshman year, his mother contacted the school counselor to discuss respondent's problems with his schoolwork. At the end of the school year, respondent was evaluated by a school psychologist. After interviewing him, examining his school records, and administering cognitive ability tests, the psychologist concluded that respondent did not need further testing for any learning disabilities or other health impairments, including attention deficit hyperactivity disorder (ADHD). The psychologist and two other school officials discussed the evaluation results with respondent's mother in June 2001, and all agreed that respondent did not qualify for special-education services. Respondent's parents did not seek review of that decision, although the hearing examiner later found that the School District's evaluation was legally inadequate because it failed to address all areas of suspected disability, including ADHD.

With extensive help from his family, respondent completed his sophomore year at Forest Grove High School, but his problems worsened during his junior year. In February 2003, respondent's parents discussed with the School District the possibility of respondent completing high school through a partnership program with the local community college. They also sought private professional advice, and in March 2003 respondent was diagnosed with ADHD and a number of disabilities related to learning and memory. Advised by the private specialist that respondent would do best in a structured, residential learning environment, respondent's parents enrolled him at a private academy that focuses on educating children with special needs.

Four days after enrolling him in private school, respondent's parents hired a lawyer to ascertain their rights and to give the School District written notice of respondent's private placement. A few weeks later, in April 2003, respondent's parents requested an administrative due process hearing regarding respondent's eligibility for special-education services. In June 2003, the District engaged a school psychologist to assist in determining whether respondent had a disability that significantly interfered with his educational performance. Respondent's parents cooperated with the District during the evaluation process. In July 2003, a multidisciplinary team met to discuss whether respondent satisfied IDEA's disability criteria and concluded that he did not because his ADHD did not have a sufficiently significant adverse impact on his educational performance. Because the School District maintained that respondent was not eligible for special-education services and therefore declined to provide an individualized education program (IEP), respondent's parents left him enrolled at the private academy for his senior year.

The administrative review process resumed in September 2003. After considering the parties' evidence, including the testimony of numerous experts, the hearing officer issued a decision in January 2004 finding that respondent's ADHD adversely affected his educational performance and that the School District failed to meet its obligations under IDEA in not identifying respondent as a student eligible for special-education services. Because the District did not offer respondent a FAPE and his private-school placement was appropriate under IDEA, the hearing officer ordered the District to reimburse respondent's parents for the cost of the private-school tuition.

The School District sought judicial review pursuant to § 1415(i)(2), arguing that the hearing officer erred in granting reimbursement. The District Court accepted the hearing officer's findings of fact but set aside the reimbursement award after finding that the 1997 Amendments categorically bar reimbursement of private-school tuition for students who have not "previously received special education and related services under the authority of a public agency." 20 U.S.C. § 1412(a)(10)(C)(ii). The District Court further held that, "[e]ven assuming that tuition reimbursement may be ordered in an extreme case for a student not receiving special education services, under general principles of equity where the need for special education was obvious to school authorities," the facts of this case do not support equitable relief.

The Court of Appeals for the Ninth Circuit reversed and remanded for further proceedings. The court first noted that, prior to the 1997 Amendments, "IDEA was silent on the subject of private school reimbursement, but courts had granted such reimbursement as 'appropriate' relief under principles of equity pursuant to 20 U.S.C. § 1415(i)(2)(C)" (citing *Burlington*, 471 U.S., at 370). It then held that the Amendments do not impose a categorical bar to reimbursement when a parent unilaterally places in private school a child who has not previously received special-education services through the public school. Rather, such students "are eligible for reimbursement, to the same extent as before the 1997 amendments, as 'appropriate' relief pursuant to § 1415(i)(2)(C)."

The Court of Appeals also rejected the District Court's analysis of the equities as resting on two legal errors. First, because it found that § 1412(a)(10)(C)(ii) generally bars relief in these circumstances, the District Court wrongly stated that relief was appropriate only if the equities were sufficient to " 'override' " that statutory limitation. The District Court also erred in asserting that reimbursement is limited to " 'extreme' " cases. The Court of Appeals therefore remanded with instructions to reexamine the equities, including the failure of respondent's parents to notify the School District before removing respondent from public school. In dissent, Judge Rymer stated her view that reimbursement is not available as an equitable remedy in this case because respondent's parents did not request an IEP before removing him from public school and respondent's right to a FAPE was therefore not at issue.

Because the Courts of Appeals that have considered this question have reached inconsistent results, we granted certiorari to determine whether § 1412(a)(10)(C) establishes a categorical bar to tuition reimbursement for students who have not previously received special-education services under the authority of a public education agency.

II

Justice Rehnquist's opinion for a unanimous Court in *Burlington* provides the pertinent background for our analysis of the question presented. In that case, respondent challenged the appropriateness of the IEP developed for his child by public-school officials. The child had previously received special-education services through the public school. While administrative review was pending, private specialists advised respondent that the child would do best in a specialized private educational setting, and respondent enrolled the child in private school without the school district's consent. The hearing officer concluded that the IEP was not adequate to meet the child's educational needs and that the school district therefore failed to provide the child a FAPE. Finding also that the private-school placement was appropriate under IDEA, the hearing officer ordered the school district to reimburse respondent for the cost of the private-school tuition.

We granted certiorari in *Burlington* to determine whether IDEA authorizes reimbursement for the cost of private education when a parent or guardian unilaterally enrolls a child in private school because the public school has proposed an inadequate IEP and thus failed to provide a FAPE. The Act at that time made no express reference to the possibility of reimbursement, but it authorized a court to "grant such relief as the court determines is appropriate." § 1415(i)(2)(C)(iii). In determining the scope of the relief authorized, we noted that "the ordinary meaning of these words confers broad discretion on the court" and that, absent any indication to the contrary, what relief is "appropriate" must be determined in light of the Act's broad purpose of providing children with disabilities a FAPE, including through publicly funded private-school placements when necessary. Accordingly, we held that the provision's grant of authority includes "the power to order school authorities to reimburse parents for their expenditures on private special-education services if the court ultimately determines that such placement, rather than a proposed IEP, is proper under the Act."

Our decision rested in part on the fact that administrative and judicial review of a parent's complaint often takes years. We concluded that, having mandated that participating States provide a FAPE for every student, Congress could not have intended to require parents to either accept an inadequate public-school education pending adjudication of their claim or bear the cost of a private education if the court ultimately determined that the private placement was proper under the Act. Eight years later, we unanimously reaffirmed the availability of reimbursement in *Florence County School Dist. Four v. Carter*, 510 U.S. 7 (1993) (holding that reimbursement may be appropriate even when a child is placed in a private school that has not been approved by the State).

The dispute giving rise to the present litigation differs from those in *Burlington* and *Carter* in that it concerns not the adequacy of a proposed IEP but the School District's failure to provide an IEP at all. And, unlike respondent, the children in those cases had previously received public special-education services. These differences are insignificant, however, because our analysis in the earlier cases depended on the language and purpose of the Act and not the particular facts involved. Moreover, when a child requires special-education services, a school district's failure to propose an IEP of any kind is at least as serious a violation of its responsibilities under IDEA as a failure to provide an adequate IEP. It is thus clear that the reasoning of *Burlington* and *Carter* applies equally to this case. The only question is whether the 1997 Amendments require a different result.

III

Congress enacted IDEA in 1970 to ensure that all children with disabilities are provided " 'a free appropriate public education which emphasizes special education and related services designed to meet their unique needs [and] to assure that the rights of [such] children and their parents or guardians are protected.' " *Burlington*, 471 U.S., at 367 (quoting 20 U.S.C. § 1400(c) (1982 ed.)). After examining the States' progress under IDEA, Congress found in 1997 that substantial gains had been made in the area of special education but that more needed to be done to guarantee children with disabilities adequate access to appropriate services. *See* S. Rep. No. 105-17, p. 5 (1997). The 1997 Amendments were intended "to place greater emphasis on improving student performance and ensuring that children with disabilities receive a quality public education."

Consistent with that goal, the Amendments preserved the Act's purpose of providing a FAPE to all children with disabilities. And they did not change the text of the provision we considered in *Burlington*, § 1415(i)(2)(C)(iii), which gives courts broad authority to grant "appropriate" relief, including reimbursement for the cost of private special education when a school district fails to provide a FAPE. "Congress is presumed to be aware of an administrative or judicial interpretation of a statute and to adopt that interpretation when it reenacts a statute without change." *Lorillard v. Pons*, 434 U.S. 575, 580 (1978). Accordingly, absent a clear expression elsewhere in the Amendments of Congress' intent to repeal some portion of that provision or to abrogate our decisions in *Burlington* and *Carter*, we will continue to read § 1415(i)(2)(C)(iii) to authorize the relief respondent seeks.

The School District and the dissent argue that one of the provisions enacted by the Amendments, § 1412(a)(10)(C), effects such a repeal. Section 1412(a)(10)(C) is entitled "Payment for education of children enrolled in private schools without consent of or referral by the public agency," and it sets forth a number of principles applicable to .public reimbursement for the costs of unilateral private-school placements. Section 1412(a)(10)(C)(i) states that IDEA "does not require a local educational agency to pay for the cost of education . . . of a child with a disability at a private school or facility if that agency made a free appropriate public education available to the child" and his parents nevertheless elected to place him in a private school. Section 1412(a)(10)(C)(ii) then provides that a "court or hearing officer may require [a public] agency to reimburse the parents for the cost of [private-school] enrollment if the court or hearing officer finds that the agency had not made a free appropriate public education available" and the child has "previously received special education and related services under the authority of [the] agency." Finally, § 1412(a)(10)(C)(iii) discusses circumstances under which the "cost of reimbursement described in clause (ii) may be reduced or denied," as when a parent fails to give 10 days' notice before removing a child from public school or refuses to make a child available for evaluation, and § 1412(a)(10)(C)(iv) lists circumstances in which a parent's failure to give notice may or must be excused.

Looking primarily to clauses (i) and (ii), the School District argues that Congress intended § 1412(a)(10)(C) to provide the exclusive source of authority for courts to order reimbursement when parents unilaterally enroll a child in private school. According to the District, clause (i) provides a safe harbor for school districts that provide a FAPE by foreclosing reimbursement in those circumstances. Clause (ii) then sets forth the circumstance in which reimbursement is appropriate — namely, when a school district fails to provide a FAPE to a child who has previously received special-education services through the public school. The District contends that because § 1412(a)(10)(C) only discusses reimbursement for children who have previously received special-education services through the public school, IDEA only authorizes reimbursement in that circumstance. The dissent agrees.

For several reasons, we find this argument unpersuasive. First, the School District's reading of the Act is not supported by its text and context, as the 1997 Amendments do not expressly prohibit reimbursement under the circumstances of this case, and the District offers no evidence that Congress intended to supersede our decisions in *Burlington* and *Carter*. Clause (i)'s safe harbor explicitly bars reimbursement only when a school district makes a FAPE available by correctly identifying a child as having a disability and proposing an IEP adequate to meet the child's needs. The clause says nothing about the availability of reimbursement when a school district fails to provide a FAPE. Indeed, its statement that reimbursement is not authorized when a school district provides a FAPE could be read to indicate that reimbursement is authorized when a school district does not fulfill that obligation.

Clause (ii) likewise does not support the District's position. Because that clause is phrased permissively, stating only that courts "may require" reimbursement in those circumstances, it does not foreclose reimbursement awards in other circumstances. Together with clauses (iii) and (iv), clause (ii) is best read as elaborating on the general rule that courts may order reimbursement when a school district fails to provide a FAPE by listing factors that may affect a reimbursement award in the common situation in which a school district has provided a child with some special-education services and the child's parents believe those services are inadequate. Referring as they do to students who have previously received special-education services through a public school, clauses (ii) through (iv) are premised on a history of cooperation and together encourage school districts and parents to continue to cooperate in developing and implementing an appropriate IEP before resorting to a unilateral private placement.[2] The clauses of § 1412(a)(10)(C) are thus best read as elucidative rather than exhaustive.[3]

This reading of § 1412(a)(10)(C) is necessary to avoid the conclusion that Congress abrogated sub silentio our decisions in *Burlington* and *Carter*. In those cases, we construed § 1415(i)(2)(C)(iii) to authorize reimbursement when a school district fails to provide a FAPE and a child's private-school placement is appropriate, without regard to the child's prior receipt of services.[4] It would take more than Congress' failure to comment on the category of cases in which a child has not previously received special-education services for us to conclude that the Amendments substantially superseded our decisions and in large part repealed § 1415(i)(2)(C)(iii). *See Branch v. Smith*, 538 U.S. 254, 273 (2003) ("[A]bsent a clearly expressed congressional intention, repeals by implication are not favored").[5] We accordingly adopt the reading of § 1412(a)(10)(C) that is consistent with those decisions.[6]

---

[2] [FN 8] The dissent asserts that, under this reading of the Act, "Congress has called for reducing reimbursement only for the most deserving . . . but provided no mechanism to reduce reimbursement to the least deserving." In addition to making unsubstantiated generalizations about the desert of parents whose children have been denied public special-education services, the dissent grossly mischaracterizes our view of § 1412(a)(10)(C). The fact that clause (iii) permits a court to reduce a reimbursement award when a parent whose child has previously received special-education services fails to give the school adequate notice of an intended private placement does not mean that it prohibits courts from similarly reducing the amount of reimbursement when a parent whose child has not previously received services fails to give such notice. Like clause (ii), clause (iii) provides guidance regarding the appropriateness of relief in a common factual scenario, and its instructions should not be understood to preclude courts and hearing officers from considering similar factors in other scenarios.

[3] [FN 9] In arguing that § 1412(a)(10)(C) is the exclusive source of authority for granting reimbursement awards to parents who unilaterally place a child in private school, the dissent neglects to explain that provision's failure to limit the type of private-school placements for which parents may be reimbursed. *School Comm. of Burlington v. Department of Ed.* held that courts may grant reimbursement under § 1415(i)(2)(C)(iii) only when a school district fails to provide a FAPE and the private-school placement is appropriate. The latter requirement is essential to ensuring that reimbursement awards are granted only when such relief furthers the purposes of the Act. That § 1412(a)(10)(C) did not codify that requirement further indicates that Congress did not intend that provision to supplant § 1415(i)(2)(C)(iii) as the sole authority on reimbursement awards but rather meant to augment the latter provision and our decisions construing it.

[4] [FN 10] As discussed above, although the children in *Burlington* and *Carter* had previously received special-education services in public school, our decisions in no way depended on their prior receipt of services. Those holdings rested instead on the breadth of the authority conferred by § 1415(i)(2)(C)(iii), the interest in providing relief consistent with the Act's purpose, and the injustice that a contrary reading would produce — considerations that were not altered by the 1997 Amendments.

[5] [FN 11] For the same reason, we reject the District's argument that because § 1412(a)(10)(C)(ii) authorizes "a court or a hearing officer" to award reimbursement for private-school tuition, whereas § 1415(i)(2)(C)(iii) only provides a general grant of remedial authority to "court[s]," the latter section cannot be read to authorize hearing officers to award reimbursement. That argument ignores our decision in *Burlington*, which interpreted § 1415(i)(2)(C)(iii) to authorize hearing officers as well as courts to award reimbursement notwithstanding the provision's silence with regard to hearing officers. When Congress amended IDEA without altering the text of § 1415(i)(2)(C)(iii), it implicitly adopted that construction of the statute. *See Lorillard v. Pons*, 434 U.S. 575, 580–581 (1978).

[6] [FN 12] Looking to the Amendments' legislative history for support, the School District cites two

Notably, the agency charged with implementing IDEA has adopted respondent's reading of the statute. In commentary to regulations implementing the 1997 Amendments, the Department of Education stated that "hearing officers and courts retain their authority, recognized in *Burlington* . . . to award 'appropriate' relief if a public agency has failed to provide FAPE, including reimbursement . . . in instances in which the child has not yet received special education and related services." 64 Fed. Reg. 12602 (1999); *see* 71 Fed. Reg. 46599 (2006).

The School District's reading of § 1412(a)(10)(C) is also at odds with the general remedial purpose underlying IDEA and the 1997 Amendments. The express purpose of the Act is to "ensure that all children with disabilities have available to them a free appropriate public education that emphasizes special education and related services designed to meet their unique needs," § 1400(d)(1)(A) — a factor we took into account in construing the scope of § 1415(i)(2)(C)(iii), *see Burlington*, 471 U.S., at 369. Without the remedy respondent seeks, a "child's right to a free appropriate education . . . would be less than complete." *Id.*, at 370. The District's position similarly conflicts with IDEA's "child find" requirement, pursuant to which States are obligated to "identif[y], locat[e], and evaluat[e]" "[a]ll children with disabilities residing in the State" to ensure that they receive needed special-education services. § 1412(a)(3)(A); *see* § 1412(a)(10)(A)(ii). A reading of the Act that left parents without an adequate remedy when a school district unreasonably failed to identify a child with disabilities would not comport with Congress' acknowledgment of the paramount importance of properly identifying each child eligible for services.

Indeed, by immunizing a school district's refusal to find a child eligible for special-education services no matter how compelling the child's need, the School District's interpretation of § 1412(a)(10)(C) would produce a rule bordering on the irrational. It would be particularly strange for the Act to provide a remedy, as all agree it does, when a school district offers a child inadequate special-education services but to leave parents without relief in the more egregious situation in which the school district unreasonably denies a child access to such services altogether. That IDEA affords parents substantial procedural safeguards, including the right to challenge a school district's eligibility determination and obtain prospective relief, is no answer. We roundly rejected that argument in *Burlington*, observing that the "review process is ponderous" and therefore inadequate to ensure that a school's failure to provide a FAPE is remedied with the speed necessary to avoid detriment to the child's education. Like *Burlington*, this case vividly demonstrates the problem of delay, as respondent's parents first sought a due process hearing in April 2003, and the District Court issued its decision in May 2005 — almost a year after respondent graduated from high school. The dissent all but ignores these shortcomings of IDEA's procedural safeguards.

House and Senate Reports that essentially restate the text of § 1412(a)(10)(C)(ii), H. R. Rep. No. 105-95, pp. 92–93 (1997); S. Rep. No. 105-17, p. 13 (1997), and a floor statement by Representative Mike Castle, 143 Cong. Rec. 8013 (1997) (stating that the "bill makes it harder for parents to unilaterally place a child in elite private schools at public taxpayer expense, lowering costs to local school districts"). Those ambiguous references do not undermine the meaning that we discern from the statute's language and context.

IV

The School District advances two additional arguments for reading the Act to foreclose reimbursement in this case. First, the District contends that because IDEA was an exercise of Congress' authority under the Spending Clause, U.S. Const., Art. I, § 8, cl. 1, any conditions attached to a State's acceptance of funds must be stated unambiguously. *See Pennhurst State School and Hospital v. Halderman*, 451 U.S. 1, 17 (1981). Applying that principle, we held in *Arlington Central School Dist. Bd. of Ed. v. Murphy*, 548 U.S. 291, 304 (2006), that IDEA's fee-shifting provision, § 1415(i)(3)(B), does not authorize courts to award expert-services fees to prevailing parents in IDEA actions because the Act does not put States on notice of the possibility of such awards. But *Arlington* is readily distinguishable from this case. In accepting IDEA funding, States expressly agree to provide a FAPE to all children with disabilities. An order awarding reimbursement of private-education costs when a school district fails to provide a FAPE merely requires the district "to belatedly pay expenses that it should have paid all along." *Burlington*, 471 U.S., at 370–371. And States have in any event been on notice at least since our decision in *Burlington* that IDEA authorizes courts to order reimbursement of the costs of private special-education services in appropriate circumstances. *Pennhurst's* notice requirement is thus clearly satisfied.

Finally, the District urges that respondent's reading of the Act will impose a substantial financial burden on public school districts and encourage parents to immediately enroll their children in private school without first endeavoring to cooperate with the school district. The dissent echoes this concern. For several reasons, those fears are unfounded. Parents "are entitled to reimbursement only if a federal court concludes both that the public placement violated IDEA and the private school placement was proper under the Act." *Carter*, 510 U.S., at 15. And even then courts retain discretion to reduce the amount of a reimbursement award if the equities so warrant — for instance, if the parents failed to give the school district adequate notice of their intent to enroll the child in private school. In considering the equities, courts should generally presume that public-school officials are properly performing their obligations under IDEA. *See Schaffer v. Weast*, 546 U.S. 49, 62–63 (2005) (STEVENS, J., concurring). As a result of these criteria and the fact that parents who " 'unilaterally change their child's placement during the pendency of review proceedings, without the consent of state or local school officials, do so at their own financial risk,' " *Carter*, 510 U.S., at 15 (quoting *Burlington*, 471 U.S., at 373–374), the incidence of private-school placement at public expense is quite small, *see* Brief for National Disability Rights Network et al. as Amici Curiae 13–14.

V

The IDEA Amendments of 1997 did not modify the text of § 1415(i)(2)(C)(iii), and we do not read § 1412(a)(10)(C) to alter that provision's meaning. Consistent with our decisions in *Burlington* and *Carter*, we conclude that IDEA authorizes reimbursement for the cost of private special-education services when a school district fails to provide a FAPE and the private-school placement is appropriate, regardless of whether the child previously received special education or related services through the public school.

When a court or hearing officer concludes that a school district failed to provide a FAPE and the private placement was suitable, it must consider all relevant factors, including the notice provided by the parents and the school district's opportunities for evaluating the child, in determining whether reimbursement for some or all of the cost of the child's private education is warranted. As the Court of Appeals noted, the District Court did not properly consider the equities in this case and will need to undertake that analysis on remand. Accordingly, the judgment of the Court of Appeals is affirmed.

JUSTICE SOUTER, with whom JUSTICE SCALIA and JUSTICE THOMAS join, dissenting.

I respectfully dissent.

School Comm. of Burlington v. Department of Ed. held that the Education of the Handicapped Act, now known as the Individuals with Disabilities Education Act, 20 authorized a district court to order reimbursement of private school tuition and expenses to parents who took their disabled child from public school because the school's special education services did not meet the child's needs. We said that, for want of any specific limitation, this remedy was within the general authorization for courts to award "such relief as [they] determin[e] is appropriate." § 1415(e)(2) (1982 ed.). In 1997, however, Congress amended the IDEA with a number of provisions explicitly addressing the issue of "[p]ayment for education of children enrolled in private schools without consent of or referral by the public agency." § 1412(a)(10)(C). These amendments generally prohibit reimbursement if the school district made a "free appropriate public education" available, § 1412(a)(10)(C)(i), and if they are to have any effect, there is no exception except by agreement, § 1412(a)(10)(B), or for a student who previously received special education services that were inadequate, § 1412(a)(10)(C)(ii). The majority says otherwise and holds that § 1412(a)(10)(C)(ii) places no limit on reimbursements for private tuition. The Court does not find the provision clear enough to affect the rule in *Burlington*, and it does not believe Congress meant to limit public reimbursement for unilaterally incurred private school tuition. But there is no authority for a heightened standard before Congress can alter a prior judicial interpretation of a statute, and the assessment of congressional policy aims falls short of trumping what seems to me to be the clear limitation imposed by § 1412(a)(10)(C)(ii).

I

In *Burlington*, parents of a child with a learning disability tried for over eight years to work out a satisfactory IEP for their son. They eventually gave up and sent the boy to a private school for disabled children, and we took the ensuing case to decide whether the Education of the Handicapped Act authorized courts to order reimbursement for private special education "if the court ultimately determines that such placement, rather than a proposed IEP, is proper under the Act." After noting various sections that "emphasiz[e] the participation of the parents in developing the child's [public] educational program," we inferred that the Act authorized reimbursement by providing that a district court shall " 'grant such relief as [it] determines is appropriate.' " We emphasized that the Act did not speak specifically to the issue of reimbursement, and held that "[a]bsent other reference," reimbursement for private tuition and expenses would be an " 'appropriate' " remedy in light of the purposes of the Act. In short, we read the general provision for ordering equitable remedies in § 1415(i)(2)(C)(iii) as authorizing a reimbursement order, in large part because Congress had not spoken more specifically to the issue.

But Congress did speak explicitly when it amended the IDEA in 1997. It first said that whenever the State or a local educational agency refers a student to private special education, the bill is a public expense. *See* 20 U.S.C. § 1412(a)(10)(B). It then included several clauses addressing "[p]ayment for education of children enrolled in private schools without consent of or referral by the public agency." § 1412(a)(10)(C). The first contrasts with the provision covering an agency referral:

> "(i) In general

> ". . . this subchapter does not require a local educational agency to pay for the cost of education . . . of a child with a disability at a private school or facility if that agency made a free appropriate public education available to the child and the parents elected to place the child in such private school or facility." § 1412(a)(10)(C).

The second clause covers the case in which the school authority failed to make a FAPE available in its schools. It does not, however, provide simply that the authority must pay in this case, no matter what. Instead it provides this:

> "(ii) Reimbursement for private school placement

> "If the parents of a child with a disability, who previously received special education and related services under the authority of a public agency, enroll the child in a private elementary school or secondary school without the consent of or referral by the public agency, a court or a hearing officer may require the agency to reimburse the parents for the cost of that enrollment if the court or hearing officer finds that the agency had not made a free appropriate public education available to the child in a timely manner prior to that enrollment." § 1412(a)(10)(C).

Two additional clauses spell out in some detail various facts upon which the reimbursement described in clause (ii) may be "reduced or denied." *See* §§ 1412(a)(10)(C)(iii) and (iv).

As a purely semantic matter, these provisions are ambiguous in their silence about the case with no previous special education services and no FAPE available. As the majority suggests, clause (i) could theoretically be understood to imply that reimbursement may be ordered whenever a school district fails to provide a FAPE, and clause (ii) could be read as merely taking care to mention one of a variety of circumstances in which such reimbursement is permitted. But this is overstretching. When permissive language covers a special case, the natural sense of it is taken to prohibit what it fails to authorize. When a mother tells a boy that he may go out and play after his homework is done, he knows what she means.

So does anyone who reads the authorization of a reimbursement order in the case of "a child with a disability, who previously received special education and related services under the authority of a public agency." § 1412(a)(10)(C)(ii). If the mother did not mean that the homework had to be done, why did she mention it at all, and if Congress did not mean to restrict reimbursement authority by reference to previous receipt of services, why did it even raise the subject? "[O]ne of the most basic interpretive canons [is] that [a] statute should be construed so that effect is given to all its provisions, so that no part will be inoperative or superfluous, void or insignificant. . . ." *Corley v. United States*, 129 S. Ct. 1558, 1566 (2009). But not on the Court's reading, under which clause (ii) does nothing but describe a particular subset of cases subject to remedial authority already given to courts by § 1415(i)(2)(C)(iii) and recognized in *Burlington*: a court may order reimbursement for a child who previously received special education related services, but it may do this for any other child, too.[7] But this is just not plausible, the notion that Congress added a new provision to the IDEA entitled "Reimbursement for private school placement" that had no effect whatsoever on reimbursement for private school placement. I would read clause (i) as written on the assumption that the school authorities can be expected to honor their obligations and as stating the general rule that unilateral placement cannot be reimbursed. *See* § 1412(a)(10)(C)(i) ("In general . . . "). And I would read clause (ii) as imposing a receipt of prior services limit on any exceptions to that general rule when school officials fall short of providing a FAPE. *See* § 1412(a)(10)(C)(ii) ("Reimbursement for private school placement . . . ").

This reading can claim the virtue of avoiding a further anomaly. Section 1412(a)(10)(C)(iii), which limits otherwise available reimbursement, is expressly directed to "[t]he cost of reimbursement described in clause (ii)." This makes perfect sense under my reading. Since clause (ii) is now the exclusive source of authority to order reimbursement, it is natural to refer to it in the clause setting out the conditions for reducing or even denying reimbursement otherwise authorized. Yet, as T.A. and the Government concede, under the majority's reading, Congress has called for reducing reimbursement only for the most deserving (parents described in clause (ii) who consult with the school district and give public special education services a try before demanding payment for private education), but provided no mechanism to reduce reimbursement to the least deserving (parents who have not given public placement a chance).

The Court responds to this point by doubling down. According to the majority, the criteria listed in clause (iii) can justify a reduction not only of "reimbursement described in clause (ii)," § 1412(a)(10)(C)(iii), but can also do so for a reimbursement order authorized elsewhere as well. That is, the majority avoids ascribing perverse

---

[7] [FN 2] The majority says that "clause (ii) is best read as elaborating on the general rule that courts may order reimbursement when a school district fails to provide a FAPE by listing factors that may affect a reimbursement award in the common situation in which a school district has provided a child with some special-education services and the child's parents believe those services are inadequate." But this is just another way of reading the provision off the books. On the majority's reading, clause (ii) states only that a court may award reimbursement when (1) there is a previous receipt of special education services and (2) a failure to provide a FAPE. Such a description of the most common subset of a category already described may be called elaboration, but it still has no effect on the statutory scheme.

motives to Congress by concluding that in both clause (ii) and clause (iii), Congress meant to add nothing to the statutory scheme. This simply leads back to the question of why Congress in § 1412(a)(10)(C) would have been so concerned with cases in which children had not previously received special education services when, on the majority's reading, the prior receipt of services has no relevance whatsoever to the subject of that provision.

Because any other interpretation would render clause (ii) pointless and clause (iii) either pointless or perverse, § 1412(a)(10)(C)(ii) must be read to allow reimbursement only for "parents of a child with a disability, who previously received special education and related services under the authority of a public agency."

II

Neither the majority's clear statement rule nor its policy considerations prevail over the better view of the 1997 Amendments.

A

The majority says that, because of our previous interpretation of the Act as authorizing reimbursement for unilateral private placement, Congress was obliged to speak with added clarity to alter the statute as so understood. The majority refers to two distinct principles for support: first, statutes are to be read with a presumption against implied repeals, and second, congressional reenactment of statutory text without change is deemed to ratify a prior judicial interpretation of it. I think neither principle is up to the task.

Section 1412(a)(10)(C) in no way repealed the provision we considered in *Burlington*.[8] The relief that "is appropriate" under § 1415(i)(2)(C)(iii) depends on the substantive provisions of the IDEA as surely as if the provision authorized equitable relief "consistent with the provisions of this statute."[9] When we applied § 1415(i)(2)(C)(iii) in *Burlington*, we expressly referred to those provisions and concluded that, in the absence of a specific rule, "appropriate" relief included the reimbursement sought. By introducing new restrictions on reimbursement, the 1997 Amendments produce a different conclusion about what relief is "appropriate." But § 1415(i)(2)(C)(iii) remains in effect, just as it would remain in effect if Congress had explicitly amended the IDEA to prohibit reimbursement absent prior receipt of services.

As for the rule that reenactment incorporates prior interpretation, the Court's reliance on it to preserve *Burlington*'s reading of § 1415(i)(2)(C)(iii) faces two hurdles. First, so far as I can tell, this maxim has never been used to impose a clear

---

[8] [FN 3] The presumption against implied repeals would not justify reading the later provision as useless even if it applied since, when two provisions are irreconcilable, the presumption against implied repeals gives way to the later enactment. *See Branch v. Smith*, 538 U.S. 254, 273 (2003) (plurality opinion).

[9] [FN 4] No one, for example, would suggest that a court could grant reimbursement under § 1415(i)(2)(C)(iii) to parents of a nondisabled child, but this is obvious only because we assume § 1415(i)(2)(C)(iii) is to be read in light of the substantive provisions of the statute.

statement rule. If Congress does not suggest otherwise, reenacted statutory language retains its old meaning; but when a new enactment includes language undermining the prior reading, there is no presumption favoring the old, and the only course open is simply to read the revised statute as a whole. This is so because there is no reason to distinguish between amendments that occur in a single clause (as if Congress had placed all the changes in § 1415(i)(2)(C)(iii)), and those that take the form of a separate section (here, § 1412(a)(10)(C)). If Congress had added a caveat within § 1415(i)(2)(C)(iii), or in an immediately neighboring provision, I assume the majority would not approach it with skepticism on the ground that it purported to modify a prior judicial interpretation.

Second, nothing in my reading of § 1412(a)(10)(C)(ii) is inconsistent with the holdings of *Burlington* and the other prior decision on the subject, *Florence County School Dist. Four v. Carter*. Our opinion in *Burlington* was expressly premised on there being no "other reference" that would govern reimbursement for private tuition, and this all but invited Congress to provide one. Congress's provision of such a reference in 1997 is, to say the very least, no reason for skepticism that Congress wished to alter the law on reimbursement. The 1997 legislation, read my way, would not, however, alter the result in either *Burlington* or *Carter*. In each case, the school district had agreed that the child was disabled, the parents had cooperated with the district and tried out an IEP, and the only question was whether parents who later resorted to a private school could be reimbursed " 'if the court ultimately determines that such placement, rather than a proposed IEP, is proper under the Act.' " *Carter, supra*, at 12. In ordering reimbursement, the Court in both *Burlington* and *Carter* emphasized that the parents took part in devising an IEP, and expressed concern for parents who had sought an IEP before placing their child in private school, but received one that was inadequate. The result in each case would have been the same under my reading of the amended Act, both sets of parents being "parents of a child with a disability, who previously received special education and related services under the authority of a public agency." § 1412(a)(10)(C)(ii). It is therefore too much to suggest that my reading of § 1412(a)(10)(C)(ii) would "abrogat[e] sub silentio our decisions in *Burlington* and *Carter*."

The majority argues that the policy concerns vindicated in *Burlington* and *Carter* justify reading those cases to authorize a reimbursement authority going beyond their facts, and would hold reimbursement possible even for parents who, like those here, unilaterally resort to a private school without first establishing at the administrative or appellate level that the child is disabled, or engaging in a collaborative process with the school officials. But how broadly one should read *Burlington* and *Carter* is beside the point, Congress having explicitly addressed the subject with statutory language that precludes the Court's result today.

B

The Court also rejects the natural sense of § 1412(a)(10)(C) as an interpretation that would be "at odds with the general remedial purpose underlying IDEA and the 1997 Amendments." The majority thinks my reading would place the school authorities in total control of parents' eligibility for reimbursement: just refuse any request for special education or services in the public school, and the prior service condition for eligibility under clause (ii) can never be satisfied. Thus, as the majority puts it, it would "borde[r] on the irrational" to "immuniz[e] a school district's refusal to find a child eligible for special-education services no matter how compelling the child's need." I agree that any such scheme would be pretty absurd, but there is no absurdity here. The majority's suggestion overlooks the terms of the IDEA process, the substantial procedures protecting a child's substantive rights under the IDEA, and the significant costs of its rule.

To start with the costs, special education can be immensely expensive, amounting to tens of billions of dollars annually and as much as 20% of public schools' general operating budgets. *See* Brief for Council of the Great City Schools as Amicus Curiae 22–23. The more private placement there is, the higher the special education bill, a fact that lends urgency to the IDEA's mandate of a collaborative process. . . .

The Act's repeated emphasis on the need for cooperative joint action by school and parent does not, however, leave the school in control if officials should wish to block effective (and expensive) action for the child's benefit, for if the collaborative approach breaks down, the IDEA provides for quick review in a "due process hearing" of the parents' claim that more services are needed to provide a FAPE than the school is willing to give. *See* § 1415(c)(2) (district must respond to due process hearing complaint within 10 days and hearing officer must assess facial validity of complaint within 5 days); § 1415(e) (mediation is available, provided it does not delay due process hearing); § 1415(f)(1)(B) (district must convene a meeting with parents within 15 days to attempt to resolve complaint); 34 CFR §§ 300.510(b)(1)–(2) (2008) (if complaint is not resolved, a hearing must be held within 30 days of complaint and a decision must be issued within 75 days of complaint). Parents who remain dissatisfied after these first two levels of process may have a right of appeal to the state educational agency and in any case may bring a court action in federal district court. This scheme of administrative and judicial review is the answer to the Court's claim that reading the prior services condition as restrictive, not illustrative, immunizes a school district's intransigence, giving it an effective veto on reimbursement for private placement.[10]

That said, the Court of course has a fair point that the prior services condition qualifies the remedial objective of the statute, and pursuing appeals to get a satisfactory IEP with special services worth accepting could be discouraging. The child who needs help does not stop needing it, or stop growing, while schools and parents argue back and forth. But we have to decide this case on the premise that most such arguments will be carried on in good faith, and even on the assumption that disagreements about the adequacy of IEPs will impose some burdens on the Act's intended beneficiaries, there is still a persuasive reason for Congress to have written the statute to mandate just what my interpretation requires. Given the

---

[10] [FN 5] The majority argues that we already rejected this process as inadequate *Burlington.* That was before the enactment of § 1412(a)(10)(C)(ii). The question in *Burlington* was whether the reimbursement there was an "appropriate" remedy under § 1415(i)(2)(C)(iii). With no statement to the contrary from Congress, the Court expressed concern over the possible length of the IDEA review process and surmised that Congress would have intended for reimbursement to be authorized. But Congress provided a statement to the contrary in 1997; the only reading that gives effect to § 1412(a)(10)(C)(ii) is that reimbursement is not permitted absent prior placement, and the only question for the Court now is whether Congress could have meant what it said.

burden of private school placement, it makes good sense to require parents to try to devise a satisfactory alternative within the public schools, by taking part in the collaborative process of developing an IEP that is the "modus operandi" of the IDEA. *Burlington*, 471 U.S., at 368. And if some time, and some educational opportunity, is lost in consequence, this only shows what we have realized before, that no policy is ever pursued to the ultimate, single-minded limit, and that "[t]he IDEA obviously does not seek to promote [its] goals at the expense of all considerations, including fiscal considerations," *Arlington Central School Dist. Bd. of Ed. v. Murphy*, 548 U.S. 291, 303 (2006).[11]

NOTES AND QUESTIONS

1.   What is the rule about reimbursement relief after *Carter*? Do you agree that the maintenance-of-placement provision and the in-conformance-with-state-law provisions were not intended to apply to parents? How important was legislative history to the reasoning of the courts in *Burlington* and *Carter*?

2.   *Forest Grove School District v. T.A.* raises the interesting possibility that Congress in its codification of the reimbursement remedy simply made a mistake in wording the statute. Should the Supreme Court fix apparent errors in the terms of statutes, or is that stepping out of the proper role of the judiciary? Are there social costs to failing to correct congressional language? To doing so? The *T.A.* case also presents an interesting question about how broad the Court's approach should have been. Should it have drawn a distinction between parents who had their children in public schools, but did not receive the evaluations or services requested (as in *T.A.*), and parents who had never placed their children in public schools, as in *Frank G. v. Bd. of Educ. of Hyde Park*, 459 F.3d 356 (2d Cir. 2006)? The ongoing and persistent involvement of the parents in *T.A.* with the public school officials prior to placing their child in a private school contrasts with the parents' refusal in *Frank G.* to place their children in a public school at all. Interestingly, the school district prevailed on remand in *T.A. Forest Grove Sch. Dist. v. T.A.*, 675 F. Supp. 2d 1063 (D. Or. Dec. 8, 2009).

3.   The scope of the tuition reimbursement or other remedy may be reduced if a court applies a statute of limitations or allows a laches defense to truncate the pre-hearing-request period for which relief can be provided. The 2004 IDEA Reauthorization affects this issue by creating a two-year default limitations for due process hearings. *See* 20 U.S.C. § 1415(b)(6)(B). Any explicit state limitation supersedes the default. An exception to the timeline applies for parents if the parent was prevented from requesting the hearing due to specific misrepresentations by the LEA that it had resolved the problem forming the basis of the complaint, or due to the LEA's withholding of information from the parent that IDEA requires to be provided to the parent. 20 U.S.C. § 1415(f)(3)(D). *See generally Draper v. Atlanta Sch. Sys.*, 518 F.3d 1275 (11th Cir. 2008) (discussing remedy for events early in

---

[11] [FN 6] *See* 143 Cong. Rec. 8013 (1997) (statement of Rep. Castle) ("This law . . . has had unintended and costly consequences. . . . It has resulted in school districts unnecessarily paying expensive private school tuition for children. It has resulted in cases where lawyers have gamed the system to the detriment of schools and children." "This bill makes it harder for parents to unilaterally place a child in elite private schools at public taxpayer expense, lowering costs to local school districts").

student's public school career), *infra* this Chapter.

4. The 2004 Reauthorization places restrictions on hearing officers with regard to the findings they may make on the basis of procedural failings on the part of the school district. A decision of a hearing officer is to be made on substantive grounds based on a determination of whether the child received a free, appropriate public education. 20 U.S.C. § 1415(f)(3)(E)(i). If the case alleges a procedural violation, the hearing officer may find that a child did not receive a free, appropriate public education only if the procedural inadequacies impeded the right to free, appropriate public education, significantly impeded the parents' opportunity to participate in the process of making decisions regarding the provision of the education to the child, or caused a deprivation of educational benefits. 20 U.S.C. § 1415(f)(3)(E)(ii). Nevertheless, the hearing officer may order the LEA to comply with procedural requirements in the future. 20 U.S.C. § 1415(f)(3)(E)(iii). What was the public policy behind this change? How might this provision affect the remedies ordered by hearing officers?

DRAPER v. ATLANTA INDEPENDENT SCHOOL SYSTEM
518 F.3d 1275 (11th Cir. 2008)

The court upheld an extensive award of compensatory education for a student who was not evaluated for learning disabilities but instead deemed to have intellectual disabilities, and who was provided deficient educational programs over a protracted period of time in the public school system

PRYOR, CIRCUIT JUDGE:

The issue in this appeal is whether the district court abused its discretion when it awarded a student who is disabled placement in a private school as compensation for violations of the Individuals with Disabilities Education Act. Jarron Draper entered the Atlanta Independent School System as a student in the second grade. After years of conflict with the School System, Draper's family requested and received an administrative hearing about his education. By then, Draper was 18 years old and in the eleventh grade, but he could read at only a third-grade level. The administrative law judge entered extensive findings and awarded Draper relief, and the district court, after both parties sought review, adopted the findings and increased the award. Draper is now 21 years old. The School System concedes that it violated some of Draper's rights and, in one year, provided him a deficient educational program, but the School System argues that other violations are either barred by the statute of limitations or not supported by the record. The School System also contends that Draper must be educated in a public school and that Draper's award is disproportionate to the violations of his rights. This appeal reminds us of words written by the late Judge John Minor Wisdom about a denial of educational opportunity in a different era: "A man should be able to find an education by taking the broad highway. He should not have to take by-roads through the woods and follow winding trails through sharp thickets, in constant tension because of the pitfalls and traps, and, after years of effort, perhaps attain the threshold of his goal when he is past caring about it." *Meredith v. Fair*, 298 F.2d

696, 703 (5th Cir. 1962). Because the district court did not abuse its broad discretion to fashion appropriate relief under the Act, we affirm.

I. BACKGROUND

A. The Individuals with Disabilities Education Act

. . . .

The Act directs the district court to base its decision on a preponderance of the evidence and to "grant such relief as the court determines is appropriate." 20 U.S.C. § 1415(i)(2)(C)(iii). "This Circuit has held compensatory education appropriate relief where responsible authorities have failed to provide a handicapped student with an appropriate education as required by [the Act]." *Todd D. ex rel. Robert D. v. Andrews*, 933 F.2d 1576, 1584 (11th Cir. 1991) (citing *Jefferson County Bd. of Educ. v. Breen*, 853 F.2d 853, 857 (11th Cir. 1988)). Compensatory education provides services "prospectively to compensate for a past deficient program." *G ex. rel. RG v. Fort Bragg Dependent Sch.*, 343 F.3d 295, 308 (4th Cir. 2003).

B. Factual Background

Draper entered the School System as a seven-year-old child in the second grade in 1994. He could not read, was writing at a kindergarten level, and did not know the sounds of the alphabet. Draper's teachers recommended that Draper be tested to determine the cause of his academic struggles in February 1995, November 1996, February 1997, and October 1997.

The School System performed an evaluation of Draper on June 1, 1998, and concluded that he had an intelligence quotient of 63. This evaluation was flawed because it failed to assess Draper for a specific learning disability even though he displayed signs of dyslexia, such as writing letters, numbers, and words backwards. Draper was 11 years old.

On January 25, 1999, Draper was placed in the most restrictive educational environment available, a self-contained classroom for children with mild intellectual disabilities. The restrictive classroom provided Draper with a functional curriculum that would not lead to a regular high school diploma. Draper's team met on April 19, 2000, and determined that he was reading at a third-grade level and spelling at a first-grade level. Draper was 13 years old. Draper remained in the restrictive classroom through the school year of 2002-03. His placement in the restrictive classroom between 1999 and 2003 was based on the 1998 evaluation.

Draper was not reevaluated until April 2003, when he was in the ninth grade and 16 years old. Under the Act, Draper should have been reevaluated by June 2001. After completing the evaluation, the school psychologist recommended further testing because discrepancies in subtest scores suggested that the evaluation did not accurately reflect Draper's intellectual potential.

The School System reevaluated Draper in July 2003. This evaluation revealed that Draper did not have mild intellectual disabilities but had a specific learning disability. The evaluation established that a full-scale intelligence quotient of 82, which is in the low-average range of intelligence, more accurately reflected Draper's intelligence. The evaluation also established that Draper was still reading at a third-grade level, performing at a third-grade level in arithmetic, and performing at a second-grade level in spelling. His reading level had not improved since April 2000.

Draper's team met several times throughout the summer and fall to modify his educational program. Draper's family made it clear to the School System that Draper wanted to receive a regular high school diploma so that he could go to college. On August 3, 2003, Draper's family requested private schooling and one-on-one tutoring to help Draper close the achievement gap in his studies. No action was taken on these requests.

On September 9, 2003, the School System modified Draper's diagnosis from mild intellectual disabilities to specific learning disability. Draper's team recommended only 1.5 hours of speech tutoring a week. On October 7, 2003, Draper's team amended the educational program to provide Draper with 19.5 hours of general education and 10.5 hours of special education a week. The School System placed Draper in regular-education classes for the first time since third grade even though a witness for the School System testified that a fifth-grade or sixth-grade reading level is required to survive academically in high school.

Draper's educational program provided that he would use the Lexia program, an instructional computer program, to improve his ability to read, but Draper was not provided the Lexia program. On November 17, 2003, the School System agreed, after mediation, to provide Draper with the Lexia program by no later than November 21, 2003. Despite the agreement, the School System did not implement the Lexia program until December 9, 2003, and, by January 12, 2004, Draper had received only 2.5 hours of instruction with the Lexia program.

On May 24, 2004, Draper was privately evaluated by the Lindamood-Bell reading program. The Lindamood-Bell Center recommended that Draper receive intensive sensory-cognitive training at a rate of 6 hours daily for a total of 360 hours. On May 26, 2004, although the School System was aware that Draper was still reading at a third grade level, Draper's team decided that he would use the Lexia program for the summer. Draper's family requested private reading services but were informed that they would have to file a formal complaint to pursue the matter.

During the summer of 2004, the School System referred Draper to Dr. Judy Wolman for an independent psychological evaluation. The evaluation established that Draper's skills in several areas were severely discrepant from his potential. Dr. Wolman concluded that Draper suffered from a specific learning disability consistent with dyslexia and recommended "intensive multi-sensory training" to remedy his academic deficits. Despite Draper's family's objections that the Lexia program was inadequate to address Draper's needs, Draper's team decided on November 18, 2004, to continue the use of the Lexia program. When Draper's team met again on May 12, 2005, Draper had failed his language-arts class and was failing the second semester of algebra.

On September 10, 2004, the Georgia Department of Education acknowledged that Draper's grades had not improved. The Department informed Draper's family that they could request a hearing if they were not satisfied with Draper's educational program. The hearing was conducted by the administrative law judge in November 2005. By then, Draper was 18 years old and in the eleventh grade.

C. Procedural History

The administrative law judge held a hearing for three days regarding Draper's education. The School System retained an expert, Dr. Barry Bogan, who had never met or spoken with Draper. Cross-examination established that Bogan's assumptions regarding Draper's diagnosis, age, and educational level were incorrect. Bogan was unaware that Draper had been diagnosed as having a specific learning disability. Bogan testified that Draper was 16 or 17 years old when in fact Draper was almost 19 years old. Bogan was of the opinion, based on his review of a single test, that Draper was reading at a sixth-grade or eighth-grade level instead of a third-grade level. Bogan opined that the School System had provided Draper an adequate education.

Draper called several experts to testify on his behalf. Both Dr. Wolman and Camilla Fletcher had spent extensive time with Draper. Wolman testified that Draper did not have the necessary skills to benefit from the Lexia program, and Fletcher testified that the use of the Lexia program for 30 minutes a day was insufficient to remedy Draper's achievement gap. After Dr. Edward Dragan spoke with Draper and reviewed his educational file, Dragan testified that the School System should have discovered that it had misdiagnosed Draper as mildly intellectually disabled much earlier than 2003. Dragan expressed serious doubt that the School System could or would provide Draper the appropriate services to remedy his educational deficits. Wolman and Fletcher both expressed concern about the ability of an expert to evaluate a student's education if the expert had never spoken with the student and was unfamiliar with the student's diagnosis.

Draper testified that the School System did not provide him with Lexia instruction 30 minutes a day for five days a week as the School System had alleged. Draper stated that his tutor, a football coach, spent much of the sessions surfing websites about football on the internet. Draper testified that his science class consisted of coloring and his math class of crossword puzzles. The administrative law judge concluded that Draper was "very articulate" and a "very impressive witness."

The administrative law judge found that the School System failed to provide Draper an adequate education for the school years of 2002-03, 2003-04, and 2004-05. The administrative law judge found that, after the School System misdiagnosed Draper in 1998, the School System failed to reevaluate him, in violation of the Act. The administrative law judge concluded that the use of an educational program that did not increase Draper's reading ability after three years failed to satisfy the Act.

The administrative law judge awarded Draper a choice of two remedial options. The first option provided Draper with substantial additional support services in the School System. The School System would have been required to provide Draper with intensive multi-sensory reading services for 60 minutes a day, five days a week;

train all of Draper's teachers in dyslexia instructional strategies; provide Draper with a one-on-one, certified, special-education teacher to support him in all his classes; provide one hour a day of tutorial services; provide services during the summer; and, during the first year, evaluate Draper's progress monthly. The second option allowed Draper to be placed in a private school and required the School System to pay his tuition, not to exceed $ 15,000 a year. These services were available until June 2009 or when Draper received a high school diploma, whichever came first.

. . . .

While the dispute was pending in the district court, Draper selected the second option, the placement in a private school, and requested placement at the Cottage School, but Draper reserved his right to argue that the second option was inadequate. The School System moved to stay the enforcement of the order of the administrative law judge so that the School System would not have to pay for Draper's placement in a private school while the district court reviewed the dispute. The district court denied the motion to stay the enforcement of the award and ruled that Draper's selection of the second option was enforceable while the dispute was pending in the district court.

In its final order, the district court ruled for Draper in part and for the School System in part. The district court concluded that the statute of limitations permitted an award for Draper's placement in the restrictive classroom in 1999 but limited compensation for the failure by the School System to reevaluate Draper for the period between November 2002 and April 2003. The district court agreed with the administrative law judge that the School System failed to provide Draper an adequate education for the school years of 2002-03, 2003-04, and 2004-05. As Draper requested, the district court modified the second option in the award by the administrative law judge. The district court awarded Draper full services at the Cottage School without the $15,000 cap and extended the time frame of the remedy to 2011 or when Draper receives a high school diploma, whichever comes first. The district court found that "there is ample evidence in the record of the types of services [Draper] will require to appropriately educate him within the meaning of the [Act]." The district court concluded that the Cottage School could address Draper's educational needs and was the "appropriate" placement.

II. STANDARDS OF REVIEW

A few standards govern our review of this appeal. Whether an educational program provided an adequate education under the Act "is a mixed question of law and fact subject to de novo review." *CP v. Leon County Sch. Bd. Fla.*, 483 F.3d 1151, 1155 (11th Cir. 2007). "Specific findings of fact are reviewed for clear error." *Id.* "To the extent that this issue involves the interpretation of a federal statute, it is a question of law which we review de novo." *Id.* We review awards under section 1415(i)(2)(B)(iii) of the Act for abuse of discretion. *See Board of Educ. v. L.M.*, 478 F.3d 307, 316 (6th Cir. 2007). If the district court finds a violation of the Act, it "shall grant such relief as the court determines is appropriate." 20 U.S.C. § 1415(i)(2)(C)(iii). The Act grants "broad discretion" to the district court. *School Comm. of Burlington v. Dep't of Educ.*, 471 U.S. 359, 369 (1985).

III. DISCUSSION

We evaluate the argument of the School System in two parts. First, we consider whether the district court abused its discretion in the light of the decision of the administrative law judge. Second, we consider whether Draper's award is disproportionate to the violations of the Act by the School System.

A. The District Court Did Not Abuse its Discretion in the Light of the Decision of the Administrative Law Judge.

The School System argues that, even if Draper was entitled to an award, the district court abused its discretion in two ways. First, the School System argues that, because the award by the administrative law judge provided Draper a placement in a public school as one option for compensation, the district court could not award Draper a placement in a private school. Second, the School System contends that Draper's award is contrary to the Act because the administrative law judge granted Draper a unilateral choice regarding his education. These arguments fail.

1. The Provision of a Public School Option by an Administrative Law Judge Does Not Preclude an Award of Placement in a Private School by a District Court.

The School System argues that Draper's award violates the Act as a matter of law because it allows a placement in a private school when the administrative law judge provided the option of a placement in a public school. The School System reads the provision of a public school option by the administrative law judge as a finding that the School System is able to educate Draper adequately. Although we doubt that the decision of the administrative law judge evinced any confidence in the ability of the School System to compensate for its failed attempt to educate Draper, we will assume, for the purpose of this discussion, that the administrative law judge found that the School System could prospectively provide an appropriate educational program for Draper. Even with that assumption, the argument of the School System fails.

The district court was free to fashion appropriate relief for Draper regardless of the options offered in the discussion of the administrative law judge. The Act requires "appropriate" relief, and "the only possible interpretation is that the relief is to be 'appropriate' in light of the purpose of the Act." *Burlington*, 471 U.S. at 369. " '[E]quitable considerations are relevant in fashioning relief,' *Burlington*, 471 U.S., at 374, and the court enjoys 'broad discretion' in so doing, *id.*, at 369." *Florence County Sch. Dist. Four v. Carter ex rel. Carter*, 510 U.S. 7, 16 (1993). "This Circuit has held compensatory education appropriate relief where responsible authorities have failed to provide a handicapped student with an appropriate education as required by [the Act]." *Andrews*, 933 F.2d at 1584.

The district court did not find that the School System could afford Draper appropriate relief. The district court, unlike the administrative law judge, did not award Draper a placement in a public school as one option for compensation. The district court awarded Draper placement in a private school.

The School System argues that a purpose of the Act, which is to make public schools the preferred setting, precludes Draper's award of placement in a private school, but we disagree. The Supreme Court has explained, "[T]he Act contemplates that such education will be provided where possible in regular public schools . . . , but the Act also provides for placement in private schools at public expense where this is not possible." *Burlington*, 471 U.S. at 369. We have recognized that the Act "reflects a structural preference in favor of providing special education in public schools," but we have explained that when a public school fails to provide an adequate education in a timely manner a placement in a private school may be appropriate. . . . "[A] disabled student is not required to demonstrate that he cannot be educated in a public setting. Under [the Act], the relevant question is not whether a student could in theory receive an appropriate education in a public setting but whether he will receive such an education." *Ridgewood Bd. of Educ. v. N.E. ex rel. M.E.*, 172 F.3d 238, 248–49 (3d Cir. 1999). . . .

The School System argues that Draper's award is different from an award of reimbursement, but reading "appropriate" as requiring prospective placement in a public school, as the School System argues, would create an anomaly in the law. If Draper's family had unilaterally placed him in the Cottage School, then an award of reimbursement would be appropriate under the Act. *See Burlington*, 471 U.S. at 370. The district court found that the School System had failed to provide Draper an adequate educational program, and the district court concluded that the Cottage School offered an appropriate placement. If the district court could not prospectively award Draper a placement in a private school, Draper would be worse off with an award of prospective education than he would be with a retroactive award of reimbursement for the same violations of the Act. The Supreme Court has recognized that "conscientious parents who have adequate means" will place their child in private school if they are "reasonably confident of their assessment" that an educational program at a public school is inadequate. *Id.* at 370. The argument of the School System would provide those wealthier parents greater benefits under the Act than poorer parents.

We do not read the Act as requiring compensatory awards of prospective education to be inferior to awards of reimbursement. The Act does not relegate families who lack the resources to place their children unilaterally in private schools to shouldering the burden of proving that the public school cannot adequately educate their child before those parents can obtain a placement in a private school. The Act instead empowers the district court to use broad discretion to fashion appropriate equitable relief. . . .

2. The Provision of Two Options for Draper by the Administrative Law Judge Does Not Affect the Validity of the Award by the District Court.

The School System also contends that Draper's award violates the Act because the administrative law judge provided Draper a unilateral choice between two options. The School System argues that Draper's award is inconsistent with "the cooperative process that [the Act] establishes between parents and schools." *Schaffer ex rel. Schaffer v. Weast*, 546 U.S. 49, 53 (2005). We disagree.

The argument of the School System is based on the erroneous premise that the district court, like the administrative law judge, awarded Draper two options for compensation when, in fact, the district court awarded Draper placement in only a private school. Whatever two options the administrative law judge awarded Draper is beside the point. We review the decision of the district court, and that decision awarded Draper his preferred form of compensation. . . .

B. The District Court Did Not Abuse Its Discretion and Enter a Disproportionate Remedy.

The School System argues that the district court abused its discretion in three ways: (1) the district court erroneously based its decision on Draper's misdiagnosis and placement in the restrictive classroom in 1998; (2) the award was a disproportionate remedy for the violations of the Act by the School System; and (3) the award constituted impermissible punitive damages. The first two arguments implicate findings of fact by the district court, which we review for clear error. We reject the arguments of the School System.

1. The District Court Did Not Abuse Its Discretion When It Considered Draper's Misdiagnosis in 1998 and His Placement in the Restrictive Classroom Between 1999 and 2003.

The School System presents two arguments about Draper's misdiagnosis. The School System contends that Draper was not misdiagnosed in 1998 but that, if he was misdiagnosed, Draper's complaint about his placement in the restrictive classroom between 1999 and 2003 is barred by the statute of limitations. We disagree on both points.

The School System contends that "there is no undisputed record evidence" of Draper's misdiagnosis, but that is not the issue. What matters is that there is substantial evidence to support the finding of the administrative law judge that Draper was misdiagnosed in 1998, and the acceptance of this factual finding by the district court was not clearly erroneous.

The administrative law judge relied on substantial evidence that the evaluation of Draper in 1998 was far from the comprehensive evaluation that was supposed to be administered. The administrative law judge found as follows that the limited evaluation failed to measure key aspects of Draper's abilities:

> Given that [Draper] had been observed writing words, letters, and numbers backwards, a classic symptom of dyslexia, and that he performed much better on verbal tasks, the evaluation performed in June 1998 was spectacularly deficient. The evaluation did not measure [Draper's] phonological processing levels (which are essential to reading) nor did the evaluator review [Draper's] receptive and expressive levels. Based on the limited evaluation performed, which essentially included an I.Q. test, the school psychologist concluded that [Draper] had a full scale I.Q. of 63.

The persistent refusal of the School System to acknowledge the substantial evidence of its misdiagnosis borders on incredible.

The district court also did not err in finding that the misplacement of Draper in the restrictive classroom between 1999 and 2002 is not barred by the statute of limitations. The Act requires parents to request a due process hearing "within 2 years of the date the parent . . . knew or should have known about the alleged action that forms the basis of the complaint." 20 U.S.C. § 1415(f)(3)(C). Draper filed his complaint in November 2004. The district court found that Draper's family did not have the facts necessary to know that Draper had been injured by his misdiagnosis and misplacement until they received the results of his evaluation in 2003.

The argument of the School System rests on the dubious proposition that Draper's family should have known that Draper had been misdiagnosed and misplaced even before the School System informed Draper's family that it had reached that conclusion. The School System argues, for example, that because the administrative law judge found it "incredulous" that anyone would consider Draper mentally retarded in 2003, Draper's family should have been "intimately aware of the particular nature — if not the precise medical classification — of his disability." The School System contends that the district court clearly erred because Draper's family should have known something that the trained professionals of the School System did not admit they knew.

This argument fails. Substantial evidence supports the finding that, until 2003, Draper's family did not know enough to realize that Draper had been injured by his misdiagnosis and misplacement by the School System. We decline the invitation of the School System to conclude, as a matter of law, that Draper's family should be blamed for not being experts about learning disabilities. The observation by the administrative law judge was a statement about an obvious failure by the School System, not a statement about a misdiagnosis by Draper's family. The district court did not clearly err by adopting the finding that Draper's family did not have reason to know of Draper's injury until 2003.

2. Draper's Award Is Not Disproportionate to the Violation by the School System.

The School System contends that Draper's award is disproportionate to the violations by the School System. The School System does not contest that it failed to provide Draper an adequate education for the school year of 2002-03, but instead challenges the findings of the administrative law judge and the district court that the School System failed to provide Draper an adequate education in the school years of 2003-04 and 2004-05. The School System contends that it provided Draper with an adequate program in reading in those years.

In our review of Draper's award, we are mindful that an award of compensation for a violation of the Act is different from the educational program ordinarily required by the Act. An educational program must be "reasonably calculated to enable the child to receive educational benefits." If there has been a violation, the district court may award "appropriate" compensatory relief. Although "ordinary [educational programs] need only provide 'some benefit,' compensatory awards must do more — they must compensate." *Reid ex rel. Reid v. Dist. of Columbia*, 401 F.3d 516, 525 (D.C. Cir. 2005). Compensatory awards should place children in the position they would have been in but for the violation of the Act. *Id.* at 518.

a. 2003-04

The School System contends that the district court erred when it found a violation for the school year of 2003-04 based on a disagreement with the use of the Lexia program, but this argument misunderstands the findings of the district court. The use of the Lexia program was one of many deficiencies in Draper's educational program during the school year of 2003-04. In September Draper's program maintained his placement in the restrictive classroom even though the evaluation in July 2003 found that Draper did not have mild intellectual disabilities. After the School System changed Draper's diagnosis, the School System provided Draper with only 1.5 hours of speech tutoring a week. On October 7, 2003, the School System was aware that Draper could read at only a third-grade level and that a fifth-grade or sixth-grade reading level was required to access the curriculum in high school, but the School System placed Draper in regular-education classes. Draper's program stated that the Lexia program would be provided to address his reading deficit, but Draper's family had to file a formal complaint before the School System actually provided the Lexia program. Even after the formal complaint, the School System did not provide Draper with the Lexia program until December 2003, and by January 2004 Draper had received only 2.5 hours of services using the Lexia program. Draper was still reading at a third-grade level at the end of the school year of 2003-04.

Substantial evidence supports the findings of the district court. The School System failed to modify Draper's educational program for several months after testing established that his placement was not appropriate, knowingly placed Draper in classes in which he could not succeed, and failed to address Draper's reading deficiency for half of the school year. The finding that the School System failed to provide Draper an adequate education for the school year of 2003-04 is not clearly erroneous.

b. 2004-05

The School System argues that the district court, in its finding about the school year of 2004-05, failed to recognize the difficulty of modifying an educational program to address a complex situation. This Court has recognized that, when a program is revised, "perfection is not required." *Loren F. v. Atlanta Indep. Sch. Sys.*, 349 F.3d at 1312. The record reflects that the district court understood this admonition.

The district court did not fault the School System because it failed to be perfect. The district court found that the School System failed to provide Draper with "the basic floor of opportunity." *JSK v. Hendry County School Bd.*, 941 F.2d at 1573. The School System was aware in the summer of 2004 that Draper was still reading at a third-grade level, and the School System was informed that Dr. Wolman recommended "intensive multi-sensory training to bring the deficient skills closer to his potential so that he can ultimately perform independently as an adult." Despite Draper's continued academic stagnation and the recommendation of Dr. Wolman, the School System continued to use the Lexia program over the objection of Draper's family. The district court did not clearly err when it found that the educational program provided by the School System failed to provide Draper with an adequate education for the school year of 2004-05.

3. Draper's Award Is Compensatory, Not Punitive.

The School System argues that both the decision of the district court and the earlier findings of the administrative law judge smack of retaliation. The School System complains of "disdainful references" to its witnesses and officials by the administrative law judge, and the School System describes as "caustic" the conclusion of the administrative law judge that the School System had "forfeited its right to continue to 'educate' [Draper]." The School System complains that the district court repeated these allegedly improper comments.

We are not in any position to disturb these findings. Unlike the administrative law judge, we have not observed the parties and witnesses who appeared and testified at Draper's hearings. There is ample evidence to support the administrative law judge's description of Draper's educational experience as a "tragic tale," and there is nothing in this record that suggests to us that the findings adopted by the district court are anything but supported in fact. Although strongly worded, the decisions of both the district court and the administrative law judge are professional and temperate.

In the light of this record, we cannot say that Draper's award was an abuse of discretion. The record supports the conclusion of the district court that Draper's award is "reasonably calculated to provide the educational benefits that likely would have accrued from special education services the school district should have supplied in the first place." *Reid*, 401 F.3d at 524. We categorically reject the assertion of the School System that Draper's award "looks suspiciously like" an award of punitive damages.

IV. CONCLUSION

We **AFFIRM** the judgment in favor of Draper.

NOTES AND QUESTIONS

1.   Courts have approved a variety of remedies other than tuition reimbursement in special education due process hearings. *See generally* MARK C. WEBER, SPECIAL EDUCATION LAW AND LITIGATION TREATISE § 20.13 (3d ed. 2008 & supps.). Besides reimbursement, the remedy receiving the most judicial attention has been requiring the provision of compensatory education to make up for failure to provide appropriate educational services in the past. Courts have approved compensatory education orders, and have held that the student age-eligibility limits in IDEA do not apply to these services. *See, e.g., M.C. v. Central Reg'l Sch. Dist.*, 81 F.3d 389, 397 (3d Cir. 1996) (refusing to require bad faith as predicate for compensatory education remedy); *Lester H. v. Gilhool*, 916 F.2d 865, 872 (3d Cir. 1990) (stating that making services continue past eligibility age constitutes proper remedy). What is the most persuasive reasoning those courts could rely on? Assuming that compensatory education is a proper remedy under the special education law, would you classify compensatory education as retrospective or prospective relief? *Cf.*

Milliken v. Bradley, 433 U.S. 267 (1977) (finding compensatory education services remedy for school segregation to be prospective for purposes of Eleventh Amendment immunity). Many hearing officers and courts award compensatory education on the basis of an hour or a day of services for each hour or day that the child was deprived of appropriate education. Some recent caselaw has challenged this approach, however, and has called for more flexible measurement of the remedy. *See, e.g., Reid v. District of Columbia*, 401 F.3d 516 (D.C. Cir. 2005) (holding that compensatory education should not be calculated based on rigid day-for-day compensation, but inquiry instead should be fact-specific, and compensatory education awards reasonably calculated to provide educational benefits that likely would have accrued from services wrongly withheld). Which approach makes more sense?

2.   Some courts have been less sympathetic than the *Draper* court to claims based on conduct that occurred early in the student's academic career, even when the conduct has lingering effects. *See, e.g., Somoza v. New York City Dep't of Educ.*, 538 F.3d 106 (2d Cir. 2008) (holding that limitations barred remedy). On limitations generally, see Notes and Questions following *Forest Grove School District v. T.A.*, *supra* this Chapter.

B.   MAINTENANCE OF PLACEMENT

IDEA provides that, "during the pendency of any proceedings, . . . unless the State or local educational agency and the parents otherwise agree, the child shall remain in the then-current educational placement of such child, . . . until all such proceedings shall have been completed." 20 U.S.C. § 1415(j). Although current law imposes some limits on this right in student discipline situations, *see generally infra* Chapter 9 (Student Discipline), in *Honig v. Doe*, 484 U.S. 305 (1988) (reprinted *supra* Chapter 1) the Supreme Court emphasized that the statutory provision means what it says and confers on parents the ability to keep the child where he or she is while a due process dispute is pending. This maintenance-of-placement or "stay-put" right may confer significant power upon the parents in a due process dispute, because as long as the parents continue to pursue appeals, the child retains whatever setting and services the current placement provides. In *Honig*, the Court stressed that Congress intended federal special education law to address the problem of arbitrary exclusion from school because of termination of services; the Court said it refused to create any exception to a key mechanism by which Congress attacked that problem. *Id.* at 324–25.

NOTES AND QUESTIONS

1.   Some cases present difficult questions about what the current educational placement of a child is and whether various actions by school districts in fact constitute a change of placement. *See, e.g., Clyde K. v. Puyallup Sch. Dists.*, 35 F.3d 1396 (9th Cir. 1994) (suggesting that current educational placement is latest uncontested one in case where district removed child from public school to self-contained placement and parents initially gave, but then withdrew, consent). An across-the-board decision, such as the closing of a particular school, would appear

to work a change in placement, but courts are nervous about applying the maintenance of placement provision to interfere with state and local educational decision making by keeping a school open, particularly if the child's program might be implemented at another school. *Compare Tilton v. Jefferson County Bd. of Educ.*, 705 F.2d 800, 804 (6th Cir. 1983) (finding that change of placement occurred, but declining to keep school open), *with Board of Educ. of Community High Sch. Dist. No. 218 v. Illinois State Bd. of Educ.*, 103 F.3d 545 (7th Cir. 1996) (affirming injunction placing student in residential program chosen by parent when previous placement excluded child and district did not offer comparable alternative placement).

2.   As the statutory provision says, the placement may be changed by agreement of the state or local educational agency and the parents. Courts have held that a decision by a state-appointed hearing officer in favor of the parents' request for a change of placement constitutes an agreement that creates a placement that must then be maintained during the remainder of the pendency of the dispute. *E.g., Murphy v. Arlington Cent. Sch. Dist.*, 297 F.3d 195 (2d Cir. 2000) (affirming preliminary injunction to establish placement); *see Burlington Sch. Comm. v. Department of Educ.*, 471 U.S. 359, 372 (1985) [reprinted *supra* Section A] (stating that state review decision in favor of parent "would seem to constitute agreement by the State to the change of placement."). Is this idea of agreement consistent with the requirement that state review officers be independent of the state educational agency?

3.   If a child is applying for initial admission to public school, the child "shall, with the consent of the parents, be placed in the public school program until all such proceedings have been completed." 20 U.S.C. § 1415(j). What this provision does not say is whether the placement should be in special education or general education, much less what the content of any special education program should be. What should the rule be? Perhaps an argument could be made that since the school district must always obtain parental consent before initiation of special education services, the default option is general education. *See* 34 C.F.R. § 300.300(b)(1). What if the child is already receiving infant and toddler services under IDEA-Part C? *Compare Pardini v. Allegheny Intermediate Unit*, 420 F.3d 181 (3d Cir. 2005) (holding that child making transition from IDEA Part C to Part B must receive conductive education provided for in individualized family service plan during pendency of proceedings over district's proposed IEP), *cert. denied*, 126 S. Ct. 1646 (2006), *with* 34 C.F.R. 300.518(c) *and D.P. v. School Bd.*, 483 F.3d 725 (11th Cir. 2007) (holding that invocation of stay-put provision did not require school district to continue providing services on triplets' IDEA Part C plans when they reached age three and school district instead offered other services under temporary IEPs). *See generally infra* Chapter 13 (discussing early childhood services).

C.   ISSUES RELATED TO SETTLEMENT

Like other civil disputes, special education cases frequently settle. Settlement mechanisms under IDEA receive a comprehensive description and general evaluation in Mark C. Weber, *Settling IDEA Cases: Making Up Is Hard to Do*, 43 Loy. L.A.   L.   Rev.   641,   *available   at*   http://papers.ssrn.com/sol3/

papers.cfm?abstract_id=1446008 A discussion of the law governing settlement embraces the topics of offer of judgment procedures, the enforcement of settlement agreements, and mediation procedures.

1.   Offers of Judgment

IDEA creates an elaborate offer-of-judgment procedure, by which attorneys' fees that the parents would otherwise be entitled to if they prevailed may be reduced due to the parents' rejection of a written settlement offer that is as favorable as what the parents ultimately obtain by litigation:

(D) Prohibition of attorneys' fees and related costs for certain services

(i) In general. Attorneys' fees may not be awarded and related costs may not be reimbursed in any action or proceeding under this section for services performed subsequent to the time of a written offer of settlement to a parent if —

(I) the offer is made within the time prescribed by Rule 68 of the Federal Rules of Civil Procedure or, in the case of an administrative proceeding, at any time more than 10 days before the proceeding begins;

(II) the offer is not accepted within 10 days; and

(III) the court or administrative hearing officer finds that the relief finally obtained by the parents is not more favorable to the parents than the offer of settlement.

(ii) IEP team meetings. Attorneys' fees may not be awarded relating to any meeting of the IEP Team unless such meeting is convened as a result of an administrative proceeding or judicial action, or, at the discretion of the State, for a mediation described in subsection (e). (iii) Opportunity to resolve complaints. A [resolution session] meeting conducted pursuant to subsection (f)(1)(B)(i) shall not be considered —

(I) a meeting convened as a result of an administrative hearing or judicial action; or

(II) an administrative hearing or judicial action for purposes of this paragraph.

(E) Exception to prohibition on attorneys' fees and related costs. Notwithstanding subparagraph (D), an award of attorneys' fees and related costs may be made to a parent who is the prevailing party and who was substantially justified in rejecting the settlement offer.

20 U.S.C. § 1415(i).

NOTES AND QUESTIONS

1.   This section of IDEA creates an administrative analogue to Fed. R. Civ. P. 68, as interpreted by *Marek v. Chesny*, 473 U.S. 1 (1985). Do you think that the offer-of-judgment provision is a good idea? Can you anticipate difficulties determining whether the result from a hearing is more or less favorable than what the school district offers? *See generally M.L. v. Fed. Way Sch. Dist.*, 401 F. Supp.2d 1158 (W.D. Wash. 2005) (finding nonmonetary aspects of result more favorable than district's offer, supporting fees award).

2.   Law and economics writers doubt that incentives applicable to only one side of the dispute (for example, in the special education law, the parents' loss of further attorneys' fees for rejecting an offer of settlement) are effective at inducing settlement. They reason that the side of the dispute that does not face the loss will simply diminish the attractiveness of its offer so as to compensate for the additional downside risk its opponent faces. The terms of settlement may be biased downward, but the likelihood of arriving at a settlement is unchanged. *See, e.g.*, Geoffrey P. Miller, *An Economic Analysis of Rule 68*, 15 J. LEG. STUD. 93 (1986). Only a two-sided offer-of-judgment rule would actually promote settlements. *See id.* By contrast, the Supreme Court has written that a one-sided offer-of-judgment rule "prompts both parties to a suit to evaluate the risks and costs of litigation, and to balance them against the likelihood of success upon trial on the merits," presumably leading to settlements of cases that otherwise would be litigated. *Marek v. Chesny*, 473 U.S. 1, 5 (1985). Which view is more likely correct? How would you test your conclusion empirically?

2.   Enforcing Settlements

The law favors settlements of disputes, but generally leaves enforcement of settlement agreements to ordinary principles of contract law. Settlements may be invalidated as contrary to public policy, but decisions overturning settlements on that basis appear to be rare. *See D.R. v. East Brunswick Bd. of Educ.*, 109 F.3d 896 (3d Cir. 1997) (upholding settlement over dissent's argument that settlement defeated statutory rights); *see also Lauren W. v. DeFlaminis*, 480 F.3d 259 (3d Cir. 2007) (ruling that parents failed on claim that school district unlawfully retaliated against them when it refused to fund unapproved private school for child with disabilities unless parents agreed to waive all federal and state claims related to child's placement for school year). Should parents have to go to due process if they contend that the school district has failed to live up to a settlement agreement, or should the parents be able to sue directly in court to enforce the settlement without exhausting administrative remedies? *Compare W.L.G. v. Houston County Bd. of Educ.*, 975 F. Supp. 1317 (M.D. Ala. 1997) (requiring exhaustion of claim that school district failed to obey settlement agreement), *and School Bd. v. M.C.*, 796 So. 2d 581 (Fla. App. 2001) (finding that hearing officer lacked jurisdiction in action to enforce settlement agreement or alternatively obtain rescission and damages), *with W.K. v. Sea Isle City Bd. of Educ.*, No. 06-1815, 2007 U.S. Dist. LEXIS 8342 (D.N.J. Feb. 5, 2007) (denying motion to dismiss action to enforce settlement approved by order of administrative law judge, finding federal jurisdiction and ability to enforce settlement pursuant to 42 U.S.C. § 1983, collecting authorities), *and Blackman v. District of Columbia,* 28 IDELR 1053 (D.D.C. 1998) (entering injunction to enforce settlement stipulations and rejecting exhaustion defense), Under IDEA as amended in 2004, written settlement agreements reached at mediation or a resolution settlement are enforceable in any state court of competent jurisdiction or in United States District Court. 20 U.S.C. §§ 1415(e)(2)(F)(iii) (mediation), 1415(f)(1)(B)(iii)(II) (resolution session).

3.   Mediation Procedures and Related Issues

IDEA establishes detailed mediation procedures to promote settlement of disputes between parents and educational agencies. The regulations provide:

Mediation.

(a) General. Each public agency must ensure that procedures are established and implemented to allow parties to disputes involving any matter under this part, including matters arising prior to the filing of a due process complaint, to resolve disputes through a mediation process.

(b) Requirements. The procedures must meet the following requirements:

(1) The procedures must ensure that the mediation process —

(i) Is voluntary on the part of the parties;

(ii) Is not used to deny or delay a parent's right to a hearing on the parent's due process complaint, or to deny any other rights afforded under Part B of the Act; and

(iii) Is conducted by a qualified and impartial mediator who is trained in effective mediation techniques.

(2) A public agency may establish procedures to offer to parents and schools that choose not to use the mediation process, an opportunity to meet, at a time and location convenient to the parents, with a disinterested party —

(i) Who is under contract with an appropriate alternative dispute resolution entity, or a parent training and information center or community parent resource center in the State . . . ; and

(ii) Who would explain the benefits of, and encourage the use of, the mediation process to the parents.

(3)(i) The State must maintain a list of individuals who are qualified mediators and knowledgeable in laws and regulations relating to the provision of special education and related services.

(ii) The SEA must select mediators on a random, rotational, or other impartial basis.

(4) The State must bear the cost of the mediation process, including the costs of meetings described in paragraph (b)(2) of this section.

(5) Each session in the mediation process must be scheduled in a timely manner and must be held in a location that is convenient to the parties to the dispute.

(6) If the parties resolve a dispute through the mediation process, the parties must execute a legally binding agreement that sets forth that resolution and that —

(i) States that all discussions that occurred during the mediation process will remain confidential and may not be used as evidence in any subsequent due process hearing or civil proceeding; and

(ii) Is signed by both the parent and a representative of the agency who has the authority to bind such agency.

(7) A written, signed mediation agreement under this paragraph is enforceable in any State court of competent jurisdiction or in a district court of the United States.

Discussions that occur during the mediation process must be confidential and may not be used as evidence in any subsequent due process hearing or civil proceeding of any Federal court or State court of a State receiving assistance under this part.

(c) Impartiality of mediator. (1) An individual who serves as a mediator under this part —

(i) May not be an employee of the SEA or the LEA that is involved in the education or care of the child; and

(ii) Must not have a personal or professional interest that conflicts with the person's objectivity.

(2) A person who otherwise qualifies as a mediator is not an employee of an LEA or State agency described under § 300.228 solely because he or she is paid by the agency to serve as a mediator.

34 C.F.R. § 300.506.

United States General Accounting Office, Special Education: Numbers of Formal Disputes are Generally Low and States are Using Mediation and Other Strategies to Resolve Conflicts 1–3 (2003)

School districts and families have at least three formal mechanisms for resolving disputes: state complaint procedures, due process hearings, and mediation. A state complaint procedure is a review by the state education agency (SEA) to determine whether a state or a local school district has violated IDEA. A due process hearing is an administrative agency process, in which an impartial hearing officer receives evidence, provides for the examination and cross-examination of witnesses by each party, and then issues a report of findings of fact and decisions. To provide an alternative mechanism for resolving conflicts in a way that may be less costly and less adversarial, the 1997 amendments to IDEA required that states offer voluntary mediation when a request for a due process hearing is filed. Mediation is a negotiating process that employs an impartial mediator to help the parties in conflict resolve their disputes with a mutually accepted written agreement. While school districts and families are not required to choose this option, the legislation strongly encouraged states to promote the use of mediation to resolve disagreements.

. . . .

While data are limited and inexact, four national studies indicate that the use of the three formal dispute resolution mechanisms has been generally low relative to the number of children with disabilities. Due process hearings, the most resource-intense dispute mechanism, were the least used nationwide. Using data from the National Association of State Directors of Special Education, we calculated that nationwide, in 2000, about 5 due process hearings were held per 10,000 students with disabilities. According to . . . these data, over three-quarters of the due process hearings had been held in five states — California, Maryland, New Jersey, New York, and Pennsylvania — and the District of Columbia. Mediation activity was also low. Another national study reported in 2003 that the median number of mediations for states was 4 for every 10,000 students with disabilities in school year 1999-2000. In May 2003, SEEP estimated that 4,266 mediation cases occurred during the 1998-99 school year, which we calculated as a rate of about 7 mediations per 10,000 students with disabilities. Also, using the latter study, we calculated that about 10 state complaints were filed for every 10,000 students with disabilities in the 1998-99 school year.

Officials in all four states we visited [California, Massachusetts, Ohio, and Texas] were emphasizing the use of mediation to resolve disputes between families and school districts, and some states had developed additional approaches for early resolution. State officials told us they found that mediation was successful in resolving disputes, strengthening relationships between families and educators, saving financial resources, and reaching resolution more quickly. The University of the Pacific reported that 93 percent of the mediation cases in California resulted in agreements between families and schools during the 2001-02 fiscal year; the cost of a mediator was about one-tenth that of a hearing officer.

NOTES AND QUESTIONS

1.   How would mediators be able to promote settlement in cases in which the parties have not reached resolution on their own? Many discussions of the effectiveness of mediators stress the mediators' ability to facilitate communications between parties, provide impartial assessments of the strength of the parties' respective cases, and propose resolutions of disputes that the parties themselves may not have previously identified as possible. *See generally* LEONARD L. RISKIN & JAMES E. WESTBROOK, DISPUTE RESOLUTION AND LAWYERS 313–36 (2d ed. 1997) (discussing diverse viewpoints about the proper roles of mediators in promoting dispute resolution). Mediation may also have the advantage over litigation of promoting cooperation between the parties as they work together in a continuing relationship. Do you think that mediation can be successful at accomplishing this goal? Are there some kinds of cases that should not be mediated?

2.   Would measures such as easing of enforcement of settlement agreements and making attorneys' fees available to parents in cases that settle at mediation increase the willingness of parents to make use of mediation procedures?

3.   Are there potential difficulties with mediators overstepping their role and improperly imposing "settlements" on unwilling parties? Try your hand at drafting a code of conduct for mediators of special education disputes.

4.   The regulations, mirroring statutory provisions, permit mediation to be invoked even in the absence of a due process complaint. This is one of the changes in the 2004 IDEA Reauthorization. 20 U.S.C. § 1415(e)(1). Do you think this is a wise innovation?

5.   For cases that are not mediated, the 2004 Reauthorization provides an elaborate "resolution session" requirement. Unless the parents and the LEA agree to use mediation or waive the resolution session, the LEA, prior to the due process hearing, must convene a meeting with the parents and the relevant member or members of the IEP team with knowledge of the facts in the due process complaint. 20 U.S.C. § 1415(f)(1)(B)(i). The meeting is to occur within 15 days of receipt of the parents' complaint and has to include a person with decision-making authority from the educational agency. The attorney for the LEA may not be included unless the parent is accompanied by an attorney. At the meeting, the parents are to discuss their complaint and the facts behind it, and the LEA is to be given the chance to resolve the complaint. If no satisfactory resolution is reached within 30 days of the receipt of the complaint, the due process hearing may occur, and all applicable timelines start again. If resolution is reached, the parties must execute a legally binding agreement signed in the same manner as a settlement reached at mediation, and the same right exists to enforce the settlement in court. Nevertheless, a party may void a settlement agreement reached following the resolution session within three business days of the execution of the agreement. States may choose to make attorney's fees available for mediation, but the resolution session is not considered an administrative hearing, judicial action, or meeting convened as a result of administrative or judicial action so as to entitle the parent to attorneys' fees. § 1415(i)(3)(D)(ii)–(iii).

6.   Discussions that occur during the mediation process must be kept confidential and may not be used as evidence in a due process or civil proceeding. 20 U.S.C. § 1415(e)(2)(G). In one case, the court refused to consider whether a written offer of settlement would be the basis for limiting the parents' attorneys' fees, on the ground that it referred to mediation discussions when it offered to settle "on the terms and conditions set forth in the settlement agreement reached but not signed at the mediation session." *J.D. v. Kanawha County Bd. of Educ.*, 571 F.3d 381 (4th Cir. 2009). Is this a reasonable interpretation of the confidentiality provision? Interestingly, there is no parallel confidentiality provision for the resolution session.

D. APPEALS AND JUDICIAL REVIEW

The IDEA regulations set out the procedures for review of hearing officer decisions in those states that maintain two-tier systems:

Finality of decision; appeal; impartial review.

(a) Finality of hearing decision. A decision made in a hearing conducted pursuant to §§ 300.507 through 300.513 or §§ 300.530 through 300.534 is final, except that any party involved in the hearing may appeal the decision under the provisions of paragraph (b) of this section and § 300.516.

(b) Appeal of decisions; impartial review.

(1) If the hearing required by § 300.511 is conducted by a public agency other than the SEA, any party aggrieved by the findings and decision in the hearing may appeal to the SEA.

(2) If there is an appeal, the SEA must conduct an impartial review of the findings and decision appealed. The official conducting the review must —

(i) Examine the entire hearing record;

(ii) Ensure that the procedures at the hearing were consistent with the requirements of due process;

(iii) Seek additional evidence if necessary. If a hearing is held to receive additional evidence, the rights in § 300.512 apply;

(iv) Afford the parties an opportunity for oral or written argument, or both, at the discretion of the reviewing official;

(v) Make an independent decision on completion of the review; and

(vi) Give a copy of the written, or, at the option of the parents, electronic findings of fact and decisions to the parties.

(c) Findings and decision to advisory panel and general public. The SEA, after deleting any personally identifiable information, must —

(1) Transmit the findings and decisions referred to in paragraph (b)(2)(vi) of this section to the State advisory panel established under § 300.167; and

(2) Make those findings and decisions available to the public.

(d) Finality of review decision. The decision made by the reviewing official is final unless a party brings a civil action. . . .

34 C.F.R. § 300.514

NOTES AND QUESTIONS

1. In some early decisions, the impartiality requirements of the state level review seemed to baffle agency officials accustomed to using final administrative decisions to make statewide educational policy. *See Burr v. Ambach*, 863 F.2d 1071 (2d Cir. 1988), *vacated*, 492 U.S. 902, *reaff'd*, 888 F.2d 258 (2d Cir. 1989) (enforcing requirement that individuals conducting reviews meet impartiality standards for hearing officers; disqualifying state commissioner of education from deciding review). The impartiality requirement for state level review has another implication: Allowing state administrative agencies to develop policy is a basis for requiring

exhaustion of disputes, but requirement that the state level hearing officer be independent from the state educational agency means that the hearing officer is not putting the agency's official interpretation into effect. Thus, state policy development is a dubious basis for exhaustion in IDEA cases.

2.   Is a two-tier or one-tier administrative process superior? Which would you propose if you were drafting your state's special education law? Why?

3.   A party to the hearing (either the parent or the district) may file an action in court to overturn the final decision in a special education case. Court proceedings are the subject of the Chapter 10.

Chapter 9

STUDENT DISCIPLINE

A. BEHAVIOR INTERVENTION AND APPROPRIATE EDUCATION IN THE LEAST RESTRICTIVE ENVIRONMENT

Ideally, school discipline is positive and not punitive. Education includes basic lessons in how to behave, and the educational setting should support children in their efforts to learn school rules and comply with them. For children whose disabilities make it difficult for them to conform to standards of proper behavior, appropriate education includes behavioral intervention to help them learn to conduct themselves in a way that facilitates learning. In the following case, the court considers the role of behavior management in a program of appropriate education in the least restrictive setting.

NEOSHO R-V SCHOOL DISTRICT v. CLARK
315 F.3d 1022 (8th Cir. 2003)

The court affirmed the district court's decision that the failure of an individualized education program to offer needed behavioral services denied the child a free, appropriate public education.

HANSEN, CIRCUIT JUDGE.

This dispute involves a disabled student's right to a free appropriate public education within the meaning of the Individuals with Disabilities Education Act (IDEA), 20 U.S.C. §§ 1400–1487 (Supp. III 1997). The Neosho R-V School District (hereinafter "the School District") appeals the district court's judgment that it failed to provide Robert Clark with a free appropriate public education and awarding attorneys' fees and costs to Robert Clark's parents (hereinafter "the Clarks"). The Clarks cross appeal the denial of their request for expert witness fees. We affirm.

Robert Clark was a twelve-year-old special education student in the Neosho R-V School District during the 1997-98 school year. Because he suffers from Autism-Asperger's Syndrome, Robert is prone to inappropriate behavior, which, when unmanaged, largely prevents him from interacting with his peers in an acceptable manner. He also is diagnosed as having a learning disability. During the 1997-98 school year, Robert's age was equal to children in the sixth grade, but he was placed in the fifth grade resource room for special education. His instructional level was that of fourth grade, but he needed assistance with this work, and the special education teacher often moved him back to third-grade level work to decrease his misbehaviors and to increase his self-confidence.

Before the school year began, Robert's parents had initiated a due process proceeding against the School District, which resulted in a settlement agreement providing that the School District would place Robert in a self-contained classroom with mainstreaming in music. The settlement agreement also provided for a full-time paraprofessional to help Robert in school and required the School District to provide specific interventions and strategies to manage Robert's inappropriate behavior. In August 1997, and again in October 1997, the School District developed Individualized Education Plans (IEPs) for Robert. Consistent with the settlement agreement, the IEPs placed Robert in a self-contained classroom except for music class, established an IEP team to meet every two weeks and consider the possibility of additional mainstreaming, and called for a full-time paraprofessional to accompany Robert in all classes. The IEPs also stated that a behavior plan was attached to them, but the attachments were merely short-term goals and objectives that did not provide specific interventions and strategies to manage Robert's behavior problems.

Robert's special education teacher, Mrs. Sweet, and his IEP-required paraprofessional, Larry Shadday, attempted to manage Robert's behavior problems to the best of their ability. They employed several methods that might be found in a behavior management plan but which had not been actually analyzed or approved by Robert's IEP team. They also used a checklist that had been included in a plan developed during the prior school year by an outside agency, the Judevine Center for Autism. The IEP team never adopted this document and had agreed that a new behavior management plan was necessary to meet Robert's needs during the 1997-98 school year. The IEP team agreed that the new plan should not be based on Robert's past behavior. Robert's special education teacher did not begin to formally chart data in a format that could be used to develop a new behavior management plan until March 1998.

As the 1997-98 school year progressed, Robert's behavior problems increased dramatically. His challenging behaviors numbered 3 in the month of August, 10 in the month of September, and 394 by March. The School District did not attempt to formulate a new behavior management plan for Robert until April 1998, close to the end of the school year. Robert's increasingly inappropriate behavior prevented him from being included in mainstreamed classes beyond music and substantially interfered with his ability to learn.

The Clarks sought an administrative hearing as provided by the IDEA. *See* 20 U.S.C. § 1415(f). Before the hearing, the Clarks were seeking, among other things, a private placement for Robert or a more inclusive placement within the district. By the time of the administrative hearing, the issues had been narrowed to the question of whether the School District had provided the required behavior management plan necessary to ensure that Robert received a free appropriate public education.

At the hearing, the Clarks presented the expert witness testimony of Dr. Lonny Morrow. In his opinion, Robert's autism and resulting challenging behavior required the adoption of a formal behavior management plan that would include a functional behavior assessment and develop consequences and reinforcements appropriate to Robert's disability. The three-member state administrative panel chose to credit this expert testimony. Based on this testimony, the panel found that although the IEPs identified some goals and strategies for dealing with Robert's behavior problems, these were insufficient to qualify as a cohesive behavior management plan. The panel also found that the School District's late-in-the-year attempt to formulate the required behavior management plan was insufficient to meet Robert's needs.

The School District contended that Robert's academic record demonstrated he had received some benefit from his education, even if the behavior plan did not meet the expert's requirements. The administrative panel did not credit that evidence, finding it contradicted by other evidence and unsupported by the record as a whole. The panel found that the conflicting evidence left it with no clear evidence from which it could determine if or to what extent Robert had progressed or obtained any educational benefit.

Thus, the administrative panel concluded that the School District failed to develop and implement the required behavior management plan calculated to meet Robert's needs and to enable him to gain an educational benefit. The panel ordered the School District to seek the expertise of a consultant or qualified expert to devise a behavior management plan including (1) an ongoing functional behavior analysis to identify causative factors and objectionable behaviors, and (2) a list of replacement behaviors and strategies to eliminate Robert's objectionable behavior and enable him to receive educational benefits. The panel also ordered the School District to provide its staff with development training for working with students who have Asperger's Syndrome and high functioning autism.

The School District brought suit in federal district court, seeking judicial review of the administrative panel's decision. *See* 20 U.S.C. § 1415(i)(2). On cross motions for summary judgment, the district court affirmed the panel decision that the School District had failed to provide Robert with a free appropriate public education. The district court concluded that the Clarks were prevailing parties and ordered the School District to pay attorneys' fees of $15,689.50. The district court denied the Clarks' request for expert witness fees. The School District now appeals, and the Clarks cross appeal the denial of their request for expert witness fees.

II

A. Free Appropriate Public Education

One purpose of the IDEA is "to ensure that all children with disabilities have available to them a free appropriate public education that emphasizes special education and related services designed to meet their unique needs." 20 U.S.C. § 1400(d)(1)(A). States accepting federal funding under the IDEA must "provide a disabled student with a free appropriate public education." *Gill v. Columbia 93 Sch. Dist.*, 217 F.3d 1027, 1034 (8th Cir. 2000); *see also* 20 U.S.C. § 1412(a). Congressional policies indicate a preference for educating disabled children in a mainstreamed classroom whenever possible. *Gill*, 217 F.3d at 1034; 20 U.S.C. § 1400(c)(5)(D). A team must develop a specialized course of instruction, known as an individualized education program, or "IEP," for each disabled student, taking into account that child's capabilities. *Gill*, 217 F.3d at 1034; 20 U.S.C. § 1414(d).

In a suit by an aggrieved party under the IDEA, the court engages in a twofold inquiry, asking (1) "has the State complied with the procedures set forth in the Act?" and (2) is the IEP "reasonably calculated to enable the child to receive educational benefits?" *Board of Educ. v. Rowley*, 458 U.S. 176, 206-07 (1982). "If these requirements are met, the State has complied with the obligations imposed by Congress and the courts can require no more." *Id.* at 207. While the IDEA requires school districts to provide disabled children with a free appropriate public education, it "does not require that a school either maximize a student's potential or provide the best possible education at public expense." *Fort Zumwalt Sch. Dist. v. Clynes*, 119 F.3d 607, 612 (8th Cir. 1997), *cert. denied*, 523 U.S. 1137 (1998). Instead, the requirements of the IDEA "are satisfied when a school district provides individualized education and services sufficient to provide disabled children with 'some educational benefit.' " *Blackmon v. Springfield R-XII Sch. Dist.*, 198 F.3d 648, 658 (8th Cir. 1999) (quoting *Rowley*, 458 U.S. at 200).

In this case, there is no contention that the school district failed to follow the procedures set forth in the IDEA. Rather, the dispute involves the second inquiry — whether the August and October 1997 IEPs were reasonably calculated to enable Robert to receive an educational benefit. The district court determined that because the IEPs required a behavior management plan and because the attachments to the IEPs did not qualify as such and no approved plan was timely developed, the IEPs were not reasonably calculated to provide an educational benefit.[1]

The School District asserts that, contrary to the district court's ultimate conclusion, Robert's IEPs were reasonably calculated to provide Robert an educational benefit. Specifically, the School District asserts (1) that the district court erred in giving deference to administrative panel findings of no educational benefit because those findings were contradicted by the evidence, (2) that the IEPs appropriately addressed Robert's behavior problems, and (3) that the district court erred in concluding that the School District denied Robert a free appropriate public education.

We review de novo, as a mixed question of law and fact, the ultimate issue of whether an IEP is reasonably calculated to provide some educational benefit. *Gill*, 217 F.3d at 1035 (citing *Fort Zumwalt*, 119 F.3d at 611, and *Yankton Sch. Dist. v.*

---

[1] [FN 3] This case is slightly different in posture from others we have seen because it involves a failure to implement a necessary provision of an otherwise appropriate IEP. *See Houston Ind. School Dist. v. Bobby R.*, 200 F.3d 341, 349 (5th Cir. 2000) (setting forth the analysis that a party who is challenging the implementation of an IEP must demonstrate that the school authorities failed to implement a substantial or significant provision of the IEP; and noting that this analysis affords schools some flexibility in implementing IEPs but still holds them accountable for material failures and for providing a meaningful educational benefit), *cert. denied*, 531 U.S. 817 (2000). While the analysis set forth in *Bobby R.* more accurately suits the posture of this case, the parties did not make this argument. Thus, we confine our analysis to the framework of *Rowley*, which considers whether the IEP was reasonably calculated to provide an educational benefit. We believe that this analysis is pliable enough to fit the situation at hand and will safeguard the same principles because we cannot conclude that an IEP is reasonably calculated to provide a free appropriate public education if there is evidence that the school actually failed to implement an essential element of the IEP that was necessary for the child to receive an educational benefit.

Schramm, 93 F.3d 1369, 1374 (8th Cir. 1996)). "[T]he district court's findings of fact are binding unless clearly erroneous." *Id.* The district court must receive the record of the state administrative proceedings and any additional evidence at the request of either party. 20 U.S.C. § 1415(i)(2)(B). Then, basing its decision on the preponderance of the evidence, the district court "shall grant such relief as the court determines is appropriate." *Id.* While courts are required to make an independent decision based upon a preponderance of the evidence, the fact that the statute requires the reviewing court to receive the administrative records "carries with it the implied requirement that *due weight* shall be given to these proceedings." *Rowley*, 458 U.S. at 206 (emphasis added), *see also Fort Zumwalt*, 119 F.3d at 610. This ensures that courts will not "substitute their own notions of sound educational policy for those of the school authorities which they review." *Rowley*, 458 U.S. at 206. Thus, the statutory obligation to grant "such relief as the court determines is appropriate" largely references the statute's procedural obligations; it does not permit the court to exercise a free hand in imposing substantive educational standards. *Id.*

We have noted that the district court's standard of review under the IDEA is less deferential than the substantial evidence test ordinarily applied in federal administrative law cases. *Blackmon*, 198 F.3d at 654. At the same time, however, courts are admonished to be mindful that they lack the specialized knowledge and experience necessary to resolve difficult questions of educational policy. *Id.* at 654–55. Additionally, a district court should give consideration to "the fact that the state hearing panel has had the opportunity to observe the demeanor of the witnesses." *Fort Zumwalt*, 119 F.3d at 610.

In this case, the district court was careful not to substitute its own notions of educational policy for those of the trained educators, and we conclude that the district court gave due weight to the administrative hearing panel's findings that Robert did not receive an educational benefit. The parties presented no additional evidence to the district court, and the district court's written order evidences an independent review of the administrative hearing record. The district court concluded that the record supported the administrative panel's decision to discount the evidence of Robert's alleged academic progress, and it gave deference to the panel's determination that the materials attached to the IEPs did not constitute a proper behavior management plan. The district court stated that because those decisions were supported by evidence in the record, to do otherwise would be "to substitute its views regarding proper educational methods and programs for the Panel's views on those topics." While the record is certainly not one-sided on the issue of whether Robert received an educational benefit, we agree that on the whole, the record supports the credibility assessments and findings made by the administrative panel and deferred to by the district court.

The School District's arguments that the IEPs appropriately addressed Robert's behavior problems and that the district court erred in concluding that the School District denied Robert a free appropriate public education are intertwined. Our independent review convinces us that because the IEPs did not appropriately address his behavior problem, Robert was denied a free appropriate public education.

The Clarks' expert witness testified that the papers attached to the IEPs were not sufficient to amount to a cohesive behavior management plan. Witnesses confirmed that such a plan was never adopted by the IEP team, in spite of the fact that Robert's behavior problem was the major concern at every IEP meeting. Although the special education teacher and the paraprofessional commendably attempted to cope with Robert's behavioral problems using methods that could have been employed in a behavior management plan, they were not professionally trained to successfully reduce the inappropriate behavior in a manner fitting to Robert's disabilities. The fact that no cohesive plan was in place to meet Robert's behavioral needs supports the ultimate conclusion that he was not able to obtain a benefit from his education.

Our review indicates that the administrative panel's decision reflects a thorough consideration of all the evidence regarding Robert's academic progress and his behavioral problems. The panel discounted the evidence of some slight academic progress, finding that this evidence of progress was contradicted by other evidence in the record. The record demonstrates that every time Robert's special education teacher advanced his work to a fifth-grade level, the stress engendered resulted in behavior problems that forced the teacher to readjust his work back to fourth-grade levels (which he needed assistance to complete) and even to third-grade levels to afford Robert a measure of success.

The School District points to report cards which assertedly indicate a measure of success sufficient to be considered an educational benefit, regardless of whether the IEP stated a behavior management plan. The administrative panel reviewed all of this evidence in a detailed fashion and discounted it because the records did not indicate at which grade level Robert was working at any given time or over any period of time. The records also indicated that work at higher levels was only possible with a great deal of help from the paraprofessional.

The special education teacher stated generally that she thought Robert had attained some benefit academically, and her records indicated that some short-term objectives had been met. She admitted, however, that whenever she attempted to advance Robert's work, his behavior problems worsened and prevented independent success at any level beyond third grade. Robert's mother also stated generally that she thought Robert had made "some" progress during the 1997-98 school year. She qualified her answer, clarifying that she sought more integration for him not because she felt Robert had progressed, but because she was certain that he could progress if given more mainstream classroom opportunities, which would only be possible with a proper behavior management plan.

Kerri Muns, the director of the Southwest Missouri Autism Project, was involved with the Judevine Center for Autism and had attended Robert's IEP meetings at the request of his parents. She testified that Robert's behavior problems always precluded him from attending a regular classroom, which was the main goal of his IEPs. She opined that Robert had progressed "in a very broad sense," noting that he now could start a conversation and look a person in the eye, which he could not do at the beginning of the year. On the other hand, his short attention span had not increased.

The administrative panel concluded that the generalized opinions of progress expressed by some witnesses at the hearing were "meaningless" in light of all the other evidence in this case. Our review of the record convinces us that the panel did not err in discounting the evidence of de minimis academic and social progress where the panel pointed to specific evidence in the record contradicting such a benefit and noted that any slight benefit obtained was lost due to behavior problems that went unchecked and interfered with his ability to obtain a benefit from his education. The district court considered not only the administrative panel's conclusions, but also the hearing record to reach its own conclusion that "the need for — and the ability to create — a proper behavior modification plan existed long before [the School District] made the effort to [create a plan]." Upon de novo review, we agree that the School District failed to provide Robert an educational benefit by not developing and implementing an appropriate behavior management plan as required by his IEPs.

. . . .

III

Accordingly, we affirm the judgment of the district court in all respects.

PRATT, DISTRICT JUDGE, concurring in part and dissenting in part. [omitted]

NOTES AND QUESTIONS

1.   Other cases that find education programs inappropriate due to an absence of behavioral intervention services include *Goleta Union Elementary School District v. Ordway*, 35 IDELR 246 (C.D. Cal. 2001), and *Chris D. v. Montgomery County Board of Education*, 743 F. Supp. 1524 (D. Ala. 1990). *See generally* 34 C.F.R. § 300.324(a)(2)(i) ("The IEP team must — In the case of a child whose behavior impedes the child's learning or that of others, consider the use of positive behavioral interventions and supports, and other strategies, to address that behavior."). Some cases find that specific behavioral strategies adopted by school districts deprive children of appropriate education. *See, e.g., Waukee Cmty. Sch. Dist. v. Douglas L.*, 51 IDELR 15 (S.D. Iowa 2008) (finding that restraint and time-out interventions reinforced problem behavior).

2.   Can you frame an argument similar to that of the court's in the principal case based on the duty to provide education in the least restrictive environment?

3.   What kinds of behavioral strategies would be effective with a student like Robert? Are there reasons that the school district might be reluctant to use these strategies?

B.   DISABILITY DISCRIMINATION CHALLENGES TO DISCIPLINE

In contrast to positive behavioral intervention, much traditional school discipline consists of temporary or long-term exclusion from classes. Students with disabilities, particularly those with emotional disturbance or developmental disabilities, are prime candidates for committing infractions that lead to exclusion. Their educational opportunities will diminish if that form of discipline is imposed on them. It is hard to reconcile that result with the mandate that all children with disabilities receive an appropriate education, and with the requirement that federally assisted education programs not be administered so as to have a discriminatory impact on people with disabilities in the absence of educational necessity. Accordingly, courts developed a rule that forbids exclusion of a child from education when the behavior that led to the suspension or expulsion is a manifestation of the child's disability.

S-1 v. TURLINGTON
635 F.2d 342 (5th Cir. 1981)

The court affirmed the entry of a preliminary injunction, holding that plaintiffs, children not classified as seriously emotionally disturbed, prevailed on their claim that failure to provide hearings before expulsion as to whether their misconduct was a manifestation of their disability violated the special education and disability discrimination laws.

HATCHETT, CIRCUIT JUDGE.

In this appeal, we are called upon to decide whether nine handicapped students were denied their rights under the provisions of the Education for All Handicapped Children Act, 20 U.S.C. §§ 1401–1415, or section 504 of the Rehabilitation Act of 1973, codified at 29 U.S.C. § 794, and their implementing regulations. The trial court found a denial of rights and entered a preliminary injunction against the state and local officials. Defendants attack the trial court's entry of a preliminary injunction as an abuse of discretion. Because we find that the trial court did not abuse its discretion in entering the preliminary injunction, we affirm.

FACTS

Plaintiffs, S-1, S-2, S-3, S-4, S-5, S-6, and S-8, were expelled from Clewiston High School, Hendry County, Florida, in the early part of the 1977-78 school year for alleged misconduct.[2] Each was expelled for the remainder of the 1977-78 school year and for the entire 1978-79 school year, the maximum time permitted by state law. All of the plaintiffs were classified as either educable mentally retarded (EMR), mildly mentally retarded, or EMR/dull normal. It is undisputed that the expelled plaintiffs were accorded the procedural protections required by *Goss v. Lopez*, 419 U.S. 565 (1975). Except for S-1, they were not given, nor did they request, hearings to determine whether their misconduct was a manifestation of their handicap. Regarding S-1, the superintendent of Hendry County Schools determined that because S-1 was not classified as seriously emotionally disturbed, his misconduct, as a matter of law, could not be a manifestation of his handicap.

At all material times, plaintiffs S-7 and S-9 were not under expulsion orders. S-7

---

[2] [FN 1] The misconduct upon which the expulsions were based ranged from masturbation or sexual acts against fellow students to willful defiance of authority, insubordination, vandalism, and the use of profane language.

was not enrolled in high school by his own choice. In October, 1978, he requested a due process hearing to determine if he had been evaluated or if he had an individualized educational program. S-9 made a similar request in October, 1978. Shortly before her request, S-9's guardian had consented to the individualized educational program being offered her during that school year. The superintendent denied both students' requests, but offered to hold conferences in order to discuss the appropriateness of their individualized educational programs.

Plaintiffs initiated this case alleging violations of their rights under the Education for all Handicapped Children Act (EHA) and section 504 of the Rehabilitation Act of 1973. Plaintiffs sought preliminary and permanent injunctive relief compelling state and local officials to provide them with the educational services and procedural rights required by the EHA, section 504, and their implementing regulations.

TRIAL COURT DECISION

The trial court found that the EHA, effective in Florida on September 1, 1978, provided all handicapped children the right to a free and appropriate public education. The court further found that the expelled students were denied this right in violation of the EHA. In addition, the trial court decided that under section 504 and the EHA, no handicapped student could be expelled for misconduct related to the handicap. That in the case of S-2, S-3, S-4, S-5, S-6, and S-8, no determination was ever made of the relationship between their handicaps and their behavioral problems. With regard to S-1, the trial court found that the superintendent's determination was insufficient under section 504 and the EHA. The court reasoned that an expulsion is a change in educational placement. That under the educational placement procedures of section 504 and the EHA, only a trained and specialized group could make this decision. For these reasons, the trial court concluded that a likelihood of success on the merits had been shown with respect to the expelled plaintiffs.

With regard to S-7 and S-9, the trial court stated that under 20 U.S.C. § 1415(b)(1)(E), students and their parents or guardians must be provided "an opportunity to present complaints with respect to any matter relating to the identification, evaluation, or educational placement of the child, or the provision of a free appropriate education to such child." That under 20 U.S.C. § 1415(b)(2), "whenever such a complaint has been received, the parents or guardians shall have an opportunity for an impartial due process hearing." The trial court found that the superintendent's failure to grant S-7 and S-9 impartial due process hearings contravened the express provisions of the EHA. The court therefore concluded that S-7 and S-9 had shown a likelihood of success on the merits of their claim.

Finally, the trial court found that the plaintiffs had suffered irreparable harm in that two years of education had been irretrievably lost. The court further determined that an injunction was necessary to ensure that plaintiffs would be provided their rights, even though the expulsions had expired at the time the injunction was entered.

STATEMENT OF ISSUES

In an appeal from an order granting preliminary relief, the applicable standard of review is whether the issuance of the injunction, in light of the applicable standard, constitutes an abuse of discretion. Therefore, in order to decide whether the trial court abused its discretion in entering the preliminary injunction, we must resolve the following issues: (1) whether an expulsion is a change in educational placement thereby invoking the procedural protections of the EHA and section 504; (2) whether the EHA, section 504, and their implementing regulations contemplate a dual system of discipline for handicapped and non-handicapped students; (3) whether the burden of raising the question, whether a student's misconduct is a manifestation of the student's handicap, is on the state and local officials or on the student; (4) whether the EHA and its implementing regulations required the local defendants to grant S-7 and S-9 due process hearings; and, (5) whether the trial judge properly entered the preliminary injunction against the state defendants.

DISCUSSION

Section 504 of the Rehabilitation Act and the EHA have been the subject of infrequent litigation. No reported appellate cases deal with these acts and the issues presented in the instant case. Therefore, a review of these statutes and their pertinent regulations is necessary to the disposition of this controversy.

Section 504, effective in Florida four months prior to the expulsions in question, provides:

> No otherwise qualified handicapped individual in the United States, as defined in section 706(7) of this title, shall, solely by reason of his handicap, be excluded from the participation in, be denied the benefits of, or be subjected to discrimination under any program or activity receiving federal financial assistance. . . .

Under 29 U.S.C. § 706(7)(B), a handicapped individual is defined as "any person who (1) has a physical or mental impairment which substantially limits one or more of such person's major life activities. . . ."

Under the EHA, 20 U.S.C. § 1412(1) and (5)(B), effective in Florida on September 1, 1978, a state receiving financial assistance under this Act is required to provide all handicapped children a free and appropriate education in the least restrictive environment. The definition of handicapped children under the EHA is similar to the definition under section 504.

Florida, and the Hendry County School Board, are recipients of federal funds under both section 504 and the EHA. The children in this suit are clearly handicapped within the meaning of both section 504 and the EHA. The parties agree that a handicapped student may not be expelled for misconduct which results from the handicap itself. It follows that an expulsion must be accompanied by a determination as to whether the handicapped student's misconduct bears a relationship to his handicap. From a practical standpoint, this is the only logical approach. How else would a school board know whether it is violating section 504?

Defendant local officials argue that they complied with section 504. As support for their position, they state that they determined, in the expulsion proceedings, that the plaintiffs were capable of understanding rules and regulations or right from wrong. They also assert that they found, based upon a psychological evaluation, that plaintiffs' handicaps were not behavioral handicaps (as it would be if plaintiffs were classified as seriously emotionally disturbed), thereby precluding any relationship between the misconduct and the applicable handicap. We cannot agree that consideration of the above factors satisfies the requirement of section 504. A determination that a handicapped student knew the difference between right and wrong is not tantamount to a determination that his misconduct was or was not a manifestation of his handicap. The second prong of the school officials' argument is unacceptable. Essentially, what the school officials assert is that a handicapped student's misconduct can never be a symptom of his handicap, unless he is classified as seriously emotionally disturbed. With regard to this argument, the trial court stated:

> The defendants concede that a handicapped student cannot be expelled for misconduct which is a manifestation of the handicap itself. However, they would limit application of this principle to those students classified as "seriously emotionally disturbed." In the Court's view such a generalization is contrary to the emphasis which Congress has placed on individualized evaluation and consideration of the problems and needs of handicapped students.

We agree. In addition, the uncontradicted testimony elicited at the preliminary injunction hearing suggests otherwise. At the hearing, a psychologist testified that a connection between the misconduct upon which the expulsions were based and the plaintiffs' handicaps may have existed. She reasoned that "a child with low intellectual functions and perhaps the lessening of control would respond to stress or respond to a threat in the only way that they feel adequate, which may be verbal aggressive behavior." She further testified that an orthopedically handicapped child, whom she had consulted,

> [w]ould behave in an extremely aggressive way towards other children and provoke fights despite the fact that he was likely to come out very much on the short end of the stick. That this was his way of dealing with stress and dealing with a feeling of physical vulnerability. He would be both aggressive and hope that he would turn off people and as a result provoke an attack on him.

The record clearly belies the school officials' contention.

FIRST ISSUE

With regard to plaintiff S-1, the trial court found that the school officials entrusted with the expulsion decision determined at the disciplinary proceedings that S-1's misconduct was unrelated to his handicap. The trial court, however, held that this determination was made by school board officials who lacked the necessary expertise to make such a determination. The trial court arrived at this conclusion by holding that an expulsion is a change in educational placement. Under 45 CFR § 121a.533(a)(3) and 45 CFR § 84.35(c)(3), evaluations and placement decisions must be made by a specialized and knowledgeable group of persons.

The trial court's finding presents the novel issue in this circuit whether an expulsion is a change in educational placement, thereby invoking the procedural protections of both the EHA and section 504 of the Rehabilitation Act. In deciding this issue, the EHA and section 504, as remedial statutes, should be broadly applied and liberally construed in favor of providing a free and appropriate education to handicapped students.

The EHA, section 504, and their implementing regulations do not provide this court any direction on this issue. We find the reasoning of the district court in *Stuart v. Nappi*, 443 F. Supp. 1235 (D. Conn. 1978), persuasive. In *Stuart*, a child was diagnosed as having a major learning disability caused by either a brain disfunction or a perceptual disorder. She challenged the use of disciplinary proceedings which, if completed, would have resulted in her expulsion for participating in a schoolwide disturbance. The trial court held that the proposed expulsion constituted a change in educational placement, thus requiring the school officials to adhere to the procedural protections of the EHA. In so holding, the court stated:

> The right to an education in the least restrictive environment may be circumvented if schools are permitted to expel handicapped children [without following the procedures prescribed by the EHA]. . . . An expulsion has the effect not only of changing a student's placement, but also of restricting the availability of alternative placements. For example, plaintiff's expulsion may well exclude her from a placement that is appropriate for her academic and social development. This result flies in the face of the explicit mandate of the handicapped act which requires that all placement decisions be made in conformity with a child's right to an education in the least restrictive environment. (Citation omitted.)

443 F. Supp. at 1242–43.

We agree with the district court in *Stuart*, and therefore hold that a termination of educational services, occasioned by an expulsion, is a change in educational placement, thereby invoking the procedural protections of the EHA.

The proposition that an expulsion is a change in educational placement has been cited with approval in *Sherry v. New York State Education Department*, 479 F. Supp. 1328 (W.D.N.Y. 1979) (legally blind and deaf student that suffered from brain damage and emotional disorder which made her self abusive suspended because of insufficient staff to care for her), and *Doe v. Koger*, 480 F. Supp. 225 (N.D. Ind. 1979) (EHA case in which mildly mentally handicapped student was expelled for the remainder of school term for disciplinary reasons pursuant to the procedures provided for all Indiana public school disciplinary expulsions). As stated by the district court in *Doe v. Koger*, our holding that expulsion of a handicapped student constitutes a change in educational placement distinguishes the handicapped student in that, "unlike any other disruptive child, before a disruptive handicapped child can be expelled, it must be determined whether the handicap is the cause of the child's propensity to disrupt. This issue must be determined through the change of placement procedures required by the handicapped act." *Doe v. Koger*, 480 F. Supp. at 229.

SECOND ISSUE

The school officials point out that a group of persons entrusted with the educational placement decision could never decide that expulsion is the correct placement for a handicapped student, thus insulating a handicapped student from expulsion as a disciplinary tool. They further state that Florida law does not contemplate this result because expulsion is specifically provided for under Florida law as a disciplinary tool for all students. While the trial court declined to decide the issue whether a handicapped student can ever be expelled, we cannot ignore the gray areas that may result if we do not decide this question. We therefore find that expulsion is still a proper disciplinary tool under the EHA and section 504 when proper procedures are utilized and under proper circumstances. We cannot, however, authorize the complete cessation of educational services during an expulsion period.

THIRD ISSUE

State defendants focus their attention on the fact that, with the exception of S-1, none of the expelled plaintiffs raised the argument, until eleven months after expulsion, that they could not be expelled unless the proper persons determined that their handicap did not bear a causal connection to their misconduct. By this assertion, we assume that state defendants contend that the handicapped students waived their right to this determination. The issue is therefore squarely presented whether the burden of raising the question whether a student's misconduct is a manifestation of the student's handicap is on the state and local officials or on the student. The EHA, section 504, and their implementing regulations do not prescribe who must raise this issue. In light of the remedial purposes of these statutes, we find that the burden is on the local and state defendants to make this determination. Our conclusion is buttressed by the fact that in most cases, the handicapped students and their parents lack the wherewithal either to know or to assert their rights under the EHA and section 504.

FOURTH ISSUE

The next issue is whether the EHA and its implementing regulations required the local defendants to grant S-7 and S-9 due process hearings. The school officials suggest that because S-7 had voluntarily withdrawn from school, he was not entitled to a due process hearings. With regard to S-9, the school officials assert that because she had previously agreed to the educational program being offered her during the school year, she was not entitled to a due process hearing. They also suggest that the conference offered by the superintendent was an adequate substitute for the due process hearings. They cite 45 CFR § 121a.506 as support for their argument. Under this regulation, the Department of Health, Education and Welfare (HEW) [now Health and Human Services], states in a comment that mediation can be used to resolve differences between parents and agencies without the development of an adversarial relationship.

The Justice Department, as amicus curiae, and the trial court, point out that under 20 U.S.C. § 1415(b)(1), parents and guardians of handicapped children must have "an opportunity to present complaints with respect to *any matter* relating to the identification, evaluation, or educational placement of the child, or the provision of a free appropriate public education to such child." (Emphasis added.) The statute also states, in section 1415(b), that "whenever a complaint has been received under paragraph (1) of this subsection, the parents or guardian shall have an opportunity for an impartial due process hearing. . . ." No exception is made for handicapped students who voluntarily withdraw from school or previously agree to an educational placement. With regard to defendants' argument under 45 CFR § 121a.506, HEW states in the same comment that mediation may not be used to deny or delay a parent's rights under this subpart. In the circumstances, the trial judge correctly found that plaintiffs S-7 and S-9 were entitled to due process hearings.

FIFTH ISSUE

State defendants advance three arguments that deserve comment. First, they assert that the trial judge erred in analyzing section 504 in light of the Supreme Court's decision in *Southeastern Community College v. Davis*, 442 U.S. 397 (1979). In that case, the issue was whether section 504, which prohibits discrimination against an otherwise qualified handicapped individual enrolled in a federally funded program, solely by reason of his handicap, forbids professional schools from imposing physical qualifications for admission to their clinical training program. The Supreme Court held that section 504 did not forbid professional schools from imposing physical qualifications for admission. Without discussing *Southeastern* any further, it is clear that it does not apply to this case. Physical qualifications are not at issue in this case. Furthermore, we do not deal here with a professional school.

Secondly, state defendants argue that the trial court erred in imposing the EHA as a requirement at the time of the expulsions because the EHA was not effective in Florida until September 1, 1978. The trial court did not impose the EHA as a requirement at the time of the expulsion. The court found that the expelled plaintiffs became entitled to the protections of the EHA on September 1, 1978. As such, the expelled plaintiffs became entitled to a free and appropriate education in the least restrictive environment. In fact, under 20 U.S.C. § 1412(3), because plaintiffs were not receiving educational services on September 1, 1978, they fell within a special class of handicapped students entitled to priority regarding the provision of a free and appropriate education. The only way in which the expulsions could have continued as of September 1, 1978, is if a qualified group of individuals determined that no relationship existed between the plaintiffs' handicap and their misconduct. Furthermore, section 504, effective at the time of the expulsions, provides protections and procedures similar to those of the EHA. *See North v. District of Columbia Board of Education*, 471 F. Supp. 136 (D.D.C. 1979).

Finally, the state officials argue that the trial court improperly entered the injunction against them. They assert that they lacked the authority to intervene in the expulsion proceedings because disciplinary matters are exclusively local. While this argument may be true regarding non-handicapped students, it is inapplicable to handicapped students. Expulsion proceedings are of the type that may serve to deny an education to those entitled to it under the EHA. Under 20 U.S.C. § 1412(6), the state educational agency is:

> Responsible for assuring that the requirements of this sub-chapter be carried out and that all educational programs for handicapped children within the state, including all such programs administered by any other state or local agency, will be under the general supervision of the persons responsible for educational programs for handicapped children in the state educational agency and shall meet educational standards of the state educational agency.

Clearly, the state officials were empowered to intervene in the expulsion proceedings under 20 U.S.C. § 1412(6).

CONCLUSION

Accordingly, we hold that under the EHA, section 504, and their implementing regulations: (1) before a handicapped student can be expelled, a trained and knowledgeable group of persons must determine whether the student's misconduct bears a relationship to his handicapping condition; (2) an expulsion is a change in educational placement thereby invoking the procedural protections of the EHA and section 504; (3) expulsion is a proper disciplinary tool under the EHA and section 504, but a complete cessation of educational services is not; (4) S-7 and S-9 were entitled to due process hearings; and, (5) the trial judge properly entered the preliminary injunction against the state defendants. In the circumstances, the trial judge did not abuse his discretion in entering the injunction.

AFFIRMED.

NOTES AND QUESTIONS

1.   Should the defendants have conceded that a student with a disability may not be expelled for misconduct that results from the disability? Is it discrimination to expel a student with a disability for conduct that would get a nondisabled student expelled? Isn't it simply equal treatment? Why?

2.   Much of *S-1* was codified, in modified form, in the Individuals with Disabilities Education Act Amendments of 1997, and then modified further in the 2004 IDEA Reauthorization. *See generally infra* Section D. The codification, however, covers only children who are eligible for services under IDEA. *S-1* also interpreted section 504 to require extensive protections. Given the 2008 amendment to the ADA broadening the coverage of section 504 (*see* Chapter 2, *supra*, discussing ADA Amendments Act of 2008), would a large category of children not eligible for services under IDEA but covered by section 504 now be entitled to manifestation review and due process-hearing rights with regard to significant disciplinary measures?

3.   Can involvement in drug dealing at school be the manifestation of a child's disability? *See School Bd. v. Malone*, 762 F.2d 1210 (4th Cir. 1985) (affirming conclusion that child's role as go-between in drug transaction stemmed from

susceptibility to peer pressure related to loss of self image due to learning disability).

4. Court decisions show a diversity of results on whether particular conduct is the manifestation of a child's disability. *Compare Randy M. v. Texas City ISD*, 93 F. Supp. 2d 1310 (S.D. Tex. 2000) (upholding determination that assault was not manifestation of disability), *with Jonathan G. v. Caddo Parish Sch. Bd.*, 875 F. Supp. 352 (W.D. La. 1994) (finding that disability led to acts of aggression).

5. Explain the decision you would reach in the following case: A child has an autoimmune disease that makes her susceptible to fatal bleeding even from a minor cut. She cuts herself accidentally in art class and, very upset, shouts several choice expletives. The school then tries to discipline her for using foul language, but she defends on the ground that she is being disciplined for conduct related to her disability. *See generally Thomas v. Davidson Acad.*, 846 F. Supp. 611 (M.D. Tenn. 1994) (entering preliminary injunction under section 504 and ADA to overturn exclusion from private school receiving federal funds).

C. PROCEDURAL CHALLENGES TO DISCIPLINE

The Individuals with Disabilities Education Act provides for impartial due process hearings to resolve disputes over issues of free, appropriate public education, and further establishes that, in general, "during the pendency of any proceedings . . . , unless the State or local educational agency and the parents otherwise agree, the child shall remain in the then-current educational placement of the child, . . . until all such proceedings shall have been completed." 20 U.S.C. § 1415(j). If parents dispute a disciplinary measure that amounts to a change in the child's educational placement, invocation of the maintenance of placement provision would stop the discipline in its tracks until the due process hearing and all appeals are over. Some courts resisted that interpretation, but the Supreme Court endorsed it in *Honig v. Doe*.

HONIG v. DOE
484 U.S. 305 (1988)

The court ruled that when a due process hearing is requested to challenge discipline that amounts to a change of a child's placement, the school must maintain the child in the current placement until the conclusion of all proceedings.

[The opinion in this case is reproduced in Chapter 1 (Core Concepts), *supra*.]

NOTES AND QUESTIONS

1. Do you agree that Congress wanted parents to be able to shunt disciplinary disputes into the due process procedure and halt the implementation of long-term suspensions or expulsions until all proceedings are completed? How should a court interpret provisions in a statute when it is not clear what individual members of Congress were thinking about when they voted for them, or whether the members of Congress were thinking about them at all?

2. In 1997, in response to expressions of concern from school personnel, Congress modified the maintenance of placement provision for cases involving drugs and weapons and for children who demonstrate dangerousness to themselves or others. These provisions were further amended in 2004 to provide special treatment when a student inflicts serious bodily injury on another person. Other changes have also been made. *See generally infra* Section D. Given the increasing concern about potentially violent students, are these changes appropriate? Are they adequate?

3. In *Goss v. Lopez*, cited in the principal case, the Supreme Court ruled that the Fourteenth Amendment's due process clause required school authorities to afford some kind of notice and hearing to a child facing a suspension of ten days for violating school rules. Can you construct an argument for the proposition that a child has a constitutional right to remain in her current educational placement until the completion of a full hearing in a case involving long-term suspension or expulsion? *Compare Goldberg v. Kelly*, 397 U.S. 254 (1970) (holding that failure to afford pre-cutoff hearing to welfare recipient violates due process), *with Ingraham v. Wright*, 430 U.S. 651 (1977) (holding that school authorities need not afford hearing rights before imposition of reasonable corporal punishment when post-punishment common law remedies exist for abuse).

4. School districts have followed *Honig*'s suggestion that they go to court, bypassing administrative procedures, to obtain injunctions to keep genuinely dangerous children out of school settings where they may harm others. In *Light v. Parkway C-2 Sch. Dist.*, 41 F.3d 1223 (8th Cir. 1994), the court issued an injunction permitting the school to place a child who had been violent in a self-contained special education program. The court applied a test that asked (1) if the child is substantially likely to cause injury, and (2) if the school district had done all it reasonably could to reduce the risk of the child causing injury. Courts have diverged on how dangerous the child needs to be before injunctive relief is justified. *Compare School Dist. v. Stephan M.*, 1997 U.S. Dist. LEXIS 2059, Case No. 97-1154 (E.D. Pa. Feb. 27, 1997) (denying injunction when student used razor to cut other student who had exposed himself and attempted to fondle her), *with Roslyn Union Free School Dist. v. Geffrey W.*, 740 N.Y.S.2d 451 (App. Div. 2002) (imposing home program placement when child ran from school near highway and hit people with papers and folders). Would an injunction have been justified in the cases of John Doe and Jack Smith? If so, what should the terms of the injunctive relief have been?

D. THE CURRENT CODIFICATION

In 1997 and again in 2004, Congress modified the maintenance of placement provision to codify *Honig* in part and to provide more generally for "placement in an appropriate interim alternative educational setting" under a variety of circumstances. 20 U.S.C. § 1415(k). Effectively, these amendments work significant change to the law articulated in *Honig* while at the same time maintaining most of the case's key principles. Subsection (k) may be analyzed by looking first at the general provisions and those relating to manifestation review, second at provisions for children not yet identified as children with disabilities, third at special provisions in the statute relating to drugs, weapons, and serious bodily injury, and fourth at requirements for interim alternative educational settings, appeals, and placement during appeals.

1.   General Provisions and Manifestation Review

The applicable federal regulation, which is substantially identical to the statute, embodies the principle from *Honig* that children with disabilities should not be cut off from educational services for any lengthy period of time:

(b) General.

(1) School personnel under this section may remove a child with a disability who violates a code of student conduct from his or her current placement to an appropriate interim alternative educational setting, another setting, or suspension, for not more than 10 consecutive school days (to the extent those alternatives are applied to children without disabilities), and for additional removals of not more than 10 consecutive school days in that same school year for separate incidents of misconduct (as long as those removals do not constitute a change of placement under § 300.536).

(2) After a child with a disability has been removed from his or her current placement for 10 school days in the same school year, during any subsequent days of removal the public agency must provide services to the extent required under paragraph (d) of this section.

(c) Additional authority. For disciplinary changes in placement that would exceed 10 consecutive school days, if the behavior that gave rise to the violation of the school code is determined not to be a manifestation of the child's disability pursuant to paragraph (e) of this section, school personnel may apply the relevant disciplinary procedures to children with disabilities in the same manner and for the same duration as the procedures would be applied to children without disabilities, except as provided in paragraph (d) of this section.

(d) Services.

(1) A child with a disability who is removed from the child's current placement pursuant to paragraphs (c), or (g) of this section must —

(i) Continue to receive educational services, as provided in § 300.101(a), so as to enable the child to continue to participate in the general education curriculum, although in another setting, and to progress toward meeting the goals set out in the child's IEP; and

(ii) Receive, as appropriate, a functional behavioral assessment, and behavioral intervention services and modifications, that are designed to address the behavior violation so that it does not recur.

(2) The services required by paragraph (d)(1), (d)(3), (d)(4), and (d)(5) of this section may be provided in an interim alternative educational setting.

(3) A public agency is only required to provide services during periods of removal to a child with a disability who has been removed from his or her current placement for 10 school days or less in that school year, if it provides services to a child without disabilities who is similarly removed.

(4) After a child with a disability has been removed from his or her current placement for 10 school days in the same school year, if the current removal is for not more than 10 consecutive school days and is not a change of placement under § 300.536, school personnel, in consultation with at least one of the child's teachers, determine the extent to which services are needed, as provided in § 300.101(a), so as to enable the child to continue to participate in the general education curriculum, although in another setting, and to progress toward meeting the goals set out in the child's IEP.

(5) If the removal is a change of placement under § 300.536, the child's IEP Team determines appropriate services under paragraph (d)(1) of this section.

34 C.F.R. § 300.530.

IDEA also codifies the concept expressed in *S-1* that children should not be suspended or expelled for conduct related to their disabilities. In fact, it extends the concept by grafting onto it additional procedural and definitional requirements. Whenever the district proposes to change a child's placement because of a violation of student conduct rules, no later than ten school days after the decision to take action, the IEP team and other qualified personnel must meet to review the relationship between the child's disability and the misbehavior. 20 U.S.C. § 1415(k)(1)(E). The regulation, largely tracking the statute, states:

(e) Manifestation determination.

(1) Within 10 school days of any decision to change the placement of a child with a disability because of a violation of a code of student conduct, the LEA, the parent, and relevant members of the child's IEP Team (as determined by the parent and the LEA) must review all relevant information in the student's file, including the child's IEP, any teacher observations, and any relevant information provided by the parents to determine —

(i) If the conduct in question was caused by, or had a direct and substantial relationship to, the child's disability; or

(ii) If the conduct in question was the direct result of the LEA's failure to implement the IEP.

(2) The conduct must be determined to be a manifestation of the child's disability if the LEA, the parent, and relevant members of the child's IEP Team determine that a condition in either paragraph (e)(1)(i) or (1)(ii) of this section was met.

(3) If the LEA, the parent, and relevant members of the child's IEP Team determine the condition described in paragraph (e)(1)(ii) of this

section was met, the LEA must take immediate steps to remedy those deficiencies.

(f) Determination that behavior was a manifestation. If the LEA, the parent, and relevant members of the IEP Team make the determination that the conduct was a manifestation of the child's disability, the IEP Team must —

(1) Either —

(i) Conduct a functional behavioral assessment, unless the LEA had conducted a functional behavioral assessment before the behavior that resulted in the change of placement occurred, and implement a behavioral intervention plan for the child; or

(ii) If a behavioral intervention plan already has been developed, review the behavioral intervention plan, and modify it, as necessary, to address the behavior; and

(2) Except as provided in paragraph (g) of this section, return the child to the placement from which the child was removed, unless the parent and the LEA agree to a change of placement as part of the modification of the behavioral intervention plan.

34 C.F.R. § 300.530.

The district does not have the option to discontinue services altogether, even if the child with a disability engaged in misconduct not related to the disability, and a child without a disability would be expelled without services for the same misconduct. 20 U.S.C. § 1412(a)(1)(A) (guaranteeing a free, appropriate education to all children with disabilities "including children with disabilities who have been suspended or expelled from school"); 34 C.F.R. § 300.530(d).

NOTES AND QUESTIONS

1. Apart from the provisions on appropriate education in general and on IEP considerations in specific, 34 C.F.R. § 300.530(d) and (f) and their statutory sources are the clearest bases in the law for a child's entitlement to a behavioral intervention plan. Does the regulation change your understanding of the behavior intervention requirements discussed in Section A of this chapter?

2. Are there practical difficulties in assembling the group needed to conduct the manifestation review and getting them the information they need? Are there district policies you might propose to solve any problems of this type?

3. Is *School Board v. Malone*, the drug distribution case discussed above after *Honig*, still good law under the present codification? How should a manifestation review meeting analyze the situation of a child with a learning disability that leads to him being taunted and consequently developing low self-esteem, inducing him to try to raise his social prestige by participating in a drug distribution transaction? Does the view that such taunting and low self esteem may lead to violent behavior affect your analysis?

4.   The regulation that governs the disciplinary removal provisions generally states that a change in placement occurs when a removal is for more than ten consecutive school days, or when:

The child has been subjected to a series of removals that constitute a pattern —

(i) Because the series of removals total more than 10 school days in a school year;

(ii) Because the child's behavior is substantially similar to the child's behavior in previous incidents that resulted in the series of removals; and

(iii) Because of such additional factors as the length of each removal, the total amount of time the child has been removed, and the proximity of the removals to one another.

34 C.F.R. § 300.536(a). The determination is to be made on a case-by-case basis, and is subject to due process and judicial review. The open-endedness of previous regulatory language has led to conflicting results in similar cases. *Compare Joshua S. v. School Bd.*, 37 IDELR 218 (S.D. Fla. 2002) (finding no change of placement despite suspensions of 26 days in one school year), *with Goleta Union Elementary School Dist. v. Ordway*, 35 IDELR 246 (C.D. Cal. 2001) (affirming hearing officer decision that suspensions totaling more than ten days in year constituted change of placement). Would a more rigid rule, such as one stating that ten days' cumulative suspension in a school year is always a change of placement, be preferable? The current regulation provides that if the child has been removed for ten school days in the same year (irrespective of whether there is deemed to be a change of placement) continuing services must be provided. 34 C.F.R. § 300.530(b)(2). This provision may diminish the importance of the issue, but disputes may still exist whether, for example, an offer of homebound tutoring services is sufficient. *See M.M. v. Special Sch. Dist. No. 1*, 512 F.3d 455, 464–65 (8th Cir. 2008) (finding no liability when school district offered homebound services and parents rejected offer).

5.   Many schools have adopted "zero-tolerance" policies, in which school authorities automatically suspend or expel children who commit specified infractions. *See, e.g., S.G. v. Sayreville Bd. of Educ.*, 333 F.3d 417 (3d Cir. 2003) (finding no violation of constitutional rights in suspension of five-year-old in general education who, while playing cops and robbers on the playground, said "I'm going to shoot you"). Do you agree with the use of zero-tolerance policies? Why are school administrators drawn to adopt them? How do zero-tolerance policies relate to special education discipline? In what seems to be a slap at zero-tolerance, the 2004 IDEA Reauthorization contains a provision requiring a case-by-case approach to changes of placement for disciplinary reasons. 20 U.S.C. § 1415(k)(1)(A).

6.   Even apart from the operation of zero-tolerance policies, has the existence of procedural protections for discipline of children with disabilities led to an unfair double standard in treatment of schoolchildren with and without disabilities who violate rules? How does this difference play out among parents and in the community? The disparity seems particularly acute in that schools can terminate services entirely for children who do not have disabilities, but cannot do so for

children with disabilities even when their misconduct is not a manifestation of the disability. *See* Anne Proffitt Dupre, *A Study in Double Standards, Discipline, and the Disabled Student*, 75 WASH. L. REV. 1 (2000) (criticizing current law). Could it be that the rules permitting complete termination of services for non-disabled students are misguided? For a thoughtful discussion of the discipline provisions in IDEA 1997, see Terry Jean Seligmann, *Not as Simple as ABC: Disciplining Children with Disabilities Under the 1997 IDEA Amendments*, 42 ARIZ. L. REV. 77 (2000).

2.   Children not Yet Classified as Children with Disabilities

It is entirely possible that a child who has not been designated by the school district as a child with disabilities could have disabilities that lead to misconduct. In fact, the first indication of behavioral and some other disabilities may be actions that violate school rules. IDEA allows children not previously determined to be eligible for special education to claim the protections of the Act if the school district had knowledge that the child was a child with a disability before the behavior that led to the disciplinary action. The regulation, building on the statute, explains the rules for determining when the district has knowledge, and what happens if a request for evaluation is made in an instance in which the district does not have knowledge:

> Protections for children not determined eligible for special education and related services
>
> (a) General. A child who has not been determined to be eligible for special education and related services under this part and who has engaged in behavior that violated a code of student conduct, may assert any of the protections provided for in this part if the public agency had knowledge (as determined in accordance with paragraph (b) of this section) that the child was a child with a disability before the behavior that precipitated the disciplinary action occurred.
>
> (b) Basis of knowledge. A public agency must be deemed to have knowledge that a child is a child with a disability if before the behavior that precipitated the disciplinary action occurred —
>
>> (1) The parent of the child expressed concern in writing to supervisory or administrative personnel of the appropriate educational agency, or a teacher of the child, that the child is in need of special education and related services;
>>
>> (2) The parent of the child requested an evaluation of the child pursuant to §§ 300.300 through 300.311; or
>>
>> (3) The teacher of the child, or other personnel of the LEA, expressed specific concerns about a pattern of behavior demonstrated by the child directly to the director of special education of the agency or to other supervisory personnel of the agency.
>
> (c) Exception. A public agency would not be deemed to have knowledge under paragraph (b) of this section if —

(1) The parent of the child —

(i) Has not allowed an evaluation of the child pursuant to §§ 300.300 through 300.311; or

(ii) Has refused services under this part; or

(2) The child has been evaluated in accordance with §§ 300.300 through 300.311 and determined to not be a child with a disability under this part.

(d) Conditions that apply if no basis of knowledge.

(1) If a public agency does not have knowledge that a child is a child with a disability (in accordance with paragraphs (b) and (c) of this section) prior to taking disciplinary measures against the child, the child may be subjected to the disciplinary measures applied to children without disabilities who engage in comparable behaviors consistent with paragraph (d)(2) of this section.

(2)(i) If a request is made for an evaluation of a child during the time period in which the child is subjected to disciplinary measures under § 300.530, the evaluation must be conducted in an expedited manner.

(ii) Until the evaluation is completed, the child remains in the educational placement determined by school authorities, which can include suspension or expulsion without educational services.

(iii) If the child is determined to be a child with a disability, taking into consideration information from the evaluation conducted by the agency and information provided by the parents, the agency must provide special education and related services in accordance with this part, including the requirements of §§ 300.530 through 300.536 and section 612(a)(1)(A) of the Act.

34 C.F.R. § 300.534. The 2004 IDEA Reauthorization amended the previous provision on this subject, and provided that the behavior or performance of the child is not sufficient, standing alone, to provide a basis for deeming knowledge on the part of the school.

NOTES AND QUESTIONS

1. Assume that you are advising a school district. What rules or procedures should it follow to reduce or eliminate the likelihood that a student could successfully claim that the district had knowledge that he or she had a disability and so cannot proceed with discipline except under the IDEA provisions?

2. The case law under the basis-of-knowledge provision remains sparse, but in one prominent case, the court ruled that the general education placement of a not-previously-eligible child had to be maintained during the pendency of expulsion proceedings for drug distribution. According to the allegations in the case, the school district personnel knew the child at one time took medication for attention deficit disorder, they knew that the child failed all of her courses in the preceding

year, and the child's teachers had met among themselves regarding her academic problems. *S.W. v. Holbrook Pub. Schs*, 221 F. Supp. 2d 222, 37 IDELR 216 (D. Mass. 2002). Some cases tend in the opposite direction. *See Mr. & Mrs. R. v. West Haven Bd. of Educ.*, 36 IDELR 211 (D. Conn. 2002) (holding that district did not have knowledge child had disability); *Long v. Board of Educ.*, 34 IDELR 232 (N.D. Ill. 2001) (finding no basis for knowledge of disability). These cases, of course, interpret the pre-2004 provision, which was somewhat laxer concerning the basis for deeming knowledge to the school district.

3. Drugs, Weapons, and Serious Bodily Injury

The present law allows school authorities to remove a child with a disability from the child's current placement and place the child in an interim alternative educational setting for no longer than 45 days, if the child with a disability does any of three things at school, on school premises, or at a school function: carries or possesses a weapon; knowingly possesses or uses illegal drugs or sells or solicits the sale of a controlled substance; or inflicts serious bodily injury upon another person. 20 U.S.C. § 1415(k)(1)(G). This removal may take place irrespective of whether the conduct was a manifestation of the disability. "Weapon," "controlled substance," and "serious bodily injury" are defined in accordance with other federal statutes. A child removed from the current placement on the basis of drugs, weapons, or serious bodily injury is to continue to receive educational services so as to keep participating in the general education curriculum and progressing toward meeting the goals in the child's IEP, and is to receive, as appropriate, a functional behavioral assessment and behavioral intervention services and modifications that are designed to address the behavior violation so that it does not recur. 20 U.S.C. § 1415(k)(1)(D).

NOTES AND QUESTIONS

1. The weapons provision incorporates by reference a definition found in the federal criminal statutes:

> The term "dangerous weapon" means a weapon, device, instrument, material or substance, animate or inanimate, that is used for or readily capable of causing death or serious injury, except that such term does not include a pocket knife with a blade of less than 21/2 inches in length.

18 U.S.C. § 930(g)(2). Could this statute cover, say, a plastic knife? A pencil? A pet? Does the exception for small pocket knives present an unreasonable risk for those who might be the victims of students armed with pocket knives? What could be the justification for the exception?

2. Removal on the basis of weapons, drugs, or serious bodily injury apparently triggers manifestation review, even though the provision allows for placement in the interim alternative educational setting for up to 45 days for behavior that is a manifestation of disability. What should be the remedy if the school fails to make the manifestation review under these circumstances? *See A.P. & M.S. v. Pemberton Twp. Bd. of Educ.*, No. 05-3780, 2006 U.S. Dist. LEXIS 32542 (D.N.J. May 15, 2006) (ruling that when child was suspended for 20 days without timely manifestation

conference on account of smoking marijuana at school, administrative law judge order requiring immediate return to school was improper, because child could be suspended up to 45 days without regard to whether behavior was manifestation of disability).

4.   Interim Alternative Educational Setting Requirements, Appeals, and Placement During Review Proceedings

Placement in an interim alternative educational setting is not supposed to be the end of free, appropriate public education, though it may lead to modification of the services that the child previously received. The regulation, again tracking the statute, provides that the child must "(i) [c]ontinue to receive educational services . . . so as to enable the child to continue to participate in the general education curriculum, although in another setting, and to progress toward meeting the goals set out in the child's IEP; and (ii) [r]eceive, as appropriate, a functional behavioral assessment, and behavioral intervention services and modifications, that are designed to address the behavior violation so that it does not recur." 34 C.F.R. § 300.530(d). The child's IEP team determines the interim alternative educational setting. 34 C.F.R. § 300.531.

Decisions about removal of a child, or denial of manifestation may be appealed. The regulation provides:

(a) General. The parent of a child with a disability who disagrees with any decision regarding placement under §§ 300.530 and 300.531, or the manifestation determination under § 300.530(e), or an LEA that believes that maintaining the current placement of the child is substantially likely to result in injury to the child or others, may appeal the decision by requesting a hearing. The hearing is requested by filing a complaint pursuant to §§ 300.507 and 300.508(a) and (b).

(b) Authority of hearing officer.

(1) A hearing officer under § 300.511 hears, and makes a determination regarding an appeal under paragraph (a) of this section.

(2) In making the determination under paragraph (b)(1) of this section, the hearing officer may —

(i) Return the child with a disability to the placement from which the child was removed if the hearing officer determines that the removal was a violation of § 300.530 or that the child's behavior was a manifestation of the child's disability; or

(ii) Order a change of placement of the child with a disability to an appropriate interim alternative educational setting for not more than 45 school days if the hearing officer determines that maintaining the current placement of the child is substantially likely to result in injury to the child or to others.

(3) The procedures under paragraphs (a) and (b)(1) and (2) of this section may be repeated, if the LEA believes that returning the child to

the original placement is substantially likely to result in injury to the child or to others.

(c) Expedited due process hearing.

(1) Whenever a hearing is requested under paragraph (a) of this section, the parents or the LEA involved in the dispute must have an opportunity for an impartial due process hearing consistent with the requirements of §§ 300.507 and 300.508(a) through (c) and §§ 300.510 through 300.514, except as provided in paragraph (c)(2) through (4) of this section.

(2) The SEA or LEA is responsible for arranging the expedited due process hearing, which must occur within 20 school days of the date the complaint requesting the hearing is filed. The hearing officer must make a determination within 10 school days after the hearing.

(3) Unless the parents and LEA agree in writing to waive the resolution meeting described in paragraph (c)(3)(i) of this section, or agree to use the mediation process described in § 300.506 —

(i) A resolution meeting must occur within seven days of receiving notice of the due process complaint; and

(ii) The due process hearing may proceed unless the matter has been resolved to the satisfaction of both parties within 15 days of the receipt of the due process complaint.

(4) A State may establish different State-imposed procedural rules for expedited due process hearings conducted under this section than it has established for other due process hearings, but, except for the timelines as modified in paragraph (c)(3) of this section, the State must ensure that the requirements in §§ 300.510 through 300.514 are met.

(5) The decisions on expedited due process hearings are appealable consistent with § 300.514.

34 C.F.R. § 300.532.

Honig's central holding that a child is to remain in the current educational placement during due process and judicial proceedings on the child's removal for disciplinary reasons is modified in a very specific way by IDEA's current codification. The regulation, adhering to the statutory provision, states:

Placement during appeals.

When an appeal under § 300.532 has been made by either the parent or the LEA, the child must remain in the interim alternative educational setting pending the decision of the hearing officer or until the expiration of the time period specified in § 300.530(c) or (g), whichever occurs first, unless the parent and the SEA or LEA agree otherwise.

34 C.F.R. § 300.533.

NOTES AND QUESTIONS

1. *In General.* What should an interim alternative educational setting look like? At the high school level, is it likely that school districts will simply shunt students into existing alternative high school programs? Or offer only homebound services? Are those courses of action consistent with the underlying goals of IDEA?

2. *Placement on Appeal.* Was it a wise decision by Congress to have children stay in the interim alternative educational setting rather than being returned to their previous placements during the pendency of appeals? Can you imagine the reasons Congress acted as it did? Will the expedited hearing provisions adequately protect children's interests?

3. *Continuing Removal.* At the conclusion of the 45 days or shorter removal period, the child's current educational placement reverts to what it was before removal. If, however, the district believes that the child is dangerous, it may propose a change in the child's placement and use expedited hearing procedures to obtain successive interim alternative educational setting periods of 45 days during the pendency of due process proceedings over the disciplinary decision. 34 C.F.R. § 300.532; *see* Notice of Proposed Rulemaking, 70 Fed. Reg. 35782, 35811 (June 21, 2005) ("We . . . clarify that in appropriate circumstances, a school district could seek a subsequent hearing to continue a child in an interim alternative educational placement if the school district believes that the child would be dangerous if returned to his or her original placement at the end of a removal that was based on a determination that maintaining the child's regular placement was substantially likely to result in injury to the child or others."). Is this provision sufficiently protective of the child's interests? Sufficiently protective of the school's safety?

4. *Corporal Punishment.* IDEA does not by its own terms prohibit corporal punishment, though the punishment may violate the terms of a child's IEP or otherwise constitute inappropriate education. *Cf. Chris D. v. Montgomery County Bd. of Educ.*, 743 F. Supp. 1524 (M.D. Ala. 1990) (finding that reaction of child to severe paddling by principal supported parents' proposal for child's educational placement). Excessive corporal punishment constitutes a denial of substantive due process, and so supports a damages claim under 42 U.S.C. § 1983. *E.g., Waechter v. School Dist. No. 14-030*, 773 F. Supp. 1005 (W.D. Mich. 1991) (denying motion to dismiss damages action based on death of child with heart defect made to run sprint as punishment for talking in line). Courts have found violations of the Fourth Amendment for the use of some punishments. *See Doe v. Hawaii Dep't of Educ.*, 334 F.3d 906 (9th Cir. 2003) (affirming denial of qualified immunity defense in case over vice-principal's taping of child's head to tree). Excessive punishment of children with disabilities may violate constitutional provisions or violate statutory provisions that protect against disability harassment, or do both. *See, e.g., Witte v. Clark County Sch. Dist.*, 197 F.3d 1271 (9th Cir. 1999) (allowing section 504 and ADA claim to proceed in case of child with multiple disabilities who was force-fed, choked, deprived of meals, and made to write "I will not tic"). *See generally* Mark C. Weber, *Disability Harassment in the Public Schools*, 43 Wm. & Mary L. Rev. 1079 (2002) (detailing causes of action and defenses for disability harassment).

5. *Calling the Police.* IDEA states that it does not prohibit a state or local educational agency from reporting crimes committed by children with disabilities to

appropriate authorities, though the district is supposed to transmit copies of the special education and disciplinary records of the child to the authorities to whom the crime is reported. 20 U.S.C. § 1415(k)(7). Although a court has ruled that before a school district files a petition in juvenile court against a child with a disability, it must afford special education procedural safeguards applicable to suspension or expulsion, *Morgan v. Chris L.*, 927 F. Supp. 267 (E.D. Tenn. 1994), *aff'd*, 106 F.3d 401 (6th Cir. 1997), other courts have disagreed with that interpretation, *In re Beau II*, 738 N.E.2d 1167 (N.Y. 2000), or found it superseded by the 1997 Amendments to IDEA, *Joseph M. v. Southeast Delco Sch. Dist.*, 2001 U.S. Dist. LEXIS 2994, Case No. 99-4645 (E.D. Pa. March 19, 2001). Nevertheless, claims may lie for Fourth Amendment violations, or for common law false imprisonment or defamation, if school authorities conspire with police to arrest a child without probable cause, or if the school officials give false information to the police to induce an arrest. *See* MICHAEL AVERY ET AL., POLICE MISCONDUCT LAW AND LITIGATION § 2.3 (3d ed. 2002). If a school district makes criminal complaints disproportionately against children with disabilities, does that constitute disability discrimination? *See Student with a Disability v. School Bd.*, 31 IDELR 209 (S.D. Fla. 1999) (denying motion to dismiss action based on section 504 and ADA alleging disproportionate criminal referrals of children with disabilities; rejecting claim based on violation of duty to provide reasonable accommodations to children with disabilities).

5.   Seclusion and Restraint

Significant criticism has been directed at schools' use of restraint and seclusion as methods of controlling student behavior due to hundreds of instances in which children have been severely injured or killed and persistent doubts about whether the practices are necessary or effective. *See, e.g.,* SCOTT F. JOHNSON, PREVENTING PHYSICAL RESTRAINTS IN SCHOOLS: A GUIDE FOR PARENTS, EDUCATORS, AND PROFESSIONALS (2004); National Disability Rights Network, *School is Not Supposed to Hurt: Investigative Report on Abusive Restraint and Seclusion in Schools* (Jan. 2009), http://www.napas.org/sr/SR-Report.pdf. Parents have challenged seclusion and restraint as violations of the Constitution or the ADA and section 504, with mixed results. *Compare C.N. v. Willmar Pub. Schs.*, 591 F.3d 624 (8th Cir. 2010) (dismissing complaint alleging that use of seclusion and restraint violated Fourth Amendment and substantive due process), *with Padilla v. School Dist. No. 1*, 233 F.3d 1268 (10th Cir. 2000) (affirming denial of motion to dismiss ADA claims for prolonged restraint in stroller in windowless room), *and Witte v. Clark County Sch. Dist.*, 197 F.3d 1271 (9th Cir. 1999) (overturning dismissal of section 504 and ADA claims for force-feeding and physical restraint), *See generally* Chapter 10, *infra* (discussing assertion of claims by children with disabilities against school districts and officials for violations of Constitution, section 504, and ADA).

As of the time of this writing (late March, 2010), the House of Representatives had passed and sent to the Senate H.R. 4247, which:

> Directs the Secretary of Education to establish minimum standards that:
> (1) prohibit elementary and secondary school personnel from managing any
> student by using any mechanical or chemical restraint, physical restraint or
> escort that restricts breathing, or aversive behavioral intervention that

compromises student health and safety; (2) prohibit such personnel from using physical restraint or seclusion, unless such measures are required to eliminate an imminent danger of physical injury to the student or others and certain precautions are taken; (3) require states to ensure that a sufficient number of school personnel receive state-approved crisis intervention training and certification in first aid and certain safe and effective student management techniques; (4) prohibit physical restraint or seclusion from being written into a student's education plan, individual safety plan, behavioral plan, or individual education program as a planned intervention; and (5) require schools to establish procedures to notify parents in a timely manner if physical restraint or seclusion is imposed on their child.

Congressional Research Service Summary of H.R. 4247 (Mar. 2, 2010),

> http://thomas.loc.gov/cgi-bin/bdquery/D?d111:2:./temp/
> ~bd7E6r:@@@D&summ2=m&|/bss/111search.html|

The House Committee Report on the bill (H.R. Rep. No. 111-417 (2010) may be found at

> http://frwebgate.access.gpo.gov/cgi-bin/
> getdoc.cgi?dbname=111_cong_reports&docid=f:hr417.111.pdf

NOTES AND QUESTIONS

1. Would adoption of the bill be a good idea? Should the legislation apply to private as well as public schools? What are the alternatives to seclusion and restraint?

2. What would a state or school district policy on the proper use of seclusion and restraint look like?

Chapter 10

COURT PROCEEDINGS

A. PROCEEDINGS UNDER SECTION 1415

Any party to a due process hearing dispute that is aggrieved by the final administrative decision may challenge the decision in court under 20 U.S.C. § 1415. In some special education disputes, the plaintiffs bring (or add) other claims, such as those provided by the Americans with Disabilities Act or section 504 of the Rehabilitation Act of 1973. They may also assert claims under the United States Constitution, using the civil rights cause-of-action statute, 42 U.S.C. § 1983. Some courts have also permitted plaintiffs to make claims to enforce the terms of the Individuals with Disabilities Education Act brought pursuant to § 1983, opening up the possibility of greater remedies than those most courts have found available under § 1415. After some preliminary discussion, this section will focus on two issues with regard to the § 1415 cause of action: evidentiary proceedings and remedies.

NOTES AND QUESTIONS

1.   As a matter of policy, even if the opportunity for a due process hearing is desirable, is it wise to create the right to go to court to challenge an individualized education program or a placement decision? Is this question made any easier by the fact that both the school district and the parent have the same rights to go to court?

2.   Administrative law writers frequently talk of "capture" of administrative agency decision making by repeat players — typically members of whatever industry or group of governmental entities the agency regulates. *E.g.*, Abram Chayes, *The Role of the Judge in Public Law Litigation*, 89 HARV. L. REV. 1281, 1310 (1976). Is the option of going to court a safeguard against the risk that the due process hearing procedure may be captured by the school systems and their allies? How would you use or respond to this idea of capture to construct an argument to Congress for or against the provision of the right to go to court in special education cases?

3.   *Jurisdiction.* Section 1415 provides specifically that the action may be brought in state or federal court. § 1415(i)(2)(A). Applying general principles of concurrent federal and state jurisdiction, courts have allowed removal of actions filed in state court to federal court pursuant to 28 U.S.C. § 1441(b). *See, e.g., Converse County Sch. Dist. No. 2 v. Pratt*, 993 F. Supp. 848 (D. Wyo. 1997). Imagine a typical IEP dispute over the intensity of services for a child with a learning disability. If a parent filed the action in state court in your locality and you represent the school district, would you remove? What if the roles were reversed?

4. *Parties.* Should a school district be able to sue its state educational agency under IDEA for its failure to provide adequate state aid so that underfunded districts could provide children with disabilities a free, appropriate public education? *See Andrews v. Ledbetter,* 880 F.2d 1287 (11th Cir. 1989) (answering no). Should a private child care facility be able to sue a school district for a declaration that the district was obligated to provide classrooms and services to educate children with disabilities at the facility? *See Family & Children's Ctr. v. School City,* 13 F.3d 1052 (7th Cir. 1994) (answering yes, relying in part on state law). Should non-attorney parents be able to sue pro se despite the general rule that parents who are unrepresented may not present their children's claims in court? *See Winkelman v. Parma City Sch. Dist.,* 127 S. Ct. 1994 (2007) (answering yes). Justice Kennedy's opinion in *Winkelman* is particularly interesting in its reasoning that IDEA has to be read as a whole, and that the statute makes parents real parties in interest who have independent, enforceable rights on substantive matters and are not merely representatives of their children in IDEA disputes. IDEA cases present many other difficult questions regarding party status, such as when children and parents may sue as a class, and when the state educational agency may be liable for a school district's violations of IDEA. *See generally* MARK C. WEBER, SPECIAL EDUCATION LAW AND LITIGATION TREATISE § 21.5 (3d ed. 2008 & supps.).

5. *Administrative deference.* According to the statute, the trial court, "basing its decision on the preponderance of the evidence, shall grant such relief as the court determines is appropriate." The law thus does not contain any explicit requirement that the court defer to the decision of the due process hearing officer or state review officer. Nevertheless, in *Board of Education v. Rowley,* 458 U.S. 176, 206 (1982) (reprinted *supra* Chapter 1), the Court determined that the requirement that the court receive the administrative record "carries with it the implied requirement that due weight should be given to those proceedings." Many courts have articulated the standard that results as de novo with due weight, *see, e.g., Fick v. Sioux Falls Sch. Dist. 49-5,* 337 F.3d 968, 970 (8th Cir. 2003), a phrasing that may be a contradiction in terms. For a critique of the due weight standard, see Thomas Guernsey, *When the Teachers and Parents Can't Agree, Who Really Decides? Burdens of Proof and Standards of Review Under the Education for All Handicapped Children Act,* 36 CLEV. ST. L. REV. 67, 84–85 (1988). When two tiers exist, courts generally have deferred to the final one. *E.g., Heather S. v. Wisconsin,* 125 F.3d 1045, 1053 (7th Cir. 1997). *But see Burke County Bd. of Educ. v. Denton,* 895 F.2d 973, 981 (4th Cir. 1990) (challenging approach of giving deference only to review decision). Given the independence of the review decision maker from the state educational agency and the absence of any requirement that the review officer have better qualifications than the hearing officer, does deference to the higher level of review make sense? What if the hearing officer heard the witnesses and the review officer did not? *See generally O'Toole v. Olathe Dist. Sch. Unified Schs. Dist. No. 233,* 144 F.3d 692 (10th Cir. 1998) (affording deference to review officer's decision except on conflicts with hearing officer on credibility issues).

1.   Evidentiary Hearings

Section 1415 provides that:

In any action brought under this paragraph, the court —

(i) shall receive the records of the administrative proceedings;

(ii) shall hear additional evidence at the request of a party; and

(iii) basing its decision on the preponderance of the evidence, shall grant such relief as the court determines is appropriate.

20 U.S.C. § 1415(i)(2)(C). The § 1415 procedure is exceptional, both in comparison to the ordinary civil case in which the action begins in the district court and proceeds to a trial in which all the evidence is heard by a jury, and in comparison to an ordinary administrative appeal, in which the judge reviewing the administrative decision typically does not accept any additional evidence at all.

Despite the mandatory-sounding language in the statute, courts have been reluctant to afford scarce trial time to litigants who could have built their record before the due process hearing officer. In the appellate court proceedings in the *Burlington School Committee* Supreme Court case (reprinted *supra* Chapter 8 with regard to due process hearing remedies), the First Circuit considered whether the district court should have heard testimony. It concluded that the district court should not rehear witnesses who testified at the due process hearing or otherwise conduct a trial de novo, but that the court does retain discretion to permit supplementation of the record when there is a justification for not having presented the testimony at the due process hearing. The Sixth Circuit, in *Metropolitan Government v. Cook*, appears to take a more liberal view concerning supplementation.

TOWN OF BURLINGTON v. DEPARTMENT OF EDUCATION
736 F.2d 773 (1st Cir. 1984), *aff'd*, 471 U.S. 359 (1985)

The court held that the statutory provision calling for courts to accept testimony does not authorize parties to have witnesses at trial repeat or embellish their prior administrative hearing testimony. The hearing is instead to be used to cover gaps in the record such as events that occurred after hearing; nevertheless, the fact that a witness testified at the due process hearing does not by itself prevent the person from testifying in court.

BOWNES, CIRCUIT JUDGE.

On appeal to this court a second time, all parties urge that the district court committed reversible errors in a case arising under the Education for All Handicapped Children Act (EAHCA or Act), 20 U.S.C. §§ 1401–1461. The first appeal generally involved motions for preliminary injunctions concerning the interim educational placement and funding for a learning disabled child, there referred to as John Doe, Jr. [S] *ee Town of Burlington v. Department of Education*, 655 F.2d 428 (1st Cir. 1981) (hereinafter *Burlington I*). The current appeal presents a wide variety of novel issues under the Act. These include: the choice of law to be utilized in the state due process hearings; the impact of a school system's regulatory violations on the validity of a child's IEP; the weight to be accorded to the state administrative record and the hearing officer's findings upon appeal; the meaning of the term "additional evidence" as used in the Act; the appropriate burden of proof at trial for the years subsequent to the contested IEP; and the significance of a diagnostic determination by the trial judge. Reimbursement issues include the effect of a unilateral parental transfer of the child to a school not authorized by the individualized educational program (IEP) formulated by the school system; the impact of parental reliance on and implementation of a state administrative decision; and bad faith as a bar to reimbursement.

In view of the protracted procedural background of the case which has included two published opinions, *see id.* and *Doe v. Anrig*, 561 F. Supp. 121 (D. Mass. 1983) (Aldrich, J., sitting by designation) (consolidated case including *Burlington I* on remand), we will first recount its procedural history. The factual background may be found in the above-cited opinions. We shall then review the alleged errors according to the chronological progression of the case beginning with those alleged to have occurred at the state administrative level.

Prior Proceedings

John had completed the third grade at a regular public school when his parents invoked the administrative appeals process in July 1979 to review an IEP and placement the Town of Burlington (Town) proposed to implement the following September. Mediation failed and in August the parents placed the child in a private school, the Carroll School. A state due process hearing was held by the Massachusetts Bureau of Special Education Appeals (BSEA) over four days in the autumn of 1979. The BSEA hearing officer rendered a decision in January 1980 in favor of the private school placement, holding the Town's IEP to be inadequate and inappropriate for the child's special needs. The Town then commenced a two-count action in the district court against the State and the Does, seeking to reverse the BSEA order on the basis of both the federal Act, 20 U.S.C. § 1415(e)(2), and the corollary state Act, Mass. Gen. Laws Ann. ch. 71B, §§ 1 *et seq.* The federal and state acts have different standards of review.

The district court denied the Town's request for a stay of the BSEA order that the Town fund the child's education at the Carroll School, and on the state count found in favor of the defendants on a motion for summary judgment.

On appeal to this court we, *inter alia*, vacated the grant of summary judgment and directed that the pendent state count be dismissed, holding that the "federal specification for review, when invoked, seems to us designed to occupy the field over an inconsistent state provision." *Burlington I*, 655 F.2d at 431. The federal claim was remanded for trial.

At the conclusion of a four-day trial, the district court, Zobel, J., reversed the State BSEA finding and held that the Town's IEP was adequate and appropriate.

The case was then transferred and consolidated with two others to determine whether the Town's remedies included reimbursement for tuition and travel expenses. The district court, Aldrich, J., sitting by designation, determined that reimbursement was available to the Town as the prevailing party. The case was transferred back to the original district court and an order issued requiring the parents to repay the Town the tuition, transportation costs, and other expenses related to the child's education at the Carroll School for the prior three years. This appeal ensued with the Department and the parents alleging both legal and factual errors in the district court. The Town cross-appeals on the limited issue of the method used to calculate the appropriate reimbursement and the amount thereby awarded. It must be emphasized that the State is not, as is usually the case, aligned with the Town on this appeal. The State's position parallels that of the Does. It urges that the district court erred in reversing the decision of the state educational agency as to the appropriate educational placement for the child.

. . . .

II. THE SCOPE OF THE DISTRICT COURT'S REVIEW

. . . .

C. *The Evidentiary Issues*

Defendants contend that the district court erroneously interpreted and applied the Act's provision for "additional evidence." They also question the weight the court gave the administrative record and the deference accorded the administrative findings. Because we consider these questions interrelated, we discuss them together.

The only statutory language directly addressed to these evidentiary matters directs that "the court shall *receive the records of the administrative proceedings, shall hear additional evidence at the request of a party,* and, basing its decision on the preponderance of the evidence, shall grant such relief as the court determines is appropriate." 20 U.S.C. § 1415(e)(2) (emphasis added). This court has described the judicial review proceedings under the Act as "something short of a trial *de novo.*" *Colin K. by John K. v. Schmidt,* 715 F.2d 1, 5 (1st Cir. 1983). The district court, however, which did not have the benefit either of the Supreme Court's decision in *Rowley* or of ours in *Colin K.* prior to trial, joined other courts in interpreting the Act to require a trial *de novo.* Pretrial Order at 6 (March 18, 1982). Consonant with this, it ruled that it was "bound to receive additional evidence offered by the parties, provided it is relevant." *Id.*

We believe that the key to the review authorized by the Act lies in the additional evidence clause. We construe "additional" in the ordinary sense of the word, *Perrin v. United States,* 444 U.S. 37, 42 (1980), to mean supplemental. Thus construed, this clause does not authorize witnesses at trial to repeat or embellish their prior administrative hearing testimony; this would be entirely inconsistent with the usual meaning of "additional." We are fortified in this interpretation because it structurally assists in giving due weight to the administrative proceeding, as *Rowley* requires. *Rowley,* 458 U.S. at 206.

A trial court must make an independent ruling based on the preponderance of the evidence, but the Act contemplates that the source of the evidence generally will be the administrative hearing record, with some supplementation at trial. The reasons for supplementation will vary; they might include gaps in the administrative transcript owing to mechanical failure, unavailability of a witness, an improper exclusion of evidence by the administrative agency, and evidence concerning relevant events occurring subsequent to the administrative hearing. The starting point for determining what additional evidence should be received, however, is the record of the administrative proceeding.

We decline to adopt the rule urged by defendants that the appropriate construction is to disallow testimony from all who did, or could have, testified before the administrative hearing. We believe that, although an appropriate limit in many cases, a rigid rule to this effect would unduly limit a court's discretion and constrict its ability to form the independent judgment Congress expressly directed. A salient effect of defendants' proposed rule would be to limit expert testimony to the administrative hearing. Our review of the cases involving the Act reveals that in many instances the district court found expert testimony helpful in illuminating the nature of the controversy and relied on it in its decisional process. There could be some valid reasons for not presenting some or all expert testimony before the state agency. Experts are expensive — the parties at the state level may feel that their cases can be adequately made with less backup, especially since the administrative hearing in Massachusetts is conducted by an expert. We also recognize that in many instances experts who have testified at the administrative hearing will be bringing the court up to date on the child's progress from the time of the hearing to the trial. It would be difficult to draw a sharp line between what had or could have been testified to at the administrative hearing and the trial testimony.

The determination of what is "additional" evidence must be left to the discretion of the trial court which must be careful not to allow such evidence to change the character of the hearing from one of review to a trial *de novo*. A practicable approach, we believe, is that an administrative hearing witness is rebuttably presumed to be foreclosed from testifying at trial. A motion may then be made to allow such a witness to testify within specified limits stating the justification for the testimony. In ruling on motions for witnesses to testify, a court should weigh heavily the important concerns of not allowing a party to undercut the statutory role of administrative expertise, the unfairness involved in one party's reserving its best evidence for trial, the reason the witness did not testify at the administrative hearing, and the conservation of judicial resources. The court should look with a critical eye on a claim, such as made here, that the credibility of a witness is a central issue. The claim of credibility should not be an "open sesame" for additional evidence. Such an approach followed by a pretrial order that identifies who may testify and limits the scope of the testimony will enable the court to avoid a trial *de novo*.

. . . .

V. CONCLUSION

We are fully aware of the time and effort that has gone into this case by two very able judges as well as the attorneys and parties, but a remand is necessary. This is, to put it mildly, a difficult Act to interpret and effectuate. Congress has combined elements of a number of different statutory schemes and visited on the judiciary the task of making them mesh. We have done our best to follow the intent and purpose of the Act to ensure "a free appropriate public education" for all handicapped children, but the path has not been easy.

Summary

On remand, the district court must review the state administrative proceedings in accord with the standards set forth herein giving due consideration to the Town's procedural violations and the state's substantive standards.

In determining whether additional evidence should be received, the court starts with the record of the administrative proceedings. From there on, the question of the admission of evidence is for the discretion of the district court within the guidelines set forth.

The district court must give the state administrative findings careful consideration bearing in mind that the state agency's decision that the Town did not meet the state's substantive and procedural requirements is entitled to deference.

The district court must make a finding as to the nature of the child's learning disabilities in order to evaluate properly the IEP.

The burden of proof as to subsequent years falls on the losing party in the dispute over the 1979-80 IEP.

Once the district court reaches it decision, it may order reimbursement in accordance with the principles discussed in section IV, *supra*.

Reversed in part. Affirmed in part. Remanded for further proceedings consistent herewith.

METROPOLITAN GOVERNMENT v. COOK
915 F.2d 232 (6th Cir. 1990)

The court held that it was proper for the district court to hear testimony regarding the appropriateness of alternative placements not considered by the due process hearing officer.

KENNEDY, CIRCUIT JUDGE.

Appellants, Sandra and Curtis Cook, appeal a District Court order vacating an administrative hearing officer's decision directing Curtis Cook to attend the Brehm School in Carbondale, Illinois for the 1989-90 school year at the expense of the local school system. Appellee, the Metropolitan Government of Nashville and Davidson County, argues that the District Court's opinion should be affirmed.

At the time of the administrative hearing, Curtis Cook was an eighteen-year-old learning-disabled student in the eleventh grade. When Curtis was in the tenth grade, he was suspended from Glencliff High School as a result of an incident unrelated to his handicapped condition. The suspension resulted in his transfer to McGavock High School, a public high school operated by appellee. During the fall semester of his junior year, Curtis began experiencing some major problems with his school work. In order to correct these problems, three multi-disciplinary team (M-team) meetings between the parents of Curtis Cook and the government's special education personnel were held pursuant to the Education For All Handicapped Children Act (the Act), 20 U.S.C. § 1400 *et seq.* (1978). The dispute between the two parties arose out of those M-team meetings. Curtis Cook's parents maintained that Curtis should be placed at the Brehm School, and the government contended that Curtis' needs could be served at McGavock.

An administrative hearing was held before a State Department of Education Administrative Law Judge (hearing officer). The hearing officer concluded that Curtis Cook should be placed at the Brehm School. In reaching her decision, the hearing officer stated:

> Intensive reading and language therapy must be provided if this young man is to make academic progress. Further, intensive tutoring in study and organizational strategies, counseling and management procedures by an individual trained and experienced in providing remedial compensatory therapy for individuals with similar language learning disabilities is necessary. The student needs to be educated not only in the acquisition of necessary academic skills: he also needs to be educated as to the nature of his handicap and effective techniques for minimizing or overcoming it in daily life.

> In terms of individualized pre-teaching and instruction in his grade level curriculum, the Hearing Officer finds that there must be extensive coordination and communication among all teachers, often on a daily basis, with a capacity to change instructional strategies quickly. Such coordination and capacity for modifying and fine-tuning this student's educational program is not simply advisable: it is critical.

The hearing officer concluded:

> Given his capacity for education and remediation as indicated by Dr. Kaas and by Ms. Cosgrove, it cannot be said that this young man has received an appropriate education within the meaning of the federal law.

> For these reasons, the Hearing Officer finds that this student should be placed at the Brehm School. The evidence elicited at the hearing indicated that this academic setting could provide the degree of intense, coordinated, flexible instruction by professionals experienced in dealing with his peculiar handicapping condition which this student needs.

> In the hearing before the hearing officer, the only placement proposed by appellee was the McGavock placement.

The government appealed the decision of the hearing officer, challenging only the placement of Curtis Cook in the Brehm School. Appellee argued that the hearing officer's decision to place Curtis in the Brehm School did not comply with the statutory requirement that the free, appropriate education required by the Act be provided in the least restrictive environment possible in light of the child's particular needs. *See* 20 U.S.C. § 1412(5)(B). The District Court agreed. The court noted that there was no testimony before the hearing officer concerning whether other placements less restrictive than Brehm could provide the services necessary to accomplish the five objectives set forth by the hearing officer. The court stated, however, that the testimony before it presented alternatives and "strongly suggested that Curtis' educational objectives, as explicated by the hearing officer could be provided in Hillwood School, where Curtis could have the opportunity to participate in the marching band and to take classes with non-handicapped children." The court also stated that the testimony suggested that Benton Hall School may meet Curtis' needs as well. Thus the court vacated the hearing officer's placement order and ordered Curtis' M-team to meet within ten days to develop a new Individualized Educational Program (IEP) incorporating the findings of the hearing officer regarding Curtis' broad educational needs and implementing a program to meet those needs in the least restrictive environment consistent with the requirements of the Act.

Appellants' sole argument on appeal is that the evidence relating to the placements at Hillwood and Benton Hall considered by the District Court was inadmissible under the additional evidence clause of 20 U.S.C. § 1415(e)(2). This section provides in part:

> In any action brought under this paragraph the court shall receive the records of the administrative proceedings, *shall hear additional evidence at the request of a party*, and, basing its decision on the preponderance of the evidence, shall grant such relief as the court determines is appropriate.

20 U.S.C. § 1415(e)(2) (emphasis added).

Appellants argue that allowing the introduction into evidence of alternative placements not reviewed during the administrative hearing is inconsistent with the Act. They assert that the school system could have addressed the Hillwood or Benton Hall placements during the administrative process yet failed to do so. They note that two of the three witnesses who testified in support of the Benton Hall and Hillwood placements at the hearing before the District Court were involved in the M-team meetings relating to Curtis Cook and that one of these witnesses testified at the administrative hearing.

Appellants base their argument on a First Circuit opinion, *Town of Burlington v. Department of Educ.*, 736 F.2d 773 (1st Cir. 1984), *aff'd on other grounds*, 471 U.S. 359 (1985). After the court noted that it found "no legislative history to guide [it] . . . on the construction to be given 'additional evidence' " (*id.* at 790 n. 20) as employed in 20 U.S.C. § 1415(e)(2), the court stated that it construed the term "additional" "in the ordinary sense of the word to mean supplemental." *Id.* (citation omitted). The court elaborated, "Thus construed, this clause does not authorize witnesses at trial to repeat or embellish their prior administrative hearing testimony. . . ." *Id.* The portion of the opinion upon which appellants most heavily rely reads as follows:

A trial court must make an independent ruling based on the preponderance of the evidence, but the Act contemplates that the source of the evidence generally will be the administrative hearing record, with some supplementation at trial. The reasons for supplementation will vary; they might include gaps in the administrative transcript owing to mechanical failure, unavailability of a witness, an improper exclusion of evidence by the administrative agency, and evidence concerning relevant events occurring subsequent to the administrative hearing. The starting point for determining what additional evidence should be received, however, is the record of the administrative proceeding.

Id. at 790 (footnote omitted).

Insofar as this language suggests that additional evidence is admissible only in limited circumstances, such as to supplement or fill in the gaps in the evidence previously introduced, we decline to adopt the position taken by the First Circuit. "Additional," in its ordinary usage, implies something that is added, or something that exists by way of addition. To "add" means to join or unite; the limitation on what can be joined inherent in the term "supplement" is not present in the term "add."

It should also be noted that appellants, in citing the above language from *Town of Burlington*, failed to consider the following statements by the court:

We decline to adopt the rule urged by defendants that the appropriate construction is to disallow testimony from all who did, or could have, testified before the administrative hearing. We believe that, although an appropriate limit in many cases, a rigid rule to this effect would unduly limit a court's discretion and constrict its ability to form the independent judgment Congress expressly directed. A salient effect of defendants' proposed rule would be to limit expert testimony to the administrative hearing. Our review of the cases involving the Act reveals that in many instances the district court found expert testimony helpful in illuminating the nature of the controversy and relied on it in its decisional process.

. . . .

The determination of what is "additional" evidence must be left to the discretion of the trial court which must be careful not to allow such evidence to change the character the hearing from one of review to a trial *de novo*. . . . In ruling on motions for witnesses to testify, a court should weigh heavily the important concerns of not allowing a party to undercut the statutory role of administrative expertise, the unfairness involved in one party's reserving its best evidence for trial, the reason the witness did not testify at the administrative hearing, and the conservation of judicial resources.

Id. at 790–91.

This portion of the opinion suggests that even the First Circuit would not have found fault with the consideration of the evidence of additional placements in the present case. *Town of Burlington* leaves the determination of what additional evidence may be admitted to the trial court. In the present case, the admission of additional evidence regarding less restrictive placements does not undercut the statutory role of administrative expertise. It is appropriate for a court that has determined that a hearing officer failed to consider the statutorily least restrictive alternative requirement to consider less restrictive placements.

Thus we agree with appellee that the admission of evidence regarding the Hillwood and Benton Hall schools was proper. We find that the District Court did not err in vacating the hearing officer's placement order and ordering the M-team to meet within ten days to develop a new IEP incorporating the findings of the hearing officer regarding Curtis' broad educational needs and implementing a program to meet those needs, in the least restrictive environment consistent with the requirements of the Act. Accordingly, we AFFIRM the judgment of the District Court.

NOTES AND QUESTIONS

1.   Can you reconcile the approaches of the First and Sixth Circuits? If not, how would you describe the conflict between the courts? Which approach is more persuasive? *Town of Burlington* represents the majority rule, though a number of courts have adopted positions closer to that of *Metropolitan Government v. Cook*; some circuits do not appear fully consistent in their rulings. *See generally* MARK C. WEBER, SPECIAL EDUCATION LAW AND LITIGATION TREATISE § 22.1(1) (3d ed. 2008 & supps.) (collecting cases).

2.   Do you think that the *Metropolitan Government* court would have ruled the same way if the case had been decided in favor of the school district at hearing and the parents sought to introduce new evidence at the trial level? What would the court of appeals do if the facts were the same as they were in the actual case, but the trial court, exercising its discretion, chose not to hear the newly proffered evidence?

3.   Both due process hearings and court proceedings frequently entail testimony from expert witnesses, whose conflicting opinions must be weighed by the decision maker. A useful discussion of the weight of an opinion of a witness offered as an expert is *Chris D. v. Montgomery County Bd. of Educ.*, 753 F. Supp. 922, 929 & n.17 (M.D. Ala. 1990) (discrediting testimony of individual who did not appear current in field).

4.   Limiting the evidence that can be presented to the court raises the stakes at the due process hearing and makes the presence of an attorney at due process critically important for both sides. Concerning congressional efforts to make attorneys' fees available to parents who prevail at due process, see Chapter 11, *infra*.

2.   Remedies

In actions brought pursuant to § 1415, the court "shall grant such relief as the court determines is appropriate." § 1415(i)(2)(B)(iii). The legislative history affirms that that this means the court "shall grant all appropriate relief." S. Conf. Rep. No.

94-455, at 50 (1975). Nevertheless, without taking a position on the matter, the Supreme Court as early as 1984 noted a consensus among lower courts that the federal special education law permits compensatory damages only under exceptional circumstances. *Smith v. Robinson*, 468 U.S. 992, 1020 n.24 (1984). Although the *Smith* case has been legislatively overruled, as noted *infra* Section B, its observation about relief remains valid. Thus the remedies afforded by courts in § 1415 cases are generally the same as those afforded by due process hearing officers, as discussed *supra* Chapter 8. The most common exception is attorneys' fees, which courts may award but which hearing officers in most states are not permitted to provide, a situation that forces parents who prevail at due process to file an action in court to obtain the fees from the due process hearing. *See generally infra* Chapter 11. Other areas in which the remedial actions of the courts differ from those of hearing officers in IDEA cases are those in which preliminary injunctive relief is appropriate and in systemic cases. *See generally* MARK C. WEBER, SPECIAL EDUCATION LAW AND LITIGATION TREATISE § 22.3 (3d ed. 2008 & supps.).

NOTES AND QUESTIONS

1.   Should damages relief be available under § 1415? Why do you think that courts have been reluctant to find a basis for damages despite the language of the statute and the legislative history's language about all appropriate relief? What sort of harms might children suffer for which compensatory damages would be appropriate?

2.   Due to the limited remedies under § 1415, parents who have sought damages for pain and suffering for their children have generally put forward claims under section 504 of the Rehabilitation Act of 1973, title II of the Americans with Disabilities Act (ADA), or the equal protection and due process clauses of the Fourteenth Amendment to the Constitution. In some circuits, however, they have been successful in asserting damages claims under IDEA, though more often by asserting the cause of action provided by 42 U.S.C. § 1983 rather than by using the claim provided directly by § 1415. These matters are discussed *infra* Sections B and C.

B.   SECTION 504 AND ADA CLAIMS

Section 504 of the Rehabilitation Act of 1973 and title II of the Americans with Disabilities Act provide a cause of action for discrimination engaged in by, respectively, entities receiving federal funding (such as state and local educational agencies) and state and local government units (such as state and local educational agencies). The claim is for discrimination, so the essence is unequal treatment of people with disabilities. A basic requirement of section 504, reinforced by title II, is that government programs must provide program accessibility to people with disabilities. Not every operation or facility must be able to be used by people with disabilities, but reasonable accommodation and general availability of services must be afforded. Segregation and denying a person with a disability the opportunity to benefit from equal services are forbidden. Practices with unjustified disparate impacts are forbidden. There are some technical differences between section 504 and title II, but the primary distinction is simply that title II extends section 504 obligations to any state and local governmental unit, irrespective of whether it receives federal funding; section 504 applies to any entity receiving federal funding, whether it is a unit of state or local government or not. *See* Mark C. Weber, *Disability Discrimination by State and Local Government: The Relationship Between Section 504 of the Rehabilitation Act and Title II of the Americans with Disabilities Act*, 36 WM. & MARY L. REV. 1089 (1995).

Early in the history of federal special education law, parents frequently attached section 504 claims to claims under the Education for All Handicapped Children's Act in order to take advantage of the Rehabilitation Act's attorneys' fees provision. In *Smith v. Robinson*, 468 U.S. 992 (1984), the Supreme Court held that Congress intended the special education law to preempt parallel claims under section 504 (and the equal protection clause of the Constitution), so the strategy failed. Two years later, however, Congress overruled *Smith* and enacted what is now 20 U.S.C. § 1415(*l*), which, as amended, provides:

> Nothing in this chapter shall be construed to restrict or limit the rights, procedures, and remedies available under the Constitution, the Americans with Disabilities Act of 1990, title V of the Rehabilitation Act of 1973, or other Federal laws protecting the rights of children with disabilities, except that before the filing of a civil action under such laws seeking relief that is also available under this part, the procedures under subsections (f) and (g) shall be exhausted to the same extent as would be required had the action been brought under this part.

Congress also enacted an attorneys' fees provision specifically for special education cases. *See generally infra* Chapter 11.

In the present era, students and their parents most frequently invoke section 504 and title II in disputes over accessibility of facilities or programs and the provisions of reasonable accommodations, in cases where the definitional provisions confer eligibility under section 504 and title II, but not IDEA (*see generally supra* Chapter 2), and in instances in which the students or parents seek damages relief. *Baird v. Rose* exemplifies a damages case brought by a child with a disabling condition who was not eligible for special education under IDEA.

BAIRD v. ROSE
192 F.3d 462 (4th Cir. 1999)

The court upheld a damages claim brought under Americans with Disabilities Act title II for a child who was not a special education student under IDEA.

WILKINS, CIRCUIT JUDGE.

Plaintiff Nancy Baird brought this action on behalf of her minor daughter Kristen Elisabeth Baird (Baird) against Baird's former teacher Susan Elizabeth Rose, Principal Inez Cohen, and the Fairfax County School Board (collectively,

"Appellees") alleging claims for discrimination under Title II of the Americans with Disabilities Act (ADA), *see* 42 U.S.C.A. § 12132 (1995), and intentional infliction of emotional distress under Virginia law. The district court granted Appellees' motion to dismiss for failure to state a claim upon which relief could be granted. *See* Fed.R.Civ.P. 12(b)(6). We reverse in part and affirm in part.

I.

Viewing Baird's complaint in the light most favorable to her, as we must, *see Mylan Labs., Inc. v. Matkari*, 7 F.3d 1130, 1134 (4th Cir. 1993), the complaint alleged the following facts. In the spring of 1996, while she was in the seventh grade at Rocky Run Middle School in Fairfax, Virginia, Baird auditioned for and was accepted to participate in show choir for the 1996-1997 school year. Show choir was a song and dance class for which grades were given; students learned song and dance routines and then performed them, sometimes in competition with other schools. Rose was the instructor for show choir.

During auditions for show choir, Rose expressed concern to Baird's father that Baird's frequent absences posed a potential problem for her participation in show choir. Baird's father informed Rose that although Baird suffered from recurrent sinus infections that caused her to miss school frequently, she would have no difficulty keeping up with show choir.

During the following school year, Baird continued to miss school regularly due to her ongoing medical problems. In January 1997, however, she auditioned for a lead role in the Rocky Run Middle School spring play, a musical. Rose and two drama teachers had joint responsibility for assigning roles. Rose advised Baird that she would not be considered for a lead role due to her frequent absences. Following the initial audition, which involved no singing but only dramatic readings, Baird was asked to return to audition for an alto role although she is a soprano. On January 30, 1997, Baird learned that she had been chosen for only a minor role.

On January 31, 1997, Baird was absent from school due to a sinus infection, and her mother telephoned Rose to confirm that Baird had a bona fide medical excuse. The following day, Baird attempted suicide by taking an overdose of ibuprofen. The attempt was triggered by Baird's belief that Rose had arranged for her to fail in her efforts to secure a lead role in the spring play by convincing the drama teachers to ask her to audition for an alto role Rose knew Baird could not perform rather than a soprano role for which she was more qualified.

On February 7, 1997, Baird was diagnosed as suffering from severe depression and was placed on a treatment plan that included medication and counseling. On February 12, 1997, Baird's mother informed a counselor at the school of Baird's diagnosis. On that day and the following day, Baird was absent from school. Baird's mother gave her permission for the counselor to inform Baird's teachers of the diagnosis, and on February 13, 1997 Rose learned that Baird had been diagnosed with severe depression. The next day, when Baird returned to school, Rose announced to the entire class that Baird would not be permitted to participate in the next show choir performance, which was scheduled for February 25, 1997, explaining to Baird that this "would be best." Rose thereafter assigned Baird's part to another student and forbade Baird to participate in rehearsal.

Baird's mother subsequently confronted Rose and asked that Baird be permitted to participate as usual. Rose stated that Baird did not know the dance routines well enough due to her absences. Baird's mother told Rose that her daughter in fact did know the routines, that she was capable of performing them, and that it was important to Baird's mental health and recovery that she be allowed to continue her participation in show choir. Baird's mother asked Rose to give Baird an opportunity to demonstrate that she was able to perform the dance routines. Rose refused, stating that she felt it would be best for Baird, given her depression, not to participate in show choir and that individuals who suffer from depression could not be counted on to meet their responsibilities.

On February 16 and 17, 1997, Baird's family doctor and psychologist submitted letters to Principal Cohen stating that Baird was fit to perform in show choir and that it could be detrimental to her mental health to be denied the opportunity to do so. On February 18, 1997, Baird's mother contacted Principal Cohen and requested, among other things, that Rose give Baird the opportunity to demonstrate her knowledge of the dance routines despite her absences and that Rose permit Baird to participate in the upcoming performance. Baird's mother stressed to Principal Cohen her concern that Rose might take further action that would cause Baird additional distress.

Instead of granting these requests, Principal Cohen informed Rose that she must either prohibit from participation in the performance all students who had been absent in accordance with Rose's written absence policy — which previously had not been enforced — or permit all students to perform. Later that day, Rose announced to the show choir class, in Baird's presence, that Rose was being forced to adhere to her previously published strict attendance policy although she did not wish to do so. Rose then pronounced that not only was Baird prohibited from participating in two of the three numbers in the upcoming performance, but three other students who had "legitimate" absences would be excluded from one number as well. Rose then asked the class members if they understood why she was being forced to adhere to the strict attendance policy, and other students commented that someone was taking advantage of the lax enforcement of the attendance policy and that someone did not know the routines and would slow down the performance of the group.

Humiliated, Baird left the class and telephoned her mother. Upon her mother's arrival at the school, Baird was exhibiting signs of severe emotional distress, crying uncontrollably and shaking. Baird's mother removed her from school for the rest of that day. After leaving school, Baird was unable to stop crying and a tranquilizer was prescribed by her doctor.

Baird's mother requested that Principal Cohen permit another adult to observe show choir class until Baird could be reassured that Rose would not embarrass her in front of her classmates again. When Baird's mother received no response, she took time off from work to observe the class herself. The following day Baird's grandmother attempted to attend show choir class but was prevented from doing so. Principal Cohen then contacted Baird's mother and informed her that she was barred from the school unless she received advance permission to be there. Rose, with Principal Cohen's approval, required Baird to sit during rehearsals through February 25, 1997. Baird also was not permitted to fully participate in the February 25 performance.

Due to the stress of this situation, Baird began to suffer severe sleeplessness, inability to sleep alone, decreased appetite, exhaustion, difficulty concentrating, fear of humiliation by other students, fear of humiliation by Rose, and a dramatic increase in the occurrence of physical illnesses. In addition, the quality of Baird's schoolwork began to suffer as a result of her exhaustion, difficulty concentrating, and increased physical illnesses. Her grades fell dramatically. Baird's mother took a leave of absence from work in order to ensure that Baird did not attempt suicide again.

Baird thereafter filed a Motion for Judgment against Appellees in state court, claiming a violation of the ADA and intentional infliction of emotional distress. Appellees removed the action to federal court, and the district court granted their motion to dismiss. See Fed.R.Civ.P. 12(b)(6). The district court concluded that the allegations of Baird's complaint demonstrated that she was not discriminated against on the basis of her depression. The court ruled as follows:

> [I]t [is] conclusive that the ultimate action of denying [Baird] . . . partici-
> pation in the school play was not based solely, if at all, on [her] alleged
> disability (viz., depression), but was supported by a valid and uniformly
> enforced policy of absenteeism. . . . Absenteeism was not only the articu-
> lated basis for defendants' initial action — before [Baird's] diagnosis with
> depression, but . . . was also the basis for excluding three other students
> from various parts of the show.

II.

This court reviews a dismissal of a claim by the district court under Rule 12(b)(6) de novo. See Mylan Labs., Inc., 7 F.3d at 1134. On appeal from an order granting a Rule 12(b)(6) motion to dismiss, this court accepts as true the facts as alleged in the complaint, views them in the light most favorable to the plaintiff, and recognizes that dismissal is inappropriate "unless it appears to a certainty that the plaintiff would be entitled to no relief under any state of facts which could be proved in support of his claim." Id. at 1134 & n. 4 (internal quotation marks omitted); see Hishon v. King & Spalding, 467 U.S. 69, 73 (1984) (explaining that dismissal for failure to state a claim is proper "only if it is clear that no relief could be granted under any set of facts that could be proved consistent with the allegations").

Pursuant to Title II of the ADA, "no qualified individual with a disability shall, by reason of such disability, be excluded from participation in or be denied the benefits of the services, programs, or activities of a public entity, or be subject to discrimination by any such entity." 42 U.S.C.A. § 12132. This court has stated that to establish a violation of the ADA, a plaintiff must show (1) that he has a disability; (2) that he is otherwise qualified for the benefit in question; and (3) that he was excluded from the benefit due to discrimination solely on the basis of the disability. See, e.g., Doe v. University of Md. Med. Sys. Corp., 50 F.3d 1261, 1265 (4th Cir. 1995). There is no dispute here that Baird has alleged adequately that she suffered from a disability — depression — or that she was otherwise qualified to participate in show choir classes or performances. The ruling of the district court and the appeal to this court focus on the third element — whether Baird was excluded from show choir "by reason of" discrimination on the basis of her depression. 42 U.S.C.A. § 12132.

A.

The reasoning of the district court was based upon a misunderstanding of Baird's factual allegations. The play for which Baird auditioned and show choir were separate activities, and it is discrimination with respect to show choir, not the play, that Baird claims. Under the facts alleged by Baird, her exclusion from show choir did not occur until after Rose had been informed of Baird's depression, and Rose expressly relied, at least in part, on Baird's depression in determining that she could not participate in show choir. Baird frequently had been absent prior to Rose's notification of Baird's disability, but Rose had never excluded her from show choir before. Further, Rose's absenteeism policy had never been enforced until after Rose made the decision to exclude Baird and was not enforced uniformly against all students who had been absent until after Principal Cohen informed Rose that she must apply the policy uniformly or not at all. Thus, we conclude that Baird's factual assertions are adequate to allege that she was excluded from show choir because of her depression.[1]

B.

Having concluded that Baird's complaint sufficiently alleges that she was discriminated against because of her depression, we turn to the question of what

---

[1] [FN 6] Approaching the issue from a slightly different perspective, Appellees assert that Baird's participation in show choir was denied on a nondiscriminatory basis — her absenteeism and her lack of knowledge of the routines — not on her disability. Appellees explain that it is undisputed that other students who had been absent were excluded along with Baird and that the application of this neutral rule means that Baird was not discriminated against. In support of this proposition, Appellees point to authority holding that the application of a neutral rule that does not distinguish between the disabled and the nondisabled does not violate the ADA. See, e.g., Sandison v. Michigan High Sch. Athletic Ass'n, 64 F.3d 1026, 1032, 1036 (6th Cir. 1995) (holding that application of a neutral rule excluding students over age 18 from participation in high school sports did not violate the ADA when applied to disabled 19-year-old high school students, even though the students were still in high school at age 19 because of their disabilities). Undoubtedly, the application of a neutral rule that applies to disabled and nondisabled individuals alike cannot be considered discrimination on the basis of disability. And, if Baird was excluded from participation because of her absences or lack of familiarity with the routines to perform them, Appellees did not violate the ADA. However, the allegations of Baird's complaint permit a conclusion that the application of the neutral absenteeism policy, which had never been applied until after Rose attempted to exclude Baird on the basis of her depression, was a pretext for discrimination and that the true reason for Baird's exclusion was her disability. The post hoc application of a neutral rule does not excuse discrimination when the neutral rule would not have been enforced but for the discrimination. And, it is inappropriate in addressing the appropriateness of a dismissal under Rule 12(b)(6) to make a determination concerning the weight of the evidence that ultimately may be presented in support of these various positions. See 5A Charles Allen Wright & Arthur R. Miller, Federal Practice & Procedure § 1356 (2d ed. 1990) (explaining that "[t]he purpose of a motion under Rule 12(b)(6) is to test the formal sufficiency of the statement of the claim for relief; it is not a procedure for resolving a contest about the facts or the merits of the case").

standard of causation is adequate to support a claim under the ADA. Appellees argue that Baird must allege that she was discriminated against "solely" on the basis of her disability and that her complaint fails to do so. Appellees rely on our decision in *Doe*, which contains language in dicta that a plaintiff must demonstrate that the discrimination was based "solely" on a disability. *Doe*, 50 F.3d at 1265. We conclude, however, that the language of *Doe* is not conclusive of the question of whether Baird adequately alleges a violation of the ADA if she claims that her disability was a motivating cause — as opposed to the sole cause — of discrimination.

In *Doe*, which involved both an ADA claim and a claim under § 504 of the Rehabilitation Act of 1973 (Rehabilitation Act), as amended, *see* 29 U.S.C.A. § 794(a) (1999), we set forth a single statement of the elements of both claims, acknowledging the general principle that "[b]ecause the language of the two statutes is substantially the same, we apply the same analysis to both." *Doe*, 50 F.3d at 1264 n. 9. The ADA and Rehabilitation Act generally are construed to impose the same requirements due to the similarity of the language of the two acts. *See Rogers v. Department of Health, Envtl. Control*, 174 F.3d 431, 433–34 (4th Cir. 1999) (noting that it is appropriate to refer to constructions of the Rehabilitation Act in determining the meaning of an ADA provision). Congress has directed courts "to construe the ADA to grant at least as much protection as provided by the regulations implementing the Rehabilitation Act." *Bragdon v. Abbott*, 524 U.S. 624 (1998); *see* 42 U.S.C.A. § 12201(a) (1995). And, Congress has instructed that interpretation of Title II of the ADA and § 504 of the Rehabilitation Act be coordinated "to 'prevent[ ] imposition of inconsistent or conflicting standards for the same requirements' under the two statutes." *Rogers*, 174 F.3d at 433 (alteration in original) (quoting 42 U.S.C.A. § 12117(b) (1995)); *see also* 42 U.S.C.A. §§ 12134(b), 12201(a) (1995). However, the ADA and the Rehabilitation Act are not exactly the same in all respects, and thus, while the two should be construed to impose the same requirements when possible, there are situations in which differences between the statutory provisions dictate different interpretations. *Cf. Woodman v. Runyon*, 132 F.3d 1330, 1343 (10th Cir. 1997) (emphasizing that a difference in statutory language between the Rehabilitation Act and the ADA dictates the imposition of a different burden on various classes of employers).

Despite the overall similarity of § 12132 of Title II of the ADA and § 504 of the Rehabilitation Act, the language of these two statutory provisions regarding the causative link between discrimination and adverse action is significantly dissimilar. Section 504 of the Rehabilitation Act states that "[n]o otherwise qualified individual with a disability . . . shall, *solely by reason of* her or his disability, be excluded from the participation in, be denied the benefits of, or be subjected to discrimination" by specified entities. 29 U.S.C.A. § 794(a) (emphasis added). In contrast, the pertinent language of the ADA prohibits discrimination against an individual "*by reason of such disability.*" 42 U.S.C.A. § 12132 (emphasis added); *see also* 42 U.S.C.A. § 12112(a) (1995) (prohibiting discrimination "because of" a disability); 42 U.S.C.A. § 12203(a) (1995) (prohibiting discrimination "against any individual because such individual has opposed any act or practice made unlawful by this chapter").

In *McNely v. Ocala Star-Banner Corp.*, 99 F.3d 1068, 1073–77 (11th Cir. 1996), the Eleventh Circuit addressed at length whether the ADA should be read to require that discrimination be the sole basis for the adverse employment action. After considering the statutory language, the legislative history, and Supreme Court precedent extant at the enactment of the ADA, the court ruled that the ADA did not impose a "solely because of" standard of causation. *See id.* We find this analysis to be well reasoned and adopt the conclusion that the ADA does not impose a "solely by reason of" standard of causation.[2]

Our decision in *Doe* does not require a different result. The statement of the elements contained in *Doe*, including the reference to causation "solely" on the basis of a disability in the third element, was adopted from an opinion addressing a claim under the Rehabilitation Act, *Gates v. Rowland*, 39 F.3d 1439, 1445 (9th Cir. 1994). *Doe*, 50 F.3d at 1265. *Doe*, however, dealt with the question of whether an HIV-positive doctor was a qualified individual. We thus were not called upon to decide the causation standard applicable under the ADA; indeed, beyond the brief reference contained in the statement of the elements, the opinion contains no discussion of the causation requirement. *See McNely*, 99 F.3d at 1076–77 (rejecting the argument that *Doe* "held that 'because of' in the ADA context means 'solely because of' " (emphasis omitted)).

Having rejected a "solely because of" standard, the question becomes what causation standard applies. For the reasons set forth below, we conclude that the causation standards applicable in Title VII actions are applicable to violations of § 12132. The remedies available for a violation of § 12132 are set forth in 42 U.S.C.A. § 12133 (1995), which in turn provides that "[t]he remedies, procedures, and rights set forth in section 794a of Title 29 shall be the remedies, procedures, and rights this subchapter provides to any person alleging discrimination on the basis of disability in violation of section 12132." *See* 42 U.S.C.A. § 12133. Section 794a specifically makes the remedies available under Title VII applicable to actions under the ADA. *See* 29 U.S.C.A. § 794a(a)(1) (1999) (incorporating "[t]he remedies, procedures, and rights set forth in . . . 42 U.S.C. 2000e-5(f) through (k)"). Generally, relief is not afforded under § 2000e-5(g) if the plaintiff was subjected to an adverse employment action "for any reason other than discrimination." 42 U.S.C.A. § 2000e-5(g)(2)(A) (1994). Title VII recognizes as an unlawful employment practice discrimination that "was a motivating factor for any employment practice, even though other factors also motivated the practice." 42 U.S.C.A. § 2000e-2(m) (1994); *see* 42 U.S.C.A. § 2000e-5(g)(2)(B) (1994). Thus, if a plaintiff claiming discrimination under § 12132 demonstrates that his or her disability played a motivating role in the employment decision, the plaintiff is entitled to relief. *See Foster v. Arthur Andersen, LLP*, 168 F.3d 1029, 1033–34 (7th Cir. 1999) (indicating that to recover under the ADA, an employee must demonstrate that impermissible discrimination was a motivating factor); *Katz v. City Metal Co.*, 87 F.3d 26, 33 (1st Cir. 1996) (same); *Buchanan v. City of San Antonio*, 85 F.3d 196, 200 (5th Cir. 1996) (same); *Pedigo v. P.A.M. Transp., Inc.*, 60 F.3d 1300, 1301 (8th Cir. 1995) (same); *see also Doane v. City of Omaha*, 115 F.3d 624, 629 (8th Cir. 1997) (recognizing that 42 U.S.C.A. §§ 2000e-2(m) & 2000e-5(g)(2)(B) apply in actions brought pursuant to the ADA). Damages

---

[2] [FN 7] The only two contrary decisions of which we are aware are *Sandison v. Michigan High School Athletic Ass'n*, 64 F.3d 1026, 1036 (6th Cir. 1995), and *Despears v. Milwaukee County*, 63 F.3d 635, 636 (7th Cir. 1995). Neither decision offers reasoning in support of the conclusion that the "solely because of" standard applies.

may not be awarded for such a violation, however, if the defendant "would have taken the same action in the absence of the impermissible motivating factor." 42 U.S.C.A. § 2000e-5(g)(2)(B); *Doane*, 115 F.3d at 629; *Buchanan*, 85 F.3d at 200; *Pedigo*, 60 F.3d at 1301. In such circumstances, relief is limited to declaratory and injunctive relief, costs, and attorney's fees. *See* 42 U.S.C.A. § 2000e-5(g)(2)(B); *Doane*, 115 F.3d at 629; *Buchanan*, 85 F.3d at 200; *Pedigo*, 60 F.3d at 1301; *cf. McNely*, 99 F.3d at 1076 ("hold[ing] that the ADA imposes liability whenever the prohibited motivation makes the difference in the employer's decisions, *i.e.*, when it is a 'but-for' cause"). Applying this legal standard, Baird's complaint contains adequate factual allegations to state a claim under the ADA — to allege that discrimination on the basis of her disability was a motivating factor in her exclusion from show choir — even though her complaint may be read to contain allegations that her absenteeism (or resulting perceived lack of ability to perform the routines) also played a role in that decision.[3]

C.

Finally, Appellees contend that Title II of the ADA does not recognize a cause of action for discrimination by private individuals, only public entities, so the district court properly dismissed Baird's ADA cause of action against Rose and Cohen in their individual capacities even if that claim should not be dismissed in its entirety. *See* 42 U.S.C.A. § 12132 (prohibiting denial of benefits of or discrimination by a "public entity"). Baird concedes this point of law, but maintains that the ADA does recognize a retaliation claim against individuals. *See* 42 U.S.C.A. § 12203(a) (stating that "[n]o *person* shall discriminate against any individual because such individual has opposed any act or practice made unlawful by this chapter" (emphasis added)); *see also* 28 C.F.R. § 35.134(b) (1998) (stating that "[n]o *private or public* entity shall coerce, intimidate, threaten, or interfere with any individual in the exercise or enjoyment of, or on account of his or her having exercised . . . any right granted or protected by the Act" (emphasis added)). Although they acknowledge that § 12203(a) may be read to prohibit retaliation against individuals for engaging in protected conduct, Appellees argue that this fact does not answer the pivotal question of whether Congress has provided individuals who have been retaliated against for engaging in conduct protected by the ADA with a private cause of action against the persons who are responsible for the retaliation in their individual capacities. Appellees assert that Congress did not supply such a cause of action and instead chose to limit the remedies available to those who have suffered retaliation

---

[3] [FN 9] Appellees also contend that the accommodation requested by Baird was not required because Appellees did not have to provide Baird with an opportunity to show that she knew the dance routines. Appellees maintain that attendance is an essential requirement for the benefit of participating in show choir and that they need not waive this requirement and provide an alternative means of assessing whether Baird was able to perform the routines. *See Tyndall v. National Educ. Ctrs., Inc. of Cal.*, 31 F.3d 209, 213 (4th Cir. 1994) (holding that "[a]n employee who cannot meet the attendance requirements of the job at issue cannot be considered a 'qualified' individual protected by the ADA"). This argument, however, is founded on the false premise that the opportunity to prove she knew the routines was an accommodation to her depression. As alleged by Baird, the request that she be permitted to show that she knew the routines was an "accommodation" to her absences due to illness, not an "accommodation" to her depression. Thus, the issue of "accommodation" is irrelevant to Baird's ADA claim.

for conduct protected by the ADA to those remedies available under Title VII. *See* 42 U.S.C.A. § 2000e-5 (1994). We agree.

The remedies available for a violation of the anti-retaliation provision of the ADA in the employment context are set forth in 42 U.S.C.A. § 12117 (1995). *See* 42 U.S.C.A. § 12203(c). Section 12117 specifically makes the remedies available under Title VII applicable to actions under the ADA. *See* 42 U.S.C.A. § 12117(a) (providing that "[t]he powers, remedies, and procedures set forth in section[] . . . 2000e-5 . . . of this title shall be the powers, remedies, and procedures this subchapter provides to . . . any person alleging discrimination on the basis of disability"). The enforcement provision of Title VII permits actions against an "employer, employment agency, labor organization, or joint labor-management committee." 42 U.S.C.A. § 2000e-5(b). Title VII and the ADA define an "employer" in pertinent part as "a person engaged in an industry affecting commerce who has fifteen or more employees." 42 U.S.C.A. § 2000e(b) (1994); *see* 42 U.S.C.A. § 12111(5)(A) (1995). We have expressly held that Title VII does not provide a remedy against individual defendants who do not qualify as "employers." *See Lissau v. Southern Food Serv., Inc.*, 159 F.3d 177, 180–81 (4th Cir. 1998) (holding that supervisors cannot be held liable in their individual capacity under Title VII because they do not fit within the definition of an employer). Because Title VII does not authorize a remedy against individuals for violation of its provisions, and because Congress has made the remedies available in Title VII applicable to ADA actions, the ADA does not permit an action against individual defendants for retaliation for conduct protected by the ADA. *See Stern v. California State Archives*, 982 F. Supp. 690, 692–94 (E.D. Cal. 1997) (holding that individuals who do not qualify as "employers" under Title VII cannot be held liable under the ADA); *cf. Hiler v. Brown*, 177 F.3d 542, 545–46 (6th Cir. 1999) (explaining that because it incorporates the remedies available under Title VII, the Rehabilitation Act does not permit actions against persons in their individual capacities). Accordingly, we hold that the district court properly dismissed Baird's action against Rose and Cohen in their individual capacities.

III.

Baird also asserts that the district court erred in dismissing her claim of intentional infliction of emotional distress. Under Virginia law, intentional infliction of emotional distress requires that (1) the wrongdoer's conduct was intentional or reckless; (2) the conduct was outrageous and intolerable in that it offends generally accepted standards of decency and morality; (3) the wrongdoer's conduct caused the emotional distress; and (4) the emotional distress was severe. *See Womack v. Eldridge*, 215 Va. 338, 210 S.E.2d 145, 148 (1974). There is no dispute that Baird adequately pled the first, third, and fourth elements of a cause of action for intentional infliction of emotional distress. The second element, that the conduct be outrageous, "is aimed at limiting frivolous suits and avoiding litigation in situations where only bad manners and mere hurt feelings are involved." *Ruth v. Fletcher*, 237 Va. 366, 377 S.E.2d 412, 413 (1989) (internal quotation marks omitted). Thus, " '[l]iability has been found only where the conduct has been so outrageous in character, and so extreme in degree, as to go beyond all possible bounds of decency, and to be regarded as atrocious, and utterly intolerable in a civilized community.' " *Russo v. White*, 241 Va. 23, 400 S.E.2d 160, 162 (1991) (quoting *Restatement*

(Second) of Torts § 46, cmt. d (1965)). Baird contends that Appellees' alleged conduct was sufficiently outrageous to survive a motion to dismiss under Rule 12(b)(6) because Rose was a school official who was abusing her position and because Rose had reason to know that Baird was particularly susceptible. *See Restatement (Second) of Torts* § 46, cmts. e, f (1965) (recognizing that "[t]he extreme and outrageous character of the conduct may arise from an abuse by the actor of a position . . . which gives him actual . . . authority over the other" and that "conduct may become heartless, flagrant, and outrageous when the actor proceeds in the face of . . . knowledge" of special susceptibility). Baird's complaint alleges, *inter alia*, that Rose — in her capacity as Baird's teacher and during a class to which Baird was assigned — intentionally attempted to humiliate Baird, a child, knowing that she was suffering from clinical depression. We cannot say, as a matter of law, that the allegations in Baird's complaint do not allege facts so outrageous as to exceed the bounds of decent society. Therefore, we reverse the decision of the district court dismissing Baird's claim for intentional infliction of emotional distress.

IV.

We hold that Baird's allegations state a claim of illegal discrimination under the ADA and that the district court erred in granting a dismissal of this claim pursuant to Rule 12(b)(6) with respect to the Fairfax County School Board and to Rose and Cohen in their official capacities. However, the district court correctly dismissed Baird's ADA retaliation claim against Rose and Cohen in their individual capacities. Finally, we conclude that the district court improperly dismissed Baird's claim of intentional infliction of emotional distress.

REVERSED IN PART; AFFIRMED IN PART; AND REMANDED FOR FURTHER PROCEEDINGS

MARK H. v. LEMAHIEU
513 F.3d 922 (9th Cir. 2008)

The court reversed and remanded a case in which the lower court had dismissed a claim for damages for failure to provide educational services to two children with disabilities. The court ruled that damages would be available in a proper case under the section 504 regulations if the plaintiffs showed deliberate indifference on the part of the defendants.

BERZON, CIRCUIT JUDGE:

In 2000, . . . the H. family sued the Hawaii Department of Education and various school officials in their official capacities (collectively, "the Agency") for damages for alleged violations of the IDEA and of § 504. Among other rulings, the district court held that "there are no rights, procedures, or remedies available under § 504 for violations of the IDEA's affirmative obligations," and that the United States Department of Education's ("U.S. DOE's") § 504 regulations are not enforceable through a private right of action. It is the relationship between the IDEA and the U.S. DOE's regulations implementing § 504 that is at the heart of this case.

As it turns out, that relationship is not straightforward. The IDEA requires, among other things, that states accepting funds under the Act provide disabled children with a "free appropriate public education" ("FAPE"). Section 504 of the Rehabilitation Act requires that disabled individuals not "be excluded from the participation in, be denied the benefits of, or be subjected to discrimination under any program or activity" that receives federal funds. The U.S. DOE regulations implementing § 504 include a requirement that disabled children in schools receiving federal funds be provided a "free appropriate public education." The parties and the district court have assumed throughout this litigation that a violation of the IDEA statutory FAPE requirement necessarily constitutes a violation of the § 504 regulations' FAPE requirement, an understandable assumption given the use of identical language. As we develop below, however, this assumption is wrong. The FAPE requirements in the IDEA and in the § 504 regulations are, in fact, overlapping but different.

This fundamental misunderstanding has complicated our resolution of the issues in this case. Additionally, Congress has clearly stated its intent to preserve all remedies under § 504 for acts that also violate the IDEA. For these two reasons, we hold the availability of relief under the IDEA does not limit the availability of a damages remedy under the § 504 FAPE regulations.

As the H. family has assumed that alleging a violation of the IDEA FAPE requirement is sufficient to allege a violation of § 504, they have not specified precisely whether they believe the U.S. DOE's § 504 FAPE regulations, as opposed to the IDEA FAPE requirement, were violated, and, if so, in what regard. Without some clarity about precisely which § 504 regulations are at stake and why, we cannot determine whether the H. family has sufficiently alleged a privately enforceable cause of action for damages. We thus reverse the order of the district court granting summary judgment to the Agency and remand for further proceedings.

BACKGROUND

I. FACTS

A. Historical Background and the *Felix* Consent Decree.

Hawaii has long struggled to provide adequate services to special needs students in compliance with state and federal law. The U.S. DOE performed a site visit to Hawaii in 1991 and determined that the Hawaii Department of Education ("Hawaii DOE") was not complying with federal law "because mental health services were not always provided to meet the needs of special education students." The U.S. DOE report found that although "[t]he [Hawaii] DOE is legally responsible for furnishing these services, . . . [t]he [Hawaii Department of Health ('Hawaii DOH')] provides some free services to these students, but only when it has the resources." The U.S. DOE warned the Hawaii DOE that it must provide or purchase appropriate mental health services for special education students.

In January of 1993, a report by the Auditor for the State of Hawaii acknowledged that efforts to coordinate among state agencies the provision of mental health services for special education students had largely failed. The report concluded that "the [Hawaii DOE] must provide or purchase mental health services for special education students when the [Hawaii DOH] cannot provide these services."

Later in 1993 a class of plaintiffs comprised of disabled children and adolescents eligible for special education and mental health services sued the Hawaii DOE and the Hawaii DOH in federal court, claiming a failure to comply with the IDEA and with § 504 of the Rehabilitation Act. *Felix v. Waihee*, CV. No. 93-00367-DAE. The district court granted summary judgment for the class on the issue of liability, finding that the agencies "ha[d] systematically failed to provide required and necessary educational and mental health services to qualified handicapped children," in violation of both federal laws. Thereafter, in 1994, the parties entered into a consent decree (the *"Felix* Decree"), which was approved by the district court.

In the *Felix* Decree, the two state agencies acknowledged that they had violated the federal IDEA and § 504 of the Rehabilitation Act. The agencies agreed that the Hawaii DOE would provide all educational services the Felix class members require; that the Hawaii DOH would provide all mental health services the class members require to benefit from the educational services; and that the two agencies would create and maintain a system of care adequate to provide a continuum of services, placements, and programs necessary for disabled students. The *Felix* Decree defined the plaintiff class as "all children and adolescents with disabilities residing in Hawaii, from birth to 20 years of age, who are eligible for and in need of education and mental health services but for whom programs, services, and placements are either unavailable, inadequate, or inappropriate because of lack of a continuum of services, programs, and placements." Autistic children fall within the *Felix* class.

B. Michelle H.

Michelle H. and Natalie H. are the children of Mark and Rie H. Michelle H. was born on February 15, 1991. In March 1994, a Hawaii DOH psychologist who examined Michelle concluded that she had "mild Autistic Spectrum Disorder (or Pervasive Developmental Disorder)." The DOH psychologist made a number of recommendations to address Michelle's limitations, including enrollment in the Hawaii DOE's Preschool Program, use of numerous autism-specific approaches, and assignment of an extra aide to work one-on-one with Michelle in the classroom. According to the Hawaii DOE, the psychologist's recommendations to deal with Michelle's autism were never implemented "because of difficulties . . . in getting appropriate personnel as well as appropriate funding."

In April 1994, the Hawaii DOE performed its own academic and psychological evaluation of Michelle to determine her early special education needs. The Hawaii DOE found Michelle eligible for early special education services under the IDEA because of "chronic emotional impairment," not because she suffered from an autism disorder. The Hawaii DOE developed an Individualized Educational Program ("IEP") for Michelle, including placement in a fully self-contained special education classroom on a regular school campus for an extended school year with special education and speech therapy services. Michelle's IEP was updated at regular intervals through 1998, but the recommendations remained substantially unchanged. No representative from DOH attended any of the IEP sessions to discuss mental health services.

In April 1997, the Hawaii DOE changed Michelle's eligibility category from "Emotional Impairment" to "Autism." The Hawaii DOE reassessed her IEP in January 1998, after the diagnosis changed. The recommendations in the new IEP remained nearly identical to those made before the change in diagnosis and included no additional individualized services related to autism.

C. Natalie H.

Natalie H. was born on August 3, 1992. In 1994, the preschool that Natalie was attending, concerned that she might have a "pervasive development disorder," referred her to the Hawaii DOH. The Hawaii DOH performed a psychological evaluation in September 1994 and determined that, at the age of two, Natalie was developmentally at the age of a one-year old overall, but that "[she] showed no symptoms of Pervasive Developmental Disorder." In early 1995, Natalie's family doctor observed developmental delays and referred her to Kaiser Permanente for a neurological evaluation. The Kaiser evaluation diagnosed Natalie with autism and recommended that she be provided with appropriate special education.

In the spring of 1995, when Natalie was nearly three, the Hawaii DOE academically evaluated her and deemed her eligible for special education services, classifying her disability as an "Early Childhood Learning Impairment," not autism. An IEP prepared for Natalie on July 7, 1995 specified that she was to be placed in a fully self-contained special education classroom on a regular school campus for an extended school year, just as Michelle was.

Natalie's next IEP assessment, in March 1996, noted that the Kaiser evaluation had concluded in February 1995 that she was autistic. Natalie's IEP was reevaluated on an annual basis through 1998, although, as with Michelle, no mental health representative attended the meetings. In March 1998, the Hawaii DOE changed Natalie's eligibility category from "Early Childhood Learning Impairment" to "Autism."

D. The Administrative Hearing.

Natalie and Michelle's parents initiated an administrative action against the Hawaii DOE in 1999, alleging that the girls were denied a free appropriate public education under the IDEA and § 504, that their IEPs were deficient, and that the Hawaii DOE had violated their procedural rights. A hearing was held, and, in a detailed decision, the administrative officer found significant violations of the IDEA. Among his factual findings were that (1) "No special (autism) services were provided from 1994 to 1998"; (2) at the elementary school the girls attended, "the principal did not include mental health services as part of the IEP" because "this had been the system . . . prior to" the *Felix* Decree "and she was not familiar at that time with the new procedures"; (3) "No IEP to the present time includes all of the mental health services that were authorized or agreed upon by the IEP team"; and (4) Natalie and Michelle's special education teacher was generally inexperienced and had no experience with autistic children prior to her current job. The administrative officer determined, based on these findings, that Natalie and Michelle had been denied a FAPE under the IDEA, that their IEPs were inadequate, and that numerous procedural violations had occurred.

The administrative officer instructed the Hawaii DOE to take a number of steps to remedy the violations. There is no contention that the Hawaii DOE has not complied with the administrative order, which was not appealed, or that Natalie and Michelle are currently being denied a FAPE as defined by the IDEA.

II. STATUTORY CONTEXT

Before recounting the procedural history of this case, we examine the two related but separate statutes central to this litigation, the IDEA and § 504 of the Rehabilitation Act. . . .

The IDEA defines a FAPE as:

> special education and related services that — (A) have been provided at public expense, under public supervision and direction, and without charge; (B) meet the standards of the State educational agency; (C) include an appropriate preschool, elementary school, or secondary school education in the State involved; and (D) are provided in conformity with the individualized education program required under section 1414(d) of this title.

20 U.S.C. § 1401(9). . . .

The IDEA creates a cause of action under which a court may grant individuals "such relief as [it] determines is appropriate" for violations of the IDEA. 20 U.S.C. § 1415(i)(2)(C)(iii). Although injunctive relief is available under the IDEA, "ordinarily monetary damages are not." *Witte v. Clark County School Dist.*, 197 F.3d 1271, 1275 (9th Cir. 1999).

While the IDEA focuses on the provision of appropriate public education to disabled children, the Rehabilitation Act of 1973 more broadly addresses the provision of state services to disabled individuals. Section 504 of the Rehabilitation Act, the Act's core provision, states that:

> No otherwise qualified individual with a disability in the United States . . . shall, solely by reason of her or his disability, be excluded from the participation in, be denied the benefits of, or be subjected to discrimination under any program or activity receiving Federal financial assistance or under any program or activity conducted by any Executive agency or by the United States Postal Service.

29 U.S.C. § 794(a). Section 504 applies to all public schools that receive federal financial assistance. . . .

As pertinent to this case, the U.S. DOE's § 504 regulations require recipients of federal funds to "provide a free appropriate public education to each qualified handicapped person," and define "appropriate education" as:

regular or special education and related aids and services that (i) are designed to meet individual educational needs of handicapped persons as adequately as the needs of nonhandicapped persons are met and (ii) are based upon adherence to procedures that satisfy the requirements of [34 C.F.R.] §§ 104.34, 104.35, and 104.36.

34 C.F.R. § 104.33(a), (b).

The first regulation cross-referenced in § 104.33, § 104.34, requires that recipients place disabled individuals in a "regular educational environment" unless it can be shown that "the education of the person in the regular environment with the use of supplementary aids and services cannot be achieved satisfactorily." When a handicapped individual is removed from a regular environment, the facility in which she is placed must be "comparable" to that used by non-disabled students. 34 C.F.R. § 104.34(c). The remaining cross-referenced regulations, 34 C.F.R. §§ 104.35 and 104.36, require evaluation and testing of all those who need or are believed to need special education, as well as the development of procedural safeguards to ensure that guardians of disabled children receive notice, access to relevant records, and an opportunity for an "impartial hearing."

Section 504 establishes an implied private right of action allowing victims of prohibited discrimination, exclusion, or denial of benefits to seek "the full panoply of remedies, including equitable relief and [compensatory] damages." *Greater L.A. Council on Deafness, Inc. v. Zolin*, 812 F.2d 1103, 1107 (9th Cir. 1987); *see also Barnes v. Gorman*, 536 U.S. 181, 189 (2002). Punitive damages are not available under § 504. *Barnes.*

In sum, the IDEA contains a statutory FAPE provision and allows private causes of action only for prospective relief. Section 504 contains a broadly-worded prohibition on discrimination against, exclusion of and denial of benefits for disabled individuals, under which the U.S. DOE has promulgated regulations containing a FAPE requirement worded somewhat differently from the IDEA FAPE requirement. Section 504 can be privately enforced to provide, in addition to prospective relief, compensatory but not punitive damages for past violations.

III. FEDERAL COURT PROCEEDINGS

. . . .

In 2000, the girls and their parents filed a federal lawsuit against the Hawaii DOE and various school officials in their official capacities for violations of the IDEA and of § 504 of the Rehabilitation Act of 1973. The complaint requested compensatory, punitive, and hedonic damages, and stated that it was authorized by § 504 of the Rehabilitation Act, the IDEA, and 42 U.S.C. § 1983. The H. family alleged, among other things, that the "[Agency]'s failure to provide autism specific services to Natalie and Michelle during the crucial years of ages three to seven through appropriately trained personnel and in appropriate classrooms was a violation of § 504, and constituted deliberate indifference to the needs and rights of these children." The complaint continued by alleging that "Michelle and Natalie have been discriminated against by the [d]efendants solely because of their disabilities."

A. October 18, 2000 Ruling on Motion to Dismiss.

The Agency moved to dismiss the complaint on several grounds. Among other contentions, the Agency maintained that the IDEA is the exclusive remedy for injuries caused by violation of its provisions. More specifically, the Agency argued that the H. family's § 504 claim is barred because (1) the H. family only litigated the IDEA claims, not the claims under § 504, in the administrative hearing; and (2) § 504 does not provide money damages for acts that also violate the IDEA. The Agency also argued that all of the claims in the complaint were barred by sovereign immunity.

The district court granted the motion to dismiss in part, and denied it in part. With respect to the exclusivity of the IDEA as a remedy, the court determined that the H. family had exhausted its administrative remedies under the IDEA, but did not address the Agency's other arguments as to why the IDEA cause of action for prospective relief is the only remedy available to the H. family. The court held that the Eleventh Amendment did not bar the § 504 claims, but did bar any claims against the state under § 1983 for money damages.

B. July 24, 2001 Summary Judgment Ruling.

The Agency then moved for summary judgment, advancing several new arguments and reiterating their earlier Eleventh Amendment arguments. The H. family filed a cross-motion for partial summary judgment, arguing (1) that the administrative hearing decision on the IDEA was res judicata with regard to the question whether the girls were denied a FAPE; and (2) that the appropriate substantive standard in an action for damages under § 504 is whether a defendant demonstrated "deliberate indifference" to the disabled individual's accommodation needs, not whether a defendant acted with discriminatory animus.

The district court granted the H. family's cross-motion in its entirety, and granted in part and denied in part the Agency's motion. In granting the motion, the court held that "[d]efendants are precluded from arguing that Michelle and Natalie were not denied FAPE." The court rejected most of the Agency's arguments on summary judgment but agreed with the Agency that non-equitable monetary damages are not available under the IDEA and that the appropriate defendant for monetary relief is the state, not state officials in their official capacities. As a result of these rulings, the only remaining claim as of 2001 was the § 504 cause of action against the state itself for monetary relief.

C. May 25, 2005 Summary Judgment Ruling.

On March 12, 2004, the case was reassigned to Judge Manuel Real. The Agency again moved for summary judgment, reasserting some arguments made earlier in its motion to dismiss and motion for summary judgment and making one new argument: that the H. family's proffered evidence failed to show the "deliberate indifference" the court had ruled was required for a § 504 violation. In a motion for partial summary judgment filed the same day, the H. family argued that Judge Ezra's prior rulings governed as law of the case, and further maintained that they were entitled to summary judgment on the issue of liability because the Agency failed to provide a FAPE and acted with deliberate indifference in doing so.

Judge Real granted the Agency's motion for summary judgment and denied the H. family's motion. He held that there is no § 504 cause of action for violation of any affirmative right to a FAPE, reasoning that "IDEA procedures remain the exclusive remedy for correcting problems within the terms of the act, and for deciding what is best suited to a free appropriate public education." Judge Real further held that (1) pursuant to *Alexander v. Sandoval*, 532 U.S. 275 (2001), the U.S. DOE's § 504 regulations can not be enforced through the right of action implied under § 504; and (2) a state's waiver of sovereign immunity under § 504 does not extend to claims for damages for failure to provide an IDEA FAPE. Finally Judge Real concluded that, even if the H. family had a valid § 504 cause of action, the state would prevail on the merits, because "the [p]laintiffs do not present any evidence that they were intentionally discriminated against, 'solely by reason of their disability.' " The case was dismissed. The H. family appeals from this final judgment.

ANALYSIS

I. EFFECT OF IDEA ON AVAILABILITY OF REMEDIES UNDER § 504 OF THE REHABILITATION ACT FOR DENIAL OF FAPE.

The district court held that the availability of injunctive relief under the IDEA precludes suits for damages under § 504 for government actions that violate both statutes. This conclusion was erroneous for two reasons.

First, the district court's conclusion assumed that FAPE in the IDEA and FAPE in the U.S. DOE § 504 regulations are identical. This assumption underlies not only the district court's ruling on the second summary judgment motion but all of the proceedings in this case. In particular, it also underlies the district court's earlier holding that the administrative hearing determination that Michelle and Natalie were denied a FAPE under the IDEA was res judicata with regard to whether they were denied a FAPE under the § 504 regulations. An examination of the definitions of FAPE in the two statutes demonstrates that this assumption is false.

FAPE under the IDEA and FAPE as defined in the § 504 regulations are similar but not identical. When it promulgated its § 504 regulations, the U.S. DOE described them as "*generally* conform[ing] to the standards established for the education of handicapped persons in . . . the [IDEA]." Department of Education, Establishment and Title and Chapters, 45 Fed. Reg. 30,802, 30,951 (May 4, 1980) (emphasis added). Although overlapping in some respects, the two requirements contain significant differences.

The most important differences are that, unlike FAPE under the IDEA, FAPE under § 504 is defined to require a comparison between the manner in which the needs of disabled and non-disabled children are met, and focuses on the "design" of a child's educational program. *See* 34 C.F.R. § 104.33(b)(1) (a FAPE requires education and services "*designed* to meet individual educational needs of handicapped persons *as adequately* as the needs of nonhandicapped persons are met" (emphasis added)).

Moreover, the U.S. DOE's § 504 regulations distinctly state that adopting a valid IDEA IEP is sufficient but not necessary to satisfy the § 504 FAPE requirements. 34 C.F.R. § 104.33(b)(2) ("Implementation of an [IEP under the IDEA] is *one means* of meeting" the substantive portion of the § 504 regulations' definition of FAPE (emphasis added)); *id.* at § 104.36 ("Compliance with the procedural safeguards of section 615 of the [IDEA] is *one means* of meeting" the § 504 procedural requirements in § 104.36) (emphasis added). Plaintiffs who allege a violation of the FAPE requirement contained in U.S. DOE's § 504 regulations, consequently, may not obtain damages simply by proving that the IDEA FAPE requirements were not met.

The district court thus erred when it held that the H. family's § 504 claim attempts "to correct what is in essence a mere violation of a [FAPE] under the IDEA," and that the IDEA is therefore the H. family's exclusive remedy. At the same time, this examination of the text of the § 504 regulations and the IDEA demonstrates that the H. family cannot rely on the administrative hearing officer's decision with regard to an IDEA FAPE as dispositive of whether a FAPE was denied under § 504. So, to the extent that the district court held, in deciding the first summary judgment motion, that the administrative hearing officer's IDEA decision precluded further litigation as to whether a FAPE was denied under the § 504 regulations, that decision is also incorrect.

Second, and as important, Congress has clearly expressed its intent that remedies be available under Title V of the Rehabilitation Act for acts that also violate the IDEA, overriding the holding of the Supreme Court in *Smith v. Robinson*, 468 U.S. 992 (1984). In *Smith*, the Court considered the relationship between the remedies available under § 504 and those available under the IDEA. Petitioners in *Smith* established that their rights under the IDEA had been violated because no FAPE was provided, and then sought payment of their attorney's fees under Title V of the Rehabilitation Act. The Court in *Smith* held that the "remedies, rights, and procedures" available under the IDEA were the exclusive relief for failure to provide a FAPE, so that remedies under Title V of the Rehabilitation Act, including payment of a prevailing party's attorney's fees, were unavailable.

Congress responded to the decision in *Smith* by adding to the IDEA what is now 20 U.S.C. § 1415(*l*), which provides:

> Nothing in this chapter shall be construed to restrict or limit the rights, procedures, and remedies available under the Constitution, the Americans with Disabilities Act of 1990, title V of the Rehabilitation Act of 1973, or other Federal laws protecting the rights of children with disabilities, except that before the filing of a civil action under such laws seeking relief that is also available under this subchapter, the procedures under subsections (f) and (g) of this section shall be exhausted to the same extent as would be required had the action been brought under this subchapter.

Despite the intervening passage of § 1415(*l*), the district court relied on the reasoning of the Supreme Court in *Smith* and held that, by bringing a damages claim under § 504 for denial of a FAPE, the H. family was impermissibly attempting to "circumvent or enlarge on the remedies available under the [IDEA] by resort to

§ 504." With regard to § 1415(*l*), the district court concluded, and the Agency here argues, that the legislative history of § 1415(*l*) of the IDEA shows that it was intended only to permit recovery of attorneys' fees under § 504, not damages.

Even if the legislative history supported this conclusion, it could not overrule the statute's plain language. The plain text of the statute preserves *all* rights and remedies under the Rehabilitation Act, not just attorneys' fees. Given the absence of any ambiguity in the statute's text, there is no need to examine its legislative history.

In any event, the statute's legislative history is not to the contrary. The district court observed that neither the Senate nor House reports discussed the possibility of monetary damages under § 1415(*l*). *See* S. REP. No. 99–112 (1986). Nowhere in the legislative history of the statute, however, does Congress state that it was intended to provide only for attorneys' fees, or that it was not intended to allow monetary damages under § 504.[4]

In sum, availability of relief under the IDEA does not limit the availability of a damages remedy under *§ 504* for failure to provide the FAPE independently required by *§ 504* and its implementing regulations.[5]

II. IMPLIED RIGHT OF ACTION TO ENFORCE § 504 REGULATIONS.

The district court further held that there is no private right of action available to enforce in any respect the U.S. DOE's § 504 regulations regarding provision of a FAPE. On examination, we observe that the district court's approach to this question did not recognize some considerations likely to be informative in determining whether there is or is not a private cause of action for damages available to enforce the § 504 FAPE regulations. As we explain below, however, we cannot determine without clarification of the H. family's allegations whether the district court's ultimate conclusion — that no cause of action for damages is available on these facts under § 504 — is correct, and so remand for further proceedings.

A.

It has long been established that § 504 contains an implied private right of action for damages to enforce its provisions. Whether the H. family can bring an action to enforce the § 504 *regulations* will depend on whether those regulations come within the § 504 implied right of action.

In *Alexander v. Sandoval*, 532 U.S. 275 (2001), the Supreme Court addressed the

---

[4] [FN10] We have recently held that, despite passage of § 1415(l), the provisions of the IDEA are not enforceable under § 1983. *Blanchard v. Morton Sch. Dist.*, 509 F.3d 934 (9th Cir. 2007). The conclusion that § 1983 actions cannot be used to enforce the IDEA does not affect our analysis in this case. Section 1415(*l*) explicitly mentions the remedies available under the Rehabilitation Act and indicates that they are preserved, but does not refer to § 1983.

[5] [FN 11] Because the § 504 FAPE requirement differs from the IDEA FAPE requirement, it is not clear how the exhaustion provision of § 1415(*l*) applies to suits for damages for failure to provide a § 504 FAPE. We need not reach this issue, because the H. family did exhaust the IDEA administrative remedies.

circumstances under which regulations can be enforced using the private right of action created by a Spending Clause-based statute. *Sandoval* held that disparate impact regulations promulgated under § 602 of Title VI of the Civil Rights Act of 1964 impose affirmative obligations that go beyond the requirements of § 601 and so do not fall within the private right of action created by the statute. According to *Sandoval*, regulations can only be enforced through the private right of action contained in a statute when they "authoritatively construe" the statute; regulations that go beyond a construction of the statute's prohibitions do not fall within the implied private right of action, even if valid. As applied here, *Sandoval* instructs that whether the § 504 regulations are privately enforceable will turn on whether their requirements fall within the scope of the prohibition contained in § 504 itself.

The district court held that § 504 "merely prohibits intentional discrimination," while the § 504 FAPE regulations purport to create "affirmative obligations." Applying *Sandoval*, the district court concluded that because the § 504 FAPE regulations uniformly impose "affirmative obligations" that are not imposed by the statute itself, they are not enforceable at all through the implied private right of action.

The district court's approach to this question fails to recognize three key features of § 504 and the § 504 FAPE regulations:

First, insofar as the district court was drawing a direct analogy to *Sandoval's* prohibition on private causes of action under a disparate impact regulation, that analogy is not entirely persuasive. The § 504 regulations in question — unlike the regulations under § 602 that the Supreme Court characterized in *Sandoval* as "disparate impact" regulations — are not fairly viewed as imposing liability based only on unintentionally created "effects" or outcomes.

The Title VI regulations at issue in *Sandoval* provided that funding recipients may not "utilize criteria or methods of administration which *have the effect* of subjecting individuals to discrimination because of their race, color, or national origin." In contrast, the § 504 FAPE regulations encompass several provisions, the central requirement being that disabled children must be provided an "education and related aids and services that (i) are designed to meet individual educational needs of handicapped persons as adequately as the needs of nonhandicapped persons are met." The plain language of this first, overarching FAPE regulation is not violated by a mere difference in educational outcomes or "effects." Rather, it is violated only if a state fails to "design" educational plans so as to meet the needs of both disabled and nondisabled children comparably. To "design" something to produce a certain, equal outcome involves some measure of intentionality. And an obligation to "design" something in a certain way is not violated simply because the actual impact of the design turns out otherwise than intended.

In contrast, a disparate effect or impact need not be the result of "design" at all, could be entirely accidental, and need not be recognized once it occurs. This much was made clear in *Alexander v. Choate*, 469 U.S. 287 (1985). In *Choate*, the Supreme Court expressed its view that, while § 504 may prohibit some disparate impacts, it is not intended to prohibit *all* such impacts. The Court repeatedly distinguished disparate impact discrimination from other forms of discrimination by noting that disparate impact discrimination arises from actions that discriminate only in "effect" rather than "design." And the Court was concerned that a prohibition on any and all disparate impacts would lead to liability for effects brought about wholly inadvertently, indeed, even for effects that agencies had acted to avoid. By requiring only appropriate "design" of programs, § 104.33 does not fall into that category of "disparate impacts" about which the Court was most concerned in *Choate*.

Second, § 104.33 requires a comparison between the treatment of disabled and nondisabled children, rather than simply requiring a certain set level of services for each disabled child. So, contrary to the district court's apparent concern that the § 504 regulations create free-floating "affirmative obligations," in fact the obligation created is a comparative one. In other words, school districts need only design education programs for disabled persons that are intended to meet their educational needs to the same degree that the needs of nondisabled students are met, not more.

Further, the regulations also prohibit separating handicapped students from nonhandicapped students unless "it is demonstrated . . . that the education of the person in the regular environment with the use of supplementary aids and services cannot be achieved satisfactorily," and require that disabled children be provided "comparable facilities" to those used by non-disabled children. Even if some of the other regulations might be characterized as imposing "affirmative obligations" rather than prohibiting discrimination, regulations aimed at preventing baseless segregation of disabled and nondisabled students clearly represent a prohibition on simple discrimination as long understood. *Cf. Brown v. Bd. of Educ.*, 347 U.S. 483, 493 (1954).

Third, regardless of whether or not the § 504 FAPE regulations can be characterized as to some degree prohibiting "disparate impacts" or imposing "affirmative obligations," the district court gave the prohibition contained in § 504 itself too cramped a reading. The text of § 504 prohibits not only "discrimination" against the disabled, but also "exclu[sion] from . . . participation in" and "deni[al] [of] the benefits of" state programs solely by reason of a disability. This language is nearly identical to the language in Title VI, and, in general, the remedies available under both § 504 and Title II of the ADA, 42 U.S.C. § 12132, are "linked" to Title VI. *Ferguson v. City of Phoenix*, 157 F.3d 668, 673 (9th Cir. 1998). *But see Choate*, 469 U.S. at 293 n.7 ("[T]oo facile an assimilation of Title VI law to § 504 must be resisted."). Nonetheless, the legislative history of the Rehabilitation Act and the nature of discrimination against disabled individuals have led us to construe the § 504 prohibition somewhat more broadly.

This court has recognized that the focus of the prohibition in § 504 is "whether disabled persons were denied 'meaningful access' to state-provided services." *Crowder v. Kitagawa*, 81 F.3d 1480, 1484 (9th Cir. 1996). Thus, although § 504 does not require "substantial adjustments in existing programs beyond those necessary to eliminate discrimination against otherwise qualified individuals," it, like the ADA, does require *reasonable* modifications necessary to correct for instances in which qualified disabled people are prevented from enjoying " 'meaningful access' to a benefit because of their disability." *Southeastern Community College v. Davis*, 442 U.S. 397, 410 (1979). Moreover, contrary to the Agency's contentions at oral argument, evidence that appropriate services were provided to *some* disabled individuals does not demonstrate that others were not denied meaningful access "solely on the basis of their disability."

The district court and the Agency appear to have forgotten the established § 504 "reasonable accommodation" and "meaningful access" requirements in evaluating whether the § 504 FAPE regulations come within § 504's substantive scope. The reason for this elision may have been a misunderstanding about the distinction between interpreting the scope of the prohibition contained in § 504 and determining the state of mind with which a violation of § 504 must be committed so as to give rise to a damages remedy.

Our cases on the appropriate *mens rea* standard for a § 504 damages remedy recognize — as they must after *Crowder* — that § 504 itself prohibits actions that deny disabled individuals "meaningful access" or "reasonable accommodation" for their disabilities. *See Duvall v. County of Kitsap*, 260 F.3d 1124, 1135–36 (9th Cir. 2001); *Ferguson*, 157 F.3d at 679. *Cf. Lovell v. Chandler*, 303 F.3d at 1054 (assuming that "meaningful access" is the appropriate standard). Those cases then go on to analyze the state of mind with regard to a denial of "meaningful access" or "reasonable accommodation" necessary to justify monetary damages. As to this latter question, we have held that plaintiffs must prove a *mens rea* of "intentional discrimination," to prevail on a § 504 claim, but that that standard may be met by showing "deliberate indifference," and not only by showing "discriminatory animus." Thus, a public entity can be liable for damages under § 504 if it intentionally or with deliberate indifference fails to provide meaningful access or reasonable accommodation to disabled persons.

For purposes of determining whether a particular regulation is ever enforceable through the implied right of action contained in a statute, the pertinent question is simply whether the regulation falls within the scope of the statute's prohibition. The *mens rea* necessary to support a damages remedy is not pertinent at that stage of the analysis. It becomes essential, instead, in determining whether damages can actually be imposed in an individual case. The district court took a misstep when it brought the *mens rea* question into the private cause of action analysis.

In sum, the § 504 FAPE regulations are somewhat different from the Title VI disparate impact regulation in *Sandoval*, because the regulations focus on "design" rather than "effect" and establish only a comparative obligation. Further, because the basic statutory prohibition has been understood somewhat differently in Title VI and § 504, to the degree the § 504 FAPE regulations that the H. family invokes can be interpreted as a variety of meaningful access regulation, they will fall within the § 504 implied cause of action. Finally, to obtain damages, the H. family will ultimately have to demonstrate that the Agency was deliberately indifferent to the violation of whatever requirements the family validly seeks to enforce.

B.

We also note that resolution of the question whether the regulations can be enforced through the right of action in § 504 will likely be dispositive of the Eleventh Amendment sovereign immunity concerns that have frequently popped up in this case. The state argues that, while states do not enjoy sovereign immunity from suits to enforce § 504 itself, the U.S. DOE's § 504 regulations cannot be enforced against states because they demand more of the states than they bargained for when they agreed to waive their Eleventh Amendment sovereign immunity.

However, as our discussion of *Sandoval* demonstrates, to be enforceable through the § 504 implied private right of action, regulations must be tightly enough linked to § 504 that they "authoritatively construe" that statutory section, rather than impose new obligations. Regulations that do not impose obligations beyond § 504's prohibition on disability-based disadvantage but instead implement that prohibition are part of the bargain struck between states and the federal government. Accordingly, those regulations that can be enforced through the § 504 private right of action under *Sandoval* are almost certainly enforceable against the states in a damages action.

C.

We do not here decide whether the H. family has alleged a privately enforceable cause of action for damages against the state. To this point, both parties have proceeded on the assumption that the IDEA and the § 504 FAPE requirements are identical, and have not litigated whether any of the § 504 FAPE regulations, as opposed to the IDEA FAPE requirements, can support a private cause of action. We therefore remand to the district court for further proceedings. On remand, the H. family should be given an opportunity to amend its complaint to specify which § 504 regulations they believe were violated and which support a privately enforceable cause of action.

For the foregoing reasons, the district court decision is REVERSED and REMANDED.

NOTES AND QUESTIONS

1. If on remand, the *Baird* case goes to trial and you represent Baird, what evidence will you introduce to show damages? If you are defending, what evidence will you adduce in response? If you are negotiating settlement, what would you demand? What would you offer?

2. The court in *Baird* does not question the proposition that damages are appropriate relief for intentional conduct that violates title II. Title II adopts the remedies of section 504, whose language parallels that of Title IX of the Education Amendments of 1972. In *Franklin v. Gwinnett County Public Schools*, the Supreme Court upheld a damages claim under that statute for intentional sex discrimination. 503 U.S. 60 (1992). As *Mark H.* notes, the Court, however, has barred a punitive damages claim against a municipality under section 504 and title II. *Barnes v. Gorman*, 536 U.S. 181 (2002). Do you think that the *Mark H.* court's approach to damages under section 504's comparability of services provision is persuasive? What proof will the family need to present at trial? How should the defendants respond? What should the measure of damages be?

3. *Baird* rejected a claim of individual liability under the retaliation provision of the ADA. *Contra Shotz v. City of Plantation*, 344 F.3d 1161 (11th Cir. 2003) (relying

on plain language of § 12203); *LaManque v. Massachusetts Dep't of Employment & Training*, 3 F. Supp. 2d 83 (D. Mass. 1998) (same).

4. *Mark H.* discusses the requirement of a showing of deliberate indifference for a damages claim under the section 504 regulations. Most, but not all, courts have required a showing of intentional conduct to support damages claims under section 504 and title II. Many courts have used the standard of gross misjudgment or bad-faith conduct as a proxy for intent in cases involving public schools and special education students. *E.g.*, *M.P. v. Independent Sch. Dist. No. 721*, 326 F.3d 975 (8th Cir. 2003) (finding that gross misjudgment-bad faith standard could be met by school's failure to respond to peer harassment of child with schizophrenia). Nevertheless, those courts are not always consistent in what they consider gross misjudgment or bad faith. *Compare Sellers v. School Bd.*, 141 F.3d 524 (4th Cir. 1998) (finding that failure to identify and evaluate child with disabilities did not meet standard), *with K.S. v. Fremont Unified Sch. Dist.*, No. C 06-07218, 2007 U.S. Dist. LEXIS 24860 (N.D. Cal. Mar. 23, 2007) (denying motion to dismiss section 504 and ADA claims under bad faith or gross misjudgment-deliberate indifference standard when child alleged various delays and problems over five school years in providing appropriate education); *McKellar v. Pennsylvania Dep't of Educ.*, No. 98-CV-4161, 1999 U.S. Dist. LEXIS 2194 (E.D. Pa. Feb. 23, 1999) (finding that gross misjudgment-bad faith standard could be met by showing denial of appropriate education and ignoring of individualized education programs).

5. As *Mark H.* explains, the Supreme Court has barred private suits for non-intentional discrimination on the basis of race, color, or national origin under title VI of the Civil Rights Act, another statute whose language parallels that of section 504 and title IX. The Court held that the statute itself reaches only intentional conduct, and Congress did not authorize suit for violations of the regulations promulgated under the statute (which bar disparate impacts as well). *Alexander v. Sandoval*, 532 U.S. 275 (2001). Thus, even when the plaintiff seeks only an injunction and no damages, he or she cannot bring a claim in court. The aggrieved party can do nothing but hope that the federal government will take action against the entity whose unintentional conduct creates a disparate impact against a racial minority. Section 504 and ADA title II differ from title VI, however, in that the Supreme Court has stated that section 504 was meant to reach at least disparate impacts that deny meaningful access to benefits. *Alexander v. Choate*, 469 U.S. 287 (1985). Courts have thus refused to bar injunctive-relief actions for conduct that has a negative impact on people with disabilities. *See, e.g., Robinson v. Kansas*, 295 F.3d 1183 (10th Cir. 2002).

6. The *Baird* court also upheld a claim under state common law for intentional infliction of emotional distress. Do you agree that the Restatement test is met on the basis of the facts alleged? In various special education cases, the facts may support claims for outrage, assault, battery, false imprisonment, defamation, or other common law torts. *See, e.g., Bowden v. Dever*, No. 00-12308-DPW, 2002 U.S. Dist. LEXIS 5203 (D. Mass. Mar. 20, 2002) (upholding tort claims based on psychological and physical abuse of children with autism).

C. CONSTITUTIONAL CLAIMS AND IDEA CLAIMS BROUGHT UNDER SECTION 1983

This discussion of § 1983 claims embraces both those brought for violations of the Constitution and those brought for violations of IDEA.

1. Constitutional Claims Brought Pursuant to 42 U.S.C. § 1983

Smith v. Robinson, discussed *supra* section B, found that federal special education law effectively preempted equal protection claims in the context of special education. Congressional overruling of that precedent opened the way for litigants to bring constitutional claims in cases involving special education students. Given the specificity of IDEA, however, plaintiffs have generally relied on IDEA and ignored constitutional claims unless the facts clearly manifest constitutional violations and the cases seem proper for compensatory damages relief not considered available under IDEA.

Some cases meet that description, and there the courts have upheld constitutional claims. For example, in *Sutton v. Utah State School for the Deaf and Blind*, 173 F.3d 1226 (10th Cir. 1999), the plaintiff had severe cerebral palsy that left him blind, mentally retarded, and unable to speak. One day, he told his mother through sign language that a large boy not in his class had touched his genital area when he was in the bathroom at school. The next morning, the mother met with the school superintendent, the principal, and the teacher, who assured her that the incident could not have occurred; students never went into the bathroom without adult supervision. A week later, an aide escorted the child to the bathroom door, but then left to answer the telephone. She returned to find the student the child had previously described now in the course of sexually attacking him. After the assault, the child experienced uncontrollable rages, nightmares, compulsive behavior, and other signs of acute mental distress. The court upheld a substantive due process claim against the principal in his individual capacity for failure to adopt or implement a policy or training program to prevent sexual assaults after being placed on notice of the danger.

Constitutional claims are usually brought against state or local government or their officials through the Civil Rights Act of 1871, 42 U.S.C. § 1983. To obtain liability under that statute against a municipal entity such as a school district, the plaintiff must show the existence of a policy or custom, rather than relying on respondeat superior, the doctrine by which employers are ordinarily liable for the on-duty torts of their employees. *Monell v. Department of Soc. Servs.*, 436 U.S. 658 (1978). A policy need not be written or officially enacted, however. A single decision of an authoritative decision-maker can constitute policy, *Pembaur v. City of Cincinnati*, 475 U.S. 469 (1986), as can inadequate training or supervision, when the conduct meets the standard of deliberate indifference, *City of Canton v. Harris*, 489 U.S. 378 (1989). Section 1983 supports compensatory and, with regard to non-governmental entities, punitive damages relief. *Smith v. Wade*, 461 U.S. 30 (1983). The United States Supreme Court has ruled that title IX of the Education Amendments of 1972, a statute whose language parallels that of section 504 of the

Rehabilitation Act, does not preempt a section 1983 claim for violations of constitutional equal protection rights in the context of sexual harassment of a student, thus permitting suit against school officials for constitutional violations as well as against the school district for violations of title IX. *Fitzgerald v. Barnstable Sch. Comm.*, 129 S. Ct. 788 (2009).

2. IDEA Claims Brought Pursuant to 42 U.S.C. § 1983

The Civil Rights Act of 1871 provides:

> Every person who, under color of any statute, ordinance, regulation, custom, or usage, of any State or Territory or the District of Columbia, subjects, or causes to be subjected, any citizen of the United States or other person within the jurisdiction thereof to the deprivation of any rights, privileges, or immunities secured by the Constitution and laws, shall be liable to the party injured in an action at law, suit in equity, or other proper proceeding for redress. . . .

42 U.S.C. § 1983. The cause of action thus embraces violations of laws, that is, statutes, as well as violations of the Constitution. *See Maine v. Thiboutot*, 448 U.S. 1 (1980) (upholding § 1983 claim for state's violation of Social Security Act). Nevertheless, in recent years, the Supreme Court has held that violations of some federal statutes are not actionable under § 1983. *See, e.g., Gonzaga Univ. v. Doe*, 536 U.S. 273 (2002) (finding that Family Educational Rights and Privacy Act nondisclosure provisions failed to create personal rights enforceable under § 1983). The test is whether the statute confers rights on a particular class of persons. *Id.* at 285. The Supreme Court has also found implicit substitution of other remedies for the § 1983 cause of action when a statute provides sufficiently comprehensive alternative mechanisms for enforcement. *See Middlesex County Sewerage Auth. v. Nat'l Sea Clammers Ass'n*, 453 U.S. 1, 20 (1981).

Courts have approved the use of § 1983 as a remedy for violations of IDEA in situations where the § 1415 cause of action seems inapplicable but some judicial response is plainly called for, as when a school district refuses to obey a final due process hearing decision. *See Robinson v. Pinderhughes*, 810 F.2d 1270 (4th Cir. 1987); *see also Marie O. v. Edgar*, 131 F.3d 610, 620–22 (7th Cir. 1997) (approving use of § 1983 cause of action in systemic case challenging failure to properly implement IDEA infant and toddler services); *Manecke v. School Bd.*, 762 F.2d 912 (11th Cir. 1985) (applying § 1983 to remedy special education law violation when district failed to act on parents' request for due process hearing). Most of these cases have involved requests for injunctive relief, but if the § 1983 cause of action exists, there would be no obvious basis on which to limit it to equitable remedies. Section 1983 provides for an action at law, and the general rule is that it provides for damages when damages are a suitable remedy. *See Smith v. Wade*, 461 U.S. 30 (1983). Accordingly, some cases have approved causes of action for damages under § 1983 for violations of IDEA. *E.g., Weixel v. Board of Educ.*, 287 F.3d 138, 151 (2d Cir. 2002). The court in one such case reasoned:

A. Section 1983 right of action

Section 1983 does not confer substantive rights, but merely redresses the deprivation of those rights elsewhere secured. Those rights may be created by the Constitution or federal statute, and hence in a § 1983 action a person may challenge federal statutory violations by state agents. *Maine v. Thiboutot*, 448 U.S. 1, 5–6 (1980) ("§ 1983 encompasses claims based on purely statutory violations of federal law").

When the rights at issue are statutory, however, a § 1983 action is impermissible when "Congress intended to foreclose such private enforcement." *Wright v. Roanoke Redevelopment & Housing Authority*, 479 U.S. 418, 423 (1987). Such an intent is generally found either in the express language of a statute or where a statutory remedial scheme is so comprehensive that an intent to prohibit enforcement other than by the statute's own means may be inferred. *Id.*

Relying on the latter exception, in 1984 the Supreme Court held that when EHA, § 504, and Equal Protection Clause claims overlap, EHA procedures are the exclusive means by which parents and children can secure a free appropriate education. *Smith v. Robinson*, 468 U.S. 992, 1012–13 (1984). In response to *Smith*, however, Congress amended the EHA to add § 1415(f), a provision which establishes that the statute's provisions are not the sole means for redress available to disabled children and their parents. *See* The Handicapped Children's Protection Act of 1986, Pub. L. No. 99-372 § 3, 100 Stat. 796 (1986).

In enacting § 1415(f), Congress specifically intended that EHA violations could be redressed by § 504 and § 1983 actions, as the legislative history reveals. The Senate Report discussed *Smith* at length, including quoting favorably from the *Smith* dissent, *see* S. Rep. No. 99-112, 99th Cong., 2d Sess. (1986), *reprinted in* 1986 U.S.C.C.A.N. 1798, 1799 ("Senate Report"). The House Conference Report stated "[i]t is the conferees' intent that actions brought under 42 U.S.C. 1983 are governed by [§ 1415(f)]." H.R. Conf. Rep. No. 99-687, 99th Cong., 2d Sess. (1986); 1986 U.S.C.C.A.N. 1807, 1809. In addition, the House Report made explicit that "since 1978, it has been Congress' intent to permit parents or guardians to pursue the rights of handicapped children through EHA, section 504, *and section 1983*. . . . Congressional intent was ignored by the U.S. Supreme Court when . . . it handed down its decision in *Smith v. Robinson*." H.R. Rep. No. 99-296, 99th Cong., 1st Sess. 4 (1985) ("House Report") (first emphasis added). Section 1415(f) was thus enacted to "reaffirm, in light of [*Smith*], the viability of section 504, 42 U.S.C 1983, and other statutes as separate vehicles for ensuring the rights of handicapped children." *Id.*

We have previously characterized the enactment of § 1415(f) as overruling *Smith. See Board of Education v. Diamond*, 808 F.2d 987, 994–95 (3d Cir. 1986). Far from inferring a congressional intent to *prevent* § 1983 actions predicated on IDEA then, we conclude that Congress explicitly *approved* such actions. Accordingly, § 1983 supplies a private right of action for the instant case.

B. Availability of damages

. . . .

2. Under IDEA

Beginning with the "traditional presumption in favor of all appropriate relief," *Franklin*, 503 U.S. at 69, we turn to the language and history of § 1983 and IDEA. First, it is axiomatic that § 1983 provides for remedies "at law . . . [or] in equity." 42 U.S.C. § 1983.

Second, even were we to limit our focus to IDEA itself, we discern nothing in the text or history suggesting that relief under IDEA is limited in any way, and certainly no "clear direction" sufficient to rebut the presumption that all relief is available. The expansive language of § 1415(f), which was enacted in the shadow of *Smith* and tracks the broad grant of remedial power allowed a district court reviewing a direct IDEA appeal, *see* 20 U.S.C. § 1415(e)(2), contains no restrictions on forms of relief. Nor does the legislative history of § 1415(f) suggest a congressional intent that damages be unavailable. In fact, Congress expressly contemplated that the courts would fashion remedies not specifically enumerated in IDEA. *See* House Report at 7 (excusing § 1415(f) exhaustion requirement where "the hearing officer lacks the authority to grant the relief sought").

Indeed, since enactment of § 1415(f), several courts of appeals have approved § 1983 actions to enforce IDEA rights. *See Angela L. v. Pasadena Independent Sch. Dist.*, 918 F.2d 1188, 1193 n. 3 (5th Cir. 1990) (§ 1983 and § 504 "permit parents to obtain relief which otherwise is unavailable from the EHA"); *Digre v. Roseville Sch. Independent Dist.*, 841 F.2d 245, 250 (8th Cir. 1988) (injunctive relief); *Mrs. W. v. Tirozzi*, 832 F.2d 748, 753 (2d Cir. 1987) (declaratory and injunctive relief); *Jackson v. Franklin County Sch. Bd.*, 806 F.2d 623, 631–32 (5th Cir. 1986) (compensatory damages or remedial education). *See also Hunt v. Bartman*, 873 F. Supp. 229, 245 (W.D. Mo. 1994) (injunctive relief). On the other hand, the Sixth Circuit has indicated skepticism that damages are available in a § 1983 action asserting violations of IDEA. *See Crocker v. Tennessee Secondary Sch. Athletic Ass'n*, 980 F.2d 382, 386–87 (6th Cir. 1992) (disabled transfer student, who was ruled ineligible to participate in school sports and missed two games, did not state a claim for damages under EHA).

Even before *Franklin*, in a § 1983 action to enforce IDEA, we held that compensatory damages are available to remedy IDEA violations. *Diamond*, 808 F.2d at 996. *See also Lester H. v. Gilhool*, 916 F.2d at 873 (in direct appeal from IDEA administrative proceeding, "Congress empowered the courts to grant a compensatory remedy"); *Muth v. Central Bucks Sch. Dist.*, 839 F.2d 113, 127 (3d Cir. 1988) ("there is case law suggesting that compensatory damages based solely on violations of a parent's procedural rights may be available under the EHA"), *rev'd on other grounds*, 491 U.S. 223 (1989); *Woods v. New Jersey Dep't of Educ.*, 796 F.

Supp. 767, 774, 776 (D.N.J. 1992) (compensatory and punitive damages available in § 1983 action for IDEA violations).

We conclude that the traditional presumption in favor of all appropriate relief is not rebutted as to § 1983 actions to enforce IDEA. Defendants have identified no "clear direction" in the text or history of IDEA indicating such a limitation, and indeed there is strong suggestion that Congress intended no such restriction. Certainly the plain language of § 1983 authorizes actions at law or equity, and our prior holding in *Diamond* compels the conclusion that, as a matter of law, an aggrieved parent or disabled child is not barred from seeking monetary damages in such an action.

We caution that in fashioning a remedy for an IDEA violation, a district court may wish to order educational services, such as compensatory education beyond a child's age of eligibility, or reimbursement for providing at private expense what should have been offered by the school, rather than compensatory damages for generalized pain and suffering. *See Lester H., supra; Puffer v. Raynolds,* 761 F. Supp. 838, 853 (D. Mass. 1988); *Jackson,* 806 F.2d at 632 (in § 1983 action alleging IDEA violations, "remedial educational services may be more valuable than any pecuniary damages that could be awarded"). However, we do not preclude the awarding of monetary damages and leave to the district court in the first instance the task of fashioning appropriate relief.

W.B. v. Matula, 67 F.3d 484, 493–95 (3d Cir. 1995).

In a few more recent cases, however, courts have argued that the legislative overruling of *Smith v. Robinson* is not as complete as the *W.B.* court suggested, and that the existence of the § 1415 cause of action should be taken as preempting the possibility of a § 1983 cause of action, at least one for damages. Thus the Third Circuit recently overruled *W.B.*, relying on the latest case in the Supreme Court's *Sea Clammers* line of authority, *City of Rancho Palos Verdes v. Abrams,* 544 U.S. 113 (2005). *A.W. v. Jersey City Pub. Sch.,* 486 F.3d 791 (3d Cir. 2007). One of the cases with the most fully developed reasoning on the subject is *Padilla v. School District No. 1.*

PADILLA v. SCHOOL DISTRICT NO. 1
233 F.3d 1268 (10th Cir. 2000)

In this case, the court refused to permit a damages claim under 42 U.S.C. § 1983 for a violation of IDEA, although it allowed the plaintiff to proceed with other claims for damages.

McKAY, CIRCUIT JUDGE.

Plaintiff, a minor with physical and developmental disabilities, formerly attended school in Denver School District No. 1. She brought an action against the school district and the board of education, alleging violations of the Americans with Disabilities Act (ADA), 42 U.S.C. §§ 12101–12213. She also brought an action against the district, the board, and several individual district employees, alleging

violations of 42 U.S.C. § 1983 based on Defendants' failure to provide rights
guaranteed by the Individuals with Disabilities Education Act (IDEA), 20 U.S.C.
§§ 1400–1487. Defendants moved to dismiss on various grounds, including qualified
immunity, but the district court denied their motion except as to one of the
individual defendants. This court has jurisdiction over the remaining individual
defendants' qualified immunity appeal pursuant to *Mitchell v. Forsyth*, 472 U.S. 511
(1985), and over the appeal of the district court's other determinations pursuant to
its certification for immediate appeal under 28 U.S.C. § 1292(b).

I.

In 1975, Congress enacted the Education of the Handicapped Act (EHA), the
IDEA's predecessor. Its primary purpose is "to assure that all children with
disabilities have available to them . . . a free appropriate public education which
emphasizes special education and related services designed to meet their unique
needs [and] to assure that the rights of children with disabilities and their parents
or guardians are protected." 20 U.S.C. § 1400(d)(1)(A)–(B). To implement these
goals, Congress mandated that state and local educational agencies receiving
assistance under the IDEA establish procedures to ensure the provision of such
services and the protection of these rights. *See id.* § 1415(a). To identify necessary
services, the IDEA requires representatives of the responsible educational agencies, in meetings with parents and teachers, to develop an individualized education
program (IEP) for each child with a disability. The IEP includes a written
statement of the present educational level of such child, of annual goals and
short-term instructional objectives, and of "specific educational services to be
provided to such child." § 1401(a)(20). Before developing or changing a child's IEP,
the agency must provide written notice to the parents. *See id.* § 1415(b)(1)(C). The
agency must also provide parents who present complaints regarding these matters
an impartial due process hearing. *See id.* § 1415(b)(1)–(2). Any party aggrieved by
the decision of a local educational agency may appeal to the state educational
agency. *See id.* § 1415(c). Further, an aggrieved party has the right to bring a civil
action with respect to its complaints if the state has not provided an administrative
appeals process or if the aggrieved party is dissatisfied with the findings or decision
of the administrative appeal agency. *See id.* § 1415(e).

II.

"Because this appeal arises on a motion to dismiss, we construe the facts, and
reasonable inferences that might be drawn from them, in favor of the plaintiff."
Breidenbach v. Bolish, 126 F.3d 1288, 1292 (10th Cir. 1997). According to Plaintiff,
during the five-year period between 1992 and 1997, Defendants failed to provide her
with the behavioral programming, augmentative communication, and tube feeding
services identified in her IEP.

She also asserts Defendants repeatedly "placed her in a windowless closet,
restrained in a stroller without supervision," contrary to her IEP. During one of
these incidents she tipped over and hit her head on the floor, suffering serious
physical injuries, including a skull fracture and exacerbation of a seizure disorder,
which kept her from attending school for the remainder of the term. The school

district thereafter failed to provide homebound schooling adequate to insure the free appropriate public education to which she was entitled.

In August 1997, Plaintiff moved to a new school district and began attending a different school, neither of which is a party to this action. In February 1998, she requested an administrative hearing from the defendant school district to "contest certain actions of . . . [district] personnel." In her request, Plaintiff sought "any relief" available through the administrative process, "including money damages and attorney fees." Plaintiff's hearing request was denied by the hearing officer, who ruled that he lacked jurisdiction "as the petitioner does not reside within the school district," and that he lacked authority to grant the requested relief.

Thereafter, Plaintiff filed the instant suit, raising two claims. First, she alleged that the school district and the board of education violated her rights under the ADA by excluding her from participation in publicly funded general and special education programs based on her disability. Second, she brought an action under 42 U.S.C. § 1983, alleging that the school district, the board of education, and several individual district employees violated her rights under the IDEA by denying her a free and appropriate public education. Plaintiff specifically seeks monetary damages for both the ADA and § 1983 claims.

Defendants moved to dismiss, arguing that (1) Plaintiff failed to exhaust her administrative remedies; (2) damages are unavailable under the IDEA and therefore unavailable in a § 1983 claim based on an IDEA violation; (3) the IDEA does not allow individual liability actions, and, therefore, individuals cannot be liable under a § 1983 claim based on an IDEA violation; and (4) the individual defendants were entitled to qualified immunity. The district court dismissed Plaintiff's § 1983 claim as it applied to one of the individual defendants but denied the motion in all other respects, and the remaining defendants brought this appeal.

III.

"We review the denial or grant of a motion to dismiss de novo, applying the same standard used by the district court." *Breidenbach*, 126 F.3d at 1291. We first address the viability of Plaintiff's IDEA-based § 1983 claims. The district court determined that the IDEA allows for damage awards and that it may be enforced against individuals. Therefore, the court reasoned, Plaintiff can likewise sue individuals and seek damages in a § 1983 suit based on the IDEA. The district court's analysis presupposes that § 1983 may be used to enforce the IDEA in the first place. This court has not previously ruled on this issue. 4 Circuits that have addressed the question have not come to the same conclusion. 5

It is well settled that § 1983 is "a generally and presumptively available remedy for claimed violations of federal law." *Livadas v. Bradshaw*, 512 U.S. 107, 133 (1994). Nonetheless, Congress can foreclose recourse to § 1983 "either by express words or by providing a comprehensive alternative enforcement scheme." *Id.; see also Blessing v. Freestone*, 520 U.S. 329, 341 (1997). Congress has not expressly prohibited § 1983 suits as remedies for IDEA violations, so we must turn to the question of whether the IDEA's administrative remedies nevertheless imply congressional intent to do so. Supreme Court precedent guides our inquiry.

In *Smith v. Robinson*, 468 U.S. 992 (1984), the Supreme Court considered whether the plaintiffs could pursue "virtually identical" claims for a free appropriate education under the EHA (IDEA's predecessor), the Rehabilitation Act, and § 1983 (based on alleged Equal Protection and Due Process deprivations). *Id.* at 1009. The Court concluded that the EHA's thorough enforcement mechanisms indicated Congress' intent to proscribe such a course of action. *See id.* at 1012–13, 1018. For example, as to the plaintiffs' § 1983 claim based on the Equal Protection Clause, the Court stated that

> where the EHA is available to a handicapped child asserting a right to a free appropriate public education, based either on the EHA or on the Equal Protection Clause of the Fourteenth Amendment, the EHA is the exclusive avenue through which the child and his parents or guardian can pursue their claim.

Id. at 1013. *Smith* did not specifically involve the question of whether the EHA precludes § 1983 suits based on EHA violations. In fact, the Court expressly recognized that the plaintiffs' § 1983 claims alleged constitutional violations, not EHA violations. *See id.* at 1008–09. Nonetheless, the Court's holding that the EHA provided a comprehensive enforcement scheme that preempted other overlapping but independent statutory or constitutional claims necessarily meant that the EHA also supplanted § 1983 claims based simply on EHA violations.

In response to *Smith*, Congress amended the EHA in 1986. *See* Pub. L. No. 99-372, 100 Stat. 796 (1986); S. Rep. No. 99-112, at 2 (1985), *reprinted in* 1986 U.S.C.C.A.N. 1798, 1799. Among other provisions, Congress added § 1415(f), which stated in pertinent part: "Nothing in this title shall be construed to restrict or limit the rights, procedures, and remedies available under the Constitution, title V of the Rehabilitation Act of 1973, or other Federal statutes protecting the rights of handicapped children and youth." This provision obviously voided *Smith's* broad holding that the EHA precludes overlapping but independent claims otherwise cognizable under the Constitution, the Rehabilitation Act, or other Federal laws. *See Hayes v. Unified Sch. Dist. No. 377*, 877 F.2d 809, 812 (10th Cir. 1989) ("Congress' amendment of the EHA makes clear that the EHA is not the exclusive remedy available to handicapped students seeking public educational benefits."); H.R. Rep. No. 99-296, at 6 (1985) (stating that § 1415(f) is intended to reaffirm "the viability of section 504 [of the Rehabilitation Act] and other federal statutes such as 42 U.S.C. § 1983 as separate from but equally viable with the EHA as vehicles for securing the rights of handicapped children and youth"). It is less obvious, however, whether Congress intended § 1415(f) to also overrule *Smith's* more narrow implication that the EHA provides a comprehensive remedial framework that forecloses recourse to § 1983 as a remedy for strictly EHA violations. This difficult question has created a split in the circuits. *Compare, e.g., Marie O. v. Edgar*, 131 F.3d 610, 622 (7th Cir. 1997) ("§ 1415(f) was enacted for the express purpose of ensuring that § 1983 claims would be available to enforce the IDEA."), *and W.B. v. Matula*, 67 F.3d 484, 494 (3d Cir. 1995) (same), *with Sellers v. School Bd.*, 141 F.3d 524, 530–32 (4th Cir. 1998) (stating that § 1415(f) does not allow plaintiffs to sue under § 1983 for an IDEA violation and that § 1415 does not overrule *Smith* on that point).

We agree with the Fourth Circuit that § 1415(f) left intact *Smith's* implication that the EHA may not provide the basis for § 1983 claims. *See Sellers*, 141 F.3d at 529–30. Post-*Smith* Supreme Court precedent compels this conclusion. Since Congress passed § 1415(f) in 1986, the Court has nevertheless cited *Smith* and the EHA/IDEA on at least two occasions as an example of an exhaustive legislative enforcement scheme that precludes § 1983 causes of action. *See Blessing*, 520 U.S. at 347–48; *Wright v. City of Roanoke Redevelopment and Housing Auth.*, 479 U.S. 418, 423–24, 427 (1987). In *Wright*, the Court noted that the EHA itself "provided for private judicial remedies, thereby evidencing congressional intent to supplant the § 1983 remedy." 479 U.S. at 427. The *Blessing* Court discussed *Smith* as one of only two cases in which it had "found a remedial scheme sufficiently comprehensive to supplant § 1983." 520 U.S. at 347. Moreover, the Court used the EHA/IDEA in both cases as a benchmark for assessing the comprehensiveness of the remedial scheme provided by the statutes in question. *See id.* at 348; *Wright*, 479 U.S. at 427. Based on these cases, it appears the Supreme Court considers *Smith* to be alive and well insofar as it asserts that § 1983 may not be used to remedy IDEA violations. Accordingly, we reverse the trial court's denial of the motion to dismiss Plaintiff's IDEA-based § 1983 claims against the school district, the board of education, and the individual defendants. This conclusion moots the qualified immunity issues. Furthermore, in light of our holding and Plaintiff's failure to make an independent IDEA claim, we need not address whether the IDEA imposes individual liability or permits damage awards.

IV.

Defendants argue that the trial court erred in denying their motion to dismiss Plaintiff's ADA claim against the school district and the board of education for failure to exhaust her administrative remedies.

Although Plaintiff proceeds under the auspices of the ADA, the IDEA nonetheless requires her to first exhaust its administrative procedures and remedies prior to commencing her ADA suit if she is "*seeking relief that is also available under*" the IDEA. 20 U.S.C. § 1415(f) (emphasis added). Like the Seventh Circuit, we understand "available" relief "to mean relief for the events, condition, or consequences of which the person complains, not necessarily relief of the kind the person prefers," *Charlie F. v. Board of Educ.*, 98 F.3d 989, 992 (7th Cir. 1996), or specifically seeks. Thus, our primary concern in determining whether a plaintiff must utilize the IDEA's administrative procedures relates to the source and nature of the alleged injuries for which he or she seeks a remedy, not the specific remedy itself. *See Hayes v. Unified Sch. Dist. No. 377*, 877 F.2d 809, 812 (10th Cir. 1989) (stating that the IDEA's remedies must be exhausted before a plaintiff files a non-IDEA suit if that "suit could have been filed under the" IDEA). In essence, the dispositive question generally is whether the plaintiff has alleged injuries that could be redressed to any degree by the IDEA's administrative procedures and remedies. If so, exhaustion of those remedies is required. If not, the claim necessarily falls outside the IDEA's scope, and exhaustion is unnecessary. Where the IDEA's ability to remedy a particular injury is unclear, exhaustion should be required in order to give educational agencies an initial opportunity to ascertain and alleviate the alleged problem. *See, e.g., Charlie F.*, 98 F.3d at 992, 993.

So far as we can tell in the instant case, Plaintiff seeks damages solely to redress the fractured skull and other physical injuries she suffered allegedly as a result of the school district's and board of education's purported ADA violations. Plaintiff makes no complaints regarding her current educational situation. Indeed, she expressly attests that her new school "meets her educational needs" and that she presently receives "the full benefits of a free and appropriate education in an integrated, least restrictive educational environment." Under these narrow circumstances, we fail to see how the IDEA's administrative remedies, oriented as they are to providing prospective educational benefits, could possibly begin to assuage Plaintiff's severe physical, and completely non-educational, injuries. That is not to say damages are unavailable under the IDEA. We have not previously addressed that question and need not to resolve this case. Our holding simply recognizes the fact that even if damages are available under the IDEA they should be awarded in civil actions, not in administrative hearings. *Cf. Covington v. Knox County Sch. Sys.*, 205 F.3d 912, 918 (6th Cir. 2000) (stating that damages are "unavailable through the [IDEA] administrative process"); *W.B. v. Matula*, 67 F.3d 484, 494–96 (3d Cir. 1995) (holding that IDEA-based § 1983 suits permit damage awards, but damages cannot be awarded during the course of the IDEA's administrative proceedings).

We affirm the district court's denial of Defendants' motion to dismiss for failure to exhaust administrative remedies. Under the narrow circumstances of this case, exhaustion was unnecessary because, so far as we can tell, Plaintiff's ADA claim is not seeking "relief that is also available" under the IDEA.

In conclusion, we note that other circuits, although employing slightly different approaches to the problem, have reached similar conclusions under similar circumstances. For example, in *Witte v. Clark County Sch. Dist.*, 197 F.3d 1271, 1275–76 (9th Cir. 1999), the Ninth Circuit held that exhaustion was not required where the plaintiff was seeking "only monetary damages" for alleged "physical abuse and injury" and "all educational issues already have been resolved to the parties' mutual satisfaction." The court noted that "[t]he remedies available under the IDEA would not appear to be well suited to addressing past physical injuries adequately; such injuries typically are remedied through an award of monetary damages." *Id.* at 1276. Likewise, in *Matula*, 67 F.3d at 496, the Third Circuit refused to require administrative exhaustion in a claim for compensatory damages in part because the parties had already settled their disputes over IDEA rights.

Moreover, circuit court cases cited by Defendants that have required plaintiffs who seek damages to exhaust their IDEA administrative remedies have done so where the plaintiffs' alleged injuries were educational in nature and therefore presumptively redressable through the IDEA's administrative procedures. *See, e.g., Thompson v. Board of Special Sch. Dist. 1*, 144 F.3d 574, 580 (8th Cir. 1998) (requiring exhaustion where plaintiff sought damages and one-on-one tutoring to remedy alleged denial of free and appropriate public education, and dismissing § 1983 claim on insufficient evidence grounds); *Charlie F.*, 98 F.3d at 993 (requiring exhaustion where the plaintiff alleged "that his education has suffered"); *N.B. by D.G. v. Alachua County Sch. Bd.*, 84 F.3d 1376, 1378 (11th Cir. 1996) (requiring exhaustion where the plaintiff's alleged injuries included segregation from non-disabled children and unnecessary absence from school). Under those distinct circumstances, we would also require exhaustion.

The denial of the motion to dismiss the § 1983 actions is REVERSED. The denial of the motion to dismiss the ADA action is AFFIRMED. The case is REMANDED for further proceedings consistent with this opinion.

NOTES AND QUESTIONS

1.   Does § 1983 provide a cause of action to assert damages claims for IDEA violations? The Supreme Court's recent decision on the ability of parents to sue pro se emphasizes that IDEA creates enforceable substantive rights. *Winkelman v. Parma City Sch. Dist.*, 127 S. Ct. 1994 (2007). Is there a theory under which § 1983 could provide a cause of action for injunctive relief in situations in which exhaustion is excused or the § 1415 action is otherwise inapplicable but still not provide for damages actions? Or a theory under which a § 1983 cause of action for damages and injunctive relief exists for claims on some issues but not on others? *See Sellers v. School Bd.*, 141 F.3d 524, 532 n.6 (4th Cir. 1998) (distinguishing enforcement of hearing officer decision in action under § 1983 from complaint over denial of appropriate education).

2.   Commentators also disagree about the appropriateness of a § 1983 damages action to enforce IDEA. *Compare* Terry Jean Seligmann, *A Diller, A Dollar: Section 1983 Damage Claims in Special Education Lawsuits*, 36 GA. L. REV. 465, 499–520 (2002) (rejecting § 1983 damage claims), *with* Mark C. Weber, *Disability Harassment in the Public Schools*, 43 WM. & MARY L. REV. 1079, 1113–19 (2002) (concluding that § 1415(*l*) preserves § 1983 damage claims for IDEA violations in harassment and other suitable cases). Both articles discuss policy considerations and evidence of legislative intent.

D.   DEFENSES

Vast numbers of what might otherwise be meritorious IDEA actions are dismissed because of defenses. The principal defenses are administrative exhaustion and limitations. Immunities also shield some defendants from damages liability.

1.   Exhaustion

The cause of action provided by § 1415 contemplates that a case will come up through the due process system and reach a final decision before being appealed to court, although the drafters of the statute anticipated that exhaustion of the process might be waived for good cause. Harrison Williams, principal author of the Education for All Handicapped Children Act, stated that "Exhaustion should not be required in cases where such exhaustion would be futile either as a legal or practical matter." 121 Cong. Rec. 37,416 (1975); *see also* 131 Cong. Rec. 21,392–93 (1985), 131 Cong. Rec. 31,376 (1985) (recording statements by sponsors of Handicapped Children's Protection Act that federal special education law excused exhaustion when services on IEP were not provided, when procedural rights were denied or abridged, when hearing officer lacked authority to give the relief sought, and in emergencies). One justification for application of exhaustion doctrine, that of affording the state the opportunity to develop special education policy through administrative decisions, is totally inapplicable under IDEA, because the due process and state review hearing officers must be independent of the state educational agency. Nevertheless, courts have enforced the exhaustion requirement strictly, and dismissed many cases despite plausible arguments that exhaustion should have been excused. *See, e.g., Polera v. Board of Educ.*, 288 F.3d 478 (2d Cir. 2002) (requiring exhaustion despite contention that district did not implement IEP; questioning legislative history statements); *Rose v. Yeaw*, 214 F.3d 206 (1st Cir. 2000) (requiring exhaustion in dispute concerning accommodations for child with asthma despite arguments about futility and emergency conditions). *But see, e.g., Weixel v. Board of Educ.*, 287 F.3d 138 (2d Cir. 2002) (excusing exhaustion for parents not notified of procedural rights).

As noted above, 20 U.S.C. § 1415(*l*) permits parents to assert causes of action other than that provided by § 1415(i), "except that before the filing of a civil action under such laws seeking relief that is also available under [§ 1415], the procedures of subsections (f) and (g) [due process hearings and state review] shall be exhausted to the same extent as would be required had the action been brought under [§ 1415]." Recall that in *Padilla, supra,* the court rejected an exhaustion defense to claims asserted under § 1415(*l*). If the consensus is that damages relief is not "also available under [§ 1415]," it would seem that no exhaustion is required for IDEA § 1983 claims, section 504-ADA claims, or constitutional claims for money damages. The case law, however, is far from uniform. In *Charlie F. v. Board of Education,* the court upholds an exhaustion defense to a section 504-ADA compensatory damages case.

CHARLIE F. v. BOARD OF EDUCATION
98 F.3d 989 (7th Cir. 1996)

The court affirmed dismissal for failure to exhaust administrative remedies of an action brought under section 504 and the Americans with Disabilities Act for the peer abuse caused by a teacher's conduct.

EASTERBROOK, CIRCUIT JUDGE.

When Charlie F. was in fourth grade, his teacher invited her pupils to vent their feelings about certain topics. One favorite topic was Charlie, whose disabilities (including attention deficit disorder and panic attacks) drew attention. According to the complaint, whose allegations we must accept, the teacher repeatedly invited her pupils to express their complaints about Charlie — and they all too willingly obliged, leading to humiliation, fistfights, mistrust, loss of confidence and self-esteem, and disruption of Charlie's educational progress. The teacher instructed her pupils to tell no one about these sessions, but Charlie's parents eventually found out and moved him to a different school. Youths from his former class still taunt and ridicule Charlie when they meet, in part because of the license they think the fourth grade teacher provided for such behavior.

Charlie has an "individual educational plan" under the auspices of the Individuals with Disabilities Education Act, 20 U.S.C. §§ 1400–1491o (IDEA). His parents are satisfied with his current placement but disgusted with what happened in fourth grade. They filed this suit on Charlie's behalf seeking damages from the teacher, the school's principal (who knew about the gripe sessions), the school district's superintendent, and the school district itself. The suit contends that the Constitution of the United States (through 42 U.S.C. § 1983), the Rehabilitation Act, 29 U.S.C. § 794, the Americans with Disabilities Act, 42 U.S.C. §§ 12101–12213, and the state law of torts all provide damages for misconceived educational strategies that injure disabled pupils. Instead of responding on the merits, however, the defendants asked the court to postpone adjudication until Charlie exhausts administrative remedies under the IDEA, a statute that he had not invoked in the first place. This unusual response depends on an unusual provision in the IDEA, which reads:

> Nothing in this chapter shall be construed to restrict or limit the rights, procedures, and remedies available under the Constitution, title V of the Rehabilitation Act of 1973, or other Federal statutes protecting the rights of children and youth with disabilities, except that before the filing of a civil action under such laws seeking relief that is available under this subchapter, the procedures under subsections (b)(2) and (c) of this section shall be exhausted to the same extent as would be required had the action been brought under this subchapter.

20 U.S.C. § 1415(f).

Thus any pupil who wants "relief that is available under" the IDEA must use the IDEA's administrative system, even if he invokes a different statute. Charlie replied that he wants money damages, which the IDEA does not supply.

The district court dismissed the federal claims for lack of subject-matter jurisdiction. (State-law claims went too, once the federal claims disappeared, for the parties are all citizens of Illinois.) The court did not say that the IDEA permits an award of money. Instead, the judge observed, the IDEA covers "any matter relating to the identification, evaluation, or educational placement of the child, or the provision of a free appropriate public education to such child." 20 U.S.C. § 1415(b)(1)(E). This led the judge to believe that the IDEA occupies the field, an untenable conclusion. Section 1415(f) provides that the IDEA does not limit relief available under other laws. Moreover, failure to exhaust administrative remedies does not deprive a court of jurisdiction; lack of exhaustion usually is waivable, as lack of jurisdiction is not. *See Air Courier Conference v. Postal Workers Union*, 498 U.S. 517, 522–23 & n. 3 (1991); *Weinberger v. Salfi*, 422 U.S. 749, 766–67 (1975); *cf. Granberry v. Greer*, 481 U.S. 129 (1987).

We must address the question the district court did not reach: whether Charlie is "seeking relief that is available under" the IDEA. *See Honig v. Doe*, 484 U.S. 305, 327 (1988). Charlie says that he wants compensatory money damages, which the IDEA does not authorize. It does not contain an explicit limit, but the structure of the statute — with its elaborate provision for educational services and payments to those who deliver them — is inconsistent with monetary awards to children and parents. So we held for the IDEA's predecessor, the Education for All Handicapped Children Act. *Anderson v. Thompson*, 658 F.2d 1205 (7th Cir. 1981). The two statutes do not differ in any way material to this question, and we conclude that damages are not "relief that is available under" the IDEA. *Accord, W.B. v. Matula*, 67 F.3d 484, 496 (3d Cir. 1995). This is the norm for social-welfare programs that specify benefits in kind at public expense, whether medical care or housing or, under the IDEA, education.

Charlie asks us to stop here: he wants compensatory money damages, the IDEA does not provide this form of relief, and that is that. Things are not so clear, however. The statute speaks of available relief, and what relief is "available" does not necessarily depend on what the aggrieved party wants. Certainly not in litigation. "Except as to a party against whom a judgment is entered by default, every final judgment shall grant the relief to which the party in whose favor it is rendered is entitled, even if the party has not demanded such relief in the party's pleadings." Fed.R.Civ.P. 54(c). The nature of the claim and the governing law determine the relief no matter what the plaintiff demands. If this principle is equally applicable for purposes of § 1415(f), then the theory behind the grievance may activate the IDEA's process, even if the plaintiff wants a form of relief that the IDEA does not supply. Several district courts have used this principle to hold that the pleadings in court do not end the analysis under § 1415(f), and we think these decisions right. *See Hoekstra v. Independent School District No. 283*, 916 F. Supp. 941 (D. Minn. 1996); *Doe v. Alfred*, 906 F. Supp. 1092 (S.D. W. Va. 1995); *Waterman v. Marquette-Alger Intermediate School District*, 739 F. Supp. 361 (W.D. Mich. 1990).

Suppose a school fails to provide a reader for a blind pupil, who as a result falls behind. The IDEA provides relief: the school can assign a reader to the pupil for the future and can provide tutors and other special instruction until the pupil catches up. If disgruntled parents spurn this solution and demand compensation, the response should be that they cannot ignore remedies available under the IDEA and insist on those of their own devising; under the IDEA, educational professionals are supposed to have at least the first crack at formulating a plan to overcome the consequences of educational shortfalls. That the educational problem has consequences outside school (for example, the child's self-esteem and ability to get along with his peers might suffer when he lags behind in class) can't be enough to avoid the statutory system. So too if parents demand either educational services that local school districts need not provide (for example, full-time attendants in private schools, *K.R. v. Anderson Community School Corp.*, 81 F.3d 673 (7th Cir. 1996)), or monetary compensation in lieu of the unavailable services. By making an unreasonable or unattainable demand parents cannot opt out of the IDEA.

Consider this from another angle. Why do Charlie's parents want money? Presumably at least in part to pay for services (such as counseling) that will assist his recovery of self-esteem and promote his progress in school. Damages could be measured by the cost of these services. Yet the school district may be able (indeed, may be obliged) to provide these services in kind under the IDEA. If it turns out that the school is *not* obliged to provide such services, that may be because Charlie's parents have exaggerated what happened in fourth grade, the consequences of those events, or both. In other words, the educational professionals and hearing officers who evaluate claims under the IDEA may conclude (a) that adequate remedial services can be provided, or (b) that Charlie does not today require services. The first outcome would show that relief is available under the IDEA; the second would provide information relevant to Charlie's claims under statutes other than the IDEA. In either event, pursuit of the administrative process would be justified. Charlie would not get the kind of relief the complaint demands, but this is not what § 1415(f) says. We read "relief available" to mean relief for the events, condition, or consequences of which the person complains, not necessarily relief of the kind the person prefers.

Well, then, does the IDEA require the school district to afford services for someone in Charlie's position? The district says yes, and Charlie no — the opposite of the usual positions in litigation under the IDEA. For if the answer is yes, the school district may be put to considerable expense, even if it would have prevailed under § 1983 and the Rehabilitation Act. If the answer is no, then Charlie is putting all his eggs in one basket, and it looks to us like an incommodious basket. As it happens, we think the school district right. The IDEA requires a school district to provide not only education but also "related services," a term defined to include

> transportation, and such developmental, corrective, and other supportive services (including speech pathology and audiology, psychological services, physical and occupational therapy, recreation, including therapeutic recreation, social work services, counseling services, including rehabilitation counseling, and medical services, except that such medical services shall be for diagnostic and evaluation purposes only) as may be required to assist a child with a disability to benefit from special education, and includes the early identification and assessment of disabling conditions in children.

20 U.S.C. § 1401(a)(17). Charlie's parents believe that his current educational program is apt, which they think means that any psychological services would not be "required to assist [Charlie] to benefit from special education." Yet the complaint they filed on his behalf deals with acts that have both an educational source and an adverse educational consequence; the complaint contends that his education has suffered as a result of the events in fourth grade; if he is doing fine in school today, then it is hard to see what this case is about. It would be odd to award damages because of deeds with so little educational effect that no ongoing steps to overcome them are warranted — and again we are unwilling to allow parents to opt out of the IDEA by proclaiming that it does not offer them anything they value, when the school district professes willingness to take corrective steps (if the facts justify them, a vital qualifier).

Charlie's parents also observe that medical services are provided for "diagnostic and evaluation purposes only," but psychological services are listed separately from medical services, and they are often essential if a plan is to have any realistic chance of facilitating education. The regulations implementing the statute provide that "psychological services" include "psychological counseling for children and parents." 34 C.F.R. § 300.16(b)(8)(v). *See also* 34 C.F.R. § 300.306(b).

Perhaps Charlie's adverse reaction to the events of fourth grade cannot be overcome by services available under the IDEA and the regulations, so that in the end money is the only balm. But parents cannot know that without asking, any more than we can. Both the genesis and the manifestations of the problem are educational; the IDEA offers comprehensive educational solutions; we conclude, therefore, that at least in principle relief is available under the IDEA.

Because the district court had subject-matter jurisdiction, its judgment is vacated. The case is remanded with instructions to dismiss for failure to use the IDEA's administrative remedies.

NOTES AND QUESTIONS

1. *Charlie F.* seems difficult to distinguish from *Padilla* (discussed in section C, *supra*). Can you define the respective positions regarding exhaustion and determine which is superior from the standpoint of legal policy? From the standpoint of faithfulness to congressional intentions? The views of scholars are as divided as those of the courts. *Compare* Terry Jean Seligmann, *A Diller, A Dollar: Section 1983 Damage Claims in Special Education Lawsuits*, 36 GA. L. REV. 465, 520–26 (2002) (defending application of strict exhaustion requirements even to damages claims), *with* Mark C. Weber, *Disability Harassment in the Public Schools*, 43 WM. & MARY L. REV. 1079, 1134–41 (2002) (arguing that policy and legislative interpretation principles support excusing exhaustion in cases such as *Charlie F.*). Weber contends that *Charlie F.* reads the words "action . . . seeking relief that is also available under [§ 1415]" out of the statute and substitutes "action . . . *not* seeking relief that is also available under [§ 1415], but for which that relief might in principle be helpful." He argues that the congressional language refers to what the parents seek in the action on file, not in a hypothetical action they could bring. *See id.* at 1137. Perhaps even he would concede, however, that Congress probably did not want parents to be able to bypass administrative procedures simply by conjuring up a damages claim and tacking it to their IDEA suit. How would you articulate a rule that is faithful to congressional intent but does not undermine the exhaustion principle?

2. As suggested by the pairing of *Padilla* with *Charlie F.*, courts' attitudes on exhaustion of non-§ 1415(i) claims vary greatly, and the facts of the specific cases may matter in ways that the courts have not yet fully articulated. *Compare Payne v. Peninsula Sch. Dist.*, 598 F.3d 1123 (9th Cir. 2010), *and Cave v. East Meadow Union Free Sch. Dist.*, 514 F.3d 240 (2d Cir. 2008), *and Robb v. Bethel Sch. Dist. No. 403*, 308 F.3d 1047 (9th Cir. 2002), *and Cudjoe v. Independent Sch. Dist. No. 12*, 297 F.3d 1058 (10th Cir. 2002), *and Frazier v. Fairhaven Sch. Comm.*, 276 F.3d 52 (1st Cir. 2002) (all requiring exhaustion), *with McCormick v. Waukegan Sch. Dist. No. 60*, 374 F.3d 564 (7th Cir. 2004), *and Covington v. Knox County Sch. Sys.*, 205 F.3d 912 (6th Cir. 2000), *and Witte v. Clark County Sch. Dist.*, 197 F.3d 1271 (9th Cir. 1999) (all refusing to require exhaustion). The cases requiring exhaustion even when the plaintiff asserts claims exclusively under section 504 or the ADA may bear closer examination in light of the emerging caselaw regarding what constitutes a claim for damages under section 504 in the education context and how that relates to a claim for violation of IDEA. *See Mark H., supra.* This issue may become increasingly important over time due to the implementation of the ADA Amendments of 2008, which expand the coverage of the ADA and section 504.

2.   Limitations

In the 2004 IDEA Reauthorization, Congress created a 90-day default statute of limitations for filing IDEA actions in court. The statute provides: "The party bringing the action shall have 90 days from the date of the decision of the hearing officer to bring such an action, or, if the State has an explicit time limitation for bringing such action under this part, in such time as the State law allows." 20 U.S.C. § 1415(i)(2). This new provision has triggered litigation over whether shorter or longer state limitations statutes are explicit enough to supplant the federal default time line. *See, e.g., T.T. v. District of Columbia*, No. 06-0207, 2006 U.S. Dist. LEXIS 42739 (D.D.C. June 26, 2006) (holding that 90-day default limitation in IDEA 2004 applies, rather than 30-day period borrowed from administrative appeals statute in previous cases; collecting cases). Before passage of the Reauthorization, courts applied the general caselaw rule providing that for claims based on federal statutes passed before 1990 that do not have their own limitations periods, the court borrows the limitations of the most closely analogous state cause of action, as long as that period is consistent with the federal statutory policy.

3. Immunities from Damages Liability

Official Immunity

Generally speaking, government officers who are sued personally for civil rights violations may escape financial liability by showing that they acted in a way that did not violate clearly established statutory or constitutional rights that a reasonable person would have known about. *See Harlow v. Fitzgerald*, 457 U.S. 800 (1982); *see also Wood v. Strickland*, 420 U.S. 308 (1975) (originally articulating principle of good-faith immunity). This official immunity is often referred to as qualified immunity, because it is not absolute, but instead depends on whether the right violated was clearly established such that a reasonable person would have known of it at the time of the violation. *See generally* RICHARD H. FALLON, ET AL., HART & WECHSLER'S THE FEDERAL COURTS AND THE FEDERAL SYSTEM 1127–34 (5th ed. 2003) (discussing distinction). Official immunity does not protect non-human defendants, such as school districts and states, or persons not sued in a personal capacity, such as government officers sued in their official capacities. *Owen v. City of Independence*, 445 U.S. 622 (1980).

NOTES AND QUESTIONS

Why would parents want to sue principals, teachers, or other school officials in their individual capacities? Recall that in order to establish § 1983 liability on the part of a school district, plaintiffs must establish intentionality, typically in the form of a policy or custom. Eleventh Amendment immunity may also create an obstacle to monetary liability from state agencies. *See generally* Jack M. Beermann, *Why Do Plaintiffs Sue Private Parties Under Section 1983?*, 26 CARDOZO L. REV. 9 (2004) (discussing civil rights damages claims against individuals).

Sovereign and Eleventh Amendment Immunities

As a general rule, states sued by private individuals in their own courts may invoke sovereign immunity, and relegate the cases to a court of claims or refuse to provide any compensation at all. *See Alden v. Maine*, 527 U.S. 706 (1999) (upholding ability of state to claim immunity from suit for back overtime pay and liquidated damages under Federal Fair Labor Standards Act). In federal court, states and their agencies may assert sovereign immunity principles recognized under Eleventh Amendment immunity. *See Seminole Tribe v. Florida*, 517 U.S. 44 (1996). Although state officers may be sued for injunctive relief to force them to comply with federal law in the future, *Ex parte Young*, 209 U.S. 123 (1908), suit for retrospective monetary relief is barred, *Edelman v. Jordan*, 415 U.S. 651 (1974). States may also assert Eleventh Amendment immunity against claims brought in federal court by private individuals for violations of state law, even when the claims are for prospective relief only. *Pennhurst State Sch. & Hosp. v. Halderman*, 465 U.S. 89 (1984).

Exceptions to the immunity barrier exist, however, if Congress, properly acting pursuant to its power to enforce the Fourteenth Amendment, abrogates the state's immunity, *Fitzpatrick v. Bitzer*, 427 U.S. 445 (1976), or if the state waives its immunity, *Lapides v. Bd. of Regents*, 535 U.S. 613 (2002). In *Dellmuth v. Muth*, 491 U.S. 223 (1989), the Supreme Court held that the Education for All Handicapped Children Act did not contain a sufficiently explicit abrogation of states' immunity, and so the Court rejected a claim for retrospective monetary relief against a state. In response, Congress prospectively abrogated state immunity in the 1990 Individuals with Disabilities Education Act. Pub. L. No. 101-476, § 604, 104 Stat. 1103, 1106 (1990). Matters may not rest there, however, for the Court in a series of recent cases has ruled that some efforts to abrogate Eleventh Amendment immunity are not effective. Congress, according to the Court's present view, lacks the ability to abrogate the immunity by exercising its ordinary Article I powers. *Seminole Tribe v. Florida, supra*. Congress may abrogate the immunity under its Fourteenth Amendment powers, but some statutes asserted to be exercises of Fourteenth Amendment authority have been found to exceed the scope of that power. *See, e.g., Board of Trustees of Univ. of Ala. v. Garrett*, 531 U.S. 356 (2001) (upholding immunity from monetary claim under title I of Americans with Disabilities Act). *But see Tennessee v. Lane*, 541 U.S. 509 (2004) (finding immunity validly abrogated for ADA title II claim relating to access to court for persons with disabilities).

Nevertheless, most courts considering the matter have ruled that acceptance of federal funds when statutes explicitly abrogate the immunity constitutes a waiver of the immunity, even if the federal activity is merely spending under Article I. Eleventh Amendment immunity thus does not protect states from suit under IDEA or section 504, which both contain abrogation provisions. *See Robinson v. Kansas*, 295 F.3d 1183 (10th Cir. 2002) (section 504); Jim C. v. United States, 235 F.3d 1079 (8th Cir. 2000) (en banc) (section 504); *Board of Educ. v. Kelly E.*, 207 F.3d 931 (7th Cir. 2000) (IDEA). *But see Garcia v. S.U.N.Y. Health Scis. Ctr.*, 280 F.3d 98 (2d Cir. 2001) (finding no effective waiver for section 504 for relevant time period).

Most authorities have held that local school districts are not state agencies and so are not protected by Eleventh Amendment immunity in any instance. *E.g., Mount Healthy City Sch. Dist Bd. of Educ. v. Doyle*, 429 U.S. 274 (1977). The Ninth Circuit Court of Appeals has departed from this view and found California school districts, though not Nevada school districts, protected. *See Eason v. Clark*

County Sch. Dist., 303 F.3d 1137 (9th Cir. 2002) (describing distinction); *see also* *Biggs v. Board of Educ.*, 229 F. Supp. 2d 437 (D. Md. 2002) (finding Maryland school districts protected by Eleventh Amendment).

State-Law Immunities

State statutes or constitutions may protect various classes of defendants, either governmental entities or individuals, from liability for claims asserted under state statutes or common law. *See, e.g., Brown v. Houston Sch. Dist.*, 704 So. 2d 1325 (Miss. 1997) (finding wrongful death action against school district barred by sovereign immunity).

Chapter 11

ATTORNEYS' FEES IN SPECIAL EDUCATION LITIGATION

A. INTRODUCTION

The Individuals with Disabilities Education Act provides that a court "may award reasonable attorneys' fees as part of the costs to the parents of a child with a disability who is the prevailing party." 20 U.S.C. § 1415(i)(3)(A). This provision extends to special education proceedings, including due process hearings. Although courts have the nominal discretion to award fees, they are to award fees as a matter of course when the parents prevail. *Mitten v. Muscogee County Sch. Dist.*, 877 F.2d 932 (11th Cir. 1989).

The presence of an attorney is important for parents, and the availability of fees is designed to make representation easier to obtain. As noted *supra* Chapter 8, having an attorney representing the parent dramatically increases the probability that the parent will prevail in a due process hearing. *See* Melanie Archer, Access and Equity in the Due Process System: Attorney Representation and Hearing Outcomes in Illinois, 1997-2002, at 4–7 (2002) (reporting that in Illinois parents with attorneys prevailed in 50.4% of due process cases, in contrast to success rate of 16.8% for parents without attorneys). Moreover, the guarantee of free education for all children with disabilities would be undermined if parents had to pay attorneys to achieve the results their children were entitled to under the statute. Just as prevailing plaintiffs in civil rights actions are entitled to fees for effectively acting as private attorneys general under 42 U.S.C. § 1988, so too parents who win at due process or in court receive comparable fee awards.

The entitlement to fees as a matter of course applies to prevailing parents. The school district or other defending parties may be entitled to fees when parents file a case in court that is frivolous. Under the 2004 IDEA Reauthorization, the school district or state may also receive attorneys' fees from parents or their lawyers in due process proceedings under some circumstances. The state or district may obtain attorneys' fees from a court against the parent's attorney when the educational agency is a prevailing party if the parent has filed a complaint or court case that is frivolous, unreasonable, or without foundation, or has continued to litigate after the litigation clearly became frivolous, unreasonable, or without foundation. 20 U.S.C. § 1415(i)(3)(B)(i)(II). The court may also award fees to a prevailing state educational agency or school district against either the parent's attorney or the parent, if the parent's complaint or subsequent court case was presented for any improper purpose, such as to cause harassment, unnecessary delay, or needless increase in the cost of litigation. 20 U.S.C. § 1415(i)(3)(B)(i)(III). Since this frivolousness standard mirrors the standard for imposing attorneys' fees on losing parties in court proceedings in general, it is quite unlike the simple "prevailing party" standard that applies for awards of fees to parents in IDEA cases. *See* 28 U.S.C. § 1927; Fed. R. Civ. P. 11 (employing frivolousness standard for award of fees to prevailing party in absence of civil rights or other express statutory authorization); *see also Christiansburg Garment Co. v. EEOC*, 434 U.S. 412 (1978) (applying frivolousness standard to defendant's request for fee award in civil rights case). Case law under the new IDEA provision is scarce, but at least one court has denied a motion to dismiss a fees counterclaim. *Taylor P. v. Missouri Dep't of Elementary & Secondary Educ.*, No. 06-4254-CV-C-NKL, 2007 U.S. Dist. LEXIS 59570 (W.D. Mo. Mar. 20, 2007) (denying parents' motion to dismiss counterclaim for fees, reasoning that facts might demonstrate improper purpose on part of parents; also granting motion to join parents' attorneys as counterclaim defendants). *But see T.S. v. District of Columbia*, No. 05-88861, 2007 U.S. Dist. LEXIS 21792 (D.D.C. Mar. 27, 2007) (denying claim for fees against parent and awarding fees to parent).

Among the more important general considerations in special education fees awards are some matters of procedure and the question of when the parents have actually prevailed.

1.   Procedural Matters

Parents may bring an action solely for fees, without bringing an appeal on the merits. *Barlow-Gresham Union High Sch. Dist. No. 2 v. Mitchell*, 940 F.2d 1280 (9th Cir. 1991). Parents do not have to be in the position of the plaintiff in order to receive fees. If, for example, the district unsuccessfully sues the parents for an injunction to keep their child from school on the basis of the child's dangerousness, the parents may receive fees. *Maine Sch. Admin. Dist. No. 35 v. Mr. & Mrs. R.*, 321 F.3d 9 (1st Cir. 2003).

2.   Procedural Victories and Partial Success

At times, parents prevail in the sense of getting what they want for their children, simply by demanding a hearing, invoking the maintenance-of-placement rule, and keeping the child in the existing placement while losing a series of proceedings over the district's proposed changes to the placement. Eventually, the child ages out of the system or the family moves to a new district. Courts have ruled that this sort of victory does not make the parents the prevailing party. *See, e.g., Board of Educ. v. Nathan R.*, 199 F.3d 377 (7th Cir. 2000). More difficult questions are presented when the parents prevail in obtaining something like an evaluation or a new consideration of evaluation data, but the causal chain between that victory and a change in the child's education program is uncertain.

G.M. v. NEW BRITAIN BOARD OF EDUCATION
173 F.3d 77 (2d Cir. 1999)

In the following case, the court determined that success in a claim for an independent educational evaluation and a subsequent modest increase in services supported a fees award.

CALABRESI, CIRCUIT JUDGE.

Plaintiff-appellant G.M., by and through his guardian and next friend, R.F., appeals from a decision of the United States District Court for the District of Connecticut (Alfred V. Covello, Chief Judge) granting summary judgment to defendant-appellee New Britain Board of Education (the "Board"). G.M.'s suit against the Board seeks to recover attorney fees and costs that G.M.'s representatives incurred in the course of an administrative proceeding brought under the Individuals with Disabilities Education Act ("IDEA"), 20 U.S.C. §§ 1400–1491o (1994), to challenge the adequacy of the special education program that the Board offered G.M. The district court found that G.M. was not a "prevailing party" in the administrative proceeding and therefore could not receive costs or attorney fees. Because the record does not support the district court's conclusion, we reverse.

BACKGROUND

During the time relevant to his action, G.M. was a seventeen-year-old student at New Britain High School, which is operated by the Board. Because G.M. has learning disabilities, the Board has provided him with various special education services. Beginning in September 1995, the Board contracted with Futures, Inc. ("Futures"), to furnish some of these.

Under the IDEA, G.M.'s planning and placement team ("PPT") is charged with developing an individual education plan ("IEP") that tailors G.M.'s educational services to his needs. *See* 20 U.S.C. § 1414(d)(1)(B) (Supp. 1998). G.M.'s PPT includes one of his teachers, his advocate (an employee of the State of Connecticut's Office of Protection and Advocacy for Persons with Disabilities), his probation officer, a pupil services coordinator, a representative from Futures, and an attorney representing the Board who attended some of the meetings.

In February 1996, Futures suggested that G.M.'s educational plan be modified to emphasize "transitional planning . . . with a focus on community-based goals and objectives." Subsequently, during a regular PPT meeting in April, G.M.'s advocate, Bruce Garrison, requested that the PPT modify G.M.'s IEP to implement a more community-based approach. At the time, the IEP included fifteen hours of special education at his high school each week and ten hours of vocational exploration in the community, provided by Futures. When G.M.'s teacher stated that he thought that G.M.'s school situation was improving, Garrison disagreed and requested an independent evaluation of G.M.'s educational needs. The Board's attorney refused to approve an independent evaluation until G.M.'s family showed that such an evaluation was needed. At the conclusion of the meeting, the PPT, with Garrison dissenting, decided that the current IEP was appropriate to G.M.'s needs.

In May, Futures submitted a proposal for a "Community-Based Alternative Curriculum" that was designed to help G.M. acquire basic work and social skills, a work ethic, and independent living skills. At the next PPT meeting, held in June, Garrison voiced his opinion that, unless this Futures proposal were adopted, G.M.'s IEP would remain inadequate. The PPT instead chose what it called an "adaptation" of the Futures proposal. This increased G.M.'s hours in Futures' vocational exploration program to fifteen per week, but still kept G.M. at the high school for fifteen hours. In July, Garrison, on behalf of G.M.'s guardian, requested a full administrative ("due process") hearing to address "the Board['s] refusal to approve an independent evaluation[and G.M.'s guardian's] disagree[ment] with [his] current placement and IEP."

The hearing began in September, but was adjourned when G.M.'s guardian and the Board reached an agreement to have Futures conduct an independent evaluation of G.M.'s educational needs. The Futures evaluation, completed in October, recommended a community-based educational program with characteristics similar to those of the May Futures proposal that the PPT had rejected in June. Later in October, the Board and G.M.'s guardian stipulated "to implement the recommendations contained in the independent evaluation." The hearing officer accepted the stipulation as the final decision in the case, retaining jurisdiction for ninety days to resolve any disagreements arising out of the stipulation.

In November, G.M. filed this action in the district court seeking costs and attorney fees incurred in the administrative proceeding. The Board and G.M. submitted cross-motions for summary judgment. The district court granted the Board's motion and denied G.M.'s motion. This appeal followed.

DISCUSSION

A. Standard of Review

In general, "[w]e review a district court's ruling on attorneys' fees for abuse of discretion." *McCardle v. Haddad*, 131 F.3d 43, 53 (2d Cir. 1997); *see also W.G. v. Senatore*, 18 F.3d 60, 63 (2d Cir. 1994) (noting same, in an IDEA case). Under the abuse of discretion standard, a district court's decision " 'cannot be set aside by a reviewing court unless it has a definite and firm conviction that the court below committed a clear error of judgment in the conclusion it reached upon a weighing of the relevant factors.' " *Carroll v. American Fed'n of Musicians*, 295 F.2d 484, 488 (2d Cir. 1961) (quoting *In re Josephson*, 218 F.2d 174, 182 (1st Cir. 1954)). Because the district court decided this case at the summary judgment stage, however, we also must reverse its decision if it required the resolution of any genuinely disputed material fact. *See Anderson v. Liberty Lobby, Inc.*, 477 U.S. 242, 247–48 (1986).

B. Merits

The IDEA ensures "all children with disabilities . . . a free appropriate public education that emphasizes special education and related services designed to meet their unique needs." 20 U.S.C. § 1400(d) (Supp. 1998). If the guardian of a child with a disability successfully enforces his or her rights under the IDEA in an administrative action, the statute authorizes courts to award reasonable attorney fees to the guardian. *See id.* § 1415(i)(3)(B). The district court held, however, that G.M. was not a "prevailing party" in the administrative proceedings and therefore could not receive attorney fees and costs.

" '[P]laintiffs may be considered "prevailing parties" for attorney's fees purposes if they succeed on any significant issue in litigation which achieves some of the benefit the parties sought in bringing the suit.'" *Texas State Teachers Ass'n v. Garland Indep. Sch. Dist.*, 489 U.S. 782, 789 (1989) (quoting *Nadeau v. Helgemoe*, 581 F.2d 275, 278–79 (1st Cir. 1978)). "A plaintiff may be considered a prevailing party even though the relief ultimately obtained is not identical to the relief demanded in the complaint, provided the relief obtained is of the same general type." *Koster v. Perales*, 903 F.2d 131, 134–35 (2d Cir. 1990). "[T]he most critical factor is the degree of success obtained." *Texas State Teachers Ass'n*, 489 U.S. at 789.

In applying the prevailing party standard to IDEA cases, we have compared the relief sought by the plaintiff with the relief obtained as a result of the suit. *See, e.g., Christopher P. v. Marcus*, 915 F.2d 794, 804 (2d Cir. 1990). Similarly, the Third Circuit has characterized the appropriate inquiry as a two-part test: "whether plaintiffs achieved relief and whether there is a causal connection between the litigation and the relief from the defendant." *Wheeler v. Towanda Area Sch. Dist.*, 950 F.2d 128, 131 (3d Cir. 1991); *see also Koster*, 903 F.2d at 135 ("To justify a fee award, 'the prevailing party must show a causal connection between the relief obtained and the litigation in which the fees are sought.'" (quoting *Gerena-Valentin v. Koch*, 739 F.2d 755, 758 (2d Cir. 1984))). The Third Circuit's explanation of the "causal connection" element of this test is instructive and particularly relevant in assessing whether a plaintiff has "prevailed" in a case resolved by settlement:

> Litigation is causally related to the relief obtained if it was a material contributing factor in bringing about the events that resulted in obtaining the desired relief. Litigation can be a material contributing factor if it changed the legal relations of the parties such that defendants were legally compelled to grant relief. Alternatively, causation can be established through a "catalyst" theory, where even though the litigation did not result in a favorable judgment, the pressure of the lawsuit was a material contributing factor in bringing about extrajudicial relief.

Wheeler, 950 F.2d at 132 (internal citations omitted); *see also Koster*, 903 F.2d at 135 ("Such a causal connection exists if the plaintiff's lawsuit was 'a catalytic, necessary, or substantial factor in attaining the relief.'" (quoting *Gerena-Valentin*, 739 F.2d at 758–59)).

In assessing G.M.'s success in accomplishing his goals in requesting an administrative hearing, the district court characterized G.M.'s requested relief in very narrow terms: (1) an independent evaluation by a particular evaluator, Dr. Ernie Panscofar; and (2) an increase in G.M.'s vocational and community-based education to 20–25 hours per week. According to the district court, because the Board and G.M. stipulated to an independent evaluation by Futures rather than by Dr. Panscofar and because Futures' October 1996 recommendations (adopted in the settlement) did not expressly specify the number of hours G.M. was to spend in vocational and community-based programming, G.M. did not obtain the relief he had sought. The district court deemed the changes made in G.M.'s educational plan as a result of the stipulation to be limited and relatively minor.

1. Independent Evaluation

As noted, the district court held that G.M. did not succeed in his request for an independent evaluation because the court characterized G.M. as seeking an evaluation specifically to be performed by Dr. Panscofar. There are two problems with this conclusion: (1) the record is not clear as to whether G.M. had insisted on an independent evaluation specifically by Dr. Panscofar or, more generally, had sought an evaluation by someone other than a Board employee; and (2) even if G.M. did initially seek an evaluation specifically by Dr. Panscofar, the result G.M. obtained — an independent evaluation by Futures — nevertheless constituted substantial success toward his goal.

Whether G.M. conditioned his request for an independent evaluation on Dr. Panscofar being the evaluator is at least a disputed issue of fact that the district court should not have resolved at summary judgment. The minutes of the April 1996 PPT meeting do indicate that Garrison's initial demand was for "an independent evaluation by Dr. Ernie Panscofar." The Board answered this by "stat[ing] that the New Britain Schools have done this type of evaluation," to which Garrison responded in turn that "Dr. Panscofar focuses on 'transitional planning.'" Later in the meeting, the Board's attorney told Garrison that G.M.'s family "would need to prove that this type of evaluation is appropriate." When Garrison subsequently requested an administrative hearing to resolve the dispute, he referred generally to "the Board['s] refusal to approve an independent evaluation."

Thus, the record is not clear as to the nature of the disagreement between Garrison and the Board. Based on the minutes of the April PPT meeting, the most reasonable interpretation of the record is that G.M.'s representatives wanted an independent evaluation of G.M.'s needs, and that the Board was unwilling to pay for any outside evaluation. In any event, we find no basis for the district court's conclusion that — as a matter of law — G.M. sought an independent evaluation only by Dr. Panscofar.

But even if at the time that Garrison initiated the hearing process G.M.'s demand for an independent evaluation had been conditioned on the evaluation being performed by Dr. Panscofar, G.M. nonetheless obtained at least partial (and meaningful) success as a result of seeking a hearing. The minutes of the April PPT meeting show that the Board was resistant to *any* additional evaluation, and certainly to an evaluation not performed by the school system. The minutes also reflect that Garrison wanted the evaluation conducted by Dr. Panscofar because of Dr. Panscofar's focus on "transitional planning" as opposed to traditional educational programs. Futures emphasizes "transitional" education — one of Futures' letters in the record describes its "Alternative Educational Program" as "real-life learning opportunities within the student's community in the areas of employment, recreation, community participation, and functional academics." Thus, Futures meets the criterion that Garrison gave in April for picking Dr. Panscofar to evaluate G.M. Perhaps most telling, however, is that the stipulation agreed to by the Board in the settlement itself expressly identifies the Futures assessment of G.M. as an "independent evaluation."

Thus, G.M. might, at trial, have been able to show that his request for an evaluation was essentially for a review conducted by any validly independent evaluator, in which case his representatives obtained total success on this issue. But even if G.M. had at such a trial been found initially to have sought an evaluation specifically by Dr. Panscofar, the result of the settlement — "the independent evaluation" by Futures — was at least substantial success. It follows that, either way, the district court abused its discretion in holding that G.M. was not a prevailing party on this issue.

2. Community-Based Programming

The district court also exceeded its discretion in concluding that G.M. did not achieve significant success regarding his goal of obtaining community-based programming. The court ruled that because the recommendations that Futures made in October 1996 "made no mention of the amount of hours [to be] spent on vocational/community based education, presumably allowing the Board to decide the appropriate number of hours," G.M. had not attained his goal of increased community-based programming.

Again, the record does not bear out the district court. At the April 1996 PPT meeting, Garrison asked the team to change G.M.'s IEP to make it a "community-based educational program." The plan that Futures proposed in May emphasized "real-life learning opportunities within [G.M.'s] community."[1] At the next meeting of the PPT, in June, the Board proposed an "adaptation" of the Futures proposal that increased G.M.'s hours of community-based programming to fifteen per week, but kept slightly over fifteen hours of in-school instruction. It was at this point that Garrison requested a hearing. When Futures conducted its evaluation of G.M. in October, its first recommendation was "[a]n alternative, community-based school program." By February 1997, Futures was providing all of G.M.'s educational services, and none of G.M.'s program took place in a school setting. Thus, the record is clear that G.M. accomplished his goal of obtaining a community-based educational program.

The Board contends that G.M. nonetheless did not prevail, because the PPT's adoption of Futures' recommendations "merely continued its existing policy of, first, retaining Futures to evaluate and provide services for G.M.; and second, to accept Futures' recommendations, conditioned on sufficient supporting information." The Board does not explain, however, why the PPT chose not to adopt Futures' recommendations in their entirety at its June 1996 meeting, but then changed its mind in the fall, after the hearing. Instead, the Board contends only that "it was foreseeable prior to the request for due process that Futures' recommendations would be followed [when Futures produced] sufficient supporting information." But whether the PPT's eventual adoption of Futures' community-based programming was "foreseeable" is not the relevant inquiry, which is, instead, whether G.M.'s request for an administrative hearing was a "materially contributing factor" in the change to his IEP, *Wheeler*, 950 F.2d at 132.

---

[1] [FN 2] One provision of the plan called for 20–25 hours per week of one-on-one instruction. There is no indication, however, that Garrison's demands to the PPT were ever phrased in terms of specific numbers of hours. The district court therefore erred in concluding that the lack of specific hours in the Futures recommendations that were adopted after the hearing means that G.M. did not prevail.

Denying attorney fees under these circumstances would impose excessively onerous burdens on litigants seeking fee awards, so that virtually anything less than perfect congruence between the relief requested and the relief obtained would defeat a fee award. Such an approach clearly contradicts the "generous formulation" of the prevailing party test that the Supreme Court set forth in *Texas State Teachers Association. See* 489 U.S. at 792.

Furthermore, accepting the district court's standard would deleteriously discourage settlement of claims that are subject to fee-shifting provisions. In settling a lawsuit, each party inevitably makes some concessions. Interpreting the prevailing party standard to require total victory creates an undesirable incentive for litigants not to settle, because, under such a harsh standard, litigants would lose an opportunity to recover their fees whenever they compromised their position even slightly. The more flexible approach enunciated in our precedents greatly lessens such disincentives.

3. Fee Award

Having concluded that G.M. "has crossed the 'statutory threshold' of prevailing party status," *Texas State Teachers Ass'n*, 489 U.S. at 789, we remand to the district court for a determination of the amount of fees and costs that he should recover. As we recently reaffirmed in *Quaratino v. Tiffany & Co.*, 166 F.3d 422 (2d Cir. 1999), the district court's analysis should follow the "lodestar" approach, whereby an attorney fee award is derived "by multiplying the number of hours reasonably expended on the litigation times a reasonable hourly rate," *Blanchard v. Bergeron*, 489 U.S. 87, 94 (1989). *See also Jason D.W. v. Houston Indep. Sch. Dist.*, 158 F.3d 205, 208 (5th Cir. 1998) (per curiam) (noting, in an IDEA fee award case, the use of the lodestar approach); *Beard v. Teska*, 31 F.3d 942, 945 (10th Cir. 1994) (same). In cases of this sort, "[t]here is . . . a strong presumption that the lodestar figure represents a reasonable fee." *Quaratino*, 166 F.3d at 425 (internal quotation marks omitted). Included in the award should be not only the time spent on the administrative proceeding, but the time expended on this suit (including this appeal) as well. *See id.* at 428.

We leave to the district court to determine whether G.M.'s fee award should encompass the supplementary administrative hearing held at G.M.'s request in April 1997. The district court, having found against G.M. on the threshold issue of whether he was a prevailing party in the administrative proceeding, did not reach this issue. G.M. depicts the hearing as a successful action to enforce the order issued in the original hearing, while the Board contends that the hearing officer largely rejected G.M.'s asserted grievances. We are unable to ascertain from the record before us precisely what transpired prior to and during the supplementary hearing, and so think it best to allow the district court to resolve this dispute.

CONCLUSION

We hold that the district exceeded its discretion in finding that G.M. did not prevail in the administrative proceedings challenging the adequacy of his individual education plan. We remand for a determination of the amount of fees that G.M. should recover.

NOTES AND QUESTIONS

1. The *G.M.* court's approach to independent educational evaluation as a substantial success is the dominant one, though some courts disagree on the issue. *Compare T.S. v. District of Columbia*, No. 05-88861, 2007 U.S. Dist. LEXIS 21792 (D.D.C. Mar. 27, 2007) (awarding fees), *and Malecki v. Board of Sch. Comm'rs*, 29 IDELR 1053 (N.D. Ala. 1999) (same), *with Jodlowski v. Valley View Community Unit Sch. Dist.*, 109 F.3d 1250 (7th Cir. 1997) (labeling success in claim for independent evaluation solely procedural).

2. As the *G.M.* court suggests, the parents are entitled to fees if they prevail on any substantial issue, but fees may be reduced if they lose on other issues. If the issues are intertwined, or the parents prevail on the central issues, the court may choose not to order a fee reduction. *See generally* MARK C. WEBER, SPECIAL EDUCATION LAW AND LITIGATION TREATISE § 23.1(2) (3d ed. 2008 & supps.) (collecting cases). Considering concerns of public policy, what is the best approach on this topic to achieve the intended results for students?

3. *Buckhannon* Issues

In *Buckhannon Board & Care Home, Inc. v. West Virginia Department of Health and Human Services*, 532 U.S. 598 (2001), the Supreme Court ruled that in order to be a prevailing party under two federal civil rights attorneys' fees laws, the claimant had to achieve a judicially sanctioned change in the legal relationship of the parties. The Court said that a judicially sanctioned change would include a judgment on the merits or a consent decree, but not a voluntary change in policy and consequent dismissal of the action. The Court overturned the "catalyst" theory, previously adopted by all but one of the courts of appeals, which had allowed a civil rights claimant to win fees if the lawsuit provided the catalyst for settlement or some other voluntary response by the defendant that gave the claimant what the claimant had wanted. *Buckhannon* involved the fees provisions of the Americans with Disabilities Act and the Fair Housing Amendments; the case on the merits was dismissed on the basis of mootness after the lawsuit prompted legislative change preventing the application of governmental rules that threatened the operation of an assisted living residence. The case left open the question whether its rule would be applied to other attorneys' fees provisions, such as that in IDEA.

T.D. v. LAGRANGE SCHOOL DISTRICT NO. 102
349 F.3d 469 (7th Cir. 2003)

In this decision, the court of appeals reversed the district court and held that Buckhannon does apply to IDEA cases, defeating an award of fees for the settlement. It also rejected an award of expert witness fees.

KANNE, CIRCUIT JUDGE.

Congress enacted the Individuals With Disabilities Education Act ("IDEA") with the primary purpose of ensuring that a "free appropriate public education" is available to all children with disabilities. 20 U.S.C. § 1400(d)(1)(A) (2003). To facilitate this goal, the IDEA requires schools to have in place procedures that allow parents to make complaints regarding "any matter relating to the identification, evaluation, or educational placement of the child, or the provision of a free appropriate public education" to their child. *Id.* § 1415(b)(6). If the parents' concerns cannot be satisfactorily resolved through informal channels, the IDEA provides parents a right to mediation or an impartial due process hearing conducted by the appropriate state educational agency. *Id.* § 1415(e)(1), (f)(1). If parents are still unsatisfied following a due process hearing, they may then bring a civil action in federal or state court. *Id.* § 1415(i)(2)(A). To ease the financial burden on parents making claims, the IDEA contains a fee-shifting provision that allows attorney's fees to the parents of a child with a disability who are the "prevailing party" in any action or proceeding brought under the IDEA. *Id.* § 1415(i)(3)(B).

In this appeal we address whether the plaintiff, T.D., is a prevailing party under this fee-shifting provision and whether T.D. is thereby eligible for attorney's fees. The district court, finding that the Supreme Court's recent decision in *Buckhannon Bd. & Care Home v. W. Va. Dep't of Health & Human Res.*, 532 U.S. 598 (2001), did not apply to the IDEA, held that T.D. was entitled to attorney's fees. We hold that *Buckhannon* does apply to the IDEA, but find that T.D. is still entitled to a portion of his attorney's fees. We also find that the district court erred in finding that T.D. was entitled to receive reimbursement under the IDEA for his expert witness fees.

I. History

A. Background

T.D., born June 24, 1991, is a strong-willed child, who was diagnosed with Attention Deficit Hyperactivity Disorder at an early age. His parents enrolled him in private pre-schools and elementary schools through the early part of 1997. On February 4, 1997, during T.D.'s kindergarten year, he was dismissed from a parochial school after the school determined that it did not have the special-education resources needed to properly educate him. The parochial school offered to refer T.D. to the local public school for services, but at that time his parents refused to allow the parochial school to make the referral.

A week after T.D. was dismissed from the parochial school, his parents took him to the University of Chicago's Hyperactivity, Attention, and Learning Problems Clinic for an independent evaluation. That evaluation recommended, *inter alia*, that T.D. attend a school with a low teacher:student ratio and noted that the best setting for T.D. would likely be a private, therapeutic day school.

In March and April of 1997, T.D.'s mother spoke at various times with the public school district's Director of Special Ed, Mary Ann Cusick. During these conversations, T.D.'s mother sought information about the school district's special-education programs and apparently expressed some reluctance to enroll T.D. in the school district, based on T.D.'s older brother's experience there. At some point during this period, T.D.'s mother visited the local public school that T.D. would attend. During this visit, she met with the principal and the kindergarten teacher, and the school provided her with further information about the special-education services that would be available to T.D. within the context of the regular classroom setting. At no point during March or April of 1997, did the school district request written consent to conduct a case-study evaluation of T.D. to determine his potential eligibility for various special-education programs.

In September 1997, T.D.'s parents enrolled him in the first grade at Acacia Academy, a private therapeutic day school. Acacia, however, would only allow T.D. to attend full-time if his parents hired a one-on-one aide to accompany him. After a short period of attending only part-time, T.D.'s parents hired an aide and thereafter T.D. attended full-time.

B. Due Process Administrative Proceedings

On August 25, 1997, approximately five months after T.D.'s mother first contacted the public school district officials, T.D.'s parents requested, through their attorney, a due process hearing before a state administrative hearing officer as provided for by § 1415(f) of the IDEA. In their hearing request, T.D.'s parents alleged that the school district had (i) "fail[ed] to evaluate T.D. despite actual notice that he may require special-education services"; (ii) "fail[ed] to notify" them that the school district "had decided not to conduct a case study evaluation"; (iii) "fail[ed] to consider their independent evaluation"; and (iv) "fail[ed] to appropriately advise them of the placement options for T.D. within the public school setting" other than "full inclusion placements, in a regular classroom setting." T.D.'s parents claimed that as a result of these failures the school district had denied T.D. the "free, appropriate public education" guaranteed by the IDEA.

Part of the relief requested by T.D.'s parents was that the school conduct an evaluation to determine T.D.'s eligibility under the IDEA for special-education services. On October 15, 1997, the hearing officer conducted a pre-hearing conference on this issue, after which the hearing officer determined that a case-study evaluation was necessary and ordered the school to conduct the evaluation. Following this order, on November 20, 1997, the school conducted the evaluation and convened an Individualized Education Program ("IEP") conference, as required by the IDEA § 1414. As a result of the evaluation and conference, T.D. was determined to have an "Emotional/Behavioral Disorder" and a "Speech and/or Language Impairment," and was found eligible for special-education services from the school district. The school district recommended that T.D. be placed at the local public school in a regular-education classroom, with supplemental special-education services to address T.D.'s special needs. T.D.'s parents rejected the recommended placement.

The administrative due process hearing commenced on December 5, 1997. The parents sought: (i) reimbursement for their placement of T.D. at Acacia for the 1997-1998 academic year; (ii) reimbursement for the one-on-one aide to assist T.D. at the private school; (iii) reimbursement for T.D.'s transportation to and from

Acacia; and (iv) reimbursement for the independent evaluation they had obtained from the University of Chicago.

In a ruling rendered on December 10, 1997, the hearing officer made findings that as of the last week of March 1997, the school district knew that T.D. might require special-education services and should have requested the parent's written consent to conduct a case-study evaluation of T.D. at that time. Further, pursuant to the case study, the school should have identified the student's needs and formulated program and service options. It was not until the hearing officer ordered the evaluation that these things were accomplished. The hearing officer found that the school district's failings contributed to the parents' need to place T.D. in the private school and to obtain a one-on-one aide. Therefore, the hearing officer ordered the school district to reimburse T.D.'s parents for their out-of-pocket costs for the one-on-one aide, a cost of about $1130 per month and for the costs of transportation to the school, a cost of about $5 per ride, from September 17 until the school district could provide the appropriate services. As to T.D.'s educational placement, however, the hearing officer found that the private school in which T.D. was enrolled could not adequately meet his needs. Therefore, he denied reimbursement for the private school tuition, and he ordered that T.D. be transferred to a regular mainstream classroom at the local public school with supplemental special-education services.

C. District Court Proceedings and Settlement

T.D. appealed to federal district court, seeking reversal of the proposed placement in a regular classroom, asking instead for continued placement at the private day school. Further, he sought reimbursement of the tuition already paid by his parents for the day school. He also asked for the relief already granted by the hearing officer, namely the reimbursement of the one-on-one aide cost and transportation costs. Finally, he sought attorney's fees and costs.

Both parties moved for summary judgment, but before the district court ruled, the parties settled. The settlement agreement provided that T.D. would be placed in a self-contained behavior disordered program (as opposed to a regular classroom) in a public school. The school district agreed to reimburse T.D.'s parents for tuition and all costs in any way resulting from or relating to T.D.'s attendance at the private day school, a total of $52,000. The parties did not reach an agreement regarding attorney's fees, specifically leaving the issue for decision by the district court.

The district court rendered its decision on attorney's fees on October 7, 2002, holding that T.D. was a "prevailing party" and therefore was entitled to attorney's fees under the IDEA's fee-shifting provision. In finding that T.D. was a prevailing party, the district court noted that he had succeeded on a significant issue when he obtained the case-study evaluation, which determined that he was eligible for special-education services. The court went on to state:

> [I]rrespective of how much Parents prevailed in the hearing or in my Court, I find that Parents obtained through settlement the balance of what they desired and TD needed. TD's placement in a self-contained behavior disordered classroom in a public school is the direct result of Parent's

litigation on the issue of TD's placement and the settlement represents a significant departure from La Grange's proposal to educate TD in a regular mainstream classroom with a one-on-one aide.

Importantly, the district court held that the Supreme Court's recent decision in *Buckhannon* did not apply to the IDEA. The district court expressly stated that it was not deciding whether attorney's fees would be appropriate under the strictures of *Buckhannon.*

The district court awarded T.D. $117,135.53 in attorney's fees and costs. The school district now appeals that decision.

II. Analysis

A. *Buckhannon* and the IDEA

The IDEA, like many other federal statutes, provides that courts may award attorney's fees to a "prevailing party":

> In any action or proceeding brought under this section, the court, in its discretion, may award reasonable attorneys' fees as part of the costs to the parents of a child with a disability who is the prevailing party.

20 U.S.C. § 1415(i)(3)(B) (2003). In *Buckhannon*, the Supreme Court limited the meaning of the term "prevailing party," by rejecting the catalyst theory as a method of attaining prevailing-party status under the Americans With Disabilities Act ("ADA") and Fair Housing Amendments Act ("FHAA"). 532 U.S. at 605. Under the catalyst theory, which had been accepted by many courts before *Buckhannon*, a plaintiff could prevail, if the plaintiff's suit was a catalyst that prompted the change that the plaintiff sought. *Buckhannon*, however, held that a party could not be a prevailing party without receiving some sort of "judicial imprimatur" on the charge. *Id.* at 605. Central to the Court's conclusion was its finding that the term "prevailing party" was "a legal term of art," which signified that the party had been granted relief by a court. *Id.* at 603. As examples of the type of relief necessary to attain "prevailing party" status, the court cited a judgment on the merits and a consent decree. *Id.* at 604.

The school district argues that since this case was ultimately resolved through a private settlement, without a judicial imprimatur, T.D. does not qualify as a "prevailing party" under the Supreme Court's explanation of that term in *Buckhannon*. T.D. counters that *Buckhannon's* rules are inapplicable to the IDEA. Therefore, the threshold issue in this case is whether *Buckhannon's* limitations on the meaning of the term "prevailing party" apply.

Although *Buckhannon* involved only claims under the "prevailing party" fee-shifting provisions of the ADA and FHAA, there is little doubt that the *Buckhannon* Court intended its interpretation of the term "prevailing party" to have broad effect upon similar fee-shifting statutes. The Court observed that Congress has passed many statutes that authorize courts to award attorney's fees to the "prevailing party," such as 42 U.S.C. § 1988, and that the Court has interpreted those fee-shifting provisions consistently across the federal statutes. *Buckhannon*, 532

U.S. at 602–03 & n. 4 (citing *Hensley v. Eckerhart*, 461 U.S. 424, 433, n. 7 (1983), which held that the standards used in interpreting the term "prevailing party" are "generally applicable in all cases in which Congress has authorized an award of fees to a 'prevailing party.'"). Moreover, as noted above, the Court described the term "prevailing party" as a "legal term of art," with the relatively fixed and accepted meaning of "a party in whose favor a judgment is rendered." *Id.* at 603 (citing BLACK'S LEGAL DICTIONARY 1145 (7th ed. 1999)). Therefore, one would conclude that if a statute contains this legal term of art that has been interpreted consistently across statutes, we should exercise great caution before we give that term a different meaning. *See Me. Sch. Admin. Dist. No. 35 v. Mr. & Mrs. R.*, 321 F.3d 9, 14 (1st Cir. 2003) ("Because [the IDEA] employs the phrase 'prevailing party' — a term of art — it must be interpreted and applied in the same manner as other federal fee-shifting statutes that use the same phraseology.").

Given these considerations, at least one circuit has interpreted *Buckhannon* as applying to all "prevailing party" fee-shifting statutes. *See Smyth v. Rivero*, 282 F.3d 268, 274 (4th Cir. 2002) (holding that *Buckhannon* applies to 42 U.S.C. § 1988 and stating "[t]he term 'prevailing party,' as used in § 1988(b) and other fee-shifting provisions, is a 'legal term of art,' and is interpreted consistently — that is, without distinctions based on the particular statutory context in which it appears.") (quotations and citations omitted). While there is some appeal to the simplicity of this position, this Court has not yet gone that far. Rather, we have left open the possibility that if the "text, structure, or legislative history" of a particular fee-shifting statute indicate that the term "prevailing party" in that statute is not meant to have its usual meaning — as defined in *Buckhannon* — then *Buckhannon*'s strictures may not apply.

We reiterate, however, that because "prevailing party" is a legal term of art that is interpreted consistently across fee-shifting statutes, there is a strong presumption that *Buckhannon* applies to each fee-shifting statute that awards fees to "prevailing parties." Consequently, for this Court to find that *Buckhannon* does not apply to the IDEA, a "prevailing party" fee-shifting statute, the "text, structure, or legislative history" would have to clearly indicate that in the IDEA, Congress did not intend to use the term "prevailing party" in its traditional "term of art" sense.

The district court below held that the text of the IDEA set it apart from other statutes. We acknowledge that the IDEA's text and structure is somewhat more complex than other "prevailing party" fee-shifting statutes because the IDEA not only states that attorney's fees are available to "prevailing parties," but it also contains limiting provisions in §§ 1415(i)(3)(D)–(G), which specify certain situations where attorney's fees are unavailable or must be reduced. For instance, § 1415(i)(3)(D)(i) provides that a party may not receive attorney's fees incurred subsequent to a settlement offer if the court or hearing officer determines that the relief finally obtained by the plaintiff is not more favorable than the settlement offer. Section 1415(i)(3)(D)(ii) provides in relevant part that attorney's fees may not be awarded (at the discretion of the state) for work done in mediation conducted before the filing of a formal request for a hearing. And § 1415(i)(3)(F)–(G) instructs district courts to reduce an attorney's fee award when the plaintiff has "unreasonably protracted the final resolution of the controversy."

T.D. argues that these provisions create an implication that Congress intended the term "prevailing party" as used in the IDEA to include more than just parties that obtain judicially sanctioned relief. The arguments are quite strained, however, as none of these provisions clearly indicate a Congressional intent about anything related to the "prevailing party" requirement. *John T. v. Del. County Intermediate Unit*, 318 F.3d 545, 557 (3d Cir. 2003). "Rather, §§ 1415(i)(3)(D) through (G) define situations in which attorney's fees may be prohibited or reduced" even for "prevailing parties." *Id.* For instance, if a plaintiff rejects a settlement offer and eventually receives a judicially sanctioned victory that is less beneficial than the settlement offer was, the plaintiff, though being a "prevailing party," may not get the fees incurred after the settlement offer. 20 U.S.C. § 1415(i)(3)(D)(i). Or, as § 1415(i)(3)(D)(ii) provides, if a party pursues an unsuccessful mediation and eventually obtains a victory with judicial imprimatur, then he may receive attorney's fees for the unsuccessful mediation if it occurred after the filing of a complaint. Or, if a plaintiff who eventually obtains judicially sanctioned success unreasonably protracted the resolution of the case, the court may reduce the attorney's fee award to account for the unreasonable delay. *Id.* § 1415(i)(3)(G).

The bottom line is that these limiting provisions do not clearly indicate that the term "prevailing party" was intended to encompass anything more in the IDEA than in any of the other "prevailing party" fee-shifting statutes. In fact, these provisions do not inform anything about the meaning of the term "prevailing party" in the IDEA because they are relevant only after a plaintiff has been deemed a "prevailing party."

We turn next to the legislative history. As both the Second and Third Circuits have recognized, the legislative history of the IDEA seems to indicate that Congress did not intend the IDEA to be interpreted any differently from other prevailing party fee-shifting statutes. *See John T.*, 318 F.3d at 557; *J.C. v. Reg'l Sch. Dist. 10*, 278 F.3d 119, 124 (2d Cir. 2002). When Congress added the fee-shifting provision to the IDEA's predecessor statute, the Education of the Handicapped Act, the Senate Committee on Labor and Human Resources provided that "it is the committee's intent that the terms 'prevailing party' and 'reasonable' be construed consistently with the U.S. Supreme Court's decision in *Hensley v. Eckerhart*," which involved 42 U.S.C. § 1988. S. Rep. No. 99-112, at 13 (1986), *reprinted* in 1986 U.S.C.C.A.N. 1798, 1803 (footnote omitted). We have followed this principle by interpreting the IDEA consistently with § 1988. *See, e.g., Bd. of Educ. v. Steven L.*, 89 F.3d 464, 468 (7th Cir. 1996) (" 'Prevailing party' has the same meaning under 20 U.S.C. § 1415(e) as 42 U.S.C. § 1988."). And importantly, *Buckhannon* made clear that its strictures applied to § 1988. *See, e.g., J.C.*, 278 F.3d at 124. From the legislative history then, it appears that *Buckhannon* should be applied to the IDEA.

In addition to the textual and legislative history arguments, T.D. makes essentially two policy arguments, which he claims show that *Buckhannon* should not be applied to the IDEA. We approach these arguments with caution because the *Buckhannon* Court itself, in analyzing the policy arguments made in that case, stated: "Given the clear meaning of 'prevailing party' in the fee-shifting statutes we need not determine which way these various policy arguments cut." 532 U.S. at 610. Consequently, it is not clear that the Supreme Court has left any room for this Court or any other "to interpret anew the term 'prevailing party' in light of the

IDEA policies." *John T.*, 318 F.3d at 558.

T.D. contends that the statute is designed to facilitate early, informal resolution of controversies between schools and students. According to T.D., this is an important goal of the IDEA because delay in finding an appropriate school setting can be detrimental to a child's development. T.D. maintains that this goal would be undermined if we found that private settlements do not entitle plaintiffs to attorney's fees because parents and attorneys would have an incentive to reject settlement offers and thereby delay the final resolution of the proceedings.

We recognize the importance and benefit of quick resolution to any litigation; particularly, litigation that involves the educational placement of a child. But many of the same factors that make quick resolution through settlement beneficial under the IDEA apply to the statutes that were at issue in *Buckhannon* as well. For instance, there are surely strong policy reasons for quickly resolving a disabled person's claims under the ADA. Nonetheless, *Buckhannon* held that ADA plaintiffs may receive attorney's fees only upon receipt of some judicially sanctioned victory. In other words, *Buckhannon* simply has closed the door on this argument. *John T.*, 318 F.3d at 557; *J.C.*, 278 F.3d at 124. Moreover, in response to the same policy argument that T.D. makes here — that settlement is to be encouraged under the IDEA and therefore we should allow attorney's fees for settlement — the Second Circuit noted:

> [I]t is difficult to reconcile [the] policy argument for awarding fees pursuant to informal settlements with the fact that, even before *Buckhannon*, Congress deliberately chose not to allow the recovery of attorneys' fees for participation in IEP proceedings that were not convened as a result of an administrative proceeding or judicial action. 20 U.S.C. § 1415(i)(3)(D)(ii). The IEP Team is a mechanism for compromise and cooperation rather than adversarial confrontation. This atmosphere would be jeopardized if we were to encourage the participation of counsel in the IEP process by awarding attorneys' fees for settlements achieved at that stage.

J.C., 278 F.3d at 124–25.

T.D.'s second policy argument centers around the stated purpose of the IDEA "to ensure that all children with disabilities have available to them a free appropriate public education . . . to meet their unique needs." 20 U.S.C. § 1400(d)(1)(A). T.D. contends that if the IDEA's "prevailing party" provision is interpreted to preclude the award of fees to parties that settle, then students who must hire an attorney and whose claims are ultimately resolved through private settlement will be denied the *free* appropriate education promised by the IDEA because they will be saddled with large legal fees.

While this is probably T.D.'s strongest argument, we are still not persuaded. We note that the IDEA only guarantees the right to a free education; it does not explicitly guarantee the right to attorney's fees incurred in pursuit of that education. *Cf. Edie F. v. River Falls Sch. Dist.*, 243 F.3d 329, 336 (7th Cir. 2001) ("Clearly . . . parents . . . have a right to champion their [child's] cause, but the right to have their attorneys fees picked up by the taxpayers is more circumspect."). Therefore, it is not clear that it would be against the purpose of the IDEA to require plaintiffs who do not achieve judicial imprimatur on their victory to bear their own attorney's fees. Furthermore, in light of *Buckhannon*, which made explicit that "prevailing party" has a clearly established meaning that overrides various policy arguments, we are constrained to reject T.D.'s contention on this point.

Moreover, we do not take lightly the fact that virtually every court to have decided the issue has determined that *Buckhannon* applies to the IDEA. For instance, the only two federal appellate courts, the Second and Third Circuits, that have squarely addressed the issue have both held *Buckhannon* applicable to the IDEA. *See John T.*, 318 F.3d at 556; *J.C.*, 278 F.3d at 125; *see also Smyth v. Rivero*, 282 F.3d 268, 274 (4th Cir. 2002) (stating that *Buckhannon* applies to all "prevailing party" fee-shifting provisions, regardless of "the particular statutory context."); *John & Leigh T. v. Iowa Dept. of Educ.*, 258 F.3d 860, 863–64 (8th Cir. 2001) (assuming that *Buckhannon* applies to the IDEA but not discussing the issue). Today, we join the Second and Third Circuits in holding that *Buckhannon* is applicable to the IDEA.

B. T.D.'s Status as a Prevailing Party Under *Buckhannon*

As noted above, *Buckhannon* held that to be a "prevailing party" a litigant must have obtained a judgment on the merits, a consent decree, or some similar form of judicially sanctioned relief. 532 U.S. at 603–04. In *Buckhannon*, the Court specifically noted that "[p]rivate settlement agreements do not entail the judicial approval and oversight involved in consent decrees. And federal jurisdiction to enforce a private contractual settlement will often be lacking unless the terms of the agreement are incorporated into the order of dismissal." 532 U.S. at 604 n. 7. Therefore, the Court left the clear impression that private settlements do not involve sufficient judicial sanction to confer "prevailing party" status. *See Christina A. v. Bloomberg*, 315 F.3d 990, 993 (8th Cir. 2003); *Smyth*, 282 F.3d at 279.

The merits of this case were ultimately resolved through a settlement between the parties. We agree with the Fourth Circuit's recent conclusion that some settlement agreements, even though not explicitly labeled as a "consent decree" may confer "prevailing party" status, if they are sufficiently analogous to a consent decree. *Smyth*, 282 F.3d at 281. For instance, "[w]here a settlement agreement is embodied in a court order such that the obligation to comply with its terms is court-ordered, the court's approval and the attendant judicial oversight (in the form of continuing jurisdiction to enforce the agreement) may be . . . functionally a consent decree." *Id.; see also John T.*, 318 F.3d at 558 (stating that "a stipulated settlement could confer prevailing party status . . . where it (1) contained mandatory language, (2) was entitled 'Order,' (3) bore the signature of the District Court judge, not the parties' counsel, and (4) provided for judicial enforcement") (emphasis omitted) (citation omitted).

The settlement agreement in this case does not bear any of the marks of a consent decree. It is not embodied in a court order or judgment. It does not bear the district court judge's signature, and the district court has no continuing jurisdiction to enforce the agreement. Rather, it was merely a private settlement agreement between the parties. T.D. argues that because the district court was actively involved in the settlement negotiations, having conducted a settlement conference in his chambers and made certain settlement suggestions, that we should find that there was sufficient "judicial imprimatur" on the settlement to confer "prevailing party" status.

Mere involvement in the settlement, however, is not enough. There must be some official judicial approval of the settlement and some level of continuing judicial oversight. *Buckhannon*, 532 U.S. at 604 n. 7; *Smyth*, 282 F.3d at 281. Therefore, we find that the settlement agreement reached in this case did not confer "prevailing party" status upon T.D.

T.D. asserts that even if he cannot be said to have prevailed via the settlement, that he was the "prevailing party" in the due process hearing and therefore should be compensated at least for that success. The parties do not dispute that the IDEA's fee-shifting provision allows courts to grant attorney's fees to parents who prevail in an administrative hearing. Indeed, we held in *Brown v. Griggsville Comm. Unit Sch. Dist. No. 4*, that the IDEA does allow fees to the prevailing party in administrative hearings. 12 F.3d 681, 683–84 (7th Cir. 1993). While we recognize that this opinion was issued before *Buckhannon*, we do not perceive that *Buckhannon* requires a different conclusion.

The IDEA's fee-shifting provision allows attorney's fees to the party that prevails "[i]n any action or proceeding" brought under the IDEA. 20 U.S.C. § 1415(i)(3)(B). As other courts have noted, the word "proceeding" as used in other parts of the statute refers to administrative or due process hearings. *See, e.g., id.* § 1415(d)(2)(F) & (k)(7)(C)(I) ("due process proceedings"); *Id.* § 1415(i)(2)(B)(i) & (i)(3)(D)(ii) ("administrative proceedings"); *L.C. v. Waterbury Bd. of Educ.*, No. 3:00 CV 580, 2002 U.S. Dist. LEXIS 6079, at *7–*8 (D. Conn. Mar. 21, 2002). And the Court in *Buckhannon* gave no indication that it intended to overturn its decision in *New York Gaslight Club, Inc. v. Carey*, 447 U.S. 54 (1980). That case held that the fee-shifting provision in Title VII, which also referred to "action or proceeding," allowed courts to award attorney's fees to the prevailing party in administrative hearings. *Id.* at 61.

The school district does not dispute that to the extent that T.D.'s parents prevailed at the due process hearing, they are eligible for fees for that success. The school district disputes only whether T.D. prevailed at the due process hearing at all. The Supreme Court has stated that a plaintiff may be considered a "prevailing party" if "they succeed on any significant issue in litigation which achieves some of the benefit the parties sought in bringing suit." *Hensley*, 461 U.S. at 433 (noting that this is a "generous formulation"). We find that while T.D. did not succeed on every issue at the due process hearing, he did prevail on certain significant issues and achieved at least some of the benefit he sought.

In his hearing request, T.D. sought to have the school district conduct a case-study evaluation to determine his eligibility for benefits under the IDEA. And he sought reimbursement for various costs incurred in attending the private day school, including tuition, a one-on-one aide, and transportation. The hearing officer granted T.D.'s request for an evaluation by the school district, ordering the school to conduct the evaluation on November 20, 1997. Significantly, the hearing officer placed blame on the school district for not requesting written consent to conduct the evaluation, even though they had notice that T.D. might have been eligible for IDEA benefits. The case-study evaluation and IEP conference that followed, determined that T.D. was in fact eligible for IDEA benefits and proposed placement of T.D. at public school in a regular-education classroom, with supplemental special-education services to address T.D.'s needs. This determination represented some success for T.D. because prior to his request for the due process hearing the school had not acknowledged that T.D. was even eligible for IDEA benefits.

The hearing officer partially granted T.D.'s requests for reimbursement for the costs of attending the private school, awarding reimbursement for the cost of the one-on-one aide and for transportation, but refusing to grant reimbursement for the cost of tuition. The hearing officer characterized this partial relief as an equitable award. He found that the private day school was not providing T.D. with an appropriate education; therefore, he did not award T.D. reimbursement for the cost of the tuition. The hearing officer, however, found that the school district was at least partly to blame for T.D.'s inappropriate placement at the private school since the school district failed to conduct an evaluation of T.D. and failed to offer T.D. any formal placement proposal before the November 20, 1997 evaluation and conference. Considering these failures, the hearing officer ordered the school district to reimburse T.D. for the cost of the one-on-one aid from the time she was hired until T.D. could be enrolled in the public school. And the cost of transportation to the private school was also ordered to be reimbursed.

T.D. succeeded in obtaining the case-study evaluation that the school previously had not conducted and that ultimately led to the determination that he was eligible for benefits under the IDEA. This success coupled with the reimbursement he received for the cost of the one-on-one aide and transportation to the private school (which together added up to nearly $1200 a month) rendered T.D. a "prevailing party" in the administrative hearing. Therefore, we find that T.D. is entitled to attorney's fees for prevailing at the administrative hearing.

C. Award of Expert Witness Fees

Finally, the school district challenges the district court's award of expert witness fees to T.D. as part of the attorney's fees and costs of the litigation. Because we determined that T.D. was a prevailing party as to the administrative hearing, we must consider whether T.D. should receive expert witness fees incurred as part of that hearing.

Title 28 U.S.C. § 1920 is the general provision that provides for the taxation of costs in federal court, and § 1920(3) allows for payment of witnesses. In 28 U.S.C. § 1821(b), Congress placed a limit on the witness fees authorized by § 1920(3), providing that "[a] witness shall be paid an attendance fee of $40 per day for each day's attendance." In *Crawford Fitting Co. v. J.T. Gibbons*, the Supreme Court held that "when a prevailing party seeks reimbursement for fees paid to its own expert witnesses, a federal court is bound by the limit of § 1821(b), absent contract or explicit statutory authority to the contrary." 482 U.S. 437, 439 (1987). Therefore, we must look to the IDEA's fee-shifting provision to determine if it contains "explicit statutory authority" for shifting of expert witness fees.

As cited above, the IDEA's fee provision states:

> In any action or proceeding brought under this section, the court, in its discretion, may award *reasonable attorney's fees as part of the costs* to the parents of a child with a disability who is the prevailing party.

20 U.S.C. § 1415(i)(3)(B) (emphasis added). T.D. relies on the italicized portion of the statute as authority to shift expert witness fees to the losing party. This provision, however, does not provide any explicit statement as to expert witness fees.

The only federal appellate court to address the issue of expert witness fees under the IDEA held that the IDEA did not contain the necessary explicit authority to exceed the amounts provided for in 28 U.S.C. § 1821(b). *Neosho R-V Sch. Dist. v. Clark*, 315 F.3d 1022, 1031 (8th Cir. 2003). We agree with the Eighth Circuit's reasoning and conclusion. In *Neosho*, the Eighth Circuit acknowledged that the construction of the IDEA's fee provision appears to contemplate that costs include something more than attorney's fees, "but [it] does not specifically authorize an award of costs or define what items are recoverable as costs." *Id.* Absent a specific authorization for the allowance of expert witness fees, "federal courts are bound by the limitations set out in 28 U.S.C. § 1821 and § 1920." *Id.* (quoting *Crawford Fitting Co.*, 482 U.S. at 445).

Furthermore, in *West Va. Univ. Hosps., Inc. v. Casey*, the Supreme Court was faced with the question of whether a former version 42 U.S.C. § 1988 gave authority to shift expert fees. 499 U.S. 83, 84 (1991). This former version of § 1988 contained a fee-shifting provision, almost identical to that in the IDEA, allowing "the prevailing party . . . a reasonable attorney's fee as part of costs."[2] 42 U.S.C. § 1988(b) (1990). The *Casey* Court held that this language was not an explicit statutory authorization that allowed shifting of expert witness fees. 499 U.S. at 10.

In so holding, the Court observed that Congress had specifically enacted several statutes that explicitly provided for the shifting of both attorney's fees and expert witness fees. *Id.* at 88–89 (noting that "[a]t least 34 statutes in 10 different titles of the U.S. Code explicitly shift attorney's fees *and* expert witness fees."). The Court concluded that if it were to interpret a statute that provides only for attorney's fees to actually allow shifting of both attorney's fees and expert fees, the "dozens of statutes referring to the two separately [would] become an inexplicable exercise in redundancy." *Id.* at 92. Obviously, these same concerns exist for the IDEA, which uses nearly identical statutory language.

T.D. argues that the legislative history of the IDEA supports allowing expert witness fees to the prevailing party. That legislative history, in the form of a House Conference report, states:

> The conferees intend that the term "attorney's fees as part of the costs" include reasonable expenses and fees of expert witnesses and the reasonable costs of any test or evaluation which is found to be necessary for the preparation of the . . . case.

---

[2] [FN 5] Following the Supreme Court's decision in *Casey*, Congress amended § 1988 by adding subsection (c), which provides: "In awarding an attorney's fee under subsection (b) of this section . . . the court in its discretion may include expert fees as part of the attorney's fee." 42 U.S.C. § 1988 (2003).

H.R. Conf. Rep. No. 99-687, at 5 (1986), reprinted in 1986 U.S.C.C.A.N. 1807, 1808. We recognize that this report does appear to support T.D.'s position. The Eighth Circuit, however, rejected this identical argument, finding that since "[n]othing in the plain language of the statute indicates that the district court is authorized to exceed the limitations set out in § 1821 and § 1920," there is no ambiguity in the statute, and therefore "no occasion to look to the legislative history." *Neosho*, 315 F.3d at 1032 (citing *Burlington N. R.R. v. Okla. Tax Comm'n*, 481 U.S. 454, 461 (1987) ("Unless exceptional circumstances dictate otherwise, when we find the terms of a statute unambiguous, judicial inquiry is complete.")).

The *Casey* Court in dicta characterized this portion of the IDEA's legislative history as "an apparent effort to depart from ordinary meaning and to define a term of art," noting that "the specification would have been quite unnecessary if the ordinary meaning of the term included those elements." 499 U.S. at 91 n. 5. We agree with the Eighth Circuit's determination that "this 'apparent effort' to define a term of art in legislative history is an unsuccessful one." *Neosho*, 315 F.3d at 1032. The Supreme Court made clear in *Crawford* that "explicit statutory authorization" was necessary to allow courts to exceed the limitations of 28 U.S.C. § 1821 and § 1920. We find no such authorization in the IDEA, particularly, in light of the fact that the Supreme Court in *Casey* found that the same words used in the former § 1988 ("reasonable attorney's fee as part of costs") did not provide the necessary explicit statutory authorization.

III. Conclusion

We hold that the Supreme Court's requirements for attaining prevailing party status set out in *Buckhannon* are applicable to the IDEA. We find that the settlement reached between the parties in this case was no more than a private agreement, lacking the judicial imprimatur to elevate T.D. to the status of prevailing party. T.D.'s success in the administrative hearing, however, does entitle him to receive attorney's fees to the extent that he prevailed in that hearing. Finally, we hold that expert witness fees are not available to T.D. under the IDEA. Therefore, we AFFIRM in part and REVERSE in part. The case is REMANDED to the district court for a determination of the amount of attorney's fees to which T.D. is entitled based on the degree of success he achieved in the administrative hearing.

NOTES AND QUESTIONS

1. The strong trend among the courts is to rule that *Buckhannon* applies to IDEA. *E.g.*, *P.N. v. Seattle School Dist. No. 1*, 474 F.3d 1165 (9th Cir. 2007); *Smith v. Fitchburg Pub. Schs.*, 401 F.3d 16 (1st Cir. 2005); *Alegria v. District of Columbia*, 391 F.3d 262 (D.C. Cir. 2004); *Doe v. Boston Pub. Schs.*, 358 F.3d 20 (1st Cir. 2004) (denying fees when case settled minutes before hearing began; hearing officer refused to read settlement into record).

2. The absence of fees for settlements may discourage settlements and induce a variety of strategic behavior by counsel that will work against IDEA's underlying policies. *See generally* Mark C. Weber, *Litigation Under the Individuals with Disabilities Education Act after* Buckhannon Board & Care Home v. West Virginia

Department of Health & Human Resources, 65 Ohio St. L.J. 357, 398–408 (2004) (discussing incentive effects of abolition of catalyst rule).

3. *Buckhannon* itself has proven highly unpopular with academic commentators. *See, e.g.*, David Luban, *Taking Out the Adversary: The Assault on Progressive Public-Interest Lawyers*, 91 Cal. L. Rev. 209, 243 (2003) ("*Buckhannon* creates another silencing doctrine. . . ."); Aviam Soifer, *Courting Anarchy*, 82 B.U. L. Rev. 699, 725 (2002) ("If there were a contest for the most preposterous decision of the Term, *Buckhannon* . . . surely ranks near the top."). One point made in the commentary is that however Congress felt about fees for settlements when it passed the original Civil Rights Attorneys Fees Act of 1976, by the time the fees statutes in the ADA and the Fair Housing Act (or, for that matter, IDEA) were adopted, Congress was well aware of the uniform interpretation of the courts of appeals embracing the catalyst theory. In fact, in 1985 Senators Hatch and Thurmond tried unsuccessfully to amend the 1976 Act to overturn the judicial gloss on the statute. At the time the later statutes were adopted, Congress certainly knew that the fees provisions would be interpreted to embrace catalyst cases; there thus was effective legislative acquiescence in the rule. *See* Weber, 65 Ohio St. L.J. at 367–68.

4. *Buckhannon* leaves open whether fees can be awarded for dispositions that are not dismissals based on mootness after legislative change (the facts of that case), but are not judgments on the merits or consent decrees, either. Hearing officers entering compromise dispositions are unlikely to label anything a "consent decree," a term generally reserved for judicial dispositions. Courts have awarded fees on the basis of agreed orders entered by hearing officers. *E.g.*, *P.N. v. Clementon Bd. of Educ.*, 442 F.3d 848 (3d Cir.) (finding consent order entered by administrative law judge adequate to support fees award even though administrative law judge lacked jurisdiction to enforce consent orders), *cert. denied*, 127 S. Ct. 189 (2006); *A.R. v. New York City Dep't of Educ.*, 407 F.3d 65, 77 (2d Cir. 2005) (declaring agreement embodied in a hearing officer order to be "the administrative analog of a consent decree" and permitting fees); *Brandon K. v. New Lenox Sch. Dist.*, 2001 U.S. Dist. LEXIS 20006 (N.D. Ill. Dec. 3, 2001). *But see P.N. v. Seattle School Dist. No. 1*, 474 F.3d 1165 (9th Cir. 2007) (holding that settlement providing for reimbursement of tuition and evaluation costs and reserving issue of attorneys' fees and costs, followed by order of administrative law judge dismissing proceeding at parent's request, failed to support fees award). Should a court award fees on the basis of a settlement reached at mediation? *Compare Ostby v. Oxnard Union High*, 209 F. Supp. 2d 1035 (C.D. Cal. 2002) (yes), *with Jose Luis R. v. Joliet Township High Sch. Dist. 204*, 2002 U.S. Dist. LEXIS 20916 (N.D. Ill. Jan. 15, 2002) (no). *See generally* Weber, 65 Ohio St. L.J. at 383–94 (discussing non-consent decree dispositions and collecting cases). Recall *G.M. v. New Britain Board of Education*, reprinted *supra*. Under current law, would fees be awarded in that case?

5. *T.D.* also presents the issue whether the fees provision in IDEA covers expert witnesses. The Supreme Court has concluded that IDEA does not permit the award of expert witness fees. Its decision employed an analysis similar to that of the Seventh Circuit opinion in *T.D.*, which interprets the IDEA provision consistently with 42 U.S.C. § 1988 (subsequently amended to overturn the Supreme Court's interpretation) and contrary to the IDEA legislative history. *Arlington Cent. Sch.*

Dist. Bd. of Educ. v. Murphy, 548 U.S. 291 (2006).

B. MEASURE OF FEES

Calculation of attorneys' fees under IDEA implicates any number of topics. After briefly discussing some of the more basic of the general considerations, this section takes up the question of measuring the respective liability of multiple defendants when they lose to parents in an IDEA case.

1. General Considerations

Fees are available for work done at or in preparation for hearings, but not for individualized education program meetings unless the meeting is conducted as a result of a judicial or administrative proceedings. 20 U.S.C. § 1415(i)(3)(D). States may make fees available for mediations. *Id.* Under the statute, the court is to base the fees on the rate prevailing in the community in which the proceeding arose for the kind and quality of services rendered; the statute does not permit bonuses or multipliers to compensate for the risk of pursuing the case. 20 U.S.C. § 1415(i)(3)(C). This approach to computing fees is called the lodestar method. Recall the discussion in *G.M.*, reprinted *supra* Section A. There are various bases for diminishing the amount of fees below the lodestar figure, such as unreasonable protraction of the case and failure to provide adequate information in the due process hearing request, though there are exceptions to the application of the reductions. 20 U.S.C. § 1415(i)(3)(F)–(G).

The statute also provides that fees accrued after timely receipt of an offer of settlement may be denied when the prevailing party rejects the offer and the litigated result is no better than the offer. 20 U.S.C. § 1415(i)(3)(D)(i). Regarding the effects of this scheme on settlement, see Chapter 8, *supra* (Due Process Hearings). As noted there, the statute effectively creates an administrative version of the interpretation of Fed. R. Civ. P. 68 found in *Marek v. Chesny,* 473 U.S. 1 (1985).

2. Apportionment of Liability

Many cases have more than one defendant. If the plaintiff parent wins, the court must determine which defendant is liable for how much of the fee award.

JOHN T. v. IOWA DEPARTMENT OF EDUCATION
258 F.3d 860 (8th Cir. 2001)

In this case, the court apportioned the liability between the state department of education and the local district, assessing the respective responsibilities of those two parties for the dispute.

MAGILL, CIRCUIT JUDGE.

Plaintiffs John and Leigh T. are the parents of Robert, a child with cerebral palsy. Robert's parents sued the Marion Independent School District and the Grant

Wood Area Education Association (together, the "Local Defendants"), as well as the Iowa Department of Education (the "Department"), alleging violations of Iowa law and the Individuals with Disabilities Education Act ("IDEA"). In a prior appeal, this Court held that the defendants violated IDEA, and remanded to the district court to implement a remedy and consider an award of attorneys' fees. *John T. v. Marion Indep. Sch. Dist.*, 173 F.3d 684, 691 (8th Cir. 1999) ("*John T. I*"). On remand, the district court held that Robert's parents were "prevailing parties" against the Department, and ordered the Department to pay a portion of the plaintiffs' attorneys' fees. The Department appeals, and we affirm the district court's holding that the plaintiffs were "prevailing parties" against the Department, but reverse the fee award and remand to the district court to subtract from the award all fees incurred during the administrative proceedings.

I.

Robert T. is a student at St. Joseph Catholic School ("St. Joseph"). The parties agree that Robert's cerebral palsy renders him disabled within the meaning of IDEA. Robert's parents asked the Local Defendants to provide a full-time instructional assistant to work with Robert at St. Joseph. After the Local Defendants denied their request, Robert's parents appealed the decision to an administrative law judge ("ALJ"), arguing that the Local Defendants' refusal to provide Robert with an assistant violated Iowa law and IDEA. Robert's parents did not name the Department as a defendant in the administrative appeal, and the Department did not participate in those proceedings. The ALJ decided that neither Iowa law nor IDEA compelled the Local Defendants to provide Robert with a classroom assistant.

Robert's parents appealed the ALJ's decision to federal district court, where their complaint named the Local Defendants and the Department as defendants, identifying the Department as "the 'state educational agency' with authority over Robert's education within the meaning of § 1401(7) of the IDEA." The complaint alleged that the Local Defendants were responsible for denying Robert an assistant, but did not claim that the Department affected the Local Defendants' decision. The Department filed a brief in the district court urging affirmance of the ALJ's decision; the Local Defendants jointly filed a separate brief. The district court reversed the ALJ's decision, holding that Iowa law required the Local Defendants to provide an assistant for Robert. The district court did not resolve the IDEA claim.

In wake of the district court's decision, Robert's parents requested attorneys' fees. The Local Defendants filed a joint response opposing the request, which the Department joined in part. The Department filed a separate response to counter the Local Defendants' argument that if the district court awarded fees, then the court should hold the Department wholly liable because the Local Defendants merely "followed state procedures and interpreted the applicable state law statute consistent with the guidelines established by the [Department.]" The district court granted Robert's parents' request, holding that their success on the state claim rendered them "prevailing parties" under IDEA. The district court also held that the Department's advocacy in support of the ALJ's decision justified imposing part of the fee award against the Department.

The Local Defendants appealed both the district court's decision on the merits and the court's decision to award fees. The Department joined the Local Defendants' appeal of the fee award, but did not challenge the district court's reversal of the ALJ's decision. Collectively defining the Local Defendants and the Department as the "School District," this court held that "the School District's actions before 1997 violated the IDEA but . . . its actions after that time did not violate the IDEA." *John T. I*, 173 F.3d at 686, 690.[3] On the attorneys' fees issue, we stated:

> We leave to the "broad discretion of the district court" the question of the remedy to which Robert's parents are entitled as a result of the School District's violations of the pre-1997 IDEA. After making this determination, the district court should reconsider whether and to what extent Robert's parents are entitled to an award of attorneys' fees under the IDEA. . . . At that time, the district court may consider the arguments between [the Local Defendants] on the one hand and [the Department] on the other regarding the proper apportionment of attorneys' fees among the three parties.

Id. at 691 & n. 4 (citation omitted).

After this court's decision in *John T. I*, Robert's parents resolved their attorneys' fees claims against the Local Defendants, but not against the Department. On remand, the district court held the Department liable for part of the plaintiffs' attorneys' fees. The district court noted that our decision in *John T. I* collectively referred to the Local Defendants and the Department as the "School District," and held that the School District violated IDEA. Therefore, the district court held that the plaintiffs were "prevailing parties" against the Department. The court then stated that since the Department

> was one of three defendants, and [was] a zealous advocate in support of affirmation of the administrative decision, it is the court's view that the appropriate share to be borne by the [Department] is 1/3 of all reasonable fees and costs through January 13, 2000. Additionally, [the Department] shall bear all reasonable costs and fees incurred thereafter (following settlement by the other two defendants).

The district court subsequently ordered the Department to pay the plaintiffs $65,431.14. The Department appeals.

II.

A. "Prevailing Party" Status

The Department first argues that the district court erred in holding that Robert's parents were "prevailing parties" against the Department. IDEA provides: "In any

---

[3] [FN 1] In 1997, Congress amended IDEA, limiting the rights of disabled children enrolled in private schools. The Individuals with Disabilities Education Act Amendments of 1997, Pub. L. No. 105-17, 111 Stat. 37 (1997); 20 U.S.C. § 1412(a)(10) (2000).

action or proceeding brought under this section, the court, in its discretion, may award reasonable attorneys' fees as part of the costs to the parents of a child with a disability who is a prevailing party." 20 U.S.C. § 1415(i)(3)(B) (2000). We review de novo whether the district court applied the correct legal standard in determining if the plaintiffs were "prevailing parties," and review the award of fees for abuse of discretion. *Warner v. Independent Sch. Dist. No. 625*, 134 F.3d 1333, 1336 (8th Cir. 1998).

The Supreme Court has explained that to qualify as a "prevailing party," a plaintiff must obtain "actual relief on the merits of his claim [that] materially alters the legal relationship between the parties by modifying the defendant's behavior in a way that directly benefits the plaintiff." *Farrar v. Hobby*, 506 U.S. 103, 111–12 (1992); *see also Buckhannon Bd. & Care Home, Inc. v. West Virginia Dep't of Health & Human Res.*, 531 U.S. 1004 (2001). The State of Iowa waived its Eleventh Amendment immunity by receiving funds appropriated under IDEA. *See Bradley v. Arkansas Dep't of Educ.*, 189 F.3d 745, 753 (8th Cir. 1999), *rev'd on other grounds sub nom. Jim C. v. United States*, 235 F.3d 1079 (8th Cir. 2000) (en banc).

We conclude that the district court correctly held that Robert's parents were "prevailing parties" against the Department. IDEA places primary responsibility on state education agencies ("State Agencies"), such as the Department, to ensure the proper education of disabled children. Section 1412 of IDEA makes State Agencies "responsible for ensuring that the requirements of this subchapter are met." 20 U.S.C. § 1412(a)(11)(A)(i) (2000). Moreover, IDEA's legislative history indicates that Congress wanted to "assure a single line of responsibility with regard to the education of handicapped children." S. Rep. No. 94-168, at 24 (1975). The Senate Report explained:

> The Committee considers the establishment of single agency responsibility for assuring the right to education of all handicapped children of para- mount importance. Without this requirement, there is an abdication of responsibility for the education of handicapped children. . . . While the Committee understands that different agencies may, in fact, deliver services, the responsibility must remain in a central agency overseeing the education of handicapped children, so that failure to deliver services or the violation of the rights of handicapped children is squarely the responsibility of one agency.

Id.; see also 34 C.F.R. § 300.401 (2000).

Indeed, several circuits have held State Agencies liable when they have failed to ensure Local Agencies' implementation of IDEA's requirements. *See, e.g., Gadsby v. Grasmick*, 109 F.3d 940 (4th Cir. 1997). In *Gadsby*, Eric Gadsby's parents requested the Baltimore Public Schools (the "Baltimore Schools"), the applicable Local Agency, to evaluate Eric for special education services. *Id.* at 945. Eric's parents initially challenged the program that the Baltimore Schools developed, but the parties settled their dispute when the Baltimore Schools agreed to pay part of Eric's tuition at a private school and to apply to the Maryland Department of Education (the "Maryland Department") for the remainder of the tuition. *Id.* However, when the Maryland Department rejected the Gadsbys' request that it pay the remainder of Eric's tuition, the Gadsbys filed suit against the Baltimore Schools and the Maryland Department. *Id.* at 946.

Thus, the question presented to the Fourth Circuit was whether the Gadsbys could assert a claim against the Maryland Department for reimbursement of Eric's tuition based on the Baltimore Schools' failure to develop a proper program for Eric. *Id.* at 951. Although acknowledging that IDEA does not explicitly state which governmental entity courts should hold liable for particular violations, *Gadsby* interpreted § 1412(a)(11)(A)(i) to permit holding a State Agency responsible for failing "to comply with its duty to assure that IDEA's substantive requirements are implemented." *Id.* at 952. Therefore, the court concluded that State Agencies are "ultimately responsible for the provision of a free appropriate public education to all of its students and may be held liable for the state's failure to assure compliance with IDEA." *Id.* at 953; *see also St. Tammany Parish Sch. Bd. v. State of Louisiana*, 142 F.3d 776, 783–85 (5th Cir. 1998) (following *Gadsby* in holding that the district court did not abuse its discretion in holding the State Agency liable for the costs of the plaintiff's education); *Kruelle v. New Castle County Sch. Dist.*, 642 F.2d 687, 696–97 (3d Cir. 1981) (affirming the district court's decision holding the State Agency responsible for providing the student with a proper educational program).

However, we do not think that § 1412(a)(11)(A)(i), by itself, permits a court to award attorneys' fees against a State Agency that has not participated in the underlying lawsuit. We thus agree with the Tenth Circuit's opinion in *Beard v. Teska*, 31 F.3d 942 (10th Cir. 1994), where the court examined the attorneys' fees request of a class of handicapped children who had successfully sued various Local and State Agencies under IDEA. *Id.* at 945. The court rejected the contention that § 1412(a)(11)(A)(i) alone renders State Agencies liable for attorneys' fees "on a respondeat superior theory." *Id.* at 954. Section 1412(a)(11)(A)(i), the court explained, "does not turn every 'local educational agency' under the statute . . . into the agent of the 'State educational agency' as a matter of federal law, so that the latter automatically becomes legally liable for all transgressions of the former." *Id.*; *see also Whitehead v. School Bd. for Hillsborough County*, 932 F. Supp. 1393, 1395–96 (M.D. Fla. 1996) ("Though the IDEA holds the state [department of education] responsible for assuring disabled children are provided a free appropriate public education, this alone does not render that agency liable for § [1415(i)(3)(B)] fees under a respondeat superior theory.").

We conclude that, in conjunction with IDEA's placement of supervisory responsibility on State Agencies, the Department's zealous opposition to the plaintiffs' position in this case permitted the district court's award of attorneys' fees against the Department. Robert's parents named the Department as a defendant in the district court. Instead of requesting the district court to dismiss it as not a real party in interest, the Department took a position adverse to the plaintiffs' claims by filing a brief with the court that urged affirmance of the ALJ's decision. This Court agreed with Robert's parents' argument that the defendants, including the Department, violated the pre-1997 IDEA. *John T. I*, 173 F.3d at 690. These facts persuade us that the district court correctly held that Robert's parents were "prevailing parties" against the Department.

Moreover, our opinion in *John T. I* affirmed the district court's decision interpreting Iowa law to require the defendants to reimburse Robert's parents for costs incurred in hiring an assistant to work with Robert at St. Joseph. *Id.* Although we remanded to the district court for the court to implement a remedy for the IDEA violation, since the district court already had reimbursed Robert's parents for their costs under Iowa law, the court apparently did not use the defendants' IDEA violation to provide a further remedy. Instead, the court only used the IDEA violation to award Robert's parents with attorneys' fees. But it was mere fortuity that the district court used Iowa law, and not IDEA, to reimburse Robert's parents for the costs they incurred; had the court not already reimbursed Robert's parents under Iowa law, it almost surely would have done so under IDEA. Since the awarding of costs against the Department "materially alter[ed] the legal relationship between the parties by modifying" the Department's behavior, we hold that the district court correctly determined that Robert's parents were "prevailing parties" against the Department. *Farrar*, 506 U.S. at 111–12.

Thus, we reject the Department's apparent belief that it may vigorously oppose a plaintiff's IDEA claim, thereby making it more difficult for the plaintiff to get relief, without facing any potentially adverse consequence. Under the Department's position, even if the court decides for the IDEA plaintiff, the court would have no power to award fees against it. Although we can see the appeal this stance holds for the Department, we think that IDEA's placement of primary responsibility on State Agencies to ensure the proper education of disabled children warrants some accountability where, as here, the plaintiff names the State Agency as a defendant and the State Agency argues in support of what a court holds to be a Local Agency's IDEA violation.

B. The Proper Allocation of Fees

Alternatively, the Department argues that we should subtract from the award all attorneys' fees stemming from the administrative proceedings, in which it did not participate, and part of the fees deriving from the initial Eighth Circuit appeal, where it did not challenge the plaintiffs' entitlement to relief on the merits of their claim.

We hold that the district court abused its discretion in awarding fees against the Defendant that were incurred during the administrative proceedings. Courts may award attorneys' fees under IDEA for legal work performed in connection with administrative proceedings. *Johnson v. Bismarck Pub. Sch. Dist.*, 949 F.2d 1000, 1003 (8th Cir. 1991). In a similar case, a Florida district court examined an attorneys' fees request under IDEA. *Whitehead*, 932 F. Supp. 1393. The plaintiffs sued the Local Agency under IDEA and prevailed in the administrative proceedings. *Id.* at 1395. The plaintiffs then sought to enforce the administrative ruling in federal district court and added the State Agency as a defendant, asking that the State Agency contribute to an award of attorneys' fees. *Id.* The district court rejected the plaintiffs' request, stating that "[a]lthough Plaintiffs prevailed in their dispute before the Administrative Hearing Officer, the style of that case clearly identified [the Local Agency] as the sole Defendant. . . . [The State Agency] was not a party to the dispute, and for this reason Plaintiffs are not entitled to attorney's fees as prevailing party over a non-defendant." *Id.; see also Reid v. Board of Educ., Lincolnshire-Prairie View Sch. Dist. 103*, 765 F. Supp. 965, 969 (N.D. Ill. 1991) (holding that the State Agency, which was not a party to the administrative proceedings, was not liable for the attorneys' fees incurred during those proceedings).

Robert's parents, however, contend that we should hold the Department liable for fees incurred at the administrative level under a respondeat superior theory. Although we acknowledge IDEA's placement of responsibility on State Agencies to ensure the proper education of disabled children, as we explain above, we do not think that this supervisory responsibility alone permits a fee award when the State Agency does not participate in the proceedings. Robert's parents also argue that we should hold the Department liable for fees incurred during the administrative proceedings because the Department "has attempted to reap the benefits of the [administrative] ruling in its briefs and filings." *K.Y. v. Maine Township High Sch. Dist. No. 207*, No. 96-C-7872, 1998 U.S. Dist. LEXIS 4468 (N.D. Ill. Mar. 31, 1998). We disagree. In short, the Department's actions in the district court had no impact on the fees Robert's parents incurred in the administrative proceedings.

Moreover, both *K.Y.* and *Robert D. v. Sobel*, 688 F. Supp. 861 (S.D.N.Y. 1988), upon which the plaintiffs also rely, are distinguishable from this case. In *K.Y.*, the Local Agency moved to join the State Agency in the administrative hearing. Here, neither the plaintiffs nor the Local Defendants sought to join the Department in the administrative proceedings. In *Robert D.*, the State Agency refused to provide the relief requested by the plaintiffs, but did not participate in the administrative proceedings. 688 F. Supp. at 863. The district court noted that the administrative hearings were held to review the State Agency's refusal to provide the plaintiffs with the requested relief and held: "Having declined to attend, the [State Agency] should not thus be able to immunize [it]self from liability for attorney's fees." *Id.* at 866–67. In this case, by contrast, the Local Defendants were the party that refused to provide the relief requested by the plaintiffs. Thus, the administrative proceedings here only examined whether the Local Defendants erred in refusing to provide the plaintiffs with the requested relief. Therefore, we reverse the district court's grant of attorneys' fees to the plaintiffs for work performed during the administrative proceedings.

Finally, we reject the Department's invitation to absolve it from paying fees incurred by the plaintiffs in defending the merits of the district court's decision in the first appeal. Although the Department restricted its arguments in the first appeal to the attorneys' fees question, the district court acted within its discretion in refusing to fine-tune the apportionment of fees based on the number of arguments made by each party. Perhaps the Department is less responsible than the Local Defendants for the attorneys' fees incurred during the first appeal but, as Judge Easterbrook noted, "allocation of this sort is invariably approximate. This allocation is defensible; no more is required." *Tonya K. v. Board of Educ. of City of Chicago*, 847 F.2d 1243, 1249 (7th Cir. 1988).

III.

We AFFIRM the district court's holding that the plaintiffs were "prevailing parties" against the Department. However, we REVERSE the district court's attorneys' fees award and REMAND for the court to subtract the fees awarded for the plaintiffs' costs in the administrative proceedings.

NOTES AND QUESTIONS

1.   You are the assistant attorney general assigned to give general guidance to the Iowa Department of Education on avoiding attorneys' fees liability. You have just read *John T.* What do you write in your memo to the head of the department regarding its posture in litigation that primarily involves disputes between parents and districts? Are there any drawbacks to adopting a hands-off policy in those cases?

2.   Did the parents make an error by settling the fees claim with the district before the decision of the Eighth Circuit on the department's appeal? Why might the parents have settled with the district when they did? Should the liability for attorneys' fees be joint and several rather than, as is effectively the case under *John T.*, purely several?

Chapter 12

CHILDREN IN PRIVATE SCHOOLS

A. INTRODUCTION

This chapter considers issues relevant to children placed by their parents in private schools in the absence of any dispute with a school district over the appropriateness of services being offered by the public school. Many parents opt for private schooling for their children for reasons of religion or perceived quality of instruction or other concerns. These children may have disabling conditions and would otherwise be entitled to a free, appropriate public education. At present, the law does not grant them an individual entitlement to such an education, though it permits school districts to provide services, including services on the site of religious and other private schools. This chapter will consider the current codification of statutory rights in IDEA and its regulations, considerations of establishment of religion insofar as the codification permits services to be delivered on the sites of religious schools, considerations of free exercise of religion insofar as the codification permits districts to limit services for private school children, and some remaining issues concerning possible discrimination between secular private schools and religious ones.

B. THE CURRENT CODIFICATION

The rights of children in private schools to receive services under IDEA are spelled out in the amendments to the statute enacted in 1997 and implementing regulations issued by the United States Department of Education. These provisions were further changed by the 2004 IDEA Reauthorization, which placed in the statute, with modifications, some of the provisions of the Department of Education's regulations. For a general discussion of the current law and issues in connection with it, see Mark C. Weber, *Services for Private School Students Under the Individuals with Disabilities Education Improvement Act: Issues of Statutory Entitlement, Religious Liberty, and Procedural Regularity*, 36 J.L. & EDUC. 163 (2007).

1. Definition of Private Schools

IDEA refers to nonpublic schools, whether sectarian or nonsectarian, as "private" schools, but does not separately define the term. This absence of a federal definition allows states to employ their own definitions. As discussed below, state definitions may not define home schooling as private school, to the dismay of home-schooling parents who want their children to be eligible for services under the private-school student provisions.

2.   Proportionate Allocation of Federal IDEA Funds

Local education agencies (LEAs, *i.e.*, public school districts) are required to expend funds for students with disabilities who attend private schools within the district "equal to a proportionate amount of Federal funds made available under [IDEA]." 20 U.S.C.§ 1412(a)(10)(A)(i)(I); *see* 34 C.F.R. § 300.133. Unlike previous law, the 2004 IDEA Reauthorization requires proportionate expenditure based on the number of children with disabilities enrolled in private schools within the district boundaries, rather than resident there. 20 U.S.C. § 1412(a)(10(A)(i)(I). Nonfederal funds may supplement the amounts. 20 U.S.C. § 1412(a)(10(A)(i)(IV).

3.   Child Find and Evaluation

The responsibilities of states to identify, locate and evaluate children with disabilities applies "with respect to children with disabilities in the State who are enrolled in private, including religious, elementary schools and secondary schools." 20 U.S.C. § 1412(a)(10)(A)(ii); *see* 34 C.F.R. § 300.131(a). The school district's child-find obligation under these provisions extends to those enrolled in private schools in the districts, whether or not they live in the district, or even in the state. 20 U.S.C. § 1412(a)(10(A)(i)(V); 34 C.F.R. § 300.131(b)–(f). The costs of child find are not part of the proportionate allocation on private school students. 20 U.S.C. § 1412(a)(10(A)(i)(IV); 34 C.F.R. § 300.131(d). Activities and timelines must be comparable to those for students attending public school. 20 U.S.C. § 1412(a)(10(A)(i)(III), (V); 34 C.F.R. § 300.131(c), (e). One of the rights in connection with evaluation under IDEA is the right to an independent educational evaluation at public expense if the parent disagrees with the evaluation provided by the public school system and the district fails to invoke a due process hearing and show its evaluation is appropriate. The Department of Education takes the position that the same independent educational evaluation rights apply to private school parents who disagree with the school district's evaluation. U.S. Dep't of Educ., Questions and Answers on Serving Children with Disabilities Placed by Their Parents at Private Schools, at F-3 (2006), at http://www.ed.gov/policy/speced/guid/faq-parent-placed.doc.

4.   Services Plan Requirement

Each private school child with a disability who has been designated to receive special education services is entitled to a services plan that "describes the specific special education and related services that the LEA will provide to the child in light of the services that the LEA has determined . . . it will make available to parentally-placed private school children with disabilities." 34 C.F.R. § 300.138(b)(1). These services plans lack the detail of IEPs, but are similar to IEPs to the extent that the plans must be developed, reviewed and revised consistent with the requirements for IEPs, to the extent appropriate. 34 C.F.R. § 300.138(b)(2); *see* 34 C.F.R. § 300.137(c) (requiring meetings to develop, review, and revise plan, and efforts to secure participation of representative of private school).

5.   Absence of an Individual Right to Services

No parentally-placed private school child with a disability "has an individual right to receive some or all of the special education and related services the child would receive if enrolled in a public school." 34 C.F.R. § 300.137(a). "Parentally-placed private school children with disabilities may receive a different amount of services than children with disabilities in public schools." 34 C.F.R. § 300.138(a)(2).

6.   Consultation with Private School Representatives

LEAs (or, where appropriate, state educational agencies) must consult with private school representatives, 20 U.S.C. § 1412(a)(10)(A)(iii), regarding such matters as the child-find process and the determination of the proportionate amount to be expended. The consultation has to include how the private school representatives and parent representatives will consult with LEAs about allocation and method of delivery of the services. 20 U.S.C. § 1412(a)(10)(A)(iii)(III)–(IV). The consultation must also include how the LEA will provide reasons for not providing direct or contract services, if the private school representatives disagree with the agency about the provision of services or type of services. 20 U.S.C. § 1412(a)(10)(A)(iii)(V). The LEA is to obtain a written affirmation from the private school representatives that the consultation has occurred; if the representatives do not oblige, the LEA must provide the state educational agency documentation of its consultation efforts. 20 U.S.C. § 1412(a)(10)(A)(iv). Private schools may complain to the state about failure to consult, and may take their complaint to the United States Secretary of Education if dissatisfied with the results. 20 U.S.C. § 1412(a)(10)(A)(v). *See generally* 34 C.F.R. §§ 300.134–.136 (recapitulating statutory provisions).

7.   Personnel Standards

Once an LEA determines to provide services to a private school child, the personnel providing those services must meet "the same standards as personnel providing services in public schools." 34 C.F.R. § 300.138(a). Nevertheless, private school personnel may be used to furnish IDEA-funded services, as long as the services are performed outside of regular hours of duty and the personnel are under public supervision and control, 34 C.F.R. § 300.142(b); when private elementary and secondary school teachers are used, they do not have to meet the highly qualified special education teacher requirements otherwise required of public school special education teachers, 34 C.F.R. § 300.138(a)(1).

8.   Permissibility of On-Site Services

Services can be provided on-site at private, including religious, schools "to the extent consistent with law." 20 U.S.C. § 1412(a)(10)(A)(i)(III); 34 C.F.R. § 300.139(a). Property, equipment and supplies may be placed by an LEA at a private school site for delivery of services to private school children; however, the items must be removed if they are no longer needed or if removal is necessary to prevent unauthorized use by the private school. 34 C.F.R. § 300.144. Funds are not permitted to be used to benefit a private school. 34 C.F.R. § 300.141. All services, wherever they are delivered, and including materials and equipment, must be secular, neutral, and nonideological. 20 U.S.C. § 1412(a)(10)(A)(v)(II); 34 C.F.R. § 300.138(c)(2).

9.   Transportation

Students in private schools whose services are provided outside the private school are entitled to transportation to the services site and back to the private school, or to the child's home. 34 C.F.R. § 300.139(b).

10.   Complaints by Private School Parents

Parents of students in private schools are not entitled to use the impartial due process hearing procedure under 20 U.S.C. § 1415(f), except to challenge a local school district's failure to properly identify, locate, or evaluate the student. *See* 34 C.F.R. § 300.140(a). These complaints are to be filed with the LEA in which the child's private school is located. 34 C.F.R. § 300.140(b). All other complaints are to be directed to the state educational agency (SEA, *e.g.*, state department of education), which must employ its complaint resolution process to address any dispute regarding denial of services or other matters. 34 C.F.R. § 300.140(c). Within 60 days of a parent filing a complaint, an SEA must conduct an investigation and submit a written decision containing whatever corrective measures are necessary. 34 C.F.R. §§ 300.151–.153. The state complaint resolution process does not have the various safeguards, participation requirements, and appeal rights of the due process mechanism.

NOTES AND QUESTIONS

1.   Before 1997, interpretations of IDEA left unclear whether students in private schools had the individual right to a free, appropriate public education from the state and the local public school district. The 1997 amendments to IDEA eliminated any right to on-site special education services in private schools and, as interpreted by the regulations, eliminated individual rights to services altogether. 34 C.F.R. § 300.454(a); *see Veschi v. Northwestern Lehigh Sch. Dist.*, 772 A.2d 469 (Pa. Commw. 2001); *see also Foley v. Special Sch. Dist. of St. Louis County*, 153 F.3d 863 (8th Cir. 1998) ("[Parents have] no right to a federal court decree mandating that services be provided at a particular location."). In *K.R. v. Anderson Community Sch. Corp.*, 125 F.3d 1017 (7th Cir. 1997), the court stated:

> [T]he [1997] Amendments unambiguously show that participating states and localities have no obligation to spend their money to ensure that disabled children who have chosen to enroll in private schools will receive publicly-funded education generally "comparable" to those provided to public-school children.

Id. at 1019. Was this a wise policy decision on the part of Congress? Why might Congress have decided to eliminate the possibility of an individual entitlement? Is the amendment inconsistent with the principle of providing a free, appropriate education to *all* children with disabilities?

2.   The definition of a school under state law typically has a number of purposes, one of which is to determine whether a child is complying with a state's compulsory attendance requirement. For example, Texas, in Tex. Educ. Code Ann. § 25.086, exempts a child from compulsory attendance laws if the child attends "a private or parochial school that includes in its course a study of good citizenship." This definition was interpreted in *Texas Education Agency v. Leeper*, 893 S.W.2d 432 (Tex. 1994), which defined home instruction as meeting the requirement for "a private school." The State of Florida permits home education for purposes of compulsory attendance laws, but does not otherwise accord a home school private school status. *Compare* Fla. Stat. Ann. § 1002.41 (stating that home-educated students must meet the requirements of a "home education program" for purposes of satisfying compulsory attendance) *with* Fla. Stat. Ann. § 1002.01 (stating that a "home education program" is explicitly excluded from the definition a "private school" which can, however, include "a parochial, religious, denominational, for-profit, or nonprofit school."). Under such a definition, what might be the implications under IDEA of home schooling not being defined as a "private school" under state law? Could home-schooled students in Florida be excluded from any IDEA benefits simply because a home-school is not a "private school"? The United States Department of Education gives states the latitude whether or not to include home schooling in their definitions of private school for purposes of IDEA, *Williams*, 18 IDELR 742 (U.S. Dep't of Educ., Office of Special Educ. Programs 1992). The Ninth Circuit has endorsed this position and ruled that for the time period relevant to its decision, Nevada did consider home instruction to be private schooling. *Hooks v. Clark County Sch. Dist.*, 228 F.3d 1036 (9th Cir. 2000). This interpretation has been criticized. *E.g.*, Samuel Ashby Lambert, Note, *Finding the Way Back Home: Funding for Home School Children Under the Individuals with Disabilities Education Act*, 101 COLUM. L. REV. 1709, 1713–29 (2001). Should the federal government deem home schools to be private schools for purposes of IDEA? A court has ruled that a public school district lacks the power to compel parents to consent to evaluation of a child in home schooling, provided that the child does not use public special education services. *Fitzgerald v. Camdenton R-III Sch. Dist.*, 439 F.3d 773 (8th Cir. 2006).

3.   In *Ullmo v. Gilmour Academy*, 273 F.3d 671 (6th Cir. 2001), parents unsuccessfully made the argument that, because a private school received federal assistance, it was liable under IDEA for not providing their child with special education services necessary to address a hearing impairment and a learning disability. The Sixth Circuit held that since only the local education agency (the public school district), not the private school, could receive funds under IDEA, only the LEA could be liable under IDEA for the child's failure to receive services. Thus, while the private school may have liability for discriminating against a child with disabilities under section 504, it could not be liable under IDEA. However, could a private school assume IDEA obligations of an LEA by entering into a contract with an LEA? *See St. Johnsbury Academy v. D.H.*, 240 F.3d 163 (2d Cir. 2001) (answering no). If such contractual obligations could be created, who should be able to enforce that contract — the SEA, the LEA, the parent, the student? *See St. Johnsbury*, 240 F.3d at 172.

4. Although the various obligations the school district must fulfill, such as consultation, seem designed to induce LEAs to distribute federally funded services to private school students in a rational manner, there does not appear to be anything in the statute or regulations that requires that ultimate result. Accordingly, there are complaints that school districts have in some instances distributed services on a first-come, first-served basis or chosen other odd methods for choosing where, when, and to whom to provide the benefits of special education. Could a school district's process for giving out services be so opaque or arbitrary as to violate due process? *See generally* Mark C. Weber, *Services for Private School Students Under the Individuals with Disabilities Education Improvement Act: Issues of Statutory Entitlement, Religious Liberty, and Procedural Regularity*, 36 J.L. & EDUC. 163, 204–10 (2007) (answering yes).

5. State law may provide an individual entitlement to publicly funded services for privately schooled children with disabilities. *See, e.g., John T. v. Marion Indep. Sch. Dist.*, 173 F.3d 684 (8th Cir. 1999) (interpreting Iowa law). In *Bay Shore Union Free School District v. T.*, 405 F. Supp. 2d 230 (E.D.N.Y. 2005), *vacated on jurisdictional grounds, sub nom. Bay Shore Union Free School District v. Kain*, 485 F.3d 730 (2d Cir. 2007), Judge Jack Weinstein concluded that state law in New York gave a child an individual entitlement to services at the child's private school when the services needed were those of an in-class one-on-one aide three hours a day. The decision interprets the state law to avoid what the judge believes could otherwise be an unconstitutional burden on the religious choice of the child's parents to send the child to a religious school. *Id.* at 247. *See generally Board of Educ. of Bay Shore Union Free Sch. Dist. v. Kain*, 14 N.Y.3d 289 (2010) (upholding due process hearing officer and state review decision requiring provision of one-on-one aide three hours per week in private, religious school to dually enrolled child, in accordance with child's individual educational needs in least restrictive environment). The question whether an unconstitutional burden applies is raised *infra* section D.

C. PERMISSIVE ACCOMMODATIONS AND THE ESTABLISHMENT CLAUSE

The First Amendment to the Constitution both forbids establishment of religion and guarantees free exercise of religion. IDEA permits services to be provided to children in private schools, including religious schools. If these services are provided on the site of the religious school, does that violate the prohibition against establishing religion?

ZOBREST v. CATALINA FOOTHILLS SCHOOL DISTRICT
509 U.S. 1 (1993)

Here, the Supreme Court held that a school district's voluntary decision to provide a sign language interpreter on-site at a religious school did not violate the establishment clause.

CHIEF JUSTICE REHNQUIST delivered the opinion of the Court.

. . . .

James Zobrest attended grades one through five in a school for the deaf, and grades six through eight in a public school operated by respondent. While he attended public school, [the school district] furnished him with a sign-language interpreter. For religious reasons, James' parents (also petitioners here) enrolled him for the ninth grade in Salpointe Catholic High School, a sectarian institution. . . .

When [the parents] requested that [the school district] supply James with an interpreter at Salpointe, [the district] . . . [relying on advice from the county and state attorneys general] declined to provide the requested interpreter.

[The parents] then instituted this action in the United States District Court for the District of Arizona under 20 U.S.C. § 1415(e)(4)(A). . . . The District Court denied [the parents'] request for a preliminary injunction finding that the provision of an interpreter at Salpointe would likely offend the Establishment Clause. . . .

The Court of Appeals affirmed by a divided vote . . . applying the three-part test announced in *Lemon v. Kurtzman*, 403 U.S. 602 (1971). It first found that the IDEA has a clear secular purpose: " 'to assist States and Localities to provide for the education of all handicapped children.' " . . . Turning to the second prong of the *Lemon* inquiry, though, the Court of Appeals determined that the IDEA, if applied as [the parents] proposed, would have the primary effect of advancing religion and thus would run afoul of the Establishment Clause. "By placing its employee in the sectarian school," the Court of Appeals reasoned, "the government would create the appearance that it was a 'joint sponsor' of the school's activities." . . . This, the court held, would create the "symbolic union of government and religion" found impermissible in *School Dist. of Grand Rapids v. Ball*, 473 U.S. 373 (1985).

. . . .

We granted certiorari, 506 U.S. 813 (1992), and now reverse.

. . . .

We have never said that "religious institutions are disabled by the First Amendment from participating in publicly sponsored social welfare programs." . . . For if the Establishment Clause did bar religious groups from receiving general government benefits, then "a church could not be protected by the police and fire departments, or have its public sidewalk kept in repair." . . . Given that a contrary rule would lead to such absurd results, we have consistently held that government programs that neutrally provide benefits to a broad class of citizens defined without reference to religion are not readily subject to an Establishment Clause challenge just because sectarian institutions may also receive an attenuated financial benefit. Nowhere have we stated this principle more clearly than in *Mueller v. Allen*, 463 U.S. 388 (1983), and *Witters v. Washington Dept. of Services for Blind*, 474 U.S. 481 (1986), two cases dealing specifically with government programs offering general educational assistance.

In *Mueller*, we rejected an Establishment Clause challenge to a Minnesota law allowing taxpayers to deduct certain educational expenses in computing their state income tax, even though the vast majority of those deductions (perhaps over 90%) went to parents whose children attended sectarian schools. . . . Two factors, aside from States' traditionally broad taxing authority, informed our decision. . . . We noted that the law "permits all parents — whether their children attend public school or private — to deduct their children's educational expenses." . . . We also pointed out that under Minnesota's scheme, public funds become available to sectarian schools "only as a result of numerous private choices of individual parents of school-age children," thus distinguishing *Mueller* from our other cases involving "the direct transmission of assistance from the State to the schools themselves." . . .

Witters was premised on virtually identical reasoning. In that case, we upheld against an Establishment Clause challenge the State of Washington's extension of vocational assistance, as part of a general state program, to a blind person studying at a private Christian college to become a pastor, missionary, or youth director. Looking at the statute as a whole, we observed that "[a]ny aid provided under Washington's program that ultimately flows to religious institutions does so only as a result of the genuinely independent and private choices of aid recipients." . . . The program, we said, "creates no financial incentive for students to undertake sectarian education." . . . We also remarked that, much like the law in *Mueller*, "Washington's program is 'made available generally without regard to the sectarian-nonsectarian, or public-nonpublic nature of the institution benefited.' "

. . . .

That same reasoning applies with equal force here. The service at issue in this case is part of a general government program that distributes benefits neutrally to any child qualifying as "disabled" under the IDEA, without regard to the "sectarian-nonsectarian, or public-nonpublic nature" of the school the child attends. By according parents freedom to select a school of their choice, the statute ensures that a government-paid interpreter will be present in a sectarian school only as a result of the private decision of individual parents. In other words, because the IDEA creates no financial incentive for parents to choose a sectarian school, an interpreter's presence there cannot be attributed to state decisionmaking. . . . Indeed, this is an even easier case than *Mueller* and *Witters* in the sense that, under the IDEA, no funds traceable to the government ever find their way into sectarian schools' coffers. The only indirect economic benefit a sectarian school might receive by dint of the IDEA is the disabled child's tuition — and that is, of course, assuming that the school makes a profit on each student; that, without an IDEA interpreter, the child would have gone to school elsewhere; and that the school, then, would have been unable to fill that child's spot.

[The school district] contends, however, that this case differs from *Mueller* and *Witters*, in that petitioners seek to have a public employee physically present in a sectarian school to assist in James' religious education. In light of this distinction, respondent argues that this case more closely resembles *Meek v. Pittenger*, 421 U.S. 349 (1975), and *School District of Grand Rapids v. Ball*, 473 U.S. 373 (1985).

[The school district's] reliance on *Meek* and *Ball* is misplaced for two reasons. First, the programs in *Meek* . . . — through direct grants of government aid —

relieved sectarian schools of costs they otherwise would have borne in educating their students. . . . For example, the religious schools in *Meek* received teaching material and equipment from the State, relieving them of an otherwise necessary cost of performing their educational function.

. . . So too was the case in *Ball*. The programs challenged there, which provided teachers in addition to instructional equipment and material, "in effect subsidize[d] the religious functions of the parochial schools by taking over a substantial portion of their responsibility for teaching secular subjects [amounting to a] . . . kind of direct aid. . . ."

The extension of aid to petitioners, however, does not amount to "an impermissible 'direct subsidy' " of Salpointe, *Witters*. Salpointe is not relieved of an expense that it otherwise would have assumed in educating its students. And, as we noted above, any attenuated financial benefit that parochial schools do ultimately receive from the IDEA is attributable to "the private choices of individual parents." *Mueller*, 463 U.S. at 400. Disabled children, not sectarian schools, are the primary beneficiaries of the IDEA; to the extent sectarian schools benefit at all from the IDEA, they are only incidental beneficiaries. . . .

Second, the task of a sign-language interpreter seems to us quite different from that of a teacher or guidance counselor. Notwithstanding the Court of Appeals' intimations to the contrary, . . . the Establishment Clause lays down no absolute bar to the placing of a public employee in a sectarian school. . . . Such a flat rule, smacking of antiquated notions of "taint," would indeed exalt form over substance. . . . Nothing in this record suggests that a sign-language interpreter would do more than accurately interpret whatever material is presented to the class as a whole. In fact, ethical guidelines require interpreters to "transmit everything that is said in exactly the same way it was intended." . . . James' parents have chosen of their own free will to place him in a pervasively sectarian environment. The sign-language interpreter they have requested will neither add to nor subtract from that environment, and hence the provision of such assistance is not barred by the Establishment Clause.

The IDEA creates a neutral government program dispensing aid not to schools but to individual handicapped children. If a handicapped child chooses to enroll in a sectarian school, we hold that the Establishment Clause does not prevent the school district from furnishing him with a sign-language interpreter there in order to facilitate his education. The judgment of the Court of Appeals is therefore

Reversed.

JUSTICE BLACKMUN filed a dissenting opinion, in which JUSTICE SOUTER joined, and in which JUSTICES STEVENS and O'CONNOR joined in part. JUSTICE O'CONNOR filed a dissenting opinion, in which JUSTICE STEVENS joined. [separate opinions omitted]

NOTES AND QUESTIONS

1. When *Zobrest* appeared in 1993, it appeared to conflict with earlier decisions forbidding remedial and other specialized public education services from being delivered on the sites of religious schools due to concerns over entanglement of the government and religion. The Court resolved the conflict by overruling those decisions in *Agostini v. Felton*, 521 U.S. 203 (1997), which held that it was permissible to have publicly paid teachers provide non-special education instruction on-site in religious schools. Since that decision, the Court has issued a number of decisions upholding public programs that provide benefits in, or to, religious schools. *E.g., Zelman v. Simmons-Harris*, 536 U.S. 639 (2002) (state-funded vouchers); *Mitchell v. Helms*, 530 U.S. 1296 (2000) (loaning of materials and supplies). *See generally* Ralph Mawdsley, *The Changing Role of Parents*, 2003 B.Y.U. EDUC. & L.J. 165; Ralph Mawdsley, *Religious Issues and Public School Instruction: The Search for Neutrality*, 167 ED. LAW REP. 573 (2002).

2. The permissibility of on-site services and other indirect benefits does not imply the permissibility of creating an entire school district to serve the special education needs of a specific religious community. In *Board of Education of Kiryas Joel Village School District v. Grumet*, 512 U.S. 687 (1994), the Court found an establishment clause violation when New York carved a new school district out of a larger one, in order to provide special education for the children of a Hasidic religious community. The new district's boundaries were defined by the reach of the religious settlement. The Court ruled that New York violated the establishment clause by delegating its civic power to an entity defined by a religious standard. *Id.* at 702.

3. Both IDEA and the establishment clause permit a federal or state government to provide on-site services in religious schools, but neither the Constitution nor the statute require it. Should IDEA be changed to require that special education services be provided on-site in religious schools?

D. MANDATORY ACCOMMODATIONS AND THE FREE EXERCISE CLAUSE

The vast majority of private schools are religious schools. IDEA permits fewer services to be provided to a child enrolled in a private school (thus, typically a religious school) and does not afford that student an individual entitlement to a publicly provided appropriate education. Does this so disadvantage the child attending a private, religious school that it impermissibly infringes the child's freedom of religion?

GARY S. v. MANCHESTER SCHOOL DISTRICT
374 F.3d 15 (1st Cir. 2004)

In this case, the First Circuit upheld the refusal of a public school district to fund special education services for a child at a private school to the same extent as for public school students.

CAMPBELL, SENIOR CIRCUIT JUDGE.

Appealing from an adverse judgment of the district court, the parents of Andrew S., a disabled child who is attending a Catholic elementary school, assert that the Individuals with Disabilities Education Act (IDEA), 20 U.S.C. §§ 1400-87, is unconstitutional as applied to their son. While he, like other disabled children who go to private schools, receives some educational services under federal and state law, he is not entitled by law to the panoply of services available to disabled public school students under the rubric of free and appropriate public education (FAPE), nor to the due process hearing provided to public school students alone. Appellants argue that the difference in treatment of their disabled son, who is attending a religious school, from other disabled students, who are attending public schools, violates the Free Exercise Clause of the First Amendment to the federal constitution, the Due Process and Equal Protection clauses of the federal constitution, and the federal Religious Freedom Restoration Act ("RFRA"), 42 U.S.C. §§ 2000bb-1 to -4.

The district court considered these contentions upon cross motions for summary judgment. Rejecting appellants' claims, it granted the appellee Manchester School District's motion for summary judgment and denied summary judgment to appellants. *Gary S. v. Manchester Sch. Dist.*, 241 F. Supp. 2d 111, 123 (D.N.H. 2003). On appeal, appellants reiterate their contentions. After carefully considering them, we find ourselves in agreement with the district court. . . .

I.

Appellants' lead argument on appeal is that the district court erred in determining that the federal law did not violate Andrew's and his parents' free exercise rights under the First Amendment. They reject the district court's assertion that the Supreme Court's decision in *Employment Div. Dep't of Human Res. of Oregon v. Smith*, 494 U.S. 872 (1990), is controlling. *Smith*, according to the district court, exempted most "neutral laws of general applicability" from the compelling interest test. In the district court's view,

> [A] law ordinarily need not be justified by a compelling interest if it is "neutral" in that it is not targeted at religiously motivated conduct and "generally applicable" in that it does not selectively burden religious conduct. *See Church of Lukumi Babalu Aye, Inc. v. City of Hialeah*, 508 U.S. 520 (1993).

Gary S., 241 F. Supp. 2d at 120–21.

IDEA and its regulations, the district court says, do not target religiously motivated conduct and is "generally applicable" in that it does not selectively burden religious conduct. For these reasons, and because appellants' First Amendment claim is not "hybrid," *i.e.* is not linked to a separate constitutional claim, the district court found no violation of free exercise rights. *Id.* We do not disagree.

Appellants reject the district court's analysis. They ask us to read *Smith* as limited to instances of socially harmful or criminal conduct. They point out that *Smith* did not purport to overrule the Supreme Court's holdings in the cases of *Hobbie v. Unemployment Appeals Comm'n*, 480 U.S. 136 (1987); *Thomas v. Review Bd. of the Indiana Employment Sec. Div.*, 450 U.S. 707 (1981), and *Sherbert v. Verner*, 374 U.S. 398 (1963). In *Hobbie* and *Sherbert*, the complainants were denied unemployment benefits following discharge because of their religiously-based refusal to work on Saturday, complainant's religion's Sabbath. In *Thomas*, the complainant was denied unemployment benefits after discharge based on his religiously-based refusal to help produce armaments. Holding that the denial of a public benefit in these circumstances burdened plaintiff's religion, the Court ruled that, in order to justify an action having such an effect under the free-exercise clause, the government had to demonstrate that the withholding of the benefit served a compelling governmental interest and was the least restrictive means to that end. *Hobbie*, 480 U.S. at 141–45; *Thomas*, 450 U.S. at 718–20; *Sherbert*, 374 U.S. at 403.

Appellants have likened the denial of educational disability benefits here to those situations, asking us similarly to apply strict scrutiny. If we do, appellants contend, we will find that Andrew's attendance at a Catholic school is mandated by his parents' sincerely-held religious beliefs. No compelling governmental interest is served, they say, by withholding from him the identical benefits granted to his peers at public schools.

It is not always easy to predict what analytical framework the Supreme Court will apply to the various, factually dissimilar free exercise cases that arise. *Smith* rejected a free exercise claim involving the religiously-based use of peyote, an illegal substance. Writing for five of the Justices, Justice Scalia endorsed the constitutionality of neutral, generally applicable laws even when they impinged incidentally upon individual religious practices. *Smith*, 494 U.S. at 881. The *Smith* majority expressly limited *Hobbie*, *Thomas*, and *Sherbert* to the unemployment compensation field. *Smith*, 494 U.S. at 883–84. While, as appellants point out, Justice Scalia in *Smith* also distinguished *Hobbie*, *Thomas*, and *Sherbert* on the narrower ground that the use of peyote was illegal, 494 U.S. at 876, the majority's overall message is unmistakably contrary to appellants' present argument that *Hobbie*, *Thomas*, and *Sherbert* — and, in particular, the "compelling interest" test — are broadly applicable here. *Smith*, insofar as can be told from reading the Court's more recent precedent, remains good law, albeit reflective when written of the thinking of a narrow majority of justices, some of whom no longer serve. *See, e.g., Watchtower Bible and Tract Soc'y of N.Y. v. Vill. of Stratton*, 536 U.S. 150, 159 (2002) (discussing in dicta that lower court relied on *Smith* standard); *City of Boerne v. Flores*, 521 U.S. 507, 536 (1997) (invalidating statute that sought to "restore the compelling interest test as set forth in *Sherbert v. Verner* . . . and *Wisconsin v. Yoder*," that had been rejected in *Smith*). . . .

We also agree, for the reasons the district court stated, that this case is not a "hybrid" one. Hence, we conclude that the district court analyzed the case under the correct standard. *Gary S.*, 241 F. Supp. 2d at 121.

While we could perhaps leave the free exercise analysis there, an even more fundamental reason causes us to reject appellants' First Amendment arguments. We cannot accept appellants' contention that providing to all disabled attendees at private schools, both sectarian and secular, fewer benefits than those granted to public school attendees is truly analogous to denying unemployment benefits to persons fired because of their religiously-inspired insistence upon celebrating the Sabbath or not producing weapons.

The state unemployment benefits denied in *Hobbie*, *Thomas*, and *Sherbert* were public benefits, available to all. Plaintiffs would have received them had their religiously-motivated refusal to work on a certain day or at a certain job not been erroneously viewed by local authorities as misconduct. While appellants say their son's attendance at a Catholic school is likewise a religiously-motivated act, there is a basic difference. He and they are not being deprived of a *generally available* public benefit. Rather, the benefits to which appellants lay claim under the First Amendment are benefits the federal government has earmarked solely for students enrolled in the nation's public schools — benefits still available for Andrew were he sent to a public school, though not otherwise. Since the early days of public education in this country, public financial aid has commonly been limited to public rather than independent schools. While the parents of private school attendees pay the same taxes as public school parents, the former's tax money normally supports their own children's education only if they transfer them to a public school. To be sure, parents have a protected right to send their children to private schools if they so desire. *Pierce v. Soc'y of Sisters*, 268 U.S. 510, 534–35 (1925) (state law compelling public school attendance "unreasonably interferes with the liberty of parents and guardians to direct the upbringing and education of children under their control"). But as the very term "private" denotes, it is not ordinarily expected that such schools will be publicly funded, and there is no precedent requiring such funding. *Norwood v. Harrison*, 413 U.S. 455, 462 (1973) (in affirming "right of private schools to exist and operate . . . [*Pierce*] said nothing of any supposed right of private or parochial schools to share with public schools in state largesse, on an equal basis or otherwise.").[1]

Given the traditional pattern that has so far prevailed of financing public education via the public schools, it would be unreasonable and inconsistent to premise a free exercise violation upon Congress's mere failure to provide to disabled children attending private religious schools the identical financial and other benefits it confers upon those attending public schools. Unlike unemployment benefits that are equally available to all, private school parents can have no legitimate expectancy that they or their children's schools will receive the same federal or state financial

---

[1] [FN 1] To be sure, the Court has recently permitted a state legislature to provide for attendance at private schools at public expense if it so desires. *Cf. Zelman v. Simmons-Harris*, 536 U.S. 639, 662–63 (2002) (Ohio pilot school voucher program in which 96% of participating students in Cleveland received publicly-funded tuition aid to attend religious schools did not violate Establishment Clause). But the voucher approach remains so far the exception rather than the rule in our nation as a whole.

benefits provided to public schools. Thus, the non-receipt of equal funding and programmatic benefits cannot be said to impose any cognizable "burden" upon the religion of those choosing to attend such schools.[2] Persons opting to attend private schools, religious or otherwise, must accept the disadvantages as well as any benefits offered by those schools. They cannot insist, as a matter of constitutional right, that the disadvantages be cured by the provision of public funding. It follows that denying the benefits here, to which appellants have no cognizable entitlement, do not burden their free exercise rights.

Indeed, if we were to find a burden here on appellants' right of free exercise, it would follow logically that we should find free exercise violations whenever a state, city or town refuses to fund programs of other types at religious schools, at least insofar as the absence of funding adversely affects students with parents who believe their faith requires attendance at a religious school.[3] Yet, as noted *supra*, it is clear there is no federal constitutional requirement that private schools be permitted to share with public schools in state largesse on an equal basis. *See, e.g., Norwood v. Harrison*, 413 U.S. at 462; *Harris v. McRae*, 448 U.S. 297, 317–18 (1980), *Maher v. Roe*, 432 U.S. 464, 477 (1977); *see also Locke*, 124 S. Ct. at 1315; *Strout v. Albanese*, 178 F.3d 57, 66 (1st Cir. 1999) (stating, "fundamental right [to direct child's upbringing and education] does not require the state to directly pay for a sectarian education").

Accordingly, we see no basis for holding that the federal government violates appellants' free exercise rights under the First Amendment by favoring disabled public school attendees in respect to the IDEA's programs and benefits. In so doing, the federal government does no more than state and local governments do everyday by funding public school programs while providing lesser or, more likely, no funding to private schools, religious and otherwise. This methodology leaves all parents with ultimate recourse to the public schools whenever the balance of services associated with attendance at a private school appears to them to be unsatisfactory; but the option thus available can necessitate their having to choose, as here, between

---

[2] [FN 2] We recognize the disability program provided to Andrew is not one furnished directly by the Catholic school, but is instead run by public authorities for children who attend private school. But we see no distinction in principle. It is, of course, also true that the federal government and state are here actually funding programs for disabled children such as Andrew, the complaint being not the total absence of a program but that Andrew's program and rights are less comprehensive than those accorded to public school students. Again, we see no difference in principle. The federal and state governments are entitled to fund programs associated with private schools if they so desire, provided they do not run afoul of the Establishment Clause. Our point is not that such funding is never allowed, but that it is not commonly expected in our society nor required.

[3] [FN 3] A further anomaly of such a holding would be that only persons such as appellants, with a declared religious belief in the necessity of sending their children to private schools, would be entitled under the First Amendment to the funding sought. Other students, including those in secular private schools, would lack a right to such funding. *Cf. Locke v. Davey*, 540 U.S. 712, 124 S. Ct. 1307, 1315 (2004) (stating, "Given the historic and substantial state interest at issue, we therefore cannot conclude that the denial of funding for vocational religious instruction alone is inherently constitutionally suspect. Without a presumption of unconstitutionality, [respondent's] claim must fail. The State's interest in not funding the pursuit of devotional degrees is substantial and the exclusion of such funding places a relatively minor burden on [those involved in the funding program]. If any room exists between the two Religion Clauses, it must be here. We need not venture further into this difficult area in order to uphold the [funding program] as currently operated by the State of Washington.").

alternatives each of which may seem imperfect. In any event, we cannot say that the federal government's structuring of benefits here violates appellants' free exercise rights.

II.

Our above-stated conclusion that no cognizable burden on religion has been caused by the federal government's failure to provide to disabled children attending Catholic schools the same benefits as it provides to disabled public school children applies with equal force to appellants' RFRA claim. 42 U.S.C. § 2000bb-1(a) (stating in part, "[g]overnment shall not substantially burden a person's exercise of religion even if the burden results from a rule of general applicability. . . .").

The district court rejected appellants' RFRA claim, finding no burden upon religion given this court's *Strout* decision that "the Catholic faith does not require parents to educate their children in Catholic schools." *Gary S.*, 241 F. Supp. 2d at 122 (citing *Strout*, 178 F.3d at 65). Appellants contend on appeal that it is irrelevant whether the Catholic religion as a whole requires Catholic parents to educate their children at religious schools. They assert that they personally believe, on religious grounds, that such a requirement exists. Their sincere personal belief is enough, they argue, to demonstrate the centrality to their faith of Catholic school attendance. *See Hernandez v. Comm'r of Internal Revenue*, 490 U.S. 680, 699 (1989) (stating, "It is not within the judicial ken to question the centrality of particular beliefs or practices to a faith, or the validity of particular litigants' interpretations of those creeds.") (citation omitted).

Assuming, without deciding, that appellants' personal religious belief suffices for RFRA purposes, they still face the insurmountable hurdle we have discussed in the previous section, namely that the mere non-funding of private secular and religious school programs does not "burden" a person's religion or the free exercise thereof. 42 U.S.C. § 42 U.S.C. 2000bb-1(a). There is no need to repeat what we have already said on this point. It suffices to say we find no cognizable "burden" being imposed here upon appellants' exercise of their religion, hence no occasion to apply RFRA.

III.

Likewise, appellants' equal protection claim fails, as the district court ruled. Appellants assert that the IDEA has infringed upon their fundamental right to direct Andrew's upbringing and education[4] because it deprives him of FAPE and a due process hearing while offering these benefits to students who receive special education services at public school and, therefore, should be subjected to strict scrutiny. *See Pierce*, 268 U.S. at 534–35.

---

[4] [FN 4] Appellants also argue that the distinctions made here deny their child the right to access an adequate education and a "basic floor of educational opportunity" and therefore should be analyzed under heightened scrutiny. They concede that the Supreme Court found there is no fundamental right to education, but argue that the Court left open the issue of whether the denial of a "minimally adequate education" would be subjected to heightened scrutiny. *See San Antonio Indep. Sch. Dist. v. Rodriguez*, 411 U.S. 1, 35 (1973). As appellants have failed to provide any precedential example of a court's actually having applied this particular mode of heightened scrutiny analysis, we decline to embark upon this path.

To be sure, if a requirement imposed by a state significantly interferes with the exercise of a fundamental right, it cannot be upheld unless it is supported by sufficiently important state interests and is closely tailored to effectuate only those interests. *See, e.g., Cruzan v. Director, Missouri Dep't of Health*, 497 U.S. 261, 303 (1990). Here, however, just as non-funding of private secular and religious school programs does not "burden" a free exercise of religion, it does not significantly interfere with the appellants' fundamental right to direct the upbringing and education of children under their control. *See Pierce*, 268 U.S. at 534–35. The Supreme Court has held "in several contexts that a legislature's decision not to subsidize the exercise of a fundamental right does not infringe the right, and thus is not subject to strict scrutiny." *Regan v. Taxation with Representation of Washington*, 461 U.S. 540, 549 (1983); *see also Buckley v. Valeo*, 424 U.S. 1, 143–44 (1976) (declining to apply strict scrutiny to statute that provides federal funds for candidates who enter primary campaigns but does not provide funds for candidates who do not run in party primaries); *Harris*, 448 U.S. at 316–18 (stating, "although government may not place obstacles in the path of a [person's] exercise . . . of freedom of [speech], it need not remove those not of its own creation."); *Maher*, 432 U.S. at 476–77.

Accordingly, we apply rational basis scrutiny to the IDEA and conclude, as did the district court, that the statutory classification at issue here between public and private school students bears a rational relationship to the furtherance of a legitimate governmental purpose. *Regan*, 461 U.S. at 547. The Equal Protection Clause requires that all persons "similarly situated should be treated alike." *Cleburne v. Cleburne Living Ctr.*, 473 U.S. 432, 437 (1985). A legislature has "substantial latitude to establish classifications that roughly approximate the nature of the problem perceived, that accommodate competing concerns both public and private, and that account for limitations on the practical ability of the State to remedy every ill." *Plyler v. Doe*, 457 U.S. 202, 216 (1982). The primary purpose of the IDEA is to guarantee a free and appropriate *public* education. *See Nieves-Marquez v. Puerto Rico*, 353 F.3d 108, 125 (7th Cir. 2003) ("We agree with the reasoning of these courts that IDEA's primary purpose is to ensure FAPE. . . ."); *Polera v. Bd. of Educ.*, 288 F.3d 478, 486 (2d Cir. 2002) (stating, "the [IDEA's] administrative system . . . is designed to ensure that disabled students receive the free appropriate public education to which they are entitled. . . ."). Accordingly, the distinctions made here between students in public school as opposed to children who are unilaterally placed in private schools are rational. The burden placed on local educational authorities to make FAPE available is heavy. Congress acted rationally when it chose not to subject local educational authorities to the even greater and perhaps overwhelming responsibility of providing the same services to disabled students enrolled unilaterally in private schools.

IV.

Lastly, we agree with the district court that appellants' substantive due process claim fails. Appellants argue that the federal law requires them to forego their religious beliefs and their right to control their child's education in order to obtain the same right to FAPE and due process that other students who receive special education services at Manchester receive. As appellants allege that the government has attempted to condition access to a government benefit on the relinquishment of a constitutional right, the district court correctly analyzed this claim under the framework of the "unconstitutional conditions" doctrine. The court noted that both the Supreme Court and the First Circuit have "consistently refused to invalidate laws which condition a parent's ability to obtain educational benefits on the parent's relinquishment of her right to send her child to private school." *See Norwood*, 413 U.S. at 462; *Strout*, 178 F.3d at 66; *Harris*, 448 U.S. at 318; *Maher*, 432 U.S. at 477. Moreover, for the reasons stated above, appellants' claim fails because appellants are not forced to forego their religious beliefs or their right to control their child's education in order to obtain these government benefits.

We AFFIRM the decision of the district court.

NOTES AND QUESTIONS

1. Are the court's efforts to distinguish *Pierce v. Society of Sisters* and the other cases upholding parents' rights to direct their children's education successful? Is the court correct in asserting that the possession of a fundamental right does not imply a right to government funding to exercise that right? Would any contrary decision call into question the validity of cases such as *Harris v. McRae*, which held that although there was a fundamental right to have an abortion, there was no constitutional right to government payment for the abortion for an indigent woman, even if the government provided comprehensive medical services other than the abortion for free?

2. Cases from the 1960s appear to impose on government a greater duty of mandatory accommodation of religionists than contemporary cases do. *Compare Sherbert v. Verner*, 374 U.S. 398 (1963) (finding a violation of free exercise rights when a state law burdened the exercise of religion and was not justified by a compelling state interest), *with Employment Div. v. Smith*, 494 U.S. 872 (1990) (holding that the right to free exercise of religion is not violated by a government requirement that is neutral and generally applicable). If the *Sherbert* test were applied, would *Gary S.* come out the same way?

E. DISCRIMINATION BETWEEN RELIGIOUS SCHOOLS AND OTHER PRIVATE SCHOOLS

Sometimes, state laws permit services to be provided to children in private schools, but specifically forbid the services to those in religious schools. The following case takes up such a situation.

PETER v. WEDL
155 F.3d 992 (8th Cir. 1998)

The court upheld a school district's refusal under IDEA to provide on-site special education services at a religious school, but remanded for a determination as to whether a state rule prohibiting services at religious schools, while permitting them at nonreligious private schools and home schools, constituted religious discrimination.

MAGILL, CIRCUIT JUDGE.

. . . .

I.

Aaron is a twelve-year-old boy who lives in Edina, Minnesota. Aaron suffers from a brain stem lesion which causes spastic quadriparesis, a partial paralysis from the eyes down. Although Aaron has normal cognitive abilities, he cannot speak, and communicates through finger signing. He breathes through a tracheostomy tube and eats through a gastrostomy tube. Because of his severe physical disabilities, Aaron requires a full-time paraprofessional while in school. The paraprofessional assists Aaron with his disabilities, translates his finger spelling, and adapts classroom tasks for Aaron. The cost of a paraprofessional is approximately $10,000 per year, and is the same whether Aaron attends a public school or a private school.

Aaron's parents wish him to attend Calvin Christian School, a K-8 private religious school in Edina. Aaron's two sisters attended Calvin Christian School, and Aaron was able to attend the school from 1991 until 1994. During this time, the Westendorps' church paid for Aaron's paraprofessional. When the Westendorps changed churches, however, the burden to pay for the paraprofessional fell on them. With help from relatives, the Westendorps could afford Aaron's tuition, but they could not afford the cost of a paraprofessional. Because ISD No. 273 would not pay for a paraprofessional for Aaron if he attended Calvin Christian School, the Westendorps were forced to transfer Aaron to a public school in Edina. Aaron has attended an Edina public school, with the services of an ISD No. 273-funded paraprofessional, from 1994 until the present.

When ISD No. 273 first refused to provide Aaron a paraprofessional if he attended Calvin Christian School, Minnesota law prohibited school districts from providing such services at private religious schools. *See* Minnesota Rule 3525.1150 subpt. 2 (allowing special education services only at a "neutral site"); Minn. Stat. § 123.932 subdivision 9 (defining "neutral site" as "a public center, a nonsectarian nonpublic school, a mobile unit located off the nonpublic school premises, or any other location off the nonpublic school premises which is neither physically nor educationally identified with the functions of the nonpublic school"). . . .

. . . [T]he Director of Special Services for ISD No. 273 acknowledged that Minnesota Rule 3525.1150 prohibited ISD No. 273 from providing services to Aaron at Calvin Christian School. . . .

. . . .

Despite its unwritten "consistent policy" of not providing special education services to students at private schools, ISD No. 273 has provided special education services to students at private nonreligious preschools. . . .

On July 26, 1996, the Westendorps brought this suit against ISD No. 273 and the State of Minnesota, seeking injunctive and declaratory relief and damages. The Westendorps were joined in their suit against the state by the parents of Sarah Peter, a disabled Minnesota child who was similarly denied special education services at a private religious school by Independent School District No. 877 (ISD No. 877).

On March 26, 1997, the district court granted summary judgment against the Westendorps on their IDEA claim. . . .

On June 23, 1997, the Supreme Court [in *Agostini v. Felton*] held that public school districts may provide secular teaching services at a private religious school without offending the Establishment Clause. . . . Following this decision, the State of Minnesota, ISD No. 273, and ISD No. 877 stipulated to an injunction against the enforcement of Minnesota Rule 3525.1150. . . . Following the district court's grant of the injunction, ISD No. 877 agreed to provide services to Sarah Peter at her private religious school, and the Westendorps and ISD No. 273 became the sole parties to this suit.

Despite the injunction and ISD No. 877's change of heart, ISD No. 273 continued to refuse to provide services to Aaron if he attended Calvin Christian School. The district court denied a preliminary injunction requiring ISD No. 273 to provide such services. . . .

The Westendorps now appeal the grant of summary judgment against them on their free speech, free exercise, equal protection, and IDEA claims. . . .

II.

. . . .

Prior to the district court's injunction against the enforcement of Minnesota Rule 3525.1150, [the rule] explicitly discriminated against children who attended private religious schools. While children who attended private nonreligious schools could receive government-funded special education services directly at their private schools, students like Aaron could not. Government discrimination based on religion violates the Free Exercise Clause of the First Amendment, *see Church of the Lukumi Babalu Aye, Inc. v. City of Hialeah*, 508 U.S. 520 (1993) ("the First Amendment forbids an official purpose to disapprove of a particular religion or of religion in general"), the Free Speech Clause of the First Amendment, *see Rosenberger v. Rector and Visitors of Univ. of Va.*, 515 U.S. 819, 830 (1995) ("ideologically driven attempts to suppress a particular point of view are presumptively unconstitutional in funding, as in other contexts" (quotations omitted)), and the Equal Protection Clause of the Fourteenth Amendment. *See Native American Council of Tribes v. Solem*, 691 F.2d 382, 384 (8th Cir. 1982); *cf. Romer v. Evans*, 517 U.S. 620, 633 (1996) ("Equal protection of the laws is not achieved through indiscriminate imposition of inequalities. . . . A law declaring that in general it shall be more difficult for one group of citizens than for all others to seek aid from the government is itself a denial of equal protection of the laws in the most literal sense." . . . "[I]f the object of a law is to infringe upon or restrict practices because of their religious motivation, the law is not neutral, and it is invalid unless it is justified by a compelling interest and is narrowly tailored to advance that interest." *Lukumi*, 508 U.S. at 533. . . . The only compelling interest identified by the State of Minnesota to justify Minnesota Rule 3525.1150 was that the rule was necessary to avoid a violation of the Establishment Clause. . . . This position was highly questionable in light of the Supreme Court's decision in *Zobrest v. Catalina Foothills School District* . . . and the State of Minnesota abandoned this argument following the Supreme Court's decision in *Agostini*. . . . Because Minnesota Rule 3525.1150 cannot be justified as a narrowly tailored means of avoiding a violation of the Establishment Clause, it violated the plaintiffs' rights to free exercise of religion, free speech, and equal protection, and the district court properly enjoined its enforcement.

If ISD No. 273 denied a paraprofessional to Aaron Westendorp at Calvin Christian School because of Minnesota Rule 3525.1150's unconstitutional distinction between private religious schools and private nonreligious schools, or otherwise because of the religious nature of Calvin Christian School, then ISD No. 273's action is illegal and the plaintiffs are entitled to the relief that they seek. . . .

ISD No. 273's invocation of a "long-standing policy" rings hollow in light of its actual practice of providing services to disabled children at private nonreligious preschools and at home schools. . . . While ISD No. 273 has alleged that it created its policy to ensure the quality and integration of services and to contain costs . . . , this appears to be a mere ad hoc rationalization of an irrational practice.

ISD has not attempted to explain how the goals of its alleged policy are served by denying services to students at private religious schools but allowing these services to students at home schools or at private nonreligious preschools, and there is no evidence that any of these goals are furthered by denying Aaron a paraprofessional at Calvin Christian School. It is undisputed that the cost to ISD No. 273 is the same whether it funds a full-time, one-on-one paraprofessional for Aaron at Calvin Christian School or at a public school, and ISD No. 273 has not argued that the services of a paraprofessional would be of a lower quality at Calvin Christian School than if they were provided by the same paraprofessional at a public school, or that the integration of Aaron's services would somehow be impaired at Calvin Christian School. . . .

Viewed in its entirety, the evidence in this case strongly suggests that ISD No. 273's policy is a mere pretext for religious discrimination. . . . [W]e remand this matter to the district court for a factual determination of whether ISD No. 273 based its denial of services to Aaron at Calvin Christian School on its purported religion-neutral policy, or if its denial was based on the religious animus contained in Minnesota Rule 3525.1150. . . .

III.

The Westendorps also appeal the district court's grant of summary judgment on their claim under IDEA. IDEA is designed to encourage states to develop special education programs for disabled students. In return for federal funding, IDEA requires participating states to have "in effect a policy that assures all children with disabilities the right to a free appropriate public education." . . . While the parties agree that Aaron has a disability and that he is entitled under IDEA to the services of a paraprofessional paid by ISD No. 273, they disagree on whether IDEA entitles him to those services at Calvin Christian School.

On June 4, 1997, three months after the district court granted summary judgment against the Westendorps on their IDEA claim, comprehensive amendments to IDEA became law. . . . In amending IDEA, Congress substantially limited the rights of disabled children enrolled by their parents in a private school. . . . (IDEA will "not require a local educational agency to pay for the cost of education, including special education and related services, of a child with a disability at a private school or facility if that agency made a free appropriate public education available to the child and the parents elected to place the child in such private school or facility"). . . . Accordingly, Aaron has no right under the 1997 Amendments to receive ISD No. 273-funded services at Calvin Christian School.

[The court found that school district had violated student's rights under the IDEA prior to the 1997 amendments and remanded for relief.]

IV.

Finally, the Westendorps argue that, even if ISD No. 273's actions were not motivated by religious animus, its refusal of a paraprofessional to Aaron at Calvin Christian School violates the constitution by conditioning the receipt of generally available government services on the Westendorps' foregoing of a constitutional right. It is undisputed that Aaron has the right to receive special education services if he attends a public school. It is also clear that the Westendorps have the constitutional right to choose the education that Aaron shall receive. *See Pierce v. Society of Sisters* . . . , *Wisconsin v. Yoder.* . . . If the Westendorps exercise their right to send Aaron to the school of their choice, however, ISD No. 273 will not provide special education services to Aaron. . . .

While "the government may not deny a benefit to a person because he exercises a constitutional right" . . . , the government's "decision not to subsidize the exercise of a fundamental right does not infringe the right, and thus is not subject to strict scrutiny." . . . Indeed, the Supreme Court has been extremely hesitant to suggest that private school students have a constitutional entitlement to the same benefits that are given to public school students by the government.

In light of our remand on other bases, however, we need not reach this issue. . . . Accordingly, we leave this matter for another day.

V.

We reverse the district court's grant of summary judgment to ISD No. 273, and we remand for a factual determination of whether ISD No. 273's denial of services to Aaron Westendorp at Calvin Christian School was motivated by religious animus. In addition, we remand this matter to the district court for a determination of the proper relief to the plaintiffs for the defendant's past violation of IDEA.

NOTES AND QUESTIONS

1.　As the court indicates, pre-1997 IDEA, if interpreted in the manner the court suggests, could provide an individual, enforceable entitlement to services to the child in a religious school, irrespective of state law limits, which limits would have to yield to the federal statute. Under the current version of IDEA, would *Peter v. Wedl* come out the same way?

2.   Could the federal by-pass provision provide a remedy to students in religious schools if the reason for not funding services at religious schools is a state constitutional provision prohibiting the expenditure of public funds for religious schools? *See* 20 U.S.C. § 1412(f) (calling for federal administration of funds for children in private schools when "a State educational agency is prohibited by law from providing for the participation in special programs of children with disabilities enrolled in private elementary and secondary schools. . . ."). Although by-passes have been implemented under the comparable provision for title I services for private school children, research has not disclosed records of any use of a bypass implemented on account of failure to provide special education services to private school children.

3.   In *Locke v. Davey*, 540 U.S. 712 (2004) (described in *Gary S.*), the U.S. Supreme Court upheld a Washington State statute prohibiting state aid to any post-secondary student pursuing a degree in theology, even though aid was probably constitutional under the federal establishment clause, and it was widely provided for non-theology programs. Thus, discrimination against support of a religious program is permissible in that context. Does the suggestion in *Peter* that it may be a violation of the Constitution to refuse to treat religious schools the same as other private schools survive *Locke v. Davey*? *See Eulitt v. Maine Dep't of Educ.*, 386 F.3d 344 (1st Cir. 2004) (upholding exclusion of sectarian schools from receipt of public funds for tuition). *See generally* Mark C. Weber, *Services for Private School Students Under the Individuals with Disabilities Education Improvement Act: Issues of Statutory Entitlement, Religious Liberty, and Procedural Regularity*, 36 J.L. & EDUC. 163, 196–204 (2007) (discussing mandatory accommodation and religious viewpoint discrimination issues in connection with denial of special education services to students in sectarian schools). In *Cain v. Horne*, 202 P.3d 1178 (Ariz. 2009), the Arizona Supreme Court ruled that a state tuition voucher program for children with disabilities and children in foster care permitting the vouchers to be used in private religious or secular schools violates the Arizona Constitution's clause prohibiting "appropriation of public money . . . in aid of any . . . private or sectarian school." Ariz. Const. art. 9, § 10.

Chapter 13

EARLY CHILDHOOD PROGRAMS

A. INTRODUCTION

This chapter focuses on educational rights of children from birth through two. In 1986, Congress created incentives for states to lower their age-eligibility for ordinary special education services to age three. At the same time, it established a new program offering money to states to serve infants and toddlers who have not reached that age. Originally called Part H of the Individuals with Disabilities Education Act, the infants and toddlers program is now found in Part C, 20 U.S.C. §§ 1431–1445. The regulations promulgated to enforce Part C are found at 34 C.F.R. §§ 303.1–.670.

Children are eligible for Part C services if they are developmentally delayed or have a diagnosis of a condition that has a high probability of resulting in developmental delay, but the states set their own standards for what degree of delay triggers the entitlement. The state may also include children at risk of developmental delay in the program. The developmental delay may be in one or more listed areas: cognitive development, physical development, including vision and hearing, psychosocial development, or self-help skills. 34 C.F.R. § 303.16. The 2004 IDEA Reauthorization allows a child to be served, with the consent of the parents, in a Part C program up to entry into kindergarten or elementary school, provided that the program includes an educational component promoting school readiness and incorporating pre-literacy, language, and numeracy skills. 20 U.S.C. § 1432(5)(B)(ii). Parents have to be given full notice if the school system wishes to use this option, and the parents may choose Part B services instead. 20 U.S.C. §§ 1432(5)(B)(iii), 1435(c)(1)–(2). If the parents choose to have the child served under Part C under this provision, the child is not guaranteed a free, appropriate public education. 20 U.S.C. § 1412(a)(1)(C). Nevertheless, the parents may prefer to maintain continuity with a Part C program if it has proven successful for the child.

The Part C program bears a strong resemblance to ordinary special education, with requirements that states serve all eligible children; that they provide each with an individual, written plan (the individualized family service plan, or IFSP); that services be delivered, to the maximum extent appropriate, in natural environments (a requirement that mirrors the least-restrictive-environment rule of Part B) and that procedural protections be afforded, including notice and hearing rights, with court review. Some major differences are that the statute does not use the term "appropriate" to describe the level or type of services, although the term is found in various places in the regulations; that parents may be charged for some of the services (though not for child find, evaluation, case management, program administration, IFSP review, or procedural protections) on a sliding scale that does not deprive anyone of services because of the inability to pay; that services may include family support; and that the time limits for evaluation of the child and implementation of services are tighter. In contrast to the IDEA Part B requirement, the state agency that receives federal funding and distributes it to entities providing services need not be the state educational agency; it may be the state department of public welfare or developmental disabilities agency, for example. Because of the absence of public school programs for very young children, agencies frequently contract with private providers to deliver the services.

Infant and toddler services established under the 1986 law supplemented those available in many places under the federally funded developmental disabilities program. Developmental disability program services, however, generally were not uniformly available throughout the participating states. When states accepted IDEA money to serve very young children, they undertook an enforceable commitment to deliver the services to every child who met eligibility standards. When states failed to do so, litigation ensued.

MARIE O. v. EDGAR

No. 94 C 1471, 1996 U.S. Dist. LEXIS 1070 (Feb. 2, 1996),
aff'd, 131 F.3d 610 (7th Cir. 1997)

The court in this case found that Illinois had failed to implement the infants and toddlers program, and that children remained on waiting lists for services. It ordered the state to serve all eligible children, though it acknowledged that perfect compliance may be impossible.

KOCORAS, DISTRICT JUDGE.

This matter is before the court on the parties' cross motions for summary judgment. For the reasons set forth below, the plaintiffs' motion is granted. The defendants' motion is denied.

BACKGROUND

This action arises out of the state of Illinois' alleged failure to provide critical early intervention services to developmentally-delayed infants and toddlers. The plaintiffs purport to represent a class of infants and toddlers who are eligible for but not receiving the educational and developmental services needed to prevent or ameliorate their developmental-delay and other disabling conditions. Part H of the Individuals with Disabilities Education Act ("IDEA"), 20 U.S.C. § 1471 *et seq.* ("Part H") provides the statutory framework around which these services are to be structured. The present case involves roughly 26,000 eligible children whom the plaintiffs maintain are not presently receiving the early intervention services to which they are allegedly entitled under Part H.

Part H is a federal program pursuant to which federal funds are granted to states developing and implementing coordinated systems for the provision of early intervention services to developmentally-delayed infants and toddlers. Congress enacted Part H for the purpose of addressing five "urgent and substantial" needs:

(1) to enhance the development of handicapped infants and toddlers and to minimize their potential for developmental delay,

(2) to reduce the educational costs to our society, including our Nation's schools, by minimizing the need for special education and related services after handicapped infants and toddlers reach school age,

(3) to minimize the likelihood of institutionalization of individuals with disabilities and maximize the potential for their independent living in society,

(4) to enhance the capacity of families to meet the special needs of their infants and toddlers with disabilities, and

(5) to enhance the capacity of State and local agencies and service providers to identify, evaluate, and meet the needs of historically unrepresented populations, particularly minority, low-income, inner city, and rural populations.

20 U.S.C. § 1471(a)(1)–(5).

In 1987, the State of Illinois opted to participate in the Part H program, and since that time, Illinois has received more than $34 million dollars in federal funds for use in planning and implementing a coordinated statewide system of service. Upon entering into its fifth year of participation in the program, Part H requires assurances in a state's application for federal funds that the state has in effect a statewide system providing early intervention services to all eligible infants and toddlers with disabilities and their families. 20 U.S.C. §§ 1475(c) and 1476(a). On September 23, 1991, the Illinois Early Intervention Services System Act, 325 ILCS 20/1 *et seq.* ("the Illinois Act"), became effective. On December 1, 1992, Illinois began its fifth year of participation in Part H, thus allegedly requiring Illinois under federal law to serve all eligible infants and toddlers.

The plaintiffs allege that Illinois has not complied with several components of Part H. Among other shortcomings, the plaintiffs allege that the state has failed "to develop policies and procedures for standards for training early intervention personnel, has not established a procedure securing timely reimbursement of funds used to provide services, and has not established a system for compiling data on the numbers of infants and toddlers with disabilities in need of services, the number served, and the types of services provided." *See* Class Action Complaint, ¶ 33. According to the plaintiffs, Illinois was required by federal law to have these policies, procedures, and services implemented at the beginning of Illinois' fifth year of participation in the Part H program. Instead, numerous eligible children have been placed on waiting lists for services. The plaintiffs allege that as a result of the state's noncompliance, the plaintiffs have been denied adequate early intervention services to which they are allegedly entitled under Part H.

The plaintiffs bring this action on their own behalf, and on behalf of all others similarly situated, seeking declaratory and injunctive relief. Plaintiffs seek a judgment declaring that the defendants' acts and omissions are in violation of the rights of the plaintiffs and other similarly situated Illinois children under both Part H and 42 U.S.C. § 1983. The plaintiffs further seek an injunction directing the defendants "to recognize Part H as an entitlement for all eligible children, begin providing early intervention services to all children entitled by law to those services, and bring the State of Illinois into compliance with the components of a statewide system of early intervention required under Part H." In addition, the plaintiffs seek an award of attorneys' fees and costs as allowed under 42 U.S.C. § 1988. Both parties have moved for summary judgment.

. . . .

DISCUSSION

The plaintiffs brought this action pursuant to 42 U.S.C. § 1983, alleging violations of Part H of the Individuals With Disabilities Education Act ("IDEA"), 20 U.S.C. § 1471 *et seq.* Section 1983 provides in relevant part:

> Every person who, under color of any statute, ordinance, regulation, custom, or usage, of any State or Territory or the District of Columbia, subjects, or causes to be subjected, any citizen of the United States or other person within the jurisdiction thereof to the deprivation of any rights, privileges, or immunities secured by the Constitution and laws, shall be liable to the party injured in an action at law, suit in equity, or other proper proceeding for redress.

42 U.S.C. § 1983. Although § 1983 does not create any new substantive rights, section 1983 nevertheless provides a federal cause of action for violations of certain federal rights. *See Chapman v. Houston Welfare Rights Org.*, 441 U.S. 600, 617–18 (1979). A § 1983 action may be used to remedy constitutional and federal statutory violations by state agents. *Maine v. Thiboutot*, 448 U.S. 1, 5–6 (1980). However, the availability of § 1983 as a mechanism by which to enforce federal statutory violations is not absolute. Specifically, no such action is available either where Congress has explicitly foreclosed enforcement of the statute in the statute itself, or where a statutory remedial scheme is so comprehensive that there exists an implication that it provides the exclusive remedy, effectively foreclosing all other remedies. *Wright v. City of Roanoke Redevelopment & Housing Authority*, 479 U.S. 418, 424–25 (1987). The existence of a comprehensive remedial scheme notwithstanding, the use of § 1983 will not be precluded where Congress explicitly states that it did not want its enactment construed to restrict or limit the remedies otherwise available. *Mrs. W. v. Tirozzi*, 832 F.2d 748, 754 (2nd Cir. 1987).

In 1984, the Supreme Court noted the extensive remedial scheme of the Education of the Handicapped Act ("EHA"), 20 U.S.C. § 1400 *et seq.* (subsequently retitled the IDEA), and concluded that the EHA was the exclusive avenue through which a plaintiff could assert an EHA claim. *Smith v. Robinson*, 468 U.S. 992 (1984). Congress swiftly responded to the Court's holding in *Smith* and enacted the Handicapped Children's Protection Act of 1986. In section 3 of that Act, Congress added a new subsection to 20 U.S.C. § 1415, specifically providing that individuals could seek redress under other federal statutes, such as section 1983:

> Nothing in this chapter shall be construed to restrict or limit the rights, procedures, and remedies available under the Constitution, title V of the

Rehabilitation Act of 1973 [29 U.S.C. § 790 *et seq.*], or other Federal statutes protecting the rights of children and youth with disabilities. . . .

20 U.S.C. § 1415(f). In passing § 1415(f), Congress expressed its intention to "reestablish statutory rights repealed by the U.S. Supreme Court in *Smith v. Robinson*" and to "reaffirm, in light of this decision, the viability of . . . 42 U.S.C. § 1983 and other statutes as separate vehicles for ensuring the rights of handicapped children." H.R. Rep. No. 296, 99th Cong., 1st Sess. 4 (1985). Congress' objectives thus could not have been more clear. Section 1415(f) of the IDEA states that nothing in this "chapter" shall be construed to restrict the rights available under federal statutes such as § 1983. *See* 20 U.S.C. § 1415(f). As we indicated earlier during the course of this litigation (*see* June 13, 1994 Memorandum Opinion), Congress explicitly used the word "chapter" in setting forth its pronouncement. Less comprehensive terms such as "section" or "subsection" were deliberately avoided. Since Congress has expressed an intention for a private right of action to exist under § 1983 for violations of the IDEA and Part H is an unequivocal component of the IDEA, we reaffirm our previous conclusion that Part H of the IDEA may be enforceable under 42 U.S.C. § 1983.

As presented by the plaintiffs, the matter before the court is simple. Illinois has voluntarily chosen to participate in Part H. As a participant in the federal program, Illinois is required to provide certain services to all eligible children. Illinois' failure to adequately accomplish this renders the state liable. Although we agree with the defendants that the realities surrounding full compliance with the mandates of Part H are not quite so straightforward as the plaintiffs suggest, we are nonetheless obligated to follow the law, and the law on the issue ultimately favors the plaintiffs.

Part H defines two groups of infants and toddlers who must be served by a state's early intervention system and one group which a state may, at its discretion, choose to serve. 20 U.S.C. § 1472(1). The two groups which must be served by a state's early intervention system are defined as "infants and toddlers with disabilities" from birth to age 2, inclusive, who need early intervention services because they —

> (A) are experiencing developmental delays, as measured by appropriate diagnostic instruments and procedures in one or more of the following areas: cognitive development, physical development, language and speech development, psychosocial development, or self-help skills, or

> (B) have a diagnosed physical or mental condition which has a high probability of resulting in developmental delay.

20 U.S.C. § 1472. In addition, a state may, at its option, elect to serve "individuals from birth to age 2, inclusive, who are at risk of having substantial developmental delays if early intervention services are not provided." 20 U.S.C. § 1472(1). The Illinois Act provides that all three groups of children are eligible for early intervention services in Illinois. 325 ILCS § 20/3.

As specified by Part H, the "early intervention services" which a state is required to provide include family training, counseling, home visits, special instruction, speech pathology and audiology, occupational therapy, physical therapy, vision services, psychological services, case management services, diagnostic medical services, assistive technology, early identification and screening services, and transportation. 20 U.S.C. § 1472(2)(E). Moreover, these services are to be provided by specially qualified personnel and at no cost (except where federal or state law provides). 20 U.S.C. § 1472(2)(B) and (F).

Section 1476(2) of the federal statute sets forth the early intervention programs which a state is to have in effect by the beginning of its fifth year of participation in Part H. According to this section, a "statewide system of coordinated, comprehensive, multidisciplinary, interagency programs providing appropriate early intervention services to all infants and toddlers with disabilities and their families shall include, . . . at a minimum":

* * *

(2) timetables for ensuring that appropriate early intervention services will be available to all infants and toddlers with disabilities in the State . . .

(3) a timely, comprehensive, multidisciplinary evaluation of the functioning of each infant and toddler with a disability in the State and the needs of the families to appropriately assist in the development of the infant or toddler with a disability,

(4) for each infant and toddler with a disability in the State, an individualized family service plan . . . including case management services in accordance with such service plan,

(5) a comprehensive child find system, . . . including a system for making referrals to service providers that includes timelines and provides for participation by primary referral sources,

(6) a public awareness program . . .

(7) a central directory which includes early intervention services, resources, and experts available in the State and research and demonstration projects being conducted in the State,

(8) a comprehensive system of personnel development,

* * *

(11) a procedure for securing timely reimbursement of funds . . .

(12) procedural safeguards with respect to the programs under this subchapter . . .

* * *

(14) a system for compiling data on the numbers of infants and toddlers with disabilities and their families in the State in need of appropriate early intervention services. . . .

20 U.S.C § 1476(b). As a prerequisite for continued federal funding under Part H (commencing the fifth year of participation and for each year thereafter), the state must file an application providing "information and assurances demonstrating to the satisfaction of the Secretary that the State has in effect the statewide system required by section 1476 of this title and a description of services to be pro-

vided. . . ." 20 U.S.C. § 1475(c). On December 1, 1992, Illinois began its fifth year of participation in Part H. Although the deficiencies in implementation to which the plaintiffs cite are necessarily detailed in the state's yearly application for funding, to date, Illinois has not been denied federal funds.

The plaintiffs set forth some disturbing statistics as to the numbers of children who are purportedly not receiving the full range of services afforded them under Part H. According to the plaintiffs, at any one point in time, only about one-fourth of the eligible population of disabled youngsters is being serviced under Part H in Illinois. Hundreds and hundreds of Illinois children are routinely placed on waiting lists for Part H services. Moreover, the state has reportedly been delinquent in its efforts to identify and evaluate the needs of all of the state's eligible children. By allowing these circumstances to exist, the plaintiffs maintain that these children have been denied early intervention services at a time critical to their future development. Supported by statements of representatives in the United States Department of Education, the plaintiffs assert that Part H is an entitlement program and that at the start of a state's fifth year of participation in Part H, a state must have in place fully implemented program under which all eligible children are receiving services.[1] This, the plaintiffs maintain, the defendants have plainly failed to do.

In establishing a statewide system of service, Part H affords a considerable amount of discretion to the state. The state may, for example, elect whether to serve children in the "at risk" population, 20 U.S.C. § 1472(1), and state law may also impact who pays for the services under Part H. 20 U.S.C. § 1472(2)(B). The Illinois Act, which went into effect on September 23, 1991, in many ways mirrors Part H and establishes as a matter of state law the system requirements embodied in Part

---

[1] [FN 1] A March, 1990 policy memorandum issued by Dr. Judy A. Schrag, former Director of the Office of Special Education Programs, United States Department of Education states:

> Part H is an entitlement program. This means that subject to specific provisions in the Act and regulations, each eligible child in a State and the child's family are entitled to receive the rights, procedural safeguards, and services that are authorized to be provided under a State's early intervention program.

> Each State must ensure that appropriate early intervention services will be available to all eligible children in the State no later than the beginning of the fifth year of a State's participation in Part H.

March 1990, Policy Memorandum by Judy A. Schrag, Ed.D, Director of Office of Special Education Programs, (1 Early Childhood Law and Policy Reporter ("ECLPR") ¶ 10) (3/20/90).

In 1988, G. Thomas Bellamey, former Director of the Office of Special Education Programs for the United States Department of Education responded to an inquiry as follows:

> Part H is interpreted to be an entitlement program on behalf of each eligible child and the child's family, based on statutory provisions.

Response by G. Thomas Bellamey, Ph.D., Director, Office of Special Education Programs (1 ECLPR ¶ 38) (12/20/88).

Finally, Dr. Thomas Hehir, the current Director of the Office of Special Education Programs of the United States Department of Education, stated the following:

> States in full implementation of the Part H early intervention program are required to provide appropriate early intervention services to all children who are eligible and their families.

Response by Thomas Hehir, Director, Office of Special Education Programs (2 ECLPR ¶ 59) (11/30/93).

H. Section 20/7 of the Illinois Act, for example, incorporates many of the requirements set forth in 20 U.S.C. § 1476(b), explicitly referencing the federal laws and regulations. 325 ILCS 20/7. The Illinois Act, however, further provides:

> Within 60 days of the effective date of this Act, a five-fiscal-year implementation plan shall be submitted to the Governor by the lead agency with the concurrence of the Interagency Council on Early Intervention. The plan shall list specific activities to be accomplished each year, with cost estimates for each activity. . . .

325 ILCS 20/7. Having become effective in late 1991, the Illinois Act, by its own terms, does not contemplate full implementation until late 1996. The defendants note that this five-year time frame for implementation has never been raised by the United States Department of Education as being inconsistent with the state's federal obligations under Part H.

Consistent with the state's ongoing efforts at implementation, a new Central Billing Office ("CBO"), designed "to receive and dispense all relevant State and federal resources, as well as local government or independent resources available, for early intervention services," is presently being developed. 325 ILCS 20/13. Under the new system, individualized family service plans ("IFSP") will be standardized state-wide, enabling the family to seek out services from any provider it chooses (whether under Part H or not). Moreover, a more equitable distribution of funds will ensue, because funds will be spent on a fee-for-service basis rather than to providers in lump sum grants. The CBO will also provide a means by which to fully utilize available Medicaid funds, significantly increasing the funds brought into the early intervention system. Although the CBO is not yet implemented, the defendants attest that the State Board is presently attempting to begin experimental operations of the CBO in certain regions of the state.

Section 1476 of Part H requires that a state have a statewide system in place to serve all eligible children. Although not yet fully implemented, the defendants attest that Illinois has a statewide system. As summarized in its Year 7 Annual Report, Illinois at present serves thousands of children in all parts of the state. Forty-five Local Interagency Councils exist throughout the state, and numerous committees are devoted to personnel standards, public awareness, and financial issues. An interagency staff team works on early intervention issues. Numerous state agency officials and departments participate in the statewide early intervention system, in addition to the over 100 providers of services (56 receiving Part H funds) throughout the state.

However, surveys conducted by the Illinois State Board of Education have indicated that the early intervention system needs more capacity. Children are routinely placed on waiting lists for services. The plaintiffs take issue with a portion of the Illinois Act which states that the Act shall be implemented "as appropriated funds become available." See 325 ILCS 20/14. However, as the defendants submit, financial considerations account for only part of the problem. It is not disputed that outside resources such as private insurance and Medicaid are tremendously under-utilized under the present system. Nevertheless, even if the federal and state funds devoted to early intervention services were greatly increased, a state and national shortage of professionally trained personnel still would remain. Moreover, even if there was sufficient personnel to accommodate the mandates of Part H, additional problems would emerge as to their proper distribution. Difficulties exist in attracting doctors to rural areas. A conspicuous consequence of this is the dearth of professionals involved in early intervention services in parts of southern Illinois.

Section 1476 declares that a statewide system must serve "all" infants and toddlers with disabilities. *See* 20 U.S.C. § 1476. However, a strict reading of the term "all" cannot conform to present realities. In a report prepared by the National Early Childhood Technical Assistance System ("NECTAS") at the University of North Carolina, an agency providing technical assistance to the states on early intervention services, a 1995 briefing paper in a section entitled "Moving Part H into the 21st Century" stated:

> The promises and expectations of Part H of IDEA, although not fully realized, have become a reality, through the development of partnerships among families, governmental agencies, and public and private providers. Through continued needed resources, the intent of the law — a contract with American citizens to meet the needs of their infants and children with disabilities and families — will be fully realized in the next century.

As indicated by this report, the notion of serving "all" eligible children is understood to be a goal to be attained in the future. It is not — and indeed cannot be — a rigid legal standard activated on a state's first day of full participation in Part H. Given the breadth of the requirements set forth in Part H, it is doubtful if any state could ever meet such a standard as the plaintiffs suggest.[2] By consistently approving the state's annual application for federal funding of its early intervention system, the federal government has not held Illinois to so rigid a standard. Given the practicalities of the situation, neither should we.

That is not to say, however, that the plaintiffs are not entitled to relief. Part H was enacted by Congress with the desire that, by encouraging states to develop and implement coordinated systems for the provision of early intervention services to developmentally-delayed infants and toddlers, the disabilities which these children ultimately experience might be lessened or suspended. In its efforts to relay the importance of these goals, Congress expressly chose to frame Part H in definite, explicit terms, declaring that, after five years, a state "shall" have in effect "at a minimum" certain programs serving "all" eligible children. Recognizing the value which such a system might provide, Illinois, in 1987, voluntarily elected to participate in Part H. Illinois subsequently set about creating a statewide system in accordance with the provisions of Part H. Illinois' efforts at implementation, however, have been far from perfect.

Section 1475 of the federal statute contemplates that, by the beginning of its fifth year of participation in Part H, a state must have in place the minimum components enumerated in 20 U.S.C. § 1476. However, as suggested above, rigid enforcement under such a timetable would render state participation in Part H a virtual impossibility. Still, the mandates of the statute must not be neglected. Meaningful

---

[2] [FN 3] Susan Mackey-Andrews, a consultant hired by the Illinois State Board of Education to assist in planning the state's early intervention system, testified that, at the present time, *no* state was serving one hundred percent of its eligible children.

compliance by the state, at the very least, should be required by the state's fifth year. Eight years into the Part H program, Illinois' efforts remain well below this standard.

The plaintiffs seek an injunction by this court, recognizing Part H as an entitlement to all eligible children and directing the state to begin providing early intervention services to all eligible children and to bring the state of Illinois into full compliance with the requirements of Part H. Although the practical impact of this court's intervention to achieve these goals remains unclear, we nevertheless are obligated under the law to honor the plaintiffs' request to become involved. The state's failure, for example, to adequately develop and implement programs which train early intervention personnel and seek out and inform eligible youngsters of available services must not be condoned. The regularity with which disabled children are placed on waiting lists for services and evaluations — some waiting for up to one year — should not be tolerated. The existence of waiting lists is especially tragic given that the time lost is so often critical to the future development of these disabled youngsters.

As the opinion above reflects, certain problems in implementation are inevitable.[3] We remain ever mindful of this reality. However, after eight years of "dragging its feet," the state needs to do better. Critical to the future of Part H is the continued participation of the state, and we recognize that judicial intervention which might ultimately threaten this participation may not be a step forward. As the above cited NECTAS report indicates, the goal of Part H is to create an entitlement which will be fully realized in the next century. That is not to say, however, that the thousands of disabled infants and toddlers in Illinois *today* are not entitled to reap the benefits of Part H. The statutory language makes no mention of the next century. To the contrary, Part H bestows upon the state five years. After eight years without meaningful compliance, court intervention has thus become justified. Summary judgment will be entered in favor of the plaintiffs. The defendants' motion for summary judgment is denied.

CONCLUSION

For the reasons set forth above, the plaintiff's motion for summary judgment is granted. The defendants motion for summary judgment is denied.

NOTES AND QUESTIONS

1. The court's decision was affirmed on appeal, with the Seventh Circuit specifically finding that the Eleventh Amendment did not bar a remedy and that the plaintiffs could sue under 42 U.S.C. § 1983. *Marie O. v. Edgar*, 131 F.3d 610 (7th Cir. 1997).

2. What should be done to serve the hundreds of children on waiting lists? Should the state have rejected the federal money if it knew that it could not serve

---

[3] [FN 4] Acknowledging our relative inexperience in the area, we defer to the experts in the field as to how Part H may best be implemented.

everyone? The court suggests that full compliance is not possible. Is that correct? Should the federal requirements acknowledge that reality, if it is true? What degree of noncompliance should be permitted?

3.   What should be done for the children who have spent time on waiting lists without services? Are they entitled to compensatory services? Money damages?

B.   INDIVIDUALIZED FAMILY SERVICE PLANS

The IFSP focuses on the family and family setting and seeks to address the services necessary for the family to facilitate a child's development. The federal regulations set out specific requirements for individualized family service plans:

Content of an IFSP.

(a) Information about the child's status.

(1) The IFSP must include a statement of the child's present levels of physical development (including vision, hearing, and health status), cognitive development, communication development, social or emotional development, and adaptive development.

(2) The statement in paragraph (a)(1) of this section must be based on professionally acceptable objective criteria.

(b) Family information. With the concurrence of the family, the IFSP must include a statement of the family's resources, priorities, and concerns related to enhancing the development of the child.

(c) Outcomes. The IFSP must include a statement of the major outcomes expected to be achieved for the child and family, and the criteria, procedures, and timeliness used to determine —

(1) The degree to which progress toward achieving the outcomes is being made; and

(2) Whether modifications or revisions of the outcomes or services are necessary.

(d) Early intervention services.

(1) The IFSP must include a statement of the specific early intervention services necessary to meet the unique needs of the child and the family to achieve the outcomes identified in paragraph (c) of this section, including —

(i) The frequency, intensity, and method of delivering the services;

(ii) The natural environments, as described in § 303.12(b) and § 303.18, in which early intervention services will be provided, and a justification of the extent, if any, to which the services will not be provided in a natural environment;

(iii) The location of the services; and

(iv) The payment arrangements, if any.

(2) As used in paragraph (d)(1)(i) of this section —

(i) Frequency and intensity mean the number of days or sessions that a service will be provided, the length of time the service is provided during each session, and whether the service is provided on an individual or group basis; and

(ii) Method means how a service is provided.

(3) As used in paragraph (d)(1)(iii) of this section, location means the actual place or places where a service will be provided.

(e) Other services.

(1) To the extent appropriate, the IFSP must include —

(i) Medical and other services that the child needs, but that are not required under this part; and

(ii) The funding sources to be used in paying for those services or the steps that will be taken to secure those services through public or private sources.

(2) The requirement in paragraph (e)(1) of this section does not apply to routine medical services (e.g., immunizations and "well-baby" care), unless a child needs those services and the services are not otherwise available or being provided.

(f) Dates; duration of services. The IFSP must include —

(1) The projected dates for initiation of the services in paragraph (d)(1) of this section as soon as possible after the IFSP meetings described in § 303.342; and

(2) The anticipated duration of those services.

(g) Service coordinator.

(1) The IFSP must include the name of the service coordinator from the profession most immediately relevant to the child's or family's needs (or who is otherwise qualified to carry out all applicable responsibilities under this part), who will be responsible for the implementation of the IFSP and coordination with other agencies and persons.

(2) In meeting the requirements in paragraph (g)(1) of this section, the public agency may —

(i) Assign the same service coordinator who was appointed at the time that the child was initially referred for evaluation to be responsible for implementing a child's and family's IFSP; or

(ii) Appoint a new service coordinator.

(3) As used in paragraph (g)(1) of this section, the term "profession" includes "service coordination."

(h) Transition from Part C services.

(1) The IFSP must include the steps to be taken to support the transition of the child, in accordance with § 303.148, to —

(i) Preschool services under Part B of the Act, to the extent that those services are appropriate; or

(ii) Other services that may be available, if appropriate.

(2) The steps required in paragraph (h)(1) of this section include —

(i) Discussions with, and training of, parents regarding future placements and other matters related to the child's transition;

(ii) Procedures to prepare the child for changes in service delivery, including steps to help the child adjust to, and function in, a new setting; and

(iii) With parental consent, the transmission of information about the child to the local educational agency, to ensure continuity of services, including evaluation and assessment information required in § 303.322, and copies of IFSPs that have been developed and implemented in accordance with §§ 303.340 through 303.346.

Note 1: With respect to the requirements in paragraph (d) of this section, the appropriate location of services for some infants and toddlers might be a hospital setting — during the period in which they require extensive medical intervention. However, for these and other eligible children, early intervention services must be provided in natural environments (e.g., the home, child-care centers, or other community settings) to the maximum extent appropriate to the needs of the child.

Note 2: Throughout the process of developing and implementing IFSPs for an eligible child and the child's family, it is important for agencies to recognize the variety of roles that family members play in enhancing the child's development. It also is important that the degree to which the needs of the family are addressed in the IFSP process is determined in a collaborative manner with the full agreement and participation of the parents of the child. Parents retain the ultimate decision in determining whether they, their child, or other family members will accept or decline services under this part.

Note 3: The early intervention services in paragraph (d) of this section are those services that a State is required to provide to a child in accordance with § 303.12.

The "other services" in paragraph (e) of this section are services that a child or family needs, but that are neither required nor covered under this part. While listing the non-required services in the IFSP does not mean that those services must be provided, their identification can be helpful to both the child's family and the service coordinator, for the following reasons: First, the IFSP would provide a comprehensive picture of the child's total service needs (including the need for medical and health services, as well as early intervention services). Second, it is appropriate for the service coordinator to assist the family in securing the non-required services (e.g., by (1) determining if there is a public agency that could provide financial assistance, if needed, (2) assisting in the preparation of eligibility claims or insurance claims, if needed, and (3) assisting the family in seeking out and arranging for the child to receive the needed medical-health services).

Thus, to the extent appropriate, it is important for a State's procedures under this part to provide for ensuring that other needs of the child, and of the family related to enhancing the development of the child, such as medical and health needs, are considered and addressed, including determining (1) who will provide each service, and when, where, and how it will be provided, and (2) how the service will be paid for (e.g., through private insurance, an existing Federal-State funding source, such as Medicaid or EPSDT, or some other funding arrangement).

Note 4: Although the IFSP must include information about each of the items in paragraphs (b) through (h) of this section, this does not mean that the IFSP must be a detailed, lengthy document. It might be a brief outline, with appropriate attachments that address each of the points in the paragraphs under this section. It is important for the IFSP itself to be clear about (a) what services are to be provided, (b) the actions that are to be taken by the service coordinator in initiating those services, and (c) what actions will be taken by the parents.

34 C.F.R. § 303.344.

The IFSP is to be developed at a meeting with the parents, other family members if the parents request, an advocate if the parents request, the case manager, a person or person directly involved in the child's evaluation, and, as appropriate, individuals who will be providing services to the child or family. 34 C.F.R. § 303.343. The team makes the ultimate decision about the services and their frequency, intensity, and methodology. The Department of Education has issued a letter stating that requiring approval from a state review panel for services above one hour per week per discipline violates the law. *Howard*, 38 IDELR 100 (U.S. Dep't of Educ., Office of Special Educ. Programs 2002).

Agencies have 45 days to develop an initial IFSP, and the IFSP must be reviewed every six months or more frequently if conditions warrant or the family requests. This review may be at a meeting or by another means acceptable to the parents and other participants. Meetings must be conducted at least annually to evaluate the IFSP. 34 C.F.R. § 303.342.

The Part C language does not include the definitional term for free, appropriate public education, nor is there a leading case, such as the *Rowley* decision, discussing the meaning of the entitlement in one or another educational context. Accordingly, the degree of adequacy of services under an IFSP remains unresolved.

DE MORA v. DEPARTMENT OF PUBLIC WELFARE
768 A.2d 904 (Pa. Commw. 2001)

In this case, the court ruled that the IFSP proposed by the public agency was not sufficient to provide adequate services for a child eligible for services under Part C.

FRIEDMAN, JUDGE.

Barbara de Mora (Petitioner) petitions for review of the December 31, 1999 order of a hearing officer, which determined that the Individualized Family Service Plan (IFSP) developed for Petitioner's daughter, Isabella, is "appropriate" under 34 C.F.R. § 303.344,[4] and, thus, Isabella is not entitled to additional hours of therapy or Lovaas-based discrete trial training.[5] We reverse and remand.

Isabella was born on April 11, 1997. As an infant, Isabella was identified as having developmental delays.[6] Before Isabella's family moved to Bucks County, Pennsylvania, in July 1999, Petitioner contacted the Bucks County Office of Mental Health and Mental Retardation (county) regarding early intervention services for Isabella. As a result, an IFSP was developed for Isabella on July 1, 1999. The IFSP was modified several times since July 1, 1999, ultimately providing Isabella with 24.25 hours per week of physical therapy, speech therapy, occupational therapy and special instruction.

In September 1999, Petitioner requested that Isabella's IFSP include additional hours for her therapy, and Petitioner expressed a preference for the Lovaas methodology of early intervention training. However, the county refused to provide more hours of therapy or a Lovaas program. Petitioner was convinced that the Lovaas methodology would benefit her daughter, and, as a result, Petitioner hired a Lovaas-trained therapist to provide a private home program for Isabella from October 8, 1999 through December 14, 1999.

Subsequently, Petitioner requested a due process hearing, and the matter was assigned to a hearing officer. The hearing officer agreed to hold a paper hearing, i.e., without live testimony, and the parties submitted various documents in support of their positions.

The hearing officer determined that the IFSP was "appropriate" and, therefore, Isabella was not entitled to additional hours of therapy or Lovaas-based training. Because of this determination, the hearing officer declined to address whether Petitioner is entitled to reimbursement for her expenses in hiring someone to provide Lovaas training. Petitioner now appeals to this court.

---

[4] [FN 1] Subsection (d)(1) of the federal regulation at 34 C.F.R. § 303.344 states that an "IFSP must include a statement of the specific early intervention services necessary to meet the unique needs of the child and the family to achieve the outcomes identified in paragraph (c) of this section. . . ." 34 C.F.R. § 303.344(d)(1) (2000).

[5] [FN 2] A Lovaas-based program involves forty hours per week of "discrete trial drilling." . . .

[6] [FN 3] Isabella has cerebral palsy, severe hearing loss in the left ear and mild to moderate hearing loss in the right ear. Isabella has a twin sister, Kristina, who also receives services for developmental delays.

Petitioner argues that the hearing officer erred in concluding that the IFSP was "appropriate" for Isabella's individual needs. In doing so, Petitioner presents this court with an issue of first impression. Although this court has examined whether individualized education programs (IEP) were "appropriate" for students under Part B of the Individuals with Disabilities Education Act (IDEA), this court has never addressed whether an IFSP was "appropriate" for an infant or toddler under Part C of the IDEA. Having considered the matter in this case, we agree that the hearing officer erred in concluding that the IFSP was "appropriate" for Isabella.

An IFSP must include "a statement of the specific early intervention services necessary to meet the unique needs of the child and the family to achieve the outcomes identified. . . ."[7] 34 C.F.R. § 303.344(d)(1) (2000). Through the IFSP process, the county is responsible for providing "appropriate" early intervention services to all handicapped infants, toddlers and their families. Sections 301 and 303(a) of the Early Intervention Services System Act, Act of December 19, 1990, P.L. 1372, 11 P.S. §§ 875-301 & 875-303(a).

For a county to meet its responsibility, the IFSP must provide services that are "likely to produce progress, not regression or trivial . . . advancement." *Polk v. Central Susquehanna Intermediate Unit 16*, 853 F.2d 171, 183 (3d Cir. 1988) (quoting *Board of Education v. Diamond*, 808 F.2d 987, 991 (3d Cir. 1986)). Where, as here, the IFSP provides for multiple types of developmental services, i.e., speech therapy, occupational therapy, physical therapy and special instruction, each of the services must be likely to produce meaningful progress. *Id.*

The assessment of a child's unique needs and of the services "appropriate" to meet those needs is an ongoing process. 34 C.F.R. § 303.322(b)(2). A review of progress made pursuant to an IFSP must be conducted every six months, or more frequently when conditions warrant or when a family requests it. 34 C.F.R. § 303.342(b)(1). Thus, to determine whether Isabella's IFSP is "appropriate" for her unique needs, we must examine whether the record shows that Isabella has made progress as a result of the services provided by her IFSP.

The hearing officer states that the county presented evidence of Isabella's progress from the services provided in her IFSP "before *and along with* Lovaas."[8]

---

[7] [FN 9] The outcomes identified in the July 1, 1999 IFSP are as follows: (1) Isabella will walk with better balance and less of a wide gait and stand in one place and will improve perceptual motor skills, visual tracking skills and problem solving skills; (2) Isabella will be able to imitate, pairing language and motor planning and will understand what is said and follow directions; (3) Isabella will talk so that she can let others know her thoughts, needs and ideas and will understand what is being said and follow directions; (4) Isabella will improve her self-help skills, including undressing, finger and spoon feeding, washing face and accepting new textures, so she can become independent; (5) Isabella will form relationships with others and interact more with her peers; and (6) Isabella will be "there" and not lost and will know that there is a world out there.

[8] [FN 10] In support of his statement, the hearing officer cites to County Exhibit A5; however, this exhibit is nothing more than a recitation of the services rendered to Isabella under the IFSP. It is *not* evidence of Isabella's progress. To the extent that the hearing officer believes that IFSP services are "appropriate" if they are merely *designed* to achieve the outcomes identified in the IFSP, we reject that notion. *Cf. Adams v. State*, 195 F.3d 1141 (9th Cir. 1999) (stating that, instead of asking whether the IFSP was adequate in light of the child's progress, a court should ask whether the IFSP was appropriately designed and implemented so as to convey a meaningful benefit).

(Hearing Officer's op. at 7) (emphasis added). However, evidence that Isabella made progress as of October 8, 1999, when she began receiving private Lovaas training *along with* the IFSP services, does *not* tend to show that Isabella made meaningful progress *solely* from the IFSP services. Therefore, in addressing whether the hearing officer erred in concluding that the IFSP was "appropriate" for Isabella, we will consider only that evidence relating to the period of time from July 1, 1999 to October 7, 1999, *before* Isabella began Lovaas training.

Certainly, the county presented substantial evidence to show that Isabella was making meaningful progress from the physical therapy that she was receiving under the IFSP. The county submitted a September 30, 1999 evaluation by the physical therapist, Michele R. Barbon, which states: "Isabella has made gains in stair climbing, walking board traversing and postural control in sitting and standing. Her greatest gain has been in her tolerance to handling and facilitation especially on unstable surfaces." Such progress is related to her goal of walking with better balance and standing in one place.

However, the county did *not* present substantial evidence to show that Isabella was making meaningful progress from the occupational therapy, speech therapy and special instruction provided to her under the IFSP. In fact, the county submitted *no* progress reports relating to Isabella's occupational therapy, and, although the county offered several progress reports from one of the speech therapists, Katharine Ferguson, those reports cover periods of time when Isabella was also receiving Lovaas training. As for the special instruction, the county presented a September 1999 progress summary by Scott Helsinger; however, it is not possible to determine from the document and its attachments whether any progress reported therein is related to Isabella's IFSP goals.

It is clear, then, that, except for the physical therapy, the county failed to prove that the IFSP services provided to Isabella from July 1, 1999 to October 7, 1999 produced meaningful progress towards the IFSP goals. Thus, the hearing officer erred in concluding that the IFSP was, in every respect, "appropriate" for Isabella.

Having made that determination, we must decide on a proper remedy for Petitioner. Although Isabella is no longer under three years of age and, thus, is no longer eligible for services under Part C of the IDEA, the issue of Petitioner's entitlement to reimbursement for expenses in providing Isabella with private Lovaas training is not moot.

Section 1439(a)(1) of the IDEA, 20 U.S.C. § 1439, states that, when a county fails to provide adequate services for a child, this court "shall grant such relief as the court determines is appropriate." Where a family has provided private services to supplement inadequate IFSP services and the child makes progress toward her goals as a result of the combination of services, it is appropriate to reimburse the family for the supplemental services.

Here, the hearing officer found that Isabella made progress toward her IFSP goals as a result of the *combination* of IFSP services and Lovaas training. This finding is supported by substantial evidence in the record. Thus, Petitioner is entitled to reimbursement for her expenses in providing Isabella with private Lovaas training for the period from October 8, 1999 to December 14, 1999. Because the hearing officer declined to address the issue, we must remand this case so that the hearing officer can make findings relating to Petitioner's actual costs in that regard.

Accordingly, we reverse and remand.

NOTES AND QUESTIONS

1. Is the court's decision consistent with the law? Is the absence of the term "appropriate" from the standard for services a meaningful elision, given its use, among other places, in section 303.322(b)(2)(i)? Did Congress intend that Bucks County could simply lower its expected outcomes for the child and accordingly provide reduced services?

2. Related litigation in the federal courts includes a decision awarding the parent the cost of her own time for providing Lovaas therapy to the child, despite her lack of professional certification. *Bucks County Dep't of Mental Health/Mental Retardation v. Pennsylvania*, 379 F.3d 61 (3d Cir. 2004). Is that remedy a proper one?

3. Eligibility for Lovaas-style services has become a major issue in special education litigation, in light of the dramatic increase in autism diagnoses in recent years and the belief of many parents that intensive programming of this type is the only intervention with a likelihood of significant success. The therapy and its variants typically include 40 hours a week of one-on-one instruction that breaks activities into discrete subtasks whose proper performance is immediately reinforced (hence the use of the terms "discrete trial training" or "applied behavioral analysis"). Cases diverge on whether children eligible under IDEA Part B must be provided the services. *Compare Board of Educ. v. Michael M.*, 95 F. Supp. 2d 600 (S.D. W. Va. 2000) (finding program that lacked discrete trial training not appropriate), *with Lt. T.B. v. Warwick Sch. Comm.*, 361 F.3d 80 (1st Cir. 2004) (finding no clear error in decision to uphold rival program).

4. There are relatively few cases on the adequacy of an individual child's services under the infant and toddlers program. Perhaps parents are generally satisfied with the services offered, or they do not develop dissatisfaction until the child is past the age of eligibility for the program. There is no explicit provision for attorneys' fees in Part C, but that would seem unlikely to discourage litigation, for fees would be available for court proceedings and all necessary administrative hearings under the Civil Rights Attorneys' Fees Act, 42 U.S.C. § 1988, if a § 1983 claim may be advanced. *See New York Gaslight Club v. Carey*, 447 U.S. 54 (1980) (permitting fees for necessary administrative proceedings in discrimination case).

C. TRANSITION ISSUES

As the IFSP regulation reproduced in section B, *supra*, makes clear, Congress intended children to have a seamless transition to special education services or other programs at age three. To further this goal, IDEA provides that children who are two or three may be served under either Part B or Part C if their birthdays fall during the course of the school year. 20 U.S.C. § 1419(a)(2). In the following case, the court considered what services needed to be provided a child turning three, when the parents invoked the due process hearing procedure and claimed a right to maintenance of placement under 20 U.S.C. § 1415(j) (discussed in detail *supra* Chapter 8).

PARDINI v. ALLEGHENY INTERMEDIATE UNIT
420 F.3d 181 (3d Cir. 2005)

In this case, the court required a school system receiving a child who turned three to provide the same services she had been receiving from her Part C provider during the pendency of due process proceedings over the Part B evaluation and proposed IEP.

McKEE, CIRCUIT JUDGE.

David and Jennifer Pardini brought this action on behalf of their minor daughter, "Georgia." They are appealing the District Court's ruling that she was not entitled to continue to receive certain educational/developmental services pursuant to the "stay-put" provision of the Individuals with Disabilities in Education Act, until the dispute over those services is resolved. For the reasons that follow, we will reverse.

I. Factual Background

Georgia Pardini was born on April 18, 2000. She has cerebral palsy, a condition that affects muscular coordination and body movement. Sometime after her first birthday, Georgia began receiving services from the Alliance for Infants and Toddlers ("AIT") in the form of an Individualized Family Service Plan ("IFSP") pursuant to the Individuals With Disabilities in Education Act, 20 U.S.C. §§ 1400-85, ("IDEA" or the "Act"). Shortly before Georgia's third birthday, as she was about to transition out of her IFSP, a dispute arose about whether the Individualized Education Program ("IEP") being developed for her by the Allegheny Intermediate Unit ("AIU") should include the conductive education Georgia had been receiving as part of her IFSP.[9]

The AIU had evaluated Georgia as part of the normal transition from an IFSP to an IEP that is mandated by the IDEA when a child turns three. The District Court found that the Pardinis received the evaluation on March 15, 2003 along with instructions telling them to "Read the report, sign the original, and return in the enclosed envelope within 5 days [and] if you disagree with any part of the report, write a statement on a separate piece of paper that describes the items with which you disagree."

The Pardinis and agents of AIU met on March 24, 2003, but the Pardinis refused to sign the IEP because it did not provide for the conductive education Georgia had been receiving under the IFSP. Rather than sign, the Pardinis requested an independent evaluation and asked AIU to continue all of the services Georgia had

---

[9] [FN 3] Conductive education is an educational approach for children with central nervous system disabilities. It is a holistic approach to help develop problem-solving skills.

been receiving pending the outcome of that evaluation. AIU responded by advising the Pardinis that it would instead seek a due process hearing pursuant to 20 U.S.C. § 1415(f) "to prove the appropriateness of their evaluation and thus, deny the public expense of the independent evaluation." The Pardinis reiterated their request that conductive education continue as Georgia's "current educational placement" in a letter dated March 25, 2003. Although AIU subsequently sent the Pardinis at least two letters, one of which was dated March 31, 2003, and the other of which was dated April 15, 2003, a second IEP meeting scheduled for April 17 was postponed because the Pardinis did not receive adequate notice. When the Pardinis thereafter demanded a written explanation of the services that would be discontinued on Georgia's third birthday, AIU responded by asserting its intent to request a due process hearing. AIU also informed the family that it would not continue the conductive education during the due process proceedings and that feature of her IFSP would be discontinued as of Georgia's third birthday.

At the May 1, 2003 IEP meeting, AIU presented a Notice of Recommended Educational Placement ("NOREP") that included only those services it deemed appropriate; it did not include conductive education. The Pardinis signed noting their objection to the absence of conductive education. The District Court summarized that meeting and AIU's refusal to subsequently provide Georgia with any services as follows: "Plaintiffs attended [the] . . . meeting . . . under protest. . . . AIU refused to offer Plaintiffs a NOREP that included all of the IFSP related services and Plaintiffs signed their objection to AIU's NOREP as such. Nevertheless, the AIU has not restarted Georgia's IDEA services."

The AIU and the Pardinis could not agree upon Georgia's IEP, and the Pardinis refused to sign a NOREP that did not include conductive education. The AIU took the position that it could not provide any services under the circumstances, and it terminated all of Georgia's services four days after her third birthday. The Pardinis responded in a letter to AIU in which they objected to AIU's actions and demanded that Georgia's services be reinstated pursuant to the "stay-put" requirement of 20 U.S.C. § 1415(j). The AIU maintained that § 1415(j) did not apply because Georgia was transitioning from an IFSP to an IEP. "The Pardinis reasonably believed that conductive education, . . . has proven . . . effective and . . . beneficial to Georgia. [] AIU . . . refused to even consider the appropriateness and effectiveness of conductive education . . . as part of its proposed IEP, prior to presenting that IEP to the parents." *Pardini*, 230 F. Supp. 2d. at 454.

While the due process hearings were proceeding to determine whether "a meaningful and appropriate IEP should include . . . conductive education . . . or whether the alternatives offered by AIU [were] adequate to insure [Georgia's] meaningful progress," *id.*, the Pardinis filed the instant action in the District Court.[10] The Hearing Officer did not specifically address the application of the stay-put rule. Rather, he relied upon the District Court's conclusion that "Georgia's

---

[10] [FN 4] At oral argument, the parties informed the court that the Pardinis eventually agreed to an IEP that did not include conductive education. However, since we conclude that Georgia was entitled to receive conductive education as a part of Georgia's IEP until the dispute was resolved, they are entitled to reimbursement of the out-of-pocket expense resulting from the AIU's failure to comply with 20 U.S.C. § 1415(j), as well as reasonable attorneys' fees. . . .

IFSP is not pendent," because she had reached her third birthday, and proceeded to address the issue of "whether the parents should receive an [Independent Educational Evaluation] at public expense." Thereafter, the District Court entered a final order ruling that § 1415(j) did not require the IEP to offer conductive education during the pendency of the administrative hearings.[11] This appeal followed.

Meanwhile, the state conducted due process hearings on June 10 and June 12, 2003 to determine if AIU was obligated to continue providing the services Georgia had received as part of her IFSP pending the resolution of the disputed IEP, as well as whether the proposed IEP was appropriate. Ultimately, the Dispute Resolution Hearing Officer ruled that AIU was not obligated to continue all of Georgia's services under the IFSP. The hearing was then continued to determine whether the Paridnis should receive an independent evaluation.

On August 29, 2003, after conducting a trial, the District Court issued a second opinion in which the court ruled that the Pardinis were not entitled to any relief. The court reasoned that the stay-put provision of the IDEA did not require AIU to provide the identical educational program that AIT had been providing under Georgia's IFSP because the AIT was a different program with a different funding stream. The court also concluded that the respective agency, not the parents, had the ultimate responsibility for deciding upon an appropriate educational program for Georgia. This appeal followed.[12]

II. Discussion

The District Court concluded that the stay-put rule of § 1415(j) does not apply to a child who has reached her third birthday and is therefore transitioning from an IFSP to an IEP. The court explained, "an IFSP is a medical model, . . . [whereas] an IEP is an educational model." The court reasoned that, since Georgia was embarking upon her first IEP and a public education, the "applicable stay-put placement . . . is the proposed public school placement and program" contained in the IEP that did not include conductive education. Accordingly, the court reasoned that the AIU was not obligated to provide for conductive education pending the outcome of the due process hearings.

In order to properly resolve this dispute, we must examine the IDEA to determine if Congress intended that disputed features of an IFSP be provided under an IEP that is offered upon a child reaching the age of three and transitioning from one part of the Act to another.

---

[11] [FN 5] The District Court noted the ongoing administrative proceedings but concluded "in light of the somewhat inexplicable communication problems and institutional stubbornness exhibited by AIU . . . that the Pardinis face a bewildering bureaucratic nightmare [that] must be particularly daunting to young parents who are financially strapped and emotionally pressed to provide for the special . . . needs of their child."

[12] [FN 6] Since the termination of Georgia's services, the Pardinis have paid for two sessions of conductive education services. They have also paid for Georgia to receive services at the Euromed Rehabilitation Center in Mielno, Poland, as well as services through United Cerebral Palsy/North Coast Ohio Conductive Education of Cleveland, and the Ronald McDonald House of Cleveland.

A. Statutory Background.

In enacting the IDEA, Congress originally only provided for children with disabilities who were between the ages 5 and 21. However, in 1986, Congress amended the Act to extend to disabled children who were between three and five years of age. Accordingly, 20 U.S.C. § 1412 declares that a state is only eligible for financial assistance when "a free appropriate public education is available to all children with disabilities residing in the State between the ages of 3 and 21. . . ."

The program providing services to children beyond their third birthday ("school-aged children") is referred to as "Part B," and the program providing services to children between the ages of three and five is known as the "Part B Preschool Program."

. . . .

The issue before us involves the Act's provisions for the child during the pendency of disputes involving the child's program or placement. At the outset, we referred to 20 U.S.C. § 1415(j) which provides in pertinent part as follows:

> During the pendency of any proceedings conducted pursuant to this section, unless the State or local educational agency and the parents . . . otherwise agree, the child shall remain in the then-current educational placement of such child, or, if applying for initial admission to a public school, shall, with the consent of the parents . . . be placed in the public school program until all such proceedings have been completed.

. . . .

In 1986, Congress amended the IDEA by adding the "Part C" Program to serve children from birth to age three. 20 U.S.C. §§ 1431–1445. Part C requires states that receive funds under the statute to provide "appropriate early intervention services as set forth in an Individualized Family Service Plan ('IFSP')." Section 1432(4) of the IDEA defines "early intervention services" as "developmental services" that "are designed to meet the developmental needs of an infant or toddler with a disability." This involves the child's physical, cognitive, communication, social or emotional, and/or adaptive development. *Id.*

Congress realized that it was important to allow for an overlap of services rather than legislate a rigid and artificial demarcation inconsistent with the reality of early development because "early intervention research indicated that certain types of services required by infants and toddlers with disabilities are comparable to . . . services required by preschoolers with disabilities that are included in their individualized family service plans." H.R. Rep. at 7.

In enacting the amendments to the IDEA, Congress stressed that the transition from Part C to Part B upon a child's third birthday was to be "a *smooth transition*." *See* 20 U.S.C. § 1412(a)(9). Congress mandated that "children participating in early-intervention programs . . . under [Part C], and who will participate in preschool programs [under Part B], experience a smooth and effective transition to those preschool programs in a manner consistent with section 1437(a)(8) of this title. By the third birthday, . . . an individualized education program or, if consistent with sections 1414(d)(2)(B) and 1436(d) . . . an individualized family service plan, has been developed and implemented. . . . "The referenced section 1437(a)(8), sets forth certain requirements that states applying for funds under the Act must include in their application. Congress required that such states include a "description of the policies and procedures [] to ensure a smooth transition." Similarly, the referenced section 1414(d)(2)(B) specifically states that "an individualized family service plan . . . may serve as the IEP" when appropriate.

Moreover, Congress has clearly recognized that realities dictate that there must often be significant overlap in services provided under Part C and Part B. Thus, Part C funds can be used from the child's third birthday to the beginning of the following school year. 20 U.S.C. § 1438(3). Conversely, a state can use Part B funds to provide services to a child who is not yet eligible for preschool early intervention services and therefore would not ordinarily qualify for funding under Part B. In addition, federal regulations explain that states shall comply with the requirement of providing a free, appropriate pubic education ("FAPE") by ensuring that an IEP *or* an IFSP is in effect for the child beginning at age three. 34 C.F.R. § 300.121(c)(1)(ii). Therefore, we think it is clear that an IFSP under Part C can serve as a child's Preschool IEP under the Part B if the agency and the parents both agree. 20 U.S.C. §§ 1414(d)(2)(A) and (B), 34 C.F.R. § 300.342(c)(1).

Thus, in Pennsylvania, the Early Intervention Services System Act ("Act 212") mandates appropriate special education programs for disabled children from birth to age five. 11 Pa. Cons. Stat. Ann. §§ 875-101 et. seq. (Purdon 2002). Under that act, the Pennsylvania Department of Education is responsible for providing services to disabled preschool children aged 3 to 5 as well as school aged children. The Department of Public Welfare is responsible for providing services to children from birth to age three.

The instant dispute over Georgia's conductive education is rooted in this administrative demarcation. The Department of Public Welfare recognizes conductive education. The Pennsylvania Department of Education does not recognize it.

B. The Application of the Stay-Put Rule to Georgia's Transition.

The Pardinis claim that the congressional concern for a smooth transition to preschool and services under Part B of the IDEA can best be accomplished through a program that includes conductive education. Moreover, since Georgia had been receiving conductive education as part of her IFSP, they claim that it was part of the "current educational placement." However, the AIU argues that Georgia's IEP should not merely mirror the services she was receiving under her IFSP because the IDEA recognizes a developmental, and educational change in focus when a child becomes three and begins preparing for school. The AIU states: "Stay-put does not apply to the initiation of services from Part C to Part B of the IDEA. The programs operate under different agencies, different eligibility requirements, and different purposes. To argue that they are the same is preposterous."

Of course, the issue here is not whether Part C and Part B are the same; they clearly are not. Rather, the issue is whether § 1415(j) required the AIU to include conductive education as part of Georgia's initial IEP until the agency and the parents could resolve their dispute over her IEP. That is a very different question.

In resolving that inquiry against the Pardinis, the District Court relied largely on *Johnson v. Special Education Hearing Office*, 287 F.3d 1176 (9th Cir. 2002). There, parents sought an administrative hearing to challenge an IEP that provided for a change in the vendor that had offered a particular service under their son's IEP. The services that were contemplated by the education agency were identical to those that had been offered under their son's IFSP before his third birthday. The agency claimed that the vendor could not continue to provide services after a child's third birthday, but the agency proposed offering the same services with a different vendor.

In the due process hearings that followed, the Hearing Officer ordered continuation of the placement and services, but concluded the school district " 'need not utilize the same vendors who provided services under that IFSP.' " The parents responded by seeking an injunctive order in the District Court requiring the Hearing Officer to "issue a new 'stay put' order [forcing the school district] to use the same tutors, vendors, and supervisory services [as those in their son's IFSP]." The District Court analyzed the dispute using the customary criteria for resolving claims for injunctive relief. That included an analysis of irreparable harm, and the likelihood of success on the merits. *Id.* Based upon that analysis, the court denied the request for injunctive relief, and the Court of Appeals affirmed citing *Thomas v. Cincinnati Bd. of Educ.*, 918 F.2d 618, 625 (6th Cir. 1990).

Here, the District Court concluded that since "Plaintiffs are in the transition process applying for initial services under Part B[]," the applicable stay-put placement for a three-year old child is the proposed public school placement and program." Quoting from *Johnson*, the District Court also held, "when responsibility transfers from one public agency to another, 'the new agency is required only to provide a program that is in conformity with the placement in the last agreed upon IEP or IFSP. The new agency need not . . . provide the exact same educational program.' " (internal citation omitted).

We do not disagree with the reasoning in *Johnson*. However, we believe the District Court misapplied that decision. The parties in *Johnson* stipulated that the child's IFSP constituted "his current educational placement for 'stay put' purposes." 287 F.3d at 1180. The parties were only disputing whether the identical services had to be provided by the same vendor who had provided them under the IFSP. Thus, to the extent that it applies to our analysis at all, *Johnson* undermines the District Court's focus on the distinction between the developmental needs of children who are less than three, and the educational needs of children who are older than three. The services offered under the IEP in *Johnson* were identical to those that had been offered under the IFSP.

The District Court cited *Johnson* in stating: "when responsibility transfers from one public agency to another, . . . 'the new agency need not, and probably could not, provide the exact same educational program.' " (quoting *Johnson*, 287 F.3d at 1181). However, since *Johnson* did not involve the child's entitlement to disputed services during the pendency of a dispute, the case is distinguishable from the circumstances before us. It is important to remember that Congress was concerned with the services and programs offered to handicapped children, not with the vendors supplying them. The District Court's failure to recognize that distinction undermines its reliance on *Thompson*.

Moreover, the District Court's error was compounded (or perhaps facilitated) by its reliance upon an analysis more appropriately utilized for ruling upon preliminary injunctions than enforcing the Act's stay-put rule. The court reasoned "that Plaintiffs would not be irreparably harmed by refusal to grant the injunction, and that the public interest would be served by permitting the . . . proceedings to continue, which would develop a full and meaningful record if further review became necessary." However, Congress has already balanced the competing harms as well as the competing equities. In *Drinker v. Colonial School Dist.*, 78 F.3d 859, 864 (3d Cir. 1996), we explained that the Act "substitutes an absolute rule in favor of the status quo for the court's discretionary consideration of the factors of irreparable harm and either a likelihood of success on the merits or a . . . balance of hardships."

Although, as we have noted, the court in *Johnson* also engaged in a traditional preliminary injunction analysis, that analysis did not involve the stay-put rule. Rather, the Hearing Officer in *Johnson* had already entered a "stay-put order" under the Act and the parents were asking a court to enjoin *that order*, not the proposed IEP. The court explained: "Here, the Hearing Officer's 'stay-put' order preserves the tutors, goals, and plan . . . it only changes the plan supervisors. . . . Thus, the 'stay put' order correctly determined [the child's] 'then current educational placement' and [the plaintiffs have] very little likelihood of success in challenging the 'stay put' order." Moreover, "because the [agency] offered comparable placement [to the child] no irreparable harm would befall [him] by denying the preliminary injunction." *Id.* Here, of course, there is no "stay-put order" in place and the Pardinis are arguing that the program the AIU is proposing is not comparable to the program Georgia had been receiving under the IFSP. Therefore, *Johnson* does not support the District Court's holding. Moreover, we cannot reconcile the District Court's analysis with our decision in *Drinker, supra*, or the Supreme Court's decision in *Honig v. Doe*, 484 U.S. 305 (1988).

In *Honig*, the Supreme Court rejected school authorities' claim that, under the circumstances there, proposed changes to a child's educational placement must remain in effect until the propriety of the placement was ultimately determined. The Court observed, "the language of § 1415(e)(3)[13] is unequivocal. It states plainly that during the pendency of any proceedings under the Act, unless the state or local educational agency and the parents agree . . . , 'the child *shall* remain in the then current educational placement." *Id.*, at 323 (emphasis in original). The facts in *Honig* dramatically underscore the impact and importance of the Court's ruling.

Honig involved two students whose individual cases were consolidated. Both students had engaged in disability-related misconduct. One student had forcefully choked a classmate and then kicked out a school window while being escorted to the principal's office. In both cases, the parents filed suit under the predecessor of the IDEA in an effort to enjoin the school district from expelling their children until appropriate placements and IEPs were agreed upon. Except for the district's

---

[13] [FN 9] 20 U.S.C. § 1415(e)(3) is the forerunner to 20 U.S.C. § 1415(f), and the two provisions are identical.

authority to impose a very brief suspension, the District Court enjoined the school district from unilaterally acting against "any disabled child for disability-related misconduct, or from effecting any other change in the educational placement . . . without parental consent pending completion of [due process] proceedings." *Id.*, at 315. The Court of Appeals affirmed but modified the District Court's order to allow for fixed suspensions of up to 30 school days. The court reasoned that the school district retained the authority to take such limited action under the stay-put rule and certain provisions of the state's Education Code.

On appeal, the school district asked the Supreme Court to read a " 'dangerousness' exception into the stay-put provision[.]" The Court refused. The Court did not accept the school's argument that Congress obviously intended for schools to retain "residual authority to . . . exclude dangerous students from the classroom[.]" *Id.* at 323. The Court did not think it obvious that Congress intended schools or educational agencies to have any such power. Rather, the Court thought it "clear[] . . . that Congress very much intended to strip schools of the *unilateral* authority they had traditionally employed to exclude disabled students, . . . from school." *Id.*, at 323 (emphasis in original).[14] The Court thus concluded that the stay-put provision "means what it says." *Id.*, at 324.

Nor are we convinced by AIU's claim that, since this was Georgia's initial IEP, it constituted the "current educational placement" for purposes of the stay-put rule. In *Drinker*, we stressed the importance of maintaining the *status quo* when identifying "the then current educational placement" for purposes of the stay-put rule. 78 F.3d at 864. We stated

> Implicit in the maintenance of the status quo is the requirement that a school district continue to finance an educational placement made by the agency and consented to by the parent before the . . . due process [procedure is invoked]. To cut off public funds would amount to a unilateral change in placement, prohibited by the Act.

Id. (brackets in original) (quoting *Zvi D. v Ambach*, 694 F.2d 904, 906 (2d. Cir. 1982)).

We are also not persuaded by AIU's claim that the demarcation between Part C and Part B of the IDEA, and the administrative and fiscal division of the providers of services offered under those respective programs, counsels against viewing the IFSP as the "current educational placement" under the circumstances of this

---

[14] [FN 10] Given this clear statutory authority, the District Court's belief in the primacy of the educational agency is somewhat puzzling. The court stated: "the responsibility for choosing the educational method most suitable to the child's needs is left to the educational agency." 280 F. Supp. 2d at 454. To the extent that this suggests a marginalized or diminished role for the parents, the court's assessment of the respective roles is erroneous. It is clear that the parents are not to be excluded from the decision, and the "responsibility" for the decision does not solely rest with the educators or an educational agency. Rather, "Congress repeatedly emphasized throughout the Act *the importance and indeed the necessity* of parental participation in both the development of the IEP and any subsequent assessments of its effectiveness." *Honig*, 108 S.Ct. at 598 (emphasis added). Although the Court was there referring to an IEP, parental involvement in an IFSP is no less important under the Act. "The Act establishes various . . . safeguards that guarantee parents both an opportunity for meaningful input into all decisions affecting their child's education and the right to seek review of any decisions they think inappropriate." *Id.*, 312–13.

dispute. This distinction simply can not negate the explicit language of the stay-put provision, Congress's concern for the child's "smooth transition," the Supreme Court's analysis in *Honig* or our decision in *Drinker*. Rather, we think it clear that "the [stay-put] provision represents Congress' policy choice that all handicapped children, regardless of whether their case is meritorious or not, are to remain in their current educational placement until the dispute with regard to their placement is ultimately resolved." *Drinker*, at 865.

Our conclusion is not altered by the fact that Part C programs are deemed "developmental" and part B programs are deemed "educational." As we explained in *Drinker*:

> Because the [current educational placement] connotes preservation of the status quo, it refers to the operative placement actually functioning at the time the dispute first arises. If an IEP has been implemented, then that program's placement will be the one subject to the stay put provision. And where . . . the dispute arises before any IEP has been implemented, the current educational placement will be the operative placement under which the child is actually receiving instruction at the time the dispute arises.

Drinker, at 867. Here, it is beyond dispute that Georgia was receiving an IFSP that included conductive education when the dispute arose. That was the "operative placement actually functioning [when, this] dispute arose." Georgia was therefore entitled to continue to receive that service as a component of her IEP until the dispute was resolved following her third birthday.

Had Congress intended a prospective IEP to govern the Act's stay put provision, as opposed to an operational placement, it could have employed the term "individualized educational program" which it had already defined. Since it did not, the term "then current educational placement" must be accorded its plain meaning. Because the term connotes preservation of the status quo, it refers to the operative placement actually functioning at the time the dispute first arises. . . . [W]here, as here, the dispute arises before any IEP has been implemented, the "current educational placement" will be the operative placement under which the child is actually receiving instruction at the time the dispute arises. *Thomas*, 918 F.2d at 625–26.

In addition, 20 U.S.C. § 1415(j) must be read in context with the rest of the IDEA statute. It is a fundamental rule of statutory construction that a statute's provisions should be read to be consistent with one another. *United Steelworkers of America v. North Star*, 5 F.3d 39, 43 (3d Cir., 1993). Instead of noting the differences between the Part B and Part C programs, we must remember that Congress sought to ensure continuity in the education of each under the IDEA. Yet, the AIU's attempt to chisel distinct barriers between services provided under Parts C and B based upon its theory of childhood development would require us to ignore the programmatic and fiscal overlap between Part C and Part B as well as the congressional mandate of a smooth transition between the two. Congress stressed that the amendments it added were "designed to promote a *seamless* system of services for children with disabilities, aged birth to five, inclusive." H.R. Rep. No. 198, 102nd Cong., 1st Sess. 1991.

Congress has clearly recognized that needs of disabled children do not fit neatly into the age-defined stages suggested by the AIU. Although Georgia was technically transitioning within the administrative and fiscal structure of IDEA's statutory scheme, her needs did not magically change on her third birthday. She still needed substantially the same services she was receiving in the days preceding her birthday. Indeed, 20 U.S.C. § 1412(a)(9) describes the transition to the preschool programs and notes that either an IEP or an IFSP may be used and implemented for the child. The Act expressly states that an IFSP may be used if it is "consistent with State policy," and "agreed to by the agency and the child's parents." Thus, the IDEA both anticipates and condones the possible interchangeability of an IFSP and IEP during transition to preschool.

Furthermore, even if we could accept the AIU's theory of "development" vs. "education," we would still be convinced that by the analysis in the cases we have discussed, that the conductive education in Georgia's IFSP was part of the status quo that should have been maintained pending resolution of the dispute over her IEP.

[C.] OSEP's Letter to Klebanoff.

The District Court also relied upon on OSEP's [Office of Special Education Programs of the U.S. Department of Education] *Letter to Klebanoff.* "The level of deference to be accorded such interpretive rules depends upon their persuasiveness." *Michael C. v. The Radnor Township School Dist.*, 202 F.3d 642, 649. In evaluating persuasiveness we consider such factors as the thoroughness, reasoning, and consistency with other agency pronouncements.

In *Letter to Klebanoff*, the OSEP answered an inquiry regarding whether the stay-put provision mandated the continuation of services a three-year old received in the Birth to Three-Year old program when the parents did not agree to the school's proposed education program. OSEP responded to the inquiry by stating it did not interpret 34 C.F.R. § 300.513 as requiring a public agency responsible for providing FAPE . . . to maintain [the] child in a program developed for a two-year old child as a means of providing that child and . . . her family appropriate early intervention services under Part H." 28 IDELR 478. However, the OSEP never explained how it reached that conclusion. Moreover, we find the discussion in *Thomas v. Cincinnati Bd. of Ed.* much more helpful. We agree that the plain meaning of "current educational placement" refers to the "operative placement actually functioning at the time the dispute first arises." 918 F.2d 618 at 625–626 (6th Cir. 1990).

In *Thomas*, an IEP was developed for a severely retarded eleven year old child, but before the services were to begin, doubts about funding caused the school to review the plan. The Court of Appeals held that the IEP could not be the "current educational placement" because it had never been implemented. Likewise, here, the proposed IEP had not been implemented when the dispute over whether it should contain conductive education arose. Rather, Georgia's operative placement consisted of the services she was receiving under her IFSP.

III. Conclusion

For the reasons set forth above, we hold that the stay-put provision of the IDEA, 20 U.S.C. § 1415(j), required Georgia to continue to receive conductive education until the dispute over its appropriateness for inclusion in her IEP was resolved. Accordingly, the Pardinis are entitled to the cost of the conductive education that they purchased before the dispute was resolved by their agreement to an IEP that did not contain it. We will therefore reverse the decision of the District Court and remand for the court to determine the amount of reimbursement the Pardinis are entitled to as well as the amount of any attorneys fees.[15]

D.P. v. SCHOOL BOARD
483 F.3d 725 (11th Cir. 2007)

Here the court disagrees with Pardini and, over a strenuous dissent, rules that children who exceed the age qualification for Part C services are not entitled to have the Part B agency continue to provide the services while a due process hearing is pending.

Cox, Circuit Judge.

We consider in these consolidated appeals whether the Individuals with Disabilities Education Act ("IDEA") requires a school board to continue providing services to children who have reached three years of age pursuant to Individualized Family Service Plans previously developed for those children under Part C of the IDEA until such time as Individualized Educational Plans are developed for the children under Part B of the IDEA. We conclude that it does not. Therefore, we affirm the district court's judgments of dismissal.

I. BACKGROUND & PROCEDURAL HISTORY

D.P., E.P., and K.P. are autistic triplets who live with their parents (collectively, "Appellants") in Broward County, Florida. Prior to their third birthday, the triplets received individualized care under the Early Intervention Program administered under Part C of the IDEA. The services provided the triplets under Part C of the IDEA were provided pursuant to Individualized Family Service Plans ("IFSPs"). Pursuant to IFSPs, disabled infants and toddlers may be provided with develop-

---

[15] [FN 13] The District Court reached the merits of the Pardinis' complaint without requiring exhaustion of administrative remedies under the IDEA because of the "bewildering bureaucratic nightmare," they had faced in dealing with the AIU. 280 F. Supp. 2d at 454. We assume that the court was concluding that exhaustion would be futile and that failure to exhaust was therefore excused. *See* W.B. v. Matula, 67 F.3d 484, 495–96 (3d. Cir. 1995). On appeal, the AIU argues that the reimbursement remedy the Pardinis are seeking "is an available administrative remedy in an administrative proceeding," and urges us to deny relief because an administrative remedy is available.

However, the issue here — the interpretation of § 1415(j) — is a purely legal one. "Courts require exhaustion where the peculiar expertise of an administrative hearing officer is necessary to develop a factual record. . . . Where the factual record is fully-developed and no evidentiary disputes remain, the court can and should decide legal issues." *Lester H. v. Gilhool*, 916 F.2d 865, 869 (3d. Cir. 1990) (citations omitted).

mental services such as speech, occupational, and physical therapy services; medical services for diagnosis and evaluation purposes; and social work services. While IFSPs may include an educational component, they do not necessarily include such a component.

On January 4, 2004, the triplets turned three and "aged out" of the Part C program. At the same time, they became eligible for services under Part B of the IDEA. Part B of the IDEA guarantees free appropriate public education ("FAPE") to disabled children older than three. Services provided under Part B of the IDEA are generally provided pursuant to Individualized Educational Plans ("IEPs") rather than IFSPs. IEPs differ from IFSPs in that they are focused on the educational needs of disabled children. However, at the time the triplets turned three, no IEPs had been developed for them.

On January 6, 2004, the Appellants initiated an administrative action by filing a due process complaint pursuant to the IDEA's provisions. The due process complaint alleged that the School Board of Broward County ("the Board") was contemplating modifying the services provided in the triplets' last IFSPs and sought an injunction requiring the Board to continue the services in the IFSPs. Appellants purported to invoke the "stay put" provision in Part B of the IDEA, 20 U.S.C. § 1415(j). On January 9, 2004, an Administrative Law Judge ("ALJ") held a telephone conference with the parties to the administrative action during which the parties agreed that no evidentiary hearings were necessary as the dispute presented only questions of law that could be resolved on papers submitted by the parties. After the matter had been fully briefed, the ALJ issued an order holding that the "stay put" provision did not require the Board to provide services pursuant to the triplets' last IFSPs. The ALJ denied Appellants' requests for injunctive relief, for reimbursement of the costs Appellants had incurred in continuing the services previously provided under the IFSPs, and for attorneys' fees and costs. Appellants appealed the ALJ's order to the federal district court in a case styled *D.P. and L.P., on behalf of E.P., D.P., and K.P. v. School Board of Broward County ("D.P. I")*. The complaint in *D.P. I* requested a declaration that the Board must continue the services provided to the triplets pursuant to the IFSPs, an injunction requiring the Board to do so, and reimbursement of the costs Appellants had incurred in continuing the services previously provided under the IFSPs.

On August 17, 2004, while *D.P. I* was still pending in the district court, Appellants filed another due process complaint alleging, among other things, that the Board had failed to have IEPs in place for the triplets on their third birthday and that, instead, the Board belatedly had developed temporary IEPs for the triplets. The temporary IEPs proposed placement of the triplets in the Baudhuin Preschool for pre-kindergarten children with autism. Appellants alleged that the temporary IEPs were invalid by reason of the parents' refusal to consent to them. This second administrative action sought a declaration that the temporary IEPs were invalid and an injunction requiring the Board to provide the triplets with services pursuant to their last IFSPs until valid IEPs were in place. It also sought reimbursement from the Board for the costs that the parents had incurred in continuing the services previously provided under the IFSPs. Appellants requested that the ALJ first resolve (without an evidentiary hearing) the legal issues of whether the temporary IEPs were invalid and, if so, what remedy was due. After receiving briefing on those questions, the ALJ determined that the temporary IEPs were invalid because the parents had never consented to them. However, the ALJ also found that nothing in the IDEA or Florida law obligated the Board, as a result of the parents' refusal to consent to the temporary IEPs, to provide the triplets with the Early Intervention Services they had been receiving previously under Part C of the IDEA. The ALJ denied Appellants' requests for reimbursement. Finally, the ALJ ordered Appellants to file a statement indicating whether, in light of the resolution of the threshold questions, Appellants believed there to be any remaining unresolved issues in their action. Appellants filed no such statement. Instead, they filed a complaint in the district court challenging the ALJ's decision.

The second district court case was styled *L.M.P. on behalf of D.P., K.P., and E.P. v. School Board of Broward County ("D.P. II")*. In *D.P. II*, Appellants claimed that the Board failed to provide the triplets with FAPE as required by the IDEA. Appellants asked the district court to declare the temporary IEPs invalid, order the Board to reimburse Appellants for the costs they had incurred in continuing the services formerly provided under the IFSPs, order the Board to continue the services provided under the IFSPs, and award Appellants attorneys' fees and costs.

The Board moved to dismiss *D.P. I* and *D.P. II*, arguing in both cases that Appellants' claims failed as a matter of law because neither the IDEA nor any other provision of law requires the Board to continue to provide services to the triplets pursuant to their IFSPs until valid IEPs are in place.

On March 8, 2005, the district court granted the Board's motion to dismiss the complaint in *D.P. I* pursuant to Fed. R. Civ. P. 12(b)(6). On August 19, 2005, the district court granted the Board's motion to dismiss in *D.P. II*, also for failure to state a claim upon which relief can be granted. Judgment was entered for the Board in both cases. Appellants appealed both judgments to this court, and we consolidated the cases on appeal.

II. CONTENTIONS OF THE PARTIES & ISSUES ON APPEAL

Appellants contend that the IDEA entitles the triplets to continued services pursuant to their IFSPs until valid IEPs are put in place for them. Appellants further contend that, because the parents did not consent to the temporary IEPs proposed by the Board, there are no valid IEPs for the triplets. They argue that the district court erred in refusing to issue an injunction requiring the Board to provide the services previously provided under the IFSPs.

The Board contends that the IDEA imposes no duty to continue to provide services under IFSPs to children who have reached age three. The Board also argues that, according to the plain language of the IDEA's "stay put" provision, because the triplets have never enrolled in public school, the proper placement for them while an IEP is not yet in place is the public school program.

III. STANDARD OF REVIEW

We review de novo the district court's grant of a motion to dismiss . . . for failure to state a claim, accepting the factual allegations in the complaint as true and construing them in the light most favorable to the plaintiff. . . . Dismissal is appropriate "when, on the basis of a dispositive issue of law, no construction of the factual allegations will support the cause of action." *Marshall County Bd. of Educ. v. Marshall County Gas Dist.*, 992 F.2d 1171, 1174 (11th Cir. 1993).

IV. DISCUSSION

In the orders granting the motions to dismiss, the district court relied on the plain language of the pendency, or "stay put," provision of the IDEA to hold that the statute does not require the Board to provide the services that had previously been provided under the IFSPs. We have said, " 'In construing a statute we must begin, and often should end as well, with the language of the statute itself.' . . . Where the language Congress chose to express its intent is clear and unambiguous, that is as far as we go to ascertain its intent because we must presume that Congress said what it meant and meant what it said." *United States v. Steele*, 147 F.3d 1316, 1318 (11th Cir. 1998) (quoting *Merritt v. Dillard*, 120 F.3d 1181, 1185 (11th Cir. 1997) (other citations omitted).

The "stay put" provision, which governs during the course of all administrative and judicial proceedings regarding a child's proper placement under Part B of the IDEA, says:

Maintenance of current educational placement

[D]uring the pendency of any proceedings conducted pursuant to this section, unless the State or local educational agency and the parents otherwise agree, the child shall remain in the then-current educational placement of the child, or, if applying for initial admission to a public school, shall, with the consent of the parents, be placed in the public school program until all such proceedings have been completed.

20 U.S.C. § 1415(j).

Appellants contend that, through use of the disjunctive "or," the statutory provision provides alternative placements for the triplets. According to Appellants, while their due process requests were pending, the triplets could have been placed in the public school program or they could have remained in their then-current educational placement. Appellants cite a Third Circuit case, *Pardini v. Allegheny Intermediate Unit*, 420 F.3d 181 (3d Cir. 2005), to support their contention that the triplets "then-current educational placement" was the last IFSP from the Early Intervention Program.

We find Appellants' argument unpersuasive in light of the unambiguous language of the statute. The disjunctive "or" does indeed provide alternatives; but, contrary to Appellants' contention, the alternatives separated by the "or" are mutually exclusive. As the district court stated, if the educational agency (here, the Board) and parents do not agree to a placement for the child, which of the other two alternatives applies depends on one fact only — whether the child is applying for initial admission to a public school. If the child is not applying for initial admission, he shall remain in his existing educational placement. *Or*, if the child is applying for initial admission, he shall be placed in the public school program. We reach this conclusion based upon the placement of the disjunctive coordinating conjunction — between the two alternatives, but before the imperative, "if applying for initial admission to a public school [the student] shall . . . be placed in the public school program."

In this case, Appellants do not contest the fact that the triplets have never been admitted to a public school program. Therefore, the triplets are "applying for initial admission to a public school." And, in the absence of an agreement otherwise between the Board and the triplets' parents, the only placement available to the triplets is the public school program. The district court properly held that the fact that the parents withheld consent to placement in the program offered by the public school (pursuant to the temporary IEPs) does not create another option for the triplets. Without the parents' consent, the triplets cannot be placed in the public school program; but, they are not entitled to an alternative placement pursuant to the statute. In other words, the IDEA does not entitle the triplets to continue receiving services pursuant to their IFSPs until such time as valid IEPs are put in place for them.[16]

We acknowledge that our decision is at odds with the Third Circuit's holding in *Pardini*. We think that case was incorrectly decided. As stated above, we base our conclusions on the plain language of the "stay put" provision. We do note, however, that our interpretation of the statute is consistent with that of the Department of Education. The implementing regulation in effect at the time Appellants filed their due process requests stated:

> If the [due process] complaint involves an application for initial admission to public school, the child, with the consent of the parents, must be placed in the public school until the completion of all the proceedings.

34 C.F.R. § 300.514(b).[17]

---

[16] [FN 1] The dissent maintains that our holding requires the triplets to enter public school, without any accommodation whatsoever and without any remedy. That conclusion is based upon neither the facts of this case nor our legal analysis. The "public school placement" that the triplets were offered by the school board is, in fact, enrollment at the Mailman Segal Institute's Baudhuin Preschool, located on the main campus of Nova Southeastern University. The Baudhuin Preschool is a private school for pre-kindergarten-aged children with autism.

The triplets' parents rejected this placement, as is their right under the IDEA. Having done so, they could have continued private services and challenged the school board's plan in a due process hearing and, if necessary, a subsequent lawsuit in which they attempted to prove that the school board had denied the triplets FAPE. Had they been successful, the parents would have been able to receive reimbursement from the school board for the costs of the private services that replaced the FAPE their children were wrongly denied. *See M.M. ex rel. C.M. v. School Bd. of Miami-Dade County, Fla.*, 437 F.3d 1085, 1098–99 (11th Cir. 2006).

However, while the triplets' parents alleged in their due process requests that their children had been denied FAPE, they chose not to present evidence supporting their FAPE allegations. Therefore, no determination has ever been made as to whether the Board denied the triplets FAPE.

[17] [FN 2] The regulation has since been revised. The same language now appears in 34 C.F.R. § 300.518(b) (effective Oct. 13, 2006). Subsection (c) of the revised regulation reads, in part:

> If the complaint involves an application for initial services under this part from a child who is transitioning from Part C of the Act to Part B and is no longer eligible for Part C services because the child has turned three, the public agency is not required to provide the Part C services that the child had been receiving.

Our interpretation is also consistent with other agency guidance on the proper pendency placement for children transitioning from Part C to Part B of the IDEA. That guidance, issued by the Office of Special Education Programs within the Office of Special Education and Rehabilitative Services of the United States Department of Education, is published in the Federal Register with the implementing regulations for the statute. It states:

> Comment: A few commenters requested that the regulation be revised to make clear that the pendency provisions of § 300.514 apply to children transitioning from early intervention services under Part C to preschool special education and related services under Part B.
>
> Discussion: The pendency provision at § 300.514(a) does not apply when a child is transitioning from a program developed under Part C to provide appropriate early intervention services into a program developed under Part B to provide FAPE. Under § 300.514(b), if the complaint requesting due process involves the child's initial admission to public school, the public agency responsible for providing FAPE to the child must place that child, with the consent of the parent, into a public preschool program if the public agency offers preschool services directly or through contract or other arrangement to nondisabled preschool-aged children until the completion of authorized review proceedings.
>
> Changes: None.

64 Fed. Reg. 12,406, 12,558 (Mar. 12, 1999).

Because we rely on the plain language of the "stay put" provision, we do not engage in analysis to determine whether the agency's interpretation of the statute is reasonable and therefore entitled to deference. *See Chevron U.S.A., Inc. v. Natural Resources Defense Council, Inc.*, 467 U.S. 837, 842–43 (1984) (stating that, where the statute is clear, that is the "end of the matter"). We simply note its consistency with our reading.

Appellants argue that they should have been granted an injunction pursuant to the "stay put" provision or Fed. R. Civ. P. 65. But, we do not find any error in the district court's denial of the injunction. As stated above, the IDEA does not provide for continued provision of services to the triplets pursuant to their IFSPs. And, for that reason, Appellants did not (and cannot) carry their burden of demonstrating a substantial likelihood of success on the merits of their claim. . . .

The dissent claims that our holding is inconsistent with *M.M. ex rel. C.M. v. School Bd. of Miami-Dade County, Fla.*, 437 F.3d 1085 (11th Cir. 2006). It is not. *M.M.* does not hold (as the dissent states) that the plaintiffs in that case were eligible for reimbursement because their child had received early intervention services. To the contrary, our opinion in that case affirmed dismissal of the plaintiffs' claim for reimbursement because the complaint failed to state a claim that the child was denied FAPE. . . . And, though *M.M.* recognizes that reimbursement may be available for services rendered after a child's third birthday, that case does not hold that a school board can be enjoined to continue providing services previously

---

34 C.F.R. § 300.518(c).

rendered pursuant to an IFSP after a child's third birthday or even that, in the case where FAPE has been denied, all services previously rendered pursuant to an IFSP are reimbursable. As stated above, whether the triplets were denied FAPE is not at issue in this case.

The dissent characterizes the result that our holding produces as "absurd," using that word at least four times. We do not agree and take comfort in the fact that the Department of Education interprets the "stay put" provision as we do.

V. CONCLUSION

For the foregoing reasons, we affirm the judgments for the Board.

AFFIRMED.

BARKETT, CIRCUIT JUDGE, dissenting:

I would agree with the majority's application of the "stay put" provision's plain language — that the pendency placement for a child applying for initial admission to public school is only the public school — if this case involved a situation for which that part of the provision was intended; that is, for a school-aged, disabled child who had never received services under the IDEA and was applying for initial admission to public school. The triplets in this case, however, were receiving services under later amendments to the IDEA, which were designed to promote the development of children before they reach school age and assure their smooth transition into school when they reach school age. Thus I believe the majority errs by finding as a matter of law that the receipt of these services did not entitle the triplets to the continuation of services pending resolution of their placement dispute.

Although we are generally to apply a statutory provision's plain language, we must read that language in context, and consider the statute's overarching purpose in order to avoid absurd results. Congress enacted "stay put" provisions under both Part C and Part B of the IDEA — each of which, when read independently, prohibit the disruption of services during a placement dispute. Moreover, Congress made clear its intent that there be a smooth transition from one part of the statute to the other. Thus, it would be absurd to apply the "stay put" provision in a manner that reaches the completely opposite result: the withdrawal of existing services to a disabled child when she reaches school age.[18] Withdrawing necessary services at the moment of transition eviscerates the procedural protections Congress afforded

---

[18] [FN 3] In this case, the School Board refused to continue, or pay for the continuation of, the "early intervention services" the triplets had been receiving when they turned 3 on January 4, 2004; that is, right in the middle of the school year.

Although the majority is correct that in this case the School Board ultimately offered the triplets placement at a private school for children with autism (in the form of a proposed "temporary" IEP about a month after refusing to continue early intervention services), no such placement is mandated by the majority's reading of "stay put." The only placement required under the majority's opinion is enrollment in the public schools. Moreover, there is no indication that the private school placement the School Board belatedly offered the triplets in this case would have included the particular one-on-one services which they had been receiving. Thus, this accommodation would not have been the same as continuing those services already deemed to be necessary and appropriate for these children. It is precisely the

parents who challenge a proposed change in services, disrupts the smooth transition Congress expressly intended for children transitioning from one program to the other, and punishes children whose disabilities have been detected and addressed early under the statute, leaving them with no accommodation pending resolution of a placement dispute. The IDEA cannot reasonably be read to permit this result. Therefore, I respectfully dissent.

The "stay put" provision at issue was enacted in 1975, at a time when the IDEA's predecessor statute provided funding for special education and related services only to school-age children and did not provide for early intervention services to infants and toddlers. *See* Education for All Handicapped Children Act of 1975, S. 6, 94th Cong., 89 Stat. 773 (1975) ("EAHCA" or "the Act"). Because the statute did not yet provide for early intervention services to disabled infants and toddlers, its provisions were drafted with only school-age children in mind. The "stay put" provision assured that, pending the resolution of a placement dispute, a school-age child applying for initial admission to public school would be guaranteed placement in the public school program (rather than be excluded on the basis of disability), and that a child already in school with an educational placement under the IDEA would be entitled to maintain that placement until the dispute was resolved. The dual purposes of this procedural safeguard were clear: to guarantee access to public school, on the one hand, and to maintain special educational services where those were already being provided, on the other. The drafters of this provision could not have intended, or even anticipated, that once Congress amended the statute to also provide grants for early intervention services to disabled infants and toddlers, this "stay put" provision would be construed against the interests of a disabled child to result in the withdrawal of services pending the resolution of a placement dispute.

More than a decade later, in 1986, Congress enacted what we now know as Part C of the IDEA to address the developmental disabilities of handicapped infants and toddlers before those children reached school age (ages birth to 2, inclusive). *See* Education of the Handicapped Act Amendments of 1986, S. 2294, 99th Cong., 100 Stat. 1145 § 101(a) (1986) ("1986 Amendments"). In passing this legislation, Congress recognized that certain special education needs could be mitigated if children's developmental disabilities were addressed before they reached the age of 3. Congress thus developed a program to help states identify handicapped infants and toddlers and provide "early intervention services" to those children and their families. . . . Entities receiving federal funding for this purpose were to develop "individualized family service plans" ("IFSPs") that would identify each child's developmental needs and the particular services required to meet those needs. . . .

Notably, as it had done more than ten years before with Part B, Congress enacted a "stay put" provision for parents who disputed a proposed change in services now provided to handicapped infants and toddlers, to assure that those services too would be maintained during any dispute.[19] . . . Congress additionally

---

continuation of services pending a placement dispute that Congress sought to protect by enacting "stay put."

[19] [FN 9] The "stay put" provision relevant to the infants and toddlers program provides:

During the pendency of any proceeding or action involving a complaint by the parents of an infant or toddler with a disability, unless the State agency and the parents otherwise agree,

required that IFSPs state "the steps to be taken supporting the transition of the handicapped toddler to [special education] services provided [to school age children] under part B" where those services would be needed, *id.* at § 677(d)(7), thereby emphasizing the importance of a smooth transition from this new program into Part B.

As of 1986, then, it was clear that Congress intended to develop a framework for the continuous provision of services to handicapped children from birth through school age in order to promote their educational development. The 1986 amendments dovetailed with the existing law (providing for services for children ages 3 and up) by providing for early intervention services for children from birth to age 2, inclusive, and increasing the incentives to provide services for children ages 3 to 5.[20] The "stay put" provision pertaining to handicapped infants and toddlers guaranteed that parents could maintain the current level of early intervention services pending resolution of any dispute. Congress therefore intended that where services were provided under the IDEA (whether under Part B or Part C of the IDEA), those services would continue to be provided if a dispute arose as to a child's proper placement, until the dispute was resolved.

Indeed, Congress recognized that where early intervention and special education services would be provided by different entities, it would be "essential that the agencies coordinate their efforts to transition the child to the special education system operated by the local educational agency." H.R. No. 99-860, at 6, *as reprinted in* 1986 U.S.C.C.A.N. at 2407. The House Report also noted that speedy resolution of placement disputes in the infant and toddler program would be essential "because an infant's development is rapid and therefore undue delay could be potentially harmful." *Id.* at 14, *as reprinted in* 1986 U.S.C.C.A.N. at 2415.

Congress' intention to ensure a smooth transition from Part C to Part B became most prominent in the IDEA's 1991 amendments. *See* Individuals with Disabilities Education Act Amendments of 1991, S. 1106, 102nd Cong., 105 Stat. 587 (1991) ("1991 Amendments"). Congress expressly crafted those amendments "to facilitate the development of a comprehensive 'seamless' system of services for children, aged birth to 5, inclusive, and their families which will ensure . . . a smooth transition for children moving from early intervention programs under [Part C] to preschool programs under part B. . . ." H.R. No. 102-198, at 4 (1991), *as reprinted in* 1991 U.S.C.C.A.N. 310, 313. The House Report found that "it is critical that there will be no gap in services when a child turns three. . . ." *Id.* at 7, *as reprinted in* 1991 U.S.C.C.A.N. at 316.

To this end, the 1991 amendments (1) require that state educational agencies

---

the infant or toddler shall continue to receive the appropriate early intervention services currently being provided or, if applying for initial services, shall receive the services not in dispute.

20 U.S.C. § 1439(b) (2005).

[20] [FN 10] The requirement that attention be paid to the transition of handicapped infants and toddlers who would continue to require services when they reached school age protected against any interruption in services necessary for the child's development and education. Early intervention services were to include case management services designed to facilitate "the development of a transition plan to preschool services" where those would be needed. H.R. No. 99-860, at 8, *as reprinted in* 1986 U.S.C.C.A.N. 2401, 2408.

establish policies and procedures for the smooth transition from early intervention services to special education services in preschool programs, including an assurance that either an IEP or an IFSP is being implemented by the disabled child's third birthday; (2) allow educational agencies, with the parents' consent, to continue using IFSPs as IEPs for children ages 3 to 5; (3) authorize states and local educational agencies to use preschool grants to provide a FAPE to 2-year old children with disabilities who will turn 3 during the school year; (4) require that personnel be trained to coordinate transition services for children moving from early intervention services to special education services in preschool programs; (5) make transition arrangements available that involve the family; and (6) guarantee the right of parents or guardians to determine whether a disabled infant or toddler will accept or decline an early intervention service without jeopardizing other early intervention services. . . .

In short, these amendments were unambiguously designed to assure continuous services to disabled children from birth through school age notwithstanding any disputes and disagreements as to a child's placement. The majority errs by reading the "stay put" provision entirely outside this context and, having done so, reaches a result that is contrary to the history, design, and purpose of the IDEA. In order avoid an absurd result and give effect to the IDEA's procedural safeguards, we cannot read the "stay put" provision in isolation.

Nowhere could the absurd consequences of our failure to consider statutory language in context be clearer than under the facts presented in this case. The majority's interpretation of "stay put" allows for the actual withdrawal of services to the triplets in the middle of a school year (when they turned 3 years old), even though the School Board failed to meet its statutory obligation to have an IEP in place for the triplets when they reached the age of 3. This ruling thus has the surely unintended effect of allowing a school board to abdicate its obligation to develop IEPs for disabled infants and toddlers about to transition, and leaving those children and their parents with no effective recourse during the pendency of a placement dispute.[21] A procedural safeguard intended to protect the rights of disabled children during a placement dispute simply cannot reasonably be read to result in the withdrawal of services already identified as necessary to a child's educational development. This result is contrary to the purpose of the IDEA.

Relying solely on part of the "plain language" of the stay-put provision to conclude that the only placement for a disabled child who has reached school age and is therefore applying for initial admission to public school is a "public school

---

[21] [FN 12] The majority contends that the reimbursement remedy is sufficient, because aggrieved parents can simply pay for private educational services on their own during the pendency of the placement dispute, and then sue to recover those expenses if it is later determined that the school denied the child a FAPE. While the Supreme Court has noted that "conscientious parents who have adequate means and who are reasonably confident of their assessment" will often choose that course, *School Committee of Town of Burlington, Mass. v. Department of Educ. of Mass.*, 471 U.S. 359, 370 (1985), this is no remedy for parents who do not have the financial means to pay for private educational services in the first place. The IDEA's procedural safeguards promote access to a free and appropriate public education by protecting disabled children's current educational placements during a dispute as well as by providing for reimbursement when children are denied a FAPE under Part B and then seek private services on their own.

program" with no accommodation, the majority rejects the argument that the existing IFSP may constitute the triplets' then-current educational placement, so as to entitle them to continuation of those services pending the resolution of their dispute with the School Board. For the foregoing reasons, concluding as a matter of law that existing IFSPs cannot constitute a current educational placement is inconsistent with the statute, when read as a whole, as well as with its intent and purpose. This conclusion is also inconsistent with our reasoning in *M.M. ex rel. C.M. v. School Bd. of Miami-Dade County, Fla.*, 437 F.3d 1085 (11th Cir. 2006). In *M.M.*, we recognized that "early intervention services" previously provided under Part C — the same type of services the triplets had been receiving here — may also constitute "special education and related services" for purposes of establishing eligibility for reimbursement for private school expenses when a child is denied a FAPE. If "early intervention services" may constitute "special education services" for purposes of establishing eligibility for reimbursement under the IDEA, then they may also constitute a child's existing "educational placement" for purposes of "stay put." Like the triplets here, C.M. (the child of M.M.) had never been enrolled in public school (by virtue of not having yet reached school age), but had been provided early intervention services under the IDEA. Even though C.M. had never been enrolled in public school, we held that her parents were eligible for reimbursement for private school expenses because the early intervention services C.M. had previously received constituted "special education and related services under the authority of a public agency" for purposes of the reimbursement provision. *M.M.*, 437 F.3d at 1098. The majority errs by finding as a matter of law that the triplets did not have a current educational placement without considering, consistent with our case law, whether the "early intervention services" they received also constituted "special education and related services."

In *Pardini v. Allegheny Intermediate Unit*, 420 F.3d 181 (3d Cir. 2005), the Third Circuit found that Part B's "stay put" provision required the continuation of early intervention services to a child transitioning from Part C to Part B pending resolution of a placement dispute, because those services constituted the child's "educational placement," even though the child had not previously been admitted to public school. In reaching that conclusion, the Third Circuit took particular note of Congress' intention that children transitioning from Part C to Part B enjoy a smooth transition.[22] *See id.* at 191 ("Congress stressed that the amendments it added [to the IDEA] were 'designed to promote a seamless system of services for children with disabilities, aged birth to five, inclusive.' ") (citation omitted). Although the majority rejects our sister Circuit's decision in *Pardini* as "incorrectly decided," it fails to address how its ruling squares with our own reasoning in *M.M.*

For these reasons, I dissent.

---

[22] [FN 15] The Third Circuit also rejected the interpretation of "stay put" by the Department of Education, finding it to be unpersuasive in light of the purpose and design of the statute. . . . Indeed, an agency interpretation is not entitled to deference when it is not based on a permissible construction of the statute. *See Chevron U.S.A. Inc. v. Natural Res. Def. Council*, 467 U.S. 837, 842–44 (1984).

NOTES AND QUESTIONS

1. In Pennsylvania and a number of other states, the state public welfare agency is responsible for IDEA Part C services. This practice allows coordination with programs administered under the Developmental Disabilities Act, Medicaid, and other programs for which the department of public welfare is responsible. On the other hand, it increases the chances of interdepartmental disputes and of children falling through the cracks when the children reach their transition dates for Part B services. Do you think having the state educational agency be the administrator of Part C is a better practice? Are there issues of state politics that might arise in the decision over which agency is to take responsibility? Is it fair to make the Part B agency unit pay for the ongoing consequences of another agency's decision? Should it have a right of recovery for its costs from the department of public welfare or some other source? At the same time, is it fair to place the child and the parents in the middle of a dispute between two agencies and have the child suffer a loss of services because the agencies cannot agree who will pay? Would it be better to have one agency pay subject to later recovery from the other agency? The child will be passing developmental milestones while the dispute continues.

2. Which opinion has the better of the argument on the statutory construction, regulatory deference, and absurd-results issues? Do you expect that the Supreme Court will resolve the dispute between the circuit courts? Will Congress? Can the Department of Education resolve the issue? *See generally* 34 C.F.R. § 300.518(c) (new regulation discussed in *D.P.*, *supra*).

3. For additional discussion of transition issues, see Mark C. Weber & Mary Binkelman, *Legal Issues in the Transition to Public School for Handicapped Infants and Children*, 19 J.L. & EDUC. 193 (1990).

Chapter 14

POST-SECONDARY EDUCATION

A. INTRODUCTION

The Individuals with Disabilities Education Act guarantees education for children with disabilities only up through high school: "The term 'free appropriate public education' means special education and related services that — . . . (C) include an appropriate preschool, elementary, or secondary school education. . . ." 20 U.S.C. § 1401(9). For students past high school who need specialized services and accommodations, or who fear discrimination on account of disability, the sources of protection are section 504 of the Rehabilitation Act of 1973 and titles II and III of the Americans with Disabilities Act ("ADA"). Title I of the ADA covers employment; title II covers state and local government services, hence public colleges and universities; title III covers privately operated public accommodations, including private schools, though not religious institutions. Religious institutions' students are protected under section 504 if their schools receive federal money (and nearly all do).

Because federal funding triggers coverage under section 504 and is a universal feature of public higher education, state colleges and universities must obey both section 504 and title II. The duties under the statutes are essentially the same, however, so most authorities speak of a section 504-title II combination, or use one statute's name as a stand-in for both. For a more thorough discussion of section 504's relationship to the ADA, see Mark C. Weber, *Disability Discrimination by State and Local Government: The Relationship Between Section 504 of the Rehabilitation Act and Title II of the Americans with Disabilities Act*, 36 WM. & MARY L. REV. 1089 (1995). Title III of the ADA has a separate provision requiring accessibility by entities that offer examinations and courses relating to credentialing and related matters. 42 U.S.C. § 12189.

This chapter considers only issues of discrimination under section 504 and the ADA. It does not take up sources of assistance for higher education that may be available to students with disabilities, though education lawyers and administrators should be aware that public sources do provide some financial and in-kind support for students with disabilities. One avenue is the federal-state rehabilitation services program established by title I of the Rehabilitation Act, 29 U.S.C. §§ 701–797b. *See generally* Kyle Murray & Lelia B. Helms, *The Buck Stops Here: Graduate Level Disability Services and the 1998 Rehabilitation Act Amendments*, 28 J.C. & U.L. 1 (2001) (discussing rehabilitation services program funding issues). This chapter also does not consider claims that students may have under state disability statutes even though they may apply the same analytical framework as the ADA in determining liability. *See Bowers v. Nat'l Collegiate Athletic Ass'n*, 475 F.3d 524,

535 n.12 (3d Cir. 2007).

NOTES AND QUESTIONS

1.   Why did Congress stop with high school education when it drafted IDEA? Could there have been a stereotype at work — an implicit assumption that students with disabilities are unfit for higher education? Or is it simply that free public education does not generally extend beyond high school? How good are typical special education programs at preparing children with disabilities for success in college?

2.   Enrollment rates of students with disabilities in higher education are 50% lower than enrollment among the general population. President's Commission on Excellence in Special Education, A New Era: Revitalizing Special Education for Children and Their Families 1 (2002), *available at* http://www.ed.gov.inits/ commissionsboards/whspecialeducation/reports.html. Although few students with mental retardation might be expected to attend traditional collegiate programs, the number of those students is small, and their presence in the population of students with disabilities accounts for only a modest portion of the discrepancy. What accounts for the remainder?

3.   Do you think that the school you attend adequately accommodates students with disabilities? Should it be doing more? Less? If more, what is the highest priority?

B.   ELIGIBILITY FOR PROTECTION UNDER TITLE II AND SECTION 504

Title II and section 504 protect any person who is a "qualified individual with a disability." The ADA provides:

The term "disability" means, with respect to an individual —

(A) a physical or mental impairment that substantially limits one or more of the major life activities of an individual;

(B) a record of such an impairment; or

(C) being regarded as having such an impairment.

42 U.S.C. § 12102(2); *see* 29 U.S.C. § 705(20)(B) (similar provision pertaining to section 504).

Title II states:

The term "qualified individual with a disability" means an individual with a disability who, with or without reasonable modifications to rules, policies, or practices, the removal of architectural, communication, or transportation barriers, or the provision of auxiliary aids and services, meets the essential eligibility requirements for the receipt of services or the participation in programs or activities provided by a public entity.

42 U.S.C. § 12131; *see* 34 C.F.R. § 104.3(*l*)(3) (parallel regulation pertaining to section 504) ("With respect to postsecondary and vocational education services, a handicapped person who meets the academic and technical standards requisite to admission or participation in the recipient's education program or activity"). The section 504 regulations retain the use of the term "handicapped."

The definition of "qualified" thus brings into play issues of reasonableness and effectiveness of modifications, barrier removal, and auxiliary services, creating a circularity: the only people entitled to reasonable accommodations are those for whom the accommodations are reasonable. Because the definition relies on the accommodation requirement, the question of who is qualified is taken up in section C, *infra* (discussing reasonable accommodations and related topics).

The underlying definition of "individual with a disability" has led to significant litigation, although a greater portion of the decisions relate to employment rather than higher education. The same definitional issues exist in higher education cases as exist in employment cases, however. An individual with a disability has a physical or mental impairment that substantially limits one or more major life activities, or has such a record, or is so regarded. "Physical or mental impairment means (A) any physiological disorder or condition, cosmetic disfigurement, or anatomical loss affecting one or more of the following body systems: neurological; musculoskeletal; special sense organs; respiratory, including speech organs; cardiovascular; reproductive, digestive, genito-urinary; hemic and lymphatic; skin; and endocrine; or (B) any mental or psychological disorder, such as mental retardation, organic brain syndrome, emotional or mental illness, and specific learning disabilities," 34 C.F.R. § 104.3(j)(2)(ii), with the important caveat that the list is not exclusive. Major life activities include "functions such as caring for one's self, performing manual tasks, walking, seeing, hearing, speaking, breathing, learning, and working," 34 C.F.R. § 104.3(j)(2)(ii), but that list is not exclusive. Note that learning is specifically listed as a major life activity, just as specific learning disabilities are included as impairments. The ADA currently provides that "major life activities include, but are not limited to, caring for oneself, performing manual tasks, seeing, hearing, eating, sleeping, walking, standing, lifting, bending, speaking, breathing, learning, reading, concentrating, thinking, communicating, and working," and that "a major life activity also includes the operation of a major bodily function, including but not limited to, functions of the immune system, normal cell growth, digestive, bowel, bladder, neurological, brain, respiratory, circulatory, endocrine, and reproductive functions." 42 U.S.C. § 12102(2).

The Supreme Court has determined that a person with asymptomatic HIV infection is covered by the statute, *Bragdon v. Abbott*, 524 U.S. 624 (1998). However, in a trio of cases in 1999, the Supreme Court considered how mitigating measures, such as appliances, medications, even the body's own compensating systems, should be treated in determining whether a person has an impairment that substantially limits major life activities, or is regarded as having such an impairment. *Sutton v. United Air Lines*, 527 U.S. 471 (1999), ruled that would-be pilots who could see normally with eyeglasses were not individuals with disabilities, despite the fact that the company excluded them from global pilot jobs because of their visual impairments. The Court also rejected the contention that the job applicants were regarded by the employer as substantially limited in the life activity of working. *Murphy v.*

United Parcel Service, Inc., 527 U.S. 516 (1999), applied the same approach and reached the same result with regard to a mechanic who lost his job because his blood pressure exceeded limits imposed by the Department of Transportation for people driving commercial vehicles. Although his condition led to the loss of the job, when he was medicated, it placed no limits on his daily activities except for a restriction on heavy lifting, and limited his working only by excluding jobs that required driving commercial vehicles. In *Albertson's, Inc. v. Kirkingburg*, 527 U.S. 555 (1999), a truck driver lost his job for failure to meet Department of Transportation standards for binocular vision, even though his brain adequately compensated for the loss of vision in one eye. The Court held that the lower court incorrectly considered his vision in its unmitigated state in evaluating whether he was disabled. The Court further ruled that the employer did not need to consider the possibility of obtaining a waiver from the federal rule when it established job standards. In another case,, the Court reversed a grant of partial summary judgment for an employee on the issue of whether her impairments substantially limited the major life activity of performing manual tasks when the lower court did not ask whether the impairments prevented or restricted the employee from performing tasks that are of central importance in daily life, *Toyota Motor Mfg., Kentucky, Inc. v. Williams*, 534 U.S. 184 (2002).

The Americans with Disabilities Act Amendments, passed in 2008 and effective January 1, 2009, specifically disapproved *Sutton* and *Williams*, and provided for significantly expanded coverage of persons with disabilities under the ADA and section 504. The Amendments adopted the list of major life activities quoted above, and further provided that the definition of disability shall be construed in favor of broad coverage, that episodic impairments and those in remission are disabilities if they would substantially limit a major life activity when active, and that mitigating measures, except for ordinary eyeglasses, are not to be considered in determining whether an impairment substantially limits a major life activity. 42 U.S.C. § 12102(4). A person meets the requirement of being regarded as having an impairment if it is established that he or she was subjected to discrimination because of an actual or perceived physical or mental impairment whether or not the impairment limits or is perceived to limit a major life activity, but the regarded-as provision does not apply to impairments that are transitory and minor. § 12102(3).

Generally speaking, students in colleges and universities have the obligation to provide documentation to establish eligibility for modifications, barrier removal, and auxiliary services. However, some documentation requirements have been found to violate the law because they are unnecessarily onerous. *See Guckenberger v. Boston Univ*, 974 F. Supp. 106 (D. Mass. 1997) (also invalidating some aspects of policy for obtaining accommodations as discriminatory); *see also Abdo v. University of Vermont*, 263 F. Supp. 2d 772 (D. Vt. 2003) (finding appropriate university's request for detailed documentation from student to demonstrate that major life function had been substantially limited, but also finding that letters from student's doctor satisfied university's request because they identified cause and nature of disability, even though they failed to recite specific diagnosis).

NOTES AND QUESTIONS

1. Why was there so much litigation on the question whether a person is disabled under the ADA? There has been no comparable spate of cases on whether, for example, someone bringing a title VII case is a member of a racial minority, even though there is no agreed-upon definition of what a racial minority is. Do you expect the litigation on the issue to continue now that the ADA Amendments Act has taken effect?

2. For purposes of coverage of a child under the Individuals with Disabilities Education Act, learning disabilities are sometimes evaluated on the basis of the discrepancy between an individual's measured ability and performance. Should this approach be used in determining coverage under the ADA or section 504? A number of courts have insisted that the comparison relevant for coverage under the ADA is the level of performance that the individual displays in comparison to the population as a whole, rather than in comparison to that person's abilities or to the performance of the population in the student's program. Thus, a pre-enrollment medical student might read very poorly in comparison to his overall cognitive ability or in comparison to other medical students, but might still be in the average range in comparison to the population as a whole, and so is not deemed disabled under the ADA. *See Betts v. Rector & Visitors of the Univ. of Va.*, 113 F. Supp. 2d 970 (W.D. Va. 2000); *see also Gonzalez v. National Bd. of Med. Exam'rs*, 225 F.3d 620 (6th Cir. 2000). For a good discussion of this comparison with regard to students already in medical school, see *Price v. National Bd. of Med. Examiners*, 966 F. Supp. 419, 427–28 (S.D. W. Va. 1997). Does this approach make sense, or should the comparison be to the individual's cognitive ability or the relevant student group?

C.   QUALIFIED INDIVIDUAL/REASONABLE ACCOMMODATION

1.   In General

Under the section 504 regulations, accommodations include academic adjustments, exemptions from rules, changes in examinations, and the furnishing of auxiliary aids. For a school, academic adjustments are "such modifications to its academic requirements as are necessary to ensure that such requirements do not discriminate or have the effect of discriminating" against a student who is qualified. "Modifications may include changes in the length of time permitted for the completion of degree requirements, substitution of specific courses required for the completion of degree requirements, and adaptation of the manner in which specific courses are conducted." 34 C.F.R. § 104.44(a). "A recipient to which this subpart applies may not impose upon handicapped students other rules, such as the prohibition of tape recorders in classrooms or of dog guides in campus buildings, that have the effect of limiting the participation of handicapped students in the recipient's education program or activity." Testing accommodations are considered *infra* section D. "Auxiliary aids may include taped texts, interpreters or other effective methods of making orally delivered materials available to students with hearing impairments, readers in libraries for students with visual impairments, classroom equipment adapted for use by students with manual impairments, and other similar services and actions. Recipients need not provide attendants, individually prescribed devices, readers for personal use or study, or other devices or services of a personal nature." 34 C.F.R. § 104.44(d)(2).

If participation of a person with a disability requires more than these sorts of modifications and would work an alteration of the program, the person is not qualified. The following case develops the contrast between required modifications and not-required program alterations, all in the context of determining whether an individual is qualified.

SOUTHEASTERN COMMUNITY COLLEGE v. DAVIS
442 U.S. 397 (1979)

In this case, the Supreme Court ruled that substitution of a portion of a nurse training program for a student who had a serious hearing impairment went beyond what section 504 requires.

JUSTICE POWELL delivered the opinion of the Court.

This case presents a matter of first impression for this Court: Whether § 504 of the Rehabilitation Act of 1973, which prohibits discrimination against an "otherwise qualified handicapped individual" in federally funded programs "solely by reason of his handicap," forbids professional schools from imposing physical qualifications for admission to their clinical training programs.

I

Respondent, who suffers from a serious hearing disability, seeks to be trained as a registered nurse. During the 1973-1974 academic year she was enrolled in the College Parallel program of Southeastern Community College, a state institution that receives federal funds. Respondent hoped to progress to Southeastern's Associate Degree Nursing program, completion of which would make her eligible for state certification as a registered nurse. In the course of her application to the nursing program, she was interviewed by a member of the nursing faculty. It became apparent that respondent had difficulty understanding questions asked, and on inquiry she acknowledged a history of hearing problems and dependence on a hearing aid. She was advised to consult an audiologist.

On the basis of an examination at Duke University Medical Center, respondent was diagnosed as having a "bilateral, sensori-neural hearing loss." A change in her hearing aid was recommended, as a result of which it was expected that she would be able to detect sounds "almost as well as a person would who has normal hearing." But this improvement would not mean that she could discriminate among sounds sufficiently to understand normal spoken speech. Her lipreading skills would remain necessary for effective communication: "While wearing the hearing aid, she is well aware of gross sounds occurring in the listening environment. However, she can only be responsible for speech spoken to her, when the talker gets her attention and allows her to look directly at the talker."

Southeastern next consulted Mary McRee, Executive Director of the North Carolina Board of Nursing. On the basis of the audiologist's report, McRee recommended that respondent not be admitted to the nursing program. In McRee's view, respondent's hearing disability made it unsafe for her to practice as a nurse.[1] In addition, it would be impossible for respondent to participate safely in the normal clinical training program, and those modifications that would be necessary to enable safe participation would prevent her from realizing the benefits of the program: "To adjust patient learning experiences in keeping with [respondent's] hearing limitations could, in fact, be the same as denying her full learning to meet the objectives of your nursing programs."

After respondent was notified that she was not qualified for nursing study because of her hearing disability, she requested reconsideration of the decision. The entire nursing staff of Southeastern was assembled, and McRee again was consulted. McRee repeated her conclusion that on the basis of the available evidence, respondent "has hearing limitations which could interfere with her safely caring for patients." Upon further deliberation, the staff voted to deny respondent admission.

Respondent then filed suit in the United States District Court for the Eastern District of North Carolina, alleging both a violation of § 504 of the Rehabilitation Act of 1973, and a denial of equal protection and due process. After a bench trial, the District Court entered judgment in favor of Southeastern. 424 F. Supp. 1341 (1976). It confirmed the findings of the audiologist that even with a hearing aid respondent cannot understand speech directed to her except through lipreading, and further found:

> "[I]n many situations such as an operation room intensive care unit, or post-natal care unit, all doctors and nurses wear surgical masks which would make lip reading impossible. Additionally, in many situations a Registered Nurse would be required to instantly follow the physician's instructions concerning procurement of various types of instruments and drugs where the physician would be unable to get the nurse's attention by other than vocal means." *Id.* at 1343.

Accordingly, the court concluded:

> "[Respondent's] handicap actually prevents her from safely performing in both her training program and her proposed profession. The trial testimony indicated numerous situations where [respondent's] particular dis-

---

[1] [FN 1] McRee also wrote that respondent's hearing disability could preclude her practicing safely in "any setting" allowed by "a license as L[icensed] P[ractical] N[urse]." Respondent contends that inasmuch as she already was licensed as a practical nurse, McRee's opinion was inherently incredible. But the record indicates that respondent had "not worked as a licensed practical nurse except to do a little bit of private duty," and had not done that for several years before applying to Southeastern. Accordingly, it is at least possible to infer that respondent in fact could not work safely as a practical nurse in spite of her license to do so. In any event, we note the finding of the District Court that "a Licensed Practical Nurse, unlike a Licensed Registered Nurse, operates under constant supervision and is not allowed to perform medical tasks which require a great degree of technical sophistication." 424 F. Supp. 1341, 1342–1343 (E.D.N.C. 1976).

ability would render her unable to function properly. Of particular concern to the court in this case is the potential of danger to future patients in such situations." *Id.* at 1345.

Based on these findings, the District Court concluded that respondent was not an "otherwise qualified handicapped individual" protected against discrimination by § 504. In its view, "[o]therwise qualified, can only be read to mean otherwise able to function sufficiently in the position sought in spite of the handicap, if proper training and facilities are suitable and available." 424 F. Supp. at 1345. Because respondent's disability would prevent her from functioning "sufficiently" in Southeastern's nursing program, the court held that the decision to exclude her was not discriminatory within the meaning of § 504.

On appeal, the Court of Appeals for the Fourth Circuit reversed. 574 F.2d 1158 (1978). It did not dispute the District Court's findings of fact, but held that the court had misconstrued § 504. In light of administrative regulations that had been promulgated while the appeal was pending, the appellate court believed that § 504 required Southeastern to "reconsider plaintiff's application for admission to the nursing program without regard to her hearing ability." 574 F.2d at 1160. It concluded that the District Court had erred in taking respondent's handicap into account in determining whether she was "otherwise qualified" for the program, rather than confining its inquiry to her "academic and technical qualifications." *Id.* at 1161. The Court of Appeals also suggested that § 504 required "affirmative conduct" on the part of Southeastern to modify its program to accommodate the disabilities of applicants, "even when such modifications become expensive." 574 F.2d at 1162.

Because of the importance of this issue to the many institutions covered by § 504, we granted certiorari. . . . We now reverse.

II

As previously noted, this is the first case in which this Court has been called upon to interpret § 504. It is elementary that "[t]he starting point in every case involving construction of a statute is the language itself." *Blue Chip Stamps v. Manor Drug Stores*, 421 U.S. 723, 756 (1975) (POWELL, J., concurring). . . . Section 504 by its terms does not compel educational institutions to disregard the disabilities of handicapped individuals or to make substantial modifications in their programs to allow disabled persons to participate. Instead, it requires only that an "otherwise qualified handicapped individual" not be excluded from participation in a federally funded program "solely by reason of his handicap," indicating only that mere possession of a handicap is not a permissible ground for assuming an inability to function in a particular context.

The court below, however, believed that the "otherwise qualified" persons protected by § 504 include those who would be able to meet the requirements of a particular program in every respect except as to limitations imposed by their handicap. *See* 574 F.2d at 1160. Taken literally, this holding would prevent an institution from taking into account any limitation resulting from the handicap, however disabling. It assumes, in effect, that a person need not meet legitimate physical requirements in order to be "otherwise qualified." We think the understanding of the District Court is closer to the plain meaning of the statutory language. An otherwise qualified person is one who is able to meet all of a program's requirements in spite of his handicap.

The regulations promulgated by the Department of HEW to interpret § 504 reinforce, rather than contradict, this conclusion. According to these regulations, a "[q]ualified handicapped person" is, "[w]ith respect to postsecondary and vocational education services, a handicapped person who meets the academic and technical standards requisite to admission or participation in the [school's] education program or activity. . . ." 45 CFR § 84.3(k)(3) (1978). An explanatory note states:

> "The term 'technical standards' refers to *all* nonacademic admissions criteria that are essential to participation in the program in question." 45 CFR pt. 84, App. A, p. 405 (1978) (emphasis supplied).

A further note emphasizes that legitimate physical qualifications may be essential to participation in particular programs.[2] We think it clear, therefore, that HEW interprets the "other" qualifications which a handicapped person may be required to meet as including necessary physical qualifications.

III

The remaining question is whether the physical qualifications Southeastern demanded of respondent might not be necessary for participation in its nursing program. It is not open to dispute that, as Southeastern's Associate Degree Nursing program currently is constituted, the ability to understand speech without reliance on lipreading is necessary for patient safety during the clinical phase of the program. As the District Court found, this ability also is indispensable for many of the functions that a registered nurse performs.

Respondent contends nevertheless that § 504, properly interpreted, compels Southeastern to undertake affirmative action that would dispense with the need for effective oral communication. First, it is suggested that respondent can be given individual supervision by faculty members whenever she attends patients directly. Moreover, certain required courses might be dispensed with altogether for respondent. It is not necessary, she argues, that Southeastern train her to undertake all the tasks a registered nurse is licensed to perform. Rather, it is sufficient to make § 504 applicable if respondent might be able to perform satisfactorily some of the

---

[2] [FN 7] The note states:

> "Paragraph (k) of § 84.3 defines the term 'qualified handicapped person.' Throughout the regulation, this term is used instead of the statutory term 'otherwise qualified handicapped person.' The Department believes that the omission of the word 'otherwise' is necessary in order to comport with the intent of the statute because, read literally, 'otherwise' qualified handicapped persons include persons who are qualified except for their handicap, rather than in spite of their handicap. Under such a literal reading, a blind person possessing all the qualifications for driving a bus except sight could be said to be 'otherwise qualified' for the job of driving. Clearly, such a result was not intended by Congress. In all other respects, the terms 'qualified' and 'otherwise qualified' are intended to be interchangeable." 45 CFR pt. 84, App. A, p. 405 (1978).

duties of a registered nurse or to hold some of the positions available to a registered nurse.[3]

Respondent finds support for this argument in portions of the HEW regulations discussed above. In particular, a provision applicable to postsecondary educational programs requires covered institutions to make "modifications" in their programs to accommodate handicapped persons, and to provide "auxiliary aids" such as sign-language interpreters. Respondent argues that this regulation imposes an obligation to ensure full participation in covered programs by handicapped individuals and, in particular, requires Southeastern to make the kind of adjustments that would be necessary to permit her safe participation in the nursing program.

We note first that on the present record it appears unlikely respondent could benefit from any affirmative action that the regulation reasonably could be interpreted as requiring. Section 84.44(d)(2), for example, explicitly excludes "devices or services of a personal nature" from the kinds of auxiliary aids a school must provide a handicapped individual. Yet the only evidence in the record indicates that nothing less than close, individual attention by a nursing instructor would be sufficient to ensure patient safety if respondent took part in the clinical phase of the nursing program. See 424 F. Supp. at 1346. Furthermore, it also is reasonably clear that § 84.44(a) does not encompass the kind of curricular changes that would be necessary to accommodate respondent in the nursing program. In light of respondent's inability to function in clinical courses without close supervision, Southeastern, with prudence, could allow her to take only academic classes. Whatever benefits respondent might realize from such a course of study, she would not receive even a rough equivalent of the training a nursing program normally gives. Such a fundamental alteration in the nature of a program is far more than the "modification" the regulation requires.

Moreover, an interpretation of the regulations that required the extensive modifications necessary to include respondent in the nursing program would raise grave doubts about their validity. If these regulations were to require substantial adjustments in existing programs beyond those necessary to eliminate discrimination against otherwise qualified individuals, they would do more than clarify the meaning of § 504. Instead, they would constitute an unauthorized extension of the obligations imposed by that statute.

The language and structure of the Rehabilitation Act of 1973 reflect a recognition

---

[3] [FN 8] The court below adopted a portion of this argument:

"[Respondent's] ability to read lips aids her in overcoming her hearing disability; however, it was argued that in certain situations such as in an operating room environment where surgical masks are used, this ability would be unavailing to her.

"Be that as it may, in the medical community, there does appear to be a number of settings in which the plaintiff could perform satisfactorily as an RN, such as in industry or perhaps a physician's office. Certainly [respondent] could be viewed as possessing extraordinary insight into the medical and emotional needs of those with hearing disabilities.

"If [respondent] meets all the other criteria for admission in the pursuit of her RN career, under the relevant North Carolina statutes, N.C. Gen. Stat. §§ 90-158, et seq., it should not be foreclosed to her simply because she may not be able to function effectively in all the roles which registered nurses may choose for their careers."

574 F.2d 1158, 1161 n. 6 (1978).

by Congress of the distinction between the evenhanded treatment of qualified handicapped persons and affirmative efforts to overcome the disabilities caused by handicaps. Section 501(b), governing the employment of handicapped individuals by the Federal Government, requires each federal agency to submit "an affirmative action program plan for the hiring, placement, and advancement of handicapped individuals. . . ." These plans "shall include a description of the extent to which and methods whereby the special needs of handicapped employees are being met." Similarly, § 503(a), governing hiring by federal contractors, requires employers to "take affirmative action to employ and advance in employment qualified handicapped individuals. . . ." The President is required to promulgate regulations to enforce this section.

Under § 501(c) of the Act, by contrast, state agencies such as Southeastern are only "encourage[d] . . . to adopt and implement such policies and procedures." Section 504 does not refer at all to affirmative action, and except as it applies to federal employers it does not provide for implementation by administrative action. A comparison of these provisions demonstrates that Congress understood accommodation of the needs of handicapped individuals may require affirmative action and knew how to provide for it in those instances where it wished to do so.

Although an agency's interpretation of the statute under which it operates is entitled to some deference, "this deference is constrained by our obligation to honor the clear meaning of a statute, as revealed by its language, purpose, and history." *Teamsters v. Daniel*, 439 U.S. 551, 566 n. 20 (1979). Here, neither the language, purpose, nor history of § 504 reveals an intent to impose an affirmative-action obligation on all recipients of federal funds. Accordingly, we hold that even if HEW has attempted to create such an obligation itself, it lacks the authority to do so.

IV

We do not suggest that the line between a lawful refusal to extend affirmative action and illegal discrimination against handicapped persons always will be clear. It is possible to envision situations where an insistence on continuing past requirements and practices might arbitrarily deprive genuinely qualified handicapped persons of the opportunity to participate in a covered program. Technological advances can be expected to enhance opportunities to rehabilitate the handicapped or otherwise to qualify them for some useful employment. Such advances also may enable attainment of these goals without imposing undue financial and administrative burdens upon a State. Thus, situations may arise where a refusal to modify an existing program might become unreasonable and discriminatory. Identification of those instances where a refusal to accommodate the needs of a disabled person amounts to discrimination against the handicapped continues to be an important responsibility of HEW.

In this case, however, it is clear that Southeastern's unwillingness to make major adjustments in its nursing program does not constitute such discrimination. The uncontroverted testimony of several members of Southeastern's staff and faculty established that the purpose of its program was to train persons who could serve the nursing profession in all customary ways. This type of purpose, far from reflecting any animus against handicapped individuals is shared by many if not most of the institutions that train persons to render professional service. It is undisputed that respondent could not participate in Southeastern's nursing program unless the standards were substantially lowered. Section 504 imposes no requirement upon an educational institution to lower or to effect substantial modifications of standards to accommodate a handicapped person.[4]

One may admire respondent's desire and determination to overcome her handicap, and there well may be various other types of service for which she can qualify. In this case, however, we hold that there was no violation of § 504 when Southeastern concluded that respondent did not qualify for admission to its program. Nothing in the language or history of § 504 reflects an intention to limit the freedom of an educational institution to require reasonable physical qualifications for admission to a clinical training program. Nor has there been any showing in this case that any action short of a substantial change in Southeastern's program would render unreasonable the qualifications it imposed.

V

Accordingly, we reverse the judgment of the court below, and remand for proceedings consistent with this opinion.

So ordered.

NOTES AND QUESTIONS

1.　In *Alexander v. Choate*, 469 U.S. 287 (1985), the Court described *Davis'* distinction between affirmative action and reasonable accommodation as one between substantial or fundamental changes and reasonable accommodations. *Id.* at 300 n.20. Does the "affirmative action" language in *Davis* clarify the relevant distinction or obscure it?

2.　Section 104.44(a) of the section 504 regulations provides that "Academic requirements that the recipient can demonstrate are essential to the instruction being pursued by such student or to any directly related licensing requirement will not be regarded as discriminatory within the meaning of this section." However, should some form of limited licensing, such as licensing for non-operating room settings, be a reasonable accommodation from a nurse licensure board for a nurse who cannot hear? If that is the case, would substitution of other activities for

---

[4] [FN 12] Respondent contends that it is unclear whether North Carolina law requires a registered nurse to be capable of performing all functions open to that profession in order to obtain a license to practice, although McRee, the Executive Director of the State Board of Nursing, had informed Southeastern that the law did so require. *See* App. 138a-139a. Respondent further argues that even if she is not capable of meeting North Carolina's present licensing requirements, she still might succeed in obtaining a license in another jurisdiction.

Respondent's argument misses the point. Southeastern's program, structured to train persons who will be able to perform all normal roles of a registered nurse, represents a legitimate academic policy, and is accepted by the State. In effect, it seeks to ensure that no graduate will pose a danger to the public in any professional role in which he or she might be cast. Even if the licensing requirements of North Carolina or some other State are less demanding, nothing in the Act requires an educational institution to lower its standards.

operating-room nursing make sense as an accommodation in a nursing education program? Most professionals recognize that broad scale licensures do not qualify them to perform all tasks for which they are licensed. For example, many, if not most persons licensed as attorneys would be hopelessly out of their depth trying a complex antitrust case or setting up an insurance company demutualization. Can a general license be given to a person who has physical limits on performing some tasks, and can the licensure system trust that the individual will respect his or her own limits? Does the analysis differ when the disabling condition is mental rather than physical?

LANE v. PENA

867 F. Supp. 1050 (D.D.C. 1994), *vacated in part*,
aff'd, No. 95-5006, 1995 U.S. App. LEXIS 20039 (D.C. Cir. June 5, 1995),
aff'd, 518 U.S. 187 (1996)

In this case, the court ruled that a student may not be excluded from the Merchant Marine Academy despite his diabetic condition.

RICHEY, DISTRICT JUDGE.

INTRODUCTION

Before the Court in the above-captioned case are the parties' cross-Motions for Summary Judgment, as well as their oppositions and replies thereto. . . .

The Plaintiff filed a preliminary injunction seeking reinstatement to the United States Merchant Marine Academy ("USMMA" or "Academy"). He was admitted to the Academy in July of 1991. Thereafter he developed diabetes but managed to complete his first year. In September of 1992, the Academy informed him that he would be disenrolled due to his medical condition. The Plaintiff argues that the Defendants' actions violate both the Maritime Education and Training Act of 1980, 46 App. U.S.C. § 1295 ("META"), and Section 504 of the Rehabilitation Act of 1973, 29 U.S.C. § 794 *et seq.* ("Section 504"). In his motion, the Plaintiff seeks a preliminary and permanent injunction requiring the Academy to reinstate Lane immediately, compensatory damages, including out-of-pocket costs, loss of professional opportunity, and pain and suffering, attorneys' fees, and costs.

The Defendants argue, in sum, that the META imposes on USMMA graduates an obligation to serve in an armed forces reserve unit upon graduation as a condition of receiving an education at the Academy. The Defendants contend that the Plaintiff cannot satisfy his reserve service obligation because he has insulin-dependent diabetes mellitus and, therefore, does not meet the physical standards established by the Department of Defense for a commission in the armed forces reserve. According to the Defendants, the Plaintiff cannot satisfy an essential statutory requirement as a condition of attending the Academy and, therefore, he cannot be considered an "otherwise qualified person with a disability" for purposes of Section 504 of the Rehabilitation Act. The Defendants further argue that the agency's interpretation of the statute warrants due deference by the Court, and assert sovereign immunity with respect to damages.

Alternatively, the Plaintiff argues, in sum, that the META nowhere authorizes the *per se* exclusion of a student simply because he has a medical condition which precludes admission into the naval reserve, when that same condition in no way limits the student's ability to serve in the merchant marine.[5] He further argues that the META mandates only that students qualify for a merchant marine license — not that they also qualify to serve in the naval reserve — and contends that he is eligible for a merchant marine license. Moreover, the Plaintiff maintains that the Court need not afford the agency deference because it has not consistently followed their alleged practice of disenrolling cadets who fail to meet the requirements for a naval reserve commission, and because the plain language of the META demonstrates that no such practice is required. Finally, the Plaintiff asserts that Section 504 was also violated because he was denied the opportunity to complete his education at a federally funded academic institution solely because he developed a disability.

Upon careful consideration of the papers filed by both parties for dispositive relief, the oral arguments of counsel, the applicable law, and the entire record in this case, the Court has determined that the Plaintiff's Motion shall be granted, and the Defendants' Motion shall be denied.

The Court finds that the Defendants violated Section 504 of the Rehabilitation Act by disenrolling Lane solely on the basis of his diabetes and without making any attempt to reasonably accommodate his disability. The Stipulated Facts reveal that James Griffin Lane has repeatedly achieved an "outstanding" rating on the physical readiness exam administered by the Academy, that it is undisputed that James Griffin Lane may qualify for a merchant marine license if he maintains control of his diabetes, that his physician has reported that his diabetes mellitus is under "extremely good control," and that the Academy has allowed students in the past with a lost limb, a lost eye, brain damage, and color blindness to remain at the Academy and graduate despite their disabilities. Nevertheless, the Defendants now refuse to acknowledge that the Rehabilitation Act requires any reasonable accommodation — or even an attempt to provide reasonable accommodation — of Lane's diabetes mellitus. The Court simply cannot accept this untenable reading of the Rehabilitation Act. The Court thus finds that the Defendants have not shown that Lane has failed to meet an essential program requirement under Section 504 or, critically, that the Academy would suffer undue hardship by reasonably accommodating the diabetes mellitus of this otherwise extremely well qualified cadet.

The Defendants argue that the META dictated their disenrollment of Lane. However, the Court further finds that the plain language of the META does no such thing. Neither the statute, the regulations promulgated thereunder, nor the agency's inconsistent practices support the Defendants' position that the Academy was obliged to disenroll Lane upon discovery of his diabetes mellitus. The Court finds that, despite the Defendants' assertions to the contrary, the META contains no requirement that cadets such as Lane meet all physical requirements for a

---

[5] [FN 1] The Plaintiff does not challenge the Department of Defense's determination that diabetes mellitus prevents an individual from meeting requisite physical qualifications for participation in the armed forces reserve. He only argues that eligibility for the reserve is not a requirement for continued enrollment in the Academy, and that he meets all necessary requirements.

commission in the armed forces reserve or suffer unconditional expulsion from the Academy. Moreover, the Court finds that the agency's reading of the META does not warrant due deference because it is contradicted by the plain language of the statute, and because the USMMA has acted inconsistently with respect to Lane and other disabled students.

Accordingly, the Court shall order the United States Merchant Marine Academy to reinstate forthwith Plaintiff James Griffin Lane as a student at the USMMA, and shall require the Defendants to take all steps necessary to permit Lane to resume his maritime training as soon as practicable. Finally, the Court finds that the Plaintiff is entitled to compensatory damages for his injuries.

. . . .

BACKGROUND

In 1990, the Plaintiff, James Griffin Lane, applied for an appointment to the U.S. Merchant Marine Academy, a federal service academy that trains men and women to serve as commercial merchant marine officers and as commissioned officers in the United States armed forces. As a condition of his appointment, the Plaintiff was required to undergo a physical examination to determine if he met the requisite physical qualifications. On November 29, 1990, the Department of Defense Medical Examination Review Board ("DODMERB") administered the examination. Two days earlier, the Plaintiff had submitted a medical history form which asked whether he had at any time "blood, protein, or sugar in urine;" to this, he answered "no." The results of a urinalysis test administered later by DODMERB were "negative" for sugar in the urine. On June 4, 1991, DODMERB stamped on the Plaintiff's medical evaluation form that he was "medically qualified" and "recommended for service academies and ROTC programs," and the Plaintiff entered the Academy the next month.

On February 1, 1991, Lane consulted a private family physician and reported excessive thirst and hunger. A test showed he had an elevated blood sugar level, and the doctor directed the Plaintiff to limit his intake of calories and take an oral hypoglycemic medication to reduce his blood sugar level. Over a period of seven weeks, Lane's blood sugar level fluctuated between the normal range and higher. In September or October of that year, the Plaintiff had the flu and began to lose weight and again experience excessive thirst and hunger. In December 1991, the Plaintiff was diagnosed with diabetes mellitus by Dr. Didace Kabatsi, a private endocrinologist, who performed several tests on blood and urine samples.

On February 11, 1992, Lane visited Dr. Daniel Kalash, Chief Medical Officer at the Academy, who recorded in his notes that the Plaintiff advised that he had an "intermittent history during [the] past several months of glycosuria [sugar in the urine] and [elevated] blood sugar" and that he had been treated for his condition. He further recorded that the Plaintiff reported he was monitoring his "blood sugar in [his] barracks" and that "all findings [were] normal." Finally, he made the following notes: "Assess: Early Diabetes type I" and "Capt. Bauer notified & communicated problem to BuMed." At that time, Bauer was the Head of the Department of Naval Science at the Academy. Dr. Kalash instructed the Plaintiff to continue observing his blood sugars and report abnormalities and symptoms, and told him that he would repeat the lab workup at the end of the Plaintiff's third class, or sophomore year.

In March 1992, the Plaintiff consulted Dr. Jay Skyler, an endocrinologist at the University of Miami, and President of the American Diabetes Association. Dr. Skyler confirmed that Lane had diabetes, recommended insulin therapy, and referred him to Dr. S. Mark Tanen, an endocrinologist in Northern Virginia. In early July 1992, shortly before commencing his second year, the Plaintiff began seeing Dr. Tanen and, upon Dr. Tanen's recommendation, began insulin therapy.

In a letter dated July 23, 1992, the Plaintiff's father, J.W. Lane, Jr., notified Paul Krinsky, the Superintendent of the Academy, that his son had began taking insulin to control his diabetes. On September 4, 1992, the Plaintiff learned that a Physical Examination Review Board ("PERB") hearing had been scheduled for September 8, 1992 to determine his "medical suitability for continuance" at the Academy. The hearing was to confirm that the Plaintiff had insulin-dependent diabetes mellitus, as indicated in his father's July 23, 1992 letter. At the hearing, which Lane attended unaccompanied, the PERB did not evaluate the particular circumstances of Lane's case other than verify his status as a diabetic.

On September 16, 1992, the PERB advised the Superintendent of the Academy that the Plaintiff had insulin-dependent diabetes and that, under U.S. Navy commissioning standards, this was "a disqualifying condition for military service" and, accordingly, that the Plaintiff "would not be commissionable in the Navy/ Merchant Marine Reserve Program." The PERB further advised, however, that Lane may not be ineligible for a Coast Guard merchant marine license as the "requirements do not seem to be as rigid as the Navy requirements but a waiver is required when an applicant is insulin-dependent and may not be automatic[;] it would depend on the specifics of the condition."

In contrast to the Department of the Navy, the United States Coast Guard grants merchant marine licenses, including those which permit holders to serve as deck officers at sea, to persons with diabetes mellitus who obtain a waiver of Coast Guard physical qualifications standards with respect to diabetes. Waivers are issued to individuals who show to the Coast Guard's satisfaction that their diabetes is under control and that they are otherwise physically qualified for a merchant marine license. As of December 1993, more than fifty persons with diabetes, some insulin-dependent, are sailing on an active merchant marine license.

On September 21, 1992, the Superintendent advised the Plaintiff that he would be separated from the Academy effective December 18, 1992, and stated that "Adult-onset (Type I) diabetes is a disqualifying condition for military service. You are not eligible for appointment as Midshipman, MMR/USNR nor for commissioning as a Naval Reserve Officer." The Superintendent advised Lane that he would be permitted to continue to take classes at the Academy through December 18, 1992, and thus complete the first half of his sophomore year. This did not include participation in shipboard training, however.

Lane achieved a 3.4 grade point average during his first year at the Academy, rowed crew, and participated in various sea-going activities, including a four to five day journey up the East Coast in a tugboat, during which storm conditions caused the boat to undergo 40 degree rolls. The Plaintiff's medical records contain no indication that he had any medical problems associated with these activities, and in November 1992, Lane achieved an "outstanding" rating on the physical readiness exam administered by the Academy, as he had achieved each time it was administered previously. In December 1992, Dr. Tanen concluded that Lane's diabetes was under "extremely good control" and noted that he had not experienced any incapacitating episodes due to his condition.

In early October 1992, the Plaintiff's father wrote to Captain Warren G. LeBack, then-Administrator of the U.S. Maritime Administration ("MARAD"), to challenge the Superintendent's decision. In a letter dated January 15, 1993, LeBack responded to the Plaintiff's request for a review of the decision, and between January 15, 1993 and April 15, 1994, the Plaintiff took steps to obtain the assurances specified in the January 15, 1993 letter.

On April 15, 1994, MARAD Administrator A.J. Herberger issued a letter to Lane stating, in part, that Lane could not meet physical qualifications standards applicable to midshipmen at the USMMA because "insulin dependent diabetes disqualifies an individual from receiving a commission in any component of the reserve of the armed forces of the United States."

The Department of the Navy has consistently applied the same physical qualifications standards with respect to diabetes mellitus, which is a disqualifying condition for commissioning in all active duty and reserve units of the armed forces. In recent years, however, students have attended and graduated from the Academy despite having developed physical disabilities while they were students, which include loss of a limb, loss of an eye, brain damage, and color blindness. Moreover, students with insulin-dependent diabetes have enrolled in and recently graduated from at least one state maritime academy, the Maine Maritime Academy.

STATUTES AND REGULATIONS APPLICABLE TO THIS CASE

The Plaintiff claims violations of both the Maritime Education and Training Act of 1980, 46 App. U.S.C. § 1295 ("META"), and Section 504 of the Rehabilitation Act of 1973, 29 U.S.C. § 794 *et seq.* ("Section 504").

I. *The META*

. . . .

The parties' main contention is over three portions of the statute which explicitly deal with the armed forces reserve. The statute requires that "[a]ny citizen of the United States selected for appointment . . . *must agree to apply for midshipman status in the United States Naval Reserve* (including the Merchant Marine Reserve, United States Naval Reserve) before being appointed as a cadet at the Academy." 46 U.S.C. App. § 1295b(b)(3)(F) (emphasis added). The final authority to appoint cadets to a reserve post lies with the Secretary of the Navy:

> Any citizen of the United States who is appointed as a cadet at the Academy *may be appointed by the Secretary of the Navy as a midshipman in the*

United States Naval Reserve (including the Merchant Marine Reserve, United States Naval Reserve).

46 U.S.C. App. § 1295b(c) (emphasis added).

The key statutory language at issue in this case, however, deals with a cadet's commitment agreements once he or she is appointed:

Each individual appointed as a cadet at the Academy . . . who is a citizen of the United States, shall as a condition of appointment to the Academy sign an agreement committing such individual —

(A) to complete the course of instruction at the Academy, unless the individual is separated by the Academy;

(B) to fulfill the requirements for a license as an officer in the merchant marine of the United States on or before the date of graduation from the Academy of such individual;

(C) to maintain a license as an officer in the merchant marine of the United States for at least 6 years following the date of graduation from the Academy of such individual;

(D) *to apply for an appointment as, to accept if tendered an appointment as, and to serve as a commissioned officer in the United States Naval Reserve* (including the Merchant Marine Reserve, United States Naval Reserve), the United States Coast Guard Reserve, or any other Reserve unit of an armed force of the United States, for at least 6 years following the date of graduation from the Academy of such individual; and

(E) to serve in the foreign or domestic commerce and the national defense of the United States for at least 5 years following the date of graduation from the Academy

(i) as a merchant marine officer;

(ii) as an employee of the United States maritime industry, if the Secretary determines that service under (i) is not available to such individual;

(iii) as a commissioned officer on active duty in the armed forces of the United States or in the National Oceanic and Atmospheric Administration; *or*

(iv) any combination of (i), (ii) or (iii).

46 U.S.C. App. § 1295b(e)(1) (emphasis added).

The Plaintiff argues that this language is conditional, such that cadets only have to apply for and, if tendered, accept a commission in the armed forces reserve. The Defendants contend that this language creates a binding obligation both to serve in the naval reserve or some other armed forces reserve unit and, by implication, to meet physical requirements for such a commission.

. . . .

In addition, the regulations provide for waiver of some medical requirements for enrolled students and applicants to the USMMA:

> (2) The requirement to meet these standards is a continuing one and shall apply through graduation from the Academy. Failure to meet the standards while attending the Academy is grounds for, and may lead to disenrollment. *Individuals who have completed at least two years of study and, as a result of an accident, illness or other cause (during official duty), fail to meet this requirement may be permitted to remain at the Academy at the discretion of, and under conditions set by, the Administrator. . . .*

46 C.F.R. § 310.56(a) (emphasis added).

Later, the regulations state:

> The Administrator *shall have the discretion to grant waivers* of the service obligation contract in cases where there would be undue hardship or impossibility of performance due to accident, illness, or other justifiable reason.

46 C.F.R. § 310.58(f).

The Plaintiff argues that, like the META, the regulations employ conditional language which, along with the allowance for waiver upon hardship, support the conclusion that the agency does not follow a hard and fast rule that all Academy students meet requirements for a naval reserve commission at all times. The Defendants, however, point to another regulatory provision in order to demonstrate that the agency policy is clear:

> Since commissioning in the United States Navy, or any other branch of the Armed Forces, is a requirement for graduation, *no waivers will be granted for medical conditions which would prevent commissioning in at least a restricted status in the U.S. Navy Reserve.*

Id. § 310.56(d) (emphasis added).

As discussed in detail below, the Court finds that the META does not contain a clear statutory requirement that every cadet both serve in, and at all times meet physical qualifications for, commissioning in the armed forces reserve. This conclusion is critical to the Court's analysis under Section 504. The Court further finds that the agency's regulatory interpretation of the META in 46 C.F.R. § 310.56(d) does not support the Defendants' contention that the META obliged them to separate Lane from the USMMA for failure to meet physical requirements for commissioning in the naval reserve.

II. *SECTION 504 OF THE REHABILITATION ACT*

. . . .

The Plaintiff argues that, here, Lane is clearly qualified to continue at the Academy. The Defendants argue that, since commissioning in a reserve unit of the armed forces is, under their reading of the META, a statutory requirement for receiving an education at the USMMA, physical qualification for such a commission is necessarily an "essential" condition which must be satisfied. The Court agrees with the Plaintiff that the Defendants have violated Section 504 by disenrolling him solely on the basis of his diabetes mellitus, without attempting to provide reasonable accommodation, and without making an individualized determination under Section 504.

. . . .

DISCUSSION

I. *THE PLAIN LANGUAGE OF THE META DOES NOT REQUIRE ALL CADETS TO BE ELIGIBLE FOR RESERVE SERVICE AT ALL TIMES*

The crux of the Defendants' argument under both statutes rests on the agency's reading of the META as expressly mandating that all USMMA students meet the physical requirements for commissioning in the armed forces reserve. The Court finds that the Defendants have unreasonably stretched the plain language of the META too far.

It is undisputed that, on its face, the META sets forth a requirement that USMMA students apply for and, if tendered, accept an appointment as a commissioned officer in the naval reserve, or another reserve unit of the armed forces. 46 U.S.C. § 1295b(e)(1). From this language, the Defendants conclude not only that the META contains an express requirement that all USMMA students serve in the armed forces reserve, but that it further contains a clear requirement that all students at all times meet physical eligibility requirements for commissioning in the reserve. The Defendants concede in their papers that the physical eligibility requirement is, at best, implied from the statute. . . . Thus there is no clear mandate from Congress that Lane or any other cadet meet physical standards for the naval reserve. Accordingly, the Court finds that the Defendants' further arguments under the META *and* Section 504 lack merit because they are based on the erroneous premise that the META contains a clear and unconditional requirement that all enrolled students meet armed forces reserve requirements.

A. The META only mandates that USMMA students qualify for a license as an officer in the merchant marine and apply for and, if tendered, accept a commission in the armed forces reserve.

The Defendants maintain that the "apply for" and "accept if tendered" language of the META requires that cadets obtain a commission in an armed forces reserve unit as a condition of receiving a taxpayer-funded education at the USMMA. 46 U.S.C. App. § 1295b(e)(1). By necessary *implication*, the Defendants argue, the statute also contains a requirement that cadets meet the physical standards to satisfy that obligation.

The Court finds, however, that the language of the META speaks for itself. The plain language of the META requires each cadet to apply for an appointment in the reserve and, if an appointment is offered, to accept it. Indeed, it is undisputed that cadets must apply for such a position. However, the only logical way to give effect to the "if tendered" language is to conclude that, *upon application* for a reserve commission, receipt of such commission becomes conditioned on an evaluation of the cadet's eligibility for a reserve unit at that time. Consequently, in section 1295b(b)(3)(F), Congress required that individuals selected for appointment at the Academy "must *agree to apply for* midshipman status in the United States Naval Reserve . . . before being appointed as a cadet at the Academy." *Id.* (emphasis added). The statute further states that individuals appointed as cadets at the Academy "*may be appointed* . . . as a midshipman in the United States Naval Reserve. . . ." 46 U.S.C. App. § 1295b(c) (emphasis added). Thus, consistently, Congress employed unconditional language only to express the requirements that cadets apply for the reserve, and conditional language to express the possibility that cadets "may be appointed" as midshipmen in the reserve upon graduation. The Court finds no support for the Defendants' suggestion that Congress did not require what the plain language expresses, namely, that all cadets apply for and accept if tendered a commission in the armed forces reserve but, rather, that Congress required that all cadets serve in, and at all times qualify for, the reserve.

Moreover, in the same subsection containing the "apply for" and "accept if tendered" language, namely, 46 U.S.C. App. § 1295b(e)(1), Congress affords cadets a *choice* in meeting their duty "to serve in the foreign or domestic commerce and the national defense" upon graduation. *Id.* § 1295b(e)(1)(E). Congress expressly provided that, as part of their commitment agreement, students must serve as *either* merchant marine officers, employees in the maritime industry, *or* commissioned officers. *Id.* The Defendants argue that the statutory active duty requirement is entirely separate from the alleged reserve service requirement, and remind the Court that statutes must be read to give meaning to every section.

This, however, is precisely what the Court intends to do. Again, the Court finds that nowhere does the META require, as the Defendants assume, that each and every cadet serve in the armed forces reserve. It only requires that students apply for a reserve commission and accept one if tendered. With respect to the META's *express active* duty requirement, however, the META gives cadets a choice. As long as each cadet serves in one of the three capacities listed in the statute, they have fulfilled their post-graduation commitment under the META. The Court finds that, given the express statutory allowance of a choice upon graduation regarding active duty, it cannot conclude that, on the other hand, Congress *impliedly* intended an unconditional requirement that all cadets serve in a reserve unit of the armed forces. Accordingly, the Court also finds that there is no merit to the Defendants' contention that the statute impliedly requires that all cadets be qualified for armed forces reserve positions throughout their training.

Furthermore, the Court observes that other subsections of the META *are un* conditional; thus Congress knew how to make an express, mandatory requirement when it wanted to. For example, in the same section which sets forth the "apply for" and "accept if tendered" language, the statute unconditionally requires cadets to complete the Academy's course of instruction, to fulfill the requirements for a license as an officer in the merchant marine of the United States, to maintain a license as an officer in the merchant marine of the United States for at least 6 years following graduation, and to serve as either a merchant marine officer, an employee in the maritime industry or as a commissioned officer in the armed forces upon graduation. 46 U.S.C. App. § 1295b(e) (1)(A)–(E).

The Court observes that, if Congress so clearly intended to make service in, and qualification for, the reserve an unconditional requirement, it would have used the unconditional language it employed throughout the rest of section 1295b(e)(1) in order to say just that. Moreover, because the statute contains a provision regarding fulfillment of the requirements for a merchant marine license, the absence of such a provision regarding the requirements for a reserve commission suggests that Congress did not intend that satisfaction of standards for service in the reserve be an absolute graduation requirement. *See I.N.S. v. Cardoza-Fonseca*, 480 U.S. 421 (1987) ("[w]here Congress includes particular language in one section of a statute but omits it in another section of the same Act, it is generally presumed that Congress acts intentionally and purposely in the disparate inclusion or exclusion") (quoting *Russello v. United States*, 464 U.S. 16, 23, (1983)).

. . . .

B. The META's language affording waivers for hardship and precluding the denial of degrees based solely on an inability to meet the physical requirements for obtaining a merchant marine license undermines the Defendants' central argument.

. . . .

C. MARAD's own regulations, and its inconsistent interpretation thereof, belie the Defendants' argument that the USMMA has an unconditional rule that all cadets meet all physical requirements for commissioning in the armed forces reserve, absent waiver late in their education.

. . . .

The Court first observes that the regulations do, in part, require candidates for admission to "meet the physical requirements . . . for appointment as Midshipman, [United States Naval Reserve,]" as well as those for obtaining a merchant marine license. 46 C.F.R. § 310.56(a). Moreover, the regulations state that failure to meet these standards "while attending the Academy is grounds for, and may lead to disenrollment." *Id.* § 310.56(a).

However, the Court finds the regulations internally inconsistent. For example, the regulations state that "[i]ndividuals who have completed at least two years of study and, as a result of an accident, illness or other cause (during official duty), fail to meet this requirement may be permitted to remain at the Academy at the discretion of, and under conditions set by, the Administrator . . . ." *Id.* Later, however, the regulations allow for waiver for hardship without imposing *any* limitation on first and second year students. *Id.* § 310.58(f).

Moreover, the Court finds that these regulations, read together with others, simply do not support the Defendants' claim that a *per se* rule exists which required Lane's disenrollment after his first year. First, the regulations properly employ the conditional language of the statute, and definitively state that cadets "are appointed at the Academy for training to prepare them to become officers in the U.S. merchant marine" and that after graduation they shall receive a merchant marine license. *Id.* § 310.52(a). Later, the regulations state that "[i]*f qualified*, an officer *may be* commissioned as an officer in a reserve component of an armed force of the United States." *Id.* (emphasis added).

. . . .

D. Because the Court finds that the Defendants' alleged policy mandating the separation of Lane from the Academy upon discovery of his diabetes is not supported by the statute or its regulations, the Court shall not defer to the Defendants' espoused reading of the META.

II. *THE COURT FINDS THAT THE DEFENDANTS VIOLATED SECTION 504 BY DISENROLLING LANE SOLELY ON THE BASIS OF HIS DIABETES MELLITUS*

A. The Defendants have not shown that meeting the physical qualifications for commissioning in the armed forces reserve is an essential program requirement of the USMMA.

It is undisputed that Section 504 is violated if (1) the claimant has a disability; (2) he or she was denied participation in a federal program because of that disability; and (3) he or she was otherwise "qualified" for the program. *See Gallagher v. Catto*, 778 F. Supp. 570, 577 (D.D.C. 1991), *aff'd*, 988 F.2d 1280 (D.C.Cir. 1993). The issue in the instant case is whether the Plaintiff was otherwise qualified to remain at the USMMA.

A qualified disabled person is one who meets all academic and non-academic qualifications that are "essential to participation in the program in question." *Southeastern Community College v. Davis*, 442 U.S. 397, 406 (1979). Further, even if the person *cannot* meet all essential qualifications, he is still "qualified" under Section 504 if reasonable modifications in the program will accommodate his disability. *School Board of Nassau County v. Arline*, 480 U.S. 273, 287 n. 17 (1987); *Davis*, 442 U.S. at 408. Such accommodations are reasonable if they do not require a "fundamental alteration in the nature of [the] program" in question or if they pose "undue financial and administrative burdens." *Arline*, 480 U.S. at 287 n. 17; *Davis*, 442 U.S. at 410, 412. The federal agency bears the burden of establishing that "further reasonable accommodation would present an undue hardship." *Catto*, 778 F. Supp. at 577–78. In addition, the Supreme Court has stressed that "in most cases" the question of whether a disabled person is qualified will involve an "individualized inquiry" and "appropriate findings of fact." *Arline*, 480 U.S. at 287. Thus a refusal to apply Section 504 to a class of disabled persons is lawful only where Congress has "specifically determined that no individualized inquiry [i]s necessary." *Traynor v. Turnage*, 485 U.S. 535, 551 n. 11 (1988).

Once again, the Defendants base their entire argument under Section 504 on the erroneous premise that Congress intended that all cadets meet the physical qualifications for commissioning in the armed forces reserve in order to remain at the Academy. The Defendants argue that, since commissioning in an armed forces reserve unit is, in their view, a statutory requirement for receiving an education at the USMMA, physical qualification for such a commission is necessarily an "essential" condition which must be satisfied. Because Lane cannot meet this essential program requirement, they reason, he is not otherwise qualified to complete his education at the USMMA. The Defendants further claim that exempting Lane from this general requirement would undermine the Academy's mission to provide trained reserve officers for military service. Because of the congressional mandate that cadets serve in, and qualify for, a reserve commission, the Defendants assert, such an accommodation would work a "fundamental alteration in the nature of the program." The Defendants therefore conclude that their actions with respect to Lane do not violate the Rehabilitation Act.

The Court cannot endorse the Defendants' position that continuous eligibility for the armed forces reserve is an essential program requirement under Section 504, or that attempting to accommodate Lane would result in undue hardship. As discussed above, the META in no way binds the Academy to the *per se* policy it purports to follow; rather, the statute merely requires cadets to apply for and, if tendered, accept a naval reserve commission, or a commission in another reserve unit of the armed forces. Moreover, the Defendants admit that such requirements, if any, do not even apply to students such as Lane who have not yet reached their third year. Consequently, the Defendants cannot simply point to that statute and definitively conclude that maintaining eligibility for such a commission is an essential requirement to remaining at the USMMA and that, therefore, their actions were consistent with Section 504.

In addition, the Court finds that, *aside from* pointing to the statute, the Defendants have not offered any explanation of how continuous eligibility for an armed forces reserve commission is an essential program requirement for purposes of Section 504. Rather, given that many people with diabetes have obtained merchant marine licenses, and at least 50 people with diabetes mellitus are currently operating under a merchant marine license at sea, the Court finds that the rigid naval reserve requirements are not "essential" to at least one purpose of the program, namely, training officers for the merchant marine.

Further, even if producing people for military reserve service were an equally important purpose under the META, the Court finds that purpose is fully satisfied without Lane through the Academy's graduation of the many other cadets who do not have diabetes. Indeed, it is undisputed that a large portion of these graduates never enter the reserve. As counsel for the Plaintiff have observed, if the situation at hand arose in a time of war, or if the Defendants could demonstrate a recognition by Congress that the supply of reserve troops was sorely insufficient when Lane was disenrolled, the Defendants' argument under Section 504 might have some merit. But here, the Defendants concede that they can "only speculate" as to the impact of allowing Lane to graduate. The Defendants have made no showing that the reason for separating Lane from the Academy was essential to the program at all.

B. The Defendants have not even attempted to make reasonable modifications in the program to accommodate Lane's disability.

Moreover, even if cadets' continuous eligibility for an armed forces reserve commission were an essential program requirement, the agency carries the burden of showing that it could not reasonably accommodate Lane's disability. *Gallagher v. Catto*, 778 F. Supp. at 577–78. The Defendants argue that any accommodation would require a fundamental alteration in the nature of its program because the physical eligibility requirement for an armed forces reserve commission is mandated by the META.

It is undisputed that, aside from his diabetes, Lane is extremely well qualified to complete his education at the USMMA. Moreover, in Lane's case, he developed the disease after enrolling in the Academy, and he has maintained an excellent record with respect to both academic *and* physical testing. This is not a case of an applicant challenging the Academy under Section 504. Rather, Lane was an enrolled student, who was fully qualified upon application, and who made a serious investment in the USMMA and in his future following his education there. In turn, the government, through tax-payer dollars, also made an investment in his training and, as Lane's record shows, their investment was a good one. It is undisputed that, if Lane continues to control his diabetic condition, he will make a fine merchant marine officer.

Accordingly, the Court finds that the Defendants have made no showing under Section 504 that the Academy cannot provide reasonable accommodation for Lane's condition. Such accommodation, as far as the Court can tell from the record before it, would amount to simply allowing Lane to graduate. Those most familiar with Lane's abilities and control over his diabetes confirm that he could complete his education and training at the Academy with little or no difficulty. . . . Moreover, the Defendants admit that, in their view, such accommodation may be made for third and fourth year students under the regulations addressing the statute's waiver provisions, and they admit that the Academy has allowed students in the past with a lost limb, a lost eye, brain damage, and color blindness to remain at the Academy and graduate despite their disabilities. The Court cannot conceive of any reason why accommodating Lane would, in contrast, cause the Academy grievous injury. Moreover, Lane developed the disease after he enrolled. Thus a finding that the Academy's act of separating Lane from the USMMA after he discovered he had diabetes mellitus would not necessarily impact the Academy's admission standards.

. . . .

C. The Court finds that the Defendants erred in failing to make an individualized inquiry into the particular facts of Lane's case.

The Court further finds that the Agency erred in failing to make an individualized inquiry into the particular facts of Lane's case. . . .

Because the Court finds that the META does not impose a requirement that all students meet eligibility standards for commissioning in the armed forces reserve, the Court determines that the facts of Lane's case did demand a more thorough inquiry than simply confirming that he had diabetes mellitus. Moreover, the Court observes that the Defendants erred in creating a blanket restriction absent a specific determination by Congress that such restriction is necessary. *See Traynor v. Turnage*, 485 U.S. 535, 551 n. 11 (1988).

. . . .

In sum, the Court finds that the Defendants have violated Section 504 of the Rehabilitation Act by separating Lane from the Academy based solely on his diabetes mellitus. In particular, the Court finds that meeting physical requirements for commissioning in the naval reserve is not an essential program requirement. Even if it were essential, however, the Court holds that the Defendants have not met their burden of showing that providing reasonable accommodation would result in undue hardship for the USMMA and, further, that the Defendants erroneously failed to make any individualized inquiry into the facts of the Plaintiff's case.

. . . .

NOTES AND QUESTIONS

1. The opinion contains extensive discussion of the propriety of a damages award. The award was later vacated on the basis of federal sovereign immunity, and the Supreme Court upheld that decision.

2. Is the court guilty of second-guessing the people who know the job best? How persuasive is the opinion on the issue of what is essential to being a student at the Merchant Marine Academy?

3. Is this case fully consistent with *Davis*?

4. Both *Southeastern Community College v. Davis* and *Lane v. Pena* dealt with traditional on-site residential programs, but an increasing number of students are taking courses, and indeed entire programs, on-line. For an example of a discrimination claim by a student in such an on-line program, see *Hartnett v. Fielding Graduate Inst.*, 198 Fed. Appx. 89 (2d Cir. 2006), which held that a student diagnosed with lupus that prevented her from traveling to monthly on-site residential cluster meetings required for accreditation purposes stated a possible section 504 claim when the on-line post-secondary institution rejected the student's request to replace the on-site participation with videoconferencing. Visually impaired students may also have discrimination claims. Most web-based materials can easily be made accessible to visually impaired individuals who use electronic reading software, as long as the text is not buried in an inaccessible graphic display. *See generally National Fed. of the Blind v. Target Corp.*, 452 F. Supp. 2d 946 (N.D. Cal. 2006) (denying motion to dismiss ADA public accommodations claim based on merchant's display of inaccessible web site).

5. Many post-secondary institutions operate overseas study programs, but the extent to which section 504 and the ADA apply to these programs has not been clearly determined. *See Bird v. Lewis and Clark Coll.*, 303 F.3d 1015 (9th Cir. 2002) (finding no section 504 or ADA violation as to semester-long overseas study biology program in Australia where, although wheelchair-using student was not able to participate in all parts of program's projects to same extent as non-disabled students, college paid for two assistants and made alternative travel arrangements so that student had "meaningful access" to most of program). Because the college prevailed on the disability claims, the Ninth Circuit in *Bird* did not address the college's claim that section 504 and ADA should not apply "extraterritorially to regulate the administration of overseas programs." What arguments can you develop supporting and refuting the college's position? For a good discussion of extraterritoriality, see Arlene S. Kantor, *The Presumption Against Extraterritoriality As Applied To Disability Discrimination Laws: Where Does It Leave Students With Disabilities Studying Abroad?*, 14 STAN. L. & POL'Y REV. 291 (2003). The Supreme Court has applied the public accommodations title of the ADA to foreign flag cruise ships that operate in United States waters. *Spector v. Norwegian Cruise Line Ltd.*, 545 U.S. 119 (2005).

6.   For students who have incurred indebtedness in securing a higher education, the process of repayment can be burdensome. Students with disabilities who have secured a higher education may find an additional barrier to repayment where the accommodations that a college or university had in place to assist the student may not be present in post-higher education employment. Securing a Chapter 7 discharge of student loans has not generally been successful for most students, because they must demonstrate that: (1) they cannot maintain a minimal standard of living for themselves, usually because of inability to secure employment; (2) their current situation is likely to continue for a significant period of the repayment period for the debt; and, (3) they have made good faith efforts to repay the loan. In *Porrazzo v. Educational Credit Management Corporation*, 307 B.R. 345 (D. Conn. 2004), a federal district court discharged the $22,747 student loan debt of Porrazzo, who had been diagnosed with Asperger's Syndrome, a form of autism that frequently manifests itself in lack of interpersonal skills and sometimes in aggressive behavior. After graduation, he had been employed, and eventually discharged, by two employers as a result of his unsupervised displays of anger towards coworkers. In his petition for discharge of his student loans, Porrazzo was able to persuade the district court that he qualified under the three criteria for discharge of his student debt. However, to what extent is Porrazzo's discharge symptomatic of a more systemic issue? Assuming that the university attended by plaintiff Porrazzo had provided close supervision to assist him in dealing with his anger towards other persons around him, should post-graduation employers be expected to provide the same measure of accommodation under the ADA in order to enable disabled employees to continue working?

2.   Academic Deference

Many courts have afforded deference to the decisions of teachers and academic administrators on whether students are qualified and what reasonable accommodations they should be permitted. In the next pair of cases, the courts wrestle with the issue of whether courts considering disability discrimination cases should defer to academic decision making, and, if so, how much deference they should give.

ZUKLE v. REGENTS OF THE UNIVERSITY OF CALIFORNIA
166 F.3d 1041 (9th Cir. 1999)

In this case, the court upheld a decision by a school to dismiss a medical student, articulating an approach to academic deference that is highly protective of the school.

O'SCANNLAIN, CIRCUIT JUDGE.

We must decide whether a medical school violated the Americans with Disabilities Act or the Rehabilitation Act when it dismissed a learning disabled student for failure to meet the school's academic standards.

I

Sherrie Lynn Zukle entered the University of California, Davis School of Medicine ("Medical School") in the fall of 1991 for a four year course of study. The first two years comprise the "basic science" or "pre-clinical" curriculum, consisting of courses in the function, design and processes of the human body. The final two years comprise the "clinical curriculum." In the third year, students take six consecutive eight-week clinical clerkships. During the fourth year, students complete clerkships of varying lengths in more advanced areas. Most clerkships involve treating patients in hospitals or clinics, and oral and written exams.

From the beginning, Zukle experienced academic difficulty. During her first quarter, she received "Y" grades in Anatomy and Biochemistry.[6] Upon reexamination, her Biochemistry grade was converted to a "D." She did not convert her Anatomy grade at that time. In her second quarter, she received a "Y" grade in Human Physiology, which she converted to a "D" upon reexamination.

In April 1992, the Medical School referred Zukle to the Student Evaluation Committee ("SEC"). Although subject to dismissal pursuant to the Medical School's bylaws, Zukle was allowed to remain in school. The SEC (1) placed Zukle on academic probation, (2) required her to retake Anatomy and Biochemistry, (3) required her to be tested for a learning disability, and (4) placed her on a "split curriculum," meaning that she was given three years to complete the pre-clinical program, instead of the usual two years. Zukle continued to experience academic difficulty. For the spring quarter of 1992 (while on academic probation) she received a "Y" grade in Neurobiology. In the fall, she received a "Y" grade in Medical Microbiology and in the winter she received a "Y" in Principles of Pharmacology. In total, Zukle received eight "Y" grades during the pre-clinical portion of her studies. Five were converted to "C" after reexamination, two to "D" and one to "F."

In November 1992, Zukle was tested for a learning disability. The results received in January 1993, revealed that Zukle suffered from a reading disability which "affects visual processing as it relates to reading comprehension and rate when under timed constraints." In short, it takes Zukle longer to read and to absorb information than the average person.[7] Zukle asked Christine O'Dell, Coordinator of the University's Learning Disability Resource Center, to inform the Medical School of her test results in mid-July 1993. O'Dell informed Gail Currie of the Office of Student Affairs in a letter dated July 21, 1993. O'Dell recommended that the Medical School make various accommodations for Zukle's disability and recommended various techniques for Zukle to try to increase her reading comprehension. The Medical School offered all of these accommodations to Zukle.

After completing the pre-clinical portion of Medical School, Zukle took the United States Medical Licensing Exam, Part I ("USMLE") in June 1994. Shortly

---

[6] [FN 1] . . . A "Y" grade in a pre-clinical course is provisional; it means that a student has earned a failing grade but will be or has been permitted to retake the exam. However, a "Y" grade in a clinical clerkship indicates unsatisfactory performance in a major portion of that clerkship and may not be converted until the student repeats that portion of the clerkship.

[7] [FN 5] Under timed conditions, Zukle's reading comprehension is in the 2nd percentile, whereas when untimed her comprehension is in the 83rd percentile.

thereafter, she began her first clinical clerkship, OB-GYN. During this clerkship, Zukle learned that she had failed the USMLE. The Medical School allowed Zukle to interrupt her OB-GYN clerkship to take a six-week review course to prepare to retake the USMLE, for which the Medical School paid.

Before leaving school to take the USMLE review course offered in southern California, Zukle asked Donald A. Walsh, the Associate Dean of Curricular Affairs, if she could rearrange her clerkship schedule. At this point, Zukle had completed the first half of her OB-GYN clerkship. She asked Dean Walsh if, instead of completing the second half of her OB-GYN clerkship upon return from retaking the USMLE, she could start the first half of a Family Practice Clerkship, and then repeat the OB-GYN clerkship in its entirety at a later date. Zukle testified that she made this request because she was concerned about how far behind she would be when she returned from the USMLE review course. She further asserted that she thought that if she started the Family Practice clerkship (which apparently requires less reading than the OB-GYN clerkship), she would be able to read for her upcoming Medicine clerkship at night. Zukle testified that Dean Walsh, and several other faculty members, including the Instructor of Record for Family Practice and the Instructor of Record for OB-GYN, initially approved her request. Later, however, Dean Walsh denied Zukle's request and informed her that she had to complete the OB-GYN clerkship before beginning another clerkship.

In September 1994, Zukle took and passed the USMLE on her second attempt. She returned to the Medical School and finished her OB-GYN clerkship. Without requesting any accommodations, she began her Medicine clerkship. During this clerkship, she learned that she had earned a "Y" grade in her OB-GYN clerkship. Because of this grade, Zukle was automatically placed back on academic probation.

Two weeks before the Medicine written exam, Zukle contacted her advisor, Dr. Joseph Silva, and expressed concern that she had not completed the required reading. Dr. Silva offered to speak with Dr. Ruth Lawrence, the Medicine Instructor of Record, on Zukle's behalf. According to Zukle, she then spoke with Dr. Lawrence in person and requested time off from the clerkship to prepare for the exam. Dr. Lawrence denied Zukle's request. Zukle passed the written exam, but failed the Medicine clerkship because of unsatisfactory clinical performance. On Zukle's grade sheet, Dr. Lawrence rated Zukle as unsatisfactory in clinical problem solving skills; data acquisition, organization and recording; and skill/ability at oral presentations. Dr. Lawrence also reported negative comments from the people who worked with Zukle during the clerkship. Because Zukle had earned a failing grade while on academic probation, she was again subject to dismissal pursuant to the Medical School's bylaws.

On January 13, 1995, Zukle appeared before the SEC. The SEC recommended that Zukle (1) drop her current clerkship, Pediatrics; (2) start reviewing for the OB-GYN exam, and retake it; (3) repeat the Medicine clerkship in its entirety; (4) obtain the approval of the SEC before enrolling in any more clerkships; and (5) remain on academic probation for the rest of her medical school career.

On January 17, 1995, the Promotions Board met to consider Zukle's case. The Promotions Board voted to dismiss Zukle from the Medical School for "failure to meet the academic standards of the School of Medicine." According to Dr. Lewis, who was a member of the Promotions Board and was present when it reached its decision, "the Promotions Board considered Plaintiff's academic performance throughout her tenure at the medical school and determined that it demonstrated an incapacity to develop or use the skills and knowledge required to competently practice medicine."

In June 1995, Zukle appealed her dismissal to an *ad hoc* Board on Student Dismissal composed of faculty and students ("the Board"). Zukle appeared before the Board on November 12, 1995, and requested that her dismissal be reconsidered and that she be given extra time to prepare prior to some of her clerkships to accommodate her disability. The Board also heard testimony from Dr. Silva, who spoke favorably on her behalf, Dr. Ernest Lewis, Associate Dean of Student Affairs and Dr. George Jordan, the Chair of the Promotions Board at the time of Zukle's dismissal. When asked about Zukle's request to remain in Medical School on a decelerated schedule, Dean Lewis testified:

> There is a certain point when everyone has to be able to respond in the same time frame. A physician does not have extra time when in the ER, for example. Speed of appropriate reaction to crisis is essential.

The Board on Student Dismissal voted unanimously to uphold the Promotions Board's decision of dismissal. . . .

The district court entered its Memorandum of Opinion and Order on August 7, 1997, granting summary judgment to The Regents on all of Zukle's claims. . . . On Zukle's Americans with Disabilities Act ("ADA") and Rehabilitation Act claims, the district court found that "[b]ecause the evidence before the court shows that Zukle could not meet the minimum standards of the UCD School of Medicine with reasonable accommodation, she is not an otherwise qualified individual with a disability under the Rehabilitation Act or the ADA." . . .

II

Zukle claims that she was dismissed from the Medical School in violation of Title II of the ADA and section 504 of the Rehabilitation Act. . . .

The Regents do not dispute that Zukle is disabled and that the Medical School receives federal financial assistance and is a public entity. The Regents argue, however, that Zukle was not "otherwise qualified" to remain at the Medical School. Zukle responds that she *was* "otherwise qualified" with the aid of reasonable accommodations and that the Medical School failed reasonably to accommodate her.

A

The ADA defines a "qualified individual with a disability" as one who "meets the essential eligibility requirements . . . for participation in [a given] program[] provided by a public entity" "*with or without reasonable modifications* to rules, policies, or practices. . . ." 42 U.S.C. § 12131(2) (emphasis added). . . .

B

In order to evaluate Zukle's claim, we must clarify the burdens of production and persuasion in cases of this type. The district court correctly noted that we have not previously addressed the allocation of the burdens of production and persuasion for the "otherwise qualified" — "reasonable accommodation" prong for a prima facie case in the school context. We have, however, recently articulated the allocation of these burdens in the employment context. *See Barnett v. U.S. Air, Inc.*, 157 F.3d 744 (9th Cir. 1998). . . .

Adopting a similar burden shifting framework in the school context, we hold that the plaintiff-student bears the initial burden of producing evidence that she is otherwise qualified. This burden includes the burden of producing evidence of the existence of a reasonable accommodation that would enable her to meet the educational institution's essential eligibility requirements. The burden then shifts to the educational institution to produce evidence that the requested accommodation would require a fundamental or substantial modification of its program or standards. The school may also meet its burden by producing evidence that the requested accommodations, regardless of whether they are reasonable, would not enable the student to meet its academic standards. However, the plaintiff-student retains the ultimate burden of persuading the court that she is otherwise qualified.

C

Before turning to the merits of Zukle's claims, we must decide whether we should accord deference to academic decisions made by the school in the context of an ADA or Rehabilitation Act claim, an issue of first impression in this circuit.

In *Regents of the Univ. of Michigan v. Ewing*, the Supreme Court analyzed the issue of the deference a court should extend to an educational institution's decision in the due process context. *See* 474 U.S. 214 (1985). In *Ewing*, the plaintiff-medical student challenged his dismissal from medical school as arbitrary and capricious in violation of his substantive due process rights. *See id.* at 217. The Court held that:

> When judges are asked to review the substance of a genuinely academic decision, such as this one, they should show great respect for the faculty's professional judgment. Plainly, they may not override it unless it is such a substantial departure from accepted academic norms as to demonstrate that the person or committee responsible did not actually exercise professional judgment.

Id. at 225 (footnote omitted).

While the Court made this statement in the context of a due process violation claim, a majority of circuits have extended judicial deference to an educational institution's academic decisions in ADA and Rehabilitation Act cases. *See Doe v. New York Univ.*, 666 F.2d 761 (2d. Cir. 1981); *McGregor v. Louisiana State Univ. Bd. of Supervisors*, 3 F.3d 850 (5th Cir. 1993); *Wynne v. Tufts Univ. Sch. of Med.* (*"Wynne I"*), 932 F.2d 19 (1st. Cir. 1991).[8] *But see Pushkin v. Regents of the Univ.*

---

[8] [FN 13] Each circuit has, however, developed its own formulation of the deference standard.

of Colorado, 658 F.2d 1372 (10th Cir. 1981) (refusing to adopt deferential, rational basis test in evaluating educational institution's decisions in Rehabilitation Act case). These courts noted the limited ability of courts, "as contrasted to that of experienced educational administrators and professionals," to determine whether a student "would meet reasonable standards for academic and professional achievement established by a university," and have concluded that " '[c]ourts are particularly ill-equipped to evaluate academic performance.' " *Doe*, 666 F.2d at 775–76 (quoting *Board of Curators of Univ. of Missouri v. Horowitz*, 435 U.S. 78, 92 (1978)).

We agree with the First, Second and Fifth circuits that an educational institution's academic decisions are entitled to deference. Thus, while we recognize that the ultimate determination of whether an individual is otherwise qualified must be made by the court, we will extend judicial deference "to the evaluation made by the institution itself, absent proof that its standards and its application of them serve no purpose other than to deny an education to handicapped persons." *Doe*, 666 F.2d at 776.

Deference is also appropriately accorded an educational institution's determination that a reasonable accommodation is not available. Therefore, we agree with the First Circuit that "a court's duty is to first find the basic facts, giving due deference to the school, and then to evaluate whether those facts add up to a professional, academic judgment that reasonable accommodation is not available." *Wynne I*, 932 F.2d at 27–28; *see also McGregor*, 3 F.3d at 859 (the court must "accord deference to [the school's] decisions not to modify its programs [when] the proposed modifications entail academic decisions").

We recognize that extending deference to educational institutions must not impede our obligation to enforce the ADA and the Rehabilitation Act. Thus, we must be careful not to allow academic decisions to disguise truly discriminatory requirements. The educational institution has a "real obligation . . . to seek suitable means of reasonably accommodating a handicapped person and to submit a factual record indicating that it conscientiously carried out this statutory obligation." *Wynne I*, 932 F.2d at 25–26. Once the educational institution has fulfilled this obligation, however, we will defer to its academic decisions.

III

Having answered several preliminary questions, we now turn to the ultimate question — did Zukle establish a prima facie case of discrimination under the ADA or the Rehabilitation Act? As noted before, only the "otherwise qualified" prong of the prima facie case requirements is disputed by the parties. Zukle argues that she was otherwise qualified to remain at the Medical School, with the aid of the three accommodations she requested. The Medical School argues that Zukle's requested accommodations were not reasonable because they would have required a funda-

---

Compare Doe, 666 F.2d at 776 (holding that in determining whether a plaintiff is otherwise qualified to attend medical school, "*considerable judicial deference* must be paid to the evaluation made by the institution itself, absent proof that its standards and its application of them serve no other purpose than to deny an education to handicapped persons." (emphasis added)), *with McGregor*, 3 F.3d at 859 ("[A]bsent evidence of discriminatory intent or disparate impact, we must accord *reasonable deference* to the [school's] academic decisions." (emphasis added)).

mental or substantial modification of its program. *See Alexander*, 469 U.S. at 300 (holding that institution subject to Rehabilitation Act may be required to make reasonable modifications to accommodate a disabled plaintiff, but need not make fundamental or substantial modifications).

Zukle bears the burden of pointing to the existence of a reasonable accommodation that would enable her to meet the Medical School's essential eligibility requirements. Once she meets this burden, the Medical School must show that Zukle's requested accommodation would fundamentally alter the nature of the school's program. We must determine, viewing the evidence in the light most favorable to Zukle, if there are any genuine issues of material fact with regard to the reasonableness of Zukle's requested accommodations. *See Margolis v. Ryan*, 140 F.3d 850, 852 (9th Cir. 1998).

We note at this stage that "[r]easonableness is not a constant. To the contrary, what is reasonable in a particular situation may not be reasonable in a different situation — even if the situational differences are relatively slight." *Wynne v. Tufts Univ. Sch. of Med. ("Wynne II")*, 976 F.2d 791, 795 (1st Cir. 1992). Thus, we must evaluate Zukle's requests in light of the totality of her circumstances. *See Barnett*, 157 F.3d at 748 ("Whether a particular accommodation is reasonable depends on the circumstances of the individual case.").

The evidence is undisputed that the Medical School offered Zukle all of the accommodations that it normally offers learning disabled students. When the Medical School first learned of Zukle's disability she was offered double time on exams, notetaking services and textbooks on audio cassettes. Further, Zukle was allowed to retake courses, proceed on a decelerated schedule and remain at the Medical School despite being subject to dismissal under the Medical School's bylaws.

Even with these accommodations, Zukle consistently failed to achieve passing grades in her courses. Though Zukle was on a decelerated schedule, she continued to receive "Y" grades in her pre-clinical years and failed the USMLE on her first attempt. Further, although she was able to remedy some of her failing grades in her pre-clinical years, she was only able to do so by retaking exams. Moreover, she received a "Y" grade in her first clinical clerkship, automatically placing her on academic probation, and an "F" in her second. Because Zukle received a failing grade while on academic probation, she was subject to dismissal pursuant to the Medical School's bylaws. Clearly, Zukle could not meet the Medical School's essential eligibility requirements without the additional accommodations she requested.

The issue, then, is whether the ADA and Rehabilitation Act required the Medical School to provide Zukle with those additional accommodations. As noted above, the Medical School was only required to provide Zukle with *reasonable* accommodations. Accordingly, we examine the reasonableness of Zukle's requested accommodations.

A

Zukle claims that the Medical School should have granted her request to modify her schedule by beginning the first half of the Family Practice Clerkship instead of finishing the second half of her OB-GYN clerkship when she returned from retaking the USMLE. She proposed that she would then begin the Medicine clerkship, and finish Family Practice and OB-GYN at a later time.

The Regents presented evidence that granting this request would require a substantial modification of its curriculum. While the Medical School has granted some students reading time prior to the commencement of a clerkship, Dean Walsh testified that once a clerkship begins "all students are expected to complete the reading and other requirements of the clerkship, including night call and ward care, and to prepare themselves for the written exam which is given only at the end of the 8-week clerkship." Zukle's request would have entailed interrupting her OB-GYN clerkship, and starting the Medicine clerkship before finishing the Family Practice clerkship. Thus, by the time Zukle began the Medicine clerkship she would have had two uncompleted clerkships.

Dean Walsh testified that the only time the Medical School allows a student to begin a clerkship, interrupt it, and then return to that clerkship at a later point is when a student has failed the USMLE and needs time off to study. However, the student is still required to return to the same clerkship. Given that no student had been allowed to rearrange her clerkships in the manner Zukle requested and that Zukle's request would entail Zukle interrupting two courses to complete them at some later date, we have little difficulty concluding that this would be a substantial alteration of the Medical School's curriculum. *See Davis*, 442 U.S. at 413 (holding that a school is not required to make substantial modifications to accommodate a handicapped student).

Zukle argues that the Medical School allowed numerous students to rearrange their clerkship schedules, and thus there is a material issue of fact as to whether her request was reasonable. However, while the students that Zukle mentions were allowed to remedy failing grades by retaking clerkships or exams, *none* was allowed to begin a clerkship, interrupt it, begin another clerkship, and retake the second half of the first clerkship at a later point. The facts are undisputed that no student had been allowed to rearrange their clerkship schedule as Zukle requested. Indeed, Zukle admitted in the district court that "no student has been permitted to finish an interrupted course in the fashion [she] requested because it would require substantial curricular alteration." We defer to the Medical School's academic decision to require students to complete courses once they are begun and conclude, therefore, that this requested accommodation was not reasonable.

B

Two weeks before the scheduled written exam in her Medicine clerkship, Zukle asked Dr. Silva, her advisor, if she could have more time to prepare for the exam because she was behind in the readings. Zukle testified that she specifically requested to leave the hospital early every day so that she could spend more time preparing for the written exam in Medicine. Dr. Silva and Zukle spoke with the

Instructor of Record in Zukle's Medicine clerkship, Dr. Lawrence. Dr. Lawrence told Zukle that she could not excuse her from the in-hospital part of the clerkship. Dr. Lawrence testified that she denied this request because she thought that it would be unfair to the other students.

The Medical School presented uncontradicted evidence that giving Zukle reduced clinical time would have fundamentally altered the nature of the Medical School curriculum. The Medical School presented the affidavit of Dean Lewis in which he explained the significance of the clinical portion of the Medical School curriculum:

> The third-year clinical clerkships are designed to simulate the practice of medicine. . . . Depending on the specialty and the setting, students are generally required to be "on call" at the hospital through an evening and night one or more times each week. Other than these call nights, students remain at the hospital or clinic during day time hours on a schedule similar to that expected of clinicians. . . . Releasing a student from a significant number of scheduled hours during the course of a rotation would compromise the clerkship's curricular purpose, i.e. the simulation of medical practice.

We defer to the Medical School's academic decision that the in-hospital portion of a clerkship is a vital part of medical education and that allowing a student to be excused from this requirement would sacrifice the integrity of its program. Thus, we conclude that neither the ADA nor the Rehabilitation Act require the Medical School to make this accommodation.

. . . .

C

Finally, after she was dismissed, Zukle requested that the *ad hoc* Board place her on a decelerated schedule during the clinical portion of her studies. Specifically, Zukle sought eight weeks off before each clerkship to read the assigned text for that clerkship in its entirety.

. . . .

We agree with the district court that the Board's denial of Zukle's request to proceed on a decelerated schedule was a "rationally justifiable conclusion." *See Wynne II*, 976 F.2d at 793 (quoting *Wynne I*, 932 F.2d at 26). The Board noted that, even on a decelerated schedule during the pre-clinical phase, Zukle experienced severe academic difficulties: Zukle earned deficient grades in five courses and failed the USMLE exam on her first attempt even though she had taken several pre-clinical courses twice. The Board noted that there is "a fair amount of overlap on written exams of material from second-year courses and that the clinical work overlaps with the written." In sum, the evidence makes clear that the decelerated schedule would not have aided Zukle in meeting the Medical School's academic standards. Given Zukle's unenviable academic record, allowing her to remain in Medical School on a decelerated schedule would have lowered the Medical School's academic standards, which it was not required to do to accommodate Zukle. *See Davis*, 442 U.S. at 413.

IV

In conclusion, we are persuaded that Zukle failed to establish that she could meet the essential eligibility requirements of the Medical School with the aid of reasonable accommodations. Accordingly, she failed to establish a prima facie case of disability discrimination under the ADA or the Rehabilitation Act.

AFFIRMED

WONG v. REGENTS OF THE UNIVERSITY OF CALIFORNIA
192 F.3d 807 (9th Cir. 1999)

In this case, the court found reasons to be less than fully deferential to university decision making, and determined that an issue of fact existed with regard to qualification and accommodation.

KRAVITCH, CIRCUIT JUDGE.

Plaintiff-appellant Andrew H.K. Wong appeals the district court's order granting summary judgment in favor of defendant-appellee Regents of the University of California ("the University") on Wong's claim that the University discriminated against him in violation of Title II of the Americans with Disabilities Act, 42 U.S.C. § 12132 ("the ADA") and section 504 of the Rehabilitation Act, 29 U.S.C. § 794. Wong alleges that the University violated the Acts when, after refusing to grant his request for accommodation of his learning disability, it dismissed him for failing to meet its academic requirements. The district court ruled that summary judgment was appropriate on two grounds: (1) the accommodation Wong requested was not reasonable, and (2) Wong was not qualified to continue his course of study in the School of Medicine because with or without accommodation, he could not perform the tasks required of an effective medical doctor. We conclude, however, that Wong created a question of fact with respect to both of these issues and that the district court therefore erred in granting the University's motion.

I. FACTS

After excelling in his undergraduate and master's degree programs, Wong entered the School of Medicine at the University of California at Davis in the fall of 1989. The School of Medicine consists of a four-year curriculum: typically, in the first two years, students take academic courses in basic sciences; in the third year, they complete six consecutive clinical "clerkships" in core areas of medical practice; and in the fourth year, they take a series of more specialized clerkships. The clinical clerkships teach the students to integrate their academic knowledge with the skills necessary to practice medicine and test them on their progress in developing these skills.

Wong completed the first two years of medical school on a normal schedule and with a grade point average slightly above a "B"; he also passed the required national board examination immediately following the second year. He began his third year on schedule, enrolling in the Surgery clerkship in the summer of 1991 and, upon its conclusion, in the Medicine clerkship. When he was approximately four weeks into the Medicine clerkship, Wong learned that he had failed Surgery. In accordance with school policy, Wong appeared before the Student Evaluation Committee ("SEC"), a body that meets with students having academic problems and makes recommendations to another group, the Promotions Board, which ultimately decides what action, if any, the school should take with respect to that student. The Promotions Board placed Wong on academic probation, decided that he should repeat the Surgery clerkship, and recommended that he continue in the Medicine clerkship at least until the midterm evaluation. Wong withdrew from the Medicine clerkship in November 1991 when his midterm evaluation showed significant problems with his performance to that point. Wong's instructor of record then assigned a senior resident to work with Wong one-on-one, focusing upon taking patient histories and making oral presentations. These sessions continued through the winter of 1992.

In March 1992, Dr. Ernest Lewis, associate dean of student affairs, granted Wong's request to take time off from school to be with his father, who had just been diagnosed with lung cancer. Wong spent at least some of this time doing extra reading in preparation for his upcoming clerkships, Psychiatry and Pediatrics. He returned to school in July 1992 and between July and December passed clerkships in Psychiatry (with a "B"), Pediatrics ("C+"), and Obstetrics/Gynecology ("C"). Wong generally received positive comments on his final evaluation forms for these courses. Instructors noted that he was "competent," "prompt," "enthusiastic," "a very hard worker," and "an extremely pleasant student who related exceptionally well with the staff"; they also stated that he had "a good fund of knowledge," "contributed meaningfully to the discussions at hand," "made astute observations of patients," and "did a good job of presenting on [gynecology] rounds." Evaluators also observed, however, that Wong "seem[ed] to have difficulty putting things together" and "limited abilities to effectively communicate his thoughts," and they recommended that he work on "organizational skills" and "setting priorities."

Wong re-enrolled in the Medicine clerkship in January 1993. Three weeks later, his father died, an event that by all accounts had a devastating impact on Wong. He continued in the Medicine clerkship for a brief period of time, but after his midterm evaluation showed a borderline performance in the first half of the clerkship, Wong, with Dean Lewis's approval, withdrew from the course and left the Davis campus to be closer to his family, who lived in the San Francisco area. In order to prevent Wong from falling further behind, Dean Lewis permitted him to take several fourth-year level clerkships at hospitals in the San Francisco area. He earned A's and B's in these courses, with positive comments. Two evaluators thought that Wong needed to improve his fund of knowledge, but both attributed the deficiency to the fact that he was taking classes in the fourth-year curriculum without having completed his third year "core" clerkships. When Wong returned to the School of Medicine at Davis in the summer of 1993, he again enrolled in Medicine. He asserts that although he did not feel prepared for this course and attempted to drop it,

Dean Lewis did not permit the withdrawal, and he ultimately failed the class, triggering another appearance before the SEC and Promotions Board.

The Promotions Board adopted strict conditions for Wong to remain a student in the School of Medicine: it required him to take only reading electives for the next three quarters; to meet again with the SEC and Dean Lewis following that period to assess his progress; and, assuming he received approval to re-enter the clerkship program, to repeat the entire third year, including the courses he already had passed. During the meeting with the Promotions Board, Wong stated that he thought he might have a learning disability and learned from members of the Promotions Board about the University's Disability Resource Center ("DRC"). DRC staff members and doctors to whom they referred Wong administered a battery of tests and concluded that Wong has a disability that affects the way he processes verbal information and expresses himself verbally.[9]

When Dean Lewis learned the results of the tests, he referred Wong to Dr. Margaret Steward, a psychologist and School of Medicine faculty member, so that she could counsel him regarding coping skills and help him determine what accommodations would allow him to complete his courses successfully. Dr. Steward suggested several strategies for Wong to employ, including telling people that he has a "hearing problem" and may need them to slow down or repeat messages; using a tape recorder; and double-checking his understanding of information he has received verbally. Dr. Steward reported to Dean Lewis in a memorandum that "[t]here is no doubt that [Wong] will need extra time to complete the clerkship years." In the same memorandum, she also specifically recommended giving Wong extra time to read before his next two clerkships, Medicine and Surgery; in a later memorandum, she informed Dean Lewis that she had discussed with Wong that he needed to pass the Medicine clerkship to provide "empirical support" for extra reading time before his next clerkship and that "if he passes Medicine that he needs to anticipate extra time in order to complete the clerkship years." Finally, Dr. Steward recommended that Dean Lewis assign Wong an "SLD [Student Learning Disability] advisor" with whom he could meet to review strategies for coping with his disability. Dean Lewis never appointed this advisor. Wong also contends (and the University does not dispute) that Dr. Steward told him that the School of Medicine "would set up a learning disability resource team to ensure that Wong received adequate accommodations," but the school never did so.

After completing the requisite three quarters of elective reading under the supervision of a faculty member, Wong planned to retake the Medicine clerkship in July 1994. After attending orientation, however, he felt unprepared for the course and asked for another eight weeks off for additional reading. Dean Lewis granted

[9] [FN 7] One of the evaluations divided Wong's disability into two categories: "[r]eceptive language" and "[e]xpressive language." Mem. from Dr. Margaret Steward to Dean Lewis (April 14, 1994). According to this description, Wong's problem with receptive language stems from his need to slow down information that others give him verbally by repeating their words to himself. Wong does not listen to the parts of the speaker's communication that occur while he is processing the previous message. With respect to expressive language, Wong sometimes cannot find the words he needs to express his thoughts quickly; to compensate, he uses gestures or substitutes generic words for technical terms. *See id.* Both aspects of the disability can result in significant miscommunication and anxiety, and having to deal with new, technical, or "not-quite-mastered" information exacerbates the problem.

this request, although he noted that he did not know how the extra time would help Wong. In September 1994, Wong took and passed Medicine, earning a "B" and receiving overwhelmingly positive comments on his grade report, including observations of his "excellent fund of knowledge," "excellent retention of new material," and compassionate manner with patients as he performed effective physical exams and formulated diagnoses. The instructor noted some difficulty in making verbal presentations, including uncertainty and taking extra time to answer, but concluded that Wong was a "solid third year medical student" who performed satisfactorily "in all areas of the clerkship." Wong then received eight weeks off to read in preparation for his Surgery clerkship, which commenced in January 1995 and in which he earned a "B." The comments on his grade report were similar to those for the preceding clerkship: generally positive remarks mitigated by reference to his need for time and a calm setting to make good oral presentations. The instructor of record concluded:

> [T]he department was very pleased with [Wong]'s performance on the clerkship. We thought that he had turned in a solid performance and that he had improved markedly over the past year. We think that he has everything it takes to become a safe and effective physician.

Before completing the Surgery clerkship, Wong contacted Dean Lewis's office and requested eight weeks off to read for his next clerkship, Pediatrics. Dean Lewis denied this request through the registrar; he has offered several different reasons for this decision, giving rise to an issue of fact on this point. In an October 1997 deposition, Dean Lewis stated that he received Wong's request through the registrar, who told him that Wong wanted time off for reading but also asked to intersperse fourth year electives with his remaining third year clerkships because he wanted to graduate on time without having to take the core clerkships in straight succession. According to Dean Lewis's testimony, he did not grant Wong's request because Wong needed to finish his third year before proceeding to fourth year courses and because giving Wong time off to read would keep him from graduating the following year. Wong denies that he pressed for permission to take fourth year courses in order to keep from delaying his graduation date; he contends that he only mentioned this alternative after Dean Lewis denied his request for eight weeks off to read for Pediatrics and told Wong that he must take courses in succession for the remainder of the year.

In the same deposition, Dean Lewis also explained his denial of Wong's request for reading time as follows: Wong already had received time off before the previous two clerkships and had passed the Pediatrics clerkship three years earlier. For these reasons, Dean Lewis opined that Wong did not need the extra time for this Pediatrics clerkship. In the course of this explanation, however, Dean Lewis again mentioned his belief that Wong wanted to graduate on time; furthermore, Dean Lewis acknowledged that Pediatrics, as well as Obstetrics/Gynecology and Psychiatry, which he expected Wong to take in succession following Pediatrics, had become much more rigorous and demanding over the past few years. Wong concurred in Dean Lewis's evaluation of the relative difficulty of the 1995 Pediatrics course as compared to the 1992 Pediatrics course.

Finally, in his December 1997 declaration, Dean Lewis repeated as reasons for denying Wong's requested accommodation that he already had granted Wong a significant amount of time off for additional reading and directed studies and that Wong previously had passed Pediatrics (and the next scheduled clerkship, Obstetrics/Gynecology) with no accommodation. Lewis also advanced a third set of explanations: "In that he was presumed to have previously read the material for those courses, I decided that allowing additional time off to read before repeating those clerkships would have been unreasonable, unfair to other students and contrary to the purposes of the curriculum."

Wong received a "Y" grade in the Pediatrics clerkship. A "Y" signifies work of failing quality in one area of a clerkship; Wong's evaluations showed that he passed the written and oral examinations but that his ward performance was unsatisfactory. His final grade sheet reported that his "clinical judgment was poor" and that his evaluators "had concerns with his ability to synthesize information." The grade sheet also noted reporting inaccuracies that in at least one instance "would have resulted in inappropriate dosages," although Wong contends that his supervisor was responsible for this particular error. Some evaluators wondered whether Wong "could safely practice clinical medicine." At the time Wong learned of his unsatisfactory performance in Pediatrics, he already had begun his Obstetrics/Gynecology clerkship. A preliminary report from his instructor in that course stated that for the first two weeks, Wong's performance had been "borderline" and "lower than expected." This evaluation particularly noted that Wong did not communicate effectively and seemed unsure of himself when examining patients, causing them to react with anger or anxiety.

Wong's "Y" grade in Pediatrics triggered another appearance before the SEC and Promotions Board. In a letter to the Promotions Board, Wong attributed his poor performance in the pediatric ward to a flu-like virus that affected him during the first two weeks of the clerkship. He stated that during this time, he was extremely ill, once requiring IV fluids, and that he fell behind in his reading which affected his performance in the wards. Wong also mentioned being preoccupied with his mother's health; she recently had been diagnosed with cancer. Wong contends that Dean Lewis's refusal to grant him an eight-week reading period prior to this clerkship also contributed to his failing grade; he did not tell the Promotions Board about the refused accommodation because, according to Wong, Dean Lewis ordered him not to mention that issue, an allegation that the University has not disputed.

The SEC recommended dismissal from the School of Medicine, and the Promotions Board concurred. Although the Promotions Board does not keep records of its proceedings, Wong was present during some of the Board's debate and contends that Dean Lewis (a member of both the SEC and Promotions Board) dominated the discussion. The written recommendation of the Promotions Board stated that it had "considered at length the academic record of Mr. Wong, [including] his current academic deficiency, a 'Y' grade in [the] Pediatrics Clerkship. . . . After a discussion, it was . . . approved to recommend Mr. Wong['s dismissal] for failure to meet the academic standards of the School of Medicine." The Dean of the School of Medicine accepted this recommendation and dismissed Wong on May 17, 1995. Wong did not appeal his dismissal through the procedure for appeal outlined in the School of Medicine Bylaws and Regulations.

II. DISCUSSION

To establish a prima facie case of discrimination based upon his disability in violation of the Acts, Wong must produce evidence that: (1) he is "disabled" as the Acts define that term; (2) he is qualified to remain a student at the School of Medicine, meaning that he can meet the essential eligibility requirements of the school with or without reasonable accommodation; (3) he "was dismissed solely because of [his] disability"; and (4) the school "receives federal financial assistance (for the Rehabilitation Act claim) or is a public entity (for the ADA claim)." *Zukle v. Regents of the Univ. of California*, 166 F.3d 1041, 1045 (9th Cir. 1999). For summary judgment purposes, the University concedes that Wong has met the first and last elements of this test. The dispute focuses upon the second element: the University argues that Wong was not qualified because he could not satisfy the academic standards of the School of Medicine, even with reasonable accommodation.

Wong bears the "initial burden of producing evidence" both that a reasonable accommodation exists and that this accommodation "would enable [him] to meet the educational institution's essential eligibility requirements." *Zukle*, 166 F.3d at 1047. Production of such evidence shifts the burden to the University to produce rebuttal evidence that either (1) the suggested accommodation is not reasonable (because it would substantially alter the academic program), or (2) that the student is not qualified (because even with the accommodation, the student could not meet the institution's academic standards). *See id.* Wong argues that, viewing the evidence in his favor, he has created an issue of fact as to whether allowing him eight weeks of additional reading time between the Surgery and Pediatrics clerkships was a reasonable modification of the School of Medicine's academic program. If extra reading time was reasonable, Wong contends, the evidence shows that he was qualified to continue in the School of Medicine because when granted that accommodation, he met the school's standards, performing satisfactorily in both the academic and interactive portions of his courses. According to the University, however, it is entitled to summary judgment because it has rebutted Wong's evidence on both of these points as a matter of law.

A. *Standards of Review*

. . . .

In this case, we must consider another standard of review as well: the degree of deference (if any) with which we should treat an educational institution's decisions involving its academic standards and curriculum. We recently observed that the Supreme Court, in the context of examining whether a university violated a student's constitutional rights to due process when it dismissed him, has held that judges "should show great respect for [a] faculty's professional judgment" when reviewing "the substance of a genuinely academic decision." *Regents of the Univ. of Michigan v. Ewing*, 474 U.S. 214, 225 (1985), *quoted in Zukle*, 166 F.3d at 1047. Extending this reasoning to the realm of the ADA and Rehabilitation Act, we concluded, as most other circuits have, "that an educational institution's academic decisions are entitled to deference." *Zukle*, 166 F.3d at 1047 (citing with approval cases from the First, Second, and Fifth Circuits). We typically defer to the judgment of academics because courts generally are "ill-equipped," as compared with experienced educators, to determine whether a student meets a university's "reasonable standards for academic and professional achievement." *Id.* (internal quotations omitted).

This deference is not absolute, however: courts still hold the final responsibility for enforcing the Acts, including determining whether an individual is qualified, with or without accommodation, for the program in question. We must ensure that educational institutions are not "disguis[ing] truly discriminatory requirements" as academic decisions; to this end, "[t]he educational institution has a 'real obligation . . . to seek suitable means of reasonably accommodating a handicapped person *and to submit a factual record indicating that it conscientiously carried out this statutory obligation.*' " *Zukle*, 166 F.3d at 1048 (quoting *Wynne v. Tufts Univ. Sch. of Med.*, 932 F.2d 19, 25–26 (1st Cir. 1991) (en banc) (*Wynne I*)) (emphasis added). Subsumed within this standard is the institution's duty to make itself aware of the nature of the student's disability; to explore alternatives for accommodating the student; and to exercise professional judgment in deciding whether the modifications under consideration would give the student the opportunity to complete the program without fundamentally or substantially modifying the school's standards. *See Wynne I*, 932 F.2d at 26 (explaining that institution needs to submit "*undisputed facts*" showing that "relevant officials" "considered alternative means, their feasibility, [and] cost and effect on the academic program") (emphasis added); *id.* at 28 (refusing to defer when institution presented no evidence regarding "who took part in the decision" and finding "simple conclusory averment" of head of institution insufficient to support deferential standard of review). We defer to the institution's academic decisions only after we determine that the school "has fulfilled this obligation." *Zukle*, 166 F.3d at 1048. Keeping these standards in mind, we examine the two issues in contention: whether the accommodation Wong requested was reasonable and whether, with accommodation, he was "qualified" to continue his studies at the School of Medicine.

B. *Reasonable Accommodation*

A public entity must "make reasonable modifications in policies, practices, or procedures when the modifications are necessary to avoid discrimination on the basis of disability." *Zukle*, 166 F.3d at 1046 (quoting 28 C.F.R. § 35.130(b)(7)). The Acts do not require an academic institution "to make fundamental or substantial modifications to its programs or standards," however. *Id.; see also Southeastern Comm. Coll. v. Davis*, 442 U.S. 397, 413 (1979) (Rehabilitation Act does not require school to substantially modify or lower its standards to accommodate disabled students). Because the issue of reasonableness depends on the individual circumstances of each case, this determination requires a fact-specific, individualized analysis of the disabled individual's circumstances and the accommodations that might allow him to meet the program's standards. *See Crowder v. Kitagawa*, 81 F.3d 1480, 1486 (9th Cir. 1996). As we have observed in the employment context, "mere[] speculat[ion] that a suggested accommodation is not feasible" falls short of the "reasonable accommodation" requirement; the Acts create "a duty to 'gather sufficient information from the [disabled individual] and qualified experts as needed to determine what accommodations are *necessary* to enable [the individual to meet the standards in question].' " *Buckingham v. United States*, 998 F.2d 735, 740 (9th Cir. 1993) (quoting *Mantolete v. Bolger*, 767 F.2d 1416, 1423 (9th Cir. 1985)).

In the typical disability discrimination case in which a plaintiff appeals a district court's entry of summary judgment in favor of the defendant, we undertake this reasonable accommodation analysis ourselves as a matter of course, examining the record and deciding whether the record reveals questions of fact as to whether the requested modification substantially alters the performance standards at issue or whether the accommodation would allow the individual to meet those requirements. In a case involving assessment of the standards of an academic institution, however, we abstain from an in-depth, *de novo* analysis of suggested accommodations that the school rejected if the institution demonstrates that it conducted such an inquiry itself and concluded that the accommodations were not feasible or would not be effective. *See supra* Part II.A. We do not defer to the academic institution's decision in the present case because the record that the University presented falls short of this requirement.

Dean Lewis's denial of Wong's requested accommodation is not entitled to deference because the University failed to present us with a record undisputedly showing that Dean Lewis investigated the proposed accommodation to determine whether the School of Medicine feasibly could implement it (or some alternative modification) without substantially altering the school's standards. First, Dean Lewis rejected Wong's request for an eight-week reading period before the Pediatrics clerkship without informing himself of Wong's need for accommodation of his learning disability. Despite Dr. Steward's earlier statement to Dean Lewis to the effect that Wong was certain to need additional time to finish the third-year clerkships, Dean Lewis failed to discuss Wong's proposal with any of the professionals who had worked with Wong to pinpoint his disability and help him develop skills to cope with it. This omission is particularly noteworthy when considered in light of the following testimony that Dean Lewis gave at his deposition:

> Q: Am I correct, Dr. Lewis, that you are the person within the School of Medicine who has the ultimate authority to determine what accommodations should be made available to students with disabilities?
>
> A: I'm not responsible for determining which accommodations will be offered to students[;] my office is responsible for seeing that the suggested accommodations are provided to the students, but we don't make the decisions as to what the accommodations are.
>
> Q: Who does?
>
> A: The Disability Resources Center.

Given Dean Lewis's own description of the limitations upon his responsibility in assessing appropriate accommodations, the fact that he simply passed messages to Wong through the registrar stating his decision to deny Wong's request — without consulting Wong or any person at the University whose job it was to formulate appropriate accommodations — strikes us as a conspicuous failure to carry out the obligation "conscientiously" to explore possible accommodations.

Second, the evidence creates real doubts that Dean Lewis gave any consideration to the effect the proposed accommodation might have upon the School of Medicine's program requirements or academic standards at the time he denied Wong's request. In his October 1997 deposition, Dean Lewis stated that he denied Wong's requested accommodation because (1) Wong wanted to graduate on time, and (2) Wong already had taken Pediatrics and had received a significant amount of time off for reading, and Dean Lewis therefore did not believe Wong needed additional time off. Neither of these reasons is relevant to the School of Medicine's curriculum or standards. Only in a declaration dated two months after this deposition did Dean Lewis assert that he denied the requested accommodation because it was "contrary to the purposes of the curriculum." A jury reasonably could find that Dean Lewis did not formulate this final rationale for denying the accommodation until long after Wong's dismissal from the School of Medicine. Such after-the-fact justification obviously does not satisfy the University's obligation to present "undisputed facts" showing that it conscientiously considered whether possible modification would fundamentally or substantially alter the school's standards when it decided that it could not reasonably accommodate the disabled student. *See Wynne I*, 932 F.2d at 26.[10] We therefore do not defer to the institution's decision; we examine the rejection of Wong's request for an eight-week reading period *de novo*.

We briefly note that both parties have met their burdens of production as to whether the accommodation was reasonable. Among other things, Wong has shown that the University granted this accommodation in the past. The University, on the other hand, has produced the testimony of Dean Lewis that the eight-week break Wong requested was unreasonable because it required the School of Medicine to alter its curriculum. It contends that the schedule was designed for students to complete consecutively to allow them to practice skills consistently and frequently and to allow the faculty to evaluate the steady development of those skills. Allowing extra time for reading before every clerkship does not comport with this goal, the University argues. Our analysis focuses upon whether this evidence shows as a matter of law that the proposed accommodation is unreasonable; we conclude for the reasons discussed below that the evidence creates an issue of fact as to the reasonableness of granting Wong an eight-week reading period prior to his Pediatrics clerkship.

First, Dr. Steward, the Coordinator of the Student Learning Disability Resource Teams and a member of the medical school faculty, informed Dean Lewis soon after Wong's diagnosis that Wong certainly would need additional time to complete the clerkship portion of the curriculum. Dr. Steward also stated that if Wong passed the Medicine clerkship after receiving additional reading time, that success would provide empirical support for Wong to receive the same accommodation for his next clerkship. A jury could have found Dr. Steward a persuasive authority on the issue whether the decelerated schedule fundamentally altered the curriculum. *See also* 34 C.F.R. § 104.44(a) (regulation interpreting Rehabilitation Act as it applies to

---

[10] [FN 30] In *Zukle*, we cited *Wynne I* with approval for the proposition that the academic institution must present a factual record that it conscientiously fulfilled its obligation to seek suitable means of accommodating disabled students. *See Zukle*, 166 F.3d at 1048. We did not delve into the particulars of what that record must show to entitle the school to deference, however, because that case did not call for any analysis of this issue: *Zukle* presented no dispute about whether the school properly had considered its ability feasibly to accommodate that disabled student.

postsecondary education stating that "[m]odifications may include changes in the *length of time* permitted for the completion of degree requirements" (emphasis added)).

Second, the School of Medicine had granted Wong this same accommodation for his two previous clerkships. An institution's past decision to make a concession to a disabled individual does not obligate it to continue to grant that accommodation in the future, nor does it render the accommodation reasonable as a matter of law. *See, e.g., Myers v. Hose*, 50 F.3d 278, 284 (4th Cir. 1995) (holding that fact that employer had offered accommodation to employees in the past did not require employer to grant same accommodation to plaintiff as a matter of federal law). The fact that the school previously made the exact modification for the Surgery and Medicine clerkships that Wong requested for the Pediatrics clerkship, however, is certainly persuasive evidence from which a jury could conclude that the accommodation was reasonable. *Cf. Hunt-Golliday v. Metropolitan Water Reclamation Dist.*, 104 F.3d 1004, 1013 (7th Cir. 1997) (observing fact that employer previously had restricted employee's lifting requirements to 50 pounds in response to back injury indicated that this accommodation was reasonable). The School of Medicine also deviated from the consecutive clerkship standard when it allowed Wong to take a leave of absence during the third year to spend time with his ailing father. Both of these occurrences imply that consecutive completion of the third-year clerkships was not an essential element of the curriculum.

Third, that Wong had earned "B's" and received generally positive comments in the Medicine and Surgery clerkships for which Dean Lewis granted him eight weeks of reading time indicates that it may have been reasonable for Wong to continue receiving this same accommodation. *Cf. Roberts v. Progressive Indep., Inc.*, 183 F.3d 1215, 1220 (10th Cir. 1999) (in the employment context, holding that "[r]easonable accommodation[s are] those accommodations which presently, or in the near future, enable the employee to perform the essential functions of his job") (internal quotations and citations omitted). From this evidence, a jury could conclude that the decelerated schedule allowed Wong to meet the substantive academic standards of the two clerkships for which he received the eight-week reading period. Allowing disabled individuals to fulfill the "essential eligibility requirements for . . . participation in programs" is, after all, the principle behind the statutory mandate that public entities provide disabled individuals with reasonable accommodations. 42 U.S.C. § 12131(2).

Our holding that Wong has created an issue of fact as to the reasonableness of an eight-week reading period between clerkships does not conflict with our opinion in *Zukle*, in which we decided that the plaintiff did not create an issue of fact as to the reasonableness of the same accommodation that Wong requested. *See* 166 F.3d at 1050–51. In *Zukle*, we reached the conclusion that a disabled medical student's requested decelerated schedule for clerkships was not a reasonable accommodation only after determining that a deferential standard of review was appropriate. We noted that the Promotions Board had considered the plaintiff's previous failure to perform adequately even when granted a decelerated schedule. *See id.* at 1050–51. Given that plaintiff's inability to perform even *with* accommodation, we concluded that the school made a rationally considered decision that allowing her to remain in the program would negatively impact the school's academic standards. Here, however, Wong has presented evidence that when granted the decelerated schedule, his performance drastically improved, and that the University failed to consider fully the effect of this modification on its program and on his abilities. *See id.* at 1048 ("[R]easonableness is not a constant. To the contrary, what is reasonable in a particular situation may not be reasonable in a different situation — even if the situational differences are relatively slight.") (internal punctuation and citation omitted).

We re-emphasize that at this stage of the litigation, we examine all of the record evidence in the light most favorable to Wong. We do not hold that allowing Wong to take eight weeks off between each of the third-year clerkships would have been a reasonable accommodation; in fact, we recognize that a jury may well find that, despite the evidence we have just discussed, this modification to the school's curriculum was not reasonable. Under the summary judgment standard, however, we do not consider whether a jury could find in favor of the defendant: we affirm the entry of summary judgment only if a jury could not find for the plaintiff. Here, a jury could decide that the modification he requested in the School of Medicine's program was reasonable. The district court erred in concluding otherwise.

C. *Qualified Individual*

The ADA provides that "no qualified individual with a disability shall, by reason of such disability, be excluded from participation in or be denied the benefits of the services, programs, or activities of a public entity. . . ." 42 U.S.C. § 12132. The statute defines a "qualified individual with a disability" as "an individual with a disability who, with or without reasonable modifications to rules, policies, or practices . . . meets the essential eligibility requirements for . . . participation in programs or activities provided by a public entity." *Id.* § 12131(2). The Rehabilitation Act creates similar rights and duties. In the context of postsecondary education, administrative regulations define "qualified" as "meet[ing] the academic and technical standards requisite to . . . participation in the . . . education program or activity." 34 C.F.R. § 104.3(k)(3). For purposes of resolving the summary judgment issue, Wong concedes that he is not qualified to continue in the School of Medicine without reasonable accommodation; the issue we must consider, therefore, is whether, with the accommodation of time off between clerkships for additional reading, Wong has created an issue of fact that he could satisfy the school's academic standards.

Again, our analysis begins with a determination of whether we defer to the University's decision to dismiss Wong for "failure to meet the academic standards of the School of Medicine." We will not defer to a school's decision if the ostensibly professional, academic judgment "disguise[s] truly discriminatory requirements." *Zukle*, 166 F.3d at 1048. Moreover, the academic institution bears the burden of presenting us with a factual record that shows it conscientiously considered all pertinent and appropriate information in making its decision. Far from demonstrating a conscientious effort to consider all relevant factors in deciding that Wong could not meet the school's academic requirements even with reasonable accommodation, the record contains evidence that the University eschewed its obligation to consider possible modifications it could make (or could have made) in the program to accommodate Wong and the past and potential effects of such accommodations (and lack thereof) on Wong's performance.

The University has not disputed Wong's assertion that Dean Lewis instructed him not to mention the requested accommodation — or Dean Lewis's denial of it — to the Promotions Board. In fact, the record contains evidence that at least two Promotions Board members believed that Dean Lewis *had* given Wong accommodations and erroneously believed that Wong had been unable to perform adequately even with those modifications. These same two individuals also identified Wong's failure of the Pediatrics clerkship as the determining factor in their decision to dismiss him. Finally, Dean Lazarus, who issued the letter formally dismissing Wong, testified that Dean Lewis told him that Wong had been accommodated and that based upon this representation and the Promotions Board's recommendation for dismissal, he issued the school's decision without considering the matter independently. The University has presented no evidence that the Promotions Board considered the fact that in his previous two clerkships, Wong had performed well after receiving an eight-week reading period as an accommodation but that in the Pediatrics clerkship, Wong performed poorly after failing to receive the same accommodation. *Cf. Zukle*, 166 F.3d at 1050–51 (in deferring to University's decision not to grant accommodation to that plaintiff, noting that Promotions Board had considered fact that the student previously had "experienced severe academic difficulties" "even on a decelerated schedule").

This failure to take Wong's disability and need for accommodation into account shows that the school's system for evaluating a learning disabled student's abilities and its own duty to make its program accessible to such individuals fell short of the standards we require to grant deference to an academic institution's decision-making process. We therefore analyze whether Wong has created an issue of fact with respect to his qualifications *de novo*.

Wong has produced enough evidence that he could meet the University's eligibility requirements to shift the burden of production to the University: his final grade sheets from the Medicine and Surgery clerkships for which he received the accommodation show that he received satisfactory grades and generally positive comments from his evaluators. The University argues, however, that an examination of Wong's entire academic record demonstrates that he did not have the capacity to become an effective physician. Evaluators from multiple courses reported flaws in his performance — such as Wong's inability to comprehend verbal information, accurately respond to questions posed to him on the wards, think on his feet, and relate to patients and staff — that the University argues could not be corrected simply by allowing Wong additional time to read before each clerkship. Thus, the University contends, Wong was not qualified because even with the accommodation he requested, he could not satisfy the School of Medicine's standards. We acknowledge that Wong's performance in some areas of the clerkship program were less than ideal, and a jury may eventually determine that Wong simply does not have and cannot acquire — even with reasonable modifications to the program — skills that are indispensable for the receipt of a license to practice medicine. For the reasons discussed below, however, we cannot say as a matter of law that he was unqualified to continue participating in the medical program.

Most importantly, a comparison of Wong's final grade sheets from his 1991 Surgery and 1993 Medicine clerkships (which he failed and for which he received no accommodation) and his 1994 Medicine and 1995 Surgery clerkships (which he passed with grades of "B" and for which he received eight weeks of reading time prior to starting) show a marked improvement, not only in Wong's performance on written and oral examinations, *but also in his performance in the clinical setting.* For example, the final grade sheet for the 1993 Medicine clerkship reported that Wong's clinical performance was "below that expected" because, for example, he could not collect data from patients and use it to formulate a diagnosis; his oral presentations were problematic; and he had difficulty with interpersonal interactions. In contrast, his 1994 Medicine clerkship evaluation stated that his clinical performance was "satisfactory in all areas." It noted some difficulty with verbal presentations, including taking a little extra time or repeating a question, but stated that he nonetheless answered questions satisfactorily. Significantly, this grade sheet reported excellent performance in two areas with which Wong earlier had struggled: interpersonal relationships (both with patients and with other professionals) and synthesizing a diagnosis while taking a patient's history.

Wong's poor performance in the 1995 Pediatrics clerkship for which he did not receive the accommodation he requested mimicked his earlier failures. The comments he received regarding his clinical performance were similar to the assessments of his work in the 1993 Medicine and 1991 Surgery clerkships: he could not synthesize information; his oral presentation skills were poor; and he lacked confidence. From all of this evidence, a reasonable jury could discern a pattern: Wong failed when he did not have extra time to prepare before a clerkship, but with the modified schedule, he succeeded in all areas of the clerkship.

. . . .

III. CONCLUSION

Faculty members and administrators of a professional school are unquestionably in the best position to set standards for the institution and to establish curricular requirements that fulfill the school's purpose of training students for the work that lies ahead of them. However, "extending deference to educational institutions must not impede our obligation to enforce the ADA and the Rehabilitation Act. . . . The educational institution has a 'real obligation . . . to seek suitable means of reasonably accommodating a handicapped person and to submit a factual record indicating that it conscientiously carried out this statutory obligation.'" *Zukle*, 166 F.3d at 1048 (quoting *Wynne I*, 932 F.2d at 25–26). Here, school administrators accepted the recommendation of a faculty member (and learning disability services coordinator) to grant Wong the schedule modification he requested for two courses, and Wong performed well with this accommodation. The School of Medicine did not present any evidence that during this time period, it believed that Wong's decelerated schedule impeded his attainment of the goals of the program or lowered the school's academic standards. Then, however, for reasons about which there is a dispute of fact, the school refused to continue granting Wong the accommodation and dismissed him when he could not perform satisfactorily without it.

The deference to which academic institutions are entitled when it comes to the

ADA is a double-edged sword. It allows them a significant amount of leeway in making decisions about their curricular requirements and their ability to structure their programs to accommodate disabled students. On the other hand, it places on an institution the weighty responsibility of carefully considering each disabled student's particular limitations and analyzing whether and how it might accommodate that student in a way that would allow the student to complete the school's program without lowering academic standards or otherwise unduly burdening the institution. Here, although the record shows that the University failed to undertake this task properly, the University still asks that we hold as a matter of law and at a very early stage of this litigation that it has satisfied its legal obligations under the ADA. Under the circumstances, we cannot grant this request. We will not sanction an academic institution's decision to refuse to accommodate a disabled student and subsequent dismissal of that student when the record contains facts from which a reasonable jury could conclude that the school made those decisions for arbitrary reasons unrelated to its academic standards.

Because genuine issues of fact remain as to both the reasonableness of the accommodation in question and Wong's qualifications, summary judgment was inappropriate. Resolving these factual disputes is the province of a jury. We REVERSE the order of the district court and REMAND this case for further proceedings consistent with this opinion.

NOTES AND QUESTIONS

1.   The concept of judicial deference, as indicated in *Regents of the University of Michigan v. Ewing*, 474 U.S. 214, 228 (1985), reflects the judiciary's respect for academics to determine their post-secondary institution's requirements for program completion. Thus, in *Ewing*, the Supreme Court upheld the university's decision to dismiss a student who failed an examination required for entry into the last two years of medical school because the university had engaged in a process of "reasoned academic decision-making." In *Guckenberger v. Boston University*, 8 F. Supp. 2d 82 (D. Mass. 1998), the federal district court in a sequel case to the one in this text afforded deference to the university's decision to deny foreign language course substitutions in one of its college programs against learning disabled students' claim that not permitting substitutions constituted a failure to accommodate under ADA and section 504. Applying the three criteria in *Wynne II, infra*, the federal district court in *Guckenberger* found that the university had engaged in "a deliberative procedure by which it considered in a timely manner both the importance of the foreign language requirement to this college and the feasibility of alternatives." *Guckenberger*, 8 F. Supp. 2d at 91. However, while not waiving the foreign language requirement, the university provided a number of other accommodations, including one-on-one instruction to learning disabled students navigating the required sequences of language classes, spelling accommodations in language classes, student tutoring at no cost to the students, additional time on tests, a reading track for French and Spanish, distraction-free testing, distribution of lecture notes in advance, and replacement of written with oral exams. How do the accommodations in *Guckenberger* that supported a finding of judicial deference differ from those in *Wong* that did not?

2.   Some courts do not afford academic deference at all. *See, e.g., Pushkin v. Regents of the University of Colo.*, 658 F.2d 1372 (10th Cir. 1981). Is there any evidence that Congress intended to treat universities differently from other federal grantees or units of state and local government? Is giving academic deference akin to giving the fox deference regarding its decisions about the chicken coop?

3.   Does *Wong* modify *Zukle*? Are the *Wong* court's efforts to reconcile *Zukle* persuasive? How do you describe the contrast between the two cases? How important are the peculiar facts of each situation? Of what significance are the particular accommodations requested and the individual and cumulative changes they might impose on the preexisting program?

4.   If you represent Wong, what evidence will you stress on remand? What if you represent the university? On remand, the court ruled against Wong on the ground that he did not have a disability within the meaning of the law, and that decision was affirmed. *Wong v. Regents of the Univ. of Cal.*, 410 F.3d 1052 (9th Cir. 2005).

5.   For a case applying academic deference to the law school context (but with less in the way of analysis than *Zukle* or *Wong*), see *Anderson v. University of Wisconsin*, 841 F.2d 737 (7th Cir. 1988) (affirming grant of summary judgment that law student with alcoholism was not qualified to continue in program).

6.   For a thoughtful treatment of the academic deference topic, see James Leonard, *Judicial Deference to Academic Standards Under Section 504 of the Rehabilitation Act and Titles II and III of the Americans with Disabilities Act*, 75 Neb. L. Rev. 27 (1996). For an interesting comparison of deference in higher education and elementary-secondary education, see Anne P. Dupre, *Disability, Deference, and the Integrity of the Academic Enterprise*, 32 Ga. L. Rev. 393 (1998).

D.   TESTING AND TESTING ACCOMMODATIONS

Schools that are federal grantees must: "provide such methods for evaluating the achievement of students who have a [disability] that impairs sensory, manual, or speaking skills as will best ensure that the results of the evaluation represent the student's achievement in the course, rather than reflecting the student's impaired sensory, manual, or speaking skills (except where such skills are the factors that the test purports to measure). 34 C.F.R. § 104.44(c).

The ADA also has a specific provision on testing and courses in title III. The provision is not limited in its scope to public accommodations, but instead covers "any person." 42 U.S.C. § 12189. Some entities are covered both by the general public accommodations provisions and by § 12189, leading to questions whether there is a broader duty under the public accommodations provisions than under the specific provision on testing. *See generally Doe v. National Bd. of Med. Exam'rs*, 199 F.3d 146 (3d Cir. 1999) (discussing overlap). The regulations promulgated under § 12189 provide:

(a) General. Any private entity that offers examinations or courses related to applications, licensing, certification, or credentialing for secondary or postsecondary education, professional, or trade purposes shall offer such examinations or courses in a place and manner accessible to persons with disabilities or offer alternative accessible arrangements for such individuals.

(b) Examinations.

(1) Any private entity offering an examination covered by this section must assure that —

(i) The examination is selected and administered so as to best ensure that, when the examination is administered to an individual with a disability that impairs sensory, manual, or speaking skills, the examination results accurately reflect the individual's aptitude or achievement level or whatever other factor the examination purports to measure, rather than reflecting the individual's impaired sensory, manual, or speaking skills (except where those skills are the factors that the examination purports to measure);

(ii) An examination that is designed for individuals with impaired sensory, manual, or speaking skills is offered at equally convenient locations, as often, and in as timely a manner as are other examinations; and

(iii) The examination is administered in facilities that are accessible to individuals with disabilities or alternative accessible arrangements are made.

(2) Required modifications to an examination may include changes in the length of time permitted for completion of the examination and adaptation of the manner in which the examination is given.

(3) A private entity offering an examination covered by this section shall provide appropriate auxiliary aids for persons with impaired sensory, manual, or speaking skills, unless that private entity can demonstrate that offering a particular auxiliary aid would fundamentally alter the measurement of the skills or knowledge the examination is intended to test or would result in an undue burden. Auxiliary aids and services required by this section may include taped examinations, interpreters or other effective methods of making orally delivered materials available to individuals with hearing impairments, Brailled or large print examinations and answer sheets or qualified readers for individuals with visual impairments or learning disabilities, transcribers for individuals with manual impairments, and other similar services and actions.

(4) Alternative accessible arrangements may include, for example, provision of an examination at an individual's home with a proctor if accessible facilities or equipment are unavailable. Alternative arrangements must provide comparable conditions to those provided for non-disabled individuals.

(c) Courses.

(1) Any private entity that offers a course covered by this section must make such modifications to that course as are necessary to ensure that the place and manner in which the course is given are accessible to individuals with disabilities.

(2) Required modifications may include changes in the length of time permitted for the completion of the course, substitution of specific requirements, or adaptation of the manner in which the course is conducted or course materials are distributed.

(3) A private entity that offers a course covered by this section shall provide appropriate auxiliary aids and services for persons with impaired sensory, manual, or speaking skills, unless the private entity can demonstrate that offering a particular auxiliary aid or service would fundamentally alter the course or would result in an undue burden. Auxiliary aids and services required by this section may include taped texts, interpreters or other effective methods of making orally delivered materials available to individuals with hearing impairments, Brailled or large print texts or qualified readers for individuals with visual impairments and learning disabilities, classroom equipment adapted for use by individuals with manual impairments, and other similar services and actions.

(4) Courses must be administered in facilities that are accessible to individuals with disabilities or alternative accessible arrangements must be made.

(5) Alternative accessible arrangements may include, for example, provision of the course through videotape, cassettes, or prepared notes. Alternative arrangements must provide comparable conditions to those provided for nondisabled individuals.

28 C.F.R. § 36.309.

For an example of a case requiring accommodations for a dyslexic student in the bar examination, see *D'Amico v. New York State Board of Law Examiners*, 813 F. Supp. 217 (W.D.N.Y. 1993). *Compare New York State Bd. of Law Exam'rs v. Bartlett*, 226 F.3d 69 (2d Cir. 2000), *on remand*, 2001 U.S. Dist. LEXIS 11926 (S.D.N.Y. 2001) (awarding a total of $7,500 damages for three state separate bar exams to plaintiff who had taken and failed exams because State Board had failed to provide reasonable accommodations), *with Cox v. Alabama State Bar*, 330 F. Supp. 2d 1265, 1268 (M.D. Ala. 2004) (denying preliminary injunction for law student diagnosed with ADD and dyslexia to have double time to take state bar exam, specifically observing that student's having had double time on exams in past, including Law School Admissions Test and exams at her law school, did not demonstrate that this accommodation was "per se reasonable in every new testing situation.").

In the following pair of cases applying section 504 to professional school testing, a medical student sought to be excused from multiple-choice testing as an accommodation to his learning disabilities. Although he won the first appeal, he lost on remand, and the court of appeals affirmed that result.

WYNNE v. TUFTS UNIVERSITY SCHOOL
OF MEDICINE ("WYNNE I")
932 F.2d 19 (1st Cir. 1991) (en banc)

The court in this case overturned a grant of summary judgment and permitted the plaintiff medical student to pursue his claim that making an exception to testing policy to permit evaluation methods other than multiple-choice examinations was a reasonable accommodation, and thus he was qualified under section 504.

COFFIN, SENIOR CIRCUIT JUDGE.

This appeal addresses the obligation of an academic institution, a university medical school, when it seeks to demonstrate as a matter of law that there is no reasonable means available to accommodate a handicapped person within the meaning of section 504 of the Rehabilitation Act of 1973, 29 U.S.C. § 794 ("the Act").

Appellant Steven Wynne was dismissed from Tufts University School of Medicine after failing numerous courses during successive attempts to complete the first-year program. Wynne, who suffers from a learning disability subsequently diagnosed as dyslexia, claims that the University unlawfully discriminated against him because of his handicap, in violation of the Act, when it refused to modify its testing methods to accommodate his difficulties. He also asserted a state civil rights claim.

The district court granted summary judgment for the University on both claims. It held, with reference to the federal claim, that Wynne was not an "otherwise qualified" handicapped person within the protection of the Act, because he was not able to meet the school's requirements. With reference to the Massachusetts civil rights claim, it held that there was no showing that Wynne had been "threatened, coerced or intimidated," as required by Mass. Gen. Laws Ann. ch. 12, §§ 11H, 11I.

A panel of this court reversed, concluding that Tufts, on the record thus far made, had failed to show as a matter of law that it had no obligation under the Act to accommodate Wynne's handicap by altering its testing methods. It also held that as to one requirement imposed on Wynne, that of auditing courses he previously had passed, there remained a factual dispute sufficient to bar summary judgment on the civil rights claim. Subsequently, Tufts' petition for rehearing en banc was granted. . . .

. . . .

I. *The Facts*

Appellant Wynne, although possessing lower MCAT (Medical College Aptitude Test) scores and undergraduate grades than most Tufts students, was admitted under the school's affirmative action program for minority applicants in 1983. In December of that year he became aware of his difficulty in dealing with written multiple choice examinations; the following spring he had conversations with school officials about his difficulty. At the end of his first year he had failed eight of fifteen courses. Although the school's guidelines provide for dismissal after five course failures, and the Student Evaluations and Promotions Committee and the Student Appeals Committee had both voted to dismiss Wynne, the dean decided to permit him to repeat the first-year program.

During the summer between his first and second years, Wynne underwent a neuropsychological evaluation at the request of the medical school, which arranged and paid for the test. The psychologist began by noting that Wynne had described having difficulties with multiple choice examination questions and experiencing more success on practicum, laboratory, or applied sections of his courses. She summarized his neuropsychological profile as follows:

> [E]valuation reveals average general cognitive abilities with marked variability among individual skills. Significant strengths were noted in conceptual thinking and reasoning abilities. In contrast, Mr. Wynne encountered serious difficulties processing discrete units of information in a variety of domains, both verbal and non-verbal. Formal language testing revealed insecurities in linguistic processing including inefficient retrieval and retention of information. This type of neuropsychological profile has been identified in the learning disabled population.[11]

The difficulties identified by the psychologist impaired Wynne's ability to answer multiple-choice questions, even though he did manage to pass several such examinations. A reading specialist who worked with him after he was dismissed from medical school observed that he had difficulty interpreting "Type K" multiple-choice questions because of their structure, which often includes passive constructions and double and triple negatives.

Wynne began his second exposure to the first-year program with the assistance of counselling, tutors, note-takers, and taped lectures, the nature, quantity, and regularity of which are presently subjects of considerable dispute. In addition to retaking the seven courses he had failed, Wynne also was required to attend classes and take exams in three courses he had passed with low-pass scores. At the end of the year he passed all but two courses, Pharmacology and Biochemistry. The Student Evaluations and Promotions Committee permitted him to take make-up exams in these two courses. He subsequently passed Pharmacology but failed Biochemistry for the third time. The two committees, Student Evaluations and Student Appeals, recommended dismissal and the dean agreed. Wynne was dismissed from the medical school in September 1985.

In 1986 Wynne filed a complaint with the United States Department of Education Office for Civil Rights alleging discrimination. On January 12, 1987 that office issued its report, finding no discrimination. A year later Wynne filed suit, alleging that Tufts' treatment of him constituted discrimination on the basis of his handicap. Although the record contains references to various supposed faults in Tufts' response to his disability, Wynne's brief on appeal ties his claim of discrimination

---

[11] [FN 1] Subsequent to Wynne's dismissal from Tufts, he underwent testing at the Massachusetts General Hospital Language Disorders Unit. In a report dated January 9, 1986, the reading therapist who evaluated Wynne observed that the 1984 neuropsychological testing, "which showed weaknesses in sequencing, memory, visual memory and part-whole relationships, taken in conjunction with his academic history, strongly suggests dyslexia."

solely to the school's failure to offer an alternative to written multiple choice examinations. We therefore treat the appeal as limited to this issue.

II. *Framing the Issue*

The district court initially denied Tufts' motion for summary judgment because "questions of fact remain regarding both the reasonableness of the accommodations made by the defendant and the extent to which defendant adhered to the program it did devise for plaintiff." Tufts moved for reconsideration, arguing that "[i]f the only remaining questions of fact concern the reasonableness of Tufts' accommodations and the extent to which Tufts adhered to those accommodations, then Tufts is entitled to judgment as a matter of law. If Mr. Wynne is not an 'otherwise qualified handicapped individual,' then it is immaterial for Rule 56 purposes whether Tufts made reasonable accommodations or adhered to them."

Wynne opposed reconsideration, arguing that "he would be able to satisfy defendant's reasonable academic requirements but for its refusal to accommodate him in the means of testing." The district court subsequently allowed the motion for reconsideration and also the motion for summary judgment, saying:

> The record is undisputed that plaintiff failed eight of fifteen courses during his first year; he again failed two of the eight when he repeated the first year and one, biochemistry, a third time. "An otherwise qualified person is one who is able to meet all of a program's requirements in spite of his handicap." *Southeastern Community College v. Davis*, 442 U.S. 397, 406 (1979). Since plaintiff clearly has not been able to meet the academic requirements of defendant school, he cannot be deemed to be "otherwise qualified." Accordingly, a cause of action under section 504 of the Rehabilitation Act of 1973, 29 U.S.C. § 794 (1987), does not lie.

The narrow issue before us is the propriety, on this record, of the grant of summary judgment to defendant on the ground that plaintiff was not an "otherwise qualified" handicapped person within the meaning of the Act and the relevant caselaw. Our task is therefore to determine, viewing the evidence in the light most favorable to Wynne, whether he has at least managed to create a genuine and material factual issue regarding his qualifications to pursue a Tufts medical education. *Anderson v. Liberty Lobby, Inc.*, 477 U.S. 242, 247–48 (1986); *Medina-Munoz v. R.J. Reynolds Tobacco Co.*, 896 F.2d 5, 7–8 (1st Cir. 1990).

. . . .

III. *The Rehabilitation Act and Caselaw: Institutional Obligations*

. . . .

Our inquiry into the meaning of "otherwise qualified" begins, but does not end, with *Southeastern Community College v. Davis*, 442 U.S. 397 (1979). That case involved a nursing school applicant who was afflicted with a serious hearing disability and whose dependence on lip reading would prevent her from clinical training and limit her in other ways. The court of appeals had set aside a district court finding that plaintiff was not an "otherwise qualified" handicapped individual, reasoning that the Act required the College to consider the application without regard to hearing ability and that it required " 'affirmative conduct' on the part of Southeastern to modify its program to accommodate the disabilities of applicants, 'even when such modifications become expensive.' " *Id.* at 404.

The Court, in reversing the judgment, addressed both propositions embraced by the court of appeals. It first rejected the idea that an institution had to disregard any limitation resulting from a handicap, saying, "[a]n otherwise qualified person is one who is able to meet all of a program's requirements in spite of his handicap." *Id.* at 406. Second, observing that no action short of a "substantial change" in Southeastern's program would accommodate plaintiff, *id.* at 414, and that the Act did not impose an affirmative action obligation on all recipients of federal funds, *id.* at 411, it held that no such "fundamental alteration" in Southeastern's program was required. *Id.* at 410. It also noted that the program, aimed at training persons for "all normal roles of a registered nurse, represents a legitimate academic policy." *Id.* at 413 n. 12. The Court did, however, leave open the possibility that an insistence on continuing past requirements notwithstanding technological advances might be "unreasonable and discriminatory." *Id.* at 412–13.

The language we have quoted, employed to deal with the absolutist views of the lower court, led other courts to seek only a rational basis for an institution's decision, without imposing any requirement to seek feasible alternative methods of accommodating the essential features of a program to a given disability. . . .

. . . .

The arguably absolutist principles of *Davis* — a handicapped person must be able to meet *all* requirements of an institution; and there is no affirmative action obligation on an institution — were meaningfully qualified by the Court in *Alexander v. Choate*, 469 U.S. 287, 105 S. Ct. 712 (1985). The Court signalled its awareness of criticism that the *Davis* pronouncement on "affirmative action" obscured the difference between "a remedial policy for the victims of past discrimination" and "the elimination of existing obstacles against the handicapped." *Id.* at 300 n. 20. It then distinguished "substantial" and "fundamental" changes (affirmative action) from "changes that would be reasonable accommodations." *Id.* It added this gloss to *Davis*:

> The balance struck in *Davis* requires that an otherwise qualified handi- capped individual must be provided with meaningful access to the benefit that the grantee offers. The benefit itself, of course, cannot be defined in a way that effectively denies otherwise qualified handicapped individuals the meaningful access to which they are entitled; to assure meaningful access, reasonable accommodations in the grantee's program or benefit may have to be made.

Id. at 301.

Thus, in determining whether an individual meets the "otherwise qualified" requirement of section 504, it is necessary to look at more than the individual's ability to meet a program's *present* requirements. As the court in *Brennan v. Stewart*[, 834 F.2d 1248 (5th Cir. 1988),] recognized:

The question after *Alexander* is the rather mushy one of whether some "reasonable accommodation" is available to satisfy the legitimate interests of both the grantee and the handicapped person. And since it is part of the "otherwise qualified" inquiry, our precedent requires that the "reasonable accommodation" question be decided as an issue of fact. . . .

834 F.2d at 1262. In *Brennan* the Fifth Circuit was considering the rejection of a totally blind applicant for a training permit as a fitter and dispenser of hearing aids because of his obvious inability to meet the requirement of making visual ear examinations. The court set aside the district court's dismissal of applicant's claim and remanded the case for a determination whether there was "some reasonable accommodation . . . which meets [claimant's] special needs without sacrificing the integrity of the Board's licensing program." *Id.*

Following on *Davis* and *Alexander*, the Court in *School Bd. of Nassau County v. Arline*, 480 U.S. 273 (1987), elaborated on how courts should deal with the "otherwise qualified-reasonable accommodation" inquiry. The case involved an elementary school teacher whose long dormant tuberculosis had recently reoccurred several times. The school board dismissed her and she brought suit under the Act. The district court, without making findings as to the duration, severity or contagiousness of the disease, or the availability of reasonable accommodation, held that an elementary school teacher with a contagious disease was not "qualified" to teach elementary school. The court of appeals reversed and remanded for findings as to the risks of infection and the possibility of making some reasonable accommodation. In affirming, the Supreme Court stated:

> The remaining question is whether Arline is otherwise qualified for the job of elementary schoolteacher. To answer this question in most cases, the District Court will need to conduct an individualized inquiry and make appropriate findings of fact. Such an inquiry is essential if § 504 is to achieve its goal of protecting handicapped individuals from deprivations based on prejudice, stereotypes, or unfounded fear, while giving appropriate weight to such legitimate concerns of grantees as avoiding exposing others to significant health and safety risks.

Id. at 287 (footnote omitted).

In addition to stressing the importance of an individual inquiry and appropriate findings of fact, the *Arline* Court gave guidance on an issue of great importance in the instant case — the deference to be given the institutional decisionmaker. The Court, recognizing that it was dealing with the grave and delicate issue of the employability of a teacher with a contagious disease in an elementary school, cited the suggestion of amicus American Medical Association that findings as to the risks involved should be "based on reasonable medical judgments given the state of medical knowledge." *Id.* at 288. The Court held that in making these findings, trial judges normally should defer to the reasonable medical judgments of public health officials. Earlier in the opinion, in responding to the argument that its decision would unwarrantably extend the Act "beyond manageable bounds," the justices also had observed that "courts may reasonably be expected normally to defer to the judgments of public health officials in determining whether an individual is otherwise qualified unless those judgments are medically unsupportable." *Id.* at 286 n. 15.

We glean additional insight on the deference issue from the Court's footnote on the limits of "reasonable accommodation," *id.* at 287–88 n. 17, which cited *Strathie v. Department of Transportation*, 716 F.2d 227, 231 (3d Cir. 1983). The Third Circuit in *Strathie*, noting that *Davis* lacked any discussion on the scope of judicial review, acknowledged the need to accord some measure of judicial deference to program administrators, but rejected a "broad judicial deference resembling that associated with the 'rational basis' test [which] would substantially undermine Congress' intent . . . that stereotypes or generalizations not deny handicapped individuals equal access to federally-funded programs." *Id.* (footnote omitted). So reasoning, the court announced the standard apparently referenced in the Court's footnote in *Arline*:

> A handicapped individual who cannot meet all of a program's requirements is not otherwise qualified if there is a factual basis in the record reasonably demonstrating that accommodating that individual would require either a modification of the essential nature of the program, or impose an undue burden on the recipient of federal funds.

Id.

What we have distilled from *Arline* and *Strathie* is consistent with the well established principle enunciated in *Regents of University of Michigan v. Ewing*, 474 U.S. 214, 225 (1985) (footnote omitted): "When judges are asked to review the substance of a genuinely academic decision, . . . they should show great respect for the faculty's professional judgment." The question in *Ewing* was whether a university had violated substantive due process (i.e., had engaged in wholly arbitrary action) in dropping plaintiff from an academic program after plaintiff had failed several subjects and received the lowest score so far recorded in the program. This was a context where no federal statutory obligation impinged on the academic administrators; their freedom to make genuine academic decisions was untrammeled. This is why the Court added to the above quoted passage the sentence: "Plainly, [judges] may not override [the faculty's professional judgment] unless it is such a substantial departure from accepted academic norms as to demonstrate that the person or committee responsible did not actually exercise professional judgment." *Id.*

In the context of an "otherwise qualified-reasonable accommodations" inquiry under the Rehabilitation Act, the same principle of respect for academic decision-making applies but with two qualifications. First, as we have noted, there is a real obligation on the academic institution to seek suitable means of reasonably accommodating a handicapped person and to submit a factual record indicating that it conscientiously carried out this statutory obligation. Second, the *Ewing* formulation, hinging judicial override on "a substantial departure from accepted academic norms," is not necessarily a helpful test in assessing whether professional judgment has been exercised in exploring reasonable alternatives for accommodating a handicapped person. We say this because such alternatives may involve new approaches or devices quite beyond "accepted academic norms." As the Court acknowledged in *Davis*, "[t]echnological advances can be expected to enhance opportunities to rehabilitate the handicapped or otherwise to qualify them for some useful employment." 442 U.S. at 412.

It seems to us that the case before us, where the adversaries are an individual and an academic institution, involves a set of conflicting concerns suggestive of those in cases where an individual seeks damages from a government official for allegedly abusing his office. *See, e.g., Anderson v. Creighton*, 483 U.S. 635, 638 (1987); *Harlow v. Fitzgerald*, 457 U.S. 800, 814 (1982). Just as in this case concern for the statutory rights of a handicapped individual is in tension with concern for the autonomy of an academic institution, so in the official conduct setting is concern for protecting individual constitutional rights in tension with concern for insulating officials from personal monetary liability and harassing litigation that would unduly inhibit discharge of their duties.

The tension has been resolved in the official conduct setting by according qualified immunity from civil damages to government officials for actions that did not violate clearly established rights. In many cases, where the material facts have not been disputed, courts have been able to determine whether qualified immunity is applicable as a matter of law without extensive proceedings. We believe a similar though not identical approach is appropriate to assess whether an academic institution adequately has explored the availability of reasonable accommodations for a handicapped individual. If the institution submits undisputed facts demonstrating that the relevant officials within the institution considered alternative means, their feasibility, cost and effect on the academic program, and came to a rationally justifiable conclusion that the available alternatives would result either in lowering academic standards or requiring substantial program alteration, the court could rule as a matter of law that the institution had met its duty of seeking reasonable accommodation. In most cases, we believe that, as in the qualified immunity context, the issue of whether the facts alleged by a university support its claim that it has met its duty of reasonable accommodation will be a "purely legal one." *See Mitchell v. Forsyth*, 472 U.S. 511, 528 n. 9 (1985). Only if essential facts were genuinely disputed or if there were significantly probative evidence of bad faith or pretext would further fact finding be necessary.

IV. *Appropriateness of Summary Judgment*

The district court, in granting Tufts' motion for summary judgment, explicitly relied on the fact that Wynne had failed eight of his first year courses, two of the eight a second time, and one a third time. Following the literal language of *Davis* that an "otherwise qualified person" must meet "all of a program's requirements," 442 U.S. at 406, the court felt compelled to grant the motion. As we have indicated in our review of the caselaw, *Alexander* in effect modified the "all" language of *Davis* and articulated the obligation to make reasonable accommodation part of the "otherwise qualified" inquiry.

If the record were crystal clear that even if reasonable alternatives to written multiple-choice examinations were available, Wynne would have no chance of meeting Tufts' standards, we might be able to affirm on a different ground from that relied on by the district court. But although Wynne has an uphill road to travel, with much to indicate that he has cognitive and other problems that are independent of his difficulties with multiple-choice examinations, we do not think the record permits this course. The results of his neuropsychological evaluation after his first year indicated average general cognitive abilities and well-developed skills in conceptual reasoning and abstract problem solving; he did pass most of his exams; he scored substantially higher in time-measured "practicum," a form of examination requiring him to apply his knowledge to a problem; he assertedly read and digested information from medical journals for his master's thesis; he read and assimilated computer-generated data in his Hematology course, which was successfully completed; experts asserted that he had the ability and motivation to improve his language skills. Whatever may be the ultimate outcome, we think that on the record as made thus far Tufts had the obligation of demonstrating that its determination that no reasonable way existed to accommodate Wynne's inability to perform adequately on written multiple-choice examinations was a reasoned, professional academic judgment, not a mere ipse dixit.

Tufts' submission on this issue consisted of an affidavit from the Dean of its School of Medicine, Dr. Henry Banks. Three paragraphs concern written multiple-choice (Type K) examinations. The first stated the test's purpose: "to measure a student's ability not only to memorize complicated material, but also to understand and assimilate it." The second, and major, paragraph stated:

> In the judgment of the professional medical educators who are responsible for determining testing procedures at Tufts, written multiple choice (Type K) examinations are important as a matter of substance, not merely of form. In our view, the ability to assimilate, interpret and analyze complex written material is necessary for the safe and responsible practice of modern medicine. It is essential for practicing physicians to keep abreast of the latest developments in written medical journals. Modern diagnostic and treatment procedures often call for the reading and assimilation of computer-generated data and other complex written materials. Frequently, and often under stressful conditions fraught with the most serious consequences, physicians are called upon to make choices and decisions based on a quick reading, understanding and interpretation of hospital charts, medical reference materials and other written resources. A degree from the Tufts University School of Medicine certifies, in part, that its holder is able to read and interpret such complicated written medical data quickly and accurately.

The third paragraph asserted that it was the judgment of "the medical educators who set Tufts' academic standards" that the above described demands "are best tested . . . by written, multiple choice examinations."

Under *Arline* a court's duty is first to find the basic facts, giving due deference to the school, and then to evaluate whether those facts add up to a professional, academic judgment that reasonable accommodation is simply not available. The above quoted affidavit, however, does not allow even the first step to be taken. There is no mention of any consideration of possible alternatives, nor reference to any discussion of the unique qualities of multiple choice examinations. There is no indication of who took part in the decision or when it was made. Were the simple conclusory averment of the head of an institution to suffice, there would be no way of ascertaining whether the institution had made a professional effort to evaluate possible ways of accommodating a handicapped student or had simply embraced what was most convenient for faculty and administration. We say this, of course, without any intent to impugn the present affiant, but only to attempt to underscore the need for a procedure that can permit the necessary minimum judicial review.

We therefore set aside the summary judgment and remand this issue for further proceedings. As is evident from our discussion, the court will be free to consider other submissions, to enter summary judgment thereon if they meet the standard we have set forth, or to proceed with further fact-finding if such should prove necessary.

V. *The State Civil Rights Claim*

[Omitted]

The action of the district court in granting summary judgment to Tufts on Count II of the complaint (Rehabilitation Act count) is reversed and the case is remanded for further proceedings in accordance with this opinion.

BREYER, CHIEF JUDGE, with whom CAMPBELL and TORRUELLA, CIRCUIT JUDGES, join (dissenting).

I agree with what I take as the majority's statement of the law. First, Tufts must make a "reasonable accommodation" to Mr. Wynne's handicap. *See Alexander v. Choate*, 469 U.S. 287, 301 (1985). Second, in determining what is "reasonable," a court must examine a host of case-specific circumstances. *See School Bd. v. Arline*, 480 U.S. 273, 287 (1987). Here, I believe those circumstances include the potential disadvantage to the disabled person, the nature of the disability, the degree of potential harm to the institution, and the comparative expertise (of courts and private parties) in making the relevant factual assessments relevant to harms, needs, and likely institutional consequences. Third, as the majority says, in the context of academic testing before us:

> If the institution submits undisputed facts demonstrating that the relevant officials within the institution considered alternative means, their feasibility, cost and effect on the academic program, and came to a rationally justifiable conclusion that the available alternatives would result either in lowering academic standards or requiring substantial program alteration, the court could rule as a matter of law that the institution had met its duty of seeking reasonable accommodation.

Fourth:

> In the context of an "otherwise qualified-reasonable accommodations" inquiry under the Rehabilitation Act, the . . . principle of respect for academic decisionmaking applies. . . .

. . . .

I disagree, however, with the majority's application of these principles to the facts in this record. The record contains an affidavit of the Dean of the Tufts

University Medical School, a conceded academic expert. That affidavit says:

> 11. The particular type and form of written, multiple choice (Type K) examinations administered to Mr. Wynne and all first year Tufts students is expressly designed to measure a student's ability not only to memorize complicated material, but also to understand and assimilate it.
>
> 12. In the judgment of the professional medical educators who are responsible for determining medical testing procedures at Tufts, written multiple choice (Type K) examinations are important as a matter of substance, not merely of form. In our view, the ability to assimilate, interpret and analyze complex written material is necessary for the safe and responsible practice of modern medicine. It is essential for practicing physicians to keep abreast of the latest developments in written medical journals. Modern diagnostic and treatment procedures often call for the reading and assimilation of computer-generated data and other complex written materials. Frequently, and often under stressful conditions fraught with the most serious consequences, physicians are called upon to make choices and decisions based on a quick reading, understanding and interpretation of hospital charts, medical reference materials and other written resources. A degree from the Tufts University School of Medicine certifies, in part, that its holder is able to read and interpret such complicated written medical data quickly and accurately.
>
> 13. It is the judgment of the medical educators who set Tufts' academic standards and requirements that this and other important aspects of medical training and education are best tested and evaluated by written, multiple choice examinations of the type given to Mr. Wynne and all of his peers.

The affidavit speaks of the "judgment of professional medical educators." It says that, in "the judgment of medical educators who set Tufts' academic standards and requirements," the demands of medicine "are *best* tested" by a multiple-choice exam. This language seems to me to say that experts considered the fairly obvious alternatives (oral exams or essay-type written exams) and concluded that written multiple-choice exams were "*best.*"

The affidavit explains *why* these educators believe that multiple-choice examinations are best. The affidavit indicates that "the unique qualit[y] of multiple choice examinations" is that these examinations are "expressly designed to measure a student's ability not only to memorize complicated material, but also to understand and assimilate it." The alternatives to written multiple-choice exams — oral or essay-type — obviously do not test reading comprehension.

. . . .

Accordingly, I would affirm. Respectfully, I dissent.

WYNNE v. TUFTS UNIVERSITY SCHOOL OF MEDICINE ("WYNNE II")

976 F.2d 791 (1st Cir. 1992)

In this decision, the court affirmed a later grant of summary judgment against the medical student seeking modification of the multiple-choice examination policy.

SELYA, CIRCUIT JUDGE.

This appeal requires us to revisit a longstanding dispute between Tufts University School of Medicine and Steven Wynne, a former student. On a previous occasion, we vacated the district court's entry of summary judgment in Tufts' favor. *See Wynne v. Tufts Univ. School of Medicine*, 932 F.2d 19 (1st Cir. 1991) (en banc). After further proceedings, the district court again entered summary judgment for the defendant. This time around, on an augmented record, we affirm.

. . . .

Prior Proceedings

In his court case, Wynne alleged that he was learning-disabled and that Tufts had discriminated against him on the basis of his handicap. In short order, Wynne refined his claim to allege that his disability placed him at an unfair disadvantage in taking written multiple-choice examinations and that Tufts, for no good reason, had stubbornly refused to test his proficiency in biochemistry by some other means. Eventually, the district court granted summary judgment in Tufts' favor on the ground that Wynne, because of his inability to pass biochemistry, was not an "otherwise qualified" handicapped person within the meaning of section 504 of the Rehabilitation Act of 1973, 29 U.S.C. § 794 (1988), as explicated by the relevant caselaw.

On appeal, a panel of this court reversed. . . . We concluded that, in determining whether an aspiring medical student meets section 504's "otherwise qualified" prong, it is necessary to take into account the extent to which reasonable accommodations that will satisfy the legitimate interests of both the school and the student are (or are not) available and, if such accommodations exist, the extent to which the institution explored those alternatives. *See Wynne*, 932 F.2d at 24–26 (citing, *inter alia*, *School Bd. of Nassau County v. Arline*, 480 U.S. 273 (1987)). Recognizing the unique considerations that come into play when the parties to a Rehabilitation Act case are a student and an academic institution, particularly a medical school training apprentice physicians, we formulated a test for determining whether the academic institution adequately explored the availability of reasonable accommodations:

> If the institution submits undisputed facts demonstrating that the relevant officials within the institution considered alternative means, their feasibility, cost and effect on the academic program, and came to a rationally justifiable conclusion that the available alternatives would result either in lowering academic standards or requiring substantial program alteration,

the court could rule as a matter of law that the institution had met its duty of seeking reasonable accommodation. In most cases, we believe that, as in the qualified immunity context, the issue of whether the facts alleged by a university support its claim that it has met its duty of reasonable accommodation will be a purely legal one. Only if essential facts were genuinely disputed or if there were significantly probative evidence of bad faith or pretext would further fact finding be necessary.

Id. at 26 (citation and internal quotation marks omitted). Because the summary judgment record did not satisfactorily address this issue, we vacated the judgment and remanded for further proceedings, leaving the district court "free to consider other submissions [and] to enter summary judgment thereon if [an expanded record] meet[s] the standard we have set forth." *Id.* at 28.

Following remand, Tufts filed a renewed motion for summary judgment accompanied by six new affidavits. The plaintiff filed a comprehensive opposition supported, *inter alia*, by his own supplemental affidavit. The court below read the briefs, heard oral argument, reviewed the parties' updated submissions, and determined that Tufts had met its burden under *Wynne*. In the lower court's view, the expanded record clearly showed that Tufts had evaluated the available alternatives to its current testing format and had reasonably concluded that it was not practicable in this instance to depart from the standard multiple-choice format. Accordingly, the court again entered summary judgment in Tufts' favor. This appeal ensued.

Issues

The principal issue on appeal is whether, given those facts not genuinely in dispute, Tufts can be said, as a matter of law, either to have provided reasonable accommodations for plaintiff's handicapping condition or to have demonstrated that it reached a rationally justifiable conclusion that accommodating plaintiff would lower academic standards or otherwise unduly affect its program. There is also a secondary issue: whether plaintiff has advanced significantly probative evidence sufficient to ground a finding that Tufts' reasons for not making further accommodations were pretextual or asserted in bad faith.

. . . .

Discussion

We have carefully reviewed the amplitudinous record and are fully satisfied that the district court did not err in granting summary judgment. Fairly read, the record presents no genuine issue as to any material fact. Because this case has consumed so many hours of judicial time, we resist the temptation to wax longiloquent. Instead, we add only a few decurtate observations embellishing what the en banc court previously wrote and remarking the significance of the new materials adduced below.

First: Following remand, Tufts satisfactorily filled the gaps that wrecked its initial effort at summary judgment. The expanded record contains undisputed facts demonstrating, in considerable detail, that Tufts' hierarchy "considered alternative means" and "came to a rationally justifiable conclusion" regarding the adverse effects of such putative accommodations. *Wynne*, 932 F.2d at 26. Tufts not only documented the importance of biochemistry in a medical school curriculum, but explained why, in the departmental chair's words, "the multiple choice format provides the fairest way to test the students' mastery of the subject matter of biochemistry." Tufts likewise explained what thought it had given to different methods of testing proficiency in biochemistry and why it eschewed alternatives to multiple-choice testing, particularly with respect to make-up examinations. In so doing, Tufts elaborated upon the unique qualities of multiple-choice examinations as they apply to biochemistry and offered an exposition of the historical record to show the background against which such tests were administered to Wynne. In short, Tufts demythologized the institutional thought processes leading to its determination that it could not deviate from its wonted format to accommodate Wynne's professed disability. It concluded that to do so would require substantial program alterations, result in lowering academic standards, and devalue Tufts' end product — highly trained physicians carrying the prized credential of a Tufts degree.

To be sure, Tufts' explanations, though plausible, are not necessarily ironclad. For instance, Wynne has offered evidence that at least one other medical school and a national testing service occasionally allow oral renderings of multiple-choice examinations in respect to dyslexic students. But, the point is not whether a medical school is "right" or "wrong" in making program-related decisions. Such absolutes rarely apply in the context of subjective decisionmaking, particularly in a scholastic setting. The point is that Tufts, after undertaking a diligent assessment of the available options, felt itself obliged to make "a professional, academic judgment that [a] reasonable accommodation [was] simply not available." *Wynne*, 932 F.2d at 27–28. Phrased another way, Tufts decided, rationally if not inevitably, that no further accommodation could be made without imposing an undue (and injurious) hardship on the academic program. With the diligence of its assessment and the justification for its judgment clearly shown in the augmented record, and with the fact of the judgment uncontroverted, the deficiency that spoiled Tufts' original effort at *brevis* disposition has been cured.

Second: The undisputed facts show that Tufts neither ignored Wynne nor turned a deaf ear to his plight. To the contrary, the defendant (a) warned Wynne in 1983 that he was failing biochemistry and suggested he defer his examination (a suggestion that Wynne scotched); (b) arranged for a complete battery of neuropsychological tests after Wynne failed eight courses in his freshman year; (c) waived the rules and permitted Wynne to repeat the first-year curriculum; (d) furnished Wynne access to tutoring, taped lectures, and the like; (e) allowed him to take untimed examinations; and (f) gave him make-up examinations in pharmacology and biochemistry after he again failed both courses. Given the other circumstances extant in this case, we do not think that a reasonable factfinder could conclude that Tufts, having volunteered such an array of remedial measures, was guilty of failing to make a reasonable accommodation merely because it did not *also* offer Wynne, unsolicited, an oral rendering of the biochemistry examination.

Third: Reasonableness is not a constant. To the contrary, what is reasonable in a particular situation may not be reasonable in a different situation — even if the situational differences are relatively slight. . . . Ultimately, what is reasonable depends on a variable mix of factors.

In the section 504 milieu, an academic institution can be expected to respond only to what it knows (or is chargeable with knowing). This means, as the Third Circuit has recently observed, that for a medical school "to be liable under the Rehabilitation Act, [it] must know or be reasonably expected to know of [a student's] handicap." *Nathanson v. Medical College of Pa.*, 926 F.2d 1368, 1381 (3d Cir. 1991). A relevant aspect of this inquiry is whether the student ever put the medical school on notice of his handicap by making "a sufficiently direct and specific request for special accommodations." *Id.* at 1386. Thus, we must view the reasonableness of Tufts' accommodations against the backdrop of what Tufts knew about Wynne's needs while he was enrolled there.

Several factors are entitled to weight in this equation, including the following: (a) Wynne was never diagnosed as dyslexic while enrolled at Tufts; (b) the school gave him a number of special dispensations and "second chances" — including virtually every accommodation that he seasonably suggested; (c) Wynne had taken, and passed, multiple-choice examinations in several courses; and (d) he never requested, at any time prior to taking and failing the third biochemistry exam, that an oral rendering be substituted for the standard version of the multiple-choice test. Under these circumstances, we do not believe a rational factfinder could conclude that Tufts' efforts at accommodation fell short of the reasonableness standard.

Fourth: Wynne's allegations of pretext do not raise prohibitory doubts about the reasonableness of Tufts' attempted accommodations or about the honesty of its assessment of alternatives to multiple-choice examinations vis-a-vis the school's educational plan. When pretext is at issue in a discrimination case, it is a plaintiff's duty to produce specific facts which, reasonably viewed, tend logically to undercut the defendant's position. *See, e.g., Villanueva v. Wellesley College*, 930 F.2d 124, 127 (1st Cir.), *cert. denied*, 502 U.S. 861 (1991); *Mack v. Great Atlantic & Pacific Tea Co.*, 871 F.2d at 181. The plaintiff may neither "rest[] merely upon conclusory allegations, improbable inferences, and unsupported speculation," *Medina-Munoz v. R.J. Reynolds Tobacco Co.*, 896 F.2d 5, 8 (1st Cir. 1990), nor measurably bolster his cause by hurling rancorous epithets and espousing tenuous insinuations. *See Mesnick v. General Electric Co.*, 950 F.2d at 826; *Yerardi's Moody St. Restaurant & Lounge, Inc. v. Board of Selectmen*, 932 F.2d 89, 92 (1st Cir. 1991).

Here, Wynne's charges comprise more cry than wool. They consist of unsubstantiated conclusions, backed only by a few uncoordinated evidentiary fragments. More is required to forestall summary judgment. . . .

Conclusion

We need go no further. In our earlier opinion, we recognized the existence of a statutory obligation on the part of an academic institution such as Tufts to consider available ways of accommodating a handicapped student and, when seeking summary judgment, to produce a factual record documenting its scrupulous attention to this obligation. Of course, the effort requires more than lip service; it must be sincerely conceived and conscientiously implemented. We think that Tufts, the second time around, has cleared the hurdle that we envisioned: the undisputed facts contained in the expanded record, when considered in the deferential light that academic decisionmaking deserves, meet the required standard.

We add a final note of caution. Although both parties to this litigation invite us to paint with a broad brush, we decline their joint invitation. The issue before us is not whether a medical student, authoritatively diagnosed as a dyslexic and known to the school to be so afflicted, is ever entitled, upon timely request, to an opportunity to take an examination orally. Rather, we are limited to the idiosyncratic facts of Wynne's case. The resulting record presents a narrower, easier issue — and we believe that the district court resolved that issue correctly.

Affirmed.

NOTES AND QUESTIONS

1.   A film critic once described the movie "Die Hard II" as less a sequel to the original than a remake of it. Can the same be said of *Wynne II* and its original? Is it fair to say that there is no genuine issue of material fact by the time of *Wynne II*?

2.   Does the qualified immunity analogy in *Wynne I* make sense? Are there additional policies at play in qualified immunity cases? Should different rules apply to accommodations from academic institutions if the case is one for damages from individuals rather than one for injunctive relief?

3.   How does *Wynne I* fit into the cases on academic deference? *Wynne II*?

4.   The court in *Wynne II* seems to caution against extending its reasoning beyond its immediate facts. Is that good advice? Why?

E.   HARASSMENT AND HOSTILE ENVIRONMENTS

GUCKENBERGER v. BOSTON UNIVERSITY
957 F. Supp. 306 (D. Mass. 1997)

Here, the court ruled that plaintiffs could state a claim under the ADA and section 504 if the defendants created a learning environment hostile to students with disabilities, but held that the facts did not support the existence of the claim. The court dismissed several of the state law claims, but upheld a claim based on breach of contract.

Saris, District Judge.

I. *INTRODUCTION*

This is a proposed class action challenging the new policy adopted by defendant Boston University ("BU") to evaluate the requests of its students to accommodate their learning disabilities. The plaintiffs — ten students with learning disabilities and four organizations — claim that the defendants[12] have violated the Americans with Disabilities Act ("ADA"), 42 U.S.C. §§ 12101 et seq., the Rehabilitation Act, 29 U.S.C. § 794, and state law. They seek injunctive, declaratory, and compensatory relief.

Plaintiffs challenge three aspects of BU's new policy as violative of state and federal anti-discrimination laws. First, they contend that BU has unreasonably erected a series of harsh eligibility requirements for students who seek accommodations for their learning disabilities, such as the requirement that all testing to document the disability must be no more than three years old and must be performed only by a licensed psychologist or a physician. Second, plaintiffs allege that BU has subjected the students' accommodation requests to an unfair evaluation and appeal procedure. Third, plaintiffs assert that the university has imposed a discriminatory blanket prohibition against course substitutions for mathematics and foreign language. In addition to the discriminatory treatment claims based on the university's new accommodations policy, plaintiffs allege that defendants have created a hostile learning environment for learning-disabled students, that the university has breached its contractual agreement to provide reasonable accommodations for such students, and that the named students with learning disabilities at BU have suffered severe emotional distress due to the university's intentional refusal to deliver on those promises.

Plaintiffs now move for class certification. Defendants oppose plaintiffs' motion and, pursuant to Fed. R. Civ. P. 12(b)(6), move to dismiss a majority of the plaintiffs' eight claims, the four associational plaintiffs, and two of the named defendants. Defendants argue that the allegations of the complaint fail to support plaintiffs' claims for hostile environment discrimination (Count IV), breach of contract (Count V), promissory estoppel (Count VI), and intentional infliction of emotional distress (Count VII). Defendants also assert that the associational plaintiffs lack standing, and that defendants Silber and Klafter are improper parties. For the reasons set forth below, defendants' motion to dismiss is *ALLOWED IN PART* and *DENIED IN PART*, and plaintiffs' motion for class certification is *ALLOWED*.

II. *FACTUAL ALLEGATIONS*

The allegations in the complaint that are relevant to the defendants' 12(b)(6) motion to dismiss and to the plaintiffs' motion for class certification are as follows.

Boston University is a private institution of higher learning that is chartered and incorporated under the law of the state of Massachusetts. Prior to the 1995-1996 school year, students with learning disabilities who sought accommodations were required to provide BU's Learning Disabilities Support Services ("LDSS") with documentation of their disability. After reviewing the documentation, LDSS would determine which accommodations were appropriate. Authorized accommodations included tape-recorded textbooks, note-taking assistance, special testing accommodations, reduced course loads, and course substitutions for the mathematics and foreign language requirements. In its promotional materials, BU represented its

---

[12] [FN 3] Boston University; Jon Westling, current president of BU; John Silber, former president and current Chancellor of BU; and Craig Klafter, assistant to President Westling.

commitment to accommodating learning-disabled students and stated that the services and accommodations provided by LDSS would be available throughout the academic career of a student with a documented learning disability.

During the 1995-1996 school year, 480 students with learning disabilities were enrolled at BU. Yet, as in prior years, only a small percentage of the total number of learning disabled students asked for and received an accommodation for their disabilities. For example, from 1990 to 1995, BU allowed an average of 15 students per year to accommodate their disabilities by substituting other courses for math and foreign language.

In December of 1995, just prior to final exams, certain BU students with learning disabilities were sent a letter from LDSS notifying them of a new policy regarding their eligibility for accommodations. Students were told that their medical documentation had to have been completed within the preceding three years by a licensed psychologist or a physician "of reputable practice," and that they had until January 8, 1996 to submit test results that satisfied this new criteria if they were to remain eligible for accommodations. BU extended the deadline for submission of new documentation to August 31, 1996 in a letter dated December 22, 1995; however, other aspects of the university's new policy went into effect during the 1995-1996 school year, including its revised evaluation procedure.

Under the new evaluation scheme, a request for accommodation that has been submitted by a student with a learning disability is subjected to several tiers of review. A student is required, first, to submit to LDSS a recent physician's or psychologist's report. LDSS reviews the documentation, makes a recommendation regarding the student's request, and forwards the application to the president's office. BU's president, currently Jon Westling, then reviews the application *de novo*. When this reevaluation is complete, the president's office notifies LDSS of the chief administrator's decision, and LDSS notifies the student of the university's position regarding accommodations for the student's disability. There is no avenue of appeal for students whose applications for accommodation have been denied by the president. Most significantly, under the new policy, a student with a learning disability will not be accommodated with a course substitution of any kind under any circumstances.

President Westling, who has no expertise in learning disabilities or accommodations, is the final arbiter of student requests under the new policy. He personally denied twenty-six out of twenty-seven student requests for accommodation under the university's new evaluation procedure during the 1995-1996 school year. Several students were denied access to the same accommodations that they had been receiving from the university prior to the implementation of the new policy.

Moreover, in two speeches, delivered in Australia and before the Heritage Foundation in Washington, D.C., President Westling referred to students with learning disabilities as "a plague," and an indication of "a silent genetic catastrophe," and he has made similar statements in letters to the New York Times, the Boston Globe, campus newspapers, and students' parents. Other administrators at BU, including Westling's assistant, Craig Klafter, have also made derogatory comments, such as referring to students with learning disabilities as "draft dodgers."

Students with learning disabilities at BU subjectively perceive the university to be a hostile educational environment for the learning-disabled. Plaintiffs claim they have suffered a loss of educational and professional opportunity, and their physical, mental, and emotional well-being has been irreparably harmed.

III. *MOTION TO DISMISS*

. . . .

1. *Hostile Learning Environment (Count IV)*

Plaintiffs contend that the defendants' derogatory speeches and discriminatory conduct have created a "hostile learning environment" for BU students with learning disabilities in violation of the ADA and the Rehabilitation Act. Cmplt. ¶ 76. Although several district courts have held that *workplace* harassment of a disabled employee violates federal law, *see, e.g., Gaither v. Barron*, 924 F. Supp. 134, 136 (M.D. Ala. 1996); *Davis v. York Int'l, Inc.*, 1993 U.S. Dist. LEXIS 17649, at *25–26 (D. Md. 1993); *Easley v. West*, 1994 U.S. Dist. LEXIS 17789, at *22 (E.D. Pa. 1994), only one federal court appears to have allowed a student to bring a hostile *educational* environment claim under the ADA or the Rehabilitation Act. *See Gaither*, 924 F. Supp. at 137 (using Title VII's hostile work environment theory to analyze a harassment claim brought by a disabled student). The threshold issue in ruling on defendants' motion to dismiss the plaintiffs' hostile learning environment claim is whether such a cause of action exists under the federal laws prohibiting discrimination against persons with disabilities.

The analysis begins, of course, with the statutory language. *See Bailey v. United States*, 516 U.S. 137 (1995). Title III of the Americans with Disabilities Act, 42 U.S.C.A. § 12182 (1988), provides that "[n]o individual shall be discriminated against on the basis of disability in the full and equal enjoyment of the goods, services, facilities, privileges, advantages, or accommodations of any place of public accommodation. . . ." The Rehabilitation Act, 29 U.S.C.A. § 794(a) (as amended 1992), states that "[n]o otherwise qualified individual with a disability . . . shall, solely by reason of her or his disability, be excluded from the participation in, be denied the benefits of, or be subjected to discrimination under any program or activity receiving Federal financial assistance." Both statutes apply to discrimination by educational facilities in receipt of federal funds, *see* 42 U.S.C. § 12181(7)(J) and 29 U.S.C. § 794(b)(2)(A), and neither limits its prohibitions to discrimination in the employment context.

The language of both Title III of the ADA and Section 504 of the Rehabilitation Act is substantially similar to Title IX of the Education Amendments of 1972, 20 U.S.C. §§ 1681–88 (1988), which courts have held is the statutory basis for hostile learning environment claims based on sexual harassment. *See, e.g., Franklin v. Gwinnett County Pub. Schs.*, 503 U.S. 60, 75 (1992) (holding that the analysis in *Meritor Sav. Bank, FSB v. Vinson*, 477 U.S. 57, 64 (1986), applies to claims of sexual harassment under Title IX); *Seamons v. Snow*, 84 F.3d 1226, 1232 (10th Cir. 1996) (finding a "sexually charged hostile environment cognizable as sexual harassment" under Title IX). . . .

Persuaded by this line of cases interpreting the analogous language and policies of Title VII and Title IX, I conclude there is a cause of action under the ADA and the Rehabilitation Act for a hostile learning environment when harassment based on a student's disability has "the purpose or effect of unreasonably interfering with [the] individual's performance or [of] creating an intimidating, hostile, or offensive environment." *Brown v. Hot, Sexy & Safer Prods.*, 68 F.3d at 540. This conclusion is consistent with the express congressional purpose in enacting the ADA to "address the major areas of discrimination faced day-to-day by people with disabilities." 42 U.S.C. § 12101(b) (1988) (ADA congressional statement of findings and purposes); *cf. Doe v. Marshall*, 882 F. Supp. 1504, 1507 (E.D. Penn. 1995) (finding that harassment of a student by a professor on the basis of her disability would "fall[] within the ambit" of the ADA and the Rehabilitation Act). Harassment based on disability is no less potent, disruptive, or discriminatory on a university campus or in a classroom than on an assembly line or in a boardroom. *See Franklin v. Gwinnett County Pub. Schs.*, 503 U.S. 60, 74–75 (1992) ("[A] student should have the same protection in school that an employee has in the workplace.")

This Court concludes, further, that the flexible Title VII standards for establishing a hostile work environment claim apply to hostile learning environment claims brought under the federal statutes prohibiting discrimination against persons with disabilities. *Brown*, 68 F.3d at 540 (applying Title VII caselaw by analogy to a hostile learning environment claim brought under Title IX); *but cf. Rowinsky v. Bryan Indep. Sch. Dist.*, 80 F.3d 1006, 1011 n. 11 (5th Cir. 1996) (noting that "importing a theory of discrimination from the adult employment context into a situation involving children is highly problematic"), *cert. denied*, 519 U.S. 861 (1996).

To state a cognizable claim for hostile learning environment harassment under the ADA and Rehabilitation Act, a plaintiff must allege: (1) that she is a member of a protected group, (2) that she has been subject to unwelcome harassment, (3) that the harassment is based on a protected characteristic, her disability, (4) that the harassment is sufficiently severe or pervasive that it alters the conditions of her education and creates an abusive educational environment, and (5) that there is a basis for institutional liability. *See Brown*, 68 F.3d at 540 (citing *Meritor Sav. Bank, FSB v. Vinson*, 477 U.S. 57, 66–73 (1986)).

Applying these standards, this Court must now decide whether the claim of hostile learning environment discrimination in this case passes muster. Here, the individual plaintiffs are BU students with learning disabilities who claim that the derogatory statements of university administrators, in particular, President Westling, combined with the university's "draconian" new accommodations policy, has created an abusive learning environment that has altered their educational and professional opportunities.

"[T]he relevant factors must be viewed both objectively and subjectively." *Brown*, 68 F.3d at 540. "[T]o state a hostile environment claim for discrimination by unlawful harassment, a plaintiff must show that the alleged harassment creates an objectively hostile or abusive . . . environment and that the putative victim subjectively perceives the environment to be abusive." *Haysman v. Food Lion, Inc.*, 893 F. Supp. 1092, 1107 (S.D. Ga. 1995); *accord Harris v. Forklift Systems*, 510 U.S. 17, 21–22 (1993). Under well-established Title VII precedent, harassment is actionable as illegal discrimination only if the environment is "permeated with 'discriminatory intimidation, ridicule, and insult.' " *Harris*, 510 U.S. at 21 (quoting *Meritor Sav. Bank*, 477 U.S. at 64–65). In evaluating a complaint pursuant to a motion to dismiss a hostile environment claim, a court should consider the "totality of the circumstances," including the frequency of the discriminatory conduct, its severity, whether the alleged conduct is "physically threatening or humiliating rather than a mere offensive utterance," and whether it interferes with the plaintiff's performance. *Brown*, 68 F.3d at 540.

The allegations of the complaint fall short of describing an objectively "hostile" educational environment for students with learning disabilities. Jon Westling's speeches, which are the only concrete examples of the alleged expressions of "scorn and hostility" toward learning disabled students made by university administrators, were delivered on only two occasions, both off-campus and in nonstudent fora. When read in context, the statements are critiques of the learning disabilities "movement" that are not focused on or addressed to particular BU students. For example, in the speech "Disabling Education: The Culture Wars Go to School," Westling explores what he identifies as "the distinction between learning disabilities *per se* and [the] ideological movement that has seized on the existence of some real disabilities and conjured up other[s]":

> We should, in my view, make a strong distinction between diagnoses that rest on clear, specific criteria and corroborating medical and epidemiological evidence, and the penumbra complaints. The latter, much larger category of alleged maladies comprises much of the repertoire of learning disabilities specialists. . . .
>
> These are, it is fair to say, fugitive disorders. For most of them there is no standard test. Their symptomatologies are as vague as those photographs taken of bank robbers by surveillance cameras. That is to say, they do occasionally identify a suspect, but more often they identify a blur. Mostly what these fugitives disorders lack is a grounding in careful medical or scientific inquiry. . . .
>
> What, then, ails the fifteen to twenty percent of the school-age population that is allegedly learning disabled? . . . Between 1977 and 1982, the number of learning disabled students in the United States more than doubled (from 797,000 to 1,627,000). What happened? Did America suffer some silent genetic catastrophe during those decades?

Although these comments, viewed objectively, may certainly be offensive to learning-disabled students, under the *Brown* standard, they are not physically threatening or humiliating. *See Brown*, 68 F.3d at 541 (finding conduct insufficiently severe, threatening, or humiliating where the "remarks were not directed specifically at plaintiffs" and were intended to educate).

The complaint is devoid of the sharply-pointed, crudely-crafted, and frequently-launched "slings and arrows" that courts have found sufficient to establish severe and pervasive harassment that alters a plaintiff's working conditions. *See, e.g., Harris*, 510 U.S. at 19–20 (describing allegations of gender-based insults, statements that made plaintiff "the target of unwanted sexual innuendos," and orders by supervisor that plaintiff retrieve coins from his front pants pocket and bend over to pick up items intentionally dropped); *Burrow v. Postville Community Sch.*, 929 F. Supp. 1193, 1198 (N.D. Iowa 1996) (recounting classmates' acts of yelling sexual obscenities at plaintiff, throwing food and spit balls at her, kicking her between the legs in a sexually suggestive manner, threatening her life, and defacing her locker and materials with sexually offensive threats); *Haysman v. Food Lion, Inc.*, 893 F. Supp. at 1098 (describing the supervisors' threatening and berating attitudes and statements, extreme profanity, and physical assaults on the disabled plaintiff); *Davis v. York Int'l, Inc.*, 1993 U.S. Dist. LEXIS 17649, at *26 (D. Md. 1993) (assessing disabled plaintiff's allegations that her supervisor mocked her speech and gait, spread myths and rumors about her condition, blamed her for other workers' errors, hovered over her excessively while she worked, threatened to remove her equipment, and denigrated her abilities privately and publicly).

One court in this district has recently held that "there is enough difference between the work and the school milieu to justify a less rigorous" threshold of offensive conduct when plaintiffs claim that sexual harassment has created a hostile educational environment than when plaintiffs seek to support a hostile workplace sexual harassment claim. *Donovan v. Mt. Ida College*, No. 96-10289 (D. Mass. 1997). Even if the measure of harassment in the educational environment is less rigorous than Title VII's requirement of "severe and pervasive" conduct, the activity alleged in this complaint would miss the hostile environment mark.

Holding a university president liable for creating a hostile learning environment solely because of an unpopular speech would also have serious First Amendment implications. *See Brown v. Trustees of Boston Univ.*, 891 F.2d 337, 351 (1st Cir. 1989) (holding that it was error to permit the speeches of a university president to be admitted as evidence of discriminatory animus because of the "chilling effect that admission of such remarks could have on academic freedom"), *cert. denied*, 496 U.S. 937 (1990); *cf. Sweezy v. State of New Hampshire*, 354 U.S. 234, 250 (1957) (concluding that "to impose any straitjacket upon the intellectual leaders in any colleges and universities would imperil the future of our nation"). The fact that a vociferous administrator with a concern about a perceived abuse of learning-disability protections is personally involved in the day-to-day implementation of the university's allegedly discriminatory accommodations policy may be of some consequence in this Court's determination of the fairness of BU's evaluation procedures. However, insensitive or politically incorrect speeches by high ranking university officials do not transform a cognizable discriminatory treatment claim into an action for hostile environment discrimination.

Assuming *arguendo* that one can state a hostile learning environment claim under Article 114 of the Amendments to the Massachusetts Constitution, plaintiffs' allegations would also fail to support such a claim. *See Layne v. Superintendent of Mass. Correctional Inst.*, 406 Mass. 156, 159, 546 N.E.2d 166, 168 (1989) (finding that "assistance in construing art. 114" can be found in case law that interprets the Rehabilitation Act "from which the language of the amendment was largely taken").

Accordingly, Count IV is *DISMISSED*.

2. Breach of Contract (Count V)

. . . .

Plaintiffs allege that BU "published and disseminated various brochures, catalogues, and promotional materials" that described accommodations that students with learning disabilities are eligible to obtain, including course substitutions in math and foreign language. Cmplt. at ¶ 84. Plaintiffs also assert that the published materials assured learning disabled students that "the services and accommodations provided by LDSS would remain available for the remainder of the student's academic career at BU," and that these promises were a "significant factor" in the students' decisions to attend the university. *Id.* at ¶¶ 84, 85. The complaint alleges that the promotional materials created a contract between the students with learning disabilities and the university, and that the university breached this agreement by prohibiting course substitutions in math and foreign language and by requiring retesting for continued eligibility for accommodations, among other things. *Id.* at ¶ 87. This Court concludes that plaintiffs have alleged facts that, if true, are sufficient to support its breach of contract claim.

Universities are capable of forming legally cognizable contractual relationships with their students. *See Russell v. Salve Regina College*, 890 F.2d 484, 488 (1st Cir. 1989), *rev'd on other grounds*, 499 U.S. 225 (1991), *and reinstated on remand*, 938 F.2d 315 (1st Cir. 1991). Brochures, policy manuals, and other advertisements can form the basis of such contractual agreements. *See id.* (discerning the terms of an agreement between a nursing student and a college "[f]rom the various catalogs, manuals, handbooks, etc., that form the contract between student and institution"); *see also Hannon v. Original Gunite Aquatech Pools, Inc.*, 385 Mass. 813, 822, 434 N.E.2d 611, 617 (1982) ("We have no doubt that express warranties can be created by an advertising brochure.").

Nonetheless, the defendants argue that the Court should exercise extreme care in deciding that the BU's relationship with its learning disabled students is subject to commercial contract doctrine. Although "there can be no doubt that courts should be slow to intrude into the sensitive area of the student-college relationship," *Russell*, 890 F.2d at 489, plaintiffs have alleged sufficient facts to establish a contract between BU and its students with learning disabilities and to support their allegation of breach. *See id.* at 488; *see also Lyons v. Salve Regina College*, 565 F.2d 200, 202 (1st Cir. 1977) ("[S]ome elements of the law of contracts are used and should be used in the analysis of the relationship between plaintiff and the university. . . ." (quoting *Slaughter v. Brigham Young Univ.*, 514 F.2d 622, 626 (10th Cir. 1975))), *cert. denied*, 435 U.S. 971 (1978).

Defendants' argument that the university has issued materials with a disclaimer statement which undermines the plaintiffs' breach of contract claim presents matters outside the four corners of the complaint and must await the summary judgment stage.

The motion to dismiss Count V of the complaint is *DENIED*.

[Discussion of promissory estoppel claim omitted.]

4. *Intentional Infliction of Emotional Distress (Count VII)*

To state a claim for intentional infliction of emotional distress under Massachusetts law, the plaintiff must allege

> (1) that the actor intended to inflict emotional distress or that he knew or should have known that emotional distress was the likely result of his conduct; (2) that the conduct was "extreme and outrageous," was "beyond all possible bounds of decency" and was "utterly intolerable in a civilized community"; (3) that the actions of the defendant were the cause of the plaintiff's distress; and (4) that the emotional distress sustained by the plaintiff was "severe" and of a nature "that no reasonable man could be expected to endure it."

Agis v. Howard Johnson Co., 371 Mass. 140, 144–45, 355 N.E.2d 315, 318–19 (1976) (citations omitted); *accord Brown v. Hearst Corp.*, 54 F.3d 21, 27 (1st Cir. 1995) (following the *Agis* standard). It is well-established that, in regard to claims of intentional infliction of emotional distress, "the door to recovery should be opened but narrowly and with due caution." *Agis*, 371 Mass. at 144, 355 N.E.2d 315 (quoting *Barnett v. Collection Serv. Co.*, 214 Iowa 1303, 1312, 242 N.W. 25, 28 (1932)). Simply stated, "liability is imposed only where the case is one in which the recitation of the facts to an average member of the community would arouse his resentment against the actor, and lead him to exclaim, 'Outrageous!' " *Borden v. Paul Revere Life Ins. Co.*, 935 F.2d 370, 380 (1st Cir. 1991); *see also Foley v. Polaroid Corp., Inc.*, 400 Mass. 82, 99, 508 N.E.2d 72, 82 (1987) (quoting Restatement (Second) of Torts, § 46, comment d (1965)).

This is not such a case. Plaintiffs claim emotional distress based on the defendants' imposition of an allegedly discriminatory accommodations policy and on the creation of an allegedly hostile environment for students with learning disabilities. Even when taken as true, the factual allegations of the complaint are not extreme and outrageous enough to give rise to liability for any resulting emotional distress. *Cf. Chakrabarti v. Cohen*, 31 F.3d 1, 6 (1st Cir. 1994) (finding that "[l]awyers, who use the term 'outrage' liberally, may become tone-deaf to the nuances" but that "an atrocity is something more than a faulty evaluation").

Plaintiffs argue that the defendants' conduct was sufficiently outrageous because the defendants knew that students with learning disabilities are particularly susceptible to emotional injury. While "the relationship of the plaintiff to the defendant and the knowledge of the plaintiff's sensitivities" is an important consideration in determining whether the challenged conduct satisfies the "extreme and outrageous" conduct requirement, *Russell*, 890 F.2d at 487 (citing Prosser and Keeton, *The Law of Torts*, § 12, at 64 (5th ed. 1984)), vulnerable plaintiffs do not state an emotional distress claim solely by demonstrating that the defendants were aware of the plaintiffs' susceptibility to emotional injury when they acted. *Cf. Fudge v. Penthouse Int'l, Ltd.*, 840 F.2d 1012, 1021 (1st Cir. 1988) ("[C]onduct that is intentional or reckless and causes severe emotional distress does not *ipso facto* constitute extreme and outrageous conduct."), *cert. denied*, 488 U.S. 821 (1988); *Foley*, 400 Mass. at 99, 508 N.E.2d at 82 (finding that liability for emotional distress cannot be based upon the tortious, criminal, or malicious intent of the defendant; rather, it is permitted only where the defendant's conduct is "so outrageous in character, and so extreme in degree, as to go beyond all possible bounds of decency" (internal quotation marks and citation omitted)). Although it is a fair inference from the allegations in the complaint that BU's administrators knew that students with learning disabilities were likely to be upset by the new accommodations procedure, the conduct is insufficiently extreme and outrageous as a matter of law to state a claim for intentional infliction of emotional distress.

Moreover, the mere fact that the defendants' conduct may turn out to be violative of the plaintiffs' civil rights does not, in and of itself, necessitate a finding that the conduct is sufficiently egregious to state a claim for intentional infliction of emotional distress. *See, e.g., Marques v. Fitzgerald*, 99 F.3d 1, 6–7 (1st Cir. 1996) (concluding that a reasonable jury may have found that the defendant's conduct violated the state whistleblower statute, but that the conduct nonetheless was insufficiently extreme and outrageous to support liability for intentional infliction of emotional distress).

The intentional infliction of emotional distress claim (Count VII) is *DISMISSED*. *See Fudge*, 840 F.2d at 1021 (affirming the dismissal of an emotional distress claim where the "facts do not allege conduct that is sufficiently extreme and outrageous to warrant the imposition of liability"); *Hoffman v. Optima Systems, Inc.*, 683 F. Supp. 865, 872–73 (D. Mass. 1988) (dismissing emotional distress claim as based on conduct that is legally insufficient).

. . . .

NOTES AND QUESTIONS

1. Assume that a university president called African-American or female students a "plague." Would the hostile-environment claims of those students be disposed of the same way they were in *Guckenberger*? How is *Guckenberger* different from that scenario?

2. What facts would be required to constitute a hostile environment in an academic setting? How relevant is the topic of academic freedom? How relevant are ongoing controversies over campus civility codes and general prohibitions on hate speech? For a provocative approach to addressing disabilities and hostile environ-ment, see Ani B. Satz, *A Jurisprudence of Dysfunction: On the Role of "Normal Species Functioning" in Disability Analysis*, 6 YALE J. HEALTH POL'Y L. & ETHICS 221 (2006). For an extended discussion of disability harassment claims and defenses and relevant policy issues, see MARK C. WEBER, DISABILITY HARASSMENT (2007).

3. If a hostile environment is found at a university, what remedies should the court provide?

4. Are damages a proper remedy for harassment? Note that a continuing controversy exists about the propriety of damages from units of state government (such as state universities) under the ADA because of Eleventh Amendment immunity. *Compare Tennessee v. Lane*, 541 U.S. 509 (2004) (upholding congres-sional abrogation of state immunity from damages for action under ADA title II implicating fundamental right of access to courts), *with Board of Trs. of Univ. of Ala. v. Garrett*, 531 U.S. 356 (2001) (finding damages action by employee under ADA

title I barred by Eleventh Amendment immunity). Several courts have found that ADA title II validly abrogates Eleventh Amendment immunity in higher education cases under *Lane*'s reasoning. *See Toledo v. Sanchez*, 454 F.3d 24 (1st Cir. 2006), *cert. denied*, 127 S. Ct. 1826 (2007); *Constantine v. Rectors & Visitors of George Mason Univ.*, 411 F.3d 474 (4th Cir. 2005); *Association for Disabled Americans v. Florida Int'l Univ.*, 405 F.3d 954 (11th Cir. 2005). *Contra Doe v. Board of Trs. of Univ. of Ill.*, 429 F. Supp. 2d 930 (N.D. Ill. 2006). *See generally supra* Chapter 10 (discussing damages remedies in special education cases). Punitive damages are not available under ADA title II or section 504. *Barnes v. Gorman*, 536 U.S. 181 (2002).

Acquired Immune Deficiency Syndrome	AIDS	A disease of the immune system caused by infection with the human immunodeficiency virus (HIV).
Administrative Law Judge	ALJ	A federal or state hearing officer who hears and makes decisions on administrative matters for a federal or state agency.
Advanced placement	AP	Advanced courses offered in high schools which, when successfully completed, offer the basis for being placed at a higher level in college. Advanced placement tests provide the basis for colleges awarding credit for such courses.
Alternative school		A school for placement of students unable to function in regular classroom settings. IDEA refers to an "alternative educational setting," 20 U.S.C. § 1415(k).
Americans with Disabilities Act	ADA	Federal law prohibiting discrimination against individuals with disabilities, 42 U.S.C. 12101 et seq.
Applied behavior analysis	ABA	A skills-based therapy that teaches socially significant behavior by applying certain psychological principles, specifically teaching skills by breaking them into small steps taught (and rewarded) one at a time. The term can encompass any method that changes behavior in a measurable, systematic way; such methods have traditionally involved learning situations free from distraction and discrete trials.
Asperger Syndrome		A developmental disability sometimes referred to as high functioning autism; Asperger Syndrome is characterized by the poor communication and social skills evident in autism, but also by at least normal intelligence and language development.

Assistive technology	AT	Equipment or technology that can improve functional capacity of individuals with disabilities including, for example, computer access aids, communication aids, hearing aids. The term is defined by statute and regulation, 20 U.S.C. § 1401(1); 28 C.F.R. § 35.104, 34 C.F.R. §§ 300.5–.6.
Attention Deficit Disorder	ADD	A disorder that involves impulsivity and attentional deficits in initiating or maintaining concentration; these difficulties often result in learning and behavioral issues; sometimes called ADD/WO meaning "without" hyperactivity.
Attention Deficit Hyperactivity Disorder	ADHD	ADD with hyperactivity, that is excessive movement and restless behavior. ADD and ADHD are not specifically included in the statutory definitional list for child with a disability but may qualify for special education under other categories where appropriate.
Autism		A neurologically based developmental disorder that affects verbal and nonverbal communication social skills. Autism is part of a spectrum of pervasive development disorders (PDD) including Autistic Disorder, Asperger Disorder, Childhood Disintegrative Disorder (CDD), Rett's Disorder, and PDD-Not Otherwise Specified (PDD-NOS). Autism is included in the definitional list for child with a disability. This term is defined by statute and regulation, 20 U.S.C. § 1401(3)(A), 34 C.F.R. § 300.8(c)(1).
Behavioral intervention plan	BIP	A written document that outlines how the IEP team and others will try to intervene with the environment and/or the student to alter problematic behaviors presented by a student and identified in the functional behavioral assessment. This term is used in IDEA at 20 U.S.C. § 1415(k)(1)(D), (F) to address an approach to a child's behavior. *See also* 34 C.F.R § 300.530(f).
Board of Cooperative	BOCES	Typically an intermediate level public Educational Services agency formed to provide shared services to school districts.
Charter school		A self-governing public school operating under its authorizing charter under state law.

Coding		In some states, term to describe designation of a student as eligible for special education.
Cognitive development		Acquisition of the ability to think, reason, and understand concepts, process information, and solve problems. *See* 20 U.S.C. §§ 1401, 1432; 34 C.F.R. § 300.8.
Compensatory education	COMP ED	Services provided beyond the time that eligibility for special education under IDEA has otherwise expired to address situation where the student can show that the program that he/she was given was inappropriate.
Conduct disorder	CD	Repetitive patterns of aggressive and severe antisocial behavior including Oppositional Defiant Disorder (ODD), Disruptive Behavior Disorder Not Otherwise Specified (DBD-NOS), Adjustment Disorder, and Child or Adolescent Antisocial Behavior.
Department of Education	DOE	There are the United States Department of Education and also various State departments, the latter sometimes referred to by variations on this name.
Diagnostic and Statistical Manual of Mental Disorders — 4th Edition	DSM-IV	Published by the American Psychiatric Association, this manual codifies diagnostic attributes for mental health disorders for both children and adults.
Discrete trial training	DTT	A skill based therapy for autistic students that uses an instruction-prompt-response-reward methodology, i.e. a stimulus, a behavior and a consequence.
Dyslexia		A neurologically-based disorder that hampers processing of language and reading ability, typically involving difficulty with phonetic mapping, spatial orientation, and sequential ordering. Dyslexia is included as a specific learning disability under 20 U.S.C. § 1401(30)(B) and 34 C.F.R. § 300.8.
Early Childhood Team	ECT	In some states, the name for the team which meets to formulate the Individual Family Service Plan.
Early Intervening Services	EIS	Services funded by up to 15% of an LEA's federal IDEA funds for children not found to be eligible for services under IDEA, pursuant to 20 U.S.C. § 1413(f) and 34 C.F.R. § 300.226. Not to be confused with early intervention services for children ages 0–2.

Education for All Handicapped Children Act	EAHCA	Enacted in 1975, Public Law 94-142, predecessor to current IDEA federal special education legislation.
Education of the Handicapped Act	EHA	Enacted in 1970, the predecessor and framework to the EAHCA.
Elementary and Secondary Education Act	ESEA	Major federal legislation focused on K12 education, initially the Elementary and Secondary Education Act of 1965 and variously amended since then. ESEA provides large amounts of federal aid to states and local districts. The best-known provision of ESEA is Title I, which directs funding to serve economically disadvantaged children. The ESEA is subject to reauthorization, the most recent reauthorization being the No Child Left Behind legislation enacted in 2001.
English as a second language; English for speakers of other languages	ESL/ESOL	A method for teaching English to limited-English-speaking students.
English language learners	ELL	A student whose first language is a language other than English; typically the term describes a student in a particular program for learning English such as bilingual education or ESL.
Extended school year	ESY	Services provided to a student during vacations and holidays.
Family Educational Rights and Privacy Act	FERPA	The federal law protecting the confidentiality of student records and providing certain parental/student rights in regard to those records for schools receiving federal financial assistance, 20 U.S.C. § 1232g; 34 C.F.R. Part 99.
Free appropriate public education	FAPE	Special education and necessary related services provided without charge in conformity with state standards and a student's IEP. This term is defined by statute and regulation, 20 U.S.C. § 1401(7); 34 C.F.R. §§ 104.33(b),(d), 300.17.
Functional behavioral assessment	FBA	A review and analysis of the student's situation to find the "functions" of that student's problem behaviors by identifying problem behaviors and the contextual factors that contribute to those behaviors. The term is used in IDEA and its implementing regulations at 20 U.S.C. § 1415(k), 34 C.F.R. § 300.530.

Head Start		Head Start is a federally sponsored program focused on preparing low-income children ages 0–5 for school, codified at 42 U.S.C. § 9831.
Homeschooling		Education at home; governed by various state laws.
Inclusion		Educating all children in the same classroom, including children with various disabilities, by adding appropriate services
Independent Educational Evaluation	IEE	An evaluation of a student for special education and related services conducted by someone other than those employed by the school district. This term is defined by statute and regulation, 20 U.S.C. § 1415(b)(1); 34 C.F.R. § 300.502.
Individualized Education Program	IEP	A single written document laying out the plan for special education and related services for a student with disabilities. This term is defined by statute and regulation, 20 U.S.C. § 1401(14); 34 C.F.R. §§ 300.320.328.
Individualized Family Service Plan	IFSP	A plan written by a multidisciplinary team to address the needs of children with disabilities ages 0–3. This term is defined by statute and regulation, 20 U.S.C. §§ 1401(15); 1436; 34 C.F.R. § 303.340(b).
Individuals with Disabilities Education Act	IDEA	Federal special education legislation, 20 U.S.C. § 1400 et seq.
Individuals with Disabilities Education Improvement Act	IDEIA	The reauthorization of IDEA in 2004 is sometimes referred to with this acronym.
Intelligence quotient	IQ	A standardized test score measuring a person's cognitive abilities in relation to his/her age. The score is calculated by dividing the "mental age" (derived from the test) by actual age.
Interim alternative educational setting	IAES	An education placement outside of the student's regular placement, authorized specifically by statute under 20 U.S.C. § 1415(k) and 34 C.F.R § 300.530(b)(1).

Learning disability	LD	This term covers a variety of conditions that affect a student's ability to learn, more particularly, ability to acquire and use verbal or nonverbal information. The IDEA speaks to "specific learning disability" as "a disorder in one or more of the basic psychological processes involved in understanding or in using language, spoken or written, that may manifest itself in an imperfect ability to listen, think, speak, read, write, spell, or to do mathematical calculations, including conditions such as perceptual disabilities, brain injury, minimal brain dysfunction, dyslexia, and developmental aphasia." 20 U.S.C. §§ 1401(3), (30); 34 C.F.R. § 300.8(c)(10); *see also* 34 C.F.R. § 104.3(j)(2); 34 C.F.R. Part 104 Appendix A.
Learning disorder		Another term for learning disability, a condition that interferes with a student's ability to learn.
Least restrictive environment	LRE	The placement of children with disabilities that allows for their being included in academic and non-academic settings "to the maximum extent appropriate" with students who are not disabled. IDEA requires that there be a continuum of placements, *see* 20 U.S.C. § 1412(a)(5); 34 C.F.R. §§ 300.114–.120.
Limited English proficiency	LEP	Students whose primary language is not English. *See generally* 20 U.S.C. § 7801(25). This term is used in IDEA as part of the definition of native language at 20 U.S.C. § 1401(20); 34 C.F.R. § 300.29.
Local education agency	LEA	Public board of education or authority that administers education in various political subdivisions. This term is defined by statute and regulation, 20 U.S.C. § 1401(19), 34 C.F.R. § 300.28.
Local Hearing Officer	LHO	A hearing officer at the local level; *see* 20 U.S.C. § 1415(f).
Lovaas	Lovaas	An intensive, early intervention behavior program for children with autism developed by and named for Dr. O. Ivar Lovaas; also known as the UCLA Model of Applied Behavioral Analysis.

Magnet School		A school with a strong emphasis in a particular subject area, for example, music, science, drama, or math. Typically students attend a magnet school by application and selection rather than attending a school that would be in their residential area.
Mainstreaming		The practice of integrating students with disabilities into regular classrooms for at least part of their school day.
Manifestation		For special education students, a determination review statutorily mandated review to ascertain whether the student's behavior is a result of his/her disability. *See* 20 U.S.C. § 1415(k)(1)(E); 34 C.F.R. § 300.530(e).
Mediation		Generally, a process where a third party neutral helps to facilitate a solution to a problem between or among other parties. Mediation is part of the dispute resolution procedures referenced by IDEA, 20 U.S.C. § 1415(e); 34 C.F.R. § 300.506, 303.419.
Multidisciplinary conference	MDC	Meeting of professionals and other educators from a variety of disciplines involved in a student's evaluation.
No Child Left Behind	NCLB	Reauthorization of the Elementary and Secondary Education Act (ESEA), the major federal funding legislation for public schools, P.L. 107-110 codified as 20 U.S.C. § 6301 et seq.
Office for Civil Rights	OCR	Part of the Department of Education, the enforcement agency for several federal civil rights statutes that prohibit discrimination including discrimination on the basis of age, disability, race, color, national origin, and sex, as well as for Title II of the ADA prohibiting discrimination on the basis of disabilities by public entities.
Office of Special Education and Rehabilitation Services	OSERS	Part of the Department of Education, OSERS includes the Office of Special Education Programs (OSEP), the National Institute on Disability and Rehabilitation Research (NIDRR), and the Rehabilitation Services Administration (RSA) and works to support programs to educate, rehabilitate and otherwise improve the lives of those with disabilities.

Office of Special Education Programs	OSEP	Part of OSERS, OSEP administers thefederal IDEA and describes itself as "dedicated to improving results for infants, toddlers, children and youth with disabilities ages birth through 21 by providing leadership and financial support to assist states and local districts."
Orton Gillingham		A specific method for teaching students with specific language or reading disabilities including dyslexics.
Picture exchange communication system	PECS	A modified applied behavioral analysis method for teaching non-verbal communication, typically used with nonverbal autistic students.
Portfolio		A collection of student work that can form the basis of assessment.
Private school		Schools that are administered primarily by other than local, state or federal government funds and which thus retain mostly separate control over their functioning. Private schools would include parochial (religiously affiliated) schools as well as various secular schools such as boarding schools, military schools, and others.
Pull-out programs		Programs that provide assistance to individual students outside of the regular classroom, i.e. by "pulling them out" of regular classes.
Pupil evaluation team	PET	Term used for IEP team in some states.
Regulation		Rule adopted by an agency to implement legislation; when properly adopted rules and regulations have the force and effect of law.
Related services		Related services include a variety of services as may be necessary for a student to benefit from special education. This term is defined by statute and regulation, 20 U.S.C. § 1401(26); 34 C.F.R. § 300.34.
Resolution Session		Meeting prior to opportunity for due process hearing, between parents and relevant IEP team members, including representative with decision-making authority, to discuss complaint and attempt to resolve it. The LEA attorney is excluded unless the parent is accompanied by an attorney. Relevant statutory and regulatory provisions are 20 U.S.C. § 1415(f)(1)(B) and 34 C.F.R. § 300.510.

Resource room		A special classroom, typically a special education classroom where additional help is provided.
Response to Intervention	RTI	Process for evaluating children suspected to have specific learning disabilities that employs systematic assessment of the student's response to high quality, research-based general education instruction. The term "Response to Instruction" is also used by some sources. The IDEA regulations provide that states must permit LEAs to use such a process. 34 C.F.R. § 300.307(a)(2); see 20 U.S.C. § 1414(b)(6)(A). For information supporting the use of RTI and selected references, see 71 Fed. Reg. 46647-59 (Aug. 14, 2006).
Section 1983	1983	42 U.S.C. § 1983, civil action for deprivation of rights.
Section 504	504	Section 504 of the Rehabilitation Act of 1973, 29 U.S.C. § 794, federal law that prohibits discrimination against disabled students.
State education agency	SEA	The State Board of Education or other similar state-level agency responsible for implementing education law and policy. This term is defined by statute, 20 U.S.C. § 1401(32).
State hearing officer, also state review officer	SHO, SRO	A state level hearing officer; in regard to special education, part of the due process provisions, see 20 U.S.C. § 1415(g).
Stay Put		Student stays in his/her "then current educational placement" while disputes are ongoing; see 20 U.S.C.A. 1415(j); 34 C.F.R. 300.518.
Title I		Refers to Title I of the Elementary and Secondary Education Act (ESEA) of 1965, which targeted federal financial resources to schools with high concentrations of economically disadvantaged students. This part of the federal legislation was also known as Chapter I.
Title I		Title I of the Americans with Disabilities Act of 1990, 42 U.S.C. §§ 12111–12117; 29 C.F.R. Part 1630 (employment).
Title II		Title II of the Americans with Disabilities Act of 1990, 42 U.S.C. §§ 12131–12134; 28 C.F.R. Part 35 (public services and transportation).

Title III		Title III of the Americans with Disabilities Act of 1990, 42 U.S.C. §§ 12181–12189; 28 C.F.R. Part 36 (public accommodations and services operated by private entities).
Title VI		Title VI of Civil Rights Act of 1964, 42 USCS § 2000d (prohibiting discrimination on the basis of race, color or national origin).
Title VII		Title VII of the Civil Rights Act of 1964, 42 U.S.C. § 2000e (Equal Employment Opportunities).
Title IX		Title IX of the Education Amendments of 1972, 20 U.S.C. § 1681 (sex discrimination).
Treatment and Education of Autistic and Related Communication Handicapped Children	TEACCH	A skill-based therapy that emphasizes teaching functional skills.

TABLE OF CASES

[References are to pages]

A

A.B. v. Lawson. 163; 184
A.P. & M.S. v. Pemberton Twp. Bd. of Educ. . . 432
A.R. v. New York City Dep't of Educ. 516
A.S. v. Norwalk Bd. of Educ. 185; 291
A.S., C.G. ex rel. v. Five Town Community School
    District. 233
A.W. v. Jersey City Pub. Sch. 479
A.W. v. Northwest R-1 Sch. Dist. . . .270; 274–276;
                     287; 317; 319
Abdo v. University of Vermont 590
Abington School District v. Schempp. 131
Adams v. State. 562
Age v. Bullitt County Pub. Schs. 164; 269
Agis v. Howard Johnson Co. 661
Agostini v. Felton 51; 534
Aguilar v. Felton. 51
Air Courier Conference v. Postal Workers Union.487
Alamo Heights Independent School Dist. v. State Bd.
    of Education. 172
Alaska Dept. of Environmental Conservation v.
    EPA. .352
Albertson's, Inc. v. Kirkingburg. 590
Alden v. Maine. 491
Alegria v. District of Columbia 515
Alexander v. Choate . . 20; 194; 470, 471; 474; 598;
                    619; 642; 647
Alexander v. Sandoval 467; 469; 474
Alvin Independent School District v. A.D. 100
Ambach v. Norwick. 131
Anderson v. Creighton. 645
Anderson v. Liberty Lobby, Inc.. . . . . . .498; 641
Anderson v. Thompson. 487
Anderson v. University of Wisconsin 636
Andree v. County of Nassau. 159
Andrews v. Ledbetter 440
Angela L. v. Pasadena Independent Sch. Dist. . . 478
Arlington Cent. Sch. Dist. Bd. of Ed. v. Murphy . 88;
                   254; 380; 387; 516
Association for Disabled Americans v. Florida Int'l
    Univ.. 663

B

Bailey v. United States. 656
Baird v. Rose. 451
Bales v. Clarke. 165
Barlow-Gresham Union High Sch. Dist. No. 2 v.
    Mitchell. 496

Barnes v. Gorman. 465; 473; 663
Barnett v. Collection Serv. Co. 661
Barnett v. U.S. Air, Inc. 617; 619
Battle v. Pennsylvania 45
Bay Shore Union Free School District v. Kain . .530
Bay Shore Union Free School District v. T. . . . 530
Beard v. Teska 502; 521
Beau II, In re. 436
Beth B. v. Van Clay 283
Bethel Sch. Dist. v. Fraser 49
Betts v. Rector & Visitors of the Univ. of Va. . . .591
Biggs v. Board of Educ.. 493
Bird v. Lewis and Clark Coll 612
Blackmon v. Springfield R-XII Sch. Dist.. .412, 413
Blanchard v. Bergeron. 502
Blanchard v. Morton Sch. Dist. 469
Blazejewski v. Board of Educ.. 183
Blessing v. Freestone. 481; 483
Blue Chip Stamps v. Manor Drug Stores. 594
Board of Curators of Univ. of Missouri v.
    Horowitz. 618
Board of Educ. v. Diamond 477, 478; 562
Board of Educ. v. Holland 289; 311; 317; 320
Board of Educ. v. Illinois State Bd. of Educ.. . .270
Board of Educ. v. Kelly 171; 492
Board of Educ. v. L.M. 392
Board of Educ. v. Michael M.. 564
Board of Educ. v. Nathan R.. 496
Board of Educ. v. Rowley . 3; 21; 99; 117; 121; 160;
      163; 183; 204; 229–231; 235, 236; 246; 253;
      265; 267; 270, 271; 273–275; 277–279; 294;
      298; 303; 305; 307, 308; 318; 321; 323; 349;
      357; 363; 366; 368; 412, 413; 440; 443
Board of Educ. v. Steven L.. 509
Board of Educ. of Bay Shore Union Free Sch. Dist. v.
    Kain. .530
Board of Educ. of Community High Sch. Dist. No.
    218 v. Illinois State Bd. of Educ. 400
Board of Educ. of Kiryas Joel Village School District
    v. Grumet. 534
Board of Educ., Sacramento Unified Sch. Dist. v.
    Rachel H. 184; 283
Board of Trustees v. Garrett. 16; 492; 662
Bobby R. v. Houston Indep. Sch. Dist.. 412
Boerne, City of v. Flores. 536
Borden v. Paul Revere Life Ins. Co. 661
Borough of (see name of borough) . . . .
Bowden v. Dever. 474

[References are to pages]

Bowen v. Massachusetts 159

Bowers v. NCAA. 587

Bradley v. Arkansas Dep't of Educ 172; 520

Bragdon v. Abbott 456; 589

Branch v. Smith. 378; 384

Brandon K. v. New Lenox Sch. Dist. 516

Breidenbach v. Bolish 480, 481

Brennan v. Stewart. 642

Briggs v. Board of Educ. 323

Brown v. Board of Education. 1; 132; 471

Brown v. Griggsville Community Unit Sch. Dist. No.
4. 512

Brown v. Hearst Corp.. 661

Brown v. Hot, Sexy & Safer Prods.. . . . .657, 658

Brown v. Houston Sch. Dist. 493

Brown v. Trustees of Boston University 659

Buchanan v. City of San Antonio 457, 458

Buckhannon Board & Care Home, Inc. v. West
Virginia Department of Health and Human
Services. 503, 504; 507; 512; 520

Buckingham v. United States 629

Buckley v. Valeo. 540

Bucks County Dep't of Mental Health/Mental
Retardation v. Pennsylvania. 171; 564

Burilovich v. Board of Educ. of Lincoln . . 172; 217

Burke County Bd. of Educ. v. Denton 440

Burlington School Committee v. Department of
Education .80; 96; 246; 259; 332; 359; 360; 362;
369; 371; 373, 374; 376; 379, 380; 387;
392–394; 400; 441; 442; 447; 584

Burlington N. R.R. v. Okla. Tax Comm'n 515

Burr v. Ambach 407

Burrow v. Postville Community Sch. 659

C

C.M., M.M. ex rel. v. School Bd. of Miami-Dade
County, Fla. 579, 580; 585

C.N. v. Willmar Pub. Sch. 436

Cain v. Horne. 546

Campbell v. Talladega City Bd. of Education. . .268

Canton, City of v. Harris. 475

Capistrano Unified Sch. Dist. v. Wartenberg . . . 172

Carnwath v. Grasmick. 346

Carroll v. American Fed'n of Musicians 498

Carter v. Florence County Sch. Dist. Four 368

Cave v. East Meadow Union Free Sch. Dist. . . .490

Cedar Rapids Community Sch. Dist. v. Garret F. by
Charlene F.. . . . . .300; 302; 357

Central Columbia School Dist. v. Polk 165

Chakrabarti v. Cohen. 661

Chapman v. Houston Welfare Rights Org. 550

Charlie F. v. Board of Educ.. . . . . . 483, 484; 486

Chester County Intermediate Unit v. Pennsylvania
Blue Shield 159

Chevron, U.S.A. Inc. v. Natural Resources Defense
Council, Inc.. . . . . .258; 580; 585

Chris D. v. Montgomery County Board of
Education 415; 435; 449

Christiansburg Garment Co. v. EEOC. 496

Christina A. v. Bloomberg. 511

Christopher P. v. Marcus. 499

Church of Lukumi Babalu Aye, Inc. v. City of
Hialeah. 535; 543

City of (see name of city). . . . .

Cleburne, City of v. Cleburne Living Center. 16; 540

Clementon Bd. of Educ. v. P. N. 516

Cleveland v. Policy Management Systems Corp.. .351

Cleveland Heights-University Heights City Sch. Dist.
v. Boss. 226; 290

Clyde K. v. Puyallup Sch. Dist., No. 3 399

Colin K. by John K. v. Schmidt. 443

Constantine v. Rectors & Visitors of George Mason
Univ.. 663

Converse County Sch. Dist. No. 2 v. Pratt 439

Corey H. v. Board of Educ.. 290

Corley v. United States 383

County of (see name of county). . . . .

County Sch. Bd. v. Z.P. 171

Covington v. Knox County Sch. Sys. 484; 490

Cox v. Alabama State Bar. 638

CP v. Leon County Sch. Bd. Fla 392

Crawford Fitting Co. v. J. T. Gibbons, Inc.. . 513, 514

Crocker v. Tennessee Secondary Sch. Athletic
Ass'n 478

Crowder v. Kitagawa. 471; 628

Cruzan v. Director, Missouri Dep't of Health. . .540

Cudjoe v. Independent Sch. Dist. 490

Cypress-Fairbanks Indep. Sch. Dist. v. Michael
F.. . . . . .246; 250; 253

D

D'Amico v. New York State Board of Law
Examiners. 638

D.D. v. New York City Bd. of Educ. 255

D.D., In re 154

D.P. v. School Bd. 400; 575; 586

D.R. v. East Brunswick Bd. of Educ.. 402

Daniel R.R. v. State Bd. of Educ . . . 248; 270, 271; 287, 288; 290; 311; 317–322
Davis v. Southeastern Community College.593; 594; 596
Davis v. York Int'l, Inc. 656; 659
De Mora v. Department of Pub. Welfare 561
De Stafney v. University of Alabama. 343
Deal v. Hamilton County Bd. of Educ.. . .171; 172; 226; 355
Debra P. v. Turlington. 199
Dellmuth v. Muth. 478; 492
Dennin v. Connecticut Interscholastic Ath. Conf..189
Department of Educ. v. Cari Rae S.. 310
Department of Educ. v. Katherine D. . 271; 287; 300
Department of Public Welfare v. Haas 48
Despears v. Milwaukee County 457
Detsel v. Board of Ed. of Auburn Enlarged City School Dist.. 303
Devries v. Fairfax County Sch. Bd. . . 287; 317, 318
Digre v. Roseville Sch. Independent Dist. 478
Doane v. City of Omaha. 457, 458
Doe v. Alfred. 488
Doe v. Anrig 362; 442
Doe v. Board of Trs. of Univ. of Ill. 663
Doe v. Boston Pub. Schs. 515
Doe v. Hawaii Dep't of Educ.. 435
Doe v. Koger. 420
Doe v. Marshall 657
Doe v. National Bd. of Med. Exam'rs 636
Doe v. New York Univ. 617, 618
Doe v. University of Md. Med. Sys. Corp..454; 456, 457
Doe, Doe ex rel. v. Bd. of Educ.. 90
Doran v. Salem Inn, Inc.. 351
Draper v. Atlanta Indep. Sch. Sys.. . .184; 387, 388
Drinker v. Colonial School Dist 571; 573
Dubois v. Connecticut State Bd. of Educ.. 294
Duvall v. County of Kitsap 472

E

Easley v. West 656
Eason v. Clark County Sch. Dist. 492
Edelman v. Jordan. 492
Edie F. v. River Falls Sch. Dist.. 510
Employment Div. Dep't of Human Res. of Oregon v. Smith. 535, 536; 541
Enterprise City Board of Education v. Miller. . .343
Ernest M., Gregory M. ex rel. v. State Bd. of Educ 90
Eulitt v. Maine Dep't of Educ. 546

Evanston Cmty. Consol. Sch. Dist. No. 65 v. Michael M 163
Ex parte (see name of relator). . . . .
Ex rel. (see name of relator). . . . .

F

Family & Children's Ctr. v. School City 440
Farrar v. Hobby. 520; 522
Ferguson v. City of Phoenix 471, 472
Fick v. Sioux Falls School District 183; 440
Fitzgerald v. Barnstable Sch. Comm.. 476
Fitzgerald v. Camdenton R-III Sch. Dist.. . 122; 529
Fitzpatrick v. Bitzer 492
Florence County Sch. Dist. Four v. Carter by & Through Carter . 96; 117; 367; 376; 380; 385; 393
Florida High School Activities Association. . . .192
Foley v. Polaroid Corp., Inc.. 661
Foley v. Special Sch. Dist. of St. Louis County . 528
Forest Grove Sch. Dist. v. T. A.. . . . .372; 387; 399
Fort Zumwalt Sch. Dist. v. Clynes 412, 413
Foster v. Arthur Andersen, LLP. 457
Frank G. v. Bd. of Educ. of Hyde Park 387
Franklin v. Gwinnett County Pub. Sch.. . .473; 478; 656, 657
Frazier v. Fairhaven Sch. Comm.. 490
Fudge v. Penthouse Int'l, Ltd. 661, 662

G

G. v. Fort Bragg Dependent Schs.. . . .164; 171; 389
G.I. Forum v. Texas Educ. Agency 200
G.M. by & Through R.F. v. New Britain Bd. of Educ.. 496
Gadsby v. Grasmick 520, 521
Gaither v. Barron. 656
Gallagher v. Catto 609, 610
Garcia v. S.U.N.Y. Health Scis. Ctr.. 492
Gary S. v. Manchester Sch. Dist. 535; 537; 539
Gaskin v. Pennsylvania 290
Gates v. Rowland. 457
Gean v. Hattaway 159
Geis v. Bd. of Educ.. 323
Gerena-Valentin v. Koch. 499
Gerstmyer v. Howard County Pub. Sch. 226
Gill v. Columbia 93 Sch. Dist 172; 411, 412
Glendale Unified Sch. Dist. v. Almasi. 347
Goldberg v. Kelly 333; 425
Gonzaga Univ. v. Doe 476
Gonzalez v. National Bd. of Med. Exam'rs. . . .591
Gonzalez v. P.R. Dep't of Educ. 86

[References are to pages]

Goss v. Lopez 49; 333; 416
Granberry v. Greer. 487
Greater L.A. Council on Deafness, Inc. v. Zolin .465
Green v. Johnson. 200
Greenland Sch. Dist. v. Amy N. 81
Greenleaf's Lessee v. Birth 353
Greer v. Rome City Sch. Dist.. . . . .270; 287, 288;
                                         318–322; 325
Guckenberger v. Boston Univ.. . . . .590; 635; 653

H

Halderman v. Pennhurst State School & Hospital . 20
Hall v. Vance County Bd. of Educ. 184
Hannon v. Original Gunite Aquatech Pools, Inc. .660
Harlow v. Fitzgerald 491; 645
Harris v. Forklift Systems 657, 658
Harris v. McRae. 538; 540, 541
Hartnett v. Fielding Graduate Inst. 612
Hayes v. Unified Sch. Dist. 482, 483
Haysman v. Food Lion, Inc.. . . . . . . 657; 659
Hazelwood Sch. Dist. v. Kuhlmeier 49
Heather S. v. Wisconsin 440
Hensley v. Eckerhart. 508; 512
Hernandez v. Commissioner. 539
Hickman v. Dothan City Board of Education. . . .343
Hiler v. Brown. 459
Hines v. Pitt County Bd. of Educ. 187
Hishon v. King & Spalding 454
Hjortness, Hjortness ex rel. v. Neenah Joint Sch.
    Dist.. 230
Hobbie v. Unemployment Appeals Comm'n . . . 536
Hoekstra v. Independent School District 488
Hoffman v. Optima Systems, Inc.. 662
Hollenbeck v. Board of Educ.. 345
Honig v. Doe . . 3; 32; 39; 305; 318; 399; 424; 487;
                                         571, 572
Hood v. Encinitas Union School District. 99
Hooks v. Clark County Sch. Dist.. 529
Hornstine v. Township of Moorestown 197
Houston Indep. Sch. Dist. v. Bobby R .250–252; 412
Houston Indep. Sch. Dist. v. VP. 242
Hunt v. Bartman 329; 478
Hunt v. Cromartie 351
Hunt-Golliday v. Metropolitan Water Reclamation
    Dist.. .631

I

I.N.S. v. Cardoza-Fonseca 608
In re (see name of party) . . . .

Independent Sch. Dist. No. 284 v. A.C.. 290
Ingraham v. Wright. 425
Inhabitants of Warren v. Inhabitants of
    Thomaston. 136
Irving Independent School District v. Tatro.279; 295;
                                      302, 303; 305–309

J

J.B. v. Killingly Bd. of Educ 188
J.C. v. Reg'l Sch. Dist. 10 509–511
J.D. v. Kanawha County Bd. of Educ. 406
J.D., J.D. ex rel. v. Pawlet Sch. Dist. 72; 90; 92
J.K., A.K. ex rel. v. Alexandria City Sch. Bd. . .232
J.L. v. Mercer Island Sch. Dist. 163
J School District v. Luke P. 165; 172
Jackson v. Franklin County Sch. Bd. 478, 479
Jason D.W. v. Houston Indep. Sch. Dist. 502
Jefferson County Bd. of Educ. v. Breen. . . .323; 389
Jenkins v. Squillacote 117
Jim C. v. United States. 492; 520
Jodlowski v. Valley View Community Unit Sch.
    Dist.. .503
John T. v. Del. County Intermediate Unit . . 509–511
John T. v. Iowa Dep't of Educ. 511; 517
John T. v. Marion Indep. Sch. Dist.. . 518, 519; 521;
                                                     530
Johnson v. Bismarck Pub. Sch. Dist. 522
Johnson v. Independent Sch. Dist. No. 4 182
Johnson v. Metro Davidson County Sch. Sys.. . . 62
Johnson v. Special Education Hearing Office. . .570
Jonathan G. v. Caddo Parish Sch. Bd.. 424
Jones v. Washington County Bd. of Educ. 345
Jose Luis R. v. Joliet Township High Sch. Dist.
    204. 516
Joseph M. v. Southeast Delco Sch. Dist. 436
Josephson, In re 498
Joshua A v. Rocklin Unified Sch. Dist.. 254
JSK v. Hendry County School Bd. 397
Juvenile, In re 154

K

K.R. v. Anderson Community School Corp..488; 528
K.S. v. Fremont Unified Sch. Dist. 474
K.Y. v. Maine Township High Sch. Dist. 523
K.Y. and Robert D. v. Sobel. 523
Katz v. City Metal Co.. 457
Kennedy v. Board of Educ. 294
Kerkam v. McKenzie. 323
Knable v. Bexley City Sch. Dist.. . . . .226; 229; 232

[References are to pages]

Koster v. Perales. 499
Kruelle v. New Castle County Sch. Dist. 521

L

L.B. v. Nebo Sch. Dist. 171; 271; 329; 345
L.C. v. Waterbury Bd. of Educ. 512
Lachman v. Illinois State Board of Education . . .274;
275; 280
LaManque v. Massachusetts Dep't of Employment &
Training. .474
Lane v. Pena. 599
Lapides v. Bd. of Regents. 492
Larry P. v. Riles 123
Lascari v. Board of Education 323, 324; 355
Lauren W. v. DeFlaminis 402
Lavine v. Milne 352
Layne v. Superintendent of Mass. Correctional
Inst. 659
Lemon v. Kurtzman 531
Lester H. v. Gilhool. 398; 478, 479; 575
Light v. Parkway C-2 Sch. Dist.. 425
Linda W. v. Indiana Dep't of Educ. 137; 290
Liscio v. Woodland Hills School Dist. 319
Lissau v. Southern Food Serv., Inc. 459
Little v. Streater 333
Little Rock School Dist. v. Mauney. 349
Livadas v. Bradshaw. 481
Locke v. Davey. 538; 546
Logwood v. Louisiana Department of Education. 196
Loren F. v. Atlanta Indep. Sch. Sys.. 397
Lorillard v. Pons 376; 378
Lovell v. Chandler. 472
Lt. T.B. v. Warwick Sch. Comm. 163; 172; 564
Lujan v. Defenders of Wildlife 351
Luke P. v. Thompson R2-J Sch. Dist. 172
Lyons v. Salve Regina College 660
Lyons v. Smith. 184

M

M.C. v. Central Reg'l Sch. Dist.. 398
M.L. v. Fed. Way Sch. Dist.. 402
M.M. v. Special Sch. Dist. No. 1 . . . . . . 358; 429
M.P. v. Independent Sch. Dist.. 474
M.S. v. Yonkers Bd. of Educ.. 290
Mack v. Great Atlantic & Pacific Tea Co. 652
Maher v. Roe 538; 540, 541
Maine v. Thiboutot 476, 477; 550
Maine Sch. Admin. Dist. No. 35 v. Mr. & Mrs.
R.. . . . . 496; 508

Manchester Sch. Dist. v. Crisman. 148
Manecke v. School Bd. 476
Mantolete v. Bolger 629
Marek v. Chesny. 402; 517
Margolis v. Ryan. 619
Marie O. v. Edgar. 476; 482; 548; 556
Mark H. v. Lemahieu. 460; 490
Marques v. Fitzgerald 662
Marshall County Bd. of Educ. v. Marshall County Gas
Dist.. 578
Martinez v. Bynum. 134; 144
Mary T. v. School Dist. 165; 310
Mathews v. Eldridge. 352
Mavis v. Sobol. 329
Max M. v. Illinois State Bd. of Education 184
Mayson v. Teague 339
McCardle v. Haddad. 498
McCormick v. Waukegan Sch. Dist.. 490
McGregor v. Louisiana State Univ. Bd. of
Supervisors 617, 618
McKellar v. Pennsylvania Dep't of Educ.. 474
McLaughlin v. Holt Pub. Schs. Bd. of Educ.. . .265
McNely v. Ocala Star-Banner Corp. 456–458
Medina-Munoz v. R.J. Reynolds Tobacco Co.. .641;
652
Meek v. Pittenger. 532
Meredith v. Fair 388
Meritor Sav. Bank, FSB v. Vinson. 656–658
Merritt v. Dillard. 578
Mesnick v. General Electric Co.. 652
Metropolitan Government of Nashville and Davidson
County v. Cook. 67; 445
Meyer v. Nebraska. 131
Middlesex County Sewerage Auth. v. Nat'l Sea
Clammers Ass'n. 476
Miener v. Missouri. 158
Milliken v. Bradley. 135; 399
Mills v. Board of Education of the District of
Columbia 1; 10; 331; 352; 366
Missouri Dep't of Elementary and Secondary Educ. v.
Springfield R-12 Sch. Dist. 163
Mitchell v. Forsyth. 480; 645
Mitchell v. Helms 534
Mitten v. Muscogee County Sch. Dist. 495
MM v. Sch. Dist.. 230
Monell v. Department of Soc. Servs. 475
Morgan v. Chris L.. 436
Morse v. Frederick. 49
Mr. I. v. Me. Sch. Admin. Dist. No. 55 79
Mrs. W. v. Tirozzi 478; 550

Mt. Healthy City Bd. of Ed. v. Doyle 351; 492
Mueller v. Allen 531; 533
Murphy v. Arlington Cent. Sch. Dist. 400
Murphy v. United Parcel Service, Inc. 589
Murray by & Through Murray v. Montrose County
  Sch. Dist. RE-1J 236
Muth v. Central Bucks Sch. Dist. 478
Myers v. Hose 631
Mylan Labs., Inc. v. Matkari. 452; 454

N

N.B. v. Hellgate Elementary Sch. Dist. 163
N.B. by D.G. v. Alachua County Sch. Bd. 484
Nadeau v. Helgemoe. 499
Nathanson v. Medical College of Pa. 652
National Fed. of the Blind v. Target Corp. 612
Native American Council of Tribes v. Solem. . .543
Neely v. Rutherford County School. 303
Neosho R-V Sch. Dist. v. Clark 409; 514, 515
New Jersey v. T.L.O. 49
New York Gaslight Club, Inc. v. Carey . . . 512; 564
New York, N. H. & H. R. Co.; United States v. .353
New York State Bd. of Law Exam'rs v. Bartlett .638
Nieves-Marquez v. Puerto Rico 540
North v. District of Columbia Board of
  Education. 422
Norwood v. Harrison 537, 538; 541

O

O'Toole v. Olathe Dist. Schs. Unified Sch. Dist..226;
  440
Oberti v. Board of Educ. of Clementon School
  Dist. . . . 287; 288; 310; 319, 320; 325–328; 355
Olmstead v. L.C. 264; 328
Ostby v. Oxnard Union High 516
Owen v. City of Independence 491

P

P. v. Newington Bd. of Educ 329
P.E.C., In re. 200
P.N. v. Clementon Bd. of Educ.. 516
P.N. v. Seattle Sch. Dist. 515, 516
P.P. v. West Chester Area Sch. Dist. 56
Pachl v. Seagren 283
Padilla v. School Dist. No. 1. . . . . . . .436; 479
Pardini v. Allegheny Intermediate Unit. . .400; 565;
  578; 585
Parents in Action on Special Education (PASE) v.
  Hannon .123

Patterson v. McLean Credit Union 305
Payne v. Peninsula Sch. Dist. 490
Pedigo v. P.A.M. Transp., Inc.. . . . . . . .457, 458
Pembaur v. City of Cincinnati. 475
Pennhurst State School v. Halderman. 160; 308; 380;
  492
Pennsylvania Association of Retarded Children v.
  Pennsylvania (PARC) 1; 3; 352; 366
Perrin v. United States. 443
Peter v. Wedl. 541
PGA Tour, Inc. v. Martin 109
Pierce v. Soc'y of Sisters. 537; 539, 540
Pitchford v. Salem-Keizer Sch. Dist. No. 24J. . .172
Planned Parenthood v. Casey 333
Plyler v. Doe 128; 147; 540
Polera v. Board of Educ.. . . . . .486; 540
Polk v. Central Susquehanna Intermediate Unit
  16. . . . . .165; 318; 320; 562
PolyMedica Corp. Sec. Litig, In re 85
Porrazzo v. Educ. Credit Mgmt. Corp. (In re
  Porrazzo) 613
Pottgen v. Missouri State High Sch. Activities
  Ass'n. 100; 188; 191; 192
Price v. National Bd. of Med. Examiners. 591
Puffer v. Raynolds. 479
Pushkin v. Regents of the Univ. of Colorado . . 617;
  636

Q

Quaratino v. Tiffany & Co. 502

R

Rabinowitz v. New Jersey State Board of
  Education 146, 147
Rancho Palos Verdes, City of v. Abrams 479
Randy M. v. Texas City ISD. 424
Regan v. Taxation with Representation of Washington
 540
Regents of University of Michigan v. Ewing . . 617;
  627; 635; 644
Reid v. Board of Educ., Lincolnshire-Prairie View
  Sch. Dist. 103. 522
Reid L. v. Illinois State Bd. of Educ.. 290
Reid, Reid ex rel. v. Dist. of Columbia. . .396; 398,
  399
Rene v. Reed. 199
Reusch v. Fountain. 182
Richardson Indep. Sch. Dist. v. Michael Z.. 165; 310
Ridgewood Bd. of Educ. v. N.E. ex rel. M.E. . . .394

[References are to pages]

Robb v. Bethel Sch. Dist. 490

Robert D., Todd D. ex rel. v. Andrews . . . 389; 393

Robert J., Adam J. ex rel. v. Keller Indep. Sch. Dist. 246

Robert M. v. Benton 343

Roberts v. Progressive Indep., Inc. 631

Robinson v. Kansas. 474; 492

Robinson v. Pinderhughes 476

Rogers v. Department of Health, Envtl. Control . 456

Roland M. v. Concord School Comm. 323

Rome Sch. Comm. v. Mrs. B 86

Romer v. Evans 543

Roncker v. Walter. . .185; 265; 274– 276; 278; 280; 287; 317; 319; 322

Rose v. Yeaw 486

Rosenberger v. Rector and Visitors of Univ. of Va. 543

Roslyn Union Free School Dist. v. Geffrey W. . .425

Rothschild v. Grottenthaler 104

Rowinsky v. Bryan Indep. Sch. Dist. 657

Rowinsky v. Bryan Indep. Sch. Dist. 657

Rowley v. Board of Educ. 162

Russell v. Salve Regina College 660, 661

Russello v. United States. 608

Russo v. White 459

Ruth v. Fletcher 459

S

S-1 v. Turlington 416

S.C. v. Deptford Township Bd. of Educ. 290

S.G. v. Sayreville Bd. of Educ. 429

S.M. v. Weast 222

S.W. v. Holbrook Pub. Schs 432

San Antonio Ind. Sch. Dist. v. Rodriguez . . 49; 131; 132; 539

Sandison v. Michigan High Sch. Athletic Ass'n . 192; 455; 457

Scanlon v. Tokarcik 297

Schaffer, Schaffer ex rel. v. Weast. . .237; 348; 380; 394

Schoenbach v. District of Columbia. 114

School Bd. v. M.C. 402

School Bd. v. Malone 423

School Bd. of Nassau County v. Arline. . .609; 643; 647; 649

School Dist. v. Stephan M. 425

School Dist. of Grand Rapids v. Ball 531, 532

Seals v. Loftis 293

Seamons v. Snow 656

Seattle Sch. Dist., No. 1 v. B.S. 110

Sellers v. School Bd. 474; 482, 483; 485

Seminole Tribe v. Florida 492

Shapiro v. Paradise Valley Unified Sch. Dist. No. 69 222

Sherbert v. Verner. 536; 541

Sherman v. Mamaroneck Union Free Sch. Dist. . 176

Sherry v. New York State Education Department. 420

Shook v. Gaston County Board of Education. . .158

Shotz v. City of Plantation. 473

Slaughter v. Brigham Young Univ. 660

Smith v. Fitchburg Pub. Sch. 515

Smith v. Robinson. . .300; 450, 451; 468; 477; 482; 550

Smith v. Wade 475, 476

Smyth v. Rivero. 508; 511, 512

Somoza v. New York City Dep't of Educ. 399

Sonkowsky v. Bd. of Educ. for Indep. No. 721 . . 71

Sonya C. v. Arizona School for Deaf & Blind . . 140

Southeastern Community College v. Davis . 98; 422; 471; 592; 609; 620; 622; 628; 641

Spector v. Norwegian Cruise Line Ltd. 612

Springdale Sch. Dist. No. 50 v. Grace 185

Springer by Springer v. Fairfax County Schoolboard 58

St. Johnsbury v. D.H. 529

St. Mary's Honor Center v. Hicks. 351

St. Tammany Parish Sch. Bd. v. State of Louisiana 521

State of (see name of state) . . . .

Steele; United States v. 578

Stephen C., Michael C. ex rel. v. Radnor Twp. Sch. Dist. 255; 574

Stern v. California State Archives. 459

Stratham Sch. Dist. v. Beth P. 294

Strathie v. Department of Transportation 644

Strout v. Albanese. 538, 539; 541

Stuart v. Nappi 420

Sutton v. United Air Lines. 57; 589

Sutton v. Utah State School for the Deaf and Blind. 475

Sweezy v. New Hampshire 659

Sytsema v. Acad. Sch. Dist. No. 20 . .227; 235, 236; 242

T

T.D. v. La Grange Sch. Dist. No. 102 503

T.H. v. Board of Educ. of Palatine Cmty. Consol. Sch. Dist. 171

T.S. v. District of Columbia 496; 503

T.T. v. District of Columbia 491

[References are to pages]

Tatro v. Texas. 296; 306

Taylor P. v. Missouri Dep't of Elementary & Secondary Educ. 496

Teamsters v. Daniel 597

Tennessee v. Lane 492; 662

Texas Educ. Agency v. Leeper. 529

Texas State Teachers Ass'n v. Garland Indep. Sch. Dist.. . . . . .499; 502

Thomas v. Cincinnati Bd. of Educ. . . .570; 573, 574

Thomas v. Davidson Acad. 424

Thomas v. Review Bd. of the Indiana Employment Sec. Div.. 536

Thompson v. Board of Special Sch. Dist. 1. . . .484

Thompson R2-J Sch. Dist. v. Luke P.. 234

Tilton v. Jefferson County Bd. of Educ.. 400

Timothy H. v. Cedar Rapids Community Sch. Dist 183

Timothy W. v. Rochester, New Hampshire, School District. 3; 39

Tinker v. Des Moines Indep. Cmty. Sch. Dist.. . .49

Tokarcik v. Forest Hills Sch. Dist.. . . . . .184; 297

Toledo v. Sanchez 663

Tonya K. v. Board of Educ. of City of Chicago . 523

Town of (see name of town). . . . .

Township of (see name of township) . . . .

Toyota v. Williams. 57; 590

Traynor v. Turnage. 609; 611

Tucker v. Bay Shore Union Free School Dist.. .368; 370

Tyler v. Northwest Indep. Sch. Dist. 172

Tyndall v. National Educ. Ctrs., Inc. of Cal. . . .458

U

Ullmo v. Gilmour Academy. 529

Union Sch. Dist. v. Smith 172; 232

United States v. (see name of defendant). . . . . .

United Steelworkers of America v. North Star . . 573

V

Van Duyn v. Baker Sch. Dist.. 358

Veschi v. Northwestern Lehigh Sch. Dist. 528

Villanueva v. Wellesley College. 652

Vlandis v. Kline 134; 144

Vogel v. School Board of Montrose. 343; 345

W

W.B. v. Matula. 479; 482; 484; 487; 575

W.G. v. Senatore. 498

W.K. v. Sea Isle City Bd. of Educ.. 402

W.L.G. v. Houston County Bd. of Educ.. 402

Waechter v. School Dist.. 435

Warner v. Independent Sch. Dist.. 520

Watchtower Bible and Tract Soc'y of N.Y. v. Vill. of Stratton .536

Waterman v. Marquette-Alger Intermediate School District. 488

Weast v. Schaffer 351; 354; 356

Weinberger v. Salfi. 487

Weixel v. Board of Educ. 98; 476; 486

West Virginia Univ. Hosps. v. Casey 514

Wharf (Holdings) Ltd. v. United Int'l Holdings, Inc.. 351

Wheeler v. Towanda Area Sch. Dist. 499; 501

White v. Ascension Parish Sch. Bd.. . . . .211; 265

Whitehead by & Through Whitehead v. School Bd.. . . . . .521, 522

Wilson v. Marana Unified School District . 274; 280; 289

Winkelman v. Parma City Sch. Dist. 440; 485

Wisconsin v. Yoder. 131

Witte v. Clark County Sch. Dist..435, 436; 464; 484; 490

Witters v. Washington Dep't of Services for Blind. .531

Womack v. Eldridge. 459

Wong v. Regents of the Univ. of Cal.. . . .622; 636

Wood v. Strickland. 491

Woodman v. Runyon. 456

Woods v. New Jersey Dep't of Educ.. 478

Wright v. Roanoke Redevelopment & Housing Authority. 477; 483; 550

Wynne v. Tufts Univ. Sch. of Med. ("Wynne I") . 617, 618; 621; 628; 630; 634; 639; 649; 651

Wynne v. Tufts Univ. Sch. of Med. ("Wynne II"). 619; 621; 649

Y

Yankton Sch. Dist. v. Schramm. 412

Yerardi's Moody St. Restaurant & Lounge, Inc. v. Board of Selectmen. 652

Villanueva Yick Wo v.Hopkins. 129

Young, Ex parte 492

Youngberg v. Romeo 264; 328; 333

Z

Zelman v. Simmons-Harris. 534; 537

Zobrest v. Catalina Foothills Sch. Dist. . . .530; 531

[References are to pages]

Zukle v. Regents of the Univ. of Cal. . 613; 627, 628; 630; 632–634

Zvi D. v. Ambach 572

TABLE OF STATUTES

[References are to pages]

ARIZONA

Arizona Revised Statutes

Sec.	Page
15-1343	141; 143–145
15-1346	143

CALIFORNIA
CALIFORNIA STATUTES

Education Code

Sec.	Page
56101	288
56101(a)	289
56101(b)	289
60851	199

COLORADO

Colorado Revised Statutes

Sec.	Page
22-20-103(18)	241

DISTRICT OF COLUMBIA

District of Columbia Code

Sec.	Page
31-201	14
31-208	11

DELAWARE

Delaware Code

Tit.:Sec.	Page
14:3140	354; 357

FLORIDA

Florida Statutes

Sec.	Page
1002.01	529

Florida Statutes—Cont.

Sec.	Page
1002.41	529

ILLINOIS

Illinois Compiled Statutes

Ch.	Page
325:20/1	549
325:20/3	551
325:20/7	554
325:20/13	554
325:20/14	554

INDIANA

Indiana Code

Sec.	Page
4-21.5-3-14	357
10-8.1-6.1-1(e)	139
20-1-6-14(a)	138
20-8.1-6.1-1.	139
20-8.1-6.1-1(b)	139

KENTUCKY

Kentucky Revised Statutes

Sec.	Page
13B.090(7)	357

LOUISIANA

Louisiana Revised Statutes

Sec.	Page
17:1943	98

MAINE

Maine Revised Statutes

Tit.:Sec.	Page
20-A:6209	91
20-A:6209(2)(A)	92
20-A:7001	90
20-A:7001(5)	93, 94

[References are to pages]

Maine Revised Statutes—Cont.

Tit.:Sec.	Page
20-A:7202(5)	93

MINNESOTA

Minnesota Statutes

Sec.	Page
123.932(9)	542
125A.091(16)	354; 357

MISSOURI

Missouri Revised Statutes

Sec.	Page
162.670	164

NEW HAMPSHIRE

New Hampshire Revised Statutes

Sec.	Page
171-A:18	154
186-C	40
186-C:1	149
186:C:1-16	154
186-C:14	150
193:12	136; 150
193:12-29	154
193:27 to 29	150
193:29	149

NEW JERSEY

New Jersey Statutes

Sec.	Page
18:46-13	164
18A:46-19.1	164

NORTH CAROLINA

North Carolina General Statutes

Tit.:Sec.	Page
90-158	596

North Carolina General Statutes—Cont.

Tit.:Sec.	Page
115C-106(a)	164

OHIO

Ohio Revised Code

Sec.	Page
3301.0710	199
3313.642	158
3323	50
4112	49

PENNSYLVANIA

Pennsylvania Consolidated Statutes

Tit.:Sec.	Page
11:875-101	569
11:875-301	562
11:875-303(a)	562

TENNESSEE

Tennessee Code

Sec.	Page
49-10-101(a)(1)	164

TEXAS

Education Code

Sec.	Page
21.031	135
21.914(c)	299
25.086	529

Texas Administrative Code

Title:Sec.	Page
19:89.223(a)(4)(C)	279

[References are to pages]

WASHINGTON

Washington Administrative Code

Sec.	Page
392-171-341	113
392-171-366	114

FEDERAL STATUTES, RULES, AND REGULATIONS

United States Constitution

Amend.	Page
amend.:1	.49; 51; 71; 351; 530–538; 543, 544; 546; 659
amend.:4	435, 436
amend.:5	15; 129
amend.:11	3; 256; 399; 466; 472, 473; 491–493; 520; 556; 662, 663
amend.:14	15, 16; 28; 128–131; 135; 147; 196; 255; 259; 264; 331; 333; 425; 450, 451; 477; 482; 492; 535; 540; 543
art.:9:10	.546
art.:I:8:1	.380

United States Code

Title:Sec.	Page
5:553	.50
5:556(d)	.351
18:930(g)(2)	432
20:34	56; 294; 569
20:504	416
20:1221e-3	.50
20:1400	.2, 3; 40; 79; 137; 212; 235; 242; 306; 367; 446; 550
20:1400 to 85	.565
20:1400 to 87	.535
20:1400 to 1461	114
20:1400 to 1485	310
20:1400 to 1487	409; 480
20:1400 to 1490	111
20:1400 to 1491o	.486; 497
20:1400(b)	.271
20:1400(c)	301; 307, 308; 323; 363; 376
20:1400(c)(5)(D)	.411
20:1400(c)(5)(E)	.163
20:1400(d)	17; 498
20:1400(d)(1)(A)	.21; 86; 92; 115; 411; 504; 510
20:1400(d)(1)(A) to (B)	.480

United States Code—Cont.

Title:Sec.	Page
20:1400(d)(2)	.115
20:1401	62; 140; 265; 318, 319; 359
20:1401(1)	299; 359
20:1401(1) to (2)	.294
20:1401(1)(B)	294
20:1401(3)	.17
20:1401(3)(A)	.68; 89
20:1401(3)(A)(i)	.56; 82; 85
20:1401(3)(A)(ii)	.56; 84; 95
20:1401(3)(B)(i)	.56
20:1401(8)(A)	115
20:1401(9)	.18; 157; 293; 464; 587
20:1401(9)(A)	.158, 159
20:1401(10)(B)	.186
20:1401(10)(C)(ii)	.186
20:1401(10)(D)	.186
20:1401(11)	.137
20:1401(14)	.158
20:1401(17)	.296; 298
20:1401(18)	.363
20:1401(20)	.367
20:1401(26)	.158; 293
20:1401(26)(A)	.94
20:1401(29)	.18; 93; 157, 158
20:1401(30)	.188
20:1401(30)(B)	.188
20:1401(36)	.148
20:1401 to 1415	416
20:1401 to 1461	441
20:1401(B)(ii)	.56
20:1401(a)(2)(C)	.225
20:1401(a)(7)	.73
20:1401(a)(8)	.73
20:1401(a)(17)	.176; 302; 304; 307; 320; 489
20:1401(a)(18)	.367
20:1401(a)(20)	.369
20:1401(a)(20)(F)	.225
20:1402(a)	.258
20:1406	.260
20:1406(a)	.260
20:1406(d)	.260
20:1406(e)	.260
20:1411(a)(1)	.79
20:1412	151; 265; 568
20:1412(1)	.22; 41; 146; 272; 297; 418
20:1412(2)(A)	170

United States Code—Cont.

Title:Sec.	Page
20:1412(2)(C)	146
20:1412(3)	422
20:1412(5)	240
20:1412(5)(B)	265; 287–289; 311; 317–320; 418; 447
20:1412(6)	423
20:1412(a)	50; 127; 214; 349; 411; 526
20:1412(a)(1)(A)	38; 85; 149; 428
20:1412(a)(1)(C)	547
20:1412(a)(3)(A)	80
20:1412(a)(5)(A)	200; 248; 262
20:1412(a)(5)(B)(i)	262
20:1412(a)(9)	568; 574
20:1412(a)(10)	372; 519
20:1412(a)(10)(A)(i)(I)	526
20:1412(a)(10)(A)(i)(III)	527
20:1412(a)(10)(A)(ii)	526
20:1412(a)(10)(A)(iii)	527
20:1412(a)(10)(A)(iii)(III) to (IV)	527
20:1412(a)(10)(A)(iii)(V)	527
20:1412(a)(10)(A)(iv)	527
20:1412(a)(10)(A)(v)	527
20:1412(a)(10)(A)(v)(II)	528
20:1412(a)(10)(B)	382
20:1412(a)(10)(B)(ii)	159
20:1412(a)(10)(C)(ii)	372; 374
20:1412(a)(10)(C)(iii)(I)(aa)	119
20:1412(a)(11)	349
20:1412(a)(11)(A)(i)	520
20:1412(a)(14)	186
20:1412(a)(14)(B)	187
20:1412(a)(15)(A)	349
20:1412(a)(15)(A)(ii)	199
20:1412(a)(16)(A)	199
20:1412(a)(16)(A) to (B)	199
20:1412(a)(16)(C)(ii)	199
20:1412(a)(16)(D)	199
20:1412(a)(24)	123
20:1412(f)	546
20:1413(a)(4)	115
20:1413(f)	56
20:1414(B)	569
20:1414(V)	207
20:1414(a)(1)(A)	138
20:1414(a)(1)(B)	121
20:1414(a)(1)(C)	110; 206
20:1414(a)(1)(C)(ii)(II)	110; 206

United States Code—Cont.

Title:Sec.	Page
20:1414(a)(1)(D)(ii)	122
20:1414(a)(5)	189; 318; 319; 367
20:1414(a) to (c)	90; 110
20:1414(b)	56
20:1414(b)(6)	124
20:1414(b)(6)(A)	123
20:1414(d)	18; 203; 412
20:1414(d)(1)(A)	115; 200; 237
20:1414(d)(1)(A)(IV)	206
20:1414(d)(1)(A)(i)	231
20:1414(d)(1)(A)(i)(III)	207
20:1414(d)(1)(A)(i)(IV)	254
20:1414(d)(1)(A)(i)(IV)(bb) to (cc)	207
20:1414(d)(1)(A)(i)(VI)	207
20:1414(d)(1)(A)(i)(VIII)	207
20:1414(d)(1)(A)(vi)	214, 215
20:1414(d)(1)(B)	80; 115; 205; 214; 497
20:1414(d)(1)(B)(vi) to (vii)	205
20:1414(d)(1)(C)(i)	206
20:1414(d)(1)(C)(ii) to (iii)	206
20:1414(d)(1)(i)(II) to (III)	197
20:1414(d)(2)(A)	115; 206; 569
20:1414(d)(2)(C)(i)(I)	260
20:1414(d)(2)(C)(i)(II)	260
20:1414(d)(3)(B)	206
20:1414(d)(3)(D)	207
20:1414(d)(4)	203
20:1414(d)(4)(A)(i)	284
20:1414(d)(5)	211
20:1414(d)(7)(A)	200
20:1414(d)(7)(B)	200
20:1414(f)	203; 206; 214
20:1415	24; 117; 241; 300; 337; 372; 439; 451; 468; 486; 550
20:1415(a)	356
20:1415(a) to (e)	272
20:1415(b)	138
20:1415(b)(1)	421
20:1415(b)(1)(E)	417; 487
20:1415(b)(2)	115; 266; 284; 339; 417
20:1415(b)(2)(A)(ii)	137
20:1415(b)(3)	372
20:1415(b)(6)	80
20:1415(b)(6)(A)	356
20:1415(b)(6)(B)	387
20:1415(b) to (d)	121
20:1415(c)	138

[References are to pages]

United States Code—Cont.

Title:Sec.	Page
20:1415(c)(2)(B)(i)(I)	353
20:1415(e)	50; 323, 324; 509
20:1415(e)(1)	406
20:1415(e)(2)	115; 267; 284; 315; 323; 360; 371; 442, 443; 447; 478
20:1415(e)(2)(F)(iii)	403
20:1415(e)(2)(G)	406
20:1415(e)(3)	32; 46; 361; 571
20:1415(e)(4)(A)	531
20:1415(f)	50; 410; 483; 487; 528; 551; 566; 571
20:1415(f)(1)(A)	80; 357
20:1415(f)(1)(B)(i)	406
20:1415(f)(2)	353
20:1415(f)(3)(A)	80; 338
20:1415(f)(3)(C)	396
20:1415(f)(3)(D)	387
20:1415(f)(3)(E)(i)	388
20:1415(f)(3)(E)(ii)	388
20:1415(f)(3)(E)(iii)	388
20:1415(f) to (g)	50
20:1415(i)	50; 401
20:1415(i)(2)	67; 411; 491
20:1415(i)(2)(A)	149
20:1415(i)(2)(B)	67; 413
20:1415(i)(2)(C)	80; 374; 441
20:1415(i)(2)(C)(iii)	96; 389; 392; 464
20:1415(i)(3)(A)	495
20:1415(i)(3)(B)	507; 512; 514; 520
20:1415(i)(3)(B)(i)(I)	241
20:1415(i)(3)(B)(i)(II)	495
20:1415(i)(3)(B)(i)(III)	495
20:1415(i)(3)(C)	517
20:1415(i)(3)(D)	517
20:1415(i)(3)(D)(i)	509; 517
20:1415(i)(3)(D)(ii)	510
20:1415(i)(3)(F) to (G)	517
20:1415(j)	255; 257; 399, 400; 424; 565, 566; 568; 573; 575, 576; 578
20:1415(k)	38; 356; 425
20:1415(k)(1)(A)	429
20:1415(k)(1)(D)	432
20:1415(k)(1)(E)	427
20:1415(k)(1)(G)	432
20:1415(k)(7)	436
20:1417	50
20:1418(d)	56
20:1419(a)(2)	564

United States Code—Cont.

Title:Sec.	Page
20:1422(5)(B)	324
20:1431 to 1445	547; 568
20:1432(5)(B)(ii)	547
20:1432(5)(B)(iii)	547
20:1435(c)(1) to (2)	547
20:1438(3)	569
20:1439	563
20:1439(b)	582
20:1471	548; 550
20:1471(a)(1) to (5)	549
20:1472	551
20:1472(1)	551; 553
20:1472(2)(B)	552, 553
20:1472(2)(E)	552
20:1472(F)	552
20:1475(c)	549; 553
20:1476	555
20:1476(a)	549
20:1476(b)	552; 554
20:1681 to 88	656
20:6301	186
20:6311(G)(i)	198
20:6311(b)(2)(C)	198
20:6311(b)(2)(I)(i)	198
20:6311(b)(3)	198
20:6311(b)(3)(C)(ix)(II)	198
20:6311(b)(3)(C)(xiii)	198
20:6311(d)	198
20:6311(h)	198
20:6311(h)(C)(viii)	198
20:6316(b)	198
20:6319(a)	186
20:6319(c)	187
20:7801	186
20:7801(11)	186
20:7801(23)	186
20:7801(23)(B)	186
20:7801(23)(C)(ii)	186
20:7801(C)	186
26:213(d)(1)	304
28:636(b)(1)(B)	80
28:1291	111; 223
28:1292(b)	480
28:1441(b)	439
28:1821	514, 515
28:1821(b)	513, 514

[References are to pages]

United States Code—Cont.

Title:Sec.	Page
28:1920	513–515
28:1927	496
29:701	77; 114
29:701 to 797b	587
29:705(20)(B)	57; 588
29:706	191
29:706(7)(B)	418
29:790	551
29:794	2; 19, 20; 40; 57; 83; 127; 191; 207; 212; 255; 296; 416; 487; 599; 603; 622; 639; 641; 649; 654
29:794(a)	104; 106; 456; 464; 656
29:794a(a)(1)	457
29:794(b)(2)(A)	656
29:1415(c)	266
42:42	539
42:1983	.40; 105; 114; 191; 212; 220; 255; 260; 402; 435; 439; 450; 465; 475–482; 487; 549–551; 556
42:1988	495; 507–509; 514; 516; 550; 564
42:1988(b)	514
42:2000bb-1	535
42:2000bb-1(a)	539
42:2000e-2	351
42:2000e-2(m)	457
42:2000e-5	459
42:2000e-5(b)	459
42:2000e-5(f) to (k)	457
42:2000e-5(g)(2)(A)	457
42:2000e-5(g)(2)(B)	457, 458
42:2000e(b)	459
42:11431(1)	72
42:11431(2)	136
42:11431(3)	72
42:12101	2; 191; 212; 654
42:12101 to 12213	479; 487
42:12101(b)	657
42:12102	19; 57, 58
42:12102(2)	588, 589
42:12102(4)	590
42:12111(5)(A)	459
42:12112(a)	456
42:12117	459
42:12117(a)	459
42:12117(b)	456
42:12131	589
42:12131(1)	19, 20; 195
42:12131(2)	103; 616; 631

United States Code—Cont.

Title:Sec.	Page
42:12131 to 12132	20; 57
42:12132	102; 194; 452; 454–456; 458; 471; 622; 632
42:12133	457
42:12134(b)	456
42:12181(6)	194
42:12181(7)	194
42:12181(7)(J)	656
42:12182	194; 656
42:12182(2)(A)(i)	20
42:12182(b)(1)(E)	20
42:12189	587; 636
42:12201(a)	456
42:12203(a)	456; 458
42:12203(c)	459
46:1295b(e)(1)	606
46:Appendix:1295	599; 603
46:Appendix:1295b(b)(3)(F)	603
46:Appendix:1295b(c)	604; 607
46:Appendix:1295b(e)(1)	604; 606, 607
46:Appendix:1295b(e)(1)(A)	607

Code of Federal Regulations

Title:Sec.	Page
28:35	20
28:35.104	57
28:35.130(b)(7)	103; 628
28:35.130(d)	264
28:35.134(b)	458
28:36	20
28:36.309	638
34:104	20; 146; 280; 321
34:104.3	589
34:104.3(2)(j)(ii)	57
34:104.3(j)(2)(ii)	589
34:104.3(k)	107
34:104.3(k)(3)	632
34:104.3(k)(4)	109
34:104.12(b)(2)	108
34:104.31	207
34:104.33 to 36	207
34:104.33(a)	77; 127; 207; 465
34:104.33(a)(2)	207
34:104.33(b)	465
34:104.33(b)(1)	77; 467
34:104.33(b)(2)	77; 468

[References are to pages]

Code of Federal Regulations—Cont.

Title:Sec.	Page
34:104.34	465
34:104.34(a)	264
34:104.34(b)	264
34:104.34(c)	264; 465
34:104.35	110; 465
34:104.36	465
34:104.37	109
34:104.44(a)	591; 630
34:104.44(c)	636
34:104.44(d)(2)	108; 592
34:104.52(d)(3)	108
34:200.6	198
34:200.6(a)(1)	198
34:200.6(a)(2)	198
34:200.7	198
34:200.8	198
34:200.13 to 21	198
34:200.13(c)(2)	199
34:200.13(c)(3) to (7)	199
34:200.33 to 53	198
34:200.55(c)	186
34:200.56	186
34:200.56(d) to (f)	187
34:200.58	187
34:200.59	187
34:300	3
34:300.5	299
34:300.7(a)(1)	59; 74
34:300.7(a)(2)	55
34:300.7(b)(9)	60
34:300.7(b)(9)(i)	61; 75
34:300.7(b)(9)(i)(B)	61
34:300.7(c)(4)	69, 70
34:300.8	90
34:300.8(a)(4)(ii)	70
34:300.8(a)(9)	71
34:300.8(c)	56; 85
34:300.8(c)(1) to (c)(13)	88, 89
34:300.8(c)(1)(i)	80; 88
34:300.13(a)	298, 299; 303
34:300.13(b)(4)	298, 299; 308
34:300.13(b)(10)	299
34:300.14	299
34:300.16(a)	302
34:300.16(b)(4)	302; 308
34:300.16(b)(8)(v)	489
34:300.16(b)(11)	302

Code of Federal Regulations—Cont.

Title:Sec.	Page
34:300.17	157
34:300.17(a)	159
34:300.34(a)	293
34:300.34(b)(1)	294
34:300.34(b)(2)	294
34:300.39(a)(2)(iii)	188
34:300.39(b)(1)	158
34:300.39(b)(3)	93
34:300.39(b)(5)	188
34:300.57	339, 340
34:300.104	290
34:300.107(a)	188
34:300.107(b)	188
34:300.111(a)(1)(i)	55
34:300.114	263
34:300.114(a)(2)	185
34:300.115	263
34:300.116(b)	263
34:300.116(b)(3)	265
34:300.116(c)	263; 265
34:300.116(d)	263
34:300.116(e)	263
34:300.117	263
34:300.118 to 120	263
34:300.121(c)(1)(ii)	569
34:300.125(a)(1)(i)	115
34:300.128	113
34:300.131 to 132	127
34:300.131(a)	526
34:300.131(b) to (f)	526
34:300.131(c)	526
34:300.131(d)	526
34:300.131(e)	526
34:300.132	364
34:300.133	526
34:300.134 to 136	527
34:300.137(a)	527
34:300.137(c)	526
34:300.138(a)	527
34:300.138(a)(1)	527
34:300.138(a)(2)	527
34:300.138(b)(1)	526
34:300.138(b)(2)	526
34:300.138(c)(2)	528
34:300.139(a)	527
34:300.139(b)	528
34:300.140(a)	528

[References are to pages]

Code of Federal Regulations—Cont.

Title:Sec.	Page
34:300.140(b)	528
34:300.140(c)	528
34:300.141	527
34:300.142(b)	527
34:300.144	527
34:300.146(c)	159
34:300.148(a)	159
34:300.151 to 153	528
34:300.154(d)(2)	158
34:300.154(e)	158
34:300.156	186
34:300.160	199
34:300.207	186
34:300.227	364
34:300.300	122; 177
34:300.300(a)(3)(ii)	115
34:300.300(b)(1)	400
34:300.301	110
34:300.301 to 311	56
34:300.304 to 305	123
34:300.304(c)(2)	123
34:300.306(b)	56; 489
34:300.307	124
34:300.307 to 311	123
34:300.307(b)	364
34:300.320(5)	207
34:300.320(7)	206
34:300.320 to 300.328	208
34:300.320(A)(1)	208
34:300.320(A)(2)(I)(A)	208
34:300.320(A)(2)(I)(B)	208
34:300.320(A)(2)(II)	209
34:300.320(A)(3)(I)	209
34:300.320(A)(3)(II)	209
34:300.320(A)(4)(I)	209
34:300.320(A)(4)(II)	209
34:300.320(A)(4)(III)	209
34:300.320(A)(5)	209
34:300.320(A)(6)(I)	209
34:300.320(A)(6)(II)(A)	210
34:300.320(A)(6)(II)(B)	210
34:300.320(A)(7)	210
34:300.320(B)(1)	210
34:300.320(B)(2)	210
34:300.320(a)	262
34:300.320(a)(3)	207
34:300.320(a)(4)	206

Code of Federal Regulations—Cont.

Title:Sec.	Page
34:300.320(a)(4)(ii) to (iii)	207
34:300.320(b)	207
34:300.321(a)	110
34:300.321(a)(7)	206
34:300.321(b)	206
34:300.322(d)	222
34:300.323(a)	226
34:300.323(c)	110
34:300.323(c)(1)	206
34:300.323(c)(2)	206; 255
34:300.323(d)	206
34:300.323(e)	260
34:300.323(f)	260
34:300.324(a)(1) to (2)	206
34:300.324(a)(2)(i)	415
34:300.325(a)	226
34:300.325(b)	226
34:300.325(c)	226
34:300.343 to 300.347	177
34:300.345	363
34:300.345(d)	224
34:300.345(d)(1) to (3)	225
34:300.347	364
34:300.347(a)	366
34:300.401	520
34:300.403	367
34:300.403(b)	365
34:300.454(a)	528
34:300.502	122
34:300.502(b)(1)	353
34:300.503	121
34:300.503(b)	113, 114
34:300.504(a)	259
34:300.506	50; 404
34:300.510(b)	348
34:300.510(b)(1) to (2)	386
34:300.511	338; 348
34:300.511(c)(ii) to (iii)	346
34:300.512	259; 347, 348
34:300.512(a)(1)	348
34:300.513	574
34:300.514	407
34:300.514(b)	579
34:300.515	347
34:300.518(b)	579
34:300.518(c)	400; 579; 586
34:300.520	211

[References are to pages]

Code of Federal Regulations—Cont.

Title:Sec.	Page
34:300.530	427, 428
34:300.530(b)(2)	429
34:300.530(d)	428; 433
34:300.530(f)	428
34:300.531	225; 433
34:300.532	434, 435
34:300.533	434
34:300.534	431
34:300.536(a)	429
34:300.551	215; 280
34:300.551(a)	320; 322
34:300.551(b)	320
34:300.551(b)(2)	320
34:300.552	215; 280; 321
34:300.552(b)	216
34:300.552(c)	216
34:300.600	257
34:300.600(b)	151
34:303.1 to 670	547
34:303.16	547
34:303.322(b)(2)	562
34:303.342	560
34:303.342(b)(1)	562
34:303.343	560

Code of Federal Regulations—Cont.

Title:Sec.	Page
34:303.344	560, 561
34:303.344(d)(1)	561, 562
34:Appendix:104:A:504	20
34:Appendix:104:D:A	127
34:Appendix:300:C	279; 320; 326
45:84.3(k)(3)	595
45:84.35(c)(3)	419
45:121a.506	421, 422
45:121a.533(a)(3)	419
45:Appendix:84:A	595
46:310.56(a)	605; 608
46:310.56(d)	605
46:310.58(f)	605

Federal Rules of Civil Procedure

Rule	Page
11	496
12(b)(6)	452; 454; 577; 654
54(b)	360
54(c)	488
65	580
68	401, 402; 517

INDEX

[References are to pages.]

A

ADA (See AMERICANS WITH DISABILITIES ACT (ADA))

AGE OF STUDENTS (See also EARLY CHILDHOOD PROGRAMS; POST-SECONDARY EDUCATION)
Free, appropriate public education, issue in . . . 187

ALTERNATIVE EDUCATIONAL SETTINGS, INTERIM
Requirements for . . . 433

AMERICANS WITH DISABILITIES ACT (ADA)
Claims . . . 450
Disability under . . . 19
Eligibility requirements . . . 57
Post-secondary students, Title II protection for . . . 588
Public entity under . . . 19
Qualified individual with a disability under . . . 20
Title II, protection of post-secondary students under . . . 588

APPEALS (See also COURT PROCEEDINGS)
Attorneys' fees (See ATTORNEYS' FEES IN SPECIAL EDUCATION LITIGATION)
Due process hearings . . . 406
Student discipline
    Generally . . . 433
    Placement during proceedings . . . 433

APPROPRIATE EDUCATION (See FREE, APPROPRIATE PUBLIC EDUCATION (FAPE))

ASSESSMENTS
District-wide . . . 198
Eligibility, evaluation to determine
    Generally . . . 110
    Private school students . . . 526
Grading . . . 197
Individual high-stakes testing . . . 198
Post-secondary education testing and testing accommodation . . . 636

ATTORNEYS' FEES IN SPECIAL EDUCATION LITIGATION
Generally . . . 495
Apportionment of liability . . . 517
Buckhannon issues . . . 503
Liability, apportionment of . . . 517
Measure of fees
    Generally . . . 517
    Apportionment of liability . . . 517
Partial success . . . 496
Procedural matters . . . 496
Procedural victories . . . 496

B

BEHAVIOR INTERVENTION
Least restrictive environment, in . . . 409

BURDEN OF PERSUASION
Due process hearings . . . 348

C

CHARTER SCHOOLS
Free, appropriate public education for students in . . . 200

CHILD FIND
Private schools, children in . . . 526

CLASS SIZE
Free, appropriate public education, issue in . . . 187

CONSTITUTION, U.S.
Establishment Clause and permissive accommodations for private school students . . . 530
Free Exercise Clause and mandatory accommodations for private school students . . . 534
Private school students
    Establishment Clause and permissive accommodations . . . 530
    Free Exercise Clause and mandatory accommodations . . . 534
Residency of student, parameters for determining . . . 128
Section 1983, claims under . . . 475
Source of disabilities education law . . . 49

CONSTITUTIONS, STATE
Sources of disabilities education law . . . 49

COURT PROCEEDINGS
Americans with Disabilities Act claims . . . 450
Attorneys' fees (See ATTORNEYS' FEES IN SPECIAL EDUCATION LITIGATION)
Constitutional claims under Section 1983 . . . 475
Damages liability, immunities from . . . 491
Defenses
    Generally . . . 485
    Exhaustion . . . 485
    Immunities from damages liability . . . 491
    Limitations . . . 490
Evidentiary hearings, Section 1415 proceedings . . . 441
Exhaustion defense . . . 485
Immunities from damages liability . . . 491
Individuals with Disabilities Education Act claims under Section 1983 . . . 476
Limitations defense . . . 490
Remedies, Section 1415 proceedings . . . 449
Section 504 claims . . . 450
Section 1415, proceedings under
    Generally . . . 439
    Evidentiary hearings . . . 441

COURT PROCEEDINGS—Cont.
Section 1415, proceedings under—Cont.
   Remedies . . . 449
Section 1983, claims under
   Constitutional claims . . . 475
   Individuals with Disabilities Education Act
     (IDEA) claims . . . 476

COURTS AS SOURCE OF LAW
Generally . . . 51
Federal court system, overview of . . . 51
Individualized education program (See INDIVIDU-
   ALIZED EDUCATION PROGRAM (IEP), sub-
   head: Court decisions)
State court systems, overview of . . . 51

CUSTODY OF CHILD, JOINT
Residency of student with disability, determining
   . . . 137

D

DAMAGES LIABILITY
Immunities from . . . 491

DEFENSES (See COURT PROCEEDINGS, subhead: Defenses)

DETENTION FACILITIES, JUVENILES IN
Free, appropriate public education for . . . 200

**DISABILITIES, EDUCATION OF STUDENTS
   WITH**
All children with disabilities, case defining educa-
   tion for . . . 39
Appropriate education (See FREE, APPROPRIATE
   PUBLIC EDUCATION (FAPE))
Cases
   Defining cases
     Generally . . . 21
     All children with disabilities, education
      for . . . 39
     Appropriate education . . . 21
     Discipline, student . . . 32
     Education for all children with disabili-
      ties . . . 39
     Maintenance of placement . . . 32
     Placement, maintenance of . . . 32
     Student discipline . . . 32
   Source of law, as . . . 51
Children not yet classified as children with disabili-
   ties, discipline of . . . 430
Constitutions as source of law, federal and state
   . . . 49
Court systems as source of law . . . 51
Discipline (See DISCIPLINE, STUDENT)
Federal sources of law
   Constitution . . . 49
   Court system . . . 51
   Regulations . . . 50
   Statutes . . . 49
Foundation cases . . . 3
Free, appropriate public education (See FREE, AP-
   PROPRIATE PUBLIC EDUCATION (FAPE))

**DISABILITIES, EDUCATION OF STUDENTS
   WITH**—Cont.
Fundamental principles . . . 1
Placement (See PLACEMENT)
Regulations as sources of law, federal and state
   . . . 50
Sources of law
   Generally . . . 49
   Caselaw . . . 51
   Constitutions, federal and state . . . 49
   Court systems, federal and state . . . 51
   Federal (See subhead: Federal sources of law)
   Regulations, federal and state . . . 50
   States (See subhead: State sources of law)
State sources of law
   Constitutions . . . 49
   Court systems . . . 51
   Regulations . . . 50
   Statutes . . . 49
Statutes as source of law, federal and state . . . 49

DISABLING CONDITIONS
Generally . . . 58

DISCIPLINE, STUDENT
Alternative educational settings, interim . . . 433
Appeals
   Generally . . . 433
   Placement during . . . 433
Behavior intervention and appropriate least restric-
   tive environment . . . 409
Bodily injury, serious . . . 432
Case defining . . . 32
Challenges to
   Disability discrimination . . . 415
   Procedural . . . 424
Children not yet classified as children with disabili-
   ties . . . 430
Disability discrimination challenges . . . 415
Drugs, possession, use or sale of . . . 432
Interim alternative educational setting requirements
   . . . 433
Least restrictive environment and behavior interven-
   tion, appropriate . . . 409
Manifestation review
   Generally . . . 426
   Appeals . . . 433
   Placement during . . . 433
Placement during review proceedings . . . 433
Procedural challenges . . . 424
Restraint . . . 436
Review proceedings
   Appeals . . . 433
   Manifestation review . . . 426
   Placement during . . . 433
Seclusion . . . 436
Serious bodily injury . . . 432
Statutes, current
   Generally . . . 425
   Appeals . . . 433
   Drugs, possession, use or sale of . . . 432
   Interim alternative educational setting require-
    ments . . . 433

[References are to pages.]

DISCIPLINE, STUDENT—Cont.

Statutes, current—Cont.

    Manifestation review . . . 426

    Placement during review proceedings . . . 433

    Restraint . . . 436

    Review proceedings

        Appeals . . . 433

        Manifestation review . . . 426

        Placement during . . . 433

    Seclusion . . . 436

    Serious bodily injury . . . 432

    Weapons, carrying or possession of . . . 432

Weapons, carrying or possession of . . . 432

DISCRIMINATION

Discipline, disability discrimination challenges to . . . 415

Religious schools and other private schools, discrimination between provision of services in . . . 541

DIVORCE

Residency of student with disability, determining . . . 137

DRUGS

Student discipline for possession, use or sale of . . . 432

DUE PROCESS HEARINGS

Appeals and judicial review . . . 406 (See also COURT PROCEEDINGS)

Attorneys' fees (See ATTORNEYS' FEES IN SPECIAL EDUCATION LITIGATION)

Burden of persuasion . . . 348

Decisions . . . 346

Discipline, challenges to

    Generally . . . 424

    Placement during review process . . . 433

Enforcement, settlement . . . 402

Impartiality requirements . . . 338

Judgment, offers of . . . 401

Mediation procedures and related issues . . . 403

Notice . . . 333

Offers of judgment . . . 401

Participation rights and decisions . . . 346

Placement, maintenance of

    Generally . . . 399

    Discipline, challenges to . . . 433

Private school parents, complaints by . . . 528

Remedies . . . 359

Rights

    Generally . . . 331

    Burden of persuasion . . . 348

    Decisions, related to . . . 346

    Impartiality requirements . . . 338

    Notice . . . 333

    Participation rights and decisions . . . 346

    Remedies . . . 359

Settlement

    Generally . . . 400

    Enforcement of . . . 402

    Mediation procedures and related issues . . . 403

DUE PROCESS HEARINGS—Cont.

Settlement—Cont.

    Offers of judgment . . . 401

E

EARLY CHILDHOOD PROGRAMS

Generally . . . 547

Individualized family service plans . . . 557

Transition issues . . . 564

ELIGIBILITY

Generally . . . 55

Activities, particular . . . 100

Americans with Disabilities Act . . . 57

Benefit from special education . . . 72

Conditions, particular . . . 100

Disabling conditions generally . . . 58

Evaluation for

    Generally . . . 110

    Private school students . . . 526

Individuals with Disabilities Education . . . 55

Particular activities and conditions . . . 100

Private school students, evaluation of . . . 526

Section 504 . . . 57

Statutory and regulatory requirements

    Generally . . . 55

    Americans with Disabilities Act (ADA) . . . 57

    Individuals with Disabilities Education (IDEA) . . . 55

    Section 504 . . . 57

EMPLOYEES

Free, appropriate public education, issue in . . . 186

Post-secondary education, deference to administrators' and teachers' decisions on student qualifications and reasonable accommodations in . . . 613

Private schools, standards for personnel providing services in . . . 527

ESTABLISHMENT CLAUSE

Private schools, permissive accommodations for children in . . . 530

EVALUATION

Generally . . . 110

Private school students . . . 526

EXHAUSTION DEFENSE

Generally . . . 485

EXTRACURRICULAR ACTIVITIES

Free, appropriate public education, issue in . . . 188

F

FAPE (See FREE, APPROPRIATE PUBLIC EDUCATION (FAPE))

FEDERAL COURTS (See COURT PROCEEDINGS; COURTS AS SOURCE OF LAW)

FEDERAL LEGISLATION

Generally . . . 49

[References are to pages.]

FEDERAL LEGISLATION—Cont.

Americans with Disabilities Act (See AMERICANS
    WITH DISABILITIES ACT (ADA))
Child with disability, defined . . . 17
Definitions
        Americans with Disabilities Act (ADA)
                Disability . . . 19
                Public entity . . . 19
                Qualified individual with a disability
                    . . . 20
        Individuals with Disabilities in Education Act
            (IDEA)
                Child with disability . . . 17
                Free, appropriate public education
                    . . . 17
                Special education . . . 18
Disability, defined . . . 19
Discipline (See DISCIPLINE, STUDENT, subhead:
    Statutes, current)
Eligibility (See ELIGIBILITY, subhead: Statutory
    and regulatory requirements)
Free, appropriate public education (See FREE, AP-
    PROPRIATE PUBLIC EDUCATION (FAPE),
    subhead: Statutes and regulations)
Individualized education program
        Individuals with Disabilities Education Act
            (IDEA) . . . 205
        Section 504 . . . 207
Individuals with Disabilities Education Act (See IN-
    DIVIDUALS WITH DISABILITIES EDUCA-
    TION ACT (IDEA))
Least restrictive environment
        Generally . . . 261
        Individuals with Disabilities Education Act
            (IDEA) . . . 261
Private schools, children in (See PRIVATE
    SCHOOLS, CHILDREN IN, subhead: Statutes,
    current)
Public entity, defined . . . 19
Qualified individual with a disability, defined
    . . . 20
Related services . . . 293
Residency of student . . . 127
Section 504 (See SECTION 504)
Section 1415, court proceedings under
        Generally . . . 439
        Evidentiary hearings . . . 441
        Remedies . . . 449
Section 1983, claims under
        Constitutional claims . . . 475
        Individuals with Disabilities Education Act
            (IDEA) claims . . . 476
Special education, defined . . . 18

FEDERAL REGULATIONS

Generally . . . 50
Free, appropriate public education (See FREE, AP-
    PROPRIATE PUBLIC EDUCATION (FAPE),
    subhead: Statutes and regulations)
Least restrictive environment
        Generally . . . 261
        Individuals with Disabilities Education Act
            (IDEA) . . . 262

FEDERAL REGULATIONS—Cont.

Least restrictive environment—Cont.
        Section 504 . . . 263

FIRST AMENDMENT

Establishment Clause and permissive accommoda-
    tions for private school students . . . 530
Free Exercise Clause and mandatory accommoda-
    tions for private school students . . . 534

**FREE, APPROPRIATE PUBLIC EDUCATION
(FAPE)**

Age of child . . . 187
Appropriate education
        Case, defining . . . 21
        Least restrictive environment, in . . . 409
        Statutory definition . . . 157
Assessments . . . 198
Cases, defining
        Generally . . . 21
        All children with disabilities, education for
            . . . 39
        Appropriate education . . . 21
        Placement, maintenance of . . . 32
        Student discipline . . . 32
Charter schools . . . 200
Class size . . . 187
Court definitions . . . 160
Definition . . . 17; 157
Detention facilities, juveniles in . . . 200
District-wide assessments . . . 198
Eligibility for (See ELIGIBILITY)
Extracurricular activities . . . 188
Free education . . . 158
Grading . . . 197
Juveniles in detention facilities . . . 200
Least restrictive environment . . . 185; 409
Less severe disabilities, children with . . . 183
Other issues
        Generally . . . 185
        Age . . . 187
        Assessments . . . 198
        Charter schools . . . 200
        Class size . . . 187
        Detention facilities, juveniles in . . . 200
        District-wide assessment . . . 198
        Extracurricular activities . . . 188
        Grading . . . 197
        Individual high-stakes testing . . . 198
        Juveniles in detention facilities . . . 200
        Personnel . . . 186
        Testing . . . 198
        Vocational education . . . 188
Personnel issues . . . 186
Public education . . . 159
Regulations (See subhead: Statutes and regulations)
Severity of disability
        Less severe disability . . . 183
        Severe disability . . . 165
Specific services . . . 172
Statutes and regulations
        Generally . . . 157
        Appropriate education . . . 157

[References are to pages.]

FREE, APPROPRIATE PUBLIC EDUCATION (FAPE)—Cont.
Statutes and regulations—Cont.
Free education . . . 158
Public education . . . 159
Testing . . . 198
Vocational education . . . 188

FREE EXERCISE CLAUSE
Private schools, mandatory accommodations for children in . . . 534

G

GRADING OF STUDENTS
Free, appropriate public education, issue in . . . 197

H

HARASSMENT
Post-secondary education learning environment . . . 653

HEARINGS (See DUE PROCESS HEARINGS)

HOSTILE ENVIRONMENTS
Post-secondary education learning environment . . . 653

I

IDEA (See INDIVIDUALS WITH DISABILITIES EDUCATION ACT (IDEA))

IEP (See INDIVIDUALIZED EDUCATION PROGRAM (IEP))

IMMUNITIES FROM DAMAGES LIABILITY
Generally . . . 491

INCLUSION IN LEAST RESTRICTIVE ENVIRONMENT (See LEAST RESTRICTIVE ENVIRONMENT)

INDIVIDUALIZED EDUCATION PROGRAM (IEP)
Generally . . . 203
Content of IEP, court decisions on . . . 242
Controlling, court decisions on IEP as . . . 255
Court decisions
Content of IEP . . . 242
Controlling, IEP as . . . 255
Implementation of IEP . . . 242
Process as opportunity to be heard . . . 211
Implementation of IEP, court decisions on . . . 242
Process, court decisions on . . . 211
Regulatory requirements
Individuals with Disabilities Education Act (IDEA) . . . 205
Section 504 . . . 207
Sample IEP . . . 208
Statutory requirements
Individuals with Disabilities Education Act (IDEA) . . . 205

INDIVIDUALIZED EDUCATION PROGRAM (IEP)—Cont.
Statutory requirements—Cont.
Section 504 . . . 207

INDIVIDUALIZED FAMILY SERVICE PLANS
Generally . . . 557

INDIVIDUALS WITH DISABILITIES EDUCATION ACT (IDEA)
Appropriate education (See FREE, APPROPRIATE PUBLIC EDUCATION (FAPE))
Cases, defining
Generally . . . 21
All children with disabilities, education for . . . 39
Appropriate education . . . 21
Placement, maintenance of . . . 32
Student discipline . . . 32
Definitions
Child with disability . . . 17
Free, appropriate public education . . . 17; 157
Special education . . . 18
Eligibility under . . . 55
Free, appropriate public education (See FREE, APPROPRIATE PUBLIC EDUCATION (FAPE))
Individualized education program requirements . . . 205
Least restrictive environment
Regulations . . . 262
Statute . . . 261
Private schools, proportionate allocation of federal funds to children in . . . 526
Purpose of . . . 16
Regulations
Generally . . . 50
Least restrictive environment . . . 262
Section 1983, claims under . . . 476

INJURY, SERIOUS BODILY
Student discipline for . . . 432

INTERIM ALTERNATIVE EDUCATIONAL SETTINGS
Requirements for . . . 433

J

JOINT CUSTODY OF CHILD
Residency of student with disability, determining . . . 137

JUDICIAL REVIEW
Generally . . . 406

JUVENILE DETENTION FACILITIES
Free, appropriate public education for students in . . . 200

L

LEAST RESTRICTIVE ENVIRONMENT
Generally . . . 261

[References are to pages.]

LEAST RESTRICTIVE ENVIRONMENT—Cont.
Application of standards for inclusion . . . 283
Behavior intervention in . . . 409
Free, appropriate public education and . . . 185;
   409
Individuals with Disabilities Education Act
      Regulations . . . 262
      Statute . . . 261
Presumptive inclusion . . . 265
Regulations
      Generally . . . 261
      Individuals with Disabilities Education Act
        (IDEA) . . . 262
      Section 504 . . . 263
Related services, relation to . . . 310
Section 504 regulations . . . 263
Standards for inclusion, application of . . . 283
Statutory provisions
      Generally . . . 261
      Individuals with Disabilities Education Act
        (IDEA) . . . 261

LIABILITY
Attorney's fees, apportionment of liability for
   . . . 517
Damages liability, immunities from . . . 491

LIMITATIONS DEFENSE
Generally . . . 490

M

MAINTENANCE OF PLACEMENT
Case, defining . . . 32
Discipline review proceedings, during . . . 433
Due process hearings process, during . . . 399

MANIFESTATION REVIEW
Generally . . . 426
Appeals . . . 433
Placement during . . . 433

MEDIATION OF DISPUTES
Procedures and related issues . . . 403

MEDICAL SERVICES
Related services, as . . . 295

N

NOTICE
Due process hearings . . . 333

P

PARENTS
Court proceedings (See COURT PROCEEDINGS)
Divorce, effect on student residency of . . . 137
Due process hearings (See DUE PROCESS HEAR-
   INGS)
Joint custody, effect on student residency of
   . . . 137
Private school parents, complaints by . . . 528

PARENTS—Cont.
Residency of student and
      Divorce, effect of . . . 137
      Joint custody, effect of . . . 137

PERSONNEL
Free, appropriate public education, issue in . . . 186
Post-secondary education, deference to administrators' and teachers' decisions on student qualifications and reasonable accommodations in . . . 613
Private schools, standards for personnel providing
   services in . . . 527

PLACEMENT
Case defining maintenance of placement . . . 32
Due process hearings process, during . . . 399
Interim alternative education settings . . . 433
Maintenance of
      Case, defining . . . 32
      Due process hearings process, during . . . 399
      Review proceedings, during . . . 433
Review proceedings, during . . . 433

POST-SECONDARY EDUCATION
Generally . . . 587
Academic administrators and teachers, deference to
   decisions of . . . 613
Americans with Disabilities Act, Title II, eligibility
   for protection under . . . 588
Harassment . . . 653
Hostile environments . . . 653
Qualified individual
      Generally . . . 591
      Academic administrators and teachers, defer-
        ence to decisions of . . . 613
Reasonable accommodation
      Generally . . . 591
      Academic deference . . . 613
Section 504, eligibility for protection under
   . . . 588
Testing and testing accommodation . . . 636
Title II, eligibility for protection under . . . 588

PRISONERS
Juveniles, free, appropriate public education for
   . . . 200

PRIVATE SCHOOLS, CHILDREN IN
Generally . . . 525
Child Find . . . 526
Constitutional issues
      Establishment Clause, permissive accommoda-
        tions and . . . 530
      Free Exercise Clause, mandatory accommoda-
        tions and . . . 534
Consultation with private school representatives
   . . . 527
Discrimination between religious schools and other
   private schools . . . 541
Establishment Clause, permissive accommodations
   and . . . 530
Evaluation of students . . . 526
Free Exercise Clause, mandatory accommodations
   and . . . 534

[References are to pages.]

PRIVATE SCHOOLS, CHILDREN IN—Cont.

Individual right to services, absence of . . . 527

Individuals with Disabilities Education Act funds, proportionate allocation of . . . 526

Mandatory accommodations and Free Exercise Clause . . . 534

On-site services, permissibility of . . . 527

Parents, complaints by . . . 528

Permissive accommodations and Establishment Clause . . . 530

Personnel standards . . . 527

Private school, defined . . . 525

Private school representatives, consultation with . . . 527

Proportionate allocation of federal IDEA funds . . . 526

Religious schools and other private schools, discrimination between . . . 541

Services plan requirement . . . 526

Statutes, current

     Generally . . . 525

     Child Find . . . 526

     Consultation with private school representatives . . . 527

     Evaluation of students . . . 526

     Individual right to services, absence of . . . 527

     Individuals with Disabilities Education Act funds, proportionate allocation of . . . 526

     On-site services, permissibility of . . . 527

     Parents, complaints by . . . 528

     Personnel standards . . . 527

     Private school, defined . . . 525

     Private school representatives, consultation with . . . 527

     Proportionate allocation of federal IDEA funds . . . 526

     Services plan requirement . . . 526

     Transportation . . . 528

Transportation . . . 528

Q

QUALIFIED INDIVIDUAL

Americans with Disabilities Act . . . 20

Post-secondary education

     Generally . . . 591

     Academic administrators and teachers, deference to decisions of . . . 613

R

RELATED SERVICES

Generally . . . 293

Eligibility for (See ELIGIBILITY)

Least restrictive environment, relation to . . . 310

Medical services exception . . . 295

Regulatory requirements . . . 293

Statutory requirements . . . 293

RELIGION

Establishment Clause, permissive accommodations for children in private schools and . . . 530

RELIGION—Cont.

Religious schools and other private schools, discrimination between . . . 541

REMEDIES

Due process hearings . . . 359

Section 1415, court proceedings under . . . 449

RESIDENCY

Constitutional parameters . . . 128

Divorce and joint custody cases . . . 137

Joint custody cases . . . 137

Regulatory requirements . . . 127

State schools and homes cases . . . 140

Statutory requirements . . . 127

Students with disabilities, cases involving

     Generally . . . 137

     Divorce and joint custody . . . 137

     Joint custody . . . 137

     State schools and homes . . . 140

S

SECTION 504

Generally . . . 18

Claims, court proceedings for . . . 450

Eligibility . . . 57

Individualized education program requirements . . . 207

Least restrictive environment regulations . . . 263

Post-secondary education eligibility for protection under . . . 588

SECTION 1415, COURT PROCEEDINGS UNDER

Generally . . . 439

Evidentiary hearings . . . 441

Remedies . . . 449

SECTION 1983, CLAIMS UNDER

Constitutional claims . . . 475

Individuals with Disabilities Education Act claims . . . 476

SERIOUS BODILY INJURY

Student discipline for . . . 432

SETTLEMENT (See DUE PROCESS HEARINGS, subhead: Settlement)

SEVERE DISABILITIES

Free, appropriate public education for children with

     Generally . . . 165

     Less severe disabilities . . . 183

SPECIAL EDUCATION

Definition . . . 18

Eligibility for (See ELIGIBILITY)

Litigation, attorneys' fees for (See ATTORNEYS' FEES IN SPECIAL EDUCATION LITIGATION)

STATE COURTS (See COURTS AS SOURCE OF LAW)

STATES, SOURCES OF LAW IN

Constitutions . . . 49

[References are to pages.]

STATES, SOURCES OF LAW IN—Cont.
Court systems . . . 51
Regulations . . . 50
Statutes . . . 49

STATE SCHOOLS AND HOMES
Residency of student with disability, determining
  . . . 140

STUDENT DISCIPLINE (See DISCIPLINE, STU-
DENT)

T

TEACHERS
Free, appropriate public education, issue in . . . 186
Post-secondary education, deference to teachers'
  decisions on student qualifications and reasonable
  accommodations in . . . 613
Private schools, standards for personnel providing
  services in . . . 527

TESTS (See ASSESSMENTS)

**TITLE II, AMERICANS WITH DISABILITIES
ACT**
Post-secondary students, protection of . . . 588

TRANSPORTATION
Private school students, for . . . 528

U

UNITED STATES CONSTITUTION (See CON-
STITUTION, U.S.)

V

VOCATIONAL EDUCATION
Free, appropriate public education, issue in . . . 200

W

WEAPONS
Student discipline for carrying or possession of
  . . . 432